MW01052412

"The approach the authors have taken presents the best ways for a person who is beginning to learn the MMPI-2 or professionals seeking to update their knowledge about the test to get an in-depth exposure to extensive research literature underlying the MMPI-2. The result is a rich resource for understanding and interpreting the instrument."

— *James N. Butcher, PhD,*
Professor Emeritus at the University of Minnesota

"Written by masters of the MMPI, this clinically informative text reveals its interpretive gold when the authors draw on relevant data, clinical lore, and personal knowledge to provide insightful and rich descriptions of 105 MMPI-2 clinical scale elevations. Each pattern is accompanied by treatment recommendations and experience informed therapeutic feedback that will be treasured by novice and seasoned clinicians alike."

— *Gregory J. Meyer, PhD, University of Toledo*

"The authors' MMPI expertise shines through in this revised edition, which retains the depth of the earlier editions while providing updated research findings and a new overview of the MMPI-2-RF. This text is a vital resource for achieving a comprehensive understanding of the MMPI and developing sensitive, meaningful, and nuanced MMPI-2/MMPI-2-RF interpretations."

— *Radhika Krishnamurthy, PsyD, ABAP,*
Clinical Psychology Professor at the Florida Institute of Technology;
Past President of the Society for Personality Assessment

Praise from the first edition:

"This MMPI text… will become the standard textbook for courses on the test. Nothing is in the running with it."

— *Paul E. Meehl, PhD, University of Minnesota*

Psychological Assessment with the MMPI-2/MMPI-2-RF

This third edition apprises users of the MMPI-2/MMPI-2-Restructured Form (RF) of the ever-changing landscape of this dynamic personality/psychopathology instrument and its expanding utility in a variety of contexts. Two new chapters addressing the RC scales and the MMPI-2-RF are included in this updated text. Additionally, over 450 new references have been incorporated into the book, with information gathered and organized for practical clinical and forensic applications. The sections in the codetype interpretation chapter have been expanded to contain more in-depth feedback information and treatment considerations for clinicians to help in facilitating the formulation of treatment recommendations and strengthening therapeutic relationships with their clients. A number of special scales with clinical and forensic applications are also covered in this edition. An important section has been added addressing the MMPI and suicide.

This new edition is a must-have resource that will inform and guide users of the MMPI-2 and MMPI-2-RF in their daily practices, and assist researchers in conceptualizing the operating characteristics and configural relationships among the various scales and indices that comprise this instrument. From simple single scale interpretation to complex configural relationships, this text addresses a broad bandwidth of interpretive information designed for test users at all levels of sophistication.

Alan F. Friedman, PhD, is a licensed clinical psychologist in full-time independent practice in Chicago, Illinois, and an Associate Clinical Professor in the Department of Psychiatry and Behavioral Sciences at the Feinberg School of Medicine, Northwestern University, Chicago, Illinois.

P. Kevin Bolinskey, PhD, is Associate Professor of Psychology at Indiana State University in Terre Haute, Indiana.

Richard W. Levak, PhD, is a licensed clinical psychologist with a practice in Del Mar, California, and a Diplomate of the American Board of Assessment Psychology.

David S. Nichols, PhD, spent his career as a clinical psychologist in the Oregon state hospital system, retiring in 1999 after 27 years, and as an Adjunct Professor at the School of Professional Psychology at Pacific University in Forest Grove, Oregon.

Psychological Assessment with the MMPI-2/MMPI-2-RF

Third Edition

Alan F. Friedman, P. Kevin Bolinskey, Richard W. Levak, and David S. Nichols

Routledge
Taylor & Francis Group

NEW YORK AND LONDON

First published 2015
by Routledge
711 Third Avenue, New York, NY 10017

and by Routledge
27 Church Road, Hove, East Sussex BN3 2FA

Routledge is an imprint of the Taylor & Francis Group, an informa business

© 2015 Routledge

Library of Congress Cataloging in Publication Data
Friedman, Alan F., author.
Psychological assessment with the MMPI-2/MMPI-2-RF / by Alan F. Friedman, P. Kevin Bolinskey, Richard W. Levak, and David S. Nichols.
– Third edition.
      p. ; cm.
Preceded by Psychological assessment with the MMPI-2 / Alan F. Friedman ... [et al.], c2001.
Includes bibliographical references and indexes.
I. Bolinskey, P. Kevin, author. II. Levak, Richard, author. III. Nichols, David S., author. IV. Title.
[DNLM: 1. MMPI. WM 145.5.M6]
RC473.M5
155.2′83–dc23   2014012402

ISBN: 978-0-415-52634-0 (hbk)
ISBN: 978-0-415-52633-3 (pbk)
ISBN: 978-0-203-11955-6 (ebk)

Typeset in Minion
by HWA Text and Data Management, London

For my children, Emily, Ben, and Marco
and for my first mentor, James A.Wakefield, Jr.
A. F. F.

In loving memory of my grandmother, Juanita E. Giles
P. K. B.

To Linda and Rachel
R. W. L.

To my first, great psychology teacher, William L. Radtke, who opened the door for me
D. S. N.

Contents

Figures

Tables

Code Pattern Look-Up Table

About the Authors

Alan F. Friedman, PhD, is a licensed clinical psychologist in full-time independent practice in Chicago and an Associate Clinical Professor in the Department of Psychiatry and Behavioral Sciences at the Feinberg School of Medicine, Northwestern University, where he has taught MMPI/MMPI-2 interpretation courses since 1983. Dr. Friedman specializes in litigation consulting and forensic assessments. He also provides consultations to mental health professionals, security specialists, human resource professionals, managers, executives, and attorneys interested in crisis prevention and management strategies for critical incidents. He regularly performs fitness-for-duty evaluations and threat assessments for law enforcement agencies, small organizations and large multinational corporations, and designs workplace violence prevention programs. Dr. Friedman is considered a leading expert in the threat assessment of potentially dangerous employees and routinely advises agencies and companies on risk management strategies. Dr. Friedman employs the only complete actuarial approach for screening new hires for police and fire positions, utilizing the MATRIX protocol with the MMPI-2. He is a Fellow of the Society for Personality Assessment and a member of the American and Illinois Psychological Associations. He has also served as a consulting editor of the journals *Assessment* and the *Journal of Personality Assessment*. He acts as a litigation consultant and expert witness in cases of employment, criminal, personal injury, and disability matters, and child custody disputes. Dr. Friedman can be contacted at 30 N. Michigan Avenue, Suite 1206, Chicago, IL 60602; (312) 368–4515; draf48@aol.com.

P. Kevin Bolinskey, PhD, is Associate Professor of Psychology at Indiana State University (ISU), where he teaches doctoral courses in Objective Personality Assessment, Theories of Personality, Advanced Assessment and Treatment, and Statistics. His research interests are in the areas of premorbid indicators of liability to psychosis and personality assessment; he maintains an active research lab at ISU and has published numerous articles and given several presentations on these topics. In addition to his academic duties, Dr. Bolinskey maintains an active clinical practice performing psychological evaluations and psychotherapy. Dr. Bolinskey credits both David S. Nichols and Robert P. Archer for nurturing and encouraging his interest in the MMPI. He can be reached via e-mail: Kevin.Bolinskey@indstate.edu.

Richard W. Levak, PhD (aka Lewak), is a licensed clinical psychologist with a practice in Del Mar, California. His area of specialty is personality assessment. He has co-authored five books on the subject, including the first MMPI feedback and treatment guide in 1990 with Philip Marks. His most recent book, *Therapeutic Feedback with the MMPI-2* (Routledge, 2011), uses a positive approach to providing feedback as a therapeutic intervention. As a personality expert, he has served as a consultant to reality television programs from the beginning of that genre, and has worked on *Survivor, The Amazing Race, The Apprentice, The Contender, Big Brother,* and others. In this role, he made predictions about contestants' behavior, based on personality assessment. He has appeared on *Larry King Live, Anderson Cooper, 20/20,* and *Nightline,* and has a weekly segment on San Diego Fox News, *Mind Matters,* educating the public about the psychology of personality. Dr. Levak also assists companies with executive hiring decisions, management development, and corporate teambuilding. He is a Fellow of the San Diego Psychological Association and the Society for Personality Assessment and a Diplomate of the American Board of Assessment Psychology. He can be reached at drlevak@drlevak.com, (858) 755-8717.

David S. Nichols, PhD, spent his career as a Clinical Psychologist in the Oregon state hospital system, retiring in 1999 after 27 years, and as an Adjunct Professor at the School of Professional Psychology at Pacific University in Forest Grove, Oregon. He is a Diplomate of the American Board of Assessment Psychology, and a Fellow of the Society of Personality Assessment, on whose Board of Trustees he served for eight years. He has also served terms as Consulting Editor and Associate Editor of the *Journal of Personality Assessment,* and Consulting Editor of *Assessment.* He describes himself as an MMPI/MMPI-2 hobbyist, his interest in the test going back 40+ years, and has pursued research and writing about it over this period, resulting in 45+ articles, reviews, monographs, chapters, and books, and has lectured and presented workshops around the U.S. and internationally. He is co-author, with Roger L. Greene, of the *MMPI-2 Structural Summary* (PAR, 1995); with Alan F. Friedman, Richard Lewak, and James T. Webb, of *Psychological Assessment with the MMPI-2* (Lawrence Erlbaum, 2001); with Richard Levak and Liza Siegel of *Therapeutic Feedback with the MMPI-2: A Positive Psychology Approach*; and recently completed the Second Edition of *Essentials on MMPI-2 Interpretation* (Wiley, 2011). He may be reached via e-mail at Davemult@aol.com.

Foreword

James N. Butcher

Change is inevitable but not all change leads to positive outcomes—change for change's sake is not a direct route to success. Equally important is the understanding and use of methods developed in the past that worked well then and continue to do so today. The third edition of this book on the MMPI-2 by Alan Friedman, Kevin Bolinskey, Richard Levak, and Dave Nichols clearly evaluates the issues surrounding the use of the MMPI-2 in 2014 and beyond. Users of the MMPI-2 will find updated research on its use published since 2001. Additionally, this text provides a critical examination of claims that a radically different methodology resulted in the "new and improved" MMPI-2-Restructured Form (RF), released in 2008, and presents an accurate description of the development and interpretation of the MMPI-2-RF scales. However, the MMPI-2 continues to be the most widely used objective personality measure, and this book goes a long way in demonstrating why.

The authors objectively deal with controversial claims made in the marketing of the MMPI-2-RF as "a new standard in adult personality assessment." Friedman et al. devote two chapters to clarifying how the new test, the MMPI-2-RF, and its core measures, the Restructured Clinical (RC) scales, share very little in common with the MMPI-2. They conclude, and I concur, that the MMPI-2-RF is a new and very different measure than MMPI-2, was developed using completely different methodologies, and has limited research support, particularly in the areas of personnel screening and forensic applications. Indeed, six years after the introduction of the MMPI-2-RF, practitioners remain more likely to rely on the MMPI-2. This is according to public records provided to me in October 2013 (i.e., the University of Minnesota receives far more gross royalty income from sales of the MMPI-2 than it does from sales of the MMPI-2-RF).

It is a great pleasure and honor for me to be invited to write a foreword to the newest edition of Alan Friedman and his colleagues' textbook on the MMPI-2. I would like to highlight the importance of this revision. The approach they have taken presents the best ways for a person who is beginning to learn the MMPI-2 or professionals seeking to update their knowledge about the test to get an in-depth exposure to extensive research literature underlying the MMPI-2. The result is a rich resource for understanding and interpreting the instrument.

In reviewing this contribution, I believe that Friedman and colleagues have brought into this latest version of this classic MMPI-2 text a substantial amount of new information and perspective on the test. All four authors are extremely well qualified to publish this comprehensive textbook on the MMPI-2. They have devoted a major part of their scholarly careers to conducting research on the MMPI and MMPI-2, and teaching others how the test is applied in clinical settings. This comprehensive coverage on test applications in diverse settings, clinical, personnel, and forensic, will be a great addition to the literature and will be welcomed by the growing number of psychologists engaging in those activities.

The serious student of the MMPI-2 will find a lot to like in this latest version of Friedman and his colleagues' book. This volume provides a valuable summary of new empirical information about the correlates of the MMPI-2 scales and codetypes and the MMPI-2-RF scales from recent research. The authors have presented a sound approach to explaining the basics of the test—administration, assessment of response attitudes, meanings of the broad variety of MMPI-2 symptom measures, and interpretive strategies, including computer-assisted interpretation. Their broad clinical backgrounds provide practitioners with insights into how the test is used, in individual assessment, treatment planning, and many more areas.

Friedman and colleagues did not shy away from dealing with the controversies surrounding the MMPI-2 over the last 10 years. The authors are to be commended for their objective and comprehensive reporting on the problems. The controversial Fake Bad Scale (FBS), also known as the Symptom Validity Scale, is a measure added to MMPI-2 scoring by the test publisher in 2007. Friedman and colleagues point out the problems with using this "malingering" scale, including descriptions of multiple court challenges that excluded it as part of expert witness testimony. They highlight the weaknesses of the FBS, how it calls many clients "faking" when they are not, and how it is biased against women, as well as people with genuine physical problems.

One of the authors of this text, Dave Nichols, recently uncovered through meticulous research that many of the symptoms referred to in the FBS items were actually identified three years earlier, in 1988, by the lead author of the FBS as components of the stresses associated with being a plaintiff in litigation. These and other symptoms were gathered into what he aptly named the Litigation Response Syndrome (LRS). Thus, the two, FBS and LRS, lead to distinctly different conclusions based on many of the same symptoms, raising further doubts about the validity of the FBS. The discovery of the LRS–FBS connection illustrates the thorough nature of this text's consideration of one of the recent changes to the MMPI-2 to help readers understand the reasons many of us recommend against the use of the FBS.

Other notable features new to this third edition are the feedback sections that have been added for each of the codetypes. These will better enable clinicians to share the MMPI-2 results with the test-taker. Also new is a section entitled "The MMPI and Suicide" that apprises readers about this important topic. Chapter 12 presents automated computer reports with detailed commentary comparing them, and useful scale comparison tables including the Structural Summary that captures and organizes a wide array of scores helping the reader to consolidate the test data in the narrative reports, and to facilitate report writing. Throughout the text there are references that will surely prove helpful to those engaged in the challenges associated with forensic assessments. With nearly 450 new references, this text lives up to its "revised" status and will prove as authoritative as the last edition.

This book holds a very important place in the teaching of personality assessment, especially for instructors who teach objective personality assessment methods and for practitioners who want to update their knowledge about the MMPI-2 research base. I am certain that the third edition of Friedman and colleagues' book will fulfill the same important role in the academic settings that the earlier editions of the book provided.

James N. Butcher, PhD
Professor Emeritus
University of Minnesota

Preface

This third edition was written to apprise users of the MMPI-2/MMPI-2-Restructured Form (RF) of the ever-changing landscape of this dynamic personality/psychopathology instrument, and its expanding utility in a variety of contexts. Since our last edition in 2001, several significant developments have required an updated text for both new and seasoned users. In 2008, the MMPI-2-RF, an abbreviated and restructured version of the MMPI-2, was released as an alternative to the original instrument. Constructed in a fashion differing substantially from that employed for the MMPI-2, it is intended not to replace the original test, but to offer a new set of measures with reduced administration time. Subsequent research and controversy about the MMPI-2-RF and its various new scales has ensued, with a vibrant interest from the research and practitioner communities. Among clinicians and researchers alike, however, there remains a strong and vital continuing interest in the MMPI-2. It appears that the MMPI has reinvented itself over the years of its existence, with many significant milestones since its original development by Hathaway and McKinley in the early 1940s; its re-standardization in 1989; and, in subsequent developments, the Restructured Clinical (RC) scales in 2003.

In addition to keeping with the mission of the previous editions to update and refresh the material gleaned from the ongoing stream of research findings and newer practical applications, we have incorporated two new chapters to address the RC scales and the MMPI-2-RF. We are delighted to welcome Kevin Bolinskey in joining this revision project as a coauthor at its inception; his participation has been an invaluable contribution for much of the new material incorporated into the text. Additionally, over 450 new references have been incorporated into the book, with information gathered and organized for practical clinical and forensic applications. The codetype interpretation chapter has expanded its sections with more in-depth feedback information and treatment considerations for clinicians, to help in facilitating the formulation of treatment recommendations and strengthening therapeutic relationships with their clients. It is hoped that these new sections will help to guide practitioners in selecting therapeutic modalities that are maximally efficacious. The chapters have been rearranged to be more reader-friendly, and a section has been added addressing the MMPI and suicide.

It is our hope that this new edition will inform and guide users of the MMPI-2 and MMPI-2-RF in their daily practices, and assist researchers in conceptualizing the operating characteristics and configural relationships among the various scales and indices that comprise this instrument. From simple single scale interpretation to complex configural relationships, this text addresses a broad bandwidth of interpretive information designed for text users at all levels of sophistication.

Acknowledgments

We wish to express our gratitude to Roger Greene for his always-present generosity regarding his data, his time, and his insight into the MMPI-2-RF. Roger is a colleague whose intellectual horsepower is matched by few, and his spirit of friendship is inspirational. Alex Caldwell, one of the pioneers in developing clinical theories for understanding the utility of the test, graciously allowed our use of his clinical data and a Caldwell Report in this text. We also extend our appreciation and thanks to Beverly Kaemmer and Tami Brown, of the University of Minnesota Press, for their permission to reproduce a number of tables and figures, as well as for the MMPI-2 and MMPI-2-RF narrative reports in the last chapter. They spent countless hours providing information to the first author about the important changes and products available for the MMPI-2-RF. Their assistance and availability made the completion of this book possible. George Zimmar, our editor, has been a strong advocate and source of encouragement since the beginning of this project. We are indebted to him for many things, not the least of which ordinarily would be called patience but, in our case, that would be an understatement. *Very high frustration tolerance* is a more apt term for this virtue of George's. Jim Butcher, whose abundant and rich research and teaching career has centered on personality and the MMPI/MMPI-2/MMPI-A, and led the re-standardization project that germinated the MMPI-2, provided invaluable access to his research publications, data, and understandings about many complex issues discussed in this edition. Jim, like Roger, is a psychologist's psychologist, and it is our good fortune to have had his guidance in this revision. Carolyn Williams made many contributions to our understanding of various special scales, and her insights are also greatly appreciated. Special thanks are extended to Deborah DeLucia, who prepared this manuscript through all of its various phases, and who has been extraordinarily conscientious throughout this project. Without her able assistance, this project would not have come to fruition. Linda Rock is also owed our gratitude for her keen editorial comments and edits of various chapters; her efforts have also greatly improved this book.

Finally, I wish to make a special mention, not often done for a coauthor. David Nichols has been my coauthor on the last two editions of this book. Dave edited each and every page of this text, and his meticulous efforts greatly enriched what is hoped to be a wealth of clinical information. Dave never denied a request to rewrite or revisit any aspect of this revision. I cannot imagine a more selfless collaborator, or a bolder one, in that Dave never compromised his intellectual rigor for expediency. His collaboration on this book made the task much less daunting and actually enjoyable! He deserves all the thanks that my coauthors and I can give him.

Alan F. Friedman, PhD
Feinberg School of Medicine
Northwestern University
Independent Practice
Chicago

1 Development of the MMPI and MMPI-2

General Description of the MMPI/MMPI-2

The Minnesota Multiphasic Personality Inventory (MMPI) and its revised forms, the MMPI-2 (Butcher, Graham, Ben-Porath, Tellegen, Dahlstrom, & Kaemmer, 2001), the MMPI-A (Butcher, Williams, Graham, Archer, Tellegen, Ben-Porath, & Kaemmer, 1992), and the MMPI-2 Restructured Form (MMPI-2-RF; Ben-Porath & Tellegen, 2008) are the most widely used objective personality adjustment inventories in the world (Archer, 2005; Butcher, 2010; Friedman, Lewak, Nichols, & Webb, 2001; Greene, 2011; Lubin, Larsen, & Matarazzo, 1984; Lubin, Larsen, Matarazzo, & Seever, 1985). Even from its beginnings, the test has enjoyed popularity and has been ranked as a leading personality instrument (Archer, 1997, 2005; Butcher, 2010; Friedman, Webb, & Lewak, 1989). Taught in the majority of clinical psychology training programs (Dahlstrom & Moreland, 1983; Friedman, Webb, Smeltzer, & Lewak, 1989; Watkins, 1991), the MMPI is used by most psychologists who conduct assessments as part of their clinical and consulting practice (Archer et al., 2006; Dahlstrom, 1992b; Moreland & Dahlstrom, 1983; Watkins, Campbell, Nieberding, & Hallmark, 1995). The MMPI and its successors have also been the subject of extensive research. Butcher (2010) estimated the number of references for the MMPI, MMPI-2, and MMPI-A at 19,000. Greene (2011) conducted an electronic search of the psychology databases in January, 2010, using the search term "MMPI," yielding 24,171 citations, and the search term "MMPI-2" produced 4,216 citations.

The widespread use and longevity of the MMPI is attributable to several factors, including its simplicity of scoring and administration, an objective response format important for research designs, a large item pool (from which at least 800 additional scales have been derived), many useful applications, the inclusion of validity scales for determining the examinee's level of cooperation, numerous translations into other languages, and thousands of empirically established correlates. In fact, it is difficult to imagine many settings in which psychologists perform assessment and treatment functions where the MMPI in its various forms has not been used. Inpatient and outpatient mental health facilities often employ psychologists to make diagnostic and treatment decisions, and the MMPI-2/MMPI-A/MMPI-2-RF is typically included in psychological test batteries or administered independently. Many clinicians routinely use the instrument to assess new patients for psychopathology in their office practices and to help formulate treatment plans, or to conduct child custody evaluations (Alan Jaffe, personal communication, May 31, 2013). Psychologists also use the test in medical settings to evaluate the presence of psychological components in physical complaints and to assist in predicting response to various treatments (Osborne, 1979).

Industrial-organizational and clinical psychologists, whose responsibilities involve matching individuals to particular employment positions or screening individuals for psychopathology, also use the MMPI-2. For example, because the MMPI-2 is sensitive to emotional maladjustment in individuals other than identified patient groups, it is often used in personnel selection situations in which high-risk occupations require careful screening of applicants (Butcher, Ones, & Cullen, 2006; Davis & Rostow, 2004; Davis, Rostow, Pinkston, Combs, & Dixon, 2004). People in positions of public trust, such as airline flight crews, law enforcement officers, firefighters, emergency dispatchers, nursing staff, ministerial candidates, and nuclear power plant operators, are typically administered the MMPI-2, not only for selection purposes but also for fitness-for-duty evaluations. Research applications with the MMPI-2, either as the sole subject of study or as one of the major dependent measures in investigation, range from cross-cultural studies of response patterns to evaluating treatment effects to making forensic decisions (Friedman, Lewak, Nichols, & Webb, 2001; Rothke & Friedman, 1994; Rothke, Friedman, Dahlstrom, Greene, Arrendondo, & Mann, 1994; Rothke, Friedman, Jaffe, Greene, Wetter, Cole, & Baker, 2000). The test is widely used in both criminal and civil forensic settings, as the MMPI-2 is often admitted as evidence in court (Pope, Butcher, & Seelen, 2006).

The original MMPI consisted of 566 numbered statements, each of which could be answered True or False on an answer sheet, or, in the original deck form, the test takers sorted the cards into True, False, or Cannot Say categories. An item was scored Cannot Say if it was marked or sorted both True *and* False, left blank, or placed into the Cannot Say pile in the original card form. There are several methods for scoring a completed test. The answer sheet is either hand scored or read by an optical scanner. Some MMPI users enter the responses from the answer sheet into a computer programmed to score and/or interpret the test. Some test takers enter their responses directly into a computer using a keyboard, which instantly scores the test.

For the original MMPI, 13 standard scales are scored, regardless of the scoring method. The following are the original three validity scales and 10 *standard* clinical scales. Note that the convention adopted here is that the eight scales numbered 1–4 and 6–9 will be referred to as the *basic* clinical scales or, more simply, as the *basic scales.* When speaking of the entire set of clinical scales displayed on the main profile form, including Masculinity-Femininity (*Mf*, or Scale 5) and Social Introversion (*Si*, or Scale 0), we refer to the *standard clinical scales* or more simply, the *standard scales.*

Original MMPI Validity Scales

- Lie (*L*)
- Infrequency (*F*)
- Correction (*K*)

Clinical Scales

- Scale 1 Hypochondriasis (*Hs*)
- Scale 2 Depression (*D*)
- Scale 3 Hysteria (*Hy*)
- Scale 4 Psychopathic Deviate (*Pd*)
- Scale 5 Masculinity-Femininity (*Mf*)

- Scale 6 Paranoia (*Pa*)
- Scale 7 Psychasthenia (*Pt*)
- Scale 8 Schizophrenia (*Sc*)
- Scale 9 Hypomania (*Ma*)
- Scale 0 Social Introversion (*Si*)

The validity scales were developed to assist in recognizing test records produced by uncooperative or deceptive participants with various test-taking attitudes (e.g. faking good or faking bad) or participants who had difficulty comprehending or reading the test items. The clinical scales were developed primarily to assist in identifying the type and severity of abnormal psychiatric conditions. A secondary goal was to provide an objective means of estimating therapeutic effects and other changes in the status of patients' conditions over time (Dahlstrom, Welsh, & Dahlstrom, 1972). The raw scores on each of the validity and clinical scales are converted to standard *T*-scores by plotting them onto a profile form, thereby rendering the raw scores comparable. It is the pattern of these *T*-scores that is usually interpreted. The *T*-scores provide the clinician with an opportunity to examine how the test taker compares to different populations, including, most importantly, a standardized group of normal individuals. A more detailed description of *T*-scores is provided later in this chapter. Initially, individual scales were interpreted to assist in psychodiagnosis, but experience showed that combinations of scales were better predictors of personality characteristics, so test users began focusing on patterns of scale scores versus individual scale elevations. "Profile" became the term used to focus on the eight basic clinical scales, and eventually, "Codetype" or "Code Pattern" analysis became the way in which interpretation of the test was described.

Historical Development of the MMPI

In an important historical overview of the MMPI, W. Grant Dahlstrom (1992b) summarized a series of studies by Carney Landis and his colleagues at the New York State Psychiatric Institute in the 1930s (Landis & Katz, 1934; Landis, Zubin, & Katz, 1935; Page, Landis, & Katz, 1934; see also Greene, 2011); these studies strongly reinforced the skepticism at that time of professionals relying on personality testing as an aid in assessment and diagnosis because existing personality tests lacked validity. Specifically, the objective tests available at the time relied on individuals' willingness and capacity to accurately report their feelings and experiences and also depended on their reading and intellectual ability to comprehend the inventory. These concerns sensitized clinicians to the need for improving the validity of objective personality tests.

Despite the tenor of the times, or perhaps because of it, Starke Rosencrans Hathaway and J. Charnley McKinley teamed up to develop a new inventory capable of overcoming the limitations inherent in the existing personality tests. Hathaway, a clinically experienced physiological psychologist, and McKinley, a neuropsychiatrist and head of the Department of Psychiatry and Neurology, both at the Medical School at the University of Minnesota, were joined in their later efforts by Paul E. Meehl. Hathaway and McKinley were originally motivated to design a test that could serve as an aid: "in diagnosing persons classified as constitutional psychopathic inferiors" (Hathaway, 1939, p. 117); assist "in assessing the psychological factors associated with physical problems or disease seen in a medical practice" (McKinley & Hathaway, 1943, p. 161); and, as a corollary, "measure the effectiveness of insulin therapy" (Hathaway, 1964, p. 204) in schizophrenia, which was in widespread use by the late 1930s. The test also came to be seen as an aid in determining levels of psychiatric impairment and changes in the patients' condition over time, as well as in measuring the effects of psychotherapy (Dahlstrom et al., 1972).

Although the MMPI was originally published in 1942 (Nichols, 2011), the authors actually began their work on the test in the late 1930s. By the end of April, 1943, the MMPI was generating enough revenue to motivate the Psychological Corporation to become its licensed distributor. In 1951 the MMPI arrived in its final form with the addition of the *Si* scale (*Si*), published in 1946 (Drake, 1946; also in Butcher, 2000). There were several subsequent revisions of the original MMPI *Manual* through 1983.

The first article describing the inception of the MMPI was published by Hathaway and McKinley in 1940: "A Multiphasic Personality Schedule (Minnesota): I. Construction of the Schedule." Hathaway and McKinley strove to correct many of the problems hampering the effectiveness of most previously existing personality inventories. These earlier personality inventories were typically constructed on a rational basis with a focus on content validity, but lacked scales designed to measure the participant's test-taking attitude (e.g. defensiveness or over-reporting of symptoms). One such inventory was the Woodworth (1920) Personal Data Sheet, also called the Psychoneurotic Inventory. World War I created a strong need to screen for maladjustment among draftees, and Woodworth developed a 116-item self-rating scale to detect neurotic maladjustment. The items consisted of statements that Woodworth believed reflected neurotic symptoms. If a participant answered a certain number of items in the neurotic direction, a psychiatric interview was conducted. A fundamental assumption inherent in the test was that the items measured what Woodworth assumed they measured. Items were chosen on rational grounds; that is, if the items appeared content-relevant to neuroticism, they were included on the scale. Over time, it became clear that items selected on a rational basis did not always indicate deviant behavior in the way Woodworth expected. Another unwarranted assumption in the Personal Data Sheet, and similar tests, was that the participant would, and could, honestly and accurately describe him- or herself. This is not always the case; self-deception and social desirability factors operate to influence the person's responses to test items. According to Hathaway (1965) and Nichols (2011), the test was limited in its success because prospective soldiers who feared combat or otherwise considered themselves in need of evaluation were inclined to declare their vulnerabilities on the test. The items were apparently too obvious in their intent to detect neuroticism. Although the Woodworth Personal Data Sheet was not completed early enough to allow its use before World War I ended, it did set the stage for other similarly constructed inventories that achieved widespread use after the war (Anastasi, 1982).

The Bell (1934) Adjustment Inventory and the Bernreuter (1933) Personality Inventory were derived from the Woodworth Personal Data Sheet and were also criticized for their excessive reliance on a rational approach to test construction and for the face-valid nature of the test items (Colligan et al., 1989). Landis and Katz (1934) and others contributed to the demise of the Bernreuter Personality Inventory by demonstrating a lack of discriminant validity between diagnostic groups. Psychotic patients, not just neurotics, showed elevations, thereby misclassifying them as neurotic (Greene, 2011).

The Humm-Wadsworth Temperament Survey (Humm & Wadsworth, 1935) was a methodological precursor of the MMPI and was cited in Hathaway's (1939) article, "The Personality Inventory as an Aid in the Diagnosis of Psychopathic Inferiors." It was the first personality questionnaire to use the actual responses of psychiatric patients to determine the direction in which items should be scored and their suitability for scale development (Nichols, 2011). The test consisted of 318 items and provided scores for seven scales. Examination of the Humm-Wadsworth items show a remarkable resemblance to at least 27 percent of the 550 MMPI items (D. S. Nichols, personal communication, April 1, 1999). Meehl (1989) also noted that many items on the MMPI were adopted from the 318-item Humm-Wadsworth Inventory. The seven components of temperament identified on the inventory were: Normal, Antisocial, Manic, Depressed, Schizoid Autistic, Paranoid, and Epileptoid. Greene (2011) provides an excellent critique of the test and states that by the early 1950s there were a total of 14 critiques on the instrument, focusing on themes of how "problem" and "satisfactory" employees had similar profiles, and how statistical analyses of new data sets were incongruent with data reported by Humm and Wadsworth. As Greene (2011) points out, even though the published research on the test disappeared by the mid-1950s, Humm and Wadsworth were innovative and contributed to aspects of the MMPI's development.

Because of Hathaway's reservations about the rational approach to inventory construction, he used an empirical method (the criterion keying method) to construct the MMPI. Nichols (2011) illuminates Hathaway's motivation for adopting this approach to constructing the MMPI. He described Hathaway as a "thoroughgoing pragmatist" with a deep distrust of theory and an abiding belief in practical experience:

> The method of contrasted groups provided Hathaway with a practical means of avoiding theory and sidestepping rational or intuitive guidance in the selection of the items for the MMPI scales. Hathaway did not pretend to know how different kinds of patients would respond to his items. The method of contrasted groups allowed him a satisfactory way of finding out: it allowed him to ask them.
>
> (Nichols, 2011, p. 2)

As Anastasi (1982) noted, the MMPI represents the outstanding example of the empirical criterion construction methodology. In this method of contrasted groups, test items are administered to two or more groups of participants—a criterion group selected for homogeneity with respect to a certain diagnosis, cluster of features, traits, or other characteristics (e.g. schizophrenia), and a normal comparison group that does not share the same characteristics or shares them only in base-rate amounts. Items to which the criterion and comparison groups respond statistically differently are included on the scale being developed, and items to which the responses of the two groups are similar are not included. Scales constructed in this fashion are typically named after the criterion group. As Butcher (2010) noted, because items are selected based on prediction of criterion variables, the scales will be heterogeneous in their content. Scoring the scales is accomplished by assigning one point to each item answered in the direction that is marked significantly more frequently by the criterion participant; that is, if a higher proportion of individuals with hysteria than normals answered an item True, a True response to that item would earn one point on the Hysteria scale, and a False response would be given zero points. The higher the raw score a person receives on a scale, the more items he or she has answered in the direction of the criterion group.

Using this contrasted group or criterion keying method, Hathaway and McKinley began their construction of the MMPI by compiling more than 1,000 self-reference statements from a wide variety of sources, including psychiatric examination forms, psychiatric textbooks, previously published attitude and personality scales, clinical reports and case summaries, and their own clinical experience. From these resources, they initially adopted an item pool of 504 separate statements that could be answered True or False. McKinley and Hathaway (1943) later added 55 items primarily related to masculinity-femininity, but eventually eliminated nine more items, resulting in a final pool of 550 separate items. Because 16 items were repeated to facilitate early mechanical scanning, the final published booklet version of the MMPI contained 566 items, with the 16 repeated items scored no more than once on the scales on which they appeared (Scales 6, 7, 8, and 0). The 16 repeated items were scored the first time they appeared in the test. The 550 statements were divided into 26 content areas, including phobias, religious attitudes, general health—including medical and neurological symptoms— political and social attitudes, family, educational and occupational experiences, and items associated with an overly virtuous self-presentation (Dahlstrom et al., 1972). The items were judged to be easily readable, written in the first person declarative form with simplified wording based on contemporary word-frequency tables. "Brevity, clarity, and simplicity were occasionally given precedence over grammatical precision. Common English slang and idioms were used, but esoteric or specialized language was avoided" (Nichols, 2011, p. 3). Using the pool of 550 items, Hathaway and McKinley proceeded to construct scales by contrasting the responses of normal and clinical criterion groups.

The normal reference group consisted of 724 friends and relatives of patients being seen at the University of Minnesota Hospital outpatient department who were willing to complete the test. These normals were all White, as few ethnic minority groups other than native Americans lived in Minnesota at that time and belonged to what was termed "the underprivileged" classes, and came from all parts of the state (Dahlstrom, Welsh, & Dahlstrom, 1972; McKinley & Hathaway, 1940). According to Dahlstrom and Welsh (1960), "the subjects were approached in the halls and in waiting rooms of the hospital, and invited to participate in the research project" (p. 44). Additional normal and patient groups consisted of high school graduates attending pre-college conferences at the University of Minnesota ($n = 265$), medical patients from the University of Minnesota Hospital ($n = 254$), skilled Work Project Administration (WPA) personnel ($n = 265$), and inpatients with varied diagnoses in the psychiatric unit (then called the Psychopathic Unit) at the University of Minnesota Hospital ($n = 221$). Normal participants (other than the medical patients) who were then under the care of a physician were excluded from the normative samples; all other participants were included. Dahlstrom et al. (1972, pp. 7–8) pointed out the importance of the normal reference groups by stating that:

the performance of these men and women on each of the component scales in the MMPI is used as the basis for the norms in the test profile. Each subject taking the MMPI, therefore, is being compared to the way a typical man or woman endorsed those items. In 1940, such a Minnesota normal adult was about 35 years old, was married, lived in a small town or rural area, had had eight years of general schooling, and worked at a skilled or semiskilled trade (or was married to a man with such an occupational level).

Hathaway and McKinley found their original sample of normals to correspond well in age, gender, and marital status to the Minnesota population in the 1930s census (Dahlstrom et al., 1972). However, it is now generally accepted that "the original MMPI norm group appears to have over-represented lower educational and occupational groups" (Dahlstrom, 1993, p. 9). It is important to note that while the original fixed reference group consisted of 724 normals, Hathaway and Briggs (1957), in the course of providing normative data on a number of additional MMPI scales, replaced many incomplete or defective protocols of the original normals. Their modified sample of 225 men and 315 women became the basis for the *T*-scores printed on the MMPI standard profile form. *T*-scores derived from norms in *An MMPI Handbook* (Dahlstrom et al., 1972, 1975) and other MMPI reference works do not necessarily match precisely the *T*-scores of the "purified" sample. Subsequently, corrected tables appeared in the MMPI-2 *Manual* revision (Butcher et al., 2001).

The clinical criterion (abnormal) groups consisted of carefully selected psychiatric patients, and participants represented the following major diagnostic categories: hypochondriasis, depression, conversion hysteria, psychopathy, paranoia, psychasthenia, schizophrenia, and hypomania. Two other groups were later added to develop additional scales for the MMPI. One of these groups consisted of normal college women used to develop a *Si* scale (Drake, 1946), and the other group consisted of "homosexual invert males" (Hathaway, 1980, p. 110) used to develop the *Mf* scale.

Very shortly after the MMPI gained widespread acceptance, criticisms were made regarding the narrowness of the original standardization group used to obtain normal values for the scales. The 724 normals who were recruited as participants while accompanying patients to the hospital, consisted of Whites, disproportionately of Scandinavian, German, and Irish descent, who were almost exclusively from the Minnesota, North Dakota, South Dakota, Iowa, and Wisconsin areas. Nichols (1992b) stated that "the phrase 'Minnesota farmers' became the standard term of opprobrium for this largely rural, eighth-grade-educated, skilled or semi-skilled, northern Midwestern group of Scandinavian origins" (p. 562). The generalizability of such norms to other areas of the country was repeatedly questioned, and the implications of such limited norms have been well described by Pancoast and Archer (1989). In general, normal groups that have taken the MMPI since its original publication have typically scored about 0.5 *SDs* (five *T*-scores) above the mean, causing test users to have to downwardly calibrate the scores of most normals so as to avoid overinterpreting or overpathologizing their test results. Pancoast and Archer combined various MMPI samples for normal men and women collected over five decades to demonstrate the inadequacy of the original norms. Their data demonstrate the relative elevation of all other normal samples above the mean of the original normals. Their results also suggest that the scores of normals subsequent to those used in the original standardization generally have not changed across five decades of MMPI use, which, when considered along with the relative elevation, underscores the fact that the original norms were not an adequate representation of the U.S. population.

Following Pancoast and Archer's (1989) demonstration of the inadequacy of the original normative sample, Greene (1990b) questioned whether similar findings would be obtained with psychiatric patients. He examined the scores of psychiatric patients over a 40-year span with the intention of discovering any appreciable changes in profiles as a function of time. Four frequently occurring code patterns were identified (Spike 4, 24/42, 27/72, and 68/86), as were the means and medians across four time periods (1950, 1960, 1970, 1980). The results show that the code patterns differed very little over time in their means and medians. His results were similar to that of Pancoast and Archer (1989), who found strong stability on the MMPI scale scores of normal adult samples across 40 years. Although Greene (1990b) did not assess the existence of similar correlates across time for those samples, he did suggest that, given his findings, the "MMPI may not be as outdated as many people have thought" (Greene, 1991a, p. 12).

Colligan and his colleagues (Colligan, Osborne, Swenson, & Offord, 1983; Colligan et al., 1989) at the Mayo Clinic in Rochester, Minnesota, attempted to provide more contemporary and accurate norms than those provided for the original group of normals. Colligan et al. (1983) tested a contemporary sample of normal individuals in rural Minnesota to compare the results with the original standardization group. In a critique of their work, Greene (1985) noted important differences between the mean scores on the standard MMPI scales for their contemporary and original samples, generally ranging from one to six *T*-scores. These differences may have occurred as a result of the different metric used by Colligan and his associates in testing their new sample of normals. Specifically, Greene (1985) pointed out that Colligan, Osborne, and Offord (1980) used normalized *T*-scores versus linear *T*-scores, which are used with the traditional MMPI profile form. Colligan et al. (1980, 1983, 1989) used normalized *T*-scores because the original norm *T*-score distributions on most MMPI scales have varying degrees of positive skew, making it difficult to accurately compare *T*-scores across scales (Miller & Streiner, 1986). Normalized *T*-scores are comparable across scales. However, Miller and Streiner (1986) found an absence of correspondence when code patterns using the original norms were compared with the new norms; this was found for both linear transformations and normalized *T*-scores. They recommended Colligan et al.'s norms be used only in conjunction with the original norms until the clinical relevance of the differences are determined. Subsequently, Greene (1991a) commented on the incongruent profiles produced by the different norm sets. He stated that although it is important to know the concordance between codetypes generated by the two sets of norms, the basic issue remains as to whether the original or contemporary norms more accurately reflect external correlates (concurrent validity). It should be noted that Colligan et al. (1989) recognized that members of their contemporary normal sample produced significantly higher profiles than the original Minnesota normal sample, suggesting more psychological or physical distress than was reported by the original normative group. They suggested that "the differences could be attributable to changes in social attitudes and perceptions since the 1930s and 1940s and hence different meanings attached to, or perceived in, items of the MMPI" (Colligan et al., 1989, p. 47).

In addition to the basic validity and clinical scales, Colligan and his colleagues have provided norms for a variety of other scales, including Wiggins' (1966) content scales (Colligan & Offord, 1988a), Barron's (1953) Ego Strength (Colligan & Offord, 1987b), and MacAndrew's (1965) Alcoholism (Colligan & Offord, 1987a). Although their norms were not widely adopted, their efforts further sensitized other MMPI researchers to the need for contemporary norms. Readers interested in studying the Colligan et al. data can do so by referring to their useful text (Colligan et al., 1989) containing numerous conversion tables that compare the original norms with their contemporary sample. However, readers should remember that their sampling is not representative of the U.S. population. Readers also may be interested in the studies of Colligan and his associates at the Mayo Clinic who examined the MMPI profiles of 50,000 medical patients in one of the largest studies ever conducted (Swenson, Pearson, & Osborne, 1973). A more recent follow-up investigation to this large scale study involved the examination of the relationship between a sample of family medicine outpatients using new normative tables of uniform T-scores. Their results showed that contemporary medical outpatients produced profiles significantly different from the general population norm for the MMPI-2 (Colligan et al., 2008). For a more representative national sample, the MMPI-2 was developed and will be described later in this chapter.

The expansion of the MMPI into settings such as general medicine, forensic evaluation, outpatient psychotherapy, assessment of disability and personnel screening, has accentuated the inadequacy of the original norms. It appears that the original normals reflected a fixed reference group rather than a true normative sample, and the practical implications of such a major deficiency are important to consider. For example, because normals would score slightly higher on the test (Pancoast & Archer, 1989), they were vulnerable to being "screened out" of sensitive employment positions (e.g. flight crews, law enforcement and firefighter candidates, and nuclear power plant operators) when strict cut scores were used. Another problem in the use of the original normal groups was the double duty they were forced to perform. That is, although the item responses by the normals provided the needed contrast for the original criterion groups on which the MMPI clinical scales were developed, this use made the normals inappropriate for the establishment of test norms:

> By making the Minnesota normals serve as both a source of contrast for pathological samples and the reference for normative standards, the latter function was compromised. Forcing the normals to perform this double duty, in effect, purged them of their normal levels of abnormality.
>
> (Nichols, 1992b, p. 562; see also Pancoast & Archer, 1989)

In reality, there was a dearth of funds available to Hathaway and McKinley to develop an adequate normative sample and to pursue further cross-validation studies because of the economic depression at that time (Butcher, Dahlstrom, Graham, Tellegen, Dahlstrom, & Kaemmer, 2001). Nevertheless, by not cross-validating using a different sample of normals to establish the normative standard, Hathaway and McKinley introduced a serious constructional deficiency in the design of the test. The importance of proper cross-validation is well recognized, but the test constructors did not cross-validate the original keying of items (Helmes & Reddon, 1993). An important consequence of omitting a cross-validation sample involves the basic metric or measurement unit that the MMPI uses to indicate deviation from the norm. Dahlstrom and Tellegen (1993, p. 3) stated:

> The effect of such an omission would be to anchor the T-score values on each of the basic scales *too low* and to employ a T-score unit that was *too short,* because the standard deviations would be artificially small on these scales. The impact of

inappropriate anchoring and scaling on the scales of the MMPI would be to introduce an excess of false positive scores (i.e. some individuals who are not pathological would earn significantly elevated *T*-scores on one or more of the profile scales.

Another factor that seems to have slightly affected the original MMPI norms relates to the frequency of items omitted by the original normals. Pancoast and Archer (1989) reported a high rate of item omissions (14 items for men and 15 items for women) as calculated from the item endorsement frequencies presented by Dahlstrom and Welsh (1960). The original MMPI test instructions permitted participants to omit items, whereas later instructions discouraged such omissions. Later samples of adult normals probably reflect an increased compliance with these later instructions, given that participants omit very few items (e.g. Clopton & Neuringer, 1977). For example, in their study of 1,243 family medicine outpatients, Colligan et al. (2008) found 47 percent of the women and 55 percent of the men left no items unanswered, and 32 percent of both men and women left fewer than five items unanswered. The effects on the original norms from item omissions are estimated to have lowered mean *T*-scores by about one *T*-score (Pancoast & Archer, 1989). This would still leave about a four *T*-score difference, on average, between subsequent groups of normals and the original group; thereby supporting the idea that the original normals were atypical of the general population.

Another important change to note is that the re-standardization sample for the MMPI-2 produced very different raw score distributions from the original standardization group. The MMPI-2 clinical scale raw-score means are generally higher than the mean values for the original sample, and the magnitude of the differences varies across scales. As Tellegen and Ben-Porath (1993) point out, "MMPI-2 *T*-score profiles are, as a result, not only less elevated than their MMPI counterparts, but MMPI and MMPI-2 profiles differ to some degree in overall configuration or shape" (p. 490). Dahlstrom and Tellegen (1993, p. 3) stated that:

> It is possible that the adults in the MMPI-2 re-standardization samples were more willing to give definitive answers to the component items in the inventory than was the case in the original normative groups. If so, this effect would also serve to raise the raw scores and lower the *T*-scores in the norms for the MMPI-2.

The differences in MMPI-2 profile codetypes produced by using a new sample of normals and a different metric (uniform v. linear *T*-scores) will be further discussed in Chapter 2.

Finally, the decision to exclude from the normal sample anyone "under a physician's care" may have contributed to the sample's problematic nature. As Nichols (1992b) pointed out, this criterion was not operative in the revision of the MMPI leading to the MMPI-2. Excluding all participants under a physician's care introduces more atypicality into the original normal group.

In addition to inappropriate and obsolete norms, other internal problems affected contemporary use of the MMPI. Many items had become outdated and difficult to understand or were objectionable to individuals completing the test. For example, many test takers found some items pertaining to bodily functions to be intrusive or offensive. Many items asking test takers about their religious beliefs were also experienced as offensive by some people. The need to modernize the language (e.g. eliminate sexist language) or improve the grammar in many items had also long been recognized. Another complaint voiced by some test takers referred to the 16 repeated items (Gallucci, 1986); these test takers were irked by their perception that these items were put into the test to entrap them (actually, as previously mentioned, the items were repeated to facilitate early machine scoring).

A problem invisible to test takers but noticeable to test interpreters was the lack of percentile equivalency across the linear T distributions for the standard scales, thereby making it difficult to make percentile inferences from scale elevations (Caldwell, 1991; Tellegen & Ben-Porath, 1992; Ward, 1991). The need for a means to directly compare scores across different scales was evident but was not possible with the original MMPI (see "Uniform T-Scores" later in this chapter for a more detailed explanation of T-scores).

Finally, the last reason for revising the MMPI stemmed from the need to revitalize the existing item pool by introducing items and scales that reflect more current diagnostic and therapeutic concerns (Duckworth, 1991a). For example, items relevant to substance abuse, family functioning, readiness for treatment or rehabilitation, and one's ability to return to work were needed. Additionally, scales that could augment the existing validity scales in detecting unreliable and invalid profiles would enhance the usefulness of the instrument. Toward all these ends, the MMPI re-standardization project was initiated.

MMPI Re-Standardization: The MMPI-2

The project to re-standardize the MMPI began in 1982 with the re-standardization committee consisting of James N. Butcher, PhD, W. Grant Dahlstrom, PhD, John R. Graham, PhD, Auke Tellegen, PhD, and Beverly Kaemmer. The MMPI-2 was published in 1989, along with new test materials that consisted of hand-scoring templates, new answer and profile forms, new test booklets, and different computer-scoring options, all of which are described in Chapter 2. A new MMPI-2 *Manual* was also published (Butcher et al., 1989, 2001). It describes the MMPI-2 as "a broad-band test designed to assess a number of the major patterns of personality and psychological disorders." The copyright holder for the test is the University of Minnesota Press and its licensed distributor is Pearson Assessments (PearsonClinical.com). The original MMPI was discontinued by the publisher in 1999 and is no longer available. The MMPI-2, which is the first revision of the test since its original publication in 1942, is intended for use with adults aged 18 and older.

The MMPI-2 is not intended for use with adolescents. It was recognized by the MMPI-2 committee that adult norms would not be applicable to adolescents (Archer, 1984, 1987, 1988, 1997). A separate revision of the test was conducted for the sole purpose of developing an adolescent instrument derived from the MMPI-2 and was named the MMPI-A (Adolescent). The committee charged with developing the MMPI-A consisted of James N. Butcher, Caroline L. Williams, John R. Graham, Robert P. Archer, Auke Tellegen, and Yossef S. Ben-Porath. The test was released in 1992 (Butcher et al., 1992). A normative sample representative of the general teenage population was recognized as important for standardizing the MMPI-A, and a shorter version of the test was also considered to be an improvement given that the basic validity and clinical scales were essentially uncompromised. The MMPI-A *Manual* contains detailed information on this instrument (Butcher et al., 1992). Readers seeking a comprehensive treatment of the MMPI-A may consult Robert Archer's (2005) *MMPI-A: Assessing Adolescent Psychopathology* (3rd ed.) and Butcher and Williams' (2000) *Essentials of MMPI-2 and MMPI-A Interpretation* (2nd ed.).

The 478-item MMPI-A is intended for adolescents between the ages of 14 and 18, although some individuals who are less than 14 years old can be administered the MMPI-A if they possess the necessary reading level and comprehension abilities, as well as the necessary attention span and willingness to complete a lengthy inventory. Archer's (2005) textbook should be consulted for MMPI-A administration guidelines. Because the adolescent norms include 18-year-olds, the clinician who is testing an 18-year-old may use either the adolescent or the adult version of the MMPI-2. A general rule as to which test to administer involves assessing characteristics such as the person's reading level and ability, as well as whether the adolescent is living at home. In general, if the 18-year-old is living outside of the home and working or attending college, the adult version of the test is indicated; whereas, if the person is not emancipated from his or her home environment, the MMPI-A should be considered.

To summarize, the MMPI-2 re-standardization project ensured continuity with the original MMPI by minimizing changes in the composition of the original validity and clinical scales. This meant leaving the *K*-correction factor intact. A contemporary sample of normals replaced earlier outdated norms with new clinical data collected concurrently to assess the validity of new and modified scales. Items were replaced or modified in accordance with the mission of modernizing the language of the test. New scales were created in order to measure contemporary clinical problems and, for this reason, new items replaced many rarely scored or obsolete items. An improved metric, uniform *T*-scores, replaced linear *T*-scores to allow test interpreters to more accurately compare scale scores and their associated percentile ranks.

The re-standardization project was successful in meeting its goal of maintaining continuity with the original test. Despite initial concerns about the MMPI-2 revision (e.g. Adler, 1990), practitioners generally have adopted the modified test. In a survey of the entire membership of the Society of Personality Assessment regarding the use of the MMPI-2, Webb, Levitt, and Rojdev (1993) found a significant adoption of the MMPI-2 since its publication, with a trend they interpreted as suggesting that the majority of practitioners would be using the instrument within 6 months of their survey. Indeed, it does appear that the majority of individuals took advantage of the changes offered by the MMPI-2 (Ben-Porath, 1993; Beverly Kaemmer, personal communication, March 25, 2013).

Experimental Form (AX) and the MMPI-2 Booklet

An experimental booklet (Form AX) was developed for the purpose of testing a new group of normal participants and was the basis for developing the new MMPI-2 booklet. Form AX included all 550 original MMPI items, followed by an additional 154 new experimental items, although some item order changes occurred. Specifically, the 16 repeated items eliminated in the Form AX left gaps in the item slots that were filled in with some of the experimental items. This was done to preserve the traditional scoring keys for the original scales (W. G. Dahlstrom, personal communication, October 29, 1994). Therefore, the flow of the original items was slightly interrupted by the introduction of the new items, although probably without much consequence.

The re-standardization committee identified several items that required modification to improve clarity. Eighty-two of the original MMPI items were rewritten for Form AX in order to improve or modernize their language and were empirically studied by Ben-Porath and Butcher (1989) to assess the psychometric impact of these modifications. These authors administered Form AX to college students along with the original MMPI one week later (in a counterbalanced design) to determine the effects of the item changes. They also administered the original test twice to a separate group of participants to serve as a baseline for comparison purposes. Although there were some minor shifts in item endorsements (only nine items), "no significant changes were noted among items rewritten due to sexist language, minor rewording, grammatical changes, ambiguous items, or religious content" (Ben-Porath & Butcher, 1989, p. 650). Their data also showed that no item-scale correlations changed significantly as a result of rewriting the items. In effect, they found that they could improve the face validity of many items without unduly affecting the operating characteristics of the scales. Ultimately, 14 of the 82 rewritten items were eliminated, leaving 68 intact in the final MMPI-2 booklet. It should also be noted that 47 of the 154 experimental items in Form AX did not survive into the final MMPI-2 booklet (Nichols, 1992b).

The MMPI-2 booklet also dropped the 16 repeated MMPI items. Often used as a measure for test response consistency (Buechley & Ball, 1952; the test-retest [TR] index), these repeated items were replaced with a new scale, the Variable Response Inconsistency scale (*VRIN*), designed to assess inconsistent responding. This scale is described in Chapter 3.

The basic validity and standard clinical scales were essentially unaffected by item deletions, even though 13 items were eliminated from the standard clinical and validity scales: four items were deleted from the *F* scale; one item was deleted from Scale 1 (*Hs*); three items were deleted from Scale 2 (*D*); four items were deleted from Scale 5 (*Mf*); and one item was deleted from Scale 0 (*Si*). Table 1.1 allows the reader to inspect the MMPI-2 changes and deletions and their effects on the standard scales.

The re-standardization committee decided that many original MMPI items that were not scored on any basic validity or clinical scale should be eliminated and replaced with newer items that would allow additional scales to be constructed. Therefore, 77 items contained in the last 167 items on the MMPI were dropped and replaced with 89 items intended for use with new scales (Greene, 1991a). The total number of items in the MMPI-2 is 567 (one item more than the original test), and 21 of the items are so-called non-working or non-scored items, that is, items not scored on any of the scales listed in the MMPI-2 *Manual* (Butcher et al., 1989). These extra items were included as "possible replacements for problematic items or as enhancements to the existing item pool" (Dahlstrom, 1993, p. 3).

The reader is reminded that it was the 704-item Form AX that was administered to the sample of normal participants in the re-standardization project. Although the revised item pool in the MMPI-2 is considered a definite improvement by most test users, the revision is not without its critics. Nichols (1992b, p. 563) stated:

> Although the new items expand clinically important areas of content like substance abuse, marital relations, and suicide, their phrasings do not always reflect the smooth, worn quality of common speech. The three new suicide statements, for

Table 1.1 Item changes and deletions and their effects on standard scales

	Number of Items			Types of Changes			
Scale	Deleted	Remaining	Changed	A	B	C	D
L		15	2	1	1		
F	4	60	12	1	5	6	
K		30	1		1		
Hs	1	32	5		1	3	1
D	3	57	2	1	1		
Hy		60	9		4	2	3
Pd		50	4		2	1	1
Mf	4	56	6	1	2	1	2
Pa		40	2	1			1
Pt		48	2			1	1
Sc		78	13		1	7	5
Ma		46	7	4	2	1	
Si	1	69	6		3	2	1
Not any of the above			16	3	7	3	3

Note: A = elimination of possibly sexist wording; B = modernization of idioms and usage; C = grammatical clarification (tense, voice, minor additions, and deletions); D = simplifications.

Source: From *MMPI®-2 (Minnesota Multiphasic Personality Inventory®-2) Manual for Administration, Scoring, and Interpretation, Revised Edition.* Copyright © 1993 by the Regents of the University of Minnesota. Used by permission of the University of Minnesota Press. All rights reserved. "MMPI" and "Minnesota Multiphasic Personality Inventory" are trademarks owned by the Regents of the University of Minnesota.

example, employ the fixed operative expression, "kill(ing) myself," in preference to more varied and less violent ones like "want to die," "end it all," "commit suicide," "get it over with." Most of the hundreds of scales developed from the original item pool are relatively intact unless they included significant religious content or were drawn mainly from the last 200 items of the original MMPI. In order to be scored, however, the older keys must be translated into MMPI-2 item numbers, a process aided by an appendix in the *Manual.*

The loss of certain items in the MMPI-2 booklet has affected some special scales that were used in the original test, as noted by Nichols (1992a, 1992b). Some of the affected scales are discussed in Chapter 8 where the supplementary scales are described in detail. Readers interested in more detailed information about MMPI-2 item characteristics are encouraged to consult Dahlstrom's (1993) supplement to the MMPI-2 *Manual.*

New Normative Sample

The most significant change in the MMPI-2 is the replacement of the earlier outdated norms. The MMPI-2 norms are based on the responses of 2,600 adults (1,462 women and 1,138 men) between the ages of 18 and 85, who were paid volunteers recruited by a variety of methods, including newspaper advertisements and random mailing solicitations from directories and advertising lists (Butcher et al., 1989). Initially, approximately 2,900 participants were tested, but the following participants were eliminated: those who omitted 40 or more of the 704 items in Form AX or those who had a very high score on the *F* scale (20 or more) or a high score on a new "back page" *F* scale, called *F*-Back (*FB*), which was designed for Form AX (*FB* is described in Chapter 3). Participants who did not provide adequate biographical information or omitted other informational forms were also excluded from the final sample. The 2,600 participants were selected from seven states: California, Minnesota, North Carolina, Ohio, Pennsylvania, Virginia, and Washington. A small proportion of the sample included participants selected from military bases and a Federal Indian Reservation. Heterosexual couples (823 men, 832 women) were included in the sample, and were administered collateral questionnaires that included a measure of significant recent life changes (completed by the total sample) and an instrument designed to measure their perception of their partner or spouse and their level of relationship satisfaction (Butcher et al.,1989). The ethnic diversity of the new sample is greater than the original sample, as it includes African Americans, Hispanics, and Native Americans. However, in comparison with the 1990 census data reported in the MMPI-2 *Manual*, it appears that Asian Americans and Hispanics are underrepresented. The age distribution also shows that men and women in the age range of 18 to 19 are underrepresented, as are older adults between the ages of 70 and 84. As noted by Friedman et al. (2001), the re-standardization project included adults as old as 85 years of age, but the 80–85 age range represented only 0.8 percent of the total sample, as compared with 1.6 percent and 2.7 percent of the 1990 census data for men and women, respectively. It appears that older adults were generally underrepresented in the new sample. As test takers approach age 70, the normative data tends to be under-representative of the true numbers of that age cohort, according to the 1980 census data. There is an impact of age on MMPI/MMPI-2 scores, with base-rate shifts reflecting the normal process of concern with physical health that is associated with aging and with the common problems of impulse control and identity concerns affecting younger populations.

Peaks on Scales 1 (*Hs*) and 2 (*D*) are relatively uncommon early in life but become more common later. The reverse is true for Scales 4 (*Pd*) and 8 (*Sc*). The reader is referred to Greene (2011), who clearly shows the relationship between age and different codetypes. In general, because older individuals obtain higher scores on scales measuring physical health concerns, a profile with moderate to marked elevations on the Depression scale and/or the Hypochondriasis scale should be adjusted and interpreted less pathologically than the same profile from a young adult. Colligan and colleagues (Colligan et al., 1989; Colligan & Offord, 1992) expressed similar concerns, and the reader is referred to their data because their contemporary normative sample much more closely matches the 1980 U.S. census data, especially as it pertains to older adults.

The most notable difference between the re-standardization group and the 1990 census data (as reported in the *Manual* revision of 2001) centers on the educational differences and the generally higher socioeconomic status (SES) of the re-standardization sample. Examination of Table 3 in the 2001 MMPI-2 *Manual* shows that well-educated participants are notably overrepresented in the new sample (as compared with 1998 census data) at the expense of individuals with a high school education or less. For example, 27.2 percent of the male and 26.7 percent of the female participants were college graduates, as compared with 15.6 percent and 14.9 percent of men and women, respectively, for the general population in 1998. This level of education of the new normative sample is vastly higher than the original norm group, which overrepresented lower educational and occupational groups (Dahlstrom, 1993) and is more than two years higher than other estimates of the mean years of education for adults over the age of 24 (Schinka & LaLone, 1997). The general skew in the new sample toward upper socioeconomic levels in the normative group is well recognized by researchers and expert users of the test. (Note: The 2001 *Manual* revision omits the data for occupations and income distribution.) However, different concerns have been expressed about the meaning of this skew. The MMPI-2 *Manual* (Butcher, Dahlstrom, Graham, Tellegen, & Kaemmer, 1989) attempts to minimize the importance of the skew by stating that "the distributions of the normative samples on these various indexes of socioeconomic status appear to be closer to those of the typical subjects currently being asked to take the MMPI in various settings around the United States" (p. 5). Precisely what constitutes the "typical" participant being asked to complete the MMPI-2 is not specified in the *Manual* and is not otherwise known. Participants being tested for Social Security benefits, or Supplementary Security Income (SSI), as well as clients in various public agencies and in state mental hospitals, typically are of a lower SES and do not match very well to the socioeconomic characteristics of the current standardization group (Caldwell, 1991; Duckworth, 1991a, 1991b).

Duckworth (1991a, 1991b) and Caldwell (1991) suggested that the higher average educational and occupational levels of the new normative sample may handicap the utility of the MMPI-2 in populations with low SES. Friedman and Jaffe (1993) studied a sample of 291 disability-benefit applicants, who had a mean educational level of 10.5 years for men and 11.0 years for women. The mean MMPI-2 F-scale linear T-score for men was 110 and 96 for women. However, when Table K in the MMPI-2 *Manual* (Butcher et al., 1989) was used to transform MMPI-2 T-scores into MMPI linear T-scores, the T-score on the F scale fell to 97 and 84 for men and women, respectively; this use of the transformation table substantially reduced the disability-benefit participants' F-scores. SES correlated negatively with F-scale elevations, a finding consistent with Dahlstrom and Tellegen's (1993) data in their manual supplement reporting the relation of MMPI-2 patterns to levels of education and occupation. When testing a low SES individual, the reader is advised to be aware that the positive skew in the MMPI-2 normative sample toward upper SES may inflate the impression of psychopathology. Dahlstrom and Tellegen's (1993) data showed distinct differences between the various socioeconomic levels of normal participants. Using a multivariate technique, they were able to estimate the influence of the differences in age, education, gender, race, and occupational level on the basic clinical and validity MMPI-2 scale scores. For 6 of the 13 standard scales (F, K, Hs, Pt, Sc, Si) Dahlstrom and Tellegen found that the largest component of variance came from the educational-level differences. For example, men and women with less education scored higher on the L and F scales and lower on the K scale, whereas on the clinical scales, men and women with less education scored significantly higher on Scales 1, 7, 8, and 0. Men and women's scores on Scale 5 (Mf) are also noticeably affected by occupational and educational status. Men with higher SES and women with less education tend to produce higher Scale 5 scores. The reader is referred to Figs. 1.1–1.4, reprinted from Dahlstrom and Tellegen (1993). These figures graphically show the differences in scores for men and women across different educational and occupational levels.

Even so, while differences between these groups do exist, they are generally small, and personality differences are more likely to account for any given MMPI-2 profile than are general background factors (Dahlstrom & Tellegen, 1993).

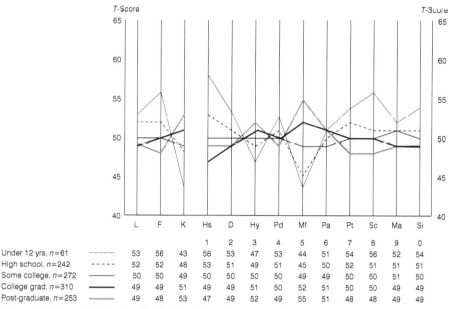

		L	F	K	Hs	D	Hy	Pd	Mf	Pa	Pt	Sc	Ma	Si
					1	2	3	4	5	6	7	8	9	0
Under 12 yrs, n=61	··············	53	56	43	58	53	47	53	44	51	54	56	52	54
High school, n=242	- - - -	52	52	48	53	51	49	51	45	50	52	51	51	51
Some college, n=272	——	50	50	49	50	50	50	50	49	49	50	50	51	50
College grad, n=310	━━━	49	49	51	49	49	51	50	52	51	50	50	49	49
Post-graduate, n=253	⚍⚍⚍	49	48	53	47	49	52	49	55	51	48	48	49	49

Figure 1.1 Mean MMPI-2 Profiles for Men by Education Level

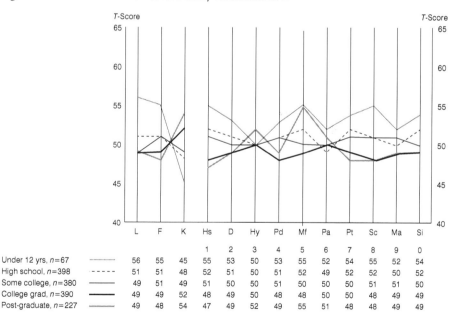

		L	F	K	Hs	D	Hy	Pd	Mf	Pa	Pt	Sc	Ma	Si
					1	2	3	4	5	6	7	8	9	0
Under 12 yrs, n=67	··············	56	55	45	55	53	50	53	55	52	54	55	52	54
High school, n=398	- - - -	51	51	48	52	51	50	51	52	49	52	52	50	52
Some college, n=380	——	49	51	49	51	50	50	51	50	50	50	51	51	50
College grad, n=390	━━━	49	49	52	48	49	50	48	48	50	50	48	49	49
Post-graduate, n=227	⚍⚍⚍	49	48	54	47	49	52	49	55	51	48	48	49	49

Figure 1.2 Mean MMPI-2 Profiles for Women by Education Level

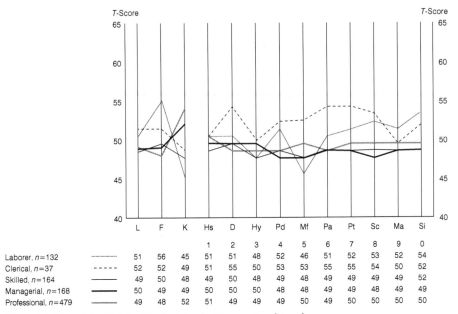

		L	F	K	Hs	D	Hy	Pd	Mf	Pa	Pt	Sc	Ma	Si
					1	2	3	4	5	6	7	8	9	0
Laborer, n=132	··············	51	56	45	51	51	48	52	46	51	52	53	52	54
Clerical, n=37	- - - - -	52	52	49	51	55	50	53	53	55	55	54	50	52
Skilled, n=164	————	49	50	48	49	50	48	49	48	49	49	49	49	52
Managerial, n=168	━━━━	50	49	49	50	50	50	48	48	49	49	48	49	49
Professional, n=479	⁓⁓⁓⁓	49	48	52	51	49	49	49	50	49	50	50	50	50

Figure 1.3 Mean MMPI-2 Profiles for Men by Occupational Level

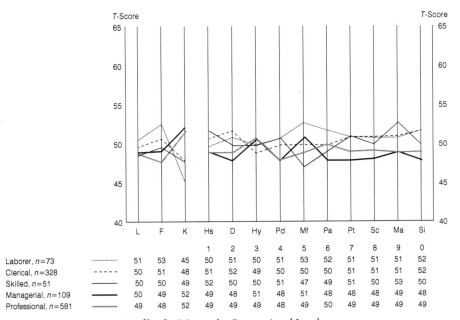

		L	F	K	Hs	D	Hy	Pd	Mf	Pa	Pt	Sc	Ma	Si
					1	2	3	4	5	6	7	8	9	0
Laborer, n=73	··············	51	53	45	50	51	50	51	53	52	51	51	51	52
Clerical, n=328	· - - - -	50	51	48	51	52	49	50	50	50	51	51	51	52
Skilled, n=51	————	50	50	49	52	50	50	51	47	49	51	50	53	50
Managerial, n=109	━━━━	50	49	52	49	48	51	48	51	48	48	48	49	48
Professional, n=581	⁓⁓⁓⁓	49	48	52	49	49	49	48	49	50	49	49	49	49

Figure 1.4 Mean MMPI-2 Profiles for Women by Occupational Level

Figures 1.3 and 1.4 source: From *Manual Supplement: Socioeconomic Status and the MMPI-2: The Relation of MMPI-2 Patterns to Levels of Education and Occupation*, by W. G. Dahlstrom & A. Tellegen, 1993, Minneapolis: University of Minnesota Press. Copyright © 1993 by the Regents of the University of Minnesota Press. All rights reserved. "MMPI" and "Minnesota Multiphasic Personality Inventory" are trademarks owned by the Regents of the University of Minnesota.

Schinka and LaLone (1997) conducted scale comparisons between the re-standardization sample and a census-matched subsample with estimates of educational level for 1993 provided by the U.S. Bureau of the Census. The census-matched subsample drawn from the larger re-standardization sample appears to accurately reflect an acceptable representation of the then current U.S. population, despite the overestimates of education previously described.

Uniform *T*-Scores

Linear vs. Uniform *T*-Scores

The raw scores of the basic MMPI/MMPI-2 scales all have different means and standard deviations as well as different ranges of scores in any normative sample. These statistics reflect differing numbers of items in the several scales as well as the frequency of item endorsement. Thus, to evaluate the clinical significance of an individual's set of scores, it is necessary to compare each score to its mean and judge the magnitude of the difference using the standard deviation. Further, to compare scores on different scales, it is desirable to transform the scores to a common metric. This has been done traditionally with the MMPI scales by converting the score on each scale to standardized *T*-scores having a mean of 50 and a standard deviation of 10. That is to say,

$$T = 50 + 10 \ (X{-}M) \ / \ SD, \tag{1}$$

where X is the raw score of a participant on the scale in question, M is the mean, and SD is the standard deviation of the scale in the normative or reference sample.

The reference sample used for the computation of *T*-scores determines the elevation and the extent of the *T*-score spread. To the extent that the normative or reference sample is inadequate, the *T*-scores will be inappropriate. As noted previously, the original normative sample differed from later normative samples, both demographically and with respect to the means and standard deviations of a number of scales.

The linear *T*-score transformation of raw scores has a number of advantages: (a) it is easy to use computationally and quickly conveys some notion of where the score stands in reference to the normative sample; (b) equal raw score differences on a particular scale are maintained as equal differences on its transformed scale; (c) all scales expressed in *T*-scores are equated with respect to their mean and standard deviation and, hence, are to some extent comparable; and (d) the linear equation allows for easy extrapolation beyond those scores actually obtained in the reference group. Such extrapolation is extremely important for tests such as the MMPI that are intended for use with pathological groups whose scores may be expected to go much higher than the reference group.

Linear *T*-scores also have two major disadvantages: (a) standardized *T*-score scales are not fully equivalent (differences in the shapes of the raw distributions as measured by skew-ness and kurtosis remain after the linear transformations), and (b) assumptions based on a normal distribution to the effect that a *T*-score of 70 or higher encompasses only about 2.5 percent of the reference population do not usually hold in non-normal distributions such as those of the MMPI/MMPI-2 basic scales. Furthermore, the percentage meeting this criterion is not the same from one scale to another when they differ in terms of skew-ness. The same linear *T*-score can correspond to different percentile ranks for different scales. In other words, linear *T*-scores from different scales are not "percentile comparable."

Normalized T-Scores

Because of the above difficulties and limitations, Colligan et al. (1980) suggested that it would be advisable to normalize scores on the clinical scales of the MMPI and developed such scores on a new reference sample of 1,408 normal men and women living in the Midwest (Colligan et al., 1983). This transformation involves fitting the raw scores of the sample to a normal distribution and then converting these scores to a mean of 50 and standard deviation of 10. They handled the problem of providing normative values for raw scores falling outside the range of values in the reference sample by using a special conversion formula based on the power transformation methods suggested by Box and Cox (1964).

The main problem with the normal transformation of scores from a raw score distribution skewed to the right (a characteristic of MMPI scores) is that it spreads out scores at the lower end of the scale while crunching together those at the upper end. Thus, the differentiation among high scores found in clinical populations is reduced.

Uniform T-Scores

The MMPI-2 re-standardization committee (Butcher et al., 1989) decided to continue using the linear rather than the normalized *T*-scale transformation, but with some modification to improve the percentile comparability of scores across scales. Changing to normalized scores would be too radical, necessitating "substantial changes in the frequencies and clinical implications of elevated *T*-scores and *T*-score profiles" (Tellegen & Ben-Porath, 1992, p. 147).

Hence, they derived a new standardized score, the uniform *T*-score, to make the percentile values of the *T*-scores more similar across the eight clinical scales (Scales 1–4 and 6–9) and between men and women, but with as little departure as possible from the original linear *T*-scores. Scales 5 and 0 were not considered clinical scales and hence were omitted from these computations. The reason given by Tellegen and Ben-Porath (1992, p. 146) for omitting these scales was that these two scales do not represent clinical constructs. They were also derived differently than were the clinical scales and are less skewed. These two scales, as well as the traditional validity scales (*L*, *F*, and *K*), continue to be transformed to linear *T*-scores. Their use in conjunction with uniform *T*-scores creates no problem according to Tellegen and Ben-Porath.

Three major steps were involved in the uniform *T*-score transformation:

1   The 16 raw-score distributions, eight scales each for men and women, were first transformed to the traditional linear *T*-scores. Then for each of the 101 percentile values (0.5, 1.0, 2.0, 3.0 ... 97.0, 98.0, 99.0, 99.5), the corresponding linear *T*-score for each of the 16 scales was obtained by interpolation. The 16 *T*-scores for each percentile value were then averaged to obtain composite scores. These 101 average *T*-score values essentially define the prototypical linear *T*-score distribution to be approximated by the uniform *T*-scores.

2. The scores resulting from Step 1 proved inadequate without further work. It was necessary to obtain the raw scores corresponding to the *T*-scores derived in Step 1. Then, by interpolation, the raw-score estimates corresponding to integer *T*-score values were derived. A round of interpolations was conducted to obtain the raw scores for each scale corresponding to the 52 integer composite scores ranging from 31 to 82 in the normative sample.

3. If uniform *T*-scores were needed for only those raw scores that actually occurred in the normative sample, it could have been accomplished at this point by further interpolation to provide integer *T*-scores for each integer raw score. However, scores well outside this range (e.g. *T* values above 90) are common in clinical samples and could not have been derived. To handle all possible raw scores, a regression equation was needed for each scale that would adequately fit the 52 target values obtained in Step 2 and would allow for extrapolation for more extreme raw-score values. For this purpose, a polynomial regression equation was sought that would become linear for high values of *X*. The equation used was as follows: .

$$\text{Uniform } T\text{-score} = B_0 + B_1 X + B_2 D^2 + B_3 D^3, \tag{2}$$

where *X* is the raw score to be transformed; B_0 is the intercept; B_1, B_2, and B_3 are regression weights, and $(D = C - X)$ if *X* is less than *C*, and 0 if *X* is greater than or equal to *C*. The value of *C* selected was the raw score for each scale corresponding to a composite *T*-score of 60. Putting it differently, the quadratic and cubic components of the above equations cease having any effect on the uniform *T*-scores above *T*-60 and thereafter, the uniform *T* values are linearly related to the raw scores.

The 16 regression equations represented by Equation 2 applied to the raw scores on each scale provide very good fits to the 52 scores of the prototype uniform *T* scale. The multiple correlations were all .998 or higher. These equations provided the non-*K*-corrected uniform *T*-score look-up tables included in the MMPI-2 *Manual*. The same method was used to derive the *K*-corrected clinical scale scores and the new content scale scores, in each case using the same target composite linear *T*-score values.

The uniform *T*-scores, like the linear *T*-scores, of the eight clinical scales are skewed to the right but, unlike the linear *T*-score scales, they are all skewed to approximately the same moderate degree. It can be argued that the moderate skew of the uniform *T*-scores is appropriate because some skew is to be expected for scales designed to tap dysfunctional attributes when used on a non-screened sample (Tellegen & Ben-Porath, 1992, pp. 150–154).

Equivalence in percentile values has been especially improved for the extremes of the distribution (see Table 1.2). For example, linear *T*-scores at the 95th percentile varied from 66 on Scale 3 to 70 on Scale 8 for men and 71 on Scale 8 for women. The corresponding range for uniform *T*-scores is 67 to 69. As Tellegen and Ben-Porath (1992) pointed out, comparability has been achieved "without requiring the marked departures from traditional linear *T*-score distributions that would have been imposed by normalization" (p. 154).

It should be noted that uniform *T*-70 is at the 96th percentile, whereas uniform *T*-65 is at the 92nd. Table 1.3 shows different uniform *T*-score values with the corresponding percentile equivalents. Butcher and Williams (1992) recommended that a uniform

Table 1.2 T-score equivalents of percentiles: ranges of obtained linear and uniform *T* (*UT*) Scores

Percentile	Range of Linear T-Scores	Range of UT Scores
10	37–40	38–39
20	41–42	41–42
30	43–45	44
40	45–18	46–47
50	48–50	48–50
60	50–52	51–52
70	53–55	54–55
80	57–59	57–59
90	62–64	62–64
95	66–71	67–69
99	73–83	77–80

Note: The ranges are those of the non-*K*-corrected *T*-scores obtained for Scales 1–4 and 6–9 in the MMPI-2 normative samples. From "The New Uniform *T* Scores for the MMPI-2: Rationale, Derivation, and Appraisal," by A. Tellegen & Y. S. Ben-Porath, 1992, *Psychological Assessment: A Journal of Consulting and Clinical Psychology, 4*, 145–155. Copyright © 1992 by the American Psychological Association. Reprinted with permission.

Table 1.3 Percentile equivalents of uniform *T* (*UT*) Scores

UT Score	Percentile Equivalent
30	<1
35	4
40	15
45	34
50	55
55	73
60	85
65	92
70	96
75	98
80	>99

Note: The percentiles are those of the targeted *UT* Scores. From "The New Uniform *T*-Scores for the MMPI-2: Rationale, Derivation, and Appraisal," by A. Tellegen & Y. S. Ben-Porath, 1992, *Psychological Assessment: A Journal of Consulting and Clinical Psychology, 4*, 145–155. Copyright © 1992 by the American Psychological Association. Reprinted with permission.

T-score of 65 or greater be used to demarcate the "clinical range." This recommendation stems from studies showing 65 to be the optimal score level for separating known clinical groups from the MMPI-2 re-standardization sample.

Although derivation of the uniform *T*-scores appears complicated, their distribution is essentially that of a composite linear MMPI *T*-score. It has been shown that relatively small differences occur, as was intended, when traditional linear *T*-scores are compared with uniform *T*-scores on the MMPI-2 for both normals (Dahlstrom & Tellegen, 1993, Figs. 1–16) and clinical participants (Edwards, Morrison, & Weissman, 1993). Much larger differences occur when linear *T*-score values derived from the original Hathaway MMPI norms are compared with either the linear *T*-scores or the uniform *T*-scores derived from the MMPI-2 re-standardization sample.

2 Administration, Scoring, and Codetyping

Forms of the MMPI-2 and MMPI-2-RF

The most commonly used version of the MMPI-2 is the printed booklet form, which appears in either softcover or hardcover form, and which contains 567 items. Both are reusable and are commonly used for individual or group administrations. The hardcover booklet is more commonly used for laptop administration when hard surfaces such as a desk are unavailable. Whereas the softcover booklet requires a separate answer sheet, the hardcover booklet uses one that is inserted over two pegs at the back, and follows a step-down format whereby each consecutive page reveals a new column of answer spaces matched to the booklet page of corresponding items. The columns use alternating shades of a light blue and non-shaded blue to assist the reader in matching the answer sheet to the appropriate page in the booklet. Because the step-down format reveals only one column of items and answer spaces at a time, the likelihood of misplacing responses to items is reduced. This is especially useful when testing confused patients or individuals unaccustomed to taking tests. The order of the items is the same in both the softcover and hardcover booklets. Separate sets of templates are needed for hand scoring these two forms of the MMPI-2. Therefore, the answer sheets for the soft- and hardcover forms are not interchangeable. Scoring the test is described in more detail later in this chapter. The usual administration time for the MMPI-2 booklet is between 90 and 120 minutes, although limited reading ability or non-cooperativeness may extend test-taking time.

The CD version of the MMPI-2 is for individuals with visual impairments, reading difficulties, and physical handicaps (a proctor can record the responses, if necessary). The MMPI-2 audio CD administration time is two hours and 15 minutes, with each item presented twice. In group administration, headphones and separate CD machines are recommended to prevent noise distraction and to allow an individual to replay unanswered items at a later time. It is also important to ensure that the participant is taught how to operate the CD player in order to pause it, for whatever reason, or to return to a previous item. Careful proctoring should be conducted in situations in which individuals are listening to the MMPI-2 CD with headphones. In one instance, a Social Security disability applicant being administered the MMPI-2 in this way replaced the MMPI-2 CD with a music CD, which the applicant found much more entertaining!

The MMPI-2-RF (described in detail in Chapter 11) has 229 fewer items than the MMPI-2, for a total of 338 items. This form is available in a softcover, or durable spiral-bound booklet, but not a hardcover step-down booklet as is available for the MMPI-2. However, a "Lap Administrator Binder" is available that provides a hard surface when a table or desk is unavailable. The MMPI-2-RF is available only in English. Test completion time of the RF for individuals with normal-range cognitive functioning and reading abilities using a booklet and answer sheet is typically 35–50 minutes, and about 25–35 minutes for a computerized administration (Ben-Porath & Tellegen, 2008, 2011). The English MMPI-2-RF audio CD has an approximate administration time of 80 minutes, with each item presented twice. Given the shortened length of the test, there is no abbreviated version for the MMPI-2-RF as there is for the MMPI-2.

Computer-based administrations are common today, and administration time varies between one to one and a half hours for the MMPI-2. One major advantage to the computer-administered MMPI-2/MMPI-2-RF is efficiency and ease of scoring, although not all participants are comfortable with this type of administration. Spinhoven, Labbe, and Rombouts (1993) reported that although most patients feel favorable about using a computer in a clinical setting, little research has been conducted to assess patient characteristics that could pose potential difficulties in computerized assessments. They suggested conducting an assessment interview to learn how a participant feels about interacting with a computer, as this may have particular importance, for example, in a case of a psychotic patient with delusions/ideas of influence.

In general, clinicians' attitudes toward computer-based testing are positive (Spielberger & Piotrowski, 1990), although questions about the comparability between computer and booklet administrations have been raised. The evidence, however, is skewed toward showing few significant differences between computer and booklet administrations (Butcher, 2009).

More recently, there has been interest in computerized adaptive testing (CAT), which involves the application of the countdown method to reduce the number of items administered in order to reduce administration time. This technique involves the presentation of scale items until the participant endorses a predetermined number that indicates that he or she has either elevated or not elevated a particular scale. Although preliminary in nature, whereas several studies have suggested that adaptive testing may have promise in the future (e.g. Ben-Porath, Slutske, & Butcher, 1989; Butcher, Keller, & Bacon, 1985; Clavelle & Butcher, 1977; Forbey & Ben-Porath, 2007; Forbey, Ben-Porath, & Gartland, 2009; Roper, Ben-Porath, & Butcher, 1991), more recent reviews have shown that this promise remains unfulfilled (Butcher, Perry, & Dean, 2009). An alternative to the countdown method for adaptive testing uses Item Response Theory (IRT). As Forbey, Ben-Porath, and Gartland (2009) point out: the IRT model does not seem to work well for the MMPI-2, most likely due to the multidimensional nature of the MMPI-2 clinical scales. It remains to be seen if IRT will be more efficacious with the more homogeneous scales on the MMPI-2-RF. See Chapter 12 for a fuller discussion of this topic.

Abbreviated and Short Forms

Because the full-length MMPI-2 can require one to one and a half hours or longer to complete, some test users have considered the length of the test prohibitive for practical application, especially with physically disabled or easily fatigued participants. The term *abbreviated form* refers to administering the first 370 items of the MMPI-2 in order to score all of the standard validity and clinical scales. The 370-item abbreviated MMPI-2 can reduce test-taking time, on average, from 20 to 40 minutes. Abbreviating the test administration in this fashion may be indicated when an elderly or enfeebled participant is physically unable to tolerate a longer sitting, or becomes less cooperative over the course of testing. Likewise, a poor reader may struggle for an excessive length of time over the test booklet before completing all of the items. A major disadvantage in eliminating the remaining items, however, is that many of the items scored on the content, Personality Psychopathology Five (PSY-5), supplemental, restructured clinical, and the newer validity scales are found later in the test booklet. It is recommended that whenever possible, the individual complete the entire inventory, even if this requires multiple sittings, unless obvious reasons contraindicate such an effort.

Short forms of the test refer to reduced sets of items on different scales that are thought to be a valid substitute for their corresponding full scales. Most short forms were developed for the original MMPI rather than MMPI-2. However, no effort was made by the MMPI re-standardization committee (Butcher et al., 1989) to preserve any of the MMPI short forms for the MMPI-2. Butcher and Hostetler (1990) concluded that short forms for the MMPI-2 were inadequate measures of the constructs assessed by the full scales. In our opinion, too many factors mitigate against the use of any of the short forms to justify their routine clinical or research use. For example, the codetype correspondence to the full-length MMPI-2 is generally poor, and in shortening the test, many items are eliminated that are needed for scoring the content and supplementary scales, the Harris-Lingoes subscales, and various other special scales.

Investigations of short forms continue to support Alker's (1978) statement that "virtually no convincing evidence is available that the short forms make contributions to clinical decision-making in a fashion that compares favorably on statistical criteria with the full MMPI" (p. 934), and that no one version is clearly superior to any other.

Dahlstrom and Archer (2000) developed a 180-item short form based on the MMPI-2 re-standardization sample and psychiatric patients. They reported the high-point agreement between the MMPI-2 and their short form to be only 50 percent, whereas 2-point codes were congruent in only about one third of the cases. Subsequent to the development of the Dahlstrom and Archer (2000) short form, McGrath, Terranova, Pogge, and Kravic (2003) examined short forms of the MMPI-2 with 216 and 297 items derived from psychiatric inpatients. They concluded that the 216-item short form was not acceptable for either identifying the single most elevated clinical scale in the complete MMPI-2 or in predicting high-point codes. However, their longer 297-item version appears to have advantages over the Dahlstrom and Archer (2000) 180 short form in terms of code pattern congruence with the MMPI-2; but, as compared to administering their first 180 items in Dahlstrom and Archer's (2000) short form, there is more scoring complexity involved in using the MMPI-297. As Cox, Weed, and Butcher (2009) note:

> The MMPI-297 produces *T*-scores that are substantially different from those derived for the complete MMPI-2 and it also demonstrates weaker convergent validity across a number of domains. Additionally, it does not produce estimates of important scales such as $F(p)$, a validity scale, or the restructured scales.

It is readily apparent that one problem common to all the short forms, whether for the original MMPI or the MMPI-2, is the failure to recapture the profile obtained from the full-length test (McLaughlin, Helmes, & Howe, 1983). Whenever a test is shortened, the issue of the effect on its reliability is raised. Streiner and Miller (1986) concluded that no shortened scale will ever favorably compare to the full-length test, and Greene (1982) suggested that we treat shortened MMPI versions as new tests that must be validated individually.

While the above described concerns regarding poor correspondence between full-scale score profiles and estimated profiles appear substantial, there still may be value in using the shortened MMPI-2 180-item form (Dahlstrom & Archer, 2000) for screening psychopathology rather than completely identifying it. Future research will determine the utility of this form, particularly for use with special populations (Friedman et al., 2001; Gass & Gonzalez, 2003).

Foreign Translations

The original MMPI was used in over 65 countries and had more than 115 translations (Butcher & Graham, 1989). The first of these were produced in Italy and Japan in 1948. Since the MMPI was re-standardized in 1989, numerous translation projects have been completed. Numerous translations for the MMPI-2 currently exist in Bulgarian, Chinese, Croatian, Czech, Danish, Dutch/Fleming, French, French-Canadian, German, Greek, Hebrew, Hmong, Hungarian, Italian, Korean, Norwegian, Polish, Swedish, and in Spanish for Spain, Mexico, South and Central America, and the U.S. The MMPI-2 is available in Spanish only in the softcover form. MMPI-2-RF translations are available in Italian, Korean, and in Spanish for Spain, South and Central America. Information about obtaining these translated versions of the test can be found at the University of Minnesota Press website, www.upress.umn.edu/tests/.

Lucio and Reyes-Lagunes (1994) developed normative data on a Mexican transliterated version of the MMPI-2 (see also Whitworth & McBlaine, 1993). Transliteration techniques follow the view that the psychological meaning of the item is more important than its literal equivalent. (For a comprehensive guide and description of general strategies for developing foreign translations of the test, see Butcher & Pancheri, 1976.) Butcher (1996) edited the comprehensive *International Adaptations of the MMPI-2*, which addresses important methodological issues in translating and adapting the MMPI-2 in foreign countries as well as presenting the results of several translation projects.

One MMPI-2 translation of potential practical importance is that for American Sign Language (ASL) for hearing-impaired persons with concurrent difficulty in reading. Brauer (1992) stated that "this language of the deaf is spatial and motile, characteristics that do not lend the language to expression in written form; therefore, an ASL translation must be captured on videotape or film" (p. 381). Results from investigations into the effectiveness of this ASL version of the MMPI-2 hold promise for its future use with deaf individuals in the U.S. (Brauer, 1988, 1992, 1993). Cross (1945) developed a Braille version of the MMPI for administration to the blind, but the publisher of the MMPI-2 does not provide versions of either the Braille or American Sign Language formats. The MMPI-2 *Manual* (Butcher et al., 2001, p. 10) does, however, address individuals with visual limitations:

> For individuals with limited vision, special provision must be made to facilitate their recording of responses and ensure adequate privacy. The use of a Braille

typewriter or a computer can be helpful in such circumstances. If this equipment is not available, it may be necessary to have visually impaired test-takers dictate their responses to a clerk or ward aide.

User Qualifications and Test Instructions

Because administering the MMPI-2/MMPI-2-RF is a relatively straightforward task, clinicians may overlook important factors that can influence participants' test-taking attitude and hence contribute to invalid results. Clinicians are urged to familiarize themselves with the MMPI-2/MMPI-2-RF test *Manuals* before administering, scoring, and interpreting the tests, as required by the *Standards for Educational and Psychological Testing* (American Educational Research Association et al., 1999). Additionally, it is recommended that there be an understanding of the relevant studies reported in the professional literature. The MMPI-2 and MMPI-2-RF *Manuals* (Ben-Porath & Tellegen, 2008, 2011; Butcher et al., 2001) specify the needed qualifications for competent test use. Among these—in addition to training, supervision, and experience in the administration, scoring, and interpretation of the MMPI tests—is graduate training in personality, psychopathology and psychological assessment, familiarity with concepts of reliability and validity (and of measurement and classification error), and the establishment of norms and their conversion to standard scores.

MMPI tests are often administered by a trained clerk, secretary, or technician. "Individuals entrusted with the responsibility of routine administration of the test must be carefully trained and well informed about the steps needed to obtain a valid and useful test protocol" (MMPI-2 *Manual*, Butcher et al., 2001, p. 8). This is quite important, particularly when the individual administering and/or scoring the test lacks a relevant professional degree or background in psychometrics. Pearson Assessments, the distributor of the tests, requires a level "C" qualification in order to purchase MMPI materials. Level "C" indicates that the purchaser must have licensure or certification to practice in their state or possess a doctorate degree in psychology, education, or closely related field with formal training in the ethical administration, scoring, and interpretation of standardized assessment tools and psychometrics.

The test should be presented to the test taker in a serious manner; too often clinicians minimize the importance of the test in an attempt to alleviate any performance anxiety. As a result, participants often believe the test is not important and, thereby, compromise their cooperation by reading the items too quickly, carelessly, skipping some, and generally lessening their investment in the task. A clear explanation of how the results will be used can help increase cooperation as well as fulfill the ethical responsibilities of the psychologist to inform consumers about the nature and purpose of an evaluation. Obtaining informed consent tells the test taker of the advantages and disadvantages of cooperating with the assessment, including how the information will be shared and used to influence decisions in treatment or a specific disposition (Nichols, 2011). It is critical to be clear about the psychologist's relationship to the test taker so there is no confusion about for whom the former is acting as an agent. Psychologists should be explicit in explaining their role in the assessment process.

Levak, Siegel, Nichols, and Stolberg (2011) and Finn (1996) present models for involving the client in the assessment task and suggest ways to increase the client's cooperation, including encouragement of questions for the examiner to jointly formulate areas of interest that the test results might address. As Levak et al. (2011) note, the latest set of ethical principles of psychologists (America Psychological Association, 2002) now specifies that all clients be given feedback about test results in a way that facilitates their comprehension. If clients are treated as collaborators in the assessment process, they are more likely to give accurate and useful information when completing the test.

Psychologists unfamiliar with professional assessment guidelines may consult the following resources: "Ethical Principles of Psychologists and Code of Conduct" (American Psychological Association, 2002); "Guidelines for Providers of Psychological Services to Ethnic, Linguistic, and Culturally Diverse Populations" (American Psychological Association, 1993); "Guidelines for Child Custody Evaluations in Divorce Proceedings" (American Psychological Association, 1994); *Standards for Providers of Psychological Services* (American Psychological Association, 1977); *Standards for Educational and Psychological Testing* (American Educational Research Association, 1999); and *Guidelines for Users of Computer-Based Tests and Interpretations* (American Psychological Association, 1986).

Instructions for completing the MMPI-2/MMPI-2-RF tests are printed on the softcover and hardcover booklet forms, and the audio instructions are presented at the beginning of the CD format. These instructions direct the test taker to decide whether an item is mostly True or mostly False as it applies to him- or herself, and encourage the test taker to try to respond to every statement. A question that commonly arises is, "Do I answer as I am currently feeling?" Most examiners encourage participants to answer as they feel at the present time, but sometimes, under special circumstances, an examiner may want to learn how participants wish to perceive themselves when they feel better, or are leaving the hospital or concluding psychotherapy. The examiner then may ask the participant to fill out the test looking ahead toward the completion of a therapy or hospital program, and answer the items in the way that he or she would expect to feel at that time. In some situations, the participant who is able to produce a less disturbed profile under such looking-ahead instructions (*projected discharge profile*), as compared with his or her admission or initial profile taken under the usual instructions, is considered to have a better prognosis (Marks et al., 1974).

In addition to the standardized instructions printed on the MMPI-2 forms, some test users and researchers use supplemental instructions and information to help answer commonly asked questions, to alleviate test anxiety, and to reduce the proportion of invalid profiles due to the over- or under-reporting of psychological strengths or problems, respectively. For example, Butcher, Morfitt, Rouse, and Holden (1997) found that a group of male job applicants for pilot positions who produced defensive MMPI-2 profiles were able, upon re-administration, to produce valid profiles after being given new test instructions. These instructions were designed to inform them that defensiveness can invalidate the test. These participants produced higher content scale scores without producing higher clinical scale scores. This study demonstrates that specialized instructions in pre-employment settings can reduce the number of profiles that may be judged invalid on the basis of defensiveness/under-reporting. Additional research is needed with other populations with high base rates for dissimulation. Examples include forensic settings, where pleas of insanity or diminished capacity are seen, or in disability and insurance compensation proceedings where claims of injury or disability are alleged.

The following example of supplemental instructions for taking the MMPI-2 is adapted from the Caldwell Report (Caldwell, 1977):

1   Answer every question as truthfully you can; that's very important for accuracy and the best use of the results.

2   Be sure to mark the correct number on the answer sheet for the question you are answering. Remember that a question marked as both "true" and "false" may be scored as "not answered," or as answered in both directions.

3   If a question seems confusing, as if it could mean different things, answer it according to the meaning that is best for you at this time.

4   Phrases like *some of the time* and words like *often* and *seldom* should be answered according to how you feel about them; it's how *you* feel about the words that matters.

5   When you have finished, take a few minutes to check your answer sheet for any missing answers, incomplete erasures, or double-answered questions.

6   Above all, relax. Numerous people have taken the MMPI-2, and all have survived.

The following answers to commonly asked questions in clinical settings are adapted from Lewak et al. (1990) and Levak et al. (2011) and from the Caldwell Report (Caldwell, 1977):

1   "What is the MMPI-2?"
Answer: The MMPI-2 is short for the Minnesota Multiphasic Personality Inventory. It is a tool used for the assessment of personality. It is approximately 70 years old and is psychology's most researched instrument.

2   "How long will this take?"
Answer: About 90 minutes to two hours, usually. Some people take longer, whereas some people finish in 60 to 75 minutes.

3   "I'm tired and not feeling well; will that affect how I do on the inventory?"
Answer: Probably not. But answer the statements in terms of how you feel most of the time. How you feel now may make you take a little longer to finish, but the results will be essentially the same as long as you answer truthfully.

4   "How do I answer the questions?"
Answer: When you take the test, answer the questions as you currently feel. Work quickly, because no one answer is "vital." It is the pattern of answers that make the difference.

5   "Do I have to answer all of the questions even if I don't know the right answer?"
Answer: Answer all of the questions. If you cannot answer all of the questions, leave no more than a few unanswered. If you are unsure of an answer, use the following rule: If the answer to a question is more true than false, answer it true. If it is more false than true, answer false. For example, the hypothetical item "I suffer from head pain frequently" could be answered as follows: I get headaches but not that often; therefore, I answer false.

6   "Will it make any difference if I skip some questions and come back to them?"
Answer: If you do it carefully, skipping some questions and returning to them probably will not make any difference. But it is easy to get mixed up in marking your answers, and that will make a difference. So it is better to do them in order, if possible.

7   "What if I do not have time to finish all the questions right now?"
     Answer: That is perfectly all right. But try to do them all now, or as soon as possible.
     Brief interruptions do not matter and will not change the results.

8   "Suppose I cannot answer all of the questions?"
     Answer: Try to answer all of them. If you omit a few items, it will not matter, but try
     to do them all.

9   "Why do so many questions seem irrelevant or just plain stupid or silly?"
     Answer: Many may seem that way, but the wording of the question often has little
     to do with how the answer is scored. Your answer is simply compared with those of
     others who have answered the same questions.

10   "Why am I taking this test? Does it mean that something is wrong with me?"
     Answer: We have asked you to take the test because it helps us to get to know you
     better in less time, and thus is cost-effective. Many who come to the clinic are asked
     to take it for this reason.

11   "But I don't have any problems. It is my child, whom I brought to the clinic, who has
     the problems. Why do I have to take the test?"
     Answer: You are asked to take the test so we know what kind of psychological
     environment your child lives in. For example, your child may possess extremely high
     energy and be very active, and you as a parent may have energy that is more in the
     average range. Knowing this helps us (and you) understand how your interactions
     with your child are affecting you both.

12   "If my wife and I take the test, I'm afraid that you will blame one of us for the
     problems we're having, and that will make things worse."
     Answer: That is a reasonable concern, but the MMPI-2 is not used to find out who
     has the most problems. What the MMPI-2 can do is help us see how two people
     might be inadvertently "pushing each other's sensitive area" and so be unable to
     communicate. The test interpretation is not meant to judge either person or to leave
     either person feeling blamed.

13   "I think I can outsmart the test. I probably can tell what the questions are getting at."
     Answer: The pattern of answers to questions rather than individual responses is what
     is important to the psychologist. Being as honest as possible will serve to make the
     test results more valid and useful to you and the psychologist interpreting the test.
     In fact, many questions that appear to be obvious are not measuring what people
     think they are measuring. People who try to outsmart the test might make it invalid,
     but often not in the direction they think and not without revealing their intention
     to do so.

14   "Why does the test ask so many questions that clearly don't apply to me?"
     Answer: The test was constructed as a general inventory; so many questions may
     not apply to you. If a question does not apply to you, simply answer false or true,
     whichever direction is most applicable for you.

15   "How can you tell anything about me from all those questions anyway?"
     Answer: After your answer sheet is finished, it is scored, and a graph is drawn to see
     how you scored on different dimensions of personality and how your scores compare
     to others. There are also scales that tell how you answered the test (cautiously,
     candidly, denying problems, or even exaggerating them). Your configuration or
     pattern of scores is what is important to us.

16   "Will I get feedback from my test?"
Answer: The actual test protocol and the graph will not be given to you in order to maintain test security. However, an explanation of the results will be provided.
17   "What if I disagree with the feedback?"
Answer: If the test results do not describe you accurately, you will have a chance to clarify how you see yourself. The value of the assessment depends on collaboration between us, so you will be able to clarify and describe the way you see yourself. When you get feedback, you may want to bring a tape recorder so that you can listen to the feedback and take some time to formulate questions that you might want to ask your therapist. Remember, the test is for your own benefit.
18   "What is the cost of the test?"
Answer: See the clinic fee schedule. The fee covers administration and scoring. Feedback will probably come in a regular session for which you pay your usual fee to your therapist.

Test Conditions

The testing environment should be comfortable, with as few distracting influences as possible. Extraneous noise should be minimized, and the participant should be isolated from others not involved in simultaneous testing. Testing is a matter involving personal or confidential issues, and, whenever possible, the participant is entitled to adequate privacy. To prevent inadvertent answer disclosure and to maintain a consistent test environment, only the test administrator and test taker should be able to see the test items and responses. Lighting should be adequate and seating comfortable, and a desk or tabletop is preferable to holding the booklet on the lap. Supplying a few extra sharpened pencils along with access to water or a beverage is often helpful (Nichols, 2011). If a participant is bedridden, the hardcover booklet is preferred. Test administrators using computer equipment to administer the test should consult the American Psychological Association *Guidelines* (1986) as well as a review by Bersoff and Hofer (1995) of legal issues in computerized psychological testing. If a monitor screen is used to present the items, correct positioning of the equipment can reduce glare or reflections from windows. An obvious but frequently neglected point is the importance of informing the participant ahead of time to bring reading glasses if they are needed.

Whether a test is group or individually administered, or presented on a monitor screen, a proctor should be available to monitor the test administration and to provide assistance when necessary and appropriate. A trained assistant to the clinician can successfully answer questions a participant raises during testing. The availability of a proctor is especially important for group administrations to ensure the privacy of responses, to help in recording responses in the appropriate spaces, and to discourage conversation. Proctors should be careful not to linger near anyone for too long, so that the individual does not become overly concerned that his or her responses are being monitored. When questions are asked about the specific meaning of an item or word, the proctor should be helpful but neutral. Specifically, dictionary definitions should be given for commonly misunderstood words such as constipation, nausea, dramatics, journalist, and brood (Dahlstrom et al., 1972). When participants question the meaning of an item itself, it is best to encourage them to interpret it in their own way. Even though the

MMPI-2/MMPI-2-RF is considered to be an objective instrument, the items pull from each participant a particular meaning that leads to an endorsement that is ultimately compared to a normative base of participants who have responded to the same items. A commonly asked question in private practice and in evaluation settings is, "Can I take the test home and complete it?" Although it may be convenient to allow this practice, it is not recommended because psychologists are ethically bound to make reasonable efforts to maintain the integrity and security of tests (see Ethical Principle 2.10 of the "Ethical Principles of Psychologists and Code of Conduct," American Psychological Association, 1992) as well as to ensure a valid result for the assessment. The psychologist cannot control the test environment when the test is taken outside of the professional setting, and there is no guarantee that the designated test taker(s) has even completed the instrument themselves. This could be particularly important in assessments when the results are used in a legal proceeding. In fact, unmonitored test administrations may be inadmissible in legal proceedings, as nonstandard administrations involve a breach in the chain of evidence because the connection between the individual and the item responses cannot be established. Another reason for avoiding an unmonitored test administration is that the presence of an individual proctoring the test is consistent with one of the elements of standardization (Pope, Butcher, & Seelen, 2006). Whenever there is a departure from the standardized procedure used in establishing the test norms, one runs the risk of losing the valid inferences drawn from the test.

Participants' Requirements

There are many important determinants for completing a valid MMPI-2/MMPI-2-RF. In addition to cooperation, one of the most important factors to assess before the test administration is the reading level of the test taker. While the intent of Hathaway and McKinley (1983) was for the original MMPI to be readable at a fifth grade level, later studies showed that a sixth grade or higher level is required to understand all of the items (Butcher et al., 2001). For example, evaluations of the MMPI/MMPI-2 item statements and vocabulary have resulted in even higher reading level recommendations, with Ward and Ward (1980) suggesting at least a seventh-grade reading level. Blanchard (1981) analyzed the MMPI for reading difficulty using readability formulas. At a criterion for comprehension between 90 percent and 100 percent, he found several items requiring tenth-grade reading skills and recommended that alternative forms of presentation be used for participants with less than tenth-grade reading skills. On average, for the original MMPI, Blanchard (1981) estimated there were about 11 words and one polysyllabic word per sentence.

The MMPI-2 *Manual* (Butcher et al., 2001) recommends that test takers have at least a sixth-grade education for a valid test administration. Studies generally have supported this recommendation (Paolo et al., 1991; Schinka & Borum, 1993), and a detailed investigation of the MMPI-2 items using different reading indexes led Dahlstrom et al. (1994) to conclude that the average difficulty level of MMPI-2 (and MMPI and MMPI-A) items is at about the sixth-grade level. They also noted that the instructions in the MMPI-2 booklet are somewhat more difficult to read than the component items; therefore, the test administrator should ensure that the participant fully understands the task. The clinician might request the test taker to read the instructions aloud and explain the meaning of the task to ensure compliance, or the clinician may elect to read the instructions aloud with the participant reading along silently.

If a test taker has less than a tenth-grade education, Schinka and Borum (1993) suggested that MMPI-2 items 114, 226, and 445 should be shown to the examinee to test their reading capability. This appears practical as these items are lengthy and have complex phrasing. More recently, Nichols (2011) usefully identified and classified MMPI-2 sample items according to grade levels and reading difficulty. Low difficulty items (grade levels 2–6) are: 8, 14, 20, 51, and 91; average difficulty items (grade levels 7–9) are: 106, 122, and 297; high difficulty items (grade levels 10–11) are: 263 and 425; and double-negative items, those that often cause difficulty for some test-takers, are: 114, 226, and 445. Dahlstrom et al. (1994, Table D.5) provided a list of the most difficult MMPI-2 items arranged by lexile scores. The following items from that list were selected because they were ranked as difficult items and appear on either the validity or clinical scales: 114, 212, 262, and 283. For persons with suspected marginal reading levels, these items could be presented prior to test administration in order to assess the participant's comprehension.

The MMPI-2-RF *Manual* (Ben-Porath & Tellegen, 2008, 2011) reports that the majority of the items for the RF require a fifth to seventh grade reading level. However, the *Manual* notes that some items on the RF, as on the MMPI-2, require a higher reading level. Therefore, setting the minimal reading level at a sixth grade equivalence for the MMPI-2, or fifth to seventh grade level for the RF, does not guarantee that the person will be able to comprehend every single item. In earlier studies, Paolo, Ryan, and Smith (1991), Dahlstrom, Archer, Hopkins, Jackson, and Dahlstrom (1994), and Schinka and Borum (1993) investigated the readability of the MMPI-2 content. In particular, Paolo et al. (1991) reported that 61 MMPI-2 special scales and subscales contained a high percentage of items requiring a reading proficiency level beyond the eighth grade. Many of the items on these scales could be difficult to understand for those individuals possessing only the minimum requisite reading level for taking the MMPI-2. They identified nine scales on which at least 25 percent of the total number of items required greater than an eighth-grade reading level: *ASP* (Antisocial Practices), *TPA* (Type A Behavior), *Hy2* (Need for Affection), *Pa3* (Naïveté), *Sc5* (Lack of Ego Mastery, Defective Inhibition), *Sc6* (Sensory Motor Dissociation), *Ma1* (Amorality), *Ma3* (Imperturbability), and *Ma4* (Ego Inflation). They suggested that *(Ma)* Hypomania be cautiously interpreted with individuals possessing less than an eighth or ninth grade education, as 66.7 percent of the *Ma1* items, 37.5 percent of the *Ma3* items, and 33.3 percent of the *Ma4* items require greater than an eighth-grade reading level. Items 250, 263, and 269 from *Ma1* illustrate the extent of the demands that these items make on the examinee.

Although a sixth-grade level is generally sufficient for the MMPI-2, it is important to note Greene's (2000) caveat that simply using completed years of education to estimate reading ability may result in gross overestimates. Similarly, Dahlstrom et al. (1994) noted the limitations of exclusively relying on "years of education" to indicate reading ability, as examinees may overstate or otherwise distort their educational histories and achievement, grades, class standing, and so forth. Hence the completed year's education index, considered in isolation, may be misleading. There are also instances in which some participants with less than a sixth-grade education may nevertheless possess the reading ability to complete the instrument.

Although the *F, FB, VRIN,* and True Response Inconsistency (*TRIN*) scales help identify MMPI-2 test administrations that are compromised by failing to understand certain items, it is obviously desirable to anticipate and screen for any comprehension problems ahead of time.

Exceeding a required sixth-grade reading level increases the probability of a valid administration. Schinka and Borum (1993) suggested using an eighth-grade level of formal education with at least average grades to ensure that participants will understand the content of the MMPI-2. If a participant has less than eight years of formal education, is not fluent in English, or is otherwise English language compromised, the examiner can either administer readability measures—such as the Gray Oral Reading Test, Forms A and B (Wiederholt & Bryant, 1986); the Woodcock-Johnson Test—Revised, Form A, Passage Comprehension; the Wechsler Individual Achievement Test, Reading Comprehension (1992); and the California Achievement Test, Reading Battery A (1993)—or the examiner can select certain items from the MMPI-2 booklet for the participant to read aloud and explain. It is not recommended that the potential test taker merely read aloud the first several items in the inventory as these items tend to be easier to read than later items. Simply reading an item may mask a problem in item comprehension; instead, more difficult items should be selected for screening purposes, as suggested earlier in this section.

If the CD form of the test is being administered to an illiterate participant or someone who cannot complete the written form, difficult items could also be read by the examiner to screen for comprehension problems. As with the MMPI-2 booklet, the examiner should not merely present the first few items from the CD form as these tend to be relatively easy items. It is also impractical to locate difficult sample items on the CD before testing, so reading them in a manner similar to the presenter's voice on the CD will suffice for screening purposes. In any case, the examiner will want to ensure that the participant adequately understands the task of listening to the CD and recording his or her responses, and should observe the first few items being recorded on the answer sheet by the participant.

It is important for the reader to note that using the CD version of the MMPI-2 may be challenging for many participants. Specifically, the items (which are presented twice) only leave, on average, four to six seconds for the test taker to respond before the next item is presented. The rapid presentation pace might interfere with responding for individuals with obsessive tendencies, depressive and concentration deficits, or those needing time to think about the double-negative statements. Therefore, it is important to ensure that the participant knows how to successfully pause the CD player while contemplating their response choice.

In most cases, CD administration is preferred to reading each item aloud to the participant, as the CD presentation of items is paced and uniform, thereby reducing inflections and fatigue in the presenter's voice. Simply reading the items represents a deviation from the standardized procedures, which could unduly influence the results of testing by introducing an interpersonal factor or other unknown elements into the process.

While some have recommended against reading the items to the participant (Ben-Porath & Tellegen, 2008, 2011), others have researched whether an oral presentation by the examiner will seriously compromise the results, provided that the items are read clearly and slowly. It could be argued that an oral administration allows the clinician the advantage of observing the client and noting any indicators of significant psychological dysfunction, such as hesitancies, emotional responses, confusion, or indecision (Edwards, Holmes, & Carvajal, 1998). In an investigation of the effects of orally administering the MMPI, Kendrick and Hatzenbuehler (1982) found that although statistical differences occurred between the standard and oral administration in a split-half design, clinically significant differences appeared minimal. Edwards et al. (1998) administered the MMPI-2 twice to college students under two conditions: standard booklet administration and oral presentation with the examiner reading the items and recording their responses. Few significant differences were found when comparing oral and booklet presentations for either men or women. *T*-scores were five to seven points lower on Scales 6 (Paranoia) and 8 (Schizophrenia) for the oral administration, suggesting the participants were hesitant to endorse more severe psychopathology in the presence of an examiner. Clinicians administering the test orally most likely will obtain results comparable with the standard administration, although more research is needed to confirm this conclusion. Specifically, it is not known whether the mere recording of responses by the examiner versus the participant makes a difference in the accuracy of the results.

Psychiatric impairment usually does not interfere with the administration of the MMPI-2/MMPI-2-RF unless the participant is too confused or agitated to cooperate. Even so, the MMPI-2 *Manual* (Butcher et al., 2001, p. 8) cautions the test administrator to be alert to any of the following physical conditions or emotional states that could impair the capacity of the participant to complete the test in a valid manner:

> Limited visual acuity, dyslexia or receptive aphasia, learning disorder, drug or alcohol intoxication or withdrawal states, toxic reactions to various infectious agents, organic deliria, disorientation arising from brain injury or confusion, post-seizure confusion in an epileptic disorder, residual neurological impairment from prolonged polydrug regimes, confusional states during catatonic episodes or bouts of hallucinations, profound psychomotor retardation of a major depressive condition, or the extreme distractibility of a manic reaction.

Because depressed patients or cognitively impaired participants may take longer than usual to complete the test (three to four hours), it is important to note the test-taking time. Too much or too little time can be of diagnostic significance for all participants (e.g. too little time may indicate impulsiveness or uncooperativeness, whereas too much time may indicate obsessiveness, psychomotor retardation, or motivational difficulties). Hospitalized psychiatric patients may require several sittings to complete the inventory because of distractibility or fatigue, or because of interruptions for treatment, medication, meals, visitations, and similar events that are common in the hospital milieu. Such interruptions can potentially add several days to the test administration. Very lengthy administrations raise the question of reliability, as such patients may undergo significant change in symptoms and mental status in the course of a few days. As Nichols (2011, p. 26) points out:

> Patients' emotional states and attitudes are always in a state of flux, and it cannot be assumed that a test result that has taken a week to produce will be the same as one

that might have been produced within a couple of hours. Nevertheless, it is almost always preferable to be flexible about allowing as much time as necessary to obtain a valid protocol, not least because such flexibility conveys the clinician's interest in test results that accurately reflect the patient's symptoms and situation.

In essence, timeliness should not be sacrificed for accuracy.

Functional intelligence as measured by a standardized IQ test, such as the Wechsler Adult Intelligence Scale-IV (WAIS-IV), should be at least in the low–average range (80–89), although participants in the borderline range (70–79) of impairment may be able to complete the task if they are properly motivated, monitored, and evaluated ahead of time for reading and comprehension. In general, an IQ score should be considered in relation to other variables (e.g. level of education, motivation, attention and concentration factors, and reading ability). For example, an individual with a Full Scale IQ (FSIQ) score of 75 without any history of central nervous system disease or brain injury may be developmentally impaired and therefore unable to complete the task, especially if he or she has reading deficits. On the other hand, an individual with an FSIQ score of 75 who premorbidly had a considerably higher IQ (perhaps as estimated from educational attainment, work record, or previous testing) is more likely to have retained the necessary reading ability to complete the MMPI-2-RF. Individuals with IQs as low as 65 and reading levels as low as the third grade can often successfully be administered the CD version of the MMPI-2 or the MMPI-2-RF (Dahlstrom et al., 1972; Greene, 2011). Participants with disabilities such as blindness, deafness, or even paralysis can successfully complete the test under certain conditions, as described earlier.

Test Scoring and Profile Plotting

Scoring the MMPI-2/MMPI-2-RF can be accomplished using handheld plastic templates or with the aid of a scanner and a computer. Pearson Assessments (www.pearsonassessments.com), the official distributor of the University of Minnesota Press trademark materials, provides scoring templates for the hard- and softcover MMPI-2 booklets, as well as interpretive software and web-based scoring services, and mail-in scoring; the reader is advised to contact the distributor for further information. Other scoring and interpretive services are available, including the Caldwell Report in Culver City, CA (phone: 877/667-4248) and Behaviordata in Cupertino, CA (phone: 800/627-2673). As previously mentioned, the scoring templates are not interchangeable. Hence, when hand scoring the MMPI-2, it is necessary to have the appropriate templates to match the soft- or hardcover form of the tests. The answer sheet designed for the softcover booklet should be used for a CD administration. Note that Scale 5 (*Mf*) on the MMPI-2 has two scoring templates, one for men and one for women, and the scorer should be careful to select the template that matches the participant's gender. The MMPI-2-RF does not use gender-specific norms; there is only one scoring template that applies to both males and females.

When using the hard- or softcover scoring keys, the marks on the bottom of the key should coincide with the marks on the answer sheets. The number of marks appearing through the transparent squares on the scoring key should be counted and recorded as the raw score in the proper place on the profile form. Omitted items are tallied by inspecting the answer sheet and should be recorded as Cannot Say (?) responses in the appropriate space provided on the profile form for the standard scales. Double-marked items (items marked as both True and False) are also recorded as Cannot Say (?) responses. These items risk being scored as a deviant response so a line should be drawn through the item so it is not inadvertently counted when a scoring template is placed over the answer sheet. Erasures usually contraindicate random responses because participants, by their modified response, are demonstrating a careful reading of the item content.

It is important to review the answer sheet before a client departs the administration site, if practical, as there may have been unintentional (or intentional) item omissions. Asking the test taker to complete the omitted items could help in producing a more valid profile. However, if it is discovered later that a participant double marked or omitted between 5 and 30 items, an augmented profile can be drawn to assist in the interpretation. Greene (2011) describes this procedure in detail and although there are no empirical data to support this method, it may lend itself to useful clinical enhancement of the interpretation of the profile. The basic method assumes that the omitted items were being avoided and that, if endorsed, the items would have been scored in the deviant direction. It is always important to inspect the omitted items for any content themes before augmenting the profile. The first step in this process is to determine which scales the omitted items are scored on, keeping in mind that some items overlap multiple scales and may be scored in opposite directions on some scales. Appendix B in the MMPI-2 *Manual* (Butcher et al., 2001) provides the scoring direction and scales on which the items are scored. The scorer adds one point for each omitted item to the raw score of the appropriate scale. Before plotting this corrected or augmented profile on the standard profile form, Greene (2011) cautioned that if the K scale has been augmented, it is important to augment all of the K-corrected scales if a K-corrected profile is being plotted. This method could change the code pattern that is interpreted, so it is important to note on the profile whether the augmented or non-augmented code pattern is being interpreted, if, in fact, they differ. As mentioned, some MMPI-2 items which overlap other scales may be scored in the opposite direction from one scale to the next. As Greene (2011, p. 46) points out, this

> double scoring of items is a logical inconsistency in this method of constructing an augmented profile; however, if it appears that the client systematically avoided the omitted items, this method represents a reasonable attempt to salvage as much clinical data as possible from an otherwise lost cause.

The MMPI-2 *Manual* (Butcher et al., 2001, Appendix C) will assist the reader in determining the scale membership for omitted items as well as the scored direction of items.

A second method described by Greene (2011) for augmenting a profile involves determining the scales with the omitted items and determining the percentage of items actually endorsed in the deviant direction on those scales. For example, if a test taker answered 20 of the 60 items on the F scale in the deviant direction and omitted 10 F items, the scorer would calculate the proportion of endorsed F items and add to that value the same proportion of omitted items on that scale. In this example, the test taker endorsed 33 percent (20 out of 60 items) of the F items, and a third of the omitted 10 items is about three items. Three items would then be added to the *F* score and plotted as an augmented *F* scale. As with the first method, it is also important to note on the profile form whether the augmented or non-augmented code pattern is being interpreted. The MMPI-2-RF can also follow the augmenting procedure just described, and the reader should consult Ben-Porath and Tellegen (2008, 2011, Appendix C) to determine scale membership and scored direction of items.

After the answer sheet has been scored for the basic validity and clinical scales, the raw scores must be carefully transferred to the profile form and converted to *T*-scores, which are located at the extreme left and right columns of the profile matrix (see Figs. 1.1–1.4). MMPI-2 *T*-scores have a mean of 50 and a standard deviation of 10 (see Chapter 1 for a detailed discussion of *T*-scores). For example, if a male participant obtains a raw score of 39 on Scale 0 (*Si*), this indicates that his *T*-score is 65, 1.5 standard deviations above the mean. Because *T*-scores differ by gender for the various MMPI-2 scales, it is important that raw scores be transferred to the appropriate side of the profile form identified as male or female (see Figs. 2.1 and 2.2). After raw scores are recorded under each scale, a different proportion of the *K* scale is added to the appropriate scales. The fraction of *K* to be added is easily computed by consulting the table listed on the MMPI-2 profile form showing all raw-score values of *K* and different proportions of those values. The scorer should draw a line under the raw score of *K* on the profile form, so that the appropriate fractions can be added to the clinical scales. The raw score plus the *K* scale addition is then plotted onto the profile form. Test users who do not wish to use the *K* correction can convert the non-*K*-corrected raw scores into appropriate *T*-scores. MMPI-2 profile forms are available from Pearson that allow plotting scores for either *K* or non-*K*-corrected profiles, although the MMPI-2-RF does not use *K*-corrections (see Figs. 2.3 and 2.4).

Within the profile matrix, the marks or dashes represent raw-score values. Each dash represents a raw-score value of 1. Each scale, except for Scale 5 (*Mf*), shows an increase in *T*-score value for each raw-score point added. The final raw score is indicated on the profile form by plotting the raw-score placement on the appropriate scale. After all the scale scores are plotted in this fashion, a solid line is drawn between the clinical scales to connect them. Likewise, the validity scales are connected. The clinical and validity scales, however, have a partition between them, and traditionally they are not connected.

The profile forms for the MMPI-2 show a darkened line for all scales at a *T*-score value of 65 to indicate scores that are within 1.5 *SD*s of the mean. Scores above this range indicate a significant deviation from the standardization group pattern of responding and are considered abnormal values. Chapter 1 provides the equation for deriving *T*-scores, but the conversions from raw scores to *T*-scores already are provided on the printed profile forms for all of the officially published scales.

Administering the test by computer that uses software that presents instructions and test items on a monitor for responses entered via keyboard has the advantage of shorter administration time, fewer item omissions, and immediate scoring once the inventory has been completed. As Nichols (2011, p. 26) states:

> Although switching formats (e.g. booklet to CD, CD to computer, etc.) once testing has begun may be inconvenient for the administrator, the publisher does not prohibit doing so. The MMPI-2 need not be administered by the clinician

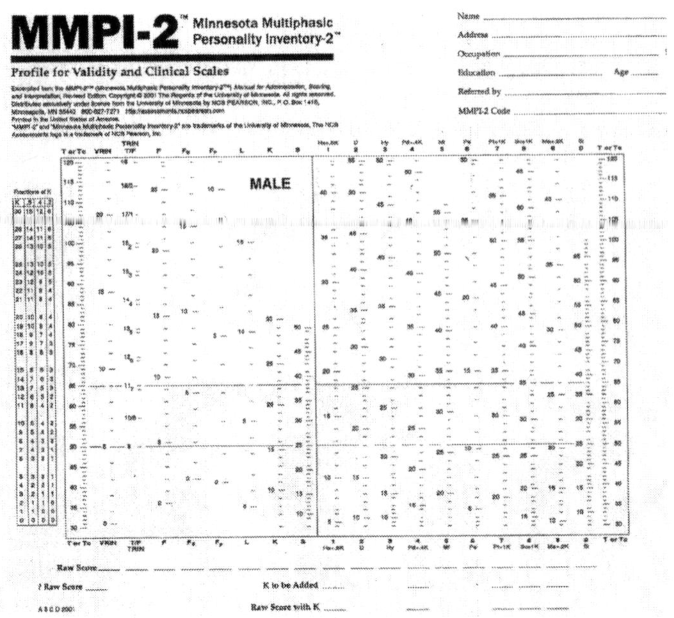

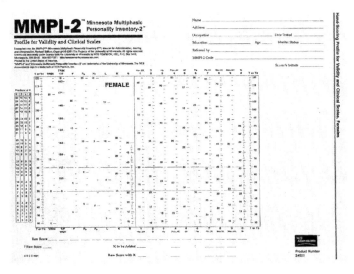

Figure 2.1 MMPI-2 Profile for Validity and Clinical Scales (Male)

Source: Excerpted from the *MMPI-2 (Minnesota Multiphasic Personality Inventory-2) Manual for Administration, Scoring, and Interpretation, Revised Edition.* Copyright © 2001 by the Regents of the University of Minnesota. All rights reserved. Used by permission of the University of Minnesota Press. "MMPI" and "Minnesota Multiphasic Personality Inventory" are registered trademarks owned by the Regents of the University of Minnesota.

Figure 2.2 MMPI-2 Profile for Validity and Clinical Scales (Female)

Source: Excerpted from the *MMPI-2 (Minnesota Multiphasic Personality Inventory-2) Manual for Administration, Scoring, and Interpretation, Revised Edition.* Copyright © 2001 by the Regents of the University of Minnesota. All rights reserved. Used by permission of the University of Minnesota Press. "MMPI" and "Minnesota Multiphasic Personality Inventory" are registered trademarks owned by the Regents of the University of Minnesota.

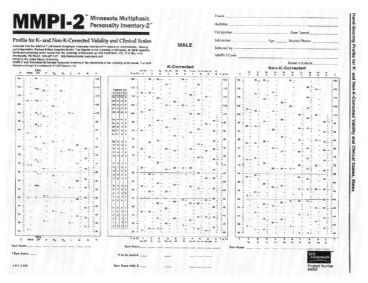

Figure 2.3 MMPI-2 Profile for *K*- and Non-*K*-Corrected Validity and Clinical Scales (Male)

Source: Excerpted from the *MMPI*-2 *(Minnesota Multiphasic Personality Inventory*-2) *Manual for Administration, Scoring, and Interpretation, Revised Edition.* Copyright © 2001 by the Regents of the University of Minnesota. All rights reserved. Used by permission of the University of Minnesota Press. "MMPI" and "Minnesota Multiphasic Personality Inventory" are registered trademarks owned by the Regents of the University of Minnesota.

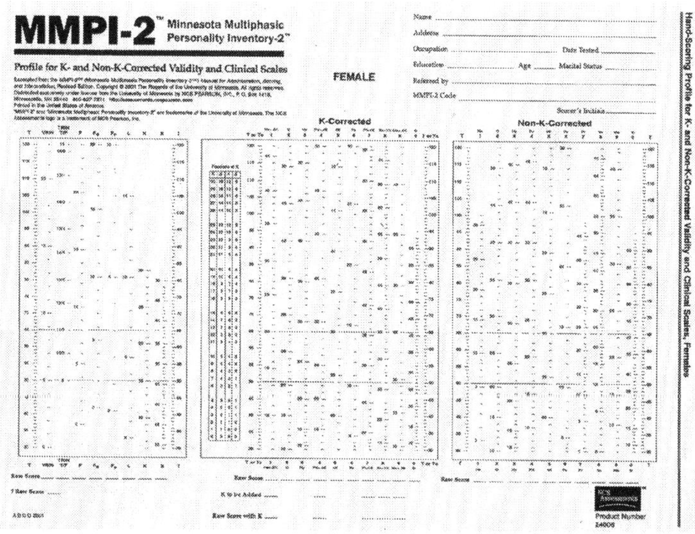

Figure 2.4 MMPI-2 Profile for *K*- and Non-*K*-Corrected Validity and Clinical Scales (Female)

Source: Excerpted from the *MMPI*-2 *(Minnesota Multiphasic Personality Inventory*-2) *Manual for Administration, Scoring, and Interpretation, Revised Edition.* Copyright © 2001 by the Regents of the University of Minnesota. All rights reserved. Used by permission of the University of Minnesota Press. "MMPI" and "Minnesota Multiphasic Personality Inventory" are registered trademarks owned by the Regents of the University of Minnesota.

who will provide test feedback on the written report; with adequate training and supervision, psychometricians or clerical/secretarial staff can handle all of the routine administration tasks,

Coding the Profile

Soon after publication of the MMPI, two systems were developed to summarize the information contained in the profile. The first system was developed by Hathaway (1947) and is summarized in Dahlstrom et al., 1972. The Hathaway system for coding the MMPI profile is illustrated in the *Atlas* (Hathaway & Meehl, 1951), a collection of clinical case summaries grouped according to their patterns of scale elevations. The second system, designed by Welsh (1948), was rapidly adopted to supplant the Hathaway system and, with a slight modification to indicate the *T*-65 cut for scores on the MMPI-2, remains the standard.

The function of coding is to provide a convenient means of identifying salient characteristics of the profile, especially with respect to profiles' shape, elevation, and scatter (the extent of variation between scale scores). Although single-scale elevations are important to examine and interpret, the emphasis in the clinical use of the test has been to interpret profile patterns, the configuration of scale scores relative to each other. By coding a profile, a test user can organize the profile information into a simple-to-read summary for clinical and research use. From the coded profile, the psychologist should be able to interpret the entire profile with most of its information, including the following: configuration or pattern of the basic clinical scales, the overall elevation of the test pattern, the range or scatter of score values, the highest and lowest scales in the profile, and the configuration of the standard validity scales.

Table 2.1 Welsh Code Symbols with Corresponding *T*-Score Values

T–Score Values	*Symbols*
>120	!!
110–119	!
100–109	**
90–99	*
80–89	"
70–79	'
65–69	+
60–64	-
50–59	/
40–49	:
30–39	#
≤ 29	(to the right of #)

The first step in the modified Welsh (1948) coding system substitutes numbers 1–0 for the 10 standard scales, in the standard profile arrangement:

Hs 1	*Pa 6*
D 2	*Pt 7*
Hy 3	*Sc 8*
Pd 4	*Ma 9*
Mf 5	*Si 0*

Recording the modified Welsh code begins by identifying the highest clinical scale *T*-score value and writing the number assigned to that scale (as in the preceding list) as the first number of the code, with the remaining scale numbers following in descending order of elevation. When two or more scales share the same elevation, they should be recorded in ordinal sequence in the profile from left (Scale 1) to right (Scale 0). The next step is to indicate the relative elevation of all scales in the profile. The *T*-score values and corresponding elevation symbols for this system are as follows (Butcher et al., 1989):

In this coding system, a double exclamation mark (!!) follows all scores at a *T*-score of 120 or above. Scores between 110 and 119 are followed by a single exclamation mark (!). A double asterisk (**) follows all scores between 100 and 109. Scores between 90 and 99 are followed by a single asterisk (*). Scores between 80 and 89 are followed by a double prime ("). A single prime (') follows score between 70 and 79. A new notation, a plus sign (+), follows scores between 65 and 69. A dash (-) follows scores between 60 and 64. A slash (/) follows scores between 50 and 59. A colon (:) follows scores between 40 and 49. The pound sign (#) follows scores between 30 and 39. Scores of 29 and below are recorded to the right of the pound sign (#). It should be noted that the validity scales are recorded to the right of the clinical scales. Traditionally, the validity and clinical scales should be separated by a space or two. Scale scores that are the same or are within one *T*-score of each other are underlined. If no scale score falls within a given interval of elevation, the appropriate symbol for the missing range is, nevertheless, recorded. When scales fall into two different ranges but remain within one *T*-score, they and the elevation symbol should be underlined. Note that it is not necessary to include a symbol to the left of the scale with the highest score or to the right of the elevation symbol following the lowest score.

The following examples illustrate the application of the modified Welsh coding system for two MMPI-2 profiles:

Example 1

	L	F	K	1	2	3	4	5	6	7	8	9	0
T-score	40	60	46	34	56	56	90	63	50	90	73	91	43

Modified Welsh code: 947*" 8´+5–236/0:1# F-/KL:

Example 2

	L	F	K	1	2	3	4	5	6	7	8	9	0
T-score	44	61	49	50	89	62	51	60	62	79	63	38	70

Modified Welsh code: 2" 70´+8365–41/:9# F-/KL:

Although the code summarizes the pattern of the MMPI-2 scores, a shorthand method is often used to describe the test record instead of the total code. Dahlstrom (1992a) has suggested that profile patterns may be briefly designated by:

- The single most elevated scale (the high-point code).
- The two highest scales (the two-point code), either with (e.g. 12, 87) or without (e.g. 12/21, 78/87) regard to order.
- The three highest scales (the three-point code).
- The highest and lowest scales (the cross-point code).

These codetype designations, often accompanied with the elevation indicators described above, permit profiles that are identical with respect to their highest or lowest scales but differing for the remaining scales to be grouped together and investigated for external correlates such as symptoms/complaints, diagnoses, and personality characteristics that may be associated with each. As a summary of the full profile code, the codetype necessarily disregards the information contained in the other scale relationships within the full code. It is also possible and often convenient to combine similar codetypes to form larger groupings, such as those contained within Lachar's (1974) neurotic, psychotic, and character disorder clusters.

MMPI/MMPI-2 Code Pattern Correspondence

Although administering, scoring, and coding an MMPI-2 is straightforward, users should be aware that there were sometimes differences in the way an MMPI-2 pattern of scores corresponded to the original MMPI pattern. Concerns were expressed about the correspondence between the new and older norms when the MMPI-2 was released in 1989. Since 1990, over 40 studies have been published on the concordance between MMPI-2 and MMPI code patterns (Greene, 2011; Greene, Gwin, & Staal, 1997) and have important practical implications. Specifically, individuals who complete the MMPI-2 and have their scores plotted on both the original and new norms, may show different profile patterns. Because different profile patterns would be associated with different correlates and interpretations, the practical question becomes which profile should the psychologist interpret. For further information, the reader is referred to Greene (1991a, p. 246) for descriptions of two different procedures for assessing congruence or concordance between the MMPI and the MMPI-2 profiles.

The reader should note that the concordance rates vary as a function of the norm shift direction; thus, the MMPI-2 and the MMPI are not expected to have perfect concordance. Greene (2011) noted that "there is a wide range of opinions on the degree of codetype comparability between the MMPI and MMPI-2, ranging from 50 percent to 90 percent using well-defined codetypes, and 40 percent to 70 percent when all codetypes are included" (p. 164). Greene also noted that rarely does the research specify whether the degree of concordance varies as a function of specific codetypes. A nonrestrictive two-point code, for example, is based on the two highest scales, regardless of other elevations. Greene (1991a, p. 249) gave the following illustration of how the norm shifts can affect code-pattern concordance:

For example, 4–8/8–4 codetypes on the MMPI have a concordance rate of 35% on the MMPI-2 in men and women, whereas 4–8/8–4 codetypes on the MMPI-2 have a concordance rate over 90% on the MMPI in men and women. Thus, 4–8/8–4 codetypes on the MMPI-2 should be a very homogeneous subset of 4–8/8–4 codetypes on the MMPI, and it would be expected that 4–8/8–4 codetypes on the MMPI-2 should have more reliable correlates since the codetype is more homogeneous.

The opposite pattern for concordance rates between the MMPI-2 and the MMPI also can be found. For example, 1–3/3–1 codetypes on the MMPI have a concordance rate over 90% on the MMPI-2 in men and women, whereas 1–3/3–1 codetypes on the MMPI-2 have a concordance rate around 50% on the MMPI in men and women. Thus, 1–3/3–1 codetypes on the MMPI-2 are a more heterogeneous subset of 1–3/3–1 codetypes on the MMPI, and it would be expected that 1–3/3–1 codetypes on the MMPI-2 should have less reliable correlates since the codetype is more heterogeneous

Dahlstrom (1992a) demonstrated that appreciable scale differences, for both men and women, occurred when their MMPI-2 scores were converted to MMPI norms. For men, Scales 1, 3, 6, and 7 appeared as the first or second high points more frequently when using the MMPI-2 norms versus the original norms. Scales 2, 4, 8, and 9 were less frequently displayed in the MMPI-2 profiles as the high point or second highest scale, and Scale 5 dropped the most in the shift. For women, similar trends were observed with Scales 1, 3, 5, 7, and 0 (particularly Scale 5), appearing more frequently as the first or second high points when using the MMPI-2 norms. Scales 2, 4, 6, 8, and 9 decreased in prominence in their profile patterns.

Dahlstrom also noted that certain code patterns showed substantial shifts in frequency of occurrence, and others did not; the most unstable patterns for men were 24/42, 25/52, 27/72, 28/82, 34/43, 45/54, 48/84, 57/75, 58/85, 59/95, and 89/98; the most unstable patterns for women were 34/43, 38/83, 30/03, 46/64, 48/84, 49/94, 40/04, 68/86, and 69/96. High-point pairs that were more stable were, for men, 12/21, 13/31, 20/02, 39/93, and 69/96 and, for women, 13/31, 26/62, 27/72, 36/63, 59/95, 70/07, and 89/98. Dahlstrom (1992a, p. 159) noted that

> the single largest increase in frequency from the original to the new norms occurred for the 13/31 code, from 28 (2.5%) to 61 (5.4%). Correspondingly, the largest drop in frequency occurred for the 59/95 code pattern, from 122 (10.7%) to 42 (3.7%).

Note that these community samples did not show either marked elevation or wide ranges of scatter in their profiles. Therefore, as Dahlstrom (1992a) stated, "they are less likely to demonstrate as much stability in their code patterns in shift in norms as would be true in records from more deviant participants with wide-ranging scores" (p. 161). Individuals such as psychiatric patients tend to produce more deviant and wide-ranging scores and therefore produce more stability in their code patterns when shifts in norms occur. The data in the MMPI-2 *Manual* (Butcher et al., 1989) show that about two thirds of patients obtained the same two-point codes when the norm shift occurred.

Greene (1991a) provided data on the concordance of specific MMPI-2 and MMPI code patterns in a sample of psychiatric inpatients and outpatients. When the two highest clinical scales had to be in the same order, the average concordance rate across all of the MMPI-2 code patterns was approximately 50 percent; this rate increased to about 65 percent when the two highest clinical scales could be in either order. Greene found the following high-point pairs in men had high concordance: 24/42, 28/82, 48/84, and 49/94. In women, the following high-point pairs had high concordance between the original and new norms: Spike 2, Spike 3, Spike 4, 48/84, 19/91, Spike 7, and Spike 0. Two-point pairs that had very low concordance rates in both men and women were the 16/61 and 26/62 patterns; 20/02, 40/04, and 69/96 were patterns of low concordance rates in men. Greene's data show that the concordance rates for specific code patterns can vary drastically, both as a function of whether the MMPI or MMPI-2 is used as the criterion, as well as the order of the scales in the codetype.

Humphrey and Dahlstrom (1995) examined the stability of MMPI and MMPI-2 *T*-score patterns within an interval of a few days. Their results showed drastic differences between using raw scores and *T*-scores for measuring stability in both high and low scale score shifts between administrations. Tellegen and Ben-Porath (1996) criticized their results on methodological grounds stating that normative differences were not the primary reason for the shifts to occur. Nonetheless, it is clear that the MMPI-2 results in lower *T*-score values (Blake et al., 1992; Friedman, 1990; Greene, 2011; Harrell, Honaker, & Parnell, 1992; Humphrey & Dahlstrom, 1995; Ward, 1991). Dahlstrom (1992a) suggested three sources of change that contribute to the differences between the original and new norms: (a) reworded or omitted items that probably do not appreciably affect any changes in code concordance, (b) uniform *T*-score values computed for the eight clinical scales, and (c) new means and standard deviations for each scale. Dahlstrom (1992a) noted that "the overall impact on the *T*-score distributions for scales 1–4 and 6–9 of the uniform *T*-score transformations was minimal, affecting primarily scores at the very ends of the distributions of *T*-scores" (p. 156). The re-standardization sample did, however, differ from the original Minnesota normative group in terms of item endorsement frequencies, which did affect the way in which the new *T*-score values were established for the MMPI-2. In essence, the general effect of the mean raw score differences between the MMPI and MMPI-2 normative samples contributed to the reduction of profile elevations on the latter, with resultant *T*-score distribution differences for the MMPI-2, due to higher raw-score values from the more heterogeneous re-standardization sample.

A major issue emerging from the concordance studies revolved around which set of *T*-scores provided the most valid pattern format from which to address the interpretive literature on code patterns as it stood prior to the release of the MMPI-2. This issue has raised significant controversy, with some researchers (e.g. Caldwell, 1997; Humphrey & Dahlstrom, 1995) recommending plotting the raw scores on both sets of norms and examining them for interpretive information, or simply interpreting the MMPI-2 on the basis of original norms. Others, in an effort to ameliorate the concordance problem, have recommended that well-defined code patterns be the only basis for the configural interpretation of MMPI-2 profiles. Well-defined code patterns tend to produce high concordance rates and, therefore, are more reliable and valid to interpret (e.g. Graham, 1990; Graham, Timbrook, Ben-Porath, & Butcher, 1991; Munley, 2002; Munley et al., 2004; Tellegen & Ben-Porath, 1993, 1996). *Well-defined codetype* or code pattern means that, for example, in a two-point code, the third scale is lower than the second scale in the high-point pair by some arbitrary value, usually five *T*-scores. According to proponents of this rule, if such separation does not meet this requirement, the profile would not be interpretable as a two-point code. Instead, they propose that the interpretation of such profiles would be limited to a scale-by-scale analysis. Dahlstrom (1992a, p. 155) has objected to this limitation on the grounds that:

> few, if any, of the research investigations that furnished the code correlates for MMPI interpretation themselves utilized such refinements in the definition of the research groups. The vast majority of studies of code patterns based on high points or high-point pairs, which presently provide the guidelines for profile pattern interpretation, were carried out without regard to such restrictions on third-scale elevation in the formation of their groupings.

Dahlstrom (1992a) also stated that "there is little empirical justification for the imposition of any arbitrary elevation gap between the first and second or the second and third or third and fourth scales in the profile code" (p. 155). A disadvantage in using such restrictive rules is that the number of interpretable profiles often drops to an impractical level. For example, Edwards, Weissman, and Morrison (1993) found that when using well-defined code patterns, the number of classifiable profiles decreased from 75 percent to 36 percent. Tellegen and Ben-Porath (1993, p. 492) argued that limiting interpretation to well-defined code patterns does not appear to exclude most profiles. They stated that:

> Graham, Timbrook, Ben-Porath, and Butcher (1991) reported that in their two psychiatric samples an average of 83% of the MMPI-2 profiles belonged to 1- or 2- or 3-point codetypes that have a 5 point definition. The corresponding average for their two normative samples is 71%. The analysis reported by Graham and colleagues (1991) did not include a fourth possible classification of codetypes as falling within normal limits (i.e. all 10 clinical scores are less than 65). When this option is added to the well-defined 1- or 3-point codetypes, the percentage of classified profiles rises to 87 in the psychiatric sample and 92 in the normative sample, where 59% of the profiles were within normal limits.

Graham et al. (1991) clearly did not think that using well-defined code patterns to interpret MMPI-2 profiles is an exclusionary process. However, McGrath, Rashid, Hayman, and Pogge (2002) studied the MMPI-2 profiles of psychiatric adult inpatients by examining four coding rules, including a minimum elevation of *T*-65 for the scales in the codetype as well as the well-defined coding rule whereby the coded scales exceed all other scales by at least five *T*-scores. They pointed out that, to date, there has never been a study examining the validity of interpreting MMPI profiles based on high-point code versus individual scale elevations. Their results supported the use of a minimum elevation rule of the scales in the codetype being at least a *T*-score of 65. However, the rule for defining a well-defined code using the third scale being at least five *T*-scores lower than the second scale in the codetype produced only equivocal findings.

More contemporary basic reference sources and texts on the MMPI-2 support the classification of codetypes using a decision rule for well-defined profiles, whereby the last scale in the code type must be at least five *T*-scores higher than the scales following it

(Butcher & Williams, 2000; Friedman et al., 2001; Graham, 2011; Greene, 2011; Nichols, 2011). Munley et al. (2004, p. 180) point out:

> Only assigning profiles to codetypes when they are well defined in terms of at least a five-point *T*-score difference, clearly seems to help protect against measurement error in code type assignment. However, it is not immediately evident whether five point code type definition is sufficient for all codetypes across all scales.

In their study of two-point codetypes that were systematically varied at different *T*-score elevation levels, Munley et al. (2004) concluded that caution is indicated in considering the five *T*-score level as the standard for profile definition and two-point code stability. As profile definition increased *above* five *T*-scores, stability increased. Specifically, there was a greater likelihood in their data set of simulated profiles for the highest two scales to change on short interval retesting with 5- to 7-point definition compared to 10- to 13-point definition and higher. The greater the profile definition, the more likely the code pattern would remain the same upon short interval retesting. Well-defined two-point codetypes with seven *T*-scores above the third highest scale achieved the same two-point codetype more than 50 percent of the time, and a difference of at least 13 *T*-scores achieved an over 75 percent concordance (Greene, 2011; Munley et al., 2004). These findings are particularly important in settings where repeated testings occur with mental health patients. It is possible that short-term code type stability will require more stringent levels of profile definition beyond the five *T*-score level of definition. The reader is referred to Greene (2011) who provides detailed information about the frequency of well-defined MMPI-2 codetypes from different clinical samples.

An important process to help resolve the issue of which profile is more valid is to conduct research that focuses on whether the specific empirical correlates of well-defined MMPI-2 code patterns differ from nonrestrictive code patterns (Greene et al., 1997; Staal & Greene, 1998). McNulty, Ben-Porath, and Graham (1998) have addressed this concern by examining the effects of profile definition on the correlates of four common MMPI-2 code patterns (13/31, 24/42, 27/72, and 46/64). The participants were 301 community mental health center outpatients with a wide range of diagnoses and diverse backgrounds. Their findings suggested that the use of more restrictive classification rules yielded more valid codetype descriptors. Although conceptually valid descriptors would also apply to nonrestrictive two-point code patterns, there were more spurious correlates. McNulty et al. (1998, p. 407) stated that for:

> profiles that are not well-defined, the list of conceptually relevant descriptors may be overinclusive. Further, the less similar the profile is to well-defined criteria, the less likely it is that such descriptors would apply. The implication for test interpretation is that clinicians should place greater confidence in the accuracy of correlates when interpreting a well-defined codetype than when interpreting a not defined one. Descriptors of individuals who produce profiles that are not well-defined should be more tenuous.

Greene (2011) summarized the empirical correlates for several MMPI-2 codetypes from four studies across different settings. (Archer et al., 1995; Aribisi, Ben-Porath, &

McNulty, 2003; Graham et al., 1999; Sellbom, Graham, & Schenk, 2005). Despite the differences in methodology and patient characteristics, Greene stated that "all these researchers concluded that the correlates for the MMPI-2 codetypes were similar to those on the MMPI" (p. 165). Greene (2011) further concludes that "clinicians can be reasonably confident in using the correlates of MMPI codetypes with MMPI-2 codetypes" (p. 165). This text's authors are in agreement with Greene's opinion that the MMPI correlates apply to the MMPI-2. We also recognize that as future empirical studies continue to focus on the MMPI-2 correlates, new findings will expand our current descriptive database for codetypes.

Codetype Stability

The stability of code-types over time is another important issue with little empirical data to indicate how consistently test takers will obtain the same codetype on successive administrations of the MMPI-2. However, as summarized in Greene (2011, p. 166):

> Clinicians should be cautious about making long-term predictions from a single administration of the MMPI-2. It appears that, even if well-defined, two-point codetypes are required, it is more likely than not that the person will have a different two-point codetype the next time that the MMPI-2 is administered. If the code-type is not well defined, the person will have a different two-point codetype three out of four times. Any MMPI-2 interpretation should be understood as reflecting how the person reports his or her behavior and symptoms *at this point in time*.

Greene (2011) concludes that when shifts do occur in codetypes, it is unclear if the changes are attributable to actual status changes in the test takers, instability of the MMPI-2, or a combination of the two. Clearly, more research is needed in this area.

Another important factor in considering codetype stability is the standard error of measurement (SEM) which is designed to establish the limits for estimated true scores with specific confidence intervals (Stanley, 1971). Munley et al. (2004) examined simulated codetypes at different *T*-score elevations, factoring in measurement error with the SEM, and found appreciably more codetype stability as the level of profile definition increased above five *T*-scores. The MMPI-2 *Manual* (Butcher et al., 2001) shows average raw-score SEMs for males to be 4.7 for the clinical scales, with females averaging higher at 5.38, for participants in the MMPI-2 normative sample. Rogers and Sewell (2006) suggest that SEM estimates should match the appropriate reference group. They also indicate that in order to gain a 95 percent confidence level (i.e. 95 percent likelihood that the true score meets the 65-*T* benchmark for clinical interpretation) that an elevation of ≥ 77 on the clinical scales is needed. In order to achieve a 95 percent confidence level for unelevated scale scores (to interpret them as within normal limits), *T*-scores of 53 or below are necessary. Without considering the SEM for the different clinical scales, they suggest that the marked variability among the clinical scales will constrain clinical interpretation. In a valid profile, this suggests that the higher the scale elevation and the greater the profile definition, the more reliable and valid will be the interpretation.

3 Measures of MMPI-2 Profile Validity

The Traditional Measures and Their Derivatives

The traditional validity measures are Cannot Say (?), *L, F,* and *K.* Three additional validity scales were published with the MMPI-2 in 1989 and are named the Variable Response Inconsistency scale (*VRIN*), the True Response Inconsistency scale (*TRIN*), and the F-Back scale (*FB*). The Infrequency-Psychopathology scale *F(p)*, Fake Bad Scale (*FBS*), and the Superlative (*S*) scales were added to the profile form after the MMPI-2 was published. All of these scales are described in this chapter. The original intent of Hathaway and McKinley in developing the traditional validity scales was to aid in determining the test-taking attitude of the subject. Some individuals are motivated to distort their responses to the test items, either to minimize the presentation of their psychological problems or to feign or exaggerate their psychopathology. Others may present a distorted picture of themselves by answering the items without fully comprehending their meaning, perhaps by simply not reading the items and responding randomly, or with a True or False response bias. It is important to ascertain the participant's test-taking disposition before interpreting the clinical scales. Although the validity scales were designed for this purpose, they have also been shown to correlate with personality traits and behaviors. Hence, these scales can enrich the clinical interpretation of the profile by providing the clinician with other psychological descriptors, as well as serving as indicators of the accuracy of the examinee's self-description.

The accurate assessment of a participant's test-taking attitude on the MMPI-2 (or any personality inventory) is complex. Some individuals believe they are giving an honest and accurate picture of themselves through their responses, but in fact may distort their presentations by an overly positive self-evaluation, exaggerated perceptions of control or mastery, or unrealistic optimism (Taylor & Brown, 1988). These self-illusions may serve them well in coping with life's stresses but will affect their responses to inventory items. Paulhus (1984) referred to those participants who believe in their positive self-reports as engaging in self-deception and those who consciously attempt to manipulate others' views of themselves as "impression managers." There appears to be a continuum of accurate self-reporting that ranges from under-reporting to over-reporting psychological problems and concerns, although Lanyon, Dannebaum, Wolf, and Brown (1989) conceptualized under-reporting and over-reporting as independent dimensions. Nichols and Greene (1997) identified several dimensions along which deceptive test-taking influences may vary, as well as the strategies test takers may adopt on the MMPI-2 to achieve these results. The reader is urged to review their article. It is up to the clinician to assess the validity of the participant's self-report before making a detailed analysis of the clinical and supplementary scale scores. To this end, the validity scales should be considered indispensable in assessing the individual's self-report style and test-taking attitude (see Chapter 4 for detailed information on the interpretation of the validity scales).

The composition of the validity scales with the scoring directions and *T*-score conversions are presented in the MMPI-2 *Manual* (Butcher et al., 2001, Appendix A, Table A-1, and Appendix B, Table B-1). The item composition and scoring directions of the supplementary validity scales, *Ds*, *Mp*, *Sd*, and *Ss* are presented in Friedman et al. (2001, Appendix A, pp. 532–538).

Cannot Say Score (?)

The Cannot Say score is the number of items the examinee left unmarked or marked both True and False, thereby leaving the response unscorable. A response may also be unscorable if it is uncertain to the test scorer whether a True or False response was given to the item. On the MMPI-2 profile form, a space is provided for recording the raw-score value of omitted or double-marked or unscorable items. The MMPI-2 *Manual* (Butcher et al., 2001) considers a profile invalid with a Cannot Say score of 30 or greater, whereas raw scores between 11 and 29 are of questionable validity. Scores between 0 and 10 are probably valid, but the psychologist should examine the content of omitted items. As all of the clinical and certain validity scales (*L*, *F*, and *K*) are scored within the first 370 items, if most of the item omissions occur later in the protocol, it is unlikely that these scales or the clinical scales will be affected (Butcher et al., 2001). However, the supplementary and content scales are likely to be impacted.

The possible reasons for the lack of a response to an item are numerous. Perhaps some of the items lack personal relevance, or an individual filling out the answer sheet may accidentally skip an item. Different motivational factors, such as test-taking resistance or suspiciousness have been associated with high Cannot Say scores (Dahlstrom et al., 1972). Not marking an item may be related to decisional ambiguity, the inability of the participant to decide how to respond to the item (Fulkerson & Willage, 1980). In addition, intellectual or reading deficits may make it difficult to comprehend an item, leading to its omission (Ball & Carroll, 1960). However, most test takers respond to all of the items, although some individuals may object to various items (Clopton & Neuringer, 1977). For example, those in personnel selection situations are more likely to react negatively to items if they feel they lack job relevance. If participants omit items, it is always desirable to encourage them to complete the omitted ones, and to assess why they chose to leave them out. Although in many cases the omission may have occurred accidentally, other omissions may have occurred because the item was ambiguous or offensive to the reader or, as implied earlier in the case of adolescence, semantically confusing. It is likely, however, that the improved item wording on the MMPI-2 has led to fewer item omissions. In fact, Greene (2011) reported that the low level of MMPI-2 item omissions in personnel settings is a function of the eliminated objectionable items from the original MMPI. Examining the item omissions among normals (Butcher et al., 1989) and for the Caldwell (2007b)[1] clinical sample, Greene reported that the most frequently omitted MMPI-2 item (215, referring to frequent brooding) is only omitted by 2.7 percent of the clinical sample: "The clinical clients were more likely to omit items than normal individuals, although these differences are very small" (Greene, 2011, p. 42). Of the 20 items Greene identified as the most frequently omitted, the content was diverse, with 4 items related to work, and another 4 items related to marital relationships. In his analysis, he reported that 74.6 percent of the normals and 66.7 percent of the clinical clients did not omit a single item.

Archer (1992) summarized the findings of Ball and Carroll (1960), who examined correlates of Cannot Say scores among 262 ninth grade, public school students in Kentucky. Archer stated that, in general, the adolescents who omitted greater numbers of MMPI items also had lower IQ scores and grades that were below average. This seems to suggest that intelligence and reading limitations are associated with Cannot Say scores at least as much as negativistic attitudes toward the testing. An inverse relationship between reading grade level and raw scores on the Cannot Say measure was also found by Archer and Gordon (1991). In a sample of 495 normal adolescents who were administered the MMPI-A and the Ohio Literacy Test, a measure of reading comprehension, they found that adolescents who have difficulty reading MMPI or MMPI-A items tend to omit items at a higher frequency than other adolescents. Archer also pointed out that, unfortunately, many adolescents also attempt to respond to items that they have difficulty reading or understanding, which often results in invalid test protocols. This emphasizes the necessity to evaluate carefully an individual's reading ability before he or she is administered the MMPI-2 (see Chapter 2).

Usually 10 or fewer omitted items will not affect the validity of the profile. When between 5 and 30 items are omitted, Greene (2011) recommended a procedure called "augmenting" the profile. In this procedure, the items that were omitted are endorsed in the deviant direction, scored, and reinterpreted. The test should also be scored without the items marked in the deviant direction so that the two profiles can be compared. More than 30 item omissions renders the test record highly suspect, if not invalid. If items are omitted, then the scale on which they are scored will be lowered, thus compromising the validity of the profile. The omission of items can also change the MMPI-2 high-point pairs (highest clinical scales), which could significantly alter the interpretation of the profile (Clopton & Neuringer, 1977).

Clopton and Neuringer (1977) conducted a two-phase study to address the issue of item omission and its effects on profile configuration. In the first phase, they examined the occurrence of omitted MMPI items from Veterans Administration (VA) psychiatric patients being admitted to the hospital, outpatients at a regional mental health center (MHC), and police and firefighter applicants who had completed the MMPI. In each of these groups, the majority of test participants completed all of the items, with the percentage of participants omitting five or fewer being 93.7 percent for the job applicants, 88.9 percent for MHC clients, and 85.6 percent for the VA patients. The corresponding number of mean items omitted was 2.45 for job applicants, 2.24 for MHC clients, and 4.68 for the VA patients.

The second phase of Clopton and Neuringer's (1977) study involved inspecting the effects of randomly omitted items on profile elevation and configuration (high-point pairs). A subset of 180 randomly selected VA patient MMPI profiles, which were completely filled out, were then rescored with 5, 30, 55, 80, 105, and 130 items randomly omitted. The original MMPI profiles were compared with the different rescored profiles with the different levels of omitted items. As more MMPI items were omitted, there was a corresponding reduction in the profile elevation and, perhaps more importantly, changes occurred in profile configurations. The mean reductions in *T*-scores across the clinical scales for the six levels of omitted items fell an average of 0.45, 2.74, 5.61, 7.70, 9.09, and 11.54 points, respectively. Randomly eliminating 30 MMPI items from complete answer sheets in their study led to a change in the high-point pair in more than 25 percent of the profiles and an average reduction of nearly three *T*-score points in the clinical profile. Thus, profile configuration, rather than specific *T*-scale scores, is more importantly affected by a large number of item omissions.

Although most people rarely omit a significant number of items, the consequences of doing so are such that the clinician should inspect the answer sheet carefully for a completed test record. Failure to check an answer sheet having a large number of item omissions can mislead the test interpreter to underestimate the degree of psychopathology revealed in the profile. As suggested earlier, whenever possible it is good practice to ask examinees why items were omitted and to encourage them to complete those items. The following example illustrates the importance of checking the answer sheet for item omissions. An MMPI-2 had been completed by a security guard applicant during a pre-employment screening. The clinical psychologist who interpreted the profile failed to examine the answer sheet and instead relied exclusively on the profile for making his recommendations. The profile was well within normal limits. However, the applicant had omitted approximately 77 of the first 370 MMPI-2 items. Because the psychologist failed to look at the answer sheet, he recommended that the security guard be hired for employment. The numerous item omissions came to the attention of this text's first author when the security guard later became involved in a shooting incident that led to litigation in which the guard was sued for excessive force. Clearly, the MMPI-2 should have been either considered invalid or given back to the job applicant to complete his responses to the items. This kind of oversight can be avoided if clinicians routinely inspect answer sheet for omissions.

Variable Response Inconsistency Scale (VRIN)

The *VRIN* scale comprises 67 pairs of items designed to detect inconsistent, contradictory responding. It was designed for the MMPI-2 and resembles in function the shorter Carelessness scale on the original MMPI developed by Greene (1978). One major difference between the *VRIN* and the Carelessness scales is the greater scale length of the former. *VRIN* is also seen as a replacement for the TR index on the MMPI, which consisted of the 16 repeated items on the original form, and for which 4 or more inconsistent responses raised the question of profile invalidity due to inconsistent responding.

The *VRIN* item pairs have similar or opposite meaning (Butcher et al., 2001). Some are scored as inconsistent if one item receives an opposite endorsement (True or False as the case may be) from the other item in the pair, whereas others are scored as inconsistent if both pairs are scored as either True or False. As Butcher et al. (2001) has stated, "the raw score in the *VRIN* scale is the total number of item pairs answered inconsistently" (p. 15). High scores raise the possibility that the test taker did not respond carefully to the content of the inventory, thereby rendering the profile uninterpretable. The scoring direction for the *VRIN* items is based on the frequency of item endorsements by the contemporary normal sample; hence, many apparently contradictory response patterns are not scored. Greene (2011) pointed out that *VRIN* actually consists of 49 pairs of unique items because two separate response patterns (i.e. True–False or False–True) are scored for 18 of these 67 pairs, as with Items 6 and 90.

Because scoring for *VRIN* is configural, the user must be especially careful if hand scoring is used because mistakes can easily be made. Iverson and Barton (1999) investigated the hand-scoring accuracy of the *VRIN* and *TRIN* scales, and compared these results to the reliabilities of the other clinical and validity scales. Despite high reliabilities across most of the scales, clerical errors were common (7 percent of the scales were scored inconsistently), although for the most part these errors only "represented one or two raw score points and did not affect the clinical interpretation of the scales" (Iverson & Barton, 1999, p. 69). However, there were three times as many scoring errors for *VRIN* than for any other scale, suggesting that the configural nature of the scale is much less of a scoring handicap if a computer-scored program is used. If this is not possible, clinicians should carefully re-check their hand scoring for this scale.

For the MMPI-2 to be clinically interpretable, it is necessary for the individual to respond to semantically similar items in similar ways (Nichols & Greene, 1995). A high rate of inconsistent responses usually indicates difficulties in understanding the content of the inventory or a lack of cooperation (non-content responding). *VRIN* (along with *TRIN*) was designed to complement the interpretation of the *L*, *F*, and *K* validity scales. The MMPI-2 *Manual* states that, for example,

> a high F score combined with a high *VRIN* score is more likely to indicate a profile that is uninterpretable owing to carelessness, confusion, etc. than if *VRIN is* not elevated. On the other hand, in the case of high F and low *VRIN,* carelessness, etc. can be ruled out and a high F score can be interpreted in terms of its actual content which could, then, reflect either true psychopathology or deliberate efforts to fake bad.
>
> (Butcher et al., 1989, p. 28)

Other research findings also support this strategy of interpreting an elevated *F* by referring to the *VRIN* score (e.g. Wetter et al., 1992).

Note that a participant may shift his or her test-taking attitude at any point during the test administration. For example, an individual could become fatigued and less motivated to read the content, and then resort to random, All-True, or All-False responding. If the participant answered cooperatively during at least the first 370 items, all of the clinical scales as well as scales *L*, *F*, and *K* can be accurately interpreted. However, after Item 370, if a participant adopts a random-response bias, the content and supplementary scales will be unduly affected. Greene (1991a) pointed out that the *VRIN* scale items are fairly evenly distributed throughout the MMPI-2. If the clinician wanted to take the care and time to score the validity scales in blocks of items rather than for the entire test, it can be determined at what point the examinee began responding randomly or inconsistently. This approach would be particularly helpful for understanding intermediate scores on the *VRIN* scale.

The MMPI-2 *Manual* (Butcher et al., 2001) suggests that a raw score of 13 ($T = 80$) on *VRIN* indicates inconsistent responding, which is in accord with the research focusing on validity scale cut scores (Berry, Wetter et al., 1991). Greene (1991a, 1991b), however, recommended a more graduated interpretation. He suggests a raw score cut of 16 for *VRIN*, and that scores between 8 and 15 can indicate either consistent or inconsistent responding, thereby necessitating the examination of other measures. Nichols and Greene (1995, p. 21) state that:

> Unfortunately for *VRIN* raw scores in the range of 11 to 16, a relatively large number of inconsistent cases may be inappropriately judged consistent, whereas many consistent cases, particularly in psychiatric samples, may be inappropriately judged inconsistent. In some cases, especially where there is a large imbalance between the proportion of items marked "true" and those marked "false," lower *VRIN* raw scores (e.g. 7–12) may lead to incorrect judgments of consistency. In these cases, *TRIN* (true response inconsistency) may prove to be a more appropriate indicator of response consistency because of its greater sensitivity to extremes and "true" versus "false" responding. Additional indices of consistency may usefully supplement *VRIN* and should always be used when *VRIN* falls within the indeterminate range of 11 to 16, inclusive, and we encourage their examination when *VRIN* exceeds a raw score of 6.

(See the section in this chapter entitled "Additional Measures of Response Style" for a discussion of other measures that can be used in conjunction with the *VRIN* scale.)

The mean number of *VRIN* items earned by men and women in the MMPI-2 standardization group was approximately 5 (SD = 2.5). Test–retest correlation coefficients for these participants over about a one-week interval was .54 for men and .51 for women (Butcher et al., 1989). A completely random pattern of item endorsements yields a raw score of 16.75 on *VRIN* as only one of the four possible combinations of True and False response patterns is scored on each of the 67 pairs of items on the *VRIN* scale (Greene, 2011).

Research data supports the validity of the *VRIN* scale. Berry et al. (1992) investigated the tendencies of normal participants who completed the MMPI-2 to randomly respond, although they were given the test with standard instructions. The participants were asked to estimate the extent to which they randomly responded to questions, and their self-reports were compared with their *VRIN*, *F*, and *FB* scores. The major findings showed that partial random responding occurred with some frequency and that self-reports of random responding correlated significantly with MMPI-2 random-responding measures. This study supports the construct validity of the *VRIN* scale and its sensitivity to random responding.

In another investigation of the sensitivity of the validity scales to detect random responding and malingering, Wetter et al. (1992) instructed college students to either randomly respond to the entire MMPI-2 or to fake various levels of psychiatric disturbance. Their results showed that the *VRIN* scale was elevated only in the random-responding group. The *F* and *FB* scales were elevated in both the random and malingering groups. It appears that the *VRIN* scale is essential to examine when the *F* or *FB* scale is elevated.

Although random responding elevates the *VRIN* scale, a high or intermediate *VRIN* score may not always indicate carelessness or uncooperativeness. Bond (1986, 1987) suggested that individuals with higher inconsistency scores tend to endorse more maladjustment items. This view is consistent with data presented by Greene (1991a), who demonstrated that 43 percent of 68/86 codetypes could result from inconsistency. In fact, he pointed out that most code patterns that include Scale 8 frequently could result from response inconsistency. This makes sense, given that seriously thought-disturbed individuals such as those obtaining the 86 or 68 profiles (e.g. individuals with schizophrenia) are likely to have difficulty maintaining the consistent set that normals do during testing. Another possible explanation for indeterminate range scores on *VRIN* (raw scores of 7 to 13) involves not carelessness or lack of cooperation, but rather indecisiveness (Bond, 1987; Fulkerson & Willage, 1980). If an item is clearly applicable or inapplicable to an individual, it will be relatively easy to respond with certainty and consistency. However, an item with ambiguous application to the person involves a complex judgment process that can change on the repeated presentation of an item. Bond (1986) studied the MMPI responses of college students and found that indecision, rather than carelessness, may be a more important determinant of inconsistency on repeated items. Even though Bond (1986) was studying the repeated items on the Carelessness scale and the TR index, it may be valid to generalize his findings about semantic inconsistency to the item pairs of the *VRIN* scale. Bond (1987) offered three possible reasons for which items may elicit indecision: (a) the degree of ambiguity in an item perceived by the respondent, (b) the perceived degree of relevance an item has to the respondent, and (c) the degree of conflict aroused in a respondent by an item that is applicable but of an undesirable nature. Whereas carelessness may be one factor for elevated scores on inconsistency measures, other factors, such as indecision and maladjustment, can also be important contributing determinants.

Examination of the MMPI-2 *Manual* (Butcher et al., 1989) shows that for contemporary normal men and women there is a small but significant correlation between *VRIN* and recent life changes and the Social Readjustment Rating Scale (SRRS). There is also a small but significant correlation between both dysphoria and hostility for a subsample of men and women, as rated by their life partners on the SSRS. The implications raised by Bond (1986, 1987) and gleaned from the MMPI-2 *Manual* data are that indeterminate scores of normals and psychiatric patients on *VRIN* may not reveal inconsistent or careless responding so much as indecisive responding, a result that would suggest quite different empirical correlates and meaning. This issue needs more study in order to make interpretive sense out of scores in the indeterminate range on *VRIN*.

True Response Inconsistency Scale (TRIN)

The *TRIN* scale consists of 23 item pairs (40 total items; 20 unique pairs) designed to assist in the interpretation of the traditional validity indicators. Like the *VRIN* scale, the *TRIN* scale reflects the tendency of a participant to respond to items in a contradictory or inconsistent fashion (Butcher et al., 2001). Although *VRIN* items can have either similar or opposite content, *TRIN* items consist exclusively of pairs that are opposite in content. According to the MMPI-2 *Manual* (Butcher et al., 2001, p. 16), inconsistency is scored as follows:

> If a test-taker responds inconsistently by answering True to both items of certain pairs, one point is added to the *TRIN* raw score; if he or she responds inconsistently

by answering False to certain item pairs, one point is subtracted. A constant is added to the raw scores to avoid negative values, and this score is converted to a *T*-score. All TRIN *T*-scores are set to be equal to or greater than 50. For example, if the original score is one standard deviation above the mean, indicating yea-saying, it will be assigned a *T*-score value of 60*T*. If the original score is one standard deviation below the mean, indicating nay-saying, it will be assigned a *T*-score value of 60*F*. The "*T*" and "*F*" notations are used in computerized scoring reports and Appendix Tables A-1 through A-4 in this manual, designating the direction of indiscriminate fixed responding found in the protocol. The hand-scored profile forms contain separate columns for TRIN True and False scores. *T*-scores greater than 79 on TRIN (in either the True or False direction) indicate an excessive level of yea- or nay-saying, raising questions about the protocol's interpretability.

Items 3 and 39 are one of the 14 item pairs to which the inconsistent response is True. A test participant endorsing both of these items would receive 1 raw-score point. Items 9 and 56 are one of the nine item pairs scored as inconsistent if both items are scored as False. For this pair, or any pair of items scored False on *VRIN*, 1 point is subtracted from the total raw score. A score of nine points is always added to the final score to avoid the possibility of negative scores (i.e. scores below *T*-50). For example, a client endorsing only falsely scored pairs of items on the *TRIN* scale and no true scored items would obtain a negative score were it not for the constant being added. Raw scores between 10 and 19 reflect a bias toward True responding, whereas raw scores between 0 and 9 reflect a bias toward False responding.

Similar to the *VRIN* item pairs, the *TRIN* item pairs were chosen on the basis of their statistical associations and semantic similarities. *TRIN* is sensitive to the acquiescence response style (and its opposite)—that is, the tendency to mark items True (or False) without regard to item content. An acquiescent (yea-saying) or non-acquiescent (nay-saying) response set is readily identified by significant deviations in the percentage of items endorsed as True or False, "with defensive protocols tending to show a low percentage of items endorsed True (and a high percentage of items endorsed False), and exaggerated protocols showing the opposite pattern" (Nichols, 2011, p. 51). It is highly likely that the test taker was not responding to the content of the items if his/her percentage of items marked "True" or "False" approaches 75 percent or greater.

The MMPI-2 *Manual* (Butcher et al., 1989) shows that the contemporary sample of men and women averaged approximately nine raw-score points on *TRIN*, corresponding to a *T*-score of 50. Test–retest reliability data in the MMPI-2 *Manual* for about a one-week interval show normal men and women to have a correlation coefficient of .34 and .52, respectively. The *Manual* also recommends that a *TRIN* score of 5 or less or 13 or greater would suggest inconsistent responding. A low raw score reflects a false-response bias, whereas higher scores reflect a true-response bias. The contemporary normal sample is used as a reference group for converting the raw scores on the *TRIN* scale to linear *T*-scores.

Interpretation of *TRIN* can often clarify the validity of a particular profile. For example, a high *F* score in conjunction with a markedly elevated *TRIN* score suggests indiscriminate responding, whereas an elevated *T*-score with a low to moderate *TRIN* score reveals a possible magnification of symptoms or marked psychopathology. The

TRIN scale, like VRIN, should always be assessed when interpreting the validity of any MMPI-2 profile.

Infrequency Scale (F)

The F scale was designed to measure the tendency of an individual to respond to the test items in an unusual manner, such as in the case of not comprehending the items. On the MMPI-2, F contains 60 items, 41 keyed True, 19 False, to which at least 90 percent of the normals in the original standardization group responded in the same direction (either True or False). However, as Greene (2011) recognized, eight of the items (12, 48, 120, 132, 204, 222, 264, and 288) fail to meet the 10 percent or below criterion for either men or women in the MMPI-2 normative sample, with an additional four items (84, 174, 306, and 343) for men also failing to meet this criterion. Whether an F scale item is answered True or False is irrelevant; the point is that the items are said to have high community agreement. According to Marks, Seeman, and Haller (1974), "every time a subject answers in the rare direction, he is deviating from the community on some subject in which it is in exceedingly high agreement" (p. 12). For this reason, the scale has come to be called the Frequency or Infrequency scale. Because the probability is about 9 in 10 that, for any given item, the normal participant will answer in the popular direction, the mean number of deviant responses for the F scale is relatively low for the MMPI-2 normative sample (mean score for men = 4.5, mean score for women = 3.7). Normal individuals responding to the test with the usual care and comprehension typically will not obtain raw-score values above six or T-score values greater than 55 on the MMPI-2. However, individuals suffering from situational distress (e.g. loss of a loved one or relationship or job-related problems) or psychopathology will often elevate their F scale score as high as T-score values of 65 or greater.

Half of the F items occur among the first 180, and all are contained within the first 361 items. The F items represent a broad range of content that obviously suggests deviant behavior, making it relatively easy for individuals either to deny symptoms or to over-claim problems, depending on their motives. The emphasis in the content is largely psychotic. Examples of F scale item content includes references to having nightmares, feeling possessed by evil spirits, hearing odd sounds, feeling depersonalized, having paranoid thoughts, schizoid apathy, cynicism, antisocial attitudes, social under-involvement, somatic symptoms, and family enmity. F underwent changes in the re-standardization, with 12 modifications to the 60 items, including six grammatical changes, five modernizations of idioms and usage, and one change in sexist wording (Dahlstrom, 1993). Because 25 of the 60 items overlap other scales, and because about one third of the scale items are scored on the so-called psychotic tetrad scales (Scales 6, 7, 8, and 9), increasing elevations on the F scale are usually associated with increasing psychotic scale elevations. Greene (2011) pointed out that 15 F items overlap with Scale 8 (Sc—Schizophrenia), 9 with Scale 6 (Pa—Paranoia), 4 with Scale 4 (Pd—Psychopathic Deviate), 14 with Infrequency-Psychopathology (F(p)), 10 with the MacAndrew (1965) Alcoholism-Revised (MAC–R) scale, and 5 with Post-Traumatic Stress Disorder—Keane (PK).

The F scale—when elevated—is considered one of the most sensitive scales of the test for indicating severity of maladjustment and generally tends to correspond to the overall elevation of the clinical scales. For this reason, seriously or acutely disturbed individuals tend to obtain elevated scores. Also, people who exaggerate their concerns and psychological problems by over-claiming symptoms elevate F due to its obvious content, whereas individuals wishing to appear free of psychological problems tend to produce low scores (Rothke, Friedman, Dahlstrom, Greene, Arrendondo, & Mann, 1994). Numerous studies have supported the validity of F in detecting people who over-claim symptoms or malinger, with the general result that F is elevated above a T score of 90 (Nichols, 2011). Greene (2011) inspected the Caldwell (2007a) clinical data set and reported that a cut score of 16 (T of 85—males; T of 92—females) on the F scale would classify approximately 10 percent of the clinical clients as simulating psychopathology, while a cut score of 29 would classify slightly less than 10 percent as simulating. Cuts vary for this scale according to the setting, but scores above 90 generally should raise the concern of the clinician to look for other indications in the MMPI-2 of exaggeration or random responding, as well as in non-test data such as interviews, life history data, and observations from people familiar with the examinee. In a review of the MMPI with a focus on the validity scales, Berry, Baer, and Harris (1991) meta-analytically reviewed 28 studies that used the MMPI to detect malingering. The multiple comparisons contrasting malingering and honest groups on raw and T-scaled F scores showed that this scale (particularly raw-score values of F) is one of the most powerful measures on the test in detecting faking. F was elevated slightly over 2 SDs above scores of participants answering honestly. Although their study identified other measures in the test for detecting malingering, the F scale was clearly the measure of choice for detecting "faking bad." It is recommended, however, that the reader not rely on any one scale in deciding about an individual's test-taking attitudes. Rather, a combination of measures coupled with non-test data should be considered in the clinical decision-making/inference process.

Elevated F scores may result from either a single factor, such as poor comprehension, random responding, severe psychosis, or malingering, or a combination of these. Accurate interpretation of F elevations requires reference to other scales, such as $VRIN$, $TRIN$, FB, $F(p)$, and the $F - K$ index. F is correlated at .80 or greater with most over-reporting scales and indices. Nichols (2011, p. 54) states:

The F scale tends to accelerate most of the clinical scales, especially scales 8, 7, 6, and 4, and may, therefore, contribute significantly to the elevation of the profile as a whole. Elevations of F also tend to drive up the content scales, especially BIZ ($BIZ1$), DEP, WRK, and LSE.

It is important to consider F as serving three important functions (Graham, 1990). First, the scale should be considered as an indication of the openness or guarded approach of the test taker. Next, if the profile appears valid and the F scale score is in the patient range, it may roughly indicate the person's level of distress or maladjustment. Last, scores on the scale can serve to suggest behavioral correlates about the individual. Numerous studies and reviews have provided useful guidelines for interpreting elevations on this scale (Bagby, Rogers, & Buis, 1994; Bagby, Rogers, Buis, & Kalemba, 1994; Berry, Baer, & Harris, 1991; Berry, Wetter, Baer, Gass, Franzen, Youngjohn et al., 1995; Lamb, Berry, Wetter, & Baer, 1994; Rogers, Bagby, & Chakraborty, 1993; Rogers, Sewell, & Salekin,

1994; Rothke et al., 1994; Sivec, Lynn, & Garske, 1994; Wetter, Baer, Berry, Robison, & Sumpter, 1993).

Test–retest correlation coefficients for 82 men and 111 women from the contemporary normative sample are reported in the MMPI-2 *Manual* (Butcher et al., 1989). These participants were retested at an average interval of 8.58 days (*Mdn* = 7 days), with men and women showing test–retest values of .78 and .69, respectively, on the *F* scale. Although the MMPI-2 *Manual* does not present similar data for psychiatric patients, Dahlstrom et al. (1975) reported test–retest coefficients for psychiatric cases on the original *F* scale that range from .80 to .81 with a one- to two-day interval between tests, and from .63 to .76 with a one-year interval between tests. In a large-scale meta-analysis of MMPI reliability studies using a wide variety of populations conducted between 1970 and 1981, Hunsley et al. (1988) found an average internal consistency for *F* of .77 across 70 studies. They also reported an average test–retest reliability of .70 for 15 studies, with time intervals from 1 day to 2 years.

F-Back Scale (FB)

The 40-item *FB* scale was developed for the MMPI-2 to operate in a manner similar to the *F* scale, but for the items appearing later in the inventory. It contains 40 items, 37 keyed True, 3 False. The 60-item *F* scale is scored within the first 361 items, with 82 percent of the items scored between Items 1 and 299. The last *F* item is 361, which indicates that this sensitive scale prematurely stops its measurement function short of the entire instrument. Therefore, the re-standardization committee for the MMPI-2 designed the *FB* scale to pick up where the *F* scale left off. *FB* begins at Item 281. Although *L*, *F*, and *K*, and the clinical scales are all scored within the first 370 items, many of the content and supplementary scale items occur after item 370. Therefore, a scale similar to the *F* scale was needed for the latter part of the test to detect random or faking-bad/faking-good tendencies that could affect content and supplementary scale scores.

The items of *FB* were selected if endorsed by less than 10 percent of the contemporary normative sample in the deviant direction. The majority (95 percent) of *FB* items are concentrated between items 300 and 567, making the scale sensitive to a response set or shift in responding due to fatigue or a change in cooperation during the latter part of an MMPI-2 administration. In this regard, the *FB* scale serves a parallel function to the earlier occurring *F* items, with a wideband sensitivity to different response sets, including symptom magnification or fabrication, random responding, and severe psychopathology (Berry et al., 1992). Thirty-seven of the 40 items are scored True and three False, making this scale susceptible to an "all True" response bias. Therefore, a very elevated score should be checked against the *TRIN* and *VRIN* scores, and the answer sheet itself.

It should be noted that *FB*, although similar in its construction to *F*, is somewhat different in its content. Whereas the predominant content theme in *F* is psychoticism, the main theme for *FB* is acute distress and depression/low self-esteem. Therefore, clinicians should consider this content difference when making any interpretive inferences from the two scales.

Because the *FB* scale was constructed to appear later in the test, it shares little item overlap with the standard clinical scales. The *FB* scale shares 2 items each with Scales 6

(Paranoia) and 7 (Psychasthenia) and 10 items with Scale 8 (Schizophrenia), and 7 items with the Infrequency-Psychopathology ($F(p)$) scale. However, because most of the items are scored between items 300 and 567, there is significant overlap with the content scales and, to a lesser degree, with the supplementary scales. For example, *FB* shares as many as 6 items with the content scales *DEP* (Depression) and *FRS* (Fears) and as few as 1 item with Social Discomfort (*SOD*), Anxiety (*ANX*), Anger (*ANG*), and Health Concerns (*HEA*). Elevations on *FB* tend to drive up virtually all of the clinical and content scales, especially *FRS* (*FRS1*), *DEP* (*DEP4*), *TRT* (Negative Treatment Indicators, and *LSE*(Low Self-Esteem). According to Nichols (2011), "the largest subset of items reflects panic/fear (9 items), with smaller subsets reflecting depression and low self-esteem (8 items), suicide/self-harm (4 items), and family estrangement (3 items). Only three items reflect psychotic processes" (p. 56).

The content differences between *F* and *FB* have interpretive importance.

> The differences in content between *F* and *FB* lead to problems with interpreting *FB*. For example, in some cases an elevated *FB* score when *F* is in an acceptable range signifies that the examinee chose to simulate mood disturbance and suicidal ideation rather than psychoticism, whereas in others this pattern of elevation reflects actual panic anxiety or depressive symptoms. Exaggeration or malingering can be safely interpreted only when *both F* and *FB* are elevated beyond acceptable limits.
>
> (Nichols, 2011, p. 56)

As mentioned above, although content differences exist between the *FB* and the *F* scales, examination of the partner ratings in the contemporary normative sample shows that *FB* is similar to *F* in that it shows significant positive correlations with dysphoria, hostility, impulsivity, and antisocial behavior, and negative correlations with sociability and conformity (Butcher et al., 1989).

Internal consistency estimates (Cronbach's coefficient alpha) for *FB* is .71 for a subsample of 82 men in the normative sample and .75 for a subsample of 111 women (Butcher et al., 1989). Test–retest reliability coefficients for the same participants are .86 and .71, for a mean test–retest interval of 8.5 days.

Although the method used for the construction of the *F* and *FB* scales was similar, the same raw score values yield more extreme *T*-scores on *FB* than on *F* because the *FB* scale has a smaller standard deviation than *F*. This is, in part, because *FB* has fewer items than *F* (40 items vs. 60) and, more importantly, because *FB*, unlike *F*, was derived on the basis of the contemporary MMPI-2 norms and as a result has a higher proportion of items with extreme endorsement frequencies (Arbisi & Ben-Porath, 1995b; A. Tellegen, personal communication, March 5, 1999).

Berry, Wetter et al. (1991b) found that a raw score of nine on *FB* out-predicted the ability of *VRIN* to detect random profiles. They had 180 college students complete the MMPI-2 under standard instructions prior to having their test booklets removed after 100, 200, 300, 400, or 500 items were completed, and the remaining blanks on the answer sheet completed randomly. The more random responses that were given, the higher the *FB* scores (as well as those for *F* and *VRIN*). Thus, the scale appears to be sensitive to random responding. Berry et al. (1992) also found *FB* to be sensitive to random responding in job applicants and community volunteers; a significant number of these normal participants taking the MMPI-2 admitted to answering some of the MMPI-2 items in a random manner. The average range of random responses was between 12 and 38. Positive correlations between *FB* (and other validity scales) and the participant's self-estimations of random responding supported the sensitivity of the *FB* scale to non-content responding.

Further support for the sensitivity of *FB* to detect not only random responding, but also malingering, comes from an investigation by Wetter, Baer, Berry, Smith, and Larsen (1992). They explored the effects of both random responding and malingering on the validity scales of the MMPI-2 using four groups of college students. One group completed the answer sheet randomly, two other groups were told to complete the MMPI-2 so as to appear moderately or severely disturbed, and the last group answered honestly. *FB* was sensitive to all four conditions and performed as well as *F*. *FB* scores increased in elevation with the level of feigned disturbance. The fake-severe disturbance group produced the highest *FB* score ($M = 119$, $SD = 4.2$), followed by random responders ($M = 116.5$, $SD = 6.0$). The values for *F* followed the same pattern, and were only slightly higher, except for the fake-severe group, which had an almost identical value ($M = 119.4$, $SD = 3.7$) to *FB*.

The efficacy of *FB* to detect the over-reporting of symptoms is further illustrated in a study by Wetter et al. (1993), who instructed two groups of normal adults about the characteristics of Post-Traumatic Stress Disorder (PTSD) and paranoid schizophrenia, and then asked them to simulate these disorders on the MMPI-2. To determine if the information about the disorders helped them to feign a realistic profile, Wetter et al. compared their scores with actual groups of paranoid schizophrenic and PTSD patients. Having specific information about the psychological disorder did not enable the fakers to simulate actual patient profiles with the validity scales, including the *FB* scale. Specifically, the PTSD patients produced a mean *FB* T-scale score of 85 ($SD = 23.6$), whereas the simulators produced a mean T-score value of 110 ($SD = 20.3$). The paranoid schizophrenic patients produced a mean T-score value of 74.2 on the *FB* scale ($SD = 19.0$), with the simulators earning a mean T-score value of 119.3 ($SD = 2.0$). Clearly, the fakers tended to grossly over-claim symptoms relative to the actual patients, a trend consistently seen in the faking-bad literature. Malingerers reliably score in the upper T-score ranges on both the *F* and *FB* scales.

Although the *FB* scale is relatively new, it has received significant research attention since publication and appears to be a useful and valuable addition to the MMPI-2. In a meta-analysis of malingering scales and indexes on the MMPI-2, Rogers et al. (1994) found that *FB* yielded strong effect sizes for controls and psychiatric comparison groups. They pointed out that several cutting scores have been proposed for *FB*, suggesting that clinicians need to exercise the same caution in interpreting this scale as they do for other validity measures. Greene (1991a) suggested interpreting the elevation on *FB* in a manner similar to that used for *F*, because the construction of the two scales is so similar. This appears to be a practical suggestion, but readers should be aware that they may encounter profiles in which *FB* is significantly more elevated than *F* (e.g. a participant may produce an *FB* T-score of 110 with an *F* T-score of 65). Such a difference may suggest the possibility of fatigue, uncooperativeness, or random responding in the latter portion of the MMPI-2 rendering the content and supplementary scales uninterpretable, but it is perhaps equally likely that this difference is driven by the greater panic-fear and depressive/low self-esteem item content on *FB*. Regardless, because the person responded consistently in the earlier part of the test, the standard clinical scales can be meaningfully analyzed. It is rare to see the converse situation—a high *F* score but a within-normal-limits *FB* score. Such a protocol would suggest standard interpretation of the content or supplementary scales, but caution in interpreting the clinical scales.

Cut scores for validity measures in the MMPI-2 vary from study to study as a function of local base rates and participant characteristics, such as educational level and intelligence. Therefore, the psychologist would be wise to examine each protocol on an individual basis while considering different factors, including, but not limited to, the participant's motivation or test-taking attitude (e.g. over-reporting in an attempt to gain sympathy or monetary gain as in a personal-injury litigation case), socioeconomic factors, reading ability (affecting comprehension), and psychopathology (which can operate independently or in concert with any of the above-mentioned factors). Guidelines for determining an invalid profile are described in this chapter and in Chapter 4; however, in general, the same *T*-score values that apply for *F* may be used for *FB* to indicate profile invalidity. As a point of reference, Greene (2011) stated that a cut score of 13 on *FB* would classify about 10 percent of the clinical clients simulating psychopathology in the Caldwell (2007b) clinical sample, and a cut score of 23 would classify one percent as simulating psychopathology.

Additional Measures of Response Style

The usefulness of the standard validity scales can be enhanced by examining additional measures of response styles, which can be roughly divided into those measuring over-reporting or self-unfavorable trends, and those reflecting under-reporting or self-favorable trends. An additional and useful comprehensive overview of the subject of deception as it relates to the MMPI-2 is available in Nichols and Greene (1997).

Self-Unfavorable Scales

The *F(p)* and Dissimulation (*Ds*) scales were designed to measure the reporting of self-unfavorable traits, attributes, and dispositions in order to magnify one's level of psychopathology, or to create the appearance of psychopathology.

Infrequency-Psychopathology Scale: F(p)

The *F(p)* scale was designed by Arbisi and Ben-Porath (1995a, 1995b) for the MMPI-2 as an additional self-unfavorable or over-reporting measure, particularly for use with patient populations in which a high rate of endorsement of psychological disturbance is expected. They suggested that *F(p)* be used to understand elevations on *F*, which may be elevated for several reasons, including random responding, poor reading comprehension, genuine psychopathology, or an attempt to fake bad (i.e. to portray one's self as more impaired than is actually the case). As previously described, the *F* scale contains items that were endorsed by less than 10 percent of the normal standardization group of the original MMPI (Hathaway & McKinley, 1943); it was not constructed of items that were endorsed infrequently by psychiatric patients (a common misconception about the scale).

Therefore, an elevated F score cannot automatically be assumed to be an indication of malingering, of illness or of an invalid profile (Friedman, Webb, & Lewak, 1989). The $F(p)$ scale is comprised of items endorsed rarely (20 percent or less in the keyed direction) by two separate groups of patients with known psychiatric disturbance, and by members of the MMPI-2 re-standardization sample. Hence, an elevated $F(p)$ score indicates that the test taker endorsed items rarely endorsed by both psychiatric patients and normals, thereby suggesting that their score was achieved by a "faking-bad" response set.

The $F(p)$ scale contains 27 items, of which 18 are True, 9 False. $F(p)$ has 15 items in common with Scale F and 7 with FB. $F(p)$ overlaps Scale 8 (Sc) by seven items, and Scale 6 (Pa) by two. Among the content scales, $F(p)$ overlaps Psychotic Symptomatology ($BIZ1$) by three items, and Generalized Fearfulness ($FRS1$) and Family Discord ($FAM1$) by two items each. The item overlap between the $F(p)$ scale and other clinical scales is substantially less than that between F and FB and these scales. Unfortunately, $F(p)$ also overlaps the Lie (L) scale by four items which, if endorsed in the scorable direction, will produce a T-score equal to or greater than 70 on $F(p)$, even if no other $F(p)$ items are endorsed; a significant weakness for this scale. The normative sample mean for men and women is approximately 1.1 with a standard deviation of about 1.32. Test–retest reliability coefficients for an interval of one week for the normative sample is .7 for men and women (Ben-Porath, Graham, & Tellegen, 2009).

Arbisi and Ben-Porath (1995b) suggested that when $F(p)$ is elevated with F, the clinician can more confidently attribute the high scores to the patient's attempt to over-report psychopathology if other validity measures, such as $VRIN$ and $TRIN$, are not elevated significantly. More recent investigations have found that $F(p)$ is less influenced by diagnostic membership and the confounding effects of distress and psychopathology than is F (with which it shares more than half of its items) and is more effective than F in distinguishing groups with genuine psychopathology from those asked to feign psychiatric impairment (Arbisi & Ben-Porath, 1997; Frueh et al., 1997; Ladd, 1998; Rothke, Friedman, Greene, Wetter, Cole, & Baker, 2000). However, Bagby et al. (1997a) found that $F(p)$ was more effective in distinguishing patients with schizophrenia from participants feigning that disorder, whereas F and FB were better able to identify patients with depression from participants feigning depression. This finding is not surprising, given that the $F(p)$ item content is more relevant to psychoticism than to major depression. Nicholson et al. (1997) found that $F(p)$ failed to outperform F in their malingering comparisons. Even so, Nicholson et al. (1997) noted "that $F(p)$ may be the preferred index of fake bad responding when the two indicators perform comparably because interpretation of elevated scores appears more straight-forward in the case of $F(p)$ than F" (p. 476). Strong, Glassmire, Frederick, and Greene (2006) also reported that $F(p)$ accurately differentiated self-unfavorably reporting forensic examinees elevated on F from bona fide psychiatric disturbances in forensic examinees.

Rothke et al. (2000) provide normative data for $F(p)$ from a large variety of clinical and forensic samples, including psychiatric inpatients with borderline personality disorder (BPD), paranoid schizophrenia, PTSD, and alcoholism, as well as pain management patients, traumatic brain injury (TBI) patients, and Social Security disability applicants. In addition, data were provided for non-litigating TBI patients and normals simulating BPD, PTSD, and paranoid schizophrenia. The results showed that $F(p)$ elevations are infrequent in most clinical samples; elevations are much more common in settings where malingering or exaggeration of psychopathology is more common. Consistent with the findings of Arbisi and Ben-Porath (1997), the Rothke et al. (2000) study supports the finding that $F(p)$ is relatively independent of psychiatric diagnoses, and is less sensitive than F or FB to specific psychopathology. It should be noted that the various scores for the different groups in this study only provide guidelines, not strict cut scores. Greene (2011) suggests a raw cut score of 6 or greater as possibly indicative of exaggeration, but states this is only a "general benchmark," not a definitive score. Nichols (2011) suggests that T-scores between 75 and 100 are optimally interpreted with reference to the range of content among the items of $F(p)$ that have been endorsed. Arbisi and Ben-Porath (1995) identified a raw score of 8 or more as suggesting exaggeration. Greene (2011) provides a useful table (3.23, p. 77) illustrating the various classification scores for personnel, normals, pain patients, clinical and psychiatric inpatients. For example, clinical patients, producing a raw score of 8 are in the 99th percentile, meaning that only 1 percent of the patients score this high. Normals scoring as high as a raw score of 5 would be unusual, as only 1 percent score this high in the standardization group. The reader is urged to consult Greene's table.

It is recommended that the $F(p)$ scale be studied further in other settings, but its applied use should be governed by using a sequence of steps, as well as observing cautions about its potential limitations. Arbisi and Ben-Porath (1995b) recommended that the following sequence be followed in interpreting an elevated F scale: (a) rule out random responding and acquiescence by eliminating profiles with elevated *VRIN* ($T \geq 100$) or *TRIN* ($T \geq 80$) scores; (b) rule out malingering or exaggeration by considering whether $F(p)$ is elevated; and (c) if the results of steps a and b are negative, then a high F scale can be considered consistent with psychopathology. An elevated FB score should be interpreted following the same sequence.

When an elevated $F(p)$ score is encountered, we recommend that the content of the endorsed items be examined before a conclusion about exaggeration or malingering is made. For example, four of the items on $F(p)$ (items 90, 192, 276, and 478) deal with participants' views of their mother and father (family enmity) and whether they love (loved) their parents and family. As is the case with the overlapping L items, described above, a score of $T \geq 70$ will be reached on $F(p)$ even if no other $F(p)$ items are endorsed. The text's first author reported a case of a patient with no other signs of malingering or secondary gain issues who endorsed all four of these items, consistent with a very significant history of impaired family relationships. Despite the fact that these items were rarely endorsed by the clinical derivation sample or the normal standardization group, we suggest that the clinician be mindful of a history of significant family problems before interpreting an $F(p)$ score inflated by the endorsement of two or more of these four items. Given that it takes very few item endorsements to inflate an $F(p)$ score, these types of concerns should be addressed to avoid over-interpreting an elevated $F(p)$ score.

Although $F(p)$ is the most sensitive and specific measure of over-reporting on the MMPI-2, the reader is cautioned that its overlap with Scale L can produce $F(p)$ scores well above T-65 for protocols in which all of these overlapping items are endorsed. As Nichols (2011, p. 58) explains:

Endorsing a few items from each of the largest areas of content within $F(p)$ is sufficient to yield very high scale elevations. For example, a raw score of five obtained on the basis of responding to two of the persecutory items and three of the family enmity items (or vice versa) yields a T-score of 77 for men and 81 for women.

Basically, Nichols (2011) cautions that when the content of the endorsed items falls into only one or two content domains, "$F(p)$ generally should not be interpreted as indicating over-reporting unless F is concurrently elevated, and F-K is high" (p. 57). The second homogeneous subset of items on $F(p)$ apart from the family enmity items reflect persecutory ideation (162, 216, 218, and 336).

It is important to recognize that, unlike F and FB, the $F(p)$ items are distributed throughout the inventory (up to item 555). An elevated $F(p)$ score may therefore be due either to item endorsements fairly evenly distributed, or concentrated early or late or even in the middle of the instrument. Recall that the MMPI-2 re-standardization committee added the FB scale to cover infrequently endorsed items that occur later in the MMPI-2 (as described earlier, the F scale stops its measurement function at item 361). This was done with the awareness that individuals may change their approach (e.g. because of fatigue, uncooperativeness, or boredom) to answering the items during the test administration. The utility of the FB scale lies in the fact that many important scales (e.g. content and supplementary) occur later in the inventory and warrant interpretive caution should FB be significantly elevated.

Arbisi and Ben-Porath (1995a) and Arbisi, McNulty, Ben-Porath, and Boyd (1999) recognized that $F(p)$ can be applied in a similar way to the F and FB scales. That is, by dividing the $F(p)$ item content into items occurring earlier versus later in the test, one may identify differences on these subcomponent scales, which can help explain an elevated FB or $F(p)$ score. Call them $F(p)1$ and $F(p)2$. The $F(p)1$ subscale begins with item 51 and ends with item 252; the $F(p)2$ subscale begins with item 270 and ends with item 501. The following examples should help illustrate how scoring for the $F(p)1$ and $F(p)2$ subscales can assist in the interpretive process. Consider a participant who obtains an acceptable $VRIN$ and $TRIN$ score, indicating consistent responding, but significantly elevates FB in the context of a normal-range F score. Examination of the $F(p)$ score for possible exaggeration might reveal a slightly elevated scale score (e.g. raw score of three or four) but not one which is considered exceedingly high in terms of a T-score value. By scoring the $F(p)1$ and $F(p)2$ subscales, the clinician can discover that all three or four items were endorsed on the $F(p)2$ subscale, thereby raising the possibility that the respondent began exaggerating his or her complaints in the latter part of the inventory. This should alert the clinician to be careful to not over-interpret the content and supplementary scales that occur later in the inventory. When the F and $F(p)$ scales are elevated without the FB scale also being elevated, an inspection of the $F(p)$ subscales can help the clinician feel confident to interpret the content and supplementary scales if the $F(p)2$ subscale is not significantly elevated.

Clearly, more research is needed to better understand the operating characteristics of these components subscales, but they appear to have promise in assisting test interpreters to identify response sets occurring early versus late in the test administration process.

It is important to remember that specific clinical settings reflect different base rates of psychopathology; it is therefore critical that clinicians understand the nature of their population with regard to frequency and type of psychopathology before interpreting $F(p)$ or any other scale score. Arbisi and Ben-Porath (1997) recommended that additional studies be conducted in settings with clear incentives to feign symptoms. Rothke et al. (2000) suggested that future investigations of samples of psychiatric or injured patients control for motivation to appear impaired (as might be the case in patients involved in litigation, seeking disability compensation, or attempting to avoid criminal responsibility) by carefully interviewing the patient or by record review, as $F(p)$ is sensitive to efforts to over-report symptoms. In the Rothke et al. (2000) study, participants who were either in the process of litigation and seeking compensation, or feigning psychiatric conditions, produced elevated $F(p)$ scores, supporting the construct validity of the scale. This is not to suggest, however, that all litigating participants exaggerate their complaints. When used with clinical judgment, the $F(p)$ scale can be a useful addition to the assessment of MMPI-2 profile validity.

Symptom Validity Scale (FBS; formerly Fake Bad Scale)

Lees-Haley, English, and Glenn (1991) developed the Fake Bad Scale (*FBS*) as a supplemental measure of validity designed to detect malingering by plaintiffs involved in personal injury litigation. It thus occupies an intermediate position among the self-unfavorable scales, comprising items that both assert symptoms as a consequence of injury or disability, and items denying unfavorable traits and behaviors that might be posed as challenges to the integrity of the examinee in order to undermine the legitimacy of claimed symptoms in support of a judgment of malingering. The *FBS* gained prominence—and notoriety (see Armstrong, 2008)—in January 2007 when the publisher of the MMPI-2, the University of Minnesota Press, decided to add the *FBS* to the official scoring program for the test. Controversy about the use of this scale intensified with this decision. Opinions as to the merits of the *FBS*, both in terms of its validity and its application, remain strongly divided. Reviews taking a favorable position on the scale include Ben-Porath, Greve, Bianchini, and Kaufmann, 2009; Greiffenstein et al., 2007; Greve and Bianchini, 2004; Nelson, Hoelzle, Sweet, Arbisi, and Demakis, 2010; and Nelson, Sweet, and Demakis, 2006. Contrasting negative positions can be found in Arbisi and Butcher, 2004; Butcher, Arbisi, Atlis, and McNulty, 2003; Butcher, Gass, Cumella, Kally, and Williams, 2008; Gass, Williams, Cumella, Butcher, and Kally, 2010; Rogers, Sewell, Martin, and Vitacco, 2003; and Williams, Butcher, Gass, Cumella, and Kally, 2009. In this section we will review the development and research on the *FBS*. Taken as a whole, this research base raises considerable questions about the construct validity of the *FBS*. Hence, as seen below, we recommend against its use.

For 17 years the *FBS* was known in the psychological literature as the Fake Bad Scale. An unprecedented and unannounced name change occurred in 2008, within a year of its adoption into the official MMPI-2 scoring program. Although its new name is Symptom Validity Scale, its abbreviation remains *FBS*. Ben-Porath, Greve et al. (2009, p. 62) subsequently explained the reason for the name change:

The *FBS* was originally labeled "Fake Bad" by Lees-Haley et al. (1991). However, shortly after it was added to the MMPI-2 standard set of validity scales, its name was changed to "Symptom Validity," to address concerns that the original label, although in keeping with a widely used nomenclature, might be viewed as prejudicial in psycho-legal assessments.

Williams and colleagues (2009) elaborated on the *FBS* name change to Symptom Validity Scale, explaining that the concerns raised by the original label were expressed in a judge's Frye (*Frye v. United States*, 1923) ruling against the admissibility of the *FBS*: The very name "Fake Bad Scale" is pejorative and derogatory and thus prejudicial (*Williams v. CSX Transportation, Inc.*, 2007). As Williams et al. (2009) point out, a simple name change is unlikely to change the fundamental use or application of this scale, which will now be described, beginning with a brief discussion of its development.

The *FBS* was developed using a convenience sample from the first author's private practice of 12 male and 13 female personal injury litigants averaging 38 years of age (range not reported) whom Lees-Haley (1991) classified as malingerers, and a comparison sample of 7 male and 13 female personal injury litigants averaging 37 years of age whom he classified as non-malingerers. The extent to which this sample is representative of personal injury litigants, whether malingering or not, is unknown, but the base rate for malingering in this combined sample appears unusually high at 56 percent (see Sharland & Gfeller, 2007, below).

FBS comprises 43 items selected rationally by Lees-Haley; 18 keyed True, 25 False. Information regarding the differential endorsement frequencies within his malingering and non-malingering groups is not provided, precluding replication, and the scale has not been subsequently cross-validated. Forty percent (17) of the items overlap one or more of the somatically-focused scales of the MMPI-2 (*Hs*—Scale 1, *Hy4*, *Sc6*, and *HEA*), with the largest number of these (14) on *HEA*. Another eight items (19 percent of *FBS*) overlap one or both of scales measuring anxiety/stress, *ANX/PK*. Twenty-one percent (nine items) negatively overlap one or more of Cyniciism (*CYN/CYN1*), Antisocial Practices (*ASP/ASP1*), or *Ho*, with the largest number of these (eight) on *ASP/ASP1*. That is, an elevated *FBS* score is most readily achieved via the endorsement of various physical/somatic and anxiety/stress complaints, while denying antisocial and cynical attitudes. Interestingly, *FBS* overlaps minimally with the other MMPI-2 over-reporting scales, with four overlaps for *F*, one of these negative, and only 1 item each for *FB* and *F(p)*.

In their initial publication, Lees-Haley et al. (1991) recommended a cutting score of 20 to identify malingering, but concluded a year later that it should be increased to 24 for men and 26 for women (Lees-Haley, 1992). In subsequent research, other cutting scores of 22, 23, 28, 29, and 30 have been recommended by various investigators, but consensus as to which of these is to be preferred for any given gender, ethnicity, age cohort, preexisting condition, or litigation status, setting, referral source, or any combinations among these has yet to be reached. The *FBS* monograph (Ben-Porath, Graham, & Tellegen, 2009, p. 13) defers to Greiffenstein, Fox, and Lees-Haley (2007), suggesting a lower-range cut ("possible" malingering) of 23 for men and 26 for women, corresponding to a *T*-score of 80 for both, and an upper-range cut of 30, corresponding to a *T*-score of ~100 for men and ~90 for women.

The lack of consensus on which cutting scores are optimal, and for whom, must be seen within the context of both the base rates for malingering in personal injury litigation, and the criteria established to define or confirm such malingering. As to the former, the precious little that is known comes from a survey of 712 members and fellows of the National Academy of Neuropsychology by Sharland and Gfeller (2007). Of the 188 (26 percent of) members responding, estimates of "definite" and "probable" malingering in the examinees seen over the past year were only 1 percent and 3 percent, respectively, this estimate rising to 20 percent when those responding were invited to "estimate the percentage of examinees, in general, who deliberately exaggerate their deficits or feign cognitive impairment in cases involving civil litigation or compensation" (p. 216). Although doubtfully reliable, it is notable that these estimates are in marked contrast to the 56 percent base rate for malingering within the Lees-Haley et al. (1991) developmental sample.

The construct validity of the *FBS* is likewise in question. For example, Butcher, Arbisi, Atlis, and McNulty (2003) examined large samples of psychiatric inpatients (n = 6,731), general medical patients (n = 5,080), chronic pain patients (n = 4,408), inmates in a correctional facility (n = 2,897), and VA inpatients (n = 901 men). They found that *FBS* scores consistently achieved lower correlations with *F* (range: .26–.34), *FB* (range: .33–.39), and *F(p)* (range: .02–.14), than with substantive symptom scales such as *Hs* (range: .60–.75), *HEA* (range: .55–.70), *D* (range: .53–.66), *DEP* (range: .40–.50), and *Hy* (range: .59–.75). These trends were similarly evident in a small sample of personal injury litigants drawn from nine forensic practices (n = 157) for which *F(p)* and content scale scores were unavailable: *F* = .53, *FB* = .55, *Hs* = .81, *D* = .84, *Hy* = .85. The lack of a significant relationship between *FBS* and *F* and *F* – *K* has been reported by Guéz, Brännström, Nyberg, Toolanen, and Hildingsson (2005).

At least two other studies raise questions about the construct validity of *FBS*. In an investigation of the factor structure of neuro-cognitive symptom validity tests (SVTs) and MMPI-2 validity scales in a forensic compensation-seeking sample, Nelson, Sweet, Berry, Bryant, and Granacher (2007) found that their SVTs and MMPI-2 scales, including *FBS*, loaded on *different* factors. Moreover, Burandt (2006) found no significant differences in the *FBS* scores among those who passed versus those who failed SVTs in a sample of 77 electrical injury patients.

Another, if indirect, indication of doubtful *FBS* construct validity is the very limited item overlap between *FBS* and two other recent MMPI-2 validity measures, one of which was constructed to predict failure on SVTs, the Response Bias scale (*RBS*; Gervais, Ben-Porath, Wygant, & Green, 2007), and the other a scale designed to measure somatic complaints infrequently endorsed by personal injury and disability claimants with histories of head injuries, the Infrequent Somatic Complaints scale (*Fs*; Wygant, 2008). *FBS* overlaps *RBS* by four items and *Fs* by three items, and *RBS* overlaps *Fs* by two items. Thus the average overlap among these three scales is only 3 items over their average 29-item length (10 percent), which, although not rare, is unusual for scales purporting to measure such similar constructs. By contrast, for example, *F* and *F(p)* overlap by 15 items over their average 43.5-item length (34 percent), *K* and *S* overlap by 9 items over their average 40-item length (23 percent), *Hs* and *HEA* by 23 over their average 34-item length (68 percent), and *BIZ* and Psychoticism (*PSYC*) by 13 over their average 24-item length (54 percent). Some, for example, Larrabee (1998), have suggested that the *FBS* specifically measures "somatic malingering," in contrast to the *F* family of scales; however, *F* itself contains nine items that reference somatic functioning (including three items that overlap *HEA*), thus *FBS* cannot be considered distinctive in this respect.

Many of the studies that have been generally supportive of the validity of the *FBS* have defined malingering or "noncredible" reporting on the basis of failure or below chance performance on one or more SVTs (e.g. Burandt, 2006; Jones, Ingram, & Ben-Porath, 2012; Larrabee, 1998; Lee, Graham, Sellbom, & Gervais, 2012; Rogers, Gillard, Berry, & Granacher, 2011; Shea, 2006; Wygant, Ben-Porath, Arbisi, Berry, Freeman, &

Heilbronner, 2009; Wygant, Sellbom, Ben-Porath, Stafford, Freeman, & Heilbronner, 2007), despite the position of the National Academy of Neuropsychology that SVT failure is not tantamount to malingering: "Invalid performance on a measure of personality does not allow for an *a priori* conclusion that the neurocognitive test results are also unreliable, and vice versa" (Bush, Ruff, Troster, Barth, Koffler, Pliskin et al., 2005, p. 424).

In short, the use of SVTs as a basis for assigning research participants to malingering or non-malingering groups may be considered instances of Meehl's (1973a, pp. 240–244) "crummy criterion fallacy." That is, studies that purport to support the validity of the *FBS* as a measure of malingering based on its relationship to various SVTs ignore Meehl's concerns from 40 years ago about faulty reasoning related to the selection of criterion measures for psychometric instruments. The use of inappropriate criterion measures in a validity study cannot be used to support the construct validity of the instrument being examined.

The differing *FBS* raw/*T*-score values for men versus women, first observed by its developer in 1991, confirmed by him in 1992, and replicated in subsequent studies (e.g., Dean, Boone, Kim, Curiel, Martin, Victor et al., 2008; Greiffenstein et al., 2007), raises the question of a structural bias in the *FBS*. That is, at any given raw-score level, women are more likely than men to be identified as malingering. Of the 43 *FBS* items, 19 show endorsement frequencies within the MMPI-2 re-standardization sample (Butcher et al., 2001, Appendix G) for women that are at least 5 percent greater (8 of these by 10 percent or greater) than those for men, whereas only 1 item shows an endorsement frequency favoring men by greater than 5 percent. In a recent report, Lee, Graham, Sellbom, and Gervais (2012) found 14 items with statistically significant endorsement frequency differences among men and women in a sample referred for worker's compensation and other medico-legal evaluations, with 11 (65 percent) of these showing significantly higher endorsement rates among women; and, excluding the personal injury sample, among the Butcher, Arbisi et al. (2003) samples described above, in which the overwhelming majority were not involved in legal cases where malingering might be a factor, 22 percent obtained *FBS* scores $\geq$ 24, whereas 18 percent of the women in these samples scored a $T > 26$, the cutting scores for malingering recommended by Lees-Haley (1992), for an overall false-positive rate of about 1 in 5.

Additionally, on Gender Role-Feminine (*GF*), a scale comprising items showing preferential endorsement rates among women, the *FBS* overlaps *GF* by two items, whereas for Gender Role-Masculine (*GM*), a scale comprising items showing preferential endorsement rates among men, *FBS* overlaps *GM* by four items, with these items being keyed *negatively*. Thus, in the context of the *GF* and *GM* scales (described in Chapter 8), female examinees appear to be disadvantaged by six (14 percent) of the *FBS* items. Moreover, the re-standardization norms for women exceed those for men by more than two raw scores. For raw scores between 20 and 35, the corresponding *T*-scores for women average 7 to 10 points lower than those for men, such that at any given raw-score level, women are more likely than men to be identified as malingering. Hence the *FBS* shows a clear intrinsic bias against women respondents.

The *FBS* may be unique among scales designed to identify potential malingering in that it contains a substantial number of items, about 20 percent of total scale length, denying antisocial beliefs, attitudes, and practices—items that are associated with a defensive response style, not malingering. It has been amply demonstrated that individuals are more likely to endorse MMPI items reflecting a defensive response style in certain settings (e.g. employment screening, child custody cases, and parole evaluations) that bear demand characteristics for one to make a favorable impression. The subset of defensive items included on the *FBS* tend to overlap positively with scales considered to measure one or another type of defensive responding such as *S*, which overlaps *FBS* by eight items (19 percent of *FBS*). Examinees in personal injury litigation are no different from individuals in these settings who may be unwilling to admit to even minor flaws like not always telling the truth (an item from the *L* scale, a well-validated measure of defensive responding, included on *FBS*). In short, involvement in adversarial litigation provides an entirely sufficient explanation for the endorsement of items denying deviant or antisocial attitudes and behaviors, making it gratuitous to include such items on the *FBS*, a purported measure of malingering.

An important and understudied issue in the research on *FBS* thus far is the potentially stressful effects of litigation itself (see, e.g., Weissman, 1990), such that regardless of the true extent of their injury/disability, plaintiffs may endorse MMPI-2 test items, including those keyed on the *FBS*, *F*, *FB*, etc., scales, on the basis of the stresses attaching to litigation, thereby raising scores on these scales. Indeed, Lees-Haley has himself acknowledged that some of the responses of those involved in litigation include anxiety-related responses, dysthymia and mood-related responses, stress-related complaints, and hysterical or hypochondriacal responses, in what he calls "Litigation Response Syndrome" (LRS; Lees-Haley, 1988). Tsushima and Tsushima (2001), for example, found that among five MMPI-2 validity scales (*F*, *FB*, *F(p)*, the MMPI-2 version of Gough's [1954] Dissimulation scale, and *FBS*), only *FBS* showed higher scores among their personal injury litigation sample (*n* = 120) than among a comparison sample of clinical patients (*n* = 208). *FBS* items such as 31T (distractibility), 39T (fitful sleep), 325T (difficulty concentrating), 339T (feeling overwhelmed), 464T (weariness), 505T (want to escape stress), 152F (fatigue), 176F (headaches), and 496F (feeling stressed) may be similarly read as plausible reactions to the stresses of litigation involvement rather than a motive to malinger.

These considerations, the relative saturation of the *FBS* with somatic symptoms and the denial of deviant attitudes, whether or not, in either case, legitimately claimed, highlight the conceptual, and clinical, difficulty in discriminating true malingering from a wide variety of conditions and response styles that, however valid or biased, contribute to scores on *FBS* that can lead unjustly to inferences of malingering. These include, but are hardly limited to, simple under- or over-reporting, or any combination of these, concurrent somatic, emotional, and situational stresses and symptoms, disability, and neuropathology, whether preexisting, acute, traumatic, or otherwise. And this is a discrimination for which the current MMPI-2 item pool, in the context of personal injury litigation, appears to be ill-equipped. Given the well documented instances of false-positive judgments of malingering (e.g. Butcher, Arbisi et al., 2003; Berry & Schipper, 2007; Clayton, 2011; Guéz et al., 2005; Iverson, Henrichs, Barton, & Allen, 2002), the risk of invalid judgments of malingering on the basis of virtually any recommended *FBS* cutting score is substantial.

The risks within the legal system posed by testimony based upon *FBS* scores have been addressed in a significant number of judicial decisions invoking the *Frye* standard, for their failure to meet criteria for admissibility in personal injury/disability cases

(*Vandergracht v. Progressive Express et al.*, 2005; *Davidson v. Strawberry Petroleum et al.*, 2007; *Williams v. CSX Transportation, Inc.*, 2007; *Nason & Nason v. Shafranski, Shafranski, & Shafranski*, 2008; *Stith v. State Farm Mutual*, 2008; *Anderson, M. et al. v. E & S International Enterprises, Inc. et al.*, 2008; *Limbaugh-Kirker v. Decosta*, 2009; and *Davis v. Bellsouth Short Term Disability Plan for Non-Salaried Employees*, 2012). In still other cases (*Solomon & Solomon v. T. K. Power & Goodwin*, 2000, *Upchurch v. School Board of Broward Co.*, 2009), testimony based on the *FBS* was voluntarily withdrawn by the defense following opposing testimony and oral arguments.

In summary, given the limited current knowledge of the true base rates for malingering, and findings demonstrating that false-positives are known to exceed available estimates (Sharland & Gfeller, 2007) of these rates in a large number of settings and conditions, the risk of invalid inferences based upon *FBS* scores appears unacceptably high, and especially so for female examinees and persons with legitimate disabilities. For this reason, further research appears unlikely to satisfactorily demonstrate the ability of the *FBS* to reliably separate validly identified malingerers (not merely inferred on the basis of SVT performances and similar criteria of convenience), from persons with medically confirmed injuries/disabilities, or malingering from more common and familiar instances of impression management, exaggeration, self-deception, over- and under-reporting, and the like. Moreover, Lees-Haley himself, the developer of the *FBS* scale, had previously listed a wide variety of symptoms and complaints, corresponding to *more than half* of the items included on *FBS*, as elements of his "Litigation Response Syndrome" construct, not as indicators of malingering (Lees-Haley, 1988). Expert testimony endorsing malingering on the basis of *FBS* scores is therefore likely to prove a hazard to the expert for being readily discredited. Thus, use of the *FBS* scale cannot be recommended, even for its limited intended purpose.

Dissimulation Scale (Ds)

The 58-item version of Gough's (1954) *Ds* scale for the MMPI-2 is a revision of the original 74-item scale that he developed for the MMPI. Gough developed *Ds* by identifying MMPI items that empirically differentiated a group of patients classified as psychoneurotic from a group of test normals (college students and professional psychologists) instructed to take the MMPI simulating the role of a neurotic patient. The items separating the simulators from the patients were further studied in cross-validation. The simulators tended to score much higher than the actual neurotic patients, suggesting that individuals' prevailing stereotypes about neuroticism were not a good fit to the actual construct of neuroticism as measured by the MMPI. (For a study of prevailing stereotypes about mental illness, see Rapport, Todd, Lumley, & Fisicaro, 1998.) There have been multiple iterations of the *Ds* scale over the years since its inception. The reader interested in these and their various designations may consult Friedman, Lewak, Nichols, and Webb (2001, pp. 68–69). For convenience, the 58-item MMPI-2 version of this scale will be simply designated *Ds* throughout this book.

Ds is intended for use in assessing the intentional overstatement of psychological disturbance or faking sick. The function of *Ds* is similar to that of the *F* and *FB* scales, although the content of *Ds* is much more subtle than the latter scales, in which "what is the rare and atypical response" (Caldwell, 1997, p. 17) is consistently obvious. "The level of psychopathology implied in these items is generally mild to moderate rather than blatant, severe, overwhelming, or grossly deviant, as is the case with the items of *F, FB,* and *F(p)*" (Nichols, 2011, p. 59). Because *Ds* does not have the extreme or psychotic-related item content of *F, FB,* and *F(p)*, it is uniquely sensitive to instances of exaggeration or malingering in which the examinee does not wish to appear psychotically disabled. It is therefore useful in assessing the intentional exaggeration of a variety of symptoms for financial gain or manipulative intent (Caldwell, 1997). Elevating *Ds* "may be more common in settings of employment and civil forensic contexts involving claims of disability based on stress and injury than in criminal forensic contexts" (Nichols, 2011, p. 59). Nichols further states that extreme elevations on *Ds* that are not accompanied by similar elevations on *F* and *F(p)* suggest an attempt to magnify selectively, or to malinger non-psychotic disability in order to bolster claims of stress or injury. However, Rogers et al. (1994) pointed out that *Ds* is multifaceted and extends beyond neurotic symptoms. Gough (1954) indicated that the items cover the following: physical complaints and dysfunctions; feelings of victimization, injustice, and discouragement; irritability, fear, and anxiety; lack of independence and self-sufficiency; discontent with childhood and family background; sexual conflicts and preoccupations; and bizarre ideation and religiosity. Few of the *Ds* items reflect severe depressive or psychotic symptoms.

Forty-eight of the 58 items are keyed True, 10 False. Of the 19 items *Ds* shares with Scale 8, 8 appear on *Sc1* (Social Alienation), 4 on *Sc5* (Lack of Ego Mastery, Defective Inhibition), and 3 on *Sc6* (Sensorimotor Dissociation). Eleven items overlap Scale *F*, 10 with *PK*, 9 with *PS*, and 8 items each with *HEA* and *FAM*. "In contrast with the other over-reporting scales, it shares no items with *BIZ* and only 2 each with *PSYC* and *RC8*" (Nichols, 2011, p. 59). The language of 11 items was updated for the MMPI-2. Generally, scores on *Ds* are raised by elevations on any of the MMPI-2 measures of general maladjustment and subjective distress.

In providing a general review of *Ds* with a few specific research examples, we wish to convey the point that the basic findings are consistent across studies; that is, *Ds* appears to measure exaggerated claims of psychopathology. There are a number of studies and reviews supporting the construct validity of the scale (e.g. Anthony, 1971; Bagby et al., 1997b; Berry, Baer, & Harris, 1991; Friedman et al., 2001; Frueh, Gold, & de Arellano, 1997; Gough, 1954, 1957; Greene, 2000, 2011; Nichols, 2011; Nichols & Greene, 1997; Rogers et al., 1994; Walters, White, & Greene, 1988; Wetter et al., 1992).

Anthony (1971) instructed 40 non-psychotic U.S. Air Force male clients, after taking the MMPI under usual administration conditions, to exaggerate the troubles that had brought them to treatment so that their re-administered MMPI would reflect a more severe condition than they were actually experiencing. They were also asked to exaggerate in a way that was not clearly obvious. The 74-item *Ds* scale was scored, and the results showed an optimum hit rate of 86 percent in identifying exaggerated MMPI profiles. This hit rate was higher than that found for *F–K* (81 percent) and raw *F* scores (81 percent). The findings supported the utility of *Ds* in discriminating exaggerated MMPIs from authentically produced deviant profiles.

Walters et al. (1988) found support for a 40-item abbreviated version of *Ds*, *Ds-r* (Gough, 1957), in an inmate population for identifying genuinely disturbed inmates. In the first part of a two-phase study, they were interested in how the standard validity and clinical scales performed against *Ds-r* and other indexes. The participants were 72 male inmates with maximum security status at a U.S. penitentiary. A structured psychiatric interview was administered to the inmates, generally within one day of an administered MMPI. A four-point rating scale was created to evaluate an inmate's proneness to exaggerate psychiatric symptomatology. The ratings were made by two psychologists familiar with both the inmates and their contact with others (e.g. work supervisors). The average length of time between the psychiatric interview and the rating assignment was 7.6 months. A rating of one on the scale reflected malingering, whereas a rating of four indicated no malingering or embellishment of symptomatology. The base-rate estimate for psychopathology in this setting was estimated to be 60 percent. An abbreviated MMPI was scored (first 400 items of MMPI Form R). Because only 28 of the 40 *Ds-r* items could be scored, prorated *T*-scores were calculated. The results showed that the MMPI validity and clinical scales (with the exception of Scale 1) could not accurately discriminate the malingerers from the non-malingerers. Although *Ds-r* failed to improve on the base-rate criterion without the inclusion of an indeterminate category, it could differentiate malingering from genuine psychopathology. Low *Ds-r* scores were predictive of authentic pathology, but high scores failed to correlate with malingering.

Berry, Baer, and Harris (1991) meta-analytically reviewed 28 studies that used the original MMPI to detect malingering. The contrasting of several malingering and honest groups on several reporting measures showed the original *Ds* scale to be one of the most effective measures in detecting over-reporting, and one of the indices of choice for identifying malingering. The mean effect size in *T*-scale value for *Ds* was approximately 2 SDs ($d = 2.17$). A raw cutting score of 35 was common across studies, showing a hit rate of about 88 percent. The corresponding cutting score for the 58-item MMPI-2 version of *Ds* is 27. The abbreviated *Ds-r* had much lower effect sizes than *Ds* when contrasting faking and honest groups, suggesting caution in its use (Berry, Baer, & Harris, 1991).

Whereas Berry, Baer, and Harris (1991) focused on findings with the original MMPI, Rogers et al. (1994) examined different faking indicators specifically for the MMPI-2. They reported that although the meta-analysis by Berry, Baer, and Harris demonstrated the efficacy of *Ds* in assessing malingering, most of the MMPI-2 studies had unfortunately relied on a shortened 34-item version of the Dissimulation scale, sometimes referred to as *Ds-r2*. The *Ds-r2* yielded only a moderate effect size in their meta-analysis. The full 58-item version of *Ds* is likely to be more discriminating in its detection of dissimulated profiles. Berry et al. (1995) found this version of *Ds* to be effective in detecting the over-reporting of closed-head injury symptoms by nonclinical participants instructed to fake such a syndrome, and by compensation-seeking (vs. non-compensation-seeking) closed-head injury patients. They cautioned that unelevated over-reporting scale scores, such as on *Ds*, do not automatically rule out the possibility of feigning neuropsychological problems.

We suggest that *Ds* is a useful addition in evaluating the validity of MMPI-2 profiles. However, more research is needed, especially with actual samples of malingerers versus analogue study participants. Research findings vary regarding cut scores as a function of the population studied, the methodology used, and the sample size employed. For these reasons, it is recommended that an assessment of protocol validity be based on the examination of multiple MMPI-2 measures as well as reliance upon other clinical data beyond the MMPI-2, such as record reviews, life history data, and interview findings.

Self-Favorable Scales

Scales *L, K, S,* Positive Malingering (*Mp*), Social Desirability (*Sd*), and Socioeconomic Status (*Ss*) all measure aspects of the display or mimicking of self-favorable traits, attributes, and dispositions. These scales are not meant to be inclusive of all available scales for use, but rather represent what we recognize to be the mainstream response-style measures.

Factor studies of various measures of self favorable responding to the MMPI have repeatedly produced findings indicating that defensiveness cannot be subsumed under a single dimension. In Wiggins' (1964) analysis and expansion of these reports, he distinguished between Alpha (Block, 1965), a dimension consistent with Edwards' (1957) interpretation of faking good on personality inventories without special instructions to do so (p. 57), and Gamma, which Wiggins (1964) interpreted as "social desirability in role-playing" (p. 555). The Alpha dimension is largely coextensive with the first factor of the MMPI/MMPI-2, with the high end of this dimension being marked by scales that reflect distress, discomfort, and maladjustment (e.g. *A* (Anxiety), *Pt, Mt* (College Maladjustment Scale), and *PK*) and the negative pole marked by scales such as *K* and *Es* (Ego Strength Scale). In the Wiggins (1964) and Paulhus (1984, 1986) analyses, this factor was marked by the *K* scale and Edwards' Social Desirability scale (*So-r*). Two scales described later, Butcher and Han's (1995) Superlative Self-Presentation scale (*S*) and Nelson's (1952) *Ss* scale, also are related to this dimension.

The Gamma dimension has been labeled variously as "lying" (Edwards, Diers, & Walker, 1962), "propagandistic bias" (Damarin & Messick, 1965) and "impression management" (Paulhus, 1984, 1986); these labels converge on the theme of a self-conscious, or intentional, motivation to promote a favorable impression of the self. Paulhus (1984, 1986) proposed a two-factor model of social desirability responding that distinguishes between self-deception, the tendency to bias inventory responses brought about by the person's belief that such responses are true and justified, and impression management ("other deception"), a self-conscious and deliberate attempt to tailor responses so as to create a favorable impression and mislead the clinician in the direction of an overly benign personality description from test results. Nichols and Greene (1988), for example, found a strong tendency for scales developed under fake-good instructional sets, "Gamma scales," to be highly correlated with each other but only weakly associated with "Alpha" scales like *K* and *A*. Two other scales, Cofer, Chance, and Judson's (1949) *Mp*, and Wiggins' (1959) *Sd*, along with *L*, marked the Gamma dimension in the Wiggins and Paulhus studies. Given the empirical support that Paulhus' distinction between self-deception and impression management has found, these tendencies appear to be a substantial advance over the earlier and simpler concept of "faking good," and so are factors important to consider in clinical, forensic, and personnel settings, where motivation can affect the test results.

Lie Scale (L)

The *L* scale contains 15 items, all keyed False. The items are phrased in a way such that a False response denies one or another moral imperfection. The scale was designed as a validity indicator to detect intentional efforts to under-report problems. Under-reporting of problems can occur in many settings and is often referred to as "faking good" or, more recently, as above, as self-deceptive or impression management styles of socially desirable responding. Circumstances and settings that may induce these response sets include personnel selection, child custody litigation and other forensic situations, prison inmates wishing a transfer to a more desirable setting, patients wanting a release from an involuntary hospitalization, and clients coerced into marital or family treatment who wish to appear psychologically healthy (Baer, Wetter, & Berry, 1992).

The rationally derived L scale items had their origin in previous research on honesty and deceit by Hartshorne and May (1928). Because the items for L were borrowed from previous work and rewritten, L is the only scale in the original MMPI that was not empirically constructed. The L scale provides 15 opportunities for the participant to endorse various improbable virtues, such as always telling the truth, never gossiping or laughing at a dirty joke, and never getting angry. The items represent socially virtuous behaviors that may be desirable, but are rarely true for most people. For this reason, the "items constituted a fairly subtle trap for anyone who wanted to give an unusually good impression of himself" (Meehl & Hathaway, 1946, as cited in Dahlstrom & Dahlstrom, 1980, p. 97). Individuals are expected to claim some feelings of virtue, and most do, in fact, answer some items in the "lie" direction. However,

the L scale items do not implicate lying as such; they merely deny minor and widespread failings of character and observance that carry little or no social opprobrium because such flaws are so widespread in Anglo-American culture that to deny such feelings may be considered naïve if not obtuse.

(Nichols, 2011, pp. 66–67)

The mean number of items answered in this direction by the contemporary normative sample was 3.5 for both men and women (Butcher et al., 2001). The original MMPI Lie scale T-score values were arbitrarily established and did not provide separate validity scale values for men and women. However, the MMPI-2 Lie scale (and other validity scales) T-score values were established in the re-standardization sample, with separate T-scores by gender.

Most often, higher raw scores on L reflect the tendency to place oneself in a favorable light. Consequently, the clinical scales will be suppressed because the individual is tending to deny basic human frailties and "look good." In addition to its sensitivity to detect obvious efforts at looking good, L may also be related to psychopathology when elevated, especially in some paranoid conditions (Coyle & Heap, 1965; Fjordbak, 1985) and certain neurotic cases; interpretive guidelines for the L scale are further discussed in Chapter 4.

Because all the items on L are keyed False, an All-False response set will elevate it, as well as Scales 1, 2, and 3, for which the deviant response is usually False. An extremely low raw score on L may likewise reflect an All-True response bias. Markedly elevated or suppressed L scores should alert the psychologist to inspect the percentage of items marked True versus False, and examine *TRIN*. In the MMPI-2 revision, L lost no items, although the sexist wording on some items was changed and one item was changed to reflect more modern usage. The majority of the items on L (nine) do not overlap the other MMPI-2 scales. The largest overlap occurs with Scales 2 and 9, each sharing two items with L.

Moderator variables (e.g. SES, education, and occupation) can greatly affect scores on *L*. Because the *L* item content is fairly obvious, sophisticated individuals rarely elevate the scale, realizing that it would be unconvincing to give such an improbable response to the items. College-educated individuals and those with a higher SES infrequently obtain *T*-scores above 50; thus an elevated *L* score for a college-educated examinee should be carefully evaluated. Greene (2011) stated that "persons with a college education who elevate the *L* scale to a *T*-score of 65 or higher are likely to display deficiencies in judgment and lack of insight into their own behavior" (p. 80). Nichols (2011) reported that given how transparent the items are, most normals and patients avoid endorsing the *L* items. "Scores are negatively correlated with education, intelligence, and cultural sophistication, so bright, well-educated, and acculturated examinees tend to obtain low scores, even when motivation to under-report is high" (Nichols, 2011, p. 67). Nevertheless, high *L* scores can be obtained from bright and educated people who have unusually rigid values (Levak et al., 2011). Individuals of lower SES with less education tend to earn higher scores on *L* because the items reflect a more obvious form of test-taking defensiveness (Dahlstrom & Tellegen, 1993).

Motives for endorsing the *L* items can be a function of an individual's concerns about how the test results are likely to be interpreted, stemming from fears of judgment about their personality functioning, or a desire to deceive the psychologist. Nichols (2011) recommends referring to scores on *Mp* and *Sd* (described later in this chapter) to help identify impression management motives as the latter scales are more sensitive in this regard than is *L*. "Scores greater than *T*-65 on *Mp* or *Sd* strongly suggest that impression management, rather than fear of moral judgment, is the motive for high *L* scores" (Nichols, 2011, p. 68).

As much as moderator variables can influence *L* scores, contextual factors are just as important to consider when interpreting the validity of an MMPI-2 profile. For example, in child custody assessments and personnel selection or employment fitness-for-duty evaluations, individuals are typically motivated to put their best "psychometric foot forward" to increase the probability of a favorable outcome. The MMPI-2 *Manual* (Butcher et al., 2001) states that in employment and child custody evaluations "moderate elevations on *L* are common and do not necessarily indicate an invalid profile" (p. 20). Cooke (2010) studied the effects of the validity scales on child custody examinees who were slightly more elevated on *L* than the normative sample. He found that a quarter of the males and a third of the females had *L* *T*-scores over 65. Carr, Moretti, and Cue (2005) studied parents at risk of losing their parenting rights who had a lower SES than did the participants in the Cooke investigation. Carr et al. found that about 27 percent of his combined sample of mothers and fathers scored at the *T*-70 threshold or greater on *L*, and about 41 percent scored at the *T*-65 threshold. Overall, these investigators concluded that the elevations on *L* (and on *K*) had a significant suppressive effect on the clinical scale scores, with approximately 60 percent of the examinee profiles compromised. The reader interested in further validity scale information for the MMPI-2 in the child custody context will find Caldwell's 2003 chapter, "How can the MMPI-2 help Child Custody Examiners?" to be illuminating.

In pre-employment selection, or in fitness-for-duty evaluations, *L* can be elevated due to defensiveness, rendering a valid clinical interpretation of an MMPI-2 profile impossible. Because it is expected that many individuals will be motivated to over-report virtues and under-report psychological problems, many psychologists use more liberal cut scores for the MMPI-2 scales, including *L*. For example, in the selection of law enforcement officers, many psychologists will allow a raw score of up to 8–10 on *L* before disqualifying the profile (Robert Davis, personal communication, September 5, 2013). Of interest is the fact that there is a robust literature demonstrating that law enforcement officers selected with elevated *L* scores manifest more performance problems than those without such elevations (Weiss, Davis, Rostow, & Kinsman, 2003). Recently, Weiss, Vivian, Weiss, Davis, and Rostow (2013) reported that law enforcement officers with *L* scale raw scores of eight or higher on their post-conditional employment MMPI-2s had significantly more performance problems than those who had scores of seven or below. Detrick and Chibnall (2008) found moralistic bias (exaggerated adjustment/ agreeableness) significantly associated with *L* in police officer applicants. Clearly, *L* has personality correlates in addition to validity implications for profile interpretation. It should be noted that in employment settings, wherein an employee is referred for a fitness-for-duty evaluation, responding to the MMPI-2 items defensively, or similar items on any other psychometric instrument, a finding of insubordination by the employer may be brought against the examinee for a lack of cooperation in the assessment process. Such a lack of cooperation disallows the clinician to make a credible finding of fit or not fit for duty, rendering the assessment useless (see *Lee v. Northwestern University*, 2012). Independent of a "fake good" approach to the inventory items, *L*

scores above *T*-65 to *T*-70 suggest naïveté or rigidity in moral outlook and a sense of constraint in self-presentation that is designed to forestall negative moral judgment, even though the examinee may exhibit significant problems, especially health concerns and dysphoria.

(Nichols, 2011, p. 68)

Typically lacking in insight and an awareness of how they impact others, they are viewed not as virtuous but rather self-centered, unoriginal, and slow to adapt to unfamiliar ideas and situations (inflexible). This style makes them vulnerable to interpersonal stress. In psychiatric settings, it is not uncommon to see patients diagnosed with somatization disorders with elevated *L* scores, coupled with elevations in the "neurotic triad," Scales 1, 2, and 3 (Nichols, 2011).

Test–retest reliability coefficients on *L* over an approximate one-week interval shows coefficients of .77 for men and .81 for women in a subset of the re-standardization sample (Butcher et al., 1989). Retest data are not available in the *Manual* for psychiatric patients on *L*, but earlier data on the original MMPI can be applied to the present MMPI-2 scale because its composition has not changed significantly. On the MMPI, *L* test–retest correlation coefficients for psychiatric cases ranged between .74 and .78 with a one- to two-day interval between tests, and between .35 and .61 with a one-year interval between administrations (Dahlstrom et al., 1975). In a large-scale meta-analysis of MMPI reliability using a wide variety of populations conducted between 1970 and 1981, Hunsley, Hanson, and Parker (1988) reported an average internal consistency for *L* of .77 across 70 studies. They also reported an average test–retest reliability of .63 for eight studies with time intervals from one to two years. Putnam et al. (1996) reported a test–retest reliability coefficient of .72 for male clergy over a four-month interval.

Additional *L* reliability data on the MMPI-2 are presented by Matz, Altepeter, and Perlman (1992), who examined the temporal stability and internal consistency of the MMPI-2 in a sample of 128 students. Moderate to high stability coefficients were obtained (range = .60 to .90, *Mdn* = .74), with alpha coefficients ranging from .39 to .91 (*Mdn* = .62).

In a meta-analysis of 25 studies in which participants who responded honestly were compared with participants who under-reported psychopathology, Baer et al. (1992) found that *L*, relative to other special scales or indexes designed to detect under-reporting, is a valid measure. In general, their review indicates that participants known to be under-reporting problems tend to score about 1 *SD* above average on *L*.

Correction Scale (K)

The original purpose for developing the *K* scale was to improve the sensitivity of the clinical scales to detect psychopathology by adding a correction or suppressor factor to the scaled scores. Without this correction factor, an excess of false negatives or low-ranging MMPI scores were found among psychiatric patients whose psychopathology should have elevated certain clinical scales. The efforts of Meehl, Hathaway, and McKinley (e.g. McKinley, Hathaway, & Meehl, 1948; Meehl, 1945b) in the development of *K* were directed primarily toward the reduction of these false negatives without significantly affecting the number of accurate diagnostic identifications, or test hits (true positives or true negatives). Experience with the MMPI also demonstrated that although both *L* and *F* were adequate in detecting extreme test-taking attitudes or distortions, they were less sensitive to more subtle expressions of defensiveness or the under-reporting of problems. Recognizing that test scores are considerably influenced by test-taking attitudes, Meehl and Hathaway (1946) identified two important general test-taking approaches: (a) the tendency to be self-critical and overly self-disclosing ("plus getting"), usually referred to as faking bad, and (b) the tendency to be defensive or to over-portray one's virtues, often referred to as faking good. Proper interpretation of the validity scales, particularly *K*, should aid in assessing the presence of a fake-bad or fake-good test attitude. Another way to conceptualize the function of the validity scales is along a continuum: one end measures an individual's willingness or capacity to be open to admitting problems, including an over-declaration of symptoms, and the other end measures the tendency to minimize problems or to be closed to admitting any problems at all. In this regard, *K* is highly negatively correlated (in the .70 to .80 range) with all of the first factor scales (*A*, Scale 7, *PK*, *PS*, *Mt*, *ANX*, *OBS* (Obsessiveness), *TRT*, *WRK* (Work Interference), and *NEGE* (Negative Emotionality/Neuroticism); Nichols, 2011).

The *K* scale was developed by selecting 25 male and 25 female psychiatric inpatients who obtained normal range scale elevations on the MMPI (no *T*-score over 70). These patients had *L* scale *T*-scores of at least 60, indicating test-taking defensiveness, and carried diagnoses primarily among the behavior disorders (e.g. alcoholism, personality disorders, or other behavioral disturbances) rather than neurotic disorders. The responses of these patients (who, based upon their *L* scores, were apparently answering the test items in a defensive manner) were compared with those of some of the cases used in the original standardization group. Item analysis yielded 22 items common to men and women that discriminated the "true and false negative profiles and their item endorsements by at least 30%" (Dahlstrom et al., 1972, p. 124). High scores on this set of items indicated more defensiveness and a greater likelihood of a false negative (e.g. a patient who should have generated an abnormal profile but who actually achieved a normal one). Low scores on these items were likewise able to detect false positives (i.e. cases in which normals obtained abnormally elevated test scores). Because this 22-item scale proved to be insensitive to some depressed and schizophrenic patients who tended to produce normal-looking profiles, an additional 8 items were added to the scale to strengthen its performance in separating the original normative group from these two patient groups, and resulted in the final 30-item *K* scale. In addition to meeting the criterion of differentiating the normals from the abnormals (e.g. schizophrenic and depressive patients), the items also had to prove insensitive to the performance of test takers instructed to fake good or fake bad, thereby implying that their content was not obvious. Thus the *K* scale should be considered subtle in nature.

By adding differential proportions of raw *K* scores to five of the clinical scales, Meehl, Hathaway, and McKinley were able to improve the ability of these scales to differentiate between the normal and criterion groups. The standard profile form is based on *T*-scores corrected for the *K* additions, and test users are advised to remember to add the *K*-correction factor to these five clinical scales. The MMPI-2 *Manual* (Butcher et al., 2001) also provides conversion tables for plotting non-*K*-corrected profiles, and many computer programs provide both *K* and non-*K*-corrected profiles for the test user. The raw *K* correction addition for Scale 1 (*Hs*) is 0.5, for Scale 4 (*Pd*) is 0.4. Scales 7 (*Pt*) and 8 (*Sc*) have the full (1.0) raw-score value of *K* added, and Scale 9 (*Ma*) receives a correction of 0.2 *K*. These *K*-correction values remain unchanged in the MMPI-2. It is important to note that the *K*-correction value for any given clinical scale is related to the proportion of subtle items it contains (McKinley et al., 1948). "In effect, the intent of *K*-correction is to lend subtlety to scales with a shortage of subtle items, and in amounts that reflect the extent of that shortage" (Nichols, 2011, p. 70). Scales 1, 4, 7, 8, and 9 all have a greater proportion of obvious items than do Scales 2, 3, and 6. Note that the MMPI-2-RF does not use *K* corrections.

Because the *K* corrections were developed with adult psychiatric patients, it may not always be appropriate to use them with dissimilar populations. Greene (2000, 2011) reviewed the literature on the use of the *K* scale in various settings and concluded that, in general, little research justifies the continued widespread use of the *K* correction for the clinical scales. Greene stated that clinicians probably need to avoid using *K* corrections in settings in which normal persons are being evaluated with the MMPI-2, but they should use it in settings in which psychopathology may be suspected, bearing in mind the potential inaccuracies that *K* corrections may introduce. As most of the codetype interpretive literature is based upon *K*-corrected profiles, omitting *K* introduces unknown effects on clinical profiles. Butcher (1994c) studied the MMPI-2 profiles of airline pilot applicants. He noted that the majority of these participants tended to score above the clinical cut of *T* = 65 on *K*, suggesting an overly favorable response pattern in a group of well-adjusted individuals. Because high *K* scale scores are common in many other personnel selection populations, the addition of the *K* correction may be inappropriate in situations assessing normals, given that the scale was developed to detect defensiveness in psychiatric populations. However, it does appear that most clinicians—and most researchers—continue to use the *K* correction despite this limitation (Colby, 1989). It is recommended for adults (e.g. those 18 years and older) that the reader apply the *K* correction and plot *T*-scores both with and without the *K* correction with normal populations until future research clarifies the appropriate parameters of its use. As Archer (1992) noted, "the raw score *K*-correction is not used in profiling *T*-scores for adolescents with either the original test instrument or the MMPI-A" (p. 84). It appears that adolescent MMPI profiles are more accurate without the *K* correction (Colligan & Offord, 1991). More specifically, Greene (2011) has recommended that the clinician plot a non-*K*-corrected profile any time the *K* score is above *T*-60 or below *T*-40, in order to avoid excessive emphasis on the clinical scales when high *K* values are added, and too little emphasis on the clinical scales when the *K*-correction value is low.

Nichols' (2011, pp. 70–71) concurs with these concerns for using the *K*-correction weights:

Little research has validated the original *K* weights, and it is likely that shifts in item response patterns in the intervening 65 years since they were devised are sufficient to have rendered these weights no longer optimal. There is even some question that the response pattern to *K* items may have shifted to a point that *K* no longer separates normals from clinical groups as satisfactorily as it did originally. Thus, revising or constructing a new *K* scale and establishing contemporary weights are important future tasks. Nevertheless, the scale's basic logic and its function as a correction to suppress the effects of over- and under-reporting among patients in psychiatric settings remain compelling.

Archer, Fontaine, and McCrae (1998) examined the accuracy of the *K*-correction procedure in a large sample of psychiatric inpatients. Their results indicated that the *K* correction with the MMPI and the MMPI-2 did not result in higher correlations with external criteria in comparison with non-*K*-corrected scores. They suggested that the reason that the original *K*-correction weights were retained for use in the MMPI-2 was because the massive research literature generated for the original MMPI was based on *K*-corrected scores. This raises a considerable dilemma, as researchers and clinicians can either use the *K*- or non-*K*-corrected scores. As they state (Archer et al., 1998, p. 98), the clinician:

can use *K*-correction procedures with standard weights, which link their results to a large research literature, or the non-*K*-corrected scores, which relate to a much smaller literature but produces stronger evidence of concurrent validity. This dilemma can be resolved if future researchers report results of analyses using non-*K*-corrected scores (perhaps in addition to *K*-corrected scores), so that a comprehensive non-*K*-corrected research literature can eventually be developed for the MMPI-2.

As pointed out by Putzke, Williams, Daniel, and Boll (1999), there is a relative dearth of studies examining the effectiveness of the *K*-correction procedure. Investigations are needed to examine various adult patient populations, as well as different clinical settings that vary in regard to the prevalence of defensiveness.

Twenty-nine of the 30 *K* items are keyed False, making the scale sensitive to the effects of an All-False or All-True response set, as well as reflecting the scale's function to measure the denial of problems. It is therefore important that the *TRIN* scale be examined for possible acquiescent or non-acquiescent response styles prior to interpreting deviant scores on *K*. The mean number of *K* items endorsed for men and women in the contemporary normative sample was approximately 15. The scale contains 6 unique (non-overlapping) items, and 19 items that overlap with one or more of the clinical scales. The overlap content of Scale *K* is summarized by Nichols (2011, p. 72):

The *K* scale shares 10 items with *S* (5-*S1*), 9 with *HyS*, 7 with *Pd-S*, 6 with *D* (5 on *D-S*), 4 each with *Hy2, Ma-S, Ma3,* and *Mp*. Overlapping items scored in reverse include 8 with *Si* (4 on *Si3*), and 5 with *CYN* (4 on *CYN1*).

The *K* scale content is thus somewhat wide-ranging, covering issues of self-control, family and interpersonal relationships, and the denial of problems. Nichols (2011) reports Caldwell's (1999) observation that *K* can be broken down into three primary sources of variance: SES, impression management, and emotional constriction. The subtle item content of *K* denies themes of negative and unstable emotionality, interpersonal problems, cynicism and mistrust, introversion, and other problems in adaptation. The *K* scale did not lose any items in the MMPI-2 revision, although one item was slightly altered to modernize language.

Test–retest correlations for *K* based on the MMPI-2 contemporary normative sample are .84 for men and .81 for women over an average interval of about one week. Internal consistency estimates (Cronbach's coefficient alpha) are .73 for men and .71 for women. The MMPI-2 *K* does not appear to have lost any reliability in the revision process as it is essentially unchanged. As expected, reliability coefficients for psychiatric patients are lower than those of normals. Test–retest correlation coefficients for psychiatric cases range between .46 and .56 for a one- to two-day interval between tests, and between .42 and .72 for a one-year interval (Dahlstrom et al., 1975). In Hunsley et al.'s (1988) large-scale meta-analysis of MMPI reliability studies using a wide variety of populations conducted between 1970 and 1981, an average internal consistency of .82 across 71 studies of *K* was reported. They also reported an average test–retest reliability of .77 for 15 studies with time intervals from one day to two years.

Various elevations on *K* are associated with different interpretations or personality correlates. Generally, in clinical settings, scores between *T*-55–65 suggest moderate self-favorableness (self-deception) rather than intentional efforts to mislead the psychologist through impression management. Very high-scoring participants (*T* = >65) are generally described as maintaining a defensive posture and unwilling to admit to psychological problems. However, well-functioning individuals also describe themselves in similar terms, which may simply reflect that their lives are in order (Butcher et al., 1989). Scores above *T*-65 in clinical settings likely will distort the reliability of an accurate personality description and clinical assessment.

At these levels, self-reported adjustment may be unrealistic and reflect a need to deny problems and weakness, and to present an image of adequacy and self-control inconsistent with—if not directly contradicted by—other clinical information.

Scores in this range usually reflect a strong bias against obvious item content, especially when *F* is in an average or low range, but they tend to stimulate elevation on most, if not all, of the *subtle* subscales. Reference to *L, Ss, S, Mp,* and *Sd* should be made to clarify the meaning and shape the interpretation of scores in this range. In addition to clarifying the motivational basis for *K* scores in this range, examining the pattern of scores on *L, Ss, Mp,* and *Sd* may reveal much about the patient's level of insight.

(Nichols, 2011, p. 74)

It is critical that *K* scores be assessed in the context of as much other information as possible, including the referral context and the person's past and current life situation. In general, elevated *K* scores are positively correlated with SES. The MMPI-2 *Manual* (Butcher et al., 1989) points out that individuals with more status stand to lose more by making disclosures that reveal incompetence, ineffectiveness, and insecurities. Therefore, these individuals may try to slant their responses in such a way as to protect their self-esteem and the impressions that others will form of them. Use of the *K* weights serves to correct for this type of defensiveness. Very-low-scoring participants (*T*-35–45) on *K* are often seen as being overly self-critical in confessing many psychological difficulties—and more pessimistic, cynical, irritable, lacking in insight, unstable, poorly defended, and possibly manifesting psychotic signs and symptoms. Scores below *T*-35 suggest over-reporting ("faking bad").

In general, elevated *K* scores are associated with lower ranging clinical scale scores, especially among the content scales, whereas the converse is true for under-elevated *K* scores. When clinical scale elevations are present in a high *K* profile, they tend to be associated with the neurotic triad (Scales 1, 2, and 3; Dahlstrom et al., 1972), whereas individuals faking bad tend to over-claim symptomatology, and the resulting low *K* scores are often associated with peaks on the psychotic tetrad scales (Scales 6, 7, 8, and 9; Dahlstrom et al., 1972).

It is important to recognize that a high *T*-score on a clinical *K*-corrected scale could be due to the addition of a large *K* correction, or to a high raw score on that scale, or both. It is therefore important to examine the raw-score values on the elevated scales, and to compare these with the added *K*-correction. For example, a *T*-score of 65 on Scale 7 (*Pt*) can be achieved in several ways. For example, one male examinee may achieve a *T*-score of 68 for Scale 7 on the basis of a non-*K*-corrected raw score of 23 on *Pt*, plus a 12-item *K*-correction, while another may achieve an identical *K*-corrected Scale 7 *T*-score on the basis of an uncorrected raw score of 12, plus a 23-item *K* correction. The latter endorsement pattern reflects significantly more defensiveness or ability to cope with symptoms than does the former pattern. Inferring worry or tension from the *T*-score of 68 in the latter case may be misleading because the individual with the lower raw-score value on Scale 7 is less likely to be experiencing worry and tension.

Interpretation of the validity scales is discussed in greater detail in Chapter 4, but it should be remembered that general psychiatric patients with bona fide disorders tend to score higher on the *K* scale than do normals instructed to feign a psychiatric disorder (Graham, Watts, & Timbrook, 1991; Wetter et al., 1992). A number of studies have supported this finding, with the implication being that *K* scores of *T*-35 or lower should be checked against other validity measures to ascertain the possibility of a faked or "over-reported" profile. A study by Lamb et al. (1994) also illustrates that when test participants are instructed to fake a closed-head injury and are given specific information on how to manipulate the validity scales (including K), they are able to lower their validity scale scores. Although these results show that coaching can have an important impact on MMPI-2 results in analogue-malingering participants, the implication is that test instructions and test-taking attitudes can greatly affect the scores that clinicians interpret. The importance of test instructions is described in Chapter 2.

Superlative Self-Presentation Scale (S)

Following the re-standardization of the MMPI, the MMPI-2, Butcher and Han (1995) developed the Superlative Self-Presentation scale, S, by contrasting the item responses of 274 male airline pilot applicants with the 1,138 men from the MMPI-2 re-standardization sample. Fifty items were identified that both differed significantly (.001) in their endorsement frequency between the two groups, and contributed to its internal consistency on the basis of item and content analyses. Six of the 50 items are keyed True, 44 False. Butcher and Han (1995) found positive correlations between S and R (Repression), Es, Re (Social Responsiblity), O-H (Overcontrolled Hostility), and L, and negative correlations with A, Pt, CYN, Mt, ANG, ANX, and Sc. These correlates indicate that S, like K, incorporates high levels of first-factor and, to a lesser extent, second-factor variance.

In separate factor analyses of the S items for the men and women of the MMPI-2 re-standardization sample, Butcher and Han (1995) developed five non-overlapping component subscales: Belief in Human Goodness ($S1$, 15 items), Serenity ($S2$, 13 items), Contentment with Life ($S3$, 8 items), Patience and Denial of Irritability and Anger ($S4$, 8 items), and Denial of Moral Flaws ($S5$, 5 items). The component subscales afford a good idea of the content of S, with their emphasis on benevolence, serenity, and freedom from impatience and irritability. These descriptors suggest a close relationship between S and K, and indeed the two scales are correlated at .88. As compared to K, the content of S is less subtle and more socially desirable, emphasizing the denial of misanthropic attitudes, cynicism, mistrust, irritability, hypersensitivity, anxiety, internal conflict or dissonance, and the assertion of a benevolent belief in the virtue, honor, and nobility of others, contentment with one's situation in life, an even temper, composure, and conformity/conventionality (Nichols, 2011). S and K may both be considered measures of defensiveness; however, the K items are restricted to the first part of the test, prior to item 366, whereas S extends through item 560. Additionally, both S and K are negatively correlated with all of the MMPI-2 content scales (Butcher, Graham, Williams, & Ben-Porath, 1990), but the correlations are generally somewhat higher for S than for K. Moreover, judging from the 39 items of S and the 30 items from K for which social desirability ratings are available (Dahlstrom et al., 1975), S appears to indicate slightly (9 percent or 10 percent) greater social desirability than does K. These factors suggest that S is somewhat more likely than K to suppress content scale scores, the endorsement of obvious items in general, and most of the clinical scales, to bias the profile toward a negative slope, and to push up scores on K, Es, GM, and similar scales. In this sense, S appears to possess good construct validity.

S shares 10 items with K (5 on $S1$, 3 on $S2$, and 1 each on $S3$ and $S4$) and 6 with Mp (4 on $S2$). Overlapping items scored in reverse include 14 with CYN (9 on $CYN1$, 5 on *CYN2*), 12 with *Ho* (10 on *S1*), 6 each with *Mt*, *ASP* (all on *ASP1*), and *TPA* (4 on *TPA1*), 5 each with *ANG* (all on *ANG2*) and *WRK*, and 4 with *GF*. High or low scores on *S1* and *S5* may thus be strongly or completely determined by scores on *CYN* and *GF*, respectively, due to overlap (Nichols, 2011).

Butcher and Han (1995) presented several empirical correlates for *S* scores gleaned from spousal ratings gathered during the MMPI-2 re-standardization project. Partners of high *S* scorers tend to describe them as pleasant and relaxed, as slow to express annoyance, as disinclined to worry or fret about minor matters or to become irritable or grouchy over such things, as not moody, and as not suspicious or argumentative in their approach to others. In other words, the unusual freedom from emotional discomfort and interpersonal conflict claimed by high *S* scorers tended to be confirmed as realistic attributes in ratings by their spouses.

Although the empirical strategy used to develop *S* is not particularly objectionable, given that the participants were all male, college educated, of higher SES, and mostly Caucasian, the scale tends to conflate the means and motives by which the pilot applicants manifested their "superlative" adjustments. Thus, some may have emphasized a deliberate strategy of claiming extraordinary adjustment; others of denying relatively common weaknesses, character flaws, worries, and habits; and still others, those of truly superior adjustment, may have merely marked the items in a manner consistent with that adjustment, without seeking to overstate it. Moreover, for those participants who may have exaggerated their adjustment, some may have approached the task in a self-conscious fashion, whereas others may have achieved similar results through less conscious, self-deceptive means (Nichols & Greene, 1997). In this sense, the construct validity of *S* remains somewhat ambiguous. Nonetheless, *S* may be the best of the self-deception scales.

Although the availability of subscales for the *S* scale affords some degree of insight into the content of the items favored by particular respondents, these subscales do not necessarily correspond well to the strategies of response undertaken by the pilot applicants to yield the different rates of endorsement that determined which items would comprise the scale as a whole. Moreover, it is difficult for scores on *S* to reach *T*-65 without drawing items from at least four of the five *S* subscales, thus examining the scatter between the subscales can aid in refining interpretation.

Regardless of these potential problems and their implications for the interpretation of *S* scores, *S* has performed well in several research trials involving the discrimination of a variety of samples instructed to fake good on the MMPI-2 from samples given standard instructions. Among these, two studies incorporated features that permitted the evaluation of the incremental contribution of several scales and indices that have been proposed for the detection of under-reporting. In hierarchical regression analyses, Baer, Wetter, Nichols et al. (1995) found that only 2 of the 11 under-reporting scales and indexes they investigated demonstrated incremental validity beyond *L* and *K*: *S* and Wiggins' *Sd*. A similar analysis by Bagby, Rogers, Nicholson et al. (1997) found that, depending on the samples compared, only *S*, *Sd*, *So-r* (Edwards' Social Desirability), and Nichols and Greene's (1991) Other Deception scale (*Od*) could demonstrate incremental validity over *L* and *K*. Moreover, in both studies, *S* was among those scales showing the largest effect sizes. Bagby, Nicholson, Buis, Radovanovic, and Fidler (1999) found that a composite based on the sum of the *S* and Sd raw scores substantially outperformed L and K in a study of under-reporting and non-under-reporting child custody litigants. The S scale thus appears to detect certain common types of under-reporting of psychopathology; however ,it will require further investigation to establish reliable empirical correlates in other samples, both normal and abnormal, and to ascertain more precisely its position in relation to other, better established response-style measures.

Positive Malingering Scale (Mp)

Cofer et al. (1949) had 81 male and female college students complete the MMPI under three instructional sets, in counterbalanced order: (1) under standard instructions (i.e. honesty) and then under instructions to malinger (to avoid induction into the Army), (2) under instructions to create the best possible impression of themselves (to be accepted into a Naval midshipman training program) as well as under standard instructions, and (3) twice under standard instructions. The second administration intended to eliminate the regression-toward-the-mean effect of the trend of slightly greater normality on the average that is expected on a second standard administration. Thirty-four items (one a duplicate) were found to be stable under the two standard administrations and the fake-bad instructions, but to be endorsed more frequently under the fake-good instructions. These constitute the 33 items of the original Mp scale. In keeping with the tendency of these items to change only under fake-good instructions, the Mp items can be understood as flaws that most people admit when responding candidly but deny when seeking to create a highly favorable impression.

The MMPI-2 version of Mp is reduced by 7 items to 26. Twenty-four items are keyed True, 9 False. It overlaps the Sd scale by 13 items, L and S by 6 items (4 on $S2$), and K by 4 items. Analyses based upon the Caldwell (2007b) data set for clinical patients compiled by Roger Greene found Mp to be highly correlated with Sd (.75) and moderately with L (.65), S (.56), and $Ma3$ (.47), and negatively correlated with $Mf2$ (−.66), APS (−.59), $NEGE$ (−.58), A (−.57), ANX (−.56), Scale 7 (−.55), WRK (−.55), Mt (−.55), OBS (−.54), $Pd5$ (−.52), PS (−.51), DEP (−.50), LSE (−.50), $LSE1$ (−.50), PK (−.50), and MDS (−.50).

Content is quite subtle and variable, with denial of worries, fears, and internal struggles or changes of heart; unusual circumspection about sexuality; high confidence in oneself and in one's leadership potential emerging, and masculine interests as discernible themes. The inclusion of the masculine interest items introduces a possible gender bias for Mp; the mean for women is about 1.33 raw scores lower than that for men. Nichols (2011) points out that this may reduce the sensitivity of Mp to impression management among women. "On the other hand, these items may increase the sensitivity of Mp for certain employment screening applications (e.g. police), as Caldwell (1988) has suggested" (Nichols, 2011, p. 84).

In their meta-analysis of MMPI under-reporting scales, Baer et al. (1992) found an average effect size of 1.42 across 11 studies, making it among the best performers among the 10 scales and indexes examined, and substantially better than L, K, and $F − K$ index, with which it was found to correlate at .94, .90, and .71, respectively. For example, Otto, Lang, Megargee, and Rosenblatt (1988) found that Mp correctly classified 80 percent of a sample of alcoholic participants, when half of the sample were instructed to conceal psychopathology, and the other half followed standard instructions.

High scores are best considered in relation to scores on the *L, K, Sd, Ss,* and *S* scales. Scores at or above *T*-60 should raise the question of a deliberate effort to exaggerate one's level of adjustment, especially when accompanied with similar elevations on *Sd*. When both *Mp* and *Sd* exceed *T* = 65 and are higher than *K*, and when *Ss* scores are average or low, a conscious attempt to fake good (i.e. impression management) is strongly suggested. High *L* scores tend to push up *Mp* and *Sd* due to thematic similarity. When scores on *L* are significantly higher than those for *Mp* and *Sd*, however, the respondent's approach may be more naïve than deliberate, a reaction to the fear of moral judgment rather than an attempt to mislead the examiner into a belief or judgment that the respondent is free of maladjustment and psychopathology. *S* scores exert considerably greater upward pressure on *K* and *Mp* than on *L* or *Sd*, such that *S* is usually high, along with *K*, when *Mp* is significantly elevated but *Sd* and *L* are not.

Social Desirability Scale (Sd)

In a study of Stanford University undergraduates, the responses of 72 males and 106 females, instructed to answer each item in terms of whether people in general would consider a True or a False response more desirable, were compared with 55 male and 85 female controls following standard instructions. Participants given the desirability instructions were further given to understand that they were to make their judgments on the basis of "the general values of American culture." Wiggins (1959) found 40 items, the *Sd* scale that separated the desirability group from the standard instruction group at .001 or less, for both men and women. In their meta-analysis, Baer et al. (1992) found an average effect size for *Sd* of 1.60 across six studies, making it the best performing of the scales and indexes they reviewed. Baer and Miller (2002) further confirmed the superiority of *Sd* for detecting under-reporting in a subsequent meta-analysis.

The MMPI-2 version of *Sd* is reduced by 7 items to 33. Eleven items are keyed True, 15 False. It overlaps *Mp* by 13 items, *L* by 7, *S* by 2 (both on *S2*), and *K* by 2 items. Correlations with these scales of .75, .55, .37, and .29, respectively, were found in a large psychiatric sample (Caldwell, 2007b, as found in Greene, 2011).

Whereas the items of *Mp* are biased toward the denial of shortcomings and distress, the items of *Sd* tend to emphasize the assertion of positive attributes. Nichols (2011, p. 85) insightfully elaborates on the differences between *Mp* and *Sd*.

Although *Mp* and *Sd* are both highly effective measures of impression management, three features of *Sd* differentiate it from *Mp*. First, unlike *Mp*, for which 58% of the items are keyed *False*, 73% of the *Sd* items are keyed *True*. Second, both *Mp* and *Sd* deny flaws and assert virtues that most people need neither to deny nor assert when taking the MMPI-2, but *Mp* emphasizes the denial of negative attributes, whereas *Sd* emphasizes the assertion of positive attributes. Thus, the images portrayed of the self in these two scales differ, with *Mp* emphasizing virtue and stability in the context of relaxed, pacific, quiet self-assurance, and a placid if not imperturbable emotionality, and *Sd* emphasizing virtue and vitality in the context of a strong-willed, outgoing, constructive, engaged, and poised social presence. Finally, *Sd* has considerably more top than *Mp*, with *T*-scores peaking above 100 vs. at about 80 for *Mp*.

The content of *Sd* affirms broad interests: conventional, if not conservative, socially responsible moral values; a high level of drive and energy; persistence and decisiveness; sociability, extraversion, and an absence of self-consciousness; and an absence of health concern. In keeping with the instructions to judge desirability in terms of the values of people in general, the content of *Sd* converges on a portrait of an idealized model citizen, one who is extraverted and outgoing, free of worry and self-doubt, assertive, self-directed and in full control of his or her mental faculties; who is orderly, confident, capable, decisive, cool under pressure, and oriented to success; and who is composed but friendly, buoyant, energetic, up-to-the-task, and actively engaged in living; but one who is also over-conventional, hypervirtuous, prudish, and unrealistic in terms of self-portrayal.

Unlike *S* and other Alpha-type scales, which appear to conceal psychopathology directly by suppressing test expressions of neuroticism and psychoticism, *Mp* and *Sd*, as measures of the Gamma dimension, appear to achieve their results by somewhat different and more indirect means. Although these means are not thoroughly understood, both scales appear to mask psychopathology through the substitution of a highly favorable social image. High scorers on *Mp* and *Sd* deny flaws and assert virtues that most people feel the need neither to deny nor assert when taking the MMPI-2. As above, in the case of *Mp*, this image emphasizes virtue and stability in the context of relaxed, pacific, quiet self-assurance, and a placid if not imperturbable emotionality, whereas the image conveyed by *Sd* emphasizes virtue and vitality in the context of a strong-willed, outgoing, constructive, engaged, and poised social presence.

As with the *Mp* scale, scores at $T = 60-65$ on *Sd* should raise the question of a deliberate attempt to portray oneself in terms of an idealized social image, and *Sd* scores that exceed scores on *K* strongly suggest such, especially when *Ss* scores are average or low.

Socioeconomic Status Scale (Ss)

Rescued from obscurity by Alex Caldwell, Nelson's (1952) *Ss* scale is a measure of attained SES as distinct from a measure of status aspiration (cf. Gough's, 1948a, 1948b, Status scale [*St*]). Its creation was inspired by the insight that various aspects of abnormal psychology and symptomatic behavior may be related to social stratification. As an example, Nelson mentioned that such behaviors as wife beating, heavy drinking, improvident spending habits, siding with and covering for children vis-à-vis school authorities, and relocating the family's domicile to avoid creditors, may be easily construed as psychopathic by mental health service providers, a group typically if not uniformly of high social status, even though such behaviors may be all but normative in some segments of the lower-lower class.

From an initial sample of 710 male patients who had been treated at the Ft. Snelling VA Hospital, Nelson simultaneously rated patients for years of education and occupational level, as determined by the Warner seven-step scale of occupational status categories. Forty-one participants with 13 or more years of education and occupations within the highest two status categories (e.g. engineer or manager) constituted the high-status group; 43 participants with 8 or fewer years of education and occupations within the lowest status category (e.g. laborer or dishwasher) constituted the low-status group.

Eighty-seven items were found to separate the two groups at the .01 level or less, and these became the *Ss* scale; 73 of these items remain on the MMPI-2. Thirteen items are keyed True, 60 False.

Ss was validated on new samples of patients for which highly significant correlations were found with education (.47), occupational level (.45), and intelligence (.41). The *Ss* scale was unrelated to age in both the scale development and later validation samples. In Nelson's cross-validation sample, *Ss* misclassified only half as many participants as Gough's (1948a, 1948b) *St* scale, although both scales correctly classified most participants. Jenkins (1952) found that *Ss* was related to better prognosis in paranoid schizophrenia.

Nelson divided *Ss* into 12 groups of items according to its wide-ranging content: physical complaints (13 items), sleep difficulties (3 items), psychological deficit (4 items), phobias and obsessive–compulsive traits (9 items), delusions and misperceptions (6 items), paranoid traits (5 items), affective states (5 items), self-insight (3 items), rigid moral code (2 items), interest in intellectual pursuits (2 items), other interests (6 items), and a miscellaneous category (15 items). The direction of scoring is such that high scorers tend to deny somatic complaints and sleep difficulties; dysphoric mood; fears and phobias; cynicism, suspiciousness, paranoia, and psychoticism; problems with cognitive functioning; nonintellectual interests and occupations that depend largely on physical (vs. mental) activity; introversion; and impulsiveness. They portray themselves as alert, concerned about their social presentation, fallible, inclined toward candor, mature, discreet, and morally flexible and tolerant.

A scale of the Alpha type, *Ss* shares considerable variance with both *K* and *S*, correlating with both at about .65, despite sharing only two items with each. Although such correlations would naturally raise the question of defensiveness, albeit of a rather subtle kind, there is little doubt that higher status members of society generally possess a degree of insulation from the stresses and sources of instability that is unavailable to those at lower socioeconomic levels. Their better reputations and the greater financial resources, and the respect these command, confer considerable flexibility and a wider range of alternatives for managing interpersonal conflict, situational difficulties, and economic reverses—indeed hardships and misfortunes of most kinds. Moreover, and in the main, such people tend to possess the kinds of abilities, intelligence, knowledge, and skills that enabled them to attain higher SES in the first place, as compared with those who fail to attain such status. In the face of difficulty, then, the higher status person tends to have a wider network and greater access to social support; better and more reliable problem-solving skills; greater access to information and expertise; more money and discretion as to how it is spent; and more time to assess, plan, and implement measures for the alleviation of a broad range of life difficulties. In the light of such advantages, it is not surprising that such persons would have a higher threshold for experiencing feelings of inadequacy and insecurity, developing symptoms of maladjustment and psychopathology, and expressing distress over their problems, even when present, than would persons lacking these advantages.

Consistent with the above description, Nichols (2011) reported a very high correlation between *Ss* and *Es* (which is sensitive to stress tolerance and to the physiologically organized responses to stress). He also reported *Ss* to be largely free of variance related to impression management (*Ss* x *Mp* = .17; *Ss* x *Sd* = .05). A significant limitation of *Ss* is its low ceiling with raw scores being exhausted at about *T*-75.

Although the validity and performance characteristics of *Ss* have been little explored since its initial development, Caldwell (1988) has argued that this scale can play a helpful role in the interpretation of *K* scores, along with the Gamma scales *L*, *Mp*, and *Sd*. When high *K* scores are accompanied by high *Ss* scores, and *L*, *Mp*, and *Sd* scores are unelevated or low, Caldwell suggests that the elevation on *K* should not be construed as a deliberate attempt to mislead the examiner or to frustrate the purposes of the evaluation; rather, the elevation should be understood to reflect the portrayal of favorable adjustment over which the examinee has little conscious control. By an extension of this reasoning, a deceptive or defensive interpretation of elevated scores on *S* should be attenuated when these are accompanied by high *Ss* scores. When the *K* score is high along with elevations on the Gamma scales and the *Ss* score is average or low, Caldwell recommends that *K* be interpreted to emphasize an impression management approach to the evaluation.

Conversely, when the *K* and *Ss* scores are both low, the *Mp*, *Sd*, and *Ds* scores are average, and *F* is not greater than T = 80, "a low-status candor, lack of sophistication, and genuine self-negativity in the absence of any 'faking bad'" (Caldwell, 1988, p. 95) is suggested. When the *K* and Gamma scale scores are low, the *F* and/or *Ds* score is high, and the *Ss* score is within an average range, Caldwell (1988) argued that there existed "an excessive self-criticalness or deliberate faking bad with the low *K* not being due to low socioeconomic status" (p. 95). In keeping with Caldwell's (1988) view that *Ss* achieves its positivizing of test performance without any conscious effort to convey a more favorable impression on the MMPI-2, it is noteworthy that its correlations with the Gamma scales are very low, if not close to 0, as above.

Nichols (2011) reported the following item overlap information and correlations for *Ss* and various scales: *Ss* shares 11 items with *Es*, 7 with *GM*, and 6 with *GF*, but only 1 item with *K*, 2 with *S*, and none with either *Mp* or *Sd*. It negatively overlaps Scale 8 (12 items, 6 on *Sc5* and 4 on *Sc1*), Scale 6 (9 items, 6 on *Pa1*), *F* (9 items), *PS* (9 items), *Ds* (8 items), *HEA* (8 items, 4 on *HEA2*), *PK* (7 items), *BIZ* (7 items, 3 on *BIZ2*), Scale 4 (6 items, 4 on *Pd-O* (Psychopathic Deviate–Obvious) and 4 on *Pd4*), *FB* (6 items), *FRS* (6 items, 3 on *FRS2*), *CYN* (6 items), Scale 9 (5 items), *PSYC* (5 items), and *Mt* (4 items).

Ss is highly correlated with *Es* (.83), and moderately correlated with *Do* (Dominance) (.72), *GM* (.67), *S* (.65), and *K* (.65). It has strong negative correlations with Scale 8 (−.83), *PS* (−.81), *PK* (−.81), *Ds* (−.80), *FB* (−.78), *PSYC* (−.78), Scale 7 (−.77), *F* (−.77), *HEA* (−.77), Scale 1 (−.76), and *BIZ* (−.76). This pattern of relationships indicates that self-sufficiency and stress tolerance (*Es*) and self-deception (*S*) can raise *Ss* scores, and that psychoticism (Scale 8, *PSYC*, *BIZ*), broad maladjustment and subjective distress (*PS*, *PK*), and symptom exaggeration and malingering (*F*, *FB*) suppress *Ss* scores.

Validity Indices

F-FB *Index*

In a valid profile, the *F* and *FB* scales should have roughly similar scores, given that both scales consist of infrequently endorsed items. Nichols and Greene (1995) recommended that the absolute raw score difference between the *F* and *FB* scales provides a crude measure of consistency of item endorsement on both halves of the test and tends to confirm indications of inconsistency from other scales, such as *VRIN* and *TRIN*. If the raw score for the *FB* scale exceeds the *F* scale by six or more and there are no content reasons to explain the difference, it becomes important to consider that the validity of the second half of the test may be compromised. As stated earlier, *F* ends with item 361 and *FB* begins at item 281. Thus *FB* can be useful for detecting random or faking-bad/faking-good tendencies that affect the content scales concentrated among the last 150 items of the inventory. It should be noted that the *F-FB* Index is confounded by the fact that the *F* items emphasize paranoid/psychotic content whereas the *FB* items emphasize panic/fear, depressive cognition, and suicidal ideation in its content. Thus, an individual with psychotic symptoms is more likely to elevate *F* over *FB*, whereas one manifesting primarily depressive symptoms will tend toward the opposite pattern.

As noted by Nichols (2011), the performance of this measure is enhanced when combined with *VRIN* (*VRIN* + |*F-FB*|) or with *F* (*F* + *FB* + |*F-FB*|; Cramer, 1995). These indices are especially valuable in determining whether a protocol has reached an excessive level of response inconsistency when scores on *VRIN* are equivocal.

On the basis of a random sort of scores for the *VRIN*, *F*, and *FB* scales, Greene (2000) reported that 75 percent of these random sorts had a raw score of seven or greater on the *F-FB* Index. With raw *VRIN* scores in the intermediate range (8–15), he reported that less than 26 percent of the random sorts had scores of six or below on this index. Greene (1991a) stated that the "clinician can be fairly confident that the client has endorsed the items consistently if this index is 6 or lower when *VRIN* is in the intermediate range of 8–15" (p. 70). It is recommended that the *F-FB* raw difference score be routinely examined in assessing the validity of an MMPI-2 profile.

Dissimulation Index (F – K)

The *F* – *K* index was derived by Gough (1947, 1950) as an additional validity indicator for the original MMPI to assist in determining whether an individual completed the test appropriately or attempted to simulate or exaggerate psychopathology. Gough found the *F* – *K* index to be a more accurate classifier of simulated or faked profiles than either *F* or *K* alone. The *F* – *K* index is derived by subtracting the raw *K* score from the raw *F* score. When the raw *F* score exceeds the raw *K* score, the index takes on a positive numerical value; when the reverse is true, the index takes on a negative numerical value. Positive *F* – *K* index values raise the question of over-reporting psychopathology, while negative values may be consistent with under-reporting. In general, elevated *F* scores can be variously ascribed to psychotic conditions, cries for help, general maladjustment, random responding, and partial or pure malingering. Participants with low *F* scores when the *K* is significantly elevated are described as free of psychological problems or denying difficulties (faking good). Elevated *K* has usually been interpreted as suggesting defensiveness, cautiousness, or emotional reserve, with low *K* scores reflecting a tell-all attitude and a lack of emotional modulation or reserve (Caldwell, 1988; Lewak, Marks, & Nelson, 1990).

In creating the index, Gough (1950, p. 408) had a group of 11 clinical workers feign two psychiatric syndromes:

The first was defined as "an acute, severe, anxiety neurosis which would lead to separation from the service, but not to commitment to a mental hospital," and the second as "a non-deteriorated, acute, paranoid schizophrenic psychosis." Skilled judges were able to identify eight of eleven psychoneurotic patterns that were intermixed with 68 authentic psychoneurotic records, and were able to identify all 11 of the psychotic simulations that were mixed among 24 authentic profiles. At the same time, a simple combination of the raw F score minus the raw K score was able to pick out ten of the eleven simulated records in each of the two situations. The $F - K$ cutting scores proposed at that time were plus 4 and greater for neurotic profiles, and plus 16 and greater for psychotic profiles.

Gough (1950) later suggested that $F - K$ scores of greater than nine indicated a fake-bad approach, with the participant attempting to present him- or herself with serious psychopathology. Scores of less than zero on the $F - K$ index indicated a fake-good profile, wherein the participant attempted to deny the presence of any type of psychological disturbance. He stated that the $F - K$ index was less efficient in detecting fake-good profiles, as compared with fake-bad profiles, at any particular cut score, and pointed out that the problem in establishing an $F - K$ cutting score is one of minimizing false positives and false negatives.

What is considered to be over- versus under-reporting is often subject to the interpretative skills of the clinician, as cut guidelines using clinical and normal groups have varied considerably among researchers and reference groups. Most investigations of the $F - K$ index have used analogue participants who were asked to simulate various disorders or normalcy, and whose profiles were then compared with those of authentic normal and patient profiles. College students have constituted the majority of these participants, and Dahlstrom et al. (1972) noted the differences in conducting faking studies with college students. For example, it is known that well-educated individuals tend to score higher on K by almost one SD. Their elevated K scores will thus tend to bias their $F - K$ index scores in the fake-good direction. Greene (2011) indicated in his discussion of the $F - K$ index that it has been difficult to identify any specific $F - K$ score for the detection of students instructed to fake good under the usual administration instructions for the MMPI/MMPI-2. Presumably, students who are, for the most part, free of psychopathology find it difficult to look even better than they already are when instructed to fake good. Greene also acknowledged another problem in detecting fake-good profiles in college students (or others): the person who is well-adjusted and effectively handling his or her problems would be expected to score low on F and high on K, indicating an absence of distress, with the result that normal persons taking the MMPI-2 often will be inappropriately classified as producing under-reported profiles.

Some important conclusions from Greene's (2011) discussion include the following: The usefulness of the $F - K$ index in detecting fake-bad profiles may be more limited with actual clinical patients who exaggerate their problems than with students. He recommends interviewing those who obtain a high F score and high $F - K$ index, to determine if the self-report of distress is accurate or exaggerated. He also questions the utility of the index in detecting fake-good profiles among psychiatric patients, pointing out that psychiatric patients and inmates have difficulty producing normal-appearing profiles when instructed to do so (Grayson & Olinger, 1957; Lawton & Kleban, 1965). However, Bagby, Rogers, Nicholson et al. (1997) found that a sample of schizophrenic outpatients in the residual phase were, in fact, able, under fake-good instructions, to reduce their clinical scale elevations as well as, if not better than, students, thereby suggesting that patients may be as capable as students in manipulating their MMPI-2 clinical scale scores. The Marks et al. (1974) study of projected discharged profiles seems to supports Greene's (2011) call for additional research to examine whether normal profiles produced by clinical participants instructed to fake good are generally positive prognostic signs.

Clear limitations have also been reported on the utility of the $F - K$ index for separating profiles of patients simulating or exaggerating illness from authentic patient profiles (Anthony, 1971). Hedlund and Won Cho (as cited by Greene, 1988b) found that psychiatric patients achieved a mean $F - K$ index score near 0, as compared to the -10 noted for normals (Osborne, Colligan, & Offord, 1986), which is clearly in contrast to what Gough (1950) had indicated earlier about the index not being affected by the presence of psychiatric disturbance per se. In light of this, the interpretation of a profile as the result of malingering or exaggerating psychopathology must be made with caution, as the presence of psychiatric disturbance has a bearing on $F - K$ scores.

It is generally reported that $F - K$ index scores increase significantly as the degree of simulated disturbance increases (Greene, 1988a; Wetter et al., 1992). Berry, Baer, and Harris (1991) conducted a meta-analysis of 28 studies that used the original MMPI to detect malingering in order to quantify how much higher malingerers or simulators score on the various over-reporting scales and indexes, including the $F - K$ index. They noted a wide variability in cut scores used across studies, with cut scores between 7 and 16 yielding the highest classification rates. On the basis of their review of various scales and indexes, the $F - K$ index was recommended for identifying malingerers. Overall, the results showed that participants malingering or over-reporting their symptoms scored almost 2 *SD*s higher on the $F - K$ index than participants answering honestly. Rogers et al. (1994) also found the $F - K$ index to be a powerful indicator of malingering in their meta-analytic study of MMPI-2 fake-bad measures, and recommended that it be used in conjunction with F and the obvious-subtle subscale differences as a screening indicator.

Along the same lines as the above-reported investigation, Baer et al. (1992) meta-analytically reviewed the empirical literature on the detection of under-reporting psychopathology (faking good) on the original MMPI. Twenty-five studies in which participants were responding honestly were compared with participants' under-reporting psychopathology. Several indexes were examined, including the $F - K$ index. By computing the mean overall hit rate (percentage of total participants correctly classified) for each index of under-reporting by collapsing across cutting scores, these investigators were able to gain a general impression of which measure best detected under-reporting participants. The $F - K$ index correctly classified 77 percent of the participants, and the highest mean overall hit rate of 84 percent was obtained for the *Sd* scale (Wiggins, 1959). As with the malingering participants reported earlier (Berry, Baer, & Harris, 1991), there was considerable variability in hit rates; the percentage of honest participants correctly classified ranging from 62 percent to 100 percent, with the best overall hit rate being 95 percent with an $F - K$ index score of -11. In general, the results indicated that under-reporting participants and honest participants differ on the $F - K$ index by just less than 1 *SD* ($d = 0.71$). Thus it appears that the $F - K$ index is less accurate in correctly classifying under-reporters versus over-reporters of psychopathology, a finding consistent with other investigations (Bagby et al., 1997b). The considerable overlap in distributions between honest and under-reporting participants is likely an important factor in these differences. The reader interested in more detail about methodologies used in these type of studies is referred to those by Baer et al. (1992); Baer, Wetter, and Berry (1995); Baer, Wetter, Nichols et al. (1995); and Berry, Baer, and Harris (1991).

The first attempt to apply the $F - K$ index to the detection of participants attempting to present an overly favorably test profile (fake good) was by Hunt (1948), who found that a cutting score of equal to or less than –11 identified 62 percent of a prison sample asked to fake good but also resulted in a 93 percent false-positive rate with psychology undergraduate students asked to produce an authentic profile. Much better results were obtained for the identification of simulators of psychiatric disorder (fake bad) using a cut of equal to or greater than 11 (a much lower 12 percent false-positive rate). Gough (1950) reanalyzed data from several studies not initially involving the $F - K$ index and found the index much more useful for correctly separating fake-bad simulators from normal and patient groups than for the discrimination of simulated fake-good profiles from authentic normal and psychiatric profiles. He also noted that the mean $F - K$ index score did not differ between normal and authentic psychiatric patients from university and VA hospital settings, suggesting that the index was not susceptible to distortion on the basis of psychiatric disturbance (a critical element for the establishment of an empirical index used to discriminate simulators of illness or wellness from genuine normal and impaired populations). Gough reported $F - K$ index data for the original normative sample of the MMPI (294 men and 397 women), noting that scores were roughly normally distributed ($M = -8.96$, $SD = 6.97$ for the composite sample; separate means by gender were not reported). Only 11 percent of the participants had an $F - K$ index equal to or greater than zero, although this may have been, in part, an artifact of the normative sample having included participants with many missing item responses (excessively disturbing or embarrassing items), thus lowering the potential F score. This was one of the issues addressed by Hathaway and Briggs (1957) in their "purification" of the original normative sample. When Gough pooled his data with data from other clinical and analogue simulator groups, he found a cutting score of seven or greater correctly identified 95 percent of normal and 75 percent of fake-bad simulators.

Note that the study and use of the $F - K$ index is primarily focused on adults. Adolescent inpatient respondents score significantly higher on F than do adult psychiatric inpatients, whereas outpatient adolescents score similarly to adult inpatients. Given the higher F scale value among teenagers, Archer (1997) suggested that the $F - K$ index criterion should be used very cautiously with these respondents when the MMPI-A is administered.

The revision of the MMPI necessitated the establishment of new norms for the $F - K$ index for several reasons. Four items were deleted from the original F scale (resulting in a scale of 60 items), and 12 modifications were made to the remaining items, including 6 grammatical changes, 5 modernizations of idioms and usage, and 1 change in sexist wording (Butcher et al., 1989; Dahlstrom, 1993). K was less affected, as it lost no items in the revision and only a single item on the scale was modified. Participants in the re-standardization normals were screened out if their F scale exceeded a raw score greater than 20). No such limitations were imposed on the collection of participants for the normative sample of the original MMPI. Inspection of the item endorsement frequencies of the contemporary and original normative groups shows distinct differences on many items, especially on K, which may reflect societal and cultural changes since the time of the development of the original MMPI.

Data are now available from several investigations of the $F - K$ index from the MMPI-2 (e.g. Baer, Wetter, Nichols et al., 1995; Graham, Watts et al., 1991; Larrabee, 2003; Lewis, Simcox, & Berry, 2002; Steffan, Morgan, Lee, & Sellbom, 2010; Sweet, Malina, & Ecklund-Johnson, 2006; Rothke et al., 1994). For example, Graham, Watts et al. (1991) examined the utility of the MMPI-2 validity scales and the $F - K$ index for identifying fake-bad and fake-good profiles. A cut score of 12 or greater for women and 17 or greater for men correctly classified 90 percent of fake-bad profiles by college students, but misclassified about 16 percent of psychiatric patients as faking bad. The index was not as useful for detecting fake-good profiles, a finding consistent with previous research with the original MMPI (e.g. Baer, Wetter, & Berry, 1992; Berry, Baer, & Harris, 1991). Other research on MMPI-2 malingering has shown that F and the $F - K$ index outperform FB in identifying over-reporting (Berry et al., 1995; Iverson, Franzen, & Hammond, 1993).

Following the release of the MMPI-2, Rothke et al. (1994) reported MMPI-2 norms for the new standardization group on the $F - K$ index and presented data for samples of psychiatric patients, litigating and non-litigating head-injured patients, individuals seeking disability benefits, job applicants for police and priest positions, and substance abusers. These investigators chose to approach the establishment of normative guidelines for detecting over- or under-reported profiles by selecting scores that separated the upper and lower 2.5 percent from the overall score distribution (i.e. ±2 SDs from the mean, assuming a normal distribution of scores). This approach is viewed as preferable to the use of cut scores derived from analogue studies (i.e. those in which participants are asked to fake bad or fake good), which assume that analogue participants actually perform as would true malingerers.

Wetter et al. (1993) noted that analogue participants often are given neither specific information about the diagnoses they are attempting to feign, nor that successful malingering involves selective rather than mass endorsement of symptoms. This may result in analogue malingerers obtaining an inflated $F - K$ index value, leading to exaggerated cut scores. Rothke et al.'s approach of setting guideline scores based on the extremes of the distribution of scores of a particular diagnostic or applicant group, versus using analogue participants, is similar to the concept of using local norms as a way of enhancing the generalizability of cut scores to an individual participant. Using non-analogue data to establish cutting scores is likely to yield more valid descriptions and predictions for clinical decision making, but also for decisions about malingering in litigation and forensic contexts, or even whether an applicant should be denied a job on the basis of an excessive denial of psychological weakness.

Table 3.1 lists the MMPI-2 $F - K$ scores at the approximate lower and upper 2.5 percentiles of the distributions reported for various samples, allowing a specific comparison of an examinee's score to the general population from which the individual derives:

These scores should not be viewed as inflexible cuts for fake good or fake bad profiles, partly because some of the samples are small in size and these "cut scores" could easily be affected by a single extreme score. These scores should serve as a reminder that $F - K$ scores will differ across clinical samples necessitating future normative studies on these clinical populations.

(Rothke et al., 1994, p. 10)

Table 3.1   MMPI-2 F – K scores at the lower and upper extremes of different diagnostic and subject groups

Subject Group	N	Approximate lower 2.5% (fake good)	Approximate upper 2.5% (fake bad)
Normals, male	1,138	–22	+4 [a]
Normals, female	1,462	–22	+3 [a]
Psychiatric, male	215	–18	+27
Psychiatric, female	241	–20	+22
Substance dependent, male	168	–19	+ 10
Substance dependent, female	96	–22	+10
Traumatic brain injury, male	50	–23	+17
Traumatic brain injury, female	29	–22	–1
SSD/SSI benefit applicants, male	217	–11	+37
SSD/SSI benefit applicants, female	74	–22	+30
Police applicants, male	49	–25	–11 [b]
Police applicants, female	12	–24	–13 [b]
Priest applicants, male	38	–25	–8 [b]
Priest applicants, female	30	–24	–7 [b]

Notes: SSD = Social Security Disability. SSI = Supplemental Security Income.
a   These "cutoffs" might have been higher had the normative group not excluded subjects with raw F scores of ≥ +20.
b   Scores in this direction more likely reflect a willingness to acknowledge difficulties (in these subject groups) than an attempt to feign a disorder.

Source: From "MMPI-2 Normative Data for the *F – K* Index: Implications for Clinical, Neuropsychological, and Forensic Practice," by S. E. Rothke, A. F. Friedman, W. G. Dahlstrom, R. L. Greene, R. Arrendondo, and A. W. Mann, 1994, *Assessment, 7*, 1–15. Copyright© 1994 by Psychological Assessment Resources. Reproduced by special permission of the Publisher, Psychological Assessment Resources, Inc., Odessa, FL, 33556. Further reproduction is prohibited without permission from PAR, Inc.

The importance of comparing a single participant's score to an appropriate reference group is suggested by Table 3.1:

For example, in a competency-to-stand trial evaluation in which the defendant presumably would have an interest in appearing impaired, it would be important to consider using *F – K* scores for psychiatric patients (if that individual had a history of psychiatric disturbance) as they may differ from those of the normative population. Thus, an interpretation of the validity of the profile should not be based solely on the guidelines for the normative population. The same would hold true of a patient with traumatic brain injury (TBI) involved in personal injury litigation; the sample scores for patients with TBI should be considered.

(Rothke et al., 1994, p. 13)

As can be seen in Table 3.1, very different conclusions can be drawn about whether a participant was feigning or exaggerating a disorder if cuts based on the normative sample are used, as opposed to making adjustments based upon a specific diagnostic group. Rothke et al. suggested that the clinician use the guidelines from the normative group, but make adjustments for the specific diagnostic group in order to address how a participant's score compares with that of the general population in a manner that is mindful of the impact of a particular condition on the $F - K$ index score. This is similar to the practice of using general cut scores on neuropsychological tests for identification of impairment, and then modifying interpretations based on adjustments for age and education, which are well known to affect neuropsychological test performance (e.g. Heaton, Grant, & Matthews, 1991).

The Rothke et al. (1994) data show the scores on the $F - K$ index are generally more in the negative or under-reporting direction on the MMPI-2 than for the original MMPI, where comparison scores were available, except for the psychiatric sample. This may be due in part because the mean raw K scale scores for the MMPI-2 re-standardization sample were approximately 15 (for both men and women), as compared with approximate means of 13 for the original normative group. This is likely to have been an effect of the MMPI-2 normative sample having a higher mean level of education than the original normative group. Rothke et al.'s findings also indicate the need to maintain separate guidelines for male and female participants in fake-bad assessments, a finding consistent with other studies.

In summary, the research to date with the $F - K$ index for both the MMPI and the MMPI-2 suggests that the index is much more useful for identifying fake-bad than fake-good profiles. The cut scores derived from the original MMPI should be replaced with cuts based upon the research literature for the MMPI-2 (see Chapter 4 for suggested cut scores).

It is recommended that a determination of profile validity not be made on the basis of a single score or index value alone. Rather, an examination of various measures, as well as of overall (e. g. mean) clinical scale elevation, in conjunction with interview findings and the participant's history and current circumstances, is recommended. Future research should focus on specific diagnostic groups in order to maximize generalizability to individual cases. This would also minimize the potential impact of differing base rates of elevated and low index scores within different groups on the sensitivity and specificity of cut guidelines (Glaros & Kline, 1988). Research exploring the outcome (e.g. treatment, job selection, and litigation status) and recovery correlates of the $F - K$ index would make it a much more useful clinical tool. Specifically, Rothke et al. (1994, p. 14) suggested that

> investigations on the use of the $F - K$ index as a validity indicator need to include independent measures (either other tests or criterion measures if available) of malingering, exaggeration of illness, defensiveness, denial of illness, and effects of litigation and/or of the job selection process on test performance.

True Percent Index (T percent)

An indication of a test-taker's approach to the MMPI-2 may be revealed, in part, by the percentage of True items endorsed. Over-declaring symptoms (e.g. faking bad), will generally produce a higher True than False percentage rate. The majority of the items on the psychotic tetrad (Scales 6–9) are keyed True (75 percent), whereas only 30 percent of the items on the neurotic triad (Scales 1–3) are keyed True. The somatic items on the test are generally keyed in the False direction. "A relatively high False percentage may stem from an emphasis on somatization in one's self-report or from a highly self-favorable response style" (Nichols and Greene, 1995, p. 22). Like Scales 6–9, the MMPI-2 content scales are also predominantly keyed True (81 percent). Higher True percentage values also tend to be associated with elevations on Scale *F*, and high False percentage endorsements are associated with Scales *L* and *K*. Nichols (2011, p. 66) provides a practical interpretive overview for the True Percent Index:

> Values for True percent (or T %) are of clinical interest only at extremes of less than 25% or more than 60% in psychiatric populations. High values reflect the acquiescence response set, which, if indiscriminate, is accompanied by high scores on TRIN. Because a bias toward endorsing items True suggests a crude approach to exaggerating symptoms, scores on F, F_B, F_P, and Ds are usually extremely high and should be checked. The only clinical group that tends to produce high values on T % without extremely high scores on F, F_B, F_P, and Ds with any consistency are bipolar maniacs. Clinical groups often producing unusually low values on this index are among the somatization disorders. Interpreting protocols with T % values exceeding 70 or less than 15 is discouraged, because these are almost always the result of a deviant response style, and the resulting profiles are so distorted as to provide a misleading basis for personality description.

It is recommended that the psychologist examine the percentage of True endorsements as another validity check with the caveats by Nichols in mind, as described above. If the computer scoring program does not provide such information, one can quickly count the True items on the answer sheet and divide by 567 to derive True percent.

Note

1 As described in Greene (2011), the Caldwell clinical sample consists of over 161,000 MMPIs from inpatients and outpatients that were submitted to the Caldwell Report for scoring and interpretive analysis. After frequency distributions on a number of scales revealed extreme scores on the validity scales, the sample size was reduced to close to 155,000 cases. The reader interested in the demographic characteristics of the Caldwell clinical sample should consult Greene's 2011 text (Tables 11.1 and 11.2, pp. 468–469).

4 Interpreting the MMPI-2 Validity Scales

Several methods and a number of basic and special scales are available to assess complex validity issues on the MMPI-2. Nine basic MMPI-2 validity measures provide the clinician with the essential frame of reference for interpreting the clinical and supplementary scales. These nine basic validity measures (*?, VRIN, TRIN, F, FB, F(p)*, *L, K,* and *S*) give some indications of (a) whether the client understood and answered all the items in a consistent fashion; (b) the extent to which the client is endorsing items claiming the experience of psychological pain and unusual, bizarre experiences, behaviors, or ideas; and (c) the extent to which the client might be trying, intentionally or unintentionally, to give a favorable or unfavorable self-portrayal. In other words, the basic validity scales are useful in determining the *consistency* and *accuracy* of reported symptoms, complaints, and traits. In addition to measuring validity, some of the validity scales also have personality correlates. The interpretations that follow, then, focus both on the *validity* aspects of the validity scales and, where applicable, the *personality* aspects. Additional special validity scale guideline ranges are presented for: *Ds, Mp, Sd, Ss, F-FB Index, Dissimulation Index (F – K),* and the *True Percent* index.

As previously described in Chapter 3, the original MMPI was constructed with three basic validity scales: *L, F,* and *K.* The *VRIN, TRIN, FB, F(p),* and *S* scales were later developed for the MMPI-2 to assist in evaluating the consistency and accuracy of a given protocol. Except for some slight differences in cut scores, minor rewordings, and the loss of four items on *F,* the three original validity scales (*L, F,* and *K*) are the same for the MMPI-2 as they were for the MMPI. The contemporary normative sample did slightly alter the *T*-score values for the *L, F,* and *K* scales.

Chapter 3 provides a detailed description of the construction methodology, psychometric operating features, and reliability and validity research for all of the scales described in this chapter. This chapter also describes various response sets (e.g. All-True, All-False, Random) and illustrates profiles with common validity patterns.

Cannot Say Score (?)

The *?* scale is misnamed in that it is not a scale, but simply a report of the number of unscorable items (i.e. double-marked or omitted items). Consequently, we refer to it as the Cannot Say score. On the MMPI-2, the number of unscorable items is recorded on the bottom left of the profile form, and no *T*-score value is assigned. The original MMPI test instructions were less stringent than those adopted for the MMPI-2, with test takers now asked to answer all of the items. The mean number of omitted items on the MMPI-2 thereby reduced and their significance is thereby increased over that for the MMPI.

Normal Range: 5 or Fewer Unscorable Items

Little, if any, validity significance is associated with the omission of five or fewer items, although examining omitted items may yield clinical hypotheses. It is unlikely that omissions in this range will distort the profile unless they are narrowly confined to a particular content area. In forensic settings, every omitted item may be significant and should be noted by the expert witness, as the opposing attorney might question the omission(s) during cross-examination. In such settings, a protocol could be returned for completion even if only four or five items are left unanswered. The psychologist should be aware that a cross-examining attorney may ask, "Did the defendant respond to all the items?" and, if the answer is no, "Which items were not answered?" Thus, if feasible, the client should be encouraged to complete the omitted items on the test, and to provide an explanation for them.

Moderate to High Range: 6 to 29 Unscorable Items

Raw scores of 6 to 29, if reading or comprehension difficulties can be ruled out, generally indicate idiosyncratic and contentious interpretation of items and/or obsessional indecision, often with extreme intellectualization. This process may be seen in the legalistic over-cautiousness of some paranoid clients or the indecision of anxious, obsessive–compulsive ones. In other individuals, this range may reflect a reticence to respond openly to test items that probe personal experiences or private feelings and experiences in particularly sensitive areas for that person. It is recommended that the clinician examine the content and scale membership(s) of omitted items.

Marked Elevation (Possibly Invalid Profile): 30 or More Unscorable Items

If more than 30 items are omitted, the elevation and the code pattern of the clinical profile is likely to be significantly lowered (except for Scale 5 for women, which could be elevated), or otherwise altered, reducing the probability of obtaining an accurate picture of the person's unique personality characteristics. Extremely high raw scores can occur among severely emotionally impaired persons, who are unable to perform the decision-making task because of profound depression, intrusive thoughts, excessive preoccupation with the exact meaning of the items, or apprehension that the items' dichotomous nature will unfairly put them in some negative or inaccurate category. It is probable, however, that such a high score indicates a resistive, uncooperative person or a person with substantial reading or comprehension problems.

The clinician should attempt to discover the reasons for the individual's Cannot Say propensity when so many items are omitted before asking the individual to retake the test. The clinician should sensitively probe the reasons for items being unanswered or double marked and reassure the individual that the assessment process is collaborative in nature—unless, of course, the client is taking the test in a litigation, personnel selection, or employment fitness-for-duty context. Even so, it is possible to interpret profiles with limited accuracy when as many as 30 items are omitted—although the attenuating effect on the profile must be considered because clinical scales can drop significantly and the code pattern can also change. Note that if the omitted items all or mostly occur after Item 370, the basic validity and clinical scales will not be affected.

If up to 30 items are omitted, Greene (2011) suggested augmenting the profile by re-plotting it after scoring the omitted or double-marked items in the keyed direction. See Chapter 2 under "Test Scoring and Profile Plotting" for a fuller description of this procedure. In general, if more than 30 items have been omitted, the profile is likely invalid.

Variable Response Inconsistency Scale (*VRIN*) (67-item pairs)

This MMPI-2 scale was designed to detect inconsistent responding. It is particularly useful when *F* and/or *FB* is elevated and there is uncertainty as to whether the elevations reflect severe psychopathology, random, or careless responding, or symptom exaggeration. In such cases, an elevated *VRIN* would suggest that the *F* and *FB* elevations are due to confusion or careless responding, whereas a low *VRIN* score would suggest that the high *F* or *FB* score is due to severe psychopathology or deliberate exaggeration of psychopathology. Cut scores for invalidity are inexact, but the following ranges provide interpretive guidelines.

Consistent Responding: Raw Scores Between 0 and 9, T-Scores Between 30 and 66

Because the determination of validity is a multivariate process, it is important to examine other indicators of response consistency when assessing the validity of the profile. Raw scores between 0 and 9 on *VRIN* typically reflect consistent responding, with a raw score of 9 equaling a *T*-score of 65 for males and 66 for females. Scores in this range suggest the test taker understood and responded to the items in a consistent manner.

Profile Indeterminate: Raw Scores Between 10 and 14, T-Scores Between 69 and 86

In this range, the profile could reflect either inconsistent or consistent responding. The MMPI-2 *Manual* (Butcher et al., 2001) suggests that a raw score of 13 or higher (*T*-score of 80 for men, 82 for women) should be the cut score for determining inconsistent responding. However, because the mean *VRIN* score for random responding is only 16.75, a cutting score of 13 may be too liberal, and raw scores above 11 should be viewed with suspicion. Examine the *TRIN*, *F*, *FB*, and *F(p)* scores to further determine the validity of the profiles. Also consider where the inconsistently-endorsed *VRIN* item pairs are concentrated, and especially on which side of item 370 the endorsements occur. An imbalance in the proportion of True to False responses could also account for scores in this range; so, the *T* percent value should be checked (see Chapter 3 and "*T* Percent Index" in this chapter). Severely disturbed individuals (whose confusion and uncertainty is part of their symptom picture), or uncooperative clients, often score in this range on the *VRIN* scale. However, if the *VRIN* score is in the upper end of this large range, it is unlikely that the MMPI-2 profile validly reflects the individual's stable personality, unless *TRIN*, *F*, *FB*, and *F(p)* appear valid.

Inconsistent Responding: Raw Scores Greater Than 14, T-Scores of 87 or Greater

Raw scores over 14 (*T-84* [males]; *T-86* [females]) on the *VRIN* scale strongly suggest that the profile is invalid due to inconsistent or random responding. At this level, it can be difficult to discern whether such random elements are caused by carelessness or by a compromised mental state characterized by confusion and uncertainty. Even if the profile is valid by *F*, *FB*, *F(p)*, *L*, and *K* criteria, the high *VRIN* score suggests so much inconsistency that the profile's validity is compromised.

True Response Inconsistency Scale (*TRIN*) (23-item pairs)

This 23-item scale developed for the MMPI-2 measures a participant's tendency to answer True or False to the MMPI-2 items without careful consideration of the meaning of the items. Some individuals may answer the items with a tendency to acquiesce, responding True (yea-saying) to the items even if their answers are inconsistent. Others respond with resistance or defensiveness, responding False (nay-saying) without full regard for the meaning of an item.

A majority of MMPI-2 items are scored in the pathological direction when marked True; thus, severely disturbed, non-defensive individuals will produce high *F* scores, high scores on Scales 6 and 8, and a higher percentage of True responses. The exception, however, are somatizing profiles (e.g. 123/321 and 13), where more of the pathological responses are False. These individuals, like others who are approaching the test with a highly positive self-presentation, will produce a higher False than True response percentage.

The *TRIN* scale can be useful in determining a yea- or nay-saying response set, especially when True or False percentages are high. The *TRIN* score is computed by adding a point for every True *TRIN* item pair endorsed and subtracting a point for every False *TRIN* pair. Nine is added to the equation to ensure there are no negative numbers. A profile is showing no evidence of yea- or nay-saying with a *TRIN* score of 9 (0 True items endorsed + 0 False items endorsed + 9 = 9). A raw score of 13 or greater suggests considerable yea-saying, and a score of five or less suggests nay-saying.

Raw Scores Between 8 and 10

If other validity indicators suggest the profile is valid, then *TRIN* scores in this range confirm it. The mean raw score for the re-standardization sample was about nine, which corresponds to a *T*-score of 50.

Raw Scores of 6 and 7, and 11 and 12

Raw scores of 6 and 7, and 11 and 12 are of uncertain significance. When *TRIN* exceeds *VRIN* and True percent is low (≤ 25 percent), raw scores of 6–7 suggest an indiscriminate preference for False-marking or nay-saying, and retesting may be warranted. Similarly, when *TRIN* exceeds *VRIN* and True percent is high (≥ 60 percent), raw scores of 11–12 suggest an acquiescent or yea-saying response style, and may also warrant retesting. In all other cases, such moderate elevations on *TRIN* may be allowed, unless *VRIN* exceeds *TRIN*, in which case the interpretation of the *VRIN* score should supersede the interpretation of *TRIN* (Nichols, 2011).

Raw Scores of 5 or Less and 13 or Greater

The profile is invalid because of excessive yea- or nay-saying and the test should be retaken with appropriate test-taking instructions and/or proctoring.

Infrequency Scale (*F*) (60 items)

The *F* items reflect the degree to which thoughts, attitudes, and experiences reported by a person differ from the normative population. Persons who randomly mark items, who cannot comprehend item content, or who consciously attempt to portray a negative image of themselves endorse *F* items to a higher degree than the general population, and usually to a higher degree than genuinely disturbed populations. However, individuals who are authentically disturbed and unhappy also elevate the *F* scale, as would persons with unusual attitudes (e.g. sociopaths) or alienating experiences (e.g. minority populations). Because about one third of the *F* items overlap with Scales 6, 7, 8, and 9, elevations on the *F* scale are often accompanied by elevations on these clinical scales, particularly Scales 6 and 8. The following descriptions deal primarily with validity issues and, to some extent, address clinical correlates. The clinical information, however, is minor compared with the validity information, and should be ignored if contradicted by the information from the basic clinical scales. As described earlier in Chapter 3, it is imperative that other validity scales be examined when *F* is elevated; particularly *VRIN*, *TRIN*, *FB*, *Ds*, *F(p)*, *F-FB*, and *F-K indices*, and the True percent index.

Low Scores: Raw Scores of 2 or Less, T-Scores Between 42 (Males) and 44 (Females)

Raw scores of two or less on *F* suggest conventionality, if not over-conventionality, in that the person is reporting few, if any, unusual thoughts, beliefs, or behaviors, and is in no particular distress at the time of testing. Individuals without elevations on the clinical scales, then, may be described as calm, dependable, sincere, unpretentious, and honest, attributes one would expect from a person who is basically psychologically healthy. For some individuals, however, the possibility exists that they are denying or minimizing problems and that they have systematically avoided admitting to distressing or unusual feelings or thoughts. The other validity scales, however, would provide a clue to the source of the low *F* scores; thus a low *L* score and a normal *K* score would suggest that the low *F* score is, in fact, reflecting mental health rather than positive malingering. Sometimes an individual obtains a very low *F* score but also obtains a moderately elevated clinical profile. This would suggest that the individual's disturbance is not acute but more longstanding, and perhaps not psychologically disorganizing.

Moderate Scores: Raw Scores Between 3 and 7, T-Scores Between 45 and 61

Raw scores between three and seven indicate acknowledgment of a number of unusual experiences, attitudes, feelings, and behaviors that differ somewhat from the norm.

With adolescents, college populations, creative persons, or moderately disturbed people, such F elevations are not atypical. Similarly, when persons become intensely involved in religious, political, or social causes that are different from the mainstream, the scores on the F scale tend to be slightly elevated. Occasionally, however, particularly in mental health settings, such scores will occur in persons with some psychopathology, but who have adjusted to chronic problems, and therefore are not in great immediate distress. Their problems are "contained" and perhaps ego-syntonic.

High Scores: Raw Scores Between 8 and 16, T-Scores Between 61 and 92

Valid raw scores between 8 and 16 suggest distress, increasing significantly toward the middle and high end of this range. Scores in this range indicate unusual or markedly unconventional thinking and attitudes, as well as psychological distress. Identity and self-esteem issues, as well as psychopathology, are indicated, and the person is likely to be described as moody, changeable, restless, unstable, dissatisfied, talkative, and opinionated but self-deprecating, all descriptions associated with psychological disturbance. The clinical scales are almost always elevated when the F scale is in this range, so the basic personality picture is described by the code pattern. The personality descriptors associated with F elevations in this range reflect general disturbance and distress. Young people struggling with identity problems and a need to define themselves through nonconformity frequently score in this range on F. Generally, as raw scores approach 16, the profile almost always reflects a serious, often panicked disturbance. F raw scores between 8 and 12 are typically seen in individuals with a longstanding and serious disturbance.

Borderline Valid Scores: Raw Scores Between 17 and 25, T-Scores Between 88 and 113 (for Men) and Between 88 and 120 (for Women)

Raw scores between 17 and 25 are in an indeterminate range and suggest the following possibilities: (a) failure of the client to understand the items; (b) resistance or lack of cooperation; (c) random or haphazard reporting of numerous F items because of delusional thinking, confusion, or other psychotic processes; (d) conscious distortion and exaggeration of psychological symptom for secondary gain; (e) panicked over-endorsement of F items, perhaps to draw attention to current fear, pain, and distress; or (f) seriously disturbed individuals, perhaps in inpatient or prison settings. As the F raw score approaches 17, the importance of all the other validity indicators to rule out symptom magnification becomes even more critical. With scores this high, the examiner should suspect that the profile is invalid and should verify this by considering the characteristics of the remainder of the profile, the actual test-taking and interview behavior, and possible motivations for exaggeration that might derive from the client's current situation. Even profiles with F scores of 25 may be occasionally interpreted in a psychiatric setting. An interpretable F score in this range is almost always associated with a profound disturbance, disorganized thinking and psychotic symptoms, although sometimes it may be a "cry for help." A clinical interview usually reveals very atypical thought processes, poor judgment, and distortions of reality, often accompanied by confusion, withdrawal, and lack of cooperation.

Interpreting a profile with an *F* score between 22 and 25 is hazardous. Certainly, in a forensic setting, the clinician would have to be armed with solid supportive evidence to withstand a cross-examination to show that such a profile is validly interpretable. Information would have to be presented from other tests, history, and interviews to paint an integrated picture of the individual so that the elevated profile has some context. For example, an expert witness psychologist might say, "Yes, by standard criteria this *F* score of 25 suggests invalidity. However the other tests suggest a serious psychotic disturbance and the patient's history confirms it. In light of such data this MMPI-2 may reflect his current psychosis." Although *F* scores in the very high range can be interpreted in some situations, they should not be interpreted if the scales showing confusion, inconsistency, or a biased response set (i.e. *VRIN, TRIN, F(p)*, and *Ds*) are also significantly elevated. Increasingly, it has been our experience that attorneys send, through a psychologist, their clients' or opponent clients' MMPI-2 to one of the computer-generated report services. These services tend to be conservative in validity cut scores so that an *F* score over 18 is ruled invalid. This may be too conservative in some cases, but the psychologist would need to be prepared to defend a claim of validity as the *F* score reaches 18 and above. It can be difficult to explain under cross-examination why a respected computer-generated report is inaccurate in suggesting that a profile is malingered or invalid and why the psychologist is accurate in suggesting it is valid. Consequently, the expert witness needs to be well prepared and have the ability to integrate the MMPI-2 data with other persuasive data if claiming an elevated *F* score is valid.

Very High/Invalid Scores: Raw Scores of 26 or Greater, T-Scores of 116 or Greater (for Men) and 120 or Greater (for Women)

Although *F* scores in the very high range (raw scores of 26 and above) sometimes can be very cautiously interpreted in situations in which there appears no motivation for malingering and a serious disturbance is suspected, generally such high scores should be considered invalid or seriously exaggerated. Information from *F* scores this high is probably not stable because it reflects an acute disturbance. Nevertheless, the test data will give information about how the individual is experiencing the world right now and how the person is presenting himself to the psychologist. Once the individual has stabilized, it may help to have the person retake the test for a more valid evaluation of his or her personality organization.

F-Back Scale (FB) (40 items)

As described earlier in Chapter 3, this 40-item scale was developed by identifying items endorsed at a frequency of 10 percent or less of the MMPI-2 normative sample. However, the MMPI-2 *Manual* (Butcher et al., 2001, Appendix G) does show that there are at least three items with an endorsement rate of 17 percent, 11 percent, and 13 percent (395, 407, and 525) in the contemporary normative sample. *FB* identifies persons whose concentration or motivation decreases during the last half of the test and who may even begin randomly marking items with little or no attention to item content. Almost half of the *FB* items occur among the final 100 items on the test, and all occur after item number 280. It is important to note that the *T*-scores for the *FB* scale rise much more quickly for a given raw score than the *T*-scores for the *F* scale. A raw score of 16 on the *FB* scale, for example, yields a *T*-score of 108, whereas the equivalent raw score on the *F* scale is a *T*-score of 85. Most items on the *FB* scale have an acute distress and depression theme (affective upheaval), whereas the major theme of the *F* items reflects psychoticism. Consequently, profiles may show quite different raw scores on the two *F* scales, depending on the kind of disturbance being evaluated. In some cases, the *FB* scale is significantly higher than the *F* scale, but this does not necessarily mean that the individual became more disturbed over the course of the test or necessarily exaggerated his or her symptoms toward the end of the test. An *FB* score higher than an *F* score may instead reflect individuals, for example, who are experiencing distress associated with drug and/or alcohol problems, and the resulting disorganization of their life and support system, rather than the psychotic-like disorganization reflected in *F* elevations. Nichols (2011, p. 57) provides greater elaboration on the differences between these two scales:

> The different content emphases between *F* and *FB* create a special dilemma when *FB* scores are elevated, but *F* scores are not. As a rule of thumb, such scores are generally acceptable if the scores on at least two of the four content scales—*DEP, LSE, WRK,* and *TRT*—exceed the score on *BIZ*, or if the scores on *ANX* and *FRS* exceed that on *BIZ*. When these conditions cannot be met, *FB* can be interpreted to reflect exaggeration of problems or a lack of care in completing the second half of the MMPI-2. In this case, the content scales and other scales that draw most of their items from this half of the test should be interpreted with caution, if at all.

Exaggeration or malingering can be safely interpreted only when both *F* and *FB* are elevated beyond acceptable limits. The following interpretive guidelines may provide a framework for determining validity. The elevation guidelines for *F*, including low scores, are generally applicable to the interpretation of *FB* scores, bearing in mind the differences in the content of the two scales.

Low Scores: Raw Scores Between 0 and 3, T-Scores Between 42 and 55

Raw scores between zero and three would suggest a well-adjusted individual if the clinical scales are not elevated and the other validity scales suggest validity. It could also reflect a possible denial of problems, especially if the other validity scales suggest under-reporting. Psychopathology, if present and reflected on the profile with an *FB* score in this range, tends to be longstanding, ego-syntonic, and nonpsychotic in nature.

High Normal to High Range: Raw Scores Between 4 and 14, T-Scores Between 58 and 100

In a valid, unelevated profile, the low end (e.g. *FB* = four) could reflect normal range distress, occasioned by perhaps, for example, chemical dependency problems. If obtained in an elevated profile, *FB* scores in the lower part of this range suggest that the disturbance is longstanding and may be ego-syntonic. As the *FB* score approaches a raw score of 14, the severity of the disturbance increases and the importance of ensuring that other validity indicators are within acceptable parameters increases.

Very High Range: Raw Scores Between 15 and 19, T-Scores Between 101 and 120

This range is often associated with chronically maladjusted and acutely disturbed individuals, as well as the range for malingered and random profiles. As scores approach 19, the probability increases that the individual is malingering, especially in cases in which there is clear secondary gain from doing so. In rare cases, scores in this range could also reflect chronic psychopathology, borderline personality functioning, panic, and chemical addiction/abuse. As described earlier, 37 of the 40 *FB* items are scored as True, so an acquiescing response bias would elevate the *FB* scale, but not without also elevating the *TRIN* score to unacceptable levels in most cases.

Extremely Elevated Scores: Raw Scores of 20 or Greater, T-Scores of 120 or Greater

The profile is very probably invalid, especially if there is any secondary gain, as in forensic and disability cases. In some psychiatric settings, *FB* scores may be as high as 21 to 24 raw-score points and reflect a severe disturbance; additionally, the accompanying profile code pattern is probably unstable. Scores in this range in a *clinical* population suggest a high degree of response atypicality, even among clinical groups. As raw scores range from 20 to 24, the probability increases that the individual is over-reporting regardless of the setting, or that the individual is panicked, pleading for help, or severely disturbed. Other validity scales should confirm the determination of whether the profile is valid.

Self-Unfavorable Scales

Infrequency-Psychopathology Scale: F(p) *(27 items)*

The *F(p)* scale (see Chapter 3) consists of very rarely endorsed items among both psychiatric patients and normals, and is useful in detecting the over-reporting of psychopathology.

Normal Range: Raw Scores of 3 and Below, T-Scores of 65 and Below

Raw scores of three and below suggest a lack of obvious over-reporting. If the other validity scales suggest invalidity, a low *F(p)* score would not change that determination.

Indeterminate Range: Raw Scores Between 4 and 9, T-Scores Between 71 and 113

Raw Scores between four and nine are in the indeterminate range, depending on the setting. If other validity indicators suggest over-reporting, then *F(p)* scores in this range would confirm it. *F(p)* scores between 71 and 113 are best interpreted with reference to the range of content among the items of *F(p)* that have been endorsed. Nichols (2011) states that when the items manifest a wide range of content, over-reporting is indicated: "when the content of the endorsed items falls into only one or two content domains, *Fp* generally should not be interpreted as indicating over-reporting unless scales *F* and *FB* are concurrently elevated, and *F-K* is high" (p. 58).

High/Invalid Range: Raw Scores of 10 or More, T-Scores of 114 or Greater

If the $F(p)$ score is a raw score of 10 or greater, the profile is probably exaggerated, even if the other validity scales are in an acceptable range.

Dissimulation Scale (Ds) (58 items)

As discussed in Chapter 3, this is a useful scale in detecting a self-unfavorable bias or over-reporting of psychopathology. The items in this scale are non-psychotic, so a significant elevation may reflect an attempt to magnify or malinger non-psychotic disabilities. When *F* is elevated, it is often difficult to determine how much of the disturbance is genuine psychopathology, with little or no exaggeration, and how much is due to over-reporting. *Ds* is often helpful in distinguishing the former from the latter.

Valid Range: Raw Scores of 18 and Below, T-Scores of 63 and Below (for Women) and 65 and Below (for Men)

Raw scores on *Ds* of 18 and below generally suggest an absence of malingering. Any psychopathology evidenced is likely accurate, even if the other validity scales suggest some exaggeration (e.g. raw $F = 20$ and $K = 10$). In general, lower scores on *Ds* suggest that the examinee has been highly discriminating in his/her responses to the test items in an effort to accurately portray themselves (Nichols, 2011). Low *Ds* scores likely accompany a good fit between the patient and the clinical profile when the latter shows a clear pattern of elevation (Caldwell, 1988). "Scores below *T*-45 suggest unusual freedom from symptoms and attitudes consistent with mental disorders and may raise the question of undue guardedness in responding to the items" (Nichols, 2011, p. 60).

Moderately Elevated Range: Raw Scores Between 19 and 27, T-Scores Between 65 and 82

Raw scores between 19 and 27 suggest some exaggeration and a tendency to present oneself from the perspective of feeling one's worst. If the other validity scales suggest validity, then the profile is likely still valid, even as raw *Ds* scores approach 27, especially in seriously disturbed and psychotic individuals. Even so, some exaggeration is likely present as raw scores approach 27. If the other validity scales suggest invalidity or exaggeration, then raw *Ds* scores at the upper end of this range support invalidity.

High Range: Raw Scores Between 28 and 33, T-Scores Between 81 and 93

Raw scores between 28 and 33 suggest the likelihood of exaggeration, even if the profile is valid by other validity criteria. Scores this high suggest that persons are consciously presenting themselves as mentally ill, and the clinician needs to determine why. Even so, in severely impaired psychiatric patients, scores this high do not always invalidate the profile, although exaggeration is likely taking place.

Very High Range: Raw Scores Between 34 and 37, T-Scores Between 92 and 101

Raw scores between 34 and 37 are high and, in almost all cases, suggest malingering, especially if the other validity scales confirm it. Even if the profile is determined valid by other validity measures, raw scores in this range suggest intentional self-unfavorable reporting and malingering.

Invalid Range: Raw Scores of 38 and Above, T-Scores Equal to or Greater Than 99

Raw scores above 38 strongly suggest that the profile is malingered, even if the other validity scales are solidly in the interpretable range. If the other validity scales suggest self-unfavorable responding, scores in this range would make a diagnosis of malingering difficult to refute.

Self-Favorable Scales

Lie Scale (L) *(15 items)*

L, an impression management scale, allows the respondent 15 opportunities to endorse transparently virtuous items which deny minor and widespread failings of character. When elevated, *L* reflects naïve or obvious attempts by a person to look unusually virtuous, culturally conservative, overly conscientious, and above moral reproach. Because frank, self-aware persons so rarely endorse such statements, *L* scores above a *T*-65 are unusual, except in persons who have cultural backgrounds that require strict cultural conformity, are in occupations (e.g. clergy) that stress narrow personal and professional virtues, or are in situations (such as a job interview, fitness-for-duty, or child custody evaluation) that prompt them to present themselves in their "best light." It is, therefore, not surprising that the mean number of *L* items reported for airline pilot applicants is about five (Butcher, 1994c). Most normals and patients tend to avoid endorsing the *L* items, with normals averaging only three to five items and patients only slightly more.

In essence, *L* is generally effective at detecting purposeful distortion in naïve, unsophisticated people in high-stakes assessment contexts. Psychologically sophisticated individuals, however, particularly persons with a college education, are often able to "see through" the items on this scale and therefore not endorse them. These individuals generally are able to admit to certain understandable moral "flaws" and understand that to deny them would make them look as if they were not being honest. They may still attempt to portray themselves as unusually virtuous on other portions of the test, which would change elevations on some of the other validity scales, but *L* would likely remain within normal limits.

Education and age must be considered when interpreting an *L* score. Individuals of less than average intelligence or less than high school education tend to score slightly higher (about five *T*-score points) than a *T*-score of 50. "Scores are negatively correlated with education, intelligence, and cultural sophistication, so bright, well-educated, and acculturated examinees tend to obtain low scores, even when motivation to underreport is high" (Nichols, 2011, p. 87). Individuals above age 50, likewise, tend to endorse more *L* items, perhaps associated with age-related increases in conservative attitudes. Elevated *L* scores (eight or higher) in persons with broadly educated backgrounds can be difficult to interpret. In some cases, these may reflect a person who, although educationally sophisticated, is quite morally and psychologically constricted and judgmental. Consider the following.

Ms. L., a successful attorney and MBA, was given the MMPI-2 as part of her treatment plan subsequent to a painful divorce. Her husband had complained in therapy prior to the divorce that his wife was a very judgmental person who had little patience with his recent business difficulties. When asked about this, Ms. L. admitted that she believed that failure was a sign of defectiveness and that she had little tolerance for people who got the "wrong answer" in life. Her MMPI-2 profile was within the normal range, but her *L* score was elevated at a *T*-score of 81 (raw score = 10). She was rigid in her views, perfectionistic, and had difficulty admitting to mistakes. She was clearly apprehensive about being judged by the therapist and stated that she thought psychological problems were a sign of weakness. Such attributes may be associated with elevated *L* scores in educated individuals who are not taking the test, for example, as part of a job evaluation or divorce custody evaluation. Educated individuals with high *L* scores lack insight and generally are psychologically naïve. When they seek treatment, it is usually only for advice for a specific problem. Insight therapy is particularly threatening to them because they feel that probing questions by the therapist are somehow searches for what is "wrong" with them. Interestingly, educated individuals with high *L* scores tend to lack anxiety (Matarazzo, 1955), perhaps reflecting the inner peace associated with moral certitude.

Table 4.1 L Scale Descriptors by *T*-Score Elevations

Raw Score	T-Score	Description
0–2	Valid 33–43	Suggests candor and a willingness to admit to common human failings. However, if the other validity scales suggest an exaggeration of psychopathology, a low score could be part of an attempt to present oneself as disturbed and without resources to be moral. In some exaggerated profiles, clients over-endorse pathological items (e.g. high *F* score), claim to have no defenses (e.g. very low *K* score), and have very low *L* scores.
3–5	Valid 47–57	This is the "normal" range for individuals taking the test in clinical settings. Individuals taking the test in forensic or job evaluation settings would typically score higher. At a *T*-score of 55, there is already a slight tendency to be putting one's best foot forward, unless the individual is from an unsophisticated background. A *T*-score of 55 might be seen in an educated, although mildly cautious, defensive individual and/or in a mildly moralistic individual. Individuals from lower SES backgrounds score in this range and the *L* score reflects traditional, if somewhat unsophisticated views.
6–7	Likely valid 61–67	These scores suggest concern and some rigidity over matters of self-control and moral values as well as a tendency to be conforming and conventional. Such preoccupation with high moral standards usually is attached to a fear of being found unacceptable by others, unless the person scrupulously adheres to rules. The defense mechanism of denial may be characteristic of these individuals. People show some lack of self-awareness and insight with *L* elevations in this range. In an educated individual or in a custody or job evaluation setting, these *L* elevations also suggest an attempt to look one's best and to deny unacceptable human impulses. The validity of the test may be somewhat compromised by elevations towards the high end of this range. Airline pilot applicants score at the lower end of this range.

Raw Score	T-Score	Description
8–10	Marked elevation 70–81	Uncommon. If scoring errors or a systematic denial response set can be ruled out, the person is denying many of the most common and obvious human failings. Such individuals have intense needs to present a good front and do so with rigidity, repression, and denial. Moral issues, as well as their own integrity and concern with scruples, permeate their lives to the point that they are typically seen as self-righteous and uncompromising. Their self-perception and lifestyle are bound by rigid moral rules, and they are sensitive to social disapproval. Some see psychological problems as a sign of moral weakness. They tend to be naïvely defensive, as though worried that their "life rules" might be "wrong" and, therefore, vulnerable to judgment. They deny or gloss over unfavorable traits in themselves, repress foibles or unacceptable urges, and have little insight into their motives or behaviors. Sometimes the elevated *L* score is a manifestation of extreme naïveté in a person from a culturally restricted environment. Other times it reflects an intentional attempt to distort the MMPI-2 profile. In either case, such persons typically make poor candidates for insight-oriented psychotherapy. Strategic or directive approaches are likely to work best. In forensic settings, these elevations would bring into doubt the veracity of the test taker. The burden of proof would be on the expert witness in claiming, for example, that an MMPI-2 profile of a divorcée seeking custody of her children was valid with a raw *L* score of 10. If the protocol is valid, then the *L* scale suggests a very moralistically rigid and psychologically naïve individual.
11–15	Likely invalid 83–105	These scores are rare. Although the profile is probably invalid, the reasons for such an elevated *L* scale need to be ascertained. Valid scores in this range may reflect (a) an overcontrolled, rigid, repressed individual lacking insight; (b) the black-and-white moralistic thinking associated with some religious orders, although having strong religious convictions will not necessarily raise the *L* score—it is the rigidity and lack of sophistication about knowing how others really behave; (c) an unsophisticated or even panicked attempt to look unusually virtuous (often found in forensic or personnel situations); or (d) a psychotic individual who has an unelevated profile, although usually the clinical profile will be close to *T*-65. In the latter case, the high *L* score reflects a paranoid rigidity and apprehension about being criticized. However, in these cases, there are usually other signs of a serious disturbance, such as the endorsement of items on the *BIZ* content scale and/or elevations on the Harris-Lingoes subscales and endorsement of relevant critical items.

Correction Scale (K) *(30 items)*

This scale was not significantly altered on the MMPI-2 except for the minor rewording of one item. Although primarily considered a validity scale, it contains substantial clinical information about ego strength, reality contact, and coping abilities, as well as about defensiveness, guardedness, and test-taking posture. The *K* scale is an empirically derived "correction" scale developed to sharpen the diagnostic accuracy of Scales 1, 4, 7, 8, and 9 with adult inpatients. Note that the *K* items are less obvious than the *L* items.

Despite the addition of the *K* corrections to these clinical scales, high *K* scores are usually associated with defensiveness and therefore lowered profiles, whereas low *K* scores are more often associated with more elevated clinical profiles. This is because elevations on *K* in general reflect poise, emotional sophistication, and an unwillingness to admit to being "knocked off balance" or distressed by emotional problems. If an individual is guarded, as reflected by an elevated *K* score, he or she is unlikely to admit to psychopathology. It is important for the clinician to examine the contribution of *K to* Scales 7 and 8 because the full amount of obtained raw *K* is added to each. The individual with an elevated Scale 8 score due to the *K* addition is different from a person whose Scale 8 score is elevated due to the contribution of mostly Scale 8 items with a small added *K* value. The high *K* person is more likely to be in control of whatever pathology exists and is often able to mask it, especially in structured situations.

The *K* scale can be thought of as representing emotional control and coping capacity. At higher elevations, it also reflects emotional constriction. In answering the items in the scored direction, the individual reveals a cautiousness about admitting extremes of emotions, whether positive or negative, or any loss of emotional control. Items keyed in the scored direction, reflect, in part, any urges to swear, or feeling vulnerable to criticism, and denials of not feeling well. People of higher SES tend to score higher on *K* because emotionally modulated responding is socially appropriate. Extremes of emotion, "making a fuss," and being too emotional are seen as inappropriate. Not all upper SES individuals have a high *K* score, however. One challenge that clinicians, especially forensic experts, encounter is how to distinguish when a high *K* score is due to genuine upper SES, poise, and emotional control, and when it is due to a conscious attempt by respondents to distort and portray themselves as psychologically healthy and emotionally balanced.

Very Low Scores: Raw Scores of 7 or Below, T-Scores Below 35

Very low scores (*T* < 35) can stem from several possibilities. If there is any secondary gain from being diagnosed with a psychiatric disturbance and other validity scales suggest self-unfavorable responding along with elevated clinical scales, consider that the profile may be intentionally exaggerated. Typically, the profile would also show exaggerated *F* and *FB* scores, and the over-endorsement of critical items. In valid profiles in which the clinical scales are elevated, such a low *K* score suggests severe disturbance with little capacity to modulate feelings and behaviors. The individual would likely need a very supportive and involved intervention, and any suicidal and/or homicidal threats should be taken seriously. These individuals experience their symptoms as frightening and feel a sense of panic and loss of control. They are self-critical and need directive, supportive, esteem-building psychotherapy.

Low Scores: Raw Scores Between 8 and 13, T-Scores Between 35 and 45 (for Men) and Between 35 and 46 (for Women)

Low scores suggest that the person's coping abilities are compromised. Their defenses may be immature, and their emotional conflicts destabilizing. Emotional-behavioral controls are likely to be poor. The low *K* score suggests that the disturbance reflected on the clinical scales will be behaviorally manifested, thus the client is also likely to admit to the symptoms and complaints associated with the profile. These individuals tend to be self-critical, have poor self-esteem, and lack confidence that they have the skills to deal with their problems.

A similar non-defensiveness and self-criticality is sometimes evident in persons engaged in the self-examination involved in insight-oriented psychotherapy. In cases in which the clinical scales show an absence of elevation, such low K scores would suggest candor and healthy openness, although often with a tendency to "wear one's feelings on one's sleeve."

Normal Elevations: Raw Scores Between 14 and 18, T-Scores Between 47 and 56

A normal K elevation indicates a person who exhibits culturally appropriate emotional control and manifests a balance between emotional spontaneity and emotional constraint. These individuals generally feel in control of their emotional life. Even if the clinical scales are elevated, K scores in this range, especially toward T-55–56, suggest some coping ability. Psychological symptoms associated with the clinical scale elevations are likely to be at least somewhat under volitional control. In general, the closer the scale approaches T-50 and higher, the more functional are the defenses and coping system. The prognosis is better for successful therapeutic interventions as the K scale approaches a T-score of 55 to 56 and above, until about a T-score of 65, when emotional overcontrol and defensiveness can inhibit therapeutic insight.

Moderate Elevations: Raw Scores Between 19 and 22, T-Scores Between 58 and 65

Moderate K elevations in the absence of elevations on the clinical scales are found in people generally described as independent, enterprising, ingenious, resourceful, enthusiastic with wide interests, and having a variety of interpersonal relationships, all attributes suggesting good mental health. Their lives are generally well managed, and they feel in control. K scores in this range, even in elevated profiles, generally contraindicate loss of control or uncontrollable acting out. The prognosis for psychological insight and change is generally better when K is in this moderate range, rather than when K is below 45 or above 65. When K is below 40 to 45, the individual is likely to be overwhelmed by the feelings and psychopathology associated with the clinical scale elevations. If K is elevated above T-65, poise and control tend to become emotional constriction and the individual resists psychological insight. If the clinical scales suggest psychopathology, moderate K scores suggest an ability to cope, with many areas of practical self-sufficiency and compensated functioning. For example, if an individual obtained a profile suggesting a serious depression with anxiety, low self-esteem, and guilt (e.g. high elevations on Scales 2, 7, and 8), but his or her K is at a T-score of 64, the individual might be able to successfully mask the full extent of his or her discomfort and work reasonably well. Such individuals can function with extended periods of efficiency and competence, even though their disturbance would be experienced by them as a loss of pleasure, underlying but managed anxiety, and periods of deep, but controlled, unhappiness.

High Scores: Raw Scores of 23 and Greater, T-Scores of 66 and Greater

High scores in clinical populations reflect people who are particularly defensive and have difficulty tolerating suggestions that they might have psychological problems. Although they may see others as having psychological problems, they view their own emotional difficulties as "under control." They tend to be uncomfortable and rejecting of unconventional or nonconformist behavior in others, and are often subtly judgmental of such behavior. Although quite concerned with being socially appropriate, they are relatively insight-less concerning their emotional effect on others. Many such persons are rigidly managerial in their attempts to control their "world," as though disorganization would create a catastrophic unraveling of their lives. They show reluctance to be seen as psychotherapy patients and reject suggestions that they might need assistance in understanding or managing their feelings or behaviors. Generally, they avoid examining problem areas because they view themselves as rational, normal, and balanced. They feel uncomfortable with any uncontrollable surges of emotion that can arise in the process of psychotherapy, and the exploration of past experiences. If they seek psychotherapy, they gravitate toward intellectual types of therapy, such as psychoanalysis, which makes few unpredictable cathartic demands on them. K scores in this high range can also be obtained in forensic (e.g. child custody) and personnel evaluation situations. In these settings, K scores of 65 to 66 and above reflect the defensiveness that is somewhat expected, and the profile is likely to underestimate psychopathology. Long-range predictions from the profile may be inaccurate.

Some individuals, usually from higher socioeconomic groups, can score at or above T-65 and obtain non-elevated clinical scales that accurately reflect a lack of psychopathology. In these cases, the K score is often reflecting the "stiff upper lip" of a basically non-pathological individual from a cultural background that frowns on any uncontrolled displays of emotion, and emphasizes that "one should always have one's life in order." K is correlated with education and upper SES, and people of upper SES tend to value emotional control and etiquette over impulsive expressions of affect. It is difficult to differentiate an elevated K scale due to high SES and non-conscious defensiveness from an elevated K scale due to conscious defensiveness. Scores on Positive Malingering (Mp), Socioeconomic Status (Ss), Social Desirability (Sd), and the Superlative Scale (S) are useful in making that differentiation and are discussed later in this chapter.

Superlative Scale (S) (50 items)

As previously described, Butcher and Han (1995) developed S by contrasting the item responses of 274 male airline pilot applicants with the 1,138 men of the MMPI-2 re-standardization sample. The scale has good external validity and appears to measure mental health, contentment with life, and an ability to get along effectively with others. Although mentally healthy people will exhibit some of these attributes, it is unlikely that many will exhibit all of them to a high degree. Consequently, high S scores ($T > 65$, raw score > 38) suggest that claims of superlative adjustment likely are exaggerated.

Butcher and Han (1995) suggested that S may operate similarly to the F scale. For example, moderate F scores suggest true distress and disturbance, but extreme scores suggest exaggeration. In the same way, moderate S (T-50–60) scores can suggest good adjustment and mental health, but as T-scores rise above 60, the claims of good adjustment may be exaggerated. When S is elevated, L, Ss, Mp, and Sd should all be examined, and a low S score should be viewed in the context of scores on F, FB, $F(p)$, Ds, and $F - K$, as well as in relation to Es, regardless of whether the score on S is high or low, using the same guidelines given for interpreting K scores. It is not uncommon to find K, S, and Mp elevated simultaneously.

In such cases, interpretive weight should be given to *Sd*, with scores greater than *T*-60 tending to support an impression management interpretation of *Mp*, but scores less than *T*-55—especially less than *T*-50—indicating the possibility that *Mp* may have been spuriously elevated by variance shared with *S* and *K*.

(Nichols, 2011, p. 78)

In the latter case, a self-deception interpretation for *S* and *K* should be considered. Butcher and Han (1995) also factorially identified five subscales for *S* scale.

S1: Belief in Human Goodness (15 items)

This subscale appears to measure the exact opposite of the Cynicism content scale (*CYN*), with items pertaining to a belief that people are decent, helpful, loyal, and fair. A raw score of 13 and 14 equals a *T*-score of 65 for men and women, respectively. Because this subscale contains only 15 items, it tops out at a *T*-score of 70. Consequently, *T*-scores over 60 (raw score > 11) should be considered high. Low scores (< *T*-40) reflect a cynical and mistrustful, if not hostile, view of others and their motives.

S2: Serenity (13 items)

This subscale appears to measure a sense of inner peace, lack of internal conflict, social comfort, and integrity. A raw score of 10 equals a *T*-score of 64 for men and 67 for women. A raw score of 13 equals a *T*-score of 75 for men and 79 for women, so *T*-scores between 64 and 79 should be considered high. Low scorers (< *T*-40) report a great deal of internal conflict and turbulence, with worries, indecision, a lack of self-confidence, and a sense of being rushed.

S3: Contentment with Life (8 items)

This subscale measures a sense of contentment with one's life choices, family, and achievements. A raw score of 7 equals a *T*-score of 65 for men and 68 for women so the scale has a low ceiling. Scores above a *T*-score of 60 should be considered high. Low scorers (< *T*-40) express a tense or strained discontent in these areas.

S4: Patience and Denial of Irritability and Anger (8 items)

This subscale includes items pertaining to being patient, not irritable or grouchy, not needing to win points with difficult people, and being accommodating when hurried or made to wait. A raw score of 7 equals a *T*-score of 63 for both men and women and endorsement of all 8 items yields a *T*-score of 68, so scores over a *T*-score of 60 should be considered high. Low scorers (< *T*-40) admit to anger, impatience, and retaliatory motives.

S5: Denial of Moral Flaws (5 items)

This very short subscale deals mainly with a denial of alcohol or marijuana abuse, denial of unusual sex practices, and claiming no secrets of which one is ashamed. Four endorsed items yields a T-score of 53 for women and 58 for men. Five endorsed items yield a T-score of 65 for men and 61 for women. Low scorers ($< T$-40) admit these items and may show a low threshold for risk-taking.

For cases in which self-favorable responding is suspected with high K scores and elevations on the Mp and Sd scales, elevations on some of the S subscales could validate the assumption of under-reporting and the exaggeration of superlative adjustments.

Future research should provide cut scores for different settings and populations, but until then, clinicians should cautiously factor scores on the S scale into their validity decisions.

Positive Malingering Scale (Mp) (26 items)

The Mp scale (Cofer et al., 1949) has been found useful in determining how much of the K elevation may be due to intentional self-favorable responding versus upper SES and self-deception. At present, only the Caldwell computerized report scores the Mp scale routinely, and uses it as an essential part of the validity write-up. Although little research exists on cut scores for the Mp scale, the following may serve as guidelines (Caldwell, 1988):

1   If both the K and Mp scales are elevated above T-scores of 60, the individual may be consciously attempting to make a good impression; the moderately elevated Mp score reflects some conscious under-reporting and attempts to look socially virtuous.
2   If K is elevated above T-60 and Mp scale is below T-60, K is probably the result of a genuine lack of introspective self-awareness and/or the "stiff upper lip" approach to life associated with upper SES. The lower the Mp score in relation to K, the more likely the K is reflecting a non-deliberate positive self-presentation.

Social Desirability Scale (Sd) (33 items)

This scale was developed by Wiggins (1959) by asking Stanford University students to respond to the MMPI as "people in general would consider desirable" (Caldwell, 1988, p. 92). The scale operates similarly to Mp, which accounts for its high correlation of .75 with that scale.

As with Mp, Sd scores should be considered in a broad context, including scores on L, K, S, and Ss. One can be more confident about interpreting elevated Sd scores when accompanied by elevations on Mp, are of greater elevation than K and S, and when Ss is below 55. Nichols (2011, p. 86)) stated:

> Spuriously high scores may be the result of extreme values for $T\%$ and generally should not be interpreted when $T\%$ exceeds 50. Such profiles are not uncommon among manics, who are prone to higher values for $T\%$ than other diagnostic

groups and whose responses to many of the highly self-positive items on *Sd* may be determined by grandiosity or psychomotor acceleration rather than by impression management.

Caldwell (1988) reasoned that raw scores on *Sd* of 18 to 20 (*T*-73–86) in the presence of a low *K* score suggest a person of lower SES who is attempting to consciously look his or her best, whereas low scores in the presence of a high *K* score suggest that the person's *K* score is reflecting mostly upper SES identification, with little, if any, conscious under-reporting. If *K* is elevated and both the *Mp* and *Sd* scales are at or below a *T*-55, the *K* elevation may well reflect education, social poise, and non-deliberate positive self-presentation. If both *Mp* and *Sd* are elevated above a *T*-60, the elevated *K* is probably reflecting self-favorable responding. The higher the *Mp* and/or *Sd* score, the more the individual is attempting to consciously look his or her best. Nichols (2011) concurs, stating that "as *Sd* scores reach *T*-65, especially when *Mp* is of equal or greater elevation, or when both exceed *K*, impression management is strongly suggested and interpretation should proceed with caution" (p. 86).

Socioeconomic Status Scale (Ss) (73 items)

This scale, developed by S. E. Nelson (1952), is described by Caldwell (1988), who viewed it as reflective of "current 'earned' (socio-economic) status" (p. 94). *Ss*, together with *Mp* and *Sd*, is used by Caldwell to fine-tune the validity section of the Caldwell Report (see Chapter 12) by determining how much of a particular *K* elevation is due to SES and how much is due to conscious or unconscious under-reporting. Caldwell reported that the scale correlates about .50 with independent measures of SES, and about .40 with IQ scores.

Although there is limited empirical research, Caldwell (1988) has made a convincing argument for using *Ss* as part of the process to partial-out an elevated *K* score of genuine emotional restraint associated with upper SES versus conscious defensiveness. For example, when *K* is elevated (e.g. *T*-65), he suggested that if *Ss* is also elevated (e.g. *T*-65), reflecting upper SES, and *Mp* and *Sd* are low (e.g. *T*-53 and 54, respectively), suggesting a lack of a conscious positive self-presentation, then the high *K* score reflects the genuine emotional control and poise associated with upper SES, without conscious positive malingering. On the other hand, if *K* is high but *Ss* is low (e.g. *T*-50–55) and the *Mp* and *Sd* scores are high, then the elevated *K* score reflects someone who is intentionally responding self-favorably or under-reporting.

Validity Indices

F-FB Index

In a valid profile, typically the *F* and *FB* scores will be elevated in more or less the same *T*-score range because both scales reflect disturbance, psychological distress, and unusual responding. As mentioned earlier, sometimes there is a valid discrepancy between *F* and *FB* scores, wherein *FB* is higher than *F* because the individual's disturbance is associated with serious depression and its resulting distress. However, if *FB* is between 15 and 19 raw scores and greater than F by 8 raw scores, and the content items do not clearly reflect drug and alcohol abuse issues or acute panic-like distress, then the second half of the test may be invalid. Therefore the content scales should not be interpreted, although the clinical scales may still be interpreted, assuming the other validity scales are not unduly elevated.

Dissimulation Index (F – K)

The $F - K$ index is a useful further check on validity. F measures severity of psychopathology and K measures defensiveness. Most bona fide psychopathology involves some attempt at compensated functioning. A very high F score and a very low K score indicates that the individual is grossly disturbed and defenseless, a condition that is rarely true. Schizophrenic individuals typically will obtain raw F scores between 10 and 18 but usually with at least some elevation on K. Conceptually, the usefulness of the $F - K$ index reflects the fact that psychopathology usually is associated with some functioning defenses, so an individual claiming extreme distress (high F) and no defenses (low K) is probably exaggerating their disturbance. Cut scores for the $F - K$ index, like all cut scores, vary according to the setting, so the following are to be used only as guidelines.

Low F – K Scores

The $F - K$ index is less accurate in correctly identifying self-favorable responders (see Chapter 3). The mean $F - K$ score is –10.77 and –11.37 for men and women, respectively, in the MMPI-2 re-standardization group. The approximate lower 2.5 percent range for the re-standardization sample is –22 for both men and women. Table 3.1 (see Chapter 3) provides a range of scores across diagnostic groups for self-favorable (fake good) responding. As the research with this index to date indicates that $F - K$ is much more useful in identifying fake-bad versus fake-good profiles, it is recommended that the reader rely upon the $F - K$ index for assistance in assessing self-unfavorable responding rather than self-favorable responding. The reader is referred to the S, Mp, Sd, and Ss scales in this chapter, and in Chapter 3 for assistance in interpreting self-favorable responding.

Normal Range: Raw Scores Between 0 and 11

Scores in this range suggest the profile is valid, especially if the other validity indicators suggest validity. If other validity measures suggest exaggeration, then an $F - K$ score of 11 and below would argue for a valid, but pathological, profile.

High Range: Raw Scores Between 12 and 16

Scores in this range suggest exaggeration or malingering, except in psychiatric patients, where $F - K$ scores up to 16 would not be uncommon. If there appears to be no secondary gain from appearing pathological, $F - K$ scores in this range may reflect the extreme pain and lack of psychological resources associated with severe psychopathology. In cases in which there may be secondary gain from appearing disturbed, $F - K$ scores in this range should act as a red flag, alerting the clinician to the possibility of symptom magnification or severe distress.

Invalid Range: Raw Scores of 17 or Greater

Scores in this range suggest invalidity, especially if there is any secondary gain from over-reporting. If the other validity indicators suggest exaggeration, scores in this range would confirm it.

True Percent Index (T percent)

The proportion of items bearing True responses affords a rough guide to a test-taker's attitude in completing the MMPI-2. Self-unfavorable reporting will generally produce a higher True than False percentage rate. Chapter 3 provides a more detailed description of the True/False item distributions across the clinical scales. In general, the majority of the items on the psychotic scales (6–9) are keyed True (75 percent), whereas only 30 percent of the items on the neurotic scales (1–3) are keyed True.

T percent less than 25 percent or more than 60 percent in psychiatric populations may suggest a response set that may be accompanied by high scores on *TRIN*. If so, scores on *F*, *FB*, *F(p)*, and *Ds* typically are also elevated and should be checked. A high False percentage may stem from clinical patients with somatization disorders or from a highly self-favorable response style. Non-psychiatric samples show T percent varying in a range of 25 percent to 50 percent, with an average between 35 percent and 40 percent (Nichols & Greene, 1995). Many automated reports record the T percent; if not, it can be easily calculated by counting the True items on the answer sheet and dividing by 567 to derive True percent.

Issues in Determining Validity

Determining the validity of a profile is often a difficult task for seasoned and novice practitioners alike. The problem is aggravated by the fact that exact cut scores are rarely given in the major textbooks on the MMPI-2 and, when they are provided, they are accompanied by the necessary disclaimers about how cut scores vary according to the setting and the motivation to over- or under-report problems. Given the expanded use of the MMPI-2 in forensic and employment settings, as well as its traditional use in diagnosis and treatment planning, it is remarkable how robust the original and supplementary scales have proven in determining test-taking attitudes across a wide range of settings. Nevertheless, it is a very complex task to be able to factor in the issues of setting and motivation with the co-varying of a number of validity scales in determining the various test-taking attitudes. The following is a summary of validity issues to remember when venturing into the challenging task of determining test-taking response sets:

1   In private practice settings, if the individual taking the test has little motivation to distort his or her adjustment, the basic validity scales, *VRIN*, *TRIN*, *F*, *FB*, *F(p)*, *L*, *K*, and *S* are often sufficient in determining test-taking attitude. In these non-forensic, mainly treatment-oriented settings, the clinician can be more liberal with cut scores before suggesting that a profile is invalid. For example, a self-referred client taking the MMPI-2 as part of treatment evaluation obtains an *FLK* configuration as follows: *F* at *T*-43, *L* at *T*-64, *K* at *T*-65, with *VRIN* and *TRIN* valid. In a forensic situation,

this validity configuration would suggest an under-reporting style. However, in a private practice setting, if there is little motivation to self-favorably report, the clinician needs to consider that the validity scales may be accurately portraying a rigid, emotionally constricted individual who lacks psychological insight and self-awareness, rather than somebody who is consciously under-reporting. In this setting, the test feedback process with the client would be helpful in arriving at a diagnosis and treatment plan, irrespective of whether the profile appeared to reflect an over- or under-reporting style, and the clinician can be less concerned about strict cutting scores for validity.

2   In settings in which other data (e.g. setting and history) suggest extreme psychopathology and distress (e.g. psychiatric inpatient unit), the validity cut scores need to be adjusted upward. For example, in such a setting, a raw F score of 28 might not be unusual, and the *VRIN* and *TRIN* scales as well as the *Ds* scale may be elevated, reflecting real confusion, panic, and yea-saying in the direction of pathology. Although the profile is unlikely to be a stable reflection of the individual's personality, it may not always be consciously exaggerated. In such settings, extreme endorsements of psychopathology may reflect genuine panic, disorientation, and extreme self-criticism, with some conscious exaggeration, reflecting a plea for help. In these cases, strict cut scores that might be used in a forensic setting would clearly be inappropriate.

3   In forensic situations in which there is high motivation to appear, or not appear, psychologically impaired, yet socially and morally above reproach, cut scores become more important and the need to use the additional measures of response style becomes more pressing. In these cases, *Ds*, *Mp*, *Sd*, *Ss*, *S*, and T percent, as well as the traditional validity scales, become very useful. Clinicians should also be aware that there is sometimes a borderline area where it is difficult to tell solely from MMPI-2 data whether a profile is clearly malingered or accurate.

4   In work settings (e.g. pre-employment screenings, fitness-for-duty evaluations, and workers' compensation assessments), motivation may be high to appear psychologically healthy and morally above reproach, so cut scores are more important and the usefulness of scores on the additional measures of response style increases. Unfortunately, giving exact cutting scores is difficult. Sometimes a profile that appears under-reported is, in fact, accurately reflecting an individual from an upper socioeconomic background and a cultural milieu that values emotional control, denial of emotions, and "getting on with life" in the face of an emotional crisis. This would be reflected in a high K score, some L elevation, and perhaps an unelevated clinical profile. Typically, the *Mp* and *Sd* scales would also be low and the *Ss* scale would be elevated, with only moderate scores on *S*. The clinician also has to weigh the evidence from interviews and other test data to determine whether a particular profile in the indeterminate area is likely invalid or likely valid. In many cases, of course, the profile is clearly invalid or valid. It is the indeterminate forensic cases that are the most difficult. Validity is determined by examining not only all the basic and supplemental validity scales, but also the likelihood that the person is motivated to malinger, the elevation of the profile, and the number of critical items endorsed. It is the overall direction of validity that is relevant. The good news for the clinician is that rarely will one validity indicator invalidate a profile; usually, there is a pattern of scale scores

that, in sum, are in accord with one another. For example, an individual may have a yea-saying response set in which he or she is saying True to many psychopathological items. This will lead to an elevated profile, a high True percentage, an elevated *TRIN* score, perhaps some *VRIN* elevation if the individual is contradictory in some of his or her responses, and high *F* and *FB* scores. The *Ds* scale would likely show an elevation, and there would be a significant number of critical items endorsed. There would be many indicators that the profile was not an accurate clinical portrayal, so the task of determining validity is not as daunting as it may appear.

Basic Validity Scale Configurations

An important validity consideration is whether a client simply marked the items at random, tended to mark most or all of them as True, or as False. Early in the MMPI's development, these response sets were examined to see how effective the validity scales were in detecting such test-taking behaviors. The configurations of the validity scales show distinctive patterns for each response bias, as do the clinical scales.

Random Response Set

Random marking results in the patterns shown in Figs. 4.1 and 4.2. However, some actual clinical situations result in a similar-looking validity scale configuration, so clinicians need to examine the actual raw- and *T*-scores for each of the validity scales before determining validity. Although the elevated clinical scales and high *F* pattern look similar to the "most open" validity scale pattern described later, it is important to note that the *L* and *F* scales are far more elevated in the randomly marked profile.

Notes

The validity configuration resulting from a random response set of an adult client (male or female) shows that *F* is much greater than *T*-120, that *L* is at *T*-65–66, and that *K* is about *T*-50. The clinical scales are characterized by a generally elevated profile with all of the clinical scales except Scale 0 at or above *T*-65 and Scale 5 at *T*-scores of 54 and 69 for men and women, respectively. A psychotic slope with a spike on Scale 8 and a subspike on Scale 6 is evident. A person responding in a random manner may adopt an idiosyncratic response pattern, such as marking a block of four or five items as True followed by another block of four items as False, or the person may mark True and False randomly. The *VRIN* scale is the most useful in determining randomness (see this chapter for cut scores). The *FB*, *VRIN*, and *TRIN* scales are at *T*-scores of 124, 96, and 71, respectively, for men, and 120, 98, and 73, respectively, for women.

Report Language

The profile is invalid because the respondent likely answered the items in a random manner. The respondent may have done this out of confusion, anger, or resistance to the testing situation. After the clinician has determined the reasons for this response pattern, the respondent should retake the test, if practical.

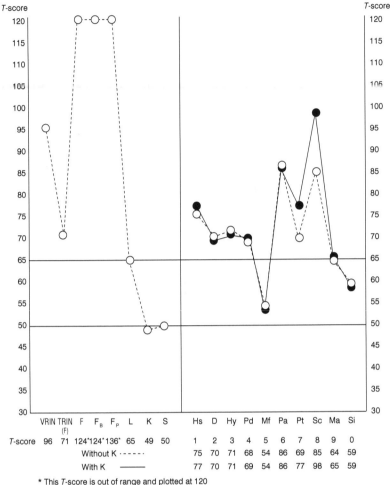

	VRIN	TRIN (F)	F	F$_B$	F$_P$	L	K	S		Hs	D	Hy	Pd	Mf	Pa	Pt	Sc	Ma	Si
T-score	96	71	124*	124*	136*	65	49	50		1	2	3	4	5	6	7	8	9	0
					Without K $\cdots\cdots$					75	70	71	68	54	86	69	85	64	59
					With K ———					77	70	71	69	54	86	77	98	65	59

* This T-score is out of range and plotted at 120

Figure 4.1 Random Response Set for Men

All-True Response Set

An All-True response set (see Figs. 4.3 and 4.4) has as its most discerning features elevated *F* and *FB* scores, with subaverage scores on *L* and *K* (usually at or below a *T*-score of 35).

Notes

The discerning features of this configuration are extremely elevated *F* and *FB* scores, usually off the top of the profile sheet, with the *L* and *K* scores well below 50. On the

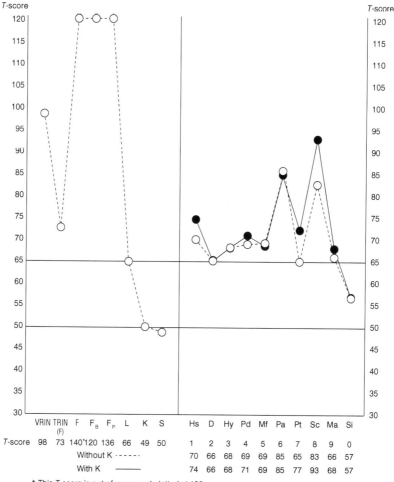

Figure 4.2 Random Response Set for Women

Source: Adapted from *Manual Supplement: Corrected Graphs for the Items in the MMPI-2: Alterations in Wording, Patterns of Interrelationships, and Changes in Endorsements,* by W. G. Dahlstrom, 1994, Minneapolis: University of Minnesota Press. Copyright © 1994 by the Regents of the University of Minnesota. Used by permission of the University of Minnesota Press. All rights reserved. "MMPI" and "Minnesota Multiphasic Personality Inventory" are trademarks owned by the Regents of the University of Minnesota.

clinical scales, a psychotic slope typically occurs, with a 68 code pattern. Scales 1, 2, 3, and 4 tend to be low relative to Scales 6, 7, 8, and 9. Whereas *VRIN T*-scores are 50 for both men and women, *FB* and *TRIN T*-scores are 192 and 149, respectively, for men, and 180 and 156, respectively, for women. A visual examination of the answer sheet or an examination of the computer printout to determine the percentages of True and False responses would quickly confirm the presence of an All-True response bias.

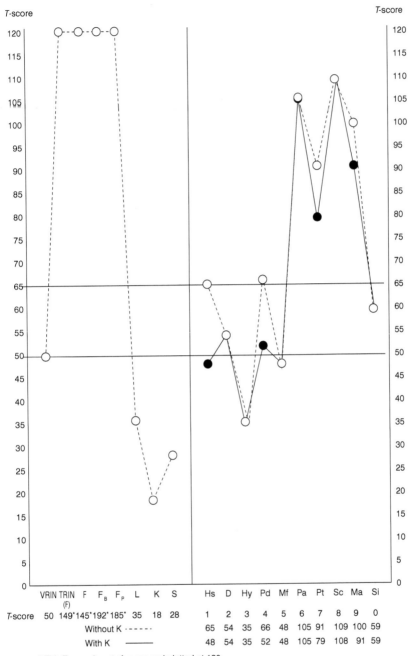

T-score (left axis)
120
115
110
105
100
95
90
85
80
75
70
65
60
55
50
45
40
35
30
25
20
15
10
5
0

	VRIN	TRIN (F)	F	F$_B$	F$_P$	L	K	S		Hs	D	Hy	Pd	Mf	Pa	Pt	Sc	Ma	Si
T-score	50	149*	145*	192*	185*	35	18	28		1	2	3	4	5	6	7	8	9	0
Without K · · · · ·										65	54	35	66	48	105	91	109	100	59
With K ———										48	54	35	52	48	105	79	108	91	59

* This T-score is out of range and plotted at 120

Figure 4.3 All-True Response Set for Men

Source: Adapted from *Manual Supplement: Corrected Graphs for the Items in the MMPI-2: Alterations in Wording, Patterns of Interrelationships, and Changes in Endorsements*, by W. G. Dahlstrom, 1994, Minneapolis: University of Minnesota Press. Copyright © 1994 by the Regents of the University of Minnesota. Used by permission of the University of Minnesota Press. All rights reserved. "MMPI" and "Minnesota Multiphasic Personality Inventory" are trademarks owned by the Regents of the University of Minnesota.

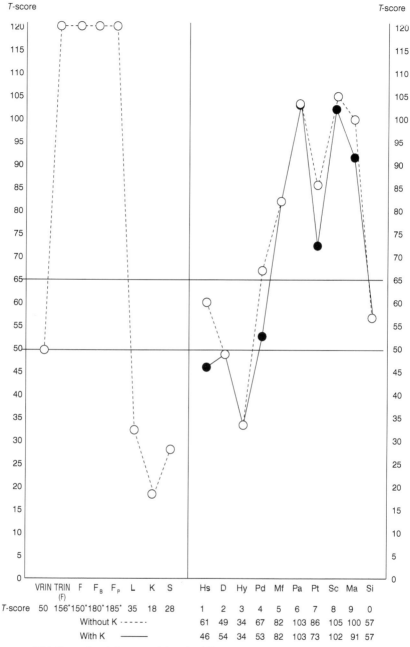

	VRIN	TRIN	F	F_B	F_P	L	K	S		Hs	D	Hy	Pd	Mf	Pa	Pt	Sc	Ma	Si
		(F)																	
T-score	50	156*	150*	180*	185*	35	18	28		1	2	3	4	5	6	7	8	9	0
Without K ------										61	49	34	67	82	103	86	105	100	57
With K ————										46	54	34	53	82	103	73	102	91	57

* This *T*-score is out of range and plotted at 120

Figure 4.4 All-True Response Set for Women

Source: Adapted from *Manual Supplement: Corrected Graphs for the Items in the MMPI-2: Alterations in Wording, Patterns of Interrelationships, and Changes in Endorsements*, by W. G. Dahlstrom, 1994, Minneapolis: University of Minnesota Press. Copyright © 1994 by the Regents of the University of Minnesota. Used by permission of the University of Minnesota Press. All rights reserved. "MMPI" and "Minnesota Multiphasic Personality Inventory" are trademarks owned by the Regents of the University of Minnesota.

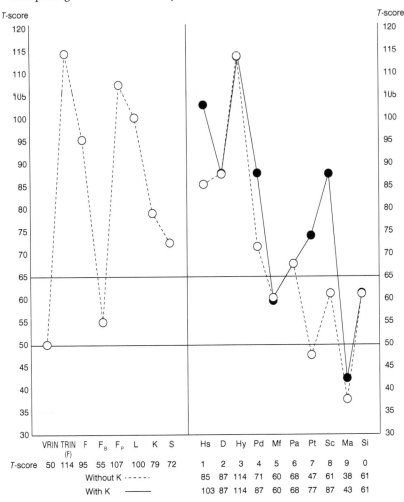

Figure 4.5 All-False Response Set for Men

Source: Adapted from *Manual Supplement: Corrected Graphs for the Items in the MMPI-2: Alterations in Wording, Patterns of Interrelationships, and Changes in Endorsements,* by W. G. Dahlstrom, 1994, Minneapolis: University of Minnesota Press. Copyright © 1994 by the Regents of the University of Minnesota. Used by permission of the University of Minnesota Press. All rights reserved. "MMPI" and "Minnesota Multiphasic Personality Inventory" are trademarks owned by the Regents of the University of Minnesota.

Report Language

The profile is likely invalid. The patient has answered most of the items in the True direction. The respondent may have done this out of confusion, anger, or fear of the testing situation. After the clinician has determined the reasons for this response pattern, the respondent could retake the test, if practical.

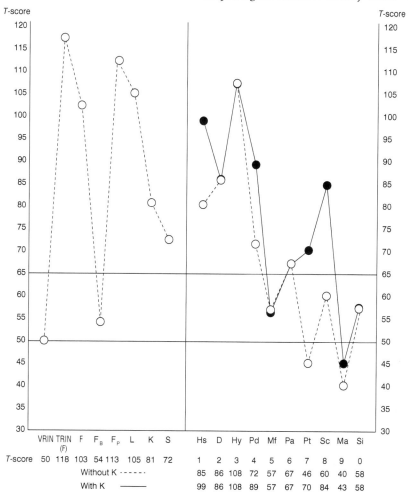

Figure 4.6 All-False Response Set for Women

Source: Adapted from *Manual Supplement: Corrected Graphs for the Items in the MMPI-2: Alterations in Wording, Patterns of Interrelationships, and Changes in Endorsements*, by W. G. Dahlstrom, 1994, Minneapolis: University of Minnesota Press. Copyright © 1994 by the Regents of the University of Minnesota. Used by permission of the University of Minnesota Press. All rights reserved. "MMPI" and "Minnesota Multiphasic Personality Inventory" are trademarks owned by the Regents of the University of Minnesota.

All-False Response Set

An All-False response set (see Figs. 4.5 and 4.6) will generate a distinctive pattern on the validity and clinical scales.

Notes

In an All-False response set, the F, L, and K scales are all elevated, with L highest, followed by F and K. This elevation on the L scale is not surprising as the L items are all scored when endorsed False, so all the *L* items are endorsed in this response set. Scales 1, 2, and 3 (neurotic scales) are elevated above Scales 6, 7, 8, and 9 (psychotic scales). Whereas *VRIN* T-scores are 50 for both men and women, *FB* T-scores are at 55 for men and 54 for women. The *FB* score is relatively low because 37 of the 40 items on this scale are scored in the True direction. *TRIN* T-scores are at 114 and 118 for men and women, respectively.

Report Language

The profile is invalid because the respondent tended to answer the items in the False direction. The respondent may have done this out of confusion, anger, or resistance to the testing situation. After the clinician has determined the reasons for this response pattern, the respondent should retake the test, if practical.

Common Validity Scale Patterns

People's responses to being questioned about various intimate aspects of their lives vary. As some reality TV shows attest, some people relish sharing even intimate aspects of their lives to the point of exaggeration, whereas others react defensively when questioned about basic human habits, foibles, or behaviors. The MMPI-2 validity scales can reflect a number of response styles on a continuum of "Most Open"—representing normal to exaggerated self-disclosure—to "Most Closed"—representing defensiveness such that little information is revealed other than a reluctance to self-disclose (see Fig. 4.7). The following descriptions apply to both men and women, in terms of disclosing emotional and psychological difficulties and human vulnerabilities.

"Most-Open" to "Most-Closed" Validity Configurations

The following basic validity scale configurations and their variants are important because they occur frequently and add substantially to the interpretations obtained through considering each validity scale separately.

"Most Open" Validity Configuration

This configuration, also referred to as an "open and self-critical," "in pain," or "plea for help" configuration, occurs when *F* is above *T*-65, and *L* and *K* are at or below *T*-50 (see Fig. 4.7). Such persons are openly admitting to psychological difficulties, doubt their ability to handle stress, and generally are amenable to professional help.

As *F* increases above *T*-80 and/or *K* decreases below *T*-45, these individuals are reporting acute and pervasive distress and an absence of coping abilities. Their level of psychological disorganization is so extreme that they are unlikely to benefit from insight-oriented therapy until crisis intervention has achieved some stability and the immediate stress is alleviated. With such a high *F* score, however, the possibility should also be considered that the person may be exaggerating his or her psychological conflicts, stress, and personal problems, sometimes as a "cry for help" in order to obtain the most immediate attention. He or she may also be attempting to simulate psychopathology. The cut scores for the validity scales are discussed earlier in this chapter.

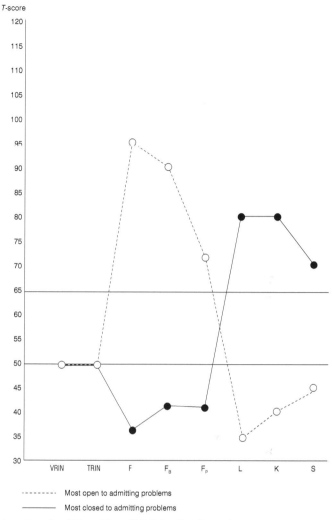

Figure 4.7 "Most-Open" to "Most-Closed" Validity Configurations

Two subtypes of the "Most Open" validity pattern (formerly referred to as the "Inverted V" configuration by Greene, 1991a) frequently occur.

In Subtype 1 (see Fig. 4.8), *L* and *K* are between *T*-50 and 65 and *F* is greater than *T*-65, and sometimes much higher.

Subtype 1

These clients, although admitting problems, are also exhibiting the defenses of denial and repression. They are often not well educated and they lack psychological-mindedness (reflected in the elevated *L* score). Often the coping attempts of such persons are limited in effectiveness, and they may have a stable but chronically maladjusted lifestyle. If *Mp*

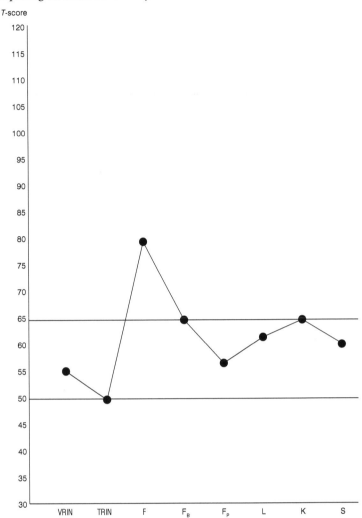

Figure 4.8 Admitting Serious Problems While Attempting to Cope and Preserve Self-Esteem

and/or *Sd* and *S* are also elevated, then the elevations on *L* and *K* are likely reflecting conscious attempts to minimize the considerable pathology being manifested.

Subtype 2 can be referred to as the "good ego strength, but experiencing problems" profile (see Fig. 4.9).

Subtype 2

This profile reflects good ego strength in a person who is experiencing problems. In this configuration, *K* is above *T*-55, *F* is at least equal to *K*, and *L* is less than *T*-50. Persons with this pattern typically cope well, as would be expected given their moderate psychopathology (moderate *F*) and good emotional control (moderate *K*). Although

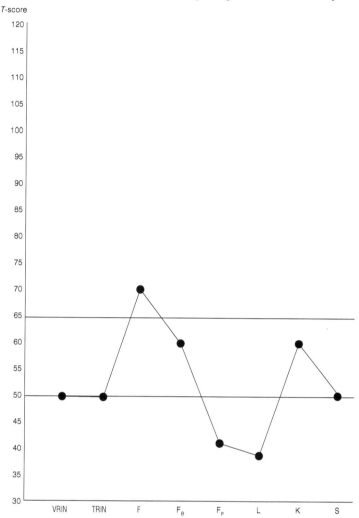

Figure 4.9 Good Ego Strength, But Experiencing Problems

they may have longstanding problems, these individuals may have adjusted to them as a chronic lifestyle so that they experience few feelings of disorganizing distress. Even as *F* rises above *T*-65–70, such persons have a functioning defense system as reflected in the elevated *K*, but simultaneously are describing a variety of problems that may be severe. If *K* is moderately elevated in the presence of high *F*, the score on Ego Strength (*Es*) can be helpful in determining the stability or fragility of the individual's coping style. For example, if *K* is at *T*-60 and *Es* is at *T*-35, the exterior poise and control reflected in *K* is probably somewhat brittle and fragile.

Validity Pattern "A" is characterized by a validity configuration wherein *K* is greater than *F* and *FB* which, in turn, are greater than *L* (see Fig. 4.10).

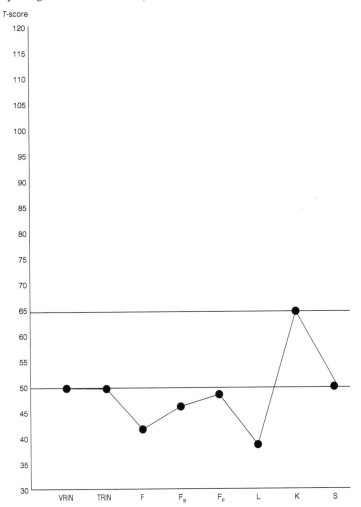

Figure 4.10 Validity Pattern "A"

Validity Pattern "A"

Generally, the *F* and *FB* *T*-scores are between 50 and 55, *L* is about 40 to 45, and *K* is about 60 to 65. Persons with such patterns usually are not in distress and have appropriate resources for dealing with any current stresses. If they do have problems, they do not feel overwhelmed by them. College-educated or other widely experienced persons are somewhat more likely to show this pattern, and it reflects the array of their coping resources. Some job applicants or normal persons in marital conflict situations may also obtain this pattern, but in such cases this may represent an attempt to portray themselves in a somewhat overly favorable light.

The "Naïve but Open" (see Fig. 4.11) validity profile, is one where the *T*-scores decrease from *L* to *F* to *K*, resulting in a linear downward trend. Generally, the *L* *T*-score is about 60 to 65, the *F* *T*-score is about 55, and the *K* *T*-score is about 45.

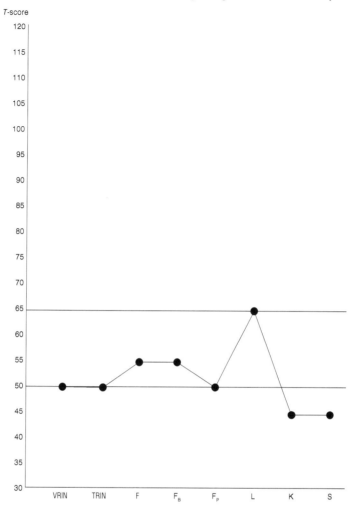

Figure 4.11 Naïve But Open Validity Configuration

"Naïve but Open"

Although such persons may be experiencing some mild situational, emotional, or interpersonal difficulties, they are usually psychologically naïve and unsophisticated, often have limited educational backgrounds, and often have lowered expectancies about the extent to which they can control or have an impact on their own feelings, impulses, or life situations. They usually are poor candidates for insight-oriented psychotherapy, preferring practical solution-oriented approaches.

"Most Closed" Validity Configuration

This pattern occurs when L and K are above T-65, with F at or below T-50 (see Fig. 4.7). The more elevated L and K, the more likely the profile is invalid and the more confidence can be put in the interpretation that such persons were strongly attempting to present themselves in an extremely favorable light by minimizing or denying problems, and unacceptable impulses and feelings. A similar, although lower, T-score validity configuration occurs often among job applicants or persons in situations (e.g. child custody evaluations) in which they wish to appear particularly well-adjusted. In inpatient settings, however, this validity scale pattern can be found sometimes in psychotic patients who are using massive denial, repression, or strong attempts at self-control. Other diagnostic groups characterized by denial and lack of insight (such as individuals with hysteria, hypochondriasis, or alcoholism, or other substance abuse problems) may occasionally show a similar pattern.

In some cases, this pattern is found in normals or clients in outpatient settings (although at a lower T-score level) who are out of touch with any emotional difficulties, who emphasize self-control, and who are repressed and inhibited. For example, they may seek therapy as part of a marriage problem, but they tend to lack psychological-mindedness and are often naïve and morally judgmental. It is hard to claim that this validity configuration invalidates a profile if it has been obtained by a bright professional who is self-referred for a marriage problem. More likely, the validity configuration reflects a rigid, inhibited, and naïve individual who lacks insight but presents with a good social facade. However, the same validity configuration in a person seeking custody of his or her children in a forensic setting would raise red flags for invalidity.

The minimizing effect reflected on the validity scales would also be reflected on the clinical scales, which would tend to be suppressed. In some cases in which defensiveness is to be expected, as in a job screening, norms have been collected to serve as a base for expected levels of defensiveness (e.g. Pope, Butcher, & Seelen, 2006). Defensive MMPI-2 profiles may be interpreted cautiously in settings in which the cost of making an error may not be high and when the test results are not likely to be subject to significant challenge. In other settings, however, defensive profiles need to be carefully integrated with historical and other data to partial-out how much of the variance is accounted for by conscious distortion versus self-deception and personality attributes. The Mp, Sd, S, and Ss scales, among others discussed earlier, can also be helpful in making such validity determinations.

Individuals with the "Most Closed" validity pattern are often self-favorably reporting. To the extent that situational causes for this pattern can be ruled out, such as job applications, fitness-for-work assessments, or child custody evaluations, this pattern is associated with persons who value control, are rigid in their views, cling to rules and regulations, and view the world and the behaviors of others in terms of extremes of value judgments (e.g. "good" vs. "bad" or "strong" vs. "weak").

5 The MMPI-2 Clinical Scales and Their Derivatives

Clinical Scale Development and Use

The MMPI-2 has 10 standard clinical scales that are universally scored. These scales were originally named after the diagnostic criterion groups (hypochondriasis, depression, etc.) used in their construction, but currently are indicated by their numbers, 1 through 9, plus 0. The last of the clinical scales to be added to the test, *Si*, is referred to as Scale 0. The original diagnostic labels from which the scale names derive can be misleading, as the behaviors expected to be associated with the scale diagnostic labels are not always observed. For this reason, referring to the clinical scales by number is less misleading in terms of what the scales are measuring. The reader is referred to the MMPI-2 *Manual* (Butcher et al., 2001), Appendix A, page 61, for the *T*-score conversions, and to Appendix B, page 85, for the item composition and the scoring direction for each item based upon the men and women of the re-standardization sample for all of the currently approved MMPI-2 scales. This information may also be found, along with similar information for many additional scales, in Friedman et al. (2001) or Greene (1991a).

The clinical scales were the first scales to be constructed from the test items and have been the focus of much of the MMPI research done over the past 70-plus years. They form the basis of all the coding systems (see Chapter 2) and the core of all the clinical uses of the MMPI-2. Traditionally, Scales 1, 2, and 3 are referred to as the *neurotic triad*, and Scales 6, 7, 8, and 9 are referred to as the *psychotic tetrad*. The modifications made in the re-standardized MMPI-2 left the clinical scales essentially intact, with only nine deleted items from Scales 1, 2, 5, and 0.

Once the clinician has ascertained through an analysis of the validity measures that a profile is valid, an interpretation of the clinical scales is possible. Such interpretation is primarily focused on scale elevation, configuration (shape), and scatter, or the spread of the scale scores, highest to lowest, with attention to item content being an important adjunct to this process. Typically, clinicians examine each scale elevation to form an initial impression of the test taker prior to examining the score combinations and the profile code. After examining the clinical scales and the "critical" items that are described in Chapter 7, the psychologist typically examines the different content and supplementary scale scores, including the Harris-Lingoes and Subtle–Obvious subscales. These subscales were derived for many of the clinical scales in order to help clarify the meaning of individual scale elevations. Because these subscales are discussed within the context of the clinical scales, we present an overview of their derivation and meaning before going on to describe the clinical scales. Moderator variables, such as age, education, and SES are discussed in relationship to MMPI-2 profiles in Chapter 9.

The *T*-score value at which clinical significance is generally assumed is 65 and greater (as compared with 70 on the original MMPI). This does not mean that individuals with scores below 65 are necessarily free of psychopathology or concerns. *T*-65 should be considered no more than a demarcation guideline to assist the clinician in interpreting the MMPI-2 profile, not an absolute standard. Although considerably less research has been conducted on low-scale elevations, it is nevertheless important to examine the lowest scores in a profile to ascertain if significance should be attached to the score (Friedman, Webb, & Lewak, 2001; Greene, 1991a, 2011). Keiller and Graham (1993) studied partner ratings in a subsample of the MMPI-2 re-standardization sample and compared low, medium, and high scores on the clinical scales. They reported that for this nonclinical sample, low scores on most of the scales provided valuable information. In general, low-scoring nonclinical participants showed positive characteristics and better than average adjustment, which will usually be opposite to the descriptions typically associated with high scores on a particular scale. Their findings did not suggest that low scores indicate negative characteristics or adjustment problems that were poorer than average.

Graham, Ben-Porath, and McNulty (1997) recognized that Keiller and Graham's (1993) findings might not generalize to clinical settings in which the MMPI-2 is most typically used. They therefore studied the meaning of low scores on both the clinical and supplementary scales in an outpatient mental health population. Low scores were defined as below a *T*-score of 41. Graham et al. (1997, p. 390) reported the following:

> Our results indicate that the meaning of low scores on the MMPI-2 scales that we were able to study differs from one scale to another. For some scales, low scores seemed to provide no useful information. For other scales, low scorers appeared to have fewer symptoms and negative characteristics than within normal limit scorers. In some cases, these characteristics are specifically related to the construct that the scales were designed to measure; in others, they indicate better overall adjustment. Perhaps the most consistent finding was that for none of the scales that we studied did low scores indicate more negative characteristics or poorer overall adjustment than within normal limit scorers.

Graham et al. (1997) therefore recommended that low MMPI-2 scales in an outpatient mental setting be interpreted cautiously, and it should usually not be assumed that a low score necessarily indicates the converse of a high score on a given scale.

More research on a variety of populations is needed to better identify reliable correlates of low scores on the clinical and supplementary scales. We believe it is important to note unusually low scores on any of the clinical or supplementary scales in any population, as these may raise important interpretive hypotheses. For example, if a psychiatric patient who recently suffered multiple losses obtained a very low score on the Depression scale, the clinician should consider whether the patient is attempting to deny depression and whether suicide precautions should be considered. Any statistically deviant score is worthy of consideration and should be understood in the particular context of the individual's situation.

Table 5.1 T-score classifications and percentile values

Uniform T-Score	Classification	Percentile Equivalent
30	Very low	<1
35		4
40	Moderately low	15
45		34
50	Average	55
55		73
60	Moderately high	85
65		92
70	High	96
75		98
80	Very high	>99
85		
90	Extremely high	

Source: From "The New Uniform T-scores for the MMPI-2: Rationale, Derivation, and Appraisal," by A. Tellegen & Y. S. Ben-Porath, 1992. Psychological Assessment: A Journal of Consulting and Clinical Psychology, 4, 145–155. Copyright © 1992 by the American Psychological Association. Adapted with permission.

On the profile form for plotting MMPI-2 scores, the scales have been limited to a lowest T-score of 30, so it is not possible to plot a lower score. However, Ward (1994) provided a table that includes T-score values below 30 for selected scales. This table is also reproduced in Friedman et al. (2001). Ward (1994) notes that the T-score cut of 30 truncates the distributions of positive traits in clinical populations, and that, although the MMPI-2 is basically a measure of psychopathology and therefore sensitive to the presence of psychiatric symptoms and maladaptive personality traits, there are a few supplementary scales that measure positive personality attributes, such as Dominance, Social Responsibility, and Ego Strength (Butcher et al., 2001). Additionally, two other scales, Gender Role—Masculine and Gender Role—Feminine, were designed to measure aspects of gender identity. Because conversion tables in the MMPI-2 *Manual* limits low scores, Ward (1994) stated that a T-score of 30 will be automatically assigned to any raw score that is more than two standard deviations below the mean. Although this is unlikely to be important with the clinical scales (except Scale 5), the positive attribute scales above may be better interpreted when they are very low by using Ward's more accurate T-score table.

Recall that the MMPI-2 profile form is graduated in uniform T-scores for the basic clinical Scales 1, 2, 3, 4, 6, 7, 8, and 9, whereas Scales 5 and 0 still follow the linear T-score conversions of the original MMPI. Describing various elevations on the scales as "high," "very high," and so on is a subjective process that varies across different interpretative manuals and clinical situations. This text uses the K-corrected T-score ranges in Table 5.1 for describing standard clinical scale elevations on the MMPI-2. These elevation descriptions are approximations for the clinical scales and relatively rough, sometimes very rough, approximations for all of the other scales. Scores on the border between classifications are particularly open to judgment.

Once a profile has been scored and plotted onto the profile form, it can be coded. Coding is a procedure used to summarize the elevation and rank order of scales using the notation system described in Chapter 2. Coding is provided by most computerized report services and is readily accomplished by hand. Coding is useful for research purposes and profile classification, such as finding similarly configured profiles. This topic, and other scoring procedures, was described in detail in Chapter 2.

Harris-Lingoes Subscales

Elevations on certain clinical scales often can be better understood by examining the subscale components to the parent scale. To this end, Harris and Lingoes (1955, 1968) devised rational, content-based subscales that are used routinely in the analysis of MMPI-2 protocols. The MMPI-2 item pool is heterogeneous or multidimensional, meaning that most of the clinical scales are diverse in content. These subscales were therefore constructed to allow for enhanced interpretive depth regarding the behavioral/emotional disturbances associated with clinical scale elevations. A particular clinical scale score can reflect different item endorsement patterns for different individuals. For example, two individuals with an identical *T*-score of 70 on Scale 2 (Depression) may have endorsed quite different areas of content areas within the Depression items. One may have endorsed many items related to depressed mood, whereas another may have emphasized items related to somatic/vegetative symptoms, both areas having different clinical implications for the description and treatment of depression. Dissimilar endorsement patterns of items within a given scale are thought to be related to relatively distinctive behavioral patterns or correlates. Harris and Lingoes developed subscales for Scales 2, 3, 4, 6, 8, and 9 after inspecting the item content of each clinical scale, and grouped these items into categories that appeared homogeneous. That is, items that appeared to reflect a single trait or attribute were grouped into subscales that Harris and Lingoes named on the basis of their item content. However, Levitt (1989) reminded that Harris and Lingoes themselves noted that other researchers would have undoubtedly assigned somewhat different names to their scales, and that several of the subscales are less homogeneous than might be desired—meaning that they are likely measuring more than one construct. Research conducted by Childs, Dahlstrom, Kemp, and Panter (1992) also suggests that many of the Harris-Lingoes subscales are likely to be multidimensional in nature. Nevertheless, the subscales do serve as a useful aide in profile interpretation. They did not develop subscales for Scales 1 and 7 as the items on these scales appeared to be related to single constructs. Scale 1 is obvious in content and relates to bodily concerns, whereas Scale 7, also obvious in content, relates to anxiety, worry, tension, and general maladjustment/subjective distress. Scales 5 and 0 are multidimensional, but Harris and Lingoes chose not to develop subscales for these, presumably because they were added later to the instrument and were not included among the original clinical scales. Scales 5 and 0 have been divided into subscales by others, and are discussed later in this chapter.

The Harris-Lingoes subscales are described under the appropriate clinical parent scale in this chapter. The *Manual* does not provide reliability coefficients for these subscales. Because the Harris-Lingoes subscale items are all contained within the first 370 items of the test, a clinician wishing to administer an abbreviated test can still derive the scores for these subscales. In the re-standardization, only one item (item 95) was dropped that affected any of the Harris-Lingoes subscales. Specifically, the Depression subscale, Psychomotor Retardation subscale (*D2*), lost 1 item, leaving it with 14 instead of 15 items.

Most interpretive and scoring services provide scores for all of the Harris-Lingoes subscales, but when hand scoring the test, the clinician is advised to score for the subscales when the clinical scale is between a *T*-score of 60 and 80. Scores much higher or lower are unlikely to reveal any significant scatter among the subscales. The reader should note that, because 11 of the subscales contain 10 or fewer items, a change in the response to even one item can produce a large shift in the *T*-score value for that particular subscale (Caldwell, 1988). Greene (2011) similarly noted that the Harris-Lingoes subscales: "… should not be interpreted unless they exceed a *T*-score of 70, because of their restricted variance; on some subscales, endorsing one additional or one fewer item will change the client's score by five to nine *T*-score points" (p. 115).

The 28 subscales derived from the clinical scales for the Harris-Lingoes subscales vary in length from 6 to 32 items, resulting in low internal consistency values for several of them (Krishnamurthy, Archer, & Huddleston, 1995). However, most have a high degree of internal consistency. The reader is referred to Graham (1990) for a listing of the internal consistency coefficients for men and women in the re-standardization. Graham (1990) also presented data on the temporal stability of the subscales. These data show that the subscales are generally less stable than their parent scales. Gotts and Knudsen (2005) also provide internal consistency coefficients for all of the Harris-Lingoes subscales in their sample consisting primarily of hospitalized psychiatric patients.

There are also considerable intercorrelations among some of the subscales because Harris and Lingoes made no effort to eliminate item overlap. Some items may overlap up to four different subscales (Caldwell, 1988). It is reasonable to assume that the high intercorrelations among the subscales are a result of this structural redundancy: "For example, all 10 items on the Brooding subscale also appear on the Subjective Depression (D_1) subscale, and 12 of the 15 items on the Mental Dullness (D_5) subscale are on the Subjective Depression (D_1) subscale" (Greene, 2011, p. 113).

McGrath, Powis, and Pogge (1998) found that scores on the subscales co-varied significantly as a function of code pattern. The MMPI-2 profiles of 483 psychiatric inpatients were analyzed, with the results indicating that code pattern was found to be a predictor of every Harris-Lingoes subscale. McGrath et al. provided a useful table presenting the mean subscale values across 14 code patterns, thereby giving the user a basis for comparing their data against a large psychiatric sample. The value in this table lies in its ability to give the reader an opportunity to compare their individual Harris-Lingoes subscale scores to normative data for a particular code pattern, thereby indicating whether or not the subscale scores are consistent with a prototypic code pattern. Greene (2011, pp. 526–580) provides prototypic scores for the Harris-Lingoes subscales for all of the single and two-point codetypes. However, more research is needed to detail score patterns within the more common three- and four-point codes.

Most interpretive guidebooks, including this one, suggest 65 as the *T*-score value at or above which a subscale score should be interpreted, although some researchers suggest a *T*-score of 70 as more appropriate (e.g. Chojnacki & Walsh, 1994; Greene, 1991a). However, there are, and should be, exceptions to any fixed cut recommendation. Krishnamurthy et al. (1995) discuss a psychometric problem posing interpretative limitations for two of the Harris-Lingoes subscales. Specifically, *Hy1* (Denial of Social Anxiety) and *Pd3* (Social Imperturbability) contain only six items each, with relatively high mean raw score values in the re-standardization sample. Consequently, as reflected in the normative tables (A-5 and A-6 in the MMPI-2 *Manual*, Butcher et al. 2001), it is not possible for an individual (male or female) to produce a *T*-score greater than 61 on *Hy1*, or for a man to exceed a score greater than 63 or a woman greater than 64 on *Pd3*. Krishnamurthy et al. (1995) correctly concluded that using a cut score of *T*-65 for interpreting all of the Harris-Lingoes subscales will, therefore, eliminate the possibility of interpreting these particular subscales which cannot elevate to a *T*-score of 65.

Because the Harris-Lingoes subscales have been used to supplement and not to replace the interpretation of the clinical scales, clinicians have generally found the Harris-Lingoes subscales to be helpful in interpreting MMPI/MMPI-2 profiles. However, there are several concerns about their reliability and validity. The most important problems are related to the ways in which the subscales were constructed. The rational method of forming the subscales by clustering items into content areas is a subjective process, the success of which may vary. Factors contributing to this success can include the number of candidate items and the adequacy of the definition of content areas selected. However, Harris and Lingoes made no attempt to cross-validate their subscales, nor to relate them to external criteria. This type of research is greatly needed. One attempt to link behavioral correlates to the subscales failed (Calvin, 1975). Another attempt (Miller & Streiner, 1985) to reproduce the Harris-Lingoes subscales, by clinicians asked to rationally group the items, failed to duplicate more than about one third of the subscales. The nine subscales of the 28 that the judges agreed reliably on were *D3*, *Hy1*, *Hy2*, *Hy4*, *Pd1*, *Pa3*, *Sc3*, *Sc6*, and *Ma1*. Their findings suggest that the subscales' reliabilities are poor and that their interpretation may be as subjective as their development.

An investigation (Foerstner, 1986) of the factor structure of various MMPI scales (including, but not limited to, the Harris-Lingoes) showed that 10 factors accounted for the majority of variance. The first factor was named Depression. The three highest loadings on this factor were *D1* (Subjective Depression), *D4* (Mental Dullness), and *D5* (Brooding). However, *D2* (Psychomotor Retardation) and *D3* (Physical Malfunctioning) did not load at all on this factor. This suggests that these subscales may not be related to the construct of depression in the specific way Harris and Lingoes (1955, 1968) assumed. For example, *D2* and *D3* may be more associated with the vegetative than the depressed mood aspects of depressive syndromes. Likewise, the study showed that other subscales failed to appear with significant factor loadings in a way that would be expected from their parent scales. This and other studies therefore suggest that the subscales under a given parent scale may be associated with heterogeneous constructs.

Krishnamurthy et al. (1995) suggested generally reexamining the utility of the subscales and their limitations. We agree with this suggestion and note that there is a conspicuous lack of diverse norms in different settings, which are needed to aid in the interpretation of the subscales. However, at least three other investigations have sought to expand our understanding of how the Harris-Lingoes subscales operate in different settings. Wrobel (1992) found support for 16 of the 28 Harris-Lingoes subscales in a study using clinicians' ratings of outpatient therapy clients; however, the remaining 12 were not supported. Almagor and Koren (2001) investigated cross-culturally the factor structure of *D*, *Hy*, *Pd*, *Pa*, *Sc*, and *Ma* to explore the adequacy of the subscales developed for these scales. Their results did not support the structural adequacy of the subscales for Scales *D*, *Pd*, *Sc*, and *Ma*, but generally supported their suitability for scales *Hy* and *Pa*. Osberg and Poland (2001) explored the ability of the Harris-Lingoes subscales to emerge as significant correlates of inmates' past offenses. *Ma1* (amorality), *Pd2* (authority problems), and *Pd5* (self-alienation) demonstrated positive associations with criminal history. It appears that this study is the first to examine the incremental validity of the Harris-Lingoes scales within a forensic sample and is worth reviewing by the interested reader. DiLalla, Gottesman, Carey, and Bouchard (1999) in recognizing an absence of research on the heritability of the Harris-Lingoes (and Subtle–Obvious) subscales attempted to fill this gap in the literature by ambitiously studying a large sample of identical and fraternal twins who had been reared apart. They sought to understand the genetic versus environmental contributions for the subscales and found significant heritability for all 28 of the subscales. Although their study used the original MMPI, they pointed out that their results were generalizable to the MMPI-2 (with the exception of the *Pd* subscales) due to the high degree of consistency between the MMPI and MMPI-2 clinical scales. The reason for the *Pd* subscales' exception, according to DiLalla et al. (1999, p. 356), was that

> the original Harris-Lingoes *Pd* subscales for the MMPI included 14 items that were on a preliminary version of the *Pd* scale, but were not included in the final scale. The MMPI-2 Harris and Lingoes *Pd* subscales do not include the 14 "off-scale" items.

It should be noted that, in earlier research, DiLalla, Carey, Gottesman, and Bouchard (1996) found significant heritability for the clinical scales and, in their investigation examining the Harris-Lingoes subscales, their estimates were of similar magnitude to those reported previously for the full-length clinical scales.

Subtle–Obvious Subscales

Another important component of the clinical scales are the Subtle–Obvious (S–O) subscales developed by Wiener and Harmon (1946) and later published (Wiener, 1948, 1956). By rationally grouping items into categories obviously reflective of psychopathology, Wiener and Harman found that they could provide additional measures useful in determining the test-taking attitude of a respondent. They created Subtle (S) and Obvious (O) subscales for Scales 2, 3, 4, 6, and 9. For these scales, the addition of the Subtle raw score to the Obvious raw score should equal the non-*K*-corrected raw score. Subtle subscales for Scales 1, 7, and 8 were abandoned as these contain mostly obvious items. The S–O subscales do not contain equal numbers of items, and no effort was made to balance them. The subscales contain 108 subtle items and 145 obvious items. Greene (1991a, p. 79) stated that the

> empirically determined deviant response for 65 (59%) of these subtle items was in the opposite direction from what would be expected by merely inspecting item

content, whereas only 8 (5%) of these obvious items were scored in the opposite direction. These findings substantiate the subtle and obvious nature of these two groups of items, respectively.

A complete listing of the subscales' composition can be found in Friedman et al. (2001), Appendix A, Table A-2, and the linear *T*-score conversions from raw scores can be found in Appendix B, Table B-6. In Wiener and Harmon's (1946) scheme, subtle items refer to less obvious measures of psychopathology or, said another way, items that lack face validity.

Although Wiener and Harmon defined item obviousness and subtlety according to the items' relationship to psychopathology, other researchers have defined the distinction in different terms. For example, Jackson (1971) defined item subtlety as involving the respondent's ability to determine the specific trait or scale to which an item corresponds. Christian, Burkhart, and Gynther (1978) defined S–O items by having college students rate all of the MMPI items in relation to psychopathology on a five-point scale ranging from one (*very subtle*) to five (*very obvious*) with the midpoint termed neutral. For example, the mean obviousness ratings for all of the MMPI scales showed that the *F* scale and Scale 8 had the highest ratings, indicating their items are obvious in nature. The mean obviousness ratings were lowest, thereby indicating subtlety, for the *Mf* and *K* scales. In still another attempt to classify S–O items, Wales and Seeman (1968) made the distinction using a statistical assignment method. They called items obvious or *X items* if a minority of the normative group's endorsements on the items were exceeded by a larger proportion of psychiatric cases. Subtle items were referred to as *0* (*zero*) *items* when items endorsed frequently by the normative participants were exceeded in endorsement frequency by the psychiatric cases. *X* (obvious) items were therefore scored as pathological when answered in the converse direction of the majority of the normative group, and 0 (subtle) items were scored as pathological because more psychiatric cases than normative participants endorsed the items.

Many different S–O distinctions have thus been made, and Dubinsky, Gamble, and Rogers (1985) provided a useful overview of the S–O literature. They stated that regardless of the item sets used, participants instructed to manipulate their MMPI scores tend to increase or decrease their obvious item scores, but their scores for subtle items tend to move in the opposite direction. In other words, it is easier for participants to more effectively manipulate the obvious than the subtle items. This so-called paradoxical effect "is a fairly robust phenomenon and occurs with fake bad and fake good instructions with normal and psychiatric (inpatient, outpatient, and forensic) populations, and with all three of the major S/O item sets" (Hollrah, Schlottmann, Scott, & Brunetti, 1995, p. 288).

Although most of the S–O research has been conducted with the MMPI, it appears safe to generalize the research findings from the MMPI to the MMPI-2, given that only 3 of the 13 items dropped from the original test were on the S–O subscales (all on Scale 2; Hollrah et al., 1995). Specifically, Scale 2 lost one item on the Obvious and two items on the Subtle subscales.

The S–O distinction has been used for two main purposes. The first is to assess the test-taking attitude of the participant. This is generally done by examining the difference scores between the Subtle and Obvious subscales. Participants who over-report or magnify their problems may substantially elevate their Obvious scores over their Subtle scores, whereas the converse is true for participants under-reporting their problems. Greene (2000) suggested that a participant who obtains *T*-scores of 90 or more on all five Obvious subscales, and *T* scores close to 40 on all five Subtle scales, may be attempting to over-report or over-declare psychological problems, whereas the converse relationship between scores on the subscales should suggest an under-reporting response set. By summing the differences between the Obvious and Subtle subscales, a single overall measure can be used to determine reporting styles. Greene (2000) described this simple method as follows: subtract the Subtle and Obvious *T*-score values for each of the five subscales, and sum them. The mean total *T*-score difference in normal samples is in the range of 0 to −30, whereas in psychiatric samples the range is 50 to 60. There is more variability in psychiatric samples because patients admit to more problems, thereby increasing their scores on the Obvious subscales. (Note that because the majority of MMPI-2 items are scoreable [i.e. pathological], when endorsed True, the percentage of items marked True provides a gross index of psychopathology that corresponds to the sum of the differences between the Obvious and Subtle subscales.) As Greene (2000) noted, it is crucial that a high score suggestive of over-reporting be verified so as not to discount the possibility of genuine psychopathology. The second way in which the subscales are used is to provide personality correlates associated with the subscale scores. To this end, Dahlstrom (1991) provided correlates for each of the Subtle and Obvious subscales derived from partner ratings on the Katz (1968) Adjustment Scales for the 841 couples in the re-standardization sample. Many of these correlates are described under the appropriate scale descriptions in this chapter.

The issue of S–O subscale effectiveness has been the focus of much controversy. Some researchers have strongly asserted that the subtle items actually diminish the efficacy of the parent scale and fail to provide valid correlates of behavior (e. g. Nelson, 1987; Nelson & Cicchetti, 1991; Weed, Ben-Porath, & Butcher, 1990). Unfortunately, many of the studies suggesting such evidence are deeply flawed conceptually, regardless of their varying merits in terms of execution. The typical format for such studies is to select some obvious criterion such as the Beck Depression Inventory (BDI), the Symptom Checklist-90 Depression scale, or the Profile of Mood State Depression scale, and to then compare the success of, say, the Depression–Obvious or Depression–Subtle subscale (and sometimes the full Depression scale) in predicting to this criterion. The typical finding, of course, is that the obvious component of the Depression scale best predicts such an obvious criterion, the subtle component predicts poorly if at all, and the full scale is somewhere in the middle.

Although the Subtle and Obvious subscales are known to have different, in some cases markedly different, social desirability values, this factor has rarely been addressed, much less controlled, in the rather long series of studies of the S–O subscales. Each Subtle and Obvious subscale has its own unique operating characteristics and should be assessed as such. Until recently, there has not been sufficient impartial analysis of this body of S–O research. Fortunately, the situation changed with the publication of Hollrah et al.'s (1995) exhaustive and balanced review of the convergent and discriminant validities of the S–O subscales. They also raised important questions in response to some of the recent contributions to the "negative" subtle items literature, such as the article by Weed et al. (1990). The following statements summarize Hollrah et al. (1995) findings, which we endorse:

After a thorough review of the literature, some uncertainty still remains regarding the validity of the MMPI subtle items. Support for the subtle item validity varies depending on the methodology used and the particular subtle subscale investigated. Of even greater clinical relevance, addressing the empirical method of test construction, and in response to the hypothesis that the subtle items were included by sampling error (e.g. Jackson, 1971), there is as yet no consistent evidence that removing the subtle items would result in MMPI scales with greater clinical validity.

It is likely that some of the subtle items were indeed included by sampling error. However, some of the subtle items may belong on the respective scales. Likewise, many obvious items may be on their scales due to sampling error, as some studies do not support their discriminative validity. Analyses to determine validity for specific items, or at least specific scales, seems more appropriate than declaring either all or none of the subtle items as valid measures (p. 295). Hollrah et al. (1995) also stated that the main support in the literature for the subtle items lies in their ability to detect fake-good profiles in psychiatric settings.

In the first and only investigation of the heritability of the S–O subscales, DiLalla et al. (1999) studied them in a large sample of identical and fraternal twins who had been reared apart in order to determine the genetic versus environmental contributions to their scores. Analyses indicated significant heritability for all five Obvious subscales (estimates ranged from .37 to .56), and for four of the five Subtle (excluding *Pa-S*) subscales (estimates ranged from .27 to .35). The significant genetic effect found for all Subtle subscales except for *Pa-S* argues against the position that the four Subtle subscales represent nothing more than random variance. DiLalla et al. (1999) determined that of the four Subtle subscales, *Ma-S* items most approximated its original purpose in contributing significantly to the Scale 9 (*Ma*) construct, and was "positively correlated with the experience of atypical symptoms, psychotic symptoms, hostility, and hypomania, and negatively associated with depression, social maladjustment, repression, and defensiveness" (p. 364). The reader is referred to the DiLalla et al. (1999) study for further details on their findings, but their analyses suggest that the Subtle subscales should not be ignored.

Overlapping Item Content

Most of the items (245, 60 percent) on the MMPI-2 basic clinical scales (1–4 and 6–9) are also scored on the others. Items unique to a particular scale are referred to as *non-overlapping items*; those scored on more than one scale are called *overlapping items*. The overlapping items within the MMPI-2 have been a source of concern to clinicians and researchers alike. The empirical criterion approach to test construction allows the total item pool to be used repeatedly with different criterion groups. An item is retained for inclusion in the scale if it discriminates a criterion group from a normal group. The number of scales that can be derived from this method is only limited by the number of available criterion groups (Stein, 1968). The concern that arose from this construction method is that although the basic MMPI scales were capable of differentiating the normals from each of the psychiatric criterion groups, these criterion groups were not contrasted with each other. Hence, there is extensive overlap (co-variation) in item content among the

Table 5.2 Item overlap and correlations among the MMPI 2 clinical scales in the Caldwell (2007b) clinical sample

	1 (Hs)	2 (D)	3 (Hy)	4 (Pd)	5 (Mff)	5 (Mfm)	6 (Pa)	7 (Pt)	8 (Sc)	9 (Ma)	0 (Si)
1 (Hs)	–	10(1)	20	1	0	0	1	2	4	0	1
2 (D)	.82	–	13	7	2	2	2	13	10(1)	5(4)	8(1)
3 (Hy)	.80	.74	–	10	4	4(1)	4	7	8	6(2)	8(7)
4 (Pd)	.55	.59	.40	–	3(1)	3(2)	8	6	10	7(1)	11(6)
5 (Mff)	.21	.27	.22	.32	–	56(4)	2	1	4(3)	3	9(3)
5 (Mfm)	–.09	–.18	–.19	–.17	–.90	–	2	1	4(1)	3	9(4)
6 (Pa)	.58	.60	.50	.66	.32	–.22	–	4	13	6(2)	5(4)
7 (Pt)	.79	.81	.53	.72	.33	–.16	.69	–	17	3	9(1)
8 (Sc)	.79	.76	.52	.75	.31	–.11	.73	.93	–	11	6(1)
9 (Ma)	.33	.13	.10	.45	.09	.06	.37	.44	.54	–	6(5)
0 (Si)	.63	.74	.34	.54	.25	–.16	.52	.80	.76	.14	–

Note: Numbers in parentheses indicate the number of items scored in the opposite direction on the two scales. For example, Scales 1 (Hs) and 2 (D) share 10 items, one of which is scored in the opposite direction; that is, it is scored True on one scale and False on the other.

Source: Greene, Roger L., *The MMPI-2/MMPI-2-RF: An Interpretive Manual*, 3rd Edition, © 2011, p. 145. Reprinted by permission of Pearson Education, Inc., Upper Saddle River, NJ.

basic scales (and others). This structural redundancy has inflated the correlations among these scales, thereby compromising their discriminant validity for differential diagnosis (Maloney & Ward, 1976; Rosen, 1962). Structurally independent scales or scales that are less highly correlated are more desirable for purposes of separating criterion groups. Furthermore, as Rosen (1962) pointed out, it would have been more logical for purposes of differential diagnosis to have used a reference group of psychiatric patients in addition to the normals employed.

Considerable range exists in the amount of item overlap among the clinical scales, but there are many more overlapping than non-overlapping items on each scale (see Table 5.2 for a description of the item overlap and correlations among the MMPI-2 clinical scales).

The shortened or non-overlap scales must suffer from lowered reliability. Among the basic clinical scales, 66 items overlap two scales, 35 items overlap three, 4 items overlap four, and 2 items overlap five of these scales. Scale 8 (*Sc*), the longest, with 78 items, has 62 overlapping items, the greatest number for any of the basic scales, whereas Scales 1 (*Hs*) and 3 (*Hy*) overlap by 20 items, the largest number shared by any two scales. Scales 7 (*Pt*) and 8 overlap by almost as many, with 17 items in common. A perusal of the items belonging to the basic clinical scales indicates that the traditional neurotic and psychotic scales share a considerable amount of item overlap. Thirty-five items appear concurrently on at least one neurotic and one psychotic scale. Within the neurotic triad, 30 items appear on at least two of the three scales and in some instances all three. Within the psychotic tetrad, 18 items are shared by at least two of the four scales that are exclusive of the neurotic scales and one item that overlaps all four psychotic scales (item 23). Only seven pairs of scales have no items in common: *L* and *Hs, Hs* and *K, Pd* and *L, Hs* and *Mf, Hs* and *Ma, L* and *Si,* and *F* and *S.*

Historically, the degree of item overlap has long been recognized. Adams and Horn (1965) developed a set of operationally independent keys for the original MMPI scales. Welsh (1956) also attempted to develop pure or non-overlapping scales but retained items scored in opposite directions for two scales.

Following the suggestions made by Anderson and Bashaw (1966) and Wakefield et al. (1975) that items common to two or more scales measure common dimensions, three new scales were developed by Friedman et al. (1983) for the purpose of differentiating groups of neurotic, psychotic, and normal individuals. These scales are collectively referred to as the Friedman Overlap Scales (FOS). The individual scales are named the psychotic overlap scale (POS), the neurotic overlap scale (NOS), and the maladjustment overlap scale (MOS). These scales were derived in a rational manner. Items that are scored on the traditional psychotic scales (scales *Pa, Sc,* and *Ma*) were counted as items on the POS if they occurred on at least two scales within the psychotic triad and did not occur on any of the neurotic scales (scales *Hs, D, Hy,* and *Pt*). This produced 18 items that are scored on the POS. Similarly, the NOS consists of items occurring on at least two scales within the traditional neurotic triad (scales *Hs, D,* and *Hy*) plus scale *Pt* and on none of the psychotic scales. This produced 30 items that are scored on the NOS. A third scale, the maladjustment scale, was developed for purposes of discriminating normal from psychotic and neurotic patients. This consists of 35 items occurring on at least one neurotic and one psychotic scale. All 83 items on the overlap scales were scored in the standard critical direction and were included only if they were scored in the same direction on the relevant scales. Scales *L, F, K, Pd, Mf,* and *Si* were excluded from consideration in the construction of these new scales. The items and keyed responses for the Friedman Overlap Scales appear in Friedman et al. (2001), Appendix F and Appendix G, and contain the *T*-score conversions for the FOS.

Friedman et al. (1983) hypothesized that the NOS and POS would discriminate normal from neurotics and psychotics, and neurotics and psychotics from each other. MMPI data from four groups of subjects were studied. Group I consisted of 101 patients hospitalized in the psychiatric unit at Ohio State University Hospital with functional psychotic diagnoses (45 males; 56 females). Group II consisted of 85 patients with neurotic diagnoses (30 males; 55 females). Group III consisted of 76 outpatients receiving treatment at the Mayo Clinic in Rochester, Minnesota, for strictly medical (non-psychiatric) problems (37 males; 39 females). Group IV consisted of 38 college students taking introductory psychology classes at a technical institute in a large Midwestern city (12 males; 26 females). Discriminant analyses of the criterion groups were performed separately for the MMPI and the FOS. The standard MMPI (566 items) correctly classified 62 percent of both the neurotic and psychotic subjects, whereas the shorter FOS (83 items) correctly classified 54 percent of the neurotics and 52 percent of the psychotics. The MMPI and FOS were equally effective in correctly classifying 88 percent of normal controls. Based on this study and others (Gentry, Wakefield, & Friedman, 1985; Wiederstein, 1986), the Friedman psychotic and neurotic overlap scales appear to measure the general constructs of psychoticism and neuroticism.

Further validation for the construct validity of overlapping items as measured by the FOS is provided by Gentry et al. (1985) making a direct comparison of the FOS, with new

MMPI scales constructed as measures of the Eysenck Personality Questionnaire (Eysenck & Eysenck, 1975, 1985) factors of Psychoticism (P), Extraversion (E), Neuroticism (N), and the EPQ Lie scale (L) by gathering the MMPI item correlates for each of the widely validated EPQ scales (e.g. Friedman, 1984; Friedman, Wakefield, Boblitt, & Surman, 1976) in a sample of 92 undergraduates. The results showed substantial correlations among like-named scales of the new MMPI scales, the EPQ factors, and the FOS, thereby supporting the construct validity of the scales. However, further research in clinical settings is needed before the FOS and the EPQ MMPI/MMPI-2 analogue scales can be considered useful for differential diagnosis.

Basic Clinical Scales

Scale 1: Hypochondriasis (Hs)

Hs was the first scale to be published on the MMPI, primarily because of the large numbers of patients with this disorder that were available, and because the diagnosis was relatively easy to establish (McKinley and Hathaway, 1940). *Hs* measures the number of bodily complaints or somatic ailments claimed by an individual or, said another way, the degree to which a person is denying good physical health. Hypochondriasis is a disturbance involving an unrealistic interpretation of physical signs or sensations as abnormal, which leads the person to fear that he or she has a serious disease (American Psychiatric Association, 2013). The criterion group consisted of 50 inpatients with only pure, uncomplicated hypochondriasis. Patients with other coexisting disorders, like a psychosis or other physical disease, were excluded from the criterion group.

Several revisions of the scale were required before it could satisfactorily make discriminations. After the criterion group was selected, the next step in the construction of the scale was to gather the normal comparisons. Various samples within the normal group used in constructing Scale 1 were also used in the construction of the remaining basic clinical scales. The first sample consisted of 109 men and 153 women of the 724 Minnesota normals, ranging in age from 26 to 43, who were visitors at the University of Minnesota Hospitals. As noted earlier (Chapter 1), participants were eliminated if they were currently under the care of a physician. The second normal sample consisted of 265 (151 men; 114 women) unmarried entering freshmen who were receiving precollege guidance counseling at the University of Minnesota Testing Bureau. Unfortunately, more is known about the demographics of the normals used in constructing Scale 1 than for the criterion participants, whose gender proportions and other information is unreported. McKinley and Hathaway (1940), however, did state that participants "were deleted, however, to exclude the extremes of age or other obviously disturbing influences" (p. 256).

The empirical method was primarily used to identify items that discriminated the normals and physically ill people from the 50 patients in the hypochondriasis criterion group. An item was considered for inclusion on the scale if the normals and patients in the criterion group differed in the frequency of response to the item by at least twice the standard error of the proportions of true-false responses of the two groups (Greene, 2011). However, McKinley and Hathaway (1940) did reject a few of the items on a non-empirical basis if they thought the item drifted too far from the construct of hypochondriasis.

An initial version of the scale consisted of 55 items, but it required further refinement because of the high numbers of psychiatric patients without clinically observed hypochondriasis who also obtained significant Scale 1 elevations. To correct for this occurrence, 50 psychiatric patients without hypochondriacal complaints, but with high scores on the initial version of Scale 1, were compared with the criterion hypochondriacs. Items that discriminated these two groups became known as the Correction for Hypochondriasis (CH) scale. The CH scale consisted of 48 items. Experimentation with the CH items by assigning them different weights failed to improve the performance of the scale. Ultimately, the maximum discrimination was achieved when CH was subtracted from the preliminary *Hs*. As Greene (2011) described it, "for each of these correction items that an individual answered in the non-hypochondriacal direction, one point was subtracted from the total score on Scale 1" (p. 8). Cross-validation with the *CH* scale reliably separated normals from hypochondriacal patients. The hospitalized medical sample demonstrated that the presence of physical disease did not significantly raise scores on the scale.

A final version of Scale 1 occurred when McKinley and Hathaway attempted to improve the separation between Scales 1 and 3. Many correction items were dropped, as were original Scale 1 items that did not stand up on further analysis. The addition of 0.5 *K* helped to improve the ability of *Hs* to make accurate diagnostic discriminations, and commercially available profile sheets provide a space to add the 0.5 *K* value to Scale 1.

The final scale consisted of 33 items related to various aspects of bodily functions, including generalized aches and pains, and concerns about different body regions. The re-standardization leading to MMPI-2 prompted the omission of one objectionable item, the modification of three items for grammatical clarification (e.g. tense), the modernization of one item for idiom or usage, and the simplification of one item. The content of the scale is considered obvious, with no subtle items, meaning that an individual wishing to deny good health can readily do so. Given its face validity, Wiener and Harmon chose not to propose S–O subscales for *Hs*. Likewise, Harris and Lingoes (1955) did not discover enough item heterogeneity to form subscales. As Greene (2011) noted, factor analyses of *Hs* in several different populations have consistently identified poor physical health and gastrointestinal difficulties as the two major factors in this scale. More generally, the items on the scale reflect head and sensory complaints, poor appetite, poor general health, upper gastrointestinal complaints, weakness, tiredness, easy fatigability, and cardiac complaints. As Nichols (2011) points out, specific complaints or symptoms exceed vague complaints on a ratio of about 2:1.

The deviant direction for 66 percent (21 of 32 items) of the items is False. Therefore, a False response set tends to elevate the scale. Most items on Scale 1 overlap the other neurotic scales, *D* and *Hy*. Only four items overlap Scale 8 (Schizophrenia); one item overlaps Scale 6 (Paranoia). Twenty of the 32 items on Scale 1 are also scored on Scale 3 (*Hy*); thus an elevated score on either scale tends to raise the other. Only eight items are unique (non-overlapping) to Scale 1. (See Table 5.2 for a description of the overlapping content for Scale 1 and the other clinical scales.)

Greene (2011) stated that the construct validity of Scale 1 is supported by the fact that Wiggins' (1966) Poor Health and Organic Symptoms content scales from the MMPI have 12 and 18 items in common, respectively, with MMPI-2 *Hs*. The MMPI-2 Health

Concerns content scale (HEA; Butcher, Graham, Williams, & Ben-Porath, 1990) shares 23 of its 36 items with Scale 1.

Increasing elevations on Scale 1 correspond to increasing bodily complaints. Neurotic individuals with bodily preoccupations tend to endorse a diffuse set of bodily complaints, whereas actually ill patients without psychological disturbance contain their item endorsements to the specific physical areas concerning them. Greene (2011) reported that physically ill patients usually obtain only moderate *T*-score elevations between 55 and 60. Patients with actual physical illness who are distressed are more likely to elevate Scale 2 (Depression) than Scale 1.

The normals in the re-standardization sample averaged a raw score of approximately five and six for men and women, respectively, on Scale 1. As normal people age, their Scale 1 scores tend to increase only slightly, approximately two to three items over the life span (Colligan et al., 1989), and five to six *T*-scores in clinical clients, as reported in Greene (2011) using a large sample from Alex Caldwell's (2007b) data base. Regarding education and Scale 1 scores, Greene reported that in both normal and clinical patients, scores on Scale 1 increase five to ten *T*-scores as the number of years of education decrease. Scale 1 elevations have also been noted to occur in chronic pain patients (who also elevate Scale 3) and have been associated with high post-treatment pain intensity and a failure to return to normal activity levels (Prokop, 1988). Generally, a high elevation on Scale 1 is a negative predictor of treatment response (Prokop, 1988). If the clinician sees an excessively low Scale 1 score, such as a raw score of zero, interpretation can range from the individual simply being unusually free of bodily complaints and concerns to being pathologically unconcerned with or unaware of his or her bodily functions. The lack of psychological-mindedness so often cited with high scores on this scale has been seen in a few rare cases with unusually low *Hs* raw scores. Such scores may also indicate the denial of any physical problems because of a counterphobic defense.

When examining Scale 1 in a profile, it is important to note the amount of *K* added. Because 0.5 *K* is added to Scale 1, a person may have important hypochondriacal concerns, despite a non-elevated score, because of a low *K* value.

Although some MMPI experts consider that Scale 1 elevations may reflect transient symptoms, such as the flu or a cold (Duckworth, 1979), it is generally considered a stable scale, with test–retest coefficients for psychiatric cases ranging from .79 to .86 for up to a two-week period and from .38 to .65 for a one-year interval (Dahlstrom et al., 1975).

Hunsley et al.'s (1988) large-scale meta-analysis of MMPI reliability studies in a wide variety of populations conducted between 1970 and 1981 found an average internal consistency of .79 across 70 studies. They also reported an average test–retest reliability of .78 for 16 studies, with time intervals from one day to two years. Butcher et al. (2001) reported reliability data for a subset of the re-standardization sample that included 82 normal men and 111 normal women retested at an average interval of 8.5 days (*Mdn* = 7 days), and found test–retest correlations for men and women of .76 and .74, respectively, again illustrating the stability or characterologic nature of the scale. Internal consistency estimates (Cronbach's coefficient alpha) of .77 and .81 were reported for men and women, respectively.

Scale 2: Depression (D)

Scale 2 (*D*) was designed to measure the presence and depth of symptomatic depression, a mood state characterized by low morale, feelings of hopelessness or worthlessness, slowing of thought and action, and occasional preoccupations with death and suicide (Dahlstrom et al., 1972). *D* is considered to be a mood scale (state vs. trait) and is therefore sensitive to transient and even very brief emotional states, including diminished morale and efficiency. For this reason, it is useful in measuring response to treatment. Scale 2 can be considered "an index of how comfortable and secure clients feel about themselves and their environment, with higher scores indicating dissatisfaction" (Greene, 2011, p. 110). In fact, the scale is generally more sensitive to bona fide health/illness states than Scale 1 scores (Nichols, 2011).

Scale 2 is the most frequently elevated scale in the MMPI-2 and the most frequent high point in adult psychiatric populations (Nichols, 1988). In adolescent patients, Scale 2 appears second only to Scale 4 (Psychopathic Deviate) in high-point frequency on the MMPI (Marks et al., 1974).

Using a large clinical sample from Caldwell (2007a), Greene (2011) listed 15 MMPI-2 scales with the highest correlations with *D*. He then organized these scales into four general categories: (1) symptoms of depression and anxiety; (2) fatigue and lack of energy; (3) general subjective distress and negative affect; and (4) poor physical health and multiple physical symptoms. Nichols (2009) has developed a revised set of subscales for Scale 2 described in the next section on the Harris-Lingoes subscales.

Five participant groups were used to construct *D*. However, most of the 60 items contained on the original scale were derived by comparing normals (i.e. participants without observable depression) with a group of 50 patients who were carefully diagnosed as being in the depressed phase of a manic-depressive psychosis (Hathaway & McKinley, 1942). Because some non-depressed participants obtained elevated scores, a correction factor was derived (as was done in the construction of Scale 1) by comparing item endorsement patterns of 40 normals, who earned elevated scores on an early version of the Depression scale, with a group of 50 patients without observable depressive signs but who also scored high. Eleven items differentiating the two groups became correction items that were included in the final scale. A depressed normal group was also used in the derivation of the scale "to help establish the meaning of more intermediate scale values between the normal and criterion groups, which would have been impossible if only the two extreme groups were contrasted" (Greene, 2011, p. 109). Hathaway and McKinley (1940, as cited in Dahlstrom & Dahlstrom, 1980, p. 26) described the final selection of *D* items in the following way:

First, each depressive item had to show a progressive increase in frequency from the normal groups through the depressed normal group to the criterion group since it was assumed that the depressed normals would be less than the criterion cases but more than the general normals. In all items primarily indicating depression, the difference in percentage between the normal and the criterion was 2.5 or more times its standard error. Second, the non-depressed group percentage for the item was required to approach that for normals. After careful analysis of all percentages for each of the 504 items, 60 items were chosen as the final depression scale.

Although the criterion group for Scale 2 consisted of individuals afflicted with a severe depressive illness characterized as psychotic, Hathaway and McKinley considered depression to be the cardinal feature of their disturbance. Dahlstrom et al. (1972, p. 187) stated that

> although the scale was devised on a largely psychotic group of patients, it became clear in the early research that the items reflected depressive mood changes on a neurotic basis in fact, any depressive reaction, no matter what the underlying character structure or adjustment status of a patient might be.

Greene (2011) stated that Scale 2 is sensitive to, but not specific to, depressive mood disorders. This explains why *D* is so often elevated in profiles where depression may not be the primary diagnosis, but is prominent in understanding the client.

The original MMPI *D* had 60 items, but the revision leading to the MMPI-2 deleted 3 items pertaining to religious matters. The resulting 57-item MMPI-2 scale also underwent modifications on 2 items, one to eliminate sexist wording and one to modernize usage. Approximately two thirds of the items are keyed False (37 False; 20 True). The All-False response set will therefore inflate Scale 2 scores, as well as the other scales in the neurotic triad (Scales 1, 2, and 3). Scale 2 shares 47 of its 57 items fairly evenly with the other clinical scales (Dahlstrom et al., 1972). Only 13 items are unique to the scale. *D* shares only 10 items with the MMPI-2 *DEP* content scale. These two scales measure different aspects of depressive symptoms, so they should not be used interchangeably. Scale 2 shares 13 items with Scales 7 and 9 and 8 items with Scales 1 and 8, respectively. Wiener and Harmon (1946) considered the majority of *D* items obvious. Thirty-nine items are obvious and 18 items are subtle, although the two sets intercorrelate at .80 (Nichols, 2011).

Test–retest reliability data for Scale 2, as reported in the *Manual* (Butcher et al., 2001), were based on 82 normal men and 111 normal women, retested at about one week, which yielded correlations of .79 and .80, respectively. Dahlstrom et al. (1972) reported lower test–retest stability data on clinical groups for MMPI Scale 2, which is expected, given the greater emotional instability of clinical patients. In Hunsley et al.'s (1988) large-scale meta-analysis of MMPI reliability studies using a wide variety of populations conducted between 1970 and 1981, an average test–retest reliability of .78 was reported for 16 studies, with time intervals from one day to two years. Hunsley et al. also reported an average internal consistency of .81 across 74 studies. Internal consistency estimates for *D* derived from the re-standardization sample (Butcher et al., 2001) yielded correlations of .59 and .64 for men and women, respectively.

The 57 *D* items reflect a number of concerns related to depression, including a loss of appetite and energy, distractibility, loss of self-confidence, lack of interest in things, denial of happiness or personal worth, and physical symptoms (e.g. sleep disturbance and gastrointestinal complaints).

In general, as Scale 2 scores elevate into the clinically significant range ($T > 65$), the greater the probability the person is suffering depressive symptoms. Severity is often a function of scale elevation, but it is also reflected in other clinical scale elevations. Rarely is Scale 2 elevated in isolation. Analysis of other clinical scale elevations, as well as the subscales and supplementary scales, helps to determine the quality of the depression.

Scale 2 not only reflects the presence and degree of various forms of symptomatic depression but also basic personality features of hyper-responsibility, high personal standards, and intro-punitiveness, which can predispose an individual to experience depression (Butcher et al., 1989; Dahlstrom et al., 1972). Individuals scoring in the extremely high range ($T \geq 91$) likely have endorsed a wide range of depressive content reflecting severe withdrawal, a dependent state, and serious suicidal risk.

Although several studies have provided correlates for high-scoring psychiatric patients, very low scores ($T < 40$) should not necessarily be interpreted in psychiatric patients as reflecting the converse of depression, such as an active, enthusiastic, optimistic, socially outgoing person. These very-low-score descriptors are more likely to apply to normals than psychiatric patients (Keiller & Graham, 1993). However, Venn (1988) reported pathological correlates in a sample of low-scoring adult men on Scales 2 and 0 (Social Introversion) who took the MMPI as part of employment screening. Low-scoring participants on both Scales 2 and 0 had indications of probable character pathology (e.g. impulsive behavior and an arrest record). As stated earlier, Keiller and Graham suggested that low scores may have different meanings for psychiatric outpatients and inpatients and that low scores may be more likely associated with unfavorable characteristics in psychiatric samples. Further research on low scores in different samples across settings (e.g. forensic, medical, and employment) is called for in order to understand the generalizability of their findings.

Harris-Lingoes Subscales

The reader is reminded to be alert about the brevity of several of the subscales and to use caution in interpreting subscale scores below a *T*-score of 70 for all of the Harris-Lingoes subscales. Harris and Lingoes (1955) developed five subscales for the Depression scale on the MMPI, which are identical on the MMPI-2. The five subscales for the *D* are: Subjective Depression (*D1*), Psychomotor Retardation (*D2*), Physical Malfunctioning (*D3*), Mental Dullness (*D4*), and Brooding (*D5*). These subscales are extensively overlapping,

> Of the 49 items that appear on one of the subscales, 23 appear on two or more, for a total of 55 overlaps. *D1*, for example, overlaps with *D2* (8 items), *D3* (3 items), and *D4* (12 items), and contains all 10 of the *D5* items. Five *D2* items overlap with *D4* and two with *D5*; *D4* and *D5* overlap by four items.
>
> (Nichols, 2011, p. 102)

Taken together, the 55 total overlaps among the *D* subscales averages 11 overlaps each which, according to Nichols (2011), is far more than for any of the other Harris-Lingoes sets. Eight (14 percent) of the Scale 2 items appear on none of the subscales. Nichols (2009) created a set of five alternative *D* subscales, named: *Dr1*—Depressed Mood; *Dr2*—Inhibition of Aggression; *Dr3*—Somatic Malaise; *Dr4*—Cognitive Infirmity; and *Dr5*—Social Vulnerability. These subscales have at least two advantages over the original Harris-Lingoes subscales.

First, the number of overlaps has been reduced to six, averaging 1.2 per scale; any given pair of scales average only 0.6 overlapping items (range: 0–3), amounting to

5 percent of the average scale length. Second, each D item appears on at least one subscale. A possible disadvantage is that two of the new subscales contain only eight items (vs. a minimum of 10 items for the Harris D subscales).

(Nichols, 2011, p. 104)

The reader interested in obtaining these alternative D subscales should contact Nichols.

D1: Subjective Depression (32 Items)

The longest of the subscales, containing more than half of the *D* items with 17 items scored False direction and 15 scored True, *D1* indicates obvious distress, such as feeling unhappy, pessimistic, suicidal, joyless, worrying; having sleeping, morale, and concentration difficulties; and generally not feeling worthwhile. Other descriptors include feeling easily hurt by criticism and a lack of energy for coping with problems (Caldwell, 1988; Nichols & Greene, 1995). Dysphoria is the mood state typified by this subscale, and diagnoses of depression or dysthymia often accompany elevations on this subscale as well as the other depression subscales (Graham, Ben-Porath, & McNulty, 1999). Caldwell (1988) stated that this subscale captures the "general misery of depression" (p. 16). The worrying aspect of the scale is found in the fact that all 10 of the items on the brooding subscale (*D5*) are contained within *D1*. Wrobel (1992) reported the following correlates to be applicable to high *D1* scorers: pessimism, poor morale, low self-esteem, lack of energy for coping, feelings of psychological inertia, and a lack of joy in doing things. Graham et al. (1999) also reported that high *D1* scorers feel overwhelmed and unable to cope with stress. The reader is referred to Nichols (2011) for an extensive listing of all the Harris-Lingoes subscales correlations, with several content and supplementary scales.

Low scorers on this subscale tend not to report a loss of interest, or general depressive feelings.

The items are predominantly obvious and *D1* is almost completely contained in and virtually identical to D-O (Nichols, 2011). As an analog of Scale 2, *D1* is likely the most sensitive MMPI-2 scale to short-term fluctuations in mood.

D2: Psychomotor Retardation (14 Items)

The items on this subscale reflect inhibited aggression and a lack of energy, vigor, and initiative (Nichols & Greene, 1995). Four of the items are scored True, 10 False. Wrobel (1992) found a low but significant correlation with a lack of participation in social interactions. Harris and Lingoes also attributed nonparticipation in social relations and immobilization to elevated scores. Nichols (2011) views *D2* as the inhibition component of Scale 2—it only weakly correlates with its contrastingly named Scale 9 counterpart, Ma, at −.15. According to Nichols (2011), the inhibitions induced appear to be more emotional than behavioral. Psychiatric outpatient women in the Graham et al. (1999) study sample were also described as being not very competitive. Nichols and Greene (1995) suggested that *D2* emphasizes social withdrawal and rigid controls against hostile or aggressive expressions. In essence, this subscale is tapping a dimension of passivity and submissiveness (Friedman et al., 2001). Caldwell (1988) asserted that elevations on

D2 may reflect indecision at least as much as physiologic slowing. This is consistent with the moderate correlation Nichols and Greene report between Mental Dullness (*D4*) and *D2*.

Levitt (1989) suggested that a low *D2* score, when other depression indexes are high, may point to a suicide potential, presumably because the person has the energy to act on his or her suicidal feelings. However, Graham et al. (1999) also found that females with high scores on *D2* were described by their therapists as having suicidal ideation.

D3: Physical Malfunctioning (11 Items)

D3 subscale encompasses the somatic component of Scale 2, although Levitt (1989) opined that it contains too few items to be useful clinically. *D3* is highly correlated with Scale 1 (*Hs*), with 7 of its 11 items overlapping Scales 1 and 3. Four of the 11 items on *D3* are keyed True, 7 False. Its content predictably reflects the vegetative features of depression, such as loss of appetite, change in weight, weakness, and constipation (Caldwell, 1988; Nichols, 2011). High scores most likely reflect a preoccupation with oneself (Wrobel, 1992). A sense of feeling unrelieved from one's discomforts and pessimistic about ever feeling well is suggested. Caldwell (1988) speculated the *D3* may touch on the fear that one may never be restored to health, that there is nothing to look forward to but further physical decline; *D3* is probably the most specific indicator of depressive somatization (Nichols & Greene, 1995). It is not surprising that the Lassitude–Malaise subscale (*Hy3*) and *D3* correlate strongly in a group of psychiatric inpatients and outpatients (Nichols & Greene, 1995).

Graham et al. (1999) reported that women psychiatric outpatients were described by their therapists as lacking energy and having a low sex drive. Furthermore, they were described as lacking interest and aspirations. Both men and women who score high on *D3* were seen as having difficulty with concentration although it is interesting to note that concentration difficulties were not generally reported by Graham et al. (1999) for patients scoring high on Mental Dullness (*D4*). Low D3 scores most likely reflect that the individual does not feel physically handicapped and may, in fact, feel very good.

D4: Mental Dullness (15 Items)

D4 reflects the cognitive enfeeblement of depression; it is the mental counterpart of *D3*. Eight of the items are keyed True, seven False. High scores imply a loss of interest, a sense of mental failure or decline, and the depletion of energy needed to accomplish mental work (Nichols, 2011). Caldwell (1988) referred to this scale as the "mental fog" (p. 17) of depression. The themes he reported in the subscale consist of: (a) "losing one's mind," that is, being easily distracted, unable to comprehend what one reads, and suffering memory and judgment problems (consistent with Wrobel's, 1992, finding of a distrust of one's psychological functioning accompanying high scores, but not with the Graham et al., 1999, investigation of psychiatric outpatients which did not reveal marked concentration difficulties in high *D4* scorers); (b) trouble initiating tasks, reduced energy, and a lack of confidence; and (c) a feeling of diminished interest and involvement in life (consistent with Wrobel's, 1992, findings of feelings of unresponsiveness and mistrust of one's psychological functioning being associated with high *D4* scores). *D4* and *D2* share five items in common. *D4* also shares four items with the Lack of Ego Mastery, Cognitive subscale (*Sc3*) and five items with the Lack of Ego Mastery, Conative subscales (*Sc4*), both reflecting mental insufficiency (Nichols and Greene, 1995). Graham et al. (1999) reported that for high *D4* scorers both men and women outpatients reported a history of physical abuse, while men reported being sexually abused. Women outpatients were also described as suspicious and as being overly sensitive to criticism. According to Caldwell (1988), low *D4* scorers do not complain that their judgment is impaired or that they are unable to be as cognitively efficient as others.

D5: Brooding (10 Items)

D5 and the *DEP* content scale for the MMPI-2 overlap by eight items. Eight of the items are keyed in the True direction, two False. The *D5* content suggests that one feels not worthwhile, useless, lacking energy and, when elevated in conjunction with a high Scale 2 score, adds to the hopelessness of the depression (Caldwell, 1988). Irritability and a proneness to rumination are likely correlates (Wrobel, 1992). Interestingly, men but not women among the Graham et al. (1999) psychiatric outpatients were described as worriers. However, Levitt (1989) was correct to report that the scale title, "Brooding," appears derived from a single item (item 215). The other seven items are the most heavily saturated with the obvious depressive content among the Scale 2 subscales.

Nichols and Greene (1995) stated that *D5* is a measure of general distress and is sensitive to anhedonia. They also note that *D5* can predict the intensity and pervasiveness of guilt, which is also reflected in the Self-Alienation subscale (*Pd5*). Specifically, guilt will be more clearly identifiable when *D5* and *Pd5* are both elevated above the *OBS* content scale, as well as above the level of other distress scales, such as Anxiety (*A*) and the following content scales: Anxiety (*ANX*), Fears (*FRS*), Depression (*DEP*), Work Interference (*WRK*), and Negative Treatment Indicators (*TRT*). Nichols and Greene (1995) underscored the fact that *D5* is saturated with first-factor variance (i.e. general maladjustment), which places an emphasis on feeling miserable and upset.

D5 is highly correlated with Scale 7 (.89), *Hy3* (.81), *Pd5* (.82), *Sc4* (.85), *ANX* (.84), *DEP* (.92), *LSE* (.80), and *NEGE* (.80). "It combines a sense of being easily upset with that of misery and agitation. For interpretive purposes, it is most useful when compared with *D1* rather than the full Scale 2" (Nichols, 2011, pp. 103–104). All 10 of the *D5* items overlap with *D1* (Subjective Depression), with *D5* expressing more anger and extra-punitiveness than *D1*. Caldwell indicated that a low *D5* score, especially with an accompanying low *T*-score on *D*, may indicate a capacity to respond with resiliency to life's stresses.

Scale 2: Subtle–Obvious Subscales

About two thirds of the 57 items on Scale 2 have obvious content. The Depression-Obvious subscale (*D-O*) has 39 items, of which 17 are keyed True, 22 False. Depression-Subtle (*D-S*) has 18 items, of which 3 are keyed True, 15 False. The item composition, scoring keys for the S–O subscales, and linear *T*-score conversions for all of the Wiener-Harmon subscales for men and women can be found in Friedman et al. (2001, Appendix A.2, pp. 539–551, and Appendix B.6, pp. 506–608).

Caldwell (1988) described the *D-O* items as covering a "broad depressive spectrum" (p. 15), including feeling unhappy, worried, and useless; crying easily; and having sleep and appetite problems. The 18 subtle items include a cluster pertaining to the inhibition of anger, aggression, and self-assertion. Nichols and Greene (1995) reported a similar description, adding that the *D-S* subscale reflects an inhibition or suppression of irritability and sadism in emotional life and fantasy. Later, Nichols (2011) was even more specific in stating that *D-S* is a subtle measure, not of depression, as such, but of the inhibition of crude affect. *D-S* reflects passivity, sub-assertiveness, and tolerance for dominance/subordination. *D-S* and Aggressiveness (*AGGR*) (low) are likely the most useful measures of inhibited aggression. *D-S* overlaps *D2* by seven items and is moderately correlated with *ANG* (–.59), *Re* (.57), *ANG1* (–.57), *Ma4* (–.57), *TPA* (–.56), *TPA2* (–.55), and *ASP* (–.55).

Other subtle items report lacking perseverance and "never feeling euphoria or even unusually good" (Caldwell, 1988, p. 15). W. G. Dahlstrom (personal communication, 1997) suggested that the subtle items may reflect a predisposition to develop the disorder that the parent scale is measuring. For example, an individual scoring low on *D-O* but high *D-S* may have a tendency to develop depression. In general, individuals with greater levels of maladjustment tend to endorse more obvious items, whereas defensive responders or persons with milder forms of psychopathology tend to endorse primarily subtle items in describing their feelings (Dahlstrom et al., 1972).

Hollrah et al.'s (1995) review of the S–O convergent validity literature led them to caution that *D-S* is not a valid measure of depression. They stated, however, that the decision to use only *D-O* should be evaluated with caution. They found *D-O* to be better than the full *D* scale when measuring obvious depression symptoms. They also reviewed studies that show support for both the full *D* scale and the discriminant validity of the *D-S* subscale.

Dahlstrom (1991) reported several correlates for men and women for each of the S–O subscales derived from partner ratings in the re-standardization sample. For *D-O*, trouble sleeping, unrealistic attitude about abilities, worries about health, a lack of energy, multiple fears, a tendency to get sad, a lack of confidence, and complaints of body aches all characterized male and female participants. For women scoring high, the following descriptors were generated: nervous, not cheerful, not pleasant or relaxed, cries easily, concerned about death, and avoiding contact with others.

D-S subscale elevations were associated with the following descriptors for both men and women: does not swear or curse, dislikes flirting, cooperative, thoughtful of others, pleasant and relaxed, and attends religious functions. Specific to women only, the following descriptions were given: self-confident, few fears and bad dreams, does not break things when angry, not lacking in emotional control, not stubborn, does not worry about the future, and gets along well with others. Men were described as: not moody or bossy, friendly, does not take prescription drugs, not argumentative or critical of others, and does not get angry and yell.

Caldwell (1988) reported that low *D-O* scores reflect an individual who has ample self-confidence and feels that life is worthwhile, whereas low *D-S* scores reflect willfulness and assertion, and the capacity to feel anger as it is situationally appropriate.

The MMPI and Suicide

It has often been reported as important to consider suicide risk when Scale 2 is prominently elevated. However, Greene (2011) reported that less than 8 percent of the clients in a large clinical sample with spike 2 codetypes actually endorsed items directly inquiring about suicidal ideation and attempts. This is less frequent than most other codetypes. Nevertheless, items 150, 303, 506, 520, 524, and 530 should be routinely reviewed regardless of the Scale 2 elevation, as these items all pertain to suicide (Glassmire, Stolberg, Greene, & Bongar 2001, Suicidal Potential Scale). Nichols (2010) developed the Hopelessness Scale (*Hp*) regarding suicide risk, as hopelessness is a strong predictor of suicidal ideation, intent, and completed suicide. His 12-item *Hp* scale was derived by inspecting item-total correlations for each of the six suicide items listed above. The reader is advised to contact Nichols for a copy of this potentially useful scale and its psychometric properties. Koss and Butcher (1973) and Koss, Butcher and Hoffmann (1976) also identified suicide items by examining the MMPI responses from 723 male Veterans Administration clients in crisis situations, including those experiencing depressed-suicidal ideation. Of their 78 critical items, 22 pertain to depressed-suicidal ideation with this item set augmented by some of the new MMPI-2 items. Four items, 303, 506, 520, and 524, indicate a self-report of past or present suicidal ideation or behavior. Because depression as measured by Scale 2 and suicide are linked, and given the extent of public concern about the high suicide rate in the the USA with suicides occurring at two to three times the rate of homicides (Friedman, 2008), it is important to briefly discuss the prediction of suicide from the MMPI-2. A fuller discussion regarding multiple MMPI-2 indices and prediction factors can be found in a review of suicide and the MMPI inventories by Friedman, Archer, and Handel (2005) from which much of the following discussion is derived.

Decades of research have shown that the MMPI cannot predict suicide, but several authors have argued that the prediction of suicide potential, rather than the prediction of actual completed suicide, remains an important assessment challenge. Clopton (1979) succinctly stated that the "...research question of most clinical relevance is whether MMPI data are of assistance in the identification of individuals who will later attempt suicide, not whether MMPI data are sufficient for such identification" (p. 162). This statement is consistent with the current literature on the prediction of dangerousness, which is based in great part on psychiatric and forensic subjects. The current thinking about risk has taught us to move away from trying to predict specific acts of dangerousness or violence in an open-ended time frame. We have come to think in terms of evaluating the probability of an individual perpetrating an act of violence in a briefer and defined window of time, dependent on the knowledge that many factors, which can shift or change rapidly, influence the propensity for violence. The move to a risk assessment model from dangerousness prediction, per se, can also be applied to MMPI-2 interpretation. As Friedman et al. (2005, p. 65) state:

Numerous factors influence an individual to think and behave in a suicidal (or homicidal) manner, including, but not limited to, changes in personal circumstances, such as loss of support from significant others, irreversible business losses, or the worsening of a medical condition with intractable pain. The exacerbation of severe psychiatric symptoms may also increase suicide risk, such as command hallucinations, intolerable depressive symptoms, or alcohol and/or drug intoxication. The value of the MMPI lies in being part of a risk assessment mosaic that includes interview data, collateral sources of information, and other psychometric data to help serve the mission of estimating suicide potential rather than the prediction of actual suicide. In this fashion, the test data can help inform and guide a risk management strategy.

The prediction of suicide is too complex a phenomenon to be measured reliably by any single variable or even a combination of indicators on the MMPI-2 or any other psychometric instrument. The low base rate problem is a critical factor to consider, but other ingredients come into play, such as an individual's motivation to report accurately their feelings and their own self-awareness of their intentions. In some cases, attempts or gestures are impulsive acts, perhaps unleashed by the disinhibiting effects of a substance such as alcohol, cocaine, or a barbiturate. The prevention of suicide or suicide attempts, commonly associated with mental illness, falls well within the province of the responsibilities of mental health practitioners. Psychologists and psychiatrists are looked on by the public and courts to make difficult decisions about the risk status of individuals, frequently as a core element in involuntary hospitalization decisions. The MMPI-2 is used clinically and forensically, and it is not uncommon for a hospital and the clinicians involved in treatment of a suicidal patient to be sued for malpractice, often resulting from incidents in which a patient, either discharged or given a leave or pass, subsequently committed suicide. As Friedman et al. (2005, p. 66) noted:

> The MMPI and other test data are usually obtained and examined following these incidents for signs or markers that could have alerted the clinicians and diagnosticians that the patient was a high-risk or at-risk candidate for attempting or completing suicide. These so-called "psychological autopsies" force clinicians to re-examine their decision-making process, and they often rely on the research literature to justify their judgments.

Nichols (1988) concluded that the many research investigations conducted during the 30 years preceding his review produced few valid correlates of, and nothing of substantive clinical value, for predicting suicide with the MMPI. If researchers are to be more productive in this area, Nichols recommended collaborative efforts to build up adequate-size samples of individuals who had completed suicide within a short time frame (e.g. one week) after having completed the MMPI. He opined that since suicide

> may more closely approximate the final common pathway of a concatenation of demographic, situational, and personologic variables than a unitary trait disposition, the constitution of suicidal and appropriate comparison groups may require the institution of more extensive and sophisticated inclusion criteria and controls than those found tolerable in previous studies.
>
> (Nichols, 1988, p. 103)

Unfortunately, few studies have been able to approach the degree of sophistication recommended by Nichols, and he pessimistically concluded that even if such work was to be done, "the clinical payoff for even valid and reliable MMPI correlates of suicide, assuming that such might eventually be found, is most unlikely to compensate the research efforts necessary to develop them" (p. 104). However, such test correlates, even if unable to accurately predict suicide, would nevertheless add to our understanding of suicidal behavior.

Suicide studies with the MMPI-2 vary along a number of dimensions. These investigations have examined MMPI/MMPI-2 data in terms of items, scales, and profile configurations or code patterns, with the subjects of these studies varying from suicide ideators, threateners, gesturers, and attempters, to successful suicides. Other important participant factors include the age, gender, and personal characteristics of the person, such as his or her voluntary versus involuntary hospitalization status (Leonard, 1977).

The available literature from the MMPI, MMPI-2, and MMPI-A provides little evidence that items, scales, or profile configurations are of practical use in the critical determination involving an adolescent's or adult's probability of engaging in suicidal behavior. Although substantial research has shown that the various forms of the MMPI are not directly useful in the prediction of suicide, numerous researchers and authors have argued that the instrument is useful in prediction to more common aspects related to suicidal phenomena, particularly the occurrence of suicidal ideation. The degree to which the endorsement of suicidal ideation on the MMPI-2/RF (or MMPI-A) is likely related to the occurrence of actual suicidal behaviors is probably mediated by numerous factors, including the individual's history or prior suicidal behaviors, family history, access to lethal methods, and the presence or absence of a variety of personality features and/or psychiatric symptoms including depression, impulsivity, alienation, and the occurrence of anger or rage. Suicidal ideation is relatively common among numerous psychiatric groups and even among adolescents in the MMPI-A normative sample. While the MMPI-2/RF (and MMPI-A) may not be able to accurately predict the occurrence of suicidal behavior, these tests have potential usefulness in uncovering the presence of suicidal ideation in adolescents and adults, and can be of significant value in performing an overall assessment of suicide risk or potential. The MMPI-2/RF should always be combined with multiple sources of other data including clinical interview, comprehensive psychosocial history taking, and results from a variety of other psychometric instruments in any evaluation of suicide issues.

Scale 3: Hysteria (Hy)

The diagnosis of hysteria, although common in the 1930s, was difficult to establish because clear-cut criteria in the clinical concept were lacking, hysterical phenomena were concurrent with other neurotic symptoms in the same individual, and there was diagnostic uncertainty of hysterical reactions in individuals who were suspected of having organic disease (McKinley & Hathaway, 1944). Thus, the 60-item *Hy* scale was originally developed to aid in the diagnosis of hysteria and to measure the degree to which a patient is likely to develop symptoms of conversion. Conversion symptoms included "fits" (e.g. fainting, blackouts, and pseudoseizures), abdominal pain, and stress vomiting; amnesia, fugue, and somnambulism; paralysis; contractures (e.g. writer's cramp); tremors; speech irregularities (e.g. aphonia/mutism, stammer, stutter, lisp, whispering, or other mannerisms/affectations); spasmodic movements; awkward or impaired gait; episodic weakness and fatigue; anesthesia, deafness, blindness, and blurred or tunnel vision; and cardiac crises (e.g. palpitations). "In fact, the range and variety of conversion symptoms are endless; hysteria has been called 'the great imitator' for its ability to simulate the signs and symptoms of organic illness" (Nichols, 2011, p. 113). The symptoms can be difficult to understand in isolation, but become less ambiguous:

a) when they are observed to be recurrent but transitory and reversible; b) when they are judged to be related to some significant emotional stress that preceded symptom onset, or to serve some communicative function (e.g. emotional appeal) or to have iconic significance; c) when the symptom appears in some way to resolve or comment on a conflict deemed to follow or be otherwise related to the precipitating stressor; or d) when the medical diagnostic pursuit of symptoms has non-confirmatory outcomes.

(Nichols, 2011, p. 113)

It should be noted that the symptom(s) may be of either recent or distant onset with the former manifesting suddenly in response to stresses that have profound emotional significance or that remind the patient of some previous emotionally traumatic event.

In cases of distant onset, the precipitating event is obscure or unknown, and the emotion surrounding it blunted. Symptoms are typically more numerous, less dramatic, and apparently disabling, and seem intended to confirm or legitimize the patient in a sick role.

(Nichols, 2011, p. 116)

La belle indifférence is typically absent, and the patient may exist as an invalid, freed of all responsibilities apart from seeking treatment. Secondary depression is often manifested, shading into the symptom pictures typical of hypochondriacal or somatization disorders. The re-standardization left the composition of *Hy* intact, with no item deletions, although nine items were modified to modernize idioms and usage, grammatical clarifications, and simplifications.

The participants in the criterion group were taken primarily from the inpatient service of the psychiatric unit at the University of Minnesota Hospitals. McKinley and Hathaway (1944, as cited in Dahlstrom & Dahlstrom, 1980, p. 46), described the criterion participants as follows:

They had each received the diagnosis psychoneurosis, hysteria, or had been especially noted as having characteristic hysterical components in the personality disturbance. In the assignment of these diagnostic terms, the neuropsychiatric staff followed, as closely as possible, current clinical practice. Where cases showed a simple conversion symptom such as aphonia, an occupational cramp, or a neurologically irrational anesthetic area, the diagnosis was usually well agreed upon. In some cases, there remained a doubt as to whether there was a true organic illness such as multiple sclerosis present or whether the syndrome reflected hypochondriasis or an early schizophrenic reaction.

Participants with less dramatic symptomatology made psychodiagnosis a more difficult and less certain task. After several attempts, a final criterion group consisting of 50 cases was selected. Although no modal description or demographic data for the *Hy* criterion hysteric patients were provided (Colligan et al., 1983), the patients included in the criterion group did manifest the "neurotic defenses of the conversion form of hysteria" (Dahlstrom et al., 1972, p. 191) or hysterical personality features. In individuals who had developed an involuntary psychogenic loss or disorder of function, the physical symptoms allowed them to evade responsibilities and to escape from stressful and unpleasant situations. It was thought that patients whose personality organization revolves around hysterical defenses tend to function adequately or even well under ordinary circumstances, but when faced with difficult situations the tenuous nature of their personality organization is taxed beyond its capacity to cope, and symptoms emerge reflecting an overburdened self (e.g. emotional lability, emotional intensity, and modulation difficulties). Dahlstrom, et al. noted that a need to detect such a predisposition for breakdown was necessary and was in part the motivation for the development of Scale 3.

It was immediately apparent to McKinley and Hathaway that *Hy* included two major categories of items. One referred to somatic complaints; the other to an extraverted social style. The bodily complaint items related to such symptoms as headaches, dizzy spells, and hand tremor. As McKinley and Hathaway (1944) pointed out, the declaration of social well-being was illustrated by the frequent endorsement of denying items declaring bashfulness, getting angry easily, and opposing bossing others, even if the demands were justified. Despite the predominance of these two types of items, several other items referred to feelings of dysphoria ("blue" or "unhappy"). Specifically, item 65 admits feeling down most of the time, whereas item 95, denies feeling generally happy. The subsets of items describing somatic complaints, and feelings of well-being and comfort, are usually independent of each other or negatively correlated in normals, but tend to be positively correlated in patients whose personality functioning is organized around hysteric psychodynamics. Generally, the more elevated and prominent the role of Scale 3 in a codetype, the less insightful the individual tends to be, and the more likely it is that physical symptoms will emerge when the individual experiences stress.

Greene (1991a, 2011) reviewed the relation of Scale 3 item content to other scales and underscored the correspondence of its content to the independent clusters of items reported by Little and Fisher (1958). The two clusters, *admission of physiologic symptoms* and *denial of symptoms*, were used to construct the Admission (*Ad*) and Denial (*Dn*) scales. Greene (2011, p. 116) stated that:

> The *Ad* scale correlates positively (.96) with Scale 1 (Hypochondriasis [*Hs*]), the two scales having 18 items in common. The *Dn* correlates positively (.84) with Correction (*K*), with which it shares 9 items. Clients who score high on *Ad* report a number of nonspecific somatic symptoms and have poor interpersonal relationships. High scorers on *Dn* are described as lacking insight into their own behavior and morally virtuous. Little and Fischer (1958) believed that when both *Ad* and *Dn* scales are elevated, the person should have conversion-reaction dynamics.

Note that the *Ad* and *Dn* scales virtually overlap the obvious and subtle components of Scale 3, respectively.

The normal group used in the construction of *Hy* consisted of 200 women and 139 men, all married and between the ages of 26 and 43, who typically had eight years of schooling, with few educated beyond high school. The second group of normals consisted of 114 women and 151 men who were entering college and included to control for age and intelligence (McKinley & Hathaway, 1944).

McKinley and Hathaway viewed *Hy* as measuring a variable trait closely related to the construct measured by Scale 1 (*Hs*). There is considerable overlap between Scales 1 and 3, 20 items, the most item overlap shared by any two clinical scales. The positive correlation between Scales 1 and 3 motivated McKinley and Hathaway to attempt to decrease this correlation by eliminating as many of the overlapping somatic items as possible. The results of this effort are best summarized by McKinley and Hathaway (1944, as cited in Dahlstrom & Dahlstrom, 1980, p. 47):

> Elimination of the somatic items resulted in a marked drop in the number of test cases identified and introduced another disturbing difficulty; if only the non-somatic items were used, there was a strong relation with age and education. The mean score was more than a half sigma higher for the college group than for older persons. These results forced the inclusion of some somatic items in the final scale with consequent high correlation (r = .52 normals and r = .71 clinic cases) between *Hs* (hypochondriasis) and *Hy* (hysteria). Some relation still remains between age and intelligence and the *Hy* score. The relation seems valid clinically.

It appears that the positive correlation between Scales 1 and 3 is not a simple artifact of the item overlap but reflects a common psychological dimension in the elevation of these two scales, apparently somatization (Friedman et al., 1983; Marks & Seeman, 1963). It is important to note that McKinley and Hathaway distinguished clinical differences between individuals when both scales were elevated but with one score higher than the other. Specifically, they identified a different prognosis and treatment for these patterns of scores (McKinley & Hathaway, 1944, as cited in Dahlstrom & Dahlstrom, 1980, p. 49):

> Where *Hs* was higher, the physical complaints were diffuse and frequently required much less study to establish the presence of an important psychological factor in the disability. On the other hand, when *Hy* was dominant, the person frequently appeared normal psychologically and his physical complaints were likely to mimic closely or be accompanied by some common physical syndrome of the type now called "psychosomatic."

As previously stated, Scale 3 is highly correlated with Scale 1 (.80) due to the overlap of somatic items and it also shares 13 items with Scale 2 (r = .72). It is also correlated with *HEA* at .70. Its configural relation to Scale 1 has a variety of implications: Scale 1 elevated greater than Scale 3 suggests more somatic complaints, greater pessimism and defeatist attitudes, and harshness in relations with others; when Scale 3 is elevated above Scale 1, the latter tends to reflect fewer somatic preoccupations, greater optimism and social adeptness, and even a seductive approach toward others.

Nichols (2011) emphasizes that the use of the ego defense mechanism of denial can be quite striking in those with prominent scale elevations. Problems and difficulties that others easily recognize as emotional or psychological in nature in the client are typically denied as having any validity.

For example, the patient may deny frank and disabling illness, documents bearing his or her signature, well-documented events in his or her history, a large dress size, pregnancy, a spouse's alcoholism or imprisonment, or divorce, even in the face of clear, graphic, and incontrovertible evidence. The patient appears simply to bypass such evidence, to glide over it in a way that prevents effective confrontation. The manner of denial generally is not to argue that the evidence is unproven, but rather is flat, unequivocal, and final. Repression (keeping painful feelings and images out of awareness) appears to be the central defensive operation in Scale 3.

(Nichols, 2011, p. 119)

Duckworth and Anderson (1995) also pointed out that denial and repression are the primary mechanisms of defense being tapped by Scale 3. Therefore, although symptoms associated with other scale scores greater than that for Scale 3 may be acknowledged by the individual, those indicated by scales with *T*-scores below that for Scale 3 may not be acknowledged and the person may show a distinct absence of insight. Greene (2011) suggested that this rule should be used cautiously, given the lack of research to support it. Note that elevations on Scales *L* and *K*, especially when combined with low scores on Scales *F*, 7, 8, and 0, emphasize the success of defensive operations in warding off anxiety.

The scoring direction for the majority of the items on Scale 3 is False. Forty-seven (78 percent) of the items are keyed False, with 13 (22 percent) keyed True. As with Scales 1 and 2, a tendency to endorse items False will also elevate Scale 3 (see Chapter 4 for a description of an All-False response set profile). Scale 3 has fairly evenly distributed overlap with the other clinical scales and also shares 15 items with *HEA* and *RC1*, and 13 with Scale 2. Although no *K* correction is added to Scale 3, there is, in effect, a built-in *K* correction factor since Scale 3 has 10 items in common with *K*. Caution is urged when examining the correlations between Scale 3 and other scales, specifically when comparing psychiatric patients to normal samples. Symptoms within such samples tend to be overweighted relative to those aspects of the scale that reflect social interest and comfort, a trusting and positive self-portrayal, and a distaste for aggression and conflict. As Nichols (2011) points out, the high (*HEA*) and moderate (*ANX, DEP, WRK*) correlations seen in psychiatric samples collapse or reverse in normal samples, whereas the negative moderate (*ANG, CYN, ASP, TPA*) content correlates within normal samples collapse or reverse in psychiatric samples.

The item content in the scale is varied, covering areas of appetite, good sleep hygiene, somatic complaints, dysphoria, anxious depression, social interest/initiative, and denial of cynicism and mistrust. High scores on Scale 3 are obtained by individuals often described as childishly self-centered with strong needs for approval and affection. They will seek reassurance that they are likable and will try to elicit it by flattering, rewarding, and complimenting others (Lewak et al., 1990; Levak et al., 2011). They tend to be cheerful, animated, and talkative, if not vivacious and flamboyant, and approving if not seductive. They are strongly oriented to present themselves as socially attractive as possible. Nichols (2011, p. 116) states that:

...there is a tendency for their expression to be exhibitionistic and toward dramatization in social situations as well as at the level of symptom(s) and mood ... suggestibility is also common, with the high scale 3 scorer being subject to influence, imitativeness, marked shifts in feeling and mood, and to the rapid embrace or abandonment of attitudes and convictions, often seemingly dependent on the person with whom the patient last spoke.

(Nichols, 2011, p. 116)

In describing the "Hysterical Style," Shapiro (1965) offers further insight into the way these individuals perceive and process information. He suggests that hysterical cognition, in general, is "relatively diffuse, and lacking in sharpness, particularly in sharp detail. In a word, it is *impressionistic*" (Shapiro, 1965, p. 111). For example, a person with distinct hysteric traits is likely to respond to questions asking for facts with not a factual answer, but rather impressions.

"These impressions may be interesting and communicative, and they are very often vivid, but they remain impressions, not detailed, not quite sharply defined, and certainly not technical" (Shapiro, 1965, p. 111). The individual, nevertheless, believes that their judgment is sound and thinking is unfettered, clear, and rational, but with a feeling that his or her mental functioning should never be put to the test. Their inability to be accurate or engage in critical thinking inclines them to embellish or fabricate events or experiences, sacrificing truth and accuracy in the hope of greater impact or appeal upon others. They are often viewed as looking but not seeing; listening not hearing, as if their information processing is hampered by sensory inhibition.

(Nichols, 2011, p. 117)

The way in which a patient presents with a significant *Hy* elevation is quite varied depending on the way in which two fairly distinct groups of items are endorsed. The somatic complaints, many with dysphoric overtones, and a second set of items, affirming freedom from emotional difficulties and a sociable orientation toward others, often differentiate and characterize differently the presentation of the patient. When the somatic items dominate in the total *Hy* score, the patient is "likely to manifest a clear somatic focus and experience significant discomfort and distress in the form of depression, anxiety, or nervousness" (Nichols, 2011, p. 114). When the somatic items are exceeded by the items emphasizing sociability, optimism, and denial of social anxiety, there is denial about somatic concerns but also a proneness to worry and inhibitions around aggression and anger. La belle indifference is the lack of worry or indifference to one's somatic symptoms and related disability, despite normal concern about other matters, and is often apparent in patients strongly endorsing the *Hy* items emphasizing well-being. Regardless of which items are endorsed, a prominent Scale 3 elevation reflects self-centeredness, but tends to be expressed demandingly when the somatic items are more frequently endorsed than the items asserting freedom from emotional difficulties, wherein the self-centeredness is expressed more appealingly or seductively.

Conformity and naïveté are characteristic, along with the absence of insight due to the predominance of denial and repression in personality organization. Fearful of emotional and physical pain, high Scale 3 scorers tend to limit their awareness, which can result in impaired reality testing under stressful circumstances (Caldwell, 1974). Levak et al. (2011) suggested that it is helpful to look for what these individuals explicitly deny because that is often at the center of their conflict. Sociable, but shallow in their relationships, high Scale 3 scorers can become resentful of perceived demands and develop somatic concerns to remove themselves from responsibilities they resent or fear being unable to handle. It is rare for high scorers to develop psychotic symptoms, although their symptom pictures can be quite pronounced when they feel overwhelmed. Although the behaviors measured by Scale 3 are trait-like in appearance, the item content reflects behaviors that can change over time. The phrasing of the items in the present tense also allows test takers to interpret the items according to their current circumstances. For these reasons, Dahlstrom et al. (1972) stated that the scale may show less test–retest agreement relative to other scales, and that split-half estimates of reliability are inappropriate or misleading for Scale 3.

The *Hy* test–retest correlations for psychiatric patients ranged between .66 and .80 for intervals between one and two weeks, and between .36 and .72 for a one-year interval between tests (Dahlstrom et al., 1975). Butcher et al. (2001) provided test–retest reliability coefficients for 82 normal men and 111 normal women retested at an average interval of about one week, with the men and women obtaining coefficients of .70 and .74, respectively. Hunsley et al.'s (1988) large-scale meta-analysis of reliability studies using a wide variety of populations conducted between 1970 and 1981 reported an average internal consistency of .78 across 70 studies, and also reported an average test–retest reliability of .74 for 15 studies with time intervals from one day to 2 years. In contrast to the Hunsley et al. internal consistency findings, Butcher et al. (2001) reported much lower estimates of internal consistency; specifically, they reported coefficient alphas of .58 and .56 for men and women, respectively, for the re-standardization sample. The much lower values reported by Butcher et al. is most likely due to the greater diversity in participants used in the Hunsley et al. meta-analysis, which included college students, psychiatric patients, medical patients, alcohol and/or drug abusers, and incarcerated criminals.

Although various correlates for Scale 3 are reported in the literature, it is important that the clinician be selective in choosing the descriptors to be applied to any one individual. Some correlates, for example, although reported to be valid, may not have the validity always ascribed to them. Hedlund (1977), in comparing the results of seven independent studies that attempted to empirically identify the behavioral or symptom correlates of individual MMPI clinical scales for psychiatric patients, found that Scale 3 did not always correlate with specific items of dissociation, amnesia, or conversion symptoms, items that might be assumed to be relevant to the hysteria construct. He did find, however, that Scale 3 was regularly related to a number of somatic complaints (e.g. diarrhea, loss of appetite, and sleep disturbance), and significantly correlated with a number of depression-related complaints. It is recommended that the clinician assess individuals on a case-by-case basis that includes an understanding of their psychosocial history and the context in which they are being evaluated, as well as carefully inspecting the various subscales and supplementary scales to better understand the meaning of the particular clinical scale elevation.

In our opinion, there is no implication that symptoms will be present at elevated scores unless these are at a sufficiently high level (e.g. *T*-75) to have forced the endorsement of some of the somatic items. Conversely, false-negative predictions can easily occur when conversions are singularly localized, and uncomplicated, even when active and manifest. Also, note that elevations on Scale 3 do not rule out medical illness. Organic pathology has been found in high rates of follow-up studies of patients diagnosed with conversion disorder (Halligan, Bass, & Marshall, 2001; Merskey, 1995).

Harris-Lingoes Subscales

Harris and Lingoes (1955, 1968) developed the following five subscales for *Hy*: Denial of Social Anxiety (*Hy1*), Need for Affection (*Hy2*), Lassitude–Malaise (*Hy3*), Somatic Complaints (*Hy4*), and Inhibition of Aggression (*Hy5*); they are entirely non-overlapping, and identical for the MMPI and MMPI-2. No items were deleted for the re-standardization, so the composition of these subscales has remained intact. It should be noted that the subscales for *Hy* are entirely non-overlapping.

Hy1: *Denial of Social Anxiety (6 Items)*

This is the shortest of the *Hy* subscales with six items keyed False. All are contained in Little and Fischer's (1958) *Dn* and in *Hy-S*. *Hy1* reflects the denial of social shyness and inhibition (social butterfly aspect of the histrionic personality emphasizing social disinhibition) and is never elevated when Scale 0 (*Si*) is elevated. Because of its limited length, it is a less reliable measure of extroversion than Scales 0 and *SOD*. Caldwell (1988) described high scorers as manifesting an "over-socialized friendliness" (p. 19) toward unfamiliar others. Nichols and Greene (1995) described high *Hy1* individuals as seeking attention, approval, support, and affection in the context of their interactions with others. Not surprisingly, *Hy1* correlates negatively with Welsh's *A* scale (Anxiety) at −.65, suggesting unusual freedom from social anxiety and fear of embarrassment. Levitt (1989) described low scorers as socially maladjusted and anxious, shy, and easily embarrassed. It appears that *Hy1* taps the personality dimension of social extraversion (when elevated) and social introversion (when submerged). Nichols and Greene suggested examining *Hy1* in the context of its relation to other measures of introversion to determine if the introversion is situational or long term. Specifically, when *Pd3* (Social Imperturbability), *Hy1*, and *Hy-S* are all low, they should be examined in relation to the *SOD* content scale, Scale 0, and Shyness/Self-Consciousness (*Si1*). Nichols and Greene (1995, p. 37) give the following configural guidelines for interpreting introversion as a state versus a trait:

> High scores on *SOD*, *Si* and *Si1* when in the context of low scores on *Pd3*, *Hy1* and *Hy-S*, suggest long term or congenital trends toward shyness and social withdrawal. When *SOD*, *Si*, and *Si1* are high, but *Pd3*, *Hy1* and *Hy-S* are in an average range, an acute or temporary withdrawal secondary to loss or distress is suggested.

It should be noted that Wrobel (1992) did not find that social introversion was linked to *Hy1* per therapist ratings of clients in psychotherapy. He suggested that the short length of the subscale or the nature of the outpatient sample may have attenuated his results.

The six items on the *Hy1* subscale are all keyed False, making this subscale susceptible to an All-False response set. The item content essentially covers the extroversive component of Scale 3. Greene (2011) issued an important interpretative caveat by stating the highest possible *T*-score for *Hy1* is 61 (due to the scale's short length) in men and women. "In this instance, clinicians should consider a *T*-score of 56 on *Hy1* as being significant because the client has endorsed five of the six items on this scale" (Greene, 2011, p. 119).

Hy2: Need for Affection (12 Items)

Hy2 is the Pollyanna component of Scale 3. The items appear to emphasize a faith and trust in people, and reflect a denial of resentment or suspicion toward others (Caldwell, 1988; Greene, 1991a, 2000; Wrobel, 1992). The items also reflect a denial of hostility, rebellious attitudes, feelings, and impulses. It appears that high scorers prefer to avoid interpersonal conflict. Graham et al. (1999) found their high scoring *Hy2* outpatient men and women to be more empathic than low scorers, and this correlate was unique to *Hy2* among the *Hy* subscales. They also reported that high scoring women were seen as moralistic by their therapists. There is a strong element of unconflicted passivity and submissiveness in *Hy2* which reflects a "go along to get along" social spirit according to Nichols and Greene (1995, p. 40), wherein high scorers believe that the consequences of self-assertion are generally not socially constructive:

> High scorers seem to believe that, if one thinks the best of others, others will oblige by behaving in accordance with a benign and benevolent set of expectations, and that argument, disagreement, challenge, and confrontation are to be rejected because they can only serve to make social relations unpleasant, create hurt feelings, and foster alienation.

They also view *Hy2* as related to an aspect of cynicism, with low scorers "disclaiming self-traits of trustworthiness and social constructiveness" (Nichols & Greene, 1995, p. 33). Caldwell (1988) described low scorers as perceiving the world as "combative" (p. 19) where one has to take care of oneself and fight for what one wants and believes.

Eleven of the 12 items on *Hy2* are keyed False, with only 1 item keyed True, making it vulnerable to the influence of an All-False response set. *Hy2* is closely related to *Pa3*—Moral Virtue (*r* = .76), with which it shares three items. Three (33 percent) of the *Pa3* items begin with "I," whereas nine (75 percent) of the *Hy2* items do so. The *Hy2* items emphasize the denial of negative traits in the self; the *Pa3* items deny negative traits in others. Thus, Nichols (2011, p. 111) states, whereas:

> ...the thrust of most of the *Pa3* items is that "Most people are virtuous and constructive," the thrust of *Hy2* is that "I am virtuous and constructive." The low level of cynicism connoted in high *Hy2* scores implies the kind of impunitive detachment and naïve lack of normal skepticism of the motives of others that some may view as immature and unrealistic. In the aggregate, these items suggest strong needs for approval, or at least an abnormally strong aversion to giving offense or to drawing negative attention from others. A high score reflects an overly gracious

and beguiling style of relating to others and apparent blind trust in their integrity and innocuousness, suggesting passivity/dependency, the lack of a sense of personal power; and an unnecessarily roundabout style when it comes to seeking affection. *Hy2* is strongly correlated with *K* (r = .77) and, negatively, with *CYN* (–.84) and *CYN1* (–.83).

Hy3: *Lassitude–Malaise (15 Items)*

Harris and Lingoes (1968) reported the content for *Hy3* as "complaints about functioning below par physically and mentally; effortful keeping up of a good front; and need for attention and reassurance." *Hy3* is clearly the depressive component of Scale 3 (Nichols, 2011). Five of the items on this subscale are keyed True, 10 False.

Elevations connote "a broad lack of vitality and physical discomfort without freedom from distress. The neurasthenic syndrome of weakness, tiredness, and easy fatigability is strongly represented in Hy3" (Nichols, 2011, p. 112). Not quite half of the items are somatic/health related, but most of these have clear depressive overtones. The somatic complaints tend to be vague rather than specific.

Although 10 of the 15 items on this scale overlap with Scale 2 (r = .90), Caldwell (1988) suggested that the scale taps less of the generalized devaluation of the self that is seen in depression, and is more of a measure of having been made to feel weak, tired, sleepless, and less interested in life by life's aggravations or one's own poor health. High scorers report not feeling like themselves physically and mentally. Nichols and Greene (1995) described *Hy3* as reflecting some depressive somatization, like *D3* (Physical Malfunctioning) with which it shares five items, but having a greater emphasis on moods than on somatic difficulty. In a sample of psychotherapy patients, Wrobel (1992) found that complaints about physical and mental functioning, and feelings of needing attention and reassurance, positively correlated with elevated *Hy3* scores, whereas efforts to keep up a good front negatively correlated with *Hy3* scores. Graham et al. (1999) found high scoring *Hy3* psychiatric men and women outpatients to have suicidal ideation.

Prokop (1986) investigated the Harris-Lingoes subscale patterns for Scale 3 in a low-back pain sample. Prokop (1986, 1988) recommended that *if Hy3* and *Hy4* are elevated (but not *Hy1*, *Hy2*, and *Hy5*), in a low-back pain population, it may be appropriate to describe the individual as abnormally focusing on his or her physical symptoms. It should be noted that *Hy1*, *Hy2*, and *Hy5* all overlap with Little and Fischer's (1958) *Dn*. Prokop (1988) cautioned against inferring the presence of conversion dynamics when only *Hy3* and *Hy4* are elevated in low-back pain patients, stating that the patient may be attempting to express his or her distress about confusing or frightening symptoms. Such patients are often diagnosed with a non-conversion-based somatoform disorder. Consistent with Prokop's (1988) contention of an abnormal focus on one's bodily functioning is Greene's (2011) description of *Hy3* having 14 of its 15 items in common with the Little and Fischer *Ad* scale. As noted earlier, Little and Fischer suggested that conversion reaction dynamics should be suspected if both the *Dn* and *Ad* scales are elevated.

Hy4: *Somatic Complaints (17 Items)*

Harris and Lingoes (1968) characterized the *Hy4* items as being "of a kind that suggest repression and conversion of affect." Six of the items are keyed True, 11 False. As the somatic conversion component of Scale 3 (Caldwell, 1988), it is not surprising that it is highly correlated with Scale 1 (*Hs*) at r = .88 (Caldwell, 2007b, as reported in Greene, 2011). Twelve of the *Hy4* 17 items are scored on Scale 1 (*Hs*) and three overlap HEA. *Hy4* correlates highly (r = .79) with *Hy* in the Caldwell (2007) clinical sample. The five items that are not scored on Scale 1 have elements of anxiety (e.g. fainting spells and "lump in my throat") that are in noteworthy contrast to the reporting of somatic dysfunction, without the explicit anxiety that characterizes Scale 1 (Caldwell, 1988, p. 20). Graham et al. (1999) reported that 17 percent of 305 psychiatric women outpatients who scored above T = 65 on *Hy4* reported current anxiolytic medication usage. Greene (1991a) pointed out that 16 of the 17 items in this scale overlap with Little and Fischer's (1958) *Ad*, and that *Ad* correlates positively (r = .89–.90) with Scale 1. With the exception of item 18, which reports attacks of nausea and vomiting, the only items missing from *Hy4* (and Scale 3) that appear on Scale 1 relate to gastrointestinal complaints. Whereas Scale 1 and the *HEA* content scale represent general physical complaints, *Hy4* (and *Hy-O*) emphasize specific, as opposed to vague, symptoms (Nichols & Greene, 1995). Low scores should be interpreted as reflecting a person free of excessive somatic concerns. Nichols (2011, p. 112) provides a description of the *Hy4* content:

> The items refer to symptoms that are fairly discrete and dramatic; specific complaints outnumber vague complaints in a ratio of about 3:1 and emphasize head complaints, pain and discomfort, and vascular and cardiorespiratory problems. About half of the items refer, implicitly or explicitly, to spells or attacks. Just over half of the symptoms lend themselves to iconic or metaphoric use, especially through wording like, "lump in my throat," "attacks of nausea," "feeling hot all over," "pains over my heart," "my muscles twitching," "a tight band around my head," "dizzy spells," "my hand shakes," "my heart pounding," and so forth. The language of these items is more dramatic—even flamboyant—than is typical for the somatic portion of the MMPI-2 item pool. These items have an arresting quality and are subject to colorful elaboration on interview. That is, they are easily pressed into service as components of a story that the patient wishes to relate, and one that is likely to have a relatively easily discernible latent message.

There is much less implied distress in *Hy4* than in *Hy3*; hence, *Hy4* greater than *Hy3* suggests a working conversion with probable la belle indifference, provided *Hy4* is not too high. However, at about five to seven raw items, *Hy4* begins to suggest somatization over conversion, regardless of the *Hy4–Hy3* difference.

Hy5: *Inhibition of Aggression (7 Items)*

Purportedly, this brief seven-item scale reflects the inhibition or suppression of aggression, irritability, and anger in emotional life and fantasy. All seven of the items are keyed False, making it vulnerable to an All-False response set. Regardless of high or low scores, the scale is a weak basis on its own for making clinical inferences. Harris and Lingoes (1968) noted that the inhibition of aggression is "expressed by concurrence with others, disavowal of violence." The scale lacks internal consistency, and only one item (item 29) appears to fit the scale title well (Levitt, 1989; Nichols, 2011).

> Judging from its correlation with *R* (.39) and *DISC* (-.28), such inhibitions as there may be appear to be biased toward the emotional. *Hy5* is only moderately-to-weakly related to measures of aggression (e.g. AGGR, -.27), anger (e.g. ANG, -.45) and hostility (e.g. TPA2, -.33); it does not appear adequate for contributing to judgments about aggression or the inhibition thereof.
>
> (Nichols, 2011, p. 112)

Nichols and Greene (1995) explained that although *Hy5* moderately correlates with measures of denial, anger or hostility, it "appears to operate more as a disgust with anger and hostility than a denial scale per se" (p. 30). At least three of the items appear to reflect distaste, abhorrence, revulsion, or noninterest in vicarious violence and aggression. Thus, the high *Hy5* scorer seems to be saying that crime news, detective stories, swearing, the sight of blood, and so on are morbid and disgusting and are implicit threats to the person's sensory inhibition (Nichols, 2011). Caldwell (1988) reported that high scorers "get upset" by aggression in others and have a "hysteroid abhorrence of violence" (p. 20) that is likely to be quite prominent if *Hy5* is elevated with a high Scale 5 (*Mf*) score in the "feminine" direction by men or women.

Low scores suggest an ability to experience anger directly; in fact, very low scores (e.g. raw score of zero or one) suggest an interest or fascination with anger or violence and its potential consequences, as well as a lower threshold for experiencing morbid or violent fantasies. Very low *Hy5* scores may particularly indicate hostility when accompanied by elevations on *ANG2* (Irritability), *TPA1* (Impatience), and *TPA2* (Competitive Drive; Nichols & Greene, 1995). It is important to note other indicators of impaired empathy when *Hy5* is very low, such as the particular code pattern and other measures (e.g. *ASP1* and *CYN*). The item content of *Hy5* is subtle, with six of its seven items overlapping *Hy-S*.

Scale 3: Subtle–Obvious Subscales

The Hysteria-Obvious subscale (*Hy-O*) has 32 items, of which 12 are keyed True, 20 False; and Hysteria-Subtle (*Hy-S*) has 28 items, of which 27 are keyed False, 1 True. The items, direction of scoring, and *T*-score conversions can be found in Friedman et al. (2001).

The *Hy-O* items appear to emphasize specific, as opposed to vague, symptoms (Nichols & Greene, 1995). In fact, as Caldwell (1988) indicated, the composition of *Hy-O* is almost identical to *Hy3* and *Hy4*, as well as Little and Fischer's (1958) *Ad*. The numerous physical concerns reflected in *Hy-O* include some items related to the construct of hysteria, such as fainting spells and hand tremors. *Hy-O* reflects somatic problems and discomforts that may also antagonize normal sleep (Nichols & Greene, 1995). A low score contraindicates depleted energies due to physical discomfort and distress.

Hy-O is highly correlated with *Hs* (.96), *HEA* (.92), *D-O* (.92), *Pt* (.84), *Sc* (.83; *Sc4*, .81; *Sc6*, .79), *ANX* (.83), and *DEP* (.80), and moderately with *K* (-.55). This subscale is highly saturated with the first factor (correlation with $A = .78$) and thus will be raised by any of the distress scales (Nichols, 2011).

Dahlstrom (1991) derived correlates for Hy-O from partner ratings on the Katz Adjustment Scales (Butcher et al., 1989) in the re-standardization sample. Men and women with high Hy-O scores were described as having trouble sleeping; worrying about their health; lacking energy and appearing worn out; lacking an interest in things; not appearing self-confident, cheerful, or pleasant; and complaining about body aches and ailments. Women in particular were seen as restless, self-blaming, worried about the future, and feeling like others do not care about them. Men in particular were seen as having a poor sense of humor; getting easily upset by small, unexpected events; having difficulty making decisions; lacking ambition; and not willing to try new things.

Caldwell (1988) pointed out that Hy-S is very similar in item content to the $Hy1$, $Hy2$, and $Hy5$ subscales, as well as virtually identical to Little and Fischer's (1958) *Dn*. Nichols and Greene (1995) viewed Hy-S as measuring a subtle and complex disposition to claim freedom from problems in adaptation, hostile feelings and impulses, cynicism and distrust, and social discomfort. An elevated Hy-S score usually is not the result of an intentional effort to mislead the psychologist. Nichols and Greene (1995, p. 34) generated several hypotheses for an elevated Hy-S score (as well as an elevated K score):

These elevations may be the product of honest but erroneous self-appraisal (self-deception); above-average adjustment, resourcefulness and resiliency; or a social advantage that confers protection or insulation from major stresses or challenges to adjustment such as great wealth, high socioeconomic status, or a close, active, and committed circle of friends or family.

They also pointed out that the full Hy scale is a somewhat less satisfactory measure of the repression construct than Hy-S, mostly because of the dysphoric content in $Hy3$.

Hy-S is highly correlated with K (.82) and negatively with CYN ($-.79$; $CYN1$, $-.77$) and A ($-.70$). Hy-S scores, thus, will be increased by K and will, in turn, suppress scores on Scales 7, 8, and 0 (Nichols, 2011).

Low Hy-S scores are likely to indicate mild cynicism. Admission to feeling somewhat beleaguered, uncomfortable with strangers, and having a view of the world as antagonistic would also characterise low scorers.

Dahlstrom (1991) provided the following correlates for the Hy-S subscales. Both men and women are perceived as being self-confident, lacking shyness, willing to try new things, getting along well with others, not being suspicious of or avoiding others, friendly, and not lacking in emotional control. Women in particular were rated as not getting very sad or bored, not lacking in energy or having many fears, being able to laugh with others, not worrying about the future, and not getting their feelings easily hurt. Men were described as not arguing about minor things, being constructive or helpful, affectionate, generous, not bossy, cooperative, and not demanding attention.

Scale 4: Psychopathic Deviate (Pd)

Scale 4 was developed to measure the "personality characteristics of the amoral and asocial subgroup of persons with psychopathic personality disorders" (Dahlstrom et al.,

1972, p. 195). The scale is named Psychopathic Deviate because McKinley and Hathaway (1944) did not expect it to differentiate all the cases of psychopathic personalities; rather, the scale was successful in identifying half or somewhat more of the cases repeatedly classified as clinical psychopathic personalities. The scale name implies "a variation in the direction of psychopathy" (p. 172), in keeping with the psychopathic personality classification of the American Psychiatric Association in use at that time, which was broad and included pathological emotionality and sexuality as well as asocial or amoral trends (McKinley & Hathaway, 1944).

The criterion group consisted of an unreported number of men and women, ranging in age from 17 to 22. The women outnumbered the men, most likely because local courts at the time diverted more of the women to the hospital and more of the men to jail. The criterion participants were referred by the courts for study in a psychiatric setting. McKinley and Hathaway (1944, as cited in Dahlstrom & Dahlstrom, 1980, pp. 57–58) provided the following description of these participants:

> The symptomatic backgrounds of the criterion cases were highly varied but can be characterized in several ways. Most often the complaint was stealing, lying, truancy, sexual promiscuity, alcoholic over-indulgence, forgery, and similar delinquencies. There were no major criminal types. Most of the behavior was poorly motivated and poorly concealed. All the criterion cases had long histories of minor delinquency. Although many of them came from broken homes or otherwise disturbed social backgrounds, there were many in whom such factors could not be seen as particularly present.

Hathaway's emphasis on the persistence and consistency of the behavior pattern, rather than on the severity of any specific aspect of conduct (e.g. theft, lying, promiscuity), appears to have been central in his conception of the scale. The common denominator across the participants seemed to be that they had low anticipation of the consequences of their behavior and could not seem to "learn those anticipatory anxieties which operate to deter most people from committing antisocial behavior" (Marks et al., 1974, p. 25). Essentially, individuals with psychopathic traits were seen as lacking in their ability to form warm and stable bonds to others, to appreciate social customs and abide by societal rules, and to profit from experiences that had negative consequences. They were, in essence, psychologically immature (McKinley, 1944). Their inability to form warm and stable attachments occasionally gives way to more durable relationships, but these typically revolve around their dependency needs and tend to be egocentric and exploitative in nature. These individuals may appear free from disabling anxiety and not be perceived as particularly troubled or disturbed until found in a situation demanding the use of inner resources that the psychopathic individual lacks. The general social maladjustment that characterizes these individuals leads to dissatisfaction with the self and others and often results in strong feelings of social and self-alienation.

Nichols (2011, p. 126) provided a comprehensive overview of Scale 4:

> The general construct embodied in Scale 4 appears to be one of an ingrained, durable, and mostly maladaptive pattern of personality organization and behavior that tends to narrow the range and stability of interpersonal satisfactions; impaired

cducational and occupational achievement; impede attainment of long-term goals; and limit the harmony, flexibility, or efficacy of social functioning. The pattern typically involves some degree of externalization such that problems and conflicts are seen as originating outside the self, especially because of unfavorable traits and motives in others or in the social environment and its organizations more broadly, dishonesty, selfishness, bias, disloyalty, malice, or rigidity—to which the subject is merely reacting. Thus the subject's attributions onto others tend to reinforce themselves as new encounters draw reactions from the social environment that are seen as confirming or validating them. This perceived confirmation, in turn, prevents new learning and renders the subject's attitudes and behaviors concerning social negotiations highly resistant to extinction.

Although Scale 4 has the word "psychopathic" in the label, the reader is urged not to interpret the construct of psychopathy as implicit in Scale 4 elevations. Psychopathy, as defined by Hare (1991) and others, is a much more psychopathologic referent group than the one used by McKinley and Hathaway (1944) to construct Scale 4 (Greene, 2011). Criminal psychopaths are known to present physical risks to others. Even though elevations on Scale 4 are correlated positively with the frequency of delinquent and criminal behaviors, Greene (2011) points out that "problematic interpersonal relations and alienation" is a more apt modernized label for Scale 4 to avoid confusion with the construct of psychopathy. This, however, is not to suggest that actual psychopaths will not elevate Scale 4, and spike Scale 4 scores should be investigated to rule out psychopathy or psychopathic tendencies, especially in a forensic context. In general, however, Scale 4 elevations constitute a greater physical risk to the examinee than to those with whom he or she may come into contact.

In terms of overall mortality/morbidity, the high Scale 4 scorer tends to be more self- than other-destructive. Substance abuse and a tendency to take imprudent risks and disregard hazards renders high scorers vulnerable to mishaps that result in injury or death. However, high scorers do constitute a greater emotional risk to others through their emotional coldness, lack of availability, selfishness, and lack of responsibility, and by their indifference to the stresses they cause others by the situation into which their behavior may place them.

(Nichols, 2011, pp. 126–127)

The normal comparison participants (294 men and 397 women) used to construct the 50-item *Pd* scale consisted of college freshmen receiving guidance counseling at the University of Minnesota and married Minnesota residents who were considerably older. The average age of these latter participants was 35, so the college sample introduced some balance. Cross-validation procedures involved 100 prisoners and 78 psychiatric inpatients diagnosed with "psychopathic personality." The scale was expected to identify only the asocial individuals. McKinley and Hathaway (1944) reported that among the prisoners, 59 percent obtained *T*-scores at or above 70 on *Pd*, whereas 45 percent of the psychiatric cases obtained scores above that level.

Five preliminary scales were developed before items were selected for the final inclusion on *Pd*. *Pd* did not lose any items in the MMPI-2 revision, although four items were changed (two items were modernized in language, one was grammatically clarified, and the wording of one item was simplified).

The item content of Scale 4 is diverse. McKinley and Hathaway (1944) initially identified the following three general groupings of item content: (a) social maladjustment items, (b) depression items, and (c) paranoid-trend items. The mixed content of the scale is reflected in factor analytic studies of the scale. For example, Dahlstrom et al. (1972) described the results of Comrey's (1958) and Astin's (1959, 1961) factor analytic investigations. They reported that hypersensitivity, poor impulse control, social maladjustment, and emotional deprivation were four of the many factors emerging from their work. Nichols and Greene (1995, p. 35) captured these factors in their poignant description of how the high *Pd* scorer tends to manifest his or her psychopathology in the environment:

> In *Pd,* an impoverished emotional life and feelings of emptiness lead the individual to make his/her mark on the social environment and to force others to acknowledge an autonomy that the individual experiences internally as incomplete and poorly consolidated. The usual result is a series of scrapes, broken promises, under-achievement, lost employment, ephemeral relationships, and legal difficulties.

Greene (2011) provides insight into the item content of Scale 4 by listing 15 scales which are highly correlated in the Caldwell (2007b) clinical sample. The three primary categories reported within these scales are: (1) alienation; (2) subjective distress and negative affect (i.e. the first factor); and (3) family/marital problems. Greene (2011) states that it is surprising that scales reflecting problems with authority figures and antisocial attitudes and behaviors are not among these 15 scales. Because the Caldwell sample consisted of clinical patients, not forensic clients with antisocial histories, it is likely that a latter sample would show higher correlations with scales measuring problems with authority and antisocial attitudes.

It should be noted that the interpretation of Scale 4 is heavily dependent on its relationships with other scales in the profile. Nichols states:

> Among the basic clinical scales, Scale 4 is most highly correlated with Scales 8 at .76 and 7 at .73. Content scale correlates of Scale 4 include *DEP* (.76) and *FAM* (.73). The correlation with *RC4* is .64. These relationships are determined by *Pd-O* and by the fact that these correlates are drawn from a psychiatric sample; in this sample, the correlation between Scale 4 and *Pd-O* is .92, whereas that with *Pd-S* is only .37. This pattern of correlations would be substantially different in a correctional sample and somewhat different in a normal sample.
>
> (Nichols, 2011, p. 123)

Harris and Lingoes (1955) also identified different subgroupings of items on Scale 4, which we describe shortly.

The critical scoring direction for Scale 4 is about evenly split between True and False responses (24 True, 26 False) for this 50-item scale. A *K*-correction of 0.4 added to *Pd* improved its ability to make diagnostic discriminations, and this value is added to the *Pd* raw score on the profile form. Ten of 50 items are non-overlapping or unique to

Scale 4, with the remaining 40 overlapping items distributed over the other clinical scales and *F* and *K*. Scale 4 shares five and seven items with *F* and *K*, respectively. It shares eight items with Scale 6, six with Scales 7, 9, *DEP*, and *FAM*, five items scored positively and six negatively with Scale 0, and five with *DISC* (Disconstraint). Scales 3 (*Hy*) and 8 (*Sc*) both share 10 items, and Scale 2 (*D*) 7 items with Scale 4. The seven Scale 4 items overlapping Scale 2 may be a reflection of the situational or state condition of the criterion participants at the time of testing. Because all were involved in legal proceedings and/or incarcerated, they may have experienced a dysphoric emotionality reflecting their situation, rather than any inherent tendency to feel depressed. Nichols (2011, p. 122) explains that

> the depressive/guilty items on the scale, mostly *Pd5*, might have differentiated the criterion group on the basis of the purely situational discomforts that attended hospitalization, or they may have represented feigned remorse and contrition calculated to mollify parents' qualms about allowing patients to return home, or to win early release.

McKinley and Hathaway (1944) originally reported a test–retest correlation of .71 for *Pd* obtained on a normal sample of 47 cases, with a time interval of a few days to more than a year. Butcher et al. (2001) reported test–retest reliability data for their community (normal) sample of 82 men ($r = .79$) and 111 women ($r = .69$) retested at an average interval of 8.6 days (*Mdn* = 7 days).

In psychiatric cases on the MMPI, the *Pd* test–retest correlations for one- to two-day intervals ranged between .69 and .75 and between .48 and .49 for one-year intervals between tests (Dahlstrom et al., 1972). Hunsley et al.'s (1988) large-scale meta-analysis of MMPI reliability studies using diverse populations conducted between 1970 and 1981, reported an average test–retest reliability of .71 for 16 studies, with time intervals from one day to two years.

Internal consistency estimates for Scale 4 were derived from the re-standardization sample (Butcher et al., 2001) and yielded coefficients of .60 and .62 for men and women, respectively. Hunsley et al. (1988) reported higher internal consistency values for Scale 4, but used a wider variety of populations (abnormal and normal) in their meta-analysis. They reported an average internal consistency of .81 across 71 studies.

Individuals with high Scale 4 scores, especially when it is the highest or second highest scale elevation in the profile, typically have shallow emotional lives that may go undetected by others until the "situation demands evidence of a sense of responsibility, appreciation of social patterns, or personal and emotional loyalties" (Dahlstrom et al., 1972, p. 195; McKinley & Hathaway, 1944). These individuals can be described as having feeling deficits as they have developed the coping mechanism of numbing out their vulnerable feelings (Levak et al., 2011). Prolonged exposure to abusive or neglectful caregivers in early life with insufficient affection, warmth, and inattention to the child's physical and emotional needs, often sets the stage for the development of a constellation of personality traits that include poor frustration tolerance, impulsiveness, antisocial attitudes, and a reduced capacity for empathy toward others. Discipline, oftentimes, was inconsistent or applied in arbitrary and controlling ways, with one or both parents possessing an authoritarian style. Nichols (2011) stated that "one or both parents may have implicitly approved of and obtained vicarious satisfaction from the child's misbehavior by repeated rescues and intercessions with authorities ('boys will be boys'), thereby reinforcing deviant social development" (p. 131). Traumatogenic experiences, such as dysfunctional childrearing, could lead to the development of a cognitive style that allows these individuals to recognize and intellectually understand their experiences, but feel emotionally cut off from their own vital resources, thereby limiting or handicapping their ability to have genuine reciprocal exchanges with others. In fact, Rathvon and Holmstrom (1996) found that Scale 4 showed a significant positive correlation with a narcissistic depletion factor. Even in so-called normal populations, such as police applicants, or among sensation seekers, such as sky divers, where the *Pd* score is the highest but still within normal limits, some of the *Pd* characteristics or trends are still observed. For example, instead of being overtly antisocial, an individual may be somewhat cynical or immature in relation to authority figures.

In the normative sample for the re-standardization, partner ratings revealed that Scale 4 appears sensitive to distress and recent life changes (Butcher et al., 1989). Participants from this sample who scored high on *Pd* were perceived by their partners to be dysphoric, antisocial, hostile, impulsive, and nonconforming. Hathaway and Meehl (1944) reported a large number of adjectives characteristic of normals with high *Pd* scores that were generated by friends of the normal participants. Overall, these high Scale 4 scorers tended to be quite socially visible. Typical descriptors applied to these normals obtaining *Pd* scores that were elevated but still within the normal range included extraverted, adventurous, enthusiastic, sarcastic, exhibitionistic, talkative, high-strung, assertive, active, energetic, immature, and irritable.

A high *Pd* score is often associated with a personality disorder diagnosis, such as narcissistic, passive-aggressive, borderline, histrionic, paranoid, dependent, or antisocial (Morey & Smith, 1988). However, the presence of a high Scale 4 elevation does not always indicate that an individual will manifest antisocial behaviors, especially if there is not a history of such actions. If Scale 9 is elevated, along with Scale 4, as a primary high point, the probability is increased for overt expressions of antisocial behavior. The reader is cautioned to be aware that negative emotionality as reflected in feelings of alienation (see *Pd4* and *Pd5*, below) is often more prominent in high Scale 4 scorers than is antisocial behavior, especially if the individual is not being assessed in the context of the correctional system. Butcher and Williams (1992) underscored this point by stating that the *ASP* content scale is only modestly correlated (.37) with *Pd*. Scale 4 has mixed content that includes, but is not limited to, measuring antisocial behavior; the *ASP* scale is a more direct measure of that construct (Butcher et al., 1990).

Emotional dysregulation is often apparent in the high Scale 4 scorer, with abrupt changes in mood. This under-regulation of emotional expression is seen, for example, when irritation becomes openly expressed anger, with anger often transmuting into aggressive verbal or physical encounters. Emotional arousal and expression tend to be poorly calibrated to the circumstances that instigate them (Nichols, 2011). Their baseline affective state is under-aroused but unstable, and tends to easily shift to restlessness or boredom, leading to sensation-seeking through activities or interpersonal turbulence. The general sense of emptiness or purposelessness they often experience in their lives leads to resentments and even bitterness, with several grievances that they can readily recall.

Duckworth and Anderson (1995) viewed "fighting something" (p. 164) as a cardinal feature of elevated *Pd*. They suggested that the individual may be in conflict with his or her parents, friends, spouse, society, or school, and that it is essential to examine the context in which the person is being assessed in order to better understand the significance of the Scale 4 elevation. Lower elevations on the scale suggest that the "fighting out" may not be expressed directly, but may instead reflect a covert attitude or feeling that something or someone other than the client needs to be changed. Duckworth and Anderson also emphasize the importance of recognizing that moderate *Pd* elevations may reflect situational stress, such as marital difficulties, rather than a personality trait disturbance.

Alcohol, drug, and polydrug abuse and addiction are often associated with high Scale 4 scores and can be conceptualized as a remedial stimulant for the feeling deficits that these individuals experience (Craig, 1984a, 1984b, 1984c, 1988; Jaffe, 1992; Jaffe & Jaffe, 1992). See the chapter by Greene and Garvin (1988, pp. 159–197) for a comprehensive review of the MMPI in drug and alcohol abuse. Although additional diagnoses, such as depression, are often given to drug and alcohol dependent individuals, it should be pointed out that if indicators in the MMPI-2 (e.g. *DEP* content scale and Scale 2) do not support such a diagnosis, a high Scale 4 scorer may not be experiencing a typical depressive feeling state, such as a sense of sadness and loss, but rather may be experiencing feelings of emptiness and alienation (Levak et al., 2011).

In addition to abusing alcohol and/or drugs as a remedial stimulant, high Scale 4 scorers, given their high need for erotic stimulation, may also focus their sexuality on sensation-seeking versus intimacy. "Sexual interaction is typically spontaneous and uninhibited but also relatively indiscriminate and promiscuous. Partners tend to be selected more for their stimulating qualities than for their suitability as companions, and selfishness and exploitativeness in this domain are common" (Nichols, 2011, p. 30).

It appears that scores on Scale 4 decrease with age by 10–12 points (two to three items) in men and women in normal, medical, and clinical populations (Colligan et al., 1983, 1989; Colligan, Osborne, Swenson, & Offord, 1984; Friedman et al., 2001; Greene, 2011). Greene (2011) suggested that this pattern most likely reflects the slow maturational changes that occur in persons with elevated scores. Archer (1997) noted that there is also clear evidence that *Pd* scores also differ as a function of adolescence versus adulthood in both normal and clinical populations. He pointed out that adolescents tend to endorse more *Pd* items than do adults, and that the normal adolescents in the MMPI-A sample would produce a mean *T*-score value of approximately 55 if scored using MMPI-2 norms. It is, therefore, not surprising that adolescent profiles typically include prominent Scale 4 elevations (Archer, Gordon, & Klinefelter, 1991; Marks et al., 1974).

Several normal groups also score in the high-normal and low-moderate range on Scale 4, including social activists, adolescents, and mental health professionals. Additionally, fire, police, airline pilots, and correctional facility applicants also tend to score in these normal ranges on Scale 4 (Aamondt, 2004; Bartol, 1991; Butcher, 1994c, 2002; Davis & Rostow, 2004; Friedman et al., 2001; Greene, 2011).

Harris-Lingoes Subscales

As previously noted, the Harris-Lingoes subscales can help identify the particular pattern of item content that characterizes a high score on the MMPI-2 parent scale. Scale 4 is particularly well served by a subscale pattern analysis as the scale is rich and varied in its content. Several *Pd* subscales assess very different aspects of psychopathy, consideration of these differences may have significant implications for clinical practice and assessment (Lilienfeld, 1999). Harris and Lingoes (1955) developed five subscales for Scale 4: Familial Discord (*Pd1*), Authority Problems (*Pd2*), Social Imperturbability (*Pd3*), Social Alienation (*Pd4*), and Self-Alienation (*Pd5*). Unlike the majority of Harris-Lingoes subscales that were unaffected by the MMPI-2 revision, several item changes and deletions on the *Pd* subscales have compromised the consistency between the MMPI and MMPI-2 for these subscales (Chojnacki & Walsh, 1994). In their original construction, Harris and Lingoes, for unexplained reasons, added from two to six items to each of the *Pd* subscales taken from an unpublished earlier version of Scale 4 (Greene, 2011; Levitt, 1990). For reasons that are likewise unclear, the MMPI-2 revision deleted these items. The only rationale provided was that these items were not included in the final version of Scale 4 (Butcher et al., 1989, p. 29), but questions about the possible advantages of retaining these "off-scale" items on the basis of their content or their contribution to enhanced subscale reliability were not addressed.

In examining the consistency between the original MMPI and the MMPI-2, Chojnacki and Walsh (1994) concluded that the shortened *Pd* subscales do not materially affect the *T*-scores for these subscales. *Pd1*, *Pd2*, *Pd3*, *Pd4*, and *Pd5* lost two, three, six, five, and three items, in the re-standardization, respectively. The Harris-Lingoes subscales for Scale 4 contain minimal overlap; three items overlap *Pd4* and *Pd5*.

Pd1: Familial Discord (9 Items)

The items in this subscale reflect current and historical problems with one's family and the accompanying feeling that one wishes to escape a loveless home (Caldwell, 1988). Five of the *Pd1* items keyed True, four False. *Pd1* has six items in common with *FAM*, three on *FAM1*, and two on *FAM2*. Levitt (1989) reported that high scorers reject a family situation that they consider affectionless, stressful, and lacking in emotional support. Wrobel's (1992) study of clinician descriptions for *Pd1* elevations showed feelings of struggle against family control to be significant. Graham et al. (1999) reported that high scoring psychiatric outpatient women on *Pd1* tended to blame their families for their difficulties, demanded much attention, and appeared argumentative. Given the item content for this subscale, it is not surprising that Pancoast and Archer (1988) found that adolescents, in contrast to adults, are particularly likely to endorse *Pd1* items. Nichols and Greene (1995) report that *Pd1* is biased toward conflict and alienation in the family of origin and viewed it as a general measure of family alienation. In fact, when *F*, *Sc1* (Social Alienation), and *Pd1* are all elevated, there is a good likelihood of the respondent making explicit statements concerning hatred toward one or both parents. Nichols (2011) described the item content in this subscale as reflecting considerable bitterness and resentment toward one's family of origin. "There is a sense of injury implicit in *Pd1* that may be the result of being controlled and disapproved of while not feeling cared for" (p. 123). *Pd1* as well as *Pd4* and *Sc1* are subscales which are sensitive to a history of abuse, both for victims and for perpetrators. Caldwell (1988) reported that low scores reflect a supportive family with genuine compatibility and strong ties or possibly a need to minimize and deny family problems.

Pd2: *Authority Problems (8 Items)*

The content of *Pd2* reflects an opposition to authority figures (reactive defiance), dislike of school, rebelliousness, a lack of constraint and a resistiveness or a sense of chafing under the constraints of custom or propriety. Two items on *Pd2* are keyed True, six False. The heterogeneous items have a strong historical bias, with an emphasis on past delinquent behavior, legal involvement, and trouble with authority. This may account for why they seem not to be suppressed by elevated *K* scores (Caldwell, 1988). Lilienfeld (1999) found *Pd2* to be more highly correlated than other *Pd* subscales with most indexes of antisocial behavior, a finding that is not surprising, given that several items refer explicitly to illegal actions. He also reported that *Pd2* may be the better marker of primary psychopathy as compared with the other *Pd* subscales, a finding generally consistent with those of Meloy and Gacono (1995) and Graham et al. (1999). Similarly, Osberg and Poland (2001) found *Pd2* related to a criminal history.

High scores reflect a lack of behavioral control or impulsivity, either in the form of "clear violations of social norms and rules or attitudes that clearly suggest a lower threshold for behavior that violates rules and brings one into conflict with others, especially those in authority" (Nichols & Greene, 1995, p. 27). Wrobel (1992) found the descriptor "resents demands and convention of parent and/or society" to apply to his sample of outpatients scoring high on *Pd2*. Levitt (1989) described high *Pd2* scorers as rebellious and having difficulty accepting standards of behavior that impose responsibilities and interfere with personal gratification.

The clinician should take note of elevated *Pd2* scores, especially if elevated with other indicators of social disinhibition, such as the *ASP* content scale or its component subscale, Antisocial Behavior (*ASP2*). *Pd2* and *ASP2* imply the direct expression of antisocial conduct, but the prediction of antisocial behavior is higher when *ASP2* is greater than *Pd2*, *Pd2* is greater than *ASP*, and *ASP* is greater than *CYN* (Cynicism; Nichols & Greene, 1995). It should be noted that *Pd2* and *ASP* share three items. Misbehavior and rule-breaking are measured by *Pd2*, but it is prudent to compare this subscale score with ego inflation (*Ma4*). "When both are elevated, issues of control avoidance, autonomy, and self-determination may be prominent" (Nichols, 2011, p. 124).

Graham et al. (1999) found that psychiatric men and women outpatients who scored high on *Pd2* reported recent alcohol and substance abuse and dependence problems. This finding is consistent with the above description of impulsive individuals with low frustration tolerance.

Low *Pd2* scorers do not admit to having difficulties with authority and tend to be socially conforming. They have a capacity for constraint that high scorers lack, and this may reflect a "mature submission to the rules and regulations that make for a sense of community with orderly and harmonious social relations among citizens" (Nichols & Greene, 1995, p. 40).

Pd3: *Social Imperturbability (6 Items)*

Originally a 12-item subscale, the removal of 6 items from the MMPI-2 version of *Pd3* left it with 6 items (shortest of the *Pd* subscales), all of which overlap *Pd-S*. *Pd3* reflects a strong extraversion tendency but without the need for affection and approval from others. All of the items are keyed False. Nichols and Greene (1995) stated that "*Pd3* reflects a highly aggressive and insouciant sociability consistent with a desire to use interpersonal relationships to manipulate, intimidate, exploit, and otherwise extract goods and services from others. There is little emphasis on social approval" (p. 37). There is a socially aggressive or impervious character to high *Pd3* scorers that is especially pronounced if signs of cynicism, hostility, and antisocial trends are present in the profile. High *Pd3* scorers (raw scores of five or greater on the MMPI-2) tend to be pushy and insensitive in their social interactions or even aggressive or overbearing (Nichols & Greene, 1995).

The Denial of Social Anxiety subscale (*Hy1*) and *Pd3* now share 67 percent of their items, making their interpretation similar. Both subscales connote an intrepid sociability. The elimination of six items in the MMPI-2 version of *Pd3* (because the items were not part of the final *Pd* scale) accounts for this increased proportion of item overlap. In effect, these two subscales reflect a social insensitivity that may constitute part of a narcissistic syndrome. Nichols (2011) emphasizes this narcissistic insensitivity by pointing out that the socially aggressive aspect of *Pd3* is also reflected in low *SOD2* scores. Consistent with this interpersonal style, Nichols states "*Pd3* correlates negatively with *A* at −.64, suggesting unusual freedom from social anxiety and fear of embarrassment, as well as an assertive, counter-anxious attitude consistent with the image of the glib, smooth operator" (Nichols, 2011, p. 124).

Low *Pd3* scorers are likely to feel uncomfortable in social situations and experience difficulty taking social initiative. When *Pd3*, *Hy1*, and *Hy-S* are all low, and there are high scores on the *SOD* content scale, *Si*, and *Si2* (Social Avoidance), there may be long-term or congenital (temperamental) trends toward shyness and social withdrawal. If, however, *Pd3*, *Hy1*, and *Hy-S* are within normal limits, but *SOD*, *Si*, and *Si1* are significantly elevated, the individual may be experiencing a temporary social withdrawal in reaction to a loss or other distress (Nichols & Greene, 1995).

Pd4: *Social Alienation (13 Items)*

Harris and Lingoes (1968) described the *Pd4* content themes as "feelings of isolation, lack of belongingness, externalization of blame for difficulties, and lack of gratification in social relations." Ten of the items are keyed True, three False. *Pd4* overlaps Scale 6 (*Pa*) by six items, all on *Pa1*, and three with *Pd5*. *Pd4* reflects a general feeling of "paranoid flavored resentments" (Caldwell, 1988). This subscale is the paranoid component of Scale 4, but with some depressive undertones. Nichols and Greene (1995) classified *Pd4* under their paranoid thought process category in their structural summary as it reflects severe alienation from others, and a sense of felt deprivation and of being given a "bum deal." There is an element of residual sadness and longing in *Pd4* that indicates a vulnerable, lonely, and unhappy self. High *Pd4* scorers have a pervasive mistrust of others, who are viewed as more depriving than hostile. Consequently, they feel that others are uncaring and cannot be counted on (Nichols & Greene, 1995). Nichols (2011) states that *Pd4* is likely the most sensitive to severe childhood deprivation and neglect, and that high scorers have come to anticipate that others will withhold affection, support, encouragement, and similar forms of emotional nourishment. Lacking an adequate holding environment in childhood causes feelings of deprivation, and neglect/mistreatment by others with a sense of feeling that one's needs have been ignored or devalued. This sense of emotional deprivation is supported by Wrobel's (1992) findings that anchored clinician ratings to patient characteristics associated with elevated *Pd4* scores. Those characteristics included feeling socially isolated, a lack of gratification in social relationships, a lack of feeling of belongingness, and externalizing blame. The finding of sadness from the Graham et al. (1999) study for male psychiatric outpatients is consistent with the lonely and unhappy individual just described. Levitt (1989) suggested examining *Pd1* when *Pd4* is elevated to ascertain if family members and intimates are the source of failed support. To this end, the clinician would want also to examine other measures, such as the *FAM* content scale. If only *Pd4* and *Pd5* (Self-Alienation) are elevated relative to the other *Pd* subscales, particularly *Pd2*, the individual may prove more likely to benefit from psychotherapy. However, research is needed to substantiate this conjecture (Lilienfeld, 1999).

Although *Pd4* and *Sc1* share identical scale titles, despite having only three items in common, the two subscales are importantly different. Nichols (2011) specified the major difference: "Whereas *Sc1* reflects a disinclination to form attachments to others, *Pd4* emphasizes an inability to do so, but with a sense of sorrow about this, unlike *Sc1*" (p. 124).

Low *Pd4* scorers feel understood, fairly treated, and enjoy a sense of belongingness in their social environments (Caldwell, 1988).

Pd5: *Self-Alienation (12 Items)*

Harris and Lingoes' (1968) items for this subscale include feeling unhappy and misunderstood as well as dissatisfied with life. Ten of the items on *Pd5* are keyed True, two False. *Pd5* overlaps *DEP* by six items and is also highly correlated with *PK* and *PS*. Wrobel (1992) described feelings of despondency as a correlate of the high *Pd5* scorer, and Caldwell (1988) and Graham et al. (1999) described a similar feeling state underscoring the guilt and self-blame, regretful feelings, and feelings of hopelessness and unhappiness so typical of these individuals. The subscale appears sensitive to the anhedonia elements inherent in Scale 4 that McKinley and Hathaway (1944) viewed as an important component of the parent scale. Hence, *Pd5* appears to be the depressive component of Scale 4. However, it should be noted that the depressive item content of *Pd5* does not appear consonant with the conventional interpretation of a high 4 (*Pd*) score (Levitt, 1989). Typically, a high 4 scorer attributes his/her dissatisfaction to the environment rather than to oneself as is the case with an elevated *Pd5* subscale score. Reported by Levitt (1989), the depression items on *Pd5* help explain the high loadings on a depression factor for both sexes in the three patient populations tested by Foerstner (1986) in her factor analytic study of MMPI special scales. Nichols (2011) concurs that the items reflect a theme of self-reproach and appear distinctly out of place in a scale intended to represent the construct of psychopathy. Voelker and Nichols (1999) showed evidence that this group of items did not contribute incrementally to the validity of

Scale 4 when compared against scores from the Psychopathy Checklist-Revised (PCL-R; Hare, 1991). Nichols (2011) sheds light on why these items appear on *Pd5* and on Scale 4. The reader will recall that many of the criterion group members for Scale 4 were hospitalized versus going to jail.

> *Pd5* appears to be an artifact of the effect of hospitalization on the criterion group cases. It may be one of the key elements in *2-4/4-2* code patterns, the so-called caught psychopath configurations. These reflect depressive phenomena that are largely inspired by situation, as a reaction to the felt need to enact mea culpa for tactical reasons, and to the inconvenience of having to live within a restrictive, style-cramping, institutional environment with its schedules, policies, rules, privilege levels, fixed menus, and so on.
>
> (Nichols, 2011, p. 125)

Nichols and Greene (1995, p. 29) believed that guilt, which can negatively affect one's capacity to enjoy life in a spontaneous and fluent fashion, is best assessed using *Pd5*. They pointed out that the level or intensity of guilt as measured by *Pd5* can be estimated from scores on *D5* (Brooding) and the *LSE* content scale. They elaborated by stating that

> it is important to discriminate guilt as a specific emotional state from states of more general upset in which guilt is only a component of distress and dysphoria. Many individuals experience guilt, regret, and remorse in the context of other, mostly unpleasant, emotions such as anxiety, fearfulness, apathy, depression, worry, and so forth. Such experiences often so obscure or obstruct the assessment of guilt per se that this emotional state and its role in the individual's psychic life are left uncertain. Guilt is most readily identified when *Pd5* and *D5* are elevated above *OBS*, as well as above the level of other distress scales such as *A*, *ANX*, *FRS*, *DEP*, *WRK*, and *TRT*.

The level or severity of the expressed guilt in high *Pd5* scorers approximates a theme of self-flagellation (with elevated *LSE*) with "exaggerated culpability and ostentatious remorse" (Nichols & Greene, 1995, p. 38). Caldwell (1988) and Nichols and Greene agreed that *Pd5* may also reflect the characteristic remorse seen in some alcoholic patterns (e.g. MMPI-2 code patterns 247/274, 427/472, and 724/742).

Low *Pd5* scorers do not report feeling unhappy, can in fact experience pleasures in life, find daily life stimulating and rewarding, do not express guilt or remorse about past misdeeds, and deny excessive use of alcohol (Graham, 1990).

Scale 4: Subtle–Obvious Subscales

The Psychopathic Deviate-Obvious subscale (*Pd-O*) has 28 items, of which 20 are keyed True, 8 False; Psychopathic Deviate-Subtle (*Pd-S*) contains 22 items, of which 4 are keyed True, 18 False. The *Pd-O* items reflect various subjective discomforts that include feeling misunderstood, unhappy, and unfairly treated, and having gotten into trouble (Caldwell, 1988). Examining the convergent validity literature, Hollrah et al. (1995) concluded that methodological problems with the MMPI S–O studies make it difficult to summarize their validity as their research results reveal different findings for different scales. They reported, however, that in isolated studies, *Pd O* docs correlate with discomfort and the admission of social nonconformity. The content of *Pd-O* suggests feeling unhappy and at odds with others and with life. Low scores suggest a closeness and warmth with others and social conformity (Caldwell, 1988).

According to Nichols (2011, p. 125):

> Two thirds of the *Pd-O* items overlap *Pd4* and *Pd5*, with the remaining one third divided about equally between *Pd1* and *Pd2*. However, *Pd-O* is thematically dominated by *Pd5* and is predominantly distressed and depressive in tone. It is highly saturated with the First Factor (correlation with *A* = .84) and thus will be raised by any of the distress scales.

Dahlstrom (1991) examined the correlates of the S–O subscales derived from partner ratings on the Katz Adjustment Scales used in the re-standardization. For both men and women, the following descriptions emerged as significant for high *Pd-O* scorers: lacks interest in things, feels others do not care about him or her, gets very sad or blue, has many fears, moody, worries about the future, takes nonprescription drugs, has been arrested or had legal difficulties, lacks social judgment, and whines and demands attention. For women only, the following represents a partial list of significant findings: poor sense of humor, restless, not affectionate, lacks energy, feelings easily hurt, easily annoyed, lacks self-confidence, lacks emotional control, argues about minor things, suspicious of others, has difficulty making decisions, and does not get along well with others. There were no unique descriptors for men.

Pd-S comprises a more mixed group of items than *Pd-O*, with an emphasis on *Pd3* (Social Imperturbability) given the items from the latter subscale. Although *Pd-S* correlates with measures of sociability/extroversions (*Pd3*, *Hy1*, and *Si1*), it does not appear to have a central theme. Nichols (2011, p. 125) describes the item content as follows:

> The items suggest an individual who is inwardly conflicted although self-controlled, and outwardly socially insouciant, carefree, and imperturbable. Many items also assert independence and self-determination in the examinee's reactions and behavior. The overall effect is one of instability or brittleness, with a potential for stubbornness or argumentative overreaction to the assertions, demands, or complaints of others.

Caldwell (1988) pointed out that some items on *Pd-S* appear nearly as obvious as the *Pd-O* items. These items report family quarrels, getting little sympathy, and wanting to leave home. The more subtle items are those reporting an absence of social anxieties, ease in talking to others, and a denial of manipulation.

Dahlstrom (1991) derived the following correlates for *Pd-S* for men and women from the partner ratings made in the re-standardization sample: moody, stubborn, easily annoyed, swears or curses, not passive and obedient, talks too much, makes big plans, and has conflicts over sex. For men only, the following correlates were derived: trouble sleeping, not shy, lacks energy, gets very sad, and has been arrested or had legal troubles. For women only, the following correlates were derived: temper tantrums, resents being told what to do, argues about minor things, nags, feels others do not care about her, gets bossy, is uncooperative, lacks emotional control, and drinks excessively.

Low *Pd-S* scores suggest self-confidence, a sense of inner calmness, and a restraint or shyness with strangers (Caldwell, 1988). However, in reviewing the literature on the Subtle subscales, Hollrah et al. (1995) were unable to find studies that supported the discriminative validity of *Pd-S*. Therefore, appropriate caution is warranted.

Scale 5: Masculinity-Femininity (MF)

The exact motivation of Hathaway and McKinley for developing Scale 5 could be somewhat unclear to readers consulting different texts, given the various accounts given to explain this scale's origins. For example, Dahlstrom et al. (1972, p. 201), generally considered the most reliable historical chroniclers of the MMPI, stated that

> Scale 5 was designed to identify the personality features related to the disorder of male sexual inversion … . Persons with this personality pattern often engage in homoerotic practices as part of their feminine emotional makeup; however, many of these men are too inhibited or full of conflict to make any overt expression of their sexual preferences.

As Colligan et al. (1983) indicated, the 1943 MMPI *Manual* describes the *Mf* scale as intending to measure "the tendency toward masculinity or femininity of interest pattern in the direction of the opposite sex" (p. 40). Clearly, the original *Manual's* description differs from the more psychopathological account given by Dahlstrom et al. (1972) in describing the origins and intent of Scale 5. Hathaway and McKinley discovered that it was too difficult in the early 1940s to obtain a large enough group of homosexual men and women possessing enough similar qualities to form suitable criterion groups (Hathaway, 1980). At least three subgroups of homosexuals were identified with different etiologies for their gender preference. One subgroup was a pseudohomosexual type with neurotic features related to inferiority; another subgroup was a psychopathic type who tended to elevate Scale 4 (*Pd*), and a third subgroup became the final reference criterion group. This group consisted of 13 homosexual men (Hathaway, 1980). Although no demographic data were reported for these participants, they were screened for gross psychological abnormalities, like psychosis, clear-cut neurotic tendencies, and psychopathy. Their homosexuality was therefore considered to rest on a constitutional basis. These individuals were seen as having a feminine emotional makeup; however, many, not surprisingly given the times, were considered too inhibited or conflicted to express their homoerotic sexual preferences. Their feminine disposition was believed to be apparent in their expressive styles, interests, and attitudes, as well as in their sexual relationships (Dahlstrom et al., 1972). Greene (2011) stated that "such persons were thought to engage in homoerotic behavior as a part of their feminine (i.e. inverted) personality characteristics" (p. 125).

Many items used to develop *Mf* were added after the original Minnesota normative group had already participated in the construction of the other clinical scales; so newly formed normal groups were selected for comparison purposes. These groups consisted of 67 female airline employees and 54 soldiers. When an item differentiated a soldier from a member of the criterion group, the item was said to be a trend in the direction of femininity (Hathaway & McKinley, 1943). A second comparison step in item selection involved identifying a group of men scoring in the "feminine" direction on an "Invert" scale derived by Terman and Miles (1936). The item endorsements of these men were then compared with a group of normals. The use of the "Invert" scale from Terman and Miles' (1936, as cited in Colligan et al., 1983) Attitude Interest Analysis Test "represents the first time that items from one diagnostic test were used to select a contrast group that was employed as an additional criterion group used for selecting items on an MMPI scale" (p. 44). A third comparison step, which appears to have been conducted initially but is considered the least important by Hathaway (1980), involved comparing the normal men (soldiers) with normal women (airline employees) to determine their response frequencies by gender.

The 60 items that survived all three comparison steps became Scale 5. Twenty-three of the Scale 5 items are borrowed from Terman and Miles (1936), whereas the other 37 items came from the MMPI item pool.

Despite some preliminary efforts, Hathaway and McKinley were unable to successfully construct an independent scale measuring female homosexual inversion. A number of subsequent studies have demonstrated that despite the efforts of the scale constructors, Scale 5 does not adequately discriminate male homosexuals from non-homosexual males, contrary to the original intent of the scale (Wong, 1984). It is therefore important not to infer homosexuality based solely on an elevated *Mf* score. In fact, it is difficult to predict homosexuality from MMPI or MMPI-2/RF data. At present, an individual's sexual orientation can generally be learned by simply asking about it, whereas this was more difficult to do when Hathaway and McKinley constructed the MMPI. The final *Mf* scale was believed to measure masculinity at one pole and femininity at the opposite pole; therefore, the scale was seen as being bipolar. However, as other researchers (e.g. Bem, 1974; Constantinople, 1973) suggested, masculinity and femininity may be more accurately assessed using separate scales for each dimension. Each may represent a different construct. On the other hand, Bem's measures of gender role are not independent of masculinity versus femininity scales, such as *Mf* (Wakefield, Sasek, Friedman, & Bowden, 1976). Also, the psychometric adequacy of Bem's Femininity scale has been criticized (Kimlicka, Wakefield, & Friedman, 1980; Kimlicka, Wakefield, & Goad, 1982). Other studies (e.g. Kimlicka, Sheppard, Wakefield, & Cross, 1987) suggest that bipolar masculinity-femininity scales have not yet been, and may not be, replaceable with separate masculine and feminine factors. However, the *Manual* (Butcher et al., 2001) describes two gender-role scales developed by Peterson and Dahlstrom (1992). These scales, Gender Role—Masculine (*GM*) and Gender Role—Feminine (*GF*), were designed as independent measures of the masculine and feminine dimensions in Scale 5. Developed on data provided by the normative sample for the MMPI-2, these scales can be useful adjuncts to aid in the interpretation of Scale 5. The *Manual* (Butcher et al., 2001) provides the psychometric data for these scales.

Because Scale 5 (and 0) were added after the initial publication of the MMPI, it took time for its assimilation into the mainstream of research and clinical practice. It was soon recognized that Scale 5 was an important measure, and research attention was eventually paid to the scale, although Harris and Lingoes (1955) and Wiener and Harmon (1946) did not develop subscales for Scale 5 (or Scale 0).

Factor analytic studies of Scale 5 indicate that the scale is not bipolar but comprises multiple factors (Graham, Schroeder, & Lilly, 1971; Sines, 1977). Graham et al. (1971) factor analyzed the responses from 422 psychiatric inpatients, outpatients, and normals, and found six factors. Serkownek (1975) later used these findings as a basis for his development of *Mf* subscales to assist in the interpretation of Scale 5: Narcissism-Hypersensitivity (*Mf1*), Stereotypic Feminine Interest (*Mf2*), Denial of Stereotypic Masculine Interests (*Mf3*), Heterosexual Discomfort-Passivity (*Mf4*), Introspective-Critical (*Mf5*), and Socially Retiring (*Mf6*). *Mf2*, *Mf4*, and *Mf5* lost only two, one, and one items, respectively, in the re-standardization. Although the Serkownek subscales remain largely intact, these have now been superseded by those of Martin and Finn (2010), described below.

Given its multidimensional character, inferences about masculinity and femininity drawn from *Mf* elevations should be made cautiously. Nonetheless, regardless of the heterogeneity of its content, *Mf* does seem to a degree to reflect, among other things, stereotypic masculine and feminine interest patterns. Items reflecting masculine–feminine interests appear to have the highest correlation with overall scale scores and are therefore considered the most differentiating items on the scale (Dahlstrom et al., 1972). Although the interest-type items are obvious or face valid, other items on the scale carry more subtle meaning. According to Nichols (2011, p. 137), Scale 5's ...

> Raw scores are normally distributed and it appears to function primarily as a measure of an individual difference variable. Scale 5 can make an important contribution to clinical descriptions, particularly in the way it may modify descriptions based on the other clinical scales and to issues related to treatment.

The *Mf* items are approximately evenly distributed between (1) sex role-related interests, activities, and vocations, and (2) an admixture of items comprised of apprehension, sexual worries, sensitivity, social reserve, and denial of cynicism and mistrust. Nichols (2011) suggested conceptualizing Scale 5 as a "family of dimensions" related to the broader construct of activity–passivity. He describes the active pole (low males, high females) as reflecting different traits, including dominance, competition, exhibitionism, intrusiveness, and acting out; whereas the passive pole (high males, low females) includes traits such as submission, dependency, cooperation, artistic, tender, verbal, and valuing nurturance, relatedness, mutuality, and style/appearance. According to Nichols (2011, p. 139):

> For both sexes, low scores tend to reflect a narrow interest pattern that may be overly tied to sex-role constraints, expectations, and identifications. High scores suggest a broader, more inclusive range of interests, which, at the extreme, may reflect identity diffusion or may become chaotic. In schizophrenia, the identity disturbance may involve a sense of uncertainty such that the boundary between what are and are not one's interests becomes highly permeable. In mania, the identity disturbance involves expanding the experience of the self to encompass an unrealistically overinclusive endorsement of interests.

Scale 5 lost four items in the MMPI-2 revision, leaving it with 56 items. The four dropped items (items 69, 70, 249, and 295) were either outdated or often considered offensive on a religious or sexual basis. Fifty two of the items on *Mf* are keyed in the same direction for men and women. An endorsement of any of these items in the keyed direction gives the respondent a point in the direction of femininity. Four of the items deal with clear sexual concerns and represent a scoring exception in that they are keyed in the opposite direction for women and men. Because of the obvious nature of these four *Mf* items, one wishing to conceal his or her sexual interests can easily do so.

In hand scoring, it is important to use the appropriate male or female template for scoring the answer sheet. For men, 25 items on *Mf* are keyed True, 31 keyed False. For women, 23 items are keyed True, 33 False. Because there is a fairly even balance between True and False keyed responses, an All-True or All-False response set will not significantly elevate scale scores. Greene (2011, p. 126) further expands on the scale's psychometric properties by stating:

> There are 33 (58.9%) items unique to Scale 5 (masculinity-femininity [MF], which is the largest percentage of unique items for any of the clinical scales. It shares no more than 4 items with any clinical scale other than Scale 0 (Social Introversion [Si] with which it shares 9 items.

Scale 5 also shares one, two, and three items with the *L*, *F*, and *K* scales, respectively, and shares the most items with Scale 0 (nine items). "With the exception of *GF* (.70) and *GM* (–.52), Scale 5 is only weakly correlated with most other MMPI-2 scales" (Nichols, 2011, p. 135).

Scale 5 uses linear *T*-scores rather than uniform *T*-score conversions. This is also the case for Scale 0 and the *L*, *F*, and *K* scales. For women, high *T*-scores on the profile sheet are associated with low raw scores, indicating a response to the items in a "masculine" direction. For men, the converse is true, with high raw scores associated with high *T*-scores. Therefore, a man with a high raw score or high *T*-score is said to be endorsing Scale 5 items the way in which women stereotypically respond. Low *T*-scores in men reflect a low endorsement of feminine-type items and indicates a more masculine interest pattern. The reason for reversing the raw scores on the profile sheet is to maintain uniformity with the other scales, in that high scores represent a form of deviation. In the case of Scale 5, elevated *T*-scores represent endorsement patterns similar to the opposite gender.

In Hunsley et al.'s (1988) large-scale meta-analysis of MMPI reliability studies using a wide variety of populations conducted between 1970 and 1981, an average internal consistency of .73 across 39 studies was reported. They also reported an average test–retest reliability of .69 for 10 studies, with time intervals from one day to two years. The *Manual* (Butcher et al., 2001) reports *Mf* reliability data for a subset of the normative sample (82 men and 111 women). An average interval of about one week shows *Mf* to have a test–retest correlation of .82 and .74 for men and women, respectively. Internal consistency estimates (coefficient alpha) for men and women were .58 and .37, respectively.

Mf is one of the scales most affected by the revision of the MMPI. It appears that men in the re-standardization group answered more items in the "feminine" direction, as compared with the original fixed reference group. This has resulted in the lowering of most men's *T* scores on *Mf* by about 10 *T*-scores (Dahlstrom & Tellegen, 1993;

Duckworth & Anderson, 1995; Friedman, 1990; Strassberg, 1991). For women, there is much less change in the endorsement frequencies of the items and women's T-scores are less dramatically affected. Another factor that influences elevations on Scale 5 is education level. In the re-standardization sample, less educated men earned lower T-score means on Scale 5 and less educated women obtained higher average T-score values. Compared to the original MMPI normals, the re-standardization normals were better educated, so that scores on Scale 5 are about 10 T-scores lower in men and 2–3 T-scores higher in women. Greene (2011) suggests that more research is needed to determine if the older correlates for the MMPI Scale 5 are applicable to the MMPI-2.

Moderator scales affecting the interpretation of Scale 5 elevations include Ss (Social Status; Nelson, 1952) and Es (Ego Strength; Barron, 1953). High scores on these scales both tend to emphasize the positive aspects of Mf scores, regardless of whether the latter are high or low. Scale 4 (Pd) is also an important moderator of Scale 5 scores. Nichols (2011, p. 135) provides a description for interpreting Scales 4 and 5 in a configural fashion:

> Scores on Scale 4 strongly influence the interpersonal aspects of high Scale 5 raw scores. For men, the strength of the patient's basic attachment to others, his commitment to the maintenance and repair of close relationships, and his capacity for trust, optimism, warmth, and forgiveness are indicated by the extent to which Scale 5 exceeds Scale 4, provided that 4 does not exceed T-55. For women, the same pattern of positive trends is given by the extent to which Scale 4 exceeds Scale 5, provided that 4 does not exceed T-60. As Scale 4 is elevated beyond these limits, especially as it exceeds Scale 5 for men, there tend to be chronic problems in the quality, strength, and stability of attachments. Such patterns tend to predict passive-aggressive struggles; significant conflicts around dependency-independency; a tendency to react to requests as if they were demands; and a quickness to feel dominated (especially with men feeling dominated by women) and to reflexively rebel against this feeling. With high scores on Scale 3, elevations on Scale 4 are more benign than otherwise. Scale 5 tends to focus the rebelliousness and authority conflict that accompany Scale 4 and give them an intellectual/philosophical basis, such that many men with this pattern are better described as anti-authoritarian rather than anti-authority.

Investigations of the correlates for high and low Mf scores in normals have been conducted by Hathaway and Meehl (1952, as cited in Dahlstrom et al., 1972) and Gough, McKee, and Yandell (1955). Hathaway and Meehl found that high Mf normal men were described by their peers as sensitive and prone to worry, idealistic and peaceable, sociable and curious, and having general aesthetic interests. Women with high Mf scores did not have correspondingly similar descriptors, but were described as adventurous. Low-scoring men were described by their peers as practical, balanced, cheerful, self-confident, and independent, whereas low-scoring women were seen as sensitive, responsive, modest, grateful, and wise.

Gough et al. (1955) described the high Scale 5 man as inner-directed and intellectually curious. Work and achievements provided these men significant gratification, and they were seen as mature, self-aware individuals. They had good judgment and common sense.

They could communicate effectively and were quite verbal. Some of the adjectives typical of these high Scale 5 men included ambitious, clear-thinking, effeminate, imaginative, nervous, organized, sensitive, and submissive. Low-scoring men were seen as lacking insight into their motives, preferring action to thought, and having narrow interests. They did not appear to have the psychological complexity or inner-directedness that the high Scale 5 men had. Nichols and Greene (1995) provided a good summary of high *Mf* scores in men (low scores in women). They stated that the *Mf* scale emphasizes passivity, sensitivity, and aesthetic and/or intellectual interests: "Sedentary activities and pastimes are preferred over those involving movement, competition, and the out-of-doors. *Mf* seems to reflect intellectualization over rationalization" (Nichols & Greene, 1995, p. 35).

Long and Graham (1991), using ratings provided by significant others, studied the descriptions of normal men with various score levels of Scale 5. The participants were 819 heterosexual couples who were included in the normative samples for the MMPI-2 (Butcher et al., 1989). In contrast to previous literature indicating high Scale 5 men to be passive, dependent, and submissive, they found that men with higher Scale 5 scores actually tended to be less passive and obedient. They found that level of education was a better predictor of certain behaviors and personality characteristics than *Mf* scores in normal men.

The correlates for high and low *Mf* scale scores vary as a function of the type of individuals being assessed. For example, high Scale 5 scores are frequently obtained by normal married men, although not for women (Dahlstrom et al., 1972). Although relatively frequent among normal men, Scale 5 is not often a high point among psychiatric patients (Tanner, 1990). Given that much of the *Mf* item content suggests mild maladjustment, Ward and Dillon (1990) investigated whether emotional distress is a correlate of the *Mf* scale in clinical populations. In studying the *Mf* raw scores and symptom ratings obtained on psychiatric patients, emotional distress correlates for Scale 5 were identified. Anxiety, depressed mood, guilt feelings, and tension were associated with high ("feminine") raw scores in both men and women. It is interesting to note that Ward and Dillon found these correlates to be largely independent of other MMPI clinical scales.

It is clear that high Scale 5 scorers, particularly men, vary in their behavioral descriptions or diagnoses as a function of their normal versus psychiatric status. High *Mf* scores in men (low *Mf* scores in women) in the normal population may indicate sensitivity, as well as aesthetic or intellectual interests, particularly if the person is college educated. Traditionally, the literature has emphasized the passivity or submissiveness often noted in high Scale 5 men, although Long and Graham (1991) found opposite trends. An underlying dimension of Scale 5 has been hypothesized to be role flexibility (Kunce & Anderson, 1976, 1984). The high Scale 5 man is able to appreciate a diversity of interests and show tolerance for differences in others. Traditional masculine interests are likely to be expressed by men who score in the *T*-46–55 range. Scores below 46 begin to suggest a more "macho" orientation, with very low scores (*T* < 40) strongly suggestive of an activity-oriented, nonverbally expressive type of individual who may be perceived as insensitive, competitive, aggressive, independent, and possibly crude, with traditional masculine–feminine views and possible underlying doubts about his own masculinity. High Scale 5 women are likely to be seen in many ways similar to low Scale 5 men, that is, as aggressive, competitive, dominating, energetic, and confident. The low Scale 5 woman may be described as hyperfeminine if her score is below a *T*-score of 40 and if she is not college educated (Graham, 1990). Between *T*-scores of 40 and 55, she is likely to be described as having stereotypically feminine interests.

Clearly, high and low *Mf* scores vary greatly in their correlates for men and women. The reader interested in more detailed descriptions of diagnostic feedback and treatment considerations is referred to Nichols (2011) and Levak et al. (2011). Overall, one's symptomatic pattern, presenting problem, interpersonal relations, history, and diagnostic considerations are strongly dependent upon the relation of *Mf* with other Scales.

Martin-Finn Subscales

A new set of seven *Mf* subscales has been developed for the MMPI-2 by Martin and Finn (Martin, 1993; Martin & Finn, 2010) using factor analytic procedures. The normative sample used in constructing these subscales was the MMPI-2 community participants (Butcher et al., 1989). These subscales are free of item overlap and have internal consistency coefficients high enough to suggest that they are cohesive measures. The first subscale, Denial of Stereotypical Masculine Interests, is a measure of lack of interest in activities typically considered male or masculine. The second subscale, Hypersensitivity-Anxiety, is a measure of self-focused worry and sensitivity. Stereotypical Feminine Interests is the third subscale and is a measure of activities typically considered female or feminine. Low Cynicism, the fourth subscale, is a measure of the lack of cynicism and suspiciousness about human motivations. Aesthetic Interest is the fifth subscale and is a measure of interest in the arts and written expression. The sixth subscale, Feminine Gender Identity, measures the wish to be female and to have interests traditionally associated with women. Restraint is the seventh subscale and is a measure of restraint from loud and aggressive interests and behaviors. Martin and Finn also provided a composite bipolar femininity–masculinity scale that is a combination of the three subscales that they believe to be the most central to the construct of masculinity–femininity (E. H. Martin, personal communication, April 8, 1996). These subscales are: Denial of Stereotypical Masculine Interests, Stereotypical Feminine Interests, and Feminine Gender Identity. Table A.2 in Appendix A (pp. 546–547) of Friedman et al. (2001) provides the item composition for these subscales, the scoring direction for the items, and the means and standard deviations for the MMPI-2 normative sample. Table B.7 in Appendix B (pp. 546–547) of Friedman et al. (2001) provides the linear *T*-score conversions for these subscales.

Scale 6: Paranoia (Pa)

There is no available information describing the exact way the paranoid criterion group was selected, nor do data exist about the demographic characteristics of the participants used in the construction of this 40-item scale. It is assumed that the usual item selection procedures were followed as with the other MMPI scales. The criterion patients, according to Hathaway (1980), carried diagnoses of paranoid state, paranoid condition, or paranoid schizophrenia, and the scale was developed to assess paranoid symptoms and features. The patients studied manifested various signs of paranoia, including ideas of reference, feelings of persecution, grandiose self-concepts, hypersensitivity, rigid thinking, and suspiciousness. There were attempts to improve the operating characteristics of the scale, but Hathaway (1980, p. 73) stated that the results were disappointing:

> As with other scales, several different scales were derived and tested by cross-validation. This cross-validation was always disappointing and the published scale was considered weak although it was the best that could be developed. One factor that seemed to justify at least temporary use of the scale was that there were few false positives. When a person had a high score, he tended to be diagnosed as paranoid or at least he was felt to be sensitive and rigid in personal relationships.

Hathaway (1980) went on to state that, as was true with Scale 8, the hope that *Pa* could be improved was not realized. "Even the *K* variable failed to sharpen the differentiation. It was felt that the *K* correction did not help because more than 20 percent of the Scale 6 items were already subtle in character" (as cited in Dahlstrom & Dahlstrom, 1980, p. 73).

Although Hathaway commented above about "few false positives" with high 6 scores (most likely due to the high concentrations of obvious items), Vestre and Watson (1972) found that 41 percent of their patients with *T*-scores greater than 75 did not have paranoid symptoms. There are, in fact, false positives associated with elevated Scale 6 scores. Nichols (2011) noted that another justification for publishing what Hathaway acknowledged as a "weak" scale was that, when sufficiently organized, paranoid patients are notoriously able to evade detection on mental status and interview. Thus, even a weak scale can add value in psychodiagnosis.

Scale 6 measures a range of chronic and acute paranoid mentation and attitudes that include frank psychotic ideation, such as delusions of control, persecutory ideas/delusions, hypersensitivity, and rigid denials of cynicism. The scale also taps externalizing processes, such as projection, hypervigilance, and scanning for "evidence" of hostile intentions or actions. According to Nichols and Greene (1995), Scale 6 is "the most general measure of projection and is sensitive to both implicit and explicit operations to place or locate motives, responsibility, and other, especially undesirable, personal attributes outside the self" (p. 36). This is consistent with Ihilevich and Gleser's (1986, 1991) definition of the projection ego-defense mechanism, which involves the attribution of negative intent or characteristics to others without substantiating evidence. Nichols (2011, p. 157) further elaborates on the defenses employed by high Scale 6 scorers:

> Rationalization of anger, resentment, and loss of control is also common if not pervasive. One sees rigid self-justification in the accumulation and hostile use of (selectively gathered) evidence to authorize suspicion, accusation, and even attack. Depending on other features of the profile, a range of secondary defenses, including intellectualization, displacement, reaction-formation, and denial, are seen.

To help determine the nature of the psychopathology, it is critical to examine the Harris-Lingoes subscales for this scale when a score is elevated. For example, an individual with no clear-cut thought disorder may appear clinically paranoid if he or she is pathologically oversensitive to others' slights or failures of consideration. Often these individuals may be diagnosed with paranoid character traits or a paranoid personality disorder. However, Morey and Smith (1988), in their comprehensive review of personality disorders, pointed out the rarity of a diagnosis of paranoid personality disorder in clinical populations with base-rate ranges between 0.9 percent and 1.4 percent. They stated that it has not been conclusively demonstrated that increasing elevations on *Pa* are associated with a paranoid personality disorder. Because individuals with this disorder are characterized as mistrustful and suspicious, it may be that they are unlikely to endorse the face-valid (obvious) items reflecting paranoia. For this reason, the *K*+ profile described by Marks et al. (1974) may reflect paranoid symptomatology in psychiatric inpatients. In the *K*+ code pattern for the MMPI, all of the clinical scales are below a *T*-score of 70, with six or more scales below a *T*-score of 60. The only prominent scale is an elevated *K*. Marks et al. (1974) found in their psychiatric inpatient sample that 18 percent of the participants with the 86/68 code pattern were diagnosed with paranoid personality disorder, whereas 68 percent were diagnosed with paranoid schizophrenia. Another code pattern that may include paranoid personality disorder features is the 248 codetype, with elevated *L* and *K* scales suggesting guardedness (Tarter & Perley, 1975). Scale *L*, which can suppress clinical profiles, sometimes acts as a proxy for Scale 6. It is interesting to note that in Goldberg's Rule 3 (Goldberg, 1965; Friedman et al., 2001), the neurotic versus psychotic index, *L* is grouped with Scales 6 and 8 for predicting a psychotic profile (see Chapter 9 where the Goldberg Rules are discussed). *L* appears to have implications for psychoticism. "In psychiatric populations, unelevated profiles with distinct elevations on *L*, especially when coded 34/43, almost invariably reflect a paranoid condition" (Nichols, 2011). It is important to note that Scale 6 may not always be elevated in paranoid-personality disordered patients, and other scales should be examined for indications of blame, anger, and mistrust (Morey & Smith, 1988).

It is important to examine the relations with other scales when *Pa* is elevated. For example, "concurrent elevations on Scales 4, 8, and 9 tend to accentuate the negative features of Scale 6 characteristics, whereas elevations on Scales 2, 3, and 7 tend to attenuate and soften them" (Nichols, 2011, p. 146). Scale 6 is most highly correlated with Scale 8, with which it shares 13 items. When Scale 8 is elevated concurrently with *Pa*, it increases the probability that greater disorganization, incoherence, and bizarre behavior will be manifested. If Scale 8 is low with a high Scale 6 elevation, delusional thinking is likely to be more systematized and focused on a specific individual or entity (e.g. the White House; the FBI). According to Nichols (2011), if Scale 3 (*Hy*) exceeds Scale 6 when both are elevated, the paranoid manifestations tend to be better socialized.

The patient manifests a socially positive and compliant attitude on the surface and rarely becomes overtly angry or hostile. Covertly, however, there are often preoccupations with control, power, and secrecy; these people command but do not inspire loyalty and tend to be seen as conniving, calculating, two-faced, and ruthless.

(Nichols, 2011, pp. 146–147)

Nichols and Greene (1995) described the cognitive operations of the high Scale 6 scorer. They stated that: "*Pa* emphasizes the rationalization of anger, resentment, and the loss of control. One sees rigid self-justification, the accumulation and hostile or self-justifying use of 'evidence' or authorization for accusation, suspicion, and attack. *Pa* seems to reflect rationalization over intellectualization" (p. 35).

It appears that the compromised rationality of the high *Pa* scorer leads them to believe that others are out to deceive or harm them, and most importantly, to undermine their dignity, and humiliate, coerce, or overpower them. There is an inherent inability to rationally overrule their own distortions by considering facts and arguments, as they believe others are motivated to discredit them. They therefore lack insight, believing that their own thinking is free of impairment and disruption. Judgment errors are usually apparent to others as reflexive and misguided.

Typically, psychiatric patients who score high on *Pa* fear moral and/or physical attacks, feel easily misunderstood, and unfairly criticized and treated, as well as self-righteous, opinionated, suspicious, and self-dissatisfied (Friedman, Webb, & Lewak, 1989; Lewak et al., 1990). Additionally, they are seen as argumentative, stubborn, self-centered and lacking in social skills. Individuals with significant dependent, dysphoric, or histrionic traits tend to better preserve close relations as they are less focused on expecting malice from others. "Although they may be rigid and self-righteous, their hypersensitivity tends to focus on rejection rather than attack, and they may make significant concessions to retain relationships of value to them" (Nichols, 2011, p. 157).

Normal men with high *Pa* elevations have been described as sensitive, sentimental, loyal, trustful, cooperative, kind, and submissive, whereas normal women have been described as emotional, soft-hearted, and sensitive (Dahlstrom et al., 1972). Individuals scoring in the normal *Pa* range (*T*-46–57) may either lack paranoid symptoms or have well-ingrained paranoid traits with sufficient reality testing to avoid endorsing the obvious items on the scale (Greene, 1991a, 1991b).

The re-standardization project examined the meaning of elevated *Pa* scores for normals who tend to be described more positively than psychiatric patients. Women in the normative sample who scored high on Scale 6 were described by their husbands as moody with a tendency to get sad and blue, lacking emotional control, having a tendency to cry easily, and being susceptible to bad dreams (Butcher & Williams, 1992). Men were not clearly differentiated in the way their partners described them, and no significant correlates were reported for them.

There is mixed information on the meaning of low scores on Scale 6. Some authors contend that low scores actually reveal the hidden presence of paranoia, as a respondent who is trying to conceal his vulnerabilities may deny any suspiciousness or hypersensitivity whatsoever (e.g. Butcher & Williams, 1992; Carson, 1969; Duckworth & Anderson, 1995; Endicott, Jortner, & Abramoff, 1969; Friedman, Webb, & Lewak, 1989; Lewak, 1993). Other researchers failed to find a consistent relationship between low *Pa* scores and paranoid symptomatology (Boerger, Graham, & Lilly, 1974; Vestre & Watson, 1972). In our experience, we have observed clinically paranoid individuals attempting to look good to obtain very low scores on Scale 6. A very low score on this scale should alert the clinician to look for other measures of suspiciousness or cynicism, such as a low score on the *Pa3* (Naïveté) subscale and/or high scores on the *CYN* (Cynicism) content scales, especially *CYN2* (Interpersonal Suspiciousness). Low *Pa* scores appear to be associated with having low empathy for others and with low motivation for making relations with others easy and comfortable.

Dahlstrom et al. (1972) reported the descriptions of Hathaway and Meehl's low-scoring normals on Scale 6. Men were described by their acquaintances as cheerful, balanced, and decisive, but also as conscienceless. These men perceived themselves as orderly and as good social mixers. Women were seen by others as serious, mature, reasonable, and trusting. They saw themselves as self-controlled, persevering, wise, loyal, and modest. Anderson (1956) found that college students in counseling with *Pa* scores below *T*-40 tended to be underachievers with low grades, and reported difficulties with their parents. All 40 of the original items in Scale 6 have been retained in the MMPI-2; however, two items were modified to eliminate sexist wording and to simplify the item meaning.

Twenty-five of the items on Scale 6 are keyed True, 15 False. Because more items are endorsed True, as is the case with the other scales of the psychotic tetrad, an All-True response set will tend to elevate this scale. Thirty-three of the Scale 6 items overlap other scales, sharing 9, 8, and 13 items, respectively, with *F* and Scales 4 and 8. Eight items overlap *BIZ*. *DEP* and Scale 6 share four items in common and Scales 3 (*Hy*) and 6 share four items. Thirteen items on Scale 6 do not overlap with the other clinical scales. Dahlstrom et al. (1972) reported early itemetric research of Little (1949) examining which Scale 6 items were the most discriminating with the highest item-total scale (biserial) correlations. The frankly paranoid item describing beliefs of being plotted against (item 138) was the most differentiating for his college-level participants with a biserial correlation of .77. Other items tended to be less related to the total scale scores. Greene (2011, pp. 130–131) reported the 15 MMPI-2 scales with the highest correlations with Scale 6 in the Caldwell (2007b) clinical sample:

> There are three primary categories represented within these scales: (1) paranoid and psychotic behavior (Paranoia, Obvious [P-O]; Persecutory Ideas [Pa1]; Scale 8 [Schizophrenia (Sc)]; (2) general subjective distress and negative affect (Post-Traumatic Stress Disorder – Keane [PK]; Scale 7 [Psychasthenia (Pt)]; Depression [DEP]; and (3) social alienation [Social Alienation (Sc1)]).

For MMPI Scale 6, the test–retest correlations for psychiatric cases ranged between .61 and .71 for a one- to two-day interval between testing, and between .59 and .65 for a one-year interval (Dahlstrom et al., 1975). In Hunsley et al.'s (1988) large-scale meta-analysis of MMPI reliability studies using various populations conducted between 1970 and 1981, an average internal consistency of .73 across 70 studies was reported. They also reported an average test–retest reliability of .69 for 15 studies over time intervals of one day to two years. For the MMPI-2, Butcher et al. (2001) reported test–retest reliability data on Scale 6 for the community (normal) sample of 82 men (*r* = .67) and 111 women (*r* = .56) retested at an average interval of 8.6 days (*Mdn* = 7 days). Scale 6 has the lowest test–retest values among the clinical scales and the lowest internal consistency estimates (Cronbach's coefficient alpha) (excluding the *Mf* scale for women) with alpha coefficients of .34 and .39 for men and women, respectively.

Harris-Lingoes Subscales

Harris and Lingoes developed three subscales for Scale 6: Ideas of External Influence (*Pa1*) (now called Persecutory Ideas), Poignancy (*Pa2*), and Moral Virtue (*Pa3*) (now called Naïveté).

Pa1· *Persecutory Ideas (17 Items)*

Sixteen of the 17 items on *Pa1* are keyed True and mostly reflect the persecutory content of Scale 6. Harris and Lingoes (1968) described the content of this subscale as consisting of "Externalization of blame for one's problems, frustrations, failures; in the extreme degree, persecutory ideas; and projection of responsibility for negative feelings." Nichols and Crowhurst (2006) described four related and somewhat overlapping subsets of items that permit a useful breakdown of *Pa1* scores: (1) *Pf1*: Resentment (items 17, 22, 42, 145, 234, and 484), reflecting fixed ideas of mistreatment and victimization with some items having a secondary depressive theme; (2) *Pf2*: Ideas of Reference (items 251, 259, 305, 333, 424, and 549); (3) *Pf3*: Delusions of Control (items 24, 144, 162, 216, 228, 336, 355, and 361), delusional items suggest that one's will and mentation are being influenced (e.g. weakened; subverted by external forces); and (4) *Pf4*: Persecutory Ideas/Delusions (items 42, 99, 138, 144, 216, 259, 333, and 314). Nichols (2011) points out that unless *Pa1* scores equal or exceed *T*-100, it is possible that the test taker may have endorsed items on only one or two of these subgroups. This suggests that a careful inspection of the endorsed *Pa1* items be conducted, as such endorsements may realistically reflect that one may actually be followed by an angry spouse's private investigator, or a claims adjustor trying to build a case against a person, the aims of a prosecuting attorney, and so on. On the other hand, item endorsements reflecting ideas of reference or delusions of control are likely to indicate a psychotic process.

Ward, Kersh, and Waxmonsky (1998) suggested that *Pa1* is the only MMPI-2 scale or subscale that measures uniquely paranoid ideas. These researchers derived a three-factor structure for the Scale 6 using substance abuse patients, and found that *Pa1* and the Paranoid factor had 14 of 16 items in common, thereby supporting the construct validity of this subscale. It should be noted that although *Pa1* substantially overlaps *PSYC* (eight items, 32 percent of *PSYC*) and *BIZ* (seven items, 30 percent of *BIZ*), the latter two scales intermix explicitly paranoid items with non-paranoid psychotic symptoms. Wrobel (1992) found projection to be a defense associated with patients having high *PA1* scores. Nichols and Greene (1995) stated that their paranoid thought process category is best represented by *Pa1* "which emphasizes persecutory ideas, resentment, and convictions of having been unfairly treated, and delusional ideas of being attacked, influenced, subverted, or undermined" (p. 32). They also noted that *Pa-O* is highly redundant with *Pa1*. High *Pa1* scorers tend to feel that the world is an unsafe or hostile place and that others are not to be trusted. "The *Pa1* items express the idea that one is the object of interest to hostile forces" (Nichols, 2011, p. 147). These forces are experienced as far more powerful than the subject. It is not surprising that *Pa1* and *Pd4* (Social Alienation) share six items in common and are highly intercorrelated in a sample of psychiatric inpatients and outpatients (Nichols & Greene, 1995). High scorers tend to blame others for their problems, feel that others have unfairly blamed or punished them, and feel misunderstood (Graham, 1990). It is not surprising to learn that high male *Pa1* scorers in the Graham et al. (1999) investigation of psychiatric outpatients tended to report a history of being physically abused as well as reporting a history of committing domestic violence, a finding generally supportive of the clinical lore and empirical data linking the two.

Low scorers do not endorse items suggesting externalization of their problems or the use of projection as their main mechanism of defense, and tend not to externalize their problems. However, Caldwell (1988) stated that raw scores as low as five or six may point to a paranoid process.

Pa2: *Poignancy (9 Items)*

This subscale appears to measure how sensitive or thin-skinned an individual is in reaction to others. Seven of the items are keyed True, two False. An All-True response set will therefore elevate *Pa1*. Harris and Lingoes (1968) provided the following content descriptors for *Pa2*: "Thinking of oneself as something special and different from other people; high-strung; cherishing of sensitive feelings; overly subjective; and thin-skinned." This subscale reflects a facet of the mood or feeling aspect of depression (Nichols & Greene, 1995). In fact, Nichols (2011) refers to *Pa2* as the depressive component of Scale 6, as the scale items connote extraordinary dysphoric vulnerability. Individuals with high scores report an unusual intensity of feelings, angry resentment, a painful sensitivity to criticism, cry easily, feel misunderstood, and feel lonely even in the presence of others (Caldwell, 1988; Graham et al., 1999). These individuals tend to see themselves as taking a longer time to heal from emotional hurts as compared to others, and recognize that they are easily wounded (Levitt, 1989). It appears that high scorers are grievance collectors who nurse grudges fueled by resentment and an inability to forgive others, most likely including empathic failures. Feeling more high-strung than others, high scorers may also tend to look for risky or exciting activities to make them feel better (Graham, 1990). Low scorers feel understood and accepted and do not experience themselves as more sensitive than others (Caldwell, 1988; Graham, 1990).

Pa3: *Naïveté (9 Items)*

Harris and Lingoes (1968) provided the following content descriptors for *Pa3*: "Affirmation of moral virtue, excessive generosity about the motives of others; righteousness about ethical matters; obtuse naiveté; and denial of distrust and hostility." Thus this subscale primarily measures how one perceives other people in terms of their trustworthiness. Eight of the nine items are keyed False, making *Pa3* susceptible to the effects of an All-False response set. High scorers tend to have optimistic and naïve attitudes about others and themselves and may have difficulty experiencing forgiveness when they feel they have been deceived or treated unfairly (Butcher et al., 2001; Caldwell, 1988; Graham, 1990).

There appears to be an underlying rigidity of opinions and attitudes that translates into a judgmental orientation toward others' behavior (e.g. good/bad, right/wrong, and moral/immoral). For this reason, Caldwell (1988) thought that *Pa3* would be better named Moral Righteousness. High scorers endorse items reflecting benign to positive expectations regarding the honesty and trustworthiness of others, denying cynical attitudes. Meehl and Hathaway (1946, as cited in Ward et al., 1998) speculated that "paranoid deviates are characterized by a tendency to give two sorts of responses, one of which is obviously paranoid, the other 'obviously' not" (p. 293). *Pa3* (and *Hy1*) are negatively correlated with *CYN* (both at –.83; Greene, 2011), and seven *Pa3* items negatively overlap *CYN*).

In outpatient mental health settings, high *Pa3* scorers tend to be viewed as hostile and as manifesting paranoid ideation despite their denial of paranoid attitudes (Graham et al., 1999). Low scorers view others as untrustworthy and motivated by self-interest, and are likely to be suspicious of their motives. Nichols and Greene (1995) suggested that a low *Pa3* score coupled with a high *Hy2* (Need for Affection) score reflects cynicism of a competitive, narcissistic, or suspicious variety.

Scale 6: Subtle–Obvious Subscales

The Paranoia–Obvious subscale (*Pa-O*) has 23 items, of which 20 are keyed True, 3 False; 15 items overlap *Pa1*. Not surprisingly, Nichols and Greene (1995) reported a high correlation (*r* = .94) between *Pa1* and *Pa-O* in a sample of psychiatric inpatients and outpatients. Paranoia-Subtle (*Pa-S*) has 17 items, of which 5 are keyed True, 12 False. *Pa-O* appears to be the psychotic component of Scale 6 as it is highly correlated with Scale 8, *PSYC*, and *BIZ*. Caldwell (1988) placed the 23 *Pa-O* items into three categories: (a) persecutory paranoid items (e.g. feeling personally mistreated and knowing who your enemies are), (b) feelings of loneliness and social isolation, and (c) self-awareness of a distressingly low threshold for emotional reactions (e.g. hypersensitivity). Overall, *Pa-O* appears to emphasize the operation of blaming and attributing hostility to others, as well as including a few oversensitive/depressive items from *Pa2*. Hollrah et al. (1995) reviewed Wrobel and Lachar's (1982) results and reported that *Pa-O* correlated positively with measures of discomfort and reality distortion. Dahlstrom et al. (1972) reported that Wiener and Harmon (1946) found that the original Minnesota normal men endorsed the *Pa-O* items much less frequently than they did those of the other obvious subscales, a finding confirmed for the re-standardization sample (see Butcher et al., 1989, pp. 81–83, Table B3). An elevated *Pa-O* score in a "normal" examinee therefore warrants a careful assessment of potential paranoid symptoms or character traits.

Dahlstrom (1991) examined the correlates of the S–O subscales derived from partner ratings on the Katz Adjustment Scales used in the re-standardization. For both men and women, the following descriptions emerged as significant for high *Pa-O* scorers: suspicious of others, poor sense of humor, lacks interest in things, feels others do not care about him or her, has many fears, experiences bad dreams, frets over little things, moody, not cheerful, complains of body aches, overly sensitive to rejection, does not show sound judgment, and gives up too easily. For men, descriptors included the following: whines and demands attention, lacks affection, bossy, unpleasant, hostile, and unfriendly. For women, descriptors included: gets very sad, thinks others are talking about her, cries easily, lacks energy, appears worn out, lacks emotional control, worries about the future, does not get along with others, and acts helpless. Caldwell (1988) suggested that low *Pa-O* scores may reflect an absence of resentments, successful social engagement, a comfort with one's own feelings, and possibly a high threshold for aggravation.

The *Pa-S* items, although classified as subtle, appear to have a few obvious items. All of the *Pa3* (Naïveté) items are contained in *Pa-S*, and there may therefore be some interpretive redundancy between high scores on these two subscales. *Pa-S* is most highly correlated (negatively) with measures of cynicism (*CYN1*, *ASP1*, *CYN*, and *ASP*) and is essentially independent of *Pa-O* and *Pa2* (Nichols, 2011). The male and female normal participants in the re-standardization sample (Butcher et al., 1989) tended to obtain a lower mean score on *Pa-S* versus the other subtle subscales. Although this could be due in part to the relatively shorter length of *Pa-S*, or to particular features of the re-standardization sample, among psychiatric patients, a high score on *Pa-S,* like *Pa-O,* warrants a careful assessment of potential paranoid symptoms or character traits. Dahlstrom (1991) found that both men and women in the re-standardization sample who elevated *Pa-S* were described by their partners as not being nervous, passive, or obedient. Women were described as not suspicious of others, showing sound judgment, not overeating, and thoughtful of others. Men were described as not lying, having a good sense of humor, not lacking an interest in things, not worrying over small things, being cooperative, and not overly sensitive to rejection.

Scale 7: Psychasthenia (Pt)

Scale 7 was designed to measure a neurotic pattern called *psychasthenia,* a now obsolescent term introduced by Pierre Janet to separate neuroses dominated by "doubting, agitation, and anxiety and by obsessional ideas" (Berrios, 1985, p. 174). Psychasthenia involves an inability to resist undesired, maladaptive behaviors, which McKinley and Hathaway (1942) described as deriving from the concept of a "weakened will" (p. 616). Preceding this concept of a weakened will was the idea of a weakened (asthenic) nervous system that was commonly referred to as neurasthenia. The catch-all diagnosis of neurasthenia applied to a syndrome with vague and variable symptoms, "particularly manifesting as extreme fatigue, insomnia, depression, headaches, dyspepsia, and a variety of non-verifiable physical complaints" (Gosling, 1987, p. 2). This diagnosis, one of the most common diagnoses in the late 19th and early 20th centuries, was given to individuals unable to keep up their former pace of life and, in fact, appeared in the second edition of the *DSM* (American Psychiatric Association, 1968) as *neurasthenic neurosis* but was subsequently dropped from the third edition of the *DSM* (American Psychiatric Association, 1980). The emphasis in this syndrome was on physical manifestations, with exhaustion, easy fatigability, and chronic weakness as the cardinal features, although proponents of the syndrome were unable to discover the pathological basis of the so-called disease (Gosling, 1987).

Rather than emphasizing physical problems, individuals classified as having psychasthenic tendencies in the initial MMPI development were described as having excessive self-doubts and worries, leading to tension, difficulty in making choices, various fears, obsessive preoccupations, compulsive urges and acts (e.g. hand washing), vague anxieties, and feelings of low self-confidence and insecurity. These individuals might find themselves ruminating about meaningless facts (like repeatedly counting unimportant objects) in an attempt to control their high anxiety levels. In the past, psychasthenic conditions were often referred to as compulsion neuroses, obsessive–compulsive states, or obsessive–ruminative tension states (McKinley, 1944). The more contemporary diagnostic category would be obsessive–compulsive disorder (DSM-5; American Psychiatric Association, 2013).

Scale 7 does not contain items reflecting specific phobias and compulsions (e.g. Scales 7 and *FRS2* share no items in common) because individual differences between participants probably failed to permit an item to be endorsed with sufficient frequency to survive the item analysis in McKinley and Hathaway's (1942) development of *Pt.* It is believed, therefore, that the underlying personality structure of psychasthenia, rather than specific fears and/or phobias, is reflected in the content of Scale 7. Marks et al.

(1974) stated that "although the specific fears, preoccupations, and compulsive acts are different from individual to individual and are potentially innumerable, the personality makeup of such persons has sufficient homogeneity to comprise a recognizable common pattern" (p. 28).

Pt was constructed with only 20 psychiatric inpatients with a diagnosis of psychasthenia constituting the criterion group. It was apparently very difficult to locate outpatients with this syndrome, and few patients were so severely handicapped by their condition as to require hospitalization. Moreover, McKinley and Hathaway (1942) admitted that even with this small group of carefully examined inpatients, there was at least one, and possibly more, who were incorrectly diagnosed.

The item endorsements of the 20 criterion cases were compared with a group of 139 normal married men ranging in age from 26 to 43 and to 200 normal married women ranging in age from 26 to 43. Additionally, 265 college students were included in a separate comparison to ascertain the effects of age on item endorsements. Because the resultant number of items discriminating the criterion from the normal groups was considered too small, these items were augmented by an additional item analysis (item-total tetrachoric correlations) performed by correlating each item with the initial set of discriminating items in a sample of 100 randomly selected psychiatric patients and 100 normals. Items were retained if they attained sufficiently high item-total correlations within either group, leading to the final 48-item composition of the scale. The resulting scale was then tested against a new sample of 50 variously diagnosed psychiatric cases. Nichols (2011, pp. 161–162) elaborated on this process by noting that…

> These were not cross-validation cases in the usual sense, and none received a final diagnosis of Psychasthenia. However, Hathaway's staff considered each to manifest "symptomatic evidence of obsessions or compulsions" (Hathaway & McKinley, 1942, p. 28). Only 10% of these cases obtained scores below the mean of a normal group of 397 women and 293 men, ages 16 to 45. The mean for these symptomatic cases was about 20% below that for the criterion psychasthenics, but 30% higher than for an unselected sample of psychiatric patients, and nearly twice that for the normal group, even though their psychasthenic symptoms were relatively mild or equivocal.

In the revision of the MMPI, Scale 7 lost no items but did have two of its items slightly rewritten for grammatical clarification.

The efforts of Hathaway seemed to pay off in the sense that *Pt* retained the homogeneity noted by Hathaway, among the highest of the clinical scales. The scale is internally consistent with split-half values that are almost as high as the test–retest coefficients. However, the efforts to lengthen the preliminary scale resulted in adding items which reflect the general maladjustment and subjective distress dimension of the MMPI, the first factor, rather than items with distinctive psychasthenic variance (see Bolinskey & Nichols, 2011). As a result, when considered in terms of its intended purpose in identifying obsessive–compulsive traits/conditions, *Pt* must be considered weak.

Greene (2011) examined the 15 scales with the highest correlations with Scale 7 in the Caldwell (2007b) clinical sample (e.g. Welsh Anxiety [*A*]; Post-Traumatic Stress

Disorder—Keane [PK]; and College Maladjustment [Mt]) and concluded that there was only one dimension represented within these scales, that of general subjective distress and negative affect. As Greene (2011) notes, "Scale 7 is a composite measure of general subjective distress and negative affect that permeates the MMPI-2 item pool" (p. 133).

Because the items on Scale 7 reflect maladjustment, the lack of item subtlety did not permit Wiener and Harmon (1946) to construct S-O subscales for it. Similarly, Harris and Lingoes found the Pt items so homogeneous as to resist separation into subcategories. True is the scoring direction for 81 percent (39) of the 48 items on Scale 7, and therefore an All-True response set would tend to elevate this scale. Nine items are keyed False. The addition of a full K raw score to Scale 7 helps to correct for a defensive response set affecting Pt scores, and a space is provided on the profile sheet to add 1.0 K to the Pt raw score.

Ten items on Scale 7 do not overlap with any of the 10 clinical scales, although they do overlap with other validity and supplementary scales. Most of the item overlap on Scale 7 is with other subjective distress scales; it shares 17 items with Scales 8 and PK, 16 items with PS, 14 with Mt, 13 with Scale 2 and A, 9 with Scale 0, DEP and RCd (Demoralization), 8 with RC7, 6 with ANX, 5 with OBS, 4 with NEGE, and 3 each with LSE and WRK. Scale 7 measures many of the tendencies and traits of the obsessive-compulsive, phobic, and generalized anxiety disorders and is also implicated in psychotic profiles (except for mania). According to Duckworth and Anderson (1995), "Kunce and Anderson (1976, 1984) have hypothesized an underlying dimension of organization for this scale that in the normal individual with moderate elevations is shown as the ability to organize and to be punctual and methodical" (p. 230).

High scores reflect negative emotionality characterized by feelings of low self-confidence and self-doubt about one's abilities, self-blame, heightened sensitivity, tension, rigid efforts to control impulses, moodiness, problems in concentration, rumination and worry, inhibition of hostility, and early insomnia, or nightmares. Somatic complaints may include racing or pounding heartbeat, fears of heart attack, asthma, tension headaches, and gastrointestinal complaints, such as acid stomach or ulcer. The primary symptom for Scale 7 is worry.

Scale 7 is the best marker for the first factor usually identified in factor analytic studies among the basic scales, and is highly correlated with Welsh's A (.90 for non-K-corrected T-scores and .55 for K-corrected T-scores), the classic marker for this factor is highly correlated with Welsh's A scale (.90 for non-K-corrected T-scores and .55 for K-corrected T-scores), which is the classic marker for the first factor. It is for this reason that Scale 7 (and Scale 2) is often referred to as a distress scale (e.g. Lachar, 1974). In general, Scale 7 is sensitive to a general dimension of cognitive inefficiency and worrying that leads to tension and the inability to relax (Friedman, Webb, & Lewak, 1989; Levak et al., 2011). Scale 7 appears to emphasize a fear or dread of some external catastrophe against which an individual might try to prepare or insulate him- or herself by rumination, obsession, and worry (Nichols & Greene, 1995). It is, therefore, not surprising that high Pt scores can be associated with sleep disturbance. Duckworth and Anderson (1995) viewed Pt as a measure of long-term distress (trait anxiety) rather than as situational stress (state anxiety). McKinley (1944) stated that the symptoms of psychasthenia become ingrained into the individual's personality, and thus they tend to last for years, although periods of acute discomfort commonly occur. Although high Pt scorers are often seen as agitated, the specific clinical manifestation will depend on other scale elevations. For example, Scale 7 is frequently elevated in the profiles of psychiatric patients (e.g. 278/728 and 87/78 profiles). When significantly elevated with Scale 2, depression and indecision are often observed, and when coupled with Scale 8 (e.g. 78/87), confusion, disorganized thinking, and feelings of depletion are manifested (Duckworth & Anderson, 1995; Friedman, Webb, & Lewak, 1989; Greene, 1991a; Rathvon & Holmstrom, 1996).

One of the most important configural relations with Scale 7 is with Scale 8 in determining a psychotic versus a non-psychotic diagnosis. Nichols (2011) recommends examining the raw scores, not the *T*-scores for Scales 7 and 8 for the MMPI-2. If the raw score on Scale 7 exceeds the raw score on Scale 8 by more than three points, *Pt* is likely reflecting a struggle against the disorganizing effects of Scale 8.

> The patient struggles to maintain relations with others, to follow a daily routine, to ignore psychotic experience (e.g. hallucinations) and to limit its effects on functioning, to live up to obligations, to maintain employment, and to retain insight. To the extent that the raw score on Scale 8 exceeds the raw score on Scale 7 by more than three, 7 is likely to reflect defeat or a yielding to psychotic influences, such that what may formerly have been experienced as struggle and resistance is now experienced more passively as apathy, anxiety, alienation, or helplessness.
>
> (Nichols, 2011, p. 163)

By examining the content scales, specifically, *ANX, FRS, OBS, DEP, HEA, LSE, WRK,* and *BIZ,* one can better infer the specific nature of the discomfort and symptomatic expression of an elevated Scale 7 score. The reader may also recall that 1.0 *K* is added to the raw patient score giving it the largest correction among the basic scales; although Scale 8 also receives 1.0 *K* added to the raw *Sc* score, *Sc* has more items, making *Pt* receive almost 40 percent more *K* correction on a per item basis. Thus, to the extent that Scale 7 is dominated by *Pt* items without much *K* correction, the total score is most likely reflecting the range and severity of symptoms; when Scale 7 is dominated by the *K* correction, personality style and traits more likely dominate the clinical focus with a relative de-emphasis on symptoms (Nichols, 2011).

Individuals scoring high on *Pt* in psychiatric settings can manifest any number of aspects of maladjustment, ranging from poor concentration, severe guilt, low energy, depressed mood, agitation, and psychotic tendencies, including hallucinations (Comrey, 1958; Graham & Butcher, 1988). High-scoring normals are generally described in more favorable terms than psychiatric patients, although women have more neurotic features typically than men. Dahlstrom et al. (1972) described peer ratings reported by Hathaway and Meehl in which high *Pt* men were described as sentimental, peaceable, good-tempered, verbal, and dissatisfied whereas women were rated as sensitive, prone to worry, emotional, and high-strung. The re-standardization participants with high *Pt* scores were rated by their spouses as having many fears, being nervous, being indecisive, lacking in self-confidence, and having sleep problems (Butcher & Williams, 1992).

Low-scoring individuals on *Pt* are often seen as relaxed and able to handle their responsibilities free of anxiety, worry, and fear. They appear self-controlled, self-confident, realistic, and able to organize themselves. However, as already mentioned, the *K* correction can greatly influence the interpretation of low *Pt* scores. *T*-scores in the range of 40–55 may result as a function of high raw scores on K with few raw Pt items. Recall that Scale 7 is likely to reflect personality traits over symptomatic features when Pt scores are dominated by the K correction. Nichols (2011, p. 171) describes in detail the importance of examining the relation of Scale 7 in proportion to both Es and K before making an interpretation.

To the extent that Es approaches or exceeds K, persons with scores in this range may be described as natural and balanced; cheerful and friendly; responsible, adaptable, and realistic; aspiring, competent, and efficient; and able to deploy their resources to address the tasks before them without inhibition or delay. This favorable pattern of traits is less convincing and partially obscured when K substantially exceeds Es. Such persons are apt to be less relaxed and flexible, and more inhibited, timid, and wary. Scorers lower than T-40 are infrequent and are achieved by lower K scores with a reappearance of raw Pt items. In this pattern, the patient appears awkward and unstable, and may exhibit obvious signs of disturbance, especially mania.

Test–retest coefficients for psychiatric patients on Pt range from .83 to .86 for one- to two-week intervals between administrations and from .49 to .58 for one-year intervals between tests (Dahlstrom et al., 1975). In Hunsley et al's. (1988) large-scale meta-analysis of MMPI reliability studies using several diverse populations conducted between 1970 and 1981, an average internal consistency of .84 across 70 studies was reported. They also reported an average test–retest reliability of .82 for 16 studies for time intervals of one day to two years. Butcher et al. (2001) reported test–retest reliability data for their community (normal) sample of 82 men ($r = .72$) and 111 women ($r = .68$) retested at an average interval of 8.6 days ($Mdn = 7$ days). Internal consistency estimates (Cronbach's coefficient alpha) for Scale 7 were also derived from the re-standardization sample (Butcher et al., 2001) and yielded coefficients of .85 and .87 for men and women, respectively.

Scale 8: Schizophrenia (Sc)

Dementia Praecox, recognized as a syndrome by Kraepelin (1893; see Kraepelin, 1919) and later named *Schizophrenia* by Bleuler (1950) in 1911, is currently recognized as a group of disorders with a biogenic etiological basis (Eysenck, Wakefield, & Friedman, 1983; Gallagher & Jones, 1987). Diagnostic criteria for a schizophrenic disorder, according to *DSM-5* (American Psychiatric Association, 2013), include impairment in various psychological processes involving thinking, perceiving, feeling, speaking and behaving, with no specific symptom considered pathognomonic of the disorder. Often deterioration from a previous level of functioning is observed, with continuous signs of the disorder necessary for at least six months. Various symptoms precede the illness (prodromal phase) or remain (residual) following the active phase of the disorder. These symptoms often vary between individuals and include social withdrawal; inappropriate affect; bizarre ideation (e.g. delusions); odd behavior; hallucinations; and digressive, vague, circumstantial or disorganized speech, which, according to Marks and Seeman (1963), can lead the clinician talking to a schizophrenic patient to often wonder "How did we get to this?" because logical thought is so circuitous and frequently interrupted.

It is not surprising that the development of *Sc* was the most difficult of the clinical scales to construct because schizophrenia involves such diverse behavioral, emotional, and cognitive symptoms. Although more research time was devoted to the development of *Sc* than the other clinical scales, it is still considered one of the weaker diagnostic scales (Marks & Seeman, 1963). Despite many efforts at refinement, the ability of *Sc* to separate the criterion schizophrenic participants from the normals (hit rate) could not be made to exceed 60 percent (Hathaway, 1956, 1980). As many as a dozen variations of the scale were attempted from four preliminary scales before the final version of *Sc* was accepted and cross-validated. These preliminary scales were derived from two partly overlapping groups of 50 patients with varying subtypes of schizophrenia (catatonic, paranoid, simple, and hebephrenic). About 60 percent of the participants were women, 40 percent men. Hathaway (1956, 1980) did not offer more specific definitional features of the criterion participants, but Dahlstrom et al. (1972, p. 215) gave the following description of schizophrenic individuals:

> Most commonly, persons showing this psychiatric reaction are characterized as constrained, cold, and apathetic or indifferent. Other people see them as remote and inaccessible, often seeming sufficient unto themselves. Delusions of varying degrees of organization, hallucinations, either fleeting or persistent and compelling, and disorientation may appear in various combinations. Inactivity or endless stereotypy, may accompany the withdrawal of interest from other people or external objects and relationships. These persons frequently perform below the levels expected of them on the basis of their training and ability.

Nichols (1988, 2011) pointed out that the criterion schizophrenic group very likely was contaminated, with a large minority of affectively disordered participants. Historically, schizophrenia had been grossly over-diagnosed in the USA, whereas affective disorders had been under-diagnosed, especially relative to schizophrenia. Pope and Lipinski's (1978) review of the extant research on the differential diagnosis of schizophrenia and manic depressive illness estimated that 40 percent of previously diagnosed American schizophrenics were misdiagnosed and suffered from affective illness, particularly mania: their findings are not surprising considering the extent of symptom overlap between the two syndromes. Therefore, many affectively disordered participants were likely inaccurately classified as schizophrenic. In contrast, few false-positive classifications were likely made in constructing the criterion group for Scale 9 (Hypomania), as manic patients with schizophrenic-like symptoms were excluded. Nichols (1988) stated that, as a result, Scale 9 was probably rendered an "unusually valid measure of the core features of the manic syndrome" (p. 80).

Despite the many efforts to improve Scale 8, it was not until the *K* scale was developed that it was considered complete. As indicated earlier, only about 60 percent of the cross-validation cases could be correctly identified with the scale when the 1.0 full *K* value was added to Scale 8. The addition of *K* helped to reduce the number of false positives or high-scoring normals from 15 percent to 2 percent. Hathaway (1956, 1980) pointed out, however, that even with the correction, a considerable number of the 91 cross-validation cases (all of which were psychiatric patients diagnosed as schizophrenic) remained below a *T*-score of 61.

The *K* value appears to work in improving the operation of Scale 8 in the following way. By adding *K* to the raw score, the *T*-scores for the criterion participants (schizophrenics) and normals were both raised, but the *T*-scores of the criterion group increased more relative to the normals. Presumably, the reason the schizophrenic participants failed initially to be identified was due to the denial or minimizing of psychopathology associated with *K*. Adding *K* to their scores is intended to correct for this minimizing tendency, which is less pronounced in the normals, who presumably have less psychopathology to minimize.

It is now customary to add 1.0 raw *K* to the raw score of Scale 8 before plotting the standard score on the profile form. It is recommended that clinicians continue to use the *K* correction for Scale 8, especially with psychiatric patients, as the vast majority of research conducted on Scale 8 has used *K*-corrected rather than non-*K*-corrected scores (Walters, 1988). Note that because one full *K* value is added to Scale 8, it is possible to obtain an elevated Scale 8 score (*T* > 65), with approximately 20 Scale 8 items endorsed in the deviant direction and an average score on the *K* scale. Therefore, it is important to examine the raw score on Scale 8 as well as the endorsed item content before inferring a diagnosis of psychosis from a high *Sc* score considered in isolation. A diagnostic conclusion of schizophrenia cannot be made solely on the basis of a Scale 8 elevation. The relationship of other scale elevations and patterns must be examined, as well as special indexes, in the context of the referral question and other clinical information in order to accurately identify an individual with schizophrenia or schizophrenic-like symptoms. Many individuals with Scale 8 as the most prominent high point in a profile are not psychotic; in some cases, an individual may be suffering from severe depression, perhaps with psychotic features and acute distress, a severe personality disorder, an organic brain disorder or some extreme sensory impairment, or have an unconventional, rebellious orientation toward society (Butcher & Williams, 1992). The diagnostic heterogeneity of the scale and the lack of specificity for psychosis in particular, is not surprising given that the psychotic content of the scale amounts to only about 10 percent of the scale items; the overlap between Scale 8 and scales explicitly developed to emphasize psychotic content such as *BIZ* (eight items) and *PSYC* (five items) is minimal (Nichols, 2011).

Scale 8 does appear to operate in a differentiating fashion in psychiatric settings. Walters (1984) found that *Sc* elevations differentiated schizophrenic and schizophrenic-spectrum disorders in general psychiatric patients. In a non-psychiatric setting, a moderately elevated *Sc* score should be interpreted with attenuated descriptors as many individuals will not present psychopathology suggestive of a schizophrenic disorder. For example, Anderson and Kunce (1984) found that in a sample of university counseling center clients with Scale 8 as their highest score at a *T*-score above 70, the majority of clients tended to feel socially isolated and had interpersonal difficulties, but only a minority were assessed as having bizarre thoughts. The case notes in the files of all of these participants indicated that the significantly elevated *Sc* score reflected stressful identity or personal crises rather than a chronic or severe psychopathological condition. Although this study demonstrates the lack of expected psychopathology associated with a Scale 8 elevation, other research has shown that although "normal" or non-psychiatric participants with high *Sc* scores may not carry a diagnosis of schizophrenia, they often share certain characteristics with the schizophrenic patients (e.g. Fine, 1973; Keane & Gibbs, 1980), thereby providing construct validity for *Sc*. For example, Keane and Gibbs tested the hypothesis that participants (university students) with elevated Scale 8 scores would exhibit qualitatively different word associations from those with normal MMPI profiles. Students with elevated profiles exhibited associations similar to those frequently observed in hospitalized schizophrenic patients, such as perseverations, self-references, and blocking. Although the students were not described as manifesting any form of a severe disturbance, Keane and Gibbs hypothesized that their associational deficits, as detected by Scale 8 elevations, could exhibit themselves in a subtle way on tasks that tap organizational ability, grammatical structure, and conventional associative linkages.

In general, researchers have found that prominent Scale 8 elevations, especially in psychiatric settings, do predict schizophrenic diagnoses, especially if there is a concurrent elevation on Scale 6 (*Pa*) or on scores in the psychotic/schizophrenic direction on certain MMPI indexes (i.e. Taulbee-Sisson signs and the Goldberg index; Walters, 1988). Marks et al. (1974) found that 68 percent of their 86/68 code pattern participants were diagnosed as psychotic (schizophrenic/paranoid), and another 18 percent were diagnosed as having paranoid personality disorders. Seventy percent of their 89/98 code pattern participants were described as psychotic (schizophrenic/mixed), whereas 58 percent of their 278/872 participants and 70 percent of their 28/82 participants were diagnosed as schizophrenic and schizophrenic/schizoaffective, respectively. Greene (2000) reported the frequency of MMPI code patterns in a large sample (*N* = 8,727) of psychiatric inpatients and outpatients collected by Hedlund and Won Cho (1979) in the 1970s. For women, some of the most frequently occurring codes were the 86, 48, and 84 code patterns (Spike 4 was the most frequent code pattern); for men, the 86 was one of the most frequently occurring code patterns. Greene provided detailed data on the frequency with which each MMPI-2 code pattern occurred in the sample of patients collected by Hedlund and Won Cho. This comparison was accomplished by eliminating the omitted 13 items from the MMPI and rescoring the data using uniform *T*-scores. Many changes in the frequency of scale elevations and code patterns resulted, but in general Scale 8 occurred less frequently in both the male and female patients. (See Greene, 2000, 2011, for a more detailed description of the code pattern frequencies for the MMPI-2, and Walters, 1988, for a review of the relation between Scale 8 and schizophrenia.) Greene (1988b, 2000, 2011) pointed out that there is considerable heterogeneity in psychiatric diagnoses within a given code pattern, as the Marks et al. (1974) data indicate. However, it does appear that Scale 8 is useful in describing the behavior of and, to a certain extent, deriving a diagnosis for individuals scoring high on this scale. Studies (e.g. Walters, 1984) consistently show that schizophrenic patients earn higher mean scores on Scale 8 relative to normals and other non-schizophrenic psychiatric patients.

Greene (2011), in examining the 15 MMPI-2 scales with the highest correlations with *Sc* in the Caldwell (2007b) clinical sample, concluded that there was only one category represented: general subjective distress and negative affect. Included in the correlated scales content were symptoms of PTSD, anxiety, depression, alienation, and social alienation. Consistent with Greene's findings, Nichols (2011) identified as a key feature of *Sc* the emphasis of its item content on the negative or deficit symptoms of schizophrenic versus positive or frank psychotic symptoms. "At least one third of the items reflect a lack of energy, interest, and motivation; a lack of pleasure in activity, and interaction; blunted, isolated, or apathetic emotionality; and social isolation if not interpersonal aversion" (Nichols, 2011, p. 176).

Disorganized thinking, impaired reality testing, and communication problems also appear to be cardinal features of high Scale 8 scorers (Friedman et al., 2001). As scores increase, the individual's logic appears less coherent and, at markedly high levels, individuals tend to have impaired communications between themselves and others.

Creating and executing rational plans is challenging for those with significant Scale 8 elevations. Nichols (2011, p. 177) provides an insightful description of the cognitive anomalies typical for those with a schizophrenic psychosis.

> Cognitive activity is effortful and unreliable, and patients are often strikingly ignorant of information needed to solve a variety of practical problems. Although intelligence and simple problem solving may be well preserved, the sustained intellectual performance required for prolonged or complex projects in the real world is out of reach. Thinking may be productive on a piecemeal basis, but the patient has difficulty organizing the materials and results of thought coherently. Information is then processed in a disorganized fashion, with elementary failures of logic and sequence; condensations, inappropriate juxtapositions, and arbitrary combinations; purposes confused with means; misplaced concreteness; the confusion of part-whole relations; fantastic intrusions; idiosyncratic biases and overvalued concepts; gaps and sudden leaps; mixed or arbitrary metaphors; metonymy; and a host of other lapses and missteps that render the products of thought labyrinthine, capricious, and impotent. Moreover, the process of thinking is subject to disruptions (e.g. blocking) that cause patients to lose their way and drift off into other directions.

The difficulties in thinking for the high Scale 8 scorer interferes with goal-directed behavior and the motivational system becomes impoverished, with escalating periods of inactivity or of actions that are repetitive, stereotyped, and even aimless, such as pacing or chanting.

Not surprisingly, Duckworth and Anderson (1995) indicated that at increasing levels of *Sc*, individuals are likely to manifest poor judgment that lands them into difficulties. Extremely high elevations (T >100) usually reflect situational stress rather than chronic disorganization, and typically individuals with identity crises ("Who am I?") score in this range. Coupled with an elevated Scale 0, the person tends to show even greater communication disturbance because of a lack of social contact with others. Nichols and Greene (1995) viewed *Sc* as a measure of the tendency to withdraw into fantasy and, at high levels ($T = 85$), to prefer the world of fantasy to real-world relationships. They provided detailed and useful information on the relation of Scale 8 to the *F* scale and to *BIZ*, stating that

> when *BIZ* (especially *BIZ1* [Psychotic Symptomatology]) is elevated along with *Sc*, the fantasy tends toward the psychotic and bizarre, with a significant breach in reality testing and in the ability to discriminate external from internal events. When *Sc* is not accompanied by elevations on *BIZ*, fantasy tends to be of a compensatory, wish-fulfillment type, in which reality adherence is relatively well preserved. These inferences may be fortified with reference to the difference between *F* and *BIZ* scores: *F* substantially greater than *BIZ* suggests social deviance and poor reality testing without bizarre aspects; a large negative difference suggests bizarre

fantasy but with relatively less impaired reality contact. A similar relationship between *F* and *Sc* scales also bears upon the expression of psychoticism. When the elevation of both scales is nearly equivalent or *F* is slightly higher than *Sc*, psychotic manifestations are apt to be public, including interpersonal bizarreness with evident emotional and motivational dyscontrol. When *Sc* is elevated, to the extent that it exceeds *F*, psychotic manifestations are apt to be of an internalized kind, such as bizarre fantasies and autism, with interpersonal detachment and withdrawal.

(Nichols & Greene, 1995, p. 36)

As discussed under Scale 7, the problems in cognitive and behavioral control can be discerned by examining the differences in elevation between Scales 8 and 7. When Scale 7 is greater than *Sc*, there is a struggle to maintain coherence and inhibit psychotic manifestations. When 8 is greater than 7, the individual loses control over inappropriate behaviors. The more 8 exceeds 7, the greater the likelihood is that the person's symptomatic expressions will be bizarre and the loss of behavioral control will be destructive to self and/or others.

Individuals with significant Scale 8 elevations tend to feel mistrustful toward others and think that people will dislike them. They tend to have long histories of social failure, as others have focused upon their appearance or behavior to hurt or reject them. Nichols (2011) stated that in response some high scale scorers would adopt a pattern of withdrawal and inaccessibility. Others would adopt an aggressive, counterphobic style in which odd features of grooming, dress, or behavior are cultivated, or accentuated, a means of "calling attention to themselves and their individualities" (Nichols, 2011, p. 182). Levak et al. (2011) and Caldwell (1984) hypothesized that Scale 8 elevations are associated with a childhood of being despised and rejected by a person on whom life and security depended:

Perhaps in some instances the child expressed some peculiar habit or eccentricities or was physically inept which led others to express anger, hatred, and resentment towards him or her. The assumption is that the child, in an act of self-protection, would shut down, that is, not think or not pay attention, which would lead in turn to faulty cognitive and emotional functioning.

(Lewak et al., 1990, p. 246)

With high Scale 8 elevations, individuals might experience hallucinations, confusion, panic, or anxiety and possibly be delusional. Scale 8 is associated with feeling unhappy, moody, inferior, and alienated, as well as with immaturity, impulsivity, and reclusion. High Scale 8 scorers are viewed by others as odd or peculiar, and shy, even schizoid at times. Low Scale 8 scorers are seen as friendly, responsible, cautious, and unimaginative in their approach to problem solving, and as practical and concrete in their thinking (Graham, 1990).

Hathaway and Meehl (1952, as cited in Dahlstrom et al., 1972) found that the normal men in their study who had elevated scores on this scale were not seen by their peers as withdrawn or deviant. Social difficulties were not perceived, although these men were seen as self-dissatisfied and prone to worry. Overall, they were described as good-tempered, verbal, enthusiastic, and having wide aesthetic interests. Peaceable, kind, and sentimental were emotional descriptors given to them. Women were described as sensitive and high-strung, as well as frank, kind, and modest. Other descriptors for normal men in a different sample provided by Gough et al. (1955) are much more negative. Terms like *hostile* and *irritable* suggest difficulties in handling aggression and imply a certain lack of control in modulating emotion.

Scale 8 lost no items in the re-standardization project, but 13 of the scale's 78 items were modified, with mostly grammatical clarifications and simplifications. As the longest clinical scale, there is considerable item overlap with other scales. Scale 8 shares the most items with Scales 7 (17 items) and F (15 items), and has more items in common with the other psychotic scales than it does with the neurotic scales. It shares 13 and 11 items, respectively, with Scales 6 and 9. Ten items are shared with Scale 4 and RC8, nine with Scale 2, eight with BIZ, and five with PSYC. Twenty-four items overlap none of the other clinical scales. As is the case for other psychotic scales, the deviant direction of endorsement for the majority of the 78 Sc items is True (76 percent); 19 (24 percent) are keyed False. Little (1949) found that item 319 describing hearing odd things has the highest correlation ($r = .70$) to the total scale, with the next highest item (item 299) describing distractibility, having a value of .67.

Test–retest correlations for a subsample of the re-standardization group (82 men and 111 women) retested at about a one-week interval were .72 and .54 for men and women, respectively (Butcher et al., 2001). In Hunsley et al.'s (1988) large-scale meta-analysis of MMPI reliability studies using a wide variety of populations conducted between 1970 and 1981, an average test–retest reliability of .78 for 17 studies was reported for time intervals for one day to two years. They also reported an average internal consistency (Cronbach's coefficient alpha) of .82 across 73 studies. Butcher et al. (2001) reported internal consistency estimates of .85 and .86 for men and women, respectively. Scales 8 and 7 had identical alpha coefficients for males and nearly identical coefficients for females, the highest for all of the validity and clinical scales. Scale 8 thus appears to be an internally consistent scale with acceptable test–retest reliability.

Harris-Lingoes Subscales

As with certain other clinical scales, it is important to examine the Harris-Lingoes subscales to help determine the meaning of a particular scale elevation. Wiener and Harmon (Wiener, 1948) did not develop Subtle and Obvious subscales for Scale 8 as the items are predominantly obvious. Harris and Lingoes developed the following subscales for Sc: Social Alienation (*Sc1*); Emotional Alienation (*Sc2*); Lack of Ego Mastery, Cognitive (*Sc3*); Lack of Ego Mastery, Conative (*Sc4*); Lack of Ego Mastery, Defective Inhibition (*Sc5*); and Bizarre Sensory Experiences (*Sc6*). Nichols (2011) noted that the Sc subscales break down into two relatively distinct divisions: detachment and disconnection, and dyscontrol and malfunction. *Sc1* and *Sc2* reflect severe alienation from others, and from the self, nonhuman environment, and the future, respectively. *Sc3*, *Sc4*, *Sc5*, and *Sc6* reflect malfunctions of cognition, motivation, impulse, and neurology, respectively.

Sc1: Social Alienation (21 Items)

Harris and Lingoes (1968) described *Sc1* as reflecting "a feeling of lack of rapport with other people; and withdrawal from meaningful relationships with others." In essence,

Sc1 consists of items reflecting emotional deprivation. Specifically, the items reflect feeling misunderstood, insulted, punished unfairly, plotted against, and detached from one's own family and others, and a sense of loneliness around others (Caldwell, 1988). Sixteen of the items are keyed True, five False. Eight items overlap Scale 6, five overlap *F*, and three overlap *Pd4*.

High *Sc1* scorers tend to lack a viable support system (Levitt, 1989). Graham et al. (1999) reported that the men in their outpatient psychiatric sample tended to report that their families lacked love and that there was a history of physical abuse. Women, in particular, admitted to more suicide attempts if they were a high versus a low scorer on *Sc1*. Although an individual may also concurrently score high on *Pd1* (Familial Discord) and *Pd4* (Social Alienation), it is important to assess these and other subscale scores separately as the clinical implications can vary. For example, a high *Sc1* score, coupled with relatively low *Sc2* (Emotional Alienation) and *Pd5* (Self-Alienation) scores, suggests that the person's sense of pessimism and hopelessness may be confined to other people, although he or she is still able to derive gratification from activities of nonsocial interests (Nichols & Greene, 1995). High *Sc1* scorers feel they have been given a "bum deal" but do not feel the residual sadness or longing that appears in *Pd4* (Nichols & Greene, 1995). To a large extent, high *Sc1* individuals prefer noninvolvement with others. *Sc1* also measures an element of paranoia in that high scorers are generally mistrustful of others (six items overlap *Pa1*). When *F*, *FAM* (six of the *Sc1* items imply strong family antipathy), and/or *Pd1* are also elevated, the person may express hatred toward one or both parents (Nichols & Greene, 1995). Nichols (2011, pp. 173–174) provided the following clinically rich description for *Sc1*:

> *Sc1* conveys an impression of irremediable social disability about which the patient is largely apathetic. The patient is cold and interpersonally adrift, and demonstrates both projected and internalized hatred. Identity is contaminated, alien, and defective. This scale is saturated with nuclear schizophrenia but also rises in suicidal depression, PTSD, and Borderline Personality Disorder. Given its heterogeneity, examining the actual items endorsed to rule out the selective endorsement of a few items (e.g. those concerning parents) that may be related only partially or indirectly to the theme of *Sc1* as a whole is helpful.

Low *Sc1* scorers tend to like others, feel attached to them, feel understood, respected, well-treated, and deny feelings of hatred/resentment toward family members (Caldwell, 1988; Graham, 1990).

Sixteen of the items on this subscale are scored in the True direction, and five items are scored in the False direction. Eight items overlap Scale 6, five items overlap *F*, and three items overlap *Pd4*.

Sc2: *Emotional Alienation (11 Items)*

Harris and Lingoes (1968) described the content of *Sc2* as including: "A feeling of lack of rapport with oneself; experiencing the self as strange; and a flattening or distortion of affect; apathy." This subscale consists of items reflecting an existence devoid of interests, engagement, or aspiration (Nichols & Greene, 1995). Eight of the 11 items are keyed True, 3 False.

Levitt (1989) thought the scale basically measured depression, and in fact, the scale does appear to measure an emotional withdrawal from life. Graham et al. (1999) reported a similar description of the high *Sc2* scorer suggesting a greater likelihood of depression as well as having few or no friends. Caldwell (1988) described high scorers as experiencing life as an "ungratifying strain" (p. 28) and as taking pleasure in hurting loved ones or being hurt by them. Graham (1990) also described high scorers as feeling apathetic and frightened. Wrobel (1992) provided correlates for *Sc2* that included feeling a lack of rapport with oneself, a flat or distorted affect, and a feeling of oneself as strange. Nichols and Greene (1995) described emotional alienation as reflecting a "pathological disengagement from life that discounts future interests, prospects, and engagements to the extent that they can no longer serve as incentives for continuing to live" (p. 29). In this regard, the high *Sc2* scorer is seen as lacking an investment in the future, which raises the possibility of suicidal behavior and thoughts, which should be further evaluated by examining critical items (150, 303, 506, 520, 524, and 530) and the suicidal ideation component *DEP4* of the *DEP* content scale described in Chapter 7 (see also Ben-Porath & Sherwood, 1993). Nichols (2011, p. 174) elaborated on the depressive core content of *Sc2*.

Along with *Sc4*, with which it shares 8 items, *Sc2* is one of the two deficit or negative symptom subscales of Scale 8. *Sc2* reflects a depressively toned, core schizoid element that other scales do not capture well. The central quality is one of emotional deadness, dysphoric detachment, and apathy, in which life is endured without any sense of participation or care. Nothing generates interest or a sense of positive anticipation. Whereas *Sc1* indicates a severe emotional withdrawal from other people, *Sc2* reflects a compromised attachment to life itself. Its outlook is bleak and pessimistic but also indifferent.

Although *Sc2* does have items reflective of unconventional thought processes, the items tend not to be as strongly suggestive of psychosis as other measures, such as Psychotic Symptomatology (*BIZ1*) or Sensorimotor Dissociation (*Sc6*; Nichols & Greene, 1995). Low *Sc2* scorers deny feelings of depression and despair, feel that life is worthwhile, and deny sadistic or masochistic needs (Graham, 1990).

Sc3: Lack of Ego Mastery, Cognitive (10 Items)

Harris and Lingoes (1968) describe the item content of *Sc3* as including: "The admission of autonomous thought processes and strange and puzzling ideas." Nine of the 10 items are keyed True, 1 False. *Sc3* has three items in common with *Sc4*, four with *D4*, and six with Scale 7. *Sc3* contains items that reflect cognitive deficits in the areas of memory, attention, and concentration. Although similar to *D4* (Mental Dullness), *Sc3* emphasizes a disruption of thought processes by the intrusion of troubling thoughts, whereas the *D4* content emphasizes disability that interferes with the completion of mental work (Nichols & Greene, 1995). The major theme of *Sc3* "is of having lost control of one's cognitive processes because of alien, unbidden, and sometimes frightening thoughts and ideas that intrude upon and disrupt thinking" (Nichols, 2011, p. 174). The high *Sc3* scorer tends to have a sense of disability where thinking is concerned (Nichols & Greene, 1995). High *Sc3* scorers tend to experience more distress or discomfort by their cognitive deficits than high *D4* scorers although the two scales frequently elevate as a pair (Levitt, 1989). High *Sc3* scores generally indicate individuals who feel they are losing their minds, report strange thought processes and feelings of unreality, and have trouble with concentration and memory functions (Graham, 1990). Graham et al. (1999) reported in their outpatient psychiatric sample that the high *Sc3* scorer was described by their therapist as suffering acute psychological turmoil and as not coping well with stress.

The MMPI-2 *HEA* content scale contains items sensitive to cognitive deficits, such as confusion and impaired judgment, but *Sc3* should exceed the score on the *HEA* scale before giving an interpretation specific to *Sc3*. Low scorers generally deny any difficulty with their thinking processes (Caldwell, 1988).

In order to maximally separate and assess two important areas of cognition, one of which is related to Sc3, Nichols (2008), inspired by Reise and Haviland (2005), created two cognitive stability scales. The first, Cognitive Problems (*CogProb*) contains 12 items reflecting more or less normal problems with attention, concentration, memory, distractibility, loss of focus, reduced cognitive initiative, and the like. These items are widely distributed across the MMPI-2 item pool, and overlap D4, Sc3, Sc4, and WRK, by five or fewer items each. *CogProb* is sensitive to the class of cognitive symptoms that commonly accumulate on both severe depression and thought disorders, with perhaps some emphasis on the former. The second scale, Disorganization (*DisOrg*), contains 11 items and overlaps *RC8* by all 11, *BIZ* by 9 (4 on *BIZ1*), *PSYC* by 7, and *Sc6* by 4, but does not include the items on *RC8* that suggest dissociation (items 168, 182, and 229). The items reflect non-paranoid experience suggestive of hallucinations, thought broadcasting, and similar relatively florid psychotic symptoms. Profiles in which *DisOrg* is greater than *T-70 and* exceeds *CogProb* suggests a strong likelihood of a psychotic condition, often schizophrenia.

Sc4: Lack of Ego Mastery, Conative (14 Items)

Conation means an inclination to act purposively, which is exactly what high *Sc4* scorer's lack. This subscale consists of items that reflect the degree of lost motivation to behave in a constructive and productive fashion (Levitt, 1989). Eleven of the items are keyed True, three False. High scorers have a sense of malfunction in their cognitive operations, such as attention, concentration, judgment, and memory, along with a withdrawal of interest, that leads to a lack of pleasure and interest in daily life (Nichols & Greene, 1995). Caldwell (1988) stated that the items reflect an inability to mobilize one's energy, that it is tough to get going and focus one's mental energy. Indeed, this subscale appears to measure the psychic equivalent of psychomotor retardation (*D2*); in fact, Nichols and Greene (1995) viewed this subscale as being sensitive to a "general psychic disability" (p. 40). Wrobel (1992) found that clinician raters found feelings of psychological weakness to be a significant correlate for high *Sc4* scorers. Typically, high scorers feel that life is a strain and may be experiencing depression, in that they have given up hope of things ever getting better (Butcher et al., 1989; Graham, 1990; Graham et al., 1999). Some items reflect a tendency to withdraw into fantasy and daydreaming as an escape from stress, and one item (item 303) raises the question of suicidal apathy or despair. Nichols (2011) likens the depression of *Sc4* to *Sc2* in that the depressiveness is apathetic rather than sad. However, *Sc4* differs from *Sc2* and *D4* in significant ways. Nichols (2011, p. 175) states:

> Unlike *Sc2* or *D4*, *Sc4*'s emphasis is not on mental breakdown but on a depleted or deanimated will (abulia), listlessness, loss of interest, and anhedonia that defeats the completion—even the initiation—of mental and behavioral projects. The high scorer is disabled by the lack of a psychic starter and lapses into regression and apathy.

The inertia and lack of initiative high scorers experience lead to severe emotional alienation; in fact *Sc4* overlaps heavily (eight items) with *Sc2*. High *Sc4* scorers, however, can differ from the pure emotional alienation that high *Sc2* scorers experience, in that *Sc4* measures a lack of sustained mental focus and passive distractibility, which proceeds more from anergy and indifference than from the cognitive disruption that is often seen in the case of *Sc3* (Nichols & Greene, 1995).

Sc4 may capture much of the essence of the *Sc* parent scale, as the two measures correlate highly ($r = .88$) in a clinical sample (Greene, 2011). Low *Sc4* scores reflect a feeling that life is worthwhile, a denial of depression and suicidal ideation, and the feeling that one has enough energy for spontaneously initiating actions. Generally, the person is happy to be alive and does not complain of cognitive deficits (Caldwell, 1988; Graham, 1990).

Sc5: Lack of Ego Mastery, Defective Inhibition (11 Items)

Harris and Lingoes (1968) used these descriptions for high *Sc5* scores: "A feeling of not being in control of one's impulses, which may be experienced as strange and alien;" "at the mercy of impulse and feeling;" and "dissociation of affect." All 11 items are keyed True and are obvious, making *Sc5* vulnerable to All-True or All-False response-style distortions. The items are heterogeneous, variously referring to losses of consciousness, depersonalization and dissociation, motor difficulties (uncontrolled movement and speech), agitation, and impulsiveness. "These disparate items converge on a theme of strong internal (and some external) menace to the patient's composure, such that he or she may be set off by even mild internal or external events" (Nichols, 2011, p. 175).

The items do, in fact, appear to emphasize a fear or dread of internal disintegration or loss of control (Graham, 1990; Nichols & Greene, 1995). Graham (1993) reported that high scorers may feel restless, hyperactive, and irritable and may have periods of laughing/crying that they cannot control, as well as having episodes during which they did not know what they were doing. High scores overpower normal defenses leading the person to feel as though they are coming apart or disintegrating (Nichols, 2011). Caldwell (1988) noted that *Sc5* shares six items with Scale 9 (*Ma*) and that *Sc5* is often elevated when Scales 8 and 9 are both elevated. Therefore, the potential for eruptions of uncontrollable rage are high when *Sc5* is elevated. When *Sc5* is elevated, the person may be vulnerable to being overwhelmed with enraged affect and other scales should be examined in relation to this subscale to assess the potential for rageful expressions. Nichols and Greene (1995, p. 30) addressed this issue in the following statement about how content scales in relation to *Sc5* can be useful in this assessment:

Relative to *ANG*, *TPA* and *Sc5* reflect a more chronic condition, one closer to concepts of hostility, rage, and resentment. Thus, *ANG* scores well above scores on *TPA* and *Sc5* imply a more state-like anger. When elevations on *TPA* and *Sc5* equal or exceed the *ANG* score, however, anger is likely to operate in a trait-like fashion, with the respondent appearing to seek opportunities for discharge or to anticipate situations in which anger in one or more of the parties involved will be stimulated, if not expressed. The relations among the three scales (*ANG*, *TPA*, and *Sc5*) provide some basis for predicting the degree of focus that will characterize angry feelings and expressions: If *ANG* is greater than *TPA* and *TPA* is greater than *Sc5*, anger is likely to be tightly focused on specific issues, perceived offenses, or persons. The reverse pattern (*Sc5* > *TPA* > *ANG*) implies blind or diffuse rage with appropriate targets determined largely by opportunity and convenience.

It should be noted that although rage is not overt in the item content, it is implicit in many of the items and appears to be unfocused and primitive unless modified by the relation of the scales described above by Nichols and Greene (1995). The Graham et al. (1999) findings of women clients with high *Sc5* scores having a higher likelihood of a borderline personality disorder diagnosis is consistent with the rage and hostility associated with elevated *Sc5* scores. Low *Sc5* scores reflect the self-perception that it takes a lot to get oneself excited, that one is well controlled and not restless or irritable (Caldwell, 1988; Graham, 1990). In essence, a low *Sc5* score may indicate good control over one's impulses.

Sc6: Bizarre Sensory Experiences (20 Items)

Harris and Lingoes (1968) provided descriptors for the content of *Sc6* that included: "A feeling of change in the perception of the self and the body image; feelings of depersonalization and estrangement." Fourteen of the items are keyed True, six False.

Sc6 covers a range of content that includes motor, sensory, and dissociative symptoms, in the form of twitchings, unusual weakness or numbness, blank spells, voice changes, loss of taste, ringing in the ears, feelings of depersonalization, fits of laughing and crying, and other unexplained bodily changes. Scores on *Sc6* can be usefully compared with the content component scales (Ben-Porath & Sherwood, 1993), such as Gastrointestinal Symptoms (*HEA1*), Neurological Symptoms (*HEA2*), and General Health Concerns (*HEA3*), to determine both the range of symptoms claimed and their level of intensity (Nichols & Greene, 1995). High *Sc6* scores reflect a deterioration of control in the way impulses are inhibited; the items reflect a certain loosening of ties to reality. However, the original and current name of the scale—Bizarre Sensory Experiences— does not appear to represent the scale content at all well, and appears to be a misnomer. Nichols and Greene (1995, p. 31) provided some much-needed clarification of this issue, stating that

in the 1955 edition of their subscale manuscript, Harris and Lingoes designated *Sc6* (*Sc3* at that time) "bizarre sensory experiences." In their 1968 revision, however, the authors renamed this subscale "sensorimotor dissociation." The revised designation corresponds far more closely to the actual content of the items comprising *Sc6*. While many of the items on this subscale are unusual and a few reflect psychoticism (311, 319, 355), only one item (355) has possible bizarre connotations. The remaining items mostly reflect soft neurologic signs: sensory (247, 252, 255, and 298), motor (23, 91, 106, 177, 179, 182, and 295), and possible dissociation (168, 182, 229, 296, and 311).

Nichols (2011) reported the correlations between *Sc6* and several scales based upon a large clinical sample provided by Caldwell (2007b). According to Nichols (2011, pp. 175–176):

Both in theme and content, the scale is largely somatic. Six of the items overlap *HEA*, all on *HEA2*, and 5 overlap *BIZ*, 4 on *BIZ2*. *Sc6* consistently achieves higher correlations with the somatic scales (*HEA2* [.86], *HEA* [.83], *Hy4* [.80], Scale 1 [.80], *RC1* [.78]) than the psychotic scales (*BIZ* [.75]; *BIZ1* [.63], *PSYC* [.72], *Pa1* [.64]), with *RC8* being the exception (.83), probably because of the dissociative content within *RC8*. The significance of *Sc6* on a scale intended to measure schizophrenia rests with the frequent reference to soft neurological signs that may be manifestations of the central neural deficit that Meehl (1962, 1972) has called "schizotaxia" and postulated as the inherited substrate for schizophrenia.

In general, high *Sc6* scorers feel their bodies are changing in strange and unusual ways. They may report skin sensitivities, voice changes, muscle twitchings, clumsiness, balance difficulties, ringing in the ears, and feelings of weakness and paralysis (Graham, 1990). Wrobel (1992) reported that a feeling of depersonalization was a significant correlate for the high *Sc6* scorer in his sample of clients in therapy in a private outpatient facility. Low scorers tend to not report the occurrence of these symptoms and experiences.

Scale 9: Hypomania (Ma)

Ma, the last of the basic scales to be developed, contains 46 items measuring the aspects of a mildly elevated mood that often is accompanied by a flight of ideas, affective lability, and psychomotor excitement. The personality pattern the scale reflects is the affective disorder termed *hypomania* (Dahlstrom et al., 1972). Hypomania indicates heightened activity levels with accompanying symptoms or traits such as easy distractibility, insomnia, over-optimism, occasional grandiosity, suspiciousness, and irascibility.

McKinley and Hathaway (1944) selected a group of 24 inpatients at the University of Minnesota Hospital as their criterion participants for constructing this scale. It took Hathaway five years to gather criterion cases that were considered sufficiently homogeneous for scale construction. Unfortunately, no available demographic data are reported on the criterion participants. Only patients with less than a full-blown manic syndrome were considered, because the more severe cases could not participate fully in the task of sorting inventory items into the appropriate True, False, and Cannot Say categories: "The clinical diagnoses were either hypomania or mild acute mania, depending on the severity of the case" (Dahlstrom & Dahlstrom, 1980, p. 52). Hence, the scale name *Hypomania* identifies this measure of a less than full-blown manic condition. It was important to derive a measure of more subtle or moderate cases of mania so that the condition could be identified early to improve the prognosis and treatment options for the patient. Patients were excluded from study if they were delirious, confused, schizophrenic, or depressed with agitation. McKinley and Hathaway (1944, as cited in Dahlstrom & Dahlstrom, 1980) recognized the small number of cases in their criterion group and conceded that "in spite of the small number of criterion and test cases available, a scale for *Hypomania* is presented. It is the best that we could derive from the patients seen over a 5-year period" (p. 57). However, the number of cases was insufficient to analyze the effects of gender, age, marital, and SES. Several preliminary scales were constructed with the final scale tested against 38 cross-validation cases, of which only five carried diagnoses of manic-depressive psychosis.

> Most carried diagnoses of Schizophrenia, but ward staff considered these patients to manifest some degree of overactivity or elation. In retrospect, many of the latter cases were probably false negatives for mania or hypomania. In evaluating the records of more than 900 clinic cases, only 30 obtained scores exceeding *T*-69, and many of these were psychopaths or chronic alcoholics, or had "organic deterioration of the brain."
>
> (Nichols, 2011, pp. 186–187)

The final scale was derived from a successful separation of the criterion and cross-validation cases from 690 of the normal and 300 randomly selected psychiatric clinic cases. Better discriminability between the groups would have been obtained had psychiatric cases been in a clearly manic or hypomanic state at the time of testing. A manic mood disorder is unstable by nature, so it is not conclusive that Scale 9 would operate more efficiently had the criterion cases been tested at the peak of the mood cycle. Capturing individuals in that mood state might have created an overly state-like measure lacking sensitivity to significant long-term and characterological aspects of the manic/hypomanic syndrome, including mood lability.

Nichols' (1988) review supporting the sensitivity and specificity of Scale 9 should be consulted for more insight into the detection ability of this measure. McKinley and Hathaway (1944, 2000) demonstrated early on that Scale 9 assisted in identifying "the juvenile delinquent, the overactive adult, and the agitated depression with ambivalent affect" (p. 42). Overall, Scale 9 scores are sensitive to state-dependent effects and tend to reflect the shifts in mood cycle commonly observed in patients with bipolar disorder. In fact, the scale may lead or follow the changes in affect such that scores may understate or overstate the clinically observed manifestations of mania at the time of testing.

Scale 9 is sensitive to expansive, elated, and euphoric mood. Additionally, Nichols and Greene (1995) stated that "*Ma* reflects the ease of access that thoughts, feelings, and impulses have to the motor system. When *Ma* is elevated, motor readiness is high" (p. 36). The higher the elevation on Scale 9, the more energetic a person tends to be and the more compelled the individual feels to act in using that energy (Duckworth & Anderson, 1995). In fact, as scale elevations increase, the more likely the person is to get overcommitted or over-involved in activities. However, Nichols (2011) noted that the "degree of elevation is not well calibrated to observed levels of activity and disturbance; some patients with scores near *T*-65 may manifest severe manic symptoms and psychosis, whereas others with higher scores may remain relatively functional and controlled" (p. 190). One method for discriminating the shading of hypomania into mania is to inspect the relative elevations of *Ma-O* and *Ma-S*. If *Ma-S* exceeds *Ma-O*, hypomania and euphoric mania are common, although irritable mania is rare. When *Ma-O* exceeds *Ma-S* the opposite pattern is likely.

Nichols (1988, p. 76) provides a useful description of manic affect for understanding Scale 9 elevations:

> Affect is characteristically elated, euphoric, enthusiastic, expansive, triumphant, and disinhibited. The patient may present as playful, jocular, quick-witted, and high-spirited, free of all normal cares and concerns, in tip-top shape, and ready for action. This picture is unstable, however, and may change suddenly into one of anger and hostility if the patient is blocked in the pursuit of some goal, has his or her self-esteem challenged, experiences a rebuff, or in some other way feels thwarted. The patient often feels highly vulnerable to real or implied personal criticism even though he or she may be quite imperturbable regarding other matters. For a large minority of patients the dominant mood is one of irritability rather than elation and affect may be somewhat dysphoric. The patient may seem cantankerous and constantly in transit between flare-ups of litigiousness, contentiousness, and antagonism. Fear may emerge in some cases, usually relatively late in the manic episode, and may be related to reverses, rejections, and alienation, secondary to the reactions of friends, family, or staff to the patient's obnoxiousness. Major lapses in judgment, including sexual or financial indiscretions occurring early in the episode, which become clear to the patient, may also stimulate a fearful response. Finally, fear may be a reaction to the realization that the manic flight will soon expire and be supplanted by depression. Not uncommonly, such fears may reach delusional proportions and involve themes of retribution or of being poisoned (by medication, i.e. being slowed down to the point that depression may catch up).

High scores on Scale 9 tend to reflect a proclivity to distance oneself from personal distress either by running away or by acting out. There is a tendency to deny emotional distress by externalizing and to shift these feelings to the motor sphere (Nichols & Greene, 1995). Nichols (2011, p. 195) elaborated on this tendency to externalize and avoid feelings:

> Acting out is common in high Scale 9 scorers, both as an outlet for high energy and as a defense against feared loss or defeat. Psychomotor acceleration may afford the patient little or no mental space for true reflection on feelings and impulses, or on the formulation of plans for dealing with them. Consequently, these feelings and impulses are rapidly shifted into the motor sphere to become manifest in behavior. In this sense, acting out may be better understood in the context of disability than in the context of defense. However, the typical behavior pattern is one in which the consumption of stimulation may be seen as a kind of race against lost opportunity, as in the case of hypersexuality, gambling, intoxication, and similar excesses; or against defeat, as in the case of hostility and assaultiveness. Sooner or later, the patient may experience the encroachment of depressed mood or begin to appreciate the destructive consequences of his or her behavior earlier in the manic cycle,

and these may stimulate acting out as a flight from insight. In hypomania, where disorganization is minimal or absent, the patient's intellectual mobility is conducive to intellectualization. Among patients without mood disorder, acting out appears to be the primary defense, but denial, rationalization, and projection are also common.

Levak et al. (2011) hypothesized that the high Scale 9 scorer is protecting him- or herself against frustration and unhappiness associated with failure. They hypothesized that these individuals may have had parents with excessively high expectations (i.e. early demands for success and achievement), which led to internalized, anxious strivings. Nichols (2011) reviewed the rearing environment studies of those with mood disorders and underscored the role of early pressures to achieve and later vulnerability to failure and loss that are not uncommon in the personal histories of bipolar patients. It is not uncommon to observe aspects of the patients' childhood experience conducive to rendering the individual vulnerable to loss or failure, such as parental death, illness or alcoholism, frequent relocations, and overindulgence.

A significant Scale 9 elevation energizes behaviors, thoughts, and emotions, particularly those associated with other clinical scale elevations. For example, when *Ma* is elevated with *Pd*, acting out may occur with an antisocial focus. However, other scales, such as *Hy*, need to be considered as *Ma* "appears to play a role in determining both the frequency of acting out and the extent to which it will take an antisocial direction" (Nichols & Greene, 1995, p. 35). Specifically, *Hy*, when elevated with *Ma*, tends to augment the expression of social interest such as through the observance of social propriety and approval seeking. When *Ma* is elevated but Scales 2 and 0 are lowest in the profiles, mood tends to be buoyant if not elated and euphoric. Scales 2 and 9, both elevated, reflects agitation and instability. Adding Scales 4, 6, and 8 tends to affect one's proneness to irritability.

Caldwell (1984) views Scale 9 elevations as reflecting the degree of fear of future frustrations, which leads to a diminished capacity to enjoy the here and now. The person cannot relax, as his or her future depends on maintaining an increasing activity level in attempt to maintain his or her reward schedule or avoid deprivation or failure (Friedman, Webb, & Lewak, 1989).

Ma scale content is heterogeneous and covers classic features of a hypomanic syndrome, including excitement, heightened activity levels, expansiveness, and overambitiousness or high aspirations (Butcher et al., 2001). Other items describe extraversion, moral attitudes, family relationships, and bodily concerns.

Patients with only mild affective symptoms may be difficult to distinguish from ambitious, energetic normals. It is therefore important to observe periods of euphoria, increased irritability, and unproductive activity to assist in making an accurate diagnosis (Lachar, 1974). Nichols (1988) pointed out the importance of retesting individuals suspected of having an affective disorder, as variability in their mood state will influence their MMPI-2 profile. For example, a psychiatric inpatient may initially test without a *Ma* elevation if he or she is depressed but, on later retesting, may show an elevated Scale 9 score suggestive of mood instability. Scale 9 does, in fact, figure prominently in code patterns associated with mood disorders, especially those with manic correlates. Code patterns 49/94, 69/96, and 89/98 are all seen in diagnosis of mania (Nichols, 1988). Setting can often determine the diagnoses associated with MMPI-2 profiles. For example, Marks et al. (1974) classified approximately 70 percent of their female psychiatric inpatients with the 89/98 code pattern as psychotic (schizophrenic/mixed) and 17 percent of them as psychoneurotic (depressive reaction). Raskin and Novacek (1989) administered MMPIs and the Narcissistic Personality Inventory to undergraduate students. The highest scorers on the measure of narcissism were best represented by the 98/89 code pattern (with an average elevated F score of T-65). Thus this code pattern in a normal population may reflect narcissism and manic defenses rather than mania per se.

Low *Ma* scores suggest a low energy or activity level. Kunce and Anderson (1976, 1984) viewed zest as an underlying dimension of Scale 9. Therefore, low *Ma* scores reflect a lack of vitality or even depression. They may feel chronically tired, have trouble performing their work, or even be temporarily ill (Duckworth & Anderson, 1995), and are unlikely to stir up excitement or be too talkative (Keiller & Graham, 1993). They may feel empty or depleted, and lack self-confidence and motivation. Levak et al. (2011, pp. 350–351) addressed low scores on Scale 9:

> Individuals with low scores on Scale 9 exhibit some of the opposite attributes associated with high 9 codetypes. In the presence of Scale 2 elevations, a low 9 may reflect the depressive side of a bipolar disorder. Sometimes, medical problems (e.g. thyroid) may be the source of low energy. In the absence of any clinical scale elevations, a low score on 9 may reflect reliable, orderly individuals who are careful not to overcommit and tend to be persevering and emotionally stable.

Dahlstrom et al. (1972) reported the correlates of Hathaway and Meehl's investigation of normal men and women. Sociability, energy, and openness appeared to be the major theme characterizing men, which is consistent with the optimism that McKinley and Hathaway (1944) described as a stable factor in normals. These men were further described as talkative, impulsive, adventurous, curious, generous, affectionate, and sentimental. Women were described similarly, and were also seen as frank, courageous, idealistic, and possessing high energy as reflected by the adjectives *talkative, enthusiastic,* and *versatile.*

Butcher and Williams (1992) reported data from the couples rating study in the re-standardization (Butcher et al., 1989). Husbands of high *Ma* scorers viewed their wives as wearing unusual clothes, talking too much, stirring up excitement, taking many risks, getting excited or happy for little reason, and telling people off. Wives viewed their high *Ma* husbands as acting bossy, talking too much, whining and demanding attention, and taking drugs other than those prescribed by a doctor.

As Duckworth and Anderson (1995) noted, it is common to see peak Scale 9 (and Scale 5 in men) scores in college students. It is important to examine the elevation of *Ma* in making an appropriate interpretation. When a person with a high score is generally well-adjusted, the appropriate descriptors for Scale 9 would be enthusiastic, eager, talkative, versatile, driven to be successful and involved, and friendly and happy. As scores increase, however, expect to see maladaptive hyperactivity and agitation.

Scores on Scale 9 tend to be related to age, with older individuals obtaining lower scores (reflecting lower energy and activity levels and more body concerns) and late-adolescent or younger participants, such as teenagers, tending to score in the upper normal to moderate range, which could be considered indicative of impulse control problems (Greene, 2011). Age should, therefore, be considered when examining *Ma* scores. Greene (2011, p. 141) offers specific useful guidelines for interpreting elevations on Scale 9:

> Scores on Scale 9 decrease significantly with increasing age. Normal individuals (Butcher et al., 1989; Colligan et al., 1983), medical patients (Swenson et al., 1973), and clinical clients (Caldwell, 2007b) under the age of 20 have average *T* scores of nearly 60, whereas normal individuals and clinical clients 70 years of age and older average around 48. (This difference of nearly 12 *T* points is about 3 to 4 items.) Thus, interpretations of high and low scores on Scale 9 must take into account these normal variations as a function of age. Clients whose scores on Scale 9 are 10 or more *T* points higher or lower (2 to 3 items) than these expected ranges should be evaluated for the presence of a mood disorder.

Consistent results have not emerged regarding the effects of race on scale scores, but Gynther (1979) described various demographic effects on MMPI scales, and African Americans do appear to score higher than Whites, although not dramatically so. Regarding gender, there are only very slight differences between males and females for Scale 9.

Ma did not lose any items in the re-standardization; however, seven items were changed, four had sexist wording modified, two were modernized, and one item had a grammatical clarification. Thirty-five of the 46 items are keyed True, 11 False. The profile forms provide for adding 0.2 *K* to Scale 9 to increase the accuracy of diagnostic discrimination. As the predominant deviant response to the items is True, as for the other psychotic tetrad scales, an All-True response set will elevate Scale 9. Other than Scale 8, with which it shares 11 items, Scale 9 shares few overlapping items relative to the other scales. Of the 11 items that overlap Scale 8, 10 appear on *Ma-O*, and 8 overlap *RC9* (Hypomanic Activation). Sixteen of the 46 items are unique to *Ma*. According to Little (1949), the highest biserial correlation for any item was .48 on the item indicating a wish to leave home (item 21), with two other items tied with similar correlations of .45. These items were related to opportunism (items 227 and 248). It is likely that these low correlations reflect the heterogeneity of the scale. Greene (2011) recognized that Scale 9 tends to have the lowest correlation with the other clinical scales.

When the MMPI was re-standardized (Butcher et al., 1989), each item was assigned a value reflecting its reading difficulty. An index, the lexile value, is derived from the sentence length, word frequency in various kinds of popular literature, and sentence complexity. The ceiling value for this index is 1,600; a value of 500 corresponds to a fifth grade reading level, 600 to a sixth grade level, and so on. A high school graduate level is 1,300. Of importance here is that, of all the clinical scales, examination of the mean lexile values for the basic scales shows Scale 9 to have the most difficult items to read and understand. For example, *Ma1* requires a ninth grade reading level. Reading level requirements are discussed in Chapter 2, but the *Manual* (Butcher et al., 2001) recommends a sixth grade reading level. However, the 1989 edition of the *Manual* recommends an *eighth* grade reading level requirement, and reports a lexile value of 825 for Scale 9, the highest for all of the basic scales. It appears that the research of Dahlstrom et al. (1994) regarding the readability level for the MMPI-2 led to a modification in the

2001 *Manual*, decreasing the overall recommendation from an eighth grade to a sixth grade reading level. Nevertheless, the higher the reading level of the test taker, the greater the likelihood that reading difficulties will not hamper effective comprehension of the items on Scale 9 and certain other subscales with more complex sentence structures.

Paolo, Ryan, and Smith (1991, p. 532) advise that for clinicians working

...with populations whose members possess average reading skills of less than eighth or ninth grade, the Hypomania (Ma) subscales, and possibly the Hypomania clinical scale itself. At the very least, clinicians should determine whether individual patients are able to read and comprehend adequately the more difficult items on these scales.

Internal consistency estimates (coefficients alpha) for *Ma* based on the re-standardization sample (Butcher et al., 2001) are .58 for men and .61 for women. Test–retest correlations over an interval of about one week are .80 for men and .65 for women. Hunsley et al.'s (1988) large-scale meta-analysis of MMPI reliability studies using a diversity of populations conducted between 1970 and 1981 reported an average internal consistency of .71 across 73 studies. They also reported an average test–retest reliability of .65 for 17 studies with time intervals from one day to two years.

Harris-Lingoes Subscales

Harris and Lingoes (1955, 1968) developed four subscales for *Ma*: Amorality (*Ma1*), Psychomotor Acceleration (*Ma2*), Imperturbability (*Ma3*), and Ego Inflation (*Ma4*). These subscales are entirely non-overlapping. Subscales *Ma2* and *Ma4* appear more distinctly related to mania than *Ma1* and *Ma3*, which may partially overlap the psychopathy construct. Only 34 of the 46 *Ma* items appear on one or another of the subscales.

Ma1: Amorality (6 Items)

This short six-item subscale has five items keyed True, one False. Descriptors provided by Harris and Lingoes for *Ma1* include: "A callousness about one's own motives and ends and those of other people; disarming frankness; and denial of guilt." Caldwell (1988) believed that the scale is better named Opportunism, given that high scorers on this subscale see others as selfish, dishonest, and opportunistic and feel justified to behave in a similar fashion. They also tend to derive vicarious gratification from the exploitive ways of others (Butcher et al., 2001). Nichols and Greene (1995) viewed *Ma1* as reflecting a kind of "thoughtless expediency" (p. 33) that can put others at a disadvantage, and as a somewhat subtle measure of cynicism. According to Levitt (1989), high scorers believe that a person is foolish not to take every possible advantage of every situation and, as selfish people, see life as an endless series of minor skirmishes in which the person who is not overburdened with scruples is usually victorious. Osberg and Poland (2001) found that *Ma1* correlated positively with a history of criminal activity. In fact, four of the *Ma1* items overlap *ASP1* (Antisocial Attitudes). "These items are attitudinal rather than behavioral in character and espouse an expedient if not opportunistic morality in which egocentric desire supplants moral scruple" (Nichols, 2011, p. 188). It is not surprising, therefore, that high scorers are unsympathetic to, if not contemptuous of, weakness in others.

Graham et al. (1999) reported the following information for high *Ma1* scorers (*T* > 65) in their sample of psychiatric outpatients. Both men and women reported a history of alcohol abuse within the last six months preceding their intake interview; women patients were more likely to have an Axis I diagnosis (*DSM III-R*) of substance abuse or dependence and an Axis II diagnosis of antisocial personality disorder. During intake interviews, men with high scores were described as having an angry mood and their therapists indicated that they had tendencies to act out. This is consistent with their higher frequency of being physically abusive, committing domestic violence, and the greater likelihood of having a domestic violence conviction. Low *Ma1* scorers (raw score of zero or one) may have moral values emphasizing individual responsibility and control over oneself (Caldwell, 1988) and may also reflect a lack of cynicism.

Ma2: Psychomotor Acceleration (11 Items)

Harris and Lingoes (1968) applied the following content descriptors to *Ma2*: "Hyperactivity, liability, flight from 'inner life' and anxiety; and pressure for action."

> *Ma2* is the core subscale of Scale 9 and reflects impulses to act in preference to contemplation or the experiencing of feelings, as a means of resolving psychomotor tension (and this would seem to include feelings of impending depression), and of breaking through perceived or anticipated obstacles.
>
> (Nichols, 2011, p. 188)

Nine of the 11 items are keyed True, 2 False.

Although the items in this subscale are manic in nature, they do not appear to reflect a negative tension state or unwanted arousal (Caldwell, 1988). Wiggins' (1966, 1969) *HYP* content scale is a better measure of excessive or undesired excitability. Although the behaviors implied by the items on *Ma2* are unusual, the item content is not strongly suggestive of psychosis (Nichols & Greene, 1995). High scorers generally report accelerated speech, thought processes, and motor activities, and may report tension, restlessness, and excitement (Butcher et al., 2001). High scorers are easily bored and may seek stimulation in order to alter their mood state. Wrobel (1992) reported hyperactivity as a significant correlate for this subscale. Levitt (1989) viewed *Ma2* as a sensation-seeking measure, with high scorers having a high optimal stimulation level. These individuals may have a significant need for a variety of experiences. If Scale 9 is significantly elevated, it is likely that *Ma2* will also be elevated (Caldwell, 1988). In fact, Greene (2011) found that *Ma2* was the third highest scale in an aggregate of 15 scales most highly correlated with Scale 9. *Ma2* correlated 73 with Scale 9 in the Caldwell clinical sample (2007b).

Graham et al. (1999) found in their sample of psychiatric outpatients that high scoring women on *Ma2* (*T* ≥ 65) were more likely to have a diagnosis of borderline personality disorder. Male patients were more likely to report a history of being physically abusive and to have a history of committing domestic violence.

Low *Ma2* scores may reflect a slow, cautious pace or tempo, and may indicate a low general level of excitement in one's life. Nichols and Greene (1995) suggested that a low

Ma2 score may indicate psychomotor retardation, whereas a low Scale 9 score, with an elevated *Ma2* score, may not suggest a loss of energy. Low *Ma2* scorers may also deny any tension or hyperactivity and not desire excitement. In fact, they may altogether avoid situations or activities involving risk or danger (Graham, 1990).

Ma3: *Imperturbability (8 Items)*

Harris and Lingoes (1968) applied the following descriptors to the content of *Ma3*: "Affirmations of confidence in social situations; denial of sensitivity; and proclamation of independence from the opinions of other people." The items on this subscale suggest that one is not bothered by interruptions, distractions, and tensions (Caldwell, 1988), and a certain quality of imperviousness is reflected in the items (Nichols & Greene, 1995). *Ma3* should be considered subtle in nature, as seven of the eight items are scored on *Ma-S*. Five of the eight items are keyed False, three True. High *Ma3* scorers deny social anxiety in a manner similar to high *Hy1* scorers (Levitt, 1989), and reflect a socially comfortable person who feels secure interacting with others with little concern about the opinions, values, and attitudes of others (Butcher et al., 2001). Extraversion appears to be related to high *Ma3* scores, although *Ma3* is not a direct measure of this factor. Nichols and Greene described the high *Ma3* scorer as not being afraid to be socially visible. They also saw *Ma3* as reflecting dispassion ("cool") and composure under difficult social stresses. Successful individuals may elevate this scale. Caldwell (1988) said that "*Ma3* is often the predominant subscale in controlled striving and performance-oriented patterns such as a relatively unelevated code 39/93 with *K* up" (p. 32). The Graham et al. (1999) investigation of MMPI-2 correlates in a psychiatric outpatient population failed to identify pathological correlates for elevated *Ma3* scores.

Ma3 appears related to both extraversion and insensitivity to others' feelings. *Ma3* overlaps *Hy1* (Denial of Social Anxiety) by two items and *Pd3* (Social Imperturbability) by three, but is less saturated with this dimension than the other two subscales. "Like *Ma1*, *Ma3* involves a denial of sensitivity to the plight of others and, like *Ma2*, involves pressures to press ahead in the face of obstacles and uncomfortable feelings" (Nichols, 2011, p. 189).

Low scores may reflect impatience at being interrupted or distracted and a self-conscious hesitation in groups (Caldwell, 1988). Low scorers often feel uncomfortable in the presence of others and are easily influenced by people's opinions, values, and attitudes. Levitt (1989) viewed low scores as reflecting anxious, shy, easy-to-embarrass individuals who are uncomfortable in social situations. Similarly, Nichols (2011) described low scorers possessing the vulnerability usually described in the Avoidant Personality Disorder.

Ma4: *Ego Inflation (9 Items)*

Harris and Lingoes (1968) stated that high scorers *Ma4* had "feelings of self-importance to the point of unrealistic grandiosity." The nine items of this relatively short subscale are all keyed True, making *Ma4* vulnerable to the All-True response set. Nichols (2011) noted that the heterogeneous content of *Ma4* defied concise thematic description; Levitt (1989) also pointed out the title of the subscale appears to derive from a single item. Indeed, this subscale reflects the grandiosity so typical of the manic or hypomanic individual, and high scorers typically have unrealistic appraisals of their own abilities and self-worth. They tend to become resentful when people make demands on them (Butcher et al., 2001) or are bossy toward them. The items appear to suggest anger when one's importance is not appreciated, and there is an underlying theme of "willful stubbornness" (Caldwell, 1988, p. 33). Nichols and Greene (1995) reported that *Ma4* reflects a quality of willfulness and bravado, and often the individual appears to be defending him or herself against passivity and dependency by behaving in a counterdependent or countersubmissive fashion (e.g. asserting dominance in an overt fashion). Consistent with Nichols and Greene (1995), Nichols (2011, p. 189) provided the following description of what *Ma4* measures:

> It reflects a tendency to resist influence and domination by experts and authority, and by others generally, and to be intolerant of and to rebel against a passive position in relationships. High scorers adhere to a defensive but pugnacious autonomy, however, moderate elevation (*T*-60 to *T*-70) may imply concerns about self-determination and a need to do things "my own way".

High *Ma4* scores also connote a sense of superiority and contempt for others.

Graham et al. (1999) found that female psychiatric outpatients with high scores on *Ma4* (*T* ≥ 65) were viewed as sociopathic by their therapists, with narcissistic and histrionic features. Difficult to motivate, they were described as easily bored and impatient.

Greene (2011) identified 15 scales with the highest correlations with Scale 9 in the Caldwell (2007b) clinical sample. He identified four categories within these 15 scales with "hypomania" being the first category. Within this grouping, *Ma4* correlated .70 with Scale 9.

Low scores reflect interpersonal submissiveness with a willingness to accept arbitrary treatment from others. A low *Ma4* score, coupled with an elevated *Sc2* (Emotional Alienation) score, suggests apathy and psychological impotence (Nichols & Greene, 1995). The low scorer is more likely to show a willingness to tolerate domineering behavior in others. There is also a certain modesty regarding their self-importance, making it easier for them to accept orders without objection (Caldwell, 1988). Low *Ma4* scores may reflect an individual who is also very self-critical (Graham, 1990).

Scale 9: Subtle–Obvious Subscales

The Hypomania-Obvious subscale (*Ma-O*) has 23 items, of which 20 are keyed True, 3 False; Hypomania-Subtle (Ma-S) also contains 23 items, of which 15 are keyed True, 8 False. The majority of obvious items on *Ma-O* pertain to episodes of intense excitement and periods of great restlessness, with excitement, impulse pressures, and vigilance predominating (Caldwell, 1988). Additionally, the items reflect tension, intense drive, impulsiveness, volatility and feelings of being out of control, both mentally and physically. Nichols (2011) stated *Ma-O* is the psychotic component of Scale 9; it is dominated by *Ma2* and is thematically distressed/dysphoric, in contrast to *Ma-S*. It should also be noted that Greene (2011) reported for the Caldwell (2007b) clinical sample that *Ma-O* correlated highly with Scale 9 (.83), reflecting a strong hypomanic component to *Ma-O*.

Hollrah et al. (1995) reviewed the research of Wrobel and Lachar (1982), examining the correlates for the S–O subscales. *Ma-O* correlated positively with the factors labeled Discomfort and Sociopathy, although discomfort was a less than optimal scale descriptor, as it correlated with all of the obvious subscales. Nevertheless, the description of the *Ma-O* item content given by Caldwell (1988) is consistent with the finding of discomfort and, to a lesser extent, with sociopathy. Other MMPI-2 measures, such as Antisocial Practices (*ASP*), Antisocial Attitudes (*ASP1*), Cynicism (*CYN*), and Disconstraint (*DISC*) should be examined to help sort out issues of sociopathy.

Dahlstrom (1991) examined the correlates of the S–O subscales derived from partner ratings on the Katz Adjustment Scales used in the re-standardization (Butcher et al., 2001). For both men and women, the following descriptors emerged as significant for high *Ma-O* scorers: nervous, does not go to religious functions, moody, and does not show sound judgment. For men only, the following descriptors were given: takes nonprescription drugs, whines and demands attention, prone to temper tantrums, suspicious of others, swears and curses, not pleasant and relaxed, upset by small unexpected events, talks back, acts without thinking, and is not thoughtful of others. For women only, the following descriptors were given: restless, has many fears, does strange things, has bad dreams, lacks emotional control, gets excited or happy for no reason, worries about the future, not helpful or constructive, talks too much, bored and restless, takes too many risks, cries easily, wears strange clothes, gives up too easily, and tells others off about their faults.

Low *Ma-O* scores suggest a constrained sense of self-importance, an absence or careful avoidance of intense excitement in one's life, and possibly a strict but integrated individual conscience (Caldwell, 1988).

Although some of the *Ma-S* items clearly reflect hypomania (e.g. item 169), other items indicating a denial of anxiety (mostly on *Ma3*) appear to be more subtle (Caldwell, 1988). Examples of such are item 200, expressing concerns about one's appearance, and item 167, indicating difficulties talking to new people. The variety in the content of the *Ma-S* subscale makes it difficult to summarize, but Caldwell (1988) stated that much of the content relates to a "heightened level of arousability and interpersonal assertiveness that is similar to but less disruptive than *Ma-O*" (p. 31). Nichols (2011) described the heterogeneous *Ma-S* item content as reflecting inflation, euphoria, and freedom from distress. *Ma-S* appears to be dominated by *Ma3* and is a more characterological than symptomatic component of Scale 9. High scorers project themselves as gregarious and strongly extraverted, emotionally resilient, morally unconstrained, full of physical energy, and disinhibited.

Hollrah et al. (1995), in a thorough review of the validity of the subtle items in the MMPI, stated that of all the subtle subscales *Ma-S* showed the best validity: "Ma-S was consistently related to scale-appropriate external measures and occasionally had more validity than Ma-full and Ma-O" (p. 293). They suggested that the convergent validity of *Ma-S* is due to the subtle items' clear relationship to hypomania. Consistent with this finding is Greene's (2011) showing that *Ma-S* correlated .64 in the Caldwell (2007b) clinical sample with Scale 9. DiLalla, Gottesman, Carey, and Bouchard (1999) studied a large sample of identical and fraternal twins who had been reared apart in order to study the "genetic and environmental architecture" of the MMPI S–O subscales. *Ma-S* "was positively correlated with the experience of atypical symptoms, psychotic symptoms, hostility, and hypomania and negatively associated with depression, social maladjustment, repression, and defensiveness. It appears that the *Ma-S* items contribute significantly to the construct validity of Scale 9" (p. 364).

Dahlstrom (1991) derived the following correlates for the *Ma-S* subscale for men and women from the partner ratings made in the re-standardization sample: not shy, talks too much, makes big plans, talks back, tells others off about their faults, stubborn, gets excited or happy for no reason, takes too many risks, and gives advice too freely. For men only, the following correlates were found: bossy, craves attention, does not lack energy, does strange things, has temper tantrums, reports bad dreams, resents being told what to do, apathetic about others' feelings, does the opposite of what is asked, takes nonprescription drugs, has been arrested or had trouble with the law, likes to flirt, acts without thinking, stirs up excitement, expresses a belief in strange things, whines and demands attention, laughs and jokes with others, volunteers for projects, and enjoys parties and friends. For women only, the following correlates were derived: wears strange clothes, tries too hard, resents being told what to do, does not avoid contact with others, does not show sound judgment, stirs up excitement, brags too much, threatens to harm others, and takes advantage of others. A low *Ma-S* score suggests a high level of interpersonal constraint and social caution consistent with a slow personal pace (Caldwell, 1988). Nichols (2011) suggested that low scorers tend toward passivity and dependency.

Scale 0: Social Introversion (Si)

The original 70-item *Si* scale was designed to evaluate an individual's degree of introversion–extraversion (Drake, 1946). The *Si* scale is the only clinical scale in the MMPI for which the criterion group was composed of a non-psychiatric (normal) sample. Its construction was motivated by the use of a test being routinely administered in the guidance program at the University of Wisconsin. This test, the Minnesota T-S-E (Thinking-Social-Emotional) Inventory, was developed by Evans and McConnell (1941). Evans and McConnell separated the character traits of introversion–extraversion into areas of thinking, social activity, and emotional expression. An individual could be considered introverted or extraverted in any of these three areas. Because the MMPI was also part of the standard battery of tests administered to students, Drake decided to devise a scale measuring social introversion from the MMPI that would produce data similar to the T-S-E Inventory. Two female criterion groups were selected. The first consisted of 50 students ranking at the 65th percentile or higher on the social introversion–extraversion dimension of the T-S-E; the second consisted of 50 students who scored below the 35th percentile. Three participants scoring high on *L* were excluded from the criterion groups. Although the scale was constructed using all females, it was later validated with men. The female students were studied in 1944 and 1945, and men were not included because of the danger that the war would have rendered male college a biased and atypical male sample on college campuses (Drake & Thiede, 1948). A later sample of men scored so similarly to the women that Drake combined the two into a single group for purposes of establishing the norms. The items that differentiated high from low scorers (after removing items with very high or very low endorsement frequencies in either or both groups) became the 70-item Social Introversion-Extraversion scale (*Si*), or Scale 0.

A new group of MMPI answer sheets was then scored for *Si*. As Drake (1946, as cited in Dahlstrom & Dahlstrom, 1980) noted, "these MMPI record sheets contain the responses of a group of students who had cleared through the testing office after the group of students who provided the data for the item analyses" (p. 77). The scores were then correlated with the T-S-E Social Introversion-Extraversion (I.E.) scores, yielding a correlation of –.72 for a sample of 87 female and –.71 for a sample of 81 male students. The correlations were negative because a low score on the T-S-E Inventory indicates introversion, whereas a high score on the *Si* indicates introversion.

Norms were reported in terms of linear *T*-scores and were based on the test records of 193 male and 350 female students. In a subsequent study, Drake and Thiede (1948) obtained additional cross-validation for Scale 0 by examining the level of high school and college activity participation in a sample of 594 female college students. Students with lower activity participation scored higher, and those participating in more activities scored lower. The developers of the Minnesota T-S-E Inventory conceptualized social introversion as withdrawal from social responsibilities and contacts, with little real interest in people, and social extraversion as involving an interest in social contact, with a strong interest in others (Dahlstrom et al., 1972). The final *Si* scale may be limited by any of the biases inherent in the T-S-E Inventory because the criterion groups were selected on the basis of its Social I.E. scores.

Elevated scores on Scale 0 (*T* > 50) indicate introversive trends, whereas scores below a *T*-50 indicate the opposite extraversive trends. The heterogeneous item content of the *Si* broadly reflects the dimension of introversion–extraversion that emerges as a primary dimension from statistical studies of the MMPI (Friedman, 1982; Gentry et al., 1985; Wakefield et al., 1975). The items reflect uneasiness in social situations; feelings of inferiority and discomfort; unhappiness, shyness, conversational reticence, circumspection, passivity, self-effacement, and hypersensitivity. Low self-confidence causes high scorers to dwell excessively on social comparisons.

> Social visibility tends to be aversive—another area of calculation in the high Scale 0 scorer's decisions about activities to be engaged in or avoided, and the amount of interaction that can be accommodated without exceeding his or her comfort level.
>
> (Nichols, 2011, p. 203)

Two broad content domains of Scale 0 have been identified as shyness and self-consciousness, the subjective aspect of introversion; and social avoidance, the objective or socially visible aspect of introversion (Nichols & Greene, 1995). Greene (2011) further validated these content domains by identifying the 15 scales from the Caldwell (2007b) clinical sample with the highest correlations with Scale 0. The two broad categories identified within these scales are shyness/self-consciousness (scales *Si1*, *SOD2*) and social avoidance/introversion (scales *Si2*, *SOD1*).

As described in the Scale 5 section of this chapter, Graham et al. (1971) factor analyzed the responses to Scale 0 from 422 psychiatric inpatients, outpatients, and normals. They identified seven Scale 0 factors, of which six were used by Serkownek (1975) to construct subscales for Scale 0. The seventh factor, Demographic Variables, was not used to construct a subscale. The Scale 0 subscales were named Inferiority-Personal Discomfort (*Si1*), Discomfort With Others (*Si2*), Staid-Personal Rigidity (*Si3*),

Hypersensitivity (*Si4*), Distrust (*Si5*), and Physical-Somatic Concerns (*Si6*). As Greene (1991a) pointed out, clinicians can continue to use the Serkownek (1975) subscales on the MMPI-2 as only 1 item has been dropped from Scale 0, which reduced *Si2* from 14 to 13 items. Graham (1987) reported test–retest reliability coefficients for men and women (over a six-week interval) provided by Moreland (1985). Over all of the Serkownek subscales, the coefficients range from .68 to .89, with an average of .77 for men, and range from .63 to .87, with an average of .76 for women. Williams (1983) reported one-week test–retest reliabilities for *Si* subscales averaging .84 for women and .68 for men.

In a large-scale study, Foerstner (1986) investigated the interrelationships among the 63 MMPI subscales developed by Serkownek (1975), Harris and Lingoes (1955), Wiggins (1966), and Wiener and Harmon (1946). Nine hundred MMPIs from male and female psychiatric inpatients, chemical-dependent residents, and private practice outpatients were analyzed. Ten factors were identified that accounted for 75.5 percent of the total variance. *Si4* (Hypersensitivity) loaded on the first factor, Depression (.67), as did *Si1* (Inferiority-Personal Discomfort; .65) and *Si5* (Distrust; .44). *Si3* (Staid-Personal Rigidity) loaded negatively on the factor named Social Introversion. *Si1* also loaded on the third factor, Agitated Hostility (.64). *Si5* loaded on the factor Cynical Distrust (.63). It is clear from the data in Foerstner's investigation that Scale 0 (like Scale 5) is multifactorial and that maladjustment is a major component of the scale. A Scale 0 score, whether high or low, may be achieved by item endorsements affecting any of a combination of at least six factors (Wong, 1984). In contrast to the non-pathological correlates for the Serkownek *Mf* subscales, the *Si* subscales, with the exception of *Si3*, appear pathology related.

Ben-Porath, Hostetler, Butcher, and Graham (1989) developed three new content-homogeneous subscales for *Si* to replace the Serkownek subscales that are generally no longer used. They used a multistage approach involving a series of empirical and rational procedures. These subscales—named Shyness/Self-Consciousness (*Si1*), Social Avoidance (*Si2*), and Self-Other Alienation (*Si3*)—were developed with data provided by college students. Data analysis with this and the re-standardization sample demonstrated that these new measures combined to contribute to the assessment of nearly 90 percent of the variance of the full *Si* scale. Validation of these subscales was provided in the results of Sieber and Meyers (1992). These investigators compared results on the *Si* subscales against self-report measures of constructs that were believed to be differentially related to the three subscales. They stated that:

> specifically, measures of self-esteem, public self-consciousness, social anxiety, and shyness were expected to correlate with *Si1*; measures of self-esteem, public self-consciousness, social anxiety, and social avoidance were expected to correlate with *Si2*; finally, measures of self-esteem, alienation, anomia, loss of control, and personal and social identity were expected to correlate with *Si3*.
>
> (Sieber & Meyers, 1992, p. 185)

These hypotheses were generally supported by the data. It appears that elevated *Si1* scores reflect shyness around others, uneasiness in social surroundings, and discomfort in unfamiliar situations. High scorers tend to lack social skills and feel disadvantaged when interacting with others, especially strangers. Low scorers are comfortable in social situations. High *Si2* scores appear to reflect an active avoidance of others, a dislike of group situations, and an aversion to social events. Low scorers are social joiners and enjoy group activities. High *Si3* scorers appear to have low self-esteem, a lack of interest in activities, low self-confidence, and to not feel in control of their life outcomes. The emphasis is on personal rather than social inadequacy, with a secondary theme of cynicism, hypersensitivity, and a sense of being at odds with others. In contrast, low scorers feel confident and are engaged with others.

In their investigation of the *Si* subscales, Ward and Perry (1998) found, as in previous research, the three *Si* subscales accounted well for the variance in *Si* scores in clinical samples. *Si3* items were found to be less obvious indicators of social introversion as compared with *Si1* and *Si2* items; *Si3* appears to be more of a measure of the general maladjustment factor of the MMPI-2. Ward and Perry cautioned users of the *Si* subscales to recognize that *Si1* and *Si2* are purer measurements of the social introversion construct, and are not reflective of negative emotionality. In fact, they pointed out that the item content of *Si1* and *Si2* is virtually the same as that from the *SOD* content scale. Nichols (2011) suggested considering *SOD* (Social Discomfort) as a purer estimate of social introversion than Scale 0. He explains that while the *Si* subscales have the advantage of high reliability and zero overlap, they account for only 39 of the 69 items on Scale 0.

Si lost one item in the revision of the MMPI-2; six items were modified to modernize idioms and usage of words, improve grammatical clarification, and simplify wording. There is a fairly even balance of True and False keyed items, with 36 keyed True, and 33 keyed False.

Scale 0 has proportionately fewer overlapping items than any other validity or clinical scale (Greene, 2000). Forty-two of the items on the scale overlap other scales, with 27 non-overlapping items. The *Pd* and *Mf* scales share the most items with *Si* (11 and 9 items, respectively). The *L* and *F* scales share no items with Scale 0. The highest net overlap with Scale 0 is found on Scales 2 and 7 with strong overlap on the following subscales: *D1* (seven items), *D5* (three items), *Hy1* (five items; negative), *Pd3* (five items; negative), and *Ma3* (three items; negative). *Si* also shares 18 items with *SOD*. Nichols (2011, p. 199) provided useful configural interpretive information for Scale 0 in relation to other scales based, in part, on the Caldwell (2007b) clinical data sample.

Among the basic clinical scales, Scale 0 is most highly correlated with Scales 7, 8, and 2, in that order. It is highly correlated with *SOD* at .89. The most important configural relationship of Scale 0 is with Scale 9, with which it correlates .14. In patients with Bipolar Disorder, these two scales often cross in the transition between depressed and manic states. Low 0 and high 9 are synergistic with respect to social hunger. When both Scales 9 and 0 are elevated, 0 tends to dominate, whereas Scale 9 features are confined to those suggested by *Ma-O*, *Ma2* and *Ma4*. When both are low, Scale 9 tends to be dominated by *Ma3* and *Ma-S*, which mostly blend in with and augment the low 0 characteristics.

It should be noted that, like Scale 5, Scale 0 uses linear, rather than uniform, *T*-scores. Introversion–extraversion is a normally distributed individual difference variable of high heritability (Scarr, 1969). Many researchers and clinicians believe strong constitutional and biological factors contribute to the introversion–extraversion dimension of personality (e.g. Eysenck, 1967; Meyer, 1983; Wakefield, Wood, Wallace, & Friedman, 1978). The stability of scores on this scale over time appear to reflect this biological and/or constitutional component. Extraverts have a need for stimulation or sensation-seeking, whereas introverts try to avoid stimulation, and there is a vast literature on the underlying neuro-cortical substrates for this phenomenon (e.g. Eysenck, 1967; Friedman, 1982). The generally high test–retest correlations support this contention. For psychiatric patients, the coefficients range from .80 to .88 for a one- to two-week interval between MMPI administrations, and from .63 to .64 for a one-year interval between tests (Dahlstrom et al., 1975). In Hunsley et al.'s (1988) large-scale meta-analysis of MMPI reliability studies using a wide variety of populations conducted between 1970 and 1981, an average test–retest reliability of .86 for 16 studies with time intervals from one day to two years was reported. Test–retest reliability data were reported for the MMPI-2 scales over about a one-week interval (Butcher et al., 2001). Test–retest *Si* correlations were .93 for men and .92 for women, and were the highest reported for any of the validity or clinical scales.

The behavioral stability for *Si*, although highly stable and persistent, does fluctuate for patients with bipolar disorder, where it is not unusual to see Scale 0 scores shift by 30 or more *T*-scores between manic and depressive states (Nichols, 2011).

In the Hunsley et al. (1988) meta-analysis of the MMPI, an average internal consistency of .81 across 41 studies was reported. The *Manual* (Butcher et al., 2001) reports internal consistency estimates (Cronbach coefficient alpha) of .82 and .84 for men and women, respectively.

The quality and type of interpersonal relations high and low scorers experience varies with their *Si* elevations as well as with other significant scores in the profile. Generally, Scale 0 reflects how comfortable an individual is around other people. High scores (introversion) reflect discomfort with others, whereas low scores (extraversion) reveal a preference for being with others. Nichols (2011, p. 203) provides an insightful overview of high Scale 0 scorers and how they experience their interpersonal world.

> High Scale 0 scorers are uncomfortable with others but do not necessarily wish to be alone or uninvolved. They form relationships slowly and deliberately, often after an initial period of considerable hesitancy and awkwardness. Once formed, however, these relationships may be highly stable, loyal, and intimate. These patients may be particularly uncomfortable dealing with members of the opposite gender, owing to deficits in heterosexual social skills that, in turn, are caused by their own shyness and past avoidance of situations (e.g. school dances) within which such skills are typically learned. In relatively close social interaction, these patients are peaceable and avoid conflict or unpleasantness. Even when safeguards are strong, they are quick to make concessions or submit, rather than expose themselves to the stimulation that comes with conflict, judging their skills as inadequate to its management. Resistance, if any, tends to be passive, and these patients may find fault with their own attitudes and conduct, or even fall into self-criticism or self-deprecation to prevent or abort confrontation.

It is important to examine other clinical scales when Scale 0 is high or low because Scale 0 can operate as an activator or inhibitor for certain behaviors. When elevated in combination with other scales, Scale 0 is most often associated with anxiety and depressive disorders, but is not uncommon in schizophrenia. For example, a high Scale 8 score will indicate more social isolation and communication problems when Scale 0 is also elevated. When Scale 7 is elevated, look for anxious, insecure, ruminative individuals who dread social attention and may exhibit social phobia. A very low Scale 0 score will accentuate the impulsivity often seen in high Scale 4 scorers and indicate a superficiality and shallowness in relationships. When *Si* is elevated with a prominent Scale 4 score, individuals are seen as sour, caustic, and uncommunicative (Levak et al., 2011). When Scale 2, *DEP*, or low Positive Emotion (*RC2*) are elevated with *Si*, consider the possibility of a long-term characterologically depressed, pessimistic, and defensively sour individual. Individuals with impoverished or compromised social relations, as often seen in schizoid, schizotypal, and avoidant personality disorders, tend to elevate Scale 0. Lewak et al. (1990, p. 273) stated that elevated *Si* scores

> may reflect a childhood characterized by an absence of warmth and physical contact from others. Elevated scores suggest that these people have extinguished their feeling response to physical touch and affection. They suffer from a form of "affect hunger" and yet, they feel conflicted about close, intimate relationships.

Low *Si* scores reflect more than just social extraversion. Low scores (*T* < 40) suggest a drive toward social interaction, sometimes, but not always, out of insecurity. "Extreme low scores may reflect not only an insatiable need to be in the spotlight but also a low level of socially acceptable embarrassment in the face of obvious self-serving and self-aggrandizing behavior" (Levak et al., 2011, p. 358).

Hathaway and Meehl (1952) examined the descriptions of high normal *Si* scorers. Men were described by their acquaintances with only one typical adjective, modest. Dahlstrom et al. (1975) suggested that perhaps the introverted personality style of these men made it difficult for others to get to know them and, therefore, to characterize them more fully. In contrast, normal women scoring high on *Si* were described as modest, serious, shy, self-effacing, and sensitive. They showed emotional warmth and had home and family interests, but did not seek out social contacts and satisfaction. Dahlstrom et al. made the important point that the personality styles of these individuals appear to reflect the basic preference for a style of life in keeping with their emotional needs, rather than individuals who are inhibited or thwarted in their efforts to have broader social contacts.

Dahlstrom et al. (1972) also presented the research descriptions of high- and low-scoring men on *Si* provided by Gough et al. (1955). Both high and low *Si* scorers are described in more unfavorable, maladjusted, terms than in the earlier Hathaway and Meehl (1952, as cited in Dahlstrom et al., 1972) depiction of the introvert. Quoting Dahlstrom et al. (1972, pp. 227–228):

> The high 0 men were described as slow in personal tempo, stereotyped, lacking originality in approach to problems. The implication seems to be that these men showed such qualities as part of a general insecurity. They were also described as unable to make decisions without vacillation, hesitation, or delay. They were seen as rigid and inflexible in thought and action, as overly controlled and inhibited, and

as lacking confidence in their own abilities. They were conforming and followed prescribed methods in the things they did. They became fussy and pedantic in even minor matters.

In their relations with others, they were seen as lacking poise and social presence, as becoming rattled and upset in a social situation. Perhaps as a consequence, these men were rated as cold and distant. They were not affected in this aloofness, however, but appeared free of pretense and conscientious and dependable in their responsibilities. They seemed to derive personal reward and pleasure from their work and placed a high value on productive achievement for its own sake.

Toward authority, these men were submissive, compliant, and overly accepting. They tended to sidestep as a way of handling troublesome situations. They either made concessions to avoid unpleasantness or passively resisted pressures by not getting involved in things. They were generally permissive and accepting, however, in their relations with others, respecting other people, and not making judgments. As a result, these high 0 men kept out of trouble and showed socially appropriate behavior. They get along well in the world as it is.

Low-scoring men (extraverts) in the normal group examined by Hathaway and Meehl (as cited in Dahlstrom et al., 1972) were described as versatile and sociable, whereas low-scoring women, also described as mixing well with others, were also seen as enthusiastic, talkative, assertive, and adventurous. The Gough et al. (1955) male low scorers were seen as expressive and colorful; they were also described as ostentatious and exhibitionistic. They ambitiously focused on success as a means for achieving status and power. Competitive and vigorous, they were dominant in relation to others, and could easily stimulate hostility and resentment around them. They could also be opportunistic in that they viewed others only in terms of what they could get from them, rather than being sensitive to their feelings. Self-indulgent and unable to delay gratification, they were often impulsive, acting without sufficient deliberation, which likely led to their being seen as immature.

6   Interpreting the MMPI-2 Codetypes

Introduction

The following code-pattern information represents an admixture of actuarial and clinical information. Actuarial data do not exist concerning all possible clinical configurations of the MMPI-2 and MMPI; however, clinical data based on observation and historical use do exist. Thus, we have integrated different sources so that the maximum number of diverse MMPI-2 profiles can be interpreted. By combining these two approaches, but using the actuarial knowledge as the basic matrix, it is possible to interpret all single and two-point codes, many three-point scale combinations, and even some four-point combinations. Because 18- and 19-year-old participants typically complete the MMPI-2, code patterns with importance to late adolescence are described when relevant.

Interpretations of code patterns are presented in a convenient lookup format (i.e. in order of the clinical scales). In addition, there is a Code-Pattern Look-Up Table immediately following the Table of Contents so that readers seeking an interpretation about a specific MMPI-2 pattern can quickly locate the pages containing interpretations associated with that pattern.

The primary sources for the present interpretations are: Archer (1992, 1997); Archer, Griffin, and Aiduk (1995); Butcher (1990b, 2011); Butcher et al. (1989); Butcher and Williams (1992); Caldwell (1988, 1997); Carkhuff, Barnett, and McCall (1965); Carson (1969); Dahlstrom et al. (1972, 1986); Drake and Oetting (1959); Duckworth and Anderson (1995); Fowler (1966); Friedman, Webb, and Lewak (1989); Friedman, Lewak, Nichols, and Webb (2001); Gilberstadt and Duker (1965); Graham (1990, 1993); Graham, Ben-Porath, and McNulty (1999); Graham and McCord (1985); Greene (1991a, 2000, 2011); Hovey and Lewis (1967); Lachar (1974); Levak, Siegel, Nichols, and Stolberg (2011); Lewak, Marks, and Nelson (1990); Marks and Seeman (1963); Marks, Seeman, and Haller (1974); Swenson, Pearson, and Osborne (1973); Van de Riet and Wolking (1969); Webb (1970a, 1970b); and Webb, McNamara, and Rodgers (1981/1986). These references are recommended as the research bases for various interpretations.

It should be noted that the correlates of the Graham et al. (1999) investigation and the Archer et al. (1995) study are based on psychiatric outpatients and psychiatric inpatients, respectively. These two extensive investigations of MMPI-2 correlates are comprehensive studies; it appears that the correlates of the MMPI-2 code patterns are similar in outpatient and inpatient psychiatric settings. Graham et al. also reported that the correlates of most MMPI-2 scales and code patterns in their study are clearly comparable with those previously identified for the original MMPI. Thus, the codetype descriptions in this chapter, including treatment and client feedback suggestions based on past MMPI and MMPI-2 research, should assist the clinician in accurately describing his or her client.

The interpretation of elevated code patterns is the primary focus of this chapter. Interpretation of normal-range *T*-scores are not described in this chapter. Normal-range correlates for the clinical scales can be found in the text by Levak et al. (2011) and, to some extent, in Chapter 5 of this textbook. Low points on several scales, however, are addressed where relevant. Few empirical studies have been conducted on the meaning of low elevations and although there is some debate regarding the interpretation of low points, low scale scores, nevertheless, can change the interpretation of a profile (see Chapters 5 and 9). As discussed previously, clinicians generally emphasize interpretation of the two-, three-, or four-point code patterns; however, elevations on other individual scales expand, modify, and color their interpretation. As described in Chapter 1, the scale elevations given here are based on *K*-corrected *T*-score ranges and are approximations for the clinical scales; scores on the border between classifications (e.g. *T*-65) are particularly open to clinical judgment.

Generally, MMPI interpretations have been developed on Caucasian participants with an IQ of 80 or above and/or education above sixth grade. Modifications of interpretations based on the different characteristics and base rates of behaviors of these various groups are sometimes included in this chapter. Even so, the reader is encouraged to become familiar with the *MMPI Patterns of American Minorities* (Dahlstrom et al., 1986) and to refer to Chapter 9 of this text, which describes moderators such as age, gender, education, race, and socioeconomic variables.

Clinical Scales and Codes

Scale 1 (Hs)

This scale reflects fears and preoccupations about physical functioning and fears of bodily damage. The more elevated the scale, the more intense and consuming the preoccupations, and the more immature, dependent, and lacking in insight the individual. Panic around physical integrity is primitive and pervasive, leaving little room for psychological insight. The lower the scale (below *T*-50), the more the individual will have a tendency to be cavalier about physical illnesses and ailments.

Spike 1

A high score in isolation (T > 65), known as the Spike 1 profile, reflects a person preoccupied with numerous physical complaints, fears, and anxieties about physical illness, injury, or decline. These individuals generally lack joy, see themselves as physically infirm, and view their bodies as sources of pain, fear, and discomfort, rather than as sources of physical pleasure. Others describe them as demanding, complaining, and egocentric, perhaps because their complaints impose demands on others. Generally, they have difficulty openly expressing anger, which tends instead to be expressed symbolically through their symptoms. Others describe them as stubborn, pessimistic, negative, and lacking in drive. Although individuals with Scale 3 elevations also exhibit numerous physical complaints, they are different from individuals with high scores on Scale 1; they are more cheerful, even blasé and denying as they complain of pain. When Scale 1 is elevated, the individual may suffer from actual physical infirmities, but their panic around these infirmities and their focus on them as the main cause of their distress differentiates them from other ill people who take a more realistic view of their symptoms. For high Scale 1 individuals, psychological conflicts and distress are expressed through the prism of physical complaints, some of which may be organic. For example, Carol, a 43-year-old, well-educated Caucasian with a Spike 1 profile, presents as constantly panicked around vague physical symptoms. After a strenuous yoga session, she experiences shoulder pain with numbness in her fingertips. She researches the symptoms on the Internet and decides she may have multiple sclerosis. Upon experiencing intense panic and fantasizing about her death and the loss of seeing her children grow up, she begins to experience tingling in her leg. Further research convinces her she has lupus and her panic increases. Carol cannot entertain the exploration of other stresses in her life because she is focused on finding the right doctors to diagnose what she is convinced is a terminal disorder.

Certain demonstrable neurological disorders can elevate Scale 1 into this range. However, it is not clear how much elevation is due to psychological factors and how much is due to neurological factors. Even in individuals with bona fide physical problems, these elevations predict a pessimistic and fearful attitude about health and a fragile trust in caregivers. Their symptoms and hypochondriacal preoccupations typically are longstanding and resistant to change. Although stress can aggravate their physical symptoms, their complaints are generally not a reaction to immediate stress—though they may be aggravated by it—but rather the result of a longstanding personality style in dealing with stress. As clients, these people can be challenging because they become easily discouraged and do not fully comply or follow through with treatment suggestions. Readily doubting a particular diagnosis and highly suggestible, they "doctor shop," their anxieties shaped by the new doctor's specialty. Although elevations on Scale 1 increase with age, they do not reach an elevation above T-65 purely due to age. When Scale 1 is above T-75, somatic concerns dominate the individual's life.

Moderately high scorers (T-55–65) may be reacting to a bona fide physical disorder; although, in such cases, they are more likely to have an accompanying elevation on Scale 2. Some physical illnesses (e.g. Lyme disease) have physical symptoms that can elevate Scale 1 into this range. Even in this moderate range, there is a tendency to be somewhat pessimistic about health, the possibility of attaining happiness, to somatize under stress, and to be somewhat repressed and inhibited in expressing negative affects.

Moderately low scores on this scale (T-35–45) suggest a person who is not overly concerned about bodily functioning and who is generally effective in daily living (if no other scales are elevated above T-60). Such individuals are seen as resilient, alert, and energetic.

Though there is little empirical data on very low scores ($T < 35$), we hypothesize that they can be obtained for a number of reasons. The individual may be reacting to a family member who used hypochondriacal illnesses in a manipulative way and now is overreacting by rejecting even normal aches and pains; or the individual may be extremely health conscious and takes pride in their health to the point of ignoring aches, pains, or illnesses until the illness is quite severe. Very low scores on Scale 1 may be meaningful in elevated depression profiles (e.g. 278 codes), where the low Scale 1 score may reflect disinterest in one's physical well-being to the point of passive resignation and indifference to one's body.

TREATMENT

Assertiveness training and education around how to deal with anger often are appropriate with this code pattern. Have the individual keep a diary of when physical symptoms seem to increase in severity and look for links between emotional stresses and physical discomfort. Supportive, non-confrontive therapies appear to work best. Look for childhood experiences of early losses or frightening illnesses in the individual or close family members and/or a family style of discouraging the expression of negative affect that may have conditioned these individuals into developing physical responses to stress.

THERAPEUTIC FEEDBACK LANGUAGE

Your profile suggests that you spend a lot of time thinking about your health, how to maintain it, avoid becoming ill, and correctly diagnosing some of your symptoms. Your health may be a source of constant worry for you and you may experience numerous vague and shifting physical symptoms that really frighten you. When stresses accumulate, your physical symptoms may increase and that increases your fear that something is very wrong with you and that nobody has diagnosed you correctly. You are not a very aggressive person and people may annoy you because they push you or try to control you. You, or somebody close to you, may have experienced physical infirmities that frightened you, leading to your adaptive response of constantly being on edge to anticipate and prevent physical problems. Keep a diary of when your symptoms become more severe and see if you can link them to stress. Work with your therapist on being more assertive and take a mindfulness class to learn how to recognize some of your more subtle emotions.

Relations with Other Scales

12/21 Codes

These individuals exhibit multiple vague and shifting physical symptoms and complaints and may experience panic about these symptoms. Sometimes there is demonstrable organic pathology, but panic around the possible dire consequences of their illness is the hallmark of the 12 codetype. The pessimism and hopelessness associated with depression is reflected in their certainty of physical decline. Their numerous somatic complaints focus on pain (e.g. headaches, stomachaches, and backaches), cardiac complaints, or gastrointestinal difficulties (e.g. anorexia, nausea, vomiting, or ulcers). Fatigue, weakness, and dizziness are often present, along with irritability and diagnoses of dysthymia and depression. If Scales 7 and/or 9 are also elevated, then restlessness and/or intense, obsessive worrying are typical.

Persons with the 12/21 codetype usually are dependent and immature, yet can be hardworking and driven. They are often conflicted about assuming responsibilities but tend to do so, albeit in a reluctant, fearful, self-effacing way. They are often sensitive to being pushed or hurried, with easily hurt feelings. They create low expectations in others, perhaps as a way of avoiding the guilt of disappointing them. They doubt their abilities, even with evidence of competence and, as a result, tend to be indecisive. Repression and denial of emotional problems is characteristic; they lack insight, even if emotionally sophisticated in other ways, and resist entertaining that their symptoms may be aggravated by emotional causes or conflicts. Understandably, if a person is convinced that they suffer from a fatal diagnosis, information from a therapist about emotional stress appears irrelevant. Internalization is common with depressive codetypes, so anger is rarely expressed directly and is experienced with associated guilt and self-disdain. Chemical use may be present as a way to medicate the depression. Medical patients with 12/21 codetypes are difficult to treat because they often have learned to live with symptoms shaped by numerous medical contacts and they engage family and friends' support in their quests for diagnosis and treatment. Generally, 12/21 individuals react to life's stresses with physiological symptoms, they are passive, and have a low sex drive. Dutiful and responsible, they typically have a stable work and marital history. Symptoms of depression occur, including sleep difficulties, low energy, and sad mood. Scale 9 below 50 would predict weight gain and further complaints of low energy and efficiency.

TREATMENT

The essence of elevated 12/21 codetypes is an underlying fear of being physically damaged, with a certainty of increasing physical illness, and even death. These clients can respond well to antidepressants. Reluctance to accept a primary diagnosis of depression is understandable, given their history of combating pain and physical infirmity, so they resist the suggestion that their medical concerns could be secondary to depression. Additional elevations on Scales 7 and 9 may require medications to treat severe agitation as well as the depression. 12/21s are vulnerable to medication dependency and side effects. Elective surgery should be avoided until the hypochondriacal aspects of the profile have been treated. Traditional insight psychotherapy tends not to work well, as they have learned to live with their complaints and tolerate high levels of discomfort. Although they may show good response to short-term treatment, symptoms are likely to return. A combination of behavioral deconditioning, Gestalt, and supportive psychotherapy seems to work best. For example, having the client's aches and pains "do the talking" may help in the expression and catharsis of blocked emotional responses. Working through early childhood losses in a supportive reparenting modality can be useful. Initially, the therapist needs to develop a therapeutic alliance by helping the client manage medical treatment and helping them avoid doctor shopping and unnecessary medical treatments. Encourage mindfulness therapies, yoga, and gentle exercise as stress relievers.

When giving feedback, discuss empathically how frightening and painful physical symptoms can be. Take a history focused on childhood illnesses and potential conditioning experiences around illness and death. Have the patient keep a diary of when physical symptoms occur and worsen to identify and educate how somatic sensitivity could be related to stress.

Your profile suggests that currently most of the time you feel little joy or happiness. You may be feeling anxious and sad, with decreased energy, sex drive, and overall efficiency. Others may see you as pessimistic and reluctant to "let go and enjoy life." Your worries make sense since you are experiencing physical symptoms that frighten or even panic you because you are fearful that they will get worse and you could die. These symptoms may become more intense when you become stressed. You are a dutiful, responsible person and you tend to feel guilty easily, so it is hard for you to assert yourself. You take on responsibilities and find it hard to say no to people who make demands on you. You may have experienced the death or illness of somebody close to you as a child, which led to your heightened sensitivity about any physical infirmity and your concerns about health. Explore any childhood memories when you felt frightened about illness and death. When your physical symptoms increase, see if you can link them to current stress. Rehearse with your therapist how you can be more assertive and learn how to deep breathe and self-soothe when you feel moments of panic.

123/213 Codes

The elevation of Scale 3 changes the interpretation of the 12/21 codetype by adding hysterical defenses; the individual shows more "niceness," repression, and inhibition, and a sense of long-suffering, almost cheerful, acceptance of physical ailments, with less of the complaining pessimism of the pure 12/21 codetype. The 213 person expresses multiple physical complaints that increase under stress, such as abdominal pain, weakness, cramping, dizziness, tingling and fatigue, low energy, low sex drive, and sleep disturbance. Somatization, anxiety, and depression, as well as conformity and cheerfulness, are primary characteristics associated with this codetype. Though fearful and even demanding because of their symptoms, passive dependency is likely to be present. Often there is real physiological breakdown because of years of tension and apprehensiveness, but their fears around the real physical symptoms become a debilitating focus. Men experience fear of sexual inadequacy and have low sex drive. Women have a somewhat conflicted attitude towards sex, at once hungry for the emotional connection but also with a prudish aversion to sex, which they may find physically painful. Confused or psychotic thinking, suicidal thoughts and obsessions are uncommon, though they do complain of depression, pessimism, hopelessness, apathy, low assertiveness, low risk taking, and feelings of being "over the hill" or in declining health. They often feel that life is a strain. Self-sacrificing, reflecting Scale 3 qualities of nurture hunger, they end up feeling unappreciated by others.

Where Scale 4 is the low point, the 123/213 codetype suggests even more passivity and lack of heterosexual drive. With a low Scale 9 ($T < 50$), it suggests a low energy level, a lack of vocational aggressiveness, and a strong tendency to "take to bed" when stresses accumulate. Low Scale 5 scores in women or high Scale 5 scores in men add to the passivity and inhibition already present in the 123/213 codetype. In their unconscious drive for emotional connection and security, they become self-sacrificing and flattering of others, and assume duties, sacrifices, and burdens to the point of guilt-inducing reciprocation by others.

If the *L* scale is elevated, moral rigidity and lack of psychological-mindedness can aggravate marital instability. Normally conscientious and concerned with social acceptance, an *L* elevation would predict even greater fears and concerns about social disapproval already present in the 123/213 codetype. Marks and Seeman (1963) reported that 85 percent of their sample had at least an average school performance in high school. Very few were either above or below average, suggesting that these individuals worked hard to fit in and did not take risks or "make waves," even during their school years. In contrast, Graham et al. (1999) reported that their participants were achievement-oriented.

TREATMENT

Therapeutic techniques should be similar to the 12/21 codetype, using assertiveness training to express anger and unblock the repressed anger and sadness around past losses and deprivations. Look for childhood experiences with early losses of loved ones and perhaps frightening physical illnesses in the patient or someone close to them. The addition of Scale 3 suggests these individuals may have dealt with these early losses by attempting to be brave and denying or repressing understandable emotions resulting from traumatic loss, perhaps out of fear of the loss of emotional support from overburdened caretakers. Allow the patient to explore potential past losses and possible recent restimulation of the "psychological scar tissue." A therapeutic goal would be to help them recognize and express anger directly over current frustrations as well as past losses and traumas, deconditioning them to the fear of loss associated with expressing anger.

THERAPEUTIC FEEDBACK LANGUAGE

Your profile suggests you are feeling much tension and sadness and experiencing physical symptoms that may be frightening to you. At the same time, you are a responsible, dutiful person who wants to be brave in the face of pain. That is why people with your profile are sometimes described as experiencing a "smiling depression," reflecting your need to be cheerful and positive in spite of pain or sadness. Sometimes people with this profile experienced traumatic losses as children or later, during which they had to be strong and repress understandable feelings of fear, anger, or sadness. Perhaps that is when you learned to put on a smile and be brave, sacrificing yourself in order to not upset others. Currently you may be experiencing stress that is affecting you physically and leading to feelings of depression and anxiety. Explore with your therapist any recent setbacks or losses. Take a mindfulness class to explore some of your subtler feelings and learn to be more assertive, asking for what you want and expressing frustration without fear that you will be rejected or abandoned. Develop a realistic medical treatment plan with a medical coach to avoid repeating diagnostic tests unnecessarily. Once you have a medical treatment plan, stick to it until it has run its full course so that you can eliminate certain diagnoses without the confusion of "doctor shopping."

1234/2134 Codes

The addition of Scale 4 modifies the interpretation of the 123/213 codetype. The expression of hostility, manipulation, self-centeredness, and alienation suggested by

Scale 4 elevations are modified by the 123/213 pattern. In some cases, Scale 4 attributes are impulsively expressed after periods of repression and inhibition. In other cases, unmet dependency needs are achieved through subtle manipulation, passive dependency and addictions, even if the *MAC–R* scale is not significantly elevated. The 1234/2134 individual is dependent and highly insecure, reflecting the basic mistrust associated with an elevated Scale 4 as well as the losses associated with unavailable caretakers in early childhood. They exhibit many of the symptoms common to the 123/213 codetype, but with added cynicism, anger, and distrust in the reliability of others' caring. The 1234 individuals feel outraged when their needs are not met, and feel entitled to love and emotional security.

Some 1234 individuals can be combative when intoxicated, especially when anticipating emotional rejection or abandonment. Men with this profile show hostility toward women, particularly when their dependency needs are frustrated or when they experience rejection. Poor work and marital adjustment are characteristic, accompanied by physical complaints (usually digestive difficulties, such as ulcers, nausea, vomiting, or anorexia), hostility, depression, tension, and perhaps insomnia. Yearning for emotional security and uncritical love appear to be related to histories of feeling rejected by unreliable, perhaps narcissistic, caretakers.

TREATMENT

In addition to the therapeutic techniques indicated with the 123/213 codetype, these patients need to recognize when tension and frustration are building and to find less impulsive ways to express them. Because they are highly dependent, yet afraid to trust, they are insistently demanding of reassurance. They need reliable, consistent therapeutic support combined with caring limit-setting to help them see how their impulsive need for instant gratification can be self-defeating and frustrating to others. Their manipulative demandingness can lead to therapist counter-transference and impatience, which can restimulate their childhood experiences of a rejecting caretaker. Insight therapy, along with behavior modification for the anger management, can help them understand how their anger is related to their unmet dependency needs in early childhood. Explore with the patient any memories of traumatic rejections and how current stressors could be restimulating past abandonment scar tissue. Antidepressants, while useful for some, usually have to be combined with cognitive behavioral therapy (CBT) since poor self-control is characterized by this codetype.

THERAPEUTIC FEEDBACK LANGUAGE

Your profile suggests you are experiencing tension, anxiety, depression, and physical symptoms such as headaches, unexplained stomach upset, weakness, and other vague symptoms that may be frightening to you. Sometimes people with your profile experienced a caretaker that was unreliable, even impatient and rejecting, so you could not trust that you were safe. You learned that you had to be a survivor, sometimes being manipulative in order for your needs to be met. Currently it is very frightening if somebody you care about is critical or rejecting of you. You may respond by feeling very angry, even explosive, and becoming controlling or demanding. When stressed, you may experience physical symptoms that shift and change; you may feel particularly alone and vulnerable to being abandoned. When you become fearful, you may do things that are self-defeating or even destructive. Rehearse with your therapist how to control your emotions when you feel rejected or criticized. Learn to express hurt feelings as "I feel" statements rather than coming across as demanding or threatening. When your physical symptoms increase in severity, explore what other emotions you may be feeling to determine how stress affects your physical well-being. Avoid chemical agents or other addictions, as they may increase your depression and volatility.

1237/2137 Codes

In addition to the 123/213 codetype correlates noted earlier (see 123/213 code interpretations), the addition of Scale 7 suggests more free-floating anxiety as well as increased tension, fearfulness, guilt, and inability to be assertive. Feelings of inadequacy and highly dependent interpersonal relationships occur together with a constant preoccupation with physical symptoms and searches for explanatory diagnoses. These individuals seek constant reassurance and caretaking from others, eliciting guilt-induced sympathy because of their litany of physical ailments. If the *OBS* content scale is elevated, decision-making and sustained concentration is difficult with the individual focusing mostly on somatic symptoms and declining health, and maintaining others' support. Helpless passivity and fears of rejection and disapproval will invite rescue, reassurance, and resentment from others. Back and chest pains, as well as epigastric complaints, are particularly common. Complaints of weakness, moodiness, fearfulness, feelings of inadequacy, and inability to cope with everyday stress and responsibility (particularly if K and ES are below T-50) are typical. This pattern predicts individuals who internalize conflict and fear even minimal confrontation. People with this profile frequently marry a dominant spouse and perpetuate a role of dependency. Chronic unemployment and chemical dependency, often with prescription medications, may occur. A lack of insight, emotional inhibition, repression, and an ingratiating, conflict-avoiding disposition characterize this profile.

TREATMENT

Because of their use of repression and denial (as expected from elevations on Scales 3 and 7), memory lapses and shifts of attention away from anxiety-loaded topics can inhibit accurate history reporting. Assertiveness training and rehearsing the expression of anger, as well as supportive self-esteem building psychotherapy, are suggested. As with any codetype in which depression and anxiety are prominent, medications may be helpful; beware of suggestibility, side effects, and habituation. These individuals are initially highly likable because of their desire to please and their ability to role-play the compliant respectful patient. They have a child-like presentation and tend to flatter the therapist, perhaps replicating how they would placate a frightening parental figure. They are quick to interpret any demands by the therapist to explore undesirable emotions or rehearse more assertive behavior as displeasure with them. This can result in premature termination. Behavioral therapies to teach self-soothing can be useful, given that many experienced chaotic childhoods with unpredictable emotional support. In childhood, they may have experienced unpredictable rages directed toward them by caretakers or siblings and peers, where they feared for their lives or the lives of their loved ones. Behavioral deconditioning of fear of anger can also be useful.

Your profile suggests that you live with an almost constant sense of tension, dread, guilt, and worry. Much of the time your body is a source of worry because you likely experience numerous physical symptoms that are frightening to you. Confronting others or expressing anger is difficult because conflict frightens you. Perhaps you have experienced somebody close to you who was unpredictably angry and rejecting and you have learned to play the right role to please others and avoid their displeasure. Asserting yourself is difficult, so you may let people control you and take advantage of you. You feel so guilty when you make a mistake that you may invite others to tell you what to do and take care of you. When stressed, your physical symptoms may increase to the point where you feel intense anxiety or panic. Explore any memories of an unpredictably angry caretaker and allow yourself to feel normal self-protective anger. Work at being more assertive and learn to switch off guilty feelings when you express irritation towards others. Using CBT, learn to soothe yourself when you experience periods of panic. Take yoga classes and use gentle exercise as a way of relieving stress.

128/218 Codes

This is primarily a depression profile, with schizoid and somatizing features. Sometimes physical complaints are odd or bizarre, reflecting the depth of the individual's depression and damaged self-esteem. Complaints of fatigue, weakness, tension, insomnia, sadness, low energy, and motivation are typical of the 12/21 codetype. The Scale 8 elevation adds an increased likelihood of motor and/or sensory complaints, and severity to the disturbance in cognitive processing associated with depression. Consequently, these individuals complain of difficulties with thinking, memory and concentration, decision making and daily organization. Some will complain that they literally feel they are "losing their mind," reflecting the primacy of cognitive problems. Feelings of alienation from others and a sense of being hopelessly broken or damaged, combined with feelings of severe physical deterioration, characterize the 28/82 codetypes. Individuals with the 128/218 codetype may become passively dependent on others because of their cognitive decline. Sexual drive tends to be low or non-existent, and emotional closeness is experienced as frightening. Some may be pre-psychotic or psychotic with somatic delusions, but most are not psychotic. Rather, the codetype suggests a severe depression with feelings of inevitable physical and cognitive decline.

Antidepressant medications are often appropriate. Insight psychotherapy should be avoided, as this type of therapy tends to be disorganizing and confirming of their negative self-esteem. Childhood histories often show cold, withdrawn caretakers and emotional deprivation. Supportive, motherly therapists that reparent the individual can be effective, although short-term treatment strategies such as cognitive restructuring, self-esteem building, and assertiveness training are also often useful. These individuals suffer from a profound negative self-image and feelings that they are hopeless, emotionally and physically damaged and unlovable, so therapies that enhance self-esteem quickly are most likely to be helpful. Do not expect, however, a quick positive transference, as these individuals fear that closeness will lead to abandonment and rejection.

THERAPEUTIC FEEDBACK LANGUAGE

Your profile suggests that you are feeling down, blue, unhappy, and unable to think as clearly as you would like. Currently it may be hard for you to focus, make decisions or be very efficient. Your sleep may be disturbed and you may have low energy. You may be experiencing physical symptoms which frighten you, and leave you preoccupied and worried. Sometimes you may feel that there is something really wrong with you because it is so hard for you to think clearly, remember things, and be efficient in your daily life. Much of the time you may feel as if you are in a mental fog, which frightens you and leads to you feel hopelessly defective. You may keep people at an emotional distance because you are afraid that you will be humiliated and rejected if you depend on others. In some cases, people with your profile grew up with caretakers who could be cold and withdrawn, even cruel. You may have learned to protect yourself by not allowing people to be close to you. Recently you may have experienced some medical problems or some other loss, leading you to feel sad, hopeless, and bad about yourself. Explore with your therapist any recent losses or setbacks which could have led to your current depression. Medication may help you to feel less sad and enable you to think more clearly. Make a list of some of your positive attributes so you can remind yourself of them when you feel hopelessly defective. Work on mindfulness so you can express how you feel to others. Develop exercises with your therapist that can help you remember better and be more efficient until medication can improve your overall efficiency.

129/219 Codes

When Scales 1, 2, and 9 are all elevated at about the same level, it is difficult to discern whether this is a primary affective disorder with mood instability creating secondary psychosomatic complaints or whether this is a somatizing depression with agitation (reflected in the Scale 9 elevation) as a secondary component. As one would expect, given the 29 component of the elevation, there is substantial mood instability and agitation. Sometimes the 29 aspect of the profile is reflected in transient mood swings. Sometimes the euphoria of the Scale 9 profile is cancelled out by the depression, and the low energy and sadness of the Scale 2 is modified by the Scale 9 attributes, leading to tension, irritability, and mood swings within a few minutes of each other, and usually precipitated by real or imagined setbacks or obstacles to goal-driven activity. Somatic concerns are greatly distressing to the 29 individual, who responds to them as virtual emergencies. Acute distress, tension, agitation, and restlessness are prominent. Headaches, insomnia, and complaints such as spastic bowel are frequent. A neurological etiology should be considered because in a minority of cases this pattern has been associated with organic brain syndrome. It is also possible that the elevation on Scale 9 reflects a hypomanic defense against depression and the somatic symptoms reflect the tension inherent in experiencing contradictory defensive responses.

TREATMENT

Psychotherapy is complicated because somatizing defenses and responses are co-morbid with a mood disorder. Where emotional lability and depressive symptoms are primary, antidepressant and mood stabilizing medications may be useful, although some clients may develop mania in response to antidepressants. A history of mood instability would suggest using a mood stabilizer, with an antidepressant added at a later date, if needed. Treatment strategies are dependent on a diagnosis that is complicated for the 129 individual. Medication may be primary if history suggests lifelong mood instability. If the precipitating event is a perceived loss, therapy to identify why the loss is experienced as catastrophic would be relevant. Help the patient to (a) identify the current loss or failure, (b) distinguish between their own wants and internalized parental expectancies for high achievement and, (c) identify the triggers for mood changes and use CBT to manage them. Usually people with this profile experience intense fears of failure and the expected resulting emotional abandonment and disapproval. Alcoholism or other addictions are associated with this codetype.

THERAPEUTIC FEEDBACK LANGUAGE

Your profile suggests that you are experiencing a great deal of internal tension, irritability, and anger, usually set off by what you see as a frustration or somebody interfering with what you want. You may find yourself experiencing mood swings, sometimes feeling highly energized and even euphoric, and then something sets you off and you become down, angry, and irritable. These mood swings can come and go within a few minutes of each other, or with longer intervals in between. You may use chemical agents or some other addictive behaviors as a way to deal with these mood swings, but they likely cause you more problems. Your tension may become so intense that you develop real physical responses to stress that frighten and preoccupy you. You may have experienced a recent setback or loss that precipitated this agitated and moody response or you may have had a tendency toward mood swings for a period of time. Your therapist may prescribe a mood stabilizing medication and explore what triggers your mood swings so you can learn to control them. In some cases, an accident or injury can precipitate some of these symptoms. In some cases people with your profile feel the need to achieve a great deal in order to feel lovable. Explore with your therapist what kind of pressure you feel to achieve great things in order to feel acceptable. Keep a diary of events that trigger your mood swings and learn to self-soothe so that you avoid catastrophizing when things go wrong. Exercise, yoga, and deep breathing can all be helpful.

120/210 Codes

Typically, the 20/02 codetype, without Scale 1 elevation, is a stable code, as is the 12/21 codetype. Taken together, these elevations predict depression, withdrawal, indecisiveness, interpersonal avoidance, and feelings of inadequacy and guilt. Somatic complaints and a quiet, defeatist, negative attitude are typical. Such persons are distinctly lacking in joy and are defensively aloof. They accept physical suffering as their lot in life, even as they can be demanding of their caretakers. Passive and attention-avoiding, unless focused on physical ailments, some can withdraw in a misanthropic or schizoid fashion, particularly if Scale 6 or 8 is also elevated. Life for the 120/210 is emotionally constricted and they have low expectations for happiness. They are irritated and even offended by demands for intimacy and the invasion of their personal space by others trying to be overly friendly.

TREATMENT

History would determine whether this is a stable, introverted, typically non-depressed personality type who has recently become depressed and somatic due to a specific perceived loss, or a profile reflecting a long history of dysphoria, somatic preoccupation and introversion. Assertiveness training and CBT with social skill building could help deal with the depression and social awkwardness which often contributes to their depression and lack of social support. Antidepressants, as with all depression profiles, could help alleviate dysphoria, although medication should be given in small doses, as these disorders tend to be longstanding and any rapid change tends to be experienced as uncomfortable. Childhood histories often reveal parental emotional and physical aloofness, and a lack of warmth, although without overt hostility. Many of these clients experienced a loss of childhood carefreeness because of demands on them to be prematurely adult and responsible, perhaps due to illness in themselves or others. Problem-focused therapies that are not demanding of intimacy tend to work best. For example, 60-year-old Steven was brought to therapy compliantly by his wife because she felt there was something wrong with him. She complained he appeared even more distant than usual. When she told him she had been diagnosed with breast cancer he had said nothing and never discussed it with her. He was a scientist at a famous California academic institution and had done very well working alone in the lab as part of a loosely structured team. Their marriage had come late in life, they had no children, and he and his wife followed the philosophy of Ayn Rand. His 210 codetype was congruent with a life of comfortable isolation and parents who rarely spoke or physically touched one another. There was no family conflict in his family of origin. They cared for his physical needs adequately and made few demands on him. He and his wife lived as comfortable roommates, with rare but mutual sexual relations and little conflict. They both worked and kept separate bank accounts, splitting their expenses down the middle. When she developed cancer and quit her work, she needed more intimacy and warmth and became more demanding. She was also introversive, but not to his extent, so the loss of her work relationships after her cancer diagnosis resulted in more demands on him. As he felt overwhelmed by her increasing criticisms of him for failing to be emotionally supportive, he became increasingly depressed and complained of constant physical ailments, which had an indeterminate diagnosis. Therapy involved teaching him how to be supportive and an available listener. He took notes, asked questions, and followed concrete advice without the destabilizing intimacy of insight therapy.

Your profile suggests you are a somewhat shy person, comfortable being alone and not needing a lot of social interaction. You might enjoy socializing with small groups of people you know well, but find social events with groups of strangers taxing and unpleasant. You are probably a dutiful, responsible, quiet person who avoids drawing attention to yourself. You may avoid conflict, at times to your detriment, and you probably are not very assertive. Currently you may feel a little down, sad, even depressed, perhaps feeling negative about your current situation. You may feel reduced energy, general efficiency, and your sleep and appetite and sex drive may be affected. You may be experiencing a number of physical symptoms that are linked to your current depression, and you may feel concerned, even defeated, by these symptoms. You have likely been a self-contained person most of your life, but you may have recently experienced some setbacks or losses which have gotten you down. Your therapist may suggest medications to help you feel better and also help you learn to deal with social situations so that they are less stressful.

13/31 Codes (see also Conversion V)

These individuals are typically preoccupied with numerous physical problems, but the most common complaint is one of pain, which usually centers on the extremities: head, back, neck, arms, eyes, and legs. A variety of specific and vague somatic worries control their lives, as they are vulnerable to developing physical symptoms in response to stress. Nausea or discomfort after eating, anorexia or bulimia, elimination difficulties and related concerns preoccupy them. Complaints of fatigue, dizziness, numbness, and tremors are common. Severe anxiety (other than that associated with physical symptoms) or complaints of depression usually are absent, although some patients report depression due to physical concerns. Sleep disturbances and low sex drive are common. The elevation on Scale 3 generally tempers the pessimistic, complaining cynicism shown by high Scale 1 individuals. If Scale 2 is coded third, then depression and pessimism are evidenced, although expressed through the defense of repression and denial, as resignation borne with long suffering niceness. If Scale 7 is elevated along with the 13/31 codetype, then anxiety, tension, and guilt also are present, with even more fears of conflict and the expression of anger. If Scale 8 is the third most elevated scale, the patient also may complain of dizziness, losses of consciousness, sexual preoccupations, and bizarre physical symptoms. If Scale 9 is elevated along with the 13/31, then there is more emotionality, approval seeking, denial, and explosiveness. Note that some 139 codetypes have been associated with chronic brain syndromes.

Few clients with 13/31 codetypes are incapacitated by their symptoms and they continue functioning, albeit at a reduced level of efficiency. Unless the *K* scale is below a *T*-score of 45, reflecting lowered emotional control, they present themselves as reasonable and responsible "good patients" who are suffering from pain and associated worries, but, in all other ways, well-adjusted. How they are seen by others is very important to them, so they often question psychological inquiry and resent the implication that their somatic concerns are "in their heads." They have a high need for social approval, and have strong values about being seen as cheerful, contented, and "brave in the face of pain." If the *L* and *K* scales are elevated, there is even more repression, denial, and fear of being judged. As a result, these individuals are difficult to engage in psychotherapy. They seek medical explanations for their problems and lack insight into psychological factors that may underlie or influence their problems. Some will exhibit demonstrable physical breakdown, perhaps a result of prolonged stress.

These individuals show a strong need for attention, affection, and sympathy, and feel insecure without them. Often their physical complaints produce secondary gains, such as caretaking behavior from others, particularly if the pattern is a Conversion V. Because these individuals are so concerned and frightened about their ailments, they need constant support and reassurance. As a result, they are described by others as immature, egocentric, dependent, and selfish.

Although generally outgoing and sociable (particularly if Scale 0 is below *T*-50), their social relations tend to be focused on meeting their needs for reassurance. Given their extreme fears regarding body damage, it is surprising that many are described as optimistic (especially if Scales 2 and 7 are within the normal range), but the description reflects their genuine desire to be acceptable and liked and not a problem for others. They do not express anger or resentment directly, so negative emotions and stress are expressed somatically. Others may judge them as passive-aggressive, perhaps experiencing their agreeableness and self-effacing demandingness as frustrating. Marital relationships, unless the spouse is a co-dependent, can become strained because of the 13 individual's incapacitation and inability to provide the reciprocal rewards necessary in a marriage. If Scale 1 is higher than Scale 3 by at least 10 *T*-scores, the codetype predicts hypochondriacal features with associated complaining and pessimism. The Scale 1 attributes are predominant and less modified by the hysterical needs for reassurance and approval. A 31 codetype with Scale 3 higher than Scale 1 by 10 *T*-scores or more will predict more ingratiating niceness and need for social approval, with physical complaints stoically suffered and activated by stress. The repression and denial driven by the need for emotional connection associated with Scale 3 predominates and Scale 1 attributes are expressed through Scale 3 defenses.

It is interesting to note that 60 percent of the individuals with 13/31 codetypes experienced the early death of a parent (Marks & Seeman, 1963). They described these parents as affectionate. Levak (Levak et al., 2011) posited that the MMPI-2 codetypes can reflect an adaptive response to a perceived stressful event, in this case the loss of a loved and possibly loving parent. This codetype suggests that in response to loss, the 31 individual adapted by being "brave" in the face of pain, and blocking the expression of anger surrounding it.

The 13/31 codetype is the second most common among parents of child psychotherapy clients. It is associated with mothers who are overprotective, extraverted and suggestible, and both mother and child tend to show improvement. The prognosis is less favorable for fathers, who exhibit immature dependency, strong needs for acceptance, and the use of subtle and indirect strategies to gain affection and attention from the child.

College women with this profile describe themselves as affectionate and thoughtful. Their peers, however, see them as somewhat selfish, self-centered, dependent, attention-seeking, irritable, emotional, high-strung, and with frequent physical complaints. Often there is a strong relationship orientation, with less academic focus, which can become a source of further stress.

College men with this profile likewise are seen as selfish, dependent, self centered, and demanding. One of their primary complaints is that they do not get enough consideration from their families. Most appear socially at ease, fluent, expressive, and confident (particularly if K is high and 0 is low). In psychological settings, they often assertively insist on knowing their test results and on being given concrete answers to their problems. They tend not to persist in insight therapy although they may find supportive problem-solving therapies useful.

TREATMENT

Although these individuals generally are reluctant to talk about possible psychological factors, it may be possible to do so if no direct link is made between their physical symptoms and the current emotional stressors. Clients with this codetype often terminate treatment prematurely if they are pressured to examine their emotional lives without a focus on their fears about physical infirmity. Clients with 13/31 codetypes are highly suggestible, and they expect therapists to provide definite answers and solutions to their physical concerns. Their symptoms can be shaped temporarily by the kinds of medical attention they receive.

Treatment should focus on finishing the mourning process around past losses, helping the client to become acclimatized to the experience of both anger and sadness. Relearning to recognize anger and sadness and finding constructive ways to express them is a productive focus of therapy. Assertiveness training, conflict resolution, and Gestalt therapy, allowing their physical symptoms to do the "talking," can help them learn to vent their feelings and negotiate their wants. If early parental illness or death occurred, help the client finish grieving. Observe during therapy how being emotionally flooded leads to somatic complaints, perhaps as a way to temporarily shift attention away from emotionally overwhelming material onto potentially soothable physical complaints.

THERAPEUTIC FEEDBACK LANGUAGE

Your profile suggests that you are a conflict avoider who prides himself on being positive, agreeable, and brave, even when experiencing severe pain and frightening physical symptoms. You like to please others and you work hard to see the best in people. Currently you appear to be experiencing numerous painful and frightening physical symptoms that are the focus of your concern. Stressful events may increase symptoms that are real, but are also linked to the way you deal with emotions. You may not notice the small ways that your body responds when you are stressed, perhaps by hunching your shoulders, holding your breath, clenching your jaw or tensing other muscle groups. Over time, these small physical responses can lead to physical breakdown, so learning not to stress your body more is a good focus for therapy. You may have learned from an early age, because of some severe loss, to be brave and not allow yourself to become flooded with sadness or anger. Your therapist may want to treat you with some medication and perhaps teach you ways to deal with conflict and stress.

Conversion V Code

A Conversion V occurs when Scales 1 and 3 are elevated above a *T*-score of 65 and Scale 2 is approximately 8 or more *T*-score points lower than Scales 1 and 3. Persons with Conversion V patterns show strong needs to interpret their psychological or interpersonal problems in ways that are socially acceptable. They deny troubles or inadequacies, and lack the expression of pessimism and depressive feelings seen in the 123/213 codetype. They seem almost indifferent or even jovial, presenting their numerous somatic complaints in a positive, almost cheerful manner. Consequently, this codetype has been described as the "beautiful indifference" or "la belle indifference." They deny psychological concerns or inadequacies, and the anxiety and depression often found in 13/31 persons without a Conversion V pattern is typically absent. If Scale 9 is distinctly elevated, then the possibility must be considered that manic defenses are being used to ward off depression, and the Conversion V pattern is likely to be somewhat less stable and likely to change when the manic defenses are insufficient for the person to cope.

Many people with Conversion V patterns develop somatic complaints or psychological symptoms of a highly reasonable and socially acceptable type that allow them to displace and externalize inadequacies or problems. They emphasize their somatic symptoms and can discuss their level of pain without the accompanying affect usually associated with people who are experiencing pain. That is not to say that they do not experience genuine pain, but repression and denial are so prevalent and needs for emotional connection are so strong, that pain is expressed with a smile. A within normal-limits conversion profile reveals a socially outgoing person who is cheerfully optimistic, responsible, sympathetic, and overcontrolled. These individuals lack insight and are quick to tire and feel poorly under stress.

TREATMENT

See Treatment section under the 13/31 codes.

THERAPEUTIC FEEDBACK LANGUAGE

See Therapeutic feedback language section under the 13/31 codes.

13/31, High K Code

If the K score is also elevated, the 13/31 profile predicts more overcontrol, inhibition, denial, and need for social acceptance. These individuals have difficulty expressing intense emotions, so the therapist will have to "multiply" the intensity of what they say in order to get a true sense of empathy for them. They are unaware of their negative impulses and emotions and are concerned with being seen as normal, responsible, helpful, and sympathetic. Often their lives are organized around ideals of service to others and contribution to community. They are genuinely caring individuals, uncomfortable with conflict to such a degree that repression of unacceptable impulses may lead to real physical breakdown. They feel judged by any suggestion that they might have psychological difficulties, which they see as a weakness. They do not tolerate the role of psychiatric patient well because they experience genuine physical distress and associated fear, and feel judged by the mental health professional as malingering. Whatever physical symptoms might exist are unlikely to be debilitating, but are the source of great concern (see also Conversion V).

TREATMENT

Although traditional insight psychotherapy is unappealing to these individuals, they can benefit from professional reassurance. Therapists may be tempted to confront patients out of a feeling that they are not doing their job if they are in some way "sympathetic" to the patients' physical complaints. However, aggressive pushing or confrontation by the therapist will lead to patient termination. The elevation on the *K* scale particularly predicts that the patient will be apprehensive to opening up and experiencing any catharsis. Assertiveness training, emotional support, and helping the client finish grieving about past losses, if done in a gradual manner, could be useful. Real physical breakdown because of the stress placed on their musculoskeletal and organ systems by the inhibition of feelings is a possibility, so relaxation training, yoga, mindfulness therapy, and assertiveness training could help.

THERAPEUTIC FEEDBACK LANGUAGE

Similar to the 13, but be mindful of the patient's increased discomfort with the exploration of intense feelings suggested by the elevated K scale.

132/312 Codes

The addition of Scale 2 as the third highest scale changes some characteristics of the 13/31 codetype. The flagrant manifestation of depression with sad mood, pessimism, and withdrawal is muted by the individual's need for emotional connection and reassurance, as suggested by the Scale 3 defenses of repression and denial. Consequently, they may be almost cheerful in their presentation, in spite of episodes of tension, distress, and complaints of weakness and fatigue. Some of these individuals deny any experience of depression, while for others it is more palpable, although explained as caused by physical suffering. Others experience periods of pain remediation, reflecting the interplay between depressive symptoms and hysterical defenses. Personality characteristics of the 13/31 codetype are also present in the 132/312. They are conventional, conforming, anxious to be liked by others, and passive, especially if Scale 4 is low. If Scale 7 is elevated, they are even more conforming, with strong needs for approval and apprehension about conflict.

TREATMENT

With the addition of Scale 2 coded third, patients may be open to hearing how their physical symptoms have "worn them out" and led to an underlying depression, which could be treated with medications. Psychotherapy should focus on how current losses and stresses replicate past childhood losses. In a supportive, nonjudgmental environment, relaxation training, CBT, and even hypnosis could be useful to help manage the symptoms of pain. During relaxation exercises, repressed feelings of anger or sadness could be stimulated, providing an opportunity to deal with past losses. See also the treatment section for the 13/31 codetype.

Your profile suggests that you are experiencing many physical symptoms. You may have low energy, feel weak and worn out, and have difficulties with memory and concentration. Sometimes people with your profile have experienced some early losses, such as a death or illness in a parent. You may have learned to be brave and to repress and smile through your sadness in order to not upset others. You dislike conflict and confrontation and your physical symptoms may increase during times of stress. Work on learning to be more assertive and finding ways to relax. Keep a diary of when your physical symptoms increase and see what could be stressing you.

134/314 Codes

Somatic complaints and impulsive, self-defeating tension reduction behaviors characterize this profile. In spite of complaints of infirmity and debilitating physical conditions, these individuals can be opinionated, demanding, argumentative, or belligerent. The addition of an elevated Scale 4 to the 13/31 codetype predicts anger, manipulative dependency, occasional impulsiveness, and emotional distrust. These individuals can manifest some of the characteristics of the 34/43 codetype, such as being explosive and manipulative. They also exhibit other 13/31 codetype characteristics, including a bland indifference toward their symptoms, role-playing for social approval, and numerous physical symptoms, which can be used to manipulate others into satisfying their dependency needs. Fears of abandonment and demands to be taken care of lead to approach-avoidance conflicts in their relations. These individuals lack insight into how they alienate others. Anger tends to be expressed either in episodic outbursts or indirectly, through passive-aggressive means.

In addition to the therapeutic strategies outlined for the 13/31 codetype, anger recognition and management is critical, so that it is expressed as it builds, rather than being overcontrolled out of fear of rejection and abandonment, and then expressed impulsively. Pay attention to what these individuals deny, as it often is the source of their conflict. Look for childhood experiences of abuse and/or rejection, which may have made them phobic about expressing anger directly toward others. In some cases, this codetype reflects an emotional shutting down, perhaps in response to some profound emotional pain. This leads these individuals to develop a role-playing approach to life whereby they fit into others' role expectations and develop physical symptoms in response to their general overcontrol and bottling up of feelings.

Your profile suggests that you are experiencing a great deal of tension and perhaps a number of physical symptoms that make it hard for you to be as productive as others expect. People with your profile often grow up with an explosive or discounting parent figure. You may have learned from an early age to play the right role and to fit in to avoid conflict and rejection. Consequently, you may have difficulty expressing anger, so that it can build up and cause you physical symptoms. Even though you are able to fit in and play the right role, it may be hard for you to trust others, so you might find yourself being manipulative and telling white lies to avoid conflict. Work with your therapist on recognizing when anger is building, learning to express it before it affects you physically.

136/316 Codes

The addition of Scale 6 to the 13/31 codetype predicts heightened sensitivity to anything that could be construed as criticism or unreasonable demands placed on them by others. These individuals exhibit many characteristics of the 13/31 codetype, but the addition of Scale 6 suggests some characteristics of a 36/63 code, such as paranoid defenses and a tendency to project their anger onto others.

These individuals are particularly sensitive to being judged by others as "mentally ill," so the suggestion that physical symptoms could be psychologically related would be threatening to them. They exhibit a strong sense of pride, a rigid morality, and a tendency to be judgmental of others. They are particularly concerned about their social image and have a strong need to be seen as attractive, conforming, reasonable, and above reproach.

Gastrointestinal problems, headaches, low back pain, and other symptoms are typical, increasing during stressful situations. Despite their physical symptoms, these individuals, particularly men with this profile, are competitive. Their competitiveness may come from a feeling that they need to be in control of situations as well as somehow having to prove themselves and "be better than others" in order to be above others' criticisms. Sometimes their need for success and control can lead them to be ruthless, justifying their ambition as a moral crusade. They lack insight into how others see them. Although their anger tends to be overcontrolled, when they feel wronged, they can be particularly focused on seeking "justice." When Scale 6 is within 8 *T*-score points of Scale 3 and both are elevated significantly above a *T* score of 65, then suspiciousness and abrupt anger reactions will be more marked. If *Pa1* is particularly elevated, hypersensitivity may shade towards overt paranoia. When Scale 3 is higher than Scale 6 by 8 or more *T*-score points, overt paranoid features are less likely and physical complaints will be more prominent. The paranoid traits will be subtler, with a tendency toward unreasonable jealousies and a sensitivity to feeling criticized or unfairly treated, but with a veneer of niceness and socially correct behavior.

TREATMENT

See also therapeutic strategies outlined for the 13/31 and 36/63 codetypes. These individuals are particularly sensitive to anything that could be construed as criticism or judgment. Before insight and catharsis can develop, these individuals need to feel that the therapist is "on their side." Explore for childhood histories of criticism or judgment, with parents' rigid adherence to high moral standards. These individuals tend to internalize their parents' strict values and have difficulty developing empathy for themselves as children who may have been severely punished for minor moral transgressions. As parents, they may replicate their own childhood experiences and be somewhat punitive, moralistic, and rigid with their own children. The primary focus in therapy should be on helping them verbalize their wants directly to others rather than allowing resentments to develop. Help them see how they judge others as a preemptive defense against being judged. Relaxation training and self-esteem building also can be helpful.

THERAPEUTIC FEEDBACK LANGUAGE

Your profile suggests that you are a person with very strong morals and values. It is disturbing to you if you perceive people as being immoral or doing the wrong thing. You have very high personal standards and others may see you as being too demanding or critical. Sometimes people who are as perfectionistic as you are develop physical symptoms in response to stress. Headaches, stomach upsets, low back pain, and other vague complaints may increase when you are stressed. Your therapist may want to work on helping you to be less self-critical and recognizing how your physical symptoms are linked to stress. Try to recall moments in your childhood when you felt punished for transgressions and see if you can develop empathy for yourself as a child who wanted to please and do the right thing. Learn to ask for what you want before you are resentful.

137 Code

Severe anxiety, panic attacks, and cardiac complaints such as tachycardia and/or epigastric distress are common with this codetype. Under stress, they develop numerous somatic complaints; although anxiety attacks are the most common, fears and phobias about illnesses are also found. The addition of Scale 7 to the 13/31 codetype adds anxiety, guilt, and profound fears of rejection to an already dependent codetype. These individuals are extremely uncomfortable with conflict and are dependent to the point that they are easily bullied or controlled. They tend to be ingratiatingly subservient.

Because of their severe anxiety, these individuals are rigid and adapt poorly to situational changes. Often they are unrealistically insecure about work and finances and depend on a dominant spouse to take responsibility for managing their lives and disciplining the children. Poor vocational adjustment because of anxiety and low self-esteem can occur.

TREATMENT

These individuals can be best understood by thinking of them as panicked, dependent children. Because they are agreeable and ingratiating, they can be likable. However, they can exhaust the therapist because of their constant need for reassurance, which has only a transitory effect on lowering their anxiety. If they perceive the therapist as impatient or angry, they become more anxious and demanding of reassurance. Look for childhood histories of unpredictably explosive and/or rejecting parents or situations. The profile reflects an individual who is constantly on guard against the onset of unpredictable, overwhelming emotional and/or physical pain. Look for traumatic experiences in which they feared for their lives, and use deconditioning therapies, such as systematic desensitization and implosion therapies, to lower their anxiety. Help them develop self-soothing strategies. Assertiveness training, relaxation training, and reparenting of their inner terrified child can be helpful.

THERAPEUTIC FEEDBACK LANGUAGE

Your profile suggests that you tend to worry and experience a great deal of anxiety. You may experience fears, phobias, anxiety attacks, and panics about your health. You dislike conflict and confrontation, so others can bully and dominate you. Perhaps you experienced unpredictable, even terrifying, events that have left you constantly on edge, wanting to make sure you don't get taken by surprise again. Perhaps you experienced an unpredictably angry or rejecting authority figure, so you go out of your way to avoid others being angry with you now. Your physical symptoms may increase during times of stress. Relaxation training and assertiveness training can help you, as well as learning to switch off panicked thoughts and be more assertive.

138/318 Codes (see also 1382 Code)

These individuals tend to have eccentric, unusual ideas and beliefs, particularly about religious and sexual topics, as well as numerous vague and bizarre somatic complaints. One example was a young woman from an upper socioeconomic background who was preoccupied with mold and had inhabited and left nine rented homes in succession, each after a brief stay, convinced she was suffering from its effects in every home. Numerous legal actions against her for breaking her leases and her countersuits for mold damages were the focus of her life. She would come to her therapy appointments with boxes of documents, neatly stapled, to substantiate her claims. She appeared logical, rational, and coherent, except for the fact that her preoccupations were bizarre and medical diagnosis had failed to find a cause for her shifting symptoms. Tremors, amnesia, blurred vision, dizziness, fainting spells, blackouts, and vague tinglings and numbnesses are often associated with neurological impairment, so 138 individuals exhaust medical diagnostic testing before being referred to a psychologist. This is an intuitively odd codetype in that it mixes both neurotic and schizoid, psychotic elements. It reflects a classical approach avoidance conflict, with high Scale 3 needs for closeness and reassurance reflecting the approach side and high Scale 8's fear of intimacy and need for self-protective distancing, the avoidance side. The hypochondriacal complaints may act as an "anchor," grounding the individual in realistic and care-eliciting concerns, preventing the disintegration into more floridly psychotic symptoms.

These individuals are quite changeable both in their moods and in their belief systems, and are therefore sometimes misdiagnosed as bipolar. When threatened, some may experience brief psychotic episodes or bizarre, loose associations that disappear once the threat is removed. Religiosity, sometimes mixed with sexuality and religious delusions, may be present. The religious preoccupations may represent a defense against the diffuse anxiety and panic associated with Scale 8, providing inner structure and meaning as a defense against the experience of anhedonia.

These individuals have difficulty concentrating. Their responses to open-ended questions tend to be confused, with loose associations, and their conversation appears oddly connected and is hard to follow. Childhood histories often show a family history of psychosis and/or severe emotional deprivation and abuse. These individuals function best in structured situations, and bizarre, confusing symptoms may increase when structure is absent. They tend to have unusual sex histories with poor childhood boundaries and sex abuse, so they are often sexually preoccupied but naïve and inhibited.

TREATMENT

Individuals with this codetype typically have severely disturbed family histories and many unresolved dependency needs. As elevations on Scale 3 would predict, they have strong needs for reassurance and closeness, but also experience great fears of rejection and closeness. Their tendency toward loose associations could be a barometer for how stressful particular avenues of psychotherapy are becoming. Therapy should be highly structured and proceed slowly. Reparenting supportive therapy in a highly structured situation would be most useful. If sexuality is explored in therapy, it should be within even more structure than typical in order to minimize transference and counter-transference.

THERAPEUTIC FEEDBACK LANGUAGE

Your profile suggests that you may be experiencing many physical symptoms that have been difficult to diagnose because they seem to shift and change over time. You probably spend a great deal of time and concern trying to determine what is wrong. You are a sensitive person, and are uncomfortable with conflict, so when you get stressed your thinking may be affected. At these times, it may be hard for you to get your thoughts out and have people understand you. You may have grown up in an environment that often felt unsafe and frightening, and you adapted by trying to stay positive and escape into your own world. Now, when you are stressed, some of your physical symptoms may increase. Relaxation training and thought stopping when your mind runs away from you can help. When you know you might become stressed, write things down you want to get across to others beforehand, so your thoughts stay clear.

1382 Code

In addition to the 138/318 codetype interpretation, depression, confused thinking, heavy drinking, and suicidal preoccupation are also likely. Social adjustment is poor and relationship problems are recurrent. Work history is also erratic, with numerous absences due to illness and stress related disorders.

TREATMENT

See treatment section under the 138/318 Code. A mixture of somatic, psychotic, hysterical, and depressive traits and symptoms manifests itself in different ways so that the depression may be expressed somatically, with loose associations masked by the somatic delusions that appear initially to have coherence. Whichever complaints and symptoms are most prominent and debilitating should be dealt with initially, dealing with the symptoms step by step. Antidepressant and anti-anxiety medications could be useful in conjunction with a reparenting supportive type of therapy, providing structure and assertiveness training as well as self-esteem building. Energizing antidepressants should be used cautiously, as they may increase cognitive disorganization.

THERAPEUTIC FEEDBACK LANGUAGE

See suggested 138 feedback language. Add: Your profile also suggests that you have periods where you feel sad, unhappy, and down. At these times it may be even harder to make decisions, recall important events, concentrate, and think clearly. Your doctor may consider medicine to help you sleep better, feel more efficient, think more clearly, and feel less down.

139 Code

Highly driven for attention and approval, these individuals tend to lack self-awareness and are surgent, opinionated, and preoccupied with physical symptoms and disabilities. They are performers and approval seekers, often exhibiting manic or hypomanic overcommitment and grandiosity. They have difficulty expressing anger in a modulated way, showing irritability, good-natured humor, hostile criticism, and explosive episodes in close proximity. After they have exploded, they tend to deny or repress the importance of the explosive episode and go back to temporary cheerful denial. Numerous somatic complaints are present, such as headaches, auditory and visual complaints, tremors, coordination difficulties, and other vague and shifting complaints. They lack self-awareness and become defensive at any criticism. They exhibit low frustration tolerance, irritability, and temper outbursts, often becoming combative or destructive (particularly if Scale 4 is also elevated and/or if *K* is low). Their agitated intensity and sudden mood shifts have been associated with an organic brain disorder, so a neurological etiology should be ruled out.

Interpersonal relations are stormy, and divorces are frequent. They are often seen as very demanding of their families and, although wanting approval and affection, they have difficulty expressing it to others. Disinhibiting agents such as alcohol can lead to impulsive aggression and subsequent amnesia around the episode. This codetype is associated most often with personality disorders or with brain syndromes associated with trauma.

TREATMENT

Look for a family history of domineering parents whose approval was dependent on performance. These individuals often internalize parental expectations and values, although resenting their control. Their physical symptoms reflect their overcontrol, combined with high energy, need for constant stimulation, and lack of self-awareness around negative emotions. Because of their need for approval, they respond well to supportive, approving therapists who can help them distinguish their own wants versus the internalized expectations of their parents. Help them realize how their strong needs for approval lead to feeling controlled and dominated by those from whom they seek approval. This dynamic replicates their experiences with their parents. Help them learn to recognize when anger and irritability are building, and help them to rehearse ways of expressing it so that negative emotions do not build, leading to explosive episodes. Exercise, mindfulness training, and insight therapy around self-esteem can be useful.

THERAPEUTIC FEEDBACK LANGUAGE

Your profile suggests you are a very driven and energetic individual who operates on two speeds: "full on" or off. You tend to be very demanding of yourself and others and you may overcommit to too many tasks and activities. You can be cheerful, humorous, and take charge easily, often expressing your opinions forcefully, but when you feel people are in your way or slowing you down you can become quite irritable, sometimes even loud and critical. It's difficult having high energy in a world you experience as moving too slowly. You may experience numerous physical symptoms that ebb and flow, depending on your level of tension and frustration. Headaches, stomach aches, numbnesses and tinglings, dizzy spells, even fainting spells have all been associated with this profile. Learning to recognize when stress is building, and relieving it through exercise as well as learning how to express anger in a non-combative way could be useful strategies in therapy. You may have grown up feeling a great deal of pressure to perform and achieve in order to experience self-esteem and you may want to discuss with your therapist what your real goals are versus what you feel you need to achieve in order to obtain others' approval.

14/41 Codes

This is a relatively rare codetype. The primary complaints tend to be somatic rather than psychopathic. Scale 1 correlates reduce the aggressive acting out usually associated with Scale 4 elevations. Rather, the acting out is manifested as manipulative dependency, with a tendency to manipulate others through physical illnesses. The addition of Scale 4 to Scale 1 aggravates the cynicism, bitterness, and pessimism already manifested by the elevation of Scale 1. These individuals are dependent and, at the same time, distrustful that others will care for them. A history of poor social adjustment and a resistance to rules, regulations, or restrictions is typical. "I'm sick and fed up, therefore the rules don't apply to me" would be a way to characterize their view of life. They tend to be negative, complaining, self-pitying, and easily upset when their immediate needs are not met. They approach life with a "who is going to help me today?" attitude centered on their physical illnesses and disabilities. They feel entitled because they are suffering and are highly dependent, although they simultaneously anticipate being let down and emotionally abandoned. Since they don't trust others to take care of them, their negativity manifests itself as stubbornness and passive resistance to being controlled. Their self-centered and demanding style, accompanied by physical complaints such as headaches and pain, makes adaptive sense for someone who is fearful of abandonment and in physical pain. Complaints of depression and anxiety as a result of their physical symptoms are associated with feelings of being defeated and helpless rather than a sense of communicative sadness.

They often exhibit socially unacceptable behavior and inadequacy in meeting the usual stresses and responsibilities of life. Excessive alcohol use or other self-soothing addictions can also be present. They have difficulty with self-discipline and decision making and exhibit poorly defined goals. They have difficulties in establishing enduring relations with members of the opposite gender. Tension, turmoil, and chronic complaining characterize family relations.

The most common three-point codetypes are 143/413 and 142/412. When Scale 3 is also elevated, manipulative role-playing and need for social approval are present. Family and marital problems are suggested. These individuals want approval and connectedness but fear abandonment, so they give very mixed messages to loved ones. The presence of Scale 3 predicts overcontrol, a tendency to mask the hostility and alienation suggested by Scale 4, and an increased likelihood that the physical symptoms reflect the overcontrol of negative impulses. Usually such code patterns show an elevated *O-H* scale.

TREATMENT

Although they may show a good response to short-term symptomatic treatment, individuals with 14/41 codetypes tend not to stay in treatment long enough to make significant personality changes because they resist demands placed on them by the therapist. They tend to be demandingly dependent individuals who want to be taken care of, but at the same time are angry and distrustful. These feelings tend to be expressed passively rather than overtly. Their tendency is to approach the therapist with a "what are you going to offer me today that probably won't work?" attitude because they see themselves as suffering and immobilized by their physical ailments. They feel in need of relief and are angry when they do not experience it.

Treatment can focus on their tendency to distrust that others really care and, consequently, to feel that they must manipulate others into taking care of them. They want to be taken care of, but are angry, anticipate abandonment, and feel justified in manipulating others as the only way they can get their needs met. Look for early childhood histories of emotional letdowns and abandonment that conditioned in them a basic mistrust. Sometimes this occurs in the context of a history of illness in themselves or in someone they were dependent on. Conceptually, this codetype reflects an immature, dependent individual who psychologically is "very young." They need to learn self-efficacy. Family therapy combined with nurturing limit setting by the therapist, and teaching loved ones how to be supportive, but not co-dependent, can be helpful. Mindfulness classes and gentle exercise can be helpful.

THERAPEUTIC FEEDBACK LANGUAGE

Your profile suggests that you are experiencing many physical symptoms that interfere with you being able to enjoy life and accomplish physical jobs and activities. You likely want loved ones to care for you, but at the same time you may be afraid to trust that they will be there for you when you need them. You may feel that you have to be a survivor, relying on manipulating those around you in order to obtain the care you need. Sometimes people like you came from a background where they felt emotionally abandoned and unable to trust authority figures to take care of them. Perhaps you were ill often and received care and special attention only when you were very sick. Now you feel dependent on others and are often impatient and irritated with how they treat you. Explore your childhood with your therapist to determine why you learned to be a survivor. Be mindful to not be manipulative with others because they will lose trust in you. Take a mindfulness class to be aware of your own and others' feelings and take time to ask others about how they are feeling. When your physical symptoms increase in intensity, don't soothe yourself with bad habits, food, or chemicals. Use deep breathing and relaxation exercises as a way to reduce stress.

15/51 Codes (see also Scales 1 and 5)

This is an uncommon codetype for men and an extremely rare code for women. Most commonly, Scale 3, 4, or 2 is the third highest scale for men.

Men with this code usually are fussy, sensitive, complaining, and passive. Somatic complaints predominate. Acting out is rare and seldom do they engage in open conflict or disagreement. Usually they are of above-average intelligence, are interested in cultural, verbal, and aesthetic pursuits and are upper SES.

In women, this uncommon codetype suggests both somatic complaints and anxieties and a self-sufficiency and assertiveness, which appear paradoxical. Scale 1 attributes such as health pessimism and immaturity coexist with interpersonal competitiveness and practical, outdoor, action-oriented activities. Sometimes women with this codetype can be emotionally domineering in their relations with others. For both men and women, this codetype is associated with multiple surgeries.

TREATMENT

Assertiveness training and catharsis can be useful treatment modalities for men. Relaxation training and yoga, as well as mindfulness, to determine what stressors increase physical symptoms could be useful for both sexes. Insight therapy is useful with 15 codetype men who are usually psychologically astute, though 15 codetype women are more practical and will be more responsive to practical solutions.

THERAPEUTIC FEEDBACK LANGUAGE

For men: Your profile suggests you are a sensitive and perceptive person who enjoys artistic, creative activities and interests. You are generally a non-aggressive person and others may feel you too readily "turn the other cheek" in response to others' anger and unreasonable demands. It may be hard for you to assert yourself, even when it would be reasonable to do so. You may experience a number of physical symptoms that cause you distress and that have been hard to diagnose. They may increase in intensity when you are stressed or angry. Assertiveness training and CBT can be helpful in decreasing some of your symptoms.

For women: Your profile suggests you are a practical, sensible, self-reliant, action-oriented woman. You can enjoy the company of men and their more traditional male activities. You also are experiencing a number of physical symptoms that may be troubling you and interfering with your activities. Perhaps you or somebody you were close to experienced frightening physical problems when you were a child or perhaps you have been through some frightening physical trauma that has caused you to become concerned about your physical health. Relaxation exercises and yoga can be useful ways to deal with stress, especially since you may be an active woman.

16/61 Codes

The addition of Scale 6 to Scale 1 adds hypersensitivity, vigilance for criticism, and a tendency to rationalize and project blame onto others to the Scale 1 somatic complaints and anxieties. These people experience physical discomfort, but are also feeling vulnerable to being blamed and criticized. Consequently, they are described as defensive, rigid, grouchy, stubborn, and sensitive to demands being made of them. They are evasive, easily wounded, take things personally, and are quick to anger. At times their sensitivity may shade towards paranoia and the misunderstanding of others' motives. Typically, they are unaware of how their irritability and hostility create a negative, defensive response from others.

Conceptually, the codetype reflects an individual who feels sick, physically infirm, unfairly treated, and angry with the world. These individuals are defensive, as if anticipating being criticized or judged because of their symptoms, and are quick to feel misunderstood.

If Scale 8 is elevated, unusual somatic preoccupations and, in some cases, somatic delusions may reflect an underlying psychotic breakdown. Bodily preoccupations may serve as a defense against overt psychosis. Psychotic behaviors are rare in a 16/61 code pattern, which itself is a rare code. The most common third highest scales for men tend to be Scales 2 and 4 and for women, Scales 3 and 8.

TREATMENT

Anticipating criticism and judgment, these individuals are defensive, resentful, and bitter. This often elicits anger and resentment from others, thereby confirming their need for preemptive self-protection. Look for childhood experiences of being criticized, judged, or physically abused. These individuals are sensitive to criticism or demands, which suggests past conditioning experiences of having been criticized, dominated, and judged. Psychotherapy needs to be supportive initially, as a therapeutic relationship is hampered by the patient's vigilance. Criticisms of other therapists should be understood by the current therapist as a sign that the patient is feeling misunderstood and unsupported by the therapist. Cognitive behavioral and dialectical behavior (DBT) therapies can help the patient to express anger directly, rather than allowing rationalized resentments to accumulate. A diary of when physical symptoms increase in intensity can be useful to see if it is linked to the buildup of anger and/or resentments. Catharsis around past criticisms and emotional wounds can also be helpful once trust is established.

THERAPEUTIC FEEDBACK LANGUAGE

Your profile suggests that you are experiencing a number of physical symptoms and concerns that may be interfering with your quality of life. At the same time, you may be feeling vulnerable to being criticized and judged right now, perhaps related to your physical worries. You are a sensitive person and people's insensitivity is especially painful to you, but currently you are feeling even more vulnerable, as if you need to protect yourself. No wonder people may see you as cautious, distrustful, and ready to protect yourself, since it's hard to know whom you can trust. Perhaps recently somebody has accused you of something unfairly, or perhaps you grew up with a controlling or abusive parent, so you learned to be vigilant for criticism and unfair punishments. Your physical symptoms may become worse when you feel angry and are unable to express it safely. Discuss with your therapist any experiences of unfair criticisms or attacks to your self-esteem. Work on asking for what you want so you don't allow resentments to accumulate.

17/71 Codes

Chronically tense and anxious as well as guilty and ruminative, these individuals manifest many tension-related complaints and physical symptoms. Obsessive concern with body functions and disorders, along with extreme intellectualization, is common. Underlying feelings of guilt, inferiority, pessimism, and difficulties in being assertive are typical symptoms. In addition to feeling insecure, inhibited, inferior, and guilty, they manifest obsessive thoughts, fears, and panic that they are "losing their health." Usually Scale 2 is also elevated since chronic anxiety can lead to depression. Typically, these individuals are passive and non-confrontational. They tend to worry about their lack of interpersonal skills and they easily feel guilty if they are demanding in any way. This codetype is more commonly obtained by men than women. For both genders, the most common three point codes are 172/712 and 173/713.

TREATMENT

This essentially is a neurotic disorder. Consequently, these self-critical and anxious individuals profit from reassurance, supportive psychotherapy, thought-stopping techniques, assertiveness training, and relaxation training. They tend to be responsible, conscientious individuals who follow recommendations. Implosive-type therapies, Gestalt therapies, and insight therapy can also be useful. Look for childhood conditioning experiences of illnesses in them or in someone close to them. The profile reflects a constant apprehensiveness about the onset of some unpredictable catastrophic illness.

THERAPEUTIC FEEDBACK LANGUAGE

Your profile suggests that you are experiencing a constant state of anxiety and worry about physical symptoms and the possibility that you have a serious disease or disorder. You may spend a great deal of time researching various symptoms and seeking medical advice so you likely experience little joy or relaxation. You are a responsible, prone to worry, dutiful person and you easily feel guilty if you feel you have been too demanding or irritated with others. Conflict is especially upsetting to you. Perhaps you have recently experienced a physical disorder that frightened you and caused you to feel in a state of constant alertness in case your symptoms worsen. Or perhaps you or somebody you depended on in childhood experienced physical trauma that was frightening to you. No wonder you responded by becoming very aware of any physical symptoms that might be associated with illness and physical decline. Your therapist may consider medicine to help you control your worst panic attacks. Learning to stop your negative thoughts while practicing deep breathing and other relaxation techniques can be helpful. Explore any childhood events that could have predisposed you to be on constant alert for danger. Notice when your thoughts are interrupted by unwanted worries about your health and explore whether you might be distracting yourself from other legitimate concerns. Learn relaxation techniques and practice assertiveness training as well as learning to distinguish between appropriate guilt and unrealistic self-criticism.

18/81 Codes

Individuals with this pattern are likely to present with somatic complaints, some of which may be odd, unlikely, and even bizarre. In some cases, they are somatic delusions; in other cases, the somatic complaints may represent a defense, a distracting focus, against the emergence of psychosis. Easily distracted and confused, difficulties with concentration, thinking, and memory are typical. These individuals may show flat affect, with generalized unhappiness and complaints of depression. Poor social and sexual adjustment is typical. They lack trust and feel alienated from others, so they keep others at a distance. They feel isolated, particularly if Scale 0 is also elevated. Some show a nomadic lifestyle with a poor work history. When stressed, these persons can become disoriented, distractible, and confused. Emotionally constricted, some may exhibit episodes of sudden belligerence if they feel cornered or threatened. Their interpersonal life is often compromised by their difficulty with intimacy and their odd somatic preoccupations. They have difficulty recognizing, labeling, and expressing complex, nuanced emotions, so their emotional life tends to be expressed symbolically through their somatic symptoms and preoccupations. The most common three-point codetypes are 182/812, 183/813, and 187/817.

TREATMENT

These clients tend to show little response to reassurance and typically do not do well with insight therapy. Look for childhood conditioning experiences of being subjected to hostility from people on whom they depended. Some of these patients were slow to mature and experienced childhood illnesses along with parental neglect that led them to feel vulnerable and unsafe. Severe teasing, put downs, or other kinds of identity-damaging experiences combined with feelings of vulnerability due to physical frailty are common with this kind of profile. Supportive, reparenting, and life skills training therapies are recommended since psychological insights tend to be interpreted by them as an attack on their self-image. Antipsychotic medication may be necessary during particularly stressful events, especially if somatic delusions are severe.

THERAPEUTIC FEEDBACK LANGUAGE

Your profile suggests you are experiencing a great deal of concern about your physical symptoms. You probably imagine many possible terrible things that could be wrong with you and these thoughts and preoccupations likely cause you great distress. Sometimes people with your profile grew up in environments where they felt vulnerable and unprotected. You may have been small for your age or perhaps experienced a number of frightening illnesses as a child that made you very sensitive to any physical sensations that could signal something is wrong with you. You may currently be feeling unsafe and vulnerable and concerned about obtaining the right diagnosis, perhaps feeling that nobody is on your side and ready to help. Make sure you get even a small amount of exercise because it will help relieve stress. When your imagination runs wild about all the things that could be wrong with you, learn to switch your mind to other things in your life. Focus on getting some small pleasure or a chore accomplished. Take a mindfulness class so you can learn to identify your feelings and express them well to others.

19/91 Codes (see also 129/219 and 139 Codes if Scales 2 and 3 are Within Five T-Score Points of Scale 9)

This profile occurs rarely. Multiple somatic complaints, a high energy level, agitation, grandiosity, argumentativeness, and attention-seeking characterize this profile. Individuals with this codetype are preoccupied with bodily malfunctions and possible disabilities and at the same time they express a cavalier attitude about those disabilities. This pattern may reflect central nervous system or endocrine dysfunction expressed in the form of a high energy level and agitation combined with numerous physical complaints. If a genetic predisposition or physical etiology has been ruled out, it's possible that the hypomania is reflecting an underlying depression (particularly if Scale 2 is below *T*-45) and that the manic defense may be indicating an attempt to deal with either dependency needs that the person finds frightening or an anticipated loss. Such persons appear extroverted, surgent, assertive, and sometimes aggressive, although they are quite dependent and need a great deal of attention and approval. Although ambitious, they often lack definite goals, or jump from goal to goal and are distractible. Most commonly, Scale 3 or 4 is the third highest elevation.

TREATMENT

Conceptually, this profile can be understood as reflecting a constant need to be productive and to protect against future frustration, perhaps out of fear of experiencing a loss and subsequent depression. The physical complaints and anxieties could be a result of extreme tension. These symptoms become a source of secondary anxiety as the hypomanic individual becomes concerned about physical impediments to maintaining control over their reward system. If mania is evident, medication is recommended. Relaxation training, managing distractibility as well as realistic goal-setting and teaching awareness of physical responses to stress can be helpful. Self-esteem building can also help the patient lower their unrealistic goals.

Your profile suggests you are an energetic, driven, ambitious person. You likely have two speeds at which you operate: off and "full on." You also appear to be experiencing a lot of physical symptoms and worries. Perhaps you have recently experienced an illness or disability and, although you want to push through the pain and discomfort, it causes you a great deal of concern. You enjoy being a "take charge" and in control person, so physical disability will be especially upsetting to you. You like to argue your point of view and enjoy attention, so you are not afraid to speak your mind. Currently, however, you may be feeling more vulnerable because of your physical concerns. Perhaps you grew up in a family where you felt a strong need to prove yourself and achieve a great deal in order to obtain your and others' approval. Perhaps that drive is adding to your physical symptoms, because you put so much stress on yourself. Work with your therapist to define what you really want versus what you think you should achieve in order to obtain others' approval. Learn to recognize physical symptoms of stress and learn relaxation techniques to relieve it. Learn to stick at a task and not become easily distracted.

10/01 Codes

This rare code is associated with persons who are socially uncomfortable, withdrawn, and suffer vague and anxiety-provoking physical symptoms. Research has suggested that introversion and extraversion are stable personality characteristics, rather than symptoms of pathology, although extreme levels of either may reflect learned behavior. Others may judge the 10/01 as aloof, passive, quiet, and unassertive. They report physical complaints and concerns but not psychological discomfort or emotional distress. These conventional, rule-abiding individuals tend to accept physical discomfort, perhaps accepting it as their lot in life. When Scale 8 is also elevated as the third highest scale, schizoid withdrawal and social inadequacies are suggested, usually combined with odd somatic complaints. Most often, Scale 2 is the third highest scale, and when elevated above T-65, the person is likely to show depression, accompanied by the lack of a social support system. Look for childhood experiences of deficient socialization and a lack of parental warmth combined with frightening experiences of illness and physical infirmity.

TREATMENT

Assertiveness training, social skill building, and teaching the recognition, labeling, and appropriate expression of anger can be helpful in dealing with their tendency toward passivity and withdrawal. If they are in a significant relationship, help them understand that others need more expressions of physical affection and social interaction. Explore any childhood memories of being ill or frightened of physical symptoms, with no one to turn to. Help them understand how physical symptoms can be linked to stress.

THERAPEUTIC FEEDBACK LANGUAGE

Your profile suggests you are comfortable in your own company and can happily spend long periods alone. When socializing, you prefer to be with small groups of close friends. Being in large groups of people you don't know or becoming the center of attention unpredictably causes you stress. There is nothing wrong with being an introvert. At the same time, you may have grown up in a family where emotions were not expressed directly, so being naturally quiet, you may have learned to withdraw in the face of conflict and keep your feelings to yourself. Currently, you appear to be experiencing some physical symptoms that are hard to diagnose fully and cause you some anxiety. You may benefit from learning how to recognize what you are feeling so you could learn to express it better to others. Notice if your physical symptoms increase in intensity when you are troubled by stressful issues and learn relaxation and deep breathing techniques. Mindfulness training can also be helpful to you, as you may have a tendency to become lost in your own thoughts.

Scale 2 (D)

Scale 2 is one of the most frequently elevated scales in clinical populations and is usually elevated together with other scales. Scale 2 is sensitive to current mood, so a grief reaction could be reflected in a Scale 2 elevation without necessarily indicating a serious depression or mood disorder. Thus, interpretation of Scale 2 elevations depends on the configuration of the rest of the profile and the clinical history. Scale 2 increases somewhat with age, perhaps reflecting pessimism about the future or the accumulation of unresolved losses. Research on optimism by Seligman (1990) and others, however, suggests that some people appear to be genetically resistant to depression, exhibiting a remarkable resilience or hardiness in the face of loss, staying positive despite setbacks and failures. Such individuals would likely exhibit low scores on Scale 2.

High scores ($T > 65$) on Scale 2 reflect people who are depressed, anxious, worried, experience low self-esteem, and are pessimistic in their outlook. Typically, they show a narrowing of interests, poor morale, and in some cases expressed irritability. They generally feel discouraged, sad, useless, and guilty. Sleep difficulty, low energy, diminished appetite and sex drive, and difficulties with memory and concentration are typical. The higher Scale 2 is above T-65, the more depressed and self-deprecating the person is likely to be. Scores above T-80 suggest a severe depression with more extreme symptoms and a marked decline in self-management and general efficiency. Normal range, slightly elevated Scale 2 (T-55–65) scores suggest individuals who are somewhat inhibited, serious, and introspective, with a tendency to take setbacks badly and with a quickness to feel guilty or self-blaming when things go wrong. They tend to lack self-confidence and to be acquiescent and passive in the face of conflict. Generally they are responsible, analytical, dutiful people who avoid risk.

Moderately low to very low scores ($T < 45$), if no other scales are elevated, suggest alertness, cheerfulness, buoyancy, self-confidence, and a good sense of humor. These individuals are seen as enthusiastic and socially outgoing, particularly if Scale 0 is low. In some people, however, a low Scale 2 score can also indicate a lack of inhibition and perhaps even impulsiveness, especially if Scale 9 is elevated, the K scale is low, and/or Scale 4 is mildly elevated. In some cases, when Scale 9 is elevated above a T-score of 65 and Scale 2 is below a T-score of 45, the low Scale 2 score may be reflecting a bipolar individual currently in a manic phase.

Treatment for depression includes medication, CBT, venting emotions and catharsis about past losses, and self-esteem building.

Spike 2

Spike 2 occurs when Scale 2 is the only scale elevated beyond *T*-65. It reflects a current depression, which may be reactive or chronic. Typically, the person feels sad and unhappy, inadequate, lacking in self-confidence, and is often anxious, self-critical, and quick to feel guilty. These individuals experience the typical symptoms of depression, including disturbances in sleep, appetite, sex drive, concentration, and memory. They can be self-punishing and self-defeating. The relative elevations on the depression subscales help to identify which depressive symptoms are the most troubling and need immediate treatment. Spike 2 individuals tend to be serious, highly responsible, and acquiescing. This is especially true if no other scales are significantly elevated.

In college students, Spike 2 profiles may reflect concern with relations with the opposite gender, learning issues, or vocational choices. Although suicide cannot be predicted by the MMPI-2 alone, responses to Items 150, 303, 506, 520, 524, and 530 on the MMPI-2 are significant because they refer directly to suicidal ideation, plans and/or suicide attempts. In some cases the Spike 2 codetype is stable; the individual has come to terms with the depression and may not even be aware of how depressed he or she is. The prognosis for a Spike 2 profile is generally good, since these individuals often respond well to medication and to a directive approach helping them to grieve past losses.

TREATMENT

There are several well-researched treatments for simple depressive disorders. Insight therapy, cognitive restructuring, psychotropic medication, assertiveness training, relaxation training, self-esteem building, and dealing with grief over past losses are all useful therapeutic modalities. (See also treatment section under the Spike 2, low Scale 9 codes.)

THERAPEUTIC FEEDBACK LANGUAGE

Your profile suggests you are a responsible, dutiful person who takes life seriously. You are cautious, avoid risk, and tend to be your own worst critic. You are quick to feel guilty and you tend to avoid celebrating your accomplishments. Currently you may be feeling quite sad and unhappy, even despondent and depressed. Perhaps a recent loss or a series of setbacks has made you feel defeated, guilty, and down on yourself. You may be experiencing sleeping problems, feeling sluggish and tired, and having difficulty remembering and focusing. Your appetite and sex drive may be affected and you may feel unable to enjoy life. Talk with your therapist if you are feeling suicidal or feel a loss of your will to live. Sometimes people with this profile experienced childhood loss of some kind with an absence of childhood carefreeness. Talk to your therapist about recent and past losses and find ways to forgive yourself for them. Learn to switch off negative thoughts and try to avoid catastrophizing. Your tendency to avoid "wanting things" or "hoping for things" is an understandable response to having experienced a severe loss. To be negative and withdrawn and to lose hope is an understandable response to a loss that feels catastrophic. Learn to switch off some of your guilty feelings and maintain a gratitude journal to remind you that things may not be as bleak as they sometimes feel.

Your therapist may suggest medication to help you obtain restful sleep and increase your energy, appetite, and positive mood.

Relations with Other Scales

Spike 2, Low 9 Code

All of the descriptors for Spike 2 apply to this profile with some additions. When Scale 2 is elevated, no other clinical scales are significantly elevated, and Scale 9 is below *T*-45, fatigue, low energy, lack of assertiveness, and a quickness to "give up" in the face of obstacles is even more pronounced. These individuals are serious, circumspect people who guard their energy resources carefully. Increased complaints of low energy, feeling easily fatigued and overwhelmed as well as a lack of willful assertiveness would be suggested by the low Scale 9. If Scale 4 is at or below *T*-50, low aggressiveness, low sex drive, and a rigid adherence to rules, regulations, duty, and responsibilities are likely.

TREATMENT

Cognitive restructuring, directive approaches, relaxation training, psychotropic medications, and finishing of grieving over past losses are all effective therapeutic strategies. These individuals follow instructions well because they are so responsible. Transference usually involves their feelings of guilt for not progressing enough, with accompanying fears of therapist impatience or abandonment.

Energizing antidepressants may be indicated for a Spike 2, low 9 codetype, though medication effects may be experienced as uncomfortable, since the profile suggests an acceptance of a high degree of unhappiness and a slow pace. Consequently, medication should be prescribed in small incremental doses, so the patient can habituate to changes in mood state and energy level.

A Spike 2, low 9 codetype may indicate the depressive phase of a bipolar disorder, so the diagnosis would need to be confirmed through a clinical history. Childhood experiences of overloads of responsibility and deficits of age-appropriate carefreeness would not be atypical for Spike 2 profile. Hyper-responsible, they may have experienced childhoods where they were expected to take on adult roles beyond their years. Helping the patient engage anger over past losses can be useful, though they would tend to avoid expressing anger towards loved ones and are more comfortable expressing anger towards themselves. Cognitive restructuring, thought stopping, relaxation training, and assertiveness training are all useful treatment modalities. Help them set up a self-reinforcement schedule after completion of their responsibilities to teach them how to celebrate their accomplishments.

THERAPEUTIC FEEDBACK LANGUAGE

Language would be the same as the Spike 2, with the following addition: Your profile suggests that your energy is currently particularly low, so even small tasks and duties take a great deal of effort. You likely resist demands on your energy and avoid taking on too much, even if some of the activities could be seen as pleasurable. Your weight may increase in response to your lowered energy level.

21 Code

The interpretation of the 21 codetype is similar to that of the 12 codetype, except that complaints of depression and anxiety are more prominent. These individuals feel burdened, tired, defeated, misunderstood, and underappreciated. They feel a sense of moral superiority because they suffer and sacrifice for their family. Others, especially family members, feel guilty because they are the focus of the 21 individual's concerns and worries. Acting out is rare, unless Scale 4 is elevated third, and then it is passive-aggressive and self-defeating. These individuals tend to have a strong work ethic, often reflected in a puritanical, self-sacrificing lifestyle. Oral-dependent and sometimes alcoholic, these individuals complain of many of the physical symptoms associated with a 12 codetype, but verbalize more of the depressive symptoms that manifest themselves as pessimism and unhappiness, rather than specific complaints about physical symptoms, which are primary for the 12 individual. This codetype is more common among men than women.

TREATMENT

See also treatment section under the 12 code. With Scale 2 elevated above Scale 1, some individuals may complain more of depressive features and be more amenable to working on finishing grieving over past losses. Others with this codetype, however, may feel defeated about their condition and therefore less motivated or trusting of the therapy process, even though they experience severe distress. Gestalt therapy to help clients express their somatic complaints through role-playing can be effective. For example, "having their symptoms do the talking" can offer them a chance to express repressed anger and sadness. Medication is often effective, but needs to be presented as a way to help them deal with their "exhaustion" due to their physical symptoms, rather than due to psychological "problems." Assertiveness training, relaxation training, and thought stopping are also useful.

THERAPEUTIC FEEDBACK LANGUAGE

See also therapeutic feedback language section under the 12 codetype. Your profile suggests that you are currently feeling down, unhappy, blue, and concerned about your physical symptoms. You are a thoughtful, responsible, and dutiful individual, and you dedicate yourself to your career and your responsibilities. You may feel others do not appreciate how much you sacrifice for them and how hard you work for others without enough reward. Currently you may be experiencing a number of physical symptoms that concern you and rob you of pleasure. Perhaps growing up you had to be dutiful and responsible because a parent was somehow unavailable due to illness or death. From an early age you learned to sacrifice yourself for others and you have continued to put responsibility and caring for others above yourself. Currently, you appear to feel somewhat worn out and exhausted, and your body is taking the strain. Your therapist may want to give you some medication to help you sleep, feel more rested, and feel more energized. Dealing with your current depression may actually help some of your physical symptoms decrease in intensity. Make a diary of when your physical symptoms are worse and examine whether you are experiencing greater stress during these times. Take a relaxation class, a mindfulness class, or perhaps yoga as a way of helping you relax. Watch your tendency to catastrophize and to see things from a negative perspective. Allow yourself to be assertive, to ask for what you want, and do not sacrifice yourself for others so much. Forgive yourself for any past losses and allow yourself to switch off your tendency to feel excessively guilty for your past mistakes.

213/231 Codes (see also 123/213 Codes)

Although interpretation of this codetype is similar to the 21/12 codetype, the elevation of Scale 3 adds other defenses, such as repression, denial, and strong needs for approval from others. These clients manifest depression and preoccupation with bodily damage, often complaining of headaches as well as chest pain, nausea, vomiting, and other vague and shifting physical symptoms. These symptoms are frightening to them and they become easily concerned about the possibility of dying due to unexplained illness. Their depressive symptomatology may, however, manifest itself as a "smiling depression," where laughing and crying at the same time manifests sadness but also their need to be pleasing to others. Anger tends to be denied, and expressing any emotion that can lead to criticism is inhibited. They have strong needs for affection, affirmation, and approval. They fear loss and abandonment, and elicit attachment responses by being self-sacrificing, but also needy and complaining. Because they are so fearful about their physical symptoms, they want others to show sympathy and support, but their demands for reassurance can become annoying to others, leading to further insecurity.

Typical symptoms are of depression, which they see as the result of poor health. Sleep and eating problems, loss of libido, and difficulties with concentration and memory are also typical. They are more likely to complain of depression as secondary to their physical concerns. They tend to be tense, nervous individuals, concerned about how others see them. Nausea or vomiting, weight loss, heart palpitations, chest pains, and forgetfulness are common. Sometimes there may be a cyclical character to these individuals' complaints. The hysterical defenses associated with Scale 3 elevations appear to operate intermittently, so that the individual may go from being outwardly smiling, pleasing and well-functioning, to being incapacitated by depression and anxiety over physical decline. Initially, the therapist may diagnose the individual as suffering from a cyclothymic disorder, but the mood swings reflect the operation of hysterical defenses and related "flights into health," followed by periods of depression and gloominess should the hysterical defenses collapse, and the patient may be overcome with fears of physical illness and decline. Genuine somatic breakdown due to years of stress and tension is typical with this profile. The individual's response to stress leads to physical breakdown, which then becomes their primary concern, leaving them less likely to tackle the psychological sources of their somatic problems/illnesses.

When Scale 7 is also elevated, anxiety and worry are greater. Histories of indifference or outright rejection from parent figures and/or traumatic loss through the death or divorce of one of their parents during childhood is typical. Childhoods are typically characterized by social participation rather than withdrawal and, especially if Scale 4 is low, they live responsible lives. They are often highly conscientious and self-sacrificing, and therefore have a tendency to induce guilt in others. As parents, they are very giving toward their families and often feel unappreciated. They do not consciously manipulate others into caring for them, but because of their early experiences of abandonment, they tend to become co-dependent and others readily take advantage of them. Consequently, they feel unloved, unappreciated, and taken for granted. Family members act out, perhaps in reaction to the 213 individual's tendency to be controlling and demanding.

TREATMENT

These individuals exhibit approach-avoidance conflicts in their primary relationships. Although they are dependent and want nurturing and emotional affirmation, they fear emotional abandonment so they can appear petulant, manipulating others into taking care of them due to their physical infirmities. Look for childhood histories of an early death of a parent and/or experiences of rejection or emotional withdrawal from a father figure. In the presence of such a history, these individuals may repeat their childhood experiences of craving emotional support from a nurturing figure, perhaps the therapist, but at the same time fearing abandonment from the therapist. They would seek to try to please the therapist, but fear the therapist becoming impatient and abandoning them. Insight therapy will not move quickly because of their tendency to deny the intensity of early childhood trauma or parental unavailability. Pushing by the therapist could lead to premature termination because it engages too intense an emotional reaction. It would be important in therapy to "go with the resistance" by validating how loving and supportive their caregivers were, but also allowing the patients to develop empathy for themselves around their early losses. Emotional catharsis can be helpful if approached gradually. Sometimes having them imagine their childhood experiences as occurring to somebody else or to one of their children can help them develop empathy for themselves, which they tend to resist since it engages frightening feelings. Relaxation training, assertiveness training, and catharsis around past losses, as well as teaching them to recognize and express anger, are helpful therapeutic strategies. Both the anger and sadness aspects of the mourning process are often blocked in this codetype. The individual has adapted to early rejection and losses by being "brave," "a good soldier," nice and acceptable to others, smiling in spite of pain, and preoccupied with avoiding further rejection.

Sometimes a "flight into health" occurs and therapy is terminated. If, during therapy, the patient begins to criticize their past therapists, they may be unconsciously venting frustration with their current therapist. Helping them to express resentment towards their current therapist could help not only model how the expression of anger and resentment need not lead to loss, but to more effective ways of expressing anger. These individuals are highly conscientious, so they are often seen as good workers, but eventually can irritate coworkers because of their taking time off due to physical complaints and their tendency to be somewhat self-sacrificing and consequently resentful. In this way, their conscientiousness backfires, as others feel they have been made to feel guilty.

As in any depression codetype, suicide assessment is important. Antidepressant medications are useful, as are insight therapy, venting, and catharsis.

THERAPEUTIC FEEDBACK LANGUAGE

Your profile suggests that you are a dutiful, responsible individual who works hard to stay positive and please others. In some cases, people with your profile experienced early childhood deprivations or losses, so that they weren't able to be as carefree and feel as secure as many children expect to be.

Perhaps you experienced a parent dying or being unavailable at an early age, and you learned that you needed to be brave, to smile through your difficulties, and to be "a good soldier." You have continued to go through life protecting yourself against disappointment and loss by not "counting your blessings," but by always being aware of what can go wrong. Your profile shows that currently you are experiencing a number of physical symptoms of stress. Headache, backache, stomach upset, feeling nauseous, and vague and shifting physical symptoms such as headache, backache, unexplained stomach upset, and nausea may cause you a great deal of anxiety. Perhaps you've become afraid that these physical symptoms will worsen and lead to infirmity or even death. At times you can smile through your difficulties, but at other times your emotions break through and you feel overwhelmed by sadness, loss, and despair. The profile suggests that you are experiencing a current depression that may be masked to others because you are trying so hard to be brave and positive. Beneath your smile you worry that people may reject or abandon you, and that you are not good enough unless you sacrifice yourself for others. A therapist may want to give you some medicine to help you sleep better, regulate your appetite, and to help you concentrate and think more clearly. Work at being more assertive and learning to ask for what you want. Work with your therapist to avoid being co-dependent with others who can take advantage of you. Talk about any past losses you experienced, perhaps of self-esteem or of child-appropriate carefreeness. Work to switch off guilty feelings that overwhelm you and try to make a gratitude list to help you realize the positive things in your life so you do not focus on the losses.

23 Code

The 23 codetype is more frequent in women. Characteristics of the 23 are depression, helplessness, apathy, fatigue, and somatic complaints, as well as emotional overcontrol and sleep disturbance, combined with a self-sacrificing, guilt-inducing lifestyle. Although Scale 1 may not be elevated the individual will complain of fatigue and vague somatic complaints, but without the intense preoccupation on physical concerns associated with Scale 1 elevations. The 23 individual is "bottled up" and consequently experiences associated physical symptoms. The combination of depression and hysteria leads to a dutiful, "nice" individual who exhibits a smiling depression, laughing and crying at the same time. Typical symptoms of depression such as low sex drive and difficulties with concentration and memory may be reported. Conflict is not expressed directly. Anxiety, when expressed, tends to be around displeasing others and somatic symptoms. Depression tends to be denied, so it is expressed as feelings of insecurity and a lack of capacity to enjoy life. These individuals generally have difficulty expressing negative emotions in any direct way. Their complaints may appear as somewhat vague dissatisfaction, unhappiness, and feelings of being unappreciated. They experience a great deal of stress around any confrontation and expression of anger. Repression and denial leaves them feeling weak, exhausted, and inefficient. Scale 9 below 50 would emphasize complaints of fatigue and low energy. These individuals are more likely to express feeling hurt, unappreciated, and unrecognized rather than expressing anger. They have learned to tolerate a high degree of unhappiness and accept that they function at a reduced level of efficiency. Though they may appear depressed, hysterical defenses may result in a pleasant, though somewhat flat, demeanor. The most frequent three-point codetypes are 231/321, 234/324, and 237/327.

People with 23 codetypes are achievement-oriented and feel a compulsive need to prove themselves. At the same time they feel that they are not recognized for their efforts. They seek out added responsibilities, which then burden them. They crave recognition and love, but then fear failure and, with it, rejection.

Marital problems may occur due to these individuals' low sex drive, and some women complain of physical pain during intercourse. Sometimes these individuals have a somewhat Victorian view of sexuality.

Although this codetype is more frequent among persons over age 25, it nonetheless occurs in adolescents and is associated with poor peer relations. These adolescents can complain of loneliness and social difficulties. Others may see them as passive, compliant, and obedient. Early childhood histories for 23 individuals in general often show an under-involved or rejecting father and an overinvolved mother. They were average, but anxious, students. Sexual acting out and drug abuse is not associated with this pattern for adolescents.

TREATMENT

Conflict and confrontation is difficult for individuals with this codetype because of their fears of rejection. Consequently they tolerate a high degree of both physical and emotional discomfort. They tend not to be psychologically introspective. Catharsis might be frightening because of their fear of loss of emotional control, but it can be quite useful, so progressive relaxation with the introduction of anxiety-loaded topics works best. Therapy should focus on helping them to gradually regain a fuller experience of their emotional life, parts of which they repress as an adaptive response to the emotional overload of loss/trauma. They deny anger towards others and are self-recriminating. Consequently, "going with the resistance" is more effective. The therapist needs to express genuine interest at understanding how they tolerate feeling unappreciated by others without also feeling anger. The therapist could express approval for how the patient continues to see "the best" and how they made "the most" out of a difficult childhood to allow them to feel empathy for themselves, and allow venting of repressed feelings. To achieve catharsis and insight, the therapist should not push the patient to "feel more," but introduce emotional awareness slowly, with the patient in control of the pace of intensity. Once they feel comfortable that the therapist is not going to push them into being angry with their loved ones, they can develop a more balanced view of their resentments, without feeling that their relationships are threatened. When a particularly painful memory is engaged, they may "shut down" and interrupt their ongoing experience in the therapy session, shifting the focus of attention to something positive. Role-playing a confrontation, "even though you may not feel any of the anger" can be helpful for them to engage the emotions they prefer to avoid. Relief usually follows after they have engaged in a role-play of expressing anger or resentment. Given their childhood histories of early traumatic loss, they are fearful of losing loved ones. Antidepressant medications, cognitive restructuring, thought stopping, and relaxation training can also be useful.

THERAPEUTIC FEEDBACK LANGUAGE

Your profile suggests that you are a very dutiful, responsible individual who generally likes to please others and avoid conflict. You tend to go the extra mile to see other peoples' perspectives and you're not afraid to sacrifice yourself for others. Sometimes people can take advantage of you because of your willingness to help and your difficulty setting limits with them. You expect that people will notice how much you give them and will be grateful, but when they are not, it deeply hurts you. From an early age you may have had to be the dutiful and responsible child, perhaps because of an early death or loss in your family, or an emotionally unavailable parent. You learned from an early age to be brave, to be a "good soldier," and not to bother the adults in your life who you felt had already suffered enough. You continue to go through life sacrificing yourself for others and finding it difficult to confront people. This may lead to stress, which can then manifest in physical symptoms such as headaches, nausea, anxiety, and exhaustion. Your therapist may want to give you some medicine to help you with some of your symptoms of depression. That may surprise you since you may have become so accustomed to feeling unhappy that you do not see yourself as depressed. Even though you smile and stay positive, you may experience some underlying depressive symptoms, including difficulties with sleep, feeling fatigued, having low energy, low sex drive, and diminished appetite. Having difficulties with concentration and memory can also be symptoms of depression. Work with your therapist on developing some empathy for yourself as a brave child who tried to take on responsibility in the face of loss. Learn how to express anger directly so that you can set limits with others without feeling that you are rejecting them. Your therapist may want you to try some medication so you can feel better.

24/42 Codes

This codetype may reflect either a chronic 24/42 lifestyle or a high Scale 4 individual who recently has experienced a situational setback and is feeling trapped, angry, and defeated. In either case, the 24 individual is feeling depressed, frustrated, dissatisfied, resentful, and pessimistic about the future. Others may see them as critical, argumentative, restless, and negative. A 24 individual can be self-defeating, often acting out impulsively when stress builds, and then feeling defeated and distressed with the consequences. They oscillate between self-blame and blaming others. Anger is episodically turned either inward, whereupon they are vulnerable to self-destructive or self-defeating behavior or, sometimes, outward and blaming, feeling that their situation can't change without others changing first. They often report feeling the unfortunate victim of circumstance, avoiding responsibility for their difficulties. For individuals with a high Scale 4 history of acting out, but currently dealing with the adverse consequences of their behavior, the 24/42 profile reflects someone who has had difficulty maintaining control over their impulses and is therefore experiencing situational and transient depression and remorse. After acting out and getting caught, they feel distress. However, this distress is the result of being caught and punished, rather than impulse-restraining guilt. Although their apparent conscience pangs may be severe, even out of proportion to the event, their acting-out behaviors are likely to recur in the future in a cyclic fashion.

Home and family problems, employment difficulties, and histories of interpersonal problems are typical for the 24/42 codetype. They are resentful of any demands placed on them. Substance abuse or alcoholism is common. In some cases, legal difficulties may also be present. Some of these individuals can manifest interpersonal relationship problems and career instabilities without any legal difficulties. For most 24 individuals, a passive-dependent adjustment pattern is predominant. They seek out relationships where someone "saves them" from the results of their impulsive behavior, gravitating towards co-dependent caretakers. After age 40, the life of poor judgment and consequent failure to achieve satisfaction can result in a deeply entrenched pattern of self-blame, depression, and self-anger, with occasional self-destructive and suicidal behavior. Suicide evaluation is important, since they may act out self-destructively, both out of a sense of defeat and as an angry response to punish others. Scale 7, 3, or 8 is often the third highest.

Adolescents with the 24 codetype are resentful of authority, argumentative, self-defeating, and lack drive. They often use chemical agents as way of medicating their dysphoria. The 24 adolescent is the "nothing to lose" teenager who feels trapped in their current predicament and may take impulsive action, such as running away, as a way of escaping a difficult situation. Adolescents with this codetype feel alienated from their family members and want to get away. They perceive their caregivers as lacking in affection and unreliable. School difficulties, with truancy and poor grades, are typical. Teenage unmarried mothers may obtain this profile, though it may be reflecting the trapped depression associated with being a caretaker with limited resources.

TREATMENT

Psychotherapy depends on whether the 24/42 individual is primarily a high 4 who has recently been caught or feels trapped between undesirable alternatives, or whether the 24/42 is reflecting a long-term personality adjustment. The high 4 individual who feels currently caught in an entrapping situation may need to experience "hitting bottom" in order to make serious changes. A subgroup of 24/42 individuals exhibits a lifestyle of chronic unhappiness, resentment, and bitterness, without antisocial acting-out behavior. They can be frustrating for their co-dependent spouses, but they do not necessarily act out antisocially. They do experience marital conflict and feel hopeless and trapped. They resist psychotherapy, often aggravating therapists because of their tendency to undermine any therapeutic suggestion with a defeated, "I've tried it, and it doesn't work" attitude. Small, concrete homework assignments in the direction of change, and holding them accountable when they do not perform these assignments, though in a gentle way, can be helpful. Help them see how they have lost trust in themselves so that, as an adaptive response, they refuse to "invest" in any change. Insight to help them see how they undermine themselves by acting out impulsively can be helpful, especially if they are bright. Look for childhood experiences of being emotionally let down and abandoned a number of times, which may have instilled in them a tendency to distrust not only relationships with others, but their own efficacy. With the high 4 individual whose 2 elevation is due to situational factors, help them see how they have "numbed themselves" as a way of surviving a childhood in which they felt defeated and trapped. Through insight, help them recognize when stress is building and rehearse ways to not act impulsively.

This codetype is the most commonly occurring one in substance abuse rehab centers. Even if the *MAC–R* scale is not elevated, the use of chemical agents should be evaluated. Although firm intentions to change may be expressed, these individuals can be quick to feel defeated. They often drop out of therapy. A combination of firm support, limits, and insight, as well as predicting how they might act out, can be helpful. It is also important for the therapist to deal with the transference, specifically, their expectation that the therapist will abandon them.

THERAPEUTIC FEEDBACK LANGUAGE

Your profile suggests that you are feeling trapped, unhappy, bitter, resentful, and unable to see a way out of your current situation. Perhaps you've recently experienced some difficulties because of your behavior and you feel angry with yourself. At other times you may feel angry with others, feeling that your situation cannot change unless others change or events beyond your control change. In some cases, people with this profile grew up in environments where authority figures were unreliable and untrustworthy. From an early age you've learned that you can't trust others, so that you've relied on yourself during times of stress. When stresses build, you can act impulsively and occasionally that gets you into the kind of trouble you may be experiencing now. Perhaps you've used chemical agents as a way of trying to feel better, or perhaps you took a shortcut that led to a series of negative events. It is no wonder you feel trapped and angry. You might want to feel like giving up or even hurting yourself. At other times you feel angry with the world and you feel unfairly treated. You may experience some feelings of depression, such as sad moods, difficulties with sleep, changes in appetite, and sex drive. You may have difficulty concentrating and completing things. When others become angry with you because you do not follow through, you may find yourself taking shortcuts, telling white lies, or even manipulating to get out of difficult situations. Currently you feel quite glum, trapped, and down on yourself. At times you feel hopeless and utterly defeated. Protecting yourself against being hopeful is understandable, given your current predicament. It is going to be hard for you to do some of the exercises your therapist wants you to do. You may find yourself agreeing to making changes, but then not being able to follow through. You may find yourself angry with your therapist for "pushing you" to do things that you feel are useless. Taking small daily steps towards a goal would be important for you. Learning to recognize when stress is building and not acting out impulsively would also be important. Try to rehearse stressful situations so that you develop habits that are not self-defeating or self-destructive. When you want to give up, force yourself not to. Working towards small goals can help you feel better about yourself. Work on avoiding chemical agents as a way of feeling better, because that may actually aggravate your depression.

243/423 Codes

The addition of Scale 3 adds hysterical defenses to the trapped, angry, self-defeating 24/42 codetype. Consequently, these individuals manifest some denial, repression, and the ability to role-play in order to avoid rejection. They are self-sacrificing, but angry about it. They feel trapped and sad, but are also inclined to relieve tension impulsively, as one would expect from Scale 4 elevation's impulsivity. The Scale 2 and 3 elevations act as a control for Scale 4 acting-out behavior. Consequently, the acting out is more interpersonal and self-centered. These individuals may have eating disorders, chemical addiction problems, and impulsive, angry episodes that they later deny. Anger tends to be expressed in more symbolic ways and through passive-aggressive behaviors and perhaps talking behind people's backs. In some people, anger might be expressed in episodic explosive episodes, especially if the *O-H* scale is elevated above a raw score of 17. The 243/423 individual tends to be oral dependent. They are depressed and hungry for love and approval, yet afraid that being emotionally vulnerable will lead to abandonment. This combination of scale elevations suggests an approach-avoidance conflict, with a desire to please others by what they perceive is self-sacrifice, but at the same, anger at not having their needs met. They go through life manipulating others to get their emotional needs met, and pretending to fit in to avoid rejection and conflict, yet distrusting others' caring towards them because they have played a role in order to obtain it. They project their own manipulativeness onto others. The 243 individual can be frustrating to live with because they crave reassurance but do not accept it, and are chronically resentful, rationalizing their acting out as a response to not having their needs met.

TREATMENT

This profile is characterized by early childhood experiences of rejection or emotional abuse and, if Scales 4 and 3 are significantly elevated, physical abuse. As an adaptive response, they learn to role-play, becoming what others expect of them to avoid rejection and conflict. Psychotherapy should focus on helping them recognize what they want versus the role they feel they have to play for others. They also need to recognize anger in themselves and express it in a modulated direct way, rather than in manipulative ways. Assertiveness training to learn not to rely solely on manipulativeness can be helpful. Catharsis around past rejections, perhaps from an explosive, discounting parent would be useful. Developing empathy towards themselves as emotionally abused children would help them recognize how they defend against "feeling" by numbing and role-playing. These individuals lack insight and can express inconsistent verbalizations. They want to please and have people like them, but at the same time, they are angry. Helping them recognize how to integrate these two sides of themselves would be important. In some cases, this is primarily a depression profile, with the 43 elevations reflecting overcontrol and role-playing, perhaps as a way of dealing with the depression. If the depression is more palpable, an antidepressant medication may be indicated.

THERAPEUTIC FEEDBACK LANGUAGE

Your profile shows that you are currently experiencing a moderate amount of distress. You may be feeling trapped and angry as well as anxious and tense. Often people with your profile grow up in environments where the caretaker was explosive, discounting, or even abusive. You may have experienced periods where you felt hopelessly trapped and unable to get your needs met. Perhaps from an early age you felt defeated and unable to think about your wants because you had to role-play being somebody that your parents wanted you to be, rather than who you were. From an early age you learned to try to please others, to fit in, and to avoid rejection by playing the correct role. You may have difficulty even knowing what you want versus what you are "supposed to do" in order to please others. You may find yourself being manipulative, trying to get others to take care of you, but at the same time not trusting them. You may be experiencing periods of depression when you feel sad, unhappy, and trapped, with low energy. Sleep and eating difficulties and disturbances in weight and sex drive can sometimes occur with this profile. You may have experienced some recent setback or loss that has left you feeling sad and unhappy, but at the same time forced to play the right role to fit in and to avoid upsetting others. You may not even recognize when anger is building inside of you, and you may express it in roundabout, symbolic, or even passive-aggressive ways. You might be so concerned that expressing what you want could lead to rejection that you feel you have to manipulate others in order to get your needs met. Your therapist may want to suggest medication to help you with some of the symptoms, particularly the sad and unhappy feelings. Talk about any recent or past experiences where you felt trapped, rejected, and discounted, so that you had to learn to play the right role in order to fit in. Learn to observe when you act impulsively to try to relieve your stress. Do you eat too much or use chemical agents as a way of self-soothing, or do you act out sexually? Talk to your therapist about what kinds of impulsive behaviors you engage in order to feel better. Learning to recognize anger and expressing it directly could be helpful to you.

247/427/472/742 Codes (see also 274/724 Codes)

This codetype reflects an anxious, acting-out and guilt-prone individual who is highly dependent on others. The 27/72 individual is characterized as being a hyper-responsible "worrier," whereas a 24/42 individual is experiencing anger and feeling defeated and depressed. The 47/74 individual shows a cyclical, almost compulsive, acting out pattern of behavior, followed by remorse and guilt. Consequently, when these patterns are combined, the codetype reflects a person who can alternate between periods of worry, anxiety, and even responsibility, followed by impulsive tension reduction as anxiety builds. After acting out, they then feel guilty, fearful, and seek reassurance. These individuals are chronically ambivalent about almost every aspect of their lives. For some it is an inability to let go of possessions, thus becoming a hoarder. For others it is holding on to relationships even as they begin new ones. Attachment to people or things engages their fear of losing them, so they derive little reward from the attachment unless it is threatened, whereupon they become energized to regain it.

These individuals are very reactive to any threats to their security and become intensely worried, with numerous anxious preoccupations, when they feel threatened. Obsessive–compulsive thoughts and behaviors are common with this codetype. In response to setbacks, they become extremely self-critical, catastrophizing the situation and seeking others' reassurance, though not profiting from it. Because they fear failure, they are quick to be self-critical, perhaps as a way of preemptively undermining the anticipated criticisms by others. They equate failure with rejection. Other people respond to the 247 individual's self-negation with reassurance and support, but eventually becoming impatient with their inability to be soothed.

These individuals are dependent, but they also fear emotional closeness and so exhibit passive-dependent manipulativeness. They invite being rescued. Family or marital problems are likely. They have difficulty expressing anger out of fear of emotional abandonment, so their anger tends to be expressed passively. 247 individuals use guilt to manipulate others and undermine others' anger towards them by their own exaggerated self-criticism. Others can find this behavior annoying. Conceptually, the way the 247 deals with anger can be seen as similar to a child breaking his own toys as a venting of frustration, and a way of punishing caregivers. These individuals feel that life is a strain, and that they are getting a raw deal. Though symptoms of depression are present, these are often secondary to the individual's interpersonal difficulties and self-defeating behaviors. Phobias, somatic complaints, anxiety, tension, worry, and feelings of inadequacy are also present. These individuals are often underachievers and have difficulty with decisions because of their fear of making a mistake and somehow failing. They often self-medicate, even when the *MAC–R* is not elevated. Suicidal ideation and discomfort with the opposite gender may be present.

Men with this codetype are often highly dependent and immature, but can become verbally hostile when stressed. Typically they marry a strong, protective, and even domineering spouse. Interestingly, a high proportion of 274 individuals are the youngest child. Most were not behavior problems as children, suggesting that Scale 4 elevations contribute alienation and emotional distrust rather than acting out. Men with this profile often show a history of a close relationship with a mother figure who tended to indulge them, but failed to teach them personal efficacy because she was dominating. Women have the same relationship, but with a male father figure, and often become involved with older married men. Some marry protective older men, reflecting their need for emotional security.

When Scale 1 is coded fourth, these individuals complain of numerous vague somatic symptoms that are stress-related. If Scale 3 is elevated, there is more overcontrol and a tendency to play a social role in order to avoid rejection.

TREATMENT

Often the precipitating event for this disturbance is the loss of dependency support by a protective caretaker, and it may replicate childhood experiences of emotional abandonment. Additionally, these individuals typically overreact to minor problems as though they were emergencies. They have difficulty expressing their emotions in a direct and clear way. Though depression is verbalized, and they may complain of sleep difficulties and other symptoms of depression, anxiety tends to be more palpable. Others tend to see them as tense, high-strung, and jumpy. The profile has been described by Alex Caldwell as the "momma's boy" profile for men and as the "daddy's girl" profile for women. This reflects that they often experienced caretakers who would indulge them, but in an unreliable way that robbed them of a sense of personal efficacy. Parental inconsistencies instilled fears of abandonment in these individuals and, at the same time, a tendency to manipulate in order to get their needs met.

In therapy, these individuals need a great deal of reassurance but, as one would expect with Scale 4 elevated, they tend not to trust it. Consequently, they constantly seek love and reassurance, but they doubt its validity or reliability. They project their own manipulativeness onto others and therefore distrust others' motives. This often reflects childhood experiences of a caregiver who was highly involved, but who was unpredictable because of their own narcissistic needs or psychiatric illness. These individuals seek a lot of reassurance from the therapist, but tend not to follow through on advice. They tend to seek help for an immediate problem, such as getting the previously supportive person who has abandoned them back into their life. Many of them experienced physical illness at a higher than average rate in childhood. They also dated less often than average. Relaxation training and teaching them to recognize when stress is building can be useful, as can rehearsing stress-relieving behaviors that are not self-defeating or self-destructive. Working on the transference is important, as the patient may withhold information from the therapist expecting the therapist to become impatient with them. If the therapist can earn the patient's trust, so that they do not selectively report, then insight therapy can help the patient develop empathy for themselves as children who could not depend upon their caretakers. Insight therapy can help them realize how they demand nurturing from others in a co-dependent way. Sometimes therapy is brief because once anxiety is alleviated, they tend to lose motivation for continuing.

THERAPEUTIC FEEDBACK LANGUAGE

Your profile suggests that currently you are feeling on edge, tense, and anxious a great deal of the time. You may find yourself constantly worrying about something, fearful that something bad might happen. You might even experience some specific phobias. When things go wrong, it is easy for you to feel a sense of panic, as if your world is about to collapse. Often people with your profile grew up in environments where parents were controlling and yet unreliable in their emotional support. One of your parents may have been ill or unavailable in some other way, but caring and hands-on when they were available. Perhaps you never knew when you could rely on them, and when they did become involved, they were often too clinging and controlling, so that you never really learned emotional self-reliance. It is no wonder that you developed a constant sense of anxiety, as if waiting for something bad to happen, because you had no one you could rely upon. You never fully developed your confidence. People with your profile often marry a nurturing and supportive person who is also controlling. You might find yourself constantly afraid to lose that person's emotional support, but at the same time resenting them, feeling that they are too controlling. It is probably hard for you to make decisions because you are afraid of loss and the guilt you feel when things go wrong, and because you see every side of an issue. As stress builds, you may find yourself doing impulsive things to feel better, such as using chemical agents or something else that ends up making you feel guilty. Your constant inner anxiety and self-doubt may leave you feeling exhausted. It is hard for you to get a good night's rest, and you may experience physical symptoms of stress. Your therapist may want you to consider medication for your anxiety and teach you ways to switch off negative thoughts. Relaxation training, deep breathing, and yoga exercises could help you relax. Mindfulness therapy can help you become more aware of the positive things in your life. Work with your therapist to develop empathy for yourself as a child, understanding how having unreliable caretakers could have made you anxious and demanding of reassurance, and yet fearful of being controlled.

248 Code

It may be difficult to determine whether this profile reflects a stable 248 personality style or whether it reflects a 48/84 individual who recently is in trouble because of acting-out behavior, with resulting elevations on Scale 2. In most cases, depression, anxiety, defensive anger, and family and interpersonal problems are present. Acting out tends to be impulsive and angry, and often self-defeating. These individuals feel very distrustful of others. They feel alienated and have difficulty reading how others are feeling. They lack a sense of empathy because they have withdrawn into a self-protective coldness, keeping others at a distance. Others are likely to judge them as moody and unpredictable. They are quick to feel slighted and can be quick to anger if they feel misunderstood. Sexual difficulties are likely, with sexuality and aggression often mixed. Suicidal ideation and multiple suicide attempts are often present.

Distrust is a central characteristic of this profile. It is manifested as a sense of alienation and disconnection from others as well as transitory episodes of diffuse paranoia. These individuals can experience periods of panic, which are manifested through irritable and hostile moods. These are usually precipitated whenever the individual feels vulnerable. Sometimes this vulnerability occurs when others are being warm and caring, and at the other times, it is when others are being controlling or demanding. Although they verbalize depression, it reflects more a sense of emptiness and disconnection from others than the sense of communicative sadness that is seen in pure depression profiles. The depression is sensitive to situational changes. These individuals can verbalize feeling anxious, but the anxiety is experienced as diffuse rather than focused, and it reflects their sense of inner emptiness and emotional disconnection from others, as one would expect from the elevation on Scale 8. These individuals are very sensitive to any demands made on them and can be passively argumentative and resistant, but at the same time are demanding of others. When frustrated, they can be self-destructive. Parents with this codetype tend to have difficulties parenting their children.

TREATMENT

Suicide attempts are common with this codetype and often occur in moments of angry desperation. They put the therapist through trust tests, reflecting their fears of emotional abandonment and rejection. Often, childhood histories of rejection, abandonment, and cold cruelty are common. Identity-damaging blows to their self-esteem may have led them to protect themselves from further hurt by keeping others at a distance. They often become involved in relationships that replicate their childhoods and are abusive or rejecting of their partners. Paternal relations were often indifferent and maternal relations were often rejecting. Early school achievement was often below average. Interestingly, in the Marks et al. (1974) study, in spite of parental rejection or indifference, 35 percent of the 482 criterion group participants received sex instruction from a family member, the highest proportion of any codetype. The 248 codetype predicts sexual difficulties with sexual aggression confusion, early childhoods of rejection (save for sexual education), and suggests poor boundaries in the family of origin.

Supportive, esteem-building psychotherapies, rather than insight-oriented ones, are most useful. These individuals can become cognitively disorganized by insight therapy.

They respond well to boundaries set by the therapist. Practical, goal-directed, supportive psychotherapies that help rebuild their self-esteem and develop coping skills are often effective. Help them recognize when impulse pressures are building so that they do not act out in self-defeating ways. Brief psychotic episodes can occur in some individuals, especially if they abuse chemical agents.

The codetype is associated with chemical addiction proneness. Avoid group psychotherapy until a trusting relationship with the primary therapist is developed. In the presence of severe depression, a sedating antidepressant may be useful.

THERAPEUTIC FEEDBACK LANGUAGE

Your profile suggests that you are experiencing periods where you feel sad, blue, and unhappy. Often people with your profile grow up in environments where you could not count on your caretakers for emotional support. Perhaps one or both of your parents were cold or rejecting, so from an early age you had to protect yourself by not letting yourself care too much. You may have even experienced periods where someone was cruel, so that you learned to protect yourself by not letting people get close. Now, when you get involved with others, you may find yourself overwhelmed by anger or mood swings and not know why. If someone is warm or kind to you, you might get angry, as if you're afraid that by letting them in you become too vulnerable to getting hurt. At other times you may become preoccupied with how someone has hurt you, and you may dwell on fantasies of how to deal with them and punish them. It may be hard for you to express yourself and to share with others what you are feeling in a way that feels satisfying. At times you may experience intense anxiety, as if the world is crumbling and you do not know whom to trust. This is because from an early age you had to learn to protect yourself, to keep a wall up around you so that you could not be hurt. You may find it difficult to open up and let people get close to you because of early childhood experiences. The therapist may want to suggest medicine to take away some of the sadness and help you sleep and feel more rested. Rehearse with your therapist what you can do when you feel stressed so that you do not act in impulsive ways that later make you feel bad about yourself. When you feel close to someone, watch your tendency to be angry and push them away, perhaps as a way of protecting yourself against getting too involved. Learn to switch off some of your dark fantasies. Learn to recognize what emotions you are feeling so that you can express them in ways that others can accept.

25/52 Codes (see also 275/725 Codes if Scale 7 is Within Five T-Score Points of Scale 5)

Men with this code are idealistic, inner-directed, unassertive, indecisive, and depressed. They care deeply about others and have a philosophical perspective. They worry about the cruelty of world events. They dislike competitiveness and at times can be passive. Acting out is unlikely and conflict tends to be handled verbally, intellectually, and with reasonableness and rationality. They are psychologically-minded and want to discuss their feelings. They are sensitive, easily hurt and can exhibit anxiety and, at times, withdraw. Some may complain of somatic symptoms and may exhibit some of the symptoms of depression, such as sleep difficulties, problems with concentration and memory, and low energy. They can be self-aware to the point of being painfully self-conscious. They are fussy and can be self-critical. Sexual adjustment may be impaired, perhaps because of their low self-esteem, sensitivity, and tendency to passivity.

This is a rare codetype among women. The high Scale 5 suggests a woman who has traditionally masculine interests and is comfortable in the world of men. She presents as depressed, inwardly focused, prone to feeling guilty, and duty-oriented. An example of a 25 woman might be somebody who enjoys outdoor activities, perhaps living and working on a farm, or perhaps a research scientist or someone who is comfortable in a practical, competitive, action-oriented, traditionally male world, such as the military. At the same time, she is circumspect and prone to periods of withdrawal and negative thinking. She is also analytical and careful to avoid attention.

Male adolescents (e.g. 18–19 years of age) with this codetype exhibit problems in their social relationships because of their sensitivity and shyness. Often interpersonally unassertive, they tend to over-intellectualize and to be perfectionistic and meticulous. Sometimes, because of stereotypes about traditional male behavior, they can be teased by their peers and called "gay" even though they may have a heterosexual orientation.

TREATMENT

Standard depression treatment such as CBT would be effective with this codetype. In some areas of the country homosexuality may still be judged negatively, so explore any issues that may be associated with this. Assertiveness training and coaching for men on how to relate intimately may be helpful. Look for childhood experiences of an opposite gender parent identification and deficits of age-appropriate childhood carefreeness. Explore the possibility of homosexual awareness from an early age and its possible resulting internal conflicts.

THERAPEUTIC FEEDBACK LANGUAGE

Your profile shows that you are a person who is dutiful, responsible, and prone to worry.

For men: You are a sensitive individual who cares about how others feel and you are prone to worry about the world and how people treat one another. You are sensitive to how things look and feel and you do not focus on just the practical aspects of life. You care about the mood and aesthetics in any situation and how things look, and you respond positively to elegance. You tend not to be very assertive. You hang back, observe, analyze, and you tend not to express anger very directly. Others may see you as quite fussy about the way things should be done, and even though you may feel critical of how others do things, it is hard for you to tell people what you think would work best because you do not want to offend them. Men with your profile are comfortable in the world of women and enjoy what may be seen as traditionally feminine interests and values. Competitiveness, harshness, and traditional male activities are less interesting to you. At times your tendency to hang back and to avoid being pushy may mean that others take advantage of you or are able to bully you into doing things you are not comfortable with. Your profile also suggests that you are somewhat quick to feel guilty and down on yourself. You are not as happy and as positive as you would like to be. Your therapist may want you to try medicine to help you sleep better, feel more rested, and increase your sense of efficiency. At the same time, work at being more assertive and learn to express what you feel more directly. Talk to your therapist about any childhood experiences where you felt you had to be dutiful and responsible, and where you felt fearful that letting down your guard could lead to some kind of loss. Learn to celebrate your accomplishments and watch your tendency to catastrophize.

For women: Your profile also suggests that you have a well-developed practical, action-oriented side, and that you are comfortable in the world of men. When a problem arises, you want to do something, rather than talk about it. No wonder that being around women with traditional feminine interests is less interesting to you than being in a world of action. At the same time, your profile suggests that you are not feeling as happy and positive as you would like. You are a dutiful, responsible, and introspective individual who can feel guilty easily when things go wrong. Your therapist may want to try you on medicine to help you sleep better, feel more rested, and increase your sense of efficiency. At the same time, work at being more assertive and learning to express what you feel more directly. Talk to your therapist about any childhood experiences where you felt you had to be dutiful and responsible, and where you felt fearful that letting down your guard could lead to some kind of loss. Learn to celebrate your accomplishments and watch your tendency to catastrophize.

26/62 Codes

This is a depression profile with underlying paranoid features. Individuals with this codetype feel trapped in a current situation, and feel their current depression is due to unfair, insensitive, and callous treatment by others, yet they feel unable to alleviate it. The elevation on Scale 6 predicts touchiness, quickness to feel hurt and take offense, and a tendency to feel victimized and self-righteously angry. These individuals have difficulty expressing resentments directly, perhaps out of fear of retaliation, so they tend to accumulate them. This leads to a self-fulfilling prophecy, whereby the resentments, when finally expressed, lead others to resenting them, confirming their view that they cannot express their feelings without retaliation.

Typical complaints for individuals with this codetype are sad moods, crying spells, worrying, somatic preoccupations, feelings of inferiority, and difficulties with sleep, concentration, memory, general efficiency, and energy. Others can view this individual as critical and bitter. Feeling trapped in a current predicament, mistreated and victimized and, at the same time, fearful about expressing their emotions, they tend to withdraw into hurt silences that are annoying to others who then judge their behavior as pouting. They misinterpret others' motives and store up and rationalize their resentments. A hypothesis is that they experienced critical and judgmental parents that they could not please. Their response was to "give up trying," but at the same time feel vigilant for evidence of how they were being mistreated as a way of preparing for retaliation. Consequently, as adults, their interpersonal relationships mimic early childhood experiences of self-protective vigilance and the accumulation of caretakers' failures of empathy. Others may see them as rigid and critical of others, though this may reflect their attempt to be preemptively critical as a defense against being criticized. Hypersensitive to judgment and therefore defensive, they are quick to look for evidence of why they are not "in the wrong." They are quick to read malevolent meaning into normal situations, and adopt a defensive, "chip on the shoulder," attitude in an attempt to protect themselves from what they perceive as attacks on them. This is rarely a psychotic profile, although paranoid defenses such as projection, rationalization, and reaction formation are typical. If Scales 4 and 8 are also elevated above *T*-65, the probability of psychosis increases.

TREATMENT

This codetype is associated with childhood experiences of feeling unfairly treated by a caretaker who could be critical, judgmental, and emotionally withholding. As an adaptive response, the 26 individual may have learned to withdraw into quiet, self-protective silence as a way of manifesting hurt anger. They likely saw the demanding caretaker as impossible to deal with. Conceptually, think of the 26 individual as someone who feels wounded and in an inescapable situation; they feel bitter and angry, and yet afraid to expose any vulnerability. They anticipate the therapist will "not understand" and will be critical. They tend to express intimate feelings in a way that others may construe as a demand or an attack that elicits from others the emotion they fear. Consequently, psychotherapy should help them learn to express underlying hurts by rehearsing expressing anger directly, without blame or judgment towards the other person. For example, they tend to express hurt in a rationalized way that comes across as blaming the person who is frustrating them. This elicits a defensive response from the person criticized, confirming the 26 individual's view that emotional vulnerability leads to being attacked. Cognitive behavioral techniques and educating the 26 individual on how to ask for what they want without criticizing the other person can be useful. Help them see that confrontations can be productive and not necessarily will-breaking. Assertiveness training, anger management, relaxation training, and working on the transference with the therapist can be useful. These clients feel vulnerable to the therapist and are on guard against being labeled or judged. They fear letting go of emotional control and expressing vulnerable feelings. If they cry during the therapy situation, they feel exposed and vulnerable. Exploring the transference after emotional catharsis would be important. These individuals anticipate being criticized, so they tend to make requests as a demand, which can incite the therapist's defensiveness. These individuals are able to verbalize how disappointed they feel with someone; but, inherent in this reaction, is judgmental and subtle blame due to the inability to directly verbalize their anger.

THERAPEUTIC FEEDBACK LANGUAGE

Your profile suggests that you are currently feeling trapped in some situation you see as difficult, even impossible. You feel angry, hurt, and even bitter that you are in this situation, but you do not know how to get out of it. You feel this entrapping situation is due to other people who are treating you unfairly, even cruelly. You are experiencing some symptoms of depression, feeling sad, unhappy, perhaps with lowered energy and difficulties with concentration, memory, and general efficiency. You feel others may judge you as "too sensitive" because you take things personally and get your feelings hurt. There is nothing wrong with being sensitive. However, currently you may be feeling easily knocked off balance by what people say to you, how they look at you, and feel that you are being judged by others. Sometimes people with your profile grew up in environments where parents were unreasonably critical and demanding. You may have learned to withdraw, stay quiet, and protect yourself by not talking, because to defend yourself would lead to being even more criticized and judged. Now, when you are angry you may withdraw into silences that others find frustrating. You may find yourself constantly attempting to analyze whether what you've said or done is reasonable and above criticism. It may be hard for you to express anger and resentment because you do not want to be attacked or criticized for doing so. Consequently you may store resentments and then, when you feel justified, express them in an outburst of hurt and anger. At other times you may stay silent, refusing to talk about things in case it leaves you vulnerable to being mistreated. Your therapist may want to suggest medication to help with some of the symptoms of depression, to sleep more, and to feel more efficient and energetic. Learn to ask for what you want and do not wait until you "deserve it," by which time you feel angry and resentful. Explore with your therapist any memories of feeling hopelessly trapped in a situation that was not of your making. Role-play with your therapist standing up for yourself so that you can experience what that feels like. Learning to relax and be mindful of what you are feeling could also be useful.

27/72 Codes

This codetype is best described as an anxious or agitated depression. It is a common codetype reflecting a hyper-responsible, prone to worry, constantly on edge, and apprehensive individual whose symptoms and complaints involve tension, depression, nervousness, anxiety, guilt, and self-devaluation. The 27 individual is painfully introspective, ruminating about his or her failings. These individuals feel inadequate, lack self-confidence, and thus are less efficient at work. They suffer from insomnia and are easily fatigued. They focus on their deficiencies, even though many are highly accomplished. As children they followed the rules and were almost never in trouble with authority. They feel obligated to take on responsibilities and then feel overwhelmed by them. Somatic complaints are common because of their high level of internal stress, even without elevations on Scale 1. They anticipate problems before they occur, but tend to panic, catastrophize, and overreact to even minor stresses. During such times they can become highly clinging and dependent, seeking reassurance at the same time as feeling guilty and unworthy of being loved. The profile reflects a defense against unpredictable loss by constantly scanning their world for danger, and rehearsing how they might deal with it. Often they develop rigid attitudes about the right and wrong way of doing things, which is heightened if Scale *L* is elevated. Internal conflicts around sexuality and fears of sexual dysfunction are common because of the person's high level of self-monitoring and fears of failure. These individuals cannot express anger directly and feel guilt whenever they assert themselves.

Work problems are common because the 27 individual tends to see every side of an issue and has difficulty making decisions. In intimate relationships, they are dependent and lack assertiveness. They often become depressed when they have overcommitted to too many responsibilities, which they feel obligated to take on. Some have phobic symptomatology. Many are compulsive, meticulous, and perfectionistic. Quick to feel guilty and self-blaming, they are slow to celebrate their accomplishments. Paradoxically, scholastic history is often average or better, though rarely below average. A high percentage of 27/72 individuals obtain a college education, and few ever act out in aggressive ways.

Suicidal ideation, however, is common, and attempts are a real possibility. This is particularly true if Scales 8 and 9 are elevated and Scale 1 and the *K* scale are low.

TREATMENT

This is one of the most prognostically favorable codetypes because these individuals are compulsive, perfectionistic, and responsible. They follow rules, feel guilty if they do not do what they are told, and are introspective. High elevations suggest a high degree of agitation, which can benefit from relaxation training and thought stopping. However, antidepressant, anti-anxiety medications may be the most efficient way to provide the 27 individual with a sense of control. Suicidal threats should be taken seriously, especially if drug abuse is present.

Early childhood histories are often associated with high levels of responsibility and a lack of age-appropriate carefreeness. A recent overload of responsibilities is often the precipitating event for a 27/72 depressive episode. Depression is also precipitated when the 27/72 individual feels that he/she have let someone down and somehow failed others.

Relaxation training, implosion therapy around fears of failure, and techniques to help them verbalize anger can be useful. Antidepressant, anti-anxiety medication, cognitive restructuring to help them turn off negative thoughts, and teaching them to switch off catastrophizing can also be useful. Help them develop a sense of empathy for themselves as highly responsible children and help them to realize how their guilt is a manifestation of their fear that they will be abandoned by loved ones unless they are perfect. Help them learn to verbalize anger towards their childhood situation, rather than at a specific parental figure, as a way of getting around their tendency to feel guilty if they express anger towards a loved one. Help them set realistic goals so that they do not overcommit. Teaching them to manage guilt through cognitive restructuring and thought stopping is important.

THERAPEUTIC FEEDBACK LANGUAGE

Your profile suggests you are a dutiful, responsible, serious individual who tends to take on too many tasks and responsibilities. People with your profile often grew up in environments where they were expected to be highly responsible at a young age. No wonder you learned to worry, think ahead, and try to anticipate all possible eventualities. Now you're going through life always analyzing almost every situation, trying to predict what can go wrong, and protect yourself against the guilt you feel when they do so. You push yourself to take on responsibilities and feel guilty if you relax or pat yourself on the back for a job most would consider well done. No wonder you wear yourself out. Your profile suggests that you may experience a constant sense of anxiety, like having butterflies in the stomach, which interferes with you relaxing and thinking clearly, and perhaps sleeping. You may have difficulties with memory and concentration, and difficulty making decisions, because you see every side of every issue. Your therapist may want to suggest medication to help you feel better, to sleep more deeply, and to be able to think without so many internal interruptions. Medication may also help you with your anxiety. Discuss with your therapist your childhood experiences of feeling that you had to be especially responsible and dutiful. Rehearse moments of patting yourself on the back for some accomplishment. Pay attention to what that feels like and watch to see if you allow yourself to experience self-praise, or if you interrupt those thoughts with minimization or guilt. Learn cognitive behavioral techniques to switch off anxiety and guilt, imagining that they are like a faulty smoke detector that you have to sometimes ignore. Learn to be more assertive so that you can say "no" to people in order to avoid overcommitting yourself and taking on too many responsibilities, without experiencing guilt afterwards for doing so.

273/723 Codes

The addition of Scale 3 to the 27 codetype adds repression, denial, and a smiling niceness, reflecting hunger for approval and the avoidance of rejection. A 27 individual is anxious, fearful, guilty, and expresses it by being constantly over-responsible. The 273 individual is highly agreeable and self-sacrificing, smiling even through tears, eliciting positive responses from others by role-playing and fitting into others' expectations. 273 individuals are fearful of being emotionally abandoned and of having people angry and disappointed in them. Consequently their attachment style is both ingratiating and hyper-responsible, and subtly guilt-inducing. However, this constant high drive state creates physical stress, which can be manifested somatically, even if Scale 1 is not significantly elevated. They set high standards for themselves, are easily persuaded and controlled by others, and highly dependent. They can often be co-dependent because of their high needs for emotional connection and reassurance. Their niceness and, when stressed, helplessness and self-deprecating attitudes, prompt others to want to protect them and give them advice. Sexual inhibition and guilt, together with unconscious seductiveness, may lead to marital difficulties. These individuals tend to be somewhat naïve and immature as well as dutiful and self-sacrificing. They go through life anticipating and preempting others' anger, and predicting possible reasons they may be rejected. As a defense, they try to placate and take care of others, inducing guilt by their self-sacrifices. They often settle with partners who are more dysfunctional than they are and become co-dependent caretakers.

TREATMENT

The addition of Scale 3 predicts repression, denial, need for reassurance, and lack of insight as well as the anxiety and depressive symptoms associated with 27 elevations. The recounting of painful events can create such anxiety that the individual may experience episodes of panic, fainting, or other somatic manifestations of emotional overload that interrupts the clinical interview. At the same time, "flights into health" are common after brief psychotherapy once a particular issue has been temporarily resolved. They return to therapy when anxiety reoccurs. These individuals lack emotional self-awareness, especially around anger and sadness. They respond well to a nurturing, non-aggressive, non-pushy therapist who takes the role of a supportive parent, viewing them as agreeable children traumatized by unpredictable catastrophic events. Help them engage self-empathy and catharsis, by exploring how repressing emotions and being "brave" was an adaptive response to overloads of emotional pain. Their transference tends to involve fearing the therapist is impatient or angry over their lack of progress. Cognitive therapy to help them recognize "reasonable" anger and rehearsing expressing it in therapy are useful. Assertiveness training and teaching self-soothing when flooded with anxiety is also helpful. Once trust and some emotional control have developed, implosion therapy can teach them anxiety control. Thought stopping, cognitive behavioral techniques, and relaxation training are all useful.

THERAPEUTIC FEEDBACK LANGUAGE

Your profile suggests that you are a dutiful, responsible, and agreeable person who avoids conflict. You'll go the extra mile to understand somebody else's perspective and meet their needs. People with your profile often experienced unpredictable anger or some other kind of unpredictable, painful losses growing up. From an early age you had to be brave, to be "a good soldier," and not let yourself feel in order to avoid more unbearable emotional pain and not upset those around you. Smiling through your difficulties and constantly rehearsing how you "should be" in order to please others have now become a pattern of behavior for you. You might find yourself taking care of others and nurturing people around you, even when they take advantage of you or try to control you. Sometimes people with your profile literally smile through their tears as they try to be nice to others, to be hyper-responsible, and in the process, not take enough care of themselves. Your therapist may suggest medication to help with some of the symptoms of depression such as sleeplessness, fatigue, physical symptoms, and anxiety. At the same time it might be useful to explore childhood moments when you felt overwhelmed by emotional pain and you had to numb yourself and smile through things. Learn to assert yourself and recognize when being angry can be reasonable so that you are able to set boundaries with people and not let them take advantage of you. Learn to stop some of your guilty thoughts and not take on too many responsibilities. Whenever your physical symptoms increase, examine whether you are experiencing stress or whether you need to express some resentment or anger toward others that you feel guilty expressing.

274/724 Codes

This codetype reflects the impulsive (high Scale 4) and, at times, self-defeating reduction of tension associated with elevations on Scales 2 and 7. These individuals act out when they are anxious, needy, bored, or emotionally unsettled. The codetype reflects a learned pattern of immediate tension reduction because childhood experiences of being soothed by caretakers were based on the caretaker's needs, not the child's needs. Anxious and needy of reassurance, insecure and anticipating emotional abandonment, they experience approach-avoidance conflicts in their primary relationships. This reflects their experience with a caretaker who would be unpredictably available and unpredictably abandoning. They do not trust that others will be emotionally available and, because of anxiety and immaturity, they make poor attachment decisions. They become tense and quickly overwhelmed; they self-soothe by acting out impulsively and, consequently, self-defeatingly—if not self-destructively. After acting out, they may feel profound guilt and invite others to rescue and reassure them. Anxiety, worry, and depression are characteristic, and are typically combined with feelings of inadequacy, low self-confidence, and of being a failure. They show exaggerated self-criticism whenever things go wrong, which undermines others' anger, but also elicits reassurance. The 24 codetype predicts self-defeating, impulsive depression, whereas the 27 codetype predicts hyper-responsible, goal-directed proneness to worry, and feelings of inadequacy. This combination of elevations portrays an individual who compulsively worries and seeks reassurance, but is unable to trust it when it is given; they then act out, feel guilty, and seek further reassurance.

Fears and phobias may be present, and the 274 individual tends to overreact to minor issues. They complain of depression, with sad moods and difficulties with sleep and general efficiency. They are high-strung, jumpy, and easily fatigued. They want to be taken care of, but distrust it when given, and easily feel trapped by the dependencies they create. They have strong needs for attention and many exhibit somatic symptoms.

Men with this profile often have histories of being emotionally rescued by their mothers and tend to replicate this pattern in adult relationships. Though seeking such dependent relationships, at the same time they resent the control that comes with them. Often they seek older, motherly partners. Women with this profile have often had close relations with their fathers, who tended to indulge them, but also unpredictably withdraw from them. These women often seek older, nurturing males and, reflecting their needs for closeness and yet fears of being controlled, many have affairs with married men. Substance abuse is common with this codetype, as one would expect with their needs for impulsive tension reduction.

TREATMENT

Usually, the precipitating event is the perceived loss of a nurturing, supportive parental figure. These individuals need a great deal of reassurance, but as expected with Scale 4 elevations, they tend not to trust it when given. Insight therapy could be useful in helping them understand how early childhood experiences of unpredictable parental withdrawal could have led them to develop the adaptive defense of constantly anticipating rejection and therefore regularly seeking reassurance. As children, few had severe behavioral problems. Many of them are the youngest siblings. Therapy should focus on helping them to identify when stress is accumulating and then rehearsing tension-reducing behaviors rather than impulsive self-defeating ones. Help them to see how they tend to panic over minor stresses and act out. Rehearse new coping strategies for stressful situations. Relaxation training, thought stopping, mindfulness therapy, and exercise can all be useful in giving them a sense of control as well as reducing anxiety.

In therapy, revisit childhood experiences of unpredictable emotional abandonment and moments when they experienced high levels of anxiety with no one to turn to. Helping them to learn self-soothing techniques in the face of panic and anxieties would be important.

THERAPEUTIC FEEDBACK LANGUAGE

Your profile shows that you are currently suffering from a high level of anxiety and worry. It is as if you're going through life constantly on edge, examining every possible situation for how it could go wrong and lead to unpredictable abandonment by the people you love. People with your profile grew up in environments where a parent was both highly protective and very involved in taking care of you, but at the same time unpredictable and occasionally abandoning you emotionally. From an early age you were never quite sure whether you could trust that your needs would be taken care of. Consequently you were always a little anxious, always feeling as if something bad was about to happen, and never quite feeling comfortable that you could relax and switch off your anticipatory worry. Now you're going through life often on edge, analyzing every situation and worrying that something bad is about to happen. As tension accumulates, you likely do something impulsive to feel better, which ends up backfiring and making you feel guilty. You want to feel close and connected to others, but at the same time you're afraid that if you trust and let down your guard, others will abandon you or attempt to control you in ways that do not help you feel safe. Consequently you find ways to be close to others, but at the same time you push them away, perhaps in your mind, because you're afraid that you're going to be controlled. If someone cares for you, it makes you wonder if you're good enough, like the famous quip about not wanting to be in a club that accepts you. You might find yourself manipulating others subtly in order to take care of you, but then pushing them away when they get close. You probably suffer from a constant sense of anxiety, as if you do not feel safe in the world. Your therapist may suggest medication to help you feel better. Sleep, concentration, memory, sex drive, and appetite may all be affected by your high level of anxiety and resulting feelings of exhaustion. Work at controlling your guilty feelings and switching them off when they are inappropriate. Rehearse with your therapist ways you can deal with anxiety and panic attacks so you do not act impulsively and later regret it. Work with your therapist on identifying times in your childhood when you felt alone and overwhelmed by anxiety, with no one to turn to. Develop some empathy for yourself as a child so that you can learn ways to soothe yourself rather than relying on being manipulative or impulsive.

275/725 (for Men) and 27, Low 5 (for Women) Codes

The addition of an elevation on Scale 5 for men, or a low Scale 5 for women, suggests increased difficulties with assertiveness and exaggerates the passivity evidenced by the 27/72 codetype. The sensitivity, fussiness, and awareness of interpersonal relationships associated with Scale 5 elevations aggravate the introspective, depressive qualities of the 27 codetype. These individuals feel they are a failure, are quick to describe themselves as inferior, and they feel guilty and inadequate. They extol others' virtues at their own expense, their submissiveness perhaps serving as a defense against others' aggression. If Scale 4 is low, they are even less assertive, and exhibit low sex drive and an even greater adherence to rules and regulations than is typical with the 27/72 codetype. It is as if these individuals are continually maintaining control over the onset of unpredictable criticism by creating relationships in which they are belittled. Sexual difficulties because of performance anxiety are common.

TREATMENT (SEE TREATMENT SECTION UNDER THE 27/72 CODETYPES)

The addition of Scale 5 for men suggests an even greater need for assertiveness training and self-esteem building. Cognitive therapy could focus on their tendency to overanalyze their interpersonal relations to the point of being immobilized by their negative introspections. Sex therapy can be an avenue to help them learn the pleasure others can experience when they are absorbed in their own sexuality.

THERAPEUTIC FEEDBACK LANGUAGE

Your profile suggests that you are a very dutiful, responsible, and prone to worry individual who dislikes conflict and tries to solve interpersonal problems by being analytical and understanding of others. However, you may hang back and not assert yourself because of not wanting others to feel in any way pushed or bullied. You are a perceptive, artistically inclined person who tends to be philosophical, thoughtful, and creative. Your deep sense of empathy may hinder you in enjoying occasional moments of self-indulgence even though others would find it rewarding to please you. (See 27/72 codetype for further feedback.)

278/728 Codes

The addition of Scale 8 to the 27/72 codetype predicts an individual who has experienced damage to their self-esteem. 278 individuals are anxious, worried, tense, and insecure, with ruminations that tend to be morbid, reflecting a basic fear that they are damaged and unlovable. They report feeling tense, anxious, depressed, and filled with self-doubt. They are constant worriers who chronically feel "a day late and a dollar short," a sense of urgency and impending doom. Many exhibit fears or phobias. They feel nervous and exhibit signs of anxiety. Sleep, concentration and memory difficulties, decreased sex drive, weight problems, and general inefficiency are typical. They feel hopeless and report difficulty in thinking, concentration, and memory. They tend to ruminate constantly, analyzing their own and others' behaviors, anticipating humiliating rejection. Suicidal thoughts, suicidal attempts, and a history of previous psychiatric hospitalizations are common. Insomnia, obsessive thinking, somatic preoccupation, fears, and phobias are also common. These individuals constantly analyze their weaknesses and vulnerabilities. Inelegantly, but descriptively, they can be described as psychological "scab pickers." Some exhibit meticulous and perfectionistic traits, and set unreasonably high standards for themselves. They feel intense guilt when they fail to meet their standards. Under the stress of anticipated failure, the 278 individual can become so cognitively disorganized by their "internal noise" that they are unable to function efficiently. Others may erroneously judge them as lazy because they are so inefficient, but their inertia reflects their psychological overload. Using a computer analogy, it is as if "all their windows" are simultaneously open so that they are overloaded with fragments of thoughts, but without any coherent cognitive stream. Excessive punitive introspection and self-criticism contribute to their difficulties with concentration and performance, which in turn aggravates their anxiety and depression.

Histories of personal isolation and withdrawal are typical. They have difficulty making emotional commitments, and tend to focus on the negative details of their relationships, analyzing what's wrong with their mate and oscillating between profound fear of rejection and fears that they are trapped with someone who must be defective if they feel love towards the 278 individual.

Suicide is a possibility as this codetype is most commonly associated with successful suicide. This is especially true if Scale 4 is coded fourth. If Scale 0 is elevated, the depression, social withdrawal, and insecurity are exacerbated by shyness and feelings of physical inferiority. If Scale 4 is below 60, passivity and submissiveness are also exaggerated, with an accompanying reduction of sexual interests. Women with 278/728 codetypes with low *T*-scores on Scale 5 will exhibit passivity to the point that they allow others to abuse them. They may complain of headaches, backaches, and sexual and intimacy problems.

TREATMENT

This codetype predicts a pervasive unhappiness and anhedonia, though palpable sadness may not be apparent to the therapist because the 278 presents as flat, almost emotionally numb, and disconnected. Because they see every side of an issue, they are highly ambivalent, and often immobilized by even small decisions. This can lead to "analysis paralysis" without any real behavioral change. Continual blunting of expressions of affect, along with difficulty dealing with emotional intimacy, leads them to have relationship problems. The observing ego tends to control them because they are so painfully self-conscious. Consequently, Gestalt therapies are particularly useful because the role-playing involved provides an opportunity for the patient to vent feelings. Taking an acting class that allows them to feel, but "feel through" somebody else's eyes may give them some relief from bottled up feelings and feelings of depersonalization. They fear being "in the moment" because they anticipate that switching off the observing ego will lead to unpredictable, humiliating emotional abandonment.

They have a fixed, negative self-image, which makes therapy difficult. Introspective insight therapies are contraindicated because of the 278 individual's tendency to intellectualize. Look for childhood experiences of feeling overwhelmed by panic anxiety with the absence of a reliable caretaker. In some cases, sexual abuse and emotional and physical abandonment are associated with this codetype. Many 278 individuals have been "only" children. Thirty-five percent of the Marks et al. (1974) sample reported deaths in the immediate family, and many reported a serious physical illness in their childhood home; 15 percent of fathers and 20 percent of mothers were sick, and 25 percent of 278s reported serious illness during their childhood. It is understandable that, as an adaptive response, they became constantly on edge, scanning the environment for danger, preparing "for the other shoe to drop." The constant edgy vigilance tends to exact a toll on their immune systems.

Interestingly, 50 percent of the Marks et al. (1974) sample reported extramarital relationships. These individuals tend to be as critical of their spouses as they are of themselves, reflecting their low self-esteem. Assertiveness training, self-esteem building, and warm, supportive, motherly type reparenting therapies can be useful therapeutic modalities. Many individuals with this codetype are diagnosed as borderline, especially when Scale 4 is elevated, but diagnoses of endogenous depression, both unipolar and bipolar, and undifferentiated schizophrenia are also common. They typically develop peculiar and esoteric personal philosophies, perhaps as a way of finding unique meaning in their lives.

THERAPEUTIC FEEDBACK LANGUAGE

Your profile suggests that you are a very analytical individual. You tend to go through life constantly observing, as if watching yourself in a movie. It is hard for you to turn off your observing self to be spontaneous and in the moment because you're always waiting for something bad to happen. It is similar to a computer freezing because too many windows are open simultaneously. The profile suggests that you are going through life as if you have "too many windows" open inside your mind, so you're seeing every side of every issue. It is as if you can't allow yourself a single train of thought without being interrupted by many competing thoughts. It is hard for you to relax and to enjoy being in the moment. It is also hard for you to enjoy your accomplishments as you are always ready to be your own worst critic. This is exhausting and leaves you feeling depressed, sad, and hopelessly defeated. Making decisions is difficult because you see all the things that could possibly go wrong so that often, even though you're anxious and worried, you can be highly inefficient and get little done. Getting going and feeling motivated is difficult. Growing up you may have felt unsafe, perhaps because of parental illness or because your parents could be unpredictably cold and emotionally withdrawn. To adapt, you developed a constant vigilance for what can go wrong, and were constantly self-critical, to make sure you never took anything for granted. It is as if you protect yourself against ever getting hopeful and enjoying the moment, because to do so would risk getting disappointed. Your therapist may suggest medication to help you sleep better, to feel more energized and rested, and help you to concentrate and think more clearly. Develop some empathy for yourself as a child who felt overwhelmed. Learn to switch off guilty thoughts and learn ways to assert yourself, asking for what you want even though you may often be confused about your own wishes. Talk to your therapist about how you feel toward him or her and discuss how hard it is for you to switch off the part of you that is always observing and self-critical, and expecting your therapist to be critical of you.

28/82 Codes

This codetype reflects severe depression, social withdrawal, and agitation, difficulties with concentration, thinking, and memory, and preoccupations with being hopelessly damaged. Sometimes this profile reflects a psychotic depression. A primary complaint for the 28/82 individual is forgetfulness and difficulties with concentration, with some reporting fears that they are "losing their mind." Cognitive impairment due to depression is often the primary complaint.

These individuals seem tense and jumpy, and they keep others at a distance. They are highly inefficient in making and carrying out plans, and may develop peculiar esoteric beliefs. Suicidal thoughts are likely. 28 individuals are extremely fearful of interpersonal intimacy and many report somatic symptoms. Problems with sleep and being easily fatigued are typical. These individuals have conflicts about emotional dependency and sexuality.

TREATMENT

Typical histories involve repeated hurts by emotional abandonment and neglect in childhood. Many adults marry after a brief courtship. Early childhood histories suggest disruption, with mental illness, in the family of origin. Look for childhood histories where they experienced hostile neglect. Sexual problems are typical because of their fears of emotional closeness.

A therapeutic relationship is hard to develop with the 28 individual because they feel broken, damaged, and unlovable, even by the therapist. They have a great deal of difficulty thinking clearly and therapy can be punctuated by long periods of silence. During these periods they are not actively processing or thinking coherently, but typically are shut down. Antidepressant medications are recommended, although these should be used in small doses, as the 28 individual is vulnerable to feeling easily knocked off balance. The 28 individual feels hopelessly defective, so reparenting, nurturing therapies are most effective. A number of initial sessions should be around rapport building, and the therapist should encourage trust by occasionally sharing his or her own vulnerabilities. 28 individuals often exhibit a long history of emotional hurt, and their adaptive response is to withdraw, shut down, and avoid emotional risks. Too much uncovering therapy is contraindicated because these individuals exhibit fragile self-esteem, which leads to them interpreting therapist insights as overwhelming criticism. Psychotherapy should be structured and concrete, using relaxation training, thought stopping, and cognitive behavioral techniques that allow the patient to maintain feelings of control, with rehearsal strategies to deal with their interpersonal anxiety. After trust is developed, insight therapy to help them develop a sense of empathy for themselves as emotionally wounded or hurt children can be effective, although the therapist should be careful to avoid the patient seeing these insights as confirming that they are hopelessly damaged due to their history. Some individuals with 28/82 codetype can manifest psychotic and even schizophrenic features. When appropriate, antipsychotic medications should be considered.

THERAPEUTIC FEEDBACK LANGUAGE

Your profile suggests that you are a very thoughtful, analytical person who tends to withdraw when confronted with severe stress. Currently, you seem to have withdrawn into yourself and you're feeling less happy, positive, and optimistic then you would like to be. It is hard for you to enjoy much, and when others try to engage you or try to get you to do something positive, you feel apathetic and low energy. It appears that it is hard right now for you to get your thinking straight and you may experience feelings that your mind is foggy, so it is hard to remember and to make decisions. You may find yourself numb and feeling empty, even in moments when others would expect you to feel positive or even joyful. You may find yourself moving slowly and at times being inefficient and not getting things accomplished. You tend to be your own worst critic and currently you're feeling bad about yourself, feeling you're unlovable, and even worthless. It is hard to have hope and feel positive. Concentrating may be particularly difficult at this time. You may find yourself easily feeling guilty and thinking about past mistakes and what a bad person you are. You may have a number of physical symptoms of stress, and you might even feel that there is something really, basically, wrong with you. It is hard to open up to people, especially strangers, and it is hard for you let people get close to you because you're afraid of being hurt. No wonder you may at times feel irritable and easily angered. Sometimes people with your profile grew up in environments where a parent was cold or even coldly cruel. From an early age, you likely learned to withdraw as a way of protecting yourself. Currently, someone you felt close to may have withdrawn from you, possibly reawakening those feelings that you are damaged and unlovable, and that the future is hopeless. You may even think about dying because life feels no longer worthwhile. It is important that you discuss these feelings with your therapist. It may be hard for you to trust your therapist and, at times, you may feel lost for words in the therapy session. Find ways to switch off negative thoughts and work with your therapist on ways to assert yourself with others. Create a list of things that might make you feel better and force yourself to get one or two of those things done, even though you may lack the motivation to do so. Your therapist may also suggest some medicine so that you can sleep better, feel more rested, think more clearly, and have more energy.

281/821 Codes

In addition to the symptoms and traits associated with the 28/82 codetype, the 281 individual is likely to complain of numerous somatic complaints that may predominate over depression complaints. Usually, these somatic complaints are rather vague and medically atypical, as one would expect with the elevation on Scale 8. Tremors, temporary losses of vision, vague numbness, paresthesia, and even somatic delusions can be present. These delusions may reflect a psychotic depression since the physical symptoms are atypical, if not implausible, but the person may not show any other obvious psychotic disturbance. These somatic preoccupations may be an attempt to defend against a more florid outbreak of psychosis.

If Scale 3 is also elevated, then the hysterical defenses associated with that scale mask the depth of the depression. The 1283 individual can exhibit 13 characteristics, with periods of smiling and crying, attempts to engage others into caretaking behavior, but also odd preoccupations and approach-avoidance conflicts in relationships.

TREATMENT (SEE 12 /21AND 28/82 TREATMENT SECTIONS)

Although the addition of Scale 1 may decrease the possibility of suicide, this effect is not robust enough to ignore the suicide items on the MMPI-2. As in all depression profiles, the potential for suicide is a risk to consider. The 281 individual may complain of side effects of any medications administered, so they should be given in small doses until the patient feels a sense of control. Antidepressant/antipsychotic medications may diminish the somatic delusions. Treatment should be similar to the 28 individual, but could also use Gestalt techniques to explore what unconscious conflicts are being expressed through the somatic symptoms.

THERAPEUTIC FEEDBACK LANGUAGE

See feedback for the 28/82 codetype. Your profile also suggests that you are experiencing a number of physical symptoms that may be quite concerning to you. These symptoms may come and go, increasing when you are stressed. At times, you may be preoccupied with physical symptoms of decline, wondering whether you are physically suffering from some severe and debilitating disease. You may find yourself thinking about disease, death, and decline, and even researching your symptoms, feeling a sense of panic about their implications. Some of these symptoms may be related to your current depression.

284/824 Codes

In addition to the 28/82 symptoms and complaints, the elevation of Scale 4 adds feelings of distrust, alienation, and a tendency to act out under stress. Individuals with these elevations act out in ways that can appear senseless and self-defeating. Sometimes the anger is turned against themselves and sometimes against others. Suicidal and self-destructive behavior is typical, and often these individuals self-medicate to deal with their anhedonia and sense of emotional disconnectedness from others. They tend to be quite impulsive, and sometimes act aggressively, towards others or themselves—especially if they feel humiliated or rejected.

The elevation on Scale 2 can act as a suppressor of antisocial acting out predicted by the Scale 4 elevation. However, when acting out does occur, it is often impulsive, poorly thought through, and sometimes bizarrely sexual, and even incomprehensible. Because these individuals are afraid of emotional involvement with others, they experience internal conflicts about sexuality and may combine and confuse sexuality and aggression. Social and marital maladjustment is typical. In some adults, this code is associated with schizoid or schizophrenic conditions, and in these cases the *F* scale is usually elevated. (If Scale 4 is within five *T*-score points of Scale 2 or 8, see the interpretation of the 482/842 codetype.) Though paranoia may be present, it is less of a fixed, rational kind and more of a diffuse sense that the world is crumbling and that people cannot be trusted. In adolescents, this code may not represent the enduring pathology indicated for adults. Instead, this code may reflect the sullen rebelliousness and alienation from social groups that is found in some adolescents, and may reflect a more situational depression. Nevertheless, poor impulse control, self-destructive and self-defeating behavior, and mental inefficiency would be present. Even if the *MAC–R* scale is not elevated above a raw score of 26, individuals with this codetype often self-medicate.

TREATMENT

In some cases, the 284/824 codetype reflects an individual who manifests a 48/84 codetype personality, but has recently become involved in a legal difficulty or difficulties with authority figures because of acting out. Their depression score is elevated because they feel trapped and bitter about their current situation. Once the situation has been resolved, these individuals continue to manifest more 48 characteristics without the depression. In other cases, this represents a stable personality pattern with chronic interpersonal difficulties, self-defeating, self-destructive behavior, profound alienation, and distrust of others. A history of rebellious, senseless, acting-out behavior would suggest a 48/84 profile with Scale 2 recently elevated if the individual is suffering from the consequences of their behavior. Antidepressant/antipsychotic medications would be less effective if the depression reflects a transitory disturbance due to acting-out behavior.

In either case, trust is a central issue for people with this codetype. The codetype reflects an individual who has experienced multiple blows to their sense of identity. Consequently, they are described as angry, alienated individuals who are cynical and lack empathy. Although these individuals are cautious about emotional ties, they also have an exaggerated need for affection. Some are diagnosed as psychotic with paranoid features, yet many do not evidence a gross or florid thought disorder. Look for childhood histories of caregiver rejection and even cruelty. In the Marks et al. (1974) sample, none reported affectionate parents. A large proportion of their sample was illegitimate and many experienced behavior problems throughout their school careers.

Conceptually, this codetype reflects the "unwanted, unloved child," with resulting craving for affection, yet a lack of trust when it is given. Consequently, they alternate between feelings of numb emptiness and episodic anger and demandingness. Reparenting, supportive therapies are usually required. These individuals have difficulty trusting the therapist and they put the therapist through "trust tests." Working on the transference is an important component of therapy. When the patient starts to cancel sessions, it is usually an indication that the intensity of the therapy is overwhelming or they are feeling the therapist "doesn't care" about them. The 284 thinks people "wear masks" and are untrustworthy, perhaps a projection of their own manipulativeness and role-playing. Behavioral techniques to help them control impulsive, self-defeating, and self-destructive behavior can be effective. Mindfulness therapy and dialectical behavior therapy can be helpful to relearn how to allow themselves to experience emotions and to label and express those emotions to others without being destructive. Rehearse ways to find emotional rewards rather than turning toward chemical agents. Though these individuals act out sexually, they tend to report little emotional satisfaction from sexuality.

THERAPEUTIC FEEDBACK LANGUAGE

Your profile suggests that you are currently somewhat trapped, down, and unhappy, so that little in life gives you pleasure. You may feel a sense of hopelessness and you may even think about dying as way of escaping. There are periods where you feel so alone and angry that you may act in self-defeating and self-destructive ways. At other times you may feel angry with others and the world in general, and you may give up and do things that get you into trouble. Sometimes people with your profile grow up with parents who were rejecting, cold, and even cruel. From an early age you learned to withdraw and to protect yourself by keeping up an emotional wall. You may now anticipate that people close to you are going to reject you and treat you cruelly. You may be demanding of others, wanting them to prove that they are trustworthy because you have been so badly hurt in the past. However, even if they do give you reason to trust them, it is hard for you to do so. At times you may feel a sense of anxiety, as if the world is a very unsafe place. At these times it may be especially hard to trust others, and you may feel that people are wearing "masks," so it is hard for you to read them and know what they are truly thinking and feeling. Your therapist may want to give you some medication to help you sleep better and feel less anxious and more rested. Medicine may help you have a clearer mind so that you can remember, concentrate, and problem solve more efficiently. Be careful not to use non-prescribed chemical agents as a way to feel better. Sometimes your sense of emptiness can be so strong that you turn to drugs and/or alcohol or perhaps sexual behavior or some other self-destructive behavior in order to feel alive. Rehearse with your therapist how you can manage stress better, anticipating the kinds of things that knock you off balance, so you do not act out in self-defeating ways. Mindfulness therapy will help you recognize and label your emotions. Learning to trust others will also be helpful.

287/827 Codes

The interpretation is similar to the 278/728 codetype, although there are some differences. The coding of Scale 8 first or second, rather than third, predicts more identity damage, alienation, and confusion, and increases the likelihood of a depression, psychotic, or borderline diagnosis. Persons with this codetype manifest depression and anxiety, but also more severe thought disturbances, with tangential and circumstantial thinking, and even more sensitivity to criticism and general distrust of others. They almost always show significant cognitive impairments, reporting concentration difficulties, confusion, insomnia, and general inefficiency. Adjustment is marginal at best. Numerous physical symptoms are also likely manifested. Labile and inappropriate emotions and even hallucinations or a thought disorder may be present. These individuals are very cautious about becoming emotionally involved with others and fear abandonment, so they maintain emotional distance. They are intensely moody and others find their moods hard to predict. Sexuality is almost always disturbed.

Suicidal thoughts, preoccupations, and verbalizations are likely. If the K scale is below a T-score of 50, and if Scales 9 and 4 are also elevated, the likelihood of self-destructive impulsiveness increases. Suicides that do occur are often poorly thought through and sometimes expressed in unusual or even bizarre ways.

TREATMENT (SEE TREATMENT SECTION UNDER THE 278/728 CODETYPE FOR RECOMMENDATIONS)

The individual experiences a damaged identity and so has difficulty with the trust and emotional closeness needed for a therapeutic relationship. Look for childhood histories similar to the 278/728 individual, with emotional withdrawal, humiliation, rejection, teasing, and putdowns, as well as cruelty from primary caretakers. Some individuals exhibited eccentricities and were slow to mature as children. The individual likely suffers from an internalized negative self-image, so that any successes they experience are discounted.

Antidepressant/antipsychotic medications should be considered. Supportive reparenting therapies are suggested. Self-esteem building, thought stopping, assertiveness training, mindfulness therapy, and CBT can all be useful. Insight therapy should be avoided as it can be destabilizing to them.

THERAPEUTIC FEEDBACK LANGUAGE

Use the same feedback as 278 codetype. Currently, you may be experiencing periods of confusion and difficulties focusing and solving problems effectively. It may be hard for you to trust others and you may feel very alone and unable to let your guard down enough to discuss with your therapist how you are feeling. You may have had parents who were cold or even cruel and rejecting. Currently you may be feeling the same sense

298 Interpreting the MMPI-2 Codetypes

of isolation and fearfulness that you experienced as a child. Discuss with your therapist if you are experiencing any loss of will to live and how you can develop techniques to switch off some of your anxiety.

29/92 Codes

This is a rare profile and it most often occurs with individuals diagnosed with bipolar disorder. The 29/92 individual may appear anxious or agitated, and can be mistakenly diagnosed as suffering from an anxiety disorder. However, this codetype suggests mood swings, irritability, and agitation, rather than anxiety. Scale 2 cancels out the euphoria of Scale 9, and Scale 9 modifies the depressive features and sadness associated with Scale 2. The 29 individual is tense, moody, irritable and, at times, grandiose, overly optimistic, and cheerful. In some cases, this profile reflects an individual whose bipolarity is shifting from either depression or mania into its opposite. A clinical history should determine whether the individual has episodes of mania and depression, or whether their codetype reflects a stable, high-strung personality type. During periods where Scale 9 appears to be dominant, they are excitable, positive, and euphoric, but can quickly become angry, upset, and despondent, triggered by small external events. Sometimes the moods can swing rapidly within a short period of time. Others view them as moody, irritable, unstable, and hard to predict. Often they exhibit temper outbursts, and people feel on edge around them. They appear inconsistent, "selling" one idea at a particular moment and then denigrating the same idea in the next. When hypomania is present, it is pressured and forced, while depression is manifested as tense and energized pessimism rather than flat and hopeless. These individuals can be impulsive and overreact to frustration.

Most often, Scale 4 or 3 is the third highest elevation. Three sub-types of 29/92 may obtain this codetype:

1 An individual with an agitated depression marked by overtly depressed behaviors, such as weeping, catastrophizing, depressive rumination, and an obsession with protecting against loss. Look for childhood histories with parents who put a great deal of emphasis on achievement and success.
2 An individual who is attempting to cope with underlying depression, using manic defenses. Grandiose thinking and overcommitment may temporarily mask the underlying depressive symptomotology.
3 This codetype has been associated with organic brain injury/disease. The 29/92 individuals may be aware of their reduced abilities and are attempting to deal with this by overactivity. In the presence of any recent head trauma, neurological and neuropsychological testing is recommended.

TREATMENT

The 29/92 individual is particularly susceptible to self-medication with alcohol. It is important to rule out bipolar disorder or a major depressive episode with agitation. The 29 individual is vulnerable to impulsive suicidal behavior, so monitor the antidepressant medications carefully, as with other depression codetypes. If Scale 4 is elevated, there is likely to be impulsiveness and increased self-defeating behavior. When a 294 individual begins to feel better, they may act out in more reckless ways. If Scale 7 is coded third, there is a great deal of fear of failure, and a tendency to develop compulsive, repetitive behaviors as a defense against anxiety. If Scale 8 is coded third, then the individual manifests an identity panic, with fears of being rejected and deemed as broken and damaged by others. Some of the hypomanic activity may be a defense against a panic resulting from a recent rejection.

Even if the *MAC–R* scale is not elevated, this codetype is associated with chemical addiction and self-medication. Some individuals with this codetype experience blackouts and mood swings while under the influence of chemical agents. Aggressive behavior is likely when intoxicated.

Explore whether the individual has experienced setbacks that led to perceived rejection by loved ones. Helping the individual set realistic goals and using CBT to enable them recognize what kind of events can trigger mood swings can be useful. Helping them learn to anticipate stress and cognitively control their mood shifts, along with relaxation training, self-esteem building, and physical exercise as a way of "burning" off excess energy can also be useful.

THERAPEUTIC FEEDBACK LANGUAGE

Your profile suggests that you are a person who can have moments of high energy, optimism, positive thinking, and productivity. However, it also suggests that small setbacks or perceived frustrations can quickly lead to you becoming down, even depressed, negative, and angry. As an analogy, you are driving through life with one foot on the accelerator, but the other foot on the brake. It is as if you are going through life driven to succeed and achieve, to prove to yourself that you are worthy of being loved, and at the same time you're looking over your shoulder to see how things can go wrong and how you can fail. This internal pressure and these mixed feelings lead to you often feeling extremely tense. Small events can switch your mood from being up and positive to down and negative. You feel your world is somewhat unpredictable and fragile, and you're constantly on edge, trying to predict how to protect against loss. Others may see your mood swings as hard to predict and find your tendency to be high-strung as difficult to deal with, perhaps even irritating.

Some people with your profile use chemical agents as a way to try to regulate their mood. You may experience a constant sense of tension as you approach goals quickly, with lots of energy, and then get defeated and feel hopeless if something goes wrong. Perhaps growing up you felt a great need to achieve and succeed, but you often felt frustrated. You may have felt that no matter what you did it wouldn't be good enough, and you felt vulnerable to losing the love of people you cared about. No wonder you go through life now always a little tense, as if afraid of loss or setback, pushing yourself hard to achieve and succeed. In some cases, your profile suggests a mood instability that may respond well to a mood stabilizing medication. In other situations, people with your profile can learn to manage their mood swings. Work with your therapist to recognize the kinds of events that can trigger your mood swings, usually an event that frightens you, because you see it as potentially catastrophic. Learn to switch off your negative thoughts and recognize when surges of excitability lead you toward overcommitment or being too positive. Avoid chemical agents other than prescription medication. Exercise, mindfulness therapy, and CBT can help you switch off negative thoughts. Should you have had any recent accidents or trauma to the head, your mood swings may be precipitated by the recent physical trauma. It would be important to discuss this with a neurologist.

20/02 Codes

This codetype predicts a socially withdrawn, introverted individual with chronic characterological depression. These individuals may manifest a lifelong genetically predisposed shyness, preferring time alone or with small groups of close friends. Symptoms of depression such as insomnia, guilt, and anxiety are almost always present. Often 20 individuals habituate to their low level of enjoyment of life and accept their condition without complaint. The 20 individual often has a phobia or an aversion to large social gatherings. They often feel physically unattractive and have lost interest in making themselves look appealing to others. Others may view them as somewhat colorless or even plain, and lacking in assertiveness. They avoid attention and are often quite passive and conventional, rarely breaking rules. In some cases, this profile reflects an individual who is genetically shy, but was parented by an emotionally aloof caretaker. Phil Marks (personal communication, 1990) has characterized the 20/02 individual as parented by the equivalent of Harlow's wire monkey (e.g. tactile deprivation). Thus, look for childhood histories in which primary caretakers provided adequate basic needs, but tended not to respond to the child emotionally.

If Scales 4 and 8 are below *T*-65, look for caretakers who were adequate, not hostile or cold, but not solicitous and affectionate. The high 20 individuals have extinguished their need for caretaking, for touch, and for being touched by others. Many report disliking physical signs of caring from others. These individuals may have learned to expect little or no emotional or physical contact from others, and may have habituated to this condition. As caregivers, consequently, they have difficulty providing tactile stimulation to their own offspring.

Typically Scale 7 or 4 is the third highest scale. Common among mothers of children receiving psychological treatment, this codetype is often associated with only moderate improvement in the child's psychological condition. The 20 individual tends to keep others at a distance and fears losing emotional control. They may have habituated to a moderate degree of unhappiness and tend not to complain of depression. They lack self-confidence and may complain of insomnia, low energy, and difficulties with cognitive processing. They feel a chronic sense of guilt. Precipitating circumstances for seeking treatment are usually new social situations, where their difficulty in reaching out to others causes them great stress. Teenagers with this profile are particularly vulnerable to social difficulties.

TREATMENT

A depression is often ego-syntonic for the 20 individual. Typically they have adjusted to a low level of pleasure and usually seek help for a specific problem. Moves, new jobs, and new relationships tend to be stressful for them because of their difficulty engaging in social interaction. Assertiveness training, role-playing, rehearsing how to deal with others, and teaching social skills are helpful. Bibliotherapy is helpful, as there are a number of books now available about introversion and how to deal with it without being self-critical. Insight therapy can help them understand how their desire for tactile contact could have been extinguished by growing up in an environment in which caregivers were caring but not emotionally expressive.

Educating them on the need for physical stimulation toward their own offspring is often important. In some cases, it is useful to help them engage memories of feeling emotionally alone and help them develop empathy for themselves as children who learned to extinguish tactile responding. If the symptoms of depression are severe enough, they may be open to antidepressant medication. These medications should be administered in small doses, as the 20/02 individual has habituated to a low level of emotional richness and can find chemically induced psychological changes highly uncomfortable. Mindfulness therapy can be helpful to increase their level of overall satisfaction. Treatments that focus on skill building tend to be more helpful than warm nurturing therapies, which can make them uncomfortable.

THERAPEUTIC FEEDBACK LANGUAGE

Your profile suggests that you are a thoughtful, circumspect, dutiful individual who tends to follow the rules. You are not an aggressive person or a risk taker. Your profile also suggests that you are somewhat shy. Research shows that shyness is an inherited trait and is not associated with any kind of mental condition. However, shy people can sometimes find transitions such as moves to a new job or neighborhood particularly difficult. You generally enjoy small groups of people you know well rather than large groups of new people. Small talk can be particularly stressful for you, as can being the center of attention or being called on to speak in a group when you're not prepared. Currently, you seem to be experiencing a period of feeling more unhappy and sad then you would like. You might experience difficulty thinking, concentrating, and remembering. You may also experience periods of low energy and difficulties getting going and being efficient. You genuinely dislike conflict and tend to hang back rather than assert yourself. However, you may recently be feeling as if you're losing out, and you may be quick to feel guilty and down on yourself. People with your profile sometimes grow up in environments where a parent was decent and took care of you, but wasn't particularly expressive or affectionate. Now you may be the kind of person who appreciates being cared for, but you may find displays of affection or warmth or praise towards you difficult to handle. Your therapist may suggest medication to help you sleep and feel less depressed. Medication may help you feel more energetic and better able to think clearly and make decisions. Learn to rehearse with your therapist things you can say when you meet new people and ways you can develop more comfortable social skills. Keep a diary of emotions you experience and discuss those emotions with your therapist so that you are better able to express yourself to close friends. Learn to recognize when you are feeling guilty and self-critical and learn to switch off those negative thoughts. Write lists of positive attributes that you like about yourself and read them when you experience periods of despondency and self-dislike.

Scale 3 (Hy)

One defense against intolerable emotionally painful conditions is to deny that they exist. Another approach is to switch the focus of attention away from something painful onto something positive, even in the face of overwhelming pain. Scale 3 measures the intensity and need for such denial and positivization. As Scale 3 is elevated over a *T*-score of 70, denial, remaining positive in the face of pain, and seeking approval from others become a core element of the individual's personality. In some situations, however, elevations on Scale 3 may reflect an individual's current level of stress, perhaps defending against an underlying depression. Scale 3 attributes are generally neurotic and so predict against psychosis, particularly when Scale 3 is one of the two most elevated scales in the profile.

High scores (*T* > 65) suggest that an individual is using repression and denial as a primary defense mechanism. These individuals are usually conforming, somewhat naïve, and can appear immature and self-centered. They also exhibit somatic preoccupations and concerns about physical illness, but generally with an absence of congruent affect. High Scale 3 individuals can appear demanding of attention, affection, approval, and support from others, but they also can be very emotionally giving to others. This reflects their needs to be nurtured and supported. They tend to be active socially and fear abandonment. Consequently, intimacy with others, while highly appealing, is also frightening to them. Because repression and denial are primary defenses, they tend to lack insight into the dynamics that drive their behavior.

Some individuals with high Scale 3 scores may be described as dramatic or exhibitionistic, perhaps reflecting the intensity of their emotional experience. Aggressive acting out is unlikely if Scale 3 is the only scale elevated above *T*-65. Elevations on Scale 3 can be viewed as reflecting an individual's fear of emotional pain. Shifting the focus onto positive events and denying anger and resentment will minimize the possibility of displeasing others and eliciting their rejection or disapproval. Because of strong needs to be liked, high Scale 3 scorers can respond enthusiastically to situations requiring their commitment. However, their difficulty in dealing with conflict and their inability to recognize and express their own resentments and anger can lead to their feeling hurt and unappreciated. Uncomfortable with anger, they tend to express it in passive ways. Lacking self-awareness, they vent their anger through humor and through somatic problems. In other words, their physical symptoms act as a symbolic expression of their underlying conflicts.

A moderately high score (*T*-55–65) on Scale 3 can reflect an individual who is optimistic and positive and could be described by others as agreeable. These individuals are people pleasers who are uncomfortable with conflict. They can develop mild physical symptoms in response to stress, which diminish once the stress has passed.

Individuals with a *T*-score less than 45 can be seen by others as somewhat cynical, although they probably see themselves as grounded and realistic. They may be seen by others as somewhat blunt and even caustic. In a flat profile with an absence of any scale elevation above a *T*-60, a low Scale 3 reflects individuals who see themselves as practical, sensible, and willing to "call a spade a spade." They lack tact, tend not to be complimentary of others, and typically express emotions without embellishment or color. When other scales are significantly elevated, a low Scale 3 score would suggest a painful awareness of emotional distress, with a lack of the potentially positive consequences of repression and denial.

Spike 3

A Spike 3 codetype (i.e. no other clinical scale above *T*-65) predicts a conventional individual who has strong needs to be accepted and liked. These individuals can lack self-assertiveness and dislike confrontations and "making waves." They play the correct social role and are threatened by any loss of social approval. When anger is expressed, it may be done in an inappropriate or impulsive way because it is poorly integrated and breaks through the individual's denial.

Backgrounds associated with a Spike 3 codetype consist of childhood homes that were unhappy, with a parent who could be explosive or episodically rejecting. In other cases, caretakers discouraged the expression of negative affect and emphasized being positive and brave in the face of distress. Because of difficulties with intimacy, the Spike 3 individual may exhibit sexual problems and a tendency to be somewhat dependent.

TREATMENT

Assertiveness training, combined with mindfulness therapy to help the individual learn to recognize negative emotions, can be helpful. Supportive, non-confrontational therapies tend to work best. Explore any past childhood experiences where they had to be "brave" and be "good soldiers" in the face of pain.

THERAPEUTIC FEEDBACK LANGUAGE

Your profile suggests that you are an agreeable individual who likes to please others and that you are a conflict avoider. You tend to see the best in people, sometimes to the point that you can deny negative things about them to your own detriment. Your tendency is to smile, conform to avoid conflict, and not assert yourself. Consequently, tensions can sometimes accumulate and some people with your profile develop physical symptoms. Low back pain, stomach upsets, headaches, episodic dizziness, nausea, and other vague and shifting physical symptoms may reflect stress that accumulates because you are working hard to please and avoid conflict. Perhaps you grew up with a parent that was episodically, frighteningly angry. Perhaps for some other reason you learned to smile, to not see the negative, and to try to focus on the positives. You may have learned from an early age that you had to be brave and soothe yourself with trying to see the positive in any situation. Work with your therapist at learning to recognize when anger or resentment is building. See if any of your physical symptoms could be tied to some frustration that you are denying. Role-play with your therapist how to get angry with someone and see if you can learn to recognize frustration so that you can manage it more effectively.

Relations with Other Scales

Spike 3, High K *Code*

An elevated *K* scale score suggests a greater need to maintain emotional control and to be seen as socially conforming. The elevation on *K* increases the need of high Scale 3 individuals to present themselves as having control over their lives and being socially exemplary. Characteristically, these individuals approach emotional situations with a determined optimism and a "stiff upper lip." They emphasize good relations and harmony with others, and avoid situations in which anger, disruptions, or hurt feelings are involved. They are often tormented when they have to reject or reprimand someone. When anger is eventually expressed, it can appear clumsy, as a breakthrough of strong and determined feelings rather than in accord with the thoughtful sensitivity that they generally exhibit.

TREATMENT

The profile reflects a well-defended, socially engaged individual. Look for childhood conditioning experiences where they were frightened by the intensity of their own emotional response to some situation. Questions such as "Do you remember a time in your life when you felt knocked off balance by the intensity of your emotional response to an event?" may engage them in understanding their discomfort with emotional intensity. Some will describe childhood histories of chaos and catastrophe within the family home, where intense emotionality was frightening to them. However, an opposite history is also possible. Individuals who grew up in homes where the expression of strong emotions and upset was discouraged can also develop a strong sense of socially appropriate, repressed emotionality. Psychotherapeutic techniques such as role-playing anger or sadness can help them become more comfortable with a wider range of emotions. Explore any early rejections or emotional traumas that could have conditioned them to avoid expressing negative emotions.

THERAPEUTIC FEEDBACK LANGUAGE

Your profile suggests that you go through life with a "stiff upper lip" approach to emotions. You are a poised individual who does not lose your head in a crisis. People have to "multiply" the intensity of what you are saying in order to get a sense of empathy for you. If you say that you are "not too happy," you might, in fact, be quite angry or upset. It may be that, from an early age, you learned to control your emotions and express them only in socially appropriate ways. Perhaps the expression of intense emotions was discouraged growing up, or perhaps it would knock you off balance when people became emotionally upset. Work with your therapist to learn how to recognize the full range of your emotions and rehearse ways to express them to others without feeling knocked off balance. Explore any memories of experiencing intense emotions and feeling out of control, or watching someone else express emotions in ways that overwhelmed you.

31 Code (see also 13/31 Codes)

In contrast to the 13 codetype, people with a 31 codetype appear more cheerful in the face of their pain. The pessimistic, negative, defeated qualities evidenced in the 13 codetype are reduced and masked by the charming attempts to please and be likable associated with Scale 3.

TREATMENT

See treatment section under the 13/31 codes.

THERAPEUTIC FEEDBACK LANGUAGE

See feedback section under the 13/31 codes.

32 Code (see also 23 Code if Scale 2 is within five T-Score points of Scale 3)

In contrast to the 23 codetype, the 32 individual evidences less overt depression and more health concerns, along with repression, inhibition, and strong needs for social approval. A smiling depression with complaints of fatigue, gastric upsets, headaches, and dizziness are common, although various other physical complaints may also be present. The depression is masked by the repression, manifesting as more vegetative symptoms. Actual physical breakdown can occur after prolonged periods of psychological stress.

While individuals with this codetype complain of anxiety, they also reveal symptoms of depression, with difficulties in concentration, memory, and generally being efficient. Even though they have physical complaints, these individuals are ambitious, conscientious, and take their responsibilities seriously. It is important for them to appear socially acceptable, and some may appear prudish. They tend to lack insight, and though reassurance about their physical concerns can be helpful, it is often difficult to engage the 32 individual in personality changing psychotherapy. For men, Scale 1, 8, or 9 is most often the third highest scale.

Women with 32 codetypes often report marital difficulties, although divorce tends to be rare. Although dutiful wives and mothers, they tend to be sexually inhibited and report decreased sexual enjoyment. This is not surprising since the 32 codetype reflects repression in addition to depression, which is associated with low sexual drive. The 32 individual is sensitive to criticism or rejection, and can become co-dependent to avoid rejection. In spite of their accomplishments, they often feel inadequate and suffer from self-doubt. Fatigue and exhaustion, perhaps associated both with the repression and the depression, are typical, as are insomnia, complaints of pain, headaches, stomach upsets, and other vague physical symptoms.

TREATMENT

The 32 individual tends to be self-sacrificing and, therefore guilt-inducing, which tends to anger those around them. Consequently, their children can become angry and resentful, especially in adolescence. Antidepressants are often quite effective, though the 32 individual is vulnerable to developing side effects. Relaxation training and assertiveness training are also useful. Beware of anxiolitics, which should be used with caution, as these individuals are vulnerable to dependency. If the *L* scale is elevated, there may be more extreme denial, moral rigidity, and a high degree of concern about being labeled as psychologically "ill." Any criticisms of other doctors to their current therapist should alert the therapist that they are experiencing frustration with him/her. These individuals have difficulties with asserting themselves and confronting transference issues. The focus in therapy tends to be on physical symptoms or on problems with their spouse or children. Gestalt therapy can help by having their physical symptoms "do the talking" as a way to get them to vent repressed anger and sadness about past hurts and losses. Childhood histories of an early death of a loved caretaker are common. The 32 codetype may reflect a repressed mourning process. The individual may have had to be brave in the face of loss and therefore unable to access the anger and sadness associated with it. Help the individual role-play being assertive or angry and, at the same time, practice relaxation techniques to decondition them to the panic they feel when they express intense negative emotions. In some cases, insight therapy can help them develop a sense of empathy with themselves as children dealing with a painful loss by having to be brave and positive in the face of pain.

THERAPEUTIC FEEDBACK LANGUAGE

See the 23 codetype. Your profile suggests that you are a dutiful, responsible, conflict avoider, whose tendency is to be agreeable and positive, even in the face of pain and physical concerns. Your profile suggests that you may be experiencing physical symptoms such as headaches, stomach upsets, low back pain, dizziness, and other vague symptoms that you are dealing with by bravely attempting to stay positive. You dislike conflict and you'll go the extra mile to avoid hurting another's feelings. It is hard for you to give yourself permission to let go and enjoy life, and you have a strong sense of responsibility and duty. You may be experiencing some symptoms of depression, such as difficulties with sleep, changes in your appetite, and a decrease in your sex drive. It is easy for you to feel guilty unless you're always taking care of others and your responsibilities. You may have experienced the early death or illness of a loved parent. Perhaps you had to stay positive in the face of pain, and you felt you had to be brave and be a "good soldier" so that you would not upset people around you. You may have continued in the role of taking care of others, sometimes at your own expense. Work with your therapist to learn to be more assertive and to recognize that when you are experiencing physical symptoms, they may be at least partly related to stress. You may also be stressed or tense about some interpersonal issue. Explore any past losses where you felt you had to be brave and shut down your emotions so as not to be negative and upset at those around you. Medication can help with some of your physical symptoms and help you with your overall energy and mood.

321 Code

The addition of Scale 1 to Scales 3 and 2 increases the hypochondriacal complaints and physical symptoms in response to stress. Constipation, diarrhea, anorexia, insomnia, muscle tension, genital pain, palpitations, and exhaustion are common. Almost every physical system, including musculoskeletal, gastrointestinal, cardiorespiratory, and genitourinary, tends to be involved. Depression and anxiety, with feelings of inferiority and hopelessness, are typical. Sleep disturbance and weight problems are common. People with this profile deny socially unacceptable impulses, particularly aggressiveness and the rejection of others.

These individuals tend to lack insight, which can lead them into self-defeating, co-dependent relationships. They suffer from guilt and can be intropunitive. If Scale 8 is also elevated, there is even more difficulty with cognitive functioning. Memory and difficulties with concentration and problem solving, as well as difficulties with history reporting, are typical. If Scale 9 is below *T*-50, the patient will complain even more of low energy and loss of drive. The 321, low 9 individual likely suffers from weight problems and feels "burned out."

The female 321 individual often reports gynecological problems and a large proportion of the Marks and Seeman (1963) sample (60 percent) had hysterectomies. The 321 was often a middle child and reported parental domination with strict discipline. Maternal relations are affectionate, but the mother is reported as strict and controlling. The 321 woman presents as tearful, crying, anxious, and depressed, with feelings of inferiority.

Men with this codetype complain of gastric distress. For both men and women, marital problems are likely, centered on conflicts over sexual intimacy and low sexual frequency.

321 individuals often were above average in school achievement. Many report a history of taking care of an ill parent.

TREATMENT

321 individuals have internalized strict parental rules and inhibitions and an uncompromising moral code. Intimate relations appear to present the biggest problem for these individuals, who crave closeness, yet are afraid of it. The focus of treatment should be on helping them process past losses and become comfortable with the expression of anger and sadness related to those losses. Mindfulness therapy can help them become more aware of their emotions and learn to express them more directly. Role-playing celebration or joy or bragging about a particular achievement can help them engage positive emotions that they have unconsciously numbed. In women, if Scale 5 is low, there is even more passivity and a fear of masculine aggressive sexuality. If Scale 0 is elevated, the individual tends to be even more of a "homebody." Usually people with this profile are relatively successful because of their conscientiousness, unless their subservience interferes with job advancement.

34/43 Codes

The 34 codetype predicts different personality attributes than the 43. However, the similarities between the two codetypes warrant discussion. Both represent emotional instability, as one would expect in the interaction between hysterical control and emotional alienation and impulsive behavior. The behavioral instability and impulsiveness suggested by the elevation on Scale 4 are modified, controlled, inhibited, and masked by the needs for approval, closeness, and validation suggested by elevations on Scale 3. The relative strength of each of those contradictory drives characterizes the similarities and differences between the 34 and 43 codetypes. Elevations on Scale 3 higher than Scale 4 would predict more overcontrol, with rare, but episodic, impulsive breaking through of strong feelings and impulsive behavior. A higher elevation on Scale 4 would suggest an edgy, poorly controlled anger with a veneer of social correctness, but more impulsive acting out. A major characteristic of both codetypes is anger and acting-out behavior. In both codetypes there are strong needs for nurturance and care from others, but also fears of closeness and needs for independence. 43 individuals are demanding of others and have high needs for validation, and yet find the demands of mutuality taxing. People with both of these codetypes place emphasis on superficial aspects of their lives and are very sensitive to social disapproval. The 34 individual is charming, but quick to feel impatient, and is subtly demanding. The 43 individual is more manipulative and uses charm to get what he or she wants. In some cases both codetypes manifest mild episodic psychosomatic complaints that reflect overcontrol and can be manipulative.

With a 43 codetype in which Scale 4 is 8 or more *T*-scores higher than Scale 3, anger is more easily and impulsively expressed. The 43/34 codetypes are associated with individuals who can, when provoked, be aggressively hostile, particularly if alcohol is involved. Angry outbursts by the 43/34 come as a buildup of internal pressure. Once anger is expressed, the individual can return to periods of socially appropriate and controlled behavior, and the outburst tends to be rationalized and even denied.

Both codetypes suggest egocentricity and immaturity as well as anger. They are both predictive of marital difficulties, sexual acting-out behavior, divorce, and generally unstable relations with others. Many have problems with substance abuse.

People with both codetypes tend to be role-players who try to "fit in" socially and seek approval from others. They tend to selectively report and subtly manipulate others into giving them approval. Sometimes this is achieved through flattery and the eliciting of approval by giving it. Often they appear quite conformist on the surface, yet their rebelliousness is manifested in subtle acting-out behavior, and in socializing with more overtly nonconformist individuals. Beneath their control they show an impatience and criticalness of others, masked by a socially appropriate veneer.

Individuals with the 34/43 codetype are quite sensitive to rejection and will respond angrily. They tend to project their own sensitivity to rejection onto others, so they have difficulty with the direct rejection of others. Hostility, especially in the 34, tends to be expressed in symbolic, roundabout ways, such as talking behind people's backs or expressing it in a sarcastic or joking way. This passive-aggressive style is captured in the statement, "I wouldn't tease you if I didn't love you." In spite of an underlying anger towards authority figures and the established way of doing things, people with 34/43 codetypes tend to be rule conscious. When Scale 3 is higher than Scale 4, acting out is sometimes denied, so the individual may actually dissociate from his or her acting-out behavior.

Women with these codetypes often place great emphasis on superficial aspects of their life and are impatient and demanding. They are unlikely to seek treatment unless experiencing a recent rejection or some intense frustration, but they tend not to seek insight therapy.

34/43 individuals value their physical appearance and are often fastidious and seductive dressers. In some cases, transitory paranoid episodes are associated with both codetypes. This is not the fixed, rational paranoia associated with Scale 6 or the sensitive emotional disintegration associated with Scale 8. Rather, it reflects a profound distrust in others that is a projection of the 34/43 individual's tendency to role-play. They occasionally experience panic around who to trust, and project their own manipulativeness onto others.

If Scale 1 is also elevated, the individual shows somatic symptoms, with a tendency to use them for secondary gain. If Scale 2 is elevated, depressive symptoms are expressed as tension and a sense of feeling trapped, bitter, resentful, and defeated. Depression may be due to the consequences of some recent acting-out behavior. It can often be self-medicated through impulsive self-defeating behaviors and addictions. If Scale 9 is elevated, energized, approval-seeking behaviors increase, with a tendency to flatter others and to seek approval through increased social role-playing. The likelihood of explosive behaviors increases.

For men, Scale 2, 5, or 6 is most often the third highest scale. For women, the third highest scale is Scale 2, 6, or 8.

Adolescents with 34/43 codetype are often referred for treatment because of conflicts with family and school authorities.

TREATMENT

Childhood histories for these individuals are associated with early rejection or being discounted by a controlling and arbitrary caregiver. In some cases, abuse precipitated the adaptive response of attempting to placate by role-playing, manipulating, and denying the emotional pain associated with the abuse. From an early age, these individuals may have learned to be survivors, subtly manipulating others and telling white lies to get their needs met. In other cases, caregivers encouraged their children to act out, perhaps in response to an overcontrolling spouse. The profile suggests a shutting down of emotional spontaneity in order to fit in and avoid rejection from an explosive and rejecting caregiver. These individuals can actually rehearse what role they want to play in a given social situation. Consequently, they often excel in sales and other people-related jobs where their ability to fit in with diverse people is rewarded.

In treatment, they are sensitive to disapproval or any suggestions that they are mentally ill. Watch for what the patient denies, as this is often the source of their conflict. The 34/43 will tend to role-play for the therapist, so in order for insight to develop, it is important to discuss the therapeutic relationship. These individuals need much approval from the therapist in order to become less defensive. Insight therapy and exploring early childhood experiences of disapproval would help in developing awareness about their tendency to role-play. Define them as people who have intense mixed feelings. On the one hand, they want to please others and, at the same time, they resent being controlled. Help them to see how this stems from a childhood in which they wanted their parents' approval and yet feared unpredictable rejection; that they had to role-play and manipulate in order to get their needs met. Help them determine how they can ask for what they want without being angry or manipulative. Giving them an exercise to express their feelings for a specific period of time, such as a day, directly and without manipulation, could help reduce overcontrol. If the patients feel criticized by the therapist, they will likely terminate therapy.

THERAPEUTIC FEEDBACK LANGUAGE

Your profile shows that you have two personality traits, which at times can feel contradictory. On the one hand, you are a people pleaser and conflict avoider. It is important for you to get along with others and to fit in and play the right social role. It is upsetting to you if people are critical or judgmental of you, and you have become skilled at "reading" what people expect of you. At the same time, you dislike being controlled and value your independence. Wanting to please and wanting to avoid making waves sometimes can be at odds with wanting to do your own thing and be free of others' control. In some cases, people with your profile have learned to play different roles according to who they are with. At times you might even find yourself rehearsing what kind of role you want to play in different social situations. At other times, you manipulate people by telling white lies or selectively reporting in order to not make waves but still get what you need. People with your profile often grew up in environments where a caretaker was emotionally explosive and, when angered, was rejecting. Early episodic angry rejections were likely quite painful for you. You learned that you had to "read" your caretakers and anticipate their moves to avoid rejection or, in some cases, even physical abuse. Learning to avoid rejection, you likely had to learn how to couch and color the truth in order to avoid their anger. Consequently, you may now be going through life playing roles and telling white lies. You may not have learned how to express your frustration and anger in a direct and honest way. Occasionally, your anger may erupt and you may express it loudly and impulsively, without realizing that tension had been building up inside of you. Work with your therapist at identifying situations from your childhood where you felt a caretaker's anger as rejecting and discounting. Explore what that felt like so that you can understand how you learned to avoid anger by playing a role. With your therapist, commit to spending a day where you keep a diary of how you are feeling, paying particular attention to feelings of anger or frustration. When you have a request of someone, rehearse with your therapist how you can ask for what you want without feeling the need to manipulate or selectively report in order to get it. Role-play with your therapist expressing anger directly. Identify with your therapist behaviors you feel reflect who you really are versus behaviors that you feel you have to role-play.

345/435/534 Codes (see also 34/43 and Scale 5 Codes)

In males, the addition of Scale 5 predicts passivity and sensitivity to rejection, with a consequent increase in the sexual difficulties that individuals with 34/43 codetypes already exhibit. Men with this profile crave approval, fear rejection, and are afraid of being trapped. They experience approach avoidance in their intimate relationships. The Scale 4 elevation suggests manipulation in the service of the drive of Scales 3 and 5 for approval and fear of rejection. The result is a charming, seductive, and role-playing individual who constantly elicits love and approval and avoids rejection by selectively reporting. The 345/435 male often seeks sexual experiences that reflect his fear of rejection and his need for nonconformist excitement. Some have engaged in exhibitionism, voyeurism, or sadomasochism. Others have homosexual fantasies or may be bisexual. Women with this combination are assertive, highly sexual, and manipulate others with their seductive sexuality.

TREATMENT

34/43 individuals fear rejection, crave approval yet dislike feeling controlled. The addition of Scale 5 for men suggests an increase in fears of rejection. Elevations of Scale 5 in females suggest an aggressive sexuality with a willingness for sexual experimentation that men often find irresistible. These women are often perceptive and use their social skills to obtain others' approval and dependency on them, which satisfies their need for approval, but elicits their fear of being controlled. Treatment should concentrate on helping these individuals deal with early caregiver rejection. Explore any specific memories when they felt startled by an abrupt, explosive parent who could otherwise be loving. Their adaptive response was to role-play and placate the rejecting parent, denying the emotional impact of the rejection and "seducing" the parent into providing love and approval by being manipulatively charming. Help them see how this adaptive response has become a lifestyle in which they constantly seduce others into relationships that then burden them. Men often had intense loving and rejecting relationships with female caretakers and women with male caretakers.

THERAPEUTIC FEEDBACK LANGUAGE

For men: Your profile suggests you are a creative, sensitive and perceptive individual who is concerned with rejection and disapproval. You have learned to avoid rejection by playing the right role. People with your profile are often good at sales because of their ability to "read" others' needs. At the same time, you fear being controlled or trapped. You may find yourself selectively reporting or lying to others to avoid them feeling rejected and, therefore, rejecting you. Your mixed feelings of wanting approval but fearing being trapped may be reflected in your sexuality. You may seek sexual experiences that allow you to feel excitement but minimize the fears of rejection. Explore with your therapist times in your childhood when you felt rejected or discounted by an opposite sex parent. Explore how this may have led to you constantly placating and seducing others, but at the same time, fearing intimacy in case you are rejected or trapped. Avoid selective reporting by telling people how you feel and what you want. If you have fears of rejection, express those directly and learn to say no to people rather than constantly trying to please others by impulsively being agreeable and then later having to manipulate out of commitments.

For women: Your profile suggests that you are comfortable with men as friends and enjoy traditionally masculine activities and interests. You can be assertive and not afraid to use your sexuality to get what you want. You probably find it easy to elicit men's approval and you can readily manipulate them into getting what you want. You have learned to avoid rejection by playing the right role. People with your profile are often good at sales because of their ability to "read" others' needs. At the same time, you fear being controlled or trapped. You may find yourself selectively reporting or lying to others to avoid them feeling rejected and, therefore, rejecting you. Your mixed feelings, wanting approval but fearing being trapped, may be reflected in your sexuality. You may seek sexual experiences that allow you to feel excitement but minimize the fears of rejection. Explore with your therapist times in your childhood when you felt rejected or discounted by an opposite sex parent. Explore how this may have led to you constantly placating and seducing others, but at the same time, fearing intimacy in case you are rejected or trapped. Avoid selective reporting by telling people how you feel and what you want. If you have fears of rejection, express those directly and learn to say no to people rather than constantly trying to please others by impulsively being agreeable and then later having to manipulate out of commitments.

346/436 Codes

The addition of Scale 6 to the 34 codetype reflects the likelihood of an accumulation of rationalized resentments. The 346 individual is socially conforming, yet seductive, often fastidious and with firmly held beliefs about what is proper, right, and correct social behavior. The addition of Scale 6 increases the 34/43 individual's sensitivity to rejection and loss of social approval. They are very sensitive to criticism, yet tend to be quite critical and judgmental of others. They are blame-oriented and often feel justified in punishing others for hurting or disappointing them. Built-up anger is expressed as an explosive, highly rationalized outburst of blame and judgment, and they often lack awareness of how their anger affects others. They rarely see shades of grey, justify their position as morally righteous, and are quite unforgiving, which is often reflected in an elevated *Pa3* score.

346 individuals are very conscious of their social role and are often seen as sexually attractive, although they may be offended when others respond to their sexuality. They fear emotional intimacy and lack psychological insight. In intimate relationships, they have difficulty articulating what they want. Rather, they allow their feelings to be hurt and then express their unfulfilled desires as resentments and demands. Blame tends to be an important part of their interpersonal style, perhaps reflecting their own fears of being blamed or judged. The 346/436 codetype has been associated with unresolved divorce custody cases.

TREATMENT

Look for childhood conditioning experiences of rejection and being discounted by authoritarian caregivers who were shaming, critical, and blaming. The 346 profile may represent an adaptive response to conditions in which the individual has learned to role-play, subtly manipulate, and be mindful of "who is to blame" in any given situation, perhaps as a way of avoiding being blamed. Insight therapy, exploring childhood memories of having been discounted, rejected, and criticized, could help them understand the origin of their tendency to repress and deny unacceptable impulses until they feel completely justified. Help them understand that by the time they feel justified in expressing their needs, they are already resentful. Give homework exercises in which they focus on asking for what they want from a loved one before they become resentful and, therefore, demanding. This can help them to see how they use moral judgment as part of their attempts to rationalize that their wants are justified. They give others the subtle message of "You ought to do this for me because this is the right thing for you to do and you owe it to me," but overtly deny that they are making a demand. By not making requests directly, instead using judgment, they protect themselves from feeling controlled by any sense of obligation. They also voice their opinion as fact, reflecting their fear of being criticized. This has the effect of eliciting others' resistance, which becomes a self-fulfilling prophecy by creating arguments, which the 346/436 individual anticipates. As they feel criticized or judged, this justifies their protecting themselves by being vigilant.

THERAPEUTIC FEEDBACK LANGUAGE

Your profile suggests that you are a sensitive person with very high standards and that you tend to be your own worst critic. It is important for you to be above criticism and judgment, so you try to do what is expected of you. You've learned how to play the right role to avoid rejection. It is hard for you to express anger or resentment to others until you feel fully justified in doing so. It is also hard for you to ask people for things directly and you try hard to make sure that when you ask for something you feel justified in doing so. However, your concern about avoiding criticism or judgment, and your desire to be above moral reproach, can mean that sometimes you may not express what you want and what you feel for long periods of time. You may wait until you feel completely justified in expressing your feelings, by which time you are quite resentful and find it hard to forgive. Sometimes people with your profile grew up in environments where parents were extremely critical and where you were forced to conform to very high moral standards. Your parents may have had a tendency to be quite critical and judgmental, and when they were disappointed in your behavior they could be rejecting and shaming. From an early age you likely learned to avoid criticism by fitting in and doing the right thing. No wonder you have a tendency to focus on who's to blame, analyzing situations to make sure that you can't be blamed, as if preparing yourself for a constant defense against a parent who is going to be critical and judgmental. Perhaps that is why it is hard for you to ask for what you want directly. You have a tendency to wait until you feel you deserve something, but by then you feel hurt or angry that your needs have not been recognized. People may see your high standards as hard to live up to, and people may see you as someone who is judgmental. Explore with your therapist any childhood events where you felt criticized, judged, and unfairly punished. Explore some of the emotions you may have experienced at that time so that you can identify how you go through life protecting yourself, as if you're about to be criticized or judged. Often when a person anticipates being criticized, they become defensive and ready to protect themselves. This may backfire because others may then become defensive in response, precipitating arguments. Learn to ask for what you want directly before you become resentful. Learn to recognize when your anger is building up so you can express it without blame or judgment.

35/53 Codes

There is limited empirical information on this codetype. Men tend to be educated and histrionic and are described as passive, fussy, and culturally, verbally, and aesthetically oriented. They are conflict avoiders and people pleasers. They see themselves as well-adjusted, happy, calm, and self-confident, although others might see them as emotionally demanding. Some can develop physical symptoms in response to stress. They are unlikely to act out in aggressive ways. They have strong needs for attention and affection, and can be somewhat inhibited and overcontrolled. Most are intellectual. If Scale 0 is also elevated, they are likely to be shy, anxious, and socially uncomfortable. If the profile is within normal limits or just above the normal range, these men are likely to be seen as peaceable, nurturing, and gentle, although with a tendency toward self-absorption.

The 35/53 codetype is also associated with the use of denial and repression as a defense. Though this codetype has been reported as rare in clinical populations, in women it is more common among those applying for reality television roles. These women are competitive and agreeable, with interests that are typically seen as masculine.

Scale 4 or 6 is usually the third highest scale in both males and females. Interpretation is best accomplished by initially ignoring the elevated Scale 5, so as to treat the three-point codetype (e.g. 354 codetype) as though it were a two-point code (e.g. 34 codetype). Subsequently, the interpretations of the elevated Scale 5 can be added. If the third highest scale is highly elevated, it should be given particular consideration in interpreting the 35/53 codetype.

TREATMENT

In men, look for a strong early son–mother identification and, for women, a daughter–father identification. The elevation on Scale 3 suggests the adaptive response of repression and denial in response to early childhood experiences of pain. Assertiveness training and insight therapy is useful in recognizing when anger is building.

THERAPEUTIC FEEDBACK LANGUAGE

For men: Your profile suggests that you are a people pleaser and conflict avoider, and that you are a sensitive, culturally and verbally-oriented individual who cares about others' feelings. You enjoy the company of creative, sensitive, non-confrontational people and you care about artistic, creative pursuits and exploring feelings. Sometimes your avoidance of conflict may lead others to see you as somewhat passive. Because you try to stay positive and avoid stressful interpersonal conflicts, your body may occasionally take the strain and you may experience some mild and shifting physical symptoms of stress. Discuss with your therapist how you can learn to recognize when you are angry and learn to express it. You will likely only recognize that you were angry in the past in any given situation rather than be aware of it in real time.

For women: Your profile suggests that you are a people pleaser and conflict avoider, and that you are an active, responsible, practical woman who is comfortable in the world of men. When you're experiencing interpersonal problems you likely want to do something about them rather than spend much time talking about them. You might not be aware of your own anger because of your concern about staying positive. Consequently, anger may build up inside of you, leading to episodic angry outbursts or perhaps to some vague and shifting physical complaints that reflect inner tension. Learning to recognize when you're angry and learning to express it before it builds up could be a focus of therapy.

36/63 Codes

A 36/63 codetype can be described as the cheerleader/beauty queen/boy scout profile. 36s are conforming, proper, nice, fastidious dressers, and highly sensitive to anything that can be construed as a criticism. These individuals are very self-conscious about their social role. Their polished, controlled demeanor reflects their fears of judgment and their need for approval. Underneath their veneer of exquisite correctness, they are somewhat distrustful and suspicious of others' motives. This may be a projection of their own tendency to be critical and judgmental, and therefore they anticipate criticism from others. Cooperative and conforming, they live their lives wanting to be above moral reproach. This means that anger and selfish feelings are repressed. They often harbor longstanding resentments, which they tend to rationalize as reasonable and morally justified, and they tend to be self-righteous and unforgiving. These individuals lack insight, living their lives to avoid criticism and judgment from others, but vigilant for how others are hurting them or in some way treating them unfairly.

In some cases, this profile is associated with brief psychotic episodes with paranoid jealousies, projections onto others, and self-righteous temper outbursts. However, this codetype is not typically associated with psychosis. The combination of Scale 3 hysteria and Scale 6 paranoia suggests a strong need for approval, sensitivity to criticism, and adherence to rigid values, perhaps as a way of protecting against rejection and criticism. The 36 individual tends to use projection as a primary defense mechanism.

Physical symptoms can reflect their overcontrol, tension, and denial. Though the 36/63 individual can complain of episodic anxiety, these anxiety attacks tend to be brief and situational, with the patient having little awareness of their precipitating cause.

These individuals have very high expectations of themselves and others. Some are rigidly religious, reflecting their overcontrol and their tendency to use moral judgment as a way of controlling others. It is not surprising that others find 36 difficult to get along with, although initially attractive and charming, because of their tendency to be so defensive and blaming.

Inhibitions and ambivalences around sexuality tend to be common with this codetype. They have a strong investment in being seen as attractive. However, the vulnerability associated with intimacy is difficult. Interpersonal problems tend to center around their feelings of being hurt and unfairly treated, and their difficulties with expressing anger and forgiving others.

Their lifestyle is characterized by self-control, the avoidance of criticism, and seeking approval. As children, they tended not to act out, and many were seen as cooperative, conscientious, and model children. A number of 36/63 women were cheerleaders and were well liked by their teachers. Men 36 individuals were described as obedient and well behaved as children (Alex Caldwell, personal communication, 1984).

When Scale 6 is significantly higher than Scale 3, then the person is likely to be more suspicious, easily hurt, and judgmental.

TREATMENT

Look for childhood conditioning experiences of being shamed into conformity by rigid, moralistic caregivers. In some cases, this may have occurred through harsh and heavily rationalized punishments, in other cases, through strong will-breaking criticisms. The 36 individual appears to have over-identified with their caregiver's values, as an adaptive defense against a retaliation response. Consequently, they have learned to judge and shame others whenever they feel that others have acted inappropriately toward them.

The 36 individual tends to be defensive in psychotherapy and perceives history taking as a probe for what is "wrong with them." Consequently, they tend to give defensive and socially correct histories, which can be frustrating for the therapist. Because of their defensiveness, they often can aggravate others into expressing anger towards them. This confirms their expectations of conflict. The therapist may feel defensive in response to the 36 self-justifications and subtle blame. They tend to be highly rational individuals who look for specific advice, the "right answer," to a specific problem. A goal of therapy would be to help them understand that feeling anger does not suggest that they are doing something wrong. They tend to see normal human emotions of anger, sexuality, jealousy, and greed as emotions that are bad, and only to be felt when clearly justified. Their childhood experiences of criticism may have taught them that certain emotions are "wrong" and "bad," which has led them into developing stress-relieving avenues to engage or express them. Exploring early experiences of having been criticized or judged, and then using Gestalt techniques to help them express anger at having been judged harshly or unfairly, could begin the process of allowing them to have empathy for themselves and to be less rigid about labeling their emotional state.

THERAPEUTIC FEEDBACK LANGUAGE

Your profile shows that you are a person with very strong values. Generally, people will see you as cheerful, polite, and socially appropriate. People with your profile are often seen as attractive and fastidious. You generally follow the rules and your teachers probably appreciated your good behavior. You are quite sensitive and you have high standards. Consequently you experience criticism quite painfully. You try hard to be above criticism and to avoid others judging you in any way. Typically, people with your profile grow up with parents who have strong values and who may have been somewhat strict, if not quite punishing. If you did something they disapproved of, they may have used shame or harsh criticism as a way to discipline you. From an early age you learned to try to do the right thing and to avoid criticism. Perhaps now you are very sensitive to what is "wrong" or "right" and you avoid expressing strong emotions until you feel you are completely justified in doing so. You may go through life unaware that you are constantly careful to avoid doing something that could be judged by others as bad. When you feel normal human emotions, such as anger, jealousy, or resentment, you may find yourself trying to analyze it away, to be rational and fair-minded. Being punished or shamed as a child has made you work very hard to be seen as always doing the right thing, and to avoid experiencing emotions that you see as bad. However, this may now lead to periods of significant stress and you may even experience stress in the form of physical symptoms. Headaches, low back pain, stomach upsets, and other vague and shifting physical symptoms may reflect how hard you've worked at trying to be perfect.

Discuss with your therapist any memories you may have of times growing up where you felt punished, humiliated, or shamed, especially if you felt that you were being misunderstood and punished unfairly. Work with your therapist to identify any "should" statements that govern your behavior in which you pass judgment on yourself or others. When you experience mild irritation or hurt feelings, experiment with verbalizing it to the person who has hurt you. Do not wait until you feel that you are justified to do so, because by then you'll be quite angry and it will be hard for you to forgive. Accept the fact that you are sensitive and do not be self-critical. Learn to accept all your emotions, not just positive ones. You could even rehearse with your therapist how to role-play being selfish and self-centered, just to see what it feels like. Since you are so sensitive when people hurt you, it is hard to forgive. If you can learn to express your emotions it will be easier to forgive others when they have disappointed or hurt you. When irritated with someone, tell them what has upset you but without having to tell them what they have done wrong.

37/73 Codes

This codetype is associated with tension, anxiety, insomnia, and psychosomatic complaints as well as with academic underachievement. Fearfulness, anxiety attacks, problems with concentration and memory, occasionally disturbed sleep, and a non-assertive, passive lifestyle characterize these individuals. The 37 individual is self-critical, guilty, and has difficulty making decisions. They catastrophize and are constantly seeking others' approval. They use repression and denial and they are highly dependent on others, sometimes to the point of being co-dependent. For both men and women, Scale 2, 4, or 1 is often the third highest scale.

The profile reflects an individual who is constantly on edge, fearing abandonment by others. The elevation of Scale 3 suggests strong needs for approval, and the elevation on Scale 7 suggests a constant sense of anticipatory dread about its loss; these individuals readily catastrophize small setbacks. They can be ingratiatingly subservient in their attempts to maintain emotional support and minimize anger or conflict. Many report a free-floating anxiety that manifests as an edgy jumpiness and occasional panic attacks.

These individuals need a great deal of reassurance and flatter others in order to get it in return. They feel guilty if they assert themselves. Any impulsive or self-centered behavior on their part is followed by guilt and looking for reassurance that they are not going to be rejected.

If Scale 2 is coded third, these individuals will exhibit the smiling depression symptoms associated with the 23/32 profile. They will also experience some symptoms of depression such as insomnia, and general inefficiency. If Scale 9 is coded third, the anxiety associated with Scale 7 tends to be focused on achievement failures and they exhibit a constant fear of unpredictable loss of approval. If *L* or *K* scale is elevated, a superficial control and poise is evidenced, with even more repression and denial than is typical of the 37 individual.

TREATMENT

Typical childhood experiences would include an unpredictably explosive or violent caregiver that terrified the individual. As children, many have been described as conforming, placating, unobtrusive, and wanting to please adults. As adults, they are highly conscientious, responsible, diligent, and anxious about financial or security setbacks. Transitions are particularly troubling for them. They do best in stable, structured, predictable environments. Relaxation training and assertiveness training can be helpful. Sometimes implosion therapy, whereby they can re-experience the terror of a child confronted by a raging parent, can help them learn not to panic about other people's anger towards them. They are suggestible and so make good hypnosis candidates, especially for deep relaxation training. They are vulnerable to experiencing medication side effects.

These individuals respond well to reassurance, so motherly, nurturing therapists can be successful. Insight therapy can be difficult because they exhibit repression and denial, but helping them develop a sense of empathy for themselves as frightened children can help them understand the origin of their panic around the threat of others' anger. Rehearsing potentially frightening situations in conjunction with relaxation therapy can help them develop a better sense of control. They tend to oscillate between acute anxiety states, where they need a great deal of reassurance, and periods of denial in which there is a "flight into health." They tend to have a pleasing, smiling disposition with a strong need for the therapist's approval, so they make good candidates for supportive therapy. During insight therapy the patient may become flooded with the accompanying emotions and frightened by their intensity. They develop a very strong positive transference, but if they feel they are disappointing their therapist, they terminate therapy prematurely.

THERAPEUTIC FEEDBACK LANGUAGE

People with your profile are described as pleasant, nice, and wanting to please others. You are seen as quick to smile and be agreeable. You avoid conflict and go the extra mile to make sure no one's feelings are hurt. When you assert yourself, or if you get angry, it is easy for you to feel guilty and become preoccupied that you have somehow offended others by your feelings. Sometimes people with your profile grew up in environments where a parent was explosive, perhaps frighteningly so. From an early age you tried to please and to predict what kind of situations would upset your parent so that you could avoid them. Maybe that is why you've learned the role of pleaser. It is as if you're always on edge, experiencing a constant sense of anxiety or even dread, worried that you're doing something wrong and that someone you care about is going to be angry with you. If you ask for what you want or are firm with someone, it is easy for you to feel guilty, as if you're going to be abandoned for doing so. Having had a parent who was explosive or frightening, you adapted by learning to avoid ever upsetting them. Now it is hard for you to upset anyone. However, it often comes at your own expense, so you are less able to assert yourself and even think about your own wants. People with your profile often experience periods of severe anxiety, especially if they feel someone is angry with them or they have somehow failed someone. Anxiety disorders are the most common problems that people face, and there are many effective well-researched treatments available. Work with your therapist to identify how you are readily overwhelmed by negative thoughts and anticipations of catastrophe. With practice you can change the negative thought patterns that lead to anxiety. Examples of an automatic negative thought include: "I will never get this right," "I should have known better," or "I'm sure that she is angry with me." Work with your therapist to see if you are currently panicked about someone being angry with you or withdrawing from you, and make sure that you're not just catastrophizing. Relaxation training, mindfulness therapy, and assertiveness training may all be helpful to you.

38/83 Codes (see also Scales 3 and 8)

This is an uncommon codetype. The Scale 3 elevation predicts hysterical defenses and a hysterical personality organization in a profile that is neurotic, whereas the elevation on Scale 8 reflects the possibility of psychotic-like thought processes. The combination of these scales is unusual, suggesting an individual who may be defending against an underlying psychotic thought process with hysterical defenses. The symptoms, complaints, and personality traits of the 38/83 codetype reflect the interaction of these two contradictory defenses.

Multiple cognitive and neuropsychological symptoms are often present. These individuals' attention span tends to be fragmented and they are often quite forgetful. Odd somatic symptoms such as loss of consciousness, dizzy spells, dissociative episodes, as well as a variety of sensorimotor and musculoskeletal symptoms are typical.

These individuals are seen as strange and peculiar, both in thought and action. An extreme example would be the giggling schizophrenic accosting people on the street corner, dressed in colorful clothes and bright lipstick, clearly psychotic. Although they fear closeness and feel alienated from others, they also have strong needs for affection. When they attempt to achieve an affectionate response from others, they typically do so in immature ways that may serve to actually push others away. They manifest loose associations, with intense and fluctuating moods that are often inappropriate, such as giggling at a sad story or getting angry at a tender moment. Some experience brief and abrupt psychotic episodes, which are characterized by feelings of unreality, emotional inappropriateness, and vague and bizarre somatic complaints. These individuals are often sexually preoccupied, though actual sexual contact is less common because of their fears of emotional closeness and its accompanying vulnerability. Psychotic episodes may disappear quickly once composure is regained, and then the episode is repressed or disassociated. Conceptually, hysterical defenses act as "ego glue," with the thought disturbances erupting occasionally when the individual feels stressed. These individuals can function relatively well and do not evidence psychotic episodes in structured situations. However, even when not stressed, they are likely to manifest dissociative symptoms, inappropriate affect, and bizarre sexualized, violent, and/or religious preoccupations. Some may occasionally experience hallucinations.

These individuals experience difficulty with spontaneous conversation. They are easily "blocked" and distracted, so that the stream of conversation tends to become interrupted and the therapist may periodically wonder, "How did we get to this point?" This "blocking" and circumstantial thinking reflects the 38 individual's tendency to experience internal interruptions around emotionally charged material. Sometimes 38 individuals become involved in bizarre religious and/or sexual activities. They commonly have problems expressing anger. Even if Scale 2 is not significantly elevated, these individuals often appear depressed, as their affect is flat. They react to frustration intropunitively, and they also experience periods of anxiety, tension, and nervousness. Easily threatened, some experience phobias. If Scale 1 is elevated, there may be more vague somatic symptoms, such as blurred vision, dizziness, numbness, and headaches (see 138/318 code).

These individuals often present with numerous physical complaints that are difficult to diagnose, and they often seek out numerous diagnostic tests. They are most often the youngest children in the family and seldom the oldest. In the Marks and Seeman (1963) sample, childhood health was reported as good, as was academic achievement, with many of them doing above-average work in school and a large proportion educated beyond the high school level. However, for many, one or both caregivers were alcoholic and some had a caregiver who was also mentally ill. Fathers tend to be affectionate, yet domineering.

TREATMENT

The profile reflects an approach-avoidance conflict in relationships. Mood disorder and schizophrenia spectrum disorder should be ruled out. The 38 individual has a strong need for affection, yet fears others' hostility and abandonment. Consequently, therapy should proceed slowly, avoiding premature warmth from the therapist. Insight therapy can be disorganizing for the 38. Consequently, supportive and practical here-and-now orientations are most successful. The therapist should be aware of areas that the patient seeks to actively avoid, as this may be a source of their internal conflict. During the course of therapy, if the patient's associations become loose and they become distracted, this should be interpreted as a signal that they are feeling stressed by the therapeutic content. Drifting into religious or sexual themes during therapy may signal that the patient is anxious or experiencing emotions they perceive as potentially threatening.

Once rapport has been established, explore childhood experiences of being frightened by an explosive or cruel parent. Rageful alcoholic outbursts or neglect directed at them or towards a loved one could have led to the adaptive response of shifting to internal distractions, away from the painful event. At the same time, the shift of focus away from reality could have resulted in poor reality testing under stress.

Mindfulness therapy and dialectical behavior therapy can be helpful for them to learn to identify their emotions and express them in a more modulated manner.

THERAPEUTIC FEEDBACK LANGUAGE

Your profile suggests that you are a creative and sensitive person who dislikes conflict and confrontation. You can think in unconventional ways and find comfort in unusual philosophies. Sometimes, when stressed, you may experience periods of anxiety to such a degree that it is hard to think clearly. During stressful times you may find yourself unable to focus, with your mind easily interrupted by thoughts that seem disconnected from what you are doing or talking about. At times your mind may "run away with you" and you may drift into thoughts that may even be a little disturbing. During these stressful times it may be hard for you to concentrate, remember things, and organize your thoughts.

Though you want closeness and connectedness with others, you are also somewhat fearful of it, perhaps concerned that the person you care about is going to hurt you or abandon you. People with your profile often grew up in an environment where a parent could be loving, but could also be angry or cruel in ways that were hard to predict and seemed odd. You may have learned to deal with them by escaping into your imagination, even as you tried to be understanding of their hurtful behavior. Perhaps you learned that you had to be strong, brave, and see what was positive about this difficult caretaker, even as they did things that hurt you. In some cases, parents like yours were alcoholics or had some other problem that made them act at times in a hurtful or neglectful manner. Now it is hard for you to deal with confrontation and conflict, and you seek comfort in philosophies that value love, sexuality, and caring. Though being sexual is important to you, it is also frightening because of your fear that you might get hurt again.

Work with your therapist to understand how stress affects you. Whenever you are around people who are angry or potentially rejecting, watch how your conversation can drift away from the subject. Some anxiety-provoking situations can lead to your being interrupted by unwanted or odd thoughts, leading you to meander off the topic. Mindfulness training may help you experience thoughts and feelings in ways that are not overwhelming, and could help you stay on topic. Identify with your therapist moments in your childhood where you were treated with coldness, hostility, or cruelty in a way that was upsetting and even panicking. With the help of your therapist, learn to soothe some of your memories so that you can now calm yourself whenever you feel overwhelmed by emotions. If you're comfortable writing stories or painting, this could be a way for you to communicate some of your feelings. Expressing yourself through art might include keeping a journal or making a collage. Learn to recognize when you are angry and practice assertiveness. Rehearse with your therapist how to tell people what you want in a clear, direct way.

39/93 Codes

Energetic, gregarious, socially outgoing, and self-assured, these individuals are also surgent, aggressive, stimulation seeking, flattering, and garrulous. They tend to be socially assertive and can be quite entertaining for brief periods of time, but can be seen as too self-centered and dominant. They are driven, ambitious, highly active individuals. They often switch discussion topics, especially when exploring an anxiety-loaded one, and they defensively extol their own virtues. They are competitive and often argue a point for the sake of being right, rather than out of a firmly held belief. Denial as a defense is associated with both Scale 3 and Scale 9. Scale 3 predicts overcontrolled "niceness" and strong needs for approval. Scale 9 also predicts needs for approval and to be the center of attention. Taken together, the 93 codetype reflects an individual who feels intense need for constant approval. Anger tends to be overcontrolled, with sudden breakthroughs of strong feeling. Such explosive episodes are usually targeted at a specific person in their environment. Usually the anger is directed at anyone trying to control or criticize them, or provide them with reality testing in response to some of their colorful exaggerations. They are described as perfectionistic, demanding and, at times, explosive, even assaultive. Repression and denial are typical defenses.

These individuals are quite excitable, but they are also vulnerable to episodic anxiety and panic attacks as repressed emotions break through their overcontrol. During times of stress, somatic complaints such as cardiac symptoms, headaches, and gastrointestinal problems reveal their high level of internal tension. They are often quite concerned about these somatic symptoms, partly because they fear that the symptoms will restrict their overactivity. If Scale 1 is elevated, somatic complaints are predominant. These, in particular, respond well to treatment, combined with reassurance. Often the *MAC–R* is elevated, so addiction proneness is likely. The 93 individual takes leadership roles and is quick to take on a cause, which provides an outlet for their energy, ambition, and needs for social prominence. As parents, they tend to be controlling and have difficulty accepting values different from their own. They are highly critical and hold others to a high standard. They lack insight and are quite argumentative when confronted with their behavior. Childhood histories suggest strong needs to prove themselves, sometimes because of parents who were controlling and demanding. Some learned that performing for praise was the way to obtain love and continue to do so. They can be demanding and exhausting spouses.

TREATMENT

In some cases this profile reflects a mood disorder. Though rare, it can also be associated with an organic brain disorder. In the absence of recent brain trauma or a mood disorder, the profile suggests a hypomanic individual who shows conflict between needs for self-assertion and needs for approval. A childhood history of caregivers who were constantly pushing for performance and achievement is typical. Help the 93 patients to develop their own goals, rather than internalized parental expectations. Help them understand how their strong needs to perform and achieve are understandable, given that approval was often dependent upon performance in their histories. Mindfulness therapy would help them identify when anger is building and learn non-impulsive ways to express it. Also help them understand how they argue instinctively, perhaps as a response to a lack of validating childhood experiences.

The 93 individual tends to experience anxiety episodically, usually around a perceived achievement failure. Consequently, they lack persistence in therapy and are easily distracted and bored. In therapy or when stressed they may appear boastful, both eliciting flattery by flattering others, and at the same time extolling their own virtues in order to gain approval. This behavior replicates their relationship with their caregivers. Rapport can develop if the therapist can find genuine ways to be approving of the positive attributes of the 93 codetype. 93 individuals need to develop a way to reward themselves for their achievements, rather than working hard for others' approval, which leaves them feeling controlled.

THERAPEUTIC FEEDBACK LANGUAGE

Your profile suggests that you are extremely energetic, driven, and ambitious. You tend to have two speeds in life, full speed and off. You may find yourself impatient with a world that moves more slowly than you do. You tend to think and move quickly, and you have a tendency to overcommit. Be careful not to confuse activity with productivity. Because of your high and often positive energy, you often see the world as full of possibilities. However, this may lead you to overcommitting and becoming distracted, not always finishing the tasks you begin. Perhaps, growing up, your parents were always motivating you by reminding you that you can do more and better. Perhaps you received praise and love for performing. You've probably always had high energy and you've probably always been competitive and driven. Your parents' tendency to try to control you, always pushing you to succeed more, has likely instilled in you a need to constantly be productive and to let people know of your success and achievements. You may find yourself becoming easily involved in arguments, especially if someone comes across strongly, perhaps because it reminds you unconsciously of a controlling parent and not being heard. You may feel a need to resist when people are pushy or bossy.

Though you are generally positive and optimistic, you can become quite upset and despondent if you feel you are failing at something. You have very high standards, so others may feel that you are critical and demanding of them, perhaps in the same way that your parents were. When stress is accumulating, you may occasionally experience periods of anxiety, physical symptoms, and increased irritability. These might be quite frightening to you. You may use chemical agents such as alcohol as a way to try to control your high energy level, but this may backfire. Be careful that you do not overdo it, and that chemical agents do not aggravate your irritability or explosiveness.

Learn to recognize when frustration and stress are building so that you can express these feelings without blowing up. Acknowledge that you have more energy than most, but also be aware that, to be successful, you have to manage your energy so you do not overcommit and become scattered and unfocused. Mindfulness training could help you by teaching you how to pay attention to the present moment in a nonjudgmental way. You do not always have to correct others, even when you are right. Learn to meditate daily so you can slow down and manage your need for constant activity. Watch your tendency to be overly optimistic and to impulsively overcommit. Your natural optimism may make you feel all things are possible, and you have a tendency to take on too much. Buy some time with the phrase, "let me check my calendar," before making a decision about a commitment until you've fully thought it through. Be mindful that your high energy can make you feel irritable, impatient, sarcastic, and verbally cutting because people are not as quick as you are. Even though you forget about your blowups quickly, others may remember them longer. Work with your therapist to determine what you want in life versus the goals and standards you think you should have. Watch your tendency to interrupt people as they talk. Whenever you feel like interrupting someone in a conversation to "correct him," take a deep breath, step back and focus on whether correcting him will be productive.

30/03 Codes

This relatively unusual code may appear contradictory in that Scale 3 suggests needs for social connection and approval, whereas Scale 0 elevations suggest social withdrawal or avoidance. Taken together, the two scales suggest a passive, dependent, unassertive, and somewhat withdrawn individual who is unassumingly "nice," but quiet. Stress may lead to episodic psychosomatic complaints, and this often is reflected in Scales 1 and 2, which frequently are the next most elevated scales. These individuals appear relatively comfortable with their level of adjustment. Their primary defenses are repression and denial.

TREATMENT

Because these individuals tend not to experience much psychological or emotional distress, they rarely seek treatment. Anxiety, although not uncommon, tends to be transitory. Social skill building, anger recognition, and assertiveness training are suggested foci of therapy. Look for childhood experiences of hostility or other emotionally painful events that have led them to feeling apprehensive, to "shut down" emotions and to be "brave" in the face of pain. In long-term therapy cases, help them re-experience any past frightening or painful events and learn to vent the appropriate anger around those events to unblock repressed anger and sadness.

THERAPEUTIC FEEDBACK LANGUAGE

Your profile suggests that you are a somewhat shy individual, comfortable with small groups of familiar people. You generally avoid conflict, and try to see situations in a positive light. Consequently, when you eventually do feel irritated or angry, it may come out more sharply than you realize. At other times, your tendency to avoid conflict and make a fuss may lead to physical symptoms of stress such as headaches, stomach upsets, low back pain, or other episodic physical symptoms. You may have experienced physical illness or other emotionally painful or frightening events that led to the adaptive response of being brave and repressing uncomfortable feelings. Social shyness is probably an inherited trait and will only cause distress if you are in a situation where you have to socialize and be more socially assertive than you enjoy. In such cases, you may apply social skill-building techniques and perhaps learn to identify when negative emotions are building so you can express them directly. Explore with your therapist any painful memories where you had to be brave and not upset people you cared about.

Scale 4 (Pd)

Scale 4 is a heterogeneous scale, so not all individuals obtaining high Scale 4 scores are necessarily antisocial or act out aggressively. Scale 4 elevations can be obtained by individuals currently experiencing alienation due to a divorce or other emotional setbacks to which they have responded by "emotional numbing." They may also be feeling anger and bitterness that is externalized. However, all individuals with Scale 4 elevations do exhibit behaviors and traits in common. Generally, they dislike rules being imposed on them, are cautious about allowing themselves to become emotionally close to others, and consequently experience problems with the trust and vulnerability required of intimacy. They dislike being controlled and yet tend to be somewhat dependent. All high Scale 4 persons can be manipulative to varying degrees and capable of selectively reporting in order to get their needs met. Although needing reassurance, they tend not to trust it. They show deficits of empathy and protect themselves against being vulnerable to getting hurt.

   Not all individuals elevated on Scale 4 necessarily overtly resist authority, although many do. SES is an important variable in how the traits and behaviors measured by Scale 4 are expressed. Educated and bright individuals with high scores on Scale 4 can act out, but often do so in controlled, deliberate, self-serving ways. In some cases they may commit white-collar crimes, such as a stock manipulator who pushes the limits of legality beyond "gray areas." It is likely that some of the individuals involved in the events leading to the financial crisis of 2008 manifested Scale 4 attributes. Bending the rules, pushing limits, and looking for immediate gratification, they exhibited classic high Scale 4 behaviors and personality traits.

   A history of acting-out behavior, rebelliousness, anger towards authority, and emotional and social alienation would suggest that a current Scale 4 elevation is characterological. In the absence of such a history and in the presence of a current or recent stressful and alienating situation, a Scale 4 elevation could reflect a situational adjustment reaction of adult life. However, even though these may not be enduring traits, an individual experiencing an adjustment reaction with Scale 4 elevated will manifest alienation, externalized anger, difficulties with emotional self-regulation, and lack trust in others.

   High scores ($T > 65$) reflect externalized anger, irritability, and a resistance to being controlled. This anger may be turned against family, society in general, or both. The manner in which antisocial or asocial impulses are expressed depends upon the elevations of other scales. If Scale 9 is elevated, the 49 individual's initial easygoing charm and glib banter can quickly become confrontational, demanding anger, whereas if Scale 8 is elevated, the acting out is senseless and self-defeating, even bizarre. Characterologically high Scale 4 individuals show impulsiveness, poor judgment, unpredictability, social alienation, and a lack of responsibility and conscience. They lack empathy and evidence poor work and marital adjustment. They sacrifice long-term goals for short-term desires and have difficulty anticipating consequences. Strong loyalties rarely develop. They can make a good first impression, but have difficulty with sustained perseverance towards goals. Not all attributes of Scale 4 are necessarily undesirable. They tend to question the established way of doing things, are willing to question authority, and often are quite adventurous. The concept of "thinking outside the box" that has been a hallmark of creativity is something that they tend to do instinctively. Substance abuse tends to be associated with high Scale 4 and increases their propensity for impulsive and poorly thought through behavior.

For individuals beyond age 40 with a high Scale 4 lifestyle, an elevated Scale 4 reflects longstanding interpersonal disaffiliation and antisocial behavior, whereas for individuals over age 60, high scores suggest alienation to the point of a sullen lack of emotional involvement.

Moderately high elevations (T-55–65) are associated with adrenaline seeking, independent thinking and subtle demandingness, as well as difficulties with emotional intimacy and a tendency to selectively report. Even in the relatively normal range, a Scale 4 elevation would predict that irritability and selective reporting readily occur under stress. In this range, for example, a person could rationalize telling white lies to "protect others" from the truth and subtly manipulate people into doing "what is good for them anyways."

Moderately low to very low scores (T < 45) are associated with conventionality, stability, and unassertiveness to the point of passivity. These individuals are not adventurous and often dependent and comfortable with routine. They generally do not question authority even when they find it onerous. They tend to not be sexually aggressive and are seen by others as reliable and stable.

Spike 4

Spike 4 occurs when Scale 4 is the only scale above T-65 (or when Scale 4 is 10 or more T-score points above all the other scales in an elevated profile). See above for associated traits. If Scale 0 is low (a T-score of 40 or below), their need for social interaction and their social ease allows them to make a good first impression, though others may sometimes see them as somewhat slick or glib.

A low tolerance for frustration, an inability to delay gratification, and a generally hedonistic approach to life are typical. Self-control is poor, and so conflicts with caregivers, family members, and authorities are common. If the K scale is above T-60, and if the individual is of above-average intelligence and education, these behaviors can be masked under a veneer of social correctness.

Extramarital relations and unusual or atypical sexual histories are common. When a Spike 4 encounters negative consequences for their actions, they often experience transitory guilt and depression, which tends to be self-pitying, with little effect on corrective behavior change. In the absence of any history of acting out or deficits of conscience, the Scale 4 elevation in the presence of a situational stress may reflect "emotional numbing." Psychotherapy in the latter case can uncover underlying blocked emotions and a second MMPI-2 testing may then reveal a different codetype.

If there is a history of acting-out behavior, the Spike 4 is characterological. Childhood histories of parents who were either overindulgent and inconsistent, or emotionally unavailable, could have created the adaptive response of emotional numbing and the development of a "survivor" profile. Manipulativeness and deviousness would make sense as an adaptive response to a situation where the individual could not trust that their emotional needs would be consistently met.

Often they exhibit conflicted marriages, though, surprisingly, not always ending in divorce. Many marry individuals who are co-dependent and tolerate their acting-out behavior.

Spike 4 is predictive of addiction-proneness, particularly if the *MAC–R* scale is elevated. They tend to externalize their problems and selectively report, even in therapy.

TREATMENT

Working on the transference is important, as they generally distrust authority figures and project their own manipulativeness onto the therapist. Asking direct questions about their experience of the therapeutic process would allow them to express criticism of the therapist without being emotionally abandoned by the therapist. This could provide a corrective emotional experience around trusting others with vulnerable feelings. Explore childhood memories of feeling alone and unable to trust the emotional stability of caretakers. Help them see how they have developed a "survivor" profile whereby they see relationships as "dog eat dog" interactions.

CBT, teaching them empathy, and rehearsing stress-reducing behaviors that are not impulsive could help them anticipate and manage impulse pressures. Help them realize how in intimate moments they experience emotional numbing.

THERAPEUTIC FEEDBACK LANGUAGE

Your profile suggests that you are an excitement-seeking, adventurous individual who is sensitive to being controlled. People with your profile often grow up in environments where, from an early age, they felt they had to be "survivors," relying on themselves emotionally because the authority figures in their lives were not trustworthy. In some cases it was because parents were self-centered and inconsistent. In others, parents abused their authority or they allowed you to get away with acting out. Perhaps that's why you learned from an early age to be somewhat manipulative and tell lies in order to get your needs met. Your profile suggests that you are able to make a good first impression with people, but persevering toward long-term goals and being reliable is more difficult. You have a tendency to be impulsive and to make decisions based on immediate desires rather than postponing gratification for long-term goals. At times, your impulsiveness may get you into trouble and you may use your manipulative skills in order to avoid negative consequences.

Though you may be skilled at getting along with people for periods of time, letting down your emotional guard and trusting those closest to you is more difficult. You might see the world as "dog eat dog place," where you need control and authority over others in order to feel safe. Work with your therapist to understand how you developed a tendency to be a "survivor," relying on yourself and your ability to manipulate others in order to get your needs met. Explore any childhood memories where you felt emotionally abandoned or mistreated and responded by numbing yourself. Anticipate situations where you might be tempted to behave impulsively and rehearse strategies to deal with stress so you do not act in self-defeating and reckless ways. People with your profile often use chemical agents as a way of "feeling alive." Discuss any chemical use with your therapist and find exciting and risk-taking activities that are not dangerous or self-destructive.

Relations with Other Scales

High 4, Low 5 Code

In men, a low Scale 5 reflects traditional male interests and activities. Typically they are action-oriented, practical, and lack psychological-mindedness. High 4 low 5 males tend to view relationships with women in terms of power and control. They also exhibit more aggressive and impulsive acting-out behavior and sexual promiscuity. Power, coarseness, and traditional masculine interests are emphasized. In working-class men without a college education, this usually reflects a traditional masculine, macho orientation. In an educated male, it would reflect an individual with non-aesthetic, traditional masculine values and interests. Regardless of educational levels, their relationship with women often is power-oriented, with attempts to control women, sometimes in a demeaning manner. The low Scale 5 increases the possibility of aggressive and impulsive acting-out behavior.

Women with a high 4, low 5 codetype are passive-dependent and/or co-dependent, and so often become involved in relationships that are self-defeating. The low Scale 5 modifies the acting out suggested by Scale 4. Alienation and anger tend to be expressed indirectly. Intimate relationships are hampered by passivity and difficulties with trust. The interaction of an elevated Scale 4 and low Scale 5 in women suggests dependency as well as anger and distrust. These women often are superficial in their relations and frequently have identified with cultural stereotypes of women who are demure, yielding, and alluring. They are often passive-aggressive, using sexuality to manipulate others. When Scale 3 is also elevated, hostility is denied. Marital and family problems are common, as is sexual dysfunction and lack of sexual enjoyment, though many of these women are sexually provocative. Headaches and backaches are also frequent. Treatment should focus on helping them recognize that their ability to achieve intimacy and closeness is hampered by their fears of emotional vulnerability.

41/14 Codes

See 14/41 Codes.

42/24 Codes

See 24/42 Codes.

43/34 Codes

See 34/43 Codes.

45/54 Codes

This codetype is usually obtained by men. However, it is also a common codetype among women applicants to reality television shows such as *Survivor, The Amazing Race,* and *America's Top Model* (Richard Levak, June 11, 2014, personal communication). The high 5, high 4 woman is assertive, sexually aggressive, manipulative, and comfortable competing with men. Males with this codetype tend to be unconventional, both in appearance and behavior. They challenge rules and rebel against social conventions. They may be intellectual rebels rather than acting-out rebels, and generally are not overtly aggressive and do not act out in obviously delinquent ways. Nevertheless, they have a low tolerance for frustration and can get into trouble because of their impulsive behavior and their tendency to use chemical agents. The elevation on Scale 5 acts as a suppressor of the aggressive, acting-out behavior that is usually associated with high Scale 4 elevations. However, some teenagers with this codetype can act out overtly in antisocial ways, perhaps by dealing drugs or cheating on tests, and other precursors to white-collar crime. The high 4, high 5 male is gregarious, extraverted, and generally well liked by his peers. In therapy they show good rapport and ego strength, and have a reasonably good prognosis.

College-educated men with this profile can exhibit narcissism and nonconformity and become involved in social protests, causes, or movements that have an anti-establishment focus. These men can be idealistic and self-aware, and are able to communicate their ideas clearly and effectively, though their anti-establishment views may provide an intellectually rationalized outlet for their anger. Others may view them as self-centered, easily hurt, demanding, and manipulatively dependent. When Scale 3 is the next highest scale, the person is more overcontrolled, passively aggressive, and less insightful (see 345/435/534 codes). When Scale 9 is coded third, these individuals emphasize action, dominance, and control of situations and people, although, unless frustrated, these individuals generally achieve this through charm.

TREATMENT

See also treatment section of Spike 4. Typical problem areas for the 45 male are intimacy, trustworthiness, and impulse control, particularly sexual acting out. The 45 codetype has been associated with male sexual offenders, reflecting immaturity and poor judgment. In men, this codetype predicts internal conflict between strong needs for ego gratification and emotional succorance, and the need for autonomy and fears of being controlled. Therapy should focus on helping them learn to express their feelings directly rather than selectively report or manipulate others. Impulse control to manage their sexual acting out could also be an appropriate focus. Look for a strong relationship with a narcissistic mother figure in which the patient felt controlled but also indulged. In women, look for a strong male figure who was controlling and unreasonable. The high 4 individual generally needs to learn how to be emotionally vulnerable, so exploring emotional trust issues would be an important focus in therapy.

45 male: Your profile suggests that you have a balance of masculine and feminine interests and values. You enjoy artistic, creative, and intellectual activities. Talking about ideas, philosophy, and how people feel is interesting to you. You tend to reject stereotypic masculine interests and values, and you enjoy the company of sensitive people. You also value your independence and resist being controlled. You tend to be a nonconformist, letting others know that you do not follow the rules like they do. You may channel some of your nonconformity and distrust of authority into an alternative lifestyle. At the same time, you have difficulties with trust and emotional intimacy, and you may occasionally act impulsively and in ways that others might see as somewhat selfish or self-absorbed. Work with your therapist to understand what situations may tempt you to be impulsive and non-empathic with others. Learn to tell the truth, even when the situation is difficult, and explore whether you resist authority instinctively, rather than thoughtfully. Explore with your therapist how you can learn to let down your guard emotionally and be more trusting of those close to you.

For 45 women: Your profile suggests that you have a balance of masculine and feminine interests and values. You might have grown up as a tomboy, comfortable with boys and doing things that boys traditionally do. You are practical and action-oriented, and you enjoy the company of men. You are independent and dislike being controlled in any way. You are competitive and a nonconformist. You can also be highly spontaneous, to the point of being impulsive and, at times, reckless. When you get in trouble, it is easy for you to bend the rules, manipulate others, and tell white lies in order to get your needs met. You may have grown up close to a male figure that was controlling and, at times, abused his authority. Work with your therapist to understand how your impulses can get you into trouble. Learn how to avoid bending the rules so that you do not get into trouble. Explore how your need for independence and your dislike of being emotionally vulnerable may hamper you in your close relationships.

46/64 Codes

The 46 codetype reflects a resentful, angry, distrustful individual who approaches life with vigilance for how others may use them or take advantage of them. Their stance in life is one of defensiveness and, though demanding of others, they are hypersensitive to demands being placed on them. They readily feel rejected or criticized, and they are quick to jump to the conclusion that others are treating them unfairly or attempting to take advantage of them. They feel chronically hurt and ruminate how others have mistreated them and how they need to protect themselves or seek revenge. They have limited awareness of how they contribute to their difficulties. They experience interpersonal problems and family conflicts, and tend to project blame onto others. This is a divorce-prone profile.

The 46 individual craves affection and validation, but demands it in ways that alienate others, who then resist giving it, thus confirming the 46 view of relationships as exploitive. They are subtly argumentative and defensive, which elicits anger from others.

Older adolescents with this codetype experience problems with their caregivers as well as with authority figures, in general, who see them as hostile, deceitful, argumentative, and blaming. 46 teenagers are highly self-indulgent and under-control their impulses. They rarely take responsibility for their behavior and are negative and argumentative.

In some cases, the extreme sensitivity of the 46 can shade towards paranoia, with jealousies, suspicions, and distrust of others. Anger is a predominant feature of this codetype. However, if Scale 6 is more elevated than Scale 4, the individual can manifest paranoid ideation and in some cases there can be psychotic symptoms.

As anger builds, the 46 individual can justify aggressive behavior, especially if they feel wronged or slighted. Threats of violence should be taken seriously. If Scale 5 is low in a 46 woman, the anger is expressed more as passive aggression and an almost masochistic interpersonal style in which they allow others to take advantage of them. The 46 low 5 codetype was well portrayed by the character of Scarlett O'Hara in *Gone With the Wind*.

TREATMENT

The 46 individual can be difficult to treat because they enter treatment defensively, and so tend to be argumentative, provoking anger or irritation in the therapist, confirming the 46 belief that they need to be defensive. In the interview situation, they might view the clinician's history taking as probing for what is "wrong with them," and so tend to be defensive. They have difficulty empathizing. When hurt, fearful, or angered, they express their feelings as a judgment or a subtle criticism of others. Rather than express their desires as requests, they frame them as owed demands. They have difficulty asking directly for what they want.

Look for childhood conditioning experiences of authoritarian, controlling caregivers who could use harsh punishments and judgment as a way to control them. Harsh criticism that often felt unfair and will-breaking punishments may have elicited from them the adaptive response of being cautious about being controlled, and approaching others with a wary defensiveness. They have difficulty being vulnerable and making requests, perhaps out of fear that to do so would give others control or power over them. This profile has been described as the "chip on the shoulder" profile, reflecting their edgy irritability and argumentativeness, which is understandable as a defense against having been harshly criticized, judged, and humiliated as a child. Others see them as "itching for a fight" and respond defensively to them. Often they experienced the more severe conflict with the opposite sex parent.

Consequently, positive regard and trust building is needed before therapy can begin. Explaining to them how they have extremely high standards and tend to be their own worst critic could help them develop a sense of empathy for themselves as children who experienced unfair and unreasonable criticism and punishments, and tried to be above criticism. Help them understand how they adapted to early humiliations and unfair punishments by being constantly prepared to defend their emotional and personal boundaries. Use CBT to help them learn to ask for what they want before they become resentful. Help them verbalize their needs and emotional vulnerabilities without expressing them as somehow owed to them by others. Cognitive behavioral training, to help them verbalize their feelings without needing to explain why those feelings are reasonable, could help them understand why others respond defensively to them. Exploring any memories where they felt particularly unfairly treated can help them unblock some of their bottled up hurt and anger and, through catharsis, help them become more comfortable exploring their emotional vulnerability.

THERAPEUTIC FEEDBACK LANGUAGE

Your profile suggests that you are going through life feeling vulnerable to being criticized, judged, controlled, or unfairly treated by others. It is as if you anticipate that other people will make unreasonable demands on you, so you feel a need to protect yourself. Sometimes people with your profile grew up in an environment where a parent was demanding, controlling, critical, and even harshly punishing. From an early age you had to learn how to protect yourself, to argue your case, and be ready to protect yourself against unfair criticism and punishment. Currently you seem to be going through life as if anticipating judgments and criticisms. Consequently, it annoys you if others make demands on you, but you are sensitive to what others owe you. It is hard for you to ask for what you want directly as a request, perhaps because you're afraid that if you do so others will somehow have control over you. You dislike owing people anything, so you resist asking for what you need because it makes you feel vulnerable to their demands for reciprocation. You generally wait until you feel irreproachably justified before you're able to express your wants or your anger, by which time you are quite angry and resentful. By the time you express your feelings, you might feel a need to explain why your feelings are "just and right," and why you deserve to feel them. However, others may feel criticized or judged, feeling that you're explaining your emotions as somehow being their fault. Inadvertently, you may end up causing just the kind of conflict you are trying to avoid. Because it is hard for you to trust others, you may feel the need to manipulate, tell white lies, or selectively report as a way of getting what you need. Talk to your therapist about any childhood experiences when you felt particularly criticized, judged, or unfairly punished. Get in touch with what that felt like, and allow yourself to have some empathy for yourself as a child. Practice ways that you can ask for what you want before you feel that you are owed it, so that you express your feelings without having to explain why they are justified or why someone else is wrong. Work at forgiving others when they have hurt you, even though your sensitivity makes you experience painful events intensely. Practice assertiveness requests with your therapist, and role-play situations where it is difficult for you to make requests in a reasonable way. Make assertive statements that begin with "I" (e.g. "I want, I feel, I think"). Also, it is important that you talk to your therapist about any feelings you have towards him or her, especially if you feel in any way criticized or judged.

462/642 Codes

The addition of Scale 2 to the 46/64 codetype adds feelings of being trapped, defeated, resentful, and, when depression is manifested, a negativistic anger and self-defeating, even self-destructive, behavior. The 462 individual feels wounded, hurt, unappreciated, and tends to be self-deprecating but, at the same time, demanding. These individuals allow others to make demands on them, but later feel used and unappreciated. Their depression is rationalized as due to other people and unreasonable circumstances, and as something that has been done "to them." Symptoms of depression such as difficulties with sleep, loss of appetite, loss of sexual interest, and lowered efficiency and energy are typical. These individuals demand attention and sympathy because of their obvious hurt and resentment, but do not trust it when it is forthcoming. They tend to be demanding of others in subtle, guilt-inducing ways, which provokes anger in others. A possible diagnosis of borderline personality is associated with this codetype. Sexual marital maladjustment and conflicts are likely.

Despite their difficulties trusting others and their resentment towards authority, they typically have an exaggerated need for affection and are dependent. They fear vulnerability and, because they crave reassurance, they often are angry with the person whose support they most covet. Interestingly, the 462/642 is often the youngest child in the family and their school achievement is below average (Marks and Seeman, 1963).

TREATMENT

Look for childhood experiences of an unavailable caretaker, perhaps due to chemical abuse. Also look for childhood experiences of caregivers being unfair, controlling, arbitrary, and punishing. Treatment should focus on the current, perceived entrapping situation and help the individual problem solve without being dependent or passive-aggressive. In some cases antidepressant medication may be useful to alleviate the depression. CBT may help them be more assertive and help them to understand how they are self-effacing and, at the same time, resentful that they are not recognized. One example of a 462 individual is a woman who was the oldest of nine children. She felt responsible for her siblings, as her mother was emotionally unavailable, and she tried to please her father by keeping the house clean. The siblings would rarely assist her, and she felt constantly, unfairly burdened. Her father would occasionally blow up at her for not keeping the house clean and did not recognize her efforts. As an adult nurse, she would volunteer for duties and responsibilities that were beyond her job description. She felt unappreciated at work and was resentful, but was also afraid to stand up for herself and continued to take on responsibilities, even when she was not asked to do so. The cycle of hurt, resentment, feeling unappreciated, and burdened, and yet being frightened to assert her wants, is a good example of the 462 individual.

THERAPEUTIC FEEDBACK LANGUAGE

Also look at 46, 24, and 26 feedback statements. Your profile suggests that you are currently feeling trapped, maybe bitter and resentful. Perhaps you have experienced some recent stress where you felt unfairly treated and you feel that you can't find a way to get your needs met. You may be experiencing some symptoms of depression, feeling sad, unhappy, low energy, and with difficulties with sleep and general efficiency. Talk to your therapist about whether you are feeling currently trapped and resentful, and practice assertiveness training so you can verbalize what you need without others feeling criticized or judged.

463/643 Codes

The addition of Scale 3 to the 46/64 codetype suggests control over the expression, and limited awareness of hostile and resentful feelings. At the same time, the Scale 3 attributes suggest a need for more interpersonal connection and approval. The 463 individual can appear charming, even seductive, and often role-plays correct social roles with hostility masked by a veneer of public correctness. The elevation of each scale in relation to the others is relevant. If the codetype is primarily a 46/64 with Scale 3 coded third and significantly lower than either Scale 4 or 6, then the classic 46/64 code attributes will be evident. Edgy suspiciousness, oversensitivity, and argumentativeness are poorly masked by Scale 3 defenses. However if Scales 4, 6, and 3 are all elevated at about the same level, then the individual presents with a good social front, conforms to role expectations, and appears socially correct, poised, and self-controlled. Anger, oversensitivity, and resentment are expressed in circuitous, perhaps sarcastic ways, as subtle judgmentalness, a sensitivity that can shade towards paranoia and a quickness to feel hurt and rejected. 463 individuals have difficulty with the constructive expression of rejection of others, projecting their own sensitivity, and avoiding conflict until resentments accumulate. When angered or feeling unfairly treated, they tend to pursue retribution with controlled, rationalized vigor. They are very sensitive to any slights or injustices they feel perpetrated against them. Anger can be particularly focused on family members and is often highly rationalized and overly justified. This profile has been associated with individuals involved in long and bitter divorce custody battles (Caldwell, 1997).

As one would expect with the elevation on Scale 3, these people have difficulties with the expression of anger. Anger tends to be expressed as judgment and blame of others, and is highly rationalized. If the *O-H* scale is elevated, they may then show infrequent, brittle, angry eruptions that are justified as self-protective. They often repress the memory of the intensity of their anger and the things they say when angered, and lack empathy for those targeted by it.

Individuals with this profile generally conform to role expectations, subtly resist authority, and resent being controlled. They can also evidence paranoid mistrust of others, reflecting their tendency to role-play, which they also expect from others. They take things personally and can easily feel jealous and possessive, but rarely acknowledge such feelings, since it would leave them open to criticism. Controlled, poised (especially if *L* and *K* are high), and observant of social etiquette, they play the correct role and subtly act out.

They demand affection and attention, yet tend to distrust it when given, so others find the 463 individual hard to please. While wanting affection and approval, their edgy vigilance for being criticized, let down, or being controlled is self-defeating, as others withhold their approval in response. They aggravate others into expressing the anger and rejection that the 463 individual expects from them. They are often seductive with the opposite sex. Marital maladjustment is likely. Physical complaints reflecting overcontrol, sexual dysfunction, headaches, and backaches are also associated with this codetype.

TREATMENT

The 463/643 codetype reflects an individual who craves attention and affection, yet distrusts its sincerity when they obtain it. This reflects childhood experiences of being harshly criticized and rejected by a displeased caretaker. Demands for strict conformity to appropriate social roles and values, and will-breaking rejections and criticisms for misbehavior would have led to the adaptive response of constantly playing a role to fit into others' expectations and therefore avoid rejection. During psychotherapy, they have difficulty expressing socially unacceptable impulses, often denying such feelings even when they appear to be expressing them. Help them to express anger as they become aware of it, rather than waiting until they feel justified before expressing it, by which time they are resentful and bitter. Have them role-play asking for what they want without using moral judgments. For example, have them repeat the phrase, "I would like you to give me ...," without having to justify it. Their defensiveness reflects childhood experiences of feeling criticized and judged, so they adapted by first justifying requests. Catharsis and insight therapy can be useful with these individuals, who tend to be quite rational and hyper-analytical.

THERAPEUTIC FEEDBACK LANGUAGE

Your profile suggests that you have very high personal standards, and for you there is a right way and a wrong way of doing things. You go through life trying to fit in to others' expectations because it is painful for you if people are critical or judgmental of you. You have a rich mixture of personality traits. On the one hand, you want to follow the rules and do the right thing, and social etiquette is important to you. At the same time, you dislike being controlled and are careful about letting down your guard and letting people too close in case you get hurt or rejected. Consequently, people with your profile often have friends who reflect different sides of your own personality. For example, you may have a socially conforming and traditional group of friends, and you also may have some friends who are more nonconformist. People with your profile often had parents who could be critical, judgmental, and rejecting when angered. From an early age you learned to play a role and do what was expected of you to avoid judgment and rejection. Perhaps you learned that you had to tell white lies in order to protect yourself. Perhaps that's why you developed an ability to conform, but at the same time, bend the rules. Because it was painful when you felt criticized or rejected, it is now hard for you to reject others unless you feel they deserve it. In fact, you may hold in negative emotions for long periods of time, wanting to be above criticism and wanting to make sure that your feelings are justified and fair. However, this may lead to anger and a buildup of resentments, so that when expressed, they come out in brittle, explosive ways. Work with your therapist to explore childhood experiences when you felt criticized and rejected. Learn to ask for what you want before you end up feeling resentful, and avoid telling people what they have done wrong. Try making "I" statements, rather than justifying your feelings based on others' bad behavior. Learn to integrate the conforming and nonconforming sides of you. Avoid selectively reporting as a way to avoid conflict.

468/648 Codes

This codetype suggests a severe and sometimes chronic disorder. Sometimes the profile is associated with a thought disorder diagnosis. These individuals are alienated, deeply resentful and suspicious of others, and are often defensively hostile. Some may show antisocial personality traits. They are hypersensitive, critical, argumentative, and evasive. Extreme sensitivity can shade to paranoid ideation. They are easily hurt by criticism, and can experience breakdowns in reality testing. They ruminate about real or imagined threats and injustices, and may show delusions or ideas of reference. Grandiosity may be present. Primary defenses are acting out, projection, reaction formation, and rationalization. Anger and rage are often rationalized as self-protective. Although complaints of depression are associated with this codetype, apathy and emotional alienation from self and others may be contributing factors.

Poor judgment, lack of insight, and impulsive angry episodes are typical. In some cases, these individuals can be assaultive. They often abuse chemical agents, which would aggravate impulsive behavior and breakdowns in reality testing. Threats of suicide or violence toward others should be taken seriously. Problems in interpersonal, marital, and sexual adjustment are common. If K is below T-50, the propensity to impulsively act out increases. If Scale 9 is also above T-65, the likelihood of acting out also increases. However, with elevated K and Es the paranoid anger can be more effectively masked and is therefore potentially more dangerous because of being less immediately obvious.

TREATMENT

This is a difficult codetype to treat because the individual is vulnerable to paranoid ideation and often feels angry, resentful, and suspicious of others. These individuals show deficits of empathy and feel emotionally isolated. Supportive non-confrontational psychotherapy is required for the development of trust. Therapists should maintain a professional but open demeanor toward the patient, avoiding being overly friendly. Help them identify and vent any injustices and hostilities they feel have been directed against them. Because of their extreme distrust, empathy from the therapist must be authentic and not role-played.

Look for childhood conditioning experiences of being treated with hostility, physical abuse, cruelty, and rejection leading to the adaptive response of constant vigilance and self-protective cruelty toward others. The expression of hurt and resentment can be helpful in a controlled, structured manner, but it can also have a disorganizing effect on them. Helping them to develop better emotional regulation using CBT could be useful.

It is important for the therapist to manage any anxiety that these individuals may elicit in them. If the therapist can remain unintimidated by the 468 individual's bristling anger, and able to validate the patient's feelings as understandable given the abuse and mistreatment they experienced, then rapport can develop. Medication is often indicated, but rapport needs to develop before it is suggested.

THERAPEUTIC FEEDBACK LANGUAGE

Your profile suggests that currently you are vulnerable to feeling criticized, judged, or even attacked. Perhaps others have mistreated you and you are therefore vigilant to maintain your self-protective guard. People with your profile sometimes grow up with a parent figure that was rejecting, hostile, or even cruel to them. From an early age you may have learned to protect yourself by keeping people at a distance, or by being cruel or angry toward them before they could hurt you. Currently you may be feeling unfairly treated, angry, resentful, and vigilant for anything that can be taken as criticism or judgment from others. You may be feeling so vulnerable that it is hard to know whom to trust. At times you may get confused about what is real, wondering whether you are seeing reality clearly. Perhaps recently you've experienced hostility from others and now feel extremely vigilant and self-protective. At times, you may even feel paranoid. When stress builds, you may find yourself unable to stop your imagination invading your mind with disturbing thoughts. You may have used chemical agents to try to feel better, which would probably aggravate your tendency to be impulsive and act out some of your anger. Rehearse with your therapist situations when you feel threatened, and anticipate how you can avoid feeling out of control and confused. Find alternative ways to deal with your emotions rather than acting out by becoming angry, argumentative, or hostile with people. Avoid chemical agents, which may increase your tendency to be destructive and impulsive.

469 Code

See 496/946 Codes.

47/74 Codes

Elevations on Scale 4 and 7 appear contradictory. Scale 4 predicts rebelliousness, acting out, deficits of empathy, and anger toward authority figures, whereas Scale 7 elevations suggest acquiescence, concern about others, guilt, anxiety, and hyper-responsibility. The 47/74 expresses these contradictory traits in a number of ways. In some cases the individual experiences periods of intense anxiety followed by impulsive tension reduction through acting out, followed by intense guilt. In other cases the 4–7 interactions are manifested as chronic approach avoidance ambivalence in many areas of their life. The presenting complaint for the 47 individual tends to be of anxiety and depression. These individuals demand reassurance from others, although reassurance tends to have little long-term soothing effect because of the mistrust associated with Scale 4.

This codetype predicts cyclical acting-out behavior. As tension and anxiety build and stresses accumulate, these individuals impulsively reduce tension, usually in self-defeating ways. The resulting consequences create more anxiety, guilt, and self-recrimination, beginning a cycle of anxiety that again leads to impulsive tension reduction. In some cases, the acting out can be compulsive, such as bulimic purging, shoplifting, binge drinking, and sexual addictions, which represent the reduction of tension by impulsive ego-gratification, followed by guilt and anxiety. Typically, others see these tension-reducing behaviors as self-indulgent and self-defeating. As one would predict with elevations on Scales 4 and 7, these individuals exhibit intense conflicts between their dependency needs and their fears of being controlled. Although they can be compulsively demanding of reassurance, they rarely profit from it. These individuals have low tolerance for frustration and have difficulty persevering toward long-term goals.

TREATMENT

Look for childhood histories of caregiver inconsistency, with overindulgence and emotional abandonment. These individuals' adaptive response is to both seek reassurance and, at the same time, anticipate its withdrawal. Consequently, they have difficulty delaying immediate gratification because they distrust the predictability of their reward system. Early childhood histories of unpredictable emotional support may have taught them to obtain what they need without regard for consequences.

Therapy should focus on helping them identify stressful situations and rehearse coping strategies that are not self-defeating. Insight-oriented therapy and restimulating past emotional abandonments may help teach them how to recognize and label experiences of anxiety and develop self-soothing coping strategies.

THERAPEUTIC FEEDBACK LANGUAGE

Your profile suggests that you go through periods when you become extremely anxious and tense. As your anxiety and tension builds, you have a tendency to act impulsively to relieve the anxiety. Sometimes this tension reduction can involve drugs or alcohol, gambling, sex or some other pleasurable activity that is ultimately self-destructive. Whenever you act impulsively, especially if you get caught, you experience anxiety, guilt, and remorse, which may change your behavior for a while. However, as stresses build, you may experience an internal struggle, wanting to act on your impulses, but also aware that to do so can cause you guilt and the loss of others' love and approval. This internal struggle can leave you feeling exhausted and even depressed. You may reach out to others and ask for reassurance and advice, but when you get it, it is hard for you to trust it. You may have grown up with inconsistent caregivers. Perhaps one of your parents would be impulsively explosive or withdraw from you in ways that felt like abandonment. Sometimes they may have been very loving, even indulgent, but you learned from an early age that you could not trust their consistency. It is no wonder that you learned to "grab what you could," when you could, rather than learning to postpone gratification in order to work toward long-term goals. Work with your therapist to identify experiences you had as a child when you felt unpredictably emotionally abandoned. Identify the feelings associated with those events so you can learn to recognize when you are becoming fearful or tense, and learn to self-soothe in healthy ways, rather than impulsively acting out. Identify people you can trust and be meticulously honest with them, rather than selectively reporting. Rehearse stressful situations and coping strategies so you do not act impulsively and later regret it. Eliminate self-destructive self-soothing behaviors.

478 Code

This profile predicts impulsive and sometimes compulsive, alienated and self-defeating acting-out behavior in order to immediately reduce tension. These individuals manifest severe anxiety, with resulting problems in concentration, memory, and general efficiency. Psychotic symptoms with disorientation and poor reality testing can occur in some cases. The addition of Scale 8 to the 47 codetype predicts a damaged identity with a history of self-esteem-damaging experiences. The intense ambivalence of the 47 is aggravated by the Scale 8 fear of emotional closeness and intimacy.

Individuals with this codetype may confuse sexuality with aggression and often exhibit sexual difficulties associated with their fears of intimacy. Addictive behaviors, odd preoccupations and ruminations, unpredictable acting out, and fears of emotional closeness are typical. Depression and emotional estrangement are also present, even if Scale 2 is not elevated above *T-65*. Look for childhood experiences of ambivalent, unpredictable, and cruel caretakers. The adaptive response in such an environment was an attempt to predict and anticipate the onset of identity damaging hostility from an unpredictably cruel caretaker. If the cruelty were inescapable, a retreat into fantasy and resulting cognitive overload would be understandable responses. Maintaining a protective emotional distance would also be understandable.

TREATMENT

These individuals tend to be manipulative because they distrust others, and may selectively report, if not lie. Because the boundary between their inner experience and reality can become blurred under stress, obtaining an accurate picture of presenting problems and stressors can be difficult and confusing. Scale 8 elevations suggest a damaged identity, indicating supportive nurturing therapies. Therapeutic structure is important since these individuals can be easily disorganized when conversations touch upon anxiety-laden topics. Relaxation training, thought stopping, and cognitive restructuring can be useful to help them manage anxiety. Because the 478 individual has experienced unpredictable, cold, rejecting hostility, their compulsive preoccupation with avoiding it makes adaptive sense. However, the cognitive disorganization associated with Scale 8 would predict poor reality testing. Helping them learn to recognize when they experience cognitive disorganization through CBT, and teaching thought-stopping techniques and relaxation can be helpful.

THERAPEUTIC FEEDBACK LANGUAGE

Your profile suggests that you are currently experiencing a great deal of anxiety. People with your profile often grow up in environments where parents were unpredictable, and sometimes cruel and coldly rejecting. From an early age you may have learned to protect yourself by withdrawing and not allowing yourself to feel vulnerable or depend on anyone emotionally. Your profile suggests that you experience periods of panic and confusion, especially if you feel somebody you depend on is angry with you or is rejecting you. When stresses accumulate, you may act out impulsively, sometimes in ways that later appear odd or self-defeating. At times it may be hard for you to think clearly or make decisions. It is as if you're going through life constantly on edge, anticipating that something bad is about to happen, and that you will be treated cruelly, rejected, or abandoned. Work with your therapist to rehearse stressful situations and coping strategies so that you do not act impulsively in difficult situations. Learn to recognize when you feel panicked and when your thinking becomes disorganized, so that you avoid impulsive decisions during these times. Learn ways to soothe yourself, to relax and control your panic, so that you can think more clearly. As you become more trusting of your therapist, talk about any events in your childhood where you felt overwhelmed by a parent's cruelty or neglect. Through therapy, learn how you can recognize when people are trustworthy so that you can begin to open up and let down your guard enough to allow yourself to depend on others.

48/84 Codes

This codetype is characterized by distrust, alienation, and a sense of emotional disconnection from others. People with this codetype have difficulties forming emotional attachments due to their profound mistrust and their difficulties with empathy. Often Scale *F* is elevated, reflecting internal turmoil and an external life that is often marginal if not largely dysfunctional. *VRIN* may also be elevated, although the elevation does not necessarily indicate invalidity as much as it reflects mental confusion. In the majority of cases, the behavior of 48/84 is consistent with the borderline personality pattern, with more or less frequent episodes in which they behave in self-defeating, if not self-destructive ways. Some may experience occasional and brief episodic breaks with reality which strikes others as unusually odd, even bizarre. Thereafter, they usually quickly reconstitute, perhaps as the stresses that led to them lift or are resolved. In some cases more persistent signs of psychosis are seen, with hallucinations, delusional thinking, aggression, and an increased likelihood of prior psychiatric hospitalization. They are often highly impulsive and unpredictable, with chaotic lives. Even when Scale 2 is not elevated, they experience anhedonia, sleep difficulties, feelings of hopelessness and defeat, and suicidal ideation. They also can be highly irritable or unable to tolerate frustration and, when frustrated, quickly become angry, if not openly hostile. Others describe them as immature, and their actions often appear odd, peculiar, and self-defeating. Chronic poor judgment often leads to a marginal social adjustment. They are described as emotionally distant, although some espouse esoteric belief systems that can be appealing to other alienated people for brief periods of time. Others may describe them as peculiar in thought and action, unpredictable and moody. Interpersonal relationships are difficult because their angry, anhedonic moods, which do not appear tied to specific external events, can be difficult to live with. Educational and occupational histories are marked by underachievement and marginal adjustments, with serious lapses in responsibility. Many 48 individuals report having been sexually abused.

Some 48/84 individuals become social isolates or nomads, whereas others become involved in antisocial or criminal activity. When these individuals commit crimes, they often seem senseless, brutal, and poorly planned and may include sexual or homicidal attacks. Individuals with this codetype often become involved with others who are equally marginally adjusted. They were often born to parents who were rejecting of them and they, in turn, often have children early and develop ambivalent attachments to them. The 48/84 has low self-esteem and so is vulnerable to being abused. They fear emotional closeness, although they can be very active sexually.

Bright, educated individuals with this codetype may not exhibit marginal social adjustment, but rather a chaotic interpersonal life, severely damaged self-esteem, periods of diffuse anxiety, a tendency to keep others at an emotional distance, and occasional breakdowns in reality testing, such as misinterpreting others' motives and paranoid thoughts. They also may experience difficulties with trust and intimacy, which may be evidenced in marital difficulties, lack of empathy, and sexual acting out.

As 48 individuals in general are anhedonic, alienated from others and can be impulsive and angry, suicide threats should be taken seriously. Chemical addiction is associated with this codetype.

In adolescents, this codetype is fairly common and may reflect a transient adjustment disorder subsequent to an identity-damaging experience. In other adolescents, however, it may reflect a pre-psychotic process. These adolescents, like their adult counterparts, are angry, distrustful, and unhappy, reveal disturbances in thinking, have interpersonal difficulties, and are impulsive and nonconforming. They keep others at a distance, and some go out of their way to appear frightening or even disgusting to others. Typically, these adolescents are academic underachievers and may be delinquent, although in some their delinquency is confined to substance abuse. Anorexia, hyperactivity, and histories of enuresis and encopresis may be present.

TREATMENT

These individuals experience disruptive, chaotic, abusive, and identity-damaging childhoods. Look for chronic family conflict, sexual abuse, alcoholism, and cruel neglect in the family of origin. Often they have been labeled as "the bad apple" in the family and are, therefore, singled out for particularly harsh treatment. The profile reflects this damaged sense of identity. As an adaptive response to hostility, the 48/84 individual may have learned to view others as untrustworthy, rejecting, hostile, or dangerous, and therefore established an enduring attitude of mistrust, and protective, hostile, emotional withdrawal from others. Many respond defensively by keeping others at a distance and lashing out at anyone who frustrates or rejects them. A therapeutic alliance is difficult, as they mistrust the therapist and are often evasive in treatment. They put the therapist through "trust tests" and, if the therapist "passes," a therapeutic alliance can develop. It would be important to discuss the transference on an ongoing basis in order to facilitate the development of trust. They are self-protectively manipulative, which reflects their experience of caretakers as having been unreliable and rejecting.

Insight therapies tend to be disorganizing to these individuals. Reparenting, supportive therapies combined with an empathic understanding of early childhood experiences of abuse or neglect can be helpful. Practical life skill training and developing basic coping strategies to avoid a marginal social adjustment may be most useful. Psychotropic medication may be appropriate, although they may have difficulty trusting the therapist enough to conform to a medication regimen.

THERAPEUTIC FEEDBACK LANGUAGE

Your profile suggests that you are feeling emotionally empty, angry, sad, and distrustful of others. It is difficult for you to become emotionally close to others and to trust that you can be vulnerable and that others won't hurt you. You see the world as a hostile place where people exploit and take advantage of each other, so you keep people at a distance, perhaps warning them to stay away from you by the way you dress and carry yourself. Perhaps through piercings or tattoos you let people know that you are someone that they should respect or fear. You can become quite hostile if you perceive others as disrespecting, threatening, or taking advantage of you. In some cases, people with your profile do not dress or act in an obviously rebellious or frightening manner. Rather, you maintain an emotional distance by treating others in a cool or aloof manner, and by finding ways to take advantage of them.

Your parents may have been cold, unavailable, or even cruel, so from an early age you learned to withdraw to protect yourself. Feeling unloved and unwanted, you found ways to be a survivor, manipulating others or becoming emotionally numb so you could not be hurt. No wonder you question all authority now, since you could not trust your parents to meet your needs.

Your profile suggests you may feel periods of emptiness, aloneness, and disconnection from others. At times, you may even feel paranoid, as if people are wearing masks and disguising how they really feel. When you are hurt, you lash out at others. Sometimes people with your profile mix aggression and sexuality, finding sweet and tender moments uncomfortable or even irritating. You may also medicate your empty, angry feelings with drugs and/or alcohol and, under the influence, you may become more volatile and mean, even to people you care about.

Explore with your therapist moments in your childhood where you felt rejected and alone. As a way of developing self-esteem, try to develop empathy for yourself as a child who felt rejected or abandoned. Avoid drugs and alcohol, especially when you are feeling angry or if you are experiencing paranoia. CBT could help you learn to manage some of your dark and negative moods by shifting your focus onto things that are positive in your life. When you experience tender or loving moments, avoid pushing the other person away. If you allow yourself to enjoy moments of emotional connection, it will help alleviate some of your empty, sad feelings. Medication could also help to soften the edges of the dark and paranoid feelings.

48/84, High F, Low 2 Code

In addition to the 48/84 characteristics, the low Scale 2 suggests the individual's sense of estrangement and alienation has become ego-syntonic. They tend to treat others as objects and often are aggressive, controlling, and quick to punish and lash out if they feel in any way mistreated. If of above-average intelligence, they can be narcissistically manipulative. Though some may complain of depression, their experience is more of a sense of existential emptiness, which reflects their distrust and alienation rather than depression. They have sexual difficulties, primarily with the confusion of aggression and sexuality, and can be quite exploitive of others. Some individuals with this pattern obtain a diagnosis of psychopathy. If Scale 7 is also low, then the lack of anxiety predicts a greater likelihood of psychopathy and un-socialized aggression.

TREATMENT

See treatment section under the 48/84 codes.

THERAPEUTIC FEEDBACK LANGUAGE

Your profile suggests that you are currently feeling very alone and disconnected from others. People with your profile have often experienced childhoods where a parent was rejecting or even cruel. From an early age you learned to protect yourself by withdrawing into your fantasy world and not allowing yourself to feel vulnerable. It is no wonder that it is hard for you to trust others now, and it is difficult to let down your guard and allow people to get close to you. In some cases, people with your profile experienced physical and/or sexual abuse that left them feeling angry and unable to trust others. In these cases, the early abuse may have created some sense of confusion between sexuality and aggression. In other cases the sexual aggression combination is similar to what they experienced in early abuse.

During times of stress, you may become preoccupied with aggressive or even frightening thoughts and your thinking may become disorganized. As stress builds, you may act out impulsively, doing something that others find disturbing, peculiar, or bizarre. Because of early neglect or abuse, you have difficulty loving yourself, so you may find it easier to be around people who live unorthodox or marginal lives rather than around people who are more conventional. Work with your therapist on how to recognize what you are feeling so that you can express feelings to others rather than withdrawing or acting out. Learn to recognize what others might be feeling so that you can respond to them with empathy. Perhaps as way of protecting yourself, you numbed your emotions, so that sometimes others may see you as cold, aloof, and uncaring. Avoid chemical agents as way of medicating your inner emptiness. Drugs and alcohol may actually increase your tendency for impulsive and even violent or illegal behavior. Work with your therapist to develop empathy for yourself as a hurt, abandoned, or neglected child.

482/842/824 Codes

Distrust and alienation characterize this codetype, along with defeated depression, anxiety, and tension, difficulties with concentration and memory, and irritability. This codetype has many similar features to the 48/84, but with the addition of depression due to some recent loss or setback. Like the 48/84 these individuals have difficulties with intimacy and keep a protective distance from others. They demand a great deal of loyalty and reassurance from others but this has little soothing effect, as they distrust it when it is given. The individual with this codetype is intensely moody and is quick to be angry, irritable, and argumentative over small, perceived slights.

As with the 48/84 codetype, these individuals' mood swings may be seen by others as inappropriate and odd, often erupting without obvious provocation or significant stress. They can show breakdowns in reality testing. Episodes of paranoia tend to be diffuse rather than fixed and rational. When stressed, they act out, either lashing out against others, or withdrawing and being self-destructive. They are extremely sensitive to any demands placed on them, and are often resentful, bitter, and feel hopeless.

These individuals experience low self-esteem, anger, which can be turned inward or outward, and anxiety around emotional involvement. At times their responses to others can appear odd or bizarre. They can be unpredictably cruel and self-protectively angry. This profile is associated with severe marital discord. They have inner conflicts around sexuality, and they have difficulty expressing emotions in any modulated or adaptive way. Suicide attempts are common, as are other self-destructive and reckless behaviors.

TREATMENT

See also treatment section under the 48/84 codetype. Similar to the 48/84, these individuals often have disastrous early childhoods. Early parental rejection and/

or domination are common, and very few report affectionate caretakers. Look for illegitimate births and a childhood in which they are labeled early as a behavioral problem, with school difficulties and education marred by truancy and absences. This profile can be understood as reflecting a childhood of being "born unwanted."

Supportive rather than insight-oriented therapy is suggested, as the latter can be psychologically disorganizing. Structured life skill therapies are recommended to help the client manage basic life skills. Dialectical behavior therapy is useful to help them recognize and label their emotions and find effective ways to express them. Learning empathy is important to help them manage interpersonal intimacy. These individuals expect rejection from the therapist and, therefore, put the therapist through trust tests, perhaps unconsciously seeking to replicate and repair their early rejection experiences with their caretakers. The prognosis is often guarded. Sedating antidepressants can be useful. Suicidality is a danger and should be monitored. Sometimes they become more self-destructive as the therapy begins to be effective.

THERAPEUTIC FEEDBACK LANGUAGE

Your profile suggests that you are currently feeling quite depressed, sad, and trapped. It is hard for you to let down your guard and to trust others because you feel others will hurt you or let you down. People with your profile often grew up with parents who were cold or even rejecting and cruel. From an early age you learned that you needed to withdraw, not allow yourself to be vulnerable, and protect yourself from feeling abandoned. You may find yourself pushing people away before they can hurt you, withdrawing to avoid rejection. If you experienced parental neglect or cruelty, you may find yourself constantly on guard, anticipating that others are going to use you or take advantage of you. You may be quick to get angry if anyone makes demands on you, and you may expect others to show you a great deal of loyalty and support before you can trust them. If they let you down in any way, you tend to push them away or punish them, and it is hard for you to give them a second chance. During times of stress you may become quite despondent, and you may even feel that life is not worth living. When stressed, it can be hard for you to feel safe. You might find yourself getting preoccupied with how people are treating you, and whether they are criticizing or judging you, or trying to hurt you. During these stressful times, you may become confused, making it hard for you to know whether you are seeing things clearly. At these times you may lash out at others or yourself. Your therapist may suggest some medications to help you feel less anxious and to take away some of the painful, sad feelings. Work with your therapist to try to understand how others see you and what they are feeling. Because from an early age you learned to numb yourself to protect yourself, it may be hard for you to "read" other people's feelings and know what they are feeling. In therapy explore how you can recognize some of the emotions you've learned to switch off so that you can talk about your feelings. CBT, relaxation training, and learning to have empathy for yourself and others can be helpful.

486/846 Codes

In addition to the 48/84 codetype characteristics, the addition of Scale 6 increases the likelihood of paranoia and other disturbances in reality testing. These individuals are suspicious, moody, and can become violent and vindictive when threatened. A preoccupation with weapons and other reflections of self-protective paranoia would not be unusual. (See also 68/86 codetype.)

489/849 Codes

Elevations on Scale 9 add energy and impulsiveness as well as surgent self-confidence to 84/48 codetype descriptors. This increases the likelihood of acting out in unsocialized, aggressive, and even cruel ways. Behavioral agitation and sudden combative or violent behaviors are suggested with this codetype.

These individuals can be quite charismatic and attractive initially, but also grandiose, manipulative, and emotionally unstable. Charles Manson is a good example of a 489 personality. In the 1960s, he persuaded a group of upper class followers to engage in a drug fuelled murder spree targeting Los Angeles socialites in an attempt to start a race war. Superficially, people with this codetype are often seen as exciting and adventurous because of their charisma. The stereotype of a gang member, such as a Hell's Angel, also fits the 489/849 code-pattern description. These individuals can be predatory, sadistic, and frightening. They resist being controlled, lack empathy, and can quickly become ruthless and coldly violent. They often dress in unusual or bizarre ways, reflecting their alienation, using fear or disgust as a way to keep others at an emotional and physical distance, yet draw attention to themselves. Often these individuals exhibit a history of verbal and physical aggression. Alcoholism and/or drug use are common and increase the possibility of unsocialized, poorly thought through behavior. If Scale 0 is low, the 489 can often be a charismatic leader, although their impulsive and bizarre ideology may eventually become self-destructive.

These individuals are sensitive to criticism or any threats to their self-esteem. If K is low, they can respond violently to threats. If K is elevated, their angry retaliation can be cunningly organized and vindictive. Sexuality and aggression tend to be fused, and they often have sadomasochistic and impersonal sexual relationships. They are often promiscuous.

Distrust is a primary feature of the profile. They fear emotional closeness and lack empathy. Projection, rationalization, externalization, and acting out are primary defenses. Numerous tattoos, body piercings, and flamboyantly bizarre clothing serve to draw attention to themselves while they keep others at a distance. Even if bright or educated, these individuals have poor and uneven achievement because of their bad judgment and impulsive behavior.

TREATMENT

Childhood histories often reveal abusive, rejecting, and cruel parenting. They have often been identified as the "bad apple" within the family. As an adaptive response they may have learned the role of a flamboyant rebel with "nothing to lose" by resisting authority. These individuals can be quite intimidating to the therapist since they are confrontational, argumentative, and lack empathy. They rarely seek help unless experiencing legal or interpersonal difficulties that require them to seek treatment. Sometimes they can benefit from a process of developing self-empathy, understanding that their angry independence makes sense given a childhood in which they had no one to turn. Describe them as highly energetic, charismatic individuals who have learned the role of an angry survivor as an adaptation. Help them realize how surges of energy can lead to impulsive, self-defeating behavior. Using cognitive behavioral techniques, teach them to recognize their feelings of intense, exciting, disorganized energy, and rehearse with them how to self-calm and not move into action in response to surges of energy. During therapy sessions, work on transference and counter-transference once trust is developed, explaining to them how they can be frightening, and explore with them how their humiliation of people can have negative long-term consequences for them. They are sensitive to any demands, so explore with them how these "hot buttons" come from childhood experiences with a rejecting, authoritarian caregiver. They have difficulty modulating their emotions, so techniques to help them vent rage can be dangerous unless they learn how to "bring themselves down" when they are highly aroused. Self-esteem building and reparenting kinds of therapies in which the therapist can play the role of the "good parent," while still setting limits, can be useful. Once a therapeutic relationship has developed, DBT can be useful to help them identify and express emotions.

THERAPEUTIC FEEDBACK LANGUAGE

Your profile suggests that you are an energetic, charismatic, excitement-seeking, and adventurous individual. People have probably always seen you as having a "wild side." You are not afraid to challenge authority, you hate to be controlled, and you enjoy the role of a colorful rebel. You have high energy and are quite excitable. Your profile also shows that you have a quick temper, and that even though you can be friendly and fun, if people cross you or get in your way, you can quickly become irritable, angry, and even dangerous. People with your profile often grew up with parents who were cruel, rejecting, and unreliable. Perhaps from an early age you learned to protect yourself by resisting and perhaps even fighting authority. From a young age you may have learned to not let yourself be vulnerable or let people get close. Learning to numb yourself emotionally may have protected you from being hurt, but it also meant that you "switched off" your ability to feel other people's feelings and have empathy for them. When somebody hurts your feelings or treats you with disrespect, you may become vindictive, hostile, even cruel, and treat them the way you were treated. When you get excited, your emotions can get the better of you and you might do impulsive and even bizarre things. Because you've learned to protect yourself against being hurt, you may take advantage of people's weaknesses and manipulate them to get what you want. It is easy for you take advantage of people and manipulate them because you see the world as a "dog eat dog" place where, unless you're top dog, you're going to be taken advantage of. People with your profile often use chemical agents as a way of feeling excitement. However, under the influence of chemical agents, you may do things that are dangerous, impulsive, and even violent. Work with your therapist to learn how to manage your high energy and your tendency to be impulsive. When you get excited, learn to recognize when your adrenaline is pumping and find ways to bring yourself down so you do not act out impulsively. Avoid drugs and alcohol. Work with your therapist to learn how other people feel so that you can develop a sense of empathy for them. Explore with your therapist any experiences as a child when you felt cruelly treated, or when you felt you had to lash out to protect yourself. Learn ways to talk about your feelings rather than impulsively lash out when you are angry.

49/94 Codes

This is a common codetype and, while 49 individuals have many traits in common, not all 49 individuals are similar. It is a codetype commonly found among criminals, police officers, fighter pilots, high profile, risk-taking businessmen, and psychopaths. Individuals who obtain this codetype question authority and have difficulties with trust, emotional closeness, and perseverance toward long-term commitments. It is the most commonly occurring profile among reality TV applicants (sensation seekers). 49/94 individuals are narcissistic, charismatic, manipulative, power-oriented, and view relationships in terms of power and control. They are arousal-seeking, self-indulgent, and resent limits, rules, or regulations. They are vulnerable to substance abuse. They can be quite focused on their own goals and wants, and are quick to get irritated and angry if they feel frustrated. They can rationalize their behavior, externalize blame when things go wrong, and they have a poorly developed conscience. Many can be quite charming and socially skilled. The absence of anxiety, especially if Scale 7 is low, allows them to create an excellent first impression, and they are quite socially perceptive, using those skills to manipulate others. Many can be quite successful until their lack of attention to detail and their manipulations catch up with them. Uneducated, lower SES, 49/94 individuals experience fighting, marital and family conflict, and underachievement. Intelligent, educated 49/94 individuals, however, benefit from having more superficial poise and social control, and many can rise quickly to positions of authority and power. While some may not act out in blatantly antisocial ways, they nevertheless bend rules, blaze new trails, and sometimes make disastrously poor decisions. The financial crisis of 2008 may have been at least partly precipitated by a number of finance professionals who embody the typical educated 49/94 descriptors.

Adolescents with this codetype have a low tolerance for frustration, experience conflicts with their caregivers and, while often successful in school early on, develop school difficulties as they reach middle and late adolescence. Adolescents, like 49/94 adults, are impulsive, reckless, provocative, and consequently experience problems with authority figures. Drug and excessive alcohol use are common both for adolescents and adults, as reflected by an often-elevated *MAC–R* scale.

If *K* is above *T*-65, overtly antisocial behavior is less likely. These individuals have a veneer of social correctness, with subtle acting-out behavior underneath. If Scale 5 is in the feminine direction, it acts as an inhibitor of aggressive, antisocial acting-out behavior, muting the overt hostility of the 49, and suggesting sexual acting out and more socialized, self-indulgent, and narcissistic behavior. Some socialized 49/94 individuals become crusaders for a cause, reflecting their need for prominence and their socialized rebelliousness.

TREATMENT

Typically, these individuals do not seek therapy unless they are required to do so, or their impulsive behavior has led to adverse consequences. They generally do not experience guilt or anxiety, and tend to externalize blame for their difficulties. They are rated low on adjectives such as tense, nervous, high-strung, anxious, shy, and inhibited. They have strong needs for immediate gratification. In psychoanalytic terms, these people are governed by the pleasure principle, and thus are described as self-indulgent, egocentric, and narcissistic. Although some do experience depression when confronted with the consequences of their behavior, it generally is of short duration and tends to not affect their subsequent behavior.

Although not all 49/94 individuals are antisocial or lack enduring adult relationships, most appear incapable of establishing any kind of non-self-serving commitment to others. Some may achieve academic success and are often quite bright. However, many become underachievers because of their acting-out behaviors and lack of discipline. The profile predicts marital conflict and sexual acting out. Look for childhood histories of dominating, narcissistic caregivers who were at times unreasonably controlling and at other times highly indulgent. These individuals learned to both fear authority and disdain it. As an adaptive response, some may have learned to be "survivors," numbing their vulnerable feelings and learning to manipulate others to get their needs met.

Working on the transference on a continuous basis is important, as these individuals tend to project onto their therapist their own tendency to "play the game" in order to get their needs met. Address their ongoing relationship with the therapist and allow them to verbalize disdain for what they may perceive as the therapist's values in order to keep them involved. Psychotherapy can help them learn how they developed a "survivor" role and, through cognitive behavioral techniques, teach them that their tendency to role-play and manipulate others may have been adaptive at some point, but can cause them ongoing interpersonal difficulties. Helping them develop discipline toward long-term goals and using cognitive behavioral strategies to help them manage impulse control can also be useful.

THERAPEUTIC FEEDBACK LANGUAGE

Your profile suggests that you are an energetic, driven, excitement-seeking individual who hates to be controlled. You live in the moment, are not afraid to take risks, and at times you can be quite impulsive. People with your profile often grew up with authoritarian parents. From an early age you learned to be a "survivor," relying on your wits and your own resources in order to get what you wanted. Perhaps one of your parents was very controlling whereas the other was indulgent. You learned to follow your impulses and to resist authority. You tend to see the world as a "dog eat dog" place, so it is important for you to be "top dog" and not let anyone have control or authority over you. Because you thought you had to be manipulative to get your needs met, you have learned to manipulate others. Telling benign or more blatant lies and bending the rules is the way you think you can get ahead. You might actually see people who follow rules as weak or stupid. Some people with your profile often do very well in life for periods of time, but events often catch up with them. Some of the ways that things can go wrong may include getting into trouble with the law or authority figures, or taking too big a risk, leading to disastrous consequences. Whatever you enjoy, you're likely to do intensely and without a great deal of discipline. Consequently, it is easy for you to become compulsive and even addicted. Talk to your therapist about your early childhood and explore whether you felt you had to be manipulative and devious in order to get your needs met. Learn to modulate your impulses so they do not get you into trouble. Pay more attention to the details of your life so that you're not reckless. Whenever you are engaged in an activity that could get you into trouble, try to imagine what it would feel like to be caught and punished. Follow through on your commitments. Be mindful to not tell lies and manipulate others, as that is likely to lead to the loss of things in your life that you want to keep. Remember that your optimism and high energy can push you into impulsive and reckless acts that will occasionally backfire, with serious negative consequences.

493/943 Codes

The addition of Scale 3 predicts needs for emotional closeness and approval, which results in a veneer of superficial niceness and role-playing social conventions. Typical 49/94 acting out will be muted, with anger expressed in disguised, perhaps in joking and sarcastic ways, or passive-aggressively. The interaction of these scales suggests individuals who have conflicts between their need for approval and acceptance from others, and at the same time, their need for autonomy. If Scale 3 is within five T-score points of Scale 4, then many of the characteristics of the 34/43 codetype may also be present. An elevated $O\text{-}H$ scale would suggest a buildup of anger due to denial, with occasional explosive outbursts, usually directed at a family member. If the $O\text{-}H$ scale is not elevated, then explosive episodes are less likely, with anger expressed as more impulsive irritability associated with 49/94 elevations. In general, the 493/943 codetype reflects individuals who have a high need for approval, success, and power, and they are willing to play manipulative social roles, and justify bending the rules in order to get their needs met.

TREATMENT

Look for early childhood experiences of rejecting, discounting, controlling parents who had a strong need for the child to succeed. Parents who themselves played correct social roles, but acted out subtly, may have modeled acting out as a way to get ahead.

Helping these individuals to recognize when anger is accumulating so they can express it directly, rather than in passive-aggressive or explosive ways, can be useful. The therapist can benefit from acting as a "coach" to the individual, validating their needs for success and approval, and helping them to identify ways to be successful without needing to manipulate others or act impulsively. These individuals are often unaware that they are role-players and manipulators, assuming or projecting that others behave as they do. The therapist should help them distinguish between their own needs versus their internalized caregiver's expectations. Help them process their conflict between needs for approval and needs for autonomy. The therapist's limit-setting needs to be mixed with approval to keep the individual involved.

THERAPEUTIC FEEDBACK LANGUAGE

Your profile suggests that you are a driven, energetic, ambitious individual. You have a strong need for approval and success, and you care about what people think of you.

However, you also have a strong need to be independent and dislike being controlled. In some ways, these traits are contradictory. The way you resolve them is by playing the right role in front of people whose approval you want, following the rules on the surface, and using your social skills to charm people, but then carefully doing what you want and bending the rules to fulfill your needs. In some ways, you can live a double life: the conformist, rule-following, nice individual, and yet somebody who can bend the rules and be subtly manipulative. You dislike hurting anyone's feelings or rejecting them, so you may express anger in roundabout, subtle ways. Perhaps you express irritation with a sarcastic, joking humor. In other cases, people with your profile do not even realize they are getting angry until they have accumulated a number of resentments and occasionally, though infrequently, explode. After you've become angry, you may feel some relief, but you might not realize how others have been negatively affected by your angry episode. In many cases, people with your profile grew up with parents who were demanding and who could be controlling, discounting, and rejecting. Perhaps from an early age you learned that playing the right role was how one got along. You may also have learned that being manipulative and getting around the rules was more effective than being direct and asking for what you wanted. Work with your therapist to recognize when anger is building. Learn to express what you want directly, and be mindful to not express your feelings in joking or sarcastic ways. Identify what you really want in life versus what you feel others expect you to do. You may have some conflict between your need for independence and your need for others' approval. Be careful not to overpromise because of your fears of rejecting others. Avoid telling white lies as a way of getting what you want, because people who care about you will eventually lose trust in what you tell them.

495/945 Codes (see also 49/94 Codes and Spike 5)

Elevations on Scale 5 in men moderate the aggressive acting out that is associated with Scales 4 and 9. High 5 males are aesthetically oriented, care about feelings, and are often educated and intellectually curious. The 49 high 5 male may be an intellectual rebel, espousing nonconformist causes, and may act out sexually, but not be antisocial. The addition of Scale 5 to the 49 codetype reflects sensitivity and aesthetic, intellectual values that others experience as self-centered and self-absorbed.

TREATMENT

Men with 495/945 codetypes tend to be more interested and responsive to psychotherapy than the 49 individual. Intellectually curious, verbal, and insightful, they are more amenable to being "coached," especially by a warm, approving psychotherapist who sets non-authoritarian, good-natured limits. Look for childhood conditioning experiences similar to the 49/94 codetype. 49 high 5 women, on the other hand, tend to be assertive, surgent, demanding, and often highly sexual. The elevation of Scale 5 predicts a practical, action-oriented female, and increases the likelihood of assertive, and even aggressive, acting-out behavior. Women with this codetype would look for practical advice rather than insight therapy.

See 49/94 codes for feedback.

496/946 Codes

The addition of Scale 6 to the 49/94 codetype predicts suspiciousness, paranoid sensitivity, and vindictiveness. Scale 6 acts as an "organizer" for the more impulsive, hedonistic live-in-the-moment qualities of the 49 individual. President Richard Nixon may have exhibited some of the qualities associated with a 496 profile. His tenacious drive, keeping of an "enemies" list, and episodes of paranoia capture the essential qualities of this codetype. These individuals are very sensitive to any slights, criticisms, or demands made on them. Some, when threatened, can be assaultive, especially if they feel they have been somehow wronged or treated with disrespect. All 496/946 individuals have a tendency to store resentments and be unforgiving and manipulatively vindictive, but not all are physically dangerous to others. They can pursue vengeance with a determination that is lacking in the pure 49/94 live-in-the-moment individual. When anger is expressed, it comes out as a dangerous breakdown of brittle control. If Scale 8 is also elevated, then episodes of bizarre violence would not be unusual. Some individuals may show brief psychotic episodes, and others can become more openly schizophrenic over time. Childhood histories often reveal arbitrary, controlling, and severely critical caregivers who may have been strict, using physical punishment and shaming as a way of controlling the child. Consequently, these individuals show a strong response to any attempts to control them, and are quick to feel criticized. They tend to have a "chip on the shoulder" attitude in life, ready to argue or fight for a cause. Educated individuals with a 496/946 codetype are argumentative, rationalizing, externalizing, and blaming, but these behaviors are expressed verbally. People with less ego strength are more prone to act out violently and impulsively when threatened.

TREATMENT

See also 49/94 codes. Anger management and impulse control strategies are most useful. Help these individuals understand how their quickness to argue and defend themselves and their tendency to obstinately "argue their position" makes adaptive sense given their childhood experiences of having been shamed and treated unfairly by authoritarian caretakers. Help them recognize how and why opinionated people can now engage them into becoming reactively argumentative. In the presence of psychosis, medication is required, although their paranoid sensitivity to being controlled would need to be managed before medication is suggested.

THERAPEUTIC FEEDBACK LANGUAGE

Your profile suggests that you are going through life on edge, as if anticipating being controlled, criticized, judged, or having unfair demands made on you. People with your profile often grew up with a parent who was controlling and unfairly punishing, or perhaps used shame to discipline. That may be why you learned to be wary of anybody trying to control or make demands on you. Currently, you appear to be feeling vulnerable to being criticized, judged, or attacked. You may fantasize about ways to protect yourself and retaliate against people you feel have hurt you. Sometimes your sensitivity to criticism and judgment may actually shade toward paranoia, and it is hard for you to know whom you can trust. When people hurt you, it is hard for you to forgive them, perhaps because you've experienced painful and unfairly inflicted wounds in the past. Others may sometimes see you as a little prickly, ready to argue and feel hurt, and sensitive to any demands being placed on you. It is as if you want others to prove that they are trustworthy before you let down your guard. Authority figures tend to make you want to resist them, and others may see you as stubborn about doing things your own way. Work with your therapist to identify childhood events where you felt unfairly judged, criticized, shamed or punished. Work on learning to ask for what you want before you feel resentful and come across as demanding. Be mindful that you may be too quick to feel hurt and angry, and that punishing people for hurting you can make them defensive and argumentative. Become aware that you are going through life overly vigilant, as if you are about to be attacked or have something taken away from you. It leads you to be defensive and argumentative in a way that makes people want to argue with you and resist your requests.

498/948 Codes (see also 489/849 Codes)

In addition to the 49/94 features, the likelihood of strange, unusual, bizarre, and/or violent behavior is high. This codetype usually represents major and enduring psychopathology. In adolescents, this codetype can be associated with situational difficulties, such as an identity crisis and adolescent rebellion, rather than the personality disorder found in adults. Nevertheless, both adults and adolescents experience intense feelings of alienation from others, family conflicts, high energy levels, difficulties with authority, and rebellious behaviors. They particularly fear feeling vulnerable and, in conversations, they are likely to jump from topic to topic to avoid talking about emotionally vulnerable issues. They can be charismatic but also bizarre, and converse casually about sexuality and aggression.

TREATMENT

See treatment section under the 489/849 codes.

40/04 Codes

This codetype predicts an individual who is alienated, distrustful, dysphoric, and lacking in empathy. They see the world as a "dog eat dog" place from which they have self-protectively withdrawn. They have difficulty expressing vulnerable emotions in a modulated way. Anger, frustration, and even attempts at intimacy can be expressed in an abrupt, interpersonally clumsy fashion. Others see them as aloof and may describe them as cold and unfeeling. They feel alienated from people and experience low self-esteem. These individuals typically act out within the family rather than resisting authority or acting in antisocial ways. They tend to be loners and have difficulty with emotional closeness and intimacy, yet are unlikely to express much psychological distress except for dysphoria and self-deprecation. They have habituated to living an isolated, emotionally self-sufficient, though alienated life.

These individuals rarely seek treatment. Therapeutic contact will likely be made due to relationship problems, dysphoria, chemical addiction, or work problems. Childhood histories of caregivers who were emotionally distant and uninvolved are typical. The high 40/04 individual has learned to be emotionally self-sufficient, perhaps as a defense against early parental withdrawal or lack of emotional availability. They have learned the role of a self-sufficient loner, and they appear to need little social interaction or validation. Practical information and advice about how others feel and interpret their behavior could be helpful. One 40 patient was discovered to have been involved with prostitutes by his distraught wife. He was angry that his apology was not enough for her to drop the matter, and that she insisted he seek therapy to understand the reasons for his infidelity. He was genuinely puzzled why an apology did not assuage her. Teaching 40/04 individuals how others feel and how to respond to loved ones can be useful. Determine how much of their self-sufficient withdrawal is constitutional and how much is a response to parental neglect in order to develop a therapeutic strategy. Using cognitive behavioral techniques to teach them how to express anger, tenderness, love, and frustration can be useful. Self-esteem building and social skill exercises can also be useful.

THERAPEUTIC FEEDBACK LANGUAGE

Your profile suggests that you are a self-sufficient, independent individual. You are shy, and find small talk and social events where you do not know people to be difficult and unpleasant. You have learned to be a survivor and to rely on your own emotional resources. In times of stress, you rarely turn to others or ask for emotional support. You see the world as a place where people do not really care for one another and where relationships are often more bother than reward. Others may see you as a little cynical, abrupt, and aloof. People may misjudge you as a snob because you do not make an effort to reach out to others. Perhaps you have always been somewhat shy and, growing up, you learned to be self-sufficient because your parents were emotionally unavailable. Now it is hard for you to connect with others emotionally, let down your guard, and feel emotionally vulnerable. You tend to be quite self-critical and, although you do not experience a great deal of joy from life, it is hard for you to feel that opening up and talking to a therapist would do much good. Work with your therapist to understand how to deal with your shyness. Learn how to recognize what other people are feeling and remember that others often need more emotional connection and support than you do. If you are involved in a relationship, learn how to talk about emotional experiences so that your partner feels a sense of connection with you.

Scale 5 (Mf)

Spike 5

A high score ($T \geq 65$) and Spike 5 codetype in a man suggests an introspective, inner-directed, and education-oriented individual who has a wide range of interests, including aesthetic and contemplative preferences. Often these men are seen as idealistic and imaginative, socially perceptive, and interpersonally sensitive. They are interested in intellectual activities, have a humanistic perspective, and value appearance, style, and intimacy. In individuals with high educational and cultural backgrounds, some of these characteristics are modal. However, this pattern may reflect a discomfort with stereotypic masculine behaviors, activities, and interests in favor of a more non-competitive, contemplative, and, at times, passive style. Because Scale 5 in men is strongly correlated with education, intelligence, and cultural breadth, high elevations should not be interpreted as pathological. In fact, adjectives used to describe high 5 men tend to be positive. Others describe them as mature, self-controlled, insightful, and self-aware. This scale tends to be at least moderately elevated for well-adjusted members of various occupational groups, such as social scientists, writers, artists, ministers, teachers, and psychologists. High scorers, with no other scales elevated, can sometimes be described as passive, particularly if Scale 9 and 4 are low, and some may exhibit mannerisms that are seen as traditionally feminine.

Elevation of Scale 5 is never sufficient to suggest homosexuality, either overt or latent. Homosexuals who wish to conceal their orientation on the MMPI-2 can readily do so. That said, when Scale 5 is above T-75 score, a male likely rejects the traditional masculine lifestyle.

Women who obtain an elevated Scale 5 above T-65 can be described as assertive, competitive, tough-minded, sensible, practical, and not particularly interested in appearing or behaving in a traditional feminine manner. Others describe them as independent, self-confident, spontaneous, dominant, and even aggressive in the pursuit of their goals. They are seen as tough-minded at times, coarse, and are comfortable in the presence of men. This may be expressed in pragmatic career and/or survival behaviors, or in traditionally masculine sports or interests.

Interestingly, the mean *Mf* scores for women applicants to the reality TV survival competition, *Survivor*, is a T-score of 60. It makes intuitive sense that women who are willing to live with no resources and compete with men over six weeks on an island would be practical, competitive, and tough-minded (Richard Levak, August 4, 2007, personal communication).

If no other scales are elevated, Scale 5 elevations in women can predict positive qualities associated with independence, self-reliance, and assertiveness. If *GF* is also elevated, the elevation on Scale 5 in women can suggest a healthy, balanced androgyny. If Scale 5 is elevated in males, and the *GM* scale is also elevated, a healthy androgyny is also suggested.

Moderately low scores (T-35–45) are interpreted differently for men and women. Low Scale 5 men show a traditionally masculine pattern of interests and behaviors. They are adventurous and enjoy action, outdoor activities, sports, and competitive or mechanical activities. They often appear rugged and can appear coarse. If educated, they gravitate toward practical, action-oriented careers rather than careers that involve nurturing or coaching others.

In women, moderately low scores (*T*-35–45) suggest sensitivity and concern about relationships, intimacy, and processing feelings. These women are usually nurturing and supportive, although as *T*-scores go below 40 this may also be accompanied by passivity. Like their high 5 male counterparts, these women are fastidious, care about their appearance, and have interests that are intellectual, academic, or aesthetic. Some are attracted to sensitive men, with whom they enjoy communicating about emotions. Professional and college-educated women tend to obtain *T*-scores in the 40 to 50 range on Scale 5, reflecting a balance between practicality and aesthetics.

When Scale 5 is very low (*T* ≤ 35), men espouse a very practical, action-oriented lifestyle and enjoy traditional masculine activities and pursuits. They have difficulty communicating feelings and are uncomfortable with discussions about emotions. When interpersonal problems arise, they want to "do something about it" rather than talk about it.

In women, very low scores (*T* ≤ 35) reflect a woman who may be so concerned about avoiding conflict and hurting others' feelings that she becomes co-dependent or allows others to take advantage of her. Her nurturing style may make it difficult for her to relate sexually to more assertive males whose sexuality she may find too rough or lacking in intimacy and finesse.

TREATMENT

Men in the high scoring range and women in the normal and low scoring range tend to be feeling-oriented, so they have an affinity for psychotherapy. They are curious about themselves and their loved ones, and enjoy the process of gaining insight. Men and women scoring in the masculine direction on Scale 5, on the other hand, tend to approach therapy looking for practical advice and feel uncomfortable with the analysis, labelling, and processing of feelings. They are looking for advice on what they need to do to solve interpersonal problems.

Males with high 5 scores and no other scales elevated generally are described in positive terms, but they may experience relationship or sexual problems because of their sensitivity and self-consciousness. They may be somewhat passive, giving in to others' expectations. In the work situation, they have difficulty asserting themselves, especially in positions of power. They tend to be democratic in their management style and they feel overwhelmed by having to be tough with others.

THERAPEUTIC FEEDBACK LANGUAGE

For men: Your profile suggests that you are a sensitive, artistically oriented man who rejects traditional stereotypic masculine interests and values. You care about peoples' feelings and are comfortable in a creative world. You might find the competitive male world less interesting in favor of a more intellectual and cooperative environment. At times, you may be passive, hanging back from expressing what you want in order to not be seen as controlling or pushy.

For women: Your profile suggests that you find the world of men interesting because you enjoy competitive, action-oriented activities and hobbies. You may find the traditional world of women less appealing. When people are upset, you want to talk about how to fix it rather than talking about feelings. You may be quite competitive, athletic and enjoy outdoor, action-oriented activities.

Relations with Other Scales

51/15 Codes

See 15/51 Codes.

52/25 Codes

See 25/52 Codes.

53/35 Codes

See 35/53 Codes.

54/45 Codes

See 45/54 Codes.

56/65 Codes

This is a rare codetype. In men, it suggests an insecure individual who fears emotional involvement with others. These men are fussy, sensitive individuals, whose feelings are easily hurt. They take things personally, and have difficulty expressing anger directly. At times, their sensitivity can shade toward paranoia, exhibiting unreasonable jealousies and projections onto others. Others see them as somewhat passive, with a tendency to accumulate resentments and hurts. They also present as rational, intellectually-oriented, intensely loyal, somewhat aloof individuals, who need a great deal of reassurance. Anger tends to be expressed in brittle, judgmental ways, once they feel justified in expressing their hurts and resentments. They are sensitive to demands being placed on them. Many have high educational and career aspirations, and they tend to be interested in cultural, verbal, and aesthetic activities. 56/65 women, on the other hand, are usually more brash and direct. When hurt or angry, they can be judgmental and abrasive. They see the world in black and white terms and can quickly take offense, which they feel justified in confronting directly. They lack insight and see themselves as "right" and others as "wrong" in any confrontation, rather than understanding conflict as representing shades of grey.

Further information can be obtained if a third scale is elevated above *T*-65 by temporarily disregarding Scale 5 and interpreting the other two scales as a two-point codetype (e.g. a 564/654 codetype can be interpreted as a 46/64 codetype with an elevated Scale 5).

TREATMENT

Because these individuals are so sensitive to criticism or demands placed on them, look for childhood histories of a caregiver who was quick to criticize or judge, and/or quick to punish. Their interpersonal gestalt is one of protecting against criticism or judgment by being highly rational and justifying their behavior and perspective and, at the same time, needing to self-protectively judge others as "wrong" or "bad." Help them find ways to express anger without judgment. Help them understand how their tendency to be judgmental was an adaptive response to unreasonably critical, shaming parents. Rehearse with them how to ask others to meet their needs directly, rather than waiting until they feel resentful or hurt before they express what they want.

THERAPEUTIC FEEDBACK LANGUAGE

For men: Your profile suggests that you are a sensitive, culturally, verbally, and aesthetically-oriented male. You value being rational, fair-minded, and analytical, and work hard to be above criticism. You have very high standards and analyze your feelings to make sure they are above reproach. At the same time, others may view you as hard to please, with a tendency to be critical or judgmental. Perhaps you grew up with a caretaker who was quick to criticize or judge, so from an early age you worked hard to be above judgment, internalizing your parents' strong values. Others may see you as a little quick to judge and slow to forgive. Because you are so sensitive, when people hurt you it takes a long time for you to forgive them. Work with your therapist on learning to recognize when you are storing up resentments, and learn to express your hurt and anger directly, without blaming. Ask for what you want without feeling you need to justify it. Sometimes people become argumentative if you ask for what you want by suggesting that others owe it to you. You may take things personally that were not meant to be a criticism. Remember that many people are less sensitive than you are, and can go through life unaware that other people are sensitive, so that they can be interpersonally clumsy but not necessarily "have it in for you."

For women: (see feedback for Scale 5 and Scale 6 spikes): Your profile suggests that you are action-oriented, highly rational, loyal, and value fairness. Even though you have a good balance of masculine and feminine values and interests, you generally enjoy the world of men and traditional male activities. You probably are competitive. Surprisingly, in spite of your resilience, you are also quite sensitive, so that your feelings may get hurt more readily than others realize. You may have grown up with a parent who had high standards and was somewhat critical or judgmental of you. You learned from an early age to avoid criticism. Before you express anger or resentment, you analyze your feelings to make sure they are justified and above reproach. By the time you express your anger, you often have stored up a number of resentments, which infrequently leads to you becoming quite angry. You may find it hard to forgive because you are sensitive, and when people hurt you, the memory lingers a long time. You may also explain to people why your feelings are justified, which can make them feel defensive. Learn to ask for what you want and express resentments as you feel them, being careful to avoid others feeling blamed. Instead of telling someone, "You are always late," for example, or "You never do your fair share," make a direct "I" statement, for example, "I would like you to help with the housework," or "I would like you to come home on time."

57/75 Codes

Men with this codetype are described as indecisive, worrying, introspective, tense, unhappy, and needing reassurance. They may experience anxious episodes characterized by obsessive rumination over inadequacies and shortcomings. They are quick to be self-critical, guilty, and self-recriminating, and some may report dysphoria as a consequence. They are easily embarrassed and bashful, get their feelings hurt easily, and frequently feel inadequate in their love relationships. Women rarely obtain this codetype, but when they do, they are more prone to guilt and anxiety than would be expected from a high Scale 5 elevation alone. Even so, they are often intellectually competitive. Considering the two-point codetype when Scale 5 is omitted may enhance the interpretation.

TREATMENT

Because of their psychological-mindedness, as predicted by the Scale 5 elevation, and their adherence to instructions, as predicted by the Scale 7 elevation, men are good psychotherapy candidates. Insightful and introspective, they do well with insight therapy as well as thought stopping, relaxation training, venting and catharsis. Self-esteem building and assertion training are useful.

THERAPEUTIC FEEDBACK LANGUAGE

For men: Your profile suggests that you are a sensitive, thoughtful, analytical man, with cultural, verbal, and aesthetic interests. You enjoy intellectual activity and are introspective, dutiful, and responsible. The profile also suggests you are prone to worry; you see every side of an issue and worry about how things can go wrong. You might even worry about philosophical issues and bigger world problems. You feel guilty easily, and can be indecisive sometimes because you're afraid of making a mistake. Perhaps you grew up with a female parent to whom you were strongly bonded, but who also demanded a lot from you. At the same time, you may have experienced unpredictable setbacks, or overloads of responsibility as a child that left you anxious in case your actions led to disappointing others. You seem to be going through life a little more on edge and anxious than perhaps you want to be. Work with your therapist at understanding why you spend so much time worrying and anticipating negative consequences. Learn to switch off negative thoughts, especially worries about not being good enough. Use CBT to manage your anxiety.

For women: Your profile shows that you are an action-oriented, direct, and assertive woman who enjoys the company of men. Practical and sensible, when a problem arises, you generally like to move into action to solve it rather than to spend too much time talking about it. At the same time, your profile suggests that you are experiencing some anxiety, with a tendency to feel guilty, worried, and tense. Perhaps growing up you were close to a male figure who took pleasure in your ability to enjoy traditional male activities. At the same time, something may have precipitated a tendency in you to worry, think ahead, plan, and be concerned that some detail that you've overlooked could lead to disaster. It is easy for you feel guilty and blame yourself when things go wrong. Work with your therapist on understanding why you spend so much time worrying and anticipating negative consequences. Learn to switch off negative thoughts, especially worries about not being good enough. Use CBT to manage your anxiety.

58/85 Codes

Men with this codetype are inner-directed and spend much time in thought, often engaging in philosophical musings or being concerned with abstract ideas about life's meaning. Most complain of feeling confused, unhappy, alienated from others, and having home conflicts. They may lack drive. (Considering the two-point codetype when Scale 5 is omitted enhances interpretation.)

Men with this codetype are likely to have family histories of alcohol abuse, mental illness, and physical abuse. Some of these men have psychiatric histories that began in childhood. Although many of them are not psychotic, they often report depression, paresthesia, and religious preoccupations. Although some can be seen as creative, others are described as odd, eccentric individuals, who have difficulties with emotional closeness. Sexual conflicts are common, as are family problems.

Women with this codetype display unusual thoughts and behaviors that often focus on issues of control of others in order to protect themselves. Typically they feel alienated. Among female adolescents, this pattern would be associated with behavioral problems at home or school, and/or legal difficulties.

TREATMENT

With men, their intellectual curiosity may make them amenable to self-analysis, but the therapist should use insight therapy judiciously since it may be disorganizing to the patient. It can also lead to endless intellectualization without behavior change. Self-esteem building, self-assertiveness training, and reparenting-type therapies are suggested for both males and females.

THERAPEUTIC FEEDBACK LANGUAGE

For men: Your profile suggests that you are a thoughtful, analytical, sensitive man, who is interested in philosophy and creative ideas. At the same time, the profile suggests that as a child you may have experienced a parent who, at times, could be somewhat cruel, cold, or rejecting. You may have responded to this adaptively by attempting to understand them and by formulating a worldview that explains why people are cruel or cold to one another. Because you are comfortable analyzing people and events, you may spend a good deal of time thinking, daydreaming, and be somewhat withdrawn from others. Others may misjudge you as a little aloof or cold. Perhaps you're also cautious about letting down your guard and letting people get close to you in case they should treat you coldly. You are quite comfortable in the world of ideas and creative, abstract thoughts. Discuss with your therapist whether you experienced moments of emotional coldness or cruelty from a parent figure that led to you "shutting down" and withdrawing into the comfort of your inner world. Learn how to be more assertive, and to recognize what is loveable about you so that you can be more comfortable allowing people to get close to you.

For women: Your profile suggests that you are comfortable in the world of men. Practical and action-oriented, you want to problem solve when you are confronted with a problem. At the same time, your profile suggests that you are somewhat cautious about letting down your guard and letting people get close to you. Perhaps growing up you had a caretaker who treated you coldly or even cruelly. You may have felt different from others and responded adaptively by developing your own personal philosophy and way of viewing the world. That may have led you to be cautious in allowing people to get too close to you. Work with your therapist on learning to like yourself so that you can allow others to care for you.

59/95 Codes

For men, the presence of an elevated Scale 5 reduces the likelihood of acting out, perhaps because of their increased capacity to intellectualize and be empathic. Some evidence suggests that men with this codetype do at least reasonably well academically. They are often colorful dressers with charismatic flair. Verbal, perceptive, and engaging, they are often seen as likable. However, they have a tendency to overcommit, (especially if the *Ma2* is elevated) and some may have difficulty with follow through. They are quite opportunistic, although not necessarily manipulative. In some cases, if Scale 9 is highly elevated, mood swings and possible mania can interfere with goal-oriented activity and interpersonal relationships. Problem areas tend to include emotional neediness and demands for constant attention. Men with this profile are driven by their need for approval, and require a great deal of reassurance. This is even more pronounced if Scale 3 is also elevated. Men with this profile can do well in people-related professions where sensitivity, empathy, and energetic charm are required, and their energy allows them to be intellectually and artistically productive.

For women, an elevated Scale 5 increases the likelihood of emotional reactivity shading toward verbal, if not physical, aggressiveness. These women typically are energetic, competitive, confident, uninhibited, adventurous, self-centered, and demanding. They can be quite intensely irritable when their goal-driven activities are thwarted or questioned.

These individuals generally do not report psychological problems or distress. Active, energetic, and easily bored, they describe themselves as self-confident and easygoing. Generally, Scale 0 is low, reflecting social comfort and the fact that they often make a good social impression. Even if the *MAC–R* scale is not elevated, both males and females can be addiction-prone, using chemical agents as a way of modulating their energy level.

TREATMENT

In the absence of mania, these hypomanic individuals are generally productive and successful. In the presence of mania, medication to stabilize energy and impulsiveness, and to prevent the possible cycling into depression is often necessary. In the absence of mania, these individuals profit from coaching types of therapy where they are held accountable for the commitments they make, but also allow them to feel validated and approved. Men and women tend to be driven by needs for approval, often reflecting internalized caregiver expectations, and their beliefs that only great success can lead to love and acceptance. Help them discover their own goals versus their beliefs about what they should do in order to obtain others' approval. For males, the mother–son relationship is sometimes a source of inner conflict. Even though they tend to extol their own virtues and appear confident, sometimes boastful, 59/95 individuals experience difficulties trusting that their accomplishments are "enough." Gestalt exercises such as role-playing "bragging" to help them engage and celebrate accomplishments can be helpful in reducing their drive to be constantly productive and validated by others. Setting realistic goals and not overcommitting out of a need to please are therapeutic goals. Women with a 59/95 codetype should explore their father–daughter relationship and its effect on their high competitive drive and need to vanquish competitors. They can also benefit from some of the above therapeutic strategies. Teach both men and women to manage their irritability when frustrated. Look for childhood histories of caregivers who were constantly motivating them to achieve and succeed. Explore childhood experiences associated with partial reinforcement reward schedules. Also, both men and women have a tendency to be quite demanding of their loved ones, demanding achievement and affection from them in ways that can lead to interpersonal conflict.

THERAPEUTIC FEEDBACK LANGUAGE

For men: Your profile suggests you are highly energetic, driven, competitive, and ambitious. You may have a tendency to overcommit. You are sensitive, creative, and intellectually curious. People with your profile are often seen as colorful, even flamboyant and charismatic. You enjoy creative and novel ideas, and you're comfortable in a sensitive, aesthetically-oriented environment. You're likely comfortable with women and enjoy some traditionally feminine activities. You may have grown up close to a female whose emotions and concerns you could readily understand. Perhaps one of your parents was always motivating you, or you felt an obligation to prove your family was successful through your efforts. You are also highly driven and impatient with a world that often moves too slowly for you. You have two speeds: "full speed" and "off." You tend to be happiest when you have slightly too much to do. Work with your therapist to determine when your energy level becomes counterproductive. Discover whether you are driven by your own ambitions or, instead, what you believe you need to achieve in order to obtain others' love and approval. Your therapist may suggest medication if your energy is counterproductive.

For women: Your profile suggests you are an energetic, ambitious woman who is comfortable in the world of men. You enjoy traditional male activities, and you are a practical, action-oriented, competitive woman who rejects stereotypic feminine interests and values. You think and move quickly, and operate at two speeds: "full speed" and "off." You probably get impatient with people who move or think more slowly than you do. People may see you as competitive to the point of being aggressive, and at times your energy is so high you may have difficulty completing things and following through on your commitments. You may have been close to a male figure growing up, and felt the need to achieve great things. Perhaps one of your parents was always motivating you or you felt an obligation to prove your family was successful through your efforts. Work with your therapist to determine whether your energy level ever becomes counterproductive.

Discover whether you are driven by your own ambitions or, instead, what you believe you need to achieve in order to obtain others' love and approval. Your therapist may suggest medication if your energy is counterproductive.

50/05 Codes

Men with this codetype are introverted, intellectual, creative, and reject stereotypical male activities and interests. They respond to stress by interpersonal and intellectual withdrawal rather than reaching out to others. They are cautious, inhibited, anxious around strangers, and are overcontrolled and over-ideational. Socially, they are awkward and have difficulty in being assertive, and some experience low self-esteem. They are embarrassed easily and do not act out. They may experience sexual difficulties due to their passivity.

Women with this codetype are typically more retiring and less assertive than one would expect from an elevated Scale 5. Some are from working-class or rural backgrounds. Others are comfortable in traditionally male occupations that require little social interaction. Women may seek careers in engineering, the armed services, or other kinds of professions where their practical, problem-solving skills are valued. They are comfortable working in relative isolation. For both men and women, further interpretation can be done by omitting Scale 5 and examining the resulting two-point codetype.

TREATMENT

Research has shown that introversion and extraversion tend to be stable, heritable traits. Assertiveness training as well as social skill building can be useful. Both males and females can profit from coming to terms with being introverts and learning social skills appropriate to their work and interpersonal circumstances.

THERAPEUTIC FEEDBACK LANGUAGE

For men: Your profile suggests that you are a sensitive, intellectual, creative, aesthetically-oriented man who is somewhat shy. You tend to avoid large groups of people you do not know, and you're most comfortable with small groups of like-minded people. You need time alone, can feel "burned out" by too much socializing, and find making small talk to be stressful. Some people with your profile are able to take on an interpersonal leadership role in front of others if it involves a structured task. At times you may hang back and lack assertiveness, not "speaking up" to protect your own interests until you feel compelled to do so. Explore with your therapist whether your shyness and empathy for others hinders you in your professional or interpersonal relationships. Rehearse certain social situations so that you become comfortable with small talk when you need to do so.

For women: Your profile suggests that you are a self-sufficient, introverted, practical, sensible, and action-oriented woman who's quite comfortable working alone. You dislike small talk and too much socializing with new people. Women with your profile are often comfortable in professions where you solve practical problems and have autonomy without the need for much social interaction. You probably have been this way most of your life, and if these traits are causing any difficulty, practice with your therapist learning how to relate to new people in unstructured social situations.

Scale 6 (Pa)

Spike 6

High scores ($T \geq 65$), a Spike 6 profile, reflects an individual who is highly sensitive, takes things personally and is suspicious of others' motives. These individuals can sometimes store resentments in a way that might be described as "injustice collecting." The interpretation of Scale 6 depends on the relative elevations of the Scale 6 subscales. In some cases, Scale 6 is elevated by mostly *Pa2* and/or *Pa3* subscales, with a lack of elevation on *Pa1*. In such cases, there is little evidence of paranoid ideation and feelings of persecution. Even without an elevation on *Pa1*, however, an elevated Scale 6 would suggest an individual whose sensitivity can shade toward paranoia when stressed, with paranoid jealousies, misunderstanding of others' motives, and ideas of reference. Projection tends to be a primary defense mechanism. When *Pa1* is also elevated, then delusions of persecution are likely. In cases with all three subscales elevated, a paranoid disorder is suggested. Some individuals, especially if they also score high on *K* and *Es*, can function relatively well for periods of time. Others may view them as "touchy," easily hurt, and quick to take retaliatory action against what might seem minor slights, but not as clearly paranoid. However, their sensitivity to criticism or any demands placed on them, and their tendency to be self-protectively argumentative about the fine points in an interaction, can eventually lead to interpersonal difficulties. A high 6 individual sees the world as a potentially dangerous place where "good people" can be trusted and "bad people" can't. Consequently, they constantly evaluate others to see where they fall on that continuum. Others may see them as rigid, judgmental, or egocentric, since they determine who is good and bad based on their own emotional needs and vulnerabilities.

High 6 individuals are argumentative and, because of this, tend to create arguments. They approach conflict as if they are defending themselves, rather than involved in a negotiation to resolve a problem for mutual satisfaction. They frame their wants, perspectives, and desires as justified on moral grounds. This leads others to argue and present the moral justification for their own perspective. A high elevation on Scale 6 with all subscales also elevated may reflect a psychotic disorder. In such cases, a preoccupation with the CIA, FBI, or even extraterrestrial malevolent forces would reflect the level of their internally experienced vulnerability, and the adaptive defensive response of appealing to higher powers and magical properties in order to protect themselves. Since the advent of reality television, there have been a number of cases of young people experiencing a paranoid reaction to stress by believing they were the stars of a reality TV show. Their paranoid construct, confirmed by what appeared to be TV episodes directed at them, maintained their belief system for long periods of time in a similar way to paranoid delusions about CIA spies shaped during the Cold War. Moderately high scores (T-55–65) reflect an individual who is sensitive, loyal, highly rational, analytical, and easily hurt by what they see as others' failures of empathy. They exhibit a tendency to take things personally and, under severe stress, misinterpret others' motives as consciously malevolent. The subscales are particularly useful in this range to tease out the relative contributions of the various components of paranoia. Sometimes Scale 6 is elevated in this range if an individual has been accused of a crime or a humiliating error. In this case it might reflect a heightened sensitivity to criticism, and feeling unfairly accused. Spike 6 individuals, even in the moderate range, can become self-defeatingly preoccupied with obtaining justice for a perceived slight or transgression. However, elevations in this range most often suggest a rational, analytical, fair-minded, and somewhat fastidious individual who can be subtly judgmental, which in turn elicits judgment from others.

Low scores ($T \leq 35$) are rare. A very low score suggests a cynical individual who sees most people as self-centered, self-absorbed, selfish, and ready to exploit any advantage over others.

TREATMENT

Since an essential issue with Spike 6 individuals is trust, the therapist has to win the patient's trust by being meticulously trustworthy. A high 6 patient will often be vigilantly aware of what the therapist says and does, and their stated procedures and therapeutic goals. Deviations from what the therapist has stated will likely be noted by the high 6 patient in anticipation of future conflict, or an injustice that may result from their therapeutic interaction. Because these patients tend to articulate their fears, concerns, and wants as rationalized demands rather than requests, they can be intimidating to treat. If the therapist views the patient in the context of their childhood conditioning experiences, this may minimize negative counter-transference. Typically, these individuals grew up in environments where a parent was extremely strict, using judgment, shame, blame, and sometimes harsh physical punishment as a way of controlling the child. In many cases, the harshness of parental discipline occurred without great hostility, but rather was administered with an air of righteousness. Repeated thrashings to "drive the devil out," and severe punishments to "teach the child a lesson," as well as verbal tongue-lashings and shaming punishments, served to instill in the child a hyper-alertness to anything that can be construed as criticism. Once the therapist sees the patient as vigilant out of fear, the therapeutic process can focus on soothing the patient's anxieties around anticipated therapist criticism or judgment. Be aware that the patient's seemingly innocuous questions about therapeutic procedures usually reflect a specific concern, and dealing with the transference on a weekly basis can be useful. Therapists must monitor their own defensiveness when the patient is subtly confrontational and critical of them. Help the patients understand that their high values and rigid moral standards are understandable, given their early conditioning experiences. Help them see how they are sensitive compared to other people, and therefore more likely to take things personally. Educate them as to how others can be insensitive out of a lack of awareness rather than willful hostility. Explore experiences of shaming punishments and unfair treatment by others, and encourage catharsis and self-empathy. Cognitive behavioral techniques can help them to be less sensitive and to take things less personally.

THERAPEUTIC FEEDBACK LANGUAGE

Your profile suggests that you are a very rational, analytical, loyal, and fair-minded person. It is important for you to be seen as doing the right thing, and you work hard to be above your own and others' criticism. You have high standards and you tend to be your own worst critic, in anticipation of how others may criticize you. People with your profile often grew up in environments where a parent may have been quite critical, shaming, judgmental, and punishing, as a means of control. From an early age you learned to try to be above criticism. You are quite sensitive, so that injustice, unfair criticism, or any kind of humiliation is particularly painful. At times people may have "accused you" of being too sensitive. Your sensitivity may well be genetic and is not a negative quality. However, many people lack your kind of sensitivity, and can often hurt you by their clumsy and unaware behavior, when they genuinely mean you no harm. Because you are sensitive and try hard to be above criticism, if others hurt your feelings it takes you a long time, if ever, to forgive them. Loyalty is very important to you, so if someone is disloyal, it is hard for you to trust them again. Since you dislike conflict and want to be above criticism, you may find yourself collecting hurts and injustices, waiting until you feel "justified" before you confront someone. By the time you are comfortable expressing your anger, hurt, and sense of being treated unfairly, you are quite angry. Because you want to be seen as fair-minded, when you are angry you try to explain to the other person what they have done "wrong." If you have a request of others, you may explain to them why what you want is reasonable and fair, and how you are not really making a request of them, but only demanding what is your right. Because you are going through life protecting yourself against criticism and judgment, others may feel criticized and feel the need to argue rather than negotiate with you. Growing up, one of your parents may have had a tendency to be quite critical, judgmental, and punish you at times that you felt were unjust. Work with your therapist to understand how you, like a number of people, experience heightened sensitivity to criticism. When you experience feelings of being wounded and unfairly treated, learn to switch these feelings off and to remind yourself that maybe your "sensitivity" is working overtime. Learn to ask for what you want before you feel resentful. When you are angry, try to tell people what you are angry about without telling them what they did wrong.

Relations with Other Scales

61/16 Codes

See 16/61 Codes.

62/26 Codes

See 26/62 Codes.

63/36 Codes

See 36/62 Codes.

64/46 Codes

See 46/64, 462/642, 463/643, and 468/648 Codes.

65/56 Codes

See 56/65 Codes.

67/76 Codes

This infrequent code most often has Scale 2 or 8 as the third or fourth highest scale. People with this profile are hypersensitive, tense, anxious, dysphoric, alienated from others, and can obsessively collect injustices. They are extremely concerned about criticism or disapproval, and are preoccupied with avoiding failure. The profile reflects an individual who is continually on edge and fearful, ruminating about how to avoid being criticized or judged. They obsess about who said what to whom, and what was really meant in relationship to them. They often present with interpersonal problems because of their extreme sensitivity, and need to constantly and defensively rationalize and justify their behaviors. Although insecure, with low self-esteem, and quick to feel guilty, they are also quick to defensively judge others. Ordinary interactions can become arguments because 67/76 individuals tend to position their requests or disappointments as resentments, perceived slights, or defensive arguments. Small misunderstandings about irrelevant details can degenerate into laborious justifications, which others perceive as subtle criticisms of them. 67 individuals experience guilt and are intropunitive. Their moods can be dysphoric due to their constant sense of apprehension. They can be distractible and indecisive since they try to see all sides of an issue, and are preoccupied with the avoidance of failure and criticism. They obsess and ruminate about how others see them, the righteousness of their own feelings, and what level of guilt or resentment they should be feeling. In rare cases, the profile can indicate a paranoid disorder. Some report intrusive ideas with religious preoccupations that reflect their needs to be absolved from guilt. They have difficulty with basic problem solving because they are both compulsive and rigid. Any perceived setbacks or shameful failures can lead to impulsive suicide, especially if suicide items are endorsed.

TREATMENT

These individuals generally have misgivings about therapy and feel very vulnerable disclosing personal and intimate details. Look for childhood experiences of being unpredictably shamed, judged, or severely punished. Supportive therapy and CBT to help them develop a more realistic self-image can be useful. Thought stopping, relaxation training, and assertiveness training can also be useful. Insight therapy can be helpful because these individuals are usually highly rational and analytical. Help them develop empathy for themselves as children who tried to be "above criticism." Help them to see how they adapted by going through life as if all interactions require them to defend themselves, rationalize their behavior, or preemptively judge others. Using CBT, work with them to understand that being constantly on guard against criticism was an adaptive response to being shamed and criticized, and that this response no longer needs to be constant and instinctive. Role-play with them how to express anger directly, without blaming others.

THERAPEUTIC FEEDBACK LANGUAGE

Your profile suggests that you are a sensitive, highly analytical, rational, and very fair-minded individual. You spend a great deal of time analyzing your own behavior to make sure it is above criticism. People with your profile often grew up in environments where a parent figure was unpredictably critical and judgmental. They had high standards and, being sensitive, criticism and judgment would make you feel guilty and ashamed. You responded adaptively by going overboard to make sure you did everything possible to avoid judgment. Now you analyze all situations to make sure that you are above criticism and have attended to your duties and responsibilities in ways that leave you beyond reproach. You may spend a great deal of time thinking about and analyzing what others think of you, what you have done in the past, and whether it leaves you open to others criticizing or judging you. It may be hard for you to make decisions, because you see every side of an issue. It may also be hard for you to tell people how you are feeling without first explaining why your feelings are reasonable and justified. When you do that, others respond to what they see as your defensiveness by being argumentative. You may experience conflicts in which you're trying to explain the righteousness of your thoughts, feelings, desires, and behaviors. Others may become defensive and focus on some minor detail of what you have said, trying to prove you wrong. Learn to express your wants, hurts, and resentments directly without explaining why your feelings are justified or why the other person is "wrong." Try to avoid using judgmental terms when you are angry with someone. Talk about your anger using "I" statements rather than "You" statements. Remember that you are sensitive and not everybody is equally sensitive. Sometimes you may take things personally when others have been clumsy or blind to your feelings, but did not intend to be mean or cruel. Talk to your therapist if you have concerns about trusting that you can open up and disclose in the therapy session. Using CBT, work on switching off your self-critical, anxious, and guilty thoughts.

68/86 Codes (see also 468/648, 486/846, and 489/849 Codes)

For both adolescents and adults, the 68/86 codetype predicts serious psychopathology and is most likely to be diagnosed with a thought disorder. It is usually accompanied by elevations on *F*, *BIZ*, *PSYC*, and *Pa1*, reflecting the psychological disorganization represented by this codetype. The *F* elevation reflects the paranoid ideation, unusual experiences, cognitive, emotional disorganization, and sense of disintegration endorsed by the individual. Psychopathology is more extreme when Scales 6 and 8 are both above *T*-65, and both are at least 10 *T*-scores above Scale 7 (sometimes called a "paranoid valley" due to the shape of the profile). A diagnosis of paranoid schizophrenia should be considered whenever the "paranoid valley" is present, and individuals with this configuration are likely to have had prior psychiatric hospitalizations, with recurrent episodes of psychosis. Since elevations on Scales 6 and 8 would suggest a severe disturbance, the lack of elevation on Scale 7, and the associated lack of anxiety would predict that the disturbance is ego-syntonic and, therefore, more resistant to treatment. These individuals experience psychotic disorganization, mental confusion, and a constant state of alertness to being attacked, judged, and criticized, which, for most people, would be highly anxiety-provoking. In the absence of such anxiety (low Scale 7), the individual appears to have habituated to a serious, disorganizing mental illness.

68/86 individuals in general are highly suspicious, distrustful, and tend to be loners. They are suspicious of others' motives and are easily cognitively disorganized by stress. They are described as moody, hostile, unpredictable, negativistic and, at times, emotionally inappropriate. They keep others at an emotional distance because of their irritability and anger and their tendency to arouse, fear, dislike, or disgust toward them in others. Affect is typically blunted, if not inappropriate. They manifest a depressed mood with apathy and anhedonia. Although they experience feelings of profound inadequacy and inferiority, they may mask it with a brittle hostility toward others. They can quickly become preoccupied with protecting themselves against real and imaginary enemies, and may avidly collect guns, knives, or other weapons. Many of these individuals are either an only child or the youngest in the family. Some may be diagnosed as bipolar because of the abruptness of their emotional reactions and sudden brittle, angry responses. (Look for elevations on Scale 9 and low scores on Scale 0 in these cases; see 698/968 codes.) Typically these mood swings are precipitated by the perception that others are threatening them. Some can become unpredictably assaultive. Many come across as eccentric or odd, with flamboyant or frightening dress and manner, perhaps because of cognitive disorganization, social alienation, and fears of emotional closeness. Tattoos, body piercing, and the brandishing of weapons may serve to keep others at a distance and remind them that the 68/86 individual is capable of self-defense. They are extremely sensitive to anything that can be construed as rejection or disrespect. Preoccupied with self-protection, they have little psychological insight.

These individuals' thought processes are characterized by overgeneralizations, misinterpretations, tangentiality/circumstantiality, and frank delusions. They have difficulties concentrating and being productive, in part because of poor reality testing and mental confusion. Depression, odd fears, phobias, and obsessions can also be present. Inner conflicts about sexuality and feelings of sexual inadequacy are a problem for these individuals. Most adults with this codetype are single and spend a great deal of time daydreaming and fantasizing. Behaviorally, these people are unpredictable, especially if Scale 4 (see 468/648 codes) or Scale 9 (see 698/968 codes) is also elevated.

Some adults with this profile reveal a history of spotty employment marked by episodic, impulsive terminations. They have difficulty controlling their anger. They exhibit episodes of fatigue, inefficiency, and difficulties with concentration. Adolescents with this codetype often show violent tempers, particularly if K is below T-50, and they have poor peer relations. They spend a great deal of time in fantasy and, not surprisingly, do poorly academically. Sometimes they are diagnosed with attention deficit disorder (ADD) and prescribed amphetamines with negative results. These teenagers often reveal a family history of having been subjected to corporal punishment and shaming.

The 68/86 individual typically has had caregivers who were rejecting, hostile or, at best, indifferent. They are particularly sensitive to hostility, perhaps because they experienced it as children, and can respond with acute outbursts of rage if they perceive themselves to be threatened.

TREATMENT

Insight therapy is contraindicated because these individuals readily become cognitively and emotionally disorganized. They may perceive the therapist as a potentially critical authority figure, possibly replicating their upbringing of having been treated coldly or cruelly. In therapy, they can easily become sidetracked and paranoid, ruminating about aggression they perceive to be directed at them by others. Psychotherapy should be nurturing and, if possible, reparenting and soothing, rather than attempting immediate behavior change. Providing structure without being overly friendly; being supportive and understanding can help the 68/86 individual feel less threatened. Antipsychotic medication is recommended. Often these individuals need assistance in meeting their basic needs, such as shelter, helping them navigate the complexities of finding employment, and managing daily affairs, such as paying bills and dealing with government agencies. Many rely on government programs for financial support. Sometimes they can become hooked in a retaliatory battle with a government employee whose rigid adherence to various bureaucratic rules appears to them as a vendetta against their rightful benefits.

THERAPEUTIC FEEDBACK LANGUAGE

Your profile suggests that currently you are feeling vulnerable to being criticized, judged, attacked, or humiliated by others. You appear to be going through life feeling unsafe, as if others are going to hurt or somehow humiliate you. You may be spending a lot of time thinking and fantasizing about who is "for" you or "against" you, and how you can protect yourself against your enemies. No wonder you do not enjoy life much of the time and feel sad, anxious, and preoccupied. Often people with your profile grew up in environments where someone was extremely critical and judgmental, or even cruel and rejecting. From an early age you learned to protect yourself, and to lash out and hurt others before they could hurt you. Perhaps one of your parents had a mental illness or some other problem that led them to be extremely strict and at times cruel, or even indifferent and uncaring. To protect yourself, you had to withdraw from others and comfort yourself by your inner world. Currently, you may be finding the world a frightening place, and it is hard for you to know whom you can trust. At times your mind might become invaded by strange and frightening thoughts, and it may be hard for you to distinguish between what is real and what is your imagination. When you are stressed, it is easy for your mind to play tricks on you, and for you to feel periods of panic and confusion about what is real and what is not. Your therapist may want to help you feel safer by suggesting medication that can take away some of the panicky feelings and confused thoughts. It is important to talk to your therapist about trust and what it will take for you to feel comfortable in therapy. Maybe you could both discuss some basic "rules of the game," so you can feel you have some control over the therapy process. If you are currently feeling afraid of being attacked and criticized, talk to your therapist about plans to defend yourself, so that you can get help to see how serious your current fears and anxieties are, and how seriously you should take some of your perceived threats.

69/96 Codes (see also 698/968 Codes)

This codetype predicts paranoid grandiosity, high energy, poor impulse control, insecurity, fear of inadequacy, and a strong need for acceptance and approval. The paranoia reflects fear of being criticized and judged. For both men and women, Scale 4 or 8 is most often the third highest scale.

People with this profile are tense, wound up, and quick to overreact to minor stressors, as though they were emergencies or potentially dangerous personal threats. These individuals live in a constant state of agitation and vigilance, feeling vulnerable to attack, criticism, and judgment from others. They have difficulty recognizing when they feel anger, so they are unable to express it in any modulated way. Anger tends to build up as an accumulation of resentments. The mania/hypomania energizes the paranoia, so the 69/96 individual is constantly alert and sees potential malevolence in almost every interaction. When anger is expressed, it tends to come as a breakdown of brittle control. These individuals often feel unfairly treated, persecuted, and thwarted in their goal-seeking activity. They are very sensitive to being controlled, and many experience family conflicts and in-law problems if married. They are rigidly moralistic and judgmental of others, perhaps as a defense against feeling judged. They defensively extol their virtues, which tend to be expressed in a competitive manner, as if they are defending themselves by revealing how others are inferior. Caldwell (personal communication, 2000) has described this codetype as reflecting the "left-out sibling" conditioning experience, in which the person has felt somehow not good enough relative to the other siblings. They develop a lifestyle that is hypomanically defensive, constantly seeking attention, approval, and acceptance, and at the same time judging others as if they were competitors for approval in a zero sum game.

People with this codetype tend to be excitable, loud, and sometimes charismatic, although also circumstantial. Paranoid defensiveness, flight of ideas, and overt psychosis also occur. The hypomania is experienced by others as intensity, irritability, impatience, suspiciousness, and resentment. These individuals can quickly become hostile if they feel threatened or criticized. Some may experience psychotic breakdowns, with hallucinations, religious visions, and delusions of grandeur and persecution. Most of the time, however, they appear to function relatively well for periods of time. This can be diagnostically confusing because the paranoid grandiosity can sometimes have some basis in reality. These individuals tend to commit to too many tasks and activities, and can be rigid and lack flexibility about doing things their own way. Often hypersexual, they can also be extremely jealous, possessive, and some may even become violent if their emotional security feels threatened. Family history often reveals a highly protective and affectionate parent who was also a strict disciplinarian. The other parent tends to be permissive or uninvolved. Both men and women with this codetype value being seen as attractive and often can be quite seductive and dress flamboyantly. However, they fear emotional involvement because of fears of rejection and demand a great deal of affection and reassurances of loyalty. If Scales 8 and 4 are also elevated, the propensity for violence increases.

TREATMENT

These individuals are defensive, seeing interactions as arguments in which they have to argue, explain, and rationalize their own behavior. Therapists may become defensive, since these patients will tend to judge and define the therapist's behavior, perhaps as a defense against being judged themselves. Even if *MAC-R* is not elevated, many have chemical addiction issues. They tend to be guarded and want to remain in control of their emotions, so articulating how they feel can be threatening to them. In some cases, a mood stabilizer can decrease the level of paranoia. Many are quite resistant to the sedating effects of antipsychotic and anti-manic agents. Therapists are most effective if they are willing to give the 69/96 individual approval and spend time listening to their elaborate hypomanic ambitions; initially taking the role of a coach rather than a therapist works best, since it avoids the stigma of a mental illness diagnosis.

Look for childhood histories of a strict, controlling, caring, but also critical, parent. Help the patient explore any memories of parent figures being harshly critical and shaming. Without criticizing the judgmental parent, help the patient experience how those moments of being criticized were particularly painful and may have felt unfair. Help them understand how their drive to be perfect and above criticism makes sense given how much they wanted to please and avoid criticism, but were, nevertheless, subjected to it. Their high drive and argumentative defensiveness makes adaptive sense given their parents' high standards and shaming criticisms. Explore how currently they may be feeling vulnerable to criticism or disapproval from others. Usually a precipitating circumstance for the increased hypomania and/or paranoia is a perceived rejection that is experienced as traumatic. If medication is indicated, help manage resistance by explaining how it could help them problem solve more efficiently. Help them distinguish between real threats and their hypervigilance.

When slighted or feeling wronged, these individuals can be dangerous, especially if they verbalize threats. It is important that the therapist does not become defensive if the patient reports feeling criticized by the therapist or becomes critical of the therapist. Genuine concern for the patient's hurt feelings as well as helping them engage in situations in which they felt particularly emotionally wounded can be productive if the therapist is sympathetic.

THERAPEUTIC FEEDBACK LANGUAGE

Your profile suggests that you are a very energetic, driven, and ambitious individual. Your mind works quickly and you tend to see the connections between things. You probably have two speeds at which you operate, "full speed ahead" and "off." You may find yourself experiencing a reduced need for sleep and periods of extremely high energy. You may feel a sense of heightened awareness and perceptiveness, feeling you possess special powers and have been chosen to accomplish great deeds. You may feel that you clearly see who is for you and who is against you. At times, your extreme sensitivity and perceptiveness may actually shade toward paranoia, so that it may be hard for you to know whom to trust, whether you're being hypersensitive or if, in fact, you are accurately "reading" people. People with your profile often grew up in environments where a parent was loving and demanding, but also critical and judgmental. Perhaps as a highly motivated child you tried extremely hard to be perfect and above criticism. Now you are particularly sensitive to people being critical or judgmental of you, especially since you have such high personal standards. You go through life trying to preempt people being critical or judgmental of you. Currently you may be feeling vulnerable to criticism, rejection, judgment, or attack from others. This may have precipitated an episode of extremely high energy spent protecting yourself against criticism by reaching for extraordinary accomplishments. At times, your sensitivity may be so acute that you actually become confused about whether you are seeing things clearly or whether you are experiencing moments of paranoia. At other times, you may feel so convinced that you have special powers and abilities that you will ignore others' advice or prohibitions. During this period of high energy, you may become irritable and angry if people block you in achieving your goals. If people are disloyal or you perceive them as in any way harming you, you may feel it necessary to protect yourself in ways that others find frightening. Talk with your therapist about whether you currently feel threatened and what may have precipitated it. In some cases, medication may help you think more clearly and allow you to use your energy productively, rather than be scattered or overcommitted.

Identify with your therapist any childhood experiences where you felt unfairly criticized or judged. Explore how that made you feel, without necessarily criticizing your parents, toward whom you may feel quite protective.

698/968 Codes

In addition to the 69/96 characteristics, the addition of Scale 8 predicts confusion, difficulties in thought and concentration, agitation, and possibly periods of intense, angry reactions and breakdowns in reality testing. Tangential and loose associations are common, as are delusions, paranoid suspiciousness, and in some cases, hallucinations. Hypomanic traits such as high energy, loud speech, and distractibility occur together with mental disorganization, so these individuals can become fixated and preoccupied with odd beliefs, religious messages, paranoid suspicions, and conspiracy theories. When Scale 8 is within five *T*-score points of Scale 6, see also 68/86 codetypes. See also 69/96 codetypes.

TREATMENT

See also the treatment sections of the 68/86 and 69/96 codetypes. In some cases, this is a manic disorder that is treated with a mood stabilizer, although in other cases an antipsychotic medication is also required. Paranoid hostility is a primary issue, as is confusion, agitation, and grandiosity, which lead to interpersonal difficulties. The therapist will need to manage the patient's anger and paranoia by being soothing and understanding, non-confrontational but limit setting. Look for early caregivers who were demanding, but hostile, possibly cruel and humiliating toward the patient. These individuals feel damaged, with hypomanic needs to prove themselves. Gentle reality testing and supportive therapy would be more useful than insight therapy.

THERAPEUTIC FEEDBACK LANGUAGE

See 69/96 and 68/86 and 89/98 codes feedback.

60/06 Codes

This is a rare codetype. These individuals experience moderate levels of distress characterized by a generally dysphoric mood, anxiety, low self-esteem, and a quick sensitivity to anything that can be construed as criticism or judgment. These individuals experience themselves as more sensitive than others, and report feeling things more intensely than others. Consequently, their feelings are easily hurt and they are inclined to take things personally. Others may see them as "touchy" and socially awkward. They readily experience feeling criticized, and see themselves as easily pushed around by others. When stressed, they may exhibit episodes of intense anger that comes as a breakdown of brittle control. These individuals tend to lack confidence. Even though they see themselves as rational, clear thinkers, with good judgment and memory, they also feel very self-conscious and socially alienated, perhaps reflecting the combination of shyness and sensitivity to being criticized. Their sensitivity can shade toward paranoia, with a misunderstanding of others' motives, unreasonable jealousies, and concerns that others are talking about them (ideas of reference). They are shy, uncomfortable in social situations, and easily embarrassed. In social events, they tend to stick to people they know and avoid spontaneously "joining in." They tend to hang back and not speak unless spoken to, and some report feeling lonely. Others may see them as honest, unassuming, reliable, and loyal once a relationship is formed. At the same time, they would be seen as somewhat prickly and unapproachable. Often they store resentments and allow them to accumulate until some particular event leads them to lash out in a highly rationalized outburst. Concerns about being sufficiently physically attractive are also common.

In some cases, a clear paranoid disorder is present, although it is not of a fragmented kind, as with schizophrenia, but a fixed, rational paranoia that is focused on a particular person or institution.

TREATMENT

Look for childhood conditioning experiences of a critical or punitive caretaker. Harsh scolding and shaming as a way of controlling the child would be typical. Help them learn to articulate needs, hurts, and resentments directly, rather than waiting until they feel justified and then expressing them as a rationalized, angry, blaming outburst. Help them understand that others' insensitivities toward them are not necessarily conscious attempts to hurt or humiliate them, and that their tendency to withdraw into hurt silence is also an expression of anger that engages others' anger toward them. Normalize introversion as a genetic trait rather than a "defect," and use assertiveness training and social skill building to decrease loneliness and social awkwardness. Prognosis should be good because they tend to follow prescriptions, but they tend to distrust and doubt the effectiveness of talk therapy, so the initial therapeutic alliance is difficult to establish. Although they would initially be uncomfortable with group therapy, a social skill-building group can be helpful. Discuss how they feel misunderstood by others and how painful it is to not be able to trust others with their intimate feelings. Encourage them to role-play "bragging" about some of their accomplishments to help them develop a better ability to accept compliments from others. Sex therapy can also be useful, as many of these individuals are afraid of letting down their guard and being vulnerable, resulting in marital discord.

THERAPEUTIC FEEDBACK LANGUAGE

Your profile suggests that you are quite shy, which means you're uncomfortable in large groups of people you do not know. People with your profile often prefer small groups of established friends or one-on-one conversations with somebody they know. You are quite sensitive, so pushy, demanding, or insensitive people can cause you a great deal of discomfort. You tend to have very high standards and are your own worst critic so others' criticisms or judgments are particularly painful, and you may find yourself ruminating about them. One of your parents may have been somewhat harsh and critical, or perhaps used shaming or severe punishments as ways to discipline you. They may also have not understood your sensitivity and how hurt you were whenever you were treated unfairly or harshly. You appear to be going through life cautious about letting down your guard, as if anticipating being criticized, judged, or unfairly treated. Sometimes it may be hard for you to distinguish between when you are being too sensitive and when, in fact, you have accurately perceived that hostility is being directed against you. Sometimes your sensitivity may lead to episodes of paranoia, where it is hard to know whom you can trust. Work with your therapist at understanding that your shyness and sensitivity are probably genetic and do not reflect that there is something wrong with you. Remember that many people are insensitive and when they hurt you, often it is out of clumsiness or lack of awareness rather than an attempt to consciously harm you. Work on expressing hurt and anger when you feel it, rather than waiting till you feel "justified" in expressing it. If you wait until you feel justified, by then you are often so angry that it is hard to forgive the other person. Perhaps join a group with other people who are also shy, so that you can realize that you are not alone, and learn some techniques for how to manage insensitive people. Learn to switch off your self-critical thoughts and use CBT techniques to manage your anxiety. You probably will feel uncomfortable engaging in psychotherapy because you are a private person who finds it difficult to discuss your feelings with a stranger. Discuss with your therapist how you can structure the therapy sessions to help you to feel most comfortable.

Scale 7 (Pt)

Spike 7

This is a relatively uncommon profile because Scale 7 has a number of items that overlap the other clinical scales, especially Scale 2 and Scale 8. High scores ($T \geq 65$) on this scale suggest an individual who is tense, anxious, guilty, and self-critically introspective. These individuals are self-conscious and feel insecure, inadequate, and inferior. A lack of self-confidence creates a tendency to procrastinate and feel overwhelmed by the responsibilities they feel obligated to undertake. They underestimate their own abilities in spite of evidence of successes. They are indecisive and suffer from "analysis paralysis" and general apprehension. In some cases, high elevations can also lead to physical symptoms associated with anxiety.

Scores in the normal range (T-55–65), the absence of a significant K elevation, would suggest an individual who takes life seriously and is prone to worry, with occasional anxious episodes as stress accumulates. Some individuals with Scale 7 in this high normal range can also exhibit obsessive–compulsive traits that others see as productive rather than disorganizing or debilitating. Others in this range may exhibit a specific fear or phobia.

Moderately low scores (*T*-35–45) in the absence of any other elevation above a *T*-score of 55 reflect an individual who is relaxed, comfortable, and without emotional distress. Generally self-confident and adaptable, others will see them as efficient and capable. However, their lack of anxiety in some cases may lead to inefficiency and missing deadlines.

TREATMENT

Scale 7 is often the most frequent high point on profiles of individuals in college counseling centers. Because of the item overlap, Scales 2 and 8 may also be elevated (see 278/728 codes). Look for childhood experiences of either a number of unpredictable traumatic or negative events, or a single traumatic unpredictable event that left them emotionally overwhelmed and panicked. In some cases, these unpredictable negative events were teasing or unpredictable explosive episodes directed at them by a caretaker. In other cases, the unpredictable event may have been the sudden loss of a parent, with the resulting loss of age-appropriate carefreeness.

Spike 7 codetypes are among the easiest to deal with therapeutically because these individuals follow advice, are disciplined, honest, and quick to feel guilty if they do not follow through on therapeutic commitments. Work on transference issues, as they expect the therapist to become impatient with them and are preoccupied with avoiding disappointing the therapist. Relaxation training, hypnosis, self-esteem building, thought stopping, and catharsis around past unpredictable traumas can be useful. Help them learn to express anger directly, without guilt or fear that anger expression could lose the support of loved ones. Also help them to develop better self-esteem. They gravitate toward taking on responsibilities out of guilt and then feel overwhelmed and panicked by the ensuing burden. They fear failure because of the shame and guilt that accompanies it.

With teenagers whose Scale 7 is significantly below *T*-50, therapy should focus on raising their level of motivation by judicious parental consequences in order for them to develop appropriate levels of anxiety.

THERAPEUTIC FEEDBACK LANGUAGE

Your profile suggests you are a dutiful, responsible, honest, and reliable person who experiences a constant level of worry and apprehension. It is as if you are always preparing for some unforeseen negative event, analyzing the future for what possibly could go wrong, and ruminating about your past behavior, usually finding something to feel guilty about. You often take on responsibilities and readily feel guilty if you make mistakes. It is hard for you to see your positive accomplishments. You often experience a sense of dread, even when you have no tangible reason to do so. It is hard for you to assert yourself and you feel guilty if you express anger toward others, even if others tell you that your anger was justified. You may have developed some rituals or behaviors that you compulsively practice, perhaps obtaining some temporary relief from anxiety in doing so.

You may have experienced some unpredictable painful events in the past, such as childhood teasing, losses of loved ones, or overloads of responsibilities to which you adapted by becoming constantly "on edge," attempting to predict and preempt guilt-inducing setbacks. Learn to recognize when you are experiencing anxiety and switch off the negative thoughts. Write down a list of your worries and preoccupations about possible future disasters and then make a list of all the things that could go well, so that you can maintain a balanced perspective. Take a meditation class and use biofeedback as a way to self-soothe. Explore with your therapist any past unpredictable events that conditioned you to preemptively worry. Develop a sense of empathy for yourself so you can begin to learn to relax and celebrate your accomplishments without guilt.

Relations with Other Scales

71/17 Codes

See 17/71 Codes.

72/27 Codes

See 27/72 Codes.

73/37 Codes

See 37/73 Codes.

74/47 Codes

See 47/74 Codes.

75/57 Codes

See 57/75 Codes.

76/67 Codes

See 67/76 Codes.

78/87 Codes

People with the 78/87 codetype have numerous symptoms and personality traits in common, but the scale order determines differences between them. When Scale 7 is higher than Scale 8, the individual is likely experiencing severe anxiety around what they perceive as a disintegration in their ability to control their thinking and feelings. A high level of anxiety in the presence of a potential thought disorder suggests an adaptive attempt at "thinking their way through" a sense of impending disorganization. When Scale 8 is elevated significantly above Scale 7, the individual has adapted to feelings of alienation and cognitive disorganization, and is no longer attempting to defensively cope. The 87 individual is, therefore, likely to be more seriously disturbed than the 78.

Individuals with the 87/78 codetype experience the following in common: They manifest worry, anxiety, dysphoria, fears and phobias, tension, obsessive thinking, and rumination. They are excessively introspective, view themselves negatively, and experience confusion and occasional breakdowns in reality testing. They experience the world as unsafe and feel a constant sense of apprehension and dread. These individuals obtain little pleasure from life. They take things personally and ruminate about how others are critical of them and do not like them. They are quick to feel irritated by minor setbacks, and see others' suggestions or advice as criticisms and judgments. These individuals tend to be passive, inviting rescue, and allowing others to control them, but then resenting it and feeling bullied. When feeling cornered, they can be explosive and, thereafter, feel humiliated. They have difficulty thinking clearly, concentrating, and effectively problem solving. They experience sleep hygiene problems and may exhibit specific fears, phobias, and compulsions. Suicidal thoughts are common. When Scale 8 is higher than Scale 7, suicide attempts can be bizarre and involve self-mutilation. Some 87 individuals can also experience hallucinations or delusions. Odd or even bizarre preoccupations are common, such as worrying about their pituitary gland or other symbolic expressions of feeling damaged. Not all 87/78 individuals show psychotic disintegration, however, although many experience at least occasional breakdowns in reality testing.

87/78 individuals lack confidence and feel inadequate. Poor sexual performance is likely since they are painfully self-aware and self-doubting. Achievement tends to be poor because of chronic low self-esteem and lack of self-confidence. Some use chemical agents as a way to medicate their anxiety.

Depersonalization and de-realization as well as isolation of affect are typical. These individuals see themselves as "damaged goods" and anticipate that they are going to be exposed as such and humiliated. They have difficulty making decisions and often feel they "lose out" because they are unable to make up their mind quickly enough. They often experience invasive thoughts interfering with concentration and memory. The 87/78 individual experiences a constant sense that he has done something wrong or that he is inherently evil. Often these individuals are quite introverted, easily embarrassed, and have poor social skills and judgment. Sexual fantasizing is common, though actual sexual contact is infrequent because of their interpersonal difficulties.

TREATMENT

These individuals generally have low motivation to seek treatment and doubt its efficacy for them, so engaging them in treatment can be difficult. Look for childhood histories of having been teased or put down, sexually abused, or experiencing some traumatic blows to their self-esteem. Some were slow to mature, which may have made them vulnerable to being teased or put down. Some may have been sickly as children and consequently felt vulnerable. Many currently experience health preoccupations and worries, perhaps reflecting a general fear that there is something seriously wrong with them. Others may have been food finicky as children, or exhibited other personal eccentricities which left them vulnerable to being teased or humiliated by siblings and peers.

If Scale 4 is coded third, the sense of alienation is increased, as is the likelihood of impulsive, self-defeating acting out to reduce tension. Young 78/87 adults experience difficulties in college because of low self-esteem and ambivalence about emancipating from a home where they were both infantilized and humiliated by their lack of self-efficacy.

Therapy should involve self-esteem building by nurturing therapists who encourage the patient to take small interpersonal risks once they have earned the patient's trust. Insight therapy tends to be disorganizing as they are self-critical and view insight as a confirmation of being "damaged goods." The 78/87 individual anticipates the therapist will take the role of an involved, caring parent who is both controlling and disappointed with them. Often they are immobilized in the therapy session, unable to collect and articulate coherent thoughts. They see themselves as defective and over-idealize the therapist. Self-revelation of personal frailties by the therapist can help the patient understand that most people experience vulnerabilities. Suicidal ideation is common. Psychopharmacologic intervention is often necessary to address their intense agitation and thought fragmentation. Assertiveness training, relaxation training and thought stopping to help manage their constant sense of panic can be useful.

THERAPEUTIC FEEDBACK LANGUAGE

Your profile suggests that you feel a constant sense of anxiety, worry, and dread, as if something terrible is about to happen. You feel self-critical and constantly guilty, as though you have done something terrible and are a condemned person. Often people with your profile grew up in environments experiencing teasing, put downs, or other unpredictable humiliations. You adapted to these events by staying constantly on guard and being careful to not allow others too close to you, lest they discover your weaknesses and exploit them to humiliate you. At times, your mind may feel as if it has a will of its own, and negative, disturbing thoughts feel as if they are invading you. It is easy to feel that others are looking at you critically and judging you, and even around strangers you likely feel sure people are feeling negatively toward you. Concentrating, remembering things, and making decisions are probably hard for you because you experience too many thoughts at once. Using a computer analogy, it is as if your mind has "too many windows" opened at once. At times, you may feel so confused that it is hard to know whether your worries and preoccupations are realistic, or if you are overblowing them. Your therapist may want to suggest medicine to help you feel a little calmer, think more clearly, sleep better, and not feel as vulnerable and unsafe. You may feel discouraged about therapy, perhaps feeling too vulnerable to open up and talk about how you are feeling. You may feel ashamed of some of your thoughts and feelings. Discuss with your therapist if you feel criticized or judged by the therapeutic experience. Talk to your therapist if you feel suicidal and plan to kill or harm yourself.

79/97 Codes

This relatively uncommon codetype often has Scales 8 or 4 as the next highest scales. It reflects an individual who is compulsively preoccupied with success and avoiding failure. The combination of Scale 7 anxiety, guilt, and apprehension is energized by hypomanic traits. In some ways, the scales are contradictory, since Scale 7 suggests insecurity, guilt, apprehension, and a lack of self-confidence while Scale 9 predicts grandiosity, overcommitment, and a buoyant self-confidence. 97/79 individuals are constantly on edge, preoccupied with avoiding loss, and maximizing rewards. They tend to be obsessive, driven, impulsive, and excitable. They are talkative, if not garrulous, and tend to switch topics readily in response to feedback from others. Some may experience somatic symptoms reflecting internal tension. Muscle spasms, backaches, insomnia, and disturbed sleep are typical. Reflecting Scale 7 and 9 traits, these individuals can present as fearful and panicked about an impending failure or loss and, at the same time, exhibit unrealistic optimism and grandiosity. They feel guilty about perceived past failures, and can exhibit both meticulous attention to detail as well as impulsiveness and procrastination. Highly overactive, 97 individuals tend to commit to too many tasks and activities. Impulsive behavior may lead to self-recriminating guilt. They are highly sensitive to being controlled. In some cases, the profile may reflect the hypomanic phase of a bipolar disorder. They exhibit conflict in intimate relationships, seek reassurance and are dependent, but at the same time resent being controlled.

TREATMENT

The central issue is a profound fear of failure and disapproval. Look for childhood conditioning experiences of parents who were constantly motivating the child to be more successful but quick to criticize their efforts when they viewed them as inadequate. In other cases, early economic deprivation may have resulted in the adoption of a constant high drive state, always seeking to maximize rewards and avoid failure. These individuals have a strong need to prove themselves. They tend to be defensive, both extolling their own virtues and preemptively protecting against criticism by exaggerated self-criticism. They oscillate between grandiosity and self-negation.

Treatment should focus on helping them define their own goals rather than internalized parental expectations. Relaxation training and thought stopping can be useful to control the severe anxiety and panic attacks. Implosion therapy can help engage their "worst fears" around failure, and being rejected and shamed because of it.

THERAPEUTIC FEEDBACK LANGUAGE

Your profile suggests that you are an extremely energetic and driven individual. You seem to work in bursts of energy, letting things pile up and then getting them done in a whirlwind of activity. Your profile also suggests that you experience periods of intense anxiety, usually centered on the pursuit of your goals. It is as if you are constantly on edge, trying to anticipate any small detail that could rob you of obtaining the maximum reward from any situation. You may experience a sense of urgency, constantly feeling like you're running late or are behind, and that somehow you have to achieve great things in order to feel lovable and worthy. If people keep you waiting or get in your way when you're focused on a task, you can become quite irritable and angry. Others may find being around you difficult because of your high energy and constant sense of anxiety. You may find yourself explaining yourself to others, sometimes talking too much or interrupting others, because "you know what they are going to say." Sometimes your mind can work quickly and you see all the connections between things, but it is hard to make a decision. Consequently, you may exhibit both compulsive and perfectionist traits and, at the same time, have areas of your life with many loose ends because you can't decide what "the perfect solution" should be. People with your profile sometimes grew up in environments where parents constantly motivate, but do not reward successes. In others cases, people with your profile grow up in environments where they were often frustrated in getting their needs met. You adapted by going on "full speed ahead" mode, constantly trying to maximize everything you do and trying to avoid the slightest setback or failure. As a result, the world moves too slowly for you, as if you're driving a sports car in rush hour traffic with one foot hard on the accelerator and the other foot hard on the brake. No wonder you experience a lot of internal tension that can result in physical symptoms of stress.

Work with your therapist to determine what you want out of life, and make sure that you identify your own goals versus goals that you think will please others. Discuss with your therapist childhood events that exemplify how you felt constantly pressured to achieve and succeed, and to avoid frustration and failure. Avoid overcommitting to too many tasks and activities. Watch your tendency to talk too much in social situations, and take some mindfulness classes to learn how to recognize when anxiety and stress are building. Find exercise programs that can help you relieve daily stress, which may improve your sleep patterns. Learn to control your anxiety by focusing on being "in the moment," rather than always thinking many steps ahead. Allow yourself to enjoy some of your past successes rather than constantly focusing on future ones.

70/07 Codes (see also Scales 7 and 0)

This is an uncommon codetype, with Scale 2 or 8 as the most commonly occurring third highest scale. It is useful to examine the two-point codetype that would result if Scale 0 were temporarily not included.

Individuals with these elevations are shy, worried, tense, and feel inadequate, especially socially. They feel insecure about their physical appearance. They tend to be obsessively self-critical, brooding, and experience difficulties with memory and concentration. The combination of scales suggests extreme social anxiety, as genetic introversion is aggravated by severe anxiety and self-doubt. These individuals lack confidence, are indecisive, and ruminate about their inadequacies. They often feel guilty, especially at the expression of anger toward others. Physical symptoms of anxiety are also common, and they may experience low energy levels in spite of feeling agitated. Even if Scale 2 is not elevated, they report feeling dysphoric. They report feeling constantly on edge, as if anticipating disaster, and are stung by minor criticism, taking setbacks badly. Problems with attention and concentration as well as difficulty in making decisions are typical. Although they gravitate toward responsibility, they are readily overwhelmed by it. Extremely shy and self-conscious, these individuals are easily embarrassed and may become "tongue-tied" in unstructured social situations. Sleep difficulties are common. While some can be obsessive, compulsive, and perfectionistic, others are unable to make decisions and tend to procrastinate.

TREATMENT

Look for a childhood history of life-long shyness, with resulting fears of being teased or humiliated. Thought stopping, relaxation training, meditation, an exercise program, self-esteem building, and social skill building can all be helpful. Mindfulness therapy can be helpful to recognize when they are experiencing overloads of stress and irritability, so they can learn to be expressive and manage their feelings with self-soothing techniques.

Your profile suggests that you are a shy person and have probably been shy most of your life. You are also a dutiful, responsible, and prone to worry individual who takes life seriously. Your profile suggests that you tend to be your own worst critic and that you are self-critical in almost all areas, even your appearance. Perhaps growing up shy you have always felt a little vulnerable in social situations. In unstructured social situations you may find yourself becoming "tongue-tied," unable to engage in small talk. Because you are prone to worry, you feel overwhelmed as responsibilities accumulate. You focus on your failures and defeats, and it is hard for you to celebrate your accomplishments. No matter how well you do at something, you can always see how it can be done better and you have a tendency to brood and ruminate about past events, criticizing yourself because you think you could have done things better.

It is often hard for you to make decisions because you're afraid of the resulting guilt if you feel you made a poor one. You tend to see the negative side of most issues, so sometimes you procrastinate, feeling paralyzed by all the possibilities and the things that can go wrong. People with your profile may experience periods of panic, and at times develop certain compulsions and obsessions, perhaps as a way of trying to reduce their anxiety. Growing up you may have felt fearful of being teased because of your shyness. You may have experienced unpredictable negative events that were traumatic, which led you to adapt by constantly trying to protect yourself against future setbacks. Work with your therapist on social skill building so you can learn to make small talk when appropriate. Work at being less self-critical. Take a mindfulness class to learn how to enjoy being in the moment and avoid looking at past events in a self-critical manner. Learn to recognize when anger is building, and rehearse ways to express it so that you do not feel guilty. Talk to your therapist about concerns you may have about therapy and feeling discouraged about the process even before you begin.

Scale 8 (Sc)

Spike 8 (T > 65)

A spike 8 profile with no other scales significantly elevated is rare and difficult to interpret. If *K* is low, so that Scale 8 is elevated mostly by the *Sc* items, it can reflect an individual who feels damaged, broken, and alienated from others. A high 8, low *K* would predict dysphoria, anhedonia, bizarre preoccupations, diffuse paranoia, and withdrawal. They have difficulty in thinking clearly and can experience psychotic breakdowns. They are unconventional in thought and action, may be socially eccentric or deviant, and are reluctant to become emotionally involved with others.

Scale 8 elevations are often associated with the need for inpatient treatment. These individuals have difficulty in communicating and their lives tend to be disorganized if not chaotic, and dysfunctional. Some exhibit periods of coherence and even productivity, but under stress they can readily decompensate. Although Scale 8 predicts schizophrenia poorly, it does predict schizophrenic-like thought processes, anhedonia, lack of social skills, and difficulties in daily functioning. These individuals tend to misunderstand others' motives and experience their inner world as outside their volitional control. Conversations with them often have a quality of being slightly "off the mark" and hard to follow. If K is elevated so that the Sc elevation is due largely to the K correction, the individual will exhibit many areas of compensated and efficient functioning. Even so, an underlying negative self-image and difficulty with intimacy can lead to interpersonal problems, even without psychosis. A high K, high 8 individual may hold eccentric beliefs and be oddly flamboyant in dress and presentation.

TREATMENT

A Spike 8 low K codetype reflects an individual who has damaged self-esteem. Look for childhood conditioning experiences of being treated with coldness, overt hostility or cruelty. In some cases, the individual was perceived as "different" from an early age. Perhaps painfully shy or with other personal eccentricities, they were vulnerable to being treated with coldness or hostility from others. In some cases, parents were overtly rejecting. The individual may have responded adaptively by withdrawing and developing behavioral habits and clothing styles that would serve to frighten others and keep them at a distance. Escapes into fantasy and emotionally "shutting down" to avoid unbearable rejection will have been an adaptive response, although at the same time limiting the individual's ability to process reality.

In therapy, these individuals may avoid eye contact and be difficult to engage. They have difficulty trusting, and anticipate the therapist rejecting them or feeling hostility toward them. Watch how the conversation may become interrupted during moments of vulnerability, as they say something distancing or odd, perhaps as an unconscious preemptive attempt to maintain distance and control. Insight therapy should be avoided as structured reparenting therapies are more appropriate. These individuals need structure because they have difficulty "reading" others' emotions. Self-esteem building and practical life-skill management are usually most appropriate. If the therapist can occasionally share minor vulnerabilities, it can help the patient feel less vulnerable to judgment for being "different."

THERAPEUTIC FEEDBACK LANGUAGE

Your profile suggests that the world currently may be somewhat frightening to you. You may be spending a lot of time thinking and daydreaming, but some of your thoughts may be frightening and you may feel that you do not have control over them. You may feel unsafe in a world that at times you find difficult to understand. People with your profile sometimes grew up in environments where a caretaker treated them coldly or cruelly. From an early age you may have learned to protect yourself by withdrawing and keeping people at a distance. Perhaps you dressed or acted in ways that frightened others, so that they would stay away from you and not invade your privacy. Currently, it may be hard for you to think clearly and make good decisions. You tend to be your own worst critic and you may be feeling that you are somehow damaged or broken, and therefore unlovable. It is hard for you to open up and allow people to get close because you are afraid they will hurt you. At times, it may feel as if your mind is playing tricks on you, so that it is hard to know what is real and what is imaginary. You may feel "invaded" by thoughts and feelings that are frightening, and even though you may want to switch off some of your thoughts, you may find it hard to do so. It may be hard to concentrate and remember things, and often your experiences may feel almost dreamlike, as if you're somehow outside your body. You may find that little in life gives you pleasure and you feel a constant sense of emptiness and dread. Your therapist may want to give you some medication that could help you organize your thoughts better and think more clearly. Work with your therapist to understand how closeness with others can be frightening to you since you grew up in an environment where you felt vulnerable to others' anger and hostility. Learn how to be more assertive so that you can tell people what you're feeling before you are angry. Learn how you keep others at a distance by some of the things you say and do, and work at finding ways to express what you are feeling in ways that others can understand.

Relations with Other Scales

81/18 Codes

Se 18/81 Codes.

82/28 Codes

See 28/82 Codes.

83/38 Codes

See 38/83 Codes.

84/48 Codes

See 48/84 Codes.

85/58 Codes

See 58/85 Codes.

86/68 Codes

See 68/86 Codes.

87/78 Codes

See 78/87 Codes.

89/98 Codes

Typically, the validity pattern with this codetype is associated with low L and low K scores with an elevated F scale, suggesting a candid, honest, somewhat panicked, "pleading for help" approach to the test items. Not surprisingly, this codetype suggests serious psychopathology, even when the scales are not highly elevated above a T-score of 65. The 89/98 individual feels inferior, inadequate, and has low self-esteem, but at the same time is disorganized, hypomanic, grandiose, and confused. They evidence hyperactivity, excitability, and disorientation. A combination of hypomania or mania, together with the Scale 8 characteristics of cognitive disorganization and damaged self-esteem, suggests an individual who is defending against feelings of inadequacy.

These individuals are highly over-ideational and spend a great deal of time in fantasy, daydreams, and rumination. They are tense and agitated, and insomnia is likely. Pressured speech, behavioral restlessness, emotional lability, and flight of ideas are likely. They are highly distractible, switching from topic to topic in response to anxiety-laden material. They have difficulties with attention and concentration. A psychosis may be present and can manifest as bizarre religious and sexual preoccupations. Physical symptoms of stress, such as gastrointestinal and neurological symptoms, may also be present, reflecting the high level of internal tension. Moods may switch from being grandiose to hostile and demanding. The 98/89 individual often exhibits a loud voice, and can also show suspiciousness and paranoid episodes. Some actually may withdraw into autistic-like episodes, although their internal thought processes can be hypomanic.

Typically, the precipitating circumstance is a perceived sexual rejection or humiliating setback. Often these individuals exhibit a history of aspirations of high achievement, but mediocre actual attainment. Perceived failure is often the precipitating cause of a hypomanic, disorganized 89/98 response. At increased elevations, there is increased likelihood of delusions and hallucinations, particularly of a religious nature. In the 1960s, this codetype was reported as common among people who experimented with LSD and had experienced a "bad trip." The term "schizo-manic episode" describes this codetype well, suggesting manic and psychotic symptoms. These individuals are extremely perfectionistic, so failure is experienced as disastrous and tends to confirm their negative self-concept. They are extremely self-critical and easily knocked off balance by rejection. The profile is often associated with an identity crisis precipitated by a failure or a rejection.

TREATMENT

Initially, treatment should focus on controlling the mania, which will diminish the psychotic symptomatology. A bipolar disorder should be considered. These individuals lack insight and resist psychological interpretation out of fear that they would be judged as defective. They need structure and support, as well as medication to manage the psychotic and manic symptomatology.

In therapy, they develop a rapid transference, with demands on the therapist, perhaps recapitulating childhood yearnings to be favored, to undo their experience of feeling put down or disfavored. Look for childhood conditioning experiences of parents who demanded a great deal of success, but could treat the child with coldness or hostility when displeased. Self-esteem building in a structured environment would be most appropriate. Help them develop realistic goals for themselves and a more realistic view of their achievements. They are extremely self-critical. Supportive therapy to help them reconstitute and feel less panicked is more useful than insight therapy.

THERAPEUTIC FEEDBACK LANGUAGE

Your profile suggests you are feeling intensely energized. You may have experienced a recent setback, perhaps a rejection by someone you cared about or a perceived failure that has left you feeling extremely agitated and anxious. You tend to be your own worst critic and you are currently experiencing a great deal of anxiety because you feel that you are a failure, are not good enough, and that the people you want to care about you will not, because you have somehow failed. You are so "wound up" it is hard for you to finish your sentences, switch off your mind, or even fall asleep when it is time to do so. You may find yourself fantasizing about doing great things, perhaps feeling that you have a special religious calling, or that somehow you have important messages to give to the world. If you have recently been taking any kind of drugs, you may be responding to their effects by becoming extremely agitated and overactive. If, in fact, you have experienced some blow to your self-esteem, this may have precipitated your current crisis. You are spending a lot of time thinking about your failures and how you need to prove yourself by doing something exceptional. However, you may find your mind racing, so that it is hard to focus and finish the things you start. Feeling this high level of tension, you might easily become irritated and angry if people get in your way or disagree with you about your insights and visions for how things should be. You may also be experiencing periods of paranoia, where you feel unsafe because you feel others are critical of you, trying to control you, or are out to get you. In some cases, people with your profile grew up with parents who demanded achievement and success, but also at times could be cold or cruel, perhaps favoring a sibling over you. You may have felt particularly controlled and, at the same time, treated unfavorably as compared to your other siblings. No wonder some recent setback could have precipitated in you a panic about your identity and a feeling that you need to do great things in order to be loved. Your therapist may want to suggest medicine to calm down your extremely high energy and feelings of panic and anxiety. Work with your therapist at seeing yourself more clearly so that you can switch off your constant self-critical thoughts. Set realistic goals for yourself and try to stick to them. Be aware that you get easily interrupted and distracted because, no matter what you are doing, you feel that maybe something more important needs to be done first. Use mindfulness therapy to observe your emotions and label them so that you can learn to express your feelings to others. Watch your tendency to interrupt others and finish their sentences or to interrupt yourself and switch from topic to topic. Learn to finish your sentences and stick to one topic until you finish exploring it.

80/08 Codes

Markedly aloof and socially withdrawn, these individuals are very uncomfortable in interpersonal relations and avoid social interaction. They tend to spend a great deal of time in personal fantasy, and their social isolation often extends to alienation from their families. They tend to describe themselves as depressed and anxious, and most report anhedonia. They describe their family life as conflicted and unsatisfying, and report having trouble making decisions because they worry that others will be critical of them. They are easily frightened and many have phobias. Extremely uncomfortable in any type of social setting, they tend to give up easily when frustrated, and avoid conflict whenever possible. Typically, they also feel worried, indecisive, and misunderstood by others. They often feel confused about what is bothering them or what they want or expect from others, and they lack assertiveness. In counseling sessions, they are likely to be largely nonverbal. They doubt therapy will work for them, and have difficulty disclosing personal information.

If a third scale is elevated within five *T*-score points of Scale 8 or 0, it is often helpful to temporarily ignore the elevation of Scale 0 and to interpret any two-point codetype that results. Scale 7 or 2 is most often the third highest scale elevation in this codetype.

TREATMENT

Because they generally are non-communicative, psychotherapeutic relationships are initially difficult. Therapist patience, without pushing the patient to speak, and a structured environment with life skill training are most useful. Gentle, supportive, esteem-building psychotherapy, along with assertiveness and social skill training, can be useful once a therapeutic alliance is developed. These clients are sensitive to anything that might be construed as criticism. Establishing rapport can perhaps be done by asking them general non-threatening questions about what foods they enjoy, or personal habits, being careful to not appear critical or "looking for what's wrong." Dialectical behavior therapy is useful. These individuals tend to be emotionally and socially isolated, so they lack the basic skills of relating to others; thus, even rudimentary rapport building can be therapeutic.

THERAPEUTIC FEEDBACK LANGUAGE

See feedback for Spike 8 and feedback for Spike 0.

Scale 9 (Ma)

Spike 9

Spike 9 individuals exhibit symptoms of hypomania and, in some cases, mania. They are energetic, excitable, over-productive, and exhibit pressured speech and superficial charm, together with a hostile, joking humor, and quick-tempered irritability if thwarted. Spike 9 individuals can often be extremely productive and successful, although impulsive behavior and lack of attention to detail can lead to self-defeating behavior. Spike 9 individuals dislike being controlled or limited, and they are often talkative, if not garrulous. Their thought processes can vary, sometimes in close proximity, from being well-organized, pressured, and somewhat grandiose, to disorganized and manically bizarre. They enjoy attention, speak with a loud-pressured voice, and readily switch topics in response to others' interests. Some are flamboyant. They tend to overcommit to tasks and activities, and they work in spurts of energy. When Spike 9 elevations are associated with mania, grandiosity with a religious flavor or messianic political fantasies and delusions can be present. Reduced sleep, and drug and/or alcohol use as way of medicating the hypomania are also common.

Moderately high scores (T-60–65) can suggest a well-adjusted energetic, outgoing, and active person who is seen by others as colorful, affable, and charismatic. They are quite achievement-oriented.

Low scores to very low scores (T < 45) suggest a lowered energy level, a lack of drive, listlessness, or even apathy. As Scale 9 is elevated, individuals appear increasingly committed to their beliefs, tend to feel that they are more perceptive and see the world more clearly than others. Some may become paranoid, feeling that others are jealous of them or getting in the way of their important world contributions. In cases of hypomania without psychosis, Spike 9 suggests an individual who superficially appears self-confident but is quite insecure and needs a great deal of approval. They tend to extol their own virtues and flatter others in order to elicit flattery in return.

TREATMENT

There may be a genetic component to high energy, hypomania, and its extreme, mania. Look for childhood histories of being active or hyperactive, with attempts by caretakers to control them. Caretakers are often constantly motivating the Spike 9 individual to achieve and succeed. In some cases they came from poor backgrounds and felt a need to enhance the family's social standing by their own success. They are very ambitious and the precipitating circumstance tends to be around the perceived failure or an obstacle to their achievement striving. In the presence of manic symptomatology, medication is recommended.

These individuals tend to be difficult to interview because of their denial and evasiveness, and their lack of focus. The therapist can develop a therapeutic alliance by giving them a great deal of praise and discussing how the intensity of their energy, while admirable, may be interfering with even better productivity. In other words, validate their self-image as needing to be productive and special, and reformulate therapy as helping them manage their intense energy so that it is more productive. Validate how they see the connections between things and their apparent social intelligence.

Once a therapeutic alliance has been established, help them to develop more realistic goals, and to differentiate between what they want for themselves and the internalized expectations of others. Help them control their impulse pressures and their tendency to switch careers or goals. Dealing with their fear of failure is a therapeutic goal.

THERAPEUTIC FEEDBACK LANGUAGE

Your profile shows that you are currently highly energetic. Your mind seems to be working unusually quickly, so you see connections between things and patterns and trends that others may not see. You may be so energized and euphoric that it is hard for you to sleep and get appropriate rest. You may feel that you have a special duty or mission in life because you see things so clearly, and you need to be a leader to help others see things as clearly as you do. Although socially skilled and charismatic, you may also show periods of intense irritability and anger, especially when people block you or get in your way when you're on a mission. You may use chemical agents as a way of trying to medicate your high, intense energy.

Your mind may work so quickly that it is hard for you to finish your sentences, and you may interrupt others without fully hearing them. You may move from topic to topic, almost as if you feel overwhelmed by all of life's possibilities. You may have grown up in an environment where you felt pressured to achieve and succeed. Perhaps recently some event occurred that made you feel a need to work harder to protect yourself against failure. Or there may have been a perceived setback or loss that precipitated a period of extremely high energy, which at times may leave you overwhelmed and unable to finish all the projects that you have undertaken. Work with your therapist to understand the pressure you feel to do great things. You may need some medication to help you make better use of your energy so that it doesn't flood your mind. Avoid chemical agents at this time, as they may interfere with clear thinking. Start a daily exercise program to blow off steam and make sure that you are getting enough sleep and rest. Work with your therapist to make a list of the things that you have accomplished successfully, so that you can set more realistic goals for yourself and also be realistic about your past successes.

Relations with Other Scales

91/19 Codes
See 19/91 Codes.

92/29 Codes
See 29/92 Codes.

93/39 Codes
See 39/93 Codes.

94/49 Codes
See 49/94 Codes.

95/59 Codes
See 59/95 Codes.

96/69 Codes
See 69/96 Codes.

97/79 Codes
See 79/97 Codes.

98/89 Codes
See 89/98 Codes.

90/09 Codes

This codetype is uncommon. A hypomanic, driven individual generally is not also shy, socially withdrawn, and socially insecure. However, this codetype does occur and describes an individual who is emotionally self-sufficient and cynical, with a tendency to obsess, ruminate, and manipulate others to get their needs met. These individuals can exhibit hypomanic traits, are readily bored, and have difficulty with attention and concentration. These individuals tend not to be depressed although they may complain of dysphoria. They are shy and withdrawn, but can be quietly egocentric and competitive. They are self-sufficient, self-directed people who can become more garrulous and talkative once they are comfortable in a small social group. In such situations they can be quite demanding of attention and extol their own virtues. People may see these individuals as somewhat aloof and disdainful toward others. This may reflect the high 9 individual's self-confidence and grandiosity. It can be helpful to initially ignore the elevated Scale 0 and to interpret the two-point codetype without the Scale 0.

TREATMENT

See treatment section under the Spike 9 codes. Social skill building may also be useful.

THERAPEUTIC FEEDBACK LANGUAGE

See Scale 9 and Scale 0 feedback.

Scale 0 (Si)

Spike 0

High scores ($T \geq 65$) and the Spike 0 codetype reflects a preference for being alone rather than with others, particularly if no other scale is elevated above T-65. Elevations on Scale 0 above T-65 suggest a person who is shy, interpersonally uncomfortable, insecure, introverted, and submissive. As the score approaches T-75, this scale also suggests an absence of social supports, perhaps even a schizoid aloofness, and problems in establishing meaningful attachments with others. Moderately high scores (T-55–65) may indicate a personality trait of being self-contained, autonomous, and quite adaptive in situations (e.g. college) requiring sustained periods of solitary activities.

Elevations of Scale 0 tend to reduce the likelihood of acting out indicated by other scale elevations (e.g. Scales 4 and 9), but may exacerbate the rumination or self-absorption indicated by, for example, Scales 2, 7, or 8.

Moderately low to very low scores ($T < 45$) are obtained by persons who prefer to be with others and feel anxious when alone. Most often they are outgoing, gregarious, friendly, enthusiastic, and have strong needs for affiliation, social recognition, and status. When scores are below T-35, their strong social presence may threaten others who may then judge them as opportunistic, manipulative, shallow, superficial, and flighty.

Usually Spike 0 persons do not seek treatment for their shyness unless they are forced by circumstances to be in situations that do not allow them personal space. If shyness is a problem, social skill building, self-esteem building, and relaxation training therapies are most useful.

THERAPEUTIC FEEDBACK LANGUAGE

Your profile suggests that you are a shy person comfortable with small groups of people you know well rather than large groups of new people. Sometimes when called upon in a social setting without being prepared, you may find yourself embarrassed or tongue-tied. Shyness tends to be a genetic trait, and as long as you're comfortable being shy, it does not reflect any mental disturbance. Work with your therapist to find a group of like-minded people to discuss ways to deal with your shyness so that you do not feel awkward and embarrassed in new social situations. Sometimes reaching out to others by asking them questions about themselves can promote a conversation so that you do not have to be at a loss for words.

THERAPEUTIC FEEDBACK LANGUAGE FOR LOW SCORES (*T* < 35)

Your profile suggests that you are an extraverted person who enjoys relating to others. You are comfortable meeting new people and even talking to people whom you've never met before. It is important for you to have time to be around people and you may become bored by spending too much time alone.

Relations with Other Scales

01/10 Codes

See 10/01 Codes.

02/20 Codes

See 20/02 Codes.

03/30 Codes

See 30/03 Codes.

04/40 Codes

See 40/04 Codes.

05/50 Codes

See 50/05 Codes.

06/60 Codes

See 60/06 Codes.

07/70 Codes

See 70/07 Codes.

08/80 Codes

See 80/08 Codes.

09/90 Codes

See 90/09 Codes.

Normal Code, High K *(K+)*

The K+ profile (Marks et al., 1974) is quite common in outpatient settings among people of upper SES and does not suggest the extent of psychopathology reflected by a similar profile in an inpatient setting. In an inpatient setting, this profile reflects a highly controlled, denying individual whose underlying psychological problems are suppressed. Profiles well within the normal limit range, with a K scale over T-65, are challenging to interpret. In some cases, they reveal a poised, emotionally sophisticated individual who approaches life with a "stiff upper lip." The archetype of British reserve and emotional control captures the high K individual. In such cases, suggesting the individual is "defensive" would be unreasonable since their emotional control and reserve may well be due to culture or personality. In other cases, a K+ profile may represent an individual who is defensive and masking inner turmoil.

On the basis of the MMPI-2 re-standardization, the following adjustments to the Marks et al. (1974) rules are suggested. Research is needed to support these modifications. In inpatient settings the following criteria should be met: F must be below T-65, L and K must be greater than F, six or more of the clinical scales must be below T-56, and K – F must be greater than five T-score points.

This profile often is produced by persons who are highly defensive about admitting psychological problems, which they view as personal weaknesses. Usually, they avoid situations in which their own performance might be compared unfavorably with others and are generally cautious, anxious, and inhibited. They are particularly influenced by others' evaluations of them and, as a result, are easily dominated, led, or controlled. Withdrawn from others, they often are seen as suspicious and fearful, with a strong schizoid component to their personality.

TREATMENT

Whether as an inpatient or outpatient, these individuals need K-lowering therapies that help them become aware of their feelings. Once rapport has developed, help them ventilate and role-play, expressing anger, sadness, and even joy, so as to lower their overcontrol.

THERAPEUTIC FEEDBACK LANGUAGE

Your profile suggests that you are a person who tends not to wear feelings on your sleeve. In a crisis when people are "losing their heads," you stay cool, calm, and collected. Others may have difficulty "reading" your emotional state. If you are angry, you might express it in a somewhat refined or controlled manner, so others will have to multiply the intensity of what you are saying in order to understand the intensity of your true feelings. Even when you experience surges of positive emotion you may not express them in ways that are obvious to others. Perhaps you grew up in a family that was highly emotional and, at times, emotionally out of control; therefore, you learned to suppress the expression of strong feelings. Perhaps at an early age, you had to stay cool, calm, and collected, because the adults in your life were emotionally volatile. In other cases, people with your personality style grew up in families where emotions were expressed in controlled and refined ways. Practice with your therapist role-playing different emotions so you can become comfortable with spontaneous emotionality. Be aware that others may have a difficult time reading you. When you do experience surges of strong emotion, learn to express your feelings in a manner that allows others to be empathetic toward you.

7 Interpreting the Content of the MMPI-2

Critical Items, Content Scales, and Subscales

Critical Items

The empirical keying or contrasted-groups methodology used by Hathaway in developing the eight basic clinical scales of the MMPI represented a significant innovation in personality inventory construction. Previous inventories relied on intuitive judgment to produce items related to a trait of interest and to combine them with other items thought to be related to the same trait to compose a scale. The items and scales thus composed tended to be highly face valid (i.e. the items tended to be obviously related to the trait to be measured). Unfortunately, they were often unsatisfactorily related to external criteria and were overly vulnerable to the test-taking attitudes of the examinee that would bias responses and potentially distort the results of testing.

The new approach required only that items selected for inclusion differentiate between normal and abnormal criterion groups empirically. The authors of the MMPI gave little consideration to the content of individual items and were concerned only that the breadth of coverage for the original item pool was sufficient to sample a wide array of attitudes and behaviors. The justification for the new empirical strategy was provided in the classic manifesto of Meehl (1945a), "The Dynamics of 'Structured' Personality Tests."

In the decades following the release of the MMPI, clinical needs and advances in psychometric theory and methods have seen a return to attaching greater importance to test item content. The "dust-bowl empiricist" rationale for proscribing the examination of item content in the clinic was succinctly stated by Meehl (1945b): "The scoring does not assume a valid self-rating to have been given" (p. 147). But studies demonstrating comparable validities for personality assessment instruments developed under both rational and empirical strategies (Hase & Goldberg, 1967), and the appearance of sophisticated positions defending the importance of test item content (Goldberg & Slovic, 1967; Jackson, 1971), were instrumental in moderating Meehl's (1945) earlier position (Meehl, 1971, 1972). These developments were predated, however, by the needs of clinicians to explore the MMPI as part of and prelude to acquiring proficiency in its use and the pressing demands of clinical work to understand patients under investigation.

Caldwell (1991) has pointed out that the basic elements of the MMPI that are subject to interpretation may be located on a gradient of increasing obviousness or transparency, with the (a) subtle components of the clinical scales and certain additional scales (e.g. *K* and, perhaps, *Mf*), (b) certain highly subtle empirically derived scales (e.g. *MAC–R* and *O-H*), and (c) the basic clinical scales having subtle components corresponding to three initial steps of this gradient. Intermediate steps would include empirically derived scales more generally, including the more obvious of the basic clinical scales. Still more obvious would be the components of the basic clinical scales and scales whose developmental methodology emphasized internal consistency standards, such as the Wiggins', the MMPI-2 content scales, and the RC scales. The top-most steps in this gradient would include scales composed of items with unusually low endorsement rates, such as the *F* and *FB* scales, and the so-called critical items. It should not be surprising that the growth in the appreciation of test item content and its potential importance in the clinic should have originated with the distinction to which Wiener and Harmon (Wiener, 1948; Wiener & Harmon, 1946) called attention, between subtle and obvious content, and critical items.

Initially, clinicians sought access to the patient's responses to certain items thought to be clearly indicative of psychopathological disturbance. Grayson (1951) gathered a set of 38 items for use with a VA population. Endorsement of any of these in the course of psychodiagnostic evaluation was considered sufficient to warrant more detailed clinical inquiry into the content area of the item, regardless of whether the MMPI profile appeared pathological. In some cases, these items were considered pathognomonic of a condition, such as delusions or suicidal ideation. In others, the item would serve as a red flag or a *stop sign*, forcing an interruption of the diagnostic process in order to explore the patient's grounds for its endorsement. These thus came to be called *stop* or *critical items*. The history of critical items actually goes back to the Woodworth (1920) Personal Data Sheet, which included 10 "neurotic tendency items." These were considered indicators of neurosis, regardless of the remainder of the individual's responses.

Although the Grayson items were widely adopted (Gravitz, 1968), particularly after being reprinted in *An MMPI Handbook* (Dahlstrom & Welsh, 1960), alert practitioners soon discovered that this group of items was overwhelmingly redundant with the *F* and *Sc* scales. Eighty-five percent (32/38) of these items were scored on one or both of these, 40 percent (16 items) on the *F* scale alone (Koss, 1979). Moreover, for 92 percent (35/38) of the items, the keyed response was True. Thus, however salient the content of the individual items might be as a springboard for investigation within the interview, it became clear that the Grayson items placed undue stress on psychoticism, to the exclusion of other problem areas; that these items, like the *F* scale itself, were sensitive to gross deviancy and to a set on the patient's part to exaggerate or conceal psychological complaints; and that they were also vulnerable to an acquiescent response style, the inclination to mark items True, regardless of their content.

Another set of critical items was selected by Caldwell (1969). Seeking a broader range of content, Caldwell chose 68 items, distributed among nine categories. As a set, the Caldwell critical items covered a wider range of problem areas than the Grayson items. Nevertheless, although not quite so dominated by psychoticism, with 56 percent (38/68) of the items overlapping *F* and *Sc* (20 items, or 33 percent, on *F* alone), these items remain relatively saturated with this source of variance. These shortcomings were in addition to the greatest concern of all: that the Grayson and Caldwell critical items, with their origins in the rational-intuitive processes of their creators, had no demonstrated empirical relationships with the symptoms and complaints they enunciated. Critiques by Greene (1980) and R. G. Evans (1984) noted the occurrence of the Grayson and Caldwell critical items in normal groups, and other contradictory evidence for their validity.

Seeking to address the external validity of critical items, Lachar and Wrobel (1979) investigated the empirical correlates of a large number of items, including those appearing in the Grayson and Caldwell lists, nominated by clinicians as relevant to 14 common problem areas for psychiatric in- and outpatients. Lachar and Wrobel ultimately settled on 111 items, distributed into 11 content areas, of which 99 achieved significant (.05) correlations with counterpart information on problems recorded in patient files; the remaining 12 items achieved acceptable correlations with closely related criteria.

An alternative approach was taken by Koss and Butcher (1973; Koss, Butcher, & Hoffmann, 1976) to ensure empirical correlates for critical items by identifying six crisis situations, each marked by a set of behaviors or complaints exhibited by patients

Table 7.1 A comparison of the content contained within three sets of critical items

Lachar–Wrobel		Caldwell		Koss–Butcher	
Content category	No. of items (MMPI/ MMPI-2)	Content category	No. of Items (MMPI/ MMPI-2)	Content category	No. of items (MMPI/ MMPI-2)
Psychological discomfort					
Anxiety and tension	11/11			Acute anxiety	9/17
Depression and worry	16/16	Distress and depression	11/11	Depressed-suicidal ideation	25/22
Sleep disturbance	6/6	Suicidal thoughts	5/5		
Reality distortion					
Deviant beliefs	15/15	Ideas of reference, persecution, and delusions	10/1	Persecutory ideas	12/11
Deviant thinking and experience	11/10	Peculiar experience and hallucinations	9/9	Mental confusion	3/11
Characterological adjustment					
Substance abuse	4/3	Alcohol and drugs	4/3	Situational stress due to alcoholism	15/7
Antisocial attitude	9/9	Authority problems	5/5		
Family conflict	4/4	Family discord	7/7		
Problematic anger	4/4			Threatened assault	3/5
Sexual concern and deviation	8/6	Sexual difficulties	7/6		
Somatic symptoms	23/23	Somatic concerns	10/10		

at the time of their admission to the hospital. After defining the crisis group, Koss and Butcher asked clinicians to identify MMPI items that corresponded to the behaviors and complaints characteristic of each of the groups. Nominated items were then cross-validated on newly admitted patients, with non-crisis psychiatric patients serving as controls.

Despite the different methods used to develop the Lachar–Wrobel, Caldwell, and Koss–Butcher critical item sets, Table 7.1 suggests a high degree of similarity in the content of the items for each set, as well as roughly comparable areas of coverage. Each critical item list references distress and dysphoria, cognitive disruption, psychotic ideation, and substance abuse. (See Table A6, pp. 569–576 in Friedman et al., 2001, for the MMPI-2 items and scoring direction for the Koss–Butcher, Lachar–Wrobel, and Nichols critical item lists.)

A fourth list was developed by Nichols (1989) when he found many of the Lachar–Wrobel critical items categories insufficiently homogeneous and those of Caldwell and of Koss and Butcher, too restricted. For example, in his consultations for a neurologist, he wanted to be able to specify the kinds of somatic complaints endorsed more precisely, both in terms of their specific content and in terms of the proportion of items endorsed within a specific content area, such as motor difficulties or genitourinary complaints. He was also discontented with the inclusion of items in categories implicating psychotic mentation that might reflect only "unusual" culturally based beliefs and experiences. For example, the item "Evil spirits possess me at times," although frequently scored on scales highly saturated with psychoticism (e.g. *F*, *Pa*, *BIZ*, *PSYC*, and *RC6*) and potentially endorsed as an acknowledgment of the kind of hallucinatory or other anomalous experience common to psychotic states, may also be endorsed at relatively high frequency by members of certain religious sects or immigrants from countries wherein a belief in spirits, evil and otherwise, is more common than in the United States. Nichols therefore devised a new set of items based on both rational and statistical considerations. Categories were initially selected from large-scale item factor analyses on a very large Midwestern psychiatric sample. These categories were then refined by subdividing many of the somatic factors into more discrete classes of symptoms by eliminating categories that essentially duplicated the content of normed scales, such as fears and phobias, and by examining patterns of item overlap among content scales and the Caldwell, Koss–Butcher, and Lachar–Wrobel lists. Because of their established validity characteristics, virtually all of the items in the Koss–Butcher and Lachar–Wrobel sets were retained on the Nichols Critical Item List (NCIL). More than any of the alternative critical item lists, the NCIL permits a more specific assessment of both the range and the intensity of symptomatic expressions, particularly within the health/somatic/neurological area. The NCIL for the MMPI-2 contains 217 items spread over four major classes and 23 specific item clusters.

Of the two chief controversies surrounding the use of critical items, one is conceptual, the other statistical. The conceptual issue is whether inventory items should be considered behavior samples or behavioral signs. According to Koss (1979), the earliest inventories viewed item responses as veridical self-reports or samples of behavior that could stand in lieu of actual interview or observational data, thereby providing a more efficient basis for clinical description. It was in part in reaction to this view, and the disappointing performance of previous inventories guided by it, that Hathaway chose to adopt an empirical approach to the composition on his scales. Abandoning the assignment of items to scales on the basis of judgments a priori, Hathaway left between-groups differences in endorsement frequency to identify each item as a sign of the criterion group, its significance to be determined by further investigation. Meehl's (1945b) enunciation of the empirical rationale emphasized the range of understandings various people might bring to test items and stressed the fact that a given statement was endorsed over the content of the statement itself. In his words, the empirical approach

> consists simply in the explicit denial that we accept a self-rating as a feeble surrogate for a behavior sample, and substitutes the assertion that a 'self-rating' constitutes an intrinsically interesting and significant bit of verbal behavior, the non-test correlates of which must be discovered by empirical means.
>
> (Meehl, 1945a, p. 297)

According to Meehl, the importance of a structured inventory response is not so much in its intrinsic semantic characteristics, its "face value," but the fact that certain kinds of people "tend to *say* certain things about themselves" (p. 298).

An unqualified allegiance to the sign approach would obviate the need for selection in gathering candidate items for the pool; any items would do. In their decision to formulate items out of their *clinical* experience, from psychiatric textbooks and interview forms and from previous personality and attitude scales, Hathaway and McKinley implicitly offered a bow to the traditional view. Their departure from it came only after the item pool was established, with the commencement of scale construction. As a result, most of the basic clinical scales of the MMPI are made up of a mix of items, some seeming to function more as samples, others apparently operating as signs. Dahlstrom (1969) called attention to this range in the way items may be understood, and his distinctions tend to parallel the distinction between obvious and subtle item content. That is, it is the obvious items that most readily conform to the behavior sample or self-report conception, whereas the subtle items, to the extent that they are valid, better fit into a conception of items as behavioral signs.

The statistical issue concerns the reliability of individual items and aggregates of items such as scales. If test–retest stability is the issue here, the MMPI-2 *Manual* (Butcher et al., 2001, Appendixes E and G) makes it clear that over short time periods, at least, the temporal stability of the majority of individual items is at least as good as that of the most commonly used scales of the MMPI-2. Nevertheless, the endorsement of individual items may occur as a result of accident, confusion, misunderstanding, or similar inadvertence. The detailed probing of critical items, even when logistically feasible, does not always correct such mishaps or yield satisfactory information. Some respondents will deny valid endorsements by claiming disability or faux pas; others may feel excessively pressed and intruded upon by close questioning of item responses. For these reasons, it is recommended that the psychologist begin any probing with the least threatening critical items and only then proceed to the more threatening content.

Proponents of the emphasis on item content (e.g. Butcher et al., 1990; Wiggins, 1966) have often focused on the internal consistency, typically measured by Cronbach's (1951) coefficient alpha, of item aggregates (i.e. scales) as an index of the adequacy of such aggregates for psychological measurement. Coefficient alpha operates as a measure of the homogeneity of item aggregates, or the degree to which the content of one item of an aggregate is similar in content to the other items included within it. Scales that have been developed using procedures designed to maximize internal consistency tend to bear a striking resemblance to aggregates derived from the factor analysis of test items (e.g. Friedman Sasek, & Wakefield, 1976; Johnson, Butcher, Null, & Johnson, 1984; Waller, 1999). In comparing scales, coefficient alpha will serve as an index of the degree of semantic spread that is observed as new items are added to a preexisting set. For example, starting with an item such as "My dad is a good fellow," the addition of a second item, "I love my dad," results in a very small enlargement of the semantic focus of the first item and a correspondingly slight decline in internal consistency. If to these two items one adds a third, "My mom is a good mother," the semantic focus is enlarged from positive sentiments about the father to similar sentiments toward parents. This will result in a further, and probably larger, increment of decline in internal consistency. The addition of a fourth item, "I enjoy kids," broadens the focus yet again from parents to parents and children or perhaps to even "people in general" and may be associated with a still larger drop in internal consistency. A fifth addition, "I like romantic movies," would suggest a very sharp broadening of semantic focus to something like "liking things and people" and would be associated with a correspondingly sharp decline in coefficient alpha. Adding a sixth item, "I hate all my relatives," might either augment both the focus of the aggregate and the value for internal consistency if it were scored "False" or essentially destroy its semantic coherence and internal consistency if scored "True." The main point is that internal consistency reflects the degree of semantic redundancy within a given set of items and, by implication, the personological redundancy (or strength, or robustness) of the attribute in the individual who achieves a high endorsement rate for the items in the set. However, coefficient alpha is always a declining function of the number of non-identical items in a set. The point at which to close a given set to additional items is therefore at least somewhat arbitrary, and there is always at least some trade-off between internal consistency and test–retest stability because internal consistency favors short scales, whereas temporal stability and classification accuracy (Emons, Sijtsma, & Meijer, 2007; Kruyen, Emon, & Sijtsma, 2012) favor long ones.

The internal consistency approach to scale development contrasts with the empirical or criterion keying approach, in which items are selected for inclusion on a given scale because they are associated with higher rates of endorsement by members of the criterion group than by groups such as normals. The values of coefficient alpha for empirically derived scales may vary considerably from one scale to the next but are generally modest in comparison with content-based scales. Each of the items included in an empirical scale is assumed to provide an increment of non-redundant criterion (e.g. diagnosis in the case of most of the basic MMPI scales) related variance that will make a unique contribution to the identification of cases similar to those comprising the criterion group. Although it is true that such scales may possess considerable common variance and yield correspondingly high estimates of internal consistency (e.g. Scales 1, 7, and 8), such variance is not a goal of the method but an artifact of major sources of variation operating within the item pool at large. In some instances, large common variances may even attenuate the validity of empirically derived scales by reducing their specificity, Scale 7, saturated as it is with the first factor, being an example.

In this context, the NCIL might be seen as a compromise between the critical item approach and the content scale approach to the analysis of content. By forming critical items into relatively many but small sets, or "miniscales," the NCIL may be less vulnerable to interpretive hypotheses based on unintentional endorsements and yield a more pointed picture of a person's symptoms and complaints than is possible when pathological responses to a small cluster of items become obscured, given that such clusters may become hidden within their parent scales.

Another set of small, highly homogeneous item clusters have been proposed as subscales for the MMPI-2 content scales (Ben-Porath & Sherwood, 1993; Sherwood & Ben-Porath, 1991) discussed below.

It is primarily in the context of other test data that sets of critical items, or any highly redundant cluster of items, have potential value to the clinician. Individual critical items and small sets thereof offer the clinician access to very highly focused components of the participant's self-report that may be obscured or lost in aggregates that approach the size of conventional scales, or even scales of high internal consistency, such as content scales. However, in the absence of supporting indicators in other features of the test, such as scale scores, profile codes, and the like, critical items are likely to over-predict the kinds of symptoms, problems, and concerns suggested by their content. It is significant that with the exception of the now rarely used Grayson items, all critical item lists subdivide their items into categories determined by content, thereby deemphasizing Grayson's initial conception of these items as stand-alone or stop items, in favor of a conception that places critical items in a position intermediate between stop items and formally developed and normed scales.

Whatever their source, critical items afford the clinician a valuable if not always reliable channel of communication with the patient. Single and small sets of items are the means by which the patient can most directly address his or her concerns to the psychologist within the context of the MMPI-2. Although the various scales and indexes of the test serve to identify those problem areas that are of significance in the patient's current life and circumstances, it is only through single-item responses that the patient can call the clinician's attention to his or her specific problems. The clinician's access to some of these responses, in the form of critical items, can help to create a channel of communication that stands to facilitate empathy between therapist and patient and build a bridge between the phases of assessment and treatment.

Content Scales

As highly homogeneous collections of items with similar content, the MMPI-2 content scales also provide a means by which the patient can communicate with the clinician. Because the most immediate access to the symptomatic behavior and concerns of the patient is through scales having a strong thematic character, content scales are designed in a way that allows them to respond directly to aspects of the examinee's self-presentation on the MMPI-2. As Wiggins, Goldberg, and Applebaum (1971) noted, the view that the MMPI constitutes "an opportunity for communication between S [subject] and the tester has much to commend it; not the least of which is the likelihood that this is the frame of reference adopted by the S himself (p. 403).

In understanding the relationship between content scales and the clinical profile, it is helpful to recall the first two levels of Leary's (1956, 1957) multilevel interpersonal diagnostic scheme. He categorized as Level I data those which are concerned with how a person is described by others or the interpersonal pressure his symptoms, complaints, preoccupations, attitudes, and traits of character exert on them (i.e. his social "stimulus value"). Data at this level are objective and public and may or may not agree with the person's own view of him- or herself or situation. It is this level that is reflected in the MMPI-2 clinical profile.

By contrast, Level II data are conscious descriptions of the person's phenomenological field, the report of his or her self-perceptions in terms of behavior, symptoms, traits, and relations with others. Content scales are especially sensitive to data at this level. Again, the person's self-report may well not coincide in its impact on or meaning to others with that anticipated by the person him- or herself.

These levels and their corresponding sets of scales reflect points of view and should not be considered mutually exclusive. Payne and Wiggins (1972) found generally excellent agreement between interpretations based on common clinical profile types and content-scale-derived personality descriptions. Butcher et al. (1990), Lachar and Alexander (1978), and Lachar, Dahlstrom, and Moreland (1986), among others, have also demonstrated meaningful and reliable Level I correlates of content scale scores.

Nevertheless, the redundancy of standard and content scales is far from perfect, and the ability to compare patterns of responses to the same item pool from both diagnostic and self-report based perspectives adds a very fruitful dimension to MMPI-2 interpretation. Each set of scales provides a useful context within which to consider the other. Comparisons between the two sets will often lead to the formulation of more detailed hypotheses regarding patterns of interpersonal functioning, psychodynamics, defensive operations and coping skills, adjustment and adaptation, and diagnosis than can be obtained from either set alone.

Taking as his starting point the 26 content categories identified by Hathaway and McKinley (1940), and treating each as a prototype scale, Wiggins (1966) developed a set of 13 content scales for the original MMPI: Poor Health (*HEA*), Depression (*DEP*), Organic Symptoms (*ORG*), Family Problems (*FAM*), Authority Conflict (*AUT*), Feminine Interests (*FEM*), Religious Fundamentalism (*REL*), Manifest Hostility (*HOS*), Poor Morale (*MOR*), Phobias (*PHO*), Psychoticism (*PSY*), Hypomania (*HYP*), and Social Maladjustment (*SOC*). Final internal consistencies ranged from about .5 to .9, with a median at .75. Research throughout the 1970s and early 1980s uniformly supported the validity of the Wiggins content scales in many different populations. (For a description of the correlates for each of the 13 Wiggins scales, see Wiggins, 1966, and Friedman, Webb, and Lewak, 1989.) Scoring keys for MMPI-2 versions of these scales may be found in Gotts and Knudsen (2005), and in Greene (2000).

With the decision of the MMPI Re-standardization Committee to replace 90 MMPI items with 107 new items came an opportunity to evaluate the content of the revised MMPI-2 item pool. Butcher et al. (1990) followed procedures similar to those of Wiggins in developing new content scales for the MMPI-2. Butcher identified 22 provisional categories of content from an examination of Hathaway and McKinley's original categories, the results of a large-scale replicated item factor analysis of the MMPI (Johnson et al., 1984), and a review of the newly written items for the MMPI-2.

He then produced definitions for each category and, with Dahlstrom and Graham, assigned items to them. Provisional content scales were established from sets of items agreed to by at least two of these three authors. They then discussed the composition of each of the provisional scales, item by item, until consensus was reached. Twenty-one revised provisional scales remained after one was dropped for an insufficient number of items. These scales were then evaluated by means of deleted item-total correlations and deleted coefficients alpha to identify items that reduced the internal consistency of the revised provisional scales so that these items could be dropped. Four of the revised provisional scales were found to have unacceptably low internal consistencies and were dropped from further development. At this stage, however, a new provisional scale, Cynicism, was added and purified, as described, bringing the number of scales for continuing investigation to 18. Computation of the correlations between the purified scales and each of the remaining items in the MMPI-AX item pool was undertaken to add new items that strengthened these scales' internal consistencies but that had not heretofore been identified as belonging to the content domain of the scale. These purified and augmented scales were then subjected to a rational review to determine if the provisional scale name and definition needed adjustment and to identify and eliminate any items having an insufficient content affinity for their parent scales, even though their statistical association was strong. At this stage, two scales were combined and two others were dropped, leaving 15 scales. In the next step, a statistical and rational review enabled the identification of items more highly correlated with other scales and their elimination or reassignment. In this stage, overlapping items were permitted so long as the scales sharing items were conceptually related. In the final steps, uniform *T*-scores were established and rational descriptions based on each scale's final item content were composed. Later, Ben-Porath and Sherwood (1993; Sherwood & Ben-Porath, 1991)

Table 7.2 The MMPI-2 content scales with numbers of items and patterns of item overlap

		FRS	OBS	DEP	HEA	BIZ	ANG	CYN	ASP	TPA	LSE	SOD	FAM	WRK	TRT
ANX	23	2												5	
FRS	23														
OBS	16													4	3
DEP	33					1				2				1	6
HEA	36														
BIZ	24											1			
ANG	16							3					1		
CYN	23						7		1				1		1
ASP	22							1							
TPA	19												2		
LSE	24												1		2
SOD	24														
FAM	25														
WRK	33														4
TRT	26														

Table 7.3 Item overlap between MMPI 2 content and component scales and the Wiggins content scales

Scale	HEA	DEP	ORG	FAM	AUT	FEM	REL	HOS	MOR	PHO	PSY	HYP	SOC
HEA	13		20										
HEA1	4		1										
HEA2			10										
HEA3	3		1										
DEP		16							5				
DEP1		5							2				
DEP2		4											
DEP3		4							2				
DEP4		2											
FAM				10									
FAM1				5									
FAM2				2									
CYN					12		2		2		2		
CYN1					10								
CYN2					2								
ASP				1	12		1						
ASP1					10								
ASP2					2								
ANG								8				1	
ANG1								3					
ANG2								4					
TPA								9				1	
TPA1								2					
TPA2								5					
LSE	1							6					
LSE1	1							5					
LSE2								1					
FRS										19			
FRS1										8			
FRS2										10			
BIZ											19		
BIZ1											9		
BIZ2				2							8		
SOD										2	1		16
SOD1										1			3
SOD2										1			6
TRT		2						2					
TRT1		2						2			1		1
TRT2													
ANX	1	6	1					3		1		1	
OBS		1						1		1			
WRK		2	1					5				2	1

developed subscales for several of the content scales that they called *components*. The
final MMPI-2 content scales are listed with their numbers of items and patterns of item
overlap in Table 7.2. (See the MMPI-2 *Manual*, Butcher et al., 2001, Tables B-4 and B-5
for a listing of the item composition and scoring directions for the MMPI-2 content and
content component scales; and Tables A-8–A-11 for the uniform *T*-score conversions
from raw scores for these scales.)

Before describing the MMPI-2 content scales in detail, it may be helpful to compare
the content domains of the MMPI and MMPI-2 with reference to the Wiggins and
MMPI-2 content scale sets (see also Kohvtek, 1992a, 1992b). Table 7.3 presents the
overlap between the MMPI-2 content scales and each of their components with the

Table 7.4 Intercorrelations of similar MMPI-2 and Wiggins content scales for re-standardization
men (and women)

MMPI-2 Somatic Content Scales			
	HEA	*ORG*	
HEA	79 (81)	82 (84)	
MMPI-2 Distress Content Scales			
	PHO	*DEP*	*MOR*
FRS	91 (92)	38 (39)	39 (39)
DEP	39 (43)	89 (91)	79 (80)
ANX	44 (47)	80 (83)	74 (77)
OBS	46 (49)	69 (75)	72 (79)
LSE	40 (41)	70 (73)	79 (83)
TRT	45 (48)	75 (76)	75 (76)
WRK	46 (46)	79 (82)	82 (85)
MMPI-2 Cynicism and Psychotic Content Scales			
	AUT	*PSY*	
CYN	84 (86)	58 (64)	
BIZ	44 (46)	84 (82)	
MMPI-2 Hostile Affect Scales			
	HOS		
ANG	79 (80)		
TPA	80 (78)		
MMPI-2 Antisocial Content Scale			
	AUT		
ASP	88 (87)		
MMPI-2 Interpersonal Content Scales			
	FAM	*SOC*	
FAM	82 (86)	23 (22)	
SOC	18 (19)	92 (92)	

Table 7.5 Similarities and differences for the MMPI-2 and Wiggins content scales

MMPI-2		Wiggins	
Content Scale	Abbreviation	Content Scale	Abbreviation
Anxiety	ANX		
Fear	FRS	Phobias	PHO
Obsessiveness	OBS		
Depression	DEP	Depression	DEP
Health Concerns	HEA	Organic Symptoms	ORG
		Poor Health	HEA
Bizarre Mentation	BIZ	Psychoticism	PSY
Anger	ANG	Manifest Hostility	HOS
Cynicism	CYN	Authority Conflict	AUT
Antisocial Practices	ASP	(Authority Conflict)	(AUT)
Type A Behavior	TPA	(Hostility)	(HOS)
Low Self-Esteem	LSE	Poor Morale	MOR
Social Discomfort	SOD	Social Maladjustment	SOC
Family Problems	FAM	Family Problems	FAM
Work Interference	WRK		
Negative Treatment Indicators	TRT		
		Feminine Interests	FEM
		Religious Fundamentalism	REL
		Hypomania	HYP

Wiggins scales. Table 7.4 presents the correlations among groups of scales from the two sets having similar item content.

Despite the similarity of the two sets of scales, differences between them often appear on examination of those scales having similar names (see Table 7.5). For example, about half (16/33) of the MMPI-2 Depression scale (*DEP*) items are retained from the Wiggins *DEP* scale, but 6 (18 percent) of the original Wiggins *DEP* items now appear on MMPI-2 Anxiety (*ANX*). Eight (24 percent) of the MMPI-2 *DEP* items are from the 107 newly written items for the MMPI-2, including 3 of 4 items bearing suicidal content. Of the 27 items on Wiggins' Manifest Hostility (*HOS*), 8 now appear on MMPI-2 Anger (*ANG*) and 9 appear on MMPI-2 Type A Behavior (*TPA*). Of the 36 items on MMPI-2 Health Concerns (*HEA*), 13 were formerly on Wiggins' Poor Health, but 20, more than half of the items on MMPI-2 *HEA*, were taken from Wiggins' Organic Symptoms (*ORG*). Nine items, including 4 with genitourinary content and 3 with bowel content, were among those dropped from the MMPI-2 item pool that were formerly on Wiggins' Poor Health.

These changes, although unsuspected from an examination of the names of the scales discussed, are apt to have significant consequences for the proper understanding of the MMPI-2 content scales, their interpretive implications, and their empirical correlates. In the case of MMPI-2 *DEP*, the loss of its "anxiety" content and the addition of items denoting suicidal ideation can only strengthen its performance as a measure of depressive symptomatology. Although not necessarily a superior measure of somatic preoccupation or over-concern than its Wiggins predecessor, MMPI-2 *HEA*, with its shift toward symptoms localized to the head and musculature and away from lower gastrointestinal and genitourinary content, must show a corresponding shift in its profile of empirical correlates. As a result of these and similar differences between the Wiggins and MMPI-2 content scales, any more than a rough equivalency between these two sets of scales should not be assumed.

The reliability of the MMPI-2 content scales is uniformly high, with internal consistencies characteristically falling into the upper end of a range of .70 to .85 and nine-day test–retest stabilities falling in the center of the range of .80 to .90. We discuss the validity characteristics of the MMPI-2 content scales for each of the scales individually (Ben-Porath, McCully, & Almagor, 1993).

The MMPI-2 content scales are organized around four themes: internal symptoms; external or aggressive tendencies; a devalued view of the self; and general problem areas, including social style, family attachment, and attitudes toward work and psychotherapeutic treatment. The internal symptoms cluster—anxiety, fears, obsessiveness, depression, health concerns, and psychotic mentation—are oriented toward Axis I syndromes. The external or aggressive tendencies cluster—anger, cynicism, antisocial practices, and Type A Behavior—is directed toward the evaluation of Axis II disorders. The devalued view of the self-category contains only one scale: Low Self-Esteem (*LSE*). Although these themes may appear conceptually distinct, they are not independent in a statistical sense. Because the MMPI-2 is geared toward the detection and description of psychopathology, the item pool is highly biased in favor of items that report symptoms and problematic attitudes and behaviors. It should not, therefore, be surprising that face-valid scales drawn from this item pool show relatively high positive intercorrelations. The largest concentration of high intercorrelations for the MMPI-2 content scales is for Anxiety (*ANX*), Obsessiveness (*OBS*), Depression (*DEP*), Low Self-Esteem (*LSE*), Work Interference (*WRK*), and Negative Treatment Indicators (*TRT*), averaging .72 in the Re-standardization Sample (range = .57–.79). These fall within a range of .40 to .49. The scales within the external-aggressive cluster are also substantially intercorrelated, averaging .58 (range = .46–.76).

Anxiety (ANX)

The *ANX* scale contains 23 items, of which 18 are keyed True, 5 False. Among the MMPI-2 clinical scales, *ANX* correlates most highly with Scale 7 (*Pt*) at .80 and with Welsh's *A* at .80. The primary theme in *ANX* is excessive worry against a background of nervous tension, disturbed sleep, and problems with attention and concentration. Subjective stress levels are already so high that decisions and disappointments are felt to carry the risk of total mental fragmentation and collapse; hence, the anxiety in question in *ANX* is close to panic. High scorers feel "stressed out" and carry a strong sense of both dread and vulnerability. The anxiety in question in *ANX* is also generalized; any and all events are seen as potentially disastrous and devastating, with tensing up and worrying providing the only insulation against the threat that a sudden unanticipated event will cause one to "go to pieces." The scale has a single item reporting somatic manifestations of anxiety: heart pounding and shortness of breath. Two of the items denote financial concerns.

Because the symptoms of anxiety captured on *ANX* tend to pervade conscious experience, they are associated with insight and a strong desire for relief. As a result, patients with high scores will generally have neither the means nor the inclination to conceal these symptoms (although they may feel reluctant to admit other symptoms, such as hallucinations).

Relations to Other Scales

Elevations on other scales in the presence of high *ANX* scores provide a basis for hypotheses about the object of anxiety and the circumstances most likely to provoke a sense of panic. For example, in the presence of an elevation on Bizarre Mentation (*BIZ*), a high *ANX* score may reflect particular concerns about anomalous experience and psychotic disintegration. With a high *LSE* score, a high *ANX* score suggests particular apprehensions around self-devaluation, narcissistic injuries, the imminent withdrawal of dependency supports, and imperiled self-esteem. With a high *DEP* score, a high *ANX* score may suggest fears of a worsening of depressive experience, falling into despair, and a collapse into helplessness and hopelessness.

Fears (FRS)

The *FRS* scale contains 23 items, 16 True, 7 False. It is one of the most independent of the content scales and achieves only modest correlations with a few of the standard MMPI-2 scales. In particular, *FRS* and *ANX* correlate at only .35. *FRS* has no counterpart among the standard clinical scales of the MMPI-2 and shares few items with them. As a result, the presence or absence of phobic symptoms cannot generally be inferred from the standard clinical profile. Excessive fearfulness and more specific phobic concerns form the primary theme of this scale. The word *fear* and its cognates (*afraid, dread*, and *frightened*) appear in more than three quarters of the items. The several groups of items include (a) specific fears of classically phobic type (e.g. darkness, heights, and open and closed spaces); (b) animals (e.g. mice, snakes, and spiders); (c) natural phenomena (e.g. earthquakes, lightning, storms, fire, and water); (d) loss of physical integrity, especially through germs and tissue damage; and (e) admissions of general neurotic fearfulness and a low threshold for feeling fearful that is likely to be incapacitating. Ben-Porath and Sherwood (1993) found statistical justification for dividing the scale into two components: *FRS1*, Generalized Fearfulness, and *FRS2*, Multiple Fears. In terms of the groups of *FRS* items described, *FRS1* encompasses most of the items in Groups a, d, and e, whereas most of the items contained in *FRS2* are from Groups b and c. The theme of *FRS1* is one of a broadly apprehensive tone in one's approach to daily life, one that places an emphasis on the dangers or potential harmfulness of objects and circumstances in the environment. Phobic anxiety appears to be the key empirical correlate of this component (Graham et al., 1999), as well as for *FRS* as a whole. Green, Archer, and Handel (2006), however, report a broader set of correlates for their inpatients based upon Brief Psychiatric Rating Scale (BPRS; Overall & Gorham, 1988), Symptom Check List

90-Revised (SCL-90-R; Derogatis, 1992), and case history data, including excitement, suspiciousness, conceptual disorganization, hallucinatory behavior, unusual thought content, and histories of sexual abuse in addition to the more expectable correlates of anxiety, tension, depressive mood, and somatic concerns. Thus it appears that *FRS1* contains non-negligible, indeed notable, psychoticism variance.

FRS2 contains no theme as such but is simply an enumeration of relatively common phobic objects and circumstances. Low scores on *FRS* connote fearlessness and the risk of reckless disregard for, or obliviousness to, danger, painful consequences or punishment such as may be found in manic-like pictures with euphoria, intrepidness, and poor judgment (high scores on Scale 9 and low scores on Scale 0 and *SOD*), or psychopathic recklessness (high scores on Scale 4, *FAM*, and *ASP* [*ASP* > *CYN*]). Low scores may also be associated with rigid attitudes regarding gender-role requirements in men, particularly macho masculinity (low scores on Scale 5 and high scores on *GM* [*GM* > *GF*]). Occasionally, low scores are seen in the context of "working" somatization pictures, with such physical complaints as abdominal pain, back pain, or visual problems.

The meaning of extreme scores on *FRS* is highly dependent on other features of the content and clinical profiles. When elevated with Scale 7, especially the 273/723 profile, *FRS* connotes phobic anxiety. In conjunction with profiles with peaks on *HEA* (and perhaps Scale 3, *Hy4*, *Sc6*, and *HEA2*), elevations on *FRS* connote a strong harm-avoidant orientation and strong fears of somatic injury, illness, or decay.

Relations to Other Scales

Both *ANX* and *FRS* tap phenomena of apprehension. In the case of *ANX*, the apprehension one feels is inchoate; one feels trepidation over the unpredictability of external and internal events that are feared to lead to disorganization and chaos. The defense against this feared breakdown in organization is active in the sense of involving preparation to contend with or absorb the threatened sudden event. With obsessive worry, one has a means of anticipating catastrophe in time to avert or avoid it. In *FRS*, however, the apprehension is condensed onto a particular object or situation, or set thereof; the focus is on the avoidance of injury and harm, and the defense against these dangers is fundamentally passive: one seeks not to contend with the feared object or situation but to avoid it; if unable to avoid, one might freeze or panic. The condensation of apprehension onto known objects and situations enables developmentally more advanced defense mechanisms to be brought to bear in the management of anxiety based on repression and displacement, measures which restore a sense of freedom from fear in those areas of life and functioning that do not risk exposure to phobic foci. This may explain, in part, why the correlation between *FRS* and *ANX* is not greater. In some patients experiencing generalized and incapacitating fear or anxiety, a score greater than *T*-70 on *FRS* or, especially, on *FRS1*, may be operating to mask more serious psychopathology, not excluding active psychosis (check *Sc*, *Sc3*, *BIZ*, *PSYC*, etc.). This is analogous to the familiar relationship between Scales 7 and 8 on the clinical profile in which the degree to which Scale 7 exceeds Scale 8, given the elevation of both scales, reflects the extent of struggle to contain psychotic expressions. In profiles with elevations on both *ANX* and *FRS*, but in which the *FRS* score is higher, the effort to use more mature defensive measures against external and internal threats is suggested, whereas the reverse pattern would suggest a reliance on more primitive defenses. *FRS* is more socially desirable and less negativistic than *ANX*, another indication that it is associated with more mature modes of defensive functioning. Along with Social Discomfort (*SOD*), *FRS* is one of the least socially undesirable among the MMPI-2 content scales. In one type of defensive paranoid patient, *FRS* may stand out as the only elevation of consequence among the content scales and be associated with an especially low Cynicism (*CYN*) score, suggesting a displacement of fears of others onto phobic objects. The patient strongly denies cynical and suspicious attitudes toward others but admits to a greater than average fearfulness of aspects of the nonhuman environment.

Obsessiveness (OBS)

The *OBS* scale contains 16 items, all keyed True. It is correlated with *Pt* in the high .70s and with *A* in the low .80s; it shares 5 items with each of these two scales. Although a few of the items do indeed seem classically obsessive in content, the modal item on this scale reflects *indecision*. The main theme, then, is one of overly busy but massively inefficient cognitive activity. Decision making becomes bogged down in detail, but this seems to occur against a background of timidity, if not dread, when faced with the necessity of taking practical action. Low scores on *OBS* suggest an opposite trend, with decisions being made with self-confidence and dispatch. Very low scores may imply overconfidence and a hasty and incautious approach to decision making.

At this time, it is unclear what relation, if any, exists between *OBS* and obsessive–compulsive disorder or, especially, obsessive–compulsive personality disorder. An appropriate scale for the identification of these disorders would need to include items having content related to such things as symmetry, checking, cleaning, ordering, perfectionism, concerns about contamination, overcontrol, restriction of affect, stinginess, over-conscientiousness, preoccupation with details, and forbidden aggressive, sexual, or sacrilegious thoughts and actions, as well as with indecision. The content of the MMPI-2 does not include a sufficient number or variety of items in these areas, and not all of those that are included found their way onto *OBS* (see, e.g. *FRS* items 322 and 447). Hence, *OBS* is a good example of a scale for which internal consistency strictures may have prevented the development of a scale having properties that would facilitate detection of obsessive syndromes. Notwithstanding these difficulties, Graham et al. (1999) did find that their high scoring outpatients did manifest "obsessive-compulsive tendencies," but did not report in what these tendencies consisted.

Relations to Other Scales

To maintain its relevance for the diagnosis of obsessional states and personality styles, it would seem important to require that *OBS* exceed both *ANX* and *FRS* by a margin of *T*-10 to ensure that *OBS* is not being pulled up by the variance it shares in common with the other two scales. (See also discussion of Harkness, McNulty, and Ben-Porath's (1995) Aggressiveness [*AGG*] and Disconstraint [*DIS*] scales, below.) The negative implications of low *OBS* scores, such as impulsive decision making, are likely to be negligible, or at least not readily apparent, unless low *OBS* scores are accompanied by a low (preferably lower) *FRS* score. Correlations in the .50 to .65 range with measures of anger and hostility, such as Wiggins' Manifest Hostility (*HOS*), the MMPI-2 Anger (*ANG*), and Type A Behavior (*TPA*), suggest that high *OBS* scores may indicate passive-aggressive motivation (i.e. using nonperformance through indecision, obsession, and preoccupation with detail as a means of coping with the demands and expectations of others and, in turn, engendering responses of impatience, frustration, and exasperation in them).

Depression (DEP)

The *DEP* scale contains 33 items, 28 True, 5 False. Among the MMPI-2 clinical scales, *DEP* correlates most highly with Scale 7 (*Pt*) at .81, and with Welsh's *A* at about .83. Sixteen of its items appear on Wiggins' *DEP*. Six of the items scored on Wiggins' *DEP* now appear on MMPI-2 *ANX*. Although the MMPI-2 and Wiggins *DEP* scales correlate at about .90, the improved separation between anxious and depressive content in the MMPI-2 content scales suggests that the current *DEP* scale is likely to have somewhat greater specificity and discriminant validity than its Wiggins predecessor, and considerable evidence for the incremental validity of *DEP* has accumulated (Bagby, Marshall, Basso, Nicholson, Bacchioch, & Miller, 2005; Barthlow, Graham, Ben-Porath, & McNulty, 1999; Ben-Porath, Butcher, & Graham, 1991; Gross, 2002; Gross, Keyes, & Greene, 2000; Hungerford, 2004; Munley, Busby, & Jaynes, 1997; Wetzler, Khadivi, & Moser, 1998).

Ben-Porath and Sherwood (1993) subdivided *DEP* into four components: lack of Drive (*DEP1*), Dysphoria (*DEP2*), Self-Depreciation (*DEP3*), and Suicidal Ideation (*DEP4*). The *DEP1* items report despair and a loss of pleasure, interest, and motivation in life, and correlates with *Sc4*, *D1*, and *D4* at .87, .86, and .86, respectively. High scores reflect apathy, anhedonia, an inability to accomplish even the routine tasks of daily life, and a sense of having given up. By contrast, low scores suggest a zestful approach to daily life in which interests, aspirations, and plans for the future have a solid role. *DEP2* reflects dysphoric/depressed mood in the form of subjective unhappiness, especially a sense of brooding and feeling blue, and of being subject to moody spells. It correlates at .86 with *D1*, and *D5*, with which it shares four of its six items. The *DEP3* items reflect self-dissatisfaction, guilt and sense of moral failure, and a negative self-concept. It correlates with both *Pd5* and *LSE1* at .83. High scorers admit to feelings of guilt, helplessness, hopelessness, regret/remorse, uselessness, and worthlessness. Low scorers deny such feelings. None of the *DEP4* items appear on Scale 2 (*D*). Although not all are explicitly suicidal in content, these items do carry the implication of a pessimism about the future that is so dire as to support a wish to die and thoughts of suicide. High scores raise the question of suicide potential, the need for its assessment, and the probable wisdom of initial precautions against suicidal acts or gestures. As Ben-Porath and Sherwood point out, *DEP1*, *DEP2*, and *DEP3* all lie close to aspects of diagnostic criteria for major depressive episode. *DEP* is highly sensitive to the cognitive and attitudinal components of depressive syndromes. High scorers (following the component scales) report despair and a loss of interest and feelings of fatigue, apathy, and exhaustion (*DEP1*); they are unhappy, blue, and quick to cry (*DEP2*); they show a collapse in self-efficacy and self-regard to the point that they feel guilt-ridden, useless, unpardonably sinful, and condemned (*DEP3*); and they feel hopeless, wish for death, and contemplate suicide (*DEP4*). The empirical correlates of high *DEP* and component scores found by Graham et al. (1999) tend to confirm this description. Their outpatients tended to have histories of prior suicide attempts and psychiatric hospitalizations, and profuse depressive symptomatology, with hopelessness, suicidal ideation, and disturbed sleep. The correlates found by Green et al. (2006), for the *DEP* component scales showed considerable overlap, but the following may be notable. For *DEP1*: Depressive mood, anxiety, irritability, feelings of hopelessness, trouble concentrating, anhedonia, feelings of worthlessness, thoughts of suicide, and a history of suicide attempts. For *DEP2*, in addition to the correlates above for *DEP1*: Sexual inadequacy, major physical problems, and financial problems as a precipitating factor leading to hospitalization. For *DEP3*: Depressive mood, guilt, self-blame, and feelings of worthlessness, and sexual inadequacy. For *DEP4*: Depressive mood, feeling that something bad is going to happen, feelings of hopelessness and worthlessness, thoughts of suicide, death and dying, and a history of suicide attempts.

Although low scores on *DEP* more clearly indicate the absence (or denial) of depressiveness than the presence of elated or expansive mood, some low scorers will be seen as defensive, euphoric, irritable, or overactive, especially in psychiatric settings.

Relations to Other Scales

DEP overlaps Scale 2 by only nine items, indicating that the two scales are likely to have significantly different patterns of empirical correlates. All of the overlapping items are found on the *D1* subscale (Subjective Depression), and eight of the nine appear on *D5* (Brooding), or 80 percent of that subscale. Convictions of worthlessness and futility, along with a view of the self as inadequate or inferior, are primary in *DEP* but secondary in Scale 2. Conversely, such syndromal characteristics of depression as psychomotor retardation, the inhibition of aggression, and vegetative symptoms (e.g. sleep disturbance, anorexia, and weight loss making up an important part of Scale 2), are largely absent from *DEP*. The relative elevations of *DEP* and Scale 2, therefore, are helpful in determining both the type and severity of depressive phenomena. To the extent that *DEP* exceeds Scale 2, a chronic condition with predominantly characterological features is suggested. To the extent that Scale 2 exceeds *DEP*, vegetative symptoms and a less complicated symptom picture are characteristic. Bagby et al. (2005) found that *DEP* better distinguished bipolar depression from schizophrenia than Scale 2, and Gross' (2002) findings likewise favored *DEP* over Scale 2 in accurately predicting a diagnosis of major depression. However, Gross et al. (2000) did not find an increase in diagnostic efficiency for *DEP* over Scale 2 in predicting depression.

Health Concerns (HEA)

The *HEA* scale contains 36 items, 14 True, 22 False. The amount of overlap between *HEA* and Scale 1 (*Hs*) is very high at 21 items, more than two thirds of *Hs*. The two scales correlate at ~.95. A majority of the items (20) appeared on Wiggins' Organic Symptoms (*ORG*); 13 on Wiggins' Poor Health. The overlap with *ORG* and the abandonment of most of the genitourinary and lower gastrointestinal items from the MMPI has made *HEA* very different from its Wiggins predecessor. The continuity of content between the two scales is largely limited to items reflecting upper gastrointestinal symptoms and concerns over one's general health status (about five items each). Not surprisingly, in contrast to Wiggins' Poor Health, *HEA* contains many items denoting complaints in and about the head, sensory and motor problems, and a few items reporting losses of consciousness. None of the items in these areas appeared on Wiggins' Poor Health scale. Complaints of pain and other somatic discomfort are more plentiful on MMPI-2 *HEA* than on Wiggins' Poor Health. The greater variety of item content in MMPI-2 *HEA* has been made explicit in the content component scales developed by Ben-Porath and Sherwood (1993). These are: Gastrointestinal Symptoms (*HEA1*), a collection of mostly upper GI items that report nausea, vomiting, stomach pain and discomfort (stomach ache), and constipation. Scale correlates of *HEA1* include *Hy4* at .74 and *D3* at .67. Neurological Symptoms (*HEA2*) covers sensory and motor problems, losses of consciousness, and other head complaints (cf. *Sc6*, with which *HEA2* correlates at .86). General Health Concerns (*HEA3*), the items of which report poor health, and health worries and preoccupations. It correlates with *Hy3*, *D3*, and *Hy4* at .78, .77, and .74, respectively.

The external correlates found for the Graham et al. (1999) outpatients included: For *HEA1*: Somatization, with multiple physical complaints and preoccupation with health problems, depression, and disturbed sleep. For *HEA2*: In addition to those of *HEA1*, developing physical symptoms in response to stress, anxious, pessimistic and overwhelmed, hopeless with suicidal ideation, and having problems in concentration. For *HEA3*: Somatization, with multiple physical complaints, developing physical symptoms in response to stress, and preoccupation with health problems, and feeling sad, depressed, anxious, pessimistic, hopeless, and overwhelmed and, for women, a history of sexual abuse. The correlates for the Green et al. (2006) inpatients were often similar, as follows. *HEA1*: Physical problems as a major problem area, physical illness as a precipitating factor, somatic concerns with nausea and numbness or tingling, and other physical problems, anxiety and depressive mood, and a history of suicide attempts and sexual abuse. *HEA2*: Physical problems as a major problem area, physical illness as a precipitating factor, motor retardation, weakness, dizziness, numbness and tingling, hot and cold spells, problems with memory, mind going blank, and symptoms of psychosis (suspiciousness and hallucinatory and/or bizarre behavior) and/or of panic or anxiety (suddenly scared for no reason, heart pounding or racing, checking behavior/ritual checking, trouble sleeping), and a history of suicide attempts. *HEA3*: Physical problems as a major problem area, physical illness as a precipitating factor, somatic concerns, feeling that something is wrong with one's body, anxiety, tension and depressive mood, and a history of suicide attempts.

Relations to Other Scales

The characterological features associated with Scale 1 are even more apparent in *HEA*. This is because of the absence of any "dampening" effect of the *K* correction applied to Scale 1. That is, the addition of 0.5 *K* to the raw score for Scale 1 tends to attenuate its association with measures of dependency, hostility, and other traits. Implications for conflicts around dependency, demandingness and the management of the demands of others, the handling of anger and frustration, and related issues are highly similar for *HEA* and the non-K-corrected version of Scale 1.

Bizarre Mentation (BIZ)

The *BIZ* scale contains 24 items, 23 True, 1 False. Its pattern of overlap with *F* (10 items), Scale 6 (8 items), and Scale 8 (8 items) would suggest that *BIZ* is the content analogue of the 86/68 profile type. About one third of the items are paranoid in content. *BIZ* is a measure of psychotic thought processes. It correlates much more highly with *PSYC* at .90, than with Scale 8 at .58 (Greene, 2011). Both *BIZ* and Scale 8 were able to separate schizophrenia and major depression in Greenblatt and Davis' (1999) sample of veterans. However, Wetzler et al. (1998) found that although *BIZ* was highly specific (i.e. tended not to elevate in non-schizophrenics, hence a high true negative rate), it lacked sensitivity. It did not separate schizophrenia from major depression in their sample, replicating earlier findings by Ben-Porath et al. (1991) and Munley et al. (1997).

Ben-Porath and Sherwood (1993) divided *BIZ* into two components: Psychotic Symptomatology (*BIZ1*), comprising items with frankly psychotic content reflecting the positive or accessory symptoms characteristic of schizophrenia and other psychotic conditions (such as auditory, visual, or olfactory hallucinations; delusions of persecution and control; and other first-rank symptoms like thought broadcasting and thought withdrawal). Nearly half of these items refer to paranoid symptomatology. The second component, Schizotypal Characteristics (*BIZ2*), contains items that are less obviously psychotic in content than *BIZ1* but are nevertheless unusual, odd, peculiar, and weird. These include ideas of reference, de-realization, intrusive thoughts, and uncanny sensory experiences such as are sometimes seen in prodromal or residual phases of schizophrenia, dissociative conditions, and mood disorders with psychotic features.

The *BIZ1* correlates for the Graham et al. (1999) outpatients included paranoid ideation and symptoms of psychosis, and those for the Green et al. (2006) inpatients were similar, including suspiciousness, unusual thought content, conceptual disorganization, disorientation, and hallucinatory behavior (auditory hallucinations and thought insertion). The correlates for *BIZ2* across these two studies were likewise similar, with Graham et al. reporting anxiety, paranoid ideation, and symptoms of psychosis including loose associations, and a history of prior psychiatric hospitalization, and Green et al. reporting anxiety, alienation, paranoia and suspiciousness, unusual, unpleasant, and/or peculiar thought content, frightening thoughts and images, conceptual disorganization, disorientation, and hallucinatory behavior (auditory hallucinations and thought insertion), expectations of bad events, feelings of deserving punishment, a belief that one's mind is disturbed, and a history of sexual abuse.

The *BIZ* items are among the most obvious items on the MMPI-2, so respondents wishing to simulate (malinger) psychosis will be drawn to these items. Conversely, respondents seeking to avoid appearing psychotic on *BIZ* (and on the MMPI-2 more generally) can do so easily, with one important exception. Because insight is often lacking in psychotic conditions, and in schizophrenia in particular, psychotic patients will commonly endorse at least a few of the *BIZ* items even when defensive motivation and guardedness are present. That is, for many patients, their lack of insight renders the psychopathological implications of certain items transparent to them, leading to the endorsement of items that guarded patients whose insight is better preserved would unhesitatingly avoid. For example, a paranoid schizophrenic patient who fears that hospital personnel have been co-opted by his primary persecutors to disable him with medications, and who therefore has every reason to attempt to convince his psychiatric captors that they have the wrong man, may see no reason not to endorse an item like 162, referencing the idea that one is the victim of another's designs to poison him/her. For this patient, the item may be said to be ego-syntonic, beyond the reach of his motivation to censor test expressions of psychopathology. Thus, high *BIZ* scores, especially when such scores are contributed to by the items of *BIZ1* (even scores above *T*-50 on *BIZ1* should be considered high in defensive profiles), carry implications that are not limited to the content of those items endorsed. Among these are impaired insight, an inability to enter into collaborative relationships, and a grandiose sense of having been selected or appointed for a secret and lofty mission or endowed with special powers. Graham et al. (1999) found relatively frequent histories of physical (men) and sexual (women) abuse among their outpatients with high *BIZ* scores.

Relations to Other Scales

One of the more important uses of *BIZ* is as an index to judge the degree to which psychotic content has contributed to elevations on *F*, Scale 6, and Scale 8. It is not at all uncommon for Scale 8 to exceed *BIZ* by a few standard deviations. Both Scales 6 and 8 have substantial depressive content and may easily elevate in major depression as well as schizophrenia (see, e.g. Bagby et al., 2005). Alienation and lowered self-esteem also may elevate Scale 8 in many different conditions. Reference to *BIZ* in profiles showing elevations on *F*, Scale 6, and Scale 8 can provide valuable guidance in interpretation by emphasizing the importance of psychotic thinking when such an emphasis can be supported by high *BIZ* (especially *BIZ1*) scores and by avoiding such emphasis when it cannot, thereby averting excessively pathological interpretations of Scale 8 elevations. The Low Self-Esteem scale (*LSE*) is very sensitive to the kinds of fixed, negative self-attitudes that often result in high Scale 8 scores. The relative elevations of *BIZ* and *LSE* can thus provide a useful index of the relative contributions of psychotic experience and impaired self-esteem to high scores on Scale 8.

Anger (ANG)

The *ANG* scale contains 16 items, 15 True, 1 False. Inexplicably, *ANG* does *not* include items 93, 102, 213, or 372, all of which reference anger/irritability more or less explicitly. It shares only two items with the standard validity and clinical scales of the MMPI-2, fewer than any other of the content scales. Eight of the items overlap Wiggins' *HOS*. *ANG* is concerned with poorly controlled anger (Schill & Wang, 1990). High scorers are irritable and volatile people who under-regulate crude affect, are intolerant of frustration, issue angry expressions at a high rate, and are prone to paroxysmal eruptions in the form of angry tirades and destructive outbursts. They have strong needs to discharge their ire, and if they feel constrained by external circumstances from discharging in expansive ways through temper tantrums, bouts of yelling and cursing, and the like, they will do so in more controlled ways through frequent bugging, nagging, picking, carping, quibbling, belittling, discrediting, deriding, needling, ridiculing, shaming, irritating, taunting, sadistic teasing, demanding, imposing, intruding, and being stubborn. As with *ANX*, high *ANG* scores are associated with a high press for expression. Indeed,

Graham et al. (1999) reported that their outpatients with high *ANG* scores were ill-tempered and had histories of being physically abusive, especially the men. The patients also showed high rates of substance abuse and dependence. Ben-Porath and Sherwood (1993) divided *ANG* into Explosive Behavior (*ANG1*) and Irritability (*ANG2*). The *ANG1* items emphasize behavior over impulse, and correlates with *AGGR* at .88. The opposite emphasis characterizes *ANG2*. *ANG2* correlates with *TPA1* (Impatience) at .79. This difference could also be conceived as a difference in the severity of anger arousal and dyscontrol between the two components. High *ANG1* scorers admit to explosive and violent episodes that have been directed to both persons and property and have likely resulted in injury or damage. The items are reminiscent of the criteria for intermittent explosive disorder. The high *ANG1* scoring outpatients studied by Graham et al. (1999) were seen as quite hostile, given to temper outbursts, with the men showing histories of convictions for domestic violence. Both the men and women had long histories of alcohol abuse, with the men showing long histories of marijuana abuse as well. The histories of the men were positive for having been physically abused, and those of women having been sexually abused and for prior suicide attempts and misdemeanor convictions. The Green et al. (2006) inpatients were described as having hostile and destructive urges, and showing antisocial behavior as a major problem area, and histories of alcohol and drug abuse, including as precipitating factors. Low *ANG1* scores emphasize the denial of under-controlled violent *expressions* over the denial of anger per se. That is, the low *ANG1* scorer is more likely to be asserting better control than an absence of angry emotionality. High *ANG2* scorers admit to a great deal of anger and irritability, but they also experience a sense of perplexity about their reactions and distress over their lack of self-control that may in some degree support the inhibition of behavioral outbursts. The emotional tone of *ANG2* is more dysphoric than hostile. Graham et al. (1999) report that their high scoring *ANG2* outpatients presented as hostile and dysthymic/depressed, and were seen by their therapists as sad, depressed, and self-degrading. The men were also seen as angry, resentful, and anxious, as having suicidal ideation, nightmares and disturbed sleep, many somatic complaints, as developing physical problems in response to stress, and as having family problems and coming from families lacking in love. The women were seen as feeling inferior, coping poorly with stress, and had histories of suicide attempts and prior outpatient treatment. The Green et al. (2006) inpatients were depressed, irritable, and hostile, with destructive urges, unpleasant thoughts, discomfort when observed, somatic concerns, depressive mood, suicide attempts, and sexual inadequacy. They had histories of alcohol and drug abuse, and such abuse was often a precipitating factor. The combination of anger and inhibition themes in *ANG2* suggests that it may be responsive to partial or attenuated expressions of anger that are emitted within a context of self-justification, such as argumentativeness, disagreeableness, annoyance, frustration, stalling, pettiness, impatience, complaining, criticism, and passive-aggressive or passive-paranoid maneuvers.

Evidence for the construct validity of *ANG* has been accumulating. For example, Clark (1994) found an association between *ANG* scores and an anger expression factor among male chronic pain patients. Kawachi, Sparrow, Spiro, Vokonas, and Weiss (1996) reported a significant relationship between *ANG* scores and risk for coronary heart disease (CHD) among older men in the VA Normative Aging Study.

Relations to Other Scales

The *ANG* items and its correlates seem to emphasize the press for discharge over hostile intent in the dynamics of anger, at least as anger is embodied in this scale. High scorers will not infrequently report a sense of being a helpless spectator to their major and minor discharges, viewing with a kind of horror their own destructiveness as they damage property or inflict physical or emotional pain and injury on others, and yet feeling unable to stop themselves. The gratification they report is in the release of anger, not in the damage occasioned by such release. For this reason, individuals scoring high on both *DEP* and *ANG* may be at special risk for dramatic suicide, including provoked homicide and murder-suicide, when they are finally rejected by the partners that they "never meant to hurt." This pattern is especially associated with scores on *ANG2*, and the configurations *ANG2* greater than *ANG1*, and *TPA1* greater than *TPA2*. There are important implications of the relationship between *ANG* and its sister scale, *TPA*. The two scales are moderately highly correlated in the high .60s, but whereas the *ANG* theme is "hot," the *TPA* theme is "cool." The implication of this difference is taken up in the Type A Behavior scale description.

Cynicism (CYN)

The *CYN* scale contains 23 items, all keyed True. Seventeen overlap the Cook and Medley (1954) Hostility scale (*Ho*) with the two scales correlating at ~.90. As a dimension, cynicism covers a broad range of sentiments from naïve altruism, an obtuse absence of skepticism regarding the motives of others, to normal prudent regard for one's vulnerability to deceit, mendacity, and chicanery at the hands of others, to the unqualified misanthropic conviction that people are dishonorable, unprincipled, dishonest, and corrupt, invariably acting out of motives that are selfish, perfidious, venal, or craven. *CYN* models this dimension well, with high scorers asserting that others are to be distrusted because they act only from self-interest, resort to honesty only to avoid detection, and act friendly only because it makes others easier to exploit. They see life as a jungle in which one must be constantly on the look-out for any competitive advantage because they expect others will use any means at their disposal to claim such advantage for themselves, given the opportunity. They therefore have no qualms about resorting to deception, misinformation, hypocrisy, subterfuge, and manipulation to get away with whatever they can. They justify their expedient, if not exploitive, approach to others with the (projective) rationalization that others are equally selfish, dishonest, and amoral. Given its very high correlation with *Ho*, it would be expected that *CYN* would be associated with the increased mortality/morbidity from coronary heart disease found in some investigations of *Ho* (Barefoot, Dahlstrom, & Williams, 1983; Barefoot, Dodge, Peterson, Dahlstrom, & Williams, 1989; Shekelle, Gale, Ostfeld, & Paul, 1983; Williams, Haney, Lee, Kong, Blumenthal, & Whalen, 1980), and indeed Almada, Zonderman, Shekelle, Dyer, Daviglus, Costa, and Stamler (1991) found high *CYN* scores were significantly associated with mortality from coronary illness and from cancer in their large sample of employed men 40 years of age and older.

Low scorers deny normal levels of skepticism regarding the good will of others by maintaining that they are completely trustworthy and driven solely by prosocial and altruistic motivations. At the same time, they portray themselves as bastions of benevolence, holders of an unshakable belief in the goodness of their fellow men and women. These sentiments are not infrequently expressed in the context of defensive response styles in which there is some focus on portraying oneself as enjoying consummately harmonious relationships, relationships in which conflict and ill will are unheard of. In some circumstances, such as when *LSE* and other signs of dependency are high, low *CYN* scores can indicate an unusual aversion to giving others offense for fear that to do so might risk rejection or the loss of dependency supports. Low scores may also be achieved by paranoid defensiveness through the specific denial of paranoid attitudes (e.g. *Pa3* and *Pdf* [paranoid defensiveness; Holroyd, 1964]). Such patients tend to produce highly defensive profiles, typically with *L* and *K* exceeding *F*. The peak among the content scales in this configuration, as mentioned earlier, is often *FRS*, possibly signifying the displacement of fears of others onto phobic objects.

Graham et al. (1999) described their high-scoring *CYN* outpatients as hostile and having paranoid ideation, but the men among them were also described as sad and depressed, and as having frequent nightmares and complaints of disturbed sleep. The women had histories of suicide attempts and made broadly negative impressions on their therapists, who described them as immature, antisocial, insight-less, and unmotivated. In a study of prison inmates, Williams (2002) found significantly greater *CYN* scores among violent than non-violent offenders.

Ben-Porath and Sherwood (1993) divided *CYN* into two components: Misanthropic Beliefs (*CYN1*) and Interpersonal Suspiciousness (*CYN2*). *CYN1* emphasizes a view of others as deceitful, selfish, untrustworthy, manipulative, unsympathetic, and disloyal. Notable scale correlates include *Pa3* at −.87, *ASP1* at .86, and *Hy2* at −.83. High scorers are likely to be "burned out" on relations with others and unwilling to exert significant efforts to improve them. Paranoid ideation was the major correlate among the Graham et al. (1999) outpatients for both *CYN1* and *CYN2*. The *CYN1* men were seen as depressed, having many nightmares, and as ruminative and socially awkward, while their women were seen as more difficult—immature, antisocial, having poor insight and a negative attitude toward treatment, lacking reliability as informants, and being difficult to motivate—as communicating poorly, having narrow interests, and lacking an orientation to work and achievement. These women failed to make a favorable first impression and were viewed as not very likable. The Green et al. (2006) inpatients showed hallucinatory behavior.

CYN2 emphasizes similar sentiments but includes a theme of feeling oneself to be a particular target of others cynical, hostile, manipulative, or exploitive actions, leading to suspicious and guarded reactions. It therefore has a more dysphoric tone than *CYN1*. The Graham et al. (1999) outpatient men were seen as dysthymic/depressed, and had histories of few or no friends, while the women were seen as undependable and lacking in insight. The Green et al. (2006) inpatients showed conceptual disorganization and hallucinatory behavior, and had histories of sexual abuse. The high *CYN2* scorer feels "under fire" and vulnerable to others, especially superiors, who are felt to be stingy with recognition and understanding, and who are trying to disadvantage him or her.

Relations to Other Scales

Butcher et al. (1990) found rather different empirical correlates for men and women on *CYN*. The re-standardization men were rated as having temper tantrums, whining, demanding, nagging, and lying but also as lacking an interest in things. The women were rated as less hostile but more psychologically disturbed. They were described as suspicious, nervous and jittery, preoccupied with death/dying, apathetic, and showing poor judgment. The pattern suggests either that among women, cynicism is more damaging to psychological functioning or that elevated *CYN* scores may be a consequence of more general or severe psychological disturbance. For men, in contrast, elevations on *CYN* appear to reflect a more specific trait disturbance that is more localized to interpersonal relations. For either gender, *CYN* is likely to interact with measures of dependency (e.g. *Si3* [Self-Other Alienation], *Do* (Dominance) [low], *GM* [low], *LSE,* and *LSE2*) and, where both are high, to signify higher levels of stress and discomfort in interpersonal functioning. Dependent high *CYN* scorers are in the position of being unable to trust those on whom they depend, and are therefore vulnerable to rapidly fluctuating levels of comfort as their psychological distance from significant others waxes and wanes. Too close and they feel the threat of engulfment and of losing autonomy; too distant and they feel vulnerable to abandonment, isolation, and loss.

As would be expected, when concurrently elevated with *ASP* and/or *BIZ,* the manifestations of high scores on *CYN* may be substantially augmented in terms of their offensiveness in the case of *CYN* with *ASP,* such as might be seen in aggressive psychopathy, or their severity in the case of *CYN* with *BIZ,* such as is not uncommon in paranoid schizophrenia.

Antisocial Practices (ASP)

The *ASP* scale contains 22 items, 21 True, 1 False. It shares 3 items with *Pd2* (Authority Problems) and 6 with *CYN1.* The latter items assert that "most people" lie and cheat to get ahead in life, steal because others tempt them, and resort to honesty chiefly to avoid trouble. These and 10 additional items form Ben-Porath and Sherwood's (1993) first *ASP* component, Antisocial Attitudes (*ASP1*). The additional items endorse a code of silence with authorities, a disdain for the rule of law, a willingness to steal given the opportunity, sympathy for those who treat others rapaciously, and a kind of vengeful joy when others are "catching it." There is thus a strong implicit theme of defective empathy in this set of items and perhaps a tertiary theme of generalized rage at others. The Graham et al. (1999) outpatients presented as hostile, but their other correlates showed significant gender differences, with the men showing poor judgment and being intolerant of frustration, having nightmares, with histories of few or no friends, while the women showed a much broader pattern of disturbance, with correlates including hallucinations and suicide attempts, antisocial/sociopathic, immature and undependable, unable to see their own limitations, having superficial relationships, being defensive, difficult to motivate, lacking insight and reliability as informants, and being unlikable. Although the data presented in Graham et al. (1999) do not implicate paranoid ideation among their high-scoring *ASP1* outpatients, the relatively high correlations between *ANG1* and *CYN2* (−.60) and *Pa1* (~.50) do suggest such trends. The correlates found for the Green et al. (2006) inpatients emphasized substance abuse, including as a precipitating factor, and a history of legal charges and incarcerations.

The five-item second component, Antisocial Practices (*ASP2*), consists of admissions of past delinquencies, including theft, truancy, school suspensions, and conflict with school and legal authorities. It correlates with *Pd2* at .71, and with *DISC* at 64. The Graham et al. (1999) outpatient correlates emphasized elements of the antisocial personality pattern, including aggression, anger/temper tantrums, hostility, resentment, impulsiveness, intolerance of frustration, stormy interpersonal relationships, polysubstance abuse, misdemeanor convictions, and multiple arrests. Additionally, their men were seen as suspicious and had histories of felony convictions, including for domestic violence, were self-indulgent and physically abusive, while their women were described as agitated, argumentative, manipulative, critical, narcissistic, paranoid, defensive and deceptive, and as having family problems and many nightmares. The Green et al. (2006) inpatients likewise had histories of legal charges and incarcerations, but their problems appeared more narrowly focused on alcohol and drug abuse, including as precipitating factors. They also showed a history of suicide attempts.

The imbalance in the length of the two *ASP* components is such that the full scale name is something of a misnomer because those items dealing with actual misbehavior (*ASP2*) come to only about one fourth of the full *ASP* scale. Moreover, *ASP2* is comparatively weakly associated with *ASP1* (about .30), a further indication that the relation of *ASP1*, and, to a lesser extent, *ASP* as a whole, to actual antisocial conduct is a tenuous one. Nevertheless, as compared with Scale 4 (*Pd*), Smith, Hilsenroth, Castlebury, and Durham (1999) found that *ASP*, but not Scale 4, was significantly correlated to DSM-IV diagnostic criteria for Antisocial Personality Disorder (APD), and was able to differentiate APD from other personality disorders. Similarly, Lilienfeld (1996) reported a stronger association for ASP than Scale 4 with measures of Machiavellianism and interviewer-rated dishonesty, and incremental validity over Scale 4 for global indexes of psychopathy and antisocial behavior. In the case of high scores on *ASP2* these features were especially pronounced, with multiple arrests, felony convictions, hostility, resentment, impulsiveness, poor frustration tolerance, temper outbursts, domestic violence, stormy and physically abusive interpersonal relationships, and diagnoses of antisocial personality disorder and substance abuse. These features were most commonly present in men but were also represented among their women outpatients, who also had histories of physical and sexual abuse, heroin abuse, family problems, and paranoid features. Williams (2002) found significantly greater *ASP* scores among prisoners convicted of violent offenses than among the non-violent offenders (see also *CYN*, above). In a study of parenting behaviors among low-income women, Bosquet and Egeland (2000) reported an association between *ASP* and parenting styles that were less understanding and more harsh and hostile.

Relations to Other Scales

The most important relative of *ASP* is *CYN*. Examination of the configuration of *CYN* versus *ASP*, *CYN1* versus *ASP1* (note the similarity of the Graham et al. [1999] correlates for these two components for their women outpatients), and *CYN2* versus *ASP2* permit fairly detailed inferences about individual sentiments and dynamics, and may be especially useful in the interpretation of the 46/64 code patterns and its variants (462, 468, and 469). For all three comparisons, a positive slope (i.e. *CYN < ASP, CYN1 < ASP1,* and *CYN2 < ASP2*) favors a psychopathic over a paranoid bias, whereas a negative slope favors the opposite bias. The within-scale configurations (e.g. *CYN2 > CYN1*) also may help to guide interpretive efforts when dealing with these issues.

Type A Behavior (TPA)

The *TPA* scale contains 19 items, all keyed True. Three overlap *ANG*, 1 on *ANG1* and 2 on *ANG2*. Nine of the *TPA* items overlap Wiggins' *HOS*, and 6 items overlap the Cook and Medley (1954) *Ho* scale (*TPA* x *Ho*: $r = \sim.75$). The concept of the Type A or coronary-prone personality as operationalized in the Jenkins Activity Survey (JAS; Jenkins, Rosenman, & Friedman, 1967) included three components: Speed and Impatience, Job Involvement, and Hard Driving Competitiveness. The first focused on the time urgency aspect of the Type A syndrome; the second with the extent of occupational demands and the person's dedication or determination to meet or exceed them; and the third with a serious, competitive, and hard-driving self-concept. The items of *TPA* fail to adequately cover this domain. First, the Job Involvement component is insufficiently represented with, at most, two items (507 and 531). Second, the Hard Driving Competitiveness component is so heavily biased toward hostility that the themes of hostile competitiveness and self-imposed demands for performance tend to recede into the background. Indeed, the only correlate found among both the male and female outpatients studied by Graham et al. (1999) to be associated with high *TPA* scores was interpersonal hostility. In a report from the VA Normative Aging Study, Kawachi et al. (1998) found moderate to poor correlations between the *TPA* and JAS total (.36), Speed and Impatience (.46), Job Involvement (.12), and Hard Driving Competitiveness (.22) scores. However, they did find that *TPA* scores were associated with events related to CHD in a community-dwelling sample of older (mean age = 61 years) men. It should also be noted that the JAS was not related to the risk of CHD in a similar cohort (Kawachi et al., 1998).

Ben-Porath and Sherwood (1993) divided *TPA* into Impatience (*TPA1*) and Competitiveness (*TPA2*) components. The *TPA1* items convey a sense of time urgency along with delay-stimulated irritability, such that having to wait in line, being interrupted, or having people on whom one depends fail do their work on time stirs one to annoyance, if not anger. *TPA1* correlates at .79 with *ANG2*. The Graham et al. (1999) outpatient correlates included high levels of hostility and developing physical symptoms in response to stress. An additional correlate for men was the display of unusual gestures at intake. The correlates for women included depression, nervousness, and worry, complaints of somatic symptoms, oversensitivity to criticism, coping poorly with stress, and being histrionic, agitated, restless, grouchy, insecure, self-degrading, socially awkward, and giving up easily. The correlates found for the Green et al. (2006) inpatients were anxiety, depressive mood, somatic concerns, and histories of sexual abuse, alcohol abuse, and suicide attempts.

The *TPA2* items convey less a spirit of competitiveness than of resentment, vengefulness, and sadism. High *TPA2* scorers admit to wanting to "win a point" against or pay back people who oppose them, opposing people for trivial reasons, relishing the misfortunes of people whom they dislike, feeling resentment when they feel taken in, and gloating over their competitive advantages. Two additional items appear thematically displaced from *TPA1* (510 and 545), and a third refers to job overinvolvement (531). *TPA2* correlates with *Ho* at .72. Graham et al. (1999) found only paranoid ideation as a general *TPA2* correlate among their outpatients, though their women were additionally described as immature and having problems with authority figures, while the Green et al. (2006) inpatients showed a history of substance abuse.

Although both components carry themes of angry emotionality, the theme of *TPA1* is "hot" and closer to the irritable-angry emotionality of *ANG*, whereas *TPA2* is "cool" and more calculating, controlled, hostile, vengeful, and sadistic than *ANG*. Because *TPA2* is the larger of the two components, containing half again as many items as *TPA1*, the quality of *TPA2* is imparted to the full *TPA* scale, making it "cooler" than the full *ANG* scale.

The question may be raised as to whether *TPA* can be presumed to be a construct valid measure of the Type A syndrome. Although there can be little doubt that the scale has *some* construct valid variance if the JAS is held as the standard, it appears on the basis of the limitations of *TPA* as a measure of Type A Behavior described earlier, and from the lack of supportive construct-related evidence from empirical investigations, that *TPA* is unlikely to function as a sufficiently sensitive and specific measure to support construct-relevant predictions in the individual case. It may be possible, however, on rational grounds, to develop a configurally-based indicator involving scores on *TPA*, its components, and other scales in a way that would combine relevant sources of variance to maximize the success of predictions of Type A Behavior. A group of hypotheses for this purpose follows.

Relations to Other Scales

Because of the overlap of three items between *TPA* and *ANG*, as well as the similarity of the content between *ANG2* and *TPA1*, these two scales must be distinguished more extensively. As noted already, *ANG* is the "hotter" of the two, and *TPA* the "cooler." That is, there is a more urgent press for the expression of affect in *ANG* than in *TPA*. The high *TPA* scorer is better controlled, more deliberate, more rigid, and less impulsive than the *ANG* scorer at comparable elevations. The high *TPA* scorer is also less dysphoric, less anhedonic, and less inclined to avoid or deny evidence of personal error or shortcomings than his or her high *ANG* counterpart. That is, *TPA* is thematically more grandiose and narcissistic than *ANG*. It is also more cynical, suspicious, self-justifying, disdainful, and control avoidant than *ANG*. Although the high *ANG* scorer is more irritable, angry, and volatile than the high *TPA* scorer, his or her enmity toward others is less persistently sadistic and domineering; it involves a lesser determination to control and inflict emotional injury on others. The greater control inherent in *TPA* is sufficient to create an impression of assertiveness at times when a comparable *ANG* score would create an impression of excessive anger.

As noted previously, one of the chief weaknesses of *TPA* is the lack of item content related to job involvement. The Work Interference scale (*WRK*) does contain content that can be considered to be at least indirectly related to this aspect of the Type A construct. Of the 33 items on *WRK*, 13 (39 percent) contain the word *work* or one of its cognates (e.g.

job). The content of *WRK* includes many items having clear relevance to job involvement and other components of the Type A construct, including eagerness or enthusiasm for work, concentration at work, self-confidence at work, perseverance, competitiveness, and coping with obstacles to work. Of these *WRK* items, about 8 are consistent with one or more of the JAS themes when endorsed in a manner consistent with the *WRK* key, and about 21 are consistent with the items on the JAS when scored in the direction opposite to those on *WRK*. With this pattern in mind, it can be hypothesized that the sign value of high *TPA* scores for the Type A Behavior pattern may be enhanced when *WRK* scores fall below *T*-60. Given the extremity of the hostile implications of *TPA2*, it is likely that the Type A Behavior pattern is more strongly suggested when scores on *TPA1* exceed those on *TPA2* than vice versa. Finally, given the high overlap between the *CYN* and *Ho* scales, which has been independently (of the JAS) shown to contain variance for coronary morbidity/mortality, *CYN* scores may support the inference of Type A dynamics when *CYN* exceeds *ASP* and when *CYN1* exceeds *CYN2*. *CYN* and *CYN1* scores that exceed *TPA2* scores might also have incremental value in identifying the Type A pattern.

Low Self-Esteem (LSE)

The *LSE* scale contains 24 items, 21 True, 3 False. It comprises items admitting personal and interpersonal shortcomings. The high scorer feels slower, less capable, less intelligent, less coordinated, less attractive, less likable, less self-confident, less resolute, and in many more general ways less adequate than others. Indeed, the high *LSE* respondent feels so overwhelmingly flawed, incompetent, and inferior to others that the independent management of life may seem out of the question, making him or her vulnerable to "charity case" dependent attachments onto others, in which dependency gratifications are paid for in the coin of self-abasement. It is the most sensitive of the content scales to ego-syntonic pathological dependency. The pattern of empirical correlates among the outpatients studied by Graham et al. (1999) appears to correspond closely to this description, but the men appeared more anxious and somatically focused, with histories of physical abuse, whereas the women were seen as more sad, dependent, isolated from others, and with histories of suicide attempts.

Ben-Porath and Sherwood (1993) divided *LSE* into Self-Doubt (*LSE1*) and Submissiveness (*LSE2*). The *LSE1* items are all negative self-attributions that are mostly phrased in such a way as to convey not self-doubt, but *conviction* that one is inferior and inadequate. That is, *LSE1* items assert negative self-attitudes that are relatively fixed and that sum to an overall negative or devalued identity. It correlates with *DEP3* at .83. The Graham et al. outpatients were described as sad/dysthymic/depressed, hopeless, feeling insecure, inferior and like a failure, self-degrading and self-doubting, interpersonally sensitive, and as coping poorly with stress, but the men were additionally described as anxious, worrying, obsessive–compulsive, histrionic, pessimistic, agitated, angry, resentful, overwhelmed, feeling that life is a strain, and having disturbed sleep and somatic complaints, while the women were seen as sensitive, passive-submissive and introversive, with narrow interests and low aspirations/achievement orientation. The correlates found for the Green et al. (2006) inpatients overlapped considerably with those they reported for *DEP* component scales, but with indecision and poorer concentration, more tension, self-consciousness, emotional withdrawal, blunted affect, loss of interest, motor retardation, feelings of inferiority, somatic concerns, and histories of sexual abuse.

The *LSE2* items reflect passivity, a servile obedience to others and, by implication, an avoidance of responsibility. In the Graham et al. (1999) outpatients, interpersonal sensitivity was the only correlate applying to both genders. Additionally, their men were described as anxious, nervous, passive, complaining of sleep disturbance, and having been physically abused, while their women were described as passive and submissive in relationships, overly compliant, neither self-reliant nor achievement oriented, having few or no friends, and with a history of suicide attempts. The Green et al. (2006) inpatients were described in terms similar to those these investigators recorded for *LSE1* but, in addition, they were described as suspicious and showing unusual thought content, hallucinatory behavior, and social/interpersonal as major problem areas.

There is an interesting tension between the two components in that, when both are elevated, the high scorer seems to be saying, "I'll gladly do whatever you tell me to, but I'm so clumsy and incompetent that you can't expect me to do anything but bollix it up." This would, among other things, suggest an affinity between *LSE* and interpersonal tactics, such as studied incompetence, that might be seen in some contexts as passive-aggressive and in others as self-defeating. However, *LSE* carries a primary implication of a collapse in normal-range defensive operations in which the ordinary maneuvers to shore up self-esteem, to put the best face on one's actions and intentions, and to save face and seek acceptable excuses for one's shortcomings are abandoned. *LSE1* contributes most directly to this aspect of *LSE*; *LSE2* extends the theme closer into the area of interpersonal interaction, where the renunciation of self-esteem culminates in an acceptance of the humiliation of servility.

Low scores on *LSE* suggest relative freedom from negative self-attitudes, especially in the context of interaction with others. Such scores affirm personal adequacy, self-confidence, competence, and independence. Within psychiatric populations, very low scores may reflect an inflated self-concept and possible grandiose ideation or delusions.

Relations to Other Scales

LSE may be contrasted with *DEP* in terms of the locus of control construct, with *LSE* being more "external" than *DEP*, whereas the high *DEP* scorer feels worthless and is more active, demanding, and relatively extra-punitive, the high *LSE* scorer feels helpless and is more passive, dependent, and intropunitive. *LSE* is highly intercorrelated with *OBS*, *DEP*, *WRK*, and *TRT*. An underlying theme in each of these scales is an inability to perform. *OBS* stresses the inability to make decisions and act on them, *DEP* stresses the inability to mobilize sufficient personal resources to engage life, *WRK* stresses the inability to produce output in the context of employment, and *TRT* stresses the inability to rise above helplessness and despair in order to grapple with personal problems. Together, these scales form a quintet for which the theme of motivational disability may be almost as significant as their common core of negative emotionality. That is, the respondent showing peaks on these scales is reporting feeling like a "basket case": depleted, immobilized, blocked, and helpless. As noted earlier, reference to *LSE* and *BIZ* can be especially useful in the interpretation of high Scale 8 scores, with these two content scales reflecting the contributions of negative self-attitudes and psychotic thinking, respectively.

Social Discomfort (SOD)

The SOD scale contains 24 items, 13 True, 11 False. Sixteen of the items overlap with Wiggins' Social Maladjustment (*SOC*). Eighteen (75 percent) of the *SOD* items overlap with Scale 0 (*Si*), 10 on *Si1* and with all 8 of the items on *Si2*, and most of the non-overlapping items express a preference for being alone; hence, the theme of interpersonal aversiveness is a good deal stronger in *SOD* than in *Si*. Like *Si*, *SOD* has a conspicuously bipolar character, with high scores connoting introversion and low scores connoting extraversion. Ben-Porath and Sherwood (1993) divided *SOD* into two components: Introversion (*SOD1*) and Shyness (*SOD2*). *SOD1* emphasizes the avoidance of group and social situations, an aversion for interpersonal interaction, and a preference for being alone. It correlates with *Si2* at .92. Very low *SOD1* scores may reflect a drive to become "lost in the crowd" and an intolerance of being alone. Containing all of the items of the *Si2* subscale (Social Avoidance), *SOD1* is the more "behavioral" of the two components. The correlates found for the Graham et al. (1999) outpatients included interpersonal sensitivity, introversion, depressed, feeling pessimistic and hopeless, and presenting with sleep disturbance and suicidal ideation, as well as, for men, insecure, suspicious, obsessive–compulsive, anxious, self-doubting, self-degrading, and self-punishing, feeling like failures, and likely to report somatic problems and physical health concerns, and for women, socially awkward, unconcerned with social status issues, neither achievement oriented, energetic, aspiring, nor extroverted, having few or no friends, diagnosed as dysthymic/depressed, and receiving anti-anxiety or antidepressant medication at the time of intake. The Green et al. (2006) inpatients showed anxiety, emotional withdrawal, guilt feelings, depressive mood, motor retardation, blunted affect, felt that doing nothing is a struggle, and had a history of sexual abuse and suicide attempts.

SOD2 is less than half the length of *SOD1* and emphasizes the more subjective and emotional features of the parent scale. It correlates with *Si1* at .94, and conveys a sense of discomfort, effort, difficulty, inhibition, and fear of embarrassment that pervades interactions with others, especially strangers, and in group situations. The correlates found for the Graham et al. outpatients included interpersonal sensitivity and, for men, passivity. Their women patients were additionally described as shy, introverted, having few interests, being non-energetic, non-competitive and neither achievement oriented nor aspiring, and failing to create a favorable first impression. The correlates found for the Green et al. inpatients essentially duplicate those these investigators found for *SOD1*.

The high *SOD2* scorer is self-consciously lacking in social skill and, although not necessarily avoidant in the way characteristic of the high *SOD1* scorer, he or she is likely to be seen as reticent and standoffish. The low *SOD2* scorer, by contrast, manifests an uninhibited sociability, enjoys high social visibility, and impresses others as socially intrepid, forward, and mixing easily. All of the *SOD2* items are contained in the *Si1* subscale (Shyness/Self-Consciousness). The high *SOD* scorer, then, seeks to stay away from others, whether individuals or groups, because he or she feels uneasy and awkward in such situations, and because being alone is felt to be happier. Thus, the high *SOD* scorer is not claiming loneliness, although this may represent a defensive denial of loneliness in some respondents. Low *SOD* scores, then, reflect a gregarious, outgoing style, the enjoyment of interaction, whether individually or in groups. Consistent with the opposite of social discomfort, the low *SOD* scorer evidences a high level of social comfort and confidence by being friendly, fun loving, talkative, participative, and flexible. Sizable *SOD2–SOD1* differences tend to identify individuals who have difficulty feeling at ease either alone or in the company of others. Ben-Porath and Sherwood have suggested that a low *SOD1* score coupled with a high *SOD2* score may reflect an aspiration to be more socially involved and a desire for an increased sense of personal comfort and control in interaction. This pattern is somewhat akin to stage fright, in which others are not rigidly avoided but simply approached with a sense of anxious trepidation. Very low scores on both components suggest a glib but superficial interactional style and are consistent with those manic/hypomanic syndromes having high social hunger (and high social turnover) as a cardinal feature.

The Graham et al. (1999) outpatients with high *SOD* scores showed interpersonal sensitivity, shyness, and social awkwardness, but they were also often seen as depressed and having suicidal ideation. The men were described in terms suggesting more severe and pervasive (e.g. suspicious, resentful, self-degrading) problems than those used to describe the women.

Relations to Other Scales

In the context of high scores on Scale 2 and low scores on Scale 9, high *SOD* scores reflect the kinds of anergic withdrawal and social anhedonia seen in depressive syndromes (see *INTR*, below). In profiles having primary elevations on *F* and Scales 6 and 8, high *SOD* scores may indicate schizophrenia spectrum interpersonal aversiveness and social withdrawal, the avoidant wariness that is grounded in paranoid suspiciousness and concerns for one's personal safety, or both. *SOD* scores in a region of T-55–65, when *SOD2* exceeds *SOD1*, are seen in borderline syndromes. Low *SOD* scores, especially when *SOD1* is low, can indicate warmth and a capacity for closeness with others when L and Scales 2, 7, and 8 are relatively low; K is in a T-55–65 range; and the raw K score exceeds the non-K-corrected raw score on *Pt*. Low *SOD* scores in which *SOD1* exceeds *SOD2* are consistent with narcissistic (check scores on *LSE* and Scale 9) and psychopathic (check scores on *Pd2*, *ASP2* [*ASP* exceeds *CYN*], *Re*, and *GF*) features, as well as with manic/hypomanic states.

Family Problems (FAM)

The *FAM* scale contains 25 items, 20 True, 5 False. *FAM* contains 10 items that appeared on the Wiggins Family Problems scale and 6 that overlap *Pd1* (Familial Discord). *FAM* items are about evenly balanced between current family and family of origin. The relatively high correlations between *FAM* and Scales 4 and 8 cannot be accounted for entirely by overlapping items, indicating that *FAM* may have a wider array of personological correlates than might be expected on the basis of its item content alone. This impression is confirmed in the findings of Butcher et al. (1990) in their ratings data from the re-standardization couples, and in the correlates Graham et al. (1999) found among their psychiatric outpatients. The re-standardization spouses rated their high *FAM* partners in terms suggesting emotional instability and loss of control; irritability, suspiciousness, hostility, and resentment; tension, worry, and fearfulness; dysphoric mood; dependency; and interpersonal ambivalence. The Graham et al. (1999) outpatients were seen as issuing from families in which emotional deprivation, discord, and abuse (men: physical; women: sexual) were common, but they were also described as depressed, hostile, resentful, and interpersonally sensitive.

The range and severity of these correlates is consistent with the view that positive emotional ties to family are essential to the kind of personal well-being that comes from feeling rooted in social life. A lack of sufficiently fostering primary relationships in childhood, and a stormy and contentious home atmosphere in particular, may bring about a level of personal deprivation and a pattern of negative social expectancies that leaves the individual ill-prepared for later developing the kinds of constructive relationships that lead to a sense of belongingness.

A substantially narrower set of correlates was found by Ben-Porath and Stafford (1993) in a forensic diagnostic sample of 113 men. Participants scoring high on *FAM* tended to show a history of poor relationships with fathers, siblings, family, spouses, and friends; had more frequently lost physical and legal custody of their children; and had been arrested while previously on probation.

High *FAM* scorers not only feel deprived and mistreated by family but also appear to have acquired or augmented a set of dispositions that maintain both intra-familial and more generalized enmity and insecurity into adulthood. They are apt to be seen by others as immature and over-reactive people who harbor grave doubts and deeply negative attitudes toward themselves but who are equally mistrustful and disparaging of others. This pattern of correlates is reminiscent of the pattern of traits in BPD. It is also a pattern that is common to alcohol and other substance abuse.

Ben-Porath and Sherwood (1993) found two *FAM* components: Family Discord (*FAM1*) and Familial Alienation (*FAM2*). The content of *FAM1* stresses intra-familial conflict and animosity, with members being seen as quarrelsome and disagreeable, oppressive and disapproving, annoying and ill-tempered. It correlates with *Pd1* at .74, and with *Sc1* at .72. The theme is one of the family as an unpleasant, noxious environment from which one would like to escape. The high *FAM1* Graham et al. (1999) outpatients were found likely to present with hostility, paranoid ideation, and interpersonal sensitivity. Additionally, their men were said to issue from families lacking in love, to have family problems and complain of family discord, to resent and blame family members for their problems, to be sad, depressed, hopeless, rejected, insecure, intolerant of frustration, to get along poorly with coworkers, and to have histories of sexual abuse, while the women were seen as critical, argumentative, grouchy, and had made suicide attempts. The Green et al. (2006) inpatients were described as hostile, suspicious, and excited, and showed histories of sexual abuse and suicide attempts.

Less than half the length of *FAM1*, *FAM2* stresses an emotional detachment from family. The items are phrased descriptively and have low emotional valences. They simply report factual states of affairs, which, in some respondents, would be associated with longing, loss, and anger, but in others with a sense of at least partial equanimity or indifference. In either case, high *FAM2* scores imply that respondents severed ties in order to cut their losses with their family because of its inability or disinclination to provide a center of belonging and emotional support. However, the empirical correlates that Graham et al. (1999) found among their outpatients suggest that for high *FAM2* scorers, the severing of emotional attachments to family is not followed by the formation of alternative attachments. Thus, in addition to having family problems and coming from families lacking in love, these patients were described as lonely, having few or no friends, and self-destructive, either through suicide attempts (women) or through chronic alcohol and marijuana abuse (men). These investigators also found histories of physical (men) and sexual (women) abuse among high *FAM2* scorers. Additionally, their men were described as experiencing family discord, being self-degrading, and abusing alcohol and marijuana, while their women were seen as narcissistic, immature, histrionic and demanding of attention, and having an exaggerated need for affection, but also as critical, argumentative, overly sensitive to criticism, having difficulty trusting others, suspicious, angry, resentful, and feeling they get a raw deal from life. The Green et al. outpatients were seen as hostile and had histories of sexual abuse and suicide attempts.

Ben-Porath and Sherwood suggested that high scores on *FAM2* when *FAM1* is (relatively) low indicate disengagement from family. This pattern would also seem to suggest a much greater sense of indifference, perhaps with some feeling of sorrow about the shortcomings of the family as a source of emotional provisions. The opposite pattern suggests the persistence of attachment in the midst of enmity and discord. When both components are elevated, a state of resentful alienation is suggested in which physical ties (i.e. association) have been severed but unresolved emotional attachments continue.

Relations to Other Scales

Despite the overlap between *FAM* and *Pdl* ($r = \sim.80$), the two scales have somewhat different interpretive implications for the primary nature and locus of family conflict. As noted previously *FAM* refers to current family and family of origin in about equal measure, whereas reference to the parental home more clearly dominates the content of *Pdl*, giving it a clear, albeit not strong, bias toward the family of origin. *Pdl* shows a relatively greater emphasis on the parents as restricting freedom, independence, and efforts toward emancipation. *FAM* conveys a relatively greater sense of family turbulence, pathology, and estrangement. As a result, scores on *FAM* exceeding those on *Pdl* may be a better reflection on current family relations, whereas the reverse pattern suggests that family strife may be largely confined to the parental home. The patient's age, family history, and current family circumstance, of course, may bear importantly on interpretations of *Pdl*, *FAM*, and the *FAM* component scales. Peak elevations on *CYN* when *FAM* is elevated imply distrust and dissatisfaction, if not enmity, with intimates that have apparently generalized to others. Distrust and dissatisfaction reach paranoid proportions when *FAM* and *BIZ* are peaked. The pattern of high scores on *FAM* and *ASP* when *ASP* exceeds *CYN* and *SOD* is low (and *SOD1* exceeds *SOD2*) appears to be the content scale equivalent of the psychopathic 49/94 profile type. Clinically, this pattern is associated with immaturity and substance abuse and with assaultiveness and destructiveness.

Work Interference (WRK)

The *WRK* scale contains 33 items, 28 True, 5 False. Twelve overlap with the 37-item Tydlaska and Mengel (1953) Work Attitude (*Wa*) scale. As noted in the discussion of *TPA*, almost 40 percent of the items contain the word *work* or one of its cognates. Of all the content scales, *WRK* is the one most saturated with first factor variance, achieving correlations with Welsh's *A* at ~.90 (8 items overlap with *A*). It is, in effect, a general measure of distress and disability that has been trimmed to the context of work, emphasizing the kinds of problems that have adverse effects on productivity. As such, it reflects an admixture of content that includes defeatist and pessimistic attitudes; anergia and impersistence; indecision and distractibility; irritability and rebelliousness; bitterness and oppositionality; a lack of initiative and ambition; a lack of enthusiasm and competitiveness; a lack of self-confidence and self-esteem; and a proneness to tension, worry, and fearfulness. Thus, the interferences covered in *WRK* include both interpersonal difficulties and the kinds of attitudes and symptoms that impair efficiency and impede output. Low scores, then, imply self-confidence, perseverance, an adequate fund of energy and the capacity to marshal one's abilities in the service of productivity on the job, a capacity for cooperative interactions with fellow employees (i.e. teamwork), and an ability to limit the influence of personal problems and symptoms on job performance. Graham et al. (1999) found that their high *WRK* scoring outpatients were described in terms indicative of depression, and as tending to lack ambition. The women presented as more passive and dependent; the men as more angry.

Relations to Other Scales

Because of its extensive shared variance with the first factor, the interpretive implications of *WRK* are most likely to be realized when it exceeds *A* in elevation. Although problems that may interfere with functioning in employment are suggested by elevations on *WRK* alone, such elevations cannot be taken to indicate occupational malfunctioning *specifically*. The requirement that *WRK* exceed *A* strengthens the implication of specific work interferences to the extent of this difference. Recalling the high intercorrelations among *OBS*, *DEP*, *LSE*, *WRK*, and *TRT*, scores on *WRK* should always be compared with those on the other scales in this group as a means of gaining additional insight into the kinds of problems that may most threaten work performance. See also *WRK* in the discussion of *TRT*, above.

Negative Treatment Indicators (TRT)

The *TRT* scale contains 26 items, 22 True, 4 False. It is highly correlated with *DEP* (.77), with which it shares 6 items (23 percent), and the empirical correlates found by Graham et al. (1999) to describe high *TRT* scorers are highly similar (often identical) to those they found to describe high *DEP* scorers. As a whole, *TRT* seems to reflect a depressive state in which apathy, despair, and helplessness reach such a level of severity as to result in immobilization. Ben-Porath and Sherwood (1993) divided *TRT* into two components: Low Motivation (*TRT1*) and Inability to Disclose (*TRT2*). The *TRT1* items connote apathy, an external locus of control, and a tendency to quickly give up in the face of obstacles because of a depletion of personal resources. It correlates with *DEP1* at .86, and with *DEP* at .85. The high *TRT1* scorer feels helpless and motivationally destitute to the point that struggle against problems and adversity, or even the formulation of plans to do so, is felt to be futile and pointless, leaving no alternative but to give up.

The Graham et al. (1999) outpatients were seen as sad and depressed, pessimistic and hopeless with suicidal ideation, anxious, insecure, coping poorly with stress, and giving up easily. In addition, their men were seen as self-degrading, obsessive–compulsive, feeling overwhelmed and that life is a strain, presenting somatic complaints, and having had prior outpatient treatment, while their women were seen as non-self-reliant, showed few interests, were not aspiring nor achievement oriented, had few or no friends, and had histories of suicide attempts. The Green et al. (2006) inpatients had a history of prior outpatient treatment and showed sexual inadequacy as a major problem, but their remaining correlates were almost identical to those these investigators found for *LSE1*.

TRT2 is less than half the length of *TRT1* and extends the theme of the futility of efforts at amelioration to the realm of discussion. It correlates with both *Si3* and *NEGE* at .64. All of the *TRT2* items reflect a disinclination to volunteer personal information and significant discomfort when one is asked to do so by others. The high *TRT2* scorer does not wish to reveal information about personal problems. Significantly, for women at least, the reasons for such disinclination and discomfort are suggested in the empirical correlates found by Graham et al. (1999) to characterize their high *TRT2* scoring female outpatients, including histories of both physical and sexual abuse, few or no friends, and prior suicide attempts and psychiatric hospitalization. Thus, for women, if not for men, high *TRT2* scorer may reason that confiding in others has not worked out well in the past and may only increase one's personal discomfort without offering any countervailing benefits. Additional correlates found by Graham et al. included, for men: depression, complaints of fatigue and sleep disturbance, and developing physical problems in response to stress; for women: shyness and introversion, not having high aspirations, and a history of alcohol abuse and misdemeanor convictions; for both: suicidal ideation, and feeling that life is a strain. The Green et al. inpatients had drug abuse as a major problem, histories of alcohol abuse, and showed anxiety, guilt feelings, motor retardation, and hallucinatory behavior.

Because both the item content and the empirical correlates of *TRT* are so heavily biased toward depression (*all* of the empirical correlates from the re-standardization couples' *TRT* ratings for women are contained within the *DEP* correlates for women; Butcher et al., 1990), it is most improbable that scores on *TRT* or its components have much to contribute to estimates of prognosis for psychotherapeutic treatments. Indeed, it is doubtful that these scores can reliably contribute to questions of psychotherapeutic outcome even in depressive states. First, muteness can be a symptom of severe depression and, in this context, may be no more predictive of psychotherapeutic outcome than other vegetative symptoms of comparable severity. Second, the prognosis for psychotherapy in depression may be quite unstable, appearing guarded to poor in the depths of depressive episodes, only to improve markedly as symptoms such as insomnia, anorexia, and psychomotor retardation subside. Thus, *TRT* scores may better serve prediction and description in the area of depressive *severity* than as a specific and reliable indicator of negative prognostic factors for the psychotherapy of depression or any other conditions commonly treated psychotherapeutically. The interpretation of low scores on *TRT* and its components is equally problematic. Because low *TRT* scorers are adequately motivated, self-confident, plan-ful, and persistent, they are likely to be less distressed and therefore less motivated for psychotherapy. Others obtaining low scores may appear grandiose, inflated, overconfident, insouciant, and unreflective in their approach to self-disclosure, and hence be potentially impervious to psychotherapeutic efforts even when tolerant of them. The mere capacity to disclose personal information affords no guarantee that the material revealed can be discussed productively, reflectively, or insightfully. Manic and psychopathic spectrum patients come easily to mind in this regard. Such patients, despite a tendency to obtain low and even very low *TRT* scores, may pose challenges to the psychotherapist that are every bit as forbidding as those posed by high *TRT* scorers. For these reasons, both the positive and the negative predictive power of *TRT* are highly suspect. In a study of male inpatients undergoing treatment for chronic pain, for example, Clark (1996) found that although high *TRT* and *TRT1* scores predicted less improvement in physical capacities over the course of treatment, they predicted greater reductions in Beck Depression Inventory (BDI) scores, the latter effect being attributed to regression to the mean. *TRT* and *TRT1* scores also predicted higher levels of post-treatment dysfunction in these patients, indicating that high scorers were more impaired to begin with. *TRT2* was not significantly associated with changes related to treatment or with post-treatment functioning. Moreover, none of the *TRT* scales were related to premature termination of treatment. To be sure, the patients and treatment examined in this study are not typical of those psychotherapy and psychiatric settings in which *TRT* may be routinely applied. Overall, the research literature on TRT may be summarized as follows: The results from studies by Garcia, Kelley, Rentz, and Lee (2011), Gilmore, Lash, Foster, and Blosser (2001), and by Kotjahasan (2005) can be considered positive, but are at a minimum counterbalanced by the negative findings of Chisholm, Crowther, and Ben-Porath (1997), Collins (1999), Craig and Olson (2004), Maiello, Salviati, De'Fornari, Del Casale, Rreli, Rusconi, and Piccione (2007), Minnix, Reitzel, Repper, Burns, Williams, Lima, Cukrowicz, Kirsch, and Joiner (2005), and by Rosik and Borisov (2010), and the mixed or equivocal findings of Coffield (2007) and Muench (1996). Indeed, in some cases, notably those of Chisholm et al. (1997), Maiello et al. (2007), and Rosik and Borisov (2010), the results suggest that, if anything, elevated scores on *TRT* are predictive of *positive* treatment outcomes or, precisely the opposite of what this scale was intended to predict. Thus until substantially more evidence of the validity of *TRT* for its intended purpose is forthcoming from traditional treatment venues, this scale should be interpreted conservatively and with due caution.

Relations to Other Scales

Recall that *TRT* is one of a cluster of scales that also includes *OBS*, *DEP*, *LSE*, and *WRK*. Of these, as noted earlier, *TRT* is most closely associated with *DEP*. Because the status of *TRT* as a predictor of problems that favor a poorer prognosis for psychotherapeutic endeavors is unknown at this time, it is premature to speculate on patterns between *TRT*, *DEP*, and other scales in this cluster.

General Principles for the Interpretation of Content Scales

Like the Wiggins content scales, scores on the MMPI-2 content scales are highly vulnerable to manipulation. The strong unithematic character of these scales, combined with the generally high obviousness or face validity of the items comprising them, places them at the ready disposal of the respondent in accordance with his or her desires.

This feature is both an asset and a liability for the assessment process. It is an asset in the sense that the homogeneity and obviousness of these scales make them suitable for a handshake across the item pool. Content scales are "user-friendly," facilitating communication between patient and clinician. Content scales, in effect, unburden the process of self-report and allow the patient greater freedom of movement within the item pool to reveal the kinds of symptoms, concerns, and attitudes considered most salient and problematic. These scales allow the patient to record the kinds of difficulties creating concern, to rank order their severity, and to contrast them with problem areas that have not given rise to concern, presumably those areas experienced by the patient to be conflict free and well within the patient's sphere of competencies to manage. In other words, the patient's control of all three features of a profile of scores—elevation, shape, and scatter—is far greater with the content scales than with other scale groupings, such as the standard clinical scales. MMPI/MMPI-2 data at the content level permit, if not encourage, a shared frame of reference between patient and clinician that, if seized by both, defines the assessment process as a collaborative enterprise; engages the trust of and promotes a sense of personal potency on the part of the patient; can be a stimulus to accurate empathy for the therapist; and can lead to a clear sense that the patient is speaking, the clinician is listening, and the two are in a state of communication. The obvious, homogeneous character of the content scales is a liability in the sense that the respondent who wishes to falsify, obscure, or otherwise present an inaccurate or deceptive account of his or her functioning and symptomatology will find few obstacles for doing so. This once again emphasizes the importance of properly preparing the patient for assessment by explaining the process and its purposes, seeking the patient's cooperation as a collaborator rather than as a subject by exploring ways that testing might help to answer questions of significance to the patient, and otherwise trying to advance the patient's individual purposes, as well as promising prompt and detailed test feedback. It is when the patient feels deprived of a stake in a collaborative relationship with the clinician and the outcome of the assessment that motivation to mislead the assessor and frustrate the goals of assessment is apt to be highest and the risk of a manipulative and deceptive response style is greatest. The patient wishing to present a distorted picture of adjustment may choose to exaggerate or minimize all manner of problems or may selectively emphasize some areas of difficulty and de-emphasize others. Some patients, typically among the most disturbed, will intentionally exaggerate or minimize some kinds of problems but inadvertently claim, or fail to claim, symptoms or complaints that disorder severity has placed outside the reach of conscious manipulation. Such cases can enormously confound and frustrate efforts at interpretation.

The extent of the patient's control of elevation in the content scales can create confusion and uncertainty to clinicians accustomed to following the distinction between elevations at or above T-65 and those failing to reach this level. Among the standard clinical scales, the operation of K, the internal corrections for some scales (e.g. Scale 2), and the inclusion of subtle item content for many scales tend to support a line of demarcation between the so-called normal and clinical ranges. The fact that the rate of endorsement for obvious items varies inversely with the endorsement rate for subtle items operates to push T-scores up when an excess of subtle items are endorsed and to decelerate elevations when obvious items are over-endorsed (Burkhart, Christian, & Gynther, 1978). For the content scales, however, these moderating factors are unavailable. As a consequence, content scale elevations are highly vulnerable to differences in response style, and both extremely high-ranging and extremely low-ranging content profiles are commonly seen. Reliance on a particular absolute elevation standard, such as T-65, as an interpretive guideline is much more hazardous in the case of content scale elevations than it is for the standard clinical scales. Instead, the appropriate interpretation of content scales depends much more heavily on *relative* elevations, regardless of whether the average elevation of these scales is high or low.

Because of the extensive shared variation among the content scales, a substantial elevation on a given scale may be required before the variance that is shared with other, similar scales can be assumed to have been exhausted and that fraction of variance unique to the scale in question may be supposed to have "kicked in." The point at which this unique variance can be considered to be in play will vary with both its absolute level of elevation and with its elevation relative to other scales with which it shares variance. For example, consider a male patient obtaining scores of T-92 on both ANX and DEP. At this level, the items on ANX have been exhausted, but five items on DEP were marked in the non-scorable direction. It may, therefore, be tentatively assumed that this pattern of scores reflects the substantial contribution of the variance that the two scales share but a relatively larger fraction of variance that is unique to ANX than that unique to DEP. The clinician would, therefore, be justified in interpreting the ANX score more aggressively than the DEP score, even though the scales are equally elevated. Consider now a female patient with a score of T-69 on ANX and of T-83 on DEP. In this case, eight items from each scale were marked in the non-scorable direction, yet the difference in elevation suggests that these scores reflect the relatively greater contribution of unique variance of DEP than that for ANX. Thus, the clinician could, with some confidence, make the assumption that the DEP score reflects a true depressive phenomenon, whereas the ANX score may indicate no more that the kind of discomfort common to both anxiety and depression, even though ANX is elevated into the "clinical range," and interpreted accordingly. Of course, it is unnecessary for any of the content scales to equal or exceed any particular level in order to be interpretable, provided that there are sufficient differences in elevation among these scales to suggest the operation of their unique variances.

Similar considerations apply to very-low-ranging content scale scores. In the great majority of cases, such scores result from a defensive approach to the content of the MMPI-2, in which an effort has been made to avoid all responses that might suggest maladjustment or psychopathology, and the clinician will have been alerted to this approach by the configuration of L, F, and K. It is, nevertheless, important to consider how successful the respondent's efforts to avoid the revelation of psychopathology have been and, where a failure to do so is indicated, to attempt identification of possible causes for such failure. For example, consider a case in which all of the content scales except ANG and TPA are below T-40. ANG is at T-43, and TPA is at T-48. Although such a profile suggests that the avoidance of pathological content has been largely realized, the avoidance of items reflecting angry or hostile content was relatively less successful. If expressions of anger and hostility are less well-contained on the MMPI-2 than other problems, a question may be raised as to whether the control of such expressions in other areas of the respondent's life are also less than fully adequate. It may be that the respondent is comfortable endorsing a few of the ANG and TPA items out of a feeling that his or her ire, when present, is never less than fully justified. In this context, the respondent may feel that his failure to endorse these few items would amount to the admission of something having worse pathological implications: cowardice, tolerance for injustice, intolerable passivity, or a lack of principle. Consider another example, in which content scale scores range from a low of *T*-30 to a high of *T*-47, but with *BIZ* having the highest score. Here, one may ask, given an obvious effort to avoid pathological content, why should failure occur on a scale having such egregious pathological implications. Because it is not unusual for psychotic ideation to underlie errors in judgment, including the kinds of social judgment that may be at play in completing the MMPI-2 (particularly in the context of ego-syntonic delusions), it is reasonable to consider the possibility of psychotic mentation in the search for an answer to this question. The reader may object, noting that a *T*-score of 47 corresponds to a raw score of only a single item. But, however well-taken, this objection does not address the question of why one of this kind of item was endorsed and not an item with less severe implications. One might also object that a single-item endorsement could be the result of an accident in marking, a distraction, a lapse in attention, a manifestation of fatigue, a temporary misalignment of test booklet and answer sheet. Indeed, these possibilities should be admitted into consideration. But the endorsement of clearly pathological content in the context of a highly defensive test protocol is always worthy of further investigation.

The interpretation of content scale scores can often be enhanced in both clarity and precision by making reference to general moderators of test performance, such as factor scales *A* and *R*, and to other gross measures of deviance (e.g. *F* and *F* – *K*), defensiveness (e.g. *K*), and behavioral dyscontrol (e.g. *DISC* [Disconstraint]). For example, a person with a score of *T*-65 on both *DEP* and *K* may be much more disabled than a person with a score of *T*-65 on *DEP*, and *T*-45 on *K*. In the first instance, *K* may be suppressing the endorsement of items reflecting depression that might otherwise be made. In the same vein, the patient who scores *T*-70 on *BIZ* and *T*-75 on *F* may be more disabled by psychosis than one who obtains an identical *BIZ* score but a score of *T*-90 on *F* because the higher *F* score provides *BIZ* greater "permission" to elevate. In other words, an individual elevating *F* at *T*-90 is likely endorsing a wide variety of unusual items but may not be responding *preferentially* to psychotic content. By contrast, in the context of a *BIZ* score at *T*-70, a much lower *F* elevation would suggest a narrow focus on the psychotic content of *F*, the content of which may be elaborated from the non-overlapping items on *BIZ*.

The Personality Psychopathology Five (PSY–5)

The MMPI re-standardization committee felt that the original MMPI item pool was inadequate to cover several assessment issues that the committee deemed important. These included suicidal ideation, substance abuse problems, accessibility to psychotherapeutic treatment, problems in the work setting, and others. The committee, therefore, generated many new items in order to expand the number of items with content related to these areas. The occasion of the re-standardization afforded the committee members a rare and possibly unique opportunity to alter an item pool that had been fixed for nearly a half-century. And given this opportunity, the members proceeded by a rational-deductive strategy, in which the formulation of new items was guided by the construct a desired future scale was intended to embody. But what of the assessor who is convinced of the merits of the rational strategy of scale construction but faced with an item pool that has been fixed, closed to new items and content? Harkness (1990) proposed that if new items could not be written in support of a construct that was not envisioned at the time the item pool became closed, the way was still open to rationally *select* items from the fixed pool to address new constructs. Specifically, Harkness proposed an approach he called *replicated rational selection*. Replicated rational selection is a rational-deductive strategy in that the scale development process begins with the specification of the construct to be measured. It is at the next step that Harkness' strategy diverges from traditional methods. Instead of deducing new items to be written for the construct, items are selected from the established pool. The process remains deductive in that the selection of candidate items follows deductively from the construct to be measured. Whereas in the usual rational-deductive sequence, items may be written by any number of contributors, from one to many, it is the essence of Harkness' procedure that many selectors, a couple of dozen or more, having been trained in the defining features of the construct, in both its convergent and discriminant aspects, nominate items to be scaled: hence his designation of the procedure as *replicated* rational selection. Candidate items are then evaluated for the degree to which each attained consensus within the group of selectors. Thus, items arrange themselves along a selection gradient that displays a range from items selected only sporadically among the cadre of selectors to those whose frequency of nomination approaches unanimity. Items for which adequate consensus is found are then subjected to expert and statistical scrutiny to ensure overall semantic consistency and adequate internal consistency reliability. No items can be added at this stage, but a few may be deleted because of ambiguous wording or keying, compound phrasing, items with a primary focus on others rather than the self, or the retention of some items leads to an unacceptable decrement in internal consistency. Following this stage, the scale is ready for empirical trials to assess its construct validity.

The PSY–5 (Harkness, McNulty, & Ben-Porath, 1995) is a set of five scales that are intended to model the domain of disordered personality. These are Aggressiveness (*AGGR*), Psychoticism (*PSYC*), Disconstraint (*DISC*), Negative Emotionality/Neuroticism (*NEGE*), and Introversion/Low Positive Emotionality (*INTR*). (See the MMPI-2 *Manual*, Table B-6 for a listing of the item composition and scoring directions for the MMPI-2 PSY–5 scales; and Tables A-12 and A-13 for the uniform *T*-score conversions from raw scores for these scales.) Despite points of similarity with five-factor models of normal personality derived from the broader lexicon of trait descriptive terms (The Big Five), Harkness and McNulty (1994) argued that measures based on such models, like the Neuroticism, Extraversion, and Openness Personality Inventory (NEO-PI), are less than optimal as applied to the routine tasks of clinical assessment and description, particularly with personality disordered patients.

The correspondence between the normal-sample-based Five Factor Model (FFM), as represented by the scales of the NEO-PI-Revised (NEO-PI-R; Costa & McCrae, 1992b, 1992c, 1992d), and the PSY–5 is as shown in Table 7.6, in descending order of their similarity.

Relationships between the NEO-PI-R and PSY–5 are further described in Bagby, Sellbom, Costa, and Widiger (2008), Egger, De Mey, Derksen, and van der Staak (2003), and Trull, Useda, Costa, and McCrae (1995).

Table 7.6 Correspondence of the PSY-5 to the Five-Factor Model (FFM)

FFM	PSY-5
Neuroticism	Negative Emotionality/Neuroticism
Extraversion	Introversion/Low Positive Emotionality (reversed)
Agreeableness	Aggressiveness (reversed)
Conscientiousness	Disconstraint (reversed)
Openness	—
—	Psychoticism

The extensive research literature on the PSY–5 scales is the subject of a recent comprehensive review by Harkness, Finn, McNulty, and Shields (2012) to which the reader is referred. In general, the research has affirmed the PSY–5 structural model as well as the psychometric properties, construct, and external validities of its component scales.

Arnau, Handel, and Archer (2005) sought to identify facet scales for the PSY–5 with a replicated principal components analysis (PCA) with tetrachoric correlations in majority outpatient samples of men and women (*Ns* = ~4300), with the number of retained components determined by parallel analysis. Thirteen facets were described, three each for *AGGR*, *PSYC*, and *INTR*, and two each for *DISC* and *NEGE*. However, Quilty and Bagby (2007), using both confirmatory and exploratory factor analysis (CFA/ EFA) were unable to affirm the stability of these facet scales in a sample of men and women psychiatric patients (*N* = 693). Wang, Zhang, Shi, Zhou, and Li (2010), following a similar methodology, likewise found the Arnau et al. facet scales to have unacceptable reliabilities and validities in a Chinese sample. Based upon these findings, the Arnau et al. PSY–5 facet scales will not be described further below.

Aggressiveness (AGGR)

The *AGGR* scale contains 18 items, 15 True, 3 False. More than a third of its items overlap with Wiggins' Manifest Hostility (*HOS*) and with Cook and Medley (1954) *Ho*. It is highly correlated with all of the scales within the aggressive tendencies cluster of the MMPI-2 content scales, ranging from a low of .45 for *ANG* to a high of .55 for *TPA*. Other correlates include *R* (−.63); Scale 9 (.56); and the Narcissistic (*NAR;* .53), Histrionic (*HST;* .40), and Antisocial (*ANT;* .37) personality disorder scales of Morey et al. (1985). Sharpe and Desai (2001) found that *AGGR* correlated .60 with the Buss and Perry (1992) Aggression Questionnaire, and −-.53 with the NEO-PI-R (Costa & McCrae [1992d]) Agreeableness, in a college sample (*N* = 234). *AGGR* is unique among MMPI/MMPI-2 scales in tapping offensive or predatory aggression. For example, it is considerably less saturated with nonspecific variance, correlating with Welsh's *A* at −.01, than scales in the aggressive tendencies cluster whose correlations with *A* are in the .45 to .60 range. In this respect, *AGGR* is much "cooler" than any of the other anger/hostility scales for the MMPI/MMPI-2, including *ANG*, *TPA*, and *Ho*. The content of *AGGR* emphasizes a theme of superiority and control avoidance, with additional subsets reflecting sadism and vindictiveness. *AGGR* expressions of aggression, hostility, and control/domination are more apt to reflect cruelty than rage and are more apt to appear calculated, deliberate, methodical, and cold. By contrast, similar expressions from, for example, high scorers on *ANG* and *TPA* are more likely to be seen as reactions to frustration or other provocation and as rash, unpremeditated, impulsive, and reckless or ill considered.

The *AGGR* scale reflects the hostile urge to antagonize, dominate, vanquish, and destroy others. Thus, it is predatory or sadistic aggression that is at stake in *AGGR* rather than the kind of (angry) aggression that is motivated by frustration in *ANG* and in *NEGE*. The self-concept is inflated, grandiose, and resentful, with a dread of being subject to the control of another and a willingness to act sadistically and vindictively in order to avoid such control. *AGGR* calls to mind several paranoid dynamisms, including the defense mechanism, identification with the aggressor, the tendency to see interactions as moves in a zero sum game and, possibly, the authoritarian complex of submissiveness with superiors and tyrannical relations with subordinates. The high *AGGR* scorer presents as controlling others through the threat of his or her temper. Relations with others are marked by aggressive efforts to control and dominate through fear and the threat of violence and by resentment, hostility, and sadism. Wygant and Sellbom (2012) found a strong association between high *AGGR* scores and their global measure of psychopathy and its components.

Low *AGGR* scores will reflect less the absence of aggression, in the sense of approach, than of the hostile orientation toward power, domination, and sadism characteristic of high *AGGR* scores. Thus, the low *AGGR* scorer may manifest an aggressive, engaging style, but one that is less pressured and that accepts relations among others on horizontal, egalitarian terms, in which the mutual achievement of individual goals is not only conceivable but also expected. The low *AGGR* scorer accepts both one-up and one-down positions in his or her relations with others, knowing that these are transitory and subject to a variety of constraints that limit arbitrary vertical action of superior on subordinate. Weisenburger, Harkness, McNulty, Graham, and Ben-Porath (2008) reported that raw scores below seven for men and six for women were associated with therapist ratings of low aggressiveness and passive and submissive features in a sample of outpatients (N: M = 188; W = 287).

Relations to Other Scales

Assessment of the degree to which hostile expressions are likely to be calculated versus precipitate may be aided by reference to the relative elevations of *AGGR* and *ANG*. *AGGR* shares some common variance with three other PSY–5 scales, Disconstraint (*DISC*; .42), and Introversion/Low Positive Emotionality (*INTR*; –.29), conceived as anergy, low activation, or low readiness to act, and Psychoticism (*PSYC*; .33), reflecting an unrealistic view of self and others and one that overemphasizes issues of power and control. The shared variance between *AGGR* and *INTR*, along with the absence of variance in common with *A*, suggests that the control, domination, and harm that issues from the high *AGGR* scorer is associated with pleasure, enjoyment, and a sense of well-being. Selfish, self-centered, and yet envious of others, the high *AGGR* scorer reflects a hostile narcissism that is heavily dependent on the attention and recognition of others. But the self-concept is so unrealistic, grandiose, and entitled that the desired reflections are forthcoming only under conditions of coercion. In this context, the combination of high *AGGR* scores with high *DISC* scores or with high *PSYC* scores would appear to be especially dangerous combinations. In the case of high *AGGR* and high *DISC* scores, there is a synergy between sadistic motivation and deficits in behavioral control. Conjoint elevations on *AGGR* and *PSYC* suggest a risk for hostile action in the context of disordered thinking, such as bizarre and violent fantasy, command hallucinations or ego-syntonic delusions, especially when *DISC* and *INTR* are high.

The *AGGR* scale has an obvious bearing on the quality and dynamics of treatment relationships, especially when *DISC* scores are high and *NEGE* scores are at least moderately high, with high scorers likely to violate treatment plans, fail to follow through on agreements, discontinue medication, and in other ways undermine therapeutic efforts.

In relation to low *AGGR* scores, low *DISC* scores suggest under-assertion, passivity, and a high threshold for resisting domination. In this context, elevations on *NEGE* (or similar distress scales, such as *A*, Scale 7, *ANX*, and *DEP*) may indicate patterns of behavior suggesting self-sabotage and self-defeat. Such a pattern would also be consistent with symptoms of obsessive–compulsive disorder. Low *AGGR* scores with low *INTR* scores would seem to create a vulnerability to being played for a patsy by misplacing trust in others and approaching situations with a kind of credulous confidence that most others would avoid.

Psychoticism (PSYC)

The *PSYC* scale contains 25 items, 23 True, 2 False. *PSYC* is strongly correlated with measures of similar constructs, including *BIZ* (.94), with which it shares 14 items, *F* (.71), and Scales 8 (.69) and 6 (.65). Additional correlates include *OBS* (.66) and *CYN* (.64), and Morey, Waugh, and Blashfield's (1985) Paranoid Personality Disorder (*PAR*; .64). The two largest groupings of items have active psychotic experience, including delusions of control, and active persecutory content, respectively. Additional subsets of items concern unusual experience/magical ideation, daydreaming, and suspiciousness. Harkness, McNulty, and Ben-Porath (1995) describe *PSYC* as assessing "the gross verisimilitude of [one's] inner models of the outer social and object world" (p. 105). Thus, it is intended to reflect the extent to which the individual's ability to conform his or her thinking to consensual views of the external world and to the human action within it—and to correct elements of thinking and interpretation that render one's model of reality a poor fit to the actual external situation—is impaired. At moderate elevations (*T*-55–65), *PSYC* may reflect little more than unusual beliefs or experiences, and perhaps a tendency to overindulge in daydreaming. Any elevation may be taken as a sign of reluctance to engage the world and other people in conventional terms. Even at mild and moderate elevations, *PSYC* reflects disharmony in one's relations with the physical and social worlds such that functioning is compromised and relationships are alienated. At these levels, the person may give the appearance of being "in the world but not of it." At higher elevations one encounters severe distortions in the way the individual interacts with his or her social and physical worlds, such that these interactions appear, respectively, hostile, provocative, offensive, inept or incompetent, irrelevant, bizarre, or self-defeating. At elevations greater than *T*-65, however, true psychotic phenomena make an appearance, including Schneiderian symptoms, fixed persecutory if not frank delusional ideation, and suspiciousness. In general, the high *PSYC* scorer presents as odd, peculiar, or weird in appearance, behavior, and belief. He or she appears to be preoccupied with fantasy and daydreaming and seems alienated and "out of touch with reality." Relations with others are apt to be minimal, distant, and covertly hostile, with a readiness to feel mistreated and resentful.

Low *PSYC* scores are largely without symptomatic significance apart from the absence of those features associated with high scores. However, in terms of its guiding construct, one would expect low *PSYC* scores to carry favorable implications regarding the individual's ability to detect and correct misimpressions in order to accommodate previous editions of his or her inner model of reality to newly apprehended features of the human and nonhuman environment.

Relations to Other Scales

Because the content of about 40 percent of the *PSYC* items is persecutory or suspicious in character, reference can be made to the *Pa1* subscale (Ideas of External Influence) to estimate the contribution of paranoid ideation to *PSYC* elevations.

Disconstraint (DISC)

The *DISC* scale contains 28 items, 17 True, 11 False. It is moderately correlated with *ASP* (.57), with which it shares eight items, and with the Morey et al. (1985) Antisocial Personality Disorder scale (*ANT*; .50). It overlaps negatively nine items with *GF* and seven items with *Re*. *DISC* is the only one of the PSY–5 scales for which age appears to be an important moderator, with scores tending to decrease with age ($r = -.24$; Harkness, Spiro, Butcher, & Ben-Porath, 1995). The largest subset of items reflects an expedient morality such that "anything goes." A somewhat smaller group of items reflects stimulation seeking. Four additional groups of items concern delinquent conduct, sexual disinhibition, activity, and the denial of heights and fire (two items). The main theme is one of under-modulation of impulse, spontaneity, broad interests, cognitive and moral flexibility, insufficient delay of gratification, and an independence from familiar if not hackneyed rubrics. High scores reflect an unconventional, intrepid, disinhibited personality structure with insufficient delay and modulation of impulse, a nonconforming and rebellious attitude toward rules and regulations, sensation seeking, shallow and self-centered loyalties, a hedonistic moral compass, indifference to, if not disdain for, legal and ethical constraints, a fearless if not reckless disregard for potential physical hazards, and a tendency to sacrifice long-term goals for short-term satisfactions. The high *DISC* scorer may present initially as energetic and spontaneous, but on closer acquaintance comes to appear unreliable, reckless, and rebellious. Relations with parents and authority figures tend to be conflicted; relations with peers and others tend to be exploitive, promiscuous, and unstable. Impulsive and antisocial acting out, a lack of loyalty, repeated lying and neglect of obligations, and a lack of shame or remorse eventually may disrupt all but correctional relationships. Wygant and Sellbom (2012) reported an association between high *DISC* scores and the behavioral features of psychopathy.

The low *DISC* scorer, by contrast, presents as conventional, conforming, and controlled. Relations with others may be quite smooth but distant, formalized, and routinized, with contacts limited to a small circle of like-minded friends. A high tolerance for boredom, sameness, and routine and a relatively rigid adherence to traditional moral standards, along with a willingness to judge others in terms of these standards, are characteristic. Very concerned with maintaining "proper" appearances, the low *DISC* scorer takes an overly deliberate if not perfectionistic, approach to problem solving.

Relations to Other Scales

DISC appears to occupy the position formerly held by Block's (1965) Ego Control (*EC-5*; scoring reversed) in the MMPI environment. The re-standardization entailed the loss of nearly a third of the *EC-5* items, with uncertain consequences for its adequacy as a marker for the second (or beta) factor of the MMPI/MMPI-2. With its emphasis on emotional inhibition, social withdrawal, and narrow interests, Repression (*R*) has been the traditional marker for this factor. An alternative marker for the same factor, *EC-5* emphasized behavioral over emotional constraint, with particular reference to rule following and social conformity. The Harkness, McNulty, and Ben-Porath (1995) Disconstraint construct is very similar to *EC-5* (reversed) and shares a similar level of association with *R*, about –.40. Because, like distress, emotional and behavioral controls are of pervasive significance in psychopathology, both *R* and *DISC* may contribute to the interpretation of most other scales. Discussion of *DISC* in relation to other scales is therefore highly selective.

In their discussion of *DISC*, Harkness, McNulty, and Ben-Porath (1995) called attention to the similarity between it and the personality disorder simplex found by Romney and Bynner (1992): both had antisocial personality at one end and compulsive personality at the other. Although it is unknown whether and to what extent *DISC* scores (when low) are sensitive to obsessive–compulsive personality disorder, for reasons having to do with the pervasiveness of the constraint dimension across a variety of psychiatric conditions, scores on this scale may well contribute to the discrimination between obsessive–compulsive disorder and obsessive–compulsive personality disorder. Along with investigation of the correlates of both high and low *DISC* scores in relevant psychiatric samples, it may also be illuminating to examine configurational relationships of *OBS* with *DISC*. For example, are small (or negative) *OBS–DISC* differences associated with obsessive–compulsive personality disorder but not with obsessive–compulsive disorder, as might be expected, whereas larger differences in the context of high *OBS* scores (and, perhaps, a relatively large *FRS–DISC* difference) show the opposite pattern?

With high *DISC* scores and moderate to high *NEGE* scores, one could anticipate contranormative approaches to coping with subjective discomfort, such as through alcoholism or other substance abuse. Harkness, Levenson et al. (1995) in a study of the Boston VA normative aging sample found that the *DISC* (formerly *CON*) and *NEGE* scales were the top-ranked variables contributing to the separation of problem and heavy drinkers from non-problem drinkers. High *DISC* scores would synergize with low *INTR* scores to produce adventurousness, sensation seeking, and sometimes recklessness. In the context of low *NEGE* scores and high *AGGR* scores, this pattern would suggest the classic amoral/asocial psychopathic picture. Low *DISC* and high

NEGE scores would appear to coincide with immaturity and a lack of responsibility and to reflect those problems of impulse control in which impulsive action is reinforced by tension reduction. High *DISC* and high *PSYC* scores may synergize to emphasize a readiness to indulge in fantasy (including bizarre fantasy) and daydreaming, especially when *INTR* scores are high. Egger, Delsing, and DeMey (2003) found that *DISC* scores were significantly higher in their Bipolar 1 patients than in their psychotics.

Negative Emotionality/Neuroticism (NEGE)

The *NEGE* scale contains 33 items, 27 True, 6 False. It is highly correlated with markers for the first factor, including *A* (.87) and Scale 7 (.84), as well as with *ANX*, *WRK*, *OBS*, and, importantly, *ANG*. Its overlap with *A*, however, is confined to only six items. The largest subset of items reflects worry, nervousness, anxiety, tension, and stress. A second subset reflects anger and emotional loss of control; six items overlap with *ANG*, three each on *ANG1* and *ANG2*. Two smaller groups of items denote guilt and fears, respectively. *NEGE* reflects the sense of being so overwhelmed with the stress of worry, nervousness, fear, and guilt that one feels "at the end of one's rope" and "quick to fly off the handle." Two themes are implicit in the item content: (a) a pervasively unpleasant and aversive emotional life, one that feels both relentless and intrusive, leading to inner agitation, and (b) a feeling that one's controls have been taxed by this relentlessly aversive emotionality to the point of collapse. The high *NEGE* scorer presents as helpless, dependent, needy, indecisive, and unstable. Relations with others are characterized by extreme passivity, fears of abandonment, and hypersensitivity to criticism. He or she may provoke exasperation in others as there may be repeated failures to take initiative to improve the situation and to act in his or her best interest. Borderline attachments to others, help-rejecting complaining-ness, and suicidal or self-mutilative behavior may be seen.

At the low end, *NEGE* reflects a relaxed and imperturbable emotionality that is so care- and worry-free as to suggest an impoverishment of internal experience and awareness, thus raising the question of repressiveness. In any case, at the extreme, low scores are likely to reflect an emotional life that is placid to the point of imperviousness. Wygant and Sellbom (2012) found an association between low *NEGE* scores and the low affectivity of the psychopathy construct.

Relations to Other Scales

As one more congener of the first factor, *NEGE* is related to distress across a wide range of manifestations.

Introversion/Low Positive Emotionality (INTR)

The *INTR* scale contains 34 items, 5 True, 29 False. Correlates with other MMPI-2 scales include Scales 2 (.79) and 0 (.76)—it shares 13 items with each—and with *DEP* (.61) and *SOD* (.73). Among the Morey et al. (1985) personality disorder scales, *INTR* has positive correlations with Avoidant (*AVD*; .68), Schizotypal (*STY*; .61) and Schizoid (*SZD*; .52), and negative correlations with Narcissistic (*NAR*; –.71) and Histrionic (*HST*;

−.64). The largest subsets of items claim dysphoria, low energy and hedonic capacity, and social avoidance/withdrawal. Three smaller groups of items deny personal adequacy, persistence, and euphoria. *INTR* reflects social disengagement and a lack of emotional buoyancy. High scores suggest not so much the presence of unpleasant or aversive emotionality, as in the case of *NEGE*, as of a depleted, impoverished, emotional life. Characteristic features include anhedonia, anergy, dissatisfaction, low self-esteem, and a tendency to give up quickly in the face of difficulty. Depending on the particular pattern of items endorsed, high *INTR* scores may reflect depressive withdrawal, schizoid under-involvement, or both. The high *INTR* scorer is uncomfortable around other people and tends to avoid social situations. Relations with others are distant, although not hostile; rather, the high *INTR* scorer tends to react to others in an impassive way when interaction cannot be avoided. A defective pleasure parameter (Meehl's 1974, 1987, anhedonia) may be at the root of the high *INTR* scorer's impoverished emotional responsiveness.

The low *INTR* scorer presents as sociable, outgoing, visible, warm, engaged, and socially attractive if not charismatic. Relations with others are warm and easygoing, based on high self-esteem, freedom from debilitating stresses, distinct pleasure in interaction with others, and mutual respect for their rights and freedoms. The low *INTR* scorer describes high self-esteem, feeling liked and accepted by others, a quickness to feel pleasure and fulfillment, a deep reservoir of energy for the pursuit of goals, and a sense of happy connection with others that includes a desire for close and intimate relationships.

Relations to Other Scales

DISC may be an important modifier of *INTR* scores, with low scores on both scales suggesting that the social buoyancy of the low *INTR* score is controlled and socially constructive. When *DISC* scores are high and *INTR* scores are low, the person's sociability is apt to be superficial and utilitarian. This combination suggests an especially high rate of social turnover, as the need for stimulation and novelty undermines loyalty and results in a lowered threshold for boredom in relationships. Conversely, low *DISC* scores in the context of high *INTR* scores reflect not only drastically curtailed social initiative, but also a high tolerance for predictability and sameness in relations with others. This is a formula for relationships that, however long-lived, may remain shallow. With moderately high *AGGR* scores, the low *INTR* scorer may be more dominant and controlling and have significant problems with joining others in compromise.

Effects of Response Styles on the PSY–5 Scales

Given their method of construction, the PSY–5 scales could not but have very high face validity. That is not to say, however, that their content will be obvious to the respondent. Whereas the items of *NEGE* and *PSYC* scores obviously refer to psychopathological disturbance, a great many if not the majority of the items on *DISC*, *AGGR*, and *INTR* scores refer to normal-range individual differences and are therefore less socially undesirable, on the whole, than *NEGE* and *PSYC*. To date, there have not been empirical investigations of the effects of response sets on the PSY–5 scales in order to gauge their susceptibility to manipulation, but on the basis of the correlates of these scales, some effects can be anticipated. Sets to exaggerate distress or psychopathology will tend to elevate *NEGE*, *INTR*, and especially *PSYC*, whereas efforts to deny or conceal symptoms and maladjustment will tend to suppress these scales.

Like the MMPI-2 content scales, the great majority of the items on the PSY–5 scales are keyed True (the exception is *INTR*, for which about 85 percent of the items are keyed False). As a consequence, these scales are vulnerable to extremes in true–false responding. A high True percentage will sharply elevate *AGGR*, *NEGE*, and especially *PSYC*, while keeping *INTR* below *T*-50. A high False percentage will sharply elevate *INTR*, and confine scores on the other four scales to the average range or below.

8   Interpreting the MMPI-2 Supplementary Scales

Introduction

Since the earliest days following its publication, investigators have selected the MMPI item pool as a source for the development of new scales for the measurement of a bewildering array of variables. Hathaway and McKinley's completion of the series of clinical scales based on pathological criterion groups produced no significant pause in scale development efforts. By the mid-1950s, these efforts had yielded a large number of scales, a plurality of which had been developed by graduates and doctoral advisees from the University of Minnesota, or by their students in turn.

Following the example of the clinical scales, some of these efforts have been focused on psychopathological syndromes, or features of them, that were formerly unavailable in sufficient numbers to permit scale development. Examples of these include low back pain, neurodermatitis, ulcer personality, alcoholism, and pedophilia. One series of scales was developed to discriminate several conditions—somatization reaction, depressive reaction, anxiety reaction, conversion reaction, and paranoid schizophrenia—not from a background sample of normals but from a reference group of general psychiatric patients (Rosen, 1962). Still other efforts sought scales to detect psychopathological syndromes but preferred a rational/statistical strategy over the empirical group contrast methodology that shaped the basic clinical scales of the MMPI. The DSM-III (American Psychiatric Association, 1980) personality disorder scales of Morey et al. (1985) are examples. However, the vast majority of new MMPI scales have been built to aid the measurement or prediction of an unusually broad range of abnormal and normal traits involving achievements, attitudes toward self and others, behavioral dispositions, styles of inventory response, and others. Dahlstrom et al. (1975) listed 455 scales, a list that was known to be incomplete at the time it was published and, among others, did not include any of the 89 basic clinical and validity scales and their derivatives that they listed in 1972. Thus, even in 1975, the total number of MMPI scales almost certainly exceeded the number of items on the test.

By far the greatest number of scales developed since the inception of the MMPI have not made their way to more than a handful of users. Many were probably never used by other than their authors. The reasons for the limited penetration of such scales are not hard to find, among them (a) scales developed for overly specific purposes; (b) the use of samples of inadequate size or representativeness; (c) inadequate or inappropriate contrast groups; (d) inadequate test–retest or internal consistency reliability; (e) inadequate concurrent or predictive validity; (f) failures on cross-validation or excessive cross-validation shrinkage;

(g) excessive redundancy with preexisting and/or better validated scales; (h) excessive redundancy with the major sources of variation within the item pool (poor discriminant validity); (i) problems with construct definition or understanding; and (j) a host of other problems including awkward, obscure, or misleading scale names, uncertainties about the availability or appropriateness of norms, difficulties in retrieval (e.g. unpublished dissertations or reports in journals of limited circulation), and simple lack (or loss) of interest. Considering the time, personnel, and support required to mount and publish investigations justifying a scale's clinical or research application, it is not surprising that so few scales have been successful.

The formation of a standard "set" of supplementary scales occurred slowly. The initial stimulus was provided by the mention of some of the newer scales in the course of MMPI presentations at seminars, colloquia, and workshops by early publicists, especially Paul Meehl and Harrison Gough. A further important impetus was the inclusion of most of them in the Welsh and Dahlstrom (1956) compendium, *Basic Readings on the MMPI in Psychology and Medicine*, and, a year later, the provision of norms for scoring them (Hathaway and Briggs, 1957). To this point, users of the MMPI could select for scoring those scales that appeared to be applicable to their particular practices and populations, ignoring the rest. It was not until the 1960s and the advent of machine scoring that scores for these scales became routinely available as a set. The first automated MMPI scoring system becoming operational at the Mayo Clinic in 1961, but The Psychological Corporation, the Consulting Psychologists Press, and many other commercial concerns made computer scoring services available shortly thereafter. These services ultimately formed what became known alternatively as the supplementary or research scales into a distinct set.

The first of the supplemental scales was actually Social Introversion (*Si*; Drake, 1946), which became formally incorporated as the last of the standard clinical scales only in 1951. The most frequently reported supplemental scales were 11 in number and usually presented in the following order: Welsh's (1956) factor scales *A* and *R*; Barron's (1953) Ego Strength scale (*Es*); Hanvik's (1949) Low Back Pain scale (*Lb*); H. L. Williams' (1952) Caudality scale (*Ca*); Navran's (1954) Dependency scale (*Dy*); Gough, McClosky, and Meehl's (1951) Social Dominance scale (*Do*); Gough, McClosky, and Meehl's (1952) Social Responsibility scale (*Re*); Gough's (1951) Prejudice scale (*Pr*); Gough's (1948a, 1948b) Social Status scale (*St*); and Cuadra's (1956) Control scale (*Cn*). Although this series persisted for many years, scale development continued apace and many services expanded to accommodate and report scores on additional supplementary scales, notably, J. A. Taylor's (1953) Manifest Anxiety scale (*At* or *MAS*); Kleinmuntz' (1961a) College Maladjustment scale (*Mt*); MacAndrew's (1965) Alcoholism scale (*Alc* or *MAC*); and Megargee, Cook, and Mendelsohn's (1967) Overcontrolled-Hostility scale (*O–H*).

There is no doubt that this list of scales, or any similar list of non-routinely interpreted scales, is somewhat arbitrary. Few if any of them had proved themselves in routine clinical applications at the time they became aggregated into a semi-standard panel of scores. Their attainment of this position of status rested on a combination of their reasonably scrupulous construction, and a degree of consensus among the MMPI opinion leaders at the time that these scales held promise for clinical decision making, application to research, or both.

The re standardization that led to the release of the MMPI-2 in 1989 created an opportunity to review an immense array of scales, those that had been available in 1975 (as compiled by Dahlstrom et al.), and those that had accumulated in the interim. Among the almost-limitless bases for the selection of a set of supplemental scales to succeed those that had become more or less standard for the MMPI environment was the effect of the 90 items that were not retained in the transition from the MMPI to the MMPI-2. The content of these discontinued items varied widely but disproportionately represented interests and hobbies (17 items); religion (16 items); interpersonal relationships (14 items); negative affects (12 items); and bodily functions, mostly urinary/excretory (9 items; Greene, 1991a). Thus, scales importantly or entirely (e.g. Wiggins, 1966, Religious Fundamentalism scale [*REL*]) consisting of such items became ineligible for retention on the MMPI-2.

A potentially important factor guiding the selection of a new set of supplemental scales was the availability of research attesting to the validity of several scales that had accumulated during the preceding 40 years. Indeed, the majority of the scales chosen for the supplemental MMPI-2 scales (*A*, *R*, *Es*, *O–H*, *Do*, *Re*, *Mt*, and *MAC–R*) appear to have been selected on this basis. These scales and others are discussed in this chapter.

The current sequence of supplemental scales for the MMPI-2 is as follows: *A*; *R*; *Es*; *Do*; *Re*; *Mt*; Keane, Malloy, and Fairbank's (1984) Post-Traumatic Stress Disorder (*PK*); Schlenger and Kulka's (1987) Post-Traumatic Stress Disorder (*PS*); Hjemboe, Butcher, and Almagor's (1992) Marital Distress (*MDS*); Cook and Medley's (1954) Hostility (*Ho*); *O–H*; *MAC–R*; Weed, Butcher, McKenna, and Ben-Porath's (1992) Addiction Admission *(AAS)* and Addiction Potential (*APS*); and Peterson and Dahlstrom's (1992) Gender Role—Masculine (*GM*) and Gender Role—Feminine (*GF*).

PK and *PS*, *MDS*, and *GM* and *GF* were, like the supplementary scales for the MMPI, selected mostly because of their judged promise for augmenting the interpretive possibilities of the test and not on the basis of accumulated research supporting their validity. (See the MMPI-2 *Manual*, Butcher et al., 2001, Table B-6 for a listing of the item composition and scoring directions for the MMPI-2 supplementary scales; and Tables A-12–A-13 for the uniform *T*-score conversions from raw scores for these scales.)

Factor Scales *A* and *R*

Welsh's purpose in developing the *A* and *R* scales was to provide a convenient means of locating respondents along the two primary dimensions that had been repeatedly identified in factor analyses of the basic clinical and validity scales of the MMPI. Although prior analyses had found varying numbers of factors, depending on the sample and the numbers of scales included in each, the primary dimension had consistently shown high positive loadings on Scales 7 and 8 and high negative loadings on *K*. Thirty-nine items (38 keyed True, 1 keyed False) that achieved a 75 percent separation between the top and bottom 10 percent of the distribution of a preliminary scale (*G*; Meehl & Hathaway, 1946) of both of two groups of male VA patients were chosen for the scale that Welsh called *A* for Anxiety. *A* became, and remains, the most widely acknowledged marker for the first factor of the MMPI/MMPI-2.

The great response style debate that raged in the decade from 1955 to 1965 was largely concerned with whether the first factor of the MMPI should have a substantive (psychopathologic) or stylistic (test-taking attitude) interpretation. Although this controversy was never fully resolved, it cooled rapidly after Block (1965) demonstrated that even when the two main stylistic features of MMPI performance (social desirability and acquiescence) were controlled, the first and second factors of the MMPI continued to be associated with highly meaningful external correlates.

Among the clinical scales, the best marker for the first factor is Scale 7 (*Pt*). It is, therefore, instructive to compare *A* with *Pt*. *Pt* is about 20 percent longer than *A*; the two scales overlap by 13 items, or one third of *A*. Of these, the content of five items is depressive, three are anxious, two are obsessive, two suggest interpersonal aversion, and one admits problems in concentration. Examining the scale as a whole, *A* overlaps *DEP* by nine items (four from *DEP2*), *ANX* by seven, and *OBS* by five. *A* overlaps Scale 8 (*Sc*) by eight items, five of which are from subscale *Sc4* (Lack of Ego Mastery, Conative). Thus, the content of *A* emphasizes disturbed concentration and decision making, as well as dysphoria, anxiety, and worry. Other content emphasizes fatigue, discouragement, and lack of initiative; inadequacy, inferiority, and sensitivity; and a sense of deviance and isolation. All of the items are obvious and socially undesirable. Despite its age and the particular circumstances of its development, *A* remains an excellent marker for the first factor. For example, it correlates at .98 with the 72 items of JBW72 (see Nichols, 2006), the set of items common to the first factor found in the replicated principal components analysis of the MMPI item pool (Johnson et al., 1984; Ns = 5,506 and 5,632), and replicated in turn by Waller (1999; N = 28,390), among the combined 25 samples reported by Rouse, Greene, Butcher, Nichols, and Williams (2008; N = 83,162).

The empirical correlates for high *A* scorers among the Graham et al. (1999) outpatients tend to confirm the description given above, but suggested relatively severe symptomatology, with many of these patients having histories of previous psychiatric hospitalizations. They presented with multiple symptoms of depression and anxiety, and were seen as sad, depressed, insecure, hopeless, self-degrading, and with suicidal ideation. In their sample of normal adults, Hoffman and Pietrzak (2012) found Adjective Check List (ACL; Gough & Heilbrun, 1983) correlates that emphasized nervousness, anxiety, worrying, confusion, immaturity, and pessimism (all > .35).

Evaluation of the discriminative validity of scales developed for assessing distress syndromes must take the first factor into account, as this source of variance can readily create an appearance of validity in single-group comparisons. Provided that one group is more distressed than another, no matter what the exact phenomenological coloring of the distress in question (whether anxious, depressed, panicky, etc.), such scales will virtually always show evidence of convergent validity. That is, scales of this kind will evidence sensitivity to distress as such but will lack the specificity to discriminate one form of distress from another.

As the major marker for the first factor of the MMPI-2, *A* plays an important dynamic role in determining the pattern of test findings. Among the basic clinical and validity scales, elevations on *A* tend to suppress *K* (and therefore the raw amounts of *K* added as corrections for five of the eight basic clinical scales), increase positive profile slope, and increase the probability that Scales 7 and especially 8 will figure in the code pattern. *A* elevations also exert widespread pressure on the content scales to enter the range above *T*-65, with its heaviest influence on *NX*, *OBS*, *DEP*, *LSE*, *WRK*, and *TRT*. Among the supplementary scales, *A* tends to exert positive pressure on *Mt*, *PK*, *PS*, and *Ho*, and negative pressure on *GM*.

The major interpretive significance of high *A* scores is that the respondent readily admits distress and maladjustment. Duckworth and Anderson (1986) asserted that *A* reflects short-term, situational (state) anxiety, in contrast to *Pt*, which they believed represents long-term, characterological (or trait) anxiety. Although their distinction is intriguing and worthy of investigation, the higher test–retest stabilities of *A* items, relative to those of *Pt*, would argue against overconfident reliance on this hypothesis. On the other hand, as Duckworth and Anderson point out, the two scales show important differences in item content. The overlap between Scales 7 and 8 at 17 items is greater than that between Scale 7 and *A*, and more than twice that between Scale 8 and *A*. This alone would suggest a tilt toward a trait interpretation of Scale 7 relative to *A*. The content of Scale 7 carries a greater emphasis on ingrained, global personal defects, such as feeling useless, lacking self-confidence, and being incapable. It also implicates more severe cognitive disruption, including problems with memory and comprehension, and fears of losing mental control, over and above the problems with concentration and indecision noted for *A*. The content on Scale 7 reflecting acute emotional instability and irrational fearfulness is entirely absent from *A*. Finally, the word *worry* (*-ied*, *-ing*) appears three times on *A* but only once on Scale 7, whereas *anxiety* (*-ious*) appears twice on Scale 7 but only once on *A*.

Regardless of the merits of assigning *A* and *Pt* state and trait implications, respectively, Caldwell (1988) cautioned that differences in their elevations may be confounded by the *K* correction for *Pt*. Thus, in comparing the scores on these two scales, it is recommended that *A* be compared only with the non-*K*-corrected version of *Pt*. However, because *A* has fewer items and is less positively skewed than Scale 7, it tops out about 10 *T*-score points lower than *Pt*. For example, the endorsement of two thirds of the items on both scales results in *T*-scores of about 78 on Scale 7 but only about 70 on *A*, with this difference increasing slightly as the proportion of the items endorsed on both scales increases. For this reason, especially when *K* is not too far below the average range, the interpretation of *A* may be undertaken confidently at somewhat lower levels of elevation than Scale 7, and protocols in which *A* exceeds Scale 7 (usually in association with elevations on Scale 0) may have particular significance.

In general, high *A* scorers may be described as uncomfortable, unhappy, and apprehensive. The anxiety they experience appears to be directed more toward a sense of their own incompetence than toward a sense of external threat. Their worry over the adequacy of their performances renders them hesitant, distractible, and vacillating, and this in turn makes them subject to the influence and suggestion of others. Under stress, they tend to become confused, disorganized, and maladaptive. They cope with their feelings of inadequacy by being cautious, standing off, maintaining their distance, avoiding initiative and involvement, and inhibiting action. In interaction with others, they tend to be timid, awkward, passive, and easily rattled.

Provided that the pattern of validity indicators is not overly defensive, low *A* scorers may be described as showing confidence in their abilities, comfortable and friendly, expressive and assertive, taking initiative, active and readily involved, vigorous and forceful, versatile and achieving. In some cases, low *A* scorers are better described as egocentric, ostentatious, overconfident, outspoken, competitive, overbearing, manipulative, reckless, and impulsive.

The items for Welsh's *R* were selected by comparing the top and bottom 10 percent of the distribution of scores on Scale 2. Forty items that achieved separations of 60 percent or more in both VA patient groups comprise R (3 of these were dropped in the transition to MMPI-2; the remaining 37 are all keyed False). Despite marking the second major source of variation among the standard validity and clinical scales of the MMPI/ MMPI-2, R achieves no better than moderate correlations with any of these scales. Its highest correlations are with Scales 2 and 9, at .30 to .40 and at −.40 to −.45, respectively. Correlations in the range of .30 to .40 are also seen for L, K, and Scale 0. Notable item overlap occurs with Scales 2 (10 items [D-O, six items; D-S, four items]) and 0 (eight items).

The content of R is fairly heterogeneous, including poor health and physical symptoms; inhibited if not blunted emotionality, particularly with respect to "negative" feelings and feelings of energy and excitement; a lack of enjoyment in and under-responsiveness to the potential stimulation of group membership and social interaction; the avoidance of conflict, competition, and social visibility; and a denial of activities and interest in pursuits that may occasion fatigue or stimulation. Taken as a whole, the content of R suggests the suppression of emotionality and the avoidance of interactions with the human and nonhuman environment that may stimulate feeling, whether positive or negative, with the tendency to refer such feeling, when it occurs, to events in the somatic sphere.

Although R scores have been available for more than 40 years, surprisingly little is known of the interpretive significance of high and low scores. Interpretations tend to converge on some notion of *control*. In his choice of Repression as the designation for R, Welsh (1956) evidently favored a construct believed to operate in an unconscious fashion. Welsh based his choice on the kinds of mental disorders associated with high and low scores on R: "The disorders exhibited by high R scorers are characterized by repression and denial; low R accompanies externalized and 'acting-out' behavior" (p. 280). More recent commentators have tended to reject the unconscious implications of Welsh's construct in favor of a kind of emotional control that is seen to operate within awareness. Thus, Duckworth and Anderson (1986, p. 245) refer to R as "a conscious repression scale (or suppression scale to be more accurate)" that reflects a coping style emphasizing limited insight, (conscious) denial and rationalization, and decisions to limit self-disclosure. Similarly, Caldwell (1988) favored an interpretation of R as *constriction*, in which the person's "range of feelings is limited and whose emotional responsiveness is constricted across a wide spectrum" (p. 76).

As noted by Nichols and Greene (1995), a comparison of the pattern of MMPI/ MMPI-2 scale correlates with R and EC-5 (Ego Control), Block's (1965) second-factor scale suggests an alternative but related interpretation of R. Whereas the correlates of EC-5 suggest the modulation and containment of impulse and aggression, a narrowing of interests, and a deliberate, conforming, prosocial, and risk-averse approach to decision making and behavioral expression, the correlates of R appear to reflect a more central locus of inhibition, one related to the strength of impulse and emotionality, and to openness to experience. Specifically, the high R scorer appears to be one who is uncomfortable with more than minimal levels of stimulation and emotionality, and who therefore prefers to operate in circumstances that are conventional, predictable, familiar, and overlearned. Such preferences, in turn, suggest limitations in the individual's capacity to become aware of, identify, differentiate, and reflect on feelings and other emotional phenomena, and it is this that is the basis for the person's constricted expression of emotionality.

By contrast, low *R* scores suggest a ready access to feeling and impulse even if not impulsively expressed; an openness to experiencing them; a prodigal and unstable pattern of interests; a high tolerance for stimulation; a willingness to entertain unfamiliar or unconventional points of view; and an ability to tolerate ambiguity, uncertainty, and conflict. Extremely low scores may be associated with chaotic emotionality, in which the individual feels flooded with emotionality or even euphoria, and is overinclusive and indiscriminate in his or her approach to expression.

Graham et al. (1999) reported only somatic symptoms and health preoccupation as broad empirical correlates of high *R* scores among their psychiatric outpatients. The normal adult ACL correlates found by Hoffman and Pietrzak (2012) included tough, show-off, flirtatious, hard-headed, daring, aggressive, loud, sly, and sociable (all –.25 to –.35).

Ego Strength Scale (*Es*)

Barron's (1953) Ego Strength scale was the product of an effort to predict the response of "psychoneurotic" outpatients to psychotherapy over a six-month period. The 68 items that discriminated the 17 patients who improved (*M* = 52.7) from the 16 who did not (*M* = 29.1) became *Es*, and these items were subdivided by Barron into eight groups based upon their content: physical functioning and physiological stability (11 items), psychasthenia and seclusiveness (10), attitudes toward religion (6), moral posture (11), sense of reality (8), personal adequacy/ability to cope (11), phobias/infantile anxieties (5), and miscellaneous (6). In the transition to the MMPI-2, *Es* lost 16 items, distributed across the above groups, respectively, as follows: 1, 1, 5, 3, 1, 2, 0, and 3. Thirty-two of the 52 items are keyed False, 20 True.

Although neither the therapists nor the type of therapy received by the patients in Barron's sample was adequately described, others have characterized the treatment as psychoanalytically oriented (e.g. Dahlstrom et al., 1975; Graham, 1990). Because this form of therapy often places rather high intellectual demands on its patients, it is notable that Barron found moderate but consistent correlations between *Es* and intelligence across a wide variety of measures. This confounding may in part help to account for the highly mixed character of the results of subsequent validity studies of *Es*. As Greene (2011) noted, "Various studies have reported positive, no, and inverse relationships between the Es scale and outcome in psychotherapy" (p. 282). It is also notable that moderate to high correlations between *Es* and various measures of the first factor (e.g. *A* and *K*) have consistently been reported, raising the question of possible differences in initial severity of psychopathology between patients showing different therapeutic outcomes. In this context, Butcher et al. (1989) reported small but significant negative correlations between *Es* and the total number of recent life changes and scores on the Social Readjustment Rating Scale (Holmes & Rahe, 1967). These data are consistent with the interpretation that if patients with high *Es* scores show greater improvement in insight-oriented psychotherapy, they do so in part because they are more intelligent and less disturbed than patients who score low.

An underappreciated part of the literature on *Es* has examined physiological stability in response to stress (Alexander, Roessler, & Greenfield, 1963; Greenfield, Alexander, & Roessler, 1963; Greenfield, Roessler, & Crosley, 1959; Roessler, Alexander, & Greenfield,

1963; Roessler, Burch, & Childers, 1966; Roessler, Burch, & Mefford, 1967; Roessler & Collins, 1970; Roessler, Greenfield, & Alexander, 1964). Using dependent measures such as catecholamine excretion, finger blood volume, heart rate, muscle potential, and skin resistance, these investigators found that participants having high *Es* scores showed evidence of greater physiological organization in their responses to stressful events than did low *Es* scorers. In the physiological reactions of these participants, there was greater evidence of the preservation of hierarchical organization ("defense in depth"), with more peripheral reactions preceding in an orderly fashion those responses more appropriate for stresses of greater severity. They also showed greater speeds of recovery following the cessation of stress. The responses of low *Es* participants were more chaotic and extreme, with a loss of hierarchical patterning and delayed recoveries. These findings suggest that the more favorable psychotherapy outcomes seen in high *Es* patients may be rooted in the greater integrity of their physiological adaptation to life stresses such that they are better able to avoid overreaction and recover more readily from stresses and setbacks. By contrast, the coping styles of low *Es* scorers would appear to be encumbered by a lack of organization and a vulnerability to overreaction, leading to distracted attempts to assess the sources and meanings of stressors, and rigid or poorly focused attempts at adaptation.

In summary, *Es* appears to serve as a measure of both control and resiliency, factors that would seem to predict successful adaptation even in the midst of significant distress. In this sense, *Es* may serve as an index of *stress tolerance*, and this may be, as Caldwell (1988) suggested, a more valuable focus for interpretive efforts than prognosis for psychotherapy. High *Es* scorers have been characteristically described as resourceful, independent, and self-reliant; as possessed of discipline and determination; as showing initiative, flexibility, and tolerance; and as creating an impression of competence and ability in others and being easily accepted by them. At times, they may be seen as aggressive, outspoken, and nonconforming if not rebellious toward authority. Thus, they would seem to be able to use psychotherapy to supplement their own problem-solving resources and to tolerate the self-scrutiny and confrontation that often occurs in this form of treatment without becoming upset or disorganized. Low *Es* scorers are unstable, over-reactive, and subject to confusion in the face of stresses; may be upset by seemingly minor matters; are less tolerant of other people, despite being suggestible and dependent; are inhibited, indecisive, and procrastinating; and are more rigid in their outlooks, in their choices of action, and in their approaches to problems. Graham et al. (1999) found that their low *Es* outpatients manifested an especially broad range of psychiatric symptoms, including depression, somatization, and psychoticism. They often had previous psychiatric hospitalizations, and were seen as insecure, hopeless, pessimistic, unambitious, and coping poorly with stress. The women often had histories of physical and sexual abuse, and of suicide attempts. In their normal adult sample, Hoffman and Pietrzak (2012) report ACL correlates suggesting that the high *Es* scorer is calm, clear-headed, ambitious, cheerful, at ease, mature, sociable, optimistic, prudent, attentive, and non-apprehensive.

As noted earlier, the interpretation of *Es* may be complicated by its co-variation with the first factor, such that *Es* and other scales having substantial first-factor variance may be mutually affected. For example, in psychiatric populations and among persons seeking mental health consultation, correlations between *Es* and *K* are commonly in a range of .50 to .60. Thus, high (low) scores on one of these scales will tend to push scores on the other up (down). As a result, a relatively low *K* score when the *Es* score is substantially higher may lead to an underestimate of stress tolerance and adaptive functioning. Conversely, a relatively high *K* score when it substantially exceeds the *Es* score may reflect a desire to portray greater adequacy in coping with problems and stresses than is justified, depleted and precarious coping resources, or both. Caldwell (1988) suggested that differences between *Es* and *K* of 10 or more *T*-score points may call for interpretive adjustments along the lines given here.

Dominance Scale (*Do*)

The Dominance scale (Gough et al., 1951) grew out of a larger project investigating political participation. The 25 items of *Do* on the MMPI-2, 6 keyed True, 19 False, form a subset of the 60-item Dominance scale (*Do*) of the California Psychological Inventory (CPI). The developers gathered peer nominations from high school and college students, with each student nominating the five most and five least dominant of their peers. The item responses of high and low dominance were compared. Care was taken to avoid confusing the construct of interest, dominance, with being domineering or autocratic and to ensure that peer ratings were based on nominees' actual behavior as opposed to how the peer thought the nominee might act, view him- or herself, and so on. Just how successful these efforts were in steering the nominations in the direction desired by the investigators is uncertain.

Although the CPI version of *Do* is one of its better validated scales (Megargee, 1972), the MMPI/MMPI-2 version has stimulated surprisingly little research, although such research has been generally supportive. Greene (2011) reports a positive correlation for *Do* with *Es* (.66), and negative correlations in a range of .65–.75 for *Pt* (highest), *A*, *WRK*, *PK*, *Mt*, *Sc*, *TRT*, *LSE*, *DEP*, and *Si*, indicating relatively high saturation with the first factor; the pattern of overlap with other MMPI/MMPI-2 scales tends to reflect extraversion and the absence of anxiety.

The textual literature of the MMPI/MMPI-2 (e.g. Butcher & Williams, 1992; Friedman, Webb, & Lewak, 1989; Graham, 1990; Greene, 2011) provides little insight into the core construct of *Do*, but describes high scorers as showing comfort, poise, initiative, and influence in social relationships; being secure, self-confident, self-assured, efficient, resourceful, persevering, and able to concentrate; and dutiful and having strong political opinions. Duckworth and Anderson (1986) described the high *Do* scorer as asserting that "he/she is able to take charge of his/her own life" (p. 273), an interpretation endorsed by Caldwell (1988) and Greene (2011). Both the descriptions and the interpretation just given appear to converge on *Do*, at least as measured in the MMPI/MMPI-2, as an indicator of *self-direction*. As a construct, self-direction would appear to encompass aspects of internal locus of control and independence of judgment, but without the implications of self-sufficiency or social distancing that these concepts sometimes carry. The high *Do* scorer tends to elicit the confidence and social approval of others that may move them in the direction of elevating the high scorer to positions of responsibility and leadership within the group. The outpatients with scores below *T*-40 studied by Graham et al. (1999) often had histories of physical abuse (for women, also sexual abuse), and a broad range of symptoms, including depression, anxiety, somatization, and social awkwardness. The ACL correlates for the high *Do* scoring normal adults studied by Hoffman and Pietrzak (2012) tend to characterize them as calm, relaxed, and comfortable, clear-headed, self-confident, ambitious, cheerful, at ease, mature, sociable, optimistic, prudent, attentive, spirited, and fearless.

Social Responsibility Scale (*Re*)

In another product of their inquiry into political participation, Gough et al. (1952) used methods similar to those used in the development of *Do* for the construction of *Re*. For samples of high school students and college members of fraternities and sororities, nominations by peers, teachers, or a high school principal identified individuals who rated as high in "a ready willingness to accept the consequences of [one's] own behavior, dependability, trustworthiness, and a sense of obligation to the group" (Gough et al., 1952, p. 74). Some effort was made to prevent the influence of extraneous characteristics, such as friendliness and popularity, on ratings of social responsibility, but it appears likely that the nominations were to at least some degree confounded with intelligence. The 30 items of *Re* for the MMPI-2, 6 keyed True, 24 False, form a subset of the 56-item Responsibility scale (*Re*) of the CPI.

The results of research with the CPI version of *Re* are mixed, with studies based on ratings of responsibility faring less well than those comparing groups based on status or performance criteria (Megargee, 1972). Studies involving antisocial and delinquent groups have been more consistently supportive. The MMPI/MMPI-2 version of *Re* has stimulated very little research, and none that has illuminated the construct measured by this version of the scale. More useful in this respect is the pattern of correlations with other MMPI scales, with moderate positive correlations being found with scales measuring academic achievement, intellectual efficiency, tolerance, and control, and moderate negative correlations with scales measuring impulsivity, hostility, antisocial attitudes, and prejudice. The correlates relating to intelligence appear, at least in part, to be an artifact both of the samples and the peer nomination methodology of scale development. An unusual and interesting correlate of *Re* is Brozek's (1955) Aging scale (*Ag*), consisting of items showing age differences in samples of high-ability college and middle-aged men. This correlate would tend to support the observations of Caldwell (1988) and Duckworth and Anderson (1986) that *Re* scores tend to increase with age.

The picture that emerges from an examination of the circumstances of its development, *Re* research to date, as well as the scale's internal MMPI/MMPI-2 correlates, suggests that the high *Re* scorer is a conventional and conforming but tolerant and even-tempered person who has benign expectations of others, exhibits self-control, is a "team player," and is able and willing to pledge allegiance to the collectives of which he or she chooses to be a part. *Re* appears to measure a form of responsibility that is most likely to be manifested in institutional settings where creative demands are low. The institution may be as small as a family or club or as large as a multinational corporation. The high *Re* scorer appears to be one whose performance and achievement are best manifested in structured settings that place a premium on cooperation with others, persistence, and a "duty-bound" variety of conscientiousness. The core construct of *Re* appears to be one of *dutifulness*. Thus, the responsible person is one on whom others can depend to observe and support the customs, norms, policies, and procedures, and advance the goals of the institution with which the individual identifies. This would account for the wide use of *Re* in employment screening (Butcher & Williams, 1992).

Duckworth and Anderson (1986) have put forward a conception of *Re* (and one that has been cited with at least some measure of approval by Caldwell, 1988; Graham, 1990; and Greene, 2011) that is similar to that offered here, but couched in terms of values. Duckworth and Anderson (1986) maintained that *Re* "measures the acceptance (high score) or rejection (low score) of a previously held value system" (p. 279) and noted that *Re* likely does not assist in identifying the nature of the particular value system that the person holds, is in transition from, or spurns. For persons under age 25, parental values are assumed to be those in question, whereas for persons over age 25, the person's current value system is not assumed to reflect parental values. According to this view, *Re* scores tend to decline during periods of transition, as previously held values become subject to increased reflection, examination, and questioning. Such periods may occur as a result of other life transitions, such as leaving home to attend college, the birth of a child, the recognition of a need to seek membership in a congregation for the benefit of a child's religious upbringing, a death in the family, shifts in occupation or employment (e.g. from sales to service), following natural disasters, and similar events. Such transitions often stimulate questions of value in their wake, just as they may lead to emotional upheaval, uncertainty, and weakened controls. Similarly, scores may fall as the person becomes disenchanted with the goals and practices of the organization to which he or she belongs.

Some of the research with delinquents reviewed by Megargee (1972) suggests that the lower ranges of *Re* are more discriminating than the higher ranges. For example, in one study reviewed, a sample of delinquents with and without actual court contact showed mean *T*-scores of 31 and 38, respectively. Duckworth and Anderson (1986) reported ranges consistent with this supposition. They stated that

> persons with elevations [of *T*-50–65] tend to accept their present value system and intend to continue using it. Persons with scores of 40 to 50 are questioning their present value system and those below 40 are rejecting their most recently held value system.
>
> (Duckworth & Anderson, 1986, p. 279)

Guidelines for interpreting *Re* scores greater than *T*-50 need further exploration and research. It appears likely, however, that as scores of about *T*-60 are exceeded, the dispositions of high *Re* scorers may be less adaptive than scores of persons closer to the average range. Duckworth and Anderson speculated that higher ranging scores may be associated with a lack of imagination and an excessive, and perhaps excessively rigid, orientation to "oughts and shoulds," giving rise to attitudes that a high *Re* scorer's associates may find annoying. Similarly, scorers in this range may be overly quick to identify with authority, regardless of its moral/ethical standing, and to sacrifice the interests of others, both within and outside of the organization in the pursuit of narrow organizational goals. For example, one would expect the "company man" to have a considerably higher *Re* score than the "whistle-blower," even though both might be seen as socially responsible.

Among the low *Re* scores studied by Graham et al. (1999), problems with substance abuse and dependence were especially prominent, and many of these outpatients had histories of one or more arrests. They were seen in largely antisocial terms, but also as resentful, suspicious, mistrustful, having family problems, and stormy relationships more generally. The ACL correlates found by Hoffman and Pietrzak (2012) for the high *Re* scoring normal adults portray them as clear-headed and realistic, but careful if not overly cautions, sober, restrained, and compliant if not obedient.

College Maladjustment Scale (*Mt*); Keane et al.'s Post-Traumatic Stress Disorder Scale (*PK*); and Schlenger and Kulka's Post-Traumatic Stress Disorder Scale (*PS*)

These three scales are discussed together because of their extensive shared variance; all are intercorrelated in the .90s. All are saturated with the major source of variation within the MMPI-2 item pool, the first factor. They show considerable item overlap and, in psychiatric samples, are intercorrelated with each other and with *A* and *Pt* (non-*K*-corrected raw scores) at > .90. As a result, all may be interpreted as global indexes of the individual's current level of distress, maladjustment, or psychopathology.

Kleinmuntz (1960, 1961a) developed the College Maladjustment scale (*Mt*) to identify college students with emotional problems of sufficient severity to impel them to seek treatment at a university mental health clinic. The item responses of students who sought counseling for emotional problems and remained for three or more sessions were compared with those of students referred to the same clinic for routine mental health screening for a teacher certification program, and who reported no previous treatment for mental health problems. Forty-three items discriminated the maladjusted from the apparently adjusted students, of which 41 are retained in the MMPI-2; 28 items are keyed True, 13 False. In a follow-up study, Kleinmuntz (1961b) found that *Mt* failed to adequately predict adjustment problems among entering college students during their first year and concluded that it is best suited to identifying current, as opposed to future, maladjustment. On the basis of *Mt* content, Kleinmuntz (1960) characterized the high scorer as an "ineffectual, pessimistic, procrastinating, anxious and worried person who tends to somatize and who finds that much of the time life is a strain" (p. 210). Low scorers, by contrast, would be considered effective, optimistic, conscientious, and free of emotional discomfort.

The similarity of the adjusted student group to groups that were provided an incentive to respond in a self-favorable manner to the items (e.g. Cofer et al., 1949) may tend to inflate scores on *Mt* in persons inclined to modesty concerning their strengths, virtues, and other positive features of outlook, character, and demeanor. By contrast, scores may be suppressed by an inclination to claim such attributes. Thus, high *K* scores may suppress, and low *K* scores inflate, *Mt* scores.

Given the extensive shared variance between *Mt* and better established markers for general maladjustment, such as *A* and *Pt* (non-*K*-corrected), and the lack of empirical data demonstrating any incremental advantages over the latter scales even in college or university settings, the continued use of *Mt* has little or nothing to recommend it.

The two PTSD scales differ primarily in terms of the contrast groups used in their development. Keane et al. (1984) compared the items of 100 male VA Vietnam combat veterans for whom diagnoses of PTSD, often among other concurrent diagnoses, had been established on the basis of structured interviews and psychophysiological measurements, with 100 veterans who carried diagnoses other than PTSD. The 49 items separating these groups, of which 46 remain in the MMPI-2, constitute *PK*. Thirty-eight items are keyed True, eight False. The empirical correlates found by Graham et al. (1999) to describe high *PK* scorers were, not surprisingly, identical to those found for high *A* scorers in most major respects.

Schlenger and associates (Schlenger & Kulka, 1987; Schlenger et al., 1989) compared the item endorsements of Vietnam veterans diagnosed with PTSD (without concurrent diagnoses) and non-patient Vietnam veterans. They found 60 items that differentiated the two groups. These items constitute *PS*, of which 47 are keyed True, 13 False. Thus, whereas the development of *PK* followed a method reminiscent of that used in the construction of the MacAndrew (1965) and Rosen (1962) scales, *PS* issued from the more conventional criterion-normal control contrast method. Despite these differences in development, the two scales are correlated to the extent allowed by their reliabilities and share 26 items in common. One could fairly consider the latter set of items as a better validated measure of PTSD than either of its parent scales. However, a scale comprising these 26 items continues to correlate at > .90 with *A* and *Pt* (non-*K*-corrected), indicating that it contains little or no specific variance for PTSD.

It is thus doubtful that either of the PTSD scales may be used to contribute to the question of diagnosis. There are both empirical and conceptual reasons for doubts concerning the utility of these scales in this context. The chief empirical problem resides in the absence of research demonstrating incremental validity for *PK* or *PS* over any of several other scales with which they share virtually all of their variance. A study by Watson, Juba, Anderson, and Manifold (1990) found only a tenuous relationship between *PK* scores and a history of trauma in a sample of normal and patient Vietnam veterans. Thus, there is an urgent need for research comparing the diagnostic efficiency of the PTSD scales with older scales, such as Welsh's *A*. As one strategy for coping with the problem of the shared variance among the *A*, non-*K*-corrected *Pt*, *Mt*, *PK*, and *PS* scales, A. B. Caldwell (personal communication, June 29, 1999) has suggested scores on the PTSD scales be required to exceed scores on *A* before diagnoses of PTSD are even entertained. Although at least minimally plausible, this suggestion also requires empirical investigation. Another empirical question that has received too little investigation concerns the specificity and positive predictive value of *PK* and *PS*, especially when traumas other than those related to military combat are at stake. Finally, in a sample of Vietnam veterans, *PK* failed to discriminate those with and without a diagnosis of PTSD (Van Atta, 1999), and there is little evidence that either of the PTSD scales contributes to the discrimination of patients with anxiety disorders and patients with known traumatic histories, but the research available to date is not encouraging (e.g. Miller, Goldberg, & Streiner, 1995). In any event, and for reasons that remain obscure, *PS*, which was included in the first edition of the MMPI-2 *Manual* (Butcher et al., 1989), was dropped in its most recent edition (Butcher et al., 2001).

Also troubling is that the status of the diagnosis of PTSD has itself not been free of controversy (Young, 1995). Apart from relatively minor terminological differences used to describe them, the symptoms of PTSD are typically indistinguishable from better established mood and anxiety disorders, at least within the context of the MMPI/MMPI-2. This circumstance has necessitated that the differential diagnosis be reckoned on the basis of etiology (i.e. putative trauma) rather than presenting symptomatology. Yet the causal relationship between the "symptoms" of PTSD and reports of traumatic events is not established (e.g. Yehuda & McFarlane, 1995), and neither is the temporal stability for recall of traumatic events themselves, even when these are combat related (Southwick, Morgan, Nicolaou, & Charney, 1997). Moreover, Litz, Orsillo, Friedman, Ehlich, and Batres (1997) reported that in a sample of Somalia peacekeepers, noncombat factors, such as a lack of pride in military service and frustration with the mission, were as important in predicting symptoms of PTSD as was combat experience. The presumption of a traumatic event as the etiological factor may not only shape the way familiar symptoms of depression, anxiety, panic, and so on are construed by both patients and clinicians so as to create confirmatory bias, it also tends to shift attention away from etiological factors, such as genetically influenced predispositions, that are better established as diatheses for such symptoms. Among veterans of military service, the population on which the vast majority of PTSD research has been conducted, the potential etiological influence of disability compensation has received inadequate research attention, although many reports (Franklin, Repasky, Thompson, Shelton, & Uddo, 2003; Frueh, Gold, & de Arellano, 1997; Frueh, Smith, & Barker, 1996; Gold & Frueh, 1999; Grubaugh, Elhai, Monnier, & Frueh, 2004; and Tolin, Maltby, Weathers, Litz, Knight, & Keane, 2004) indicate that compensation-seeking veterans obtain higher scores on one or more of the over-reporting scales[1] and indices than do non-compensation-seeking veterans. Even this finding is not uniform, however (see, e.g. DeViva & Bloem, 2003; and Tolin, Steenkamp, Marx, & Litz, 2010). Pending the clarification of these empirical and conceptual issues, the clinical utility of *PK* and *PS* will remain most doubtful.

Marital Distress Scale (*MDS*)

The availability of data gathered from couples in the course of the MMPI-2 re-standardization project provided a suitable comparison group for a sample of 150 distressed couples involved in marital counseling. Test data for the distressed couples were gathered from 21 clinicians, most of whom practiced privately in the Minneapolis-St. Paul area. A few practiced in Scottsdale, Arizona.

An initial pool of potential items was selected on the basis of the strength of correlations between the 567 MMPI-2 items and scores on the 31-item Dyadic Adjustment Scale (DAS; Spanier, 1976) separately for the men and women in the marital counseling sample. The same correlations were then gathered from 392 of the couples from the re-standardization sample. Significant (.001) correlations were found between the DAS scores and 17 MMPI-2 items for the men and women of both the counselee and the re-standardization normal couples. Of these 17 items, 2 were dropped for their failure to replicate in the 384 normal cross-validation couples and 1 was dropped for "extraneous content" (Hjemboe et al., 1992, p. 144), leaving a final scale of 14 items, of which 8 are keyed True, 6 False. The items tend to be dysphoric in tone, and *MDS* is correlated with *Pd, Pt, Sc, DEP, FAM, WRK, TRT, A, Mt,* and *PK* at ~.80.

Because *MDS* overlaps substantially with Scale 4 (eight items), *Pd1* (Familial Discord; four items), and *FAM* (six items), Hjemboe et al. (1992) undertook multiple regression analyses to evaluate the relative value of the four scales in predicting DAS scores. *MDS* emerged as the best predictor in both their clinical and nonclinical samples. Further analyses evaluated the performance of these four scales in contingency tables with respect to hit rate, positive predictive value, and sensitivity. *MDS* alone exceeded the base rate in the overall accuracy of classification, and in achieving a better than chance level of positive predictive value. However, none of these scales identified more than half of the participants scoring in the distressed range of the DAS. In attempting to account for this apparent lack of sensitivity, Hjemboe et al. compared the DAS scores of the true-positive and false-negative cases and found, as expected, that the DAS scores were significantly lower (poorer adjustment) for the former group than for the latter group. One hypothesis that is consistent with this finding is that *MDS* scores may be suppressed by an overall tendency to underreport psychopathology. That the social desirability ratings of the nine *MDS* items for which such ratings are available (Butcher et al., 1989) average only 2.53 (where neutral desirability is 5.00) would seem to lend plausibility to this hypothesis.

Although *MDS* showed a higher than desirable false-negative rate and a lower than desirable true-positive rate at a *T*-score of 60 on the basis of an estimated rate of marital maladjustment in the general population of 18 percent, the level of *T*-60 did perform favorably in some of the other Hjemboe et al. (1992) analyses. These suggested that an even lower score (e.g. *T*-58) may improve predictive accuracy in outpatient and other settings having a higher base rate for problems in marital adjustment. On the other hand, in settings having a low base rate for persons of married (or the equivalent) status and/or a high base rate for general interpersonal conflict, the predictive accuracy of *MDS* could fall off sharply. Perhaps in recognition of this problem, Butcher (1993) suggested that *MDS* be interpreted *only* when the examinee is a member of a couple.

Graham et al. (1999) found that their high *MDS*-scoring outpatients were depressed and interpersonally sensitive. They often had few or no friends, and tended to be described in terms suggesting anger and resentment as well as dysphoria. The normal adult ACL correlates found by Hoffman and Pietrzak (2012) suggest confusion, dissatisfaction, and worry, pessimism, immaturity, bitterness, apathy, and low self-confidence.

For some purposes, however, the clinician may wish to disregard this limitation. One virtue of the *MDS* is its focus on discord within current, as opposed to past, family relationships. In this respect, it may provide a useful contrast with *Pd1*, which is biased toward discord within the family of origin. Thus, the two scales can be used configurally with *FAM* to help refine hypotheses involving family conflict.

Hostility Scale (*Ho*)

The Hostility scale (Cook & Medley, 1954) was developed on the basis of contrasts of teachers scoring low versus high on the Minnesota Teacher Attitude Inventory (MTAI; Cook, Leeds, & Callis, 1951), a 150 Likert item survey of teachers' attitudes toward students and career satisfaction that seeks to get at the teacher's sense of rapport, understanding, cooperation, and sense of common purpose with students. On the basis of a combined empirical-rational methodology, 50 items were selected to form *Ho*, of which 47 items are keyed True, 3 False. It positively overlaps *CYN* by 17 items (10 on *CYN1*; 7 on *CYN2*), *Si* by 9 (5 on *Si3*), Wiggins *HOS* by 8, *ASP* by 7 (all on *ASP1*), *AGGR* by 7, and *TPA* by 6 (4 on *TPA2*); and negatively overlaps *S* by 11 items (9 on *S1*), *K* by 8, *Hy* by 8 (7 on *Hy2*), and *Pa* by 5 (all on *Pa3*). The major MMPI-2 scale correlates of *Ho* include *CYN* at .91, and *S* and *K* at ~.85 (Greene, 2011). Han, Weed, Calhoun, and Butcher (1995) found four principal components: cynicism, hypersensitivity, aggressive responding, and social avoidance. Studies addressing the construct validity have been generally positive (e.g. Pope, Smith, & Rhodewalt, 1990; Smith & Frohm, 1985). Despite the extensive shared variance with *CYN*, emphasizing a more passive misanthropic alienation from others, *Ho* conveys a greater sense of *activated* enmity or antipathy toward them, with vengefulness and a willingness to engage others antagonistically, given the opportunity.

Largely absent from the research literature following its creation, a resurgence of interest in *Ho* came with a report by Williams et al. (1980), which found a relationship between *Ho* scores and coronary atherosclerosis, and subsequently confirmed by Barefoot et al. (1989), and Shekelle et al. (1983). McCrae, Costa, Dahlstrom, Barefoot, Siegler, and Williams (1989) found an association between *Ho* scores and mortality from all causes. Other studies, however, have either failed to confirm these findings (e.g. Hearn, Murray, & Luepker, 1989; Leon, Finn, Murray, & Bailey, 1988, 1990), or reported equivocally (Friedman & Booth-Kewley, 1987). Illustrative of the status of the evidence of *Ho* in relation to CHD and mortality are the 25-year follow-up studies of physicians by Barefoot et al. (1983; $N = 255$), and by McCranie, Watkins, Brandsma, Sisson (1986; $N = 478$), in which the former investigators found *Ho* scores to be associated with both increased mortality and CHD, while the latter found *Ho* scores to predict neither. It may be that the differences in the outcomes in studies of *Ho* represent only random sampling fluctuations, as Friedman and Booth-Kewley (1987) have suggested, and Colligan and Offord (1988a) found significant overlap in distributions of *Ho* scores for normals, medical patients, and earlier CHD study participants. Another possibility is that, in relation to CHD, the *Ho* construct may be overly broad, and that only those components of the scale focused on cynicism, antagonism, hostile affect, and aggressiveness may show a robust relationship to CHD (Barefoot et al., 1989; Costa, Zonderman, McCrae, & Williams, 1986), or even that *Ho* be replaced by *CYN* in future studies of coronary disease (Mittag & Maurischat, 2004).

Ho scores appear related to race, education, gender, SES, and self-care, with non-whites, men, poorer, the less educated (Barefoot, Peterson, Dahlstrom, Siegler, Anderson, & Williams, 1991), and those with worse health habits (Leiker & Hailey, 1988) tending to achieve higher scores. Further, in evaluating scores on *Ho*, the clinician should be alert to scores on *K* ($K \times Ho = -.83$; Greene, 2011), and on the True/False balance of the protocol, as either or both elevations on *K* and a bias toward False responding will suppress *Ho* scores. Contrastingly, low *K* scores and/or a True response bias will inflate them.

In general, high *Ho* scorers tend to be cynical and mistrustful, seeing others as selfish, manipulative, morally corrupt, and undeserving of sympathy or understanding. They are quick to attribute malintent to others' actions, viewing them as deliberately hostile or provocative, and taking the position that others "deserve what they get." These trends are likely to be somewhat attenuated in women, with the latter tending to describe others in terms like "mean" and "ugly," and to appear more distressed, long-suffering, resentful, and unforgiving. Neither is likely to have many close friends. It is best to compare *Ho* scores with those on *ANG*, *CYN*, *TPA* (especially *TPA2*), and *AGGR*, as the relative elevations among these can usefully guide interpretive emphases. For example, when *ANG1* is highest among these, the emotional lability and hotheaded aspect of *Ho* would appear to be emphasized, whereas when *TPA2* and *AGGR* are comparably elevated with *Ho*, a more predatory and vindictive hostility is suggested.

Overcontrolled-Hostility Scale (O-H)

The stimulus for the development of the Overcontrolled-Hostility scale (Megargee et al., 1967) was the failure of 12 previously identified MMPI scales to achieve satisfactory identifications among a sample of male criminals who had been subdivided into extremely assaultive, moderately assaultive, and non-assaultive groups (Megargee and Mendelsohn, 1962). Moreover, there was a clear trend for the extremely assaultive criminals to score *lower* on these measures than the other two groups, suggesting that the controls (or levels of hostility) in the extremely assaultive group were, if anything, better than in the comparison groups. Megargee reasoned that the group of extremely assaultive criminals might contain a subgroup of individuals that, far from fitting the stereotype of the habitually aggressive and impulsive person who manifests a low threshold for responding with hostility to frustrating events and provocations, characteristically do *not* react to such instigations. He posited that extremely assaultive individuals could be divided into under-controlled and overcontrolled types, with the overcontrolled group characterized by high levels of hostile impulse existing side by side with massive, rigid, and unconscious inhibitions against hostile expression. For these individuals, assaultiveness was an atypical response that would occur only rarely and unexpectedly, in circumstances of sufficient moment that the individual's normally hypertrophic defenses against the expression of hostility could be overcome. Whereas in the under-controlled individual the hostile reaction was typically seen to be in some sense proportional to its instigation, the overcontrolled hostile reaction was often seen as poorly calibrated to instigating events, thereby increasing the importance of being able to identify the overcontrolled hostile individual.

The O-H scale was derived to identify this overcontrolled hostile reaction type. Megargee et al. (1967) compared the responses of extremely assaultive ($n = 14$), moderately assaultive ($n = 25$), and non-assaultive ($n = 25$) male prisoners and a group of noncriminal men ($n = 46$). Item analysis yielded 55 items that separated the assaultive from the non-assaultive participants. These were then cross-validated on new samples of extremely assaultive, moderately assaultive, and non-assaultive prisoners. On the basis of the examination of prison records, Megargee et al. also compared the responses of prisoners who had histories of violence and were identified as conforming to the overcontrolled pattern with inmates with an under-controlled pattern of violence. Thirty-one of the 55 items survived cross-validation to become O-H. In the transition to the MMPI-2, O-H lost three items. Of the remaining 28, 21 are keyed False, 7 True. This T/F imbalance was suggested by Deiker (1974) to potentially account for the O-H score differences found between his most versus least violent criminals, that simple naysaying, i.e. the preference for responding False, could more parsimoniously account for the variance in O-H. In response, Megargee and Cook (1975) constructed four T/F balanced variants of O-H, and compared their performance in his derivation samples (Megargee et al., 1967). One of these actually improved upon the performance of O-H, indicating that the latter's T/F balance effect is likely negligible.

Like most scales constructed using the method of contrasted groups, the item content of O-H is quite heterogeneous, with few if any identifiable themes. An examination of the structure of the MMPI version of O-H among 200 state penitentiary inmates found five factors (Walters & Greene, 1983), but subsequent analyses of other samples by

R. L. Greene and D. S. Nichols (personal communication, March 1, 1999) cast doubt on the stability and coherence of the earlier solution. *O-H* shares three items each with the *L, K,* and *Es* (scored in reverse) scales and four with *S* and *Hy*. It overlaps minimally with the MMPI-2 content scales; two items (scored in reverse) are shared with *ANG* and *WRK*. Among psychiatric patients, *O-H* is most highly correlated with scores on *S* and *K* (both ~.55), and *ANG* and *TPA* (both ~-.55). As Greene (2011) pointed out, it is unusual for a scale to share so few items with other scales, suggesting that *O-H* may be tapping a unique source of variance. On the basis of an examination of item content, the high *O-H* scorer portrays him- or herself as (a) free of tension and internal conflict, although not of occasional worries and fears; (b) emotionally self-contained and impassive, if not under-expressive and imperturbable, and avoidant of stimulation and emotional or physical exertion (they deny impatience, irritability, and anger, portray themselves as relaxed, and are tolerant of boredom and frustrations); and (c) noncompetitive, as well as avoidant of willfulness and interpersonal conflict (but nonetheless socially interested and comfortable), and able to seek advice and assistance from others. Gearing (1979), following Davis (1971), Davis and Sines (1971), and Persons and Marks (1971), noted the similarity of the personality descriptions for the *O-H* syndrome and the 4'3 MMPI codetype, and this suggestion was followed up in investigations by Walters, Greene, and Solomon (1982), and Walters, Solomon, and Greene (1982), who were able to confirm that despite important differences, the two indicators appeared to reflect the general similarity of their associated personality patterns.

The research on *O-H* has generally been supportive of its construct validity among male forensic psychiatric patients when administered within the context of the full MMPI (Lane & Kling, 1979; Quinsey, Maguire, & Varney, 1983; Schmalz, Fehr, & Dalby, 1989; and White & Heilbrun, 1995). Quinsey, et al. (1983), in particular, and consistent with Megargee's view, found both significant mean differences and substantial effect sizes for *O-H* between groups of murderers classified as overcontrolled versus under-controlled. Findings among youthful offenders are mixed, with both positive (White, 1975; and White, McAdoo, & Megargee, 1973) and negative (Truscott, 1990) results reported.

The findings from various other investigations include higher *O-H* scores among driving-while-intoxicated offenders (Caviaola, Strohmetz, Wolf, & Lavender, 2003), child custody litigants (Bathurst, Gottfried, & Gottfried, 1997), hospitalized sex offending Roman Catholic priests (Plante, Manuel, & Bryant, 1996), and Black than White forensic psychiatric inpatients (Hutton, Miner, Blades, & Langfeldt, 1992). Research on the validity of *O-H* among women is disappointingly meager, although a preliminary investigation (Jensen, 2004) found support for extending Megargee's overcontrolled typology to women. Investigations into the performance of *O-H* within non-forensic psychiatric populations are similarly much needed, and the findings thus far are not encouraging (Werner, Becker, & Yesavage, 1983).

Although the research tends to support Megargee's distinction between persons prone to overcontrolled versus under-controlled patterns of violence, it is much less clearly related to the propensity for violence as such, including murder. Group differences between violent and nonviolent groups have characteristically been small, compromising the predictive validity of *O-H* as applied to the individual case when the purpose of the assessment bears on the issue of dangerousness.

Given its origins, a major application of *O-H* is in the classification of male prisoners convicted of violent offenses. That is, the value of *O-H* primarily belongs in the postdictive context, providing a means for construing and classifying offenders following incidents of extreme assault. Because of the low base rates for violence in most other populations, it is unsuitable as a basis for predictions of assault, violence, or dangerousness. Data associating high *O-H* scores with violence in other than correctional populations are meager. Nevertheless, *O-H* scores may be suitable for inferring the presence or absence of a pattern of personality dynamics consisting of both hostile alienation and excessive inhibitions around the expression of aggressive or hostile impulses, both of which reside largely if not entirely outside of awareness. Quinsey et al. (1983) reported that their overcontrolled murderers lacked assertiveness and suggested that assertiveness training might be indicated as a means of altering the overcontrolled hostile pattern.

This pattern would appear to predict a vulnerability to accumulating resentments over time and to a potential for releasing them in an explosive manner when provocations are great or when controls are diminished (e.g. because of intoxication). Fixed cutting scores have not been developed for *O-H*, and Megargee et al. (1967) recommended that cuts be established by setting on the basis of local norms and the utilities attaching to false-positive versus false-negative decisions. For purposes of orientation, however, among White men, raw scores of 15 or greater should raise the question of overcontrolled personality dynamics, with scores of 18 clearly indicating such dynamics, particularly when test indicators of self-favorable responding and/or False percentage are no more than moderately elevated. Scores of 21 and above appear to be associated with strong external evidence of these dynamics, regardless of response style. African Americans and women may score somewhat higher on *O-H*, suggesting the need to adjust these scores upward before inferring overcontrolled dynamics among members of these groups. Because *O-H* reflects a syndrome (hostility/resentment + impulse overcontrol + lack of awareness of these), low scores are largely without interpretive significance. That is, a low score might signify the absence of any or all of these elements. Thus, person A might be inhibited and overcontrolled but neither hostile nor resentful, whereas person B might be hostile and resentful but neither inhibited nor overcontrolled.

Substance Abuse Measures: The MacAndrew Alcoholism Scale (*MAC/MAC–R*); the Addiction Admission Scale (*AAS*); and the Addiction Potential Scale (*APS*)

Few scales in the history of the MMPI/MMPI-2 have been the subject of more research investigation than MacAndrew's (1965) Alcoholism scale (*MAC*). This research has been organized and summarized in many reviews (e.g. Allen, 1991; Apfeldorf, 1978; Craig, 2005; Friedman et al., 1989a; Gottesman & Prescott, 1989; Greene, 1994; Graham & Strenger, 1988; Greene & Garvin, 1988; MacAndrew, 1981; Megargee, 1985; Weed, Butcher, & Ben-Porath, 1995; Young & Weed, 2006), to which the reader is referred for more detailed coverage of *MAC/MAC–R*.

Several prior attempts to develop a scale for the prediction of alcoholism had been made in the 1950s (Hampton, 1951; Holmes, 1953; Hoyt & Sedlacek, 1958), but their development typically involved comparisons between alcoholics and normals. Because discomfort and disturbance were more frequent in the alcoholic samples, these scales tended to reflect general maladjustment, i.e. to be saturated with nonspecific variance related to the first factor.

The method used by MacAndrew (1965) controlled this source of variation. He compared the item responses of 200 alcoholic outpatients with those of 200 psychiatric outpatients with problems other than alcoholism. Differentiating items were then cross-validated on another 100 members of each of these two groups. Fifty-one items survived cross-validation, of which 49 did not include content related to alcohol consumption. Although the two obvious items provided the best discrimination between his groups, MacAndrew decided not to include them on the final scale because they could be easily dissimulated. He found that a cutting score of 24 correctly classified about 82 percent of both his initial and cross-validation samples. In the transition to the MMPI-2, four items (three with religious content) were dropped. Because of the tradition of interpreting *MAC* on the basis of *raw* scores, these items were replaced with four new items that were found to discriminate alcoholic from nonalcoholic psychiatric patients (McKenna & Butcher, 1987); the revised scale was designated *MAC-R*. Thirty-eight of the items on *MAC-R* are keyed True, 11 False. *MAC-R* shares nine items with *Re* (keyed oppositely) and the Addiction Potential scale (*APS*; see below); eight items each with *Sc* and *Si*, keyed oppositely on both; and six items with *R* and *Do*, likewise keyed oppositely on both. It is moderately correlated with *Re*, *Ma* (non-*K*-corrected), *ASP*, and *DISC* in a range of .50–.55.

The use of raw cutting scores has been tellingly criticized by Gottesman and Prescott (1989). Because the base rate for alcoholism in MacAndrew's (1965) derivation research was 50 percent, his cutting score of 24 is likely to produce an excess of false positives in most clinical and nonclinical settings. For example, in their exhaustive review of studies on *MAC*, Greene and Garvin (1988) reported weighted means for White alcoholic men and women of 28.41 ($SD = 5.45$) and 25.33 ($SD = 4.28$), respectively. The corresponding false negative rates were 20.4 and 46.5, respectively. They reported a weighted average for normal White men, the group from which White adult alcoholic men are most readily discriminated by *MAC*, of 23.13 ($SD = 4.31$), with a false-positive rate of 26.5 percent. For White male psychiatric patients, the comparable figures are 23.30 ($SD = 4.60$), and a false-positive rate of 31.4 percent. The weighted means for both of the latter groups are uncomfortably close to MacAndrew's recommended cutting score. Because the comparable scores for White normal and psychiatric women are about two raw score points below those of White men, their false-positive rate is correspondingly lower—about 20 percent. What little data are available for ethnic minorities suggest that ethnicity can exert a significant influence in the diagnostic efficiency of *MAC*. Wood (2008), for example, found that *MAC-R*, *AAS*, nor *APS* predicted lifetime alcohol or drug dependency in his sample of Native Americans. Greene and Garvin (1988) found a weighted mean score of 26.32 ($SD = 4.86$) for the few available studies involving African American male psychiatric patients; for this group the rate of false positives reached 59.5 percent.

The foregoing values provide an inadequate picture of the ability of *MAC* to identify alcoholic individuals, however. Studies of *MAC* usually involve participant samples the composition of which is widely divergent from the typical base rates seen in both normal and psychiatric settings, when these can be determined at all. Gottesman and Prescott (1989) identified several groups for which classification on the basis of *MAC* scores is subject to large error rates. The first of these is members of the normal population, such as those that may be tested as a part of employment screening or in the course of child custody disputes. For such persons, the use of MacAndrew's (1965) recommended cutting score may result in as many as three to six times as many false as true positives. The situation for normal women is much worse. Because the base rate for alcoholism among women in the general population is only about half of that for men (roughly 4 percent vs. 8 percent), the likelihood that a positive (i.e. a score at or above even a cutting score favoring high specificity, such as 24) will be a *true* positive may drop to as low as 1 in 14. Gottesman and Prescott's discussion of *MAC* in relation to adolescents and ethnic minorities is to similar cautionary effect (e.g. Wood, 2008). Moreover, the manipulation of cutting scores to reduce the proportion of false positives can only be achieved at the cost of increasing the number of alcoholic individuals who will go undetected, i.e. false negatives. Even in settings with relatively high base rates for alcohol abuse, such as among psychiatric patients or correctional inmates, the development of local cutting scores is recommended to minimize misclassification. In settings with relatively high base rates for alcohol abuse, such as among psychiatric patients or correctional inmates, *MAC–R* scores may inadequately separate substance abusers from non-abusers (e.g. Gripshover & Dacey, 1994). *MAC–R* may likewise perform poorly when base rates are low, as among college students (e.g. Svanum & Ehrmann, 1993), although Svanum, McGrew, and Ehrmann (1994), in a similar sample, found that *AAS* showed a moderate ability to identify substance use disorder, primarily alcoholism, while their findings for *MAC–R* and *APS* were, at best, marginal. These kinds of findings can only emphasize the importance of developing local cutting scores within settings where *MAC–R* is to be given diagnostic weight in order to minimize misclassification rates.

To complicate matters further, Greene (1990a) and Archer and Klinefelter (1992) have reported that profile configuration also can significantly influence *MAC–R* scores. In Greene's analysis, code patterns dominated by Scales 4, 6, and especially 9, tended to have substantially higher *MAC–R* scores than code patterns dominated by Scales 1, 3, 7, and especially 2, for reasons that are elaborated later. As a result, for example, for any given cutting score, 49/94 code patterns will be associated with a relatively high false-positive rate and 27/72 code patterns will be associated with a relatively high false-negative rate. On the other hand, scores below such a cutting score in the first instance, or above it in the second, are significantly more likely to be true negatives and true positives, respectively.

Finally, there may be some false-negative cases that *MAC/MAC–R should* miss. MacAndrew (1981) proposed a distinction between two kinds of alcoholism, reflecting "two fundamentally different character orientations" (p. 620). The first he designated as *primary alcoholics*, those true positives identified by *MAC*. From these, he distinguished a much smaller group of *secondary or reactive alcoholics*, whom he characterized as "neurotics-who-also-happen-to-drink-too-much" (p. 620). In a study by Tarter, McBride, Buonpane, and Schneider (1978), the reactive alcoholic group not only scored significantly lower on *MAC* (M = 23.3, SD =3.1) than the primary alcoholic group (M = 28.5, SD = 3.7), they also reported less than half as many relatives with a history of heavy drinking and only one quarter as many symptoms of "minimal brain dysfunction" (accident proneness, lack of popularity with peers, unresponsiveness to discipline, vandalism, short attention span, fidgeting, inability to complete projects, inability to sit still, not working up to ability, ease of frustration, intolerance of delay, demanding of attention/affection, withdrawal, poor handwriting, overactivity, and impulsiveness). MacAndrew's distinction is also supported in the findings of Svanum and Ehrmann (1992) and Ward and Jackson (1990), in which primary alcoholics obtained higher *MAC* scores than secondary alcoholics; in those of Humphrey (1999) in a sample of driving-under-the-influence (DUI) offenders; and by those of Knowles and Schroeder (1990) in which undergraduates with a positive family history for alcoholism scored higher than those with a negative family history.

Although 30 years of research have amply attested to the validity of *MAC* for identifying at least so-called primary alcoholics, there has been a steady accumulation of evidence (Allen, Faded, Rawlings, & Miller, 1991; Finney, Smith, Skeeters, & Auvenshine, 1971; Levinson et al., 1990; MacAndrew, 1981) that *MAC* appears to be measuring a much broader and more fundamental bipolar personality dimension. Recall that because both the alcoholic and comparison groups used by MacAndrew (1965) to derive *MAC* were psychiatric patients, his design may be presumed to have exerted significant control over the influence of first-factor variation. Under these circumstances, the next most pervasive source of variance in the MMPI item pool, the second factor, could have been influential in the separation of his groups. The finding of Schwartz and Graham (1979) that *MAC* was significantly correlated with Wiggins' (1966) Authority Conflict (.61) and Hypomania (.55) content scales, with Welsh's *R* (−.62), and with Scale 9 (.55), all of which typically load on the second factor, confirms this expectation and is consistent with the Greene (1990b) and the Archer and Klinefelter (1992) findings, described earlier, that code pattern influences *MAC–R* scores. Hence, it should not be surprising that whatever variance possessed by *MAC–R* that is specific to the abuse/non-abuse of alcohol is secondary to a personality/life style that constitutes a risk factor for such abuse (see, e.g. Allen, Faden, Rawlings, & Miller, 1991; Earleywine & Finn, 1991; Hoffman & Pietrzak, 2012; Patton, Barnes, & Murray, 1993; Smith & Hilsenroth, 2001). The consensus of the research to date suggests that the high *MAC–R* scorer is characterized as bold and energetic; assertive and self-confident; extraverted and sociable; uninhibited and impulsive; pleasure and sensation seeking; aggressive, rebellious, and resentful of authority; and having been arrested or in trouble with the law. Several studies (Craig, 2005; Fowler, 1975; Kranitz, 1972; Lachar, Berman, Grisell, & Schoof, 1976; Rhodes & Chang, 1978; Sutker, Archer, Brantley, & Kilpatrick, 1979) have reported that drug abusers of various kinds (mostly heroin addicts) typically produce scores on *MAC* in the same range as alcoholics, and Graham (1978) found similar scores in a sample of pathological gamblers. The outpatients studied by Graham et al. (1999) tended to conform in most respects with previous expectations regarding the empirical correlates of high scorers. Their patients, 75 percent of whom were Caucasian, tended to have long histories of abusing alcohol, marijuana, and/or cocaine. Although both men and women were seen as antisocial, acting out, and having conflicts with authority, these characteristics appeared especially strong among their women patients, who often had histories of many arrests, misdemeanor and felony convictions, impulsiveness, and a low tolerance for frustration.

The cluster of traits associated with *MAC/MAC–R* is relatively stable over time. Hoffmann, Loper, and Kammeier (1974), for example, compared the MMPIs of 25 alcoholic men in treatment in a state hospital and the MMPIs these patients had completed as entering freshmen at the University of Minnesota. They found no differences in the *MAC* scores of these men, despite an average of 13 years between test administrations. A number of studies (Chang, Caldwell, & Moss, 1973; Gallucci, Kay, & Thornby, 1989; Huber & Danahy, 1975; Rohan, 1972; Rohan, Tatro, & Rotman, 1969) have reported that *MAC* scores show no change over the course of treatment or on follow-up. These findings, of course, provide yet another reason for caution in the interpretation of *MAC* scores. The risk of misidentification cannot, in general, be circumvented through the use of softened locutions such as "potential for alcoholism" or "addiction prone," as such attributions may be equally harmful in their consequences, particularly among normals such as job applicants.

Although there is little doubt of the validity of *MAC/MAC-R* as a general measure of surgency, the bulk of research on its use for the detection of alcoholism or addiction proneness is equivocal, particularly for populations other than adult White men. Under these circumstances, the use of *MAC-R* scores for the prediction of substance abuse (or a liability thereto) in the individual case must be undertaken with caution. Friedman et al. (2001) suggested that the diagnostic efficiency of the scale may be enhanced by seeking support for the implications of *MAC-R* elevations among items with obvious content related to substance abuse, such as those found on the Addiction Admission scale (*AAS*). Although this suggestion is both plausible and has received some research support (Dwyer, 1996; Stein et al., 1999), such a practice raises the question of the incremental validity of *MAC-R* or any similar scale, i.e. what is *MAC-R*'s (or *APS*'s) role in the prediction of substance abuse if the examinee endorses test items that explicitly admit such abuse? This is a question for future research to address. It is possible, however, that if MacAndrew's (1981) distinction between primary and secondary alcoholism becomes more fully corroborated, *MAC-R* may retain a useful role in the subclassification of alcoholic individuals who endorse item content admitting substance abuse.

MAC/MAC-R scores may also be used to modify the interpretation of scales such as *Pd* and *Ma*. Because both of the latter scales may be elevated into an interpretable range on the basis of their respective first-factor components, largely *Pd4* (Social Alienation), *Pd5* (Self-Alienation), and *Ma2* (Psychomotor Acceleration), the empirical correlates of *Pd* and *Ma* may not apply, or may apply less strongly, when elevations on these scales are achieved on the basis of items distributed more widely across their subscales. In such cases, reference may be made to *MAC-R* scores, with high scores tending to support the application of the usual correlates associated with these scales and low scores emphasizing aspects of negative emotionality, such as dysphoria, guilt, agitation, and identity concerns. *MAC-R* scores may also moderate the interpretation of many other scales, such as *R*, *O-H*, and varieties of the content scales.

Weed et al. (1992) developed two new substance abuse measures, the Addiction Admission scale (*AAS*) and the Addiction Potential scale (*APS*), taking advantage of a wider range of item content related to substance use in the MMPI-2 item pool. *AAS* is a refinement of 14 initial items with content thought to be obviously related to substance abuse. Three of its items were deleted for degrading the internal consistency of the remaining items, and two items were added following a search of the total item pool for items with consistent content that achieved high point-biserial correlations with the 11-item core scale. Ten of the 13 *AAS* items are keyed True, 3 False. Clements and Heintz

(2002) found two principal components: acknowledgment of alcohol/drug problems and positive alcohol expectancies.

Weed et al. (1992) reported an internal consistency estimate (coefficient alpha) for *AAS* of .74. Three reports (Dwyer, 1996; Rouse, Butcher, & Miller, 1999; Stein, Graham, Ben-Porath, & McNulty, 1999) provide evidence that *AAS* is superior to *MAC–R* and *APS* in the prediction of substance abuse among dually diagnosed psychiatric patients, private psychotherapy clients, and public mental health outpatients, respectively. For most comparisons across these studies, *AAS* was associated with higher values for sensitivity, specificity, positive predictive power, negative predictive power, and correct classification rate than those for *MAC–R* and *APS* for both women and men. Moreover, they found that the incremental variance that *AAS* brought to predictions of substance abuse was substantial, whereas the incremental validity of the other two scales over *AAS* was modest and, in the case of *APS*, negligible. The correlates of high *AAS* scores among the Graham et al. (1999) outpatients reflected diagnoses and histories of substance abuse for both men and women, but whereas the men were generally seen as depressed, insecure, and intropunitive, the women were described as antisocial, impulsive, argumentative, sarcastic, and cynical.

AAS functions essentially as a critical item list, but with the advantage of scaled scores, to detect substance abuse among persons who are able (insightful) and willing to admit such problems. Although intercorrelated at about .5, there is reason to think that conjoint use of *AAS* and *MAC–R* may be attended by an increase in diagnostic efficiency in the identification of substance abuse among non-psychiatric patients and strong reason to anticipate differences in treatment readiness among substance abusers. When *AAS* is high and *MAC–R* (or *APS*) is unelevated, abuse may be largely situational and therefore carry a highly favorable prognosis. When *AAS* and *MAC–R* (or *APS*) are both elevated, the presence of personality and lifestyle features disposing to substance abuse and the admission of such abuse combine to suggest a less favorable prognosis but a potential readiness to engage in treatment. When *MAC–R* (or *APS*) is high but *AAS* is unelevated, the prognosis for treatment, at least among true positives, may be poorer because of the person's reluctance to confide substance abuse.

APS would appear to function much as other empirically derived scales, including *MAC–R*. The basic strategy for its development required that potential items discriminate a substance abuse sample from both the MMPI-2 re-standardization sample and a mixed psychiatric sample. Participants from all the samples were subdivided on the basis of gender. Each item was subjected to four comparisons: male substance abusers versus male normals, male substance abusers versus male psychiatric patients, female substance abusers versus female normals, and female substance abusers versus female psychiatric patients. An initial item set comprising 51 items were found significantly discriminating in three of these four comparisons. Ten additional items were added on the grounds that they were strongly discriminating in two of the four comparisons and overlapped the (original) *MAC* scale. Twenty-two items were then discarded because their endorsement frequencies were intermediate to those of normals and psychiatric patients, their content was obviously related to substance abuse, or they degraded the internal consistency of the remaining items. Like *MAC–R* then, *APS* is subtle in the sense of excluding items with content related to substance abuse like those on *AAS*. On cross-validation, the final 39-item *APS* scale achieved separations of about 1.5 *SD* units in the same four comparisons. In an independent replication, Greene, Weed, Butcher, Arredondo, and Davis (1992) found that *APS* separated substance abusers from psychiatric patients at just under 1 *SD* unit, the shrinkage owing in part to an estimated 10 percent to 20 percent rate of substance abuse in the psychiatric sample. Twenty-three of the *APS* items are keyed True, 16 False. The major content domains of *APS* are suggested in the five principal components (with Varimax rotation) found by Sawrie, Kabat, Dietz, Greene, Arrendondo, and Mann (1996) in a sample of 264 alcoholic and 456 psychiatric inpatients: satisfaction/dissatisfaction with self, powerlessness/lack of self-efficacy, antisocial acting-out, surgency, and risk-taking/recklessness. A similar analysis by Clements and Heintz (2002) in a sample of 87 male and 251 female undergraduates substantially corroborated the former findings in four components: satisfaction with self, cynicism/pessimism, impulsivity, and risk-taking.

APS performed better than *MAC–R* in both the Weed et al. (1992) and Greene et al. (1992) studies, particularly among women, but it performed less well than *MAC–R* among the Graham et al. (1999) outpatients. It remains to be seen if any advantage favoring *APS* over *MAC–R* can be extended to the detection of substance abuse problems in patients with comorbid psychiatric disorders. Research is needed on both scales that incorporates the main features of MacAndrew's (1965) design, especially the comparison of alcoholic individuals having comorbid psychiatric disorders with nonalcoholic psychiatric patients. On the whole, however, the research to date (see Clements & Heintz, 2002; Demir, Uluğ, Batur, & Mercan, 2002; Devlin, 1998; Dwyer, 1996; Rostami, Nosratabadi, & Mohammadi, 2007; Rouse, et al., 1999; Stein et al., 1999) suggests that *APS* is the weakest of the three MMPI-2 substance abuse measures.

Further research is also needed to evaluate the personality characteristics of high and low *APS* scorers and the patterns and implications of co-variation between *APS* and other MMPI-2 scales and indexes. Such research would help to illuminate whether, like *MAC–R*, *APS* can be considered a general dimension of personality or is better treated as a measure, the utility of which extends no farther than that anticipated at the time of its construction: a subtle measure of substance abuse.

Gender Role—Masculine (*GM*) and Gender Role—Feminine (*GF*) Scales

In developing the gender-role scales, Peterson (1991; Peterson & Dahlstrom, 1992) sought to apply research and theory supporting a conception of masculinity and femininity as independent attributes of personality that could contribute to the understanding of both men and women. Her approach was intended as both a contrast and a supplement to the traditional bipolar measurement of masculinity–femininity embodied in the MMPI-2 *Mf* scale. The availability of scales for the independent measurement of masculinity and femininity would enable the identification of androgynous (high scores on both scales) and undifferentiated (low scores on both) gender-role styles. That is, such scales would allow inferences regarding androgyny or a lack of gender-role differentiation, patterns that would otherwise be concealed by mid-range *Mf* scores. The ability to distinguish between androgynous and undifferentiated gender-role styles is, of course, of some significance clinically, as androgyny is typically aligned with favorable emotional adjustments, whereas a lack of gender-role differentiation is associated with more fragile and unstable adjustments.

Using the MMPI-2 re-standardization sample, items were selected for each of the gender-role scales if endorsed by at least 70 percent of the members of one gender and by at least 10 percent fewer of the opposite gender. Items thus selected were then grouped into two scales. Those endorsed more commonly by men and less commonly by women comprise the 47-item *GM* scale (19 items are keyed True, 28 False). Those with the opposite trend comprise the 46-item *GF* scale (15 True, 31 False). Peterson's aspiration of independence for *GM* and *GF* was substantially realized in that the scales were found to correlate at only –.10 in the re-standardization sample (Peterson & Dahlstrom, 1992) and .05 in a large psychiatric sample (R. L. Greene, personal communication, March 6, 1998). Among members of the same psychiatric sample, *Mf* and *GM* correlated at –.39 and –.23, for men and women, respectively; *Mf* and *GF* correlated at .37 and .46, for men and women, respectively.

Although Peterson (1991) found some differences between men and women in the characteristics empirically associated with *GM* and *GF* scores, most are similar. High *GM* scores are associated with traditional attributes of masculine strength, such as emotional stability; self-confidence; forthrightness; goal persistence; and freedom from fears, worries, self-consciousness, and social inhibition. These characteristics are substantially confirmed in the ACL correlates reported by Hoffman and Pietrzak (2012). The major MMPI-2 scale correlates include *Pt* (non-*K*-corrected), and *A* at ~–.80, *Es* at ~.80, and *FRS* at ~.70, with which it shares 10 items, scored oppositely.

High *GF* scores tend to deny masculine interests and assert a feminine gender identity, and are associated with traditional feminine attributes of social circumspection, agreeableness, trust, loyalty, and the avoidance of conflict and impropriety. The ACL correlates of *GF* found for normal adults by Hoffman and Pietrzak (2012) included aggressive, rebellious, tough, and vindictive, all in a range of –.24–25. The major MMPI-2 scale correlates include *DISC* and *ASP* at ~–.50, and *Re* at .43. The attributes associated with *GM* appeared to fit both men and women more comfortably than those of *GF*. Butcher et al. (1989) found that men with high *GF* scores appeared somewhat less comfortable than women with high *GM* scores, being often described as bossy, fault-finding, and given to outbursts of temper; they were also more often described as religious and unlikely to engage in swearing. Somewhat surprisingly, both men and women with high *GF* scores were described as prone to misuse alcohol and nonprescription drugs. A few reports have found both *GM* and *GF* to be correlates of psychological well-being (Castlebury & Durham, 1997; Johnson, Jones, & Brems, 1996), but perhaps stronger in the case of *GM* (Woo & Oei, 2006). Peterson and Dahlstrom (1992) did not present empirical correlates for men or women scoring high or low on both *GM* and *GF*.

The gender-role scales have as yet to stimulate much research, and the correlates reported by Peterson and Dahlstrom (1992) are in need of replication, especially those that are counterintuitive like the abuse of alcohol and nonprescription drugs for *GF*. Nevertheless, these scales appear to serve a useful purpose, potentially confirming the usual meanings that attach to very high or very low *Mf* scores, and allowing tentative inferences concerning gender role when *Mf* scores fall into a middle range. Even in advance of further evidence bearing on the relations between *GM* and *GF* and gender-role correlates, the moderate to high correlations between these scales and *FRS, Es,*

LSE, non-*K*-corrected *Pt, WRK, Si,* and *Do,* and *DISC, ASP, Re, MAC–R*, and *Pd2*, respectively, permit a glimpse of the general trend of correlates that are likely to be found for each, whether or not these may be seen to conform to gender-role expectations and stereotypes.

The alert reader will not have missed the apparent relationship between *GM* and *GF* and the two major sources of variance in the MMPI-2 item pool. That is, the correlates of *GM* appear substantially consistent with an absence of general maladjustment or subjective distress (first factor—low), whereas the correlates of *GF*, at least for women, reflect emotional and behavioral control (second factor—high). From this perspective, one can better appreciate how high *GF* scores for men may more readily conflict with common masculine role expectations than do high *GM* scores among women, i.e. women may more readily achieve a comfortable balance between personal ambition and those traits such as loyalty and consideration that are necessary to maintain good relations with others. As in the case of other scales sharing considerable first-factor variance, *GM* is relatively sensitive to distortion through response style, with a bias toward over-reporting psychopathology tending to suppress scores and under-reporting tending to elevate them.

Unfortunately, the utility of the gender-role scales does not extend to predictions regarding the respondent's pattern of leisure and occupational interests. Users of the MMPI long ago noted that *Mf* scores, even when relatively extreme, often afforded a misleading picture of interests. Because only about half of the *Mf* items carry interest-related content, men may achieve high *Mf* scores and still endorse many more traditional masculine interests than traditional feminine interests. Similarly, women may achieve high *Mf* scores and still endorse many more traditional feminine interests than traditional masculine interests. The *GM* and *GF* scales do little to clarify this matter. In the MMPI environment, the Serkownek (1975) subscales for *Mf* provided scores for ascertaining the relative balance of masculine and feminine interests. However, these subscales were not retained in the MMPI-2. Martin and Finn (1992) developed new *Mf* subscales (scoring keys available in Friedman et al., 2001; Greene, 2000), and it is hoped that these will eventually become available for routine use. These subscales are described in detail in Chapter 5.

Note

1 Elhai, Ruggiero, Frueh, Beckham, and Gold, (2002) developed a new scale, F_{ptsd}, to discriminate simulated from genuinely reported PTSD in a sample of combat veterans. The results of subsequent validity studies on this scale have been mixed, with positive findings reported by Elhai, Naifeh, Zucker, Gold, Deitsch, and Frueh, (2004a; see also Elhai, Naifeh, Zucker, Gold, Deitsch, and Frueh, 2004b), and by Tolin, et al. (2010), and negative findings by Marshall and Bagby (2006).

9 Interpretation and Report Writing

Clinical and Actuarial Approaches to Interpretation

Although specific detailed approaches to interpretation of MMPI-2 profiles are discussed in subsequent sections, it is first necessary to have a basic understanding of actuarial and clinical approaches to the interpretation of tests such as the MMPI-2. Misunderstanding the differences in these two approaches can lead a professional to make clinical errors.

Some mental-health professionals rely solely on clinical approaches to test interpretation, even though the power of actuarial methods in psychological assessment has been demonstrated repeatedly and convincingly (e.g. Goldberg, 1965; Grove & Meehl, 1996; Grove, Zald, Lebow, Snitz, & Nelson, 2000; Marks & Seeman, 1963; Marks et al., 1974; Meehl, 1970, 1997; Quinsey, Harris, Rice, & Cormier, 1998; Sawyer, 1966).

Clinical approaches to interpretation are those that come from a professional's personal and professional experience, and in this approach, clinicians base their conclusions on intuition, experience, and clinical judgment. For example, such a clinician may draw conclusions on the basis of a Draw a Person Test with little supporting empirical evidence. On the other hand, the clinician who uses actuarial data suspends making inferences from a test until the actuarial data are consulted, and interpretations are derived by following empirically validated rules, using clinical judgment to supplement these rules. In today's litigious society, psychology, like any other profession, must withstand the rigor of legal and public scrutiny. Clinicians who use tests to make important decisions that affect peoples' lives must be able to justify their decisions based on scientific data, relying solely on clinical judgment only when other methods are unavailable or impractical.

In the first half century of psychology, clinical judgment was considered to be the skill of central importance. Clinical judgment was based on professionally accrued experience with clinical information, such as presenting symptoms, personality attributes, and past history, and rested heavily on the internal norms about patients and people in general that the practitioner developed over time. Years and varieties of clinical experience were valued by clinicians because only then, it was believed, could one develop the depth of knowledge necessary to successfully consider the complex nuances that compose personality and psychopathology. Personality was felt to be too complex to be represented adequately and accurately by test scores. Results from psychological tests, although viewed as helpful adjuncts, were characteristically treated as secondary in importance as compared with an experienced clinician's judgments. In terms of persuasiveness, test data often yielded to clinical impressions.

In the face of such a longstanding tradition, the MMPI was developed in the 1940s largely as an empirical answer to the questions being raised by the apparent unreliability of clinicians' judgments. The need for an objective and reliable measure of personality, independent of clinicians' personal impressions, became clear as empirical studies revealed the inadequacy of tests developed on the basis of clinicians' judgment alone. Although the MMPI was developed empirically, in the first several years of use it often was interpreted without clear actuarial rules, and clinicians made many false assumptions when using it. For example, empirical conclusions were derived and validated for one population (e.g. psychiatric inpatients) but not validated for other populations (e.g. outpatients, adolescents, and marriage counselees). In these first few years of MMPI use, generalizations from one population to another were often made with insufficient empirical support. It was this lack of empirical support that led groups such as Marks and his colleagues (Marks & Seeman, 1963; Marks, Seeman, & Haller, 1974), as well as Gilberstadt and Duker (1965), to begin the systematic empirical investigations of actuarial interpretation of the MMPI which provide the basis for much of the interpretive literature for the MMPI-2.

Development of Actuarial Rules

In the 1950s, practitioners usually interpreted the MMPI by analyzing each of the clinical scales in isolation and then attempting to combine these into a clinically-meaningful interpretation. Perhaps because the information from the co-varying of so many scales was complex, clinical lore was generated at a quicker rate than research could verify. Although information from clinical interpretations added richness and breadth to the use of the MMPI, questions arose as to whether they added substantial error variance at the same time.

In 1954, Paul Meehl recognized that skilled clinicians followed definable rules in their diagnosis decisions that could be articulated and taught. Furthermore, he discovered numerous studies showing that diagnostic judgments following objective, specifiable rules were superior in most instances to those of the clinicians. The result was his publication "Wanted—A Good Cookbook" (Meehl, 1956). In this article, Meehl proposed that an actuarial, rather than a clinical, approach should be used wherever possible. Subsequent research has supported this view repeatedly (e.g. Grove et al., 2000; Marks et al., 1974; Meehl, 1970). Although the term *actuary* is heard more in the context of the insurance business, it is also particularly relevant to psychological assessment. In the insurance industry, certain definable and measurable factors are statistically associated with risks. For example, age, blood pressure, lifestyle, longevity of parents, and occupation are all associated with risks of mortality, and that risk can be expressed in terms of a probability statement using mathematical relationships. Little judgment is involved. Insurance companies have found that when judgment is added (e.g. "But he seems to be particularly healthy"), the accuracy of predictions generally becomes worse.

The same findings have occurred in psychology (e.g. Goldberg, 1965; Meehl, 1954; Sawyer, 1966). Despite historical emphasis on clinical judgment, clinicians repeatedly have fared worse than the actuarial rules. In a meta-analysis of 20 studies of prediction using clinical and actuarial means, Meehl (1954) found that, "in about half of the studies, the two methods were equal; in the other half, the clinician is definitely inferior. No ...

fully acceptable study puts him clearly ahead" (p. 119). Similarly, Sawyer analyzed 45 studies and substantiated Meehl's (1954) findings that the actuarial approaches showed clear and repeated superiority over clinical judgment in numerous situations with diverse types of data. Clearly the actuary is of greater assistance to the clinician than the clinician is to the actuary, at least in day-to-day clinical practice. Meehl (1970, p. 9) stated that:

> *It is difficult to come up with so much as one single research study in which the clinician's predictions are better than the statistical table or formula; in most studies, the clinician is significantly* worse [italics added]. There are few domains of social science in which so sizeable a body of evidence is so consistently in the same direction.

Meehl (1997, p. 95) later strongly echoed the same opinion:

> I am unaware of any controversy in psychology or sociology in which the data are as massive, varied, and uniform as this. Nevertheless, the majority of clinicians continue to act as if these data do not exist, and the majority of textbooks misinform the student that the controversy "remains unsettled."

Using the MMPI, actuarial approaches to personality description have shown superiority over clinical judgments ranging from a 19 percent to 38 percent improvement in accuracy (Marks et al., 1974).

In their overview of clinical judgment difficulties, Quinsey et al. (1998, p. 56) pointed out that people appear unable to adjust their predictions according to the interrelationships among predictive variables:

> In practical terms, this means that people often think they have more information (or are using more information) than they actually have, they are therefore willing to make more extreme judgments than warranted, and they have more confidence than justified (Einhorn & Hogarth, 1978; Kahneman & Tversky, 1973; Wiggins, 1973).

Quinsey et al. (1998, pp. 55–56) further elaborated that

> when people are asked to make judgments on the basis of probabilistic data (as when a clinician tries to predict which persons will commit violence, or when a sports fan tries to predict which teams will have winning seasons), a variety of task features can lead them to make systematic and gross errors. Laboratory studies of probability learning and other tasks involving the combination of probabilistic data to arrive at a prediction have convincingly demonstrated that people make predictions on the basis of the frequencies of various individual events and not on their actual probabilities: Specifically, people do not take into account the opportunities an event has to occur, only how often it does occur (Estes, 1976). Thus, accuracy in judgment is possible only when the alternative events have equal opportunities to occur. Needless to say, this rarely occurs under natural circumstances. In addition, accuracy in judgment is possible only when the various events are equally attended to and equally remembered.

Finally, in an exhaustive meta-analytic review of 136 studies, Grove et al. (2000, p. 25) supported Meehl's (1954) contention that clinical prediction is just as effective as actuarial prediction about half of the time, and better than actuarial prediction in only a few instances. Most importantly, they note,

> The only design variable that substantially influenced the relative efficacy of the mechanical- and clinical-prediction methods was whether the clinicians had access to a clinical interview. Alas, clinical predictions were outperformed by a substantially greater margin when such data was available to the clinician.

Actuarial Data and Base Rates

To understand actuarial approaches in prediction, personality description, psychological test interpretation, and diagnosis, one must first understand the differences and interrelations between cookbook and clinical and actuarial approaches to interpretation. Cookbook approaches describe any systematic approach, or recipe, for arriving at a diagnostic conclusion and/or personality formulation. Some cookbook approaches have been adapted to computers, such that the decision logic mimics an "automated clinician." Examples of this are the Minnesota Report and the Caldwell Report, both of which are based primarily, although not exclusively, on actuarial data. In other automated cookbooks systems, recipes for diagnosis and description are based primarily on clinical judgment or when actuarial and clinical approaches are mixed in unspecified ways.

The core concept of actuarial description is well described by Marks et al. (1974, pp. 35–36):

> Actuarial descriptions consist of a set of descriptive attributes … assigned to individuals on the basis of … explicit … rules derived from experimentally-statistically demonstrated associations between data (e.g. MMPI profiles) and the descriptive statements.

The demonstrated association between a set of data and certain personality descriptions implies some relation. That is, given scores are associated with certain personality traits or behaviors only if they exceed the ordinary base rate.

Base rates refer to the frequency with which a behavior or characteristic exists within a given population. Some behaviors have such a high base rate of occurrence that they cannot distinguish among people in meaningful ways, even though they may be true. These have sometimes been referred to as "Aunt Fanny" statements; that is, they are true about you, about me, and about my Aunt Fanny (Tallent, 1983). An example would be, "Sometimes I do not say all that is on my mind" or "My moods may change depending on what is happening in my life." Meehl (1973) also labeled this phenomenon the *Barnum effect* because many professionals apparently attempt to raise their appearance of credibility through frequent use of very high base-rate statements. For a good discussion about the Barnum effect and the validity of computer-based test interpretations, refer to Guastello and Rieke's 1990 article in *Psychological Assessment: A Journal of Consulting and Clinical Psychology*.

More meaningful are base rates that are less common, or even comparatively rare, and thus allow for distinguishing between individuals or groups of individuals. Sometimes the base rates are so low that one can "play the base rates" in arriving at a professional judgment or conclusion and have virtual certainty of being correct. For example, the incidence—or base rate—of suicide among five-year-old girls attending kindergarten is virtually nil—certainly less than 1 in 100,000. Knowing nothing else about the person other than age, gender, and enrollment in public school, one could confidently predict an absence of suicidal risk with an accuracy rate of 99.999 percent or better—a rate that could hardly be improved on by the addition of any psychological test data. Consequently, development of a test to predict suicide in five-year-old girls would be virtually impossible and would not usefully improve on a prediction made simply from the base-rate information alone. Psychological test data have the greatest potential for improving accuracy over the base-rate predictions (i.e. providing incremental validity) when the base rate is not extreme in either direction but is closer to 50:50.

Base rates change with different groupings and for different populations. For example, the base rate of suicide increases with age, reported depression, loss of social support or job, or history of recent suicide attempts. In another example, diagnosing brain disorder is extremely hazardous among executive candidates for senior job opportunities in business, simply because of the rarity. To do so in such a setting would require virtually overwhelmingly clear and convincing evidence of central nervous system dysfunction. The same diagnosis of brain disorder would be considered with far greater confidence when working with patients on a neurology inpatient ward simply because you are not "fighting the base rate" in your search for accuracy of diagnosis. In other words, the issue of base rates is primarily an issue of setting and recent history because scores often have different meaning depending on the setting. For this reason, MMPI-2 and MMPI-2-RF reports should not be written without knowing from which setting it came. An elevation on Scales 4 and 9, for example, would almost certainly predict antisocial behavior if obtained in a prison setting, but not necessarily if obtained from a college counselee.

The point, then, is that base rates for different disorders differ across groups, thereby directly affecting the description and prediction process. Thus, actuarial tables derived accurately for one group (e.g. medical patients) may be less accurate with other groups (e.g. psychiatric patients). For these reasons, careful thought must be given even when using actuarially based cookbook interpretations of the MMPI-2. Particular attention must be paid to recognizing when a given client differs from those on whom the actuarial interpretations were derived (Ehrenworth & Archer, 1985). Naïve applications of any system can result in situations such as a 24-year-old inpatient being diagnosed as suffering involutional depression simply because his MMPI-2 profile configuration suggested it.

Despite the power of the actuarial approach, it is still a "work in progress." The actuarial approach to MMPI-2 interpretation is indeed powerful, but only if the actuary has access to relevant data about the client. For these reasons, a cookbook or computerized interpretation system, although powerful and efficient, is not always sufficient. The MMPI-2 user should be particularly alert to the need to modify MMPI-2 clinical interpretations because of a person's age, intelligence, social or ethnic class, educational level, health status, medication influences, prior life traumas, and current situational difficulties. Such potent factors clearly must modify many interpretations made of MMPI-2 profile configurations because the existing knowledge does not yet allow these factors to be considered by the actuarial systems (Pancoast, Archer, & Gordon, 1988).

The Importance of Referral Data

Because many MMPI-2 interpretive statements are empirically generated, individuals sharing the same code pattern will exhibit many of the same symptoms, complaints, behaviors, and personality traits. It is unlikely that individuals will obtain a valid elevated profile without exhibiting the primary typical characteristics associated with that profile. For example, persons with an elevated Scale 2 at a *T*-score of 90 will be depressed, will exhibit varied symptoms of depression, and will be ruminative and guilt prone. However, the exact manifestations of these symptoms and complaints will vary across populations and will be modified by variables such as SES, intelligence, education, recent life events, and other personality traits. For example, most persons with 27/72 codes will be compulsive, depressed, perfectionistic, and worry prone. However, one individual with a 27/72 code may be more aware of anxiety and guilt and complain somewhat less of depression, whereas another may experience the depressive symptoms more intensely, with guilt and anxiety as secondary.

Elevations on the other clinical, supplementary, and content scales will aid in predicting these differences, but intelligence, education, and socioeconomic variables also will partly determine how individuals experience their symptoms and articulate their complaints. For example, an uneducated person with a 27/72 code likely would describe psychological problems in a different way than an educated individual of higher SES who had a similar 27/72 code. In another example, one individual, elevated on Scales 4 and 9, may be a successful businesswoman, charismatic, energetic, and enterprising, although impulse prone and with intimacy difficulties, whereas another woman with the same scores on Scales 4 and 9 may be a drug-addicted, marginally adjusted individual. They share many similarities: both will find rules to be irritating; are likely to have difficulties with intimacy and long-term relationships, and will manifest impulse-control problems, difficulties with authority, and the postponement of gratification. These attributes will manifest themselves, however, quite differently. The successful businesswoman may have higher intellectual functioning and SES which will perhaps be reflected in her MMPI-2 by elevations on the *K* scale and on the *Es* scale, and perhaps on the *Ss* scale, all suggesting self-control, social poise, and sophistication. The educated, intelligent individual with a 49/94 code is more likely able to control her impulses well enough to effectively use her manipulative qualities—or to use them in a sophisticated manner—whereas the other individual with lower intelligence and lower ego strength is unable to use these qualities in socially adaptive ways.

Not factoring in the moderator variables, which often are reflected in elevations on some of the supplementary scales, can also lead to mistakes in MMPI-2 interpretation. For example, on seeing a 49/94 elevation at *T*-75, the novice clinician may assume sociopathy and a life of crime, which is not necessarily true. In one case, an unskilled psychologist's report stated that there was evidence from the MMPI-2 results that the father, who was seeking visitation rights with his children subsequent to a divorce, exhibited antisocial criminal behaviors and personality traits. In fact, the father was a successful malpractice attorney, never in trouble with the law. A recovering alcoholic, he was prominent in the community as a leader of various causes. He had a tendency to externalize and had difficulties with impulse control. His children saw him as somewhat unreliable, although often warm and playful. He had managed, however, to create a successful business, channeling his aggressive, competitive impulses in mostly appropriate ways, except for difficulties in his marital life.

Not ascertaining the population from which the 49/94 code profile originated led to a poorly worded report and an angry father who was able to cast doubt on the whole evaluation because a clearly refutable statement (about his "criminal tendencies") had been made by the psychologist in the report. Obtaining a referral question, a brief history and background information from the referral source would have helped to avoid such a mistake. The referring colleague might have requested an evaluation with a statement such as the following:

> Please evaluate this bright young attorney with a successful practice. He is recently divorced and in a post-decree custody dispute with his ex-wife. He is successful, but I'm wondering if there's any legitimacy to his wife's complaints that he's devious, manipulative, and controlling, even though others see him as successful, charming, and likeable. Can you evaluate him as part of the custody evaluation?

Thus, the report could have addressed the tendency for educated persons with 49/94 codes to come across as charming and poised, showing poor impulse control, but not necessarily as antisocial or manifesting criminal behavior. Therefore, test reports should never be written "blind," without any knowledge about an individual. At least a basic referral question is needed, as well as some population parameters. As described in Chapter 12, psychologists are increasingly using computer-generated reports as an aid in their evaluations, but most computer-generated reports incorporate extremely little background information, often only age, education, setting, and occasionally race. Currently, few computer-generated reports specifically address a particular referral question, although some computer reports vary their interpretations depending on whether the client is from a forensic setting, general medical setting, or an outpatient or inpatient mental health setting. Consequently, the psychologist must use clinical skills and information from other data to create a useful report and should not rely solely on a computer-generated report. It is the skill and judgment of the clinician that takes computer-generated statements and fits them for a particular individual, taking into consideration the referral question and the individual's history, achievements, and other intervening variables. Chapter 12 offers more detailed information about widely used computer-generated reports with examples.

Another consideration is that patients sometimes produce profiles that initially appear more pathological than is warranted once the referral question, current situation, and background information are obtained. For example, a client with an MMPI-2 profile peaking on Scale 4 with *T*-scores about 70 may be experiencing a difficult divorce. Somewhat alienated and having difficulties with trust, this individual may be responding understandably to his or her current difficulties. In another example, a client with a profile elevated on Scales 2 and 7 may show a chronic life history of compulsive, anxious, and depressive behaviors or the client may be responding to a recent catastrophic or unpredictable loss but have a history of fairly healthy adjustment.

A report using only an actuarial cookbook approach generally will describe the client accurately regarding current functioning, behaviors, and symptoms. The diagnosis, therapeutic suggestions, and the usefulness of the report may be compromised, however, unless the clinician simultaneously considers the referral question, current life situation, and background information. A key aspect of the background information is the client's demographic information because each demographic variable may influence, to some degree, how a particular set of scores is interpreted.

Demographic Variables

Age

As people age, significant changes occur. People generally become less aggressive and less risk taking with age, as well as slightly more conservative. They also tend to worry more about health and illness and show some slight decrease in optimism. These changes are reflected in the empirical research on the effects of age on MMPI/MMPI-2 code patterns. Although age effects on the MMPI/MMPI-2 have been studied infrequently, the studies nevertheless confirm the general research on aging. One of the first large-scale studies (Aaronson, 1958), using 871 normals and the original MMPI, confirmed that with aging there is a tendency to become more preoccupied with health and illness, as well as somewhat more pessimistic. These issues were reflected in average increases in elevation of five or more T-score points on the L scale and Scales 1 and 2 for both men and women. Decreases in alienation and acting out and a slight decrease in energy were reflected in a similar drop in elevations on Scales 4 and 9 for both men and women.

Other findings (Greene, 2011) for the MMPI-2 are summarized below:

1   Psychopathology tends to diminish with age. Elevations across most scales drift down as a function of age by a significant, although small, number of T-scores, except for the L scale and Scales 1 and 2, which tend to ascend.
2   Scores on Scales 4 and 9 tend to decrease more than the other scales as a function of age, confirming the clinical observation that sociopaths "burn out" with age.
3   The K scale and Scale 0, scales which may have a genetic component (Caldwell, personal communication, June 1994), tend to stay stable across all groups over time.

Aaronson, Dent, Webb, and Kline (1996) demonstrated that the endorsement of MMPI-2 critical items decreased with age, a finding which replicated the findings of Webb, Fowler, and Miller (1971) regarding critical items in the original MMPI. Both studies showed that as age increased, patients endorsed fewer items of overt pathology or distress and that this decrease was virtually linear from age 25 onward.

Two-point code-pattern frequencies likewise vary according to age. Webb's (1970a) analysis of over 12,000 patients showed that clients above age 27 obtained the following codes significantly more frequently than younger patients: 02/20, 12/21, 13/31, 23/32, 27/72, 34/43, and 36/63. Patients below age 27 obtained the following codes more frequently: 47/74, 48/84, 49/94, 68/86, 78/87, and 89/98. Although Webb's analysis has limited generalizability due to his use of a median split resulting in a cut at age 27, his point remains valid: age is a moderator variable, with younger patients showing more acting out and psychotic code patterns and older patients showing more anxious, depressed, and somatizing codes.

Gynther (1979, p. 64) similarly observed that

> younger patients and normals obtain more peaks and higher scores on scales measuring nonconformity, rebelliousness, alienation, and energy level. Older patients and normals obtain more peaks and high scores on scales measuring concern with health, introversion, and to a lesser extent, scales involving depression and immaturity.

Age, then, can affect interpretation of profiles. For example, a profile with moderate elevations on the *D* or *Hs* scales from a person over age 70 might be interpreted less pathologically than the same profile from a young adult.

On the other hand, studies comparing the average *T*-scores for various age categories in the MMPI-2 normative sample failed to show systematic scale variations by age (Dahlstrom & Tellegen, 1993; see also Fig. 1.1). Although there are definite aging effects on MMPI-2 scores, the effects vary, and by small amounts, so that age-corrected norms are difficult to generate and are probably not needed; an exception is for adolescents, which is accomplished by using the MMPI-A. The MMPI-2 is probably robust enough that the slight changes due to aging do not make a great deal of difference clinically except at the extremes.

Greene (2011, Table 4.3, p. 147) also provides the correlations for different ages and the MMPI-2 scales for the normative group and psychiatric patients. He summarizes the effects of age for the clinical scales somewhat differently from Dahlstrom and Tellegen (1993):

> Scales 4 (Psychopathic Deviate [*Pd*]) and 9 (Hypomania [*Ma*]) have the largest correlations with age in normal individuals. Individuals 80 years of age and older in the MMPI-2 normative group had a mean *T*-score of 41.0 and 46.2 on these two scales, respectively; whereas individuals 20 to 29 years of age had a mean *T*-score of 51.5 and 53.1, respectively (Table 11.4, p. 470). Thus, age will modify any clinical scale less than seven or eight *T* points, at the most, and less than five *T* points more typically. The correlations with age are smaller in the clinical clients than in the normal individuals. The largest correlations in the clinical clients were on Scales 1 (Hypochondriasis [*Hs*]), 2 (Depression [*D*]), and 3 (Hysteria [*Hy*]). There were approximately five to eight *T* point differences between clients 70 years of age and older, and clients 20 to 29 years old.
>
> (Greene, 2011, p. 145).

The interested reader is also directed to Greene (2011, Table 3.22, p. 75) for information about the relationship between age and self-unfavorable reporting in a clinical psychiatric sample. Greene reports that there are no effects of age on any of a number of self-unfavorable scales and indices (*F*, *FB*, *F(p)*, *Ds*, *F – K*, True percent, *RBS*, and *FBS*) beyond age 20. Likewise, he (2011, Table 3.30, p. 91) reports for self-favorable scales (*L*, *ODecp* Other Deception), *Sd*, *K*, *S*, *So* (Social Desirability, and False percent) that there are no effects of age on any of these scales beyond age 20.

Codetypes also vary as a function of age. Greene (2011, Table 11.6, p. 474) provides frequently occurring MMPI-2 codetypes within eight age ranges (18–80+) for the Caldwell (2007b) clinical sample. According to Greene (2011, p. 473):

> 1-3/3-1 codetypes were the most frequent codetype in all age ranges except for the 18- to 19-year-olds; their frequency increased from 8.2 percent in the 20 to 29 age range to over 20 percent in the four oldest age ranges. Spike 1, 1-2/2-1, and 2-3/3-2 showed similar increases in frequency with age, with Spike 1 codetypes approaching 5 percent and 1-2/2-1 and 2-3/3-2 codetypes approaching 10 percent in the two oldest age ranges. The 6-8/8-6 codetypes also occurred frequently, particularly in the 18-19 (9.9%) and to 20 to 29 (6.5%) age ranges and they decreased in frequency with age. There were a number of frequently occurring codetypes that were relatively stable across these eight age ranges: 2-4/4-2; 2-6/6-2; 2-7/7-2; 2-8/8-2; Spike 6; and 7-8/8-7.

Gender

Early in the development of the MMPI, different norms for men and women were developed for all of the clinical scales (except Scales 6, 9, and 0) because of the different patterns of endorsement of items for the two genders on some of the scales. Different gender norms were not developed for the original validity scales. In addition, Scales 3 (*Hy*) and 6 (*Pa*) were more often high-point elevations for women, whereas Scales 1 (*Hs*) and 7 (*Pt*) were more often highest for men (Webb, 1971). Subsequently, it was also suggested that MMPI scale elevations had different correlates for the two genders (Dahlstrom et al., 1972). That is, elevations on Scale 6 did not necessarily mean the same for men as for women. However, little research has been published on whether gender differences occur in the empirical correlates of code patterns. Greene (1991a) stated that the dearth of research could reflect that gender differences are rarely found or that there has been an absence of research in this area.

The MMPI-2 also uses different *T*-scores for men and women, although the MMPI-2-RF uses non-gendered norms. What has not yet been adequately considered in interpreting MMPI-2 patterns are the gender-related specific situations that may need to be considered in understanding the clinical significance of an MMPI-2 profile. For example, spousal abuse is disproportionately an occurrence with wives, and the knowledge that a woman is being abused would make the anger reflected in an MMPI-2 pattern more understandable. Similarly, the frustrations of a competent, independent woman who is experiencing the glass ceiling in the business world could be reflected in portions of the MMPI-2 profile, reflecting the situation rather than enduring pathology. The clinician must be sensitive to such gender issues to effectively interpret MMPI-2 code patterns. Although the MMPI-2 is robust enough that it is not likely that these gender issues invalidate interpretation, more research is clearly needed.

Greene (2011) provides a number of comparison tables for mean scale scores by gender, covering both normals (Butcher et al., 1989) and clinical patients (Caldwell, 2007b). His comparisons show minimal effects on any of the validity scales in these two samples. Greene does show somewhat larger effects of gender on the clinical scales, with women endorsing more items on Scales 1, 2, 3, and 7, and obviously on Scale 5 (*Mf*). The differences were small, however, with never more than two to three items across all of the clinical scales (except for Scale 5 [*Mf*]). Greene (2011, p. 489) also provides frequency data (Tables 11.23, 11.24, p. 490) for MMPI-2 codetypes by gender using Caldwell's (2007b) clinical sample for these comparisons:

> Several codetypes (6-8/8-6; 7-8/8-7; Spike 9) occurred more often in men, whereas several other codetypes (1-2/2-1; 1-3/3-1; 2-7/7-2) occurred more often in women. Spike 5 and 2-3/3-2 codetypes occurred about twice as often in women as in men. Most of the codetypes, however, occurred about equally often in men and women.

Education

Beyond the matter of a basic comprehension of the MMPI-2 items, education also is associated with certain scale elevations. On the original MMPI, higher education levels were associated with decreases in elevation on the *F* and *Si* scales and increases on the *K* scale. Likewise, men with higher education showed fairly strong elevations on Scale 5 (*Mf*; Gulas, 1973), and women with similarly high education showed moderately low scores on Scale 5 (Dahlstrom et al., 1986; Graham & Tisdale, 1983). These patterns on Scale 5 are also associated with increased intelligence test scores, and generally these findings exist regardless of age or ethnic group membership (Dahlstrom et al., 1986). As Dahlstrom et al. (1986, p. 123) noted,

> In general, then, all subjects who report some education beyond the level of high school graduation are more likely to answer the MMPI in less deviant ways. Their scores are consistent with greater personal effectiveness, fewer interpersonal and emotional difficulties, and better morale.

This statement is consistent with the findings of Webb et al. (1971) that MMPI critical items were endorsed significantly less frequently as education increased, regardless of age.

The effects of education on scale elevations are quite different for the MMPI-2, as opposed to the MMPI, because the MMPI-2 normative group averaged almost 15 years of education, whereas the original normative sample had approximately eight years of education. If the original "normals" deserved the sobriquet "Minnesota farmer," the new "normals" could be considered "yuppies." Consequently, a typical individual taking the MMPI-2 will score lower on the *K* scale and Scale 5 and higher on the *L* scale than they would on the MMPI, as they are being compared with an educated normative group, whereas previously they were compared with a group of less educated individuals. In an attempt to counter the concern that the new "over"-educated normals would adversely affect code-pattern data, Butcher (1990a) grouped the MMPI-2 normative sample into five groups on the basis of education and examined mean *T*-scores. His data suggested that education had no significant impact on *T*-score elevations because all five groups' mean profiles were around a *T*-score of 50. Similarly, Greene (2011) examined the impact of education on MMPI-2 scales in a clinical sample (Caldwell, 2007b) using three categories of education: (1) 6–12 years; (2) 13–16 years; and (3) 17 and greater. He noted that sores on the MMPI-2 scales tend to decrease 5 to 10 *T*-points on a majority of the clinical scales as the number of years of education increases. Also, "any age effects tend to be smaller in clients with 17 or more years of education, as compared to clients with 12 or fewer years of education" (Greene, 2011, p. 494).

Race

Numerous studies reviewing the original MMPI have shown significant differences between scores of African Americans and whites on the MMPI. Many studies have found the *F* scale and Scales 8 (*Sc*) and 9 (*Ma*) to be significantly higher in African Americans, with other studies also showing the *K* scale and Scale 5 (*Mf*) to be lower. Some evidence (Dahlstrom et al., 1986), however, strongly suggests that most of these apparent differences have resulted from influences of other variables, such as education, age, and rural/urban residence. At higher levels of SES, racial differences virtually disappeared. Within racial groups, scale score differences between higher and lower socioeconomic groups were much greater than any differences between racial groups. Clearly socioeconomic variables played a bigger role than the racial variable.

Hall, Bansal, and Lopez (1999) performed a meta-analysis that included 25 studies of male African Americans versus European Americans, and 12 studies of female African Americans versus European Americans. With regard to males, their findings, indeed, demonstrated that African American males scored higher than their European American counterparts on Scales *F*, *8*, and *9*. Within the female studies, the only reliable difference was found on Scale 9, on which African American females scored higher. However, the aggregate effect size (Cohen's *d*) ranged from .17 to .24, which equates to a difference of less than three *T* points. In other words, these differences are statistically, yet not clinically, significant.

Gynther (1979) suggested that this pattern of results appears to reflect differences in values and perceptions, rather than differences in psychological adjustment. Many studies, according to Gynther, revealed that the principal factor distinguishing between African Americans and Whites was estrangement and mistrust of society, which was reflected on Scales 4 (*Pd*) and 8 (*Sc*). Indeed, Dahlstrom et al. (1986) noted that "by no means are all deviations (as reflected in elevated MMPI scores or in similar measures) evidence for disorder" (p. 202). Even so, these elevations and profile configurations are instructive. As Dahlstrom et al. (1986, p. 202) concluded,

> the MMPI may be useful in the task of characterizing the various coping and defense mechanisms to which minority individuals may resort in their efforts to deal with the special circumstances that they all too often encounter in America today.

In a forensic setting, Shondrick, Ben-Porath, and Stafford (1992) compared African American and White men who had been ordered by the court to take the MMPI-2 as part of their pretrial evaluation. The group mean profiles of both sets of defendants revealed few scale elevation differences between the groups. Scale 9 and the *CYN* and *ASP* scales were significantly more elevated for African Americans than for Whites, however. The differences were so slight that it is difficult to interpret, especially because the socioeconomic variables were not taken into account. The slight differences, however, are consistent with previous differences between African American and Whites found on the MMPI.

Greene (2011) carefully reviewed a number of Black/White comparison studies with the MMPI-2 and concluded that there are no viable differences between the groups, albeit there are a limited number of studies. Importantly, Greene notes that "the finding of no differences in the external correlates between blacks and whites makes this conclusion very straightforward" (p. 508).

Comparisons with Hispanics and other minority groups also suggest some differences in average MMPI scores. In reviewing these studies, Greene (1980) was not able, however, to discern any clear pattern of differences on the clinical scales, although some validity scale differences appeared on the L and K scales. His review suggested that the differences on the MMPI between Hispanic populations and Whites were less than the differences between African Americans and Whites. Dahlstrom et al. (1986) made similar observations and additionally noted that acculturation generally reduced the differences between the MMPI scores of Hispanic and White populations. Hall et al. (1999) were unable to find a sufficient number of studies comparing Latina women to European American women, but were able to find a sufficient number comparing men. Their meta-analysis indicated that Latino men score about two points higher than European American men on the L scale (Cohen's $d = .21$) and about 3.5 points lower on Scale 5. More recently, Greene (2011) recognized that there have been too few studies of Hispanic–White comparisons in both normal and clinical groups to conclude anything other than the need for more research in this area.

There is a relative dearth of literature examining MMPI/MMPI-2 scores among Native Americans. However, Robin et al. (2003) have provided data using two samples comprised of Southwestern and Plains American Indian tribal members with contrasting sociocultural and historical origins. Comparisons using a matched sample of 512 Native Americans and 512 individuals from the MMPI-2 Normative sample revealed some substantial differences. The Native American sample scored more than eight points higher on L, seven points higher on F, six points higher on Scales 4 and 8, five points higher on Scale 9, four points higher on Scale 3, and three points higher on Scale 2. In addition, there were several differences noted on clinical subscales, supplementary scales, and content scales. Robin et al. suggest the fact, contrary to Dahlstrom et al.'s (1986) suggestion, that the differences did not disappear when a matched sample was incorporated may reflect that these Native Americans "have suffered more economic and social hardship, trauma, and violence even when they are matched with the MMPI-2 normative group on demographic variables" (p. 356). Greene (2011) reviewed three Native American–White comparison studies and concluded that "Native Americans will have higher scores on the MMPI-2 than Whites, although less confidence can be placed in exactly which of the validity and clinical scales will demonstrate these differences" (p. 508).

Tsai and Pike (2000) investigated the effect of acculturation on the MMPI-2 results of Asian American students. They found that the level of acculturation was related to the degree to which MMPI-2 scores of Asian American students differed from those of Whites. Compared to Whites, low-acculturated Asian Americans scored significantly higher on nine scales (L, F, 1, 2, 5, 6, 7, 8, and 0). Bicultural Asian Americans scored higher than Whites on five scales (*F*, *2*, *6*, *8*, and *0*) and lower on 1 (*K*). Further, these differences were clinically meaningful, ranging from 6.5 to 21.7 *T*-score points. There were no significant differences, however, between high-acculturated Asian Americans and Whites.

Although caution should be used when interpreting MMPI-2 profiles from ethnic groups, Greene (1987, 2011), in a comprehensive review regarding ethnicity and the MMPI, suggested that too much has been made of average differences between ethnic groups' MMPI scores. His review suggested that there was a "failure to find a consistent pattern of scale differences between any two ethnic groups in any population" (Greene, 1987, p. 509). Instead, as he pointed out, "it appears that moderator variables such as socioeconomic status, education, and intelligence, as well as profile validity are more important determinants of MMPI performance than ethnic status" (p. 509). As Greene (2011) and Dahlstrom et al. (1986) both noted, researchers should focus on the empirical correlates associated with specific patterns and elevations on the MMPI-2 for various ethnic subpopulations, rather than reporting small mean differences between various poorly defined ethnic groups. Also, researchers need to establish whether a particular individual identifies with an ethnic group, rather than assuming that identification with the minority culture is defined by a person's race or surname, and assess the person's perception of estrangement from the majority culture at that time.

Even more caution, of course, should be incorporated when interpreting a version of the MMPI-2, or any other psychological test, that has been translated into another language. Butcher and colleagues (Butcher, Cheung, Lim, 2003; Butcher, Derksen, Sloore, & Sirigatti, 2003) have examined the adaptability of the MMPI-2 in European and Asian cultures. Considering all of the available data with regard to cross-cultural use of the MMPI-2, Butcher (2004, p. 94) has suggested the following guidelines for successful international adaptation of an instrument for cross-cultural personality assessment research:

1   The instrument should have a substantial established database to allow comparisons.
2   It is valuable for the test to have successful existing translations in other languages and cultures.
3   The instrument should have a developed "translation lore" (e.g. typically difficult items to translate, acceptable item content substitutions, etc.) to provide effective developmental strategies to guide new projects.
4   The instrument should have available interpretive textbooks that focus on interpretation that can be translated into the language of the target country.
5   It is usually valuable to provide training workshops on the use of the instrument for clinical practitioners.

Socioeconomic Variables

The major dimensions that define SES in White participants can be matched only roughly to similar dimensions for participants who are African American or are from other ethnic groups. Thus, it is hazardous to make generalizations concerning MMPI-2 patterns that might be associated with socioeconomic variables (Dahlstrom et al., 1986). Even so, some patterns seem sufficiently consistent to warrant specific mention.

Normal participants from low socioeconomic groups, regardless of race or gender, tend to score higher on the *F* scale and on Scale 0 (*Si*) of the MMPI-2, whereas participants from higher socioeconomic backgrounds tend to score higher on the *K* scale (Dahlstrom et al., 1986; Duckworth & Anderson, 1986). For men, Scale 8 (*Sc*) decreases and Scale 5 (*Mf*) increases as SES increases, whereas for women, Scales 2 (*D*) and 5 (*Mf*) decrease as SES increases. SES is fundamentally composed of, and confounded with, such dimensions as education, age, gender, and ethnicity. Thus, it is no surprise that SES must provide a basic life pattern within which to interpret the MMPI-2. As noted earlier, although the MMPI-2 normative group had a mean level of education of 15 years, compared with 8 years for the MMPI normals, education as a variable does not significantly affect profile elevation. The exception to this was the *K* scale, for both men and women, and Scale 5, surprisingly only for men. Between socioeconomic groups generally, it is interesting that major differences emerged on the validity scales and Scale 5. The group with the lowest education (part high school) had higher *F* (about eight *T*-score points) and *L* (about five *T*-score points) scores and lower *K* scores (about nine *T*-score points) when compared with the group with the highest education level.

Overall, despite individual differences for certain clinical and validity scales and moderator variables, multivariate regressions of age, education, gender, ethnicity, and occupation

> have shown that the percentage of variance accounted for by any of these variables does not exceed 10 percent for any MMPI-2 scale; the only exception to this generalization is Scale 5 (Masculinity-Femininity [*Mf*]) in which slightly over 50 percent of the variance is accounted for by gender.
>
> (Greene, 2011, p. 494)

Interpretive Steps

Preparing a written report is an important part of many psychologists' work. Yet it is a procedure that has typically received insufficient emphasis in graduate schools, has been little researched, is often perceived as tedious to do, and consequently is often poorly done (Ownby, 1987). Writing a report involves two steps of which the first is the most important because, if it is done poorly, the second step becomes irrelevant. First, the psychologist needs to organize the raw data so that inferences can be developed from it, allowing for an accurate conceptualization of the testee. The second step involves crafting these inferences into a report that is empirically grounded and yet creates a picture of the testee that is accurate and useful to the reader.

Initially, most psychologists have difficulty in integrating the vast array of MMPI-2 data. At times, it can be daunting. Demographic and referral question variables are the backdrop against which 10 clinical and 9 (or more) validity scales co-vary across a wide possible range of *T*-scores. When supplementary and content scales are added to the equation, sometimes yielding information that appears contradictory, it is little wonder that integrating the information in order to write an MMPI-2 report is seen as a complex and tedious task.

The following discussions include a step-by-step approach to interpreting an MMPI-2 profile as well as addressing actual report writing, outlining some common pitfalls and suggested remedies so that MMPI-2 reports are empirically grounded yet capture the psychological richness of the individual described.

The interpretive steps outlined here assume that the interpretation is being made "blind," that is, without the benefit of other test data or clinical and historical data. Although this goes against usual and ethical clinical practice, MMPI-2 data is isolated from other data in this chapter in order to better explicate the interpretive process without the reader being burdened by the additional task of integrating other test data. Usually, however, MMPI-2 data is part of a complete battery of psychological tests and/or life history data, interview(s), and presenting complaints and referral questions.

The interpretation of the profile should be preceded by the steps described in Chapter 2. These steps include noting the test-taking time of the testee, as well as examining the answer sheet for erasures, omissions, and double-marked answers. Additionally, it is important to administer the appropriate version of the test (e.g. language and form) and to provide the testee with the appropriate instructions. Proper scoring techniques and conditions for testing are also described in Chapter 2.

The actual interpretive task should begin with determining the setting in which the profile was administered. First, obtain basic demographic data, such as gender, age, ethnicity, and years of education, as well as referral question information. Is this a profile of a client from an inpatient setting or a prison setting? Is it a divorce/custody evaluation or a self-referred private practice individual? Is it a profile of an African American or someone from a different ethnic background? What is the client's age? Even when interpreting a profile "blindly," these demographic and referral information and moderator variables are necessary because they set the stage for the way a profile is interpreted. If the setting suggests that there is either no or great motivation toward positive or negative self-presentation, then the criteria for validity are affected. Greene (2011, Table 11.37, p. 512) provides a useful comparison table showing the effects of settings on the validity and clinical scales; the reader will be well served to examine the table. As described previously, there are no exact cut scores for determining validity. Rather, the clinician has to examine the entire profile, the setting, and any motivation to over- or understate problems in order to arrive at an interpretive understanding of the profile. For example, in a custody evaluation setting, an L score of T-65, an F score of T-40, and a K score of T-65 would suggest a self-favorable presentation and a possibility that the test is invalid. In a private practice setting, however, a client without motivation for a self-favorable presentation and who is presenting as out of touch with his or her feelings, may, in fact, generate scores accurately reflecting a rigid, overcontrolled, and inhibited individual. Other validity indicators, such as the Mp and Sd scales, could help in determining the interpretation of such a profile.

The second step in profile interpretation is to verify that the client has answered the items in a consistent and accurate manner. If $VRIN$ and $TRIN$ are not within the acceptable range, no further clinical interpretation is warranted, as the profile is invalid.

If, however, these scales indicate consistent responding and the elevations on the F, FB, $F(p)$, L, K, S, and other supplementary validity scales are in the acceptable range, then the profile is valid. Sometimes profiles are not clearly invalid, although they suggest a positive or negative self-presentation. In these cases, the clinician has to determine whether the distorted self-presentation is intentional (other deception) or unintentional (self-deception). In either case, the clinician has to determine if the distortion in self-presentation is extreme enough to invalidate the test. For example, in some cases, individuals may present themselves in a somewhat favorable or unfavorable light, but the test can still be interpreted, with some caveats. An example would be a profile in which the *K* score of a custody evaluation client is *T*-63 and the *L* score is *T*-60. In examining the supplementary validity scales, the psychologist may determine that the individual "put his or her best foot forward" so that the test may underestimate any psychopathology. Nevertheless, the clinician may decide that the profile can be cautiously interpreted, especially because most child custody litigants show elevated *L* and *K* scores (Bathurst, Gottfried, & Gottfried, 1997). In addition, the *F(p)*, *F – K* index, *Ds*, *Mp*, and *Sd* scales, among others, can be helpful in determining if the positive or negative self-presentation is a function of impression management or self-deception.

Sometimes profiles are consistent, but clearly the individual is presenting with an overly unfavorable self-presentation. In settings in which there is little reason for the client to malinger, cautiously interpreting an exaggerated profile can be useful, even if only to obtain an understanding of how the client wanted to portray him- or herself to the clinician. Exaggerated profiles can serve as a road map for a dialogue with the client. For example, the clinician might state,

> The way you answered the test suggests that you went out of your way to let me know how distressed you feel, even to the point of overemphasizing some of your difficulties or fears. Did you do that intentionally? What difficulties or feelings did you want to make sure I knew about?

However, as previously stated, no profile should be interpreted if the *VRIN* and *TRIN* scales show clear-cut inconsistency and possible confusion.

The third step in interpreting a profile is to examine each of the clinical scale scores individually, noting each *T*-score and determining if the profile is a recognizable code pattern. Chapter 2 describes in detail the method for coding a profile. Before mastery of the MMPI-2 has been achieved, it is difficult to recognize a code pattern and certainly difficult to know precisely what correlates are associated with a particular code pattern without looking it up. Once familiar with the MMPI-2, clinicians will find some codetypes easily recognizable. Usually two, three, or four of the clinical scales are clearly elevated above the rest and are at more or less the same level above a *T*-score of 65. In this case, turn to Chapter 6 and read the descriptors associated with a spike, two-, three-, or four-point code pattern.

The more distinctive (well-defined) and elevated the code pattern, the greater the confidence the clinician will have about the validity of the descriptive statements. For example, a profile in which Scales 2, 7, and 8 are all elevated at *T*-80, and no other scales are elevated above 65, is a distinct and elevated code pattern. A profile in which Scales 2, 3, 4, 6, 8, 9, and 0 are all elevated between a *T*-score of 64 and 66, is a moderately elevated and non-well-defined profile, making it more difficult to interpret. The higher the scale elevations, the more confidence the clinician can have that the descriptive statements are both true and salient.

Once a codetype is identified, refer to the Code-Pattern Look-Up Table and write down the descriptions associated with the pattern. Beginning clinicians are often needlessly cautious about making strong inferences from the code-pattern data. This often reflects distrust in the test and in the clinician's abilities. It is important to remember that it is very unlikely that an individual will obtain a valid elevated code pattern, particularly a well-defined one, and not exhibit the symptoms, complaints, and personality traits associated with that code pattern. For example, an individual obtaining a Scale 2 *T*-score of 90 *will* likely be depressed and *will* likely exhibit the symptoms of depression, even if they are not (and this would be very rare) consciously aware and complaining of feeling depressed.

Psychologists are often apprehensive about copying from the textbook the descriptions associated with the code pattern. There is no danger of being accused of plagiarism, however, in copying the descriptions out of a codetype table, as these descriptions are empirically and clinically derived; however, attempting to describe the individual in a different lexicon from that of the "cookbooks" might lead to interpretive errors. Some graduate students complain that writing reports this way leaves little room for clinical and interpretive skills. However, the skill of the clinician is needed in determining which descriptors fit for a particular individual and how to combine descriptors in complex profiles.

Common Code Patterns

Over the past seven decades of MMPI and MMPI-2 use, a number of commonly occurring scale configurations or code patterns have been described and have become part of the MMPI-2 lexicon. These commonly occurring *K*-corrected patterns are summarized here:

1 *Conversion V* (see Fig. 9.1). The Conversion V occurs when Scales 1 and 3 are greater than Scale 2 by eight or more *T*-score points and when Scales 1 and 3 are at least a *T*-score of 65. In the classic Conversion V, other scales may be elevated, but not as high as Scales 1 and 3. The Conversion V is a distinctive pattern with notable personality features (see 13/31 codes in Chapter 6).
2 *Paranoid Valley or Psychotic V* (see Fig. 9.2). This profile occurs when Scales 6 and 8 are equal to or greater than Scale 7 by eight or more *T*-score points and when Scales 6 and 8 are at or above a *T*-score of 65.
3 *Spike Profiles* (see Fig. 9.3). A spike profile occurs when any scale is over 65, and higher than all other scales by at least eight *T*-score points.
4 *Psychotic versus Neurotic Slope.* A vertical line through Scale 5 would divide the MMPI-2 profile roughly between the neurotic, left-hand side of the profile and the psychotic, right-hand side of the profile. A positive slope occurs when the psychotic scales are well elevated (above *T*-65) and clearly higher than the neurotic scales that are below 65 (see Fig. 9.4). This predicts a psychotic adjustment. A negative slope occurs when the left, or neurotic, side of the profile is well elevated and the psychotic scales are relatively low (see Fig. 9.5). This generally predicts a neurotic adjustment. No clinician, however, should assume that a profile indicates a psychotic or neurotic adjustment only by the slope of the profile. The neurotic- versus psychotic-slope concept is useful only as a starting point in a diagnostic decision process that asks the question, "Am I looking at a neurotic or a psychotic profile?" Definitively determining psychotic versus neurotic adjustment is accomplished by referring

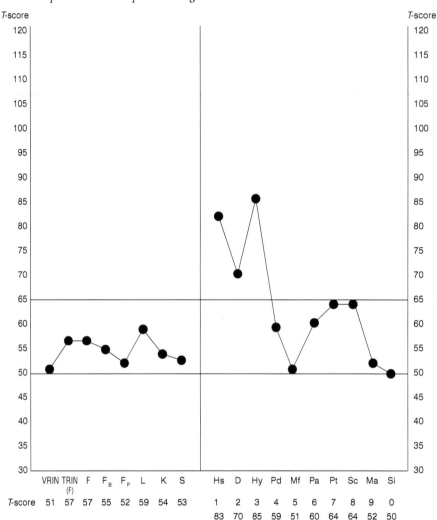

Figure 9.1 Conversion V

to the various scale elevations, scale configurations, the Goldberg index, and the critical items, with all aspects being viewed within the context of the person's behavior and history.

5   *Passive-aggressive V* (see Fig. 9.6). This profile occurs when Scales 4 and 6 are elevated at or above *T*-65 and Scale 5 is close to or below *T*-50. The profile suggests a passive-aggressive personality disorder or trait disturbance. Because of its shape, it is

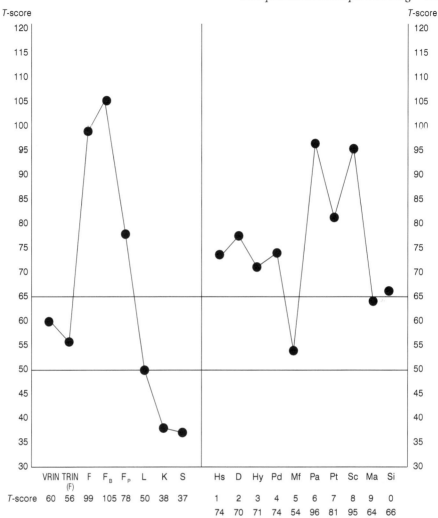

T-score

	VRIN	TRIN (F)	F	F_B	F_P	L	K	S		Hs	D	Hy	Pd	Mf	Pa	Pt	Sc	Ma	Si
T-score	60	56	99	105	78	50	38	37		1	2	3	4	5	6	7	8	9	0
										74	70	71	74	54	96	81	95	64	66

Figure 9.2 Paranoid Valley or Psychotic V

often called the passive-aggressive V. The lower the Scale 5, the more passively self-defeating is the woman. The passive-aggressive V is associated with women because the low Scale 5 score often predicts passivity. In the presence of both paranoid and aggressive traits (46/64), this passivity becomes passive aggression and wounded pride. Men who score high on Scales 4 and 6, as well as Scale 5, are also often seen as passive-aggressive, angry, and hypersensitive; however, the elevations of Scales 4, 5, and 6 do not lend themselves to the characterization of the 46/64 V women

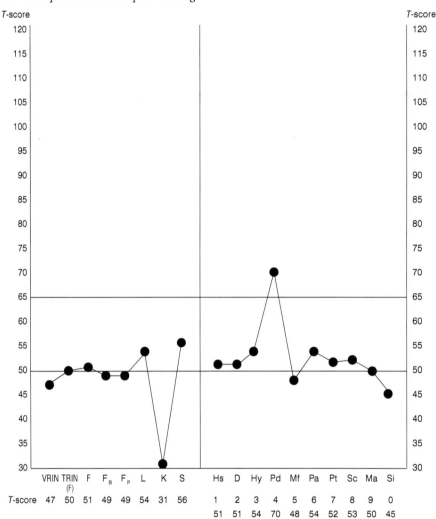

Figure 9.3 Spike 4 Profile

Source: MMPI-2 Validity and Clinical Scales Profile. Adapted from the *MMPI-2 (Minnesota Multiphasic Personality Inventory-2) Manual for Administration, Scoring, and Interpretation, Revised Edition.* Copyright © 2001 by the Regents of the University of Minnesota. All rights reserved. Used by permission of the University of Minnesota Press. "MMPI" and "Minnesota Multiphasic Personality Inventory" are registered trademarks owned by the Regents of the University of Minnesota.

because Scale 5 is elevated in men. Men who do obtain a 46/64 V pattern are likely to be aggressive, paranoid, and possibly paranoid schizophrenic. Scale 5 in the "masculine" direction (low) would increase the likelihood of acting out, whereas high Scale 5 scores in men would have the effect of inhibiting overt acting out.

6   *K+ Profile* (see Fig. 9.7). In this configuration, no clinical scales are above a *T*-score of 65, and six or more clinical scales are below or equal to a *T*-score of 56. In the *K*+ profile, the *L* and *K* scales are greater than the *F* scale. The *K* scale is also higher than

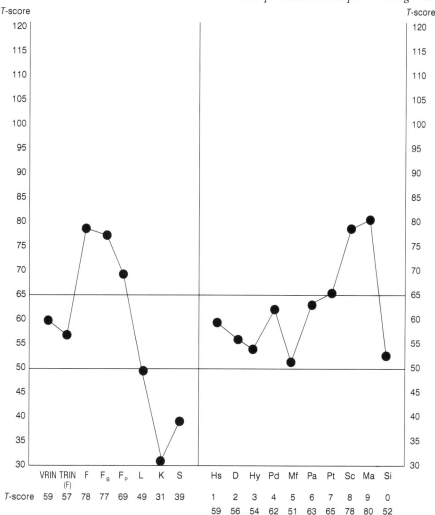

Figure 9.4 Positive or Psychotic Slope

the *F* scale by at least five *T*-score points and is *above* a *T*-score of 60. The *K+* profile was identified by Marks et al. (1974) in an inpatient psychotic population only. In other words, this profile occurred in patients whose test results were considered a false negative (test miss). The inpatient responder had gone through a minefield of test items and somehow managed to avoid raising a red flag on any of the clinical scales. In an inpatient setting, Marks et al. found that 48 percent of these responders were psychotic. Thus, if a *K+* profile is obtained by a person in an inpatient setting,

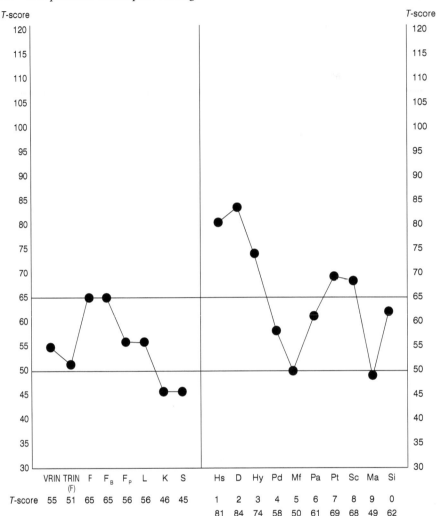

Figure 9.5 Negative or Neurotic Slope

the clinician should describe the client's failure to report psychological pain and distress with the likelihood of overcontrol, emotional shutdown, and conscious or unconscious denial of problems. This information should be integrated with what is known about the patient's history, behavioral observations, or other psychological test data. A possible way of dealing with a *K*+ profile is to ask clients to retake the test, answering the test from the perspective of how they feel at their worst. Psychologists are urged to remember that the *K*+ profile occurs in many different settings and in

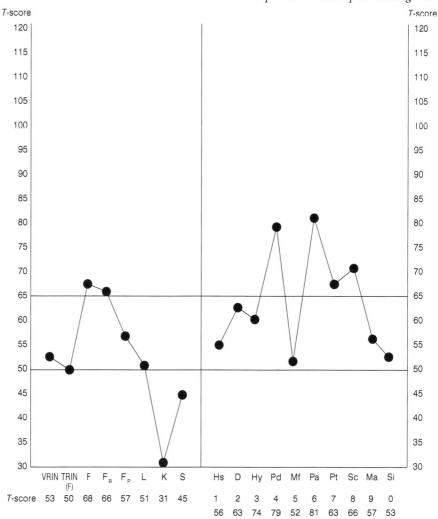

Figure 9.6 Passive-Aggressive V

both men and women. However, the *K+* correlates were derived specifically within a psychiatric inpatient setting; thus, caution should be used in applying these correlates to populations other than psychiatric inpatients (Duckworth & Barley, 1988). This kind of defensive profile without clinical elevations also often occurs in private practice settings and may suggest a well-adjusted, although somewhat overcontrolled individual. The supplemental validity scales such as *Mp, Sd,* and *SES* could assist in determining whether the profile is intentionally or unintentionally self-favorable.

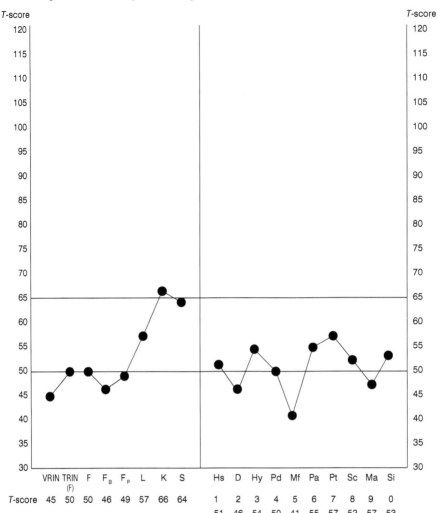

Figure 9.7 K+ Profile

7   *Floating Profile* (see Fig. 9.8). In this profile, all or most scores on Scales 1–9 are equal to or exceed a *T*-score of 65 and are usually accompanied by an extreme elevation on the *F* scale (Friedman, Webb, & Lewak, 1989; Newmark, Chassin, Evans, & Gentry, 1984). This profile is difficult to interpret, as no well-defined code pattern emerges for easy interpretation. Of all the code patterns, this is the code with the lowest congruence with original MMPI profiles. The two highest

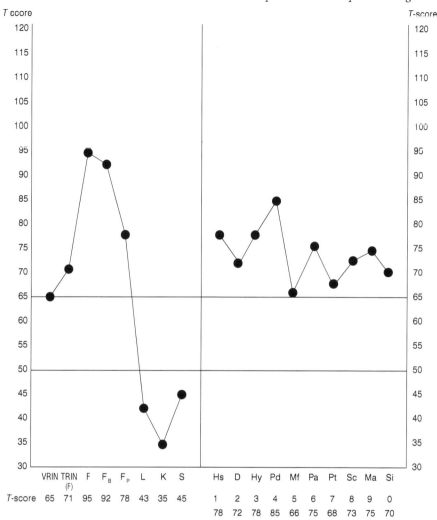

Figure 9.8 Floating Profile

scales are highly likely to be quite different when translated back to an original MMPI. The interpretive process involves breaking down this complex profile into two-point code patterns, which lend themselves to being interpreted (see section in this chapter – Interpretation of "Complex Profiles"). It is likely, although not certain, that a significant number of floating profiles are generally obtained by patients with Borderline Personality Disorder. Individuals who obtain this profile experience a great deal of tension and turmoil, but no predominant defensive pattern emerges. Rather, they experience moodiness, reflected in the elevations of Scales 2 and 9; anxiety, tension, and self-doubt, reflected in the elevations of Scales 7, 8, and 9; and the development of somatic and repressive defenses, reflected in the elevations of Scales 1, 2, and 3; as well as episodic acting out, reflected in the elevations of Scales 4, 8, and 9. The interpretation of the content and supplementary scales, as well as the critical items, will hone the interpretation of these complex profiles.

Code Patterns, Elevation, and Additional Scales

The code pattern (27, 49, etc.) defines a particular set of behaviors, symptoms, and experiential domains, irrespective of elevation. For example, people obtaining their highest scores on Scales 4 and 9 will generally be alienated from society, impulsive, and superficially charming but with a poor frustration tolerance. These characteristics will be fundamentally consistent across all 49 profile elevations, whether T-scores are between 80 and 90 or between 65 and 80, and are even mildly applicable for T-score elevations between 59 and 65. In other words, the personality picture is basically similar for all 49s. However, the elevation of a profile predicts the intensity and severity of the symptoms. The higher the profile, the more severe the symptoms and the more a person's thoughts, feelings, and behaviors are likely to be dominated by the psychopathology predicted by the particular code pattern. For example, within the normal range (e.g. Scales 4 and 9 at T-60), the 49 code suggests some propensity for impulsivity and the probability of an energetic and potentially charming individual who exhibits some frustration intolerance and occasional difficulties with intimacy. However, many of these traits will be well within the normal range and will be exhibited more as personality traits rather than as psychopathology.

In another example, a 27 code above T-80 is quite likely to reflect a person who is experiencing a severe, agitated depression that thoroughly permeates daily life. Another person with a 27 profile at T-65 will likely show periods of despondency, agitation, and depression, followed by periods of feeling less depressed and anxious. Persons with a T-score elevation at 60 on Scales 2 and 7 will generally show good adjustment, with only occasional periods of agitation, anxiety, and sad moods. Their personality style will likely be that of a prone-to-worry, responsible person.

In each case, the personality traits are the same, although the elevation predicts the intensity, duration, and pervasiveness of symptoms and pathological traits. In general, we suggest that a profile elevation between 60 and 64 predicts a mild disturbance, profiles between 65 and 74 predict a moderate disturbance, and profiles over 75 predict a severe disturbance. When a profile is severely elevated, a code pattern may be less important than just the elevation. For example, for someone who obtains a T-score of 90 on Scale 2, a prediction of depression with all the classic symptoms of depression will fit, regardless of whether the code pattern is a 27, a 29, or a 28. However, elevations on the other scales help greatly in defining the kind of depression (anxious depression [27/72], psychotic depression [28/82], and so on).

Interpretations in the normal range of 50 to 59 rely less on the elevation of any particular scale and much more on the basis of code pattern and content and supplementary scales (see Chapters 7 and 8). For example, a 27 profile at *T*-60 will predict a person who is prone to worry, experience anxiety over responsibility, be seen as responsible, and cautious about taking risks; however, a diagnosis of depression is not certain, although possible. In other words, profiles in the normal range can be understood as identifying personality traits rather than psychopathology. Duckworth and Barley's (1988) caution, however, is noteworthy. Although within normal limits profiles may often correctly identify a healthy person, such profiles can often generate false negatives (i.e. overlook pathology), particularly within the following populations: (a) psychiatric inpatients whose *K* scores are greater than *T*-65, (b) inmates, and (c) participants with observed psychopathology but who lack insight or accurate self-appraisal. As a result, profiles of persons in psychiatric settings often need to be interpreted with caution if the validity scales suggest a self-favorable response set. In these situations, the interplay of defensiveness and psychopathology needs to be carefully teased out because the person's psychopathology may be masked by defensive overcontrol, denial, and a lack of appropriate emotional outlets, factors represented by the elevation on the validity scales. For example, a profile with both Scales 9 and 6 elevated at *T*-64, with the *L* and *K* scales near *T*-60, could reflect a controlled, rigid, tense, and brittle person who might become quite hostile, agitated, and even paranoid under stress. The moderate elevations on the validity scales add more overcontrol to an already overcontrolled and brittle 69 profile. Butcher (1990b) suggested that if all the clinical scales are between *T*-scores of 60 and 64, content scales may be better sources of personality descriptions than are the clinical scales. Usually, however, information from all the scales is integrated in order to form a rich personality picture.

Usually, the content scale data confirm the code-pattern data and sharpen the interpretation. For example, a 278 profile might also exhibit elevations on the Anxiety (*ANX*) and Depression (*DEP*) content scales. Also, one would expect the Low Self-Esteem (*LSE*) and Work Interference (*WRK*) scales to be elevated, confirming the picture of a depressed, anxious, ruminative, procrastinating, and low-self-esteem individual; a picture already painted by the 278 code. If in this hypothetical example, the *DEP* and *LSE* scales were not elevated, the description would change significantly. The 278 depression might be less characterological, more situational, less angry, and with a better prognosis. Although there is not much information available about the meaning of low clinical scale scores, or the lowest scale in a code pattern, these scores can also be a source of rich interpretive material (see Chapter 5). For example, an individual with a spike 2 code (e.g. Scale 2 at *T*-85) is likely experiencing a severe depression. If Scale 9 were also elevated at *T*-65, the depression would exhibit different characteristics than if Scale 9 were elevated at *T*-40. In the first example, the moderate elevation on Scale 9 would predict agitation, moodiness, and irritability, whereas in the second example, the elevation on Scale 9 at *T*-40 would predict a more collapsed depression with low energy, low motivation, and less agitation. In another example, a 489 elevated code could be seen as more pathological if Scale 7 were below *T*-50 than if Scale 7 were coded fourth, giving a 4897 profile. The low score on Scale 7 in such a code pattern would suggest that the callous, angry sociopathy of the 489 profile was unhindered by any anxiety, remorse, or guilt. Finally, the task is to look at critical items, which usually confirms the hypotheses already generated (see Chapter 7). Critical items can also highlight aspects of statements already made about the individual. For example, an individual who is severely depressed and angry (24 code) might also be elevated on the *MAC–R* scale. The clinician may make a statement about the susceptibility of the individual to substance abuse and may then draw attention to this problem by quoting from the critical items: "The individual's response to Item 489, admitting a drug/alcohol problem suggests a careful evaluation of his or her current alcohol use." This should also be considered for suicide items or mental confusion items.

The next task is to organize the inferences into a written format that flows from paragraph to paragraph and captures the essential qualities of the test taker. Graduate students and clinicians often have trouble with report writing because they have difficulty conceptualizing the individual and organizing the inferences about him or her in a way that integrates contradictory descriptors to paint a realistic and accurate picture of the person. Once this is done well, writing the report is not difficult.

Organizing the Data

The next step in interpreting an MMPI-2 is to examine and organize the data gathered from the validity, clinical, content, and supplementary scales (and subscales), the code patterns, and the low-point elevations.

A useful organizational framework for MMPI-2 data was developed by Nichols and Greene (1995) and is entitled, *MMPI-2 Structural Summary: Interpretive manual*. It was rationally and statistically constructed and is intended to expedite interpretational report writing. Nichols and Greene (1995, p. 3) explain the rationale of their tool:

> The Structural Summary facilitates the efficient review of MMPI-2 findings by providing a set of clinically relevant categories into which disparate names, types, and origins can be sorted. This organization maximizes the extraction of test information, while minimizing the amount of time required to do so. It achieves these goals by enabling the most salient factors in test performance to stand out, allowing a rapid appraisal of the robustness of trends in MMPI-2 data, and by following a sequence of topics that facilitate the preparation of interpretive reports.

One distinct advantage in using this tool is that regardless of whether a profile has a well or poorly defined codetype, the Summary will tend to highlight trends in the MMPI-2 protocol that may be of clinical relevance. It can be daunting for the clinician when inspecting an array of scale scores to make sense out of data that are inconsistent, such as having a high score on one depression measure, but a low score on another. The number of scale and indices measuring similar dimensions is most efficiently organized by creating categories reflecting dimensions of variation within the total item pool; in this fashion, measures possessing relatively high intercorrelations can be readily inspected for convergence or divergence, allowing for more accurate interpretive inferences.

The six general categories under which the clinician completes the scores consist of the following: test-taking attitudes, factor scales, moods, cognitions, interpersonal relations, and other problem areas (i.e. substance abuse, sleep disturbances). Each category has from 2 to 12 subsections, with some containing further subdivisions. For example, Depression has a category called Depressed Mood/Dysphoria, under which is listed three Harris-Lingoes Subscales: *D1*, *D5*, and *Pa2*. Another category, Vegetative Signs, provides recording opportunities for four Harris-Lingoes Subscales (*D3*, *Hy3*, *D2*, *and Ma2*), one content scale (*IIEA*), and two areas of critical items (sexual concerns and sleep disturbance). The reader is encouraged to inspect an example of the Structural Summary in Chapter 12 of this text where a case is presented. When engaging in clinical or forensic work, using the Nichols and Greene Structural Summary is quite helpful— even in further understanding automated computerized reports—with or without narrative interpretations.

Although most of the information collected will be consistent and fit together using the Structured Summary, some of it will appear contradictory. For example, the clinician may have determined that a particular profile is valid, although slightly self-favorable; that the setting from which it came would predict some self-favorable responding (e.g. a custody setting); and that the individual has significant scale elevations (e.g. on Scales 4 and 9 at *T*-65). Having identified in the Code-Pattern Look-Up Table some descriptors for a 49 profile, the clinician would likely draw inferences that the profile is that of someone who is generally energetic, positive, and superficially charming, although with some impulse problems and some difficulties with intimacy. If in this hypothetical case there was also an elevation on Scale 7 at *T*-64 and an elevation on Scale 2 at *T*-60, the information from the elevations on Scales 7 and 2 would appear contradictory to the earlier hypothesis generated for a 49 code. Integrating the contradictory data is difficult, and some clinicians are tempted to ignore it and write a report based only on the code-pattern data (in this case, the 49 data). A report written this way will be only partially accurate and be lacking in richness and complexity. The secondary elevations on Scales 7 and 2 would predict guilt, anxiety, and angry remorse over acting out behavior, and perhaps obsessive ruminations about how to avoid acting out, but little long-term behavioral change.

Some computer-generated reports use only code-pattern information, that is, information generated from the highest 1, 2, or 3 scales. Information from other scales that are elevated are then reported using single-scale descriptors, and often no attempt is made to integrate them into the body of the code-pattern description. For example, an individual with significant scale elevations on Scales 4 and 9 would be described using 49 descriptors. Statements associated with the mild elevations on Scales 2 and 7, suggesting that the individual had some proneness to worry, to be somewhat anxious and guilty, and for episodic "down" times, would be indicated later in the report but not integrated into the personality picture. The clinician reading the computer-generated report would be responsible for determining how these statements fit into the overall profile. Thus, it is the skill of the clinician to then integrate this contradictory data into a personality picture.

After the clinician has determined profile validity and written down a series of descriptors generated from the code-pattern elevations and other elevated clinical scales and low-point scales, the next step is to examine the content and supplementary scales, as well as the Subtle–Obvious and Harris-Lingoes subscales. Usually the data from all of the extra scales confirms the inferences generated from the code pattern. In some cases, however, the material is contradictory and these contradictions have to be understood and integrated into the assessment.

In selecting the appropriate descriptors for a particular code, there are several issues to consider. In many cases, the order of elevation of a two- or three-point code is not critical. For example, it is not critical whether the profile is a 13 or 31 code pattern.

Although it is true, for example, that a 31 individual may exhibit more of the hysterical symptoms and less of the obviously negativistic and complaining attributes of the 13 individual, for most reports the order of the elevation is not critical. In other cases, however, the differences in elevations are very relevant, as in a 78 code versus an 87 code, or a 34 versus a 43 code. A second issue in interpreting code patterns involves elevation. Most interpretive guides provide descriptors only for profiles above *T*-65 but do not distinguish between various elevations above *T*-65. It is up to the clinician to make appropriate adjustments in descriptors for the level of severity of disturbance. The more elevated the profile, usually the more severe, and sometimes acute, the disturbance.

Writing the Report

In beginning to use the MMPI-2, most clinicians have difficulty integrating the personality descriptors into a coherent report. A common error is to list all the adjectives associated with elevations in the code pattern and single scales. Reports written in this manner present a string of disconnected adjectives, describing symptoms and behaviors that can confuse the reader. For example, a report based on the code pattern 278, all at *T*-80 and with Scales 4 and 9 elevated at *T*-75, might read as follows: "This individual is likely anxious, ruminative, depressed, and with low self-esteem (278 descriptor). He or she may also be hypomanic, acting out, and impulsive (94 descriptor)." Although these adjectives describe the individual, they are not integrated into a coherent picture and may be confusing. A more integrated description would describe an anxious, ruminative, depressed individual who also experiences mood swings and occasional acting out in self-defeating ways. The skill of the clinician is to understand, for example, how Scale 4 elevations in the context of 278 elevations predict self-defeating, negativistic behaviors and attitudes and how Scale 9 elevations predict moodiness and agitation, as well as increase the likelihood of impulsive, self-destructive behavior (as the depression and anger are energized by Scale 9).

When writing a report, begin by summarizing the *essence* of the profile. With what symptoms will the client present? Which symptoms or behaviors will be "glaring"? For example, a profile with the highest elevation on Scale 9 at *T*-90 will predict hypomania. The symptoms will likely be obvious. Is this a profile that indicates primarily a mood disturbance? If so, what kind of disturbance? On the other hand, is it a profile of an acting-out, rebellious, angry person? If so, what kind of acting-out behaviors are suggested (sexual, passive-aggressive, self-defeating, etc.)? Is it a profile of a confused and paranoid person? If so, is it a transitory psychotic disturbance or a longstanding one? How will the person's conflicts or personality characteristics likely manifest themselves in various situations, such as on the job or with family? What is it about the person's characteristics that prevent that person from achieving a resolution of the problems? The report should describe the code pattern before the remaining single-scale high-point and low-point information is discussed.

The following section is meant as a guide to beginning a report, often the most difficult part for psychologists. These statements are designed as *report openers*, which set the stage for the rest of the report. The first paragraph of the report should discuss the consistency and test-taking attitude and resulting validity of the profile. The second paragraph of the report should open with a statement describing the client's primary symptoms and complaints. The following descriptors/symptoms have been written as though the profile was at least moderately elevated (*T*-65). Modifications in some of the language would be needed if the profiles were more or less elevated, even though the basic characteristics would remain the same.

Guidelines for Beginning a Report

Code pattern: Spike 1	Descriptors/Symptoms
Scale 1 elevated above *T*-65	1. Somatizing
All other scales below *Hs*	2. Fearful
	3. Immature
	4. Passive
	5. Psychologically unsophisticated

This is essentially a profile reflecting a [mild/moderate/severe] somatizing disorder in a dependent, fearful, immature, and passive individual with low psychological sophistication. Typically these individuals complain of [list symptoms]. Behaviors associated with this profile are [list behaviors]. Traits associated with this profile are [list traits].

Code pattern: 12	Descriptors/Symptoms
Scale 1 highest:	1. Somatizing
Scale 2 added	2. Depressed
	3. Despondent
	4. Dependent
	5. Passive
	6. Moody

The profile suggests a [mild/moderate/severe] somatizing depression in a passive, dependent, and moody individual. Other symptoms associated with this profile are [list symptoms]. Behaviors associated with this profile are [list behaviors]. Traits associated with this profile are [list traits].

Code pattern: 13	Descriptors/Symptoms
Scale 1 highest	1. Hysterical/somatizing
Scale 3 added	2. Overcontrolled
	3. Psychologically naïve
	4. Dependent
	5. "La belle indifference"

This profile, sometimes called la belle indifference, reflects a [mild/moderate/severe] somatizing disorder in an overcontrolled, psychologically naïve, and dependent personality. Other symptoms frequently associated with this profile are [list symptoms].

Behaviors associated with this profile are [list behaviors]. Traits associated with this profile are [list traits].

Code pattern: 14	Descriptors/Symptoms
Scale 1 highest	1. Dependent
Scale 4 added	2. Manipulative
	3. Immature
	4. Passive-aggressive

The profile reflects a [mild/moderate/severe] disorder in a somatizing, dependent, manipulative, immature, passive-aggressive individual. Other symptoms often associated with the profile are [list symptoms]. Behaviors associated with this profile are [list behaviors]. Traits associated with this profile are [list traits].

Code pattern: 16	Descriptors/Symptoms
Scale 1 highest	1. Somatizing
Scale 6 added	2. Paranoid
	3. Suspicious
	4. Angry
	5. Blaming, externalizing

This is essentially a [mild/moderate/severe] somatizing disorder in a paranoid, suspicious, angry, and externalizing individual. Such persons typically show other symptoms such as [list symptoms]. Other symptoms often associated with the profile are [list symptoms]. Behaviors associated with this profile are [list behaviors]. Traits associated with this profile are [list traits].

Code pattern: 17	Descriptors/Symptoms
Scale 1 highest	1. Somatizing
Scale 7 added	2. Anxious
	3. Tense
	4. Hyper-responsible
	5. Preoccupied
	6. Obsessive–compulsive traits and behaviors

The profile suggests a [mild/moderate/severe] somatizing disorder in an anxious, tense, preoccupied, and obsessive–compulsive individual. Other symptoms typically associated with such profiles are [list symptoms]. Behaviors associated with this profile are [list behaviors]. Traits associated with this profile are [list traits].

Code pattern. 18	Descriptors/Symptoms
Scale 1 highest	1. Somatic
Scale 8 added	2. Confused
	3. Schizoid
	4. Immature
	5. Possibly psychotic

The profile suggests a [mild/moderate/severe] somatizing disorder in a confused, immature, and schizoid individual. This person will likely show additional symptoms such as [list symptoms]. Behaviors associated with this profile are [list behaviors]. Traits associated with this profile are [list traits].

Code pattern: 19/91	Descriptors/Symptoms
Scale 1 highest	1. Somatizing
Scale 9 added	2. Tense
	3. Driven
	4. Explosive

This profile suggests a [mild/moderate/severe] somatizing disorder in a tense, driven, hypomanic personality. Other symptoms often associated with such profiles are [list symptoms]. Behaviors associated with this profile are [list behaviors]. Traits associated with this profile are [list traits].

Code pattern: Spike 2	Descriptors/Symptoms
Scale 2 highest and above *T*-65	1. Vegetative symptoms [poor sleep, low sex drive, low energy]
All other scales below Scale 2	2. Depression
	3. Guilt
	4. Anxiety
	5. Low self-esteem

The profile suggests a [mild/moderate/severe] depression with vegetative symptoms of depression, disturbance in mood, feelings of guilt, anxiety, and low self-esteem. Other symptoms often associated with such profiles are [list symptoms]. Behaviors associated with this profile are [list behaviors]. Traits associated with this profile are [list traits].

Code pattern: 23	Descriptors/Symptoms
Scale 2 highest and above *T*-65	1. Depression
Scale 3 above *T*-65	2. Somatic symptoms
	3. Low psychological-mindedness
	4. Immaturity
	5. Secondary gain
	6. Guilt inducing and self-sacrificing

The profile suggests a [mild/moderate/severe] depression in a dependent, somatizing, and immature individual. Other symptoms often associated with this profile are [list symptoms]. Behaviors associated with this profile are [list behaviors]. Traits associated with this profile are [list traits].

Code pattern: 24	Descriptors/Symptoms
Scale 2 highest and above *T*-65	1. Angry
Scale 4 in second place and above *T*-65	2. Self-defeating
	3. Suicidal
	4. Dependent
	5. Manipulative

The profile suggests a [mild/moderate/severe] depression in an angry, self-defeating, dependent, and possibly suicidal individual. Other symptoms often associated with this profile are [list symptoms]. Behaviors associated with this profile are [list behaviors]. Traits associated with this profile are [list traits].

Code pattern: 25	Descriptors/Symptoms
Scale 2 highest and above *T*-65	1. Passive
Scale 5 above *T*-65 for men, below *T*-40 for women	2. Dependent
	3. Hypersensitive
	4. Indecisive

The profile suggests a [mild/moderate/severe] depression in a passive, dependent, and hypersensitive individual. Other symptoms also likely are [list symptoms]. Behaviors associated with this profile are [list behaviors]. Traits associated with this profile are [list traits].

Code pattern: 26	Descriptors/Symptoms
Scale 2 highest and above *T*-65	1. Depressed
Scale 6 in second place and above *T*-65	2. Paranoid
	3. Externalizing
	4. Resentful
	5. Bitter

The profile suggests a [mild/moderate/severe] depression in a hypersensitive, potentially paranoid, and externalizing individual. Other symptoms often associated with this profile are [list symptoms]. Behaviors associated with this profile are [list behaviors]. Traits associated with this profile are [list traits].

Code pattern: 27	Descriptors/Symptoms
Scale 2 highest and above *T*-65	1. Anxiety
Scale 7 in second place and above *T*-65	2. Depression
	3. Guilt
	4. Low self-esteem
	5. Passiveness

This profile suggests a [mild/moderate/severe] anxious depression in a passive individual who is guilt-ridden and has low self-esteem. Other symptoms often associated with this profile are [list symptoms]. Behaviors associated with this profile are [list behaviors]. Traits associated with this profile are [list traits].

Code pattern: 28	Descriptors/Symptoms
Scale 2 highest and above *T*-65	1. Depression
Scale 8 in second place and above *T*-65	2. Anxiety
	3. Agitation
	4. Withdrawal
	5. Inefficiency
	6. Fears of emotional involvement
	7. Possibly psychotic depression

This profile suggests a [mild/moderate/severe] depression in an anxious, withdrawn individual who is likely to complain of memory and concentration difficulties and have problems with general efficiency. Other symptoms often associated with this profile are [list symptoms]. Behaviors associated with this profile are [list behaviors]. Traits associated with this profile are [list traits].

Code pattern: 29	Descriptors/Symptoms
Scale 2 above *T*-65	1. Labile
Scale 9 in second place and above *T*-65	2. Explosive
	3. Moody
	4. Irritable
	5. Mood disorder

This profile suggests a [mild/moderate/severe] affective disorder with irritability, lability, and possible explosiveness. Other symptoms often associated with this profile are [list symptoms]. Behaviors associated with this profile are [list behaviors]. Traits associated with this profile are [list traits].

Code pattern: Spike 3	Descriptors/Symptoms
Scale 3 above *T*-65	1. Naïve
All other scales below *T*-65	2. Dependent
	3. Somatizing
	4. Immature
	5. Self-centered
	6. Lacking in insight

The profile suggests a [mild/moderate/severe] somatizing disorder in an immature, psychologically naïve, dependent person. Other symptoms often associated with this pattern are [list symptoms]. Behaviors associated with this profile are [list behaviors]. Traits associated with this profile are [list traits].

Code pattern: 34	Descriptors/Symptoms
Scale 3 highest and above *T*-65	1. Overcontrolled
Scale 4 in second place and above *T*-65	2. Role playing
	3. Manipulative, impulsive
	4. Explosive
	5. Lacking in insight

The profile suggests a [mild/moderate/severe] overcontrolled personality disorder in a person who is likely to present as conforming and cooperative but will exhibit episodic, impulsive, and, at times, explosive episodes. Other symptoms often associated with this profile are [list symptoms]. Behaviors associated with this profile are [list behaviors]. Traits associated with this profile are [list traits].

Code pattern: 36	Descriptors/Symptoms
Scale 3 highest and above *T*-65	1. Paranoid
Scale 6 in second place and above *T*-65	2. Controlled
	3. Conforming
	4. Projecting
	5. Denying

The profile suggests a [mild/moderate/severe] paranoid disorder in an individual who is typically overcontrolled, inhibited, disavowing, and who uses projection as a primary defense mechanism. Other symptoms often associated with this profile are [list symptoms]. Behaviors associated with this profile are [list behaviors]. Traits associated with this profile are [list traits].

Code pattern: 37	Descriptors/Symptoms
Scale 3 highest and above *T*-65	1. Overcontrolled
Scale 7 in second place and above *T*-65	2. Tense
	3. Anxious
	4. Passive
	5. Ingratiating
	6. Somatizing

The profile suggests a [mild/moderate/severe] anxiety disorder in a denying, psychologically naïve, anxious, and ingratiating individual who is likely to develop hysterical symptomatology in response to psychological stress. Other symptoms often associated with this profile are [list symptoms]. Behaviors associated with this profile are [list behaviors]. Traits associated with this profile are [list traits].

Code pattern: 38	Descriptors/Symptoms
Scale 3 highest and above *T*-65	1. Confused
Scale 8 in second place and above *T*-65	2. Sexually preoccupied
	3. Possible hallucinations
	4. Dissociative episodes

The profile suggests a [mild/moderate/severe] disturbance in an individual who will present as confused, sexually preoccupied, and dissociative and who may exhibit psychotic episodes. Other symptoms often associated with this profile are [list symptoms]. Behaviors associated with this profile are [list behaviors]. Traits associated with this profile are [list traits].

Code pattern: 39	Descriptors/Symptoms
Scale 3 highest and above *T*-65	1. Hypomanic
Scale 9 above *T*-65	2. Overcontrolled
	3. Demanding
	4. Attention seeking
	5. Somatizing

The profile suggests a [mild/moderate/severe] hypomanic disturbance in an overcontrolled, demanding, approval-seeking, and somatizing individual. Such individuals are likely to exhibit explosive episodes whenever their goal-directed behavior is blocked. Other symptoms frequently associated with this profile are [list symptoms]. Behaviors associated with this profile are [list behaviors]. Traits associated with this profile are [list traits].

Code pattern: Spike 4	Descriptors/Symptoms
Scale 4 highest and above *T*-65	1. Immature
No other scales elevated	2. Passively dependent
	3. Manipulatively dependent
	4. Angry
	5. Can act out [depends on other scales]

The profile suggests a [mild/moderate/severe] personality disorder in an immature, passively dependent, manipulative, and angry individual.

Code pattern: 45 (men)	Descriptors/Symptoms
Scale 4 highest and above *T*-65	1. Passive
Scale 5 in second place and above *T*-65	2. Dependent
	3. Manipulative
	4. Potential sexual dysfunction
	5. Passive-aggressive

The profile suggests a [mild/moderate/severe] disorder in an immature and dependent individual who is likely to have conflicts with unresolved dependency needs and will exhibit sexual and intimacy problems. The likelihood of a personality disorder should be considered. Other symptoms frequently associated with this profile are [list symptoms]. Behaviors associated with this profile are [list behaviors]. Traits associated with this profile are [list traits].

Code pattern: 45 (women)	Descriptors/Symptoms
Scale 4 highest and above *T*-65	1. Aggressive
Scale 5 in second place and above *T*-65	2. Acting out
	3. Manipulative
	4. Sexual acting-out problems

This is a rare profile in women. Women with this elevation are aggressive, act out, resist being controlled, and tend to have intimacy and sexual problems. Other symptoms frequently associated with this profile are [list symptoms]. Behaviors associated with this profile are [list behaviors]. Traits associated with this profile are [list traits].

Code pattern: 46	Descriptors/Symptoms
Scale 4 highest and above *T*-65	1. Angry
Scale 6 in second place and above *T*-65	2. Passive-aggressive
	3. Suspicious
	4. "Victim" and "chip on the shoulder" attitude
	5. Argumentative

The profile suggests a [mild/moderate/severe] disorder. Typically these individuals are angry, suspicious, and argumentative and maintain a "chip on the shoulder" attitude toward others. Typically, their lifestyle is that of a "victim," and they tend to be vigilant for any demands made on them. Other symptoms frequently associated with this profile are [list symptoms]. Behaviors associated with this profile are [list behaviors]. Traits associated with this profile are [list traits].

Code pattern: 47	Descriptors/Symptoms
Scale 4 highest and above *T*-65	1. Low frustration tolerance
Scale 7 in second place and above *T*-65	2. Impulsive tension reduction
	3. Anxiety that leads to acting out
	4. Immaturity
	5. Dependent

The profile suggests a [mild/moderate/severe] personality disorder. Typical symptoms associated with this profile are a low frustration tolerance and a tendency to impulsively reduce anxiety and frustration through acting out behavior. Manipulatively dependent, they present with cyclical patterns of acting out. Other symptoms associated with this profile are [list symptoms]. Behaviors associated with this profile are [list behaviors]. Traits associated with this profile are [list traits].

Code pattern: 48	Descriptors/Symptoms
Scale 4 highest and above *T*-65	1. Impulsive
Scale 8 in second place and above *T*-65	2. Alienated
	3. Distrustful
	4. Lacking in empathy
	5. Poor judgment and confusion
	6. Drug and alcohol problems
	7. Sexual aggression

The profile suggests a [mild/moderate/severe] personality disorder—or possibly a psychotic diagnosis—in an alienated, acting-out, angry individual who exhibits empathy deficits and is inclined to fuse sexuality and aggression. Other symptoms often associated with this profile are [list symptoms]. Behaviors associated with this profile are [list behaviors]. Traits associated with this profile are [list traits].

Code pattern: 49	Descriptors/Symptoms
Scale 4 highest and above *T*-65	1. Superficially charming
Scale 9 in second place and above *T*-65	2. Impulsive
	3. Acting out
	4. Self-centered
	5. Manipulative

The profile suggests a [mild/moderate/severe] personality disorder. Typically, these individuals are superficially charming, although often self-centered, impulsive, manipulative, and capable of acting out. Other symptoms often associated with this profile are [list symptoms]. Behaviors associated with this profile are [list behaviors]. Traits associated with this profile are [list traits].

Code pattern: Spike 6	Descriptors/Symptoms
Scale 6 highest and above *T*-65	1. Suspicious
No other scales above *T*-65	2. Overly sensitive
	3. Self-righteous
	4. Paranoid

The profile reflects a [mild/moderate/severe] elevation and suggests a paranoid individual who is likely to present as guarded, suspicious, and overly sensitive and may exhibit overt and subtle paranoid symptomatology. Other symptoms often associated with this profile are [list symptoms]. Behaviors associated with this profile are [list behaviors]. Traits associated with this profile are [list traits].

Code pattern: 67	Descriptors/Symptoms
Scale 6 highest and above *T*-65	1. Tense
Scale 7 in second place and above *T*-65	2. Overly sensitive
	3. Fearful of criticism
	4. Argumentative
	5. Anger problems

This is a rare profile. The profile suggests a [mild/moderate/severe] disturbance with symptoms of tension, hypersensitivity, and fears of criticism and failure. Other symptoms often associated with this profile are [list symptoms]. Behaviors associated with this profile are [list behaviors]. Traits associated with this profile are [list traits].

Code pattern: 68	Descriptors/Symptoms
Scale 6 highest and above *T*-65	1. Marginal psychological adjustment
Scale 8 in second place and above *T*-65	2. Intense feelings of inferiority and insecurity
	3. Distrustful
	4. Unstable
	5. Possibly psychotic

This profile suggests a [mild/moderate/severe] disorder. Typically, these individuals exhibit marginal psychological adjustment, harbor intense feelings of inferiority and insecurity, and are suspicious and distrustful of others. They avoid deep emotional ties and are emotionally unstable. This is often a psychotic profile. Other symptoms often associated with this profile are [list symptoms]. Behaviors associated with this profile are [list behaviors]. Traits associated with this profile are [list traits].

Code pattern: 69	Descriptors/Symptoms
Scale 6 highest and above *T*-65	1. Paranoid
Scale 9 in second place and above *T*-65	2. Grandiose
	3. High-strung
	4. Explosive
	5. Extremely sensitive to criticism

This profile suggests a [mild/moderate/severe] disturbance. Some individuals with this profile can exhibit paranoid traits. Often grandiose, they are high-strung and extremely sensitive to criticism. They tend to have difficulties with anger, are often explosive, and use projection as a defense mechanism. Other symptoms often associated with this profile are [list symptoms]. Behaviors associated with this profile are [list behaviors]. Traits associated with this profile are [list traits].

Code pattern: Spike 7	Descriptors/Symptoms
Scale 7 highest and above *T*-65	1. Tense
No other scales above *T*-65	2. Worried
	3. Guilty
	4. Poor self-image
	5. Apprehensive
	6. Compulsive
	7. Possibly phobic

This profile suggests a [mild/moderate/severe] disorder in an anxious, tense, worried, guilty, and dependent individual. Many of these individuals exhibit obsessive–compulsive behaviors, and most have poor self-esteem. Other symptoms often associated with this profile are [list symptoms]. Behaviors associated with this profile are [list behaviors]. Traits associated with this profile are [list traits].

Code pattern: 78	Descriptors/Symptoms
Scale 7 highest and above *T*-65	1. Worried
Scale 8 in second place and above *T*-65	2. Low self-esteem
	3. Tense
	4. Withdrawn
	5. Nervous
	6. Insecure
	7. Indecisive

This profile suggests a [mild/moderate/severe] disorder. Typically, these individuals exhibit extremely low self-esteem and are irritable, worried, insecure, and indecisive. Nervous and with strong feelings of inadequacy, many complain of depersonalization and many exhibit symptoms of withdrawal and apathy. Other symptoms often associated with this profile are [list symptoms]. Behaviors associated with this profile are [list behaviors]. Traits associated with this profile are [list traits].

Code pattern: Spike 9	Descriptors/Symptoms
Scale 9 highest and above *T*-65	1. Hypomanic
No other scale elevated above *T*-65	2. Emotionally labile
	3. Flight of ideas
	4. Good-humored euphoria
	5. Irritable with outbursts of anger
	6. Moodiness

This profile suggests a [mild/moderate/severe] disorder. Persons with this profile can exhibit good-natured euphoria, followed by mood lability, irritability, overcommitment for too many tasks and activities, and flight of ideas. Denial tends to be a major defense. Some are diagnosed as manic. Other symptoms often associated with this profile are [list symptoms]. Behaviors associated with this profile are [list behaviors]. Traits associated with this profile are [list traits].

Code pattern: 92	Descriptors/Symptoms
Scale 9 highest and above *T*-65	1. Possible agitated depression
Scale 2 in second place and above *T*-65	2. Insecure
	3. Irritable and labile
	4. Possibly alcoholic

This profile suggests a [mild/moderate/severe] disorder. It is difficult to determine whether this profile suggests a manic-depressive disorder or an agitated depression. Typically, these individuals are labile and irritable and may use chemical agents as a way of medicating their mood disorder. Other symptoms often associated with this profile are [list symptoms]. Behaviors associated with this profile are [list behaviors]. Traits associated with this profile are [list traits].

Code pattern: 98	Descriptors/Symptoms
Scale 9 highest and above *T*-65	1. Confused, disoriented
Scale 8 in second place and above *T*-65	2. Hyperactive
	3. Emotionally labile
	4. Poor sexual adjustment
	5. Flight of ideas
	6. Hostile

This profile suggests a [mild/moderate/severe] disturbance in a confused, disoriented, hyperactive, and emotionally labile individual. Typically, they have poor sexual adjustment and fears of intimacy. They often talk with a loud voice and can be hostile. Other symptoms often associated with this profile are [list symptoms]. Behaviors associated with this profile are [list behaviors]. Traits associated with this profile are [list traits].

Code pattern: 90	Descriptors/Symptoms
Scale 9 highest and above *T*-65	1. Agitated
Scale 0 in second place and above *T*-65	2. Introverted
	3. Tense
	4. Insecure

Not commonly seen, this profile suggests a [mild/moderate/severe] disturbance. Individuals with this profile tend to be tense, introverted, and withdrawn, although they are agitated and can exhibit hypomanic traits. Other symptoms often associated with this profile are [list symptoms]. Behaviors associated with this profile are [list behaviors]. Traits associated with this profile are [list traits].

You have now written an opening paragraph on the validity of the profile and the test-taking attitude of the respondent. You have begun the body of your report with an opening statement that summarizes the essence of the code pattern. Your next statements should go on to list other likely complaints, symptoms, conflicts, and so on for the code obtained from Chapter 6. It is customary to report MMPI-2 data objectively, making statements such as "Typically, these individuals are depressed, ruminative, and anxious" (e.g. a 27 profile) or "Others are likely to describe these individuals as demanding, critical and unreasonable, although they are very sensitive to any demands placed on them" (e.g. a 46 profile). Reporting statistical data is also acceptable, although not mandatory in a report; for example, "A high percentage of these individuals tend to be unmarried and of those who are married, Marks and Seeman reported that 70 percent reported marital discord" (e.g. a 48 code). When writing an MMPI-2 report, it is not customary to integrate actuarial data obtained from the Code-Pattern Look-Up Table or a cookbook with data generated from the referral question, background and history, and current life situation of the individual being tested. This kind of integration is usually reserved for the discussion section of a test report. It is important that the reader of an MMPI-2 report understands that the report is being generated in a way that emphasizes empirical and actuarial data, even though it may include clinical or historical data.

Once you have described the symptoms, behaviors, defenses, and other correlates of the elevated code pattern, look up the correlates for the next highest scale in the configuration. Repeat this for all the scales that are elevated above *T*-65 in descending order of elevation. Upon completion of this task, look up the correlates for any scale below *T*-50, if they are available (see Chapter 5). For example, look at Fig. 9.9. The profile is that of a 26/62 code pattern. Look up the correlates for the 26/62 code above *T*-65 in Chapter 6. The next highest scale is Scale 7, which adds anxiety, self-doubt, guilt, and rumination to the symptom picture of a 26 trapped, depression. The next highest scale is Scale 0, which predicts introversion and social unease. There are no other scales above *T*-65, but Scale 9 is below *T*-50. This indicates low energy and intensifies the low-energy symptoms of depression but reduces the likelihood of acting out.

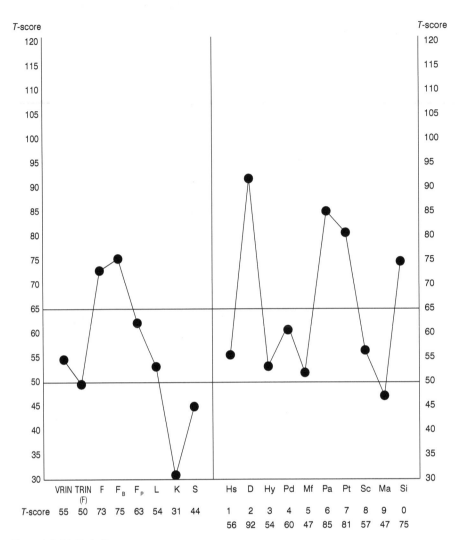

Figure 9.9 26 Code Pattern

Source: MMPI-2 Validity and Clinical Scales Profile. Adapted from the *MMPI-2 (Minnesota Multiphasic Personality Inventory-2) Manual for Administration, Scoring, and Interpretation, Revised Edition.* Copyright © 2001 by the Regents of the University of Minnesota. All rights reserved. Used by permission of the University of Minnesota Press. "MMPI" and "Minnesota Multiphasic Personality Inventory" are registered trademarks owned by the Regents of the University of Minnesota.

Organization of the Report

Reports should be organized into paragraphs that flow logically one from the other. The opening paragraph could have a separate heading, such as "Validity" or "Test-Taking Attitude." You may or may not wish to formally label sections in your report. Different settings encourage or discourage such separate labels. After you have written a brief description of the validity and test-taking attitude, begin the interpretation section as a separate paragraph, which also may have a separate heading. You may label this second part of the report "Personality Profile" or "Symptoms, Behaviors, and Personality Traits." You may also have a third section labeled "Lifestyle and Family Background" (such as in the automated Caldwell Report) or a heading called "Background Experiences." Usually a fourth section is labeled "Diagnostic Impressions," in which the possible diagnoses associated with the profile are listed. A fifth section could be labeled "Treatment Recommendations." This section would contain treatment recommendations, warnings about possible suicidality, and suggestions for medication. A final section could be labeled, "Feedback Statement," containing language for apprising the test taker of their test results. Chapter 12 presents computer reports with varied formats, any of which may appeal to the organizational inclinations of the reader.

It is not plagiarism to copy from any of the standard textbooks a list of symptoms, behaviors, and personality traits associated with a particular profile. These are generally empirically generated descriptors. The art of writing an MMPI-2 report flows from integrating descriptors from all of the scales into a coherent report. It would be plagiarism, however, to copy verbatim a computer-generated report as if it were generated by the psychologist. However, quoting from a report is acceptable if appropriately acknowledged.

Another way of organizing the data generated from an MMPI-2 is to break it down into a series of paragraphs, each one dealing with a particular aspect of psychological functioning. The following list, adapted from Graham (1990) and Levak et al. (2011), may serve as a guide in organizing a report:

1   Symptoms, complaints, and personality traits
2   Self-concept
3   Perception of the environment
4   Interpersonal relationships
5   Behaviors
6   Emotional control and response to stress
7   Psychological resources
8   Dynamics/etiology
9   Diagnostic impressions
10   Treatment implications

Symptoms, Complaints, and Personality Traits

After an opening statement that summarizes the essence of the profile, list the symptoms and complaints associated with the code and then the symptoms and complaints associated with the other elevated clinical scales. Generate hypotheses from scales below

T-50 (e.g. Scale 4 at *T*-30 suggests low aggressiveness and conformity). As part of the process of generating descriptors for this section, also look at the supplementary and content scales, as well as the various Harris-Lingoes and Subtle–Obvious subscales. For example, if a profile is within the normal range and Scale 2 is at a *T*-score of 60, the clinician may assume that a diagnosis of depression is not warranted. However, should the DEP scale be elevated above *T*-65, then symptoms of depression and complaints of difficulties with concentration and memory would be warranted. Remember that symptoms are behavioral manifestations of the disorder that are noted by the clinician, whereas complaints emanate from the client. This paragraph should also describe personality traits associated with the profile. For example, 27s are hyper-responsible and prone to worry and respond to minor threats as if they are emergencies.

Self-Concept

Once you have described the symptoms, complaints, and personality traits, describe the way the person sees him- or herself. In some cases, a sentence or two is all that is needed because the disturbance is mainly characterized by acting-out behavior or a projection of blame onto others with little self-awareness (e.g. a 49/94 profile), so the self-concept would tend to be egocentric and grandiose. In other cases, however, this will be a particularly important paragraph because the disturbance is primarily around self-image and self-dislike (e.g. 278/728, 86/68, and 89/98 profiles). This paragraph could start with a sentence such as, "Typically, these individuals see themselves as defective, damaged, and unlikable" (high scores on Scale 8). On the other hand, a statement about self-concept with an acting-out profile (49/94 or 46/64) might start off as follows: "The client is unlikely to see himself as responsible for his present difficulties. He is likely to see his difficulties as due to other people, difficult situations or bad luck, and he will tend to project blame onto others."

Perception of the Environment

In this section, describe how the person sees the outside world. For example, 68/86 persons see it as hostile, dangerous, and confusing. High scorers on Scales 2 and 7 see the world as a frightening place, and they tend to overreact to situations as if they were emergencies. They see themselves as vulnerable to threat and loss of social approval. 48/84 persons see the world as hostile and uncaring, so they maintain a self-protective, angry, defensive style. They have difficulty empathizing with others and accurately interpreting other's responses to them. On the other hand, 46/64 individuals are vigilant for any demands being placed on them and they are likely to be guarded and protective of their autonomy, often feeling "cheated by life." As you read the descriptors in Chapter 6, tease out the relevant sentences for each of your paragraphs.

It is not always necessary to organize your paragraphs according to this outline, but use the outline to make sure that you have covered as many facets of a personality description as possible, and refer to the Nichols and Greene Structural Summary, described in this chapter and illustrated in Chapter 12, for help in organizing your data.

Interpersonal Relationships

Given the previous perceptions of self and of others, describe how this affects the testee's interpersonal relationships. Descriptions of interpersonal relationships also will vary in length depending on the code pattern. For some profiles, a primary problem area will be interpersonal (e.g. in the 49/94 or 46/64 types), but for other profiles (e.g. 27/72) the problems are more of an intrapersonal nature. A possible opening statement for this paragraph could be, "The client's interpersonal relationships are apt to be characterized by painful misunderstandings (as in 78/87 elevations), exaggerated demands for affection (as in 46/64 elevations), or explosive irritability and narcissism (as in 49/94 elevations)."

Behaviors

People's behaviors result at least partly from their self-concept, perceptions of the environment, and interpersonal relationships. In a sense, interpersonal relationships are manifested in behaviors, so you may have already covered some of this in the preceding paragraph. A good opening sentence for this section might start as follows: "Typical behaviors associated with this profile are [list items]." For example, a person scoring high on Scale 2, with complaints of fatigue and with difficulties in concentration, guilt, anxiety, and sleeping will show behaviors such as apathy, a general loss in alertness and drive, and a slowed-down tempo. The behaviors you describe for a particular elevation ought to be linked in a meaningful way to the preceding symptoms, self-concept, and perception of the environment. Therefore, a person elevated on Scale 2 is likely to present with a slow interpersonal tempo, slow speech, and poor eye contact. Such a person would also likely withdraw from conflict and generally avoid assertive or purposeful behavior. Using a different example involving a Spike 4 elevation, you are unlikely to have a very long list of complaints because high scorers on Scale 4 often do not have complaints as such (although others may have many complaints about them). Often they are in therapy because of impulsive behavior that has led them into trouble or marital discord. In these cases, statements about their behaviors will predominate, so you might state

> They are likely to be in trouble because of sexual or other acting-out behavior problems. They are self-centered individuals who blame their problems on outside circumstances or difficult situations but rarely take responsibility for their behaviors. Typically, they are alienated people who exhibit an adolescent type of rebellion and nonconformity to accepted social norms and values. Rarely loyal, they see the world as a "dog eat dog" place where they have to have the "upper hand" in order to avoid being exploited. Typical behaviors are lying, impulsivity, poor frustration tolerance, and poor long-term planning. Marital difficulties are suggested, along with difficulties in accepting routine and conforming to structured work situations.

In sum, some code patterns generate a longer list of symptoms than complaints. Other codes generate longer lists of symptoms and complaints than descriptions of behaviors.

Table 9.1 Code patterns and associated stressors

Code pattern	Stressor
27/72	Accumulation of responsibilities
28/82	Perceived withdrawal of emotional support from previously supportive person
43/34	Rejection or being discounted
46/64	Demands being placed on them
49/94	The imposition of controls on their behavior
93/39	Disapproval and/or being controlled

Emotional Control and Response to Stress

Whenever people experience stress, typically they will show an increase in defensive behaviors, and therefore an increase in symptoms; as the stress increases, the maturity of their defensive behaviors decreases. The clinical and validity scales of the MMPI-2 are reflective of defensive behaviors. The clinical and validity scales of the MMPI-2 reflect not only the types of defenses that individuals are likely to use but also their level of coping skills and their levels of overall distress. Elevations on the *K* and *Es* scales suggest better coping ability than lower scores on these scales, especially if the clinical scales are elevated. High *F* and high *FB* scores, as well as elevations on Scales 6, 8, and the *BIZ* scale, suggest distress and psychological disorganization. Low scores on Scale 0 generally indicate a broader array of social and interpersonal supports as well as a history of comfortable socialization. Clinical scale configurations are often associated with varying amounts of emotional control or responses to stress. For some codetypes, increases in stress can lead to dangerous behaviors. For example, 68/86 types can become combative under stress, and 24/42 persons who have been threatening suicide can actually attempt it. High Scale 9 individuals can become increasingly manic or suddenly depressed under stress.

In this section, discuss what kinds of stressors are most likely to lead to a breakdown of adaptive defenses. Table 9.1 offers some examples, drawn from our experience, of stressors associated with particular code patterns.

Psychological Resources

Some of this section will overlap with the preceding section. Material for this section comes primarily from the code pattern and from scores on the validity scales, the *Es* scale, and the supplementary and content scales. High *Es* scores predict adequate psychological resources to deal with stress. For example, a person obtaining a 48/84 profile at an elevation of *T*-75 with an *Es* *T*-score of 65, a *K* *T*-score of 65, and an *LSE* *T*-score of 40, is probably coping with life better than a person with a 48/84 profile in which the *K* and *Es* scales are below *T*-50 and the *LSE* scale is at *T*-75. In the latter case, the sense of alienation and estrangement could result in impulsive and even bizarre acting out, whereas in the previous example, high *K* and *Es* scores would predict many areas of compensated functioning, with the alienation and estrangement being acted out in a more controlled way. However, it is nonetheless likely that in both cases the individual will be experiencing interpersonal conflicts, turmoil, and a lack of adequate emotional fulfillment in his or her interpersonal relationships. The individual with an elevated 48 code pattern, with high *K* and *Es* scores, is unlikely to present as psychotic or act out in impulsive ways because the *K* and *Es* scores predict control and the ability to handle stress. The more controlled 48 could be more potentially dangerous (e.g. Jeffrey Dahmer, who was able to lure his victims to their death with an apparent relaxed, easy charm). In another example, the higher the *F* score, in conjunction with lower *K* and *Es* scores, the less psychological resources a person has available to deal with the stress exhibited in the clinical profile elevation. Conversely, the higher the *K* and *Es* scores, the more coping resources that are available to the person.

The relationship between *K* elevations and psychological resources is curvilinear. The lower the *K* score, the less ego strength and the lower the self-concept. In the midranges, with the *K* scale at *T*-59–64, a person has adequate psychological resources to deal with stress. At elevations over a *T*-score of 65, a person is likely to be more rigid and out of touch with feelings, and therefore less flexible and less able to tolerate psychological self-exploration.

Dynamics/Etiology

Some report writers may divide their profile at this point with a heading such as "Dynamics/Etiology." In this section discuss any possible background and childhood experiences that may be associated with a particular code pattern. Marks et al. (1974) described typical background experiences associated with a particular codetype. If these characteristics are available, then begin this section with a statement such as (in the case of a 48/84 code pattern), "Persons with this profile pattern often come from backgrounds in which there was deprivation, hostility, and sexual abuse." When there are empirically relevant background experiences, include them.

Diagnostic Impressions

This is probably the most difficult part of report writing because the MMPI-2 is neither diagnostically pure nor efficient. If one scale is particularly elevated over the others, then that scale usually determines or highly colors the diagnostic picture; even so, it is rare that one scale is uniquely more elevated than the others. Therefore, a definitive diagnosis of depression, paranoia, personality disorder, and so on is not always possible using such an approach because several elevated scales will need to be considered. Therefore, the following guidelines to diagnosis are offered:

1   The highest scale predicts the type of diagnosis (Scale 2 = depression, Scale 7 = anxiety, Scale 9 = hypomania, etc.) when one scale is singularly elevated.
2   The slope of the profile suggests whether the diagnosis will fall in the neurotic or psychotic realm. Is it a neurotic slope (negative slope) or a psychotic slope (positive slope)?
3   Consider strongly the diagnoses actuarially associated most frequently with the two- or three-point code or with the configuration (e.g. Conversion V). Where evidence exists, these have been listed under each code pattern in Chapter 6.

4   Compute the Goldberg index. Is it in the psychotic or the neurotic direction? The Goldberg index is discussed in Table 9.2 and provides a description of how to properly use the Goldberg rules; the typical Goldberg index values associated with each code pattern are presented in Table 9.3.

5   When writing an MMPI-2 report, give a number of possible diagnoses associated with the code pattern. The MMPI-2 is usually administered as part of a test battery, so the clinician will have other test data, as well as extra test data, that will help him or her to make an accurate diagnosis. It is permissible when writing the MMPI-2 section of a test battery to state the typical diagnoses associated with the code pattern, although these diagnoses might not "survive" when the clinician is writing the actual diagnosis for an individual based on the complete test battery, history, and presenting problem. For example, a discussion section in a psychological evaluation may state, "Although the individual obtained an MMPI-2 profile that is typically associated with personality disorder diagnoses, the data from the other tests and the individual's history and clinical presentation do not suggest a personality disorder diagnosis." Usually, the code pattern is not diagnostically definitive and historical; behavioral and other test data can aid in making an accurate diagnosis. For example, an adolescent 89/98 profile might indicate a panic around a drug reaction or it might indicate a severe identity disturbance. Schizophrenia could be a possible diagnosis, but tell the reader what to look for in the client's history. Using the 89/98 adolescent (e.g. 19 years old) as an example, the diagnosis section of an MMPI-2 report could contain a statement such as,

> A history of schizophrenia in the family of origin would make the prognosis more guarded. If the history does not suggest a chemically induced disturbance or a recent blow to the individual's self-esteem, this profile could reflect a schizophrenic disorder.

This kind of statement would be appropriate in the diagnostic section of the MMPI-2 part of a test battery but would probably be less appropriate in the final diagnostic section of a test battery, where a more definitive diagnosis is usually helpful.

Treatment Implications

MMPI-2 users will have to use their clinical experience and the treatment literature (see treatment sections in Chapter 6) to write this last section of the MMPI-2 report. The symptoms and complaints described will demand some kind of treatment modality. There are many empirically supported treatment approaches available for dealing with different kinds of psychopathology. For example, for depression, cognitive restructuring, self-esteem building, and medication, have all proved effective (see Levak et al., 2011, for more treatment information).

The MMPI-2 can also provide some clues as to the client's treatability. Issues that are likely to arise in treatment, such as transference and defensive styles, and types of therapeutic intervention that are more or less likely to be effective should be included in this section if material is available. The K scale is generally a good indicator of therapy suitability. Extremely low K scores (below T-40) suggest low self-esteem and low ego strength (and therefore psychological accessibility for treatment) but is often a poor prognosis because of a lack of psychological inner resources. T-scores in the range of 50

Table 9.2 Notes for the clinical use of the Goldberg rules

The Goldberg rules are a set of three linear indexes, each of which uses a combination of K-corrected MMPI-2 T-scores in an equation for which a sign value (cutting score) has been established. The Goldberg rules were developed using K-corrected MMPI T-score values. Although there have been normative changes in the transition from the MMPI to the MMP-2, the cutting scores for the Goldberg rules still appear to apply to the MMPI-2. All of the Goldberg rules were developed using regression procedures on large data sets. Rules I and II were derived from 208 of the group profiles from Lanyon (1968), and Rule III (Index) emerged from the analysis of 861 individual male profiles collected from seven psychiatric centers (mostly Veterans Affairs [VA] and university hospital inpatients) previously used in Meehl and Dahlstrom's (1960) study of configural rules for discriminating psychotic from neurotic profiles. The methods and data on which these indexes are based have immediate implications for their use in clinical practice. The important point is that the Goldberg rules do not lend themselves to straightforward use in decisions involving the individual case. The differences in base rates between various kinds of settings (e.g. clinics, private practice, and college counseling centers, VA hospitals, state mental hospitals, job screening, and prisons) will have large effects on the rate of correct decisions if the cutting scores for the three rules are held constant. Another thing to bear in mind is that the Goldberg rules show a different range of values for each of the common two- or three-point profile types (see Table 9.3, which shows index values for a sample of cases provided by Alex B. Caldwell and corresponding values for profiles in the Marks & Seeman, 1963, and Gilberstadt & Duker, 1965, code books). Take Goldberg Rule III, for example: Code patterns 138 and 86 are both associated with a high frequency of psychosis, yet the ranges of values for Rule III are almost completely non-overlapping. The typical range of values for 138 profiles for Rule III is from 35 to 55, whereas that for 86 profiles is 65 to 90. Thus, decisions based solely on the Rule III cutting score of 45 will result in too many 86 profiles being called psychotic, whereas too few of the patients with 138 profiles will be called psychotic. As a result of these problems, the Goldberg rules are probably best thought of as a means of classifying large groups of patients or profile types rather than as a way of classifying individual profiles.

Let us now consider each rule separately:

Rule I: Normal versus Deviant ($Hs + 2Pd-Ma$)—Using K-Corrected T-Scores

Scores above 123.5 are called deviant, whereas scores below 123.5 are considered normal. This rule probably performs best in populations or settings with a high base rate (say, at least 30%) for psychological normality, such as general medical patients, college counseling centers, police applicants, and Peace Corps volunteers. It should be applied with considerable caution to outpatients and should be avoided completely in inpatient psychiatric settings. Among the latter group, false negatives (patients erroneously classified as normal) occur at a particularly high rate among patients with code patterns in which Scale 9 is one of the two high points or as Scale 9 equals or exceeds T-65. This rule appears to work better in outpatient settings when applied only to those profiles that do not fulfill the inclusion criteria for the normal $K+$ profile, that have no more than two scales greater than T-70, and in which Scale 9 is no greater than third highest. In inpatient settings, Rule I may be thought of as a mania versus other indicator. Scores of 123 and below are obtained by patients with high activity levels who are less ambivalent, apathetic, and depressed than patients in general and who do not manifest a sense of inadequacy/inferiority (Lane & Lachar, 1979). Manic cases typically show Rule I below 123.5 and Rule III above 45.

Rule II: Psychiatric Versus Sociopathic Personality Disordered ($2Pd - Hy - Sc$)— Using K-corrected T-scores

Scores above 11 are considered sociopathic, whereas scores below 11 are called psychiatric. This rule corresponds roughly to the *Diagnostic and Statistical Manual of Mental Disorders* (4th ed.; American Psychiatric Association, 1994) distinction between Axis I (clinical syndromes) and Axis II (personality disorders). The assignment of separate axes to these two kinds of disorders by the American Psychiatric Association Task Force on Nomenclature

continued...

Table 9.2 continued

and Statistics was decided on for the explicit purpose of encouraging, where appropriate, simultaneous classification. The implication for the practical utility of Rule II is that values exceeding the cutting score should serve to alert the clinician to the likely presence of a personality disorder rather than as a device to classify the individual patient. Rule II is relatively more sensitive in detecting those personality disorders lying at the more unstable end of the over-control/under-control continuum, such as antisocial and narcissistic personality disorder, while being correspondingly less sensitive to those at the more constricted end of this continuum, such as dependent or obsessive-compulsive personality disorders.

Classification accuracy is undoubtedly best for this rule in settings with high base rates for character pathology, such as prisons, and drug and alcohol treatment or rehabilitation programs. In clinic and psychiatric settings, this rule results in an intolerably high false-negative rate for neurotic and especially for psychotic conditions. The problem is that as Scale 4 reaches about T-80, the profile tends to be classified as sociopathic, regardless of its total configuration. The 46/64 codetype is the outstanding miss for this rule but 48/84, 482/428, 274/742/472, 96/69, and 94 are also frequently misclassified as personality disordered.

Rule III: Neurotic Versus Psychotic ($L + Pa + Sc - Hy - Pt$)—Using K-Corrected T-Scores

Scores at 45 or above are considered psychotic, whereas scores below 45 are called neurotic. This rule is commonly referred to as the *Goldberg index*. Great caution should be exercised in applying this rule outside formal psychiatric settings. Because scores are obtained by subtracting the sum of two scales from the sum of three different scales, and because the average score for normals for each scale is near T-50, the majority of individuals in unselected samples will obtain scores on the Goldberg index well within the psychotic range. It is, therefore, inappropriate to compute this index in presumptively normal samples, such as applicants for employment, general medical patients, and college counselees. Rule III is unique among the three Goldberg indexes in having some intelligible dynamic meaning in terms of the patient's psychological distance from others. High values are likely to reflect a marked distrust of others and strong needs for insulation, detachment, and withdrawal in interpersonal relations. Low values suggest over-attachment with dependency and clinging.

All of the profiles in the original data set were collected prior to 1960 and most prior to 1955, so it is very unlikely that affective disorders were fairly represented in the criterion diagnoses. Major depressions were almost certainly overrepresented in the neurotic group and underrepresented in the psychotic group at a period when schizophrenia was overly diagnosed in the United States. As a consequence, Rule III will almost certainly show greater sensitivity and specificity for schizophrenia than for affective disorders. Frequent misclassifications occur with the 278, 29/92, and 78/87 profile codes; 278s are misclassified as psychotic and as neurotic with about equal frequency, whereas 29/92s are called neurotic too often and 78/87s are called psychotic too often. Elevations on L and endorsements of most of the dozen or so somatic items on Scale 8 will result in some 13/31 profiles (especially those of female patients) being erroneously called psychotic. As suggested earlier, the 138 profile is the classic miss for Rule III, with the majority of patients with this code misclassified as neurotic.

Note: These notes on using the Goldberg rules were written by David S. Nichols and are reproduced with his permission.

Table 9.3 Mean Goldberg (N–P) index values by codetype

Codetype	Caldwell Report Index Values[a]	Gilberstadt & Duker (1965)[b]	Marks & Seeman (1963)[b]
123′[a]	34	18	
13′ or 31′	32	24	40
231′ or 213′	30	16[b]	30
26′ or 62′	62		
27′ or 72′, basically 273′ and not 274′ or 278′	26	14	28
274′, any order	36	26	36
278′, any order	46	45	48
28′ or 82′	58		58
29′or 92′	43		
321′	28		23
34′or 43′	40	33	
36′ or 63′	53		
37′, 73′, or 137′, any order	25	19[c]	
38′, 83′, or 138′, any order	44	36	53
39′or 93′	37	34[d]	
4′ and ('A–B) > 10[e]	48	45	
46′ or 64′	66		65[f]
48′ or 84′, not 489′[h]	58	56[g]	56
49′or 94′, not 489′	49	45	53
489′, any order	60		
68′ or 86′	77	99[i]	92[i]
69′ or 96′	70		78
78′ or 87′	49	42	
89′ or 98′	62	71	68
9′, B < 70, 2 < 50[j]	54	55	

a Derived from a file sequential sampling of adult cases processed by the Caldwell Report. Cases included psychotherapy outpatients; psychiatric inpatients; workers' compensation and other forensic evaluations; parents in child custody cases; and a diversity of normals, including police and other job applicants. For further information, contact Alex B. Caldwell, Caldwell Report, 5839 Green Valley Circle, Suite 203, Culver City, CA 90230; Phone: (310) 670-2874.
b Goldberg index values were derived from each corresponding adult psychiatric mean profile by codetype.
c Primed codes were used; the mean *N–P* index values for unelevated profiles are usually quite similar, with no consistent pattern of differences.
d Codetype 1237′/2137′.
e Codetype 137′ or 13′7.
f Codetype 139, 1 or 3 or 9 > *T*-70.
g (*A–B*) > 10 indicates Scale 4 minus the next highest of the eight clinical scales is more than 10 points. Gilberstadt and Duker specified 4 > *T*-70 and no other scale *T*-70.
h 65 is the average of Codetype 46/64, mean *N–P* index 78, plus Codetype 462/642, mean index 52.
i Codetype 824(7).
j Codetype 482/842/824.
High *F* scores were not excluded, nor was the *N–P* index adjusted for excessive *F* elevations; B < 70 indicates the second highest of the eight clinical scales is below *T*-70, and Scale 2 must be less than *T*-50.

to 65 typically predict a good therapeutic outcome, whereas *T*-scores above 65 predict emotional rigidity and constriction. In this case, a poor therapeutic outcome could be due to client difficulties in opening up. The TRT content scale can also be useful in determining if the client is cynical about the effectiveness of "talk therapy."

Some code patterns reflect behaviors that are more amenable to treatment than other scales. For example, the 27//2 code predicts amenability to treatment because these individuals tend to be conscientious, reasonable, and follow treatment suggestions. On the other hand, elevations on Scale 4 predict a slow response to treatment, whether it is pharmacological or psychotherapeutic. Spike 4, 48/84, 46/64, 43/34, and 49/94 are all configurations that predict a relatively enduring personality picture that is difficult to change. The exception to this is when elevations on Scale 4 are the result of a recent letdown or psychological trauma, such as divorce or loss of job. In this case, a history of good adjustment prior to the precipitating circumstance would suggest a good response to treatment. A lifelong history of passive-aggressive or acting-out behavior in the presence of elevations on Scale 4, however, would suggest a slow treatment response. Beginning users of the MMPI-2 who have limited clinical experience should attempt to build a database of treatment suggestions by reading standard books on personality and psychopathology and associating them with basic configural code patterns (see also the Code-Pattern Look-Up Table for treatment suggestions).

Interpretation of "Complex Profiles"

Some profiles do not fit cleanly into a recognizable code pattern. In this case, you need to divide the profile into manageable, recognizable entities and then build a composite personality picture. Consider the following complex profile with similar scale elevations in which all of the clinical scales are elevated above *T*-65. The scales shown below are ranked from highest to lowest *T*-scores. This ranking of scale scores is used as an example for describing how to deconstruct a profile into its basic constituent parts. This strategy, adopted from the A-B-C-D Caldwell (1998) paradigm, is to divide the profile into high-point pairs in order to generate a set of descriptors for each pair. First, write down, in order of elevations, all of the elevated scales. Derived from the example below, the following rank-ordered list is generated: 3 1 6 2 7 9 4 5 8 0. Under each number, write the corresponding letter of the alphabet as far as the fourth highest elevation:

3	1	6	2	7	9	4	5	8	0
A	B	C	D						

Then divide the profile and interpret in high-point pairs as follows: A-B, which is 3-1. Then interpret A-C, which is 3-6. Then interpret B-C, which is 1-6, followed by A-D. After that, take the correlates for each of the scales in descending order. In this case, the anchor (primary codetype) for the interpretation is the 3-1 (i.e. 13/31 two-point) code. Looking up the 13/31 code in Chapter 6 reveals that these individuals tend to be somatizing, dependent, psychologically naïve, and immature and as having difficulty facing anger directly. Descriptors for elevations on Scales 3 and 6 (see 36/63 code pattern) reveal persons who are hypersensitive to criticism, distrustful, and occasionally suspicious, with somatic symptoms. Looking up correlates for 1-6 reveals that these individuals tend to be rigid, grouchy, stubborn, hypersensitive to criticism, and quick to place blame on others.

The profile that emerges so far is that of a hypersensitive, somatizing, tense, possibly suspicious individual. Next, add the correlates for the single scales, starting with Scale 2. Elevations at this *T*-score level suggest sadness, apathy, guilt, and depression. As the basic two-point codetype for the personality picture is the 13/31 profile, the symptoms of depression will be manifested as somatic complaints, tension, and negativity, covered over with hysterical blandness. The correlates for Scale 7, the next highest scale, predicts anxiety, tension, and guilt. Given the 13/31 backdrop, the person is unlikely to be aware of guilt and anxiety; rather he or she experiences it as tension and somatic complaints, especially when responsibilities accumulate. Correlates for the next highest scale, Scale 4, suggest agitation, lability, and impulsivity, but against the backdrop of the 3-1, 3-6, and 1-6 configurations, which suggests extreme inner tension and explosiveness. This is because the primary elevations form the basis of the personality picture, and the other scales modify that base. The 3-1 pattern contraindicates aggression. Consequently, the acting out associated with Scales 4 and 9 will be modified and expressed as passive resistance, self-defeating behavior, and manipulative dependency.

To begin the integration process, write down all of your descriptors. Attempt to group similar descriptors together. Any descriptors that are contradictory to the primary and secondary code configurations need to be integrated. In our experience, psychologists rarely go to this next step of attempting to understand how contradictory traits are integrated against the backdrop of a primary code pattern. This is where the skill of a psychologist is involved because most cookbooks do not give descriptors for four-, five-, or six-point code patterns. The Structural Summary format can be useful in this process. A report that describes only the two- or three-point code is acceptable in most settings. However, learning to write reports that integrate contradictory data is the art of personality assessment. In complex profiles, the primary two or three scale elevations become the context within which the fourth, fifth, and all other individual clinical scales (including content and supplementary scales) are interpreted. Your purpose will be to make sense of the contradictions and to add those symptoms and descriptions that confirm each other so that you can use them in the report with a higher degree of certainty.

Scale 5

Elevations on Scale 5 (*Mf*) will modify the profile interpretation. For men, elevations on Scale 5 will mitigate against aggressive acting-out behaviors and will modify the scales that otherwise would predict such behaviors. Because elevated scores on this scale for men are associated with sensitivity, intellectual interests, and non-aggressiveness, it acts as a suppressor variable for acting-out behaviors. For example, a male profile elevated on Scales 4, 8, and 9, with Scale 5 elevated, would predict a charismatic, but self-centered, angry person whose acting out is likely to be in indirect antisocial ways, such as through white-collar types of crime or unusual sexual behaviors. Scale 5 correlates with education and intelligence, so elevations on that scale will modify the profile in the same way that these demographic variables would.

Low Scale 5 scores in women (below a *T*-score of 40) suggest a strong feminine identification and a rejection of competitive, aggressive values. This would increase the likelihood of passive-aggressiveness in profiles that would otherwise suggest direct anger. For example, in women, the addition of a low Scale 5 score to a 49/94 profile would suggest more sexual than antisocial acting-out behaviors in the same way that a high Scale 5 score would for a high 49 man.

Scale 0

Low scores on Scale 0 (*Si*) predict the need for and comfort with social interaction, and thus modify other aspects of profile interpretation. For example, for some codes (e.g. 278), interpersonal relationships and intimacy are a problem; when Scale 0 is additionally elevated, these interpersonal problems are even more striking. In another example, a 68/86 profile, Scale 0 is at or below *T*-50 and would appear contradictory because the person apparently has a drive toward social interactions yet is hostile, guarded, and suspicious. Whether that suggests a better or worse prognosis is difficult to ascertain. Another example is that of the 49/94 code pattern. When Scale 0 is elevated, the person is less likely to blatantly act out in an aggressive fashion and is more likely to be sullenly asocial. If Scale 0 is low, the person would be more likely to act out but in socially skillful ways that may be effective in manipulating others.

Energizers and Suppressors

Some scales act as *energizer* variables, whereas other scales act as *suppressor* variables. An energizer variable is one that increases the likelihood that the attributes of a particular code pattern will be manifested behaviorally. For example, a 24/42 code, with Scale 9 coded third and above *T*-65 would increase the likelihood of impulsive, self-destructive, or self-defeating behaviors. Similarly, elevations on Scales 4 and 8 would predict an angry, alienated, and confused individual. Adding Scale 9 coded third and above *T*-65 would predict impulsive, antisocial, and bizarre acting-out behavior as the alienation and anger are energized by *Ma*. Scales 4, 8, and 9 can be considered energizers. Scale 4 predicts poor impulse control, and thus increases the likelihood that behaviors will get acted out impulsively. Elevations on Scale 8 also predict poor impulse control due to disordered thinking.

Suppressor variables are those that inhibit the likelihood of a particular code being expressed in overt behaviors. Scales 2, 5, and 0 act as suppressor variables. For example, a 49/94 profile, with Scales 5 and 0 coded third and fourth, respectively, and above *T*-65, would predict an angry person, but one who is not likely to act out. Rather, Scales 5 and 0 would suggest a sensitive individual who tends toward introversion and whose acting-out behavior would more likely manifest itself in some kind of intellectual rebelliousness, or perhaps in a controlled way, such as passive-aggressiveness or conflict within the family.

Providing Feedback to the Client

The Health Insurance Portability and Accountability Act of 1996 (HIPAA) and American Psychological Association (APA) ethics mandate that clients have access to their psychological records and results of their psychological testing. Consequently, reports should be written in jargon-free, non-judgmental language, providing concrete recommendations and empathic, collaborative feedback (Groth-Marnat, 2009). Knowing that collaborative feedback will be available can minimize client apprehension about the assessment process and, if done well, can be therapeutic (see Finn & Tonsager, 1992; Levak et al., 2011; Lewak et al., 1990; Pope, 1992). The language of psychopathology permeates most MMPI-2 texts and, therefore, is not conducive to client candor or to the building of a therapeutic alliance. This is because the test was conceived as a clinical instrument designed to identify psychopathology in an era where clients were perceived as resistant to insight and unable to collaborate in the understanding of their psychological makeup. Most of the clinical scales were constructed with clinical groups to diagnose clinical problems characterized in clinical terms. The clinical scales were developed as measures of pathology or its absence, not as measures of personality. Their mainstream use continues to be in evaluating abnormal, maladaptive, or undesirable aspects of personality and behavioral functioning rather than normal, adaptive, or desirable ones. Terms such as *hostile, dependent, secondary gain, demanding, manipulative*, and *acting out*, are commonly used MMPI-2 textbook descriptors, although some clinicians have voiced concern that they are antithetical to a therapeutic relationship and may, at times, rise to the level of character assassination (Erdberg, 1979; Finn & Tonsager, 1992; Levak et al., 2011). A therapeutic alliance is more likely if clients feel understood, and that their complaints and fears are validated. In fact, Finn and Tonsager (1992) have shown that individuals provided with even one feedback session about their MMPI-2 results showed improvement in symptomatology when compared with individuals who had no feedback. Finn & Tonsager (1992) developed the concept of therapeutic assessment in which assessment is seen as a collaborative process. Levak et al. (2011) developed the concept of therapeutic feedback in which they provide the language and framework for a feedback approach based upon empirically generated MMPI-2 test data. This book has used the Levak et al. paradigm to provide feedback statements for most of the codetypes described, and the authors hope this will inspire researchers and clinicians to evaluate the clinical and therapeutic utility of various feedback paradigms.

The phenomenological, therapeutic-feedback approach developed by Lewak et al. (1990) and Levak et al. (2011) views personality as reflecting the interplay of genetic and environmental factors. Maladaptive behavior is seen as a product of stress (fear) operating within an individual who has a diathesis (i.e. a predisposition or set of vulnerabilities) for the type of disorder that occurs. From their perspective, it is assumed that each person has a repertoire of available psychological defenses against stress that is a function of both genetic and environmental factors. Under increased stress, those defenses that effectively reduce stress become fixed and maintained in accordance with their reinforcing value. In this model, any particular defense can be understood in the context of the stress that initially induced it. The reader interested in the association between stress and defense mechanisms is encouraged to see the excellent texts by Ihilevich and Gleser (1986, 1991).

Using Scale 1 (*Hs*) as an example, individuals with elevations are typically described as immature, dependent, psychologically naïve, and preoccupied with somatic concerns. In the Levak et al. (2011) approach, the judgmental descriptors described as maladaptive such as *immature, dependent, somatizing, psychologically naïve*, and so on can be seen as adaptive when understood in the context of the conditioning experiences that induced them. Levak et al. suggest that from the client's perspective, a constant

Table 9.4 MMPI-2 scales and associated fear-conditioned defensive responses

Scale	Fear	Response
1	Death, physical attack, illness, or pain	Maintaining physical integrity by overprotecting the body
2	Irretrievable and significant loss	Blocking wanting or needing in order to avoid further loss
3	Emotional pain	Positivizing painful emotional experiences by selectively blocking inputs (i.e. disavowal, blindness, numbness)
4	Rejection, being unwanted, or abandoned	"Numbing out" emotional responding, not allowing oneself to get emotionally involved to avoid letdown
6	Humiliation, being criticized, evaluated	Maintaining constant vigilance against attack/criticism
7	Shock, unexpected events	Thinking ahead and worrying to anticipate and prevent onset of shock
8	Hostility, being disliked or despised by those on whom one depends	"Shutting down" cognitive processing to avoid unbearable reality
9	Reward deprivation or failure	Increasing activity level in an attempt to maintain reward schedule

Source: Based on Alex B. Caldwell's unpublished theory.

preoccupation with physical health may have been an adaptive response to a perceived overwhelming threat to his or her physical integrity. Staying in bed, worrying about deteriorating health, and being preoccupied with the availability of medical health care makes sense from the perspective of the client who is terrified of bodily damage or death. Levak et al. have developed a feedback approach based on Caldwell's hypothesis that the eight clinical scales reflect different fear-conditioned (defensive) avoidant behaviors. Scales 5 and 0 do not represent conditioned fear-avoidance responses but rather personality traits. The clinical scales and their associated fears and defenses are summarized in Table 9.4. As shown in this table, for example, clients who score high on Scale 2 may have experienced significant and irretrievable loss. They may have responded by blocking needs or wants in order to avoid further loss. Similarly, according to this view, clients with a Spike 7 profile are preoccupied with avoiding the onset of shock or startle. This makes adaptive sense if they have experienced episodes of unpredictable negative events such as teasings or severe anxiety associated with an overload of childhood responsibilities.

According to this approach, the more elevated a scale, and the more scales that are elevated in the profile, the more of the client's life will be devoted to self-protective defensive behaviors. A given scale elevation determines the class of stress to which a client is most susceptible, and predicts how much of the individual's personality resources are allocated to producing defensive behavior. For example, an individual with a highly elevated 278 profile will be constantly preoccupied with avoiding the onset of unpredictable, humiliating loss. The client's history will reveal which conditioning experiences may have led to the adaptive responses reflected in the 278 configuration.

The types of defenses observed should be understood in relationship to the events that precipitated them. For example, high Scale 7 individuals fear unpredictable negative events. The defenses of being obsessive, compulsive, constantly attempting to anticipate the future (e.g. worrying), and feeling guilty when things go wrong, make sense when understood as an adaptive response to forestall future unpredictable negative events. The therapist then seeks to answer the question "What events could have conditioned such a fear?" A clinical history will reveal that there are certain early traumatic experiences that lead to the formation of a kind of psychological "scar tissue" so that current situations touching upon those earlier experiences or that reactivate the feelings associated with those earlier experiences can lead to highly defensive behavior. For example, Marks et al. (1974) reported that 60 percent of individuals with a 31 codetype experienced the death of a parent in childhood. These individuals could thus be more vulnerable to an adult experience of loss than those who had not experienced the early loss of a parent. They also reported 60 percent of the individuals with a 28 codetype experienced a significant disruption in their family of origin (e.g. due to parental mental illness). Perhaps a significant disruption in the clients' adult life would make them more susceptible to feeling depressed and hopeless, given their early experiences. Of course, some individuals develop more hardy coping mechanisms than others, leading to resilience and even post-traumatic growth (Tedeschi & Calhoun, 1995; Tedeschi, Park, & Calhoun, 1998).

Most clients desire feedback because feeling understood by a trained therapist can, in itself, be of substantial value (Erdberg, 1979; Finn & Tonsager, 1992). The general approach to giving feedback should be empathic and we provide suggested feedback language for most of the codetypes described earlier.

Guidelines for Giving Feedback

We suggest the following approach when giving feedback to clients about their MMPI-2 profiles:

1   Therapeutic assessment begins when the purpose for testing and the individual's concerns about how the test results will be used are addressed. Any past negative experiences with mental health professionals in general and negative assessment experiences in particular should be addressed before the assessment begins. Collaboratively discussing possible questions the individual seeks to answer through the MMPI-2 testing also helps to begin the process of therapeutic assessment. The assessment environment should be comfortable and private, and an individual competent to answer any questions that arise during the MMPI-2 administration should be available. A date should also be set for the feedback as well.

2   In the feedback session, the scored MMPI-2 profile is turned toward the client as he or she is told,

> You answered many questions, some of which may have seemed unusual or not applicable to you. That is because the questions were developed to assess a broad variety of experiences. [The therapeutic assessment paradigm involves

the assumption that all aspects of the client–assessor interactions are potentially therapeutic, so discussions about the client's experience of the MMPI-2 questions or the process should be seen in that context.] All of the questions you answered were scored, and we divided your personality into 10 dimensions as follows …
The client observes as the clinician counts from Scale 1 to Scale 0. This allows the client to examine the shape of the graph.

3   Next, the client is told,

> Here, on the left side [the clinician points to the validity scales], are some scores that tell me the way in which you answered the test. For example, were you self-critical, eager to tell me how you are feeling, or did you approach the test in a "stiff upper lip" manner? Are you the kind of person that readily expresses their feelings, or are you more private (see feedback statements for the validity scales)?

Be mindful not to share any information about how the validity scales operate so as to maintain the security of the test.

4   The client is then told that each clinical scale represents a dimension of personality. The lines at T-40 and T-65 represent statistical boundaries that define the average or typical range for each scale. The assessor may explain that the more elevated a scale, the more feelings and behaviors the individual experiences in that dimension. Some elevations also reveal discomfort, pain, and distress, so suggestions of pathology or deviance are avoided. Upon seeing an elevated profile, some people respond by interpreting the elevations as showing obvious deviousness and pathology. This can provide an opportunity for exploring the client's fears, anxieties, and concerns about their psychological issues or about being judged by the assessment results. The MMPI-2 should be viewed as a road map for a therapeutic exploration rather than a hierarchically explicated process. The actual profile graph does not always have to be shared with the client.

5   Use everyday language to describe the profile. Remember that many clients are cautious and defensive, anticipating being judged. Client resistance would suggest the feedback is creating defensiveness. If the client disagrees with the feedback, see it as an opportunity to engage in a therapeutic dialogue. For example, a client with an elevation on Scale 9 might be described as energetic, ambitious, and driven, but with a tendency to overcommit. In a hypothetical example, a high 9 client might resist and state they almost never overcommit and they have a reputation for reliable completion of all their commitments. Rather than becoming defensive, the psychologist could respond "Tell me about your energy level" or "Help me understand your energy level and how it affects your productivity." The feedback process needs to be a collaborative dialogue so that statements made by the therapist can be modified, enhanced, or dismissed based on the feedback from the client. The feedback is woven into a dialogue, rather than the client passively receiving the information from the clinician. Some clients want to hear all of the feedback issues before responding, perhaps to see how accurate the test is, or perhaps to see what they "need to defend themselves against." Encourage a dialogue. Give the feedback as questions more often than as statements of fact. Use the profile as a "road map" for asking the right questions (Levak et al., 2011).

6 Be empathic and understanding, and help clients see how what may appear as maladaptive behavior makes sense when understood in light of their history, past trauma, and current precipitating difficulties. For example, a person scoring high on Scale 2 experiences sadness and despondency much of the time, so it would be appropriate to inquire about past and recent losses that may have precipitated the adaptive response of withdrawal. Watch for when clients "shut down" or stop listening, or when they interrupt and divert attention or the conversation to another topic. Allow them to "take a breather" from the feedback, since their interruptions or distractions are cues that they have assimilated as much information as they are ready to process, that the feedback is not accurate, or that it is being experienced as criticism. Try to organize feedback by focusing first on a few anchor statements that are likely to validate a client's current experience of themselves. For example, all the different depression profiles (e.g. 27, 247, 278, etc.) will likely be associated with clients who experience symptoms of depression. Feedback that discusses how they are currently feeling less happy and positive than they would like would be endorsed by most individuals with any high 2 profile, regardless of which other scales are elevated. The feedback collaboration then hones the variable experiences associated with different types of depression and the types of conditioning experiences that precipitated the particular codetype. For example, persons scoring high on Scale 4 often respond to an initial feedback statement of "Your profile suggests that you are a survivor and that right now you are being cautious about letting yourself get emotionally involved in case you are let down and disappointed." The clinician could then ask, "Are you being cautious? Why?" After the client has responded to this, other feedback can be explored, but the clinician can return to this basic theme later as it relates to other issues being discussed during the session. For example, in the case of high 4 individuals, their difficulties in being intimate and trusting others could be discussed.

7 It is often useful at the end of the feedback session to ask the client to "summarize what you have heard today." This can be done in the last 10 minutes of the session so that any misunderstandings can be clarified and/or corrected. Clinicians can modify their feedback, depending on the purpose of the MMPI-2 testing. In some cases, it may be used as part of a diagnostic and treatment planning process. In others, it may be used during the course of treatment. For example, a second MMPI-2 given some time into therapy may reveal that a client is feeling more despondent and self-disliking than had been indicated on the initial MMPI-2. This, shared with the client, could then open up questions such as, "Is the client responding to reawakened, old memories brought alive by the therapy?" or "Is therapy actually being counterproductive?" On the basis of the feedback, the results can be used as a stimulus to refocus the therapy.

In brief treatment approaches, clients could be given feedback from the MMPI-2 so that specific behavioral corrective measures can be applied to alleviate the present distress. For example, a client scoring high on Scales 2 and 7 can be given specific behavioral techniques for working at lowering anxiety without further psychological intervention if that is not desirable or possible.

Feedback about the Feedback

In some cases it may be desirable to replicate the feedback paragraphs described in Chapter 6 of this book (or see Levak et al., 2011) that correspond to the client's code type. The client can then respond to each feedback statement for homework, providing a template for further exploration of the individual's make-up. The client's feedback about *their* feedback allows for an ongoing, collaborative, therapeutic engagement.

10 The Restructured Clinical (RC) Scales

Introduction

One of the more sweeping revisions to the standard MMPI-2 form came in 2003 with the introduction of the Restructured Clinical (RC) scales (Tellegen et al., 2003). These scales constitute the core set of scales of the latest form of the instrument, MMPI-2-RF, which will be discussed in the next chapter. Because the RC scales now comprise part of the standard MMPI-2 protocol, they will be discussed separately from form RF.

Among the reasons for creating the MMPI-2 RC scales was a desire to correct the longstanding problem of extensive co-variation among the clinical scales of the basic MMPI (Hathaway & McKinley, 1940) and MMPI-2 (Butcher, Dahlstrom, Graham, Tellegen, Dahlstrom, & Kaemmer, 2001)) which can make interpretation of the instrument somewhat difficult.

One source of the co-variation among the clinical scales is that the criterion-keying method of item selection employed by Hathaway and McKinley (1943) to select items for scale membership did not preclude them from appearing on scales that purportedly assess different diagnostic constructs. The item overlap among the clinical scales is not trivial, but substantial. If one considers only clinical Scales 1 through 4 and 6 through 9 (i.e. those scales with RC scale analogues), of the 259 items scored on one or more of these eight scales, 101 (39 percent) overlap at least one other scale. Of these, 66 items overlap only one other scale, 29 items are scored on three scales, 4 items are scored on four, and 2 items are scored on five. If one counts the actual number of overlaps between any two of the clinical scales, rather than the number of overlapping items, the total is 197 (see Table 10.1).

Table 10.1 Item overlap among MMPI-2 clinical scales

Scale	1	2	3	4	6	7	8	9
1	32							
2	9	57						
3	20	13	60					
4	1	7	10	50				
6	1	2	4	8	40			
7	2	13	7	6	4	48		
8	4	9	8	10	13	17	78	
9	0	1	4	6	4	3	11	46

Note: Values on diagonal are the number of items on each scale.

Among the number of reasons for item overlap across the clinical scales, two[1] are likely most responsible: (1) symptom overlap among psychiatric syndromes (Friedman, Gleser, Smeltzer, Wakefield, & Schwartz, 1983), and (2) shared first-factor variance. Each of these will be addressed below.

As there is a great deal of symptom overlap among psychiatric syndromes, it makes sense that overlapping items on scales that reflect syndromes with overlapping symptom presentations would lead to increased sensitivity of the scales; this increase in sensitivity, though, comes at the price of lowered specificity for the individual scales. Nichols (2006), in fact, has pointed out that within some samples, a pair of scales such as clinical Scale 7, viewed as a "neurotic" scale, and clinical Scale 8, viewed as a "psychotic" scale, might share close to 75 percent of their variance, although he further notes that this is not entirely surprising when one considers that the percentage of Scale 8 items that describe psychotic phenomena and the percentage that overlap Scale 7 are roughly equivalent. Both Goldberg (1965) and Dahlstrom (1969), however, have demonstrated that the configural pattern of scales with overlapping items can lead to enhanced predictability and classification. Thus, the historical shift from single-scale to codetype interpretation may be seen as an early attempt to compensate for the limited discriminant validity inherent in the clinical scales.

The second issue that affects item overlap among the clinical scales is that of shared first-factor variance. This factor reflects the major source of co-variation among MMPI/MMPI-2 scales and items and represents the broad, nonspecific general maladjustment or subjective distress dimension that has been given various labels, including Anxiety (Welsh, 1956) and Demoralization (Tellegen et al., 2003). This factor is pervasive throughout the MMPI/MMPI-2 item pools and serves to inflate the correlations among many, if not most, of the scales and, in turn, compromises their discriminant validity. The first factor is marked by a variety of item content including anxiety, tension, depression, and worry; reduced self-confidence/self-esteem; submissiveness or yielding in the face of obstacles; oversensitivity and irritability; and problems in concentration, memory, and initiative.

Given the substantial lack of specificity in the clinical scales, the RC scales project set out to create a set of scales that would better reflect the "…conceptually meaningful and clinically important constructs" (Tellegen et al., 2003, p. 11) represented by the original clinical scales.

Creation of the RC Scales

The construction of the RC scales proceeded in four steps. Although each of these steps will be briefly outlined below, the reader is encouraged to refer to Chapter 3 of the RC scales manual (Tellegen et al., 2003) for a more thorough description of the process.

The first step in the creation of the RC scales was to identify a subset of items to reliably measure the first factor and to create a new scale, termed *Demoralization*, to embody those items. The process undertaken by Tellegen et al. (2003) was informed by Watson and Tellegen's (1985) model of affect and based on Tellegen's (1985) assertion that the first-factor variance of the MMPI corresponded to the pleasantness–unpleasantness (PU) dimension of that model.

To create the Demoralization scale, Tellegen et al. (2003) first combined the items from clinical Scales 2 (Depression) and 7 (Psychasthenia), the scales they judged to be most saturated with the PU dimension. They then performed two dimension-reduction analyses of these items using principal components analysis with varimax rotation (PCA/V): once to identify items with high (at least |.50|) loadings on the first factor in each of four data sets, and again to identify items achieving high loadings on two other factors identified in the same data sets—Positive Emotionality (PEM) and Negative Emotionality (NEM). Ten items survived in both analyses. Items not appearing on Scales 2 and 7 were drawn from the remainder of the MMPI-2 item pool and added to these 10 items on the basis of their correlations with the PEM and NEM measures, yielding a Demoralization (*Dem*) scale of 23 items.

In Step 2, Tellegen et al. (2003) attempted to remove the covariance marked by *Dem* from each of the clinical scales. First, the *Dem* items were appended to each of the clinical scales, and the combined item set for each scale was subjected to PCA/V analysis to yield from two to five factors. Using this method, items from each scale that reflected PU variance would gravitate toward the *Dem* items and load on the first factor; items from each scale loading on this factor were then eliminated from the scale. Tellegen et al. then selected from their exploratory solutions a dimension judged to reflect a "substantive core" for each scale that remained "distinctive from demoralization and from the identified core components of the other Clinical Scales" (2003, p.15).

In Step 3, Tellegen et al. (2003) selected 158 of the original clinical scale items as candidates for membership in various "seed scales" that consisted of those items reflecting the distinctive core component of each clinical scale, as determined in Step 2. These seed scales were then refined to reduce overlap and increase internal consistency. From the remaining items, a second set of seed scales was derived to which items were either added to or eliminated from in order to increase the distinctiveness of the core component of each scale. The 73 items surviving these procedures were then sorted into a final set of seed scales for *RC1* through *RC9*. A seed scale for a revision of *Dem*, to be designated *RCd*, was also devised using 17 items of the original *Dem* scale.

In Step 4, the seed scales were augmented by items drawn from the entire MMPI-2 item pool. In short, an item was added to a seed scale if it demonstrated good convergence with the seed scale, as well as good discrimination from other seed scales. Items were deleted from seed scales if their inclusion led to reduced internal consistency or if they did not demonstrate adequate correlations with external validity criteria. These procedures culminated in the final RC scales, which are presented in Table 10.2, along with their corresponding clinical scales. Table 10.3 enables a comparison between the clinical, RC, and seed scales in terms of length and the extent to which items from the clinical scales persist in their RC versions and overlap with MMPI-2 content-based scales.

RC scales were not created for clinical Scales 5 and 0, as the core components of these scales were not judged to reflect psychopathology. Seed scales, however, were created for each of the core components (two core components in the case of clinical Scale 5); it was determined to focus on development of restructured versions of clinical Scales 5 and 0 at a later date.

Table 10.2 MMPI-2 RC scales and corresponding clinical scales

RC Scale	Clinical Scale
RCd Demoralization	
RC1 Somatic Complaints	Scale 1 Hypochondriasis
RC2 Low Positive Emotions	Scale 2 Depression
RC3 Cynicism	Scale 3 Hysteria
RC4 Antisocial Behavior	Scale 4 Psychopathic Deviate
RC6 Ideas of Persecution	Scale 6 Paranoia
RC7 Dysfunctional Negative Emotions	Scale 7 Psychasthenia
RC8 Aberrant Experiences	Scale 8 Schizophrenia
RC9 Hypomanic Activation	Scale 9 Hypomania

Table 10.3 Item composition and overlap for the clinical, seed, RC, and selected first factor and content-based scales

Length		Item Overlap (%)			
Scale	Clinical/RC	Seed Items	Clinical Scale Items	Off-Scale Items	Items from Content-Based Scales
RC1	32/27	15 (56%)	20 (74%)	7 (26%)	HEA: 20 (74%)
RC2	57/17	4 (24%)	8 (47%)	9 (53%)	INTR: 9 (53%); DEP: 2 (12%)
RC3	60/15	5 (33%)	5 (33%)	10 (67%)	CYN: 12 (80%); HEA: 0 (0%)
RC4	50/22	5 (23%)	9 (41%)	13 (59%)	DISC: 8 (36%); ASP: 6 (31%); AAS: 7 (32%)
RC6	40/17	6 (37%)	13 (76%)	4 (24%)	BIZ: 10 (59%); PSYC: 10 (59%)
RC7	48/24	7 (29%)	8 (33%)	16 (67%)	A: 10 (42%); ANG: 4 (17%); OBS: 3 (13%); ANX: 2 (8%)
RC8	78/18	6 (33%)	10 (56%)	8 (44%)	BIZ: 12 (67%); PSYC: 8 (44%)
RC9	46/28	8 (29%)	8 (29%)	20 (71%)	AGGR: 7 (25%); ANG: 4 (14%); TPA: 4 (14%)
RCd	–/24	17 (71%)	13 (54%)	11 (46%)	DEP: 11 (46%); NEGE: 1 (4%)

Notes: Decimals omitted. *RC1* = Somatic Complaints; *HEA* = Health Concerns; *RC2* = Low Positive Emotions; *INTR* = Introversion/Low Positive Emotionality; *DEP* = Depression; *RC3* = Cynicism; CYN = Cynicism; *RC4* = Antisocial Behavior; *DISC* = Disconstraint; *ASP* = Antisocial Practices; *AAS* = Addiction Admission Scale; *RC6* = Ideas of Persecution; *BIZ* = Bizarre Mentation; *PSYC* = Psychoticism; *RC7* = Dysfunctional Negative Emotions; *ANG* = Anger; *OBS* = Obsessiveness; *ANX* = Anxiety; *RC8* = Aberrant Experiences; *RC9* = Hypomanic Activation; *AGGR* = Aggressiveness; *TPA* = Type A; *RCd* = Demoralization; *NEGE* = Negative Emotionality/Neuroticism.

Source: Table adapted from Nichols (2006).

Psychometric Properties of the RC Scales

The RC scales have demonstrated good internal consistency (coefficient alpha) across multiple samples. Tellegen et al. (2003) reported internal consistency estimates ranging from .70 to .95 for males and .71 to .95 for females across various settings. As one might expect, given the core components' focus on psychopathology, internal consistency estimates were nominally higher among inpatient samples than within the normative sample.

Handel and Archer (2008) reported alpha estimates ranging from .83 to .94 for men and .82 to .94 for women among psychiatric inpatients. Simms et al. (2005) reported mean coefficient alpha estimates of .83 (range = .76 to .94) and .79 (range = .73 to .93) for clients at an outpatient psychology clinic and for military veterans, respectively. Rouse, Greene, Butcher, Nichols, and Williams (2008) reported mean alpha coefficients ranging from .70 to .90 across a variety of samples. Wygant, Boutacoff et al. (2007) reported coefficient alpha estimates ranging from .57 (*RC6*) to .89 (*RCd*) among candidates being evaluated for bariatric surgery. Similarly, van der Heijden, Egger, and Derksen (2008) reported alpha estimates ranging from .55 (*RC6*) to .87 (*RCd*) in the Dutch normative sample; alpha estimates in a Dutch clinical sample, however, ranged slightly higher, from .71 (*RC6*) to .91 (*RCd*). Finally, in a non-clinical sample of college students, Forbey and Ben-Porath (2008) reported alpha estimates ranging from .62 (*RC6*) to .87 (*RCd*) for males and .59 (*RC6*) to .89 (*RCd*) for females.

With regard to test–retest reliability, there has been little published research at the time of this writing. Tellegen et al. (2003), however, reported one-week test–retest correlations ranging from .76 to .91 for men and .54 to .90 for women in the MMPI-2 normative sample.

Scoring the RC Scales

The MMPI-2 re-standardization sample (Butcher et al., 2001) was used to develop gender-specific scoring norms and uniform *T*-score conversions. In addition to the traditional gender-specific scoring norms, non-gendered *T*-score conversions are available from the test publisher and are routinely scored by the Q Local scoring program offered by Pearson Assessments.

Scoring for the RC scales is accomplished in the same manner as with the clinical scales. As the RC scales now comprise part of the standard MMPI-2 protocol, they are routinely scored as part of a computer-based scoring or administration. Hand scoring templates, as well as gender-specific and non-gendered profile sheets, which are appropriate for personnel selection applications, are available from Pearson Assessments.

Using the RC Scales

In this section, each of the RC scales will be introduced. A description of the "core component" of each scale will be given. Additionally, the research surrounding each scale's correlates will be summarized. Finally, interpretative suggestions for high and low scores, when appropriate, will be offered.

First, a word about similarities and differences in relation to elevations on clinical and RC scales is warranted. In a valid profile when the elevation patterns match (i.e. no elevation on a clinical scale or its corresponding RC scale—or, conversely, elevations on each) one can be more confident in interpreting these scores. The approach may be less apparent, though, when discrepancies exist. Graham (2012) suggests that when the clinical scale is elevated, but the corresponding RC scale is not, one should use caution in making inferences about the test taker that reflect the core construct associated with the clinical scale, as their clinical scale elevation may reflect first-factor concerns. Graham notes that in many of these cases, *RCd* is likely to be elevated. He further suggests that with profiles in which the RC scale is elevated, but the corresponding clinical scale is not, one can reliably make inferences based on the core construct assessed by the RC scale and that, in these cases, there are likely to be less first-factor concerns.

Demoralization (*RCd*)

The *RCd* scale serves as a measure of general distress and emotional discomfort/turmoil that an individual is experiencing. The scale contains 24 items, with 22 keyed True. Thus, elevations on this scale can be affected by an All-True or All-False response set. Males in the normative sample scored significantly lower than females, although the effect size for the difference is small (see Table 10.4).

Correlates

Among psychiatric inpatients, Handel and Archer (2008) found that elevated *RCd* scores were positively related to suicide attempts, as well as to depression, anxiety, guilt, and blunted affect, as measured by the Brief Psychiatric Rating Scale (BPRS; Overall & Gorham, 1988). Arbisi, Sellbom, and Ben-Porath (2008) also found positive correlations with suicidal ideation and attempts, decreased energy, depression, anxiety, decreased sleep, and hopelessness among male VA inpatients and male and female community medical center inpatients. Tellegen and Ben-Porath reported the following correlates for inpatient men and women: cocaine abuse; depression and tearfulness; suicidality; decreased sleep, appetite, and energy; feelings of guilt, hopelessness, and worthlessness; poor concentration; loss of interest; and antidepressant medication.

Among those seeking outpatient psychiatric or psychological care, Sellbom, Graham, and Schenk (2006) found moderate to strong positive relationships between *RCd* scores and depression, somatization, paranoia, anxiety, and mania. Sellbom, Ben-Porath, and Graham (2006) found small, but significant, relationships between *RCd* and current Global Assessment of Function scores (this was a negative relationship), depression, interpersonal sensitivity, and insecurity. Binford and Liljequist (2008) found positive relationships between *RCd* scores and depressed mood, suicidal ideation, and sleep problems. Simms et al. (2005) found positive correlations for *RCd* scores and negative temperament, mistrust, and self-harm, as measured by the Schedule for Nonadaptive and Adaptive Personality (SNAP) (Clark, 1993), in samples of military veterans and college psychology clinic clients. Tellegen and Ben-Porath (2011) reported that *RCd* scores are positively correlated with descriptions of insecure, anxious, pessimistic, and depressed for males. Correlates for outpatient females included depressed. Among non-patients, Forbey and Ben-Porath (2008) reported

Table 10.4 Univariate statistics for RC raw scale scores by gender within the MMPI-2 normative sample

Scale	Sex	M	SD	F	d
RCd	Male	4.23	4.41	29.69	0.22
	Female	5.27	5.13		
RC1	Male	3.06	2.96	41.19	0.25
	Female	3.90	3.56		
RC2	Male	4.09	2.73	1.61	0.05
	Female	3.96	2.48		
RC3	Male	6.13	3.60	14.81	0.15
	Female	5.59	3.51		
RC4	Male	5.41	3.62	138.39	0.47
	Female	3.87	3.05		
RC6	Male	0.92	1.44	10.99	0.13
	Female	0.74	1.32		
RC7	Male	5.56	4.12	61.15	0.31
	Female	6.91	4.55		
RC8	Male	2.03	2.24	0.00	0.00
	Female	2.03	2.26		
RC9	Male	12.32	5.04	61.16	0.31
	Female	10.86	4.46		

Notes: For males, $N = 1,138$; for females, $N = 1,462$. d = Cohen's d, calculated by the formula $d = \dfrac{M_1 - M_2}{S_{Pooled}}$ where $s_{Pooled} = \sqrt{\dfrac{df_1}{df_{Total}}(s_1^2) + \dfrac{df_2}{df_{Total}}(s_2^2)}$

moderate to strong relationships between *RCd* scores and measures of depression and anxiety. Among the earlier MMPI-2 scales, *RCd* is highly correlated with *DEP* at .94 and non-*K*-corrected *Pt* at .93 (Greene, 2011).

Interpretation

In general, non-elevated scores on *RCd* indicate someone who is not experiencing a significant amount of psychological distress. As scores begin to elevate above a *T*-score of 65, individuals tend to report more dissatisfaction with their current situation and are likely to feel sad and anxious. Individuals with scores in this range see little chance of their situation improving in the future.

As scores increase, above a *T*-score of 75 we are likely to encounter individuals who feel unable to cope or are overwhelmed with their current situation, and are experiencing significant clinical distress and turmoil. Even more so than those with scores below 75, they feel that their future is bleak. Depression is more likely when scores are this high. Individuals with scores in this range should be thoroughly evaluated for suicide risk.

Somatic Complaints (RC1)

Tellegen et al. (2003, p. 54) noted that the RC1 scale "bears the strongest resemblance to its Clinical Scale counterpart" (*Hs*). *RC1* contains 27 items, 20 of which are shared with clinical Scale 1, with which it correlates at .96, and with *HEA* at .95 (Greene, 2011). The seven new items' content refers to head pain, muscle or movement dysfunction, speech problems, and having a lump in one's throat. Eleven items are keyed True and the remaining 16 keyed False. Thus, this scale is not particularly susceptible to an All-True or All-False response set. Females in the normative sample scored significantly higher than males, although the effect size for the difference was small (see Table 10.4).

Correlates

Among the correlates for psychiatric inpatients are chronic pain, along with decreased sleep, energy, and appetite (Arbisi et al., 2008). Handel and Archer (2008) reported physical illness, physical problems, somatic concerns, and suicide attempts among the correlates of higher scores on *RC1*. Tellegen and Ben-Porath (2011) reported that *RC1* scores were positively correlated with problems of suicidality and depression, along with antidepressant medication among inpatient women at the time of admission, but not in outpatient men. Correlates for inpatient men included decreased sleep, appetite, and energy among those treated at a community hospital, and chronic pain in those treated at a VA medical center. Additional correlates for females treated at a community hospital include depressed mood; decreased sleep, appetite, and energy; suicidal ideation; and chronic pain.

Somatization, depression, and anxiety were reported by Sellbom and colleagues (Sellbom, Ben-Porath, & Graham, 2006; Sellbom, Graham, & Schenk, 2006) among outpatient clients. Simms et al. (2005) reported moderate positive correlations between *RC1* scores and negative temperament and self-harm on the SNAP among their two samples. Tellegen and Ben-Porath (2011) included correlates of anxious, pessimistic, depressed, and somatic symptoms for both male and female outpatients. Forbey and Ben-Porath (2008) reported a moderate correlation between *RC1* scores and scores on a somatization screening instrument among non-patient college students.

Interpretation

In general, this scale reflects a preoccupation with physical functioning, although some studies have shown depressive and suicidal correlates. Elevations on *RC1* can occur when an individual has genuine physical or somatic complaints; thus, an elevation on this scale should not automatically lead one to assume hypochondriasis or a somatization disorder.

Non-elevated scores on this scale usually reflect an absence of significant physical complaints, whereas elevated scores reflect their presence. These are often of a gastrointestinal or neurological nature. Complaints of head pain are not uncommon, nor are complaints of fatigue and a loss of energy. Subjective reports of depression are also associated with high scores. As scores elevate above a *T*-score of 75, we begin to see individuals who are more likely to respond to psychological distress with physical symptoms; further, they are likely to reject psychological explanations for their symptoms, especially if *RC1* is elevated in isolation. The degree to which individuals with elevations in this range are preoccupied with their physical functioning is unusual among individuals with bona fide physical problems.

Low Positive Emotions (*RC2*)

As *RCd* corresponds to the negative emotionality aspect of Watson and Tellegen's (1985) model of affect, *RC2* corresponds to positive emotionality aspect, specifically, the relative lack of positive emotions. According to this model, negative affect is associated with both depression and anxiety, but a lack of positive affect is a distinguishing feature of depression (Watson, Clark, & Carey, 1988). When extracting items for the seed scale, two clear dimensions emerged from clinical Scale 2: a demoralization dimension, and a positive dimension that was negatively keyed. Of the 57 items on clinical Scale 2, only 8 are shared with *RC2*, or just under 50 percent of *RC2*'s items.

   RC2 contains 17 items, all keyed False; thus, this scale is particularly susceptible to an All-False response set. There was no significant difference on raw scores between females and males in the normative sample (see Table 10.4). Among other scales of the MMPI-2, *RC2* is correlated with *INTR* at .88 (Greene, 2011).

Correlates

Handel and Archer (2008) noted positive relationships with suicide attempts, depression, psychomotor retardation, blunted affect, and emotional withdrawal among psychiatric inpatients. Arbisi et al. (2008) reported depression and a wide range of accessory symptoms among inpatients at a community medical center; among male VA psychiatric inpatients, however, only depression was associated with *RC2* scores. Tellegen and Ben-Porath report positive correlations between *RC2* scores and depression, suicidality, and antidepressant medication in male and female inpatients. Additional correlates for males and females at a community hospital include decreased sleep, loss of interest, anhedonia, decreased energy, poor concentration, suicidal ideation, and feeling helpless, hopeless, and/or worthless. High *RC2* scores were associated with a history of a suicide attempts in men; in women, high scores were associated with a history of a suicide plan, although not with a history of attempts.

   Among outpatients, depression has been positively correlated with scores on *RC2* (Binford & Liljequist, 2008; Sellbom, Ben-Porath, Graham, 2006; Sellbom, Graham, Schenk, 2006). Other correlates include suicidal ideation, sleep problems (Binford & Liljequist, 2008), negative temperament (Simms et al., 2005), worries about the future (Forbey & Ben-Porath, 2007); loss of motivation (Forbey & Ben-Porath, 2007; Sellbom, Graham, & Schenk, 2006), and introversion (Sellbom, Graham, & Schenk, 2006). Tellegen and Ben-Porath (2011) include the following among the correlates for *RC2* scores in outpatient men: anxious, depressed, sad, self-doubting, self-degrading, self-punishing, preoccupied with health concerns, multiple somatic complaints, fatigue, acute psychological turmoil, difficulty concentrating, self-doubting, feels that life is a strain, fear of losing control, sleep disturbance, lonely, worrier, feels pessimistic and hopeless, feels like a failure, and feeling one is getting a raw deal from life. For women, the correlates include: sad, tearful, feels pessimistic and hopeless, self-doubting, self-degrading, self-punishing, feels like a failure, feels that life is a strain, socially awkward and insecure, lonely, sleep disturbance, and fatigue.

Ranson, Nichols, Rouse, and Harrington (2009) reported that in two large samples of Midwestern undergraduates (Total N = 1,202) *RC2* and *Si* predicted scores on the Wisconsin Physical and Social Anhedonia Scales (Kwapil, Chapman, & Chapman, 1999) about equally well, and less well than *INTR*, respectively, across all comparisons.

Interpretation

The scale essentially measures a lack of engagement in the positive emotional aspects of life, as well as in the types of activities associated with positive emotionality. Individuals scoring low (T < 39) are often described as confident, energetic, socially engaged, and optimistic. Individuals with elevated scores (T > 65) are at increased risk for depression. They find little pleasure in the activities of their lives or in social interactions. They may appear to be disengaged from those whom they have been close to in the past. They worry about a future that they view as bleak, and see little possibility for improving the future; thus, they have little motivation to effect change. They report a lack of energy, yet have difficulties with sleep; they may evidence psychomotor retardation. As scores increase beyond a T of 75, the possibility of major depression increases, as does the likelihood of suicidal ideation. Individuals scoring high on this scale should be carefully screened for suicidal thoughts.

Cynicism (*RC3*)

Tellegen et al. (2003, p. 55) described *RC3* as "represent[ing] a circumscribed component of clinical Scale 3 that we singled out as distinctive." All 15 items are keyed True; thus it is quite sensitive to an All-True response set. *RC3* shares 5 items with *Hy* (all from *Hy2*, Need for Affection), and 12 items with the Cynicism (*CYN*) content scale (11 of which appear on *CYN1*, Misanthropic Beliefs), with which it correlates at .93 to .95 among the Tellegen and Ben-Porath samples), and 10 items with the Hostility (*Ho*) scale, with which it correlates .85 (Greene, 2011). In addition, it shares four items with *Pa3*, Naïveté. Note that the items on *RC3* are reverse-scored as compared to clinical Scale 3, as Tellegen et al. stated a wish for higher scores to reflect higher levels of cynicism; thus, scores on *RC3* may be inversely related to scores on *Hy*. Males in the normative sample scored significantly higher than females, although the effect size for the difference was small (see Table 10.4).

Correlates

No correlates of moderate or greater strength have been reported among inpatient samples for *RC3* (Arbisi et al., 2008; Handel & Archer, 2008; Tellegen & Ben-Porath, 2011). Among outpatients, modest positive relationships have been reported for mistrust (Sellbom, Ben-Porath, & Bagby, 2008; Sellbom, Graham, & Schenk, 2006;

Simms et al., 2005), sleep disturbance in men (Tellegen & Ben-Porath, 2011), and anger (Sellbom et al., 2008) as well as high scores on the SNAP paranoid, schizotypal, borderline, and narcissistic personality disorder scales (Simms et al., 2005). Scores on RC3 were found to be negatively related to measures of agreeableness (Sellbom et al., 2008) and needs to achieve. Among non-patients, negativism has been shown to be moderately correlated (Forbey & Ben-Porath, 2008; Sellbom & Ben-Porath, 2005) with scores on RC3, as has Machiavellianism (Ingram, Kelso, & McCord, 2011) and alienation (Ingram et al., 2011; Sellbom & Ben-Porath, 2005). In addition, Sellbom and Ben-Porath have noted that positive well-being is negatively correlated with RC3 scores.

Greene (2011) has suggested that although few correlates exist for RC3, the theme of the items is one of occasional anger. Unlike the items on RC6, which will be discussed later, the items on RC3 are not self-referential.

Interpretation

Individuals who score low ($T < 39$) on RC3 have been described as seeing others as trustworthy. Low scores on this scale may also reflect naïveté or gullibility. High scorers, on the other hand, are described as being hostile and seeing others as essentially untrustworthy. They may feel alienated from others and, because of their inability to trust others, may have difficulty forming therapeutic alliances with caregivers. Because they often see others as essentially "being in it only for themselves," they may also be willing to take advantage of others.

Antisocial Behavior (RC4)

Tellegen et al. (2003) suggested that clinical Scale 4 contained an abundance of items pertaining to feelings of alienation and demoralization, and that RC4 provides "an unconfounded assessment of an individual's antisocial tendencies" (p. 56). RC4 contains 22 items, with 16 keyed True. Nine items remain from clinical Scale 4, eight items are shared with the Disconstraint PSY–5 scale (DISC; four of these also overlap clinical Scale 4), and seven items are shared with the Addiction Acknowledgement supplemental scale (AAS; two of these also overlap with clinical Scale 4), with which it correlates at .79 (Greene, 2011). Males in the normative sample scored significantly higher than females; the effect size for the difference was moderate (see Table 10.4).

Greene (2011) has suggested that RC4 correlates with scales in four categories: (1) antisocial attitudes and behaviors, (2) disconstraint, (3) substance abuse, and (4) family problems. Bolinskey and Nichols (2011) have expressed concern that the addition of items clearly related to substance abuse, in particular, may have caused an unintended "drift" away from the construct measured by the seed items (i.e. antisocial behavior) and made it possible for elevations on the scale to occur solely as a result of substance-related problems. Tellegen and Ben-Porath (2011), in fact, reported higher correlations for substance abuse problems and diagnoses than for any history of legal issues or diagnosis of antisocial personality disorder for both males and females, and in both outpatient and inpatient samples. Bolinskey, Trumbetta, Hanson, and Gottesman (2010), however, reported modest positive correlations between RC4 scores in adolescence and criminal behavior as an adult.

Correlates

Among inpatients, positive correlations have been found between *RC4* score and substance issues (Arbisi et al., 2008; Ben-Porath & Tellegen, 2008; Handel & Archer, 2008). Legal issues have also been associated with higher scores on *RC4* (Arbisi et al., 2008; Ben-Porath & Tellegen, 2008; Handel & Archer, 2008). Handel and Archer (2008) also noted a positive correlation with hostility. Ben-Porath and Tellegen (2011) reported that higher scores are associated with abusive behavior in men, but not in women. Tellegen and Ben-Porath (2011) note a positive correlation between *RC4* scores and suicidal ideation.

In outpatient samples, the primary *RC4* correlates have been found to be substance issues (Binford & Liljequist, 2008; Sellbom, Ben-Porath, & Graham, 2006), depression (Binford & Liljequist, 2008), mistrust, and manipulativeness (Simms et al., 2005). Tellegen and Ben-Porath (2011) found that both males and females with high scores on *RC4* were more likely to have been the victims of physical abuse than individuals with low scores; males were more likely to be physically abusive. Women with high scores were more likely to have been victims of sexual abuse. Tellegen and Ben-Porath also reported that both men and women felt that their family lacked love.

Interpretation

Individuals scoring low ($T < 39$) on *RC4* report a below average history of antisocial behavior and substance abuse. Individuals with elevated ($T > 65$) scores, however, are more likely to have a history of antisocial behavior and/or substance abuse. They are likely to have a history of failing to conform to social rules and norms, and to be described as argumentative, critical, or antagonistic in their relations with others. Thus, they often have a poor history of interpersonal relationships. Their family relationships tend to be strained or distant. They frequently have a history of poor achievement.

Ideas of Persecution (RC6)

RC6 contains 17 items, with 16 keyed True; as such, it is susceptible to an All-True response set. *RC6* shares 13 items with clinical Scale 6 (12 on *Pa1*, Persecutory Ideas, with which it correlates at .83 to .92 among the Tellegen and Ben-Porath [2011] samples), 10 with Bizarre Mentation (*BIZ*; 8 of these also appear on clinical Scale 6), and 10 with the PSY–5 Psychoticism scale (*PSYC*; 9 of these also appear on clinical Scale 6). Males in the normative sample endorsed significantly more items than did females, although the magnitude of the difference was small (see Table 10.4).

All but one of the *RC6* items are self-referential, in contrast to the items on *RC3* which are not. Tellegen et al. (2003) note that, as compared to clinical Scale 6, *RC6* is less saturated with demoralization and that an elevation of clinical Scale 6 in the absence of an elevation of *RC6* would suggest that the respondent is not experiencing clear persecutory ideation. Greene (2011) has suggested that the scale broadly correlates with measures of psychoticism and infrequent responses.

Correlates

Behavioral correlates that have been reported among inpatient samples include paranoid suspicions, delusions, and hallucinations (Arbisi, Sellbom, & Ben-Porath, 2008). Handel and Archer (2008) reported conceptual disorganization, suspiciousness, and hallucinatory behavior in their inpatient sample. Tellegen and Ben-Porath (2011) reported positive correlations for suspiciousness, ideas of reference, delusions, and hallucinations among inpatient men and women.

Among individuals seeking outpatient treatment, Sellbom, Graham, and Schenk (2006) reported a positive relationship between mistrust and RC6 scores. Simms et al. (2005) reported positive correlations between RC6 scores and measures of mistrust and eccentric perceptions. Sellbom, Ben-Porath, and Graham (2006) reported modest correlations with depression, global psychopathology, interpersonal sensitivity, anxiousness, and insecurity; interestingly, they did not report a significant relationship with suspiciousness. Tellegen and Ben-Porath (2011) reported the following correlates for males: feels that life is a strain, does not get along with coworkers, depressed, and self-degrading; they reported a negative relationship with high achievement needs. For women, they reported negative relationships with high aspirations, achievement needs, communication effectiveness, likability, having many interests, and creating a good impression.

Among non-patients, Forbey and Ben-Porath (2008) reported modest positive relationships between RC6 scores and measures of somatization, depression, and magical thinking. Sellbom et al. (2008) reported a negative relationship between RC6 scores and a measure of trust.

Interpretation

Low scores on RC6 are not interpreted. High scores may reflect significant persecutory ideation, such as the belief that others are out to harm one's self. As scores increase, the probability of paranoid delusions or other psychotic symptoms increases.

Individuals who score high on RC6 are often described as being suspicious of others and their motives. They see malicious intent in the actions of others and often blame others for their difficulties. Their mistrust of others can cause difficulties in interpersonal relationships; thus, these individuals are often alienated from others. As the T-score increases above 80, the individual should be carefully assessed for paranoid delusions and hallucinations.

Dysfunctional Negative Emotions (RC7)

RC7 was conceptualized as a scale to measure reports of negative emotional experiences, such as anxiety, anger, or fear. Of the 24 items in RC7, 8 are shared with clinical Scale 7, and 10 with Welsh's A (4 of these items also overlap clinical Scale 7). Greene (2011) reports a correlation between RC7 and A of .90 and notes that the various scales with which RC7 evidences very high (i.e. > .80) correlations represent only the broad category of general distress. Indeed, Bolinskey and Nichols (2011) have suggested that RC7 may be even more saturated with first-factor variance than clinical Scale 7, which they attribute as much to difficulties in the creation of the original scale as to problems unique to *RC7*. The saturation of *RC7* with the first-factor variance is not unexpected, given that all seven of its seed items overlap by at least one and as many as six items (*M* = 2.1) with three independent first-factor markers described by Nichols (2006).

RC7 contains 24 items, all keyed True. As with other scales, one should carefully evaluate the effects of response sets when interpreting elevations on this scale. Females in the normative sample evidenced a small, but significant, effect for endorsing more items than did their male counterparts (see Table 10.4).

Correlates

Handel and Archer (2008) reported positive relationships between *RC7* scores and anxiety, somatic concerns, and a history of sexual abuse among inpatients. Arbisi, Sellbom, and Ben-Porath (2008) reported decreased sleep, flashbacks, suicidal ideation, and antidepressant medication among the correlates of *RC7* scores among inpatients. Tellegen and Ben-Porath (2011) list antidepressant medication among the correlates for men, and antidepressant medication, depression, and suicidal ideation among the correlates for women in an inpatient setting.

Among those seeking outpatient treatment, Sellbom, Graham, and Schenk (2006) found *RC7* scores to be positively related to mistrust, depression, anxiety, and somatization. Simms et al. (2005) reported correlates of negative temperament, mistrust, manipulativeness, aggression, self-harm, eccentric perceptions, and detachment, as measured by the SNAP, within an outpatient sample. Scores on *RC7* were also positively related to scores on the paranoid, schizotypal, borderline, narcissistic, avoidant, and dependent personality scales of the SNAP. Within their sample of outpatients, Ben-Porath and Graham (2006) reported moderate correlates of global psychopathology, depression, interpersonal sensitivity, anxiety and insecurity. Among the correlates for outpatient men offered by Tellegen and Ben-Porath (2011) were acute psychological turmoil; anxiety; insecurity; sadness; tearfulness; moodiness; pessimism; preoccupation with health problems; difficulty concentrating; feeling overwhelmed, lonely, inferior, like a failure, and that one gets a raw deal from life; feeling as though one's family is lacking in love and resenting family members; keeping others at a distance; and being self-punishing and self-degrading. Poor stress tolerance was also positively correlated with *RC7* scores. For outpatient females, Tellegen and Ben-Porath reported positive relationships with the tendency to give up easily, as well as with suicidal ideation. Negative relationships were reported with stress tolerance, self-reliance, high aspirations, and having many interests.

Among non-patients, *RC7* scores have been correlated with measures of trait anxiety, trait anger, obsessive–compulsiveness, and social phobia (Forbey & Ben-Porath, 2008). Sellbom et al. (2008) reported positive relationships with anxiety, angry-hostility, self-consciousness, and vulnerability. They reported negative relationships with trust, conscientiousness, and competence.

Interpretation

Greene (2011) suggests that due to the high correlation between *RC7* and other measures of first-factor distress, only one such scale should be interpreted. We agree with this observation and note, again, that one should never use a score as confirming evidence for a high score on a scale with which it is redundant.

Low scores (*T* < 39) on *RC7* are obtained from individuals who report little or no general distress. High scores, on the other hand, reflect significant negative emotional experiences, such as anxiety, fear, or irritability. Individuals who score high on *RC7* can often be described as feeling sad and unhappy. They are prone to guilt and have a tendency to be self-critical. They worry excessively and are very insecure; as such, they are prone to perceive criticism where it may not exist. They are pessimistic; they expect to fail and believe that they have failed. They frequently worry and have sleep difficulties, including nightmares. They may feel overwhelmed and incapable of coping with their current situation. Particularly high scores (*T* > 80) reflect significant emotional discomfort and helplessness; a referral for medication evaluation may be warranted.

Aberrant Experiences (*RC8*)

Tellegen et al. (2003) noted that the *RC8* items describe a wide variety of symptoms, including sensory, perceptual, cognitive, and motor disturbances. *RC8* is much less saturated with first-factor variance than is its clinical Scale 8 counterpart. Further, unlike scales such as *BIZ* or *PSYC*, the items of *RC8* do not include paranoid content, as that construct was confined to *RC6*. *RC8* contains 18 items, with 17 keyed True; thus, elevations are particularly sensitive to an acquiescent or All-True response set. Of these 18 items, 10 appear on clinical Scale 8, 8 on *PSYC*, and 12 on *BIZ* (4 on *BIZ-1* and 6 on *BIZ-2*). No difference in mean item endorsement was observed between males and females in the normative sample (see Table 10.4).

Nichols (2006) observed that *RC8* reflects a good balance in content reflecting anomalous experience (e.g. de-realization and hallucinations) and Schneider's (1959) First Rank symptoms, such as thought broadcasting. He noted that there is no other MMPI-2 scale in which this content is better represented and concentrated. Greene (2011) reported a correlation between *RC8* and *BIZ* of .91, and noted that the defining characteristics of those scales with which *RC8* highly correlates are psychotic behaviors and symptoms, infrequent responses, and general distress.

Correlates

Handel and Archer (2008) reported that *RC8* scores were positively related to ratings of conceptual disorganization, hallucinatory behavior, and unusual thought content among psychiatric inpatients. Others (Arbisi, Sellbom, & Ben-Porath, 2008) have also reported that hallucinations are associated with *RC8* elevations in inpatient men and women.

Sellbom, Graham, and Schenk (2006) reported *RC8* correlates among outpatients that included bizarre experiences, paranoia, panic, anxiety, and mania. Simms et al. (2005) reported that *RC8* scores were moderately correlated with ratings of negative temperament, mistrust, and eccentric perceptions. Among the correlates for male outpatients reported by Tellegen and Ben-Porath (2011) are anxiety, depression, somatic complaints, low achievement-oriented, sleep disturbance, feelings of failure, and difficulty making decisions. Correlates reported for female outpatients included a history of suicide attempts and sexual abuse, hallucinations, feeling disoriented, and a poor ability to cope with stress.

Among non-patients, Forbey and Ben-Porath (2008) noted that *RC8* scores were positively correlated with scores on the Magical Ideation (Eckblad & Chapman, 1983) and Perceptual Aberration (Chapman, Chapman, & Raulin, 1978) scales. Sellbom et al. (2008) reported that higher scores on *RC8* were associated with lower scores on trust.

Interpretation

Low scores on *RC8* should not be interpreted. Individuals who produce moderately elevated *T*-scores in the range of 65 to 74 may be exhibiting schizotypal characteristics. They are reporting unusual perceptions and thought processes, which may include hallucinations and/or delusional beliefs. They may exhibit impaired reality testing. They are often described as anxious or depressed. They have difficulty trusting others and are also likely to have difficulties in interpersonal and occupational functioning. As *T*-scores elevate above 75, the possibility of schizophrenia or another psychotic disorder increases, along with the degree of thought and perceptual disturbance. Referral for a medication evaluation, hospitalization, or intensive therapy should be considered.

Hypomanic Activation (*RC9*)

The items in *RC9* have been described as measuring behaviors such as racing thoughts, increased energy, expanded mood, heightened self-regard, sensation-seeking, and irritability—all behaviors associated with hypomanic activation (Tellegen et al., 2003). *RC9* contains 28 items, with all but one keyed True; it is therefore particularly sensitive to All-True or All-False response sets. It shares eight items with clinical Scale 9 and seven with the Aggressiveness (*AGGR*) PSY-5 scale (one of these items also overlaps clinical Scale 9). Males evidence a small, but significant effect for endorsing more items than their female counterparts in the normative sample (see Table 10.4).

Greene (2011) has observed that scores on *RC9* correlate most highly with scales that measure antisocial attitudes and behaviors, hypomania, and aggression. Bolinskey and Nichols (2011) suggested that the hypomanic activation core present in the seed items for *RC9* may have been significantly diluted by the angry, vindictive, and aggressive content recruited into the scale in Step 4 of the RC scales' development. As a consequence, in some profiles an elevation on *RC9* may be generated more on the basis of this scale's hostile content than by its hypomanic content.

Correlates

Tellegen and Ben-Porath (2011) report a history of cocaine abuse and a history of violent behavior among the correlates of *RC9* scores for inpatient men. For inpatient women, they reported correlates of histories of substance abuse, and cocaine abuse, as well as a diagnosis of substance abuse or dependence. Handel and Archer (2008) reported substance abuse, conceptual disorganization, and excitement among the correlates of *RC9* in a sample of psychiatric inpatients. Arbisi, Sellbom, and Ben-Porath (2008) reported that cocaine use was positively correlated with *RC9* scores.

In a sample of individuals seeking outpatient treatment, Simms et al. (2005) reported manipulativeness, aggression, and disinhibition among the correlates of *RC9* scores. Scores on *RC9* were also strongly correlated with scales associated with antisocial, borderline, histrionic, and narcissistic personality disorders. Sellbom, Ben-Porath, and Graham (2006) reported that elevated *RC9* scores were correlated with descriptions of clients as antisocial and aggressive. Sellbom, Graham, and Schenk (2006) reported mistrust and mania were associated with higher scores on *RC9*.

Among non-patients, Forbey and Ben-Porath (2008) reported that higher *RC9* scores were associated with higher scores on measures of general impulsivity, motor impulsivity, and activation. Sellbom et al. (2008) reported that *RC9* scores were positively correlated with measures of angry-hostility, impulsiveness, and excitement-seeking. *RC9* scores were negatively associated with scores on measures of agreeableness, trust, straightforwardness, compliance, modesty, and deliberation.

Interpretation

Individuals who score low (*T* < 39) on *RC9* are reporting low levels of hostility, energy, and engagement with the environment. Individuals with elevated scores may be described as irritable or hostile. They report increased levels of energy and may experience racing thoughts. Individuals with high scores are likely to be high in sensation-seeking; they may have poor impulse control and be more inclined to engage in antagonistic and/or risky behaviors. They may exhibit antisocial behaviors and have problems with substance abuse. As *T*-scores increase above 75, the likelihood of a manic episode increases. A referral for a medication evaluation should be considered.

A Final Word on Interpretation

It can be expected that clinicians familiar with the MMPI-2 and the codetype approach to its interpretation may well wish to know how the codetype strategy might be applied to the profile of RC scale scores. At present, the RC/RF authors have not recommended such an application, and data bearing on the correspondence of clinical scale and RC scale profiles is in short supply. One obvious point of discrepancy is with respect to the *Hy* and *RC3* scales, with the former emphasizing the denial of cynical traits and attitudes (see *Hy2*, from which all of the *RC3* seed items were drawn), and the latter affirming such traits/attitudes. However, even if *Hy* and *RC3* are dropped from consideration, the correlations in the Tellegen et al. (2003) samples between *Hs* and *RC1*, *D* and *RC2*, *Pd* and *RC4*, *Pa* and *RC6*, *Pt* and *RC7*, *Sc* and *RC8*, and *Ma* and *RC9*, average only .76 (range: .62 for *RC6* to .94 for *RC1*), indicating that the RC scales account for less that 60 percent of the variance of the clinical scales. As a consequence, the pattern of elevations on the profile of RC scale scores may be expected to differ both widely and frequently from the codetype patterns formed by the clinical scales.

Although there are as yet no rules of thumb available for reconciling clinical scale and RC scale profiles when these are discrepant, it can be suggested that the clinician turn to the RC scale/content-based correlates identified by Rouse et al. (2008) and by Greene (2011). Thus, for example, *RC1* may be compared with *HEA*, *RC2* with *INTR*, *RC3* with *CYN1*, *RC4* with *AAS*, *RC6* with *Pa1*, *RC7* with *NEGE*, *RC8* with *BIZ*, and *RC9* with *AGGR*. Across the same samples as above, Tellegen and Ben-Porath (2011) report correlational values for each of these scale pairs averaging .85 (range: .67 for *RC9/AGGR* to .94 for *RC3/CYN1*), or about 11 percent higher than for the correlations between the RC scales and their parent clinical scales (excluding *Hy/RC3*). This increase in the magnitude of association between content-based MMPI-2 scales and the RC scales is only to be expected, as the RC scales are themselves content driven.

In summary, at the present state of knowledge, seeking to expect equivalence between the pattern of scores and their respective codetypes for the clinical scales, on the one hand, and the RC scales, on the other, is ill-advised. Rather, it is recommended that the clinician treat the RC scales as new content-based measures that are likely to find better accord with other content-based scales than with their clinical scale parents. And it is with these measures that correspondences should be sought, not with the clinical scales. As to which of *any* pattern of scores, clinical scale, content scale, RC scale, PSY–5 scale, or others, the clinician must judge the accuracy of "fit" for the patient in the usual manner, against interview and case history findings, the reports of informants, contemporary behavioral observations and ratings, and so on.

Criticisms of the RC Scales

The introduction of the RC scales has not been without controversy. Indeed, at least two of the authors of this book (i.e. Bolinskey and Nichols) have published works that urge caution in interpreting elevations on some scales. Further, James N. Butcher, the primary architect of the revision of the MMPI that led to MMPI-2, has written that he does not recommend the RC scales for clinical use (Butcher, 2011). Others, of course—chief among them Auke Tellegen and Yosef S. Ben-Porath, who were also heavily involved in the creation of MMPI-2—have published an even greater number of works purporting to provide evidence of the scales' clinical utility. Although a complete review of the extant literature concerning use of the RC scales is beyond the scope of this chapter, we will attempt to summarize the literature from both points of view. Finally, we will attempt to offer a bit of perspective.

Empirical Tradition

Butcher (2011) has criticized the *method* of the RC scales' creation, noting that Tellegen et al. (2003) essentially abandoned the empirical method of test construction on which the MMPI/MMPI-2 was based. Caldwell (2006) noted that the difference between factorially-derived scales and empirically-derived scales is that of "maximal" (i.e. to measure something very well) versus "meaningful" measurement, which can be thought of in terms of criterion discrimination. The MMPI and MMPI-2 scales, of course, were based on the latter method of test construction, whereas the RC scales were based on the former.

Theoretical Basis

Some have questioned the appropriateness of Watson and Tellegen's (1985) hierarchical model of mood as the starting point for the development of the RC scales, opening this model to criticism on the basis of its performance in subsequent empirical investigations of mood. Indeed, following an analysis of this literature, Ranson, Nichols, Rouse, and Harrington (2009) concluded that the Watson–Tellegen model is neither convincingly corroborated, nor has it performed advantageously relative to competing models of mood such as the circumplex model of Russell (1980). Despite the appropriate and well-ordered series of steps employed in the construction of the RC scales following the initial creation of the *Dem* marker for Watson and Tellegen's PU dimension, it is unclear how any deficiencies of the Watson–Tellegen model—and the representation of its PU dimension in *Dem*/*RCd* (including the omission of a replication of the RC authors' Step 2 using *RCd* following its revision from *Dem*)—may have affected the final versions of the RC scales.

Redundancy

Rouse et al. (2008) found that each of the RC scales correlate more highly with a supplementary, content, or PSY-5 scale than with its parent clinical scale. They further argued that over half of the *RC* scales (e.g. *RCd*, *RC1*, *RC3*, *RC7*, *RC8*, and *RC9*) were redundant with existing MMPI-2 scales due to the extraordinarily high correlations they evidence with those scales. Tellegen, Ben-Porath, and Sellbom (2009), however, countered the first argument by noting that the RC scales were not created to mimic the clinical scales; they noted that, rather than trying to capture the divergent and overlapping content of the clinical scales, the *RC* scales were created to measure a distinctive core component of each clinical scale. To the second argument, they note that the proposed "proxy" scales with which Rouse et al. (2008) argued that the RC are redundant are less distinguishable from one another than are the RC scales; they further argued that the RC scales better account for variance in the clinical scales than do the proposed proxies. Greene, Rouse, Butcher, Nichols, and Williams (2009) offered a rejoinder in which they, again, demonstrated the high correlations of the RC scales with extant MMPI-2 scales and noted that the MMPI-2-RF Technical Manual (Tellegen and Ben-Porath, 2011), also demonstrates the same high correlations as noted by Rouse et al.

Construct Drift

Nichols (2006) used the term "construct drift" to refer to the possibility that adding items that correlated with seed items (i.e. in Step 4 of the RC scales' creation) risked the drift of the selected core construct in the direction of substantive content areas at variance with this core. Among the RC scales for which the possibility of construct drift has attracted some empirical attention are RC3, RC4, RC7, and RC9.

With regard to RC3, Butcher (2011, p. 182) has noted that the "rich descriptors" associated with clinical Scale 3 and its associated codetypes are lost when using RC3. Thomas and Youngjohn (2009) have further noted that RC3 is not particularly useful as a marker of somatization among traumatic brain injury patients. It has been suggested (Butcher, Hamilton, Rouse, & Cumella, 2006; Nichols, 2006) that RC3 has essentially drifted to the point of being an entirely different scale from clinical Scale 3, and one that is redundant with CYN/CYN1.

With respect to this criticism, it is worth noting that this differentiation of RC3 from clinical Scale 3 was not unintentional, a fact acknowledged by Nichols (2006). Tellegen et al. (2003) clearly stated the intention to concentrate somatic concerns on RC1, which left a smaller proportion of items from which to extract a unique core component. They also noted a decision to reverse-score the items in order to reflect more clinical concerns. With regard to redundancy, Tellegen et al. (2006) noted that item overlap works in both directions. They pointed out that while 80 percent of RC3 items appear on CYN, only 52 percent of CYN items appear on RC3. The CYN items that do not appear on RC3 are self-referential items, which reflect a construct that was isolated to RC6. The item overlap of RC3 and CYN occurs primarily with CYN1, which overlaps RC3 by 11 items.

The primary area for concern regarding RC4 has been its high degree of correlation with substance abuse. Caldwell (2006, p. 194) noted that clinical Scale 4 was created to identify "the asocial and amoral type of psychopathic personality." Although Nichols (2006) initially suggested that RC4 may be an improvement over previous scales, he also expressed concern that the high proportion of substance abuse items may "risk false positive inferences of broad antisocial dispositions and behavior based on substance abuse alone" (p. 135); this concern was later echoed by Bolinskey and Nichols (2011). Indeed, as pointed out earlier, RC4 scores consistently demonstrate higher positive correlations with substance use than with legal difficulties (see, e.g. Tellegen et al., 2003).

The solution to such an apparent impasse might be found if we simply consider the respective reported purposes of clinical Scale 4 and *RC4*. As Caldwell (2006) notes, clinical Scale 4 was designed to measure a type of personality; Nichols (2006, p. 123) referred to this aspect of the clinical scales as their "syndromal complexity." The RC scales, however, were never designed to measure this type of syndromal complexity; Weed (2006), in fact, questions whether this complexity is worth preserving. The stated purpose of *RC4* is the assessment of past and current antisocial behavior, rather than a type of personality. One could certainly argue that substance issues would fall under the former umbrella; Ben-Porath and Tellegen (2008, 2011), in fact, list substance abuse as a correlate of *RC4* in the MMPI-2-RF Interpretive *Manual*. Even if one does not wish to include substance abuse as a manifestation of antisocial behavior—thus raising the question of false positives based on *RC4* scores—clinical Scale 4 was by no means immune to false positives; in the latter case, however, false positives may have arisen as a consequence of demoralization/first factor variance.

With regard to *RC7*, the focus of criticism has been as much on its redundancy with other first-factor scales as on its drift away from the original construct of psychasthenia. Bolinskey and Nichols (2011) have recently suggested that this drift may have actually occurred as much during the creation of the original clinical Scale 7 as in the creation of *RC7*. Regardless of when such drift occurred, it appears that *RC7*, like its predecessor, remains saturated with first-factor variance. We suggest that the reader heed Greene's (2011) caution regarding the interpretation of redundant scales.

The empirical correlates of *RC9* lend support to Nichols' (2006; Bolinskey & Nichols 2011) suggestion that the aggressive content in *RC9* may overpower the manic content on some profiles. That is not to suggest that elevations on *RC9* are necessarily not associated with hypomanic activation—as Tellegen et al. (2006) point out, agitation and irritability are among the diagnostic criteria for mania, but were not included among Hathaway and McKinley's (1943) criterion group's symptoms—but simply to serve as a reminder for caution when interpreting elevated scores on *RC9*.

Sensitivity

Homogeneous scales with obvious item content, of which the RC and MMPI-2 content scales are examples, tend to be somewhat more vulnerable to both under- and over-reporting than are the more complex, multivariate MMPI-2 clinical scales. Studies using a variety of samples have found that the RC scales elevate less readily, that is to say are less sensitive, or more prone to false negatives, than are the MMPI-2 clinical scales (Binford & Liljequist, 2008; Cumella, Kally, & Butcher, 2009; Gordon, Stoffey, & Perkins, 2013; Gucker, Kreuch, & Butcher, 2009; Haas & Saborio, 2012; Megargee, 2006; Pizitz & McCullaugh, 2011; Rogers, Sewell, Harrison, & Jordan, 2006; Sellbom, Ben-Porath, McNulty, Arbisi, & Graham, 2006; Wallace & Liljequist, 2005; but see also Osberg, Haseley, & Kamas, 2008). The findings reported by Megargee and by Pizitz and McCullaugh are particularly concerning in this respect. In a large (> 2,000) sample of incarcerated felons, Megargee found that their mean scores on the RC scales were, on the average, lower than the mean RC scores of the MMPI-2 re-standardization sample, and all were below a T-score of 56, including *RC4* (Antisocial Behavior), a scale one would expect to be significantly elevated among prison inmates. Pizitz and McCullaugh, in a sample of convicted male stalkers, found that five of the RC scales (*RC2, RC3, RC7, RC8,* and *RC9*) showed a mean T-score below 50, and that the mean T-score for *RC4*, a scale that one would expect to be elevated in such a sample, was only 51.7, more than a standard deviation below that obtained by these men on Scale 4. Converting the MMPI-2 to the MMPI-2-RF, these investigators found that of the 42 substantive (i.e. non-validity) scales on this form, only 8 achieved mean scores greater than T-50, the highest of these being on Mechanical-Physical Interests (MEC; see Chapter 11), at a T-score of 57, for this all-male criminal sample.

The reasons for this apparent lack of sensitivity of the RC scales are not difficult to find. Like those of the MMPI-2 content scales, the vast majority of the RC items are content-obvious, and thus readily avoided. Additionally, like the content scales, for which the keyed response is True for 297 of their 366 total items (81 percent), $M = 21$ items per scale, the keyed response for the RC scales (*RC1–RC4* and *RC6–RC9*) is True for 126 of their 168 total items (75 percent), $M = 21$ items per scale. These patterns are in substantial contrast with the MMPI-2 clinical scales, those representing psychiatric syndromes (*Hs, D, Hy, Pd, Pa, Pt, Sc,* and *Ma*). Of the 411 items that are scored on one or more of these scales, the keyed response is True for 228 items (55 percent), $M = 51$ items per scale. Thus the examinee who wishes to minimize the possibility of psychopathology being detected on the RC scales, as on the content scales, may readily do so by generally avoiding True responses, whereas this strategy will be less successful as applied to the more evenly True/False balanced MMPI-2 clinical scales.

The assessment of potentially false negative RC scale scores and/or patterns may proceed with reference to the customary validity scales and indicators. In general, RC false negatives appear to occur most frequently in the context of at least one or more indications of under-reporting/defensiveness, such as elevations on one or more of *L, K, S, Mp,* and *Sd,* or on negative values for the $F - K$ index, –10 to –20, or less. Additionally, a bias favoring False responding can often be detected by the True/False balance, with a relatively high False percent, greater than, say, 60 percent False, suggesting, and greater than 70 percent, strongly suggesting, such bias. Finally, of course, it behooves the psychologist to seek to reconcile RC scales that appear to be under-elevated with any reliable extra-test data supporting the presence of bona fide psychological disturbance.

Perspective

Archer and Newsom (2000) noted that there had been little change in psychologists' tests over the course of four decades. They further noted that although this lack of change reflected, to some degree, the robustness of the tests employed by psychologists, it spoke as well to the rather slow pace of change in the field of clinical assessment. We are all creatures of habit; we are comfortable with what we know and change is difficult. However, as Rogers and Sewell (2006, pp. 177–178) remind us, "One should not be a slave to the best test-construction practices of 1940."

Archer (2006) noted that it was precisely the desire to maintain continuity with the previous version of the instrument that led to the relatively modest revision that resulted in MMPI-2. This effort at moderation, however, did not assuage those who felt that the MMPI-2 represented too radical a departure from the original version (Adler, 1990). In the case of the RC scales, although there was some effort made to preserve some continuity with the original clinical scales with the decision to base each of the RC scales on a core component of a clinical scale, this effort was far less than that made in the MMPI-2 revision. However, it appears that the effort to maintain this level of continuity may have backfired to some extent. Whereas some (Rogers and Sewell, 2006) question the logic of basing the RC scales only upon distinctive core components of the eight clinical scales, others (e.g. Butcher, 2011; Nichols, 2006; Rouse et al., 2008) point out that the RC scales often do not correlate highly with their parent clinical scales.

We are reminded of Meehl's (1959) observation that the point of psychological testing should not be to predict what the psychiatrist down the hall would say. In that same vein, we would offer the reminder—as Tellegen et al. (2003) noted and have continued to point out—that the purpose of the RC scales was not to have them align perfectly with the clinical scales. Such an exercise would have been pointless. Rather, the RC scales were designed to measure different, but related constructs—maximal measurement, if you will, but not meaningless. We should acknowledge that the RC scales are different than the clinical scales and will not provide identical measures of the same constructs as the earlier scales. Likewise, we must accept that they are imperfect measures of the constructs they were designed to assess—and may, in fact, contain more "syndromal complexity" than was intended (e.g. see *RC4* and *RC9*). The goal of future research should be to help us understand what the RC scales *do* rather than do *not* measure. As with any psychometric instrument, the burden ultimately lies with the user to fully understand the research with regard to both the concurrent and predictive validity of an instrument before incorporating that measure into their clinical practice.

Note

1   One might argue that a third reason for item overlap is error (i.e. an item falling on a scale due to a spurious correlation between the criterion and item endorsement frequency). Such an argument, however, is beyond the scope of the present discussion.

11 The Restructured Form of the MMPI-2 (MMPI-2-RF)

The MMPI-2-RF

The Restructured Form of the MMPI-2 (MMPI-2-RF; Ben-Porath & Tellegen, 2011; Tellegen & Ben-Porath, 2011) is a 338-item, self-report measure consisting of 51 new and revised Validity and Substantive scales, with the Restructured Clinical (RC) scales as its foundation. The MMPI-2-RF was developed with the support of the University of Minnesota Press, the copyright holder of the MMPI-2, following the publication of the RC scales. Each of the MMPI-2-RF items appears on the 567-item MMPI-2; thus, dual scoring is possible when the respondent was initially administered the MMPI-2 using item-conversion tables available in the *MMPI-2-RF Manual for Administration, Scoring, and Interpretation* (Ben-Porath & Tellegen, 2011). As of the time of this writing, the MMPI-2-RF is being offered as an alternative to, but not a replacement for, the MMPI-2; the MMPI-2 continues to be fully supported by the test publisher (Ben-Porath & Tellegen, 2011).

Tellegen et al. (2003), in concluding their introduction of the RC scales, noted that creation of those scales might instigate research into the creation of additional scales to measure important clinical aspects beyond those captured by the clinical scales, and which may also be confounded by a demoralization component. Such research culminated in the release of the MMPI-2-RF, which Ben-Porath and Tellegen (2011, p. 1) state was "designed to provide an exhaustive and efficient assessment of the clinically relevant variables measureable with the instrument's item pool."

As noted above, the core of the instrument consists of the nine RC scales, introduced in Chapter 10. Beyond the RC scales, MMPI-2-RF contains 9 validity scales, 3 higher-order scales, 23 specific problem scales, 2 interest scales, and the revised PSY–5 (PSY–5-r) scales. In total, the MMPI-2-RF comprises 51 scales. Each of these will be described within a section devoted to a general discussion of their group.

In addition to its reduced length and administration time, as compared with the MMPI-2, the 42 substantive scales (i.e. excluding the validity/response style scales) of the MMPI-2-RF, the average scale length is 14 items, and the average proportion of items keyed True for these scales is 73 percent. By contrast, for the 103 substantive (again excluding the validity/response style scales) MMPI-2 scales included in the most recent edition (Butcher et al., 2001) of the MMPI-2 *Manual*, the average scale length is 22 items, and the average proportion of items keyed True for these scales is 63 percent. In brief, the scales of the MMPI-2-RF average 36 percent fewer items and 14 percent more items keyed in the True direction than the comparable substantive scales of the MMPI-2.

As of the time of this writing (the first quarter of 2013), there remains a dearth of research specifically devoted to the interpretation of the MMPI-2-RF, although substantial interpretive guidance can be found in Ben-Porath (2012). Unless otherwise noted, the correlates and interpretive suggestions offered for this instrument are derived from this source and from the two MMPI-2-RF *Manuals* (Ben-Porath & Tellegen, 2011; Tellegen & Ben-Porath, 2011); the reader is encouraged to keep abreast of new reports in the psychological assessment literature that will undoubtedly add to our body of knowledge regarding this relatively new instrument.

Administration

Test User Considerations

Qualifications for administration, scoring, and interpretation of the MMPI-2-RF are the same as for the standard MMPI-2, described in Chapter 2. The reader is urged to review the chapter on administration and scoring the MMPI-2 at this time. The reader is also encouraged to review and abide by the American Psychological Association's "Ethical Principles of Psychologists and Code of Conduct," specifically Standard 9, which pertains to psychological assessment.

Test-Taker Considerations

The MMPI-2-RF is designed to be used with adults, aged 18 years and older. It is not recommended to be used, nor is its use supported, with individuals younger than 18 years.

Ben-Porath and Tellegen (2011) recommend that the test taker has at least a sixth-grade reading level to complete either the booklet or computerized administrations of the MMPI-2-RF. If there is doubt about the test-taker's ability to adequately read and understand the items, they recommend that a standardized test of reading ability be administered. If the test taker does not possess an adequate reading level or if it is not possible to perform an assessment of reading level, they recommend that a standardized audio version of the test be administered using either the audio CD or computerized version available from the test publisher. They further note that if an individual who does not possess adequate reading ability is nonetheless administered a written version of the test, it is very likely that the inconsistency scales will detect the difficulty.

Available Formats

As of the time of this writing, the MMPI-2-RF is available only in English. Translations into other languages are not yet available. As with MMPI-2, both softcover and spiral-bound booklets are available for pencil and paper administration. Both require a separate answer sheet and are reusable. Given the popularity of computer-based administration, the MMPI-2-RF can be used with administrative and scoring software available through Pearson Assessments. Additionally, an audio CD is available for use with individuals who do not meet the minimum reading ability requirements for the test.

Scoring

Normative Sample

The normative sample for the MMPI-2-RF is a subset of the MMPI-2 re-standardization sample of 1,138 men and 1,462 women. Because of the authors' desire to create non-gender specific *T*-scores for MMPI-2-RF, the larger re-standardization female sample was reduced by randomly selecting a subsample of 1,138 women to yield a total normative sample of 2,276 for the MMPI-2-RF. The ethnicity, education, and age distributions of the MMPI-2-RF normative sample very closely resemble those of the MMPI-2 re-standardization sample. The reader is referred to the test manual (Ben-Porath and Tellegen, 2011) for a further description of the normative sample.

T-score Conversions

As noted above, the MMPI-2-RF incorporates only non-gendered norms. The use of non-gendered norms complies with the provision of the Civil Rights Act of 1991 prohibiting the consideration of sex in employment practices. Some (e.g. Butcher & Williams, 2012; Nichols, 2011) have criticized the decision to use non-gendered norms. A comparison of gender-specific versus non-gendered norms for the MMPI-2 scales conducted by Ben-Porath and Forbey (2003) revealed a dearth of significant differences, with most *T*-score differences falling within a range of three points.

Uniform *T*-scores (see Chapter 1) are incorporated for the majority of the MMPI-2-RF scales. The only exceptions to this are for the validity scales and the interest scales, for which linear *T*-score transformations are incorporated.

Protocol Scoring

Protocols can either be scored by hand or by proprietary Q Local computer software available through Pearson Assessments, or their online scoring and report service, Q Global. When scoring by hand, raw scores for each scale are first calculated using individual scoring templates available from the test publisher for use with official scoring sheets. Ben-Porath and Tellegen (2011) note that due to the time commitment involved in scoring 51 scales by hand, clinicians might be tempted to not score the full profile, which they caution against. Once raw scores are calculated for each scale, they are transferred to a profile sheet, enabling their transformation into *T*-scores.

Computerized scoring is available in several formats. If the test taker was administered the test using the Q Local software, scoring is performed automatically and a score report can be printed from the test administration software. If the test responses were administered on paper, they can be manually entered into the Q Local software so that a scored protocol can be generated. Finally, response sheets can be scanned into the Q Local software and scored protocols will be generated from the scanned responses.

Validity Scales

The MMPI-2-RF validity scales (see Table 11.1) consist of eight revised forms of their counterparts on the standard MMPI-2, and one new validity scale created specifically for

Table 11.1 MMPI-2-RF validity scales

Abbreviation	Name
VRIN-r	Variable Response Inconsistency
TRIN-r	True Response Inconsistency
F-r	Infrequent Responses
Fp-r	Infrequent Psychopathology Responses
Fs	Infrequent Somatic Responses
FBS-r	Symptom Validity
RBS	Response Bias Scale
L-r	Uncommon Virtues
K-r	Adjustment Validity

MMPI-2-RF. These scales can be grouped into those measuring response consistency, self-unfavorable reporting, and self-favorable reporting. As the majority (eight of nine) of these scales are similar to their MMPI-2 predecessors, the reader is referred back to the earlier chapters on the validity scales and their interpretation (Chapters 3 and 4) for a more thorough discussion of those earlier scales. This chapter will highlight the revisions that these scales have undergone and provide guidelines for their interpretation on the MMPI-2-RF.

Item Omissions

In general, respondents who have been adequately prepared to complete the MMPI-2-RF will omit very few items. Still, Greene (2011) points out that even relatively few omitted items can have rather consequential effects on scale *T*-scores, given the relatively few items on the scales of the MMPI-2-RF (an average of 14 items per scale, with some having as few as 4 or 5). Ben-Porath and Tellegen (2011) suggest that even when fewer than 15 items are omitted, some shorter scales may be invalid, although the protocol may still be interpreted with the understanding that some scale scores may underestimate the dimensions or problems measured by that scale. When more than 15 items are omitted, caution should be used when interpreting the profile. If more than 10 percent of a scale's items are omitted, that scale should not be interpreted.

Response Consistency

The Variable Response Inconsistency (*VRIN-r*) and True Response Inconsistency (*TRIN-r*) scales comprise the measures of response consistency on the MMPI-2-RF. A rigorous, five-criterion methodology was used for selecting items for the response consistency scales, and the reader is urged to review the MMPI-2-RF *Technical Manual* (Tellegen & Ben-Porath, 2011) for a complete explanation of the methodology. Although the method for selecting items for *VRIN-r* and *TRIN-r* was somewhat different from the method used for creating *VRIN* and *TRIN* for MMPI-2, the overall similarity in the scales would suggest that they can be interpreted in much the same manner as before. This suggestion is supported by limited empirical research (Handel, Ben-Porath, Tellegen, & Archer, 2010) demonstrating that *VRIN-r* and *VRIN* respond similarly to random responses, while *TRIN-r* and *TRIN* respond similarly to fixed response patterns.

Variable Response Inconsistency (VRIN-r)

This scale contains 53 item pairs, as opposed to the 67 item pairs that comprise the *VRIN* scale for MMPI-2. Only 13 item pairs correspond between the MMPI-2 and MMPI-2-RF versions of the scale. Although it is an oversimplification of the scoring procedure, it is illustrative to state that item pairs are scored when the test taker responds inconsistently (one item True and one item False) in a particular manner to selected pairs of items with consistent semantic meaning. Scoring can be complicated by the fact that in only six of the item pairs does the particular direction of the inconsistency (i.e. True–False vs. False–True) have no bearing on scoring.

Interpretation

Scores below a *T* of 39 indicate a very deliberate approach to the assessment procedure, with less inconsistency than is normally expected. Scores in this range suggest that the protocol is interpretable if other validity indicators do not suggest invalidity. Greene (2011) suggests that *T*-scores in this range may be indicative of a respondent making a self-favorable report.

VRIN-r T-scores between 39 and 69 also suggest consistent reporting. These scores fall within the average range. The protocol is valid as long as other validity indicators do not suggest otherwise.

Scores in the range of *T*-70 to 79 on *VRIN-r* indicate a degree of inconsistent responding beyond what is usually seen. This inconsistency could be due to a variety of reasons, including reading or language difficulties, response errors, carelessness, distraction, or fatigue. The administrator should try to ascertain if the test taker experienced any difficulties in completing the instrument.

VRIN-r scores above *T*-80 generally indicate markedly inconsistent responding to the stimulus items. Profiles with scores in this range are considered invalid. If the administrator is able to ascertain the cause for the inconsistent response patterns and take actions to correct the situation (e.g. administering the protocol via audiotape), a re-administration may be attempted.

Greene (2011) has noted that 18–19-year-olds in a clinical sample scored about four *T* points above the mean on *VRIN-r*. This effect was not found in any other age group.

True Response Inconsistency (TRIN-r)

The *TRIN-r* scale contains 26 item-pairs, whereas the MMPI-2 *TRIN* scale contains 23 pairs. Only five pairs of items overlap the two versions of the scale. Whereas *VRIN-r* assesses the tendency to respond dissimilarly to similar items, *TRIN-r* measures the tendency to respond similarly to dissimilar items. The item pairs were chosen to be essentially reversals in content. The items are scored such that each individual begins with a raw score of 11. One point is added for each item pair that is answered True–True and one point is subtracted for each pair that is answered False–False. Raw scores above 11 indicate responding in the True direction, whereas raw scores below 11 indicate a tendency to respond in the False direction. As with *TRIN*, *T*-scores are calculated using linear *T*-scores, with the caveat that scores below 50 are "reflected" to indicate a higher *T*-score (i.e. a raw score that would normally result in a *T*-score of 40, or one standard deviation below the mean, is converted to a *T*-score of 60, or one standard deviation above the mean). Response direction is indicated by appending either a T or F to the standardized score.

Interpretation

Profiles with *TRIN-r T*-scores ≥ 80F (raw score ≤ 7) evidence considerable nay-saying; these profiles are considered invalid and should not be interpreted. The MMPI-2-RF can be re-administered after the clinician ascertains the reason for the invalidity and takes corrective action.

   TRIN-r scores in range of *T*-70 to 79F (raw scores = 8) indicate significant nay-saying and may be invalid. The individual's response set should be investigated, and the test could be retaken after corrective action, or cautiously interpreted, depending on the setting.

   Scores in the range of *T*-50 to 69 (raw scores = 9 to 13) suggest that the respondent was not answering in a fixed manner. If other validity indicators suggest the profile is valid, then *TRIN-r* scores in this range confirm it.

   TRIN-r scores in range of *T*-70 to 79T (raw scores = 14) indicate significant yea-saying and may be invalid. The clinician should proceed in a manner similar to that described above for scores in this range in the False direction.

   Profiles with *TRIN-r* scores ≥ 80T (raw score ≥ 15) evidence considerable yea-saying and are considered invalid. These protocols should not be interpreted. As with scores in this range in the False direction, the MMPI-2-RF may be re-administered once the clinician ascertains the reason for the invalidity and takes corrective action to guard against it.

Self-Unfavorable Reporting

Scales that assess self-unfavorable reporting on the MMPI-2-RF include the Infrequent Responses (*F-r*), Infrequent Psychopathology Responses (*Fp-r*), Infrequent Somatic Responses (*Fs-r*), and Symptom Validity (*FBS-r*) scales. Of these scales *F-r*, *Fp-r*, and *FBS-r* represent revisions of an extant MMPI-2 scale; *Fs-r*, on the other hand, is a new scale, created for MMPI-2-RF. The broad purpose of these scales is to assess for over-reporting of psychological or other difficulties. Each of these scales will be addressed, in turn.

Infrequent Responses (F-r)

The *F-r* scale assesses the degree to which a respondent endorses items that are infrequently endorsed in the normative sample. *F-r* consists of 32 items, whereas its MMPI-2 analogue, the Infrequency (*F*) scale, consists of 60. *F-r* shares 11 items with *F* and 10 items with *FB* (Back Infrequency), and is thus largely a hybrid of these scales on the MMPI-2. Each of the *F-r* items was endorsed by less than 10 percent of the MMPI-2-RF normative sample; these items refer to a broad range of psychological, somatic, and cognitive symptoms. The items of *F-r* overlap, to varying degrees, with eight of the nine RC scales; three items appear on *RCd*, four items are common to *RC1*, two items overlap *RC2*, three items are shared with *RC4*, six items are shared with *RC6*, two items are common with *RC7*, five items appear on *RC8*, and one item appears on *RC9*.

Up to a certain degree of elevation, *F-r* scores can serve as a rough indicator of the degree of psychological distress that an individual is experiencing. However, the item content of *F-r*, as with *F*, is rather obvious, which can make it relatively easy for individuals to either deny symptoms or to over-report problems. Interpretation for various score ranges is given below.

Interpretation

Low scores on *F-r* (*T* ≤ 44) are obtained by individuals who report less socially unacceptable content or unusual experiences than normal. Greene (2011) cautions that such profiles may indicate an individual who is attempting to appear in a positive light, or may simply represent an individual who is very conventional. Other validity scales should be carefully examined in order to ascertain the meaning of low *F-r* scores.

Average scores on *F-r* (*T*-45 to 60) are seen in individuals who are reporting an average number of unusual experiences. The profile can be safely interpreted if other validity indicators suggest that it is valid.

Moderately high scores on *F-r* (*T*-61 to 79) occur among individuals who report a slightly higher number of unusual experiences, attitudes, feelings, and behaviors than is the norm. Occasionally, scores in this range occur in individuals with some psychopathology who have adjusted to their chronic problems, and therefore are not in great immediate distress. Scores in this range can serve as an indicator of the degree of clinical distress an individual is experiencing. Rogers, Gillard, Berry, and Granacher (2011) found that scores in this range, or below, were exceedingly rare among individuals feigning mental disorders.

High *F-r* scores (*T*-83 to 106) often indicate serious psychopathology, especially if other validity indicators do not suggest invalidity. *VRIN-r* and *TRIN-r* should be examined for response consistency and yea-saying; *Fp-r*, in particular (see below), should be examined to determine whether the obtained elevation represents true disturbance or an attempt to present oneself in a negative light. If it is determined that the score reflects a true psychological disturbance, the level of elevation can, to some degree, indicate the severity of disturbance; at the upper end of this range, however, one may to see some exaggeration of the level of disturbance, even in a profile that is not necessarily invalid.

Very high scores on *F-r* (*T* ≥ 111) are associated with profiles that are generally uninterpretable. Check other validity indicators (e.g. *VRIN-r*, *TRIN-r*, and *Fp-r*) for evidence of invalidity. Occasionally, one will come across a score in the lower portion of this range (*T*-109 to 119) in an otherwise valid profile. In such cases, the score is likely to be obtained from an individual with an acute psychotic disturbance. However, individuals such as this can usually be readily ascertained in an interview; the resulting profiles are usually so unstable as to be interpretatively meaningless, other than as a reflection of their current experience. The clinician is urged to use extreme caution in choosing to interpret such profiles, especially if there is any likelihood of forensic involvement. Scores greater than *T*-119 should be considered invalid and the profile should not be interpreted even if the scores on other validity indicators are within acceptable ranges.

Infrequent Psychopathology Responses (Fp-r)

Whereas *F-r* measures an individual's tendency to endorse items that are infrequently endorsed within the normative sample—and can thus function as a rough measure of psychopathology—*Fp-r* measures an individual's tendency to respond to items that were infrequently endorsed among individuals with significant psychopathology. *Fp-r* is a revised version of the *F(p)* scale which is described in Chapter 3 on MMPI-2 validity scales; the reader is encouraged to refer to that chapter for an explanation of the derivation of *F(p)* and a review of the relevant research surrounding its use.

Whereas the items of *F-r* overlap several RC scales, *Fp-r* shows overlap with only *RC6*, with which it shares five items. *Fp-r* contains 21 items, whereas *F(p)* contains 27; 17 items are common to both scales. Tellegen and Ben-Porath (2011) explained that four items were dropped from the revised version of the scale due to their concomitant appearance on the MMPI-2 *L* scale—which conflicted with their stated goal of creating scales of maximal distinction—and noted that some moderate elevations on *F(p)* could be due to endorsement of only those items (see also, Gass & Luis, 2001). Likewise, three *F(p)* items were dropped from *Fp-r*, due their appearance on the *Fs-r* scale, which is discussed below. Two additional items were dropped due to analyses that suggested that they did not perform as well as other scale items. Three new items were added to the revised version, as their inclusion improved performance of the scale. Overall, *Fp-r* appears to be a distinct improvement over its MMPI-2 counterpart.

Several recent studies have examined the effectiveness of the *Fp-r* scale. Marion, Sellbom, and Bagby (2011) reported that *Fp-r* was the most effective of the MMPI-2-RF over-reporting scales at discriminating individuals instructed to simulate psychopathology (including a sophisticated simulators group) from patients. Likewise, Sellbom and Bagby (2010) reported that *Fp-r* was the most effective of the validity scales in differentiating the profiles of individuals instructed to feign psychopathology from a group of psychiatric inpatients. Rogers et al. (2011) reported that an *Fp-r* *T*-score above 90 was slightly more effective than *F-r* in distinguishing individuals feigning mental disorders from those with psychopathology while reducing the rate of false-positives for feigning. Purdon, Purser, and Goddard (2011) reported that *Fp-r* elevations were associated with clinician ratings of positive symptoms among individuals admitted to a first-episode psychosis clinic; they were unsure whether this represented over-reporting on the part of the patients or an effect of clinical symptoms on their scores. Greene (2011) cautions that individuals scoring above *T*-81 on *Fp-r* are likely to prematurely end treatment despite having serious psychopathology; he suggests discussing this issue with clients obtaining scores in this range.

Interpretation

Average scores on *Fp-r* (*T* ≤ 59) are seen in individuals who endorse an average number of infrequently-endorsed items pertaining to odd or unusual experiences. Greene

(2011), however, cautions that scores below *T*-44 may indicate a tendency toward a self-favorable report; other validity indicators should be examined to determine if this is the case. The profile can be safely interpreted if other validity indicators suggest that it is valid.

Moderately high scores on *Fp-r* (*T*-60 to 77) are seen in individuals who may be accurately endorsing a slightly higher number of unusual experiences, attitudes, feelings, and behaviors than is the norm, especially toward the lower end of this range. Scores above 70 are associated with clinical distress, as well as the tendency for a test taker to respond in self-unfavorable manner. The client's clinical history and presenting problem should help to clarify whether the profile represents over-reporting. Other validity scales should be examined to determine profile validity; if other scales suggest validity, a score in this range would not necessarily invalidate the profile.

High *Fp-r* scores (*T*-85 to 94) often indicate serious psychopathology, especially if other validity indicators do not suggest invalidity. *VRIN-r* and *TRIN-r* should be examined for response consistency and yea-saying. Even if it is determined that the score reflects a true psychological disturbance, the level of elevation can, to some degree, indicate possible exaggeration of the extent of psychological disturbance, even in a profile that is not necessarily invalid.

Very high scores on *Fp-r* (*T* ≥ 102) should be considered invalid and the profile should not be interpreted even if other validity indicators suggest that the profile is valid.

Infrequent Somatic Responses (Fs-r)

The *Fs-r* scale was developed by Wygant and colleagues (Wygant, 2007; Wygant, Ben-Porath, & Arbisi, 2004) to aid in the identification of individuals endorsing infrequent somatic complaints. The scale consists of 16 items, with 12 keyed True. The items chosen for inclusion in the scale were endorsed by no more than 25 percent of the medical patients comprising several large samples. Tellegen and Ben-Porath (2011, p. 15) suggest that the *Fs-r* scale works in a complementary manner to *FBS-r* (described below), with "each scale outperforming the other in some settings and tasks." Greene (2011) has noted that it was unusual for individuals in any of five samples (including the MMPI-2 re-standardization sample, a clinical sample, a pain sample, and two samples of personal injury litigants) to attain *T*-scores above 74 on *Fs-r*. Thus, he suggested that scores higher than this should raise concerns that the respondent is endorsing a number of somatic symptoms that are not generally reported by individuals being treated for known medical issues. Schroeder et al. (2012) have suggested that a cut score of *T* ≥ 83 be used to minimize the risk of false positives with regard to symptom exaggeration among those undergoing neuropsychological examination. Sellbom, Wygant, and Bagby (2012) reported that among the MMPI-2-RF over-reporting scales, *Fs-r* was most sensitive to somatic malingering within three samples consisting of individuals who had been instructed to feign physical health problems as if they were participating in a disability evaluation, medical patients who were not involved in litigation, and individuals who had been carefully diagnosed with a somatoform disorder. Wygant et al. (2009) found *Fs-r* effective in identifying over-reporting among individuals in both medical simulation and head injury simulation samples.

Interpretation

Low to moderately high scores (T < 74) show no evidence of invalidity; the profile can be interpreted if other indicators suggest that it is valid. Toward the upper end of this range (T > 58), individuals are endorsing more physical complaints than is the norm, but this may well reflect genuine physical issues in individuals with medical conditions.

High scores (T-74 to 99) may reflect inconsistent responding (check *VRIN-r* and *TRIN-r*), over-reporting of somatic complaints, or significant medical symptoms. Scores in this range likely reflect over-reporting of somatic complaints when they occur in an individual without a history or evidence of physical health problems. Even in individuals with genuine medical issues, scores at the upper end of this range likely reflect some exaggeration. Scores on the somatic scales should be interpreted cautiously if the clinician chooses to proceed with interpretation.

Very high scores ($T \geq 100$) usually indicate inconsistent responding or over-reporting of somatic complaints. The other validity scales should be examined for evidence of inconsistent responding. If there is no evidence of inconsistent responding, one can proceed with interpretation, although scores on the somatic scales should be interpreted in light of this likely exaggeration of symptoms.

Symptom Validity (FBS-r)

The *FBS-r* scale for MMPI-2-RF is a revised version of the *FBS* scale that was added to the standard MMPI-2 form in 2007. The scale was originally designed to assist in identifying malingering in personal injury litigation. *FBS-r* contains 30 items, all of which overlap the 43-item version on the MMPI-2. The original version of the scale is discussed in detail in Chapter 3 on MMPI-2 validity scales and the reader is encouraged to review that section for further information on the development of *FBS*, its use, and the controversy surrounding its use. As compared with the original MMPI-2 version of the scale, *FBS-r* contains 19 items (63 percent of *FBS-r*) that overlap with the symptoms described in Lees-Haley's (1988) Litigation Response Syndrome, a proportion greater than that found on the original scale (53 percent). Additionally, the proportion of the *GM* and *GF* items on *FBS-r*, one positively for women and four negatively for women, is greater at 17 percent, versus 14 percent for *FBS*, thereby slightly increasing the gender bias against women for the RF version. In sum, the risk for false positives for malingering, especially for women, appears, if anything, to be greater for the revised *FBS-r* than for the original *FBS*; thus, its interpretation should be avoided.

Response Bias Scale (RBS)

The RBS was developed by Gervais, Ben-Porath, Wygant, and Green (2007) to detect a tendency toward over-reporting of symptoms in forensic neuropsychological or disability evaluation settings. The scale contains 28 items, 19 keyed True, and was added to the MMPI-2-RF in 2011. It overlaps *F-r*, *FBS-r*, *RC1*, and Cognitive Complaints (*COG*) by four items each, *Fs* by two items, and Neurological Complaints (*NUC*) and Head Pain (*HPC*) by one item each.

Gervais et al. (2007) reported that *RBS* consistently outperformed *F*, *F(p)*, and *FBS* at identifying individuals in forensic neuropsychological and disability evaluation settings who failed other commonly-used tests of response bias or symptom malingering-neuropsychological symptom validity tests (SVTs). Gervais, Ben-Porath, Wygant, and Green (2008), incorporating archival MMPI-2 and Memory Complaints Inventory (MCI; Green, 2004) data from non-head-injury, disability-related evaluations, found that the *RBS* was a better predictor of the mean memory complaints score than the *F*, *FB*, *F(p)*, or *FBS*. Gervais, Ben-Porath, Wygant, and Sellbom (2010) demonstrated the incremental validity of *RBS* in assessing memory complaints. Wygant et al (2010) reported that *RBS* was effective at detecting cognitive response bias in separate forensic samples composed of disability claimants and criminal defendants. They further provided evidence of the scale's incremental validity beyond the traditional MMPI-2 and MMPI-2-RF over-reporting validity scales in their disability sample. Schroeder et al. (2012) reported that a cut score of $T \geq 92$ was sensitive to symptom exaggeration in 43 percent of neuropsychological cases, with a specificity rate of 92 percent, whereas Wygant et al. (2011) reported 70 percent sensitivity and 76 percent specificity for a score of $T \geq 90$ in individuals undergoing compensation evaluations.

Interpretation

Low scores ($T < 50$) are generally considered to indicate a lack of conscious over-reporting of memory or other cognitive symptoms. The clinician should consider denial or an overly positive presentation, if cognitive testing reveals deficits. If other validity indicators suggest validity, the clinician can proceed with interpretation.

Average scores (T-50 to 63) are associated with reports of minor memory or cognitive symptoms that are consistent with cognitive test results. If other validity scales suggest possible exaggeration, symptom exaggeration is possible. If other validity indicators do not suggest exaggeration and cognitive test results do not indicate any difficulties, the clinician should consider the possibility of emotional factors (e.g. depression) contributing to memory complaints.

Moderately high scores (T-67 to 76) are associated with increasing memory complaints. If other over-reporting validity scales do not suggest exaggeration, these complaints are likely related to emotional factors. If other over-reporting validity scales suggest exaggeration, the clinician should consider the possibility of an intentional effort to exaggerate symptoms.

High scores (T-80 to 97) reflect a much higher than average number of non-credible memory complaints than is normally endorsed by individuals with genuine memory problems. This could be due to inconsistent responding, significant medical symptoms, or over-reporting. Other validity indicators should be examined to assess validity. If other indicators indicate the profile is valid, interpretation can proceed, although the test manual encourages the clinician to be alert to the possibility of over-reporting when interpreting the cognitive complaints scales.

Very high scores ($T \geq 101$) are generally considered to reflect either inconsistent responding or over-reporting of memory complaints. Other validity indicators should be examined for evidence of an inconsistent response pattern or over-reporting. Even if *VRIN-r* and *TRIN-r* do not suggest inconsistent responding and other validity indicators do not suggest over-responding, the clinician is cautioned that this level of symptom report is extremely unusual among those with substantial emotional dysfunction who report credible symptoms. If a clinician chooses to proceed with interpretation, they should be mindful of the substantial possibility of over-reporting of memory symptoms when interpreting the cognitive scales.

Self-Favorable Reporting

Scales that assess self-favorable reporting on the MMPI-2-RF include the Uncommon Virtues (*L-r*) and Adjustment Validity (*K-r*) scales. Although each of these scales represents, to some degree, a revision of an extant MMPI-2 scale, Tellegen and Ben-Porath (2011) state that the scales were created by factor-analyzing the three self-favorable validity scales of the MMPI-2 (i.e. *L*, *K*, and *S*), along with Wiggins' (1959) Social Desirability (*Sd*) scale and creating non-overlapping scales representing the two primary factors. The broad purpose of these scales is to assess for under-reporting of psychological or other difficulties. The two scales will be addressed, individually.

Uncommon Virtues (L-r)

The *L-r* scale contains 14 items, 11 of which are shared with *L* and keyed False, and 3 of which appear on *Sd* and are keyed True. Briefly, the scale is designed to assess the tendency to engage in positive self-presentation to the degree that one is unwilling to admit to even common shortcomings. Elevations on this scale often reflect a naïve or obvious attempt by the respondent to appear unusually virtuous, culturally conservative, overly conscientious, and above moral reproach.

Interpretation

Low scores ($T \leq 42$) are generally considered to indicate candor and a willingness to admit to common shortcomings. However, if the other validity scales suggest over-reporting of psychopathology, a score in this range could be part of an attempt to present oneself as disturbed and without moral resources.

Average scores (*T*-47 to 57) are associated with individuals who display a balance of admitting to and denying common shortcomings. The upper end of this range of scores may be indicative of a mildly cautious, defensive and/or moralistic individual, especially as the education level of the respondent increases. Scores at the upper end of this range are not uncommon among psychologically unsophisticated individuals.

Moderately high scores (*T*-62 to 66) suggest some concern and rigidity over matters of self-control and moral values, as well as a tendency to be conforming and conventional. Individuals with scores in this range may fear that knowledge of their shortcomings may cause others to find them unacceptable or unworthy. A lack of psychological insight and self-awareness is common among individuals with *L-r* elevations in this range. In an educated individual, or in a custody or job evaluation setting, an elevation in this range may represent an attempt to look one's best and to deny unacceptable human impulses.

High scores (*T*-71 to 76) are fairly uncommon. Check other validity scales for inconsistent responding. If inconsistent responding can be ruled out, these scores are associated with the denial of many of the most common and obvious human failings. Such individuals have intense needs to present a good front. They are typically seen as self-righteous and uncompromising and are sensitive to social disapproval. Some see psychological problems as a sign of moral weakness. A score in this range can reflect extreme naïveté in a person from a culturally restricted environment. Other times it reflects a conscious attempt to distort the MMPI-2-RF results.

Very high scores ($T \geq 81$) are generally considered invalid. Even if inconsistent responding can be ruled out, the respondent is engaged in positive impression management to such a degree that interpretation of the substantive scales is not recommended. Even if scores on the substantive scales are elevated, the degree of under-reporting suggested by *L-r* would likely mean that they greatly underestimate the respondent's true symptom level.

Adjustment Validity (K-r)

The *K-r* scale contains 14 items, 12 keyed False, each appearing on the original *K* scale; five of these items also appear on *S*. One item (item 202) is scored in the opposite direction from its scoring on *K*. Tellegen and Ben-Porath (2011) note that this was one of the correction items added to the original *K* scale as a means of addressing concerns that individuals with psychopathology produced low scores on *K*, thus lowering their *K*-corrected scores on other scales. Essentially, *K-r* is a measure of the respondent's self-reported level of adjustment, with higher scores representing a higher level of self-reported adjustment.

Interpretation

Very low scores ($T < 35$) occur for several reasons. If there is the possibility of secondary gain from being diagnosed with a psychiatric disorder, the clinician should consider the possibility that the profile may be intentionally exaggerated. Check the self-unfavorable validity scales for evidence of exaggeration or over-reporting. In valid profiles in which the clinical scales are elevated, a *K-r* score in this range would suggest a severe disturbance, with little capacity to modulate emotions and behaviors.

Low scores (*T*-35 to 42) suggest that the test-taker's coping skills are somewhat compromised. Individuals with scores in this range tend to be self-critical, have poor self-esteem, and lack confidence in their own ability to successfully deal with their problems. If substantive scales are elevated, the client is likely to admit to the symptoms and complaints associated with the profile. Greene (2011) suggests that in clients of lower SES, scores in this range reflect a moderate disturbance; in clients of higher SES, however, scores in this range reflect poor coping skills and a more serious disturbance. In cases in which no substantive scales are elevated, scores in this range would suggest candor and openness.

Average scores (*T*-45 to 55) are seen in individuals who exhibit culturally-appropriate emotional restraint and generally feel in control of their emotions. Even if the substantive scales are elevated, scores in this range, especially toward the upper end of the range, suggest that the respondent maintains some coping skills. The prognosis is better for successful therapeutic interventions when *K-r* is in this range. Greene (2011) suggests that, even in this range, some degree of distress will be evidenced by respondents of higher SES.

Moderately high scores (*T*-59 to 62) are associated with two differing interpretations. In individuals of lower SES, elevations in this range may already be associated with defensiveness and denial. Among individuals of higher SES, however, scores in this range are associated with descriptions of individuals as independent, enterprising and resourceful, who feel in control of their lives.

High scores (*T* > 65) in clinical samples are generally associated with individuals who are particularly defensive and have a serious lack of insight into their psychological problems. Because of their unwillingness to acknowledge their own difficulties, prognosis for therapy can be poor. *K-r* scores in this high range that are obtained in forensic and personnel evaluation situations may reflect the defensiveness that is somewhat expected, given the situation. However, the resultant profile is likely to underestimate psychopathology. Finally, some individuals, usually from higher socioeconomic groups, may score at, or above, a *T*-score of 65 on *K-r* and obtain a non-elevated profile that accurately reflects a lack of psychopathology. In these cases, the *K-r* score may reflect

Higher-Order Scales

The higher-order scales were created by Tellegen and Ben-Porath (2011) to capture a set of clinically-meaningful dimensions that could provide an organizational structure in which to integrate the conceptualization of the substantive scales of the MMPI-2-RF. Among the first attempts to extract higher-order dimensions in the MMPI were those of Welsh (1956) in his creation of the *A* and *R* scales, which were discussed in Chapter 8. Tellegen and Ben-Porath suggest that *A* has been conceptualized as being a similar construct to Eysenck's neuroticism dimension, while *R* has been conceptualized as a reciprocal measure of extraversion, although Greene (2011, p. 267) has provided evidence that calls this conceptualization into question. Tellegen and Ben-Porath (2011) further suggest that a "third" dimension of psychoticism has been missing in factor studies of the MMPI, due to the heterogeneous nature of the scales that best measured psychotic experience (clinical Scales 6 and 8). However, such dimensions have been prominent in several previous factor studies (cf. Costa et al., 1985; Eichman, 1961; Johnson et al., 1984; Waller, 1999; Welsh, 1952).

Tellegen and Ben-Porath (2011) repeatedly extracted three dimensions representing emotional/internalizing, thought, and externalizing dysfunctions within three separate clinical samples. The RC scales showing the highest loadings on each of the three dimensions were as follows: for the emotional/internalizing dysfunction factor, the highest scale loadings were found for *RCd*, *RC2*, and *RC7*; for the thought dysfunction factor, the highest scale loadings were found for *RC6* and *RC8*; and for the behavioral/externalizing factor, the highest scale loadings were found for *RC4* and *RC9*.

Scales for each of these dimensions were created by obtaining a three-factor structure and corresponding factor scores from the combined items of each of the scales listed above within three samples. These obtained factor scores were correlated with each of the 567 items in the MMPI-2 pool. From those correlations, a set of non-overlapping (among the three higher-order scales) items was chosen for each of the three dimensions; these items make up the three higher-order scales. The clinician is urged to remember that these scales represent broad, domain-level function; an absence of an elevation on a higher-order scale does not negate the possibility of specific dysfunction within that domain. Each of the scales will be discussed individually.

Emotional/Internalizing Dysfunction (EID)

The *EID* scale contains 41 items, with 23 keyed True. Thirty-two of the items appear on *RCd*, *RC2*, or *RC7*, with the remaining nine items appearing on other scales. Tellegen and Ben-Porath (2011) have suggested that this scale represents, in a broad form, the basic character of the 2-7 MMPI-2 codetype. Specific dysfunctions associated with *EID* can be assessed by examining *RCd*, *RC2*, *RC7*, Negative Emotionality/Neuroticism-Revised (*NEGE-r*), Introversion/Low Positive Emotionality-Revised (*INTR-r*), and the internalizing scales on the MMPI-2-RF.

Greene (2011) states that *EID* is redundant with *RCd*, being correlated at .95 in a large (*N* = 161,239) clinical sample. Tellegen and Ben-Porath (2011) cite correlations between *EID* and *RCd* of .88 to .95 across a variety of samples. In addition to the high correlations with *RCd*, the scale is highly positively correlated with *RC2* (.61 to .85, with higher correlations in clinical samples), *RC7* (.73 to .81), Self-Doubt (*SFD*; .72 to .87), Inefficacy (*NFC*; .60 to .82); Stress/Worry (*STW*; .65 to .75); and Negative Emotionality/Neuroticism-Revised (*NEGE-r*; .73 to .81). It is negatively correlated with *K-r* (−.69 to −.76).

Tellegen and Ben-Porath report a one-week test–retest correlation of .90 within a subset of the normative sample. Internal consistency (Cronbach's alpha) estimates ranged from .86 to .95 across a variety of samples.

Interpretation

Low scores ($T \leq 43$) are seen in individuals who report less subjective distress than is usually seen, especially in a clinical setting. Greene (2011) suggests that individuals scoring in this range may be extraverted or impulsive.

Average scores (*T*-45 to 57) are associated with an average degree of subjective distress and emotional discomfort.

Moderately high scores (*T*-58 to 64) are associated with slightly more reports of subjective distress and emotional discomfort than average. Their distress may lead them to seek treatment.

High scores (*T*-65 to 79) are associated with significant emotional distress. Among the correlates of scores in this range are depression, sleep disturbance, hopelessness, and pessimism for both men and women. Suicidal ideation has been associated with scores in this range for women.

Very high scores ($T > 80$) may be associated with symptom exaggeration. If validity indicators do not indicate over-reporting or exaggeration, scores in this range may represent an emotional response to a crisis.

Thought Dysfunction (THD)

The *THD* scale represents a dimensional measure of thought dysfunction associated with the 8-6 codetype. The scale contains 26 items, with 24 keyed True, of which 13 overlap *RC6* and 13 overlap *RC8*. Tellegen and Ben-Porath (2011) report a one-week test–retest correlation of .71 within a subset of the normative sample. Internal consistency estimates ranged from .69 to .95 across a variety of samples, with nominally higher estimates of internal consistency observed within clinical samples.

The clinician is strongly urged to note that 22 items also overlap the PSY–5 *PSYC-r* scale, which contains 26 items, as well. Because of this *extremely* high percentage of item overlap between *THD* and *PSYC-r*, scores on these scales will highly correlate ($r = .85$)[1] even in the case of random responding. Greene (2011) reports an actual correlation of .96 between these two scales, and correlations between *THD* and *BIZ* and *PSYC* of .90 and .89, respectively, in a large clinical sample; Tellegen and Ben-Porath (2011) reported correlations ranging from .95 to .98 in both men and women, across a variety of treatment settings and within the normative sample. Thus, interpretive information is essentially identical and it is unnecessary to interpret both scales. Specific dysfunctions associated with *THD* can be assessed by examining *RC6* and *RC8*.

Interpretation

Average scores ($T \leq 63$) are seen in individuals who are not reporting any type of persecutory thought or perceptual disturbances.

High scores (T-67 to 77) are seen among individuals who are experiencing significant dysfunction in their thought processes. Scores on *RC6* and *RC8* should be examined for additional information regarding how this dysfunction might be manifested. Greene (2011) suggests that T-scores in this range are seen in individuals in the early stages of psychotic processes, as well as in individuals with chronic psychoses who have adjusted to their dysfunction.

Very high scores ($T \geq 81$) are associated with serious thought dysfunction if validity indicators do not indicate over-reporting or exaggeration. Ideas of reference, odd thinking, paranoid ideation, and auditory and/or visual hallucinations are seen in individuals scoring in this range. The clinician is urged to assess the respondent for a psychotic disorder or associated personality disorder.

Behavioral/Externalizing Dysfunction (BXD)

The *BXD* scale was designed to provide an overall gauge of an individual's behavioral acting-out tendencies, and represents a dimensional measure of the 4-9 codetype. *BXD* contains 23 items, 20 keyed True, 13 of which appear on *RC4*, and 9 on *RC9*. With regard to overlap with the PSY–5 scales, 15 items are shared with Disconstraint-Revised (*DISC-r*) and 4 overlap Aggressiveness-Revised (*AGGR-r*). Greene (2011) reports correlations of .91 between *BXD* and *DISC-r*, and of .72 between *BXD* and *DISC*, in a large clinical sample. Tellegen and Ben-Porath (2011) report a one-week test–retest correlation of .71 within a subset of the normative sample. Cronbach's alpha estimates of internal consistency ranged from .74 to .84 across a variety of samples.

Individuals who score high on this scale present with a broad range of difficulties, with an emphasis on poor impulse control. A history of criminal behavior, as well as violent and abusive behavior is correlated with elevated scores. Mattson, Powers, Halfaker, Akeson, and Ben-Porath (2012) have reported that in a sample of individuals identified as being at risk for failure to complete a court-ordered drug treatment program, elevated scores on *BXD* and its associated scales (especially if *T* > 75) were associated with such failure. The specific dysfunctions associated with elevated *BXD* scores can be assessed by examining *RC4*, *RC9*, and the externalizing scales, as well as *DISC-r* and *AGGR-r*.

Interpretation

Low scores (*T* ≤ 43) are seen in individuals who are fairly unlikely to engage in acting-out behaviors. These individuals are often described as passive and inhibited.

Average scores (*T*-46 to 63) are seen in individuals who report an average number of externalizing behaviors. These individuals could be described as maintaining adequate behavioral control.

High scores (*T*-65 to 78) are seen among individuals who are likely to have engaged in significant acting-out behavior; they are likely to have experienced some type of repercussions as a result of their behaviors. Scores on *RC4*, *RC9*, and the externalizing scales should be examined for additional information regarding how this dysfunction might be manifested.

Very high scores (*T* ≥ 81) are seen in individuals who are reporting substantial acting-out, externalizing behaviors. They are very likely to have gotten into trouble as a result of their behaviors. Substance abuse and illegal or criminal behaviors become more likely as scores elevate into this range. Clinicians should be alert to the possibility of antisocial, borderline, or narcissistic traits in individuals scoring in this range. Clients should be assessed for substance abuse issues.

Restructured Clinical (RC) Scales

The RC scales were discussed in Chapter 10. The reader is referred to that chapter for information regarding derivation of the scales, as well as interpretive statements. The RC scales appear on the MMPI-2-RF in essentially the same form as they appear on MMPI-2, with one exception: Gender-based norms are not available on MMPI-2-RF. All norms on MMPI-2-RF are non-gendered and a single set of *T*-score transformations are incorporated.

Specific Problems (*SP*) Scales

The SP scales (see Table 11.2) were created as a way to delineate important individual issues and characteristics that comprise the population of problems assessed by one of the broader RC scales (such as substance abuse, which is subsumed by the broader *RC4*), as well as clinically-relevant issues that are *not* directly measured by any of the RC scales, such as suicidal ideation or shyness.

Tellegen and Ben-Porath do not fully describe the methodology used to derive the SP scales, which were created conjointly with the interest scales. As noted in the previous chapter devoted to the RC scales, although RC scales were not created for clinical Scales 5 and 0, as the core components of these scales were not judged to reflect psychopathology, seed scales were created for two core components for clinical Scale 5 and one core component of clinical Scale 0. These components later formed the basis of three of the SP and interest scales.

Table 11.2 MMPI-2-RF Specific Problem Scales

Somatic/Cognitive Scales	
MLS	Malaise
GIC	Gastrointestinal Complaints
HPC	Head Pain Complaints
NUC	Neurological Complaints
COG	Cognitive Complaints
Internalizing Scales	
SUI	Suicidal/Death Ideation
HLP	Helplessness/Hopelessness
SFD	Self-Doubt
NFC	Inefficacy
STW	Stress/Worry
AXY	Anxiety
ANP	Anger Proneness
BRF	Behavior-Restricting Fears
MSF	Multiple Specific Fears
Externalizing Scales	
JCP	Juvenile Conduct Problems
SUB	Substance Abuse
AGG	Aggression
ACT	Activation
Interpersonal Scales	
FML	Family Problems
IPP	Interpersonal Passivity
SAV	Social Avoidance
SHY	Shyness
DSF	Disaffiliativeness

According to Tellegen and Ben-Porath (2011, p. 18), "a systematic examination of other MMPI-2 scales yielded a substantial number of additional targets for scale construction." Initially, 14 additional scales were created, beyond the three identified above. Three additional scales were added based on initial feedback and these 20 scales were then reviewed by unidentified "experts" who suggested additional clinically significant content that they felt should be assessed. Ultimately, 25 new scales, 23 SP scales, and 2 interest scales were created. These scales do not overlap with one another, although they do overlap with higher-order, RC, and PSY–5 scales. Each of the scales is fairly short, averaging 7.52 items each and ranging from 4 to 10 items. Because of their brief length, Cronbach's alpha estimates are fairly low for some of the shorter scales; average inter-item correlations, which may provide a more appropriate measure of internal consistency with shorter scales (Clark & Watson, 1995), were not reported. Tellegen and Ben-Porath, however, report that standard errors of measurement are in the acceptable range.

The SP scales are grouped into four problem areas: somatic, internalizing, externalizing, and interpersonal. Discussion of the individual scales will follow this sequence.

Somatic/Cognitive Scales

The somatic scales consist of five individual scales that were designed to assess preoccupation with health functioning, somatic symptoms, and cognitive complaints. Graham (2012) notes that the very brevity of each of the scales and the homogeneity of their item content essentially means that high scores on any of the scales reflect likely endorsement of item content consistent with the name of the scale. Ben-Porath and Tellegen (2011) caution that each of the scales should be interpreted in light of the respondent's scores on *Fs-r*, *FBS-r*, and *RBS*, though with the caveat that elevated scores on these validity scales do not necessarily imply that the respondent is intentionally over-reporting symptoms. However, they suggest that when scores on one of these validity scales exceed *T*-100, the clinician should incorporate content-based descriptors to characterize the respondent's subjective symptom presentation, but avoid the use of empirical correlates.

Malaise (MLS)

The *MLS* scale is described as measuring a general sense of poor health and physical debilitation. The scale contains eight items, all of which overlap *Hy3*; seven are keyed False. Tellegen and Ben-Porath (2011) report a one-week test–retest correlation of .82. Internal consistency (Cronbach's alpha) estimates ranged from .59 to .82 across a variety of samples, with nominally higher estimates obtained within clinical samples. Youngjohn, Wershba, Stevenson, Sturgeon, and Thomas (2011) found that *MLS* was the single best predictor, among all MMPI-2-RF validity and somatic/cognitive scales, of failure on cognitive effort tests among individuals seeking compensation because of a reported traumatic brain injury. Elevated scores are associated with a preoccupation with health problems, multiple somatic complaints, reports of sleep disturbance, and depression in both men and women.

INTERPRETATION

Low scores (*T*-38) are associated with a general sense of physical well-being. Elevated scores (*T* ≥ 65) are associated with increasing complaints of poor health, along with feelings of tiredness, decreased energy, and weakness. Reports of sleep problems and sexual dysfunction are associated with elevated scores. As *T* increases above 80, the reports of poor health become more prominent and preoccupying. The respondent may report feeling incapacitated by some physical malady. If a physical cause for the somatic complaints has been ruled out, the clinician should consider a diagnosis of a somatoform disorder. Individuals with elevations on this scale may have difficulty participating in therapy due to their malaise.

Gastrointestinal Complaints (GIC)

The *GIC* scale contains five items, four of which are keyed True. *GIC* overlaps *HEA* by four items, three on *HEA1*. Tellegen and Ben-Porath (2011) report a one-week test-retest correlation of .75. Internal consistency (Cronbach's alpha) estimates ranged from .64 to .79 across a variety of samples.

The *GIC* items describe problems related to upset stomach, nausea, vomiting, and poor appetite. High scores have been associated with a preoccupation with health problems and complaints of depression in both men and women. In addition, high scores in men are associated with complaints of sleep disturbance, hopelessness, and difficulty with concentration. High scores in women have been associated with poor coping abilities, suicidal ideation, and multiple somatic complaints.

INTERPRETATION

Non-elevated ($T < 65$) scores are not interpreted. Elevated scores ($T \geq 65$) are associated with a greater than average number of gastrointestinal complaints. Individuals with elevated scores often have a history of gastrointestinal problems and are preoccupied with their health. As T increases above 90, the reports of gastrointestinal problems increase. They may complain of multiple physical ailments and see little hope for future improvement. If a physical cause for the somatic complaints has been ruled out, the clinician should consider a diagnosis of a somatoform disorder.

Head Pain Complaints (HPC)

The *HPC* scale contains six items, equally balanced between True and False. *HPC* overlaps *HEA* by five items. Tellegen and Ben-Porath (2011) report a test–retest correlation of .78. Internal consistency estimates ranged from .59 to .77 across a variety of samples.

The *HPC* items refer broadly to head and neck pain, as well as to the tendency to develop head pain when upset. Both men and women with elevated scores tend to be preoccupied with their physical health and may present with multiple somatic complaints; they often report feelings of hopelessness. In addition, high scores in men have been associated with complaints of sleep disturbance, depression, and anxiety. High scores in women have been associated with poor coping skills, decreased energy, and suicidal ideation.

Interpretation

Non-elevated scores ($T < 65$) are not interpreted. Elevated scores ($T \geq 65$) are associated with reports of head pain. As the T-score increases above 80, there are increasing reports of diffuse head and neck pain, and head pain associated with stress. They may present with multiple somatic complaints and be preoccupied with their physical functioning. They may have poor coping skills and see the future as not improving. If a physical cause for the complaints has been ruled out, the clinician should consider a diagnosis of a somatoform disorder.

Neurological Complaints (NUC)

The *NUC* scale contains 10 items, with 7 keyed False. *NUC* overlaps *Sc6* by seven items, and *HEA2* by six. This scale may reflect state-like problems, rather than trait-level concerns, as Tellegen and Ben-Porath (2011) report a one-week test–retest correlation of .54 within a subset of the normative sample. Cronbach's alpha estimates ranged from .52 to .75 across a variety of samples, with nominally higher internal consistency observed within clinical samples.

The items refer to a broad range of complaints, such as dizziness, numbness, muscle weakness, paralysis, and loss of motor control. Elevated scores have been associated with multiple somatic complaints, a preoccupation with health concerns, developing physical symptoms in response to stress, and complaints of fatigue and reports of depression in both men and women. Locke et al. (2010) found that a *T*-score ≥ 65 identified approximately 91 percent of individuals with psychogenic non-epileptic seizures, but also misclassified 73 percent of individuals with epilepsy as having psychogenic non-epileptic seizures, leading to an overall accuracy of 59 percent. Increasing the cut score to $T \geq 85$ increased overall accuracy to 67 percent, but decreased sensitivity to 53 percent while increasing specificity to 81 percent.

INTERPRETATION

Non-elevated scores ($T < 65$) are not interpreted. Elevated scores (*T*-65 to 91) are associated with vague reports of neurological symptoms. Individuals with elevated scores tend to be preoccupied with their physical health and may present with multiple somatic complaints. They are likely to be experiencing some psychological stress that is expressed through physical complaints. As the *T*-score increases above 92, there are increasing reports of neurological symptoms, such as those described above. If a physical cause for the complaints has been ruled out, the clinician should consider a diagnosis of a somatoform disorder or a neurological/neuropsychological referral.

Cognitive Complaints (COG)

The *COG* scale contains 10 items, with 8 keyed True. *COG* overlaps *Sc3* by six items and *D4* by three. The items refer to a broad range of cognitive complaints, including memory and concentration difficulties, confusion, and intellectual limitations. Tellegen and Ben-Porath (2011) report a one-week test–retest correlation of .74. Internal consistency estimates ranged from .64 to .82 across a variety of samples, with nominally higher estimates obtained within clinical samples. High scores are associated with concentration difficulties, low frustration tolerance, memory complaints, a preoccupation with health concerns, and stress and worry.

Gervais, Ben-Porath, and Wygant (2009) report that elevated scores on *COG* are associated with *complaints* of memory problems or other cognitive difficulties, but not necessarily with objectively assessed cognitive deficits. They note that *COG* scores are not an effective predictor of objectively assessed cognitive function and suggest that *T*-scores should be interpreted as a measure of subjective complaints, primarily associated with emotional distress rather than with neurological symptoms.

INTERPRETATION

Non-elevated scores ($T < 65$) are not interpreted. Elevated scores (T-65 to 80) are associated with reports of cognitive complaints. Individuals with elevated scores tend to be preoccupied with their physical health and may present with multiple somatic complaints. As the T score increases above 82, there are increasing reports of cognitive complaints, such as those described above. High scores should alert the clinician to the possibility of memory or other cognitive difficulties, which might require formal neuropsychological assessment.

Internalizing Scales

The internalizing scales were created to address specific areas of interest related to elevations on the *EID* Higher-Order scale, as well as *RCd*, *RC2*, and *RC7* among the RC scales. The nine internalizing scales range in length from four to nine items. Graham (2012) notes that the brevity and homogeneity of each scale's content means that high scores on any of the scales reflect likely endorsement of item content consistent with the name of the scale. Ben-Porath and Tellegen (2011) suggest that although the correlations among the scales are quite high, the presence of unique empirical correlates allows the scales to be used as substantive measures on their own, rather than merely as interpretive aids for elevations on other scales.

Suicidal/Death Ideation (SUI)

The *SUI* contains five items, all keyed True. Tellegen and Ben-Porath (2011) report a test–retest correlation of .68 within a subset of the normative sample. Cronbach's alpha estimates ranged from .41 to .81 across a variety of samples, with higher internal consistency estimates observed within clinical samples.

Four of the scale's five items appear on *DEP4* and on Greene and Nichols' (1995) Structural Summary for the MMPI-2 among five specific MMPI-2 items serving as markers of depressed ideation and attitudes. Additionally, two are those that Sepaher, Bongar, and Greene (1999) identified as the "I mean business" suicide items. High scores have been associated with suicidal ideation, depression, hopelessness, and complaints of sleep disturbance in both men and women.

Ben-Porath and Tellegen (2011) note that because these items were endorsed so infrequently in the normative sample, endorsement of only one item results in an elevated score and indicates the need for an immediate suicide risk assessment. This recommendation parallels that found in Sepaher et al. (1999). The item content of the *SUI* scale is considered critical; thus, the automated scoring program available from Pearson Assessments prints the items endorsed on this scale. In the case of a clinician choosing to engage in hand scoring, it is recommended that they carefully review the responses for any items on this scale that are endorsed by the respondent. In the case of either automated or hand scoring, this content should be reviewed with the respondent as part of a suicide risk assessment.

As noted above, an endorsement of any item results in an elevated ($T \geq 65$) score. Elevated scores are associated with a preoccupation with suicide and death. Individuals with elevated *SUI* scores may have recently attempted suicide or be contemplating an attempt. They are described as feeling helpless and hopeless. As T-scores increase above 100, individuals are likely reporting a history of suicidal ideation and/or attempts, along with current suicidal ideation. Ben-Porath and Tellegen (2011) note that suicidal risk is elevated if there is evidence of poor impulse control or substance abuse (see scales *BXD*, *RC4*, *RC9*, *DISC-r*, and Substance Abuse [*SUB*]). The clinician should conduct an immediate and thorough suicide risk assessment in the presence of an elevated score on *SUI*.

Helplessness/Hopelessness (HLP)

The items of the *HLP* scale reflect the belief that one lacks the ability to make the necessary changes in their life to help them overcome their current difficulties and achieve their goals. *HLP* contains five items, of which four are keyed True. Four items overlap *TRT*, three on *TRT1*. Elevated scores are associated with feelings of depression, hopelessness, and pessimism about the future in both men and women. In addition, high scores in men are associated with sleep disturbance, feeling overwhelmed, and feeling like a failure. High scores in women are associated with poor sexual adjustment, low energy, and suicidal ideation.

Tellegen and Ben-Porath (2011) report a one-week test–retest correlation of .65. Internal consistency (Cronbach's alpha) estimates ranged from .39 to .75 across a variety of samples, with nominally higher estimates obtained within clinical samples.

Non-elevated ($T < 65$) scores are not interpreted. Elevated scores ($T \geq 65$) are seen in individuals who are reporting a belief that the future will be unpleasant. They feel overwhelmed by their current situation and believe that life treats them unfairly. As T-scores increase above 80, individuals are reporting that they believe they are powerless to effect change in their lives. They tend to see negative outcomes as perhaps inevitable. Given their sense of powerlessness and the inevitability of negative outcomes, they are often lacking in motivation to attempt change.

Self-Doubt (SFD)

The *SFD* scale is the shortest of the internalizing scales, consisting of only four items, all keyed True. All overlap *LSE1*, and two overlap *DEP3*. It is impossible to obtain a T-score greater than 76 on this scale; endorsement of three items results in a T-score of 65. Tellegen and Ben-Porath (2011) report a test–retest correlation of .81. Cronbach's alpha estimates ranged from .67 to .84 across a variety of samples. The theme of the *SFD* items reflects a lack of confidence and a feeling of uselessness. Elevated scores are associated with self-degradation, as well as feelings of depression, hopelessness, self-doubt, and failure in both men and women.

INTERPRETATION

Non-elevated ($T < 65$) scores on *SFD* are not interpreted. Elevated scores ($T \geq 65$) are seen in individuals who may report feeling insecure or inferior. They tend to lack self-confidence and may blame themselves for their shortcomings. They tend to ruminate over their perceived failings. A *T*-score of 76 indicates that these concerns are more prominent

Inefficacy (NFC)

The *NFC* scale reflects a belief that one lacks the ability to effectively deal with both major and minor crises. *NFC* contains nine items, all keyed True. Four *NFC* items overlap each *Si*, *OBS*, and *TRT*; three items overlap *TRT*, with two of these on *TRT1*. Tellegen and Ben-Porath (2011) report a one-week test–retest correlation of .82 within a subset of the clinical sample. Internal consistency estimates ranged from .69 to .83 across a variety of samples.

It is one of only three internalizing scales on which low scores are interpreted. High scores are associated with hopelessness, low energy, a lack of self-reliance, and passivity in both males and females.

INTERPRETATION

Low scores (*T*-36) are associated with self-reliance and an orientation toward power. Scores in the average range (*T*-43 to 64) reflect a relatively healthy balance of confidence and self-doubt. Elevated scores ($T > 65$) are seen in individuals who report being passive. They have difficulty making decisions and doubt their abilities to effectively deal with life's unpleasant situations. They tend to give up easily when confronted with difficulties. When the *NFC T*-score reaches 80, these concerns are more prominent. Individuals scoring at this level report even greater difficulty with decision making and report being unable to effectively deal with even small crises.

Stress/Worry (STW)

The *STW* scale contains seven items, of which five are keyed True. *STW* overlaps *ANX* by five items, *NEGE* by four, and *TPA* by two items. Tellegen and Ben-Porath (2011) report a test–retest correlation of .77. Cronbach's alpha estimates ranged from .52 to .69 across a variety of samples.

The item content of *STW* includes financial concerns, time pressure worries, and a preoccupation with disappointments. Elevated scores have been associated with worry, anxiousness, depression, and feeling overwhelmed in both men and women. High scores in men are also associated with multiple somatic complaints and the development of physical symptoms in response to stress. High scores in women are associated with feeling as if life is a strain, complaints of sleep disturbance, and reports of suicidal ideation.

INTERPRETATION

Low scores (*T*-36) are associated with less stress and worry than is normally reported. Scores in the average range (*T*-43 to 57) reflect unremarkable levels of stress. Elevated scores ($T > 65$) are seen in individuals who report an above-average amount of stress and worry. These individuals could be described as anxious or nervous. They may feel a time pressure to accomplish tasks. They may be concerned about financial matters. These individuals are prone to worry about situations and may ruminate over their concerns. They may develop physical symptoms in response to psychological stressors. If the *STW* *T*-score = 81, these concerns are more prominent and may involve multiple stressors. Individuals with elevated scores should be assessed for suicidal ideation.

Anxiety (AXY)

The *AXY* scale contains five items, all keyed True, that are "clearly indicative of anxiety" (Ben-Porath & Tellegen, 2011, p. 52). *AXY* overlaps *ANX* by three items, and *FRS1* and *NEGE* by two items each. Tellegen and Ben-Porath (2011) report a one-week test–retest correlation of .71. Internal consistency estimates ranged from .42 to .71 across a variety of samples, with nominally higher estimates observed within clinical samples.

Each of the scale's items was infrequently endorsed in the normative sample; thus, endorsement of two items produces an elevated *T*-score. Because the item content of the *AXY* scale is considered critical, the automated scoring program prints endorsed items from this scale. If the clinician chooses to engage in hand scoring, it is recommended that they carefully check the *ANX* items endorsed by the respondent. In the case of either automated or hand scoring, this content should be reviewed with the respondent.

Elevated scores are associated with post-traumatic stress disorder in trauma victims, but are not necessarily indicative of post-traumatic stress disorder. High scores have been associated with suicidal ideation, complaints of sleep disturbance, nightmares, hopelessness, worry, and depression in both men and women.

INTERPRETATION

Non-elevated ($T < 65$) scores are not interpreted. Elevated scores ($T \geq 65$) are associated with anxiousness. Individuals with elevated scores may be experiencing sleep disturbances or nightmares. They do not cope well with stress and report significant anxiety, as well as problems associated with anxiety. Reports of suicidal ideation are associated with elevated *T*-scores on *AXY*. They may experience intrusive thoughts. When *T* reaches 100, reports of these problems escalate. At this level of elevation, respondents may be described as being anxious almost all the time. They may report having a sense of foreboding regarding some dire consequence. Sleep disturbances and nightmares are common at this level of elevation.

Anger Proneness (ANP)

The items of the *ANP* scale focus on the negative emotional experience and expression of irritability, anger, and impatience with others, as well as the tendency to be easily upset or angered. *ANP* contains seven items, with five keyed True. *ANP* overlaps *NEGE* by four items, *ANG* by three, and *TPA1* by two. Tellegen and Ben-Porath (2011) report a one-week test–retest correlation of .81. Cronbach's alpha estimates ranged from .71 to .80 across a variety of samples.

The correlates for men and women are quite different. Elevated scores in men have been associated with sleep disturbance, temper tantrums, low frustration tolerance, anger, agitation, and resentment, as well as the development of physical symptoms in response to stress and a preoccupation with physical concerns. Elevated scores in women are associated with poor coping abilities when faced with stress.

INTERPRETATION

Non-elevated scores ($T < 65$) are not interpreted. Elevated scores ($T \geq 65$) are associated with individuals who are argumentative and hold grudges. They are often described as being irritable and having low frustration tolerance. They tend to be quick to anger and are likely to have temper tantrums when angry, especially if male. As T elevates to a score of 80, these problems become more pronounced. Individuals scoring at this level may report being overcome by their anger.

Behavior-Restricting Fears (BRF)

The *BRF* scale contains nine items, all of which appear on *FRS1*. Eight of the items are keyed True. Tellegen and Ben-Porath (2011) report a one-week test–retest correlation of .67. Internal consistency estimates ranged from .44 to .63 across a variety of samples.

The item content of *BRF* generally refers to fears that restrict one's involvement in activities both within and outside of the home. Ben-Porath and Tellegen (2011) note that elevated scores are associated with agoraphobia, as well as with general fearfulness. High scores in men have been associated with low competitiveness, low achievement needs, and low self-reliance. High scores in women have been associated with multiple fears, nightmares, nervousness, and suicidal ideation.

INTERPRETATION

Non-elevated ($T < 65$) scores are not interpreted. Elevated ($T \geq 65$) scores on *BRF* are associated with fearfulness to the degree that it restricts one's activities. Individuals with elevated scores may report generalized anxiety and subjective depression. They may feel anxious when away from home. They may be uncompetitive and have low needs to achieve; such individuals are usually not work-oriented. As the T-score increases above 90, these reports become more widespread. Individuals scoring in this range may report multiple fears that interfere with their daily lives.

Multiple Specific Fears (MSF)

MSF contains nine items, with five keyed False. All overlap *FRS*, with eight on *FRS2*. Tellegen and Ben-Porath (2011) report a one-week test–retest correlation of .85. Cronbach's alpha estimates ranged from .69 to .72 across a variety of samples. The item content of the *MSF* scale describes unrelated fears of various animals and natural phenomena, such as floods, fire, and blood and item endorsement may indicate an elevated risk for specific phobias. No empirical correlates have been found for elevated scores in men; thus, we recommend interpreting elevations for men only in terms of their self-report. High scores in women are associated with low aspirations and achievement needs, low competitiveness, stereotypical gender interests, and low energy.

Low scores ($T < 39$) are seen in individuals who report fewer specific fears than average. Scores in the average range (T-42 to 59) reflect an unremarkable number of specific fears and are not generally interpreted. Elevated scores ($T \geq 65$) are seen in individuals who may be described as risk-aversive. They report multiple fears regarding various animals and acts of nature, including thunder, natural disasters, and fire. Women may tend to be passive and harm-avoidant.

Externalizing Scales

According to Ben-Porath and Tellegen (2011), the externalizing scales were created to address specific facets of *RC4* and *RC9* on the RC scales. Two scales, Juvenile Conduct Problems (*JCP*) and Substance Abuse (*SUB*) specifically address the two broad content areas of *RC4*. Likewise, two scales, Aggression (*AGG*) and Activation (*ACT*) measure the two specific areas of interest assessed by *RC9*; low scores are interpretable on these latter two scales. Thus, these scales may be useful in helping the clinician clarify the specific problems leading to elevations on *RC4* or *RC9*, which has been suggested as an area of concern, given the breadth of the item content in the two scales (cf. Bolinskey & Nichols, 2011; Nichols, 2006). Ben-Porath and Tellegen suggest that the externalizing scales can be interpreted even in the absence of elevations on *RC4* or *RC9*. However, Graham (2012) suggests that the discriminant validity among the externalizing scales is not very good.

Juvenile Conduct Problems (JCP)

The items of the *JCP* scale refer to a history of legal trouble and conduct problems when young. *JCP* contains six items, all keyed True. Five items overlap with *DISC*, four each with *ASP2* and *MAC–R*, and three with *Pd* (two of these on *Pd2*). Tellegen and Ben-Porath (2011) report a one-week test–retest correlation of .85 within a subset of the normative sample. Internal consistency (Cronbach's alpha) estimates ranged from .56 to .75 across a variety of samples.

Elevated scores are associated with antisocial behavior, holding grudges, and feeling that one's family lacks love among both men and women. Additional correlates of elevated scores in men are being physically abusive, angry, and aggressive, temper tantrums, and a history of stormy interpersonal relationships. High scores in women are also associated with trust difficulties, superficial relationships, deception, and low frustration tolerance.

Non-elevated ($T < 65$) scores are not interpreted. Elevated ($T \geq 65$) scores on *JCP* are associated with reports of conduct behaviors in school. They may have histories of illegal behavior as adolescents, as well as additional legal trouble as adults. They tend to have problems with authority figures, in general, and may especially report conflictual relationships with members of their family. Physical abuse of others is more common among men. As the *T*-score increases above 80, these reports become more widespread. It is impossible to score above *T*-84 on this scale.

Substance Abuse (SUB)

The *SUB* scale contains seven items, all of which overlap *AAS*, with six keyed True. Tellegen and Ben-Porath (2011) report a test–retest correlation of .87. Internal consistency estimates ranged from .62 to .77 across a variety of samples. The items broadly refer to significant abuse of substances—either currently or in the past—with alcohol-related items being predominant. Elevations on *SUB* have been associated with sensation-seeking, risk for substance-use problems, difficulty trusting others, and self-defeating behaviors.

The item content of *SUB* has been identified as possibly requiring immediate attention by the tests' authors. Because of this, the automated scoring program prints the responses answered in the keyed direction when the scale is elevated. When not using an automated scoring program, it is suggested that the clinician manually review the endorsed items when the scale is elevated. These items should then be reviewed with the respondent.

INTERPRETATION

Non-elevated (*T* < 65) scores are not interpreted. Elevated (*T* ≥ 65) scores on *SUB* are associated with frank admissions of past and/or current substance use. As the score elevates above *T*-80, the possibility of current substance abuse is greater. These individuals are reporting more frequent use of substances and may find it difficult to relax without the use of substances. Thus, they may experience more difficulties in their interpersonal relationships. They may be described as argumentative and may be physically aggressive with others, especially if the respondent is male.

Aggression (AGG)

The nine items comprising the *AGG* scale reflect physically aggressive behavior; all are keyed True. Six of the *AGG* items overlap *AGGR* and *ANG*, five on *ANG1*. Tellegen and Ben-Porath (2011) report a one-week test–retest correlation of .78. Cronbach's alpha estimates ranged from .58 to .76 across a variety of samples.

Temper tantrums are associated with elevated scores in both men and women. In addition, high scores in men are associated with holding grudges, resentment, stormy interpersonal relationships, and physical abuse of others. Elevated scores in women are associated with trust difficulties, grouchiness, and cynicism. As elevated scores may be associated with a history of violence and abusive behavior, this scale is deemed to contain critical content. Thus, the automated scoring program will print endorsed items if the scale score is elevated. The clinician is urged to manually check for endorsed item content if hand scoring is used. This is one of two Eexternalizing scales for which low scores are interpreted.

Low (T < 39) scores are associated with a below average level of aggressive behavior, as long as the self-favorable validity scales (*L-r*, *K-r*) do not suggest a tendency to under-report problems. Average elevations (*T*-45 to 61) are not interpreted. Elevated ($T \geq 65$) scores are seen in individuals who report acting aggressively toward others. They may be physically aggressive and violent. They may have histories of legal difficulties and behavioral problems in school. As scores elevate above *T*-80, these behaviors become more prominent. Such individuals may enjoy intimidating others or causing others to fear them.

Activation (ACT)

The *ACT* scale contains eight items, all keyed True. *ACT* overlaps *Pt*, *Ma* (two of these on *Ma2*), and *APS* by three items each; it overlaps *Sc5* by two items. Tellegen and Ben-Porath (2011) report a test–retest correlation of .77 within a subset of the normative sample. Internal consistency (Cronbach's alpha) estimates ranged from .59 to .75 across a variety of samples.

The items address broad aspects associated with hypomanic activation, including a decreased need for sleep, mood swings, and heightened excitement and energy. Tellegen and Ben-Porath (2011) caution that the possibility that elevations on this scale may reflect substance-induced problems should be evaluated by the clinician; the clinician may find it useful, then, to interpret elevations on this scale in light of scores on *SUB*. Tellegen and Ben-Porath reported no empirical correlates above |.20| for elevations on *ACT*. Thus, elevations on this scale should only be interpreted as reflecting the respondent's self-report.

Low (T < 39) scores indicate that the respondent endorsed a below-average number of items reflecting increased energy or excitement. The clinician is encouraged to consider scores on *RCd*, *RC2*, and the internalizing scales to assess for the possibility of depression. Average elevations (*T*-44 to 59) are not interpreted. These scores reflect the endorsement of an average number of items reflecting increased energy or excitement. Elevated scores ($T \geq 65$) indicate that the respondent endorsed items reflecting increased excitement and energy. They may be reporting a decreased need for sleep. As scores elevate above *T*-80, these reports become more predominant. When scores reach this level, the respondent is indicating that they experience uncontrollable mood swings. They are reporting an increased energy level and a decreased need for sleep, such that the clinician would be well-advised to assess for other signs of mania or hypomania, including pressured speech or flight of ideas, expansive mood, and an increased focus in pleasurable activities.

Interpersonal Scales

The interpersonal scales consist of five scales whose primary focus is on interpersonal functioning. They are Family Problems (*FML*), Interpersonal Passivity (*IPP*), Social Avoidance (*SAV*), Shyness (*SHY*), and Disaffiliativeness (*DSF*). Tellegen and Ben-Porath (2011) report low to moderate correlations among these scales within the normative sample.

Family Problems (FML)

The *FML* scale includes 10 items, 7 keyed True. Nine of these items overlap *FAM* (five on *FAM1*, two on *FAM2*), and two each with *Mf*, *Pd1*, and *Sc1*. Tellegen and Ben-Porath (2011) report a one-week test–retest correlation of .78. Cronbach's alpha estimates ranged from .64 to .78 across a variety of samples.

These items refer to a variety of familial issues, such as dislike of one's family members, feeling unappreciated by one's family, and feeling that one cannot count on one's family. High scores are associated with familial discord, family resentment, blaming one's family for one's difficulties, and feeling as if one's family lacks love, in both men and women.

INTERPRETATION

Low ($T < 39$) scores are associated with individuals who report that their past and present relationships with their family are relatively conflict-free. Individuals with scores in this range do not tend to blame their families for any difficulties they might be experiencing. Average (T-40 to 63) scores are not interpreted. These individuals are reporting an unremarkable number of family conflicts. Elevated scores ($T \geq 65$) are associated with reports of family discord. These individuals tend to feel that their family does not provide them the type of support and understanding that they deserve; they may blame their family for their current and past difficulties. As scores elevate above T-80, the amount of discord within the family, as well as the amount of resentment and blame on the part of the respondent, are likely to increase.

Interpersonal Passivity (IPP)

The *IPP* scale contains items that broadly refer to unassertive or submissive behavior in interpersonal interactions. The scale contains 10 items, of which 9 are keyed False. Four items overlap with *R*, two with *Si*. Tellegen and Ben-Porath (2011) report a one-week test–retest correlation of .78. Internal consistency estimates ranged from .68 to .77 across a variety of samples.

High scores are associated with passivity in both men and women and are negatively related to extroversion. Elevated *IPP* scores are associated with poor sexual adjustment, a low sex drive, self-doubt, perfectionism, and pessimism in men. High scores in women are associated with introversion, social awkwardness, and submissiveness.

Low scores ($T < 39$) are seen in individuals who describe themselves as assertive and someone who will stand up for themselves. They often see themselves as leaders, although others may see them as domineering or self-centered. Average elevations (T-43 to 62) are not interpreted. Individuals with scores in this range are reporting an average balance of assertiveness and passivity. Elevated ($T \geq 65$) scores on *IPP* are associated with individuals who describe themselves as unassertive. They often lack confidence in themselves and report a dislike for leadership roles. As scores increase above T-80, this unassertiveness becomes more pronounced. Individuals with scores in this range do not like being in social situations and may be viewed as awkward or shy by others. They are often submissive in interpersonal relationships.

Social Avoidance (SAV)

The *SAV* scale contains 10 items, with 9 keyed False. All items overlap *Si* (seven on *Si1*, three on *Si2*) and *SOD* (nine on *SOD1*, one on *SOD2*), and six items overlap *INTR*. Tellegen and Ben-Porath (2011) report a one-week test–retest correlation of .84. Internal consistency (Cronbach's alpha) estimates ranged from .77 to .86 across a variety of samples.

The content of the *SAV* items reflects the respondent's report of not enjoying social interactions and actively avoiding them. High scores in both men and women are associated with feelings of hopelessness, sadness, and depression, as well as with introversion. Elevated scores in men are also associated with sleep disturbance, feeling like a failure, self-doubt, and feeling that life is a strain. Elevated scores in women are associated with low energy and aspirations, shyness, and social awkwardness. Ben-Porath and Tellegen (2011) suggest that elevations on *SAV* in the presence of a non-elevated Shyness (*SHY*) score may suggest the presence of avoidant personality, rather than social anxiety, particularly if Self-Doubt (*SFD*) and Inefficacy (*NFC*) are elevated.

Low scores ($T < 39$) are seen in individuals who describe themselves as enjoying social interactions. They may engage in a variety of social events. Average elevations (T-44 to 59) are not interpreted. Elevated ($T \geq 65$) scores on *SAV* are associated with individuals who describe not enjoying social activities and interactions. They may be described as introverted. As with individuals scoring high on *IPP*, they may suffer from a lack of self-confidence and avoid positions of leadership. They are often passive in interpersonal relationships. As scores increase above T-80, their difficulties increase in magnitude. They may report feelings of sadness and depression. They may feel hopeless and that they have little power to effect positive change.

Shyness (SHY)

The items of the Shyness (*SHY*) scale refer to various ways in which social anxiety may be manifested, such as embarrassment and discomfort in social situations. The scale contains seven items, six of which are keyed True. All items overlap *Si1*, five overlap *SOD* (four on *SOD2*, one on *SOD1*), and three overlap *Pt*. Tellegen and Ben-Porath (2011) report a test–retest correlation of .88. Internal consistency estimates ranged from .74 to .80 across a variety of samples.

High scores in men are associated with anxiousness, depression, worry, reports of sleep disturbance, passivity, feeling overwhelmed, self-doubt, and discomfort around women. High scores in women are associated with introversion, low energy, passivity, shyness, poor sexual adjustment, and social awkwardness. It is impossible to score above *T*-75 on this scale.

INTERPRETATION

Low (*T* < 39) scores are associated with reports of little or no social anxiety. These individuals may be described as feeling very comfortable in social situations. Average (*T*-44 to 57) elevations are not interpreted. These individuals are reporting an unremarkable balance of comfort and anxiety in social situations. Elevated (*T* ≥ 65) scores are associated with reports of shyness. These individuals are uncomfortable being around others in social situations, especially members of the opposite sex. They may be described as being socially awkward or introverted.

Disaffiliativeness (DSF)

The *DSF* scale contains only six items, five keyed True. Scores below *T*-44 cannot be obtained on this scale. *DSF* overlaps *SOD1* by three items, and *FB* and *Sc1* by two items each. Tellegen and Ben-Porath (2011) report a one-week test–retest correlation of .60 within a subset of the normative sample, which may suggest a state-like quality to the concerns measured by this scale, or may be an artifact of the scale having so few items. Internal consistency estimates ranged from .43 to .65 across a variety of samples, which may, again, reflect the small number of items on the scale.

The *DSF* items refer to a dislike of people, having never had a close relationship, and a preference for solitude. Elevated scores reflect an asocial individual, although extremely high scores may be associated with schizoid personality. High scores in men have been associated with complaints of sleep disturbance, including nightmares; feelings of failure; hopelessness; depression; and a preoccupation with health problems. No empirical correlates have been reported for women; thus, we recommend that elevated scores in women be interpreted only in the context of self-report.

INTERPRETATION

Average (*T*-44 to 58) elevations are not interpreted. These individuals are reporting neither a preference for solitude nor a dislike of others. Elevated (*T* ≥ 65) scores are seen in individuals who report that they dislike being around others. As the *T*-score increases, this dislike for social involvement becomes more pronounced and individuals tend to prefer solitude. Men may be experiencing symptoms of depression, including sleep disturbance and hopelessness. Extremely elevated (*T* > 100) scores may be associated with individuals who have never had a close relationship. When

T is elevated to this level, the clinician should consider evaluating for schizoid personality disorder.

Interest Scales

As noted in the previous chapter on the RC scales, seed items for two scales were derived from clinical Scale 5 (Masculinity-Femininity) during the course of the derivation of the RC scales. These seed items formed the basis of the interest scales, which consist of the Aesthetic-Literary Interests (*AES*) and Mechanical-Physical Interests (*MEC*) scales. The scales are essentially uncorrelated with one another, which means that an individual can score high on both, low on both, or high on one and low on the other. Ben-Porath and Tellegen (2011) suggest that low scores on both scales may reflect a lack of outside interests; in some cases, low scores on both scales may indicate psychological disengagement from the environment.

Aesthetic-Literary Interests (AES)

The *AES* scale contains seven items, with each keyed True. All overlap *Mf*, with five appearing on *Mf4* and two on *Mf3*. Tellegen and Ben-Porath (2011) report a test–retest correlation of .86 within a subset of the normative sample. Cronbach's alpha estimates ranged from .49 to .66 across a variety of samples.

The items of *AES* reflect an interest in occupations or activities of an aesthetic or literary nature, such as working in a library or with flowers. Elevated scores are associated with stereotypic feminine behavior and a rejection of traditional gender roles in men. No empirical correlates have been found for high scores among women. For this reason, we suggest that elevated scores in women be interpreted only in terms of self-report of item content.

Interpretation

Low scores (*T* < 39) indicate a lack of interest in occupations or activities associated with the arts or of an aesthetic nature. Average (*T*-39 to 62) elevations are not interpreted. Elevated (*T* ≥ 65) scores are associated with a reported interest in aesthetic or literary activities or occupations. Individuals scoring in this range are often described as being empathic. Males are described as not having stereotypical gender interests. It is impossible to score above *T*-73 on this scale.

Mechanical-Physical Interests (MEC)

The items of the *MEC* scale refer broadly to an interest in activities or occupations of a mechanical or physical nature. Such activities include building things, sports, and other outdoor activities. High scores on *MEC* in men are associated with stereotypical masculine interests, few concerns about homosexuality, low self-doubt, and little difficulty making decisions. As with *AES*, no empirical correlates have been found for high scores among women. For this reason, we suggest that elevated scores in women be interpreted only in terms of self-report of item content.

MEC contains nine items, all keyed True. All overlap *Mf1*, and two items each overlap *MAC-R* and *DISC*. Tellegen and Ben-Porath (2011) report a one-week test–retest correlation of .92. Internal consistency (Cronbach's alpha) estimates ranged from .55 to .64 across a variety of samples.

Interpretation

Low scores (*T* < 39) are associated with a lack of interest in activities or occupations of a mechanical or physical nature. Average (*T*-39 to 62) elevations are not interpreted. Elevated (*T* ≥ 65) scores are associated with an above-average interest in physical or mechanical activities or occupations. Individuals scoring in this range may be described as having stereotypically masculine interests. They may be high in sensation-seeking or adventurousness.

Personality Psychopathology Five (PSY–5) Scales

The MMPI-2 PSY–5 scales (Harkness, McNulty, & Ben-Porath, 1995) reflect a dimensional five-factor trait model developed specifically for application to personality pathology. The PSY–5 constructs were originally developed by Harkness and McNulty (1994) from normal personality terms and from descriptors of abnormal personality taken from the *Diagnostic and Statistical Manual of Mental Disorders III—Revised* (*DSM-III-R*; American Psychiatric Association, 1987), as an aid for the description of normal personality and to provide a dimensional complement to the diagnosis of personality disorders. The MMPI-2 scales were developed using a combination of rational and statistical procedures, termed *replicated rational selection*, to select MMPI-2 items that measured each of the PSY–5 constructs. The resultant MMPI-2 PSY–5 scales were named Aggressiveness (*AGGR*), Psychoticism (*PSYC*), Disconstraint (*DISC*), Negative Emotionality/Neuroticism (*NEGE*), and Introversion/Low Positive Emotionality (*INTR*). The reader is encouraged to read the recent review of these scales by Harkness, Finn, McNulty, and Shields (2012).

Although there are some similarities between the constructs of the Five-Factor Model (FFM), as measured by instruments such as the NEO-PI-R (Costa & McCrae, 1992a) and the PSY–5 scales, there are also important differences, and these differences have important implications for psychological assessment. For example, as the PSY–5 scales are intended to measure the domains of disordered personality, some scales, such as *PSYC*, have no direct correspondent among the NEO-PI-R scales, just as the NEO-PI-R *Openness* scale has no direct PSY–5 correspondent. Although there is some overlap among the remaining scales in the two instruments, it is important to note that even for the PSY–5 scales that show conceptual and empirical overlap with the FFM constructs, the PSY–5 scales tend to have a higher "ceiling" for maladaptive levels of the personality traits. Commenting specifically on the PSY–5's inclusion of a psychoticism factor, Krueger et al. (2011, p. 182) have suggested that the "… PSY-5 is a highly prescient model in this regard and aligns closely with a model suitable for DSM-5."

The reader is encouraged to review the earlier description of the development of the MMPI-2 PSY–5 scales and their clinical correlates for additional information regarding their clinical utility. This section will focus on the creation of a revised group of PSY–5 scales for MMPI-2-RF.

To adapt the PSY–5 scales for MMPI-2, Harkness and McNulty (2007) first began with the 96 items (of the original 138 MMPI-2 PSY–5 items) that remained in the 338-item MMPI-2-RF pool. Incorporating a dual-method of item-scale and item-criterion analyses, Harkness and McNulty dropped 22 of the surviving items from the revised scale and added 30 items that had not previously appeared on any of the PSY–5 scales (although they were available in the MMPI-2 item pool). The resultant scales consist of 104 items; there is no item overlap among the revised PSY–5 scales, although there is substantial overlap with other MMPI-2-RF scales. The revised scales are known as Aggressiveness-Revised (*AGGR-r*), Psychoticism-Revised (*PSYC-r*), Disconstraint-Revised (*DISC-r*), Negative Emotionality/Neuroticism-Revised (*NEGE-r*), and Introversion/Low Positive Emotionality-Revised (*INTR-r*). Each will be described individually.

Aggressiveness-Revised (AGGR-r)

The *AGGR-r* scale contains 18 items referring to "aggressively assertive behavior" (Ben-Porath & Tellegen, 2011), with 16 of these keyed True. Fourteen items are common to the MMPI-2 *AGGR* scale, whereas four are unique to *AGGR-r*. Of the four items appearing on *AGGR*, but not on *AGGR-r*, two were lost from the MMPI-2-RF item pool and two were dropped from the revised scale.

Tellegen and Ben-Porath (2011) report very strong negative correlations, ranging from –.87 to –.89, between *AGGR-r* and Interpersonal Passivity (*IPP*) in both men and women, across a variety of treatment settings and within the normative sample. Moderate positive correlations, ranging from .56 to .68, were reported with *RC9*. Internal consistency estimates (Cronbach's alpha) ranged from .71 to .75 within these same samples. The test–retest coefficient within a subset of the normative sample was .84.

High scores are associated with antisocial behavior, aggressiveness, extraversion, and assertiveness. Low scores are associated with passivity, submissiveness, and proneness to guilt.

Interpretation

Low (*T* < 39) scores are associated with a lack of assertiveness. These individuals may be described as being submissive in interpersonal relationships. They prefer to let others take the lead and rarely stand up for themselves. They tend to blame themselves for their shortcomings.

Average (*T*-41 to 60) elevations are not interpreted. Individuals scoring in this range are reporting a balance between passivity and assertiveness.

Elevated (*T* ≥ 65) scores may reflect assertiveness and self-confidence at the lower end of the elevated range. They may be extraverted and view themselves as having leadership qualities. As *T* elevates above 70, however, the likelihood of aggressive and domineering behavior increases. These individuals may have a history of physical or instrumental aggression and they may try to intimidate others through the threat of aggression. At this level, the positive self-impression seen in lower elevations takes on a narcissistic quality. High scores are associated with the absences of feelings of guilt or remorse.

Psychoticism-Revised (PSYC-r)

The 26 items of the *PSYC-r* scale refer to experiences that are associated with thought disturbance; 25 of these items are keyed True. *PSYC-r* shares 17 items with the MMPI-2 *PSYC* scale, which contains 25 items; 9 items appearing on *PSYC-r* were not included on *PSYC*. Of the eight items appearing on *PSYC*, but not on *PSYC-r*, five do not appear in the MMPI-2-RF item pool, whereas three were not included on the revised scale. As noted in the discussion of the higher-order scales, *PSYC-r* shares 22 items with *THD*, which essentially makes it more similar to another scale appearing on MMPI-2-RF than the scale upon which it was based. Whereas one would expect a correlation of .85 between *PSYC-r* and *THD* on the basis of item overlap, the correlation between *PSYC-r* and *PSYC* would be only .67. For this reason, we reiterate our earlier warning that *PSYC-R* and *THD* are redundant; thus, the clinician should interpret only one of these scales and should never use an elevated score on one of these scales as independent confirmation of traits or symptoms suggested by an elevated score on the other.

As noted in the discussion of *THD*, Tellegen and Ben-Porath (2011) report very strong positive correlations, ranging from .95 to .98 between *PSYC-r* and *THD* in both men and women, across a variety of treatment settings and within the normative sample. Additionally, *PSYC-r* scores were highly related to *RC8* scores, with correlations ranging from .87 to .90, in these same samples. Cronbach's alpha estimates ranged from .69 to .88 within these samples, with nominally higher estimates seen among psychiatric patients than within non-patient samples. The test–retest coefficient within a subset of the normative sample was .76.

High scores are associated with a variety of unusual thoughts and perceptual experiences, along with a feeling of alienation from others. Low scores are associated with an absence of these experiences and feelings.

Interpretation

Low (*T* < 39) scores are associated with denial of any type of perceptual disturbance, unusual thoughts, or feelings of alienation.

Average (*T*-47 to 63) elevations are not interpreted. Individuals scoring in this range are reporting an unremarkable number of unusual perceptual experiences and thoughts.

Elevated (*T* ≥ 65) scores are associated with unrealistic thinking. They are reporting some unusual thoughts and perceptual disturbances. These individuals may feel that life is a strain and have difficulty coping with the demands of their daily lives. As the score elevates above *T*-75, the magnitude of the disturbance increases. These individuals are reporting a greater likelihood of psychotic symptoms, such as delusional beliefs or hallucinations. They may exhibit impaired reality testing. They are often described as anxious or depressed. They are likely to have difficulties with interpersonal functioning. The clinician should evaluate for the presence of a psychotic disorder or an associated personality disorder.

Disconstraint-Revised (DISC-r)

The *DISC-r* scale contains 20 items, with 17 keyed True, which refer broadly to impulsiveness and risk-taking. Of the 20 items on *DISC-r*, 13 are common to the MMPI-

2 *DISC* scale, which contains 29 items, whereas 7 items are unique to *DISC-r*. Of the 16 items that appear on *DISC*, but not on *DISC-r*, 11 were not included in the MMPI-2-RF item pool and 5 were dropped from the revised scale. As noted previously in the discussion of the higher-order scales, *DISC-r* shares 15 items with *BXD*, which means that it has more overlap with another MMPI-2-RF scale than with its namesake MMPI-2 scale. On the basis of item overlap alone, one would expect a correlation of .70 between *DISC-r* and *BXD*, as opposed to a correlation of .54 between *DISC-r* and *DISC*.

As might be expected, given the substantial item overlap, Tellegen and Ben-Porath (2011) report correlations, ranging from .89 to 92, between *DISC-r* and *BXD* across a variety of treatment settings and within the normative sample. Further, correlations ranging from .76 to .83 were reported in these samples for *DISC-r* and *RC4*, although only three items are shared between the two scales. Moderate positive correlations, ranging from .57 to .62, were reported with *RC9*, with which *DISC-r* shares five items. *DISC-r* and *AGGR-r* had positive correlations ranging from .22 to .50. Cronbach's alpha estimates ranged from .69 to .75 within these same samples. The test–retest coefficient within a subset of the normative sample was .93. Given the substantial item overlap and high correlations between *DISC-r* and *BXD*, it is not necessary to interpret both scales. High scores on *DISC-r* have been associated with antisocial behavior, lack of impulse control, narcissism, deception, and superficial relationships.

Interpretation

Low (*T* < 39) scores on *DISC-r* are associated with reports of overly constrained behavior. These individuals may be described as being inhibited and over-conventional.

Average (*T*-41 to 63) elevations are not interpreted. Individuals scoring in this range are reporting an unremarkable balance between behavioral constraint and disconstraint.

Elevated (*T* ≥ 65) scores are associated with behavioral disconstraint. Individuals at the lower end of the elevated range may be described as impulsive, nonconformist, or sensation-seeking. As scores elevate above *T* ≥ 75, however, this lack of behavioral constraint becomes more severe, as do the problems and consequences associated with it. Individuals scoring in this range show a decreasing ability to use good judgment. They are often described as rule-breakers and may have significant histories of legal difficulties and behavioral problems in school. They have narcissistic tendencies and may manipulate or deceive others in order to get what they want. The clinician should evaluate for narcissistic or antisocial personality disorder. Individuals with elevated scores are not often motivated to engage in treatment and are unlikely to initiate treatment of their own accord. Once enrolled in treatment, they tend to be non-compliant and/or to drop out of treatment early.

Negative Emotionality/Neuroticism-Revised (NEGE-r)

The items of the *NEGE-r* scale reflect a variety of negative emotional experiences and are associated with the Neuroticism dimension of the five-factor model of personality. *NEGE-r* contains 20 items, with 15 keyed True. *NEGE-r* shares 14 items with the 33-item MMPI-2 *NEGE* scale; 6 of the *NEGE-r* items are not included on *NEGE*. Of the 19 items appearing on *NEGE*, but not on *NEGE-r*, 11 are not in the MMPI-2-RF item pool, whereas 8 items were dropped from the revised scale. *NEGE-r* shares five items with the *EID* Higher-Order scale and six with *RC7*.

Even with the fairly low number of shared items, Tellegen and Ben-Porath note large positive correlations of *NEGE-r* scores with both *EID* and *RC7*, ranging from .73 to .81 and from .82 to .87, respectively, in both men and women across a variety of samples. Cronbach's alpha estimates ranged from .76 to .84 within these samples. The test retest coefficient within a subset of the normative sample was .85.

High scores are associated with anxiety, depression, insecurity, and worry. High scores are also associated with the tendency to feel hopeless, to feel as if one's family lacked love, and to develop physical responses to stress. Low scores are associated with a lack of negative emotions, as well as feeling energetic.

Interpretation

Low (*T* < 39) scores reflect the absence of negative emotionality. Individuals scoring in this range can be described as being essentially free from worry. They report having good energy and having a positive outlook on life. They report a good capability to cope with stress.

Average (*T*-40 to 62) elevations are not interpreted. Individuals scoring in this range are reporting an unremarkable number of negative emotional experiences.

Elevated (*T* ≥ 65) scores are associated with reports of emotional distress. These individuals may be described as "worriers." They have a tendency to expect the worst and may blame themselves if it comes to pass. As scores elevate above *T*-75, this anxiousness becomes more predominant. Individuals scoring in this range may find themselves behaviorally inhibited due to excessive anxiety regarding possible negative consequences. They may develop physical complaints in response to stressors; thus, the clinician is urged to examine *RC1* and the somatic scales for possible elevations.

Introversion/Low Positive Emotionality (**INTR-r**)

INTR-r contains 20 items, all keyed False. The items reflect the broad category of a dearth of positive emotional experiences, as well as avoidance of social interaction. *INTR-r* shares 16 items with the MMPI-2 *INTR* scale, which contains 34 items; 4 items appear on *INTR-r*, but are not included on *INTR*. Of the 18 *INTR* items not included in *INTR-r*, 13 do not appear in the MMPI-2-RF item pool and 5 were not included in the revised scale. *INTR-r* shares 10 items with *RC2*, 8 with *EID*, and 5 (reverse keyed) with *RC9*.

Given the number of shared items between *INTR-r* and the scales noted above, one would expect to find significant relationships. The pattern of relationships reported by Tellegen and Ben-Porath is interesting, and bears examination. Within the non-clinical normative sample, moderate sized correlations of −.52 for men and −.46 for women were reported with *RC9*. However, within clinical samples, these correlations were nominally smaller, ranging from −.35 to −.38. An opposite pattern is observed, however, with regard to *EID* and *INTR-r*. In the normative sample, *EID* correlated with *INTR-r* at only .34 for men and .37 for women; in the clinical samples, however, this correlation was substantially larger, ranging from .63 to .65. The effect was similar, although not as dramatic for *RC2*, as the normative sample evidenced a correlation of .74 for men and .69

for women, but the clinical samples evidenced correlations ranging from .84 to .86. That similarities increase as a function of clinical distress is not surprising, and may indicate that *EID* and *INTR-r*, in particular, measure separate facets of the same construct.

High scores on *INTR-r* have been associated with feeling depressed, anxious, hopeless, and like a failure. Low scores are associated with optimism, extraversion, and feeling energetic.

Interpretation

Low ($T \leq 39$) scores are associated with individuals who report more positive emotional experiences than average. Individuals scoring in this range can be described as knowing what they want and having the energy to go after it. They enjoy social interactions and have confidence in their social skills. They report having a good ability to cope with stress.

Average (T-42 to 64) elevations are generally not interpreted. These scores are obtained by individuals who endorse an unremarkable number of positive emotional experiences.

Elevated ($T \geq 65$) scores are associated with individuals who report fewer positive emotional experiences than average. They are likely to present as socially awkward or introverted; they have little confidence in their social skills. As scores elevate into the range of T-75, the lack of positive emotional experiences becomes more prominent. Such individuals may appear anhedonic and lacking in energy. They may experience significant depression and anxiety. These individuals are likely to feel overwhelmed by the difficulties they are facing. They tend to feel like a failure and have little faith in their ability to effect positive change in their lives. Given their pessimism and poor self-concept, it may be difficult to engage them in psychotherapy.

Perspective

As noted earlier, the MMPI-2-RF *Manual* notes that the instrument is not being marketed as a replacement for MMPI-2, but as an alternate version of the form (Ben-Porath & Tellegen, 2011), although its creators tout its purported psychometric superiority over the earlier form. The MMPI-2-RF shares some similarities to the earlier form, especially with regard to the validity scales and the RC scales, but also contains many unique features that reflect the particular goals of its authors, among which were improved psychometric characteristics and the creation of non-overlapping scales within content areas.

Given the overwhelming and enduring popularity of the MMPI-2 and its forerunner, the MMPI, it should be expected that the introduction of the MMPI-2-RF has been met with its share of detractors. Greene (2011, p. 22), in fact, has argued that the "MMPI-2-RF should *not* be conceptualized as a revised or restructured form of the MMPI-2, but as a *new* self-report inventory that chose to select its items from the MMPI-2 item pool and to use its normative group" (emphasis in original). This chapter is not the place for a thorough review of all of the criticisms and defenses of the MMPI-2-RF; the reader is encouraged to review Butcher and Williams' (2012) criticism, as well as Ben-Porath and Flens' (2012) response.

It has been observed that a great strength can also be a weakness. Among the advantages of the MMPI-2-RF is its substantially shorter length (338 items) in comparison to the standard MMPI-2 (567 items). As noted by Graham (2012), many test takers may find the abbreviated length more manageable, especially if they are being asked to complete a battery of multiple assessments. However, with decreased length comes decreased coverage, although the creators of MMPI-2-RF claim that they adequately covered all substantive content areas of the MMPI-2 item pool.

Another advantage of the MMPI-2-RF is that it is laid out in somewhat of a top-down approach with higher-order scales and specific problems scales. As both Graham (2012) and Greene (2011) note, this arrangement can make interpretation much simpler and less time-consuming than with the standard MMPI-2. It can also greatly decrease the learning curve for students.

One issue that, from our experience, appears to be a common misunderstanding with regard to MMPI-2-RF is the belief that the MMPI-2-RF is composed of completely non-overlapping scales. It should be noted that Tellegen and Ben-Porath (2011) are quite clear with respect to this issue; the fault for this misunderstanding does not lie with them. Although the scales within each area (i.e. higher-order, RC, specific problem, PSY–5 scales) do not share items, there is *substantial* item overlap across areas. As noted above, the *PSYC-r* PSY–5 scale shares more items with *THD*, an MMPI-2-RF higher-order scale, than with the original *PSYC* scale as it appears on MMPI-2. This issue, of course, is not unique to MMPI-2-RF, as the scales of MMPI-2 also show substantial overlap. There are few scales, however, that overlap to the extent of *PSYC-r* and *THD*. The clinician has a responsibility to be aware of the issue of item overlap and scale redundancy when interpreting the MMPI-2-RF.

One of the primary concerns with regard to the use of MMPI-2-RF concerns the lack of empirical support for its use relative to the amount of empirical support available for use of the MMPI-2 (Graham, 2012). The MMPI-2-RF was introduced in 2008, with a minor update in 2011. The RC scales, which comprise the core of the RF, were introduced in 2003. Given the relatively brief time that the RC scales and form RF have been available in comparison to MMPI /MMPI-2, it is not surprising that they do not have the wealth of empirical literature to support their use that is enjoyed by the earlier versions of the MMPI. A PsycINFO search performed on September 15, 2013, revealed 122 hits for a search of "MMPI-2" and "RC," 101 hits for a search of "MMPI-2" and "RF," and 176 hits for a search of "MMPI-2" and "Restructured;" note that there is undoubtedly some overlap among the obtained results. In comparison, a search of "MMPI-2" revealed 2,503 hits. Again, there is undoubtedly some overlap with the prior searches; nevertheless, it is clear that there remains substantially more empirical support for the standard MMPI-2 than for MMPI-2-RF.

There is no doubt that with the passage of time the research base will increase with regard to empirical correlates for MMPI-2-RF scales. At the present time, however, there appears to be limited specificity with regard to empirical content for several of the MMPI-2-RF scales, even within the *Technical Manual* (Tellegen & Ben-Porath, 2011). An example of this phenomenon can be seen in the somatic/cognitive scales in which nearly every scale has correlates of multiple somatic complaints and a preoccupation with physical symptoms. Although the item content of the scales may address different phenomena, the correlates for each of the scales are substantively similar and not especially clinically informative. Thus, these scales can best be interpreted only as a respondent's self-report. A similar phenomenon is observed with regard to the *ACT* scale, for which no empirical correlates have been reported, as well as *DSF*, *AES*, and *MEC*, for which no empirical correlates have been reported for women. The reader is encouraged to keep this in mind when interpreting these scales until such time as more research is available with regard to empirically supported correlates.

Graham (2012, p. 415), who, it should be noted, is one of the authors of the MMPI-2 RC scales, which enjoy pride of place on the MMPI-2-RF, suggested that interpretations based on the MMPI-2 "can yield a more in-depth analysis of personality and psychopathology" than interpretation based on MMPI-2-RF. He suggested that the MMPI-2-RF is preferable when brevity is a primary concern or when a screening instrument is desired. At the present time, the authors of this text partially concur with that statement; we agree that the MMPI-2-RF is best incorporated as a screening instrument or situations wherein administration of the 567-item MMPI-2 is impractical; however, we note that the MMPI-2-RF contains only 32 fewer items than the MMPI-2 370 form, whereas the latter enjoys the advantage of the extensively researched clinical scales and the literature on clinical interpretation of codetypes.

We are reminded of Alexander Pope's words from *An Essay on Criticism*, in 1711: "Be not the first by whom the new are tried, nor yet the last to lay the old aside." For now, however, we would encourage clinicians to administer the full MMPI-2 item pool, as doing so allows for scoring of both the MMPI-2 and MMPI-2-RF profiles. Tellegen and Ben-Porath (2011), as well as van der Heijden, Egger, and Derksen (2010), have reported that MMPI-2-RF scale scores obtained from an MMPI-2 administration are comparable to those obtained with the MMPI-2-RF booklet. By scoring both forms, the clinician who chooses to base their interpretation on the MMPI-2-RF scales has the MMPI-2 profile available if they are faced with interpreting an MMPI-2-RF profile containing elevations only on those scales for which limited empirical support is available. Moreover, the availability of the MMPI-2 scores and profile will often enable the clinician to place noteworthy MMPI-2-RF scores within a broader and potentially more useful context. Given the comparability of MMPI-2-RF scores obtained in this manner, extant databases—those that have given us our rich empirical knowledge base for the MMPI-2—can be mined for additional correlates for MMPI-2-RF scales.

Despite the MMPI-2 designation for both the standard MMPI-2 and MMPI-2-RF versions, the RF form should be considered to be an essentially new instrument, as distinct from a mere revision or updating of the MMPI-2, as was the case in its transition from the original MMPI. To be sure, the RF does have its roots in the MMPI-2 item pool, the 1989 norms gathered for the MMPI-2, similar (and, in at least one case, improved, see *Fp-r*) validity scales, and revisions of the MMPI-2 PSY–5 scales. However, the substitution of a theory-driven methodology for one that was empirically-driven in the construction of the RF's central set of scales, the RC scales, marks a significant departure from MMPI/MMPI-2 tradition and, in turn, a significant obstacle in applying to the RF form the vast research literature for the MMPI/MMPI-2 that has accumulated over the past 70 years. In short, the MMPI-2-RF is a new psychometric instrument and does not yet have the wealth of empirical support and interpretive data enjoyed by the MMPI-2. With time, we will surely come to develop a complete understanding of the MMPI-2-RF; for now, however, its strengths and weaknesses, and the patterns thereof, largely remain to be clarified in research efforts that the future must await.

Note

1 Using the Guilford's (1936) formula for a baseline correlation due to shared items,

$$r = \frac{N_s}{\sqrt{A_u + N_s} \cdot \sqrt{B_u + N_s}}$$, where N_s = the number of shared items between scales A and B,

A_u = the number of unique items in scale A, and B_u = the number of unique items in scale B. Shared items equals the number of items scored in the same direction minus the number of items scored in the opposite direction. Unique items for each scale equals the number of items on that scale that do not appear on the opposite scale, regardless of scoring direction.

12 Automated Interpretation of the MMPI-2 and the MMPI-2-RF

Computer-Based Test Interpretation (CBTI)

Computer applications in psychology grew remarkably during the last half of the 20th century (Bartram & Hambleton, 2006). Initially used primarily for scoring test items on academic and achievement tests, computers have increasingly been used for more complex processes in ways that not only are more reliable than similar tasks done by humans, but also more cost-effective. As summarized by Butcher (2009):

> In the 1960s, practitioners began to capitalize on computers' capabilities to assist with data interpretation as well. Optical scanners that "read" answer sheets and tabulated responses were connected with programs written to analyze the scores and report the results in a clinically meaningful way (Fowler, 1967). Today, scoring is made even easier through the use of online testing which can provide for the nearly instant computerized tabulation of results (Baker, 2007).

At present, numerous programs for CBTI are available, covering a range of popular personality tests, including the MMPI-2 and MMPI-2-RF, the Sixteen Personality Factor Questionnaire (16 PF), the Personality Assessment Inventory (PAI), the Millon Clinical Multiaxial Inventory (MCMI-III), the Emotional Quotient-Inventory (EQ-i), and the MATRIX Predictive Uniform Law Enforcement Selection Evaluation Inventory (M-PULSE Inventory). Despite initial reluctance, the psychological and psychiatric community has shown widespread acceptance of such computer uses. Indeed, by 1969, approximately one fourth of the eligible psychologists and psychiatrists in the United States used one such CBTI interpretation service (Fowler, 1969), and the proportion of such professionals using CBTI systems has continued to increase markedly (Butcher, 2009; Spielberger & Piotrowski, 1990). Likewise, computer-based interpretation and administration of psychological tests has gained increasing acceptance within the professional community (Atlis, Hahn, & Butcher, 2006; Ben-Porath & Butcher, 1986; Butcher, 1994a, 2013; Butcher, Perry, & Atlis, 2000; Butcher, Perry, & Dean, 2009; Carr & Ghosh, 1983; Fowler, 1985; Greist, Klein, Erdman, & Jefferson, 1983; Spinhoven, Labbe, & Rombouts, 1993; Williams & Weed, 2004).

The widespread use of CBTI systems has not been without controversy, however. Controversies have focused primarily on three areas:

1   whether there are important differences between computer versus booklet administrations. Watson et al. (1990), Watson, Manifold et al. (1992), Schuldberg

(1990), and Butcher (2009) all agree that the evidence shows that the two versions are generally equivalent and any differences between these administrations are typically small and inconsequential;

2   whether CBTI systems have demonstrated validity (Matarazzo, 1986; Moreland, 1985, 1990); and relatedly,

3   whether psychological assessment is being inappropriately supplanted by formula-driven testing (Tallent, 1987).

Butcher et al. (2009) provide an overview of critical questions to consider in evaluating the adequacy of computerized testing services. These include: Does the test on which the computer interpretation is based have an adequate network of established validity research? Is there a published user's guide to explain the test and system variables? Is the computer-based report based on the most widely validated measures available on the test? How frequently is the system revised to incorporate new empirical data on the test? How closely does the system conform to empirically validated test correlates? All of these important questions should be considered by clinicians in choosing the specific reports upon which they rely in their clinical decision making.

Regarding the important area of validity, the usefulness of CBTI systems would seem assured to the extent that such systems relied exclusively on actuarially-derived data. Certainly, as discussed earlier in this book, the evidence overwhelmingly supports actuarially-based interpretation as compared with clinical interpretation. However, not all aspects of CBTI systems are actuarially based. Although most computer-generated MMPI-2 reports are based upon actuarial findings, they are only partially so, and the accuracy of their non-actuarially derived elements is only as good as the interpretive skills of the CBTI program's architects.

Further, an actuarial system can consider only empirical data that have been incorporated into the system's algorithms, and these are limited by the population(s) from which the actuarial data have been derived. Because clinical situations frequently are far more complex, and one size does not fit all, it is seldom the case that all, or even most, relevant personal and contextual data will be considered by any CBTI system for interpreting the MMPI-2 and MMPI-2-RF. Problems such as these prompted Rodgers (1972) to state, "I regard them [computerized interpretations] as basically dangerous except in the hands of a person who is sufficiently expert with the MMPI that he probably will not utilize the computer printout" (p. 245). Others, such as Eichman (1972) and Tallent (1987), have raised concerns that a computer report in the hands of a psychometrically unsophisticated professional might be substituted for clinical judgment, rather than supplementing it. In using CBTI reports, Fowler and Butcher's (1986) statement that "there must be a clinician between the computer and the client" (p. 95) continues to be relevant.

Despite these concerns, even early studies found that professional consumers rated the accuracy of CBTI MMPI reports as satisfactory (Webb, 1970b; Webb, Miller, & Fowler, 1969; Webb et al., 1970). Subsequent studies (Moreland, 1985; Williams & Weed, 2004) have likewise supported the accuracy of computer-generated narrative reports for the MMPI and MMPI-2, even though the inter-rater reliability coefficients often have been so low as to limit estimates of validity. The variety of available CBTI reports makes research comparing programs difficult, as some reports rely more than others on actuarial formulas versus clinical expertise, utilize different scales in the generation of the reports, and vary widely in their complexity and coverage, with some even excluding diagnostic impressions.

Williams and Weed (2004) provide a concise overview of the methodological limitations in conducting comparison research among eight computer-generated MMPI-2 reports. They provide practical findings from their investigation of these commercially available MMPI-2 reports in order to determine their efficacy across difficult dimensions rated by practitioners. Their ratings included their clinical usefulness and the accuracy of the information contained in the reports, as well as the appropriateness of the diagnoses they contained, as judged by the practitioners. Reports generated from actual MMPI-2 profiles were compared to reports derived from modal profiles. All eight of the authentic computer-generated reports were apprised as more accurate and useful than the modal reports. The individual differences between the eight reports varied, and the interested reader is urged to read their results.

Advantages and Disadvantages of CBTI

Despite these cautionary notes, it is clear that computer scoring and interpretation of the MMPI-2 is here to stay and, in fact, will likely increase in use. It has become evident that there are several distinct advantages of computer-generated psychological reports (Butcher, 1987a, 1994b; Spielberger & Piotrowski, 1990), including the following:

1 *Reliability.* The computer has far fewer bad days than humans, and the same input results in the same output.
2 *Memory.* The computer can store and more rapidly retrieve information with accuracy far more detailed than the human, especially if that human does not have ready access to a library.
3 *Objectivity.* Interpreter bias is minimized in computer-generated reports. Once the interpretation rules are programmed, they are applied automatically and consistently to specified cases, regardless of extraneous circumstances.
4 *Rapidity.* The speed of computer processing and printing is extremely high. The computer can score, interpret, and print psychological reports for several thousand tests a day, a feat far beyond human capability, or to interpret a single test within seconds of the test administration, saving valuable professional time.
5 *Cost-efficiency.* Because of these factors, the computer-generated reports are clearly cost-efficient and will undoubtedly become more so in the decades to come.

Of course, there are disadvantages as well (Butcher, 1987a, 1987b, 2009; Butcher et al., 2009; Matarazzo, 1986; Spielberger & Piotrowski, 1990), including the following:

1 *Excessive generality.* Matarazzo (1986) pointed out that computer-generated reports rely on modal descriptions and do not do justice to the individual aspects of a person. However, as noted in Chapter 9, the actuarial approach, based on just such descriptions, continues to regularly exceed the skills of human clinicians. Even so, the relevant dimensions that modify interpretations of tests (e.g. SES,

education, recent job loss) are not routinely included for consideration by most computerized interpretation programs.

2   *Algorithm limitations.* A related criticism, then, is that the objectivity and accuracy of the computer is only as good as the objectivity and accuracy of the person who developed and programmed the CBTI system.

3   *Secrecy of the algorithms.* Because CBTI systems are generally proprietary, its algorithms are generally unavailable to others. Some, perhaps most, systems employ a panel of expert consultants, who review the interpretive algorithms in private and then issue reassurances to consumers that the interpretations appear valid.

4   *Potential for misuse.* Because of their ease of use and apparent reliability, there is an added possibility for overreliance on the reports, as well as the possibility of unqualified users having access to any personal data input to the system.

5   *Confusing abundance of packages.* Because of the large number of computer-assisted test-interpretation packages, the clinician often has difficulty in selecting among the offerings. This is made even more difficult because most of these packages were developed in a proprietary fashion and, unlike data in the public domain, the algorithms used by the computer in scoring and interpretation are private and not open to ordinary inspection or peer review.

Standards on the use of computers in psychological testing and assessment have been developed by the American Psychological Association, and the reader is encouraged to become familiar with the *Guidelines for Users of Computer-Based Tests and Interpretations,* available from the American Psychological Association (1986). In these standards, the point is clearly made that the user of a computerized interpretation service remains just as professionally responsible as if that user had interpreted the test without assistance.

To address the base-rate difficulties encountered within different populations, some CBTI programs for interpreting the MMPI-2 and MMPI-2-RF now generate different computer reports depending on the subpopulation to which a person is being compared. Thus, one may select, for example, a computer-generated MMPI-2/MMPI-2-RF interpretation based on norms from mental health clinic outpatients, psychiatric and forensic outpatients, general medical patients, and personnel being evaluated for various safety-sensitive positions, such as pilots, police, and firefighter candidates. Other population subsets undoubtedly will be developed as it becomes clear that their base rates differ in substantive ways from the basic norms for the MMPI-2 and MMPI-2-RF.

Computerized Adaptive (CA) testing is an innovation that has met with limited success in the area of personality testing. In essence, CA administration of an instrument presents only those items to the respondent needed for the specific referred question. By reducing the number of items administered, the CA approach is potentially more time-efficient. One approach, called the Countdown Method, involves two ways of classifying individuals. The first, the Classification Method (Butcher, Keller, & Bacon, 1985), stops the presentation of scale items once an elevation threshold is either met or ruled out. The second technique, the Full Scores on Elevated Scales (FSES) approach (Ben-Porath, Slutske, & Butcher, 1989), allows all remaining items on a scale to be administered if the elevation threshold cut-score is reached. While there is limited support for adaptive testing modalities (e.g. Forbey & Ben-Porath, 2007), it appears that for the MMPI-2 clinical scales, composed as they are of heterogeneous items, the time saving is not worth the reduction in validity. For content homogeneous scales such as the MMPI-2 content, PSY–5, and RC scales, however, CA may have some advantages in time savings, but these must be balanced against the lowered reliabilities that are characteristic of scales of limited length. Many of the Harris-Lingoes and RF scales, while suitably homogeneous, contain fewer than 10 items each, and may therefore be poorly suited to CA administration.

The first computer-assisted MMPI interpretative system was developed at the Mayo Clinic (Rome et al., 1962; Swenson & Pearson, 1964). Early MMPI interpretative systems were based upon simple pairings of clinical scales, which allowed for efficient screening. The next generation (Butcher et al., 2009) of applied interpretive programs focused on creating clinically useful narrative reports, with a major objective of helping clinicians determine psychiatric diagnoses. Fowler's (e.g. 1967, 1969) program developed for Roche Laboratories received widespread attention, as it included interpretation of the test-taker's attitude as well as interpretive statements flowing both from basic clinical scale configurations and decision rules for special scales. Other report systems were developed, including the Caldwell (1971), Greene & Brown (1990), and Lachar (1974) reports. The reader is referred to Butcher (1987b) for an excellent overview of the limitations associated with the early MMPI programs, including their inclusion of measures that lacked validity. In 1982, the Minnesota Report was published by National Computer Systems, now owned by Pearson Assessments, and is the most widely-used among clinicians today. It includes scores for validity, clinical, content, and widely-researched supplementary scales, and can be purchased as an extended score report only or with various interpretive reports, such as personnel and clinical narratives.

Test and Narrative Report Comparisons: A Case Example

To provide a comparison of scoring and narrative report interpretation services, the same clinical answer sheet was sent to each of two widely-used services for computerized interpretation of the MMPI-2 and MMPI-2-RF. Along with the answer sheet, the following information was provided (the reader is urged to read both reports for comparative purposes).

Client: Roseanne Valenda
Age: 23
Date of Assessment: 2/22/2011 to 3/1/2011
Referred by: Self

Reason for Referral:

Ms. Valenda was seen for assessment at a student counseling center of a Midwestern university for assessment in order to aid in determination of whether she met criteria for a diagnosis of ADHD.

Background:

Ms. Valenda is currently a graduate student working on a second attempt to complete a Master's thesis. She had "worked on and off on the first one for two years" before shifting her focus to another project. At the time of testing, Ms. Valenda was hoping to be granted an extension on her defense date because of her self-reported difficulties with concentration and focus.

Ms. Valenda stated that she had always been "flighty" and related having difficulty completing ordinary tasks. For example, she stated that it may take her "half an hour" to tie her shoes, as she would become distracted by other things.

During the interview, Ms. Valenda displayed thinking that was fairly rigid and concrete. For example, she was unable to entertain the possibility of a future in which she did not complete her thesis, nor could she accept the notion that being in graduate school was a choice, rather than a necessity. Her affective reactions to these notions were suggestive of anger and distress.

When questioned about her difficulties, Ms. Valenda was very vague, other than to repeatedly state that she could not focus her attention and would become distracted very easily. She stated that she was not sleeping very well, as she had a tendency to ruminate over things that were not going well in her life, and to specifically "stress" over the need to complete her thesis.

With regard to a history of academic problems resulting from difficulties with attention and concentration, Ms. Valenda was only able to relate a single instance. She reported that in high school she received a C grade on a paper, and the teacher told her that it appeared that she had not put forth good effort on the assignment. She did not report any history of disciplinary issues, other academic problems, or significant medical history.

With the client's permission, Ms. Valenda's mother was contacted and she, however, reported a somewhat different history with regard to academic functioning, discipline problems and, in particular, Roseanne's medical history.

Mrs. Valenda reported that Roseanne began to experience significant, frequent headaches, mimicking the symptoms of migraines, beginning around the age of three years. Mrs. Valenda reported that by the time Roseanne began school, these headaches had increased in both frequency and severity. According to Mrs.

Valenda, the pain from these headaches caused Roseanne to cry out in class which, in turn, led to her being viewed as a discipline problem by her teachers and other school officials, as well as to being somewhat ostracized by her classmates. Mrs. Valenda reported that Roseanne remains somewhat guarded in her interpersonal interactions to this day, and that she believes this to be a result of her being picked on as a child.

Mrs. Valenda reported that the headaches continued to increase in frequency and severity into puberty. She stated that the family took Roseanne to a neurologist at an out-of-state head pain clinic, and even to an orthodontist in an effort to discover the cause of these nearly disabling headaches. Mrs. Valenda stated that all of these efforts proved fruitless until they finally took Roseanne to an endocrinologist who discovered a 10mm brain tumor (location uncertain) that was the cause of her headaches. He placed Roseanne on medication that was successful in shrinking the tumor by 1mm, but which had no further effect. Several treatment options have been presented to Roseanne, including surgery but, according to Mrs. Valenda, Roseanne has so far not agreed to more aggressive treatment.

With regard to personality and interpersonal functioning, Mrs. Valenda stated, as noted above, that Roseanne was picked on quite a bit as a child as a result of her medical problems. She stated that Roseanne is very guarded with information regarding her medical history and difficulties, and that it was very likely that she hadn't told her therapist or the author of this report about them. She stated that Roseanne did not have a lot of trust in other people.

Behavioral Observations:

Ms. Valenda appeared to be in good general health on each of the assessment days, and the examiner noted no overt physical difficulties on the client's part. Ms. Valenda was aware of the purpose of the assessment and rapport was easily established. Her speech patterns were within normal limits, and the examiner noted no evidence of disrupted thought patterns or of Ms. Valenda attending to internal stimuli.

On each day Ms. Valenda arrived on time for the examination and appeared to be comfortable with the examiner and the testing situation. She was appropriately dressed in khakis and a shirt. The client did not wear glasses.

Ms. Valenda appeared to give good effort on each of the cognitive subtests and, in fact, was very interested in what each of the tasks was designed to measure. The examiner promised the client that he would explain the tests after completion of each task and this satisfied the client.

The assessment was performed over two sessions in an effort to prevent fatigue on the client's part. Ms. Valenda's work style was steady, and in no way appeared impulsive. Overall, her level of activity was within age/situational appropriate levels, and she reacted appropriately to failure. Given her good effort and comfort with the testing situation, the results of the assessment are considered valid.

MMPI-2 VALIDITY AND CLINICAL SCALES PROFILE

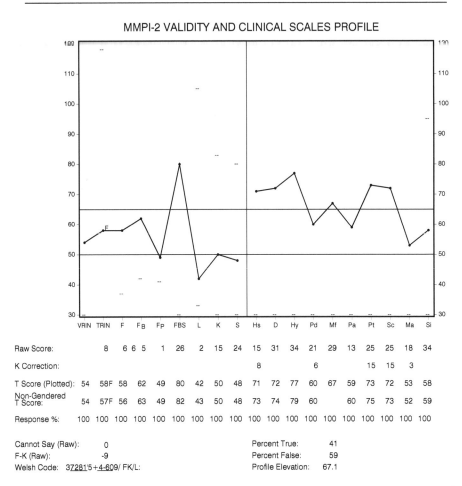

		VRIN	TRIN	F	F_B	Fp	FBS	L	K	S	Hs	D	Hy	Pd	Mf	Pa	Pt	Sc	Ma	Si
Raw Score:		8	6 6	5	1	26	2	15	24	15	31	34	21	29	13	25	25	18	34
K Correction:										8			6		15	15	3		
T Score (Plotted):	54	58F	58	62	49	80	42	50	48	71	72	77	60	67	59	73	72	53	58
Non-Gendered T Score:	54	57F	56	63	49	82	43	50	48	73	74	79	60		60	75	73	52	59
Response %:	100	100	100	100	100	100	100	100	100	100	100	100	100	100	100	100	100	100	100

Cannot Say (Raw):   0
F-K (Raw):   -9
Welsh Code: 37281'5+4-609/ FK/L:

Percent True: 41
Percent False: 59
Profile Elevation: 67.1

The highest and lowest T scores possible on each scale are indicated by a "--".

For information on FBS, see Ben-Porath, Y. S., & Tellegen, A. (2006). The FBS: Current Status, a report on the Pearson web site (www.pearsonassessments.com/tests/mmpi_2.htm).

Figure 12.1 MMPI-2 Extended Score Report: Validity and Clinical Scales Profile

MMPI-2 and MMPI-2-RF Score and Automated Interpretive Reports for Ms. Valenda

The MMPI-2 answer sheet Ms. Valenda completed at the time of her assessment was subsequently submitted to two commercial scoring services. Her answer sheet was sent to Pearson Assessments to obtain an *Extended Score Report*, and *The Minnesota Report™: Adult Clinical System-Revised, 4th Edition* by James N. Butcher, PhD, entitled *Outpatient Mental Health Interpretive Report*. The same answer sheet was simultaneously sent to Caldwell Report. Her answer sheet was then translated into a form suitable for scoring the MMPI-2-RF, which generated an MMPI-2-RF Score Report entitled, *Interpretive Report: Clinical Settings* (Ben-Porath & Tellegen), obtained through Pearson Assessments.

Because of the extensive overlap in the reporting of scores across these various reports, and to record her scores on many scales not included in the output provided by these commercial services, two tables were prepared: one for the MMPI-2 (Table 12.1); the second for the MMPI-2-RF (Table 12.2), to economize on space. Scores and indices have also been organized into a revised format of the MMPI-2 Structural Summary (Nichols & Greene, 1995). These materials will be presented in the following sequence. First, the MMPI-2 validity and clinical scale profiles; then, Table 12.1, reporting the remaining MMPI-2 scores, these then to be followed by the MMPI-2 Structural Summary and, finally, the Outpatient Mental Health Interpretive Report. The sequence for the MMPI-2-RF is similar, with the validity and Restructured Clinical (RC) scale profiles followed by Table 12.2, reporting the scores for the MMPI-2-RF Special Problem scales, and ending with the Interpretive Report: Clinical Settings.

Before turning to their respective interpretive narratives, it is suggested that readers may wish to carefully review the MMPI-2 and MMPI-2-RF scores and their patterns in order to form their own impressions about the response styles, symptom and personality characteristics, and diagnostic possibilities that emerge from this client's performance on the two measures, later to compare them with those enunciated in the automated reports.

Table 12.1 Additional MMPI-2 scales

Harris-Lingoes, Martin-Finn *Mf*, and *Si* subscales

	Raw Score	T-Score
D1 Subjective Depression	15	67
D2 Psychomotor Retardation	9	68
D3 Physical Malfunctioning	5	63
D4 Mental Dullness	8	75
D5 Brooding	4	58
Hy1 Denial of Social Anxiety	4	51
Hy2 Need for Affection	7	50
Hy3 Lassitude-Malaise	11	83
Hy4 Somatic Complaints	6	61
Hy5 Inhibition of Aggression	4	54
Pd1 Familial Discord	3	56
Pd2 Authority Problems	2	46
Pd3 Social Imperturbability	4	52
Pd4 Social Alienation	5	54
Pd5 Self-Alienation	7	68
Mf1 Denial of Stereotypic Masculine Interests	5	34
Mf2 Hypersensitivity-Anxiety	4	42
Mf3 Stereotypical Feminine Interests	1	35
Mf4 Low Cynicism	4	47
Mf5 Aesthetic Interests	0	31
Mf6 Feminine Gender Identity	4	46
Mf7 Restraint	5	55
Mf10 Composite Femininity-Masculinity	9	25
Pa1 Persecutory Ideas	3	57
Pa2 Poignancy	3	53
Pa3 Naïveté	4	45
Sc1 Social Alienation	4	53
Sc2 Emotional Alienation	2	58
Sc3 Lack of Ego Mastery, Cognitive	7	86
Sc4 Lack of Ego Mastery, Conative	8	80
Sc5 Lack of Ego Mastery, Defective Inhibition	3	59
Sc6 Bizarre Sensory Experiences	8	77
Ma1 Amorality	0	37
Ma2 Psychomotor Acceleration	5	50
Ma3 Imperturbability	4	56
Ma4 Ego Inflation	3	49
Si1 Shyness/Self-Consciousness	6	52
Si2 Social Avoidance	7	69
Si3 Alienation—Self and Others	8	58

MMPI-2 Restructured Clinical Scales

	RCd	RC1	RC2	RC3	RC4	RC6	RC7	RC8	RC9
	dem	*som*	*lpe*	*cyn*	*asb*	*per*	*dne*	*abx*	*hpm*
Raw Score	11	10	7	6	3	3	5	7	10
T-Score	60	66	62	50	48	67	47	69	48

MMPI-2 Content and Content Component Scales

	ANX	FRS	OBS	DEP	HEA	BIZ	ANG	CYN	ASP	TPA	LSE	SOD	FAM	WRK	TRT
Raw:	10	2	10	8	14	7	7	11	7	5	6	16	6	10	4
T-Scr:	56	38	63	55	66	67	53	53	52	43	52	68	50	52	49

	Raw Score	T-Score
FRS1 Generalized Fearfulness	1	48
FRS2 Multiple Fears	1	33
DEP1 Lack of Drive	3	55
DEP2 Dysphoria	2	53
DEP3 Self-Depreciation	3	61
DEP4 Suicidal Ideation	0	45
HEA1 Gastrointestinal Symptoms	1	54
HEA2 Neurological Symptoms	6	72
HEA3 General Health Concerns	3	64
BIZ1 Psychotic Symptomatology	2	65
BIZ2 Schizotypal Characteristics	4	66
ANG1 Explosive Behavior	3	61
ANG2 Irritability	3	49
CYN1 Misanthropic Beliefs	8	56
CYN2 Interpersonal Suspiciousness	3	49
ASP1 Antisocial Attitudes	7	55
ASP2 Antisocial Behavior	0	42
TPA1 Impatience	1	40
TPA2 Competitive Drive	1	40
LSE1 Self-Doubt	4	57
LSE2 Submissiveness	0	39
SOD1 Introversion	13	76
SOD2 Shyness	3	50
FAM1 Family Discord	3	47
FAM2 Familial Alienation	2	59
TRT1 Low Motivation	1	46
TRT2 Inability to Disclose	0	38

Note: Uniform T-scores are used for the clinical scales, the content and content component scales, and the PSY–5 scales. The remaining scales and subscales use linear T-scores.

continued …

Table 12.1 continued

MMPI-2 Supplementary Scales

	A	R	Es	Do	Re	Mt	PK	MDS	Ho	O-H	MAC-R	AAS	APS	GM	GF
Raw Score	16	19	25	16	24	28	23	5	16	13	16	0	25	39	35
T-Score	56	57	31	49	59	72	72	59	49	48	42		39	55	66	43

MMPI-2 PSY–5 Scales

	AGGR	PSYC	DISC	NEGE	INTR
Raw Score	8	8	8	10	18
T-Score	53	66	44	48	68

Special MMPI-2 Scales

	Raw Score	T-Score
Supplemental Validity Measures		
Ds Dissimulation	13	54
Mp Positive Malingering	7	46
Sd Social Desirability	11	47
Ss Socioeconomic Status	47	35
Revised D Subscales		
Dr1 Depressed Mood	10	68
Dr2 Inhibition of Aggression	7	47
Dr3 Somatic Malaise	5	62
Dr4 Cognitive Infirmity	5	75
Dr5 Social Vulnerability	2	48
Hp Hopelessness	0	43
Paranoia Factors		
Pf1 Resentment	0	45
Pf2 Ideas of Reference	2	57
Pf3 Delusions of Control	0	47
Pf4 Persecutory Ideas/Delusions	2	69
Cognitive Stability Scales		
CogProb Cognitive Problems	11	86
DisOrg Disorganization	4	69

Sources: MMPI-2 Harris-Lingoes Subscales. Scale name and scores taken from pages 8–9 report output for R V dated 3/3/11. *MMPI*®*-2 Outpatient Mental Health Interpretive Report The Minnesota Report™: Adult Clinical System-Revised*, 4th Edition, James N. Butcher, PhD. Copyright © 1989, 1993, 2001, 2005 by the Regents of the University of Minnesota. Excerpted from the *MMPI-2 Manual for Administration, Scoring, and Interpretation*, Revised Edition. Copyright © 2001 by the Regents of the University of Minnesota. All rights reserved. Reproduced by permission of the University of Minnesota.
MMPI-2 RC Scales, Content and Component Scales, Supplementary Scales, PSY–5 Scales. Scale names and scores taken from pages 4, 7, 9 of the report output for R V dated 3/3/11. MMPI®-2 Extended Score Report Copyright © 1989, 1994, 2000, 2003, 2006 by the Regents of the University of Minnesota. Excerpted from the *MMPI-2 Manual for Administration, Scoring, and Interpretation*, Revised Edition. Copyright © 2001 by the Regents of the University of Minnesota. All rights reserved. Reproduced by permission of the University of Minnesota Press.
Martin-Finn *Mf* Subscales. Martin, H., & Finn, S. E. (2010). *Masculinity and femininity in the MMPI-2 and MMPI-A*. Minneapolis, MN: University of Minnesota Press.

MMPI-2 Structural Summary

Nichols = Revision of Greene & Nichols (1995)
Profile Code: 37281'5+4-609/ FK/L;

TEST-TAKING ATTITUDES

1. Omissions: _0_ **2. Consistency**: VRIN_54_TRIN_58F_ **3. T%/F% Balance**: _41/59_
4. Accuracy:
A. Self-Unfavorable: F(raw)_6_F_58_Fb_62_Fp_49*_O-S_69_Ds_54_F – K(raw)_-9
L&W_37/107 K-B_27/73 * _0_ of 4 family items; _0_ of 4 L items
B. Self-Favorable: 1) Self-Deception: K_50_S_48_Ss_35_False%_59_
S subscales: S1_45_S2_56_S3_36_S4_58_S5_45_
2) Impression Management: L_42_Sd_47_Mp_46_
5. Subjective vs. Objective Coping: K – Es_19_

FACTOR SCALES

1. **First Factor Scales**: A_56_Pt*_67_RCd_60_RC7_47_PK_72_Mt_72_WRK_52_
NEGE_48_ANX_56_DEP_55_TRT_49_LSE_52_[GM]_66_[K]_50_[S]_48_[Es]_31_
2. **Second Factor Scales**:
A. Emotional Overcontrol: R_57_D2_68_D-S_53_Dr2_47_[TPA]_43_[ANG1]_61_
Hy5_54_
B. Behavioral Overcontrol: [DISC]_44_[RC9]_48_[Pd2]_46_Dr2_47_Re_59_GF_43_
[MAC–R]_42_[ASP]_52_[Pd-O]_65_O-H_48_

SOMATIC

1. **Somatization**: RC1_66_HEA_66_Hs*_69_Hy4_61_Dr3_62_Hy-O_75_Sc6_77_
D3_63_L&W_12/23
2. **Neurological**: HEA2_72_Sc6_77_
* Non-K-Corrected T-Score
NOTE: Scales in brackets ([]) indicate that <u>low</u> scores are consistent with the symptom
or trait.

MOOD

1. **Depression**:
A. Depressed Mood/Dysphoria: Dr1_68_DEP2_53_D1_67_D5_58_Pa2_53_
B. Depressed Ideation/Attitudes: DEP_55_DEP1_55_Sc2_58_K-B_7/22 L&W_7/15
Items 150, 303, 506, 520, 524, 530 (Circle)-**None**
C. Mental Insufficiency: Dr4_75_D4_75_DEP1_55_Sc3_86_Sc4_80_D2_68_
D. Vegetative Signs: Dr3_62_D3_63_Hy3_83_Hy4_61_D2_68_HEA_66_[Ma2]_50_
L&W_0/6-Sex L&W_4/6-Sleep
2. **Dysphoria**: Dr1_68_DEP2_53_
3. **Elation**: Ma*_53_[Dr1]_68_[DEP2]_53_D_72_Ma4_49_[RC2]_62_[LSE1]_57_
[FRS]_38_[DEP]_55_

4. **Anhedonia**: *INTR_68_RC2_62_DEP1_55_D4_75_ SOD1_76_Sc4_80_Sc2_58_ D2_68_ Pd5_68_*
5. **Hopelessness**: *Hp_43_*
6. **Guilt**: *Guilt_53_Pd5_68_LSE1_57_D5_58_*
7. **Anxiety**: *ANX_56_Pt*_67_FRS1_48_K-B_9/17 L&W_4/11*
8. **Fearfulness/Apprehension**: *FRS1_48_*
9. **Fears/Phobias**: *FRS2_33_FRS_38_[GM]_66_[Es]_31_Pt*_67_Sc*_67_Sc5_59_*
10. **Irritability**: *ANG2_49_TPA1_40_NEGE_48_*
11. **Anger**: *ANG_53_ANG2_49_ANG1_61_NEGE_48_TPA1_40_K-B_1/5
Items 150, 540, 542, 548 (Circle)*
12. **Resentment**: *Pf1_45_Sc1 _53_Pd4_54_*
13. **Hostile Aggression**: *AGGR_53_TPA2_40_RC9_48_*
14. **Inhibition of Aggression**: *Dr2_47_D2_68_D-S_53_[Sc5]_59_Hy-5_54_*
15. **Overcontrolled Hostility**: *O-H_48_*
16. **Impulsivity**: *ASP2_42_ASP_52_ANG_53_DISC_44_*
17. **Fearlessness/Recklessness**: *[FRS]_38_Ma*_53_DISC_44_ASP_52_*
18. **Emotional Alienation**: *Sc2_58_Pd5_68_Sc1_53_*

COGNITION

1. **Unconventional Thought Processes**: *Sc2_58_Ma2_50_F_58_*
2. **Psychotic Thought Processes**: *DisOrg_69_RC8_69_BIZ_67_PSYC_66_BIZ1_65_ BIZ2_66_Sc*_67_Sc3_86_Sc6_77_F_58_FRS1_48_Pf3_47_K-B_6/11 L&W_5/10*
3. **Persecutory Thought Processes**: *Pf4_69_RC6_67_Pa1_57_ BIZ2_66_Pa-O_60_ PSYC_66_BIZ_67_Pa_59_Sc1_53_CYN2_49_Pd4_54_K-B_2/16 L&W_2/15*
4. **Ideas of Reference**: *Pf2_57_BIZ2_66_*
5. **Cynicism/Mistrust**: *CYN_53_RC3_50_CYN1_56_CYN2_49_[S]_48_[Pa3]_45_ [Hy2]_50_[S1]_45_[Mf4]_47_ASP1_55_[Hy-S]_54_Ma1_37_Ho_49_*
6. **Grandiosity**: *Ma4_49_[LSE]_52_*
7. **Ideas of Worthlessness**: *DEP3_61_LSE1_57_TRT1_46_*
8. **Obsessions/Ruminations**: *OBS_63_Pt*_67_[Es]_31_*
9. **Memory/Attention/Concentration**: *CogProb_86_D4_75_Sc3_86_Sc4_80_ K-B_6/11*
10. **Indecision**: *OBS_63_WRK_52_NEGE_48_TRIN_58_(False)*

COGNITION—DEFENSE

1. **Suppression/Repression/Constriction**: *R_57_[DISC]_44_Hy-S_54_K_50_D-S_53_ Mf7_55_*
2. **Denial**: *L_42_K_50_False%_59_*
3. **Fantasy**: *Sc*_67_PSYC_66_BIZ_67_Sc4_80_*
4. **Rationalization/Intellectualization**: *Pa_59_Mf_67_Pd*_60_Pt*_67_*
5. **Externalization**: *Hy_77_Pd*_60_Pa_59_Ma*_53_*
6. **Identification w/Aggressor**: *Pa3_45_[CYN1]_56_*
7. **Projection**: *Pa_59_Pa-O_60_Pa1_57_ Pf2_57_ Pf3_47_Pf4_69_Pd4_54_*
8. **Acting Out**: *Ma*_53_DISC_44_MAC-R_42_Pd*_60_ASP_52_Pd2_46_Sc5_59_ Sc6_77_*

INTERPERSONAL RELATIONS

1. **Extraversion/Introversion**:
A. Extraversion: *Pd3_52_Hy1_51_[INTR]_68_[SOD2]_51_[Si]_58_Ma3_56_
[SOD]_68_Hy-S_54_[Dr5]_48_*
B. Introversion: *SOD_68_SOD1_76_Si_58_INTR_68_[Hy1]_51_[Pd3]_52_*
2. **Social Alienation**: *Sc1_53_Pd4_54_Sc*_67_Pd-O_65_Si3_58_Pd*_60_Si2_69_
Dr5_48*
3. **Self-Alienation**: *LSE_52_Pd5_68_Sc2_58_[Ma4]_49_*
4. **Family Alienation**: *FAM_50_FAM1_47_Pd1_56_Sc1_53_FAM2_59_L&W_2/4*
5. **Delinquency/Antisocial Conduct**: *DISC_44_ASP2_42_Pd2_46_RC4_48_[GF]_43_
[Re]_59_L&W_0/9*
6. **Authority Conflict/Antisocial Attitudes**: *ASP1_55_ASP_52_CYN1_56_[Hy2]_50_
[Re]_59_*
7. **Masculinity/Femininity**:
A. Masculinity: *[Mf1]_34_[Mf10]_25_[GF]_43_[Mf6]_46_GM_66_*
B. Femininity: *Mf3_35_Mf10_25_GF_43_Mf6_46_Mf5_31_[GM]_66_*
8. **Passivity/Submissiveness**: *LSE2_39_[GM]_66_[TPA1]_40_Hy2_50_Dr2_47_
D2_68_[Ma4]_49_*
9. **Dependency**: *Si3_58_LSE_52_WRK_52_[GM]_66_Hy1_51_[Pd3]_52_*
10. **Hypersensitivity**: *Pa2_53_Mf2_42_*
11. **Passive/Aggressive Struggles**: *Ma4_49_Sc4_80_TPA_43_OBS_63_CYN2_49_
[D-S]_53_LSE2_39_*
12. **Dominance/Assertiveness**: *Do_49_[WRK]_52_[AGGR]_53_[Si3]_58_[LSE]_52_
[Si]_58_Es_31_[OBS]_63_[NEGE]_48_Pd3_52_GM_66_[Si1]_52_[O-H]_48_*
13. **Narcissism**: *Pd3_52_[Si1]_52_[SOD]_68_[LSE]_52_TPA_43_*

OTHER PROBLEM AREAS

1. **Substance Abuse**: *AAS_39_MAC–R_42_RC4_48_APS_55_Pd5_68_K-B_2/7
L&W_1/3*
2. **Sexual Difficulties**: *L&W_0/6 Sc*_67_*
3. **Suicidal Ideation**: *DEP4_45_Sc2_58_Sc4_80_D5_58_Hp_43_*
Items 150, 303, 506, 520, 524, 530 (Circle) -**None**
4. **Sleep Disturbance**: *L&W_4/6 ANX_56_Hy-O_75_Pt*_67_D-O_71_*

PSYCHOSIS INDICATORS

Goldberg Index: $(L + Pa + Sc) - (Hy + Pt) = 23$

MMPI-2 Outpatient Mental Health Interpretive Report

PROFILE VALIDITY

This client's approach to the MMPI-2 was open and cooperative. The resulting clinical and content scale profiles are valid and are probably a good indication of her present level of personality functioning. This cooperative performance may be viewed as a positive indication of her involvement with the evaluation.

She has not indicated the highest level of education she has attained. The Minnesota Report has been processed as though she has completed a 12-year high school education. If the education level is actually different from high school, then the Minnesota Report, particularly interpretations related to educational background such as those based on the Mf scale, should be carefully evaluated and modified accordingly.

She has not indicated her present marital status. The Minnesota Report has been processed as though her marital status is single, never married. If her marital status is actually different from single, then the Minnesota Report should be adjusted accordingly.

The clinical setting in which this MMPI-2 was taken has not been indicated. The report has been processed as though "Outpatient Mental Health Program" was indicated. The report may not be as specific as it would have been if the actual assessment setting had been designated.

SYMPTOMATIC PATTERNS

The clinical scale prototype used to develop this report incorporates correlates of Hy and Pt. Because these scales are not well defined in the clinical profile (the highest scales are relatively close in elevation), interpretation of the clinical profile should not ignore the adjacent scales in the profile code. The client has a somewhat mixed pattern of psychological problems. Her profile suggests an unusual pattern of symptoms rarely found in mental health assessment settings. She is presenting a picture of denial and repression along with intense anxiety and possible somatic problems. She appears to be rigid, perfectionistic, and somewhat moralistic, trying to deny problems or psychological frailties. At the same time, she is presently feeling much psychological stress and believes that her problems are unmanageable. She may also be concerned about sudden fatal illness and other vague worries about sickness and death, fears that may motivate her to seek reassurance frequently.

The client has diverse interests that include activities that are not traditionally associated with her gender. Women who score high on Mf are somewhat unusual compared with other women. They endorse item content that is typically seen as representing extreme masculine interests.

In addition, the following description is suggested by the client's scores on the content scales. She has difficulty managing routine affairs, and the items she endorsed suggest a poor memory, concentration problems, and an inability to make decisions. She appears to be immobilized and withdrawn and has no energy for life. She endorsed a number of unusual, bizarre ideas that suggest some difficulties with her thinking.

Although she is describing her present problem situation largely in terms of vague physical complaints, her PSY-5 scores suggest some long-term personality characteristics that can influence her adjustment. She shows a meager capacity to experience pleasure in life. Persons with high scores on the INTR

Figure 12.2   MMPI-2 Outpatient Mental Health Interpretive Report

Source: Pages 5–7 of the *MMPI®-2 Outpatient Mental Health Interpretive Report. The Minnesota Report™: Adult Clinical System-Revised*, 4th Edition, James N. Butcher, PhD Copyright © 1989, 1993, 2001, 2005 by the Regents of the University of Minnesota. All rights reserved. Portions reproduced from the MMPI-2 test booklet. Copyright © 1942, 1943 (renewed 1970), 1989 by the Regents of the University of Minnesota. All rights reserved. Portions excerpted from the *MMPI-2 Manual for Administration, Scoring, and Interpretation*, Revised Edition. Copyright © 2001 by the Regents of the University of Minnesota. All rights reserved. Reproduced by permission of the University of Minnesota Press.

(Introversion/Low Positive Emotionality) scale tend to be pessimistic. Her pervasive physical problem presentation could result, in part, from this characteristic personality deficit. Moreover, she apparently holds some unusual beliefs that suggest that at times she becomes disconnected from reality. The extent to which her physical complaints have a delusional basis should be evaluated further. Her high score on the PSYC (Psychoticism) scale suggests that she often feels alienated from others and might experience unusual symptoms such as delusional beliefs, circumstantial and tangential thinking, and loosening of associations.

PROFILE FREQUENCY

It is usually valuable in MMPI-2 clinical profile interpretation to consider the relative frequency of a given profile pattern in various settings. The client's MMPI-2 high-point clinical scale score (Hy) was found in 10.5% of the MMPI-2 normative sample of women. However, only 3.7% of the sample had Hy as the peak score at or above a T score of 65, and only 2.1% had well-defined Hy spikes. This elevated MMPI-2 profile configuration (3-7/7-3) is very rare in samples of normals, occurring in less than 1% of the MMPI-2 normative sample of women.

The relative frequency of this profile in various outpatient settings is informative. In the Pearson female outpatient sample, this MMPI-2 high-point clinical scale score (Hy) was the second most frequent peak, occurring in 17.2% of the women. Moreover, 13.3% of the outpatient women had the Hy scale spike at or above a T score of 65, and 7.5% had well-defined Hy peaks. This elevated MMPI-2 profile configuration (3-7/7-3) is rare in samples of outpatient women, occurring in only 1.3% of the women in the Pearson outpatient sample.

PROFILE STABILITY

The relative elevation of her clinical scale scores suggests that her profile is not as well defined as many other profiles. There could be some shifting of the most prominent scale elevations in the profile code if she were to be retested. The difference between the profile type used to develop the present report (involving Hy and Pt) and the next highest scale in the profile code was 1 point. So, for example, if the client is tested at a later date, her profile might involve more behavioral elements related to elevations on D. If so, then on retesting, pronounced complaints of depressed mood and low morale might become more prominent.

INTERPERSONAL RELATIONS

She tends to be somewhat rigid and dependent in interpersonal relationships. Many women with this profile have difficulties with sexual relationships because they are overly concerned with their health and preoccupied with physical problems.

continued …

Figure 12.2 continued

DIAGNOSTIC CONSIDERATIONS

Several diagnostic possibilities are presented: she may be experiencing a Somatoform Disorder, an Anxiety Disorder, or a Post-Traumatic Stress Disorder (if a clear precipitating event can be identified). Individuals with this profile may have an underlying Personality Disorder, such as a Histrionic Personality or a Compulsive Personality. Her scores on the content scales suggest that her unusual thinking and bizarre ideas need to be taken into consideration in any diagnostic formulation.

TREATMENT CONSIDERATIONS

Verbal, insight-oriented psychotherapy, if attempted, might be difficult at first owing to her typical pattern of defensiveness. The client might be more interested, at present, in medical treatment for her perceived somatic problems. She may also respond to reassurance and behavioral management techniques such as relaxation, desensitization, or stress-management training.

CALDWELL REPORT
5839 Green Valley Circle
Suite 203
Culver City, CA 90230
310-670-2874
FAX 310-670-7907

October 3, 2013

NAME: R.V.

AGE: 23

SEX: Female

EDUCATION: 18 years

MARITAL STATUS: Single

REFERRED BY: ------------------

DATE TESTED: March 3, 2011

TEST ADMINISTERED: Minnesota Multiphasic Personality Inventory-2 (MMPI-2)

TEST TAKING ATTITUDE

Attention and Comprehension: Her score on the Variable Response
Inconsistency scale (VRIN) was unelevated; her item responses were self-
consistent throughout the inventory. This suggests that she was clearly
able to read and comprehend the test items, that she was attentive in
considering her responses, and that she consistently matched the item
numbers in the booklet to the corresponding numbers on the answer sheet.
She does not appear to have had any difficulties in understanding the
content or responding to the format of the inventory.

Attitude and Approach: Considering scales L, F, and K, her approach to the
inventory was generally straightforward without being unduly self-favorable
or self-critical. The profile appears valid by the usual criteria for these
scales.

    She made a few atypical and rarely given responses to the items
occurring in the last half of the inventory (scale F-back). These were not
notably disproportionate to her frequency of atypical responses to the
earlier MMPI-2 items (scale F). The profile does not appear to be of
questionable validity because of atypical responding.

Socio-cultural Influences vs. Conscious Distortion: The supplemental
validity scales showed a clearly below average score on the scale (Ss)
measuring her level of currently attained, recently experienced, or self-
perceived socioeconomic status. She did not show any significant amount of

continued ...

Figure 12.3 Caldwell Report

Source: Reproduced by permission of Caldwell Report, 5839 Green Valley Circle, Suite 203, Culver City, CA, 90230.

Figure 12.3 continued

conscious defensiveness. Her K score was higher than would have been
expected for her Ss score; that is, this low level of socioeconomic status
identification is usually associated with a lower level of sophistication on
K.

SYMPTOMS AND PERSONALITY CHARACTERISTICS

Moderate anxiety, tension, and apprehensions about handling her
responsibilities are indicated. Decisions, demands to perform, and time
pressures would be particularly threatening to her. Such concerns are
likely to be appropriate to the situations but more intense than would be
the reactions of most people. Her symptoms are apt to have an hysterically
dramatic quality involving specific fears or phobias, acute physical anxiety
symptoms, or repetitive reactions to threatening situations in her life.
These could erupt as episodes of diffuse anxiety or as panic attacks. Her
responses suggest that a posttraumatic stress disorder is apt to be
contributory to her clinical picture, such as having suffered an acute
emotional shock with major somatic repercussions. The current level of her
day-to-day coping and immediate practical self-sufficiency tests as quite
uneven and as partially disorganized in a variety of areas.

Her profile indicates a general repressiveness and apprehensive
avoidance of engaging her angry feelings and sexual desires. She would be
seen as inhibited emotionally and as lacking in insight in many areas.
Episodes of petulant and egocentric behavior would be rationalized and
poorly integrated into her self-image. Sexual passivity and inhibitions are
also likely. Her interests and attitudes appear unusually masculine;
esthetic sensitivities and abstract verbal pursuits would have little appeal
to her. Shyness, introversion, and social inhibitions could make her appear
modest if not timid and self-effacing.

Her diffuse anxiety would be experienced as somewhat ego-alien in
contrast to the internalized self-devaluations of primarily depressed
patients. However, definite secondary depressive trends are also indicated,
suggesting indecisiveness, ambivalences, self-doubts, and periods of
depressed moods. She would be seen as worrying, unhappy, and as suffering
from tension-related insomnia. These depressive elements also are apt to be
reflected by disturbances of her usual appetite, weight, and sleep patterns.

Episodes in which she is acutely distraught or "attacks" in which
intense apprehensions are focused on somatic sensations would not be unusual
with this pattern. Impulsive and egocentric gratifications are likely to be
followed by inhibited phases or a conversion of her anxiety and guilt. The
profile suggests a few scattered somatic complaints that would be seen as
having a significant psychological involvement (e.g., driven by fear) if not
as at least partly hysterical in origin, and she could focus persistently on
their dramatic physical aspects. Gastrointestinal symptoms and headaches
would be typical as would such complaints as pain, dizziness, weakness, and

fatigue. She may be seen as phobic about physical illnesses and feared disabilities. Older patients with similar profiles have shown a high frequency of vascular disorders and other physiological breakdowns, especially in periods of major stress.

Family conflicts and unreleased resentments would be excused and rationalized in many ways. Her dependency needs would interfere with self-assertiveness and lead to repeated difficulties in the handling of acting out by family members. She would be seen as easily frustrated with only superficially satisfying family relationships but with repeated manipulations of family members around her symptoms. At times she may be seen as unexpectedly regressive and dependent on her friends or family members with many ways of gaining help, special favors, and other evidences of emotional support or substitutes for it. She may be seen as especially unrealistic about money matters. She may be drawn to attractive and adequate men in notably contrasting and complementary relationships. Her denial anticipates a tendency to cover over the degree of dependency, especially in initial interviews.

Separation anxieties and strongly conditioned fears around losses of psychological support are apt to be central in her life style. As a child she may have been painfully sensitized to fears of rejection, abandonment, hostile criticism and otherwise being caused intense emotional pain by loved ones. Fears of body breakdown and of increasing disability are also indicated. That is, if she has had experiences of unpredictable physical upheavals or breakdowns, she could have come to live under a cloud of immediately renewable apprehension of new crises or downturns. Her sense of unlikeableness and tendency to see herself as somehow psychologically deficient or defective would add to the undermining of her self-confidence. In many of these cases the needs for attention, affection, and support in making decisions had been fostered by parental overprotection along with physical symptoms or other circumstances that had kept the patients in dependent roles as children. As children they were described as having been unobtrusive and conforming, as seeking to please adults, as wanting to be liked, and usually as accepted by their peers. Although seeing themselves as conscientious workers as adults, they suffered a painful vulnerability to feel distraught about job and family responsibilities. They learned many ways of gaining reassurances from authority figures, too readily obtaining loans and seeking special favors in a clinging way. Some did have effective vocational skills, but they were often described as fixated at a childish level of engaging in hobbies of limited practical value and income production rather than in obtaining and sustaining steady employment. Promotions, other job changes, and moving to new homes were particularly stressful to them, and such changes often appeared to have precipitated the current psychological upheaval. In a few cases with recently acute or severe traumas (and posttraumatic stress disorder contributions to the clinical picture), these developmental elements were less evident or not reported. Not infrequently, however, similar early experiences had "set up" the person to be deeply affected by the more recent trauma.

continued ...

Figure 12.3 continued

DIAGNOSTIC IMPRESSION

Diagnoses of generalized anxiety disorders and obsessive-compulsive
disorders are the most typical with this pattern. A diagnosis reflecting
hysterical conversion elements would not be ruled out. Diagnoses of
depressive disorders are also seen with this pattern along with diagnoses of
dissociative disorders. Her profile is relatively mixed and complex.

TREATMENT CONSIDERATIONS

If not already expressed in the interview, the therapist may wish to
follow up the patient's "true" response to the following item:

"People say insulting and vulgar things about me."

She tests as significantly vulnerable to increasing medical invalidism.
The pattern would recommend caution toward any extensive medical workups or
elective surgical procedures that could enhance such an invalid role. If
surgery were necessary at some time, the pathology may be negative and the
recovery is apt to be complicated, prolonged, and unsatisfactory. She would
probably need extensive postoperative pushing in order to return to her
normal level of functioning. She could readily develop a chronic pain
syndrome. Even though justified by her level of disorganization and
impairment, disability payments could also support or even "fix" a chronic
medical patient role. Reductions of stress such as staying home from work
because of her physical symptoms also would readily support an increasingly
chronic medical patient role.

Her hysterical repressiveness and denial would interfere with her
becoming fully involved in psychotherapy. She may show a pervasive lack of
psychological-mindedness. Her masculine attitudes and emphasis on action
would conflict with introspection and with "talking about feelings". Her
continuation in longterm psychotherapy is likely to be uneven despite the
acuteness of her episodic distress. She appears prone to wish for or
daydream about something that would give her immediate symptomatic relief
and to focus on externalized situational problems, partly to escape the pain
of facing her internal and emotion-laden conflicts. It would not be unusual
for her to abruptly drop out of treatment and then return after a subsequent
recurrence of her symptoms. In some cases this cycle of terminating and re-
entering treatment was repeated several times, so that therapeutic progress
was "up and down" and involvement was dependent on the current status of the
patient's symptoms. Despite her smiles and her apparent desires to
cooperate, good rapport could be slow to develop.

Similar patients were strongly home and family oriented, and because of
this they were particularly reluctant to face the full intensity of
currently negative feelings toward various members of their families. They
also had strong needs to cover over unhappy childhoods, painful family
memories, and unresolved grief over deaths in the family, and related
painful and unexpected losses. In a few cases the selective encouragement

of counter-phobic behaviors was described as helping the patients to confront situations that they had repeatedly avoided. Her denial would make it more than usually valuable to interview family members in order to evaluate the severity of her symptoms and any problem areas she would avoid discussing or even bringing up.

The profile predicts a positive short-term response to symptom oriented treatment unless the primary symptoms are clearly fixed and longstanding. She would benefit from ventilation and emotional catharsis around frustrations and grief over her family difficulties. She should also respond positively to reassurances that others have similar sexual urges and aggressive and egocentric wishes. Negative reactions to the therapist would be expressed through indirect and passive resistances; it could be important to actively draw out these negative transference feelings relatively early in treatment. The working through of her repressed feelings and of her inhibiting fears could lead to a reduction in her avoidance of her negative emotional reactions and stabilizing of more assertive means of self-expression. Successful therapy is likely to be quite gradual and extended over time.

Thank you for this referral.

    Alex B. Caldwell, Ph.D.
Diplomate in Clinical Psychology

    The preceding analysis is basically actuarial and probabilistic in nature in that the symptoms and personality characteristics presented in the report have been identified as disproportionately frequent among individuals obtaining similar scores and patterns of scores on the MMPI-2 (tm). The diagnosis of any individual, however, needs to be based on the integration of information from personal contacts, the person's history, other test results, and whatever independent data are relevant and available.

    This report has an overall focus on psychotherapy intake, differential diagnosis, treatment planning, and related personality-dependent determinations. It provides assistance in the diagnostic process by providing an extended set of clinical hypotheses, the largest part of the basis for which is data from traditional psychiatric settings. The application of these hypotheses to an individual requires independent confirmation of them by the clinician and an allowance for the specific context of testing if it differs substantially from the primarily psychotherapeutic database.

continued …

Figure 12.3 continued

THE ADAPTATION AND ATTACHMENT HYPOTHESES SUPPLEMENT:

The following paragraphs present my current hypotheses as to etiologic and developmental factors that likely contribute to the behaviors associated with the codetype to which this profile best conforms. The following description characterizes a relatively serious if not severe level of disturbance. Typically an individual with a moderate although not severely elevated profile will show an intermediate level of sensitization so that the adaptive responses to the aversive shaping experiences described below are demanding of but not overwhelming of the person's attentional energy and somewhat less disruptive of day-to-day functioning. THIS DESCRIPTION IS NOT MODIFIED OR ADJUSTED TO THE LEVEL OF DISTURBANCE OR SECONDARY VARIATIONS OF THIS PERSON'S PROFILE: IT IS AN ETIOLOGIC PROTOTYPE FOR ANYONE WITH THIS GENERAL PATTERN TYPE. It is intended to generate hypotheses as to how the individual "got this way". This prototype material will always be the same for any profile corresponding to her code type. At least three fourths of the reports currently processed will have these paragraphs--the other quarter are of more or less rarely occurring codes, and for want of code-specific data they will not have these paragraphs at this time.

My belief is that all behaviors are adaptive given the person's biologic/constitutional makeup and life experiences. An awareness of adaptational benefits is potentially helpful: (1) in understanding the origins and adaptive self-protections of the person's present behaviors, (2) in providing test-result feedback to the client as well as in explaining the person's conduct to judges and any other parties appropriately involved, and (3) in guiding psychotherapeutic intervention. These inductive hypotheses are based on an extensive searching for developmental information on pattern-matched cases. Some interpretations are supported by published data (e.g., Gilberstadt & Duker, 1965, Hathaway & Meehl, 1951, Marks & Seeman, 1963), etc., and others are based on clinically examining any cases I have been able to access on whom pertinent information has been available. Your feedback to me will be much appreciated regarding: (1) whatever in the material that follows is clearly a misfit to this individual, (2) more precisely targeted word choices, phrasing, and especially the person's own words for crucial experiences, and (3) behavioral characteristics that are likely to generalize to the code type but are missing here. For everyone's sakes, don't hesitate to send me a note.

PROPOSED DIAGNOSIS: DIFFUSE, SOMATICALLY EMPHASIZED ANXIETY ADAPTATION TO: devastating and unpredictable separation and loss-of-emotional-support experiences
TRADITIONAL DIAGNOSIS: generalized anxiety disorder (a good fit although actually diagnosed GAD cases are more heterogeneous)

PROTOTYPIC CHARACTERISTICS: episodes or "attacks" of diffuse anxiety and worrying (overlapping with but differentiable from the extreme

continued …

physiologic aspects of one or a few panic attacks with resulting fears of
leaving home lest another attack occur, etc., which latter on limited data
seem more code 23 associated). The worrying seems to others to be about
less important or "off-target" concerns rather than the person's realistic
frustrations and interpersonal issues, and the anxieties are seen as
substantially disproportionate to the event. For example, a physician who
mostly delivered babies almost dropped a (slippery) newborn; he ceased
working due to his anxiety not long after that. His hands trembled doing
the block design test; I said, "you look nervous". He exclaimed, "Wouldn't
you be nervous if your hands shook like that"? There may be much anxiety
about anxiety or sometimes vague and non-specific future unpredictable
crises. But there is often an obtuse insightlessness into the personally
internal generations of the feelings of anxiety. Strong needs for
repetitive "showings of support" from others may lead to what are seen as
clinging and reassurance-dependent (or reassurance-desperate) behaviors.
Poor financial management along with these reassurance needs can lead to a
repeated seeking of extra bits of money from others. They are attracted to
hobbies that facilitate daydreaming (e.g., persistently preoccupied with an
elaborate adult train set). When married (they usually are), the spouse is
often seen in sharp contrast as a capable and "together" person.

CONTRIBUTORY SHAPING HISTORY: childhood histories vary from one
extreme of having been babied and catered to a contrasting extreme of having
been severely rejected, particularly by punitive, brutal, and/or alcoholic
fathers. The hypothesis is that rejections and punishments were
unpredictable to the child along with strong family pressures to inhibit
direct expressions of distress and anger. The held-in tension (note the
connection of scale 1 with the freeze response) together with an unstable
physiology, especially of the vascular system (intense reactions when
startled), is associated with bodily/health breakdowns. The unpredictability
of the breakdowns makes the person phobic about unexpected illnesses. In
general the fears are seen as rational but diffuse (e.g., worrying about
worrying, the startle avoidance of scale 7 and the avoidance of confronting
and re-experiencing pain and suffering of scale 3). Facing past acutely
startling and panic-provoking occasions then seems like "more than my system
could possibly bear". Perhaps if one whistles past the cemetery, the threat
will never materialize. Sometimes the mother was very frightened that her
child might be injured, and she was highly protective of the child. As
adults, these 1-3-7's are notably dependent on their spouses and/or other
responsible figures at times of change, e.g., moving residences and changing
jobs can precipitate episodes of intense or even temporarily disabling
anxiety. Thus, any cues to possible withdrawals of protection and support
can elicit marked lowerings of the threshold for anxiety about a wide range
of displaced points of focus. Survival is how you manage your relationships
with authority figures, how you ingratiate them, sustain their nurturance
toward you, and never turn them against you.

This is a relatively infrequent pattern. The cases I have known about
seemed consistently to have longstanding anxieties. I have no data base on
adult onset in the absence of any earlier history of anxieties. I would

hypothesize that if there were a low biologic threshold for anxiety along with prior occasions of acute insecurity, it is possible that a mixture of unforseen health and financial setbacks in adult life could precipitate these sorts of anxiety symptoms even though they had not previously been noted.

RX: the case of the physician noted above was an employment disability insurance suit. As with the other somatically focused fear patterns, the intensity of the fears the person expresses is not well correlated with the severity of the proximal event(s) that precipitated the disability or other downturn in the person's life. Proximal fear-inducing experiences may trigger a disproportionately intense response, and a constitutionally low biologic threshold for anxiety would add to the vulnerability to this and perhaps the longer term continuation of distress. Thus, the relationship of event to level of distress would merit careful evaluation. If the raw 1-Hs is high, then the FBS scale score is likely to be inflated, so FBS would have to be interpreted cautiously, and FBS may be less definitive than with most other code types. In custody cases, as can be seen from the the above the loss of support would be strongly threatening, even if the focus of conscious anxiety is on some other narrower issue or point of worry. the spouse may have tired of what has been experienced as a parent-surrogate role. Identified parenting as well as financial and other responsibilities will need a careful disentangling.

For codetype information see Gilberstadt and Duker, 1965

continued …

MMPI-2-RF Interpretive Report: Validity, Higher-Order, and RC Scales

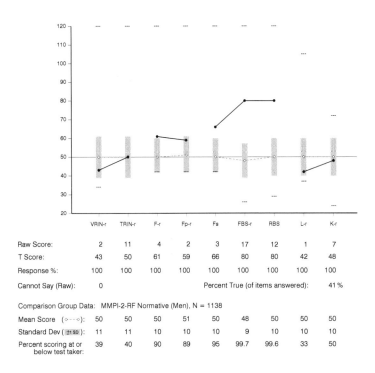

MMPI-2-RF Validity Scales

	VRIN-r	TRIN-r	F-r	Fp-r	Fs	FBS-r	RBS	L-r	K-r
Raw Score:	2	11	4	2	3	17	12	1	7
T Score:	43	50	61	59	66	80	80	42	48
Response %:	100	100	100	100	100	100	100	100	100

Cannot Say (Raw):   0   Percent True (of items answered):   41 %

Comparison Group Data: MMPI-2-RF Normative (Men), N = 1138

	VRIN-r	TRIN-r	F-r	Fp-r	Fs	FBS-r	RBS	L-r	K-r
Mean Score (◇---◇):	50	50	50	51	50	48	50	50	50
Standard Dev (±1 SD):	11	11	10	10	10	9	10	10	10
Percent scoring at or below test taker:	39	40	90	89	95	99.7	99.6	33	50

The highest and lowest T scores possible on each scale are indicated by a "---"; MMPI-2-RF T scores are non-gendered.

VRIN-r	Variable Response Inconsistency	Fs	Infrequent Somatic Responses	L-r	Uncommon Virtues
TRIN-r	True Response Inconsistency	FBS-r	Symptom Validity	K-r	Adjustment Validity
F-r	Infrequent Responses	RBS	Response Bias Scale		
Fp-r	Infrequent Psychopathology Responses				

Figure 12.4 MMPI-2-RF Interpretive Report: Validity, Higher-Order, and RC Scales

MMPI-2-RF Higher-Order (H-O) and Restructured Clinical (RC) Scales

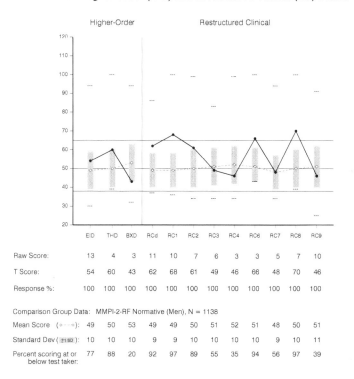

	EID	THD	BXD	RCd	RC1	RC2	RC3	RC4	RC6	RC7	RC8	RC9
Raw Score:	13	4	3	11	10	7	6	3	3	5	7	10
T Score:	54	60	43	62	68	61	49	46	66	48	70	46
Response %:	100	100	100	100	100	100	100	100	100	100	100	100

Comparison Group Data: MMPI-2-RF Normative (Men), N = 1138

	EID	THD	BXD	RCd	RC1	RC2	RC3	RC4	RC6	RC7	RC8	RC9
Mean Score (∘--∘):	49	50	53	49	49	50	51	52	51	48	50	51
Standard Dev (±1SD):	10	10	10	9	9	10	10	10	10	9	10	11
Percent scoring at or below test taker:	77	88	20	92	97	89	55	35	94	56	97	39

The highest and lowest T scores possible on each scale are indicated by a "---"; MMPI-2-RF T scores are non-gendered.

EID Emotional/Internalizing Dysfunction	RCd Demoralization	RC6 Ideas of Persecution
THD Thought Dysfunction	RC1 Somatic Complaints	RC7 Dysfunctional Negative Emotions
BXD Behavioral/Externalizing Dysfunction	RC2 Low Positive Emotions	RC8 Aberrant Experiences
	RC3 Cynicism	RC9 Hypomanic Activation
	RC4 Antisocial Behavior	

Table 12.2 MMPI-2-RF Special Problem Scale scores

	Number of Items	Raw Score	T-Score
Somatic/Cognitive			
MLS Malaise	8	6	75
GIC Gastrointestinal Complaints	5	2	72
HPC Head Pain Complaints	6	4	72
NUC Neurological Complaints	10	2	59
COG Cognitive Complaints	10	6	75
Internalizing			
SUI Suicidal/Death Ideation	5	0	
HLP Helplessness/Hopelessness	5	0	40
SFD Self-Doubt	4	2	56
NFC Inefficacy	9	5	58
STW Stress/Worry	7	1	43
AXY Anxiety	5	1	59
ANP Anger Proneness	7	0	39
BRF Behavior-Restricting Fears	9	0	43
MSF Multiple Specific Fears	9	0	36
Externalizing			
JCP Juvenile Conduct Problems	6	0	40
SUB Substance Abuse	7	0	41
AGG Aggression	9	4	61
ACT Activation	8	7	75
Interpersonal			
FML Family Problems	10	2	49
IPP Interpersonal Passivity	10	2	43
SAV Social Avoidance	10	8	70
SHY Shyness	7	3	50
DSF Disaffiliativeness	6	3	78
Interest			
AES Aesthetic-Literary Interests	7	0	33
MEC Mechanical-Physical Interests	9	3	52

MMPI 2 RF Interpretive Report: Clinical Settings

MMPI-2-RF® Interpretive Report: Clinical Settings ID:FriedTxt
03/03/2011, Page 8 R V

This interpretive report is intended for use by a professional qualified to interpret the MMPI 2 RF. The information it contains should be considered in the context of the test taker's background, the circumstances of the assessment, and other available information.

SYNOPSIS

Scores on the MMPI-2-RF validity scales raise concerns about the possible impact of over-reporting (specifically, of somatic and/or cognitive symptoms) on the validity of this protocol. With that caution noted, scores on the substantive scales indicate somatic and cognitive complaints, and thought, behavioral, and interpersonal dysfunction. Somatic complaints include preoccupation with poor health, malaise, head pain, and gastrointestinal problems. Cognitive complaints include difficulties in memory and concentration. Dysfunctional thinking findings include ideas of persecution and aberrant perceptions and thoughts. Behavioral-externalizing problems relate to excessive activation. Interpersonal difficulties include social avoidance and a dislike of people and being around them.

PROTOCOL VALIDITY

Content Non-Responsiveness

There are no problems with unscorable items in this protocol. The test taker responded relevantly to the items on the basis of their content.

Over-Reporting

The test taker provided an unusual combination of responses that is associated with non-credible reporting of somatic and/or cognitive symptoms. This combination of responses may occur in individuals with substantial medical problems who report credible symptoms, but it could also reflect exaggeration[1]. She also provided an unusual combination of responses that is associated with non-credible memory complaints. This combination of responses may occur in individuals with significant emotional dysfunction, but it could also reflect exaggeration[2]. Scores on the somatic scales--Somatic Complaints (RC1), Malaise (MLS), Gastrointestinal Complaints (GIC), Head Pain Complaints (HPC), and Neurological Complaints (NUC)--and the Cognitive Complaints (COG) scale should be interpreted in light of this caution[3].

Under-Reporting

There are no indications of under-reporting in this protocol.

Figure 12.5 MMPI-2-RF Interpretive Report: Clinical Settings

SUBSTANTIVE SCALE INTERPRETATION

Clinical symptoms, personality characteristics, and behavioral tendencies of the test taker are described in this section and organized according to an empirically guided framework. Statements containing the word "reports" are based on the item content of MMPI-2-RF scales, whereas statements that include the word "likely" are based on empirical correlates of scale scores. Specific sources for each statement can be viewed with the annotation features of this report.

The following interpretation needs to be considered in light of cautions noted about the possible impact of over-reporting on the validity of this protocol.

Somatic/Cognitive Dysfunction

The test taker reports multiple somatic complaints[4] including head pain[5] and a number of gastrointestinal complaints[6]. She is indeed likely to have a history of gastrointestinal problems[7]. She is also likely to be prone to developing physical symptoms in response to stress[8]. She also reports experiencing poor health and feeling weak or tired[9]. She is indeed likely to be preoccupied with poor health[10] and to complain of sleep disturbance[11], fatigue[12], and sexual dysfunction[11].

She reports a diffuse pattern of cognitive difficulties[13]. She is likely to complain about memory problems[14], to have low tolerance for frustration[15], not to cope well with stress[15], and to experience difficulties in concentration[16].

Emotional Dysfunction

There are no indications of emotional-internalizing dysfunction in this protocol. The test taker reports a lower than average number of specific fears[17].

Thought Dysfunction

The test taker reports unusual thought processes[18]. She is likely to experience thought disorganization[19], to engage in unrealistic thinking[20], and to believe she has unusual sensory-perceptual abilities[21]. Her aberrant experiences may include somatic delusions[22].

She reports significant persecutory ideation such as believing that others seek to harm her[23]. She is likely to be suspicious of and alienated from others[24], to experience interpersonal difficulties as a result of suspiciousness[25], and to lack insight[25].

Behavioral Dysfunction

The test taker reports episodes of over-activation such as heightened excitation and energy level[26] and may have a history of symptoms associated with manic or hypomanic episodes[27].

Interpersonal Functioning Scales

The test taker reports not enjoying social events and avoiding social situations[28]. She is likely to be introverted[29], to have difficulty forming close relationships[30], and to be emotionally restricted[31]. She also reports disliking people and being around them[32], and is likely to be asocial[33].

Interest Scales

The test taker reports an average number of interests in activities or occupations of a mechanical or physical nature (e.g., fixing and building things, the outdoors, sports)[34]. She indicates little or no interest in activities or occupations of an aesthetic or literary nature (e.g., writing, music, the theater)[35]

DIAGNOSTIC CONSIDERATIONS

This section provides recommendations for psychodiagnostic assessment based on the test taker's MMPI-2-RF results. It is recommended that she be evaluated for the following:

Emotional-Internalizing Disorders

- Somatoform disorder[36] and/or conditions involving somatic delusions[37]; malaise[38], head pain complaints[39], and gastrointestinal complaints[40] also suggest a possible somatoform disorder if physical origins for them have been ruled out
- Cycling mood disorder[41]

Thought Disorders

- Disorders manifesting psychotic symptoms[42]
- Personality disorders manifesting unusual thoughts and perceptions[43]
- Disorders involving persecutory ideation[44]

Behavioral-Externalizing Disorders

- Manic or hypomanic episode or other conditions associated with excessive energy and activation[45]

Interpersonal Disorders

- Disorders associated with social avoidance such as avoidant personality disorder[46]

TREATMENT CONSIDERATIONS

This section provides inferential treatment-related recommendations based on the test taker's MMPI-2-RF scores.

Areas for Further Evaluation

- Need for mood-stabilizing medication[47].
- Extent to which genuine physical health problems contribute to the score on the Somatic Complaints (RC1) scale[48].
- Origin of head pain complaints[39].
- Origin of gastrointestinal complaints[49].
- Origin of malaise complaints[50].
- Origin of cognitive complaints[51], bearing in mind possible over-reporting[52]. May require a neuropsychological evaluation.

continued …

Figure 12.3 continued

Psychotherapy Process Issues

- Likely to reject psychological interpretations of somatic complaints[48].
- Malaise may impede her willingness or ability to engage in treatment[50].
- Impaired thinking may disrupt treatment[53].
- Persecutory ideation may interfere with forming a therapeutic relationship and treatment compliance[54].
- Excessive behavioral activation may interfere with treatment[47].
- Her aversive response to close relationships may make it difficult to form a therapeutic alliance and achieve progress in treatment[55].

Possible Targets for Treatment

- Pain management for head pain complaints[39]
- Stress reduction for gastrointestinal complaints if stress-related[49]
- Persecutory ideation[54]
- Difficulties associated with social avoidance[56]

ITEM-LEVEL INFORMATION

Unscorable Responses

The test taker produced scorable responses to all the MMPI-2-RF items.

Critical Responses

Seven MMPI-2-RF scales--Suicidal/Death Ideation (SUI), Helplessness/Hopelessness (HLP), Anxiety (AXY), Ideas of Persecution (RC6), Aberrant Experiences (RC8), Substance Abuse (SUB), and Aggression (AGG)--have been designated by the test authors as having critical item content that may require immediate attention and follow-up. Items answered by the individual in the keyed direction (True or False) on a critical scale are listed below if her T score on that scale is 65 or higher. The percentage of the MMPI-2-RF normative sample (NS) and of the MMPI-2-RF Normative (Men) comparison group (CG) that answered each item in the keyed direction are provided in parentheses following the item content.

Ideas of Persecution (RC6, T Score = 66)

    34. Item content intentionally omitted. (True; NS 10.6%, CG 12.3%)
   194. Item content intentionally omitted. (True; NS 17.1%, CG 18.4%)
   233. Item content intentionally omitted. (True; NS 5.5%, CG 6.2%)

Aberrant Experiences (RC8, T Score = 70)

   32. Item content intentionally omitted. (True; NS 21.1%, CG 23.7%)
   46. Item content intentionally omitted. (True; NS 2.2%, CG 2.5%)
 106. Item content intentionally omitted. (True; NS 8.7%, CG 9.2%)
 179. Item content intentionally omitted. (True; NS 12.6%, CG 11.2%)

Commentary on the Interpretive Reports

Before conducting an analysis and comparison of the three preceding automated reports, based, in part, upon the Structural Summary and Tables 12.1 and 12.2, it may be helpful to briefly review the case itself in terms of a basic demographic description and, given that description, what is known and what may be reasonably expected from the MMPI-2 and MMPI-2-RF findings. That is, how may this case be reasonably conceptualized *going in* to the assessment? The idea is not, of course, to set any arbitrary or a priori limits upon what the assessment may find; it is merely to recognize that, as the saying goes, if you live in the American Midwest and hear hoof beats behind you, it is better to think of horses than zebras.

We have a 23-year-old unmarried graduate student who, on her own initiative, is seeking an assessment to see if she may warrant a diagnosis of ADHD (attention deficit hyperactivity disorder). She apparently deems this diagnosis plausible on the basis of both historical and current difficulties in task completion; attention, concentration, focus, and distractibility; and being "flighty," as reported in the case description. Also noted in her self-report on interview were problems with poor sleep, and rumination "over things that were not going well in her life." Likewise, on interview, the examining psychologist reports rigidity, concreteness, anger, and distress on the basis of behavioral observation.

This history was augmented by an informant, the client's mother, who reported a number of matters in the client's history that were not confided by the client herself. Most notable among these were frequent and severe headaches "mimicking the symptoms of migraines" going back to age three, and continuing at least into puberty, ultimately with incomplete relief, following diagnosis and medication treatment for a brain tumor. Secondary to her headache symptoms were problems in academic functioning, class disruption, and discipline while attending school, as she would "cry out" in pain. These problems, in turn, according to her mother, led to acts of ostracism and being "picked on quite a bit" by her classmates and perhaps other peers. In reaction, the mother describes her daughter as "somewhat guarded ... to this day" in her interactions with others, in whom she does "not have a lot of trust," and is very guarded in revealing her medical history.

Given the above information, what may be expected in terms of this client's performance on the MMPI-2 and MMPI-2-RF?

First, given her educational level, it is anticipated that she is able to read and comprehend the MMPI-2/MMPI-2-RF items without difficulty, leading to an adequate level of consistency such that scores on *VRIN*, *TRIN*, *VRIN-r*, and *TRIN-r* will all be within acceptable ranges, rendering both the MMPI-2 and MMPI-2-RF interpretable.

Second, her presenting complaints and difficulties around attention, memory, concentration, focus, distractibility/being "flighty," rumination, and decision making lead to the expectation of elevations on *FBS*, *D4*, *Sc3*, *CogProb*, and *OBS* on the MMPI-2, and on *FBS-r*, *RBS*, and *COG* on the MMPI-2-RF.

Third, her history of headache and related pain and discomfort would seem likely to elevate scores on *FBS*, *Hs*, *Hy4*, *HEA*, and *RC1* on the MMPI-2, and *FBS-r*, *RBS*, *RC1*, and *HPC* on the MMPI-2-RF.

Fourth, her complaints of poor sleep/insomnia, and the potential resulting weakness/tiredness/fatigue resulting therefrom, may contribute (minimally) to elevations on scales like *D3* and *Pt* on the MMPI-2, and *EID* and *RC2* on the MMPI-2-RF and, more robustly, to *Hy3* on the MMPI-2, and *MLS* on the MMPI-2-RF.

Finally, the behavioral observations of the examining psychologist regarding her rigidity, concreteness, anger, and distress, combined with the information provided by her mother concerning the client's guardedness and lack of trust in others, and her history of being ostracized and picked on by her peers, would raise questions of current emotional distress/turmoil, cynicism, and discomfort in her personal relationships and in her general social interactions, possibly including relative isolation from others. These issues lead to an expectation of elevations on scales such as *Pt, Sc, Si, ANX, DEP, ANG, CYN, SOD, WRK, TRT, A, Mt, PK, NEGE, INTR, RCd, RC2, RC3,* and *RC7* on the MMPI-2, and on *RCd, RC2, RC3, RC7, EID, STW, AXY, ANP, SAV, SHY, DSF, NEGE-r,* and *INTR-r* on the MMPI-2-RF.

Now, a word about what is *not* to be expected in this client's test findings. Although at age 23 she falls within the middle of the range for the average age of onset for both schizophrenia (e.g. Sham, MacLean, & Kendler, 1994) and bipolar disorder (e.g. Leboyer, Henry, Paillere-Martinot, & Bellivier, 2005), the base rate for these disorders among graduate students is very low (e.g. Benton, Robertson, Tseng, Newton, & Benton, 2003), hence test findings suggesting major mental disorder would be more likely to be false- than true-positives.

Turning to the automated reports themselves, and how they confirm, augment, or appear to contradict the expectations described above: at the outset, it may be said that all three of these automated reports confirm the first expectation that the assessment has resulted in interpretable protocols on the basis of the client's scores on the measures of response consistency.

Comparing the Minnesota and Caldwell Reports, both indicate that the client's approach to the test was cooperative and straightforward, neither over- nor under-reporting psychopathology. By contrast, the MMPI-2-RF report, while acknowledging the absence of under-reporting, raises the question of exaggeration in the form of "non-credible … somatic and/or cognitive symptoms," and "non-credible memory complaints." These cautions appear to be largely driven by the client's scores on *FBS-r* and *RBS*, scales that include a significant proportion of items reflecting the client's presenting attention/concentration complaints, and her history of head pain.

The extent of these complaints is likewise reflected, as expected, in her scores on *D4, Sc3, CogProb* (11 of 12 items), and *OBS* on the MMPI-2, and on *COG* in the MMPI-2-RF, consistent with her presenting complaint. The manner in which these complaints are acknowledged differs somewhat among the three interpretive narratives, with both of the Minnesota reports mentioning problems with memory and concentration, problems not explicitly mentioned in the Caldwell Report, and both of the MMPI-2 reports mentioning problems in decision making, a problem not explicitly mentioned in the MMPI-2-RF report.

Also as expected, her complaints of headache pain/discomfort are seen as contributing to elevations on *Hs, Hy4, HEA,* and *RC1* on the MMPI-2, and *FBS-r, RBS, RC1,* and *HPC* on the MMPI-2-RF. These symptoms are mentioned in both the Caldwell and MMPI-2-RF reports, but with greater emphasis in the latter, but are not explicitly reflected in the MMPI-2 Minnesota narrative.

This client's complaints of poor sleep, again as expected, appear to contribute to her elevations on *D3, Pt,* and especially to *Hy3* on the MMPI-2, and *MLS* on the MMPI-2-

RF. Reference to these and related problems is found in the Caldwell and MMPI 2 RF reports, but with greater emphasis in the latter, but are not explicitly stated in the MMPI-2 Minnesota narrative.

Lastly, the test findings that bear on her level of emotional distress and turmoil, and on the character of her social relationships, are considerably more varied than anticipated. With respect to the MMPI-2 scales known to be saturated with the first factor, she elevates *Pt*, *Mt*, and *PK* to an average *T*-score of 72, whereas her scores on *ANX*, *DEP*, *WRK*, *TRT*, *RCd*, *RC7*, *A*, and *NEGE*, average only *T*-53. In order to achieve some insight into the kinds of items that she was endorsing, we examined the 14 items overlapping scales *Pt* and *Mt*, the 16 items overlapping *Pt* and *PK*, and the 9 items overlapping *Mt* and *PK*. Of these 39 total overlaps, 25 of the items are distinct, and of these she endorsed 16 items (True: 16, 23, 31, 38, 56, 130, 196, 218, 273, 316, 325, 328; False: 3, 9, 95, 140), or about two thirds. Nine of these 16 items overlap *Sc*, three on *Sc3* and four on *Sc4*, seven overlap *D*, three on *D4*, six overlap *DEP*, three of these on *DEP1*, five overlap *Hy*, all on *Hy3*, and four overlap *ANX*. About half of 16 items either state or connote problems in cognitive control and efficiency, consistent with her clearly elevated scores on *D4*, *Sc3*, and *Sc4*. Thus her sense of distress appears related at least as much to difficulties around her cognitive as to her emotional experience.

The MMPI-2-RF appears to get at these matters just as efficiently. While her scores on *EID*, *RCd*, *RC7*, *STW*, and *NEGE-r* average a *T*-score of only 50, she shows clear elevations on *MLS* and *COG*, both at *T*-75. However, all three of the automated reports provide comments regarding the level and character of her distress, and some of its consequences in her day-to-day functioning.

As for her interpersonal and social functioning, the MMPI-2 scales related to problems with anger, irritability, cynicism, and the like are all within normal limits; however, she does elevate *Si2*, *SOD*, and *SOD1* in the context of comparatively low scores on *Si1* and *SOD2*. The pattern of scores on the MMPI-2-RF is comparable, with elevations on *SAV* and *DSF*, and a comparatively low score on *SHY*. Thus while shyness and self-consciousness are largely denied, she does express an aversion to group situations and interacting with others, and a preference for avoiding them. These problems are addressed in all of the automated reports, albeit somewhat more generally in the MMPI-2 narratives, and more narrowly in the MMPI-2-RF report.

We may now address the scores and the report commentary for the client that were *not* anticipated in the context of this assessment. First, her elevations on MMPI-2 *Mf*, *Mf* subscales *Mf1*, *Mf3*, *Mf5*, *Mf6*, and *Mf10*, and MMPI-2-RF *AES* and *MEC*, suggest a dearth of traditional feminine interests, and the MMPI-2 score pattern of *GM* and *GF* reflects, in a way consistent with her *Mf* score, a masculinized (or defeminized) gender identity. The interpretive commentary for all three automated reports acknowledges these trends in their text.

Also, and surprisingly, she shows elevated scores on several scales associated, at least by name, with major psychiatric disorders, e.g. *Sc*, *Pf4*, *DisOrg*, *RC6*, *RC8*, *BIZ*, *BIZ1*, *BIZ2*, and *PSYC* on the MMPI-2, and *RC6*, *RC8*, and *PSYC-r* on the MMPI-2-RF. In no case are these scales grossly elevated. The MMPI-2 scales above average a *T*-score of 68. The comparable value for the MMPI-2-RF scales named is also 68. Nevertheless, both the MMPI-2 and MMPI-2-RF reports mention, at a minimum, the possibility of, and in the case of the MMPI-2-RF, the likelihood of, psychotic symptoms. The MMPI-2 report mentions "bizarre ideas," "becomes disconnected from reality," the possibility that "her physical complaints have a delusional basis," "delusional beliefs," "circumstantial and tangential thinking," and "loosening of associations," whereas the MMPI-2-RF report speaks of "dysfunctional thinking," "ideas of persecution," "aberrant perceptions and thoughts," "she is likely to experience thought disorganization," "engage in unrealistic thinking," "believe she has unusual sensory-perceptual abilities," and "somatic delusions." The Caldwell Report is, by contrast, silent on such symptoms, apparently finding insufficient strength in the relevant MMPI-2 scores/indicators to make note of them.

What to make of these differences? First, the absence of any of these symptoms on interview or within the client's mother's report is hardly sufficient to rule them out. Nevertheless, their lack of appearance or suggestion in this context is by no means confirming of their presence or likelihood. Moreover, considering this client's basic demographics, as described above, such symptoms would all have unusually low base rates. Finally, given her mean elevations for the scales enumerated in the previous paragraph, her scores, even though often marginally outside the normal range, must be achieved on the basis of relatively few raw items. Take, for example, items 259 and 333, both of which this client endorsed. Item 259 appears on *Pd, Pa, Pa1, Pf4, BIZ2, Ho,* and *PSYC*. Item 333 appears on *FB, Pa, Pa1, Pf4, Sc,* and *BIZ2*. Both items appear on *RC6*. These items both admit to a conviction that one is being talked about and, in the second instance, in vulgar and insulting ways. Thus, these items are, on balance, closer in their sense to ideas of reference than to ideas/delusions of persecution. And, given her scores on MMPI-2 *Si2, SOD,* and *SOD1*, and MMPI-2-RF *SAV* and *DSF*, her responses to items 259 and 333 could be more parsimoniously understood within the context of alienating herself from others, and perhaps feeling more vulnerable and *conspicuous* as the "loner" she seeks to be. In this context, interpreting her responses within a paranoid/persecutory frame might be, and perhaps should be, considered somewhat arbitrary, particularly in view of the fact that the Goldberg Neurotic-Psychotic Index for this case is only 23, even lower than the 25.1 average value for the 37/73 profile type (Greene, 2011, p. 549).

None of this should be taken as a critique of either the Minnesota MMPI-2 or MMPI-2-RF interpretive reports. Both assume that the venues for which these reports are provided are clinical (outpatient in the case of the MMPI-2 report) settings, within which the base rates for psychotic symptomatology are substantially higher than within a university counseling center. Indeed, the MMPI-2 Minnesota Report explicitly warns that "The report may not be as specific as it would have been if the actual assessment setting had been designated." This discussion does, however, illustrate some of the limits of automated reports in which, in a sense, "one size must fit all," and some of the interpretive problems that can arise when automated inferences issue from only a minimal number of endorsed items, regardless of their pathological content. In settings for which psychotic symptoms have very low base rates, a single or couple of pathological items may have been endorsed not on the basis of their substantive content and implication, but as a consequence of a momentary lapse wherein a misunderstanding or mismarking occurs in the test taker. Or, in the phrasing of a familiar Wechsler item, "One swallow does not make a summer."

It can be readily seen that whereas the MMPI-2 Minnesota Report is somewhat more cautious than the MMPI-2-RF report in the interpretive weight assigned to inferences relating to psychotic phenomena, whereas the language of the latter represents such symptoms as likely or taken for granted (e.g. under the headings Psychotherapy Process Issues and Possible Targets for Treatment).

In closing, it may be appropriate to offer a few general remarks about the three automated reports gathered for this case example. The MMPI-2 Minnesota Report and the MMPI-2-RF reports may best be considered in the context of screening and disposition. Both are relatively specific as regards their descriptions, diagnostic possibilities, and recommendations, and both provide adequate coverage of their respective item pools. The Minnesota Report appears overall to be more sensitive to the numerous inter-scale relationships in the formation of its interpretive inferences, including, but not limited to, codetype. In contrast, the MMPI-2-RF report, despite its considerably reduced item pool, generates highly specific inferences, just as would be expected from its emphasis on the relatively discrete content domains comprising its scales. Thus, in a general way, the MMPI-2 may be preferable in contexts where initial screening is desired, and a somewhat greater value is placed on sensitivity than on specificity. Given this characteristic, one can imagine cases in which the MMPI-2-RF could be a productive follow-up to the MMPI-2, just as tests of high sensitivity are commonly followed up with tests of high specificity in medical practice (e.g. in HIV-AIDS).

The Caldwell Report, in contrast, is both more searching and more speculative in its language and recommendations and, in particular, offers a great deal more interpretive commentary that allows its inferences to be placed within an etiological context. As such, and while embodying the sensitivity and descriptive coverage of the MMPI-2 Minnesota Report, it appears to offer considerable advantages that go beyond screening, in the form of commentary that may be highly useful when the client/patient is already in a treatment relationship, or is being actively considered for such a relationship.

References

Aamondt, M. G. (2004). Special issue on using MMPI-2 scale configuration in law enforcement selection: introduction and meta-analysis. *Applied H. R. M. Research, 9,* 41–52.

Aaronson, A. L. (1958). Age and sex influence on MMPI profile peak distributions in an abnormal population. *Journal of Consulting Psychology, 22,* 203–206.

Aaronson, A. L., Dent, O. B., Webb, J. T., & Kline, C. D. (1996). Graying of the critical items: Effects of aging on responding to MMPI-2 critical items. *Journal of Personality Assessment, 66,* 169–176.

Adams, D. K., & Horn, J. L. (1965). Nonoverlapping keys for the MMPI scales. *Journal of Consulting Psychology, 29,* 284.

Adler, T. (1990). Does the "new" MMPI beat the classic? *The APA Monitor, 21(4),* 18–19.

Alexander, A. A., Roessler, R., & Greenfield, N. S. (1963). Ego strength and physiological responsivity: HI. The relationship between the Barron Ego Strength scale to spontaneous periodical activity in skin resistance, finger blood volume, heart rate, and muscle potential. *Archives of General Psychiatry, 9,* 58–61.

Alker, H. A. (1978). Minnesota Multiphasic Personality Inventory. In O. K. Buros (Ed.), *Eighth mental measurements yearbook* (pp. 931–935). Highland Park, NJ: Gryphon Press.

Allen, J. P. (1991). Personality correlates of the MacAndrew alcoholism scale: A review of the literature. *Psychology of Addictive Behaviors, 5,* 59–65.

Allen, J. P., Faden, V. B., Rawlings, R. R., & Miller, A. (1991). Personality differences associated with MacAndrew scores. *Psychological Reports, 66,* 691–698.

Almada, S. J., Zonderman, A. B., Shekelle, R. B., Dyer, A. R., Daviglus, M. L., Costa, P. T., & Stamler, J. (1991). Neuroticism and cynicism and risk of death in middle-aged men: The Western Electric Study. *Psychosomatic Medicine, 53,* 165–175.

Almagor, M., & Koren, D. (2001). The adequacy of the MMPI-2 Harris-Lingoes subscales: A cross-cultural factor analytic study of Scales D, Hy, Pd, Sc, and Ma. *Psychological Assessment, 13(2),* 199–215.

American Educational Research Association (1999). *Standards for educational and psychological testing.* Washington, DC: Author.

American Psychiatric Association. (1968). *Diagnostic and statistical manual of mental disorders* (2nd ed.). Washington, DC: Author.

American Psychiatric Association. (1980). *Diagnostic and statistical manual of mental disorders* (3rd ed.). Washington, DC: Author.

American Psychiatric Association. (1987). *Diagnostic and statistical manual of mental disorders III—Revised.* Washington, DC: Author.

American Psychiatric Association. (1994). *Diagnostic and statistical manual of mental disorders* (4th ed.). Washington, DC: Author.

American Psychiatric Association. (2013). *Diagnostic and statistical manual of mental disorders* (5th ed.). Washington: Author.

American Psychological Association. (1977). *Standards for providers of psychological services.* Washington, DC: Author

American Psychological Association. (1986). *Guidelines for users of computer-based tests and interpretations.* Washington, DC: Author.

American Psychological Association. (1993). Guidelines for providers of psychological services to ethnic, linguistic, and culturally diverse populations. *American Psychologist, 48,* 45–48.

American Psychological Association. (2002). Ethical principles of psychologists and code of conduct. *American Psychologist, 57,* 1060–1073.

Anastasi, A. (1982). *Psychological testing* (5th ed.). New York: Macmillan.

Anderson v. E & S International Enterprises, Inc., Case No. RG05 211076, Alameda County, 7/29/08.

Anderson, H. E., & Bashaw, W. L. (1966). Further comments on the internal structure of the MMPI. *Psychological Bulletin, 66,* 211–213.

Anderson, W. (1956). The MMPI: Low *Pa* scores. *Journal of Counseling Psychology, 3,* 226–228.

Anderson, W. P., & Kunce, J. T. (1984). Diagnostic implication of markedly elevated MMPI *Sc* scale scores for non-hospitalized clients. *Journal of Clinical Psychology, 40,* 925–930.

Anthony, N. (1971). Comparison of clients' standard, exaggerated and matching MMPI profiles. *Journal of Consulting and Clinical Psychology, 36,* 100–103.

Apfeldorf, M. (1978). Alcoholism scales of the MMPI: Contributions and future directions. *International Journal of the Addictions, 13,* 17–55.

Arbisi, P. A., & Ben-Porath, Y. S. (1995a, March). *Identifying changes in infrequent responding to the MMPI-2.* Paper presented at the 30th Annual Symposium on Recent Developments in the Use of the MMPI-2, St. Petersburg, FL.

Arbisi, P. A., & Ben-Porath, Y. S. (1995b). An MMPI-2 infrequent response scale for use with psychopathological populations. The Infrequency-Psychopathology scale, *F(p). Psychological Assessment: A Journal of Consulting and Clinical Psychology, 7,* 424–431.

Arbisi, P. A., & Ben-Porath, Y. S. (1997). Characteristics of the MMPI-2 *F(p)* scale as a function of diagnosis in an inpatient sample of veterans. *Psychological Assessment: A Journal of Consulting and Clinical Psychology, 9,* 102–105.

Arbisi, P. A., & Butcher, J. N. (2004). Failure of the FBS to predict malingering of somatic symptoms: Response to critiques by Greve and Bianchini and Lees Haley and Fox. *Archives of Clinical Neuropsychology, 19,* 341–345.

Arbisi, P. A., Ben-Porath, Y. S., & McNulty, J. L. (2003). Empirical correlates of common MMPI-2 two-point codes in male psychiatric patients. *Assessment, 10,* 237–247.

Arbisi, P. A., McNulty, J. L., Ben-Porath, Y. S., & Boyd, J. (1999, April). *Detection of partial fake bad responding on the MMPI-2.* Paper presented at the 34th Annual Symposium on Recent Developments in the Use of the MMPI-2 and MMPI-A, Huntington Beach, CA.

Arbisi, P. A., Sellbom, M., & Ben-Porath, Y. S. (2008). Empirical correlates of the MMPI-2 Restructured Clinical (RC) scales in psychiatric inpatients. *Journal of Personality Assessment, 90,* 122–128.

Archer, R. P. (1984). Use of the MMPI with adolescents: A review of salient issues. *Clinical Psychology Review, 4,* 241–251.

Archer, R. P. (1987). *Using the MMPI with adolescents.* Hillsdale, NJ: Lawrence Erlbaum Associates.

Archer, R. P. (1988). Using the MMPI with adolescents. In C. D. Spielberger & J. N. Butcher (Eds.), *Advances in personality assessment* (Vol. 7, pp. 103–126). Hillsdale, NJ: Lawrence Erlbaum Associates.

Archer, R. P. (1992). *The MMPI-A: Assessing adolescent psychopathology.* Hillsdale, NJ: Lawrence Erlbaum Associates.

Archer, R. P. (1997). *MMPI-A: Assessing adolescent psychopathology* (2nd ed.). Mahwah, NJ: Lawrence Erlbaum Associates.

Archer, R. P. (2005). *The MMPI-A: Assessing adolescent psychopathology* (3rd ed.). New York: Routledge.

Archer, R. P. (2006). A perspective on the Restructured Clinical (RC) Scale Project. *Journal of Personality Assessment, 87*, 179–185.

Archer, R. P., Buffington-Vollum, J. K., Stredny, R. V., & Handel, R. W. (2006). A survey of psychological test use patterns among forensic psychologists. *Journal of Personality Assessment, 87*, 84–94.

Archer, R. P., Fontaine, J., & McCrae, R. R. (1998). Effects of two MMPI-2 validity scales on basic scale relations to external criteria. *Journal of Personality Assessment, 70*, 87–102.

Archer, R. P., & Gordon, R. A. (1991). [Correlational analysis of the MMPI-A normative data set]. Unpublished raw data.

Archer, R. P., Gordon, R. A., & Klinefelter, D. (1991). [Analyses of the frequency of MMPI and MMPI-A profile assignments for 1762 adolescent patients]. Unpublished raw data.

Archer, R. P., Griffin, R., & Aiduk, R. (1995). MMPI-2 clinical correlates for ten common codes. *Journal of Personality Assessment, 65*, 391–407.

Archer, R. P., & Klinefelter, D. (1992). Relationships between MMPI codetypes and MAC scale elevations in adolescent psychiatric samples. *Journal of Personality Assessment, 58*, 149–159.

Archer, R. P., & Newsom, C. (2000). Psychological test usage with adolescent clients: Survey update. *Assessment, 7*, 227–235.

Armstrong, D. (2008, March 5). Personality check: Malingerer test roils personal-injury law. *Wall Street Journal*, p. 1.

Arnau, R. C., Handel, R. W., & Archer, R. P. (2005). Principal components analysis of the PSY–5 scales: Identification of facet scales. *Assessment, 12*, 186–198.

Astin, A. W. (1959). A factor study of the MMPI Psychopathic Deviate scale. *Journal of Consulting Psychology, 23*, 550–554.

Astin, A. W. (1961). A note on the MMPI Psychopathic Deviate scale. *Educational and Psychological Measurement, 21*, 895–897.

Atlis, M. M., Hahn, J., & Butcher, J. N. (2006). Computer-based assessment with the MMPI-2. In J. N. Butcher (Ed.), *MMPI-2: The practitioner's handbook* (pp. 445–476). Washington, DC: American Psychological Association.

Baer, R. A., & Miller, J. (2002). Underreporting of psychopathology on the MMPI-2: A meta-analytic review. *Psychological Assessment, 14*, 16–26.

Baer, R. A., Wetter, M. W., & Berry, D. T. R. (1992). Detection of underreporting of psychopathology on the MMPI: A meta-analysis. *Clinical Psychology Review, 12*, 509–525.

Baer, R. A., Wetter, M. W., & Berry, D. T. R. (1995). Effects of information about validity scales on underreporting of symptoms on the MMPI-2: An analogue investigation. *Assessment, 2*, 189–200.

Baer, R. A., Wetter, M. W., Nichols, D. S., Greene, R. L., & Berry, D. T. R. (1995). Sensitivity of MMPI-2 validity scales to underreporting of symptoms. *Psychological Assessment: A Journal of Consulting and Clinical Psychology, 7*, 419–423.

Bagby, R. M., Marshall, M. B., Basso, M. R., Nicholson, R. A., Bacchiochi, J., & Miller, L. S. (2005). Distinguishing bipolar depression, major depression, and schizophrenia with the MMPI-2 Clinical and Content scales. *Journal of Personality Assessment, 84*, 89–95.

Bagby, R. M., Nicholson, R. A., Buis, T., Radovanovic, H., & Fidler, B. J. (1999). Defensive responding on the MMPI-2 in family custody and access evaluations. *Psychological Assessment: A Journal of Consulting and Clinical Psychology, 11*, 24–28.

Bagby, R. M., Rogers, R., & Buis, T. (1994). Detecting malingered and defensive responding on the MMPI-2 in a forensic inpatient sample. *Journal of Personality Assessment, 62*, 191–203.

Bagby, R. M., Rogers, R., Buis, T., & Kalemba, V. (1994). Malingered and defensive response styles on the MMPI-2: An examination of validity scales. *Assessment, 1*, 31–38

Bagby, R. M., Rogers, R., Buis, T., Nicholson, R. A., Cameron, S. L., Rector, N. A., Schuller, D. R., & Seeman, M. V. (1997a). Detecting feigned depression and schizophrenia on the MMPI-2. *Journal of Personality Assessment, 68*, 650–664.

Bagby, R. M., Rogers, R., Nicholson, R. A., Buis, T., Seeman, M. V., & Rector, N. A. (1997b). Effectiveness of the MMPI-2 validity indicators in the detection of defensive responding in clinical and nonclinical samples. *Psychological Assessment: A Journal of Consulting and Clinical Psychology, 9*, 406–413.

Bagby, R. M., Sellbom, M., Costa, P. T., Jr., & Widiger, T. A. (2008). Predicting Diagnostic and Statistical Manual of Mental Disorders-IV personality disorders with the five-factor model of personality and the personality psychopathology five. *Personality and Mental Health, 2*, 55–69.

Baker, J. D. (2007). Queendom Online Test Respository. In R. A. Reynolds, R. Woods, & J. D. Baker (Eds.), *Handbook of research on electronic surveys and measurements* (pp. 352–354). Hershey, PA: Iea group reference/IGI Global.

Ball, J. C., & Carroll, D. (1960). Analysis of MMPI Cannot Say score in an adolescent population. *Journal of Clinical Psychology, 16*, 30–31.

Barefoot, J. C., Dahlstrom, W. G., & Williams, R. B. (1983). Hostility, CHD incidence, and total mortality: A 25-yr follow-up study of 255 physicians. *Psychosomatic Medicine, 45*, 59–63.

Barefoot, J. C., Dodge, K. A., Peterson, B. L., Dahlstrom, W. G., & Williams, R. B. (1989). The Cook-Medley Hostility scale: Item content and ability to predict survival. *Psychosomatic Medicine, 51*, 46–57.

Barefoot, J. C., Peterson, B. L., Dahlstrom, W. G., Siegler, I. C., Anderson, N. B., & Williams, R. B., Jr. (1991). Hostility patterns and health implications: Correlates of Cook-Medley Hostility Scale scores in a national survey. *Health Psychology, 10*, 18–24.

Barron, F. (1953). An ego-strength scale which predicts response to psychotherapy. *Journal of Consulting Psychology, 17*, 327–333.

Barthlow, D. L., Graham, J. R., Ben-Porath, Y. S., & McNulty, J. L. (1999). Incremental validity of the MMPI-2 content scales in an outpatient mental health setting. *Psychological Assessment: A Journal of Consulting and Clinical Psychology, 11*, 39–47.

Bartol, C. R. (1991). Predictive validation of the MMPI for small-town police officers who fail. *Professional Psychology: Research and Practice, 22*, 127–132.

Bartram, D., & Hambleton, R. K. (2006). *Computer-based testing and the internet.* New York: John Wiley & Sons.

Bathurst, K., Gottfried, A. W., & Gottfried, A. E. (1997). Normative data for the MMPI-2 in child custody litigation. *Psychological Assessment: A Journal of Consulting and Clinical Psychology, 9*, 205–211.

Bell, H. M. (1934). *Adjustment Inventory.* Stanford, CA: Stanford University Press.

Bem, S. L. (1974). The measurement of psychological androgyny. *Journal of Consulting and Clinical Psychology, 42*, 152–162.

Ben-Porath, Y. S. (1993, June). MMPI-2 items. *MMPI-2 and MMPI-A: News and Profiles, 4*, 7.

Ben-Porath, Y. S. (2012). *Interpreting the MMPI-2-RF.* Minneapolis, MN: University of Minnesota Press.

Ben-Porath, Y. S., & Butcher, J. N. (1986). Computers in personality assessment: A brief past, an ebullient present, and an expanding future. *Computers in Human Behavior, 2*, 167–182.

Ben-Porath, Y. S., & Butcher, J. N. (1989). Psychometric stability of rewritten MMPI items. *Journal of Personality Assessment, 53*, 645–653.

Ben-Porath, Y. S., Butcher, J. N., & Graham, J. R. (1991). Contribution of the MMPI-2 content scales to the differential diagnosis of schizophrenia and major depression. *Psychological Assessment: A Journal of Consulting and Clinical Psychology, 3*, 634–640.

Ben-Porath, Y. S., & Flens, J. R. (2012). Butcher and Williams's (this issue) critique of the MMPI-2-RF is slanted and misleading. *Journal of Child Custody: Research, Issues, and Practices, 9(4)*, 223–232.

Ben-Porath, Y. S., & Forbey, J. D. (2003). *Non-gendered norms for the MMPI-2*. Minneapolis, MN: University of Minnesota Press.

Ben-Porath, Y. S., Graham, J. R., & Tellegen, A. (2009). *The MMPI-2 Symptom Validity (FBS) scale: Development, research findings, and interpretive recommendations*. Minneapolis, MN: University of Minnesota Press.

Ben-Porath, Y. S., Greve, K. W., Bianchini, K. J., & Kaufmann, P. M. (2009). The MMPI-2 symptom validity scale (FBS) is an empirically validated measure of over-reporting in personal injury litigants and claimants: Reply to Butcher et al. (2008). *Psychological Injury and Law, 2*, 62–85.

Ben-Porath, Y. S., Hostetler, K., Butcher, J. N., & Graham, J. R. (1989). New subscales for the MMPI-2 Social Introversion scale. *Psychological Assessment: A Journal of Consulting and Clinical Psychology, 1*, 169–174.

Ben-Porath, Y. S., McCully, E., & Almagor, M. (1993). Incremental validity of the MMPI-2 content scales in the assessment of personality and psychopathology by self-report. *Journal of Personality Assessment, 61*, 557–575.

Ben-Porath, Y. S., & Sherwood, N. E. (1993). *The MMPI-2 content component scales: Development, psychometric characteristics and clinical application*. Minneapolis, MN: University of Minnesota Press.

Ben-Porath, Y. S., Slutske, W. S., & Butcher, J. N. (1989). A real-data simulation of computerized adaptive administration of the MMPI. *Psychological Assessment: A Journal of Consulting and Clinical Psychology, 1*, 18–22.

Ben-Porath, Y. S., & Stafford, K. P. (1993, August). *Empirical correlates of MMPI-2 scales in a forensic diagnostic sample: An interim report*. Paper presented at the 101st Annual Convention of the American Psychological Association, Toronto, Ontario, Canada.

Ben-Porath, Y. S., & Tellegen, A. (2008). MMPI-2 *Restructured Form: Manual for administration, scoring, and interpretation*. Minneapolis, MN: University of Minnesota Press.

Ben-Porath, Y. S., & Tellegen, A. (2011). *Minnesota Multiphasic Personality Inventory – 2 Restructured Form: Manual for administration, scoring, and interpretation*. Minneapolis, MN: University of Minnesota Press.

Benton, S. A., Robertson, J. M., Tseng, W. C., Newton, F. B., & Benton, S. L. (2003). Changes in counseling center client problems across 13 years. *Professional Psychology: Research and Practice, 34*, 66–72.

Bernreuter, R. G. (1933). The theory and construction of the Personality Inventory. *Journal of Social Psychology, 4*, 387–404.

Berrios, G. E. (1985). Obsessional disorders during the nineteenth century: Terminological and classificatory issues. In W. F. Brynum, R. Porter, & M. Shepherd (Eds.), *The anatomy of madness: Essays in the history of psychiatry: Vol. 1. People and Ideas* (pp. 166–187). London, England: Tavistock.

Berry, D. T. R., Baer, R. A., & Harris, M. J. (1991). Detection of malingering on the MMPI: A meta-analysis. *Clinical Psychology Review, 11*, 585–598.

Berry, D. T. R., & Schipper, L. J. (2007). Detection of feigned psychiatric symptoms during forensic neuropsychological examinations. In G. J. Larrabee (Ed.), *Assessment of malingered neuropsychological deficits* (pp. 226–263). New York: Oxford University Press.

Berry, D. T. R., Wetter, M. W., Baer, R. A., Gass, C. S., Franzen, M. D., Youngjohn, J. R., Lomb, D. G., MacInnes, W. D., & Buchholz, D. (1995). Overreporting of closed-head injury symptoms on the MMPI-2. *Psychological Assessment: A Journal of Consulting and Clinical Psychology, 7*, 517–523.

Berry, D., Wetter, M., Baer, R., Larsen, L., Clark, C., & Monroe, K. (1992). MMPI-2 random responding indices: Validation using a self-report methodology. *Psychological Assessment: A Journal of Consulting and Clinical Psychology, 4*, 340–345.

Berry, D. T. R., Wetter, M. W., Baer, R. A., Widiger, T. A., Sumpter, J. C., Reynolds, S. K., & Hallam, R. A. (1991). Detection of random responding on the MMPI-2: Utility of F, back F, and VRIN scales. *Psychological Assessment: A Journal of Consulting and Clinical Psychology, 3*, 418–423.

Bersoff, D. N., & Hofer, P. J. (1995). Legal issues in computerized psychological testing. In D. N. Bersoff (Ed.), *Ethical conflicts in psychology* (pp. 291–294). Washington, DC: American Psychological Association.

Binford, A., & Liljequist, L. (2008). Behavioral correlates of selected MMPI-2 Clinical, Content, and Restructured Clinical scales. *Journal of Personality Assessment, 90*, 608–614.

Blake, D. D., Penk, W. E., Mori, D. L., Kleespies, P. M., Walsh, S. S., & Keane, T. M. (1992). Validity and clinical scale comparison between the MMPI and MMPI-2 with psychiatric inpatients. *Psychological Reports, 70*, 323–332.

Blanchard, J. S. (1981). Readability of the MMPI. *Perceptual and Motor Skills, 52*, 985–986.

Bleuler, E. (1950). *Dementia praecox; or the group of schizophrenias.* New York: International Universities Press.

Block, J. (1965). *The challenge of response sets: Unconfounding meaning, acquiescence, and social desirability in the MMPI.* New York: Appleton-Century-Crofts.

Boerger, A. R., Graham, J. R., & Lilly, R. S. (1974). Behavioral correlates of single-scale MMPI-codetypes. *Journal of Consulting and Clinical Psychology, 42*, 398–402.

Bolinskey, P. K., & Nichols, D. S. (2011). Construct drift in the MMPI-2 Restructured Clinical (RC) scales: Further evidence and a possible historic example. *Journal of Clinical Psychology, 67(9)*, 907–917.

Bolinskey, P. K., Trumbetta, S. L., Hanson, D. R., & Gottesman, I. I. (2010). Predicting adult psychopathology from adolescent MMPIs: Some victories. *Personality and Individual Differences, 49*, 324–330.

Bond, J. A. (1986). Inconsistent responding to repeated MMPI items: Is its major cause really carelessness? *Journal of Personality Assessment, 50*, 50–64.

Bond, J. A. (1987). The process of responding to personality items: Inconsistent responses to repeated presentation of identical items. *Personality and Individual Differences, 8*, 409–417.

Bosquet, M., & Egeland, B. (2000). Predicting parenting behaviors from Antisocial Practices content scale scores of the MMPI-2 administered during pregnancy. *Journal of Personality Assessment, 74*, 146–162.

Box, G. E. P., & Cox, D. R. (1964). An analysis of transformations. *Journal of the Royal Statistical Society, 59*, 211–243.

Brauer, B. A. (1988). Substudies developed during the psychological instruments translation study. In R. C. Johnson, D. L. Smith, & S. Davies (Eds.), *A tradition of discovery.* Washington, DC: Gallaudet University, Gallaudet Research Institute.

Brauer, B. A. (1992). The signer effect on MMPI performance of deaf respondents. *Journal of Personality Assessment, 58*, 380–388.

Brauer, B. A. (1993). Adequacy of a translation of the MMPI into American Sign Language for use with deaf individuals: Linguistic equivalency issues. *Rehabilitation Psychology, 38(4)*, 247–260.

Brozek, J. (1955). Personality changes with age: An item analysis of the MMPI. *Journal of Gerontology, 10*, 194–206.

Buechley, R., & Ball, H. (1952). A new test of "validity" for the group MMPI. *Journal of Consulting Psychology, 16*, 299–301.

Burandt, C. A. (2006). Detecting incomplete effort on the MMPI-2: An examination of the Fake-Bad Scale in electrical injury. *Dissertation Abstracts International: Section B: The Sciences and Engineering, 67(4-B)*, 2216.

Burkhart, B. R., Christian, W. L., & Gynther, M. D. (1978). Item subtlety and faking on the MMPI: A paradoxical relationship. *Journal of Personality Assessment, 42,* 76–80.

Bush, S. S., Ruff, R. M., Troster, A. I., Barth, J. T., Koffler, S. P., Pliskin, N. H., Reynolds, C. R., & Silver, C. H. (2005). NAN position paper: Symptom validity assessment: Practice issues and medical necessity. *Archives of Clinical Neuropsychology, 20,* 419–426.

Buss, A. H., & Perry, M. (1992). The aggression questionnaire. *Journal of Personality and Social Psychology,* 63, 452–459.

Butcher, J. N. (1987a). Computerized clinical and personality assessment using the MMPI. In J. N. Butcher (Ed.), *Computerized psychological assessment: A practitioner's guide* (pp. 161–197). New York: Basic Books.

Butcher, J. N. (Ed.). (1987b). *Computerized psychological assessment: A practitioner's guide.* New York: Basic Books.

Butcher, J. N. (1990a, August). Education level and MMPI-2 measured psychopathology: A case of negligible influence. *MMPI-2: News and Profiles, 1,* 2.

Butcher, J. N. (1990b). *Use of the MMPI-2 in treatment planning.* New York: Oxford University Press.

Butcher, J. N. (1992, October). International developments with the MMPI-2. *MMPI-2: News and Profiles, 3,* 4–5.

Butcher, J. N. (1993). *The Minnesota report: Adult clinical system—revised user's guide.* Minneapolis, MN: National Computer Systems.

Butcher, J. N. (1994a). Psychological assessment by computer: Potential gains and problems to avoid. *Psychiatric Annals, 20,* 20–24.

Butcher, J. N. (1994b). Important considerations in the use of automated MMPI-2 reports. In J. N. Butcher & J. R. Graham (Eds.), *Topics in MMPI-2 and MMPI-A interpretation.* Minneapolis, MN: University of Minnesota, Department of Psychology.

Butcher, J. N. (1994c). Psychological assessment of airline pilot applicants with the MMPI-2. *Journal of Personality Assessment, 62,* 31–44.

Butcher, J. N. (Ed.). (1996). *International adaptations of the MMPI-2.* Minneapolis, MN: University of Minnesota Press.

Butcher, J. N. (Ed.) (2000). *Basic sources on the MMPI-2.* Minneapolis, MN: University of Minnesota Press.

Butcher, J. N. (2002, March/June). Assessing pilots with the "wrong stuff": A call for research on emotional health factors in commercial aviators. *International Journal of Selection and Assessment, 10(1/2),* 168.

Butcher, J. N. (2004). Personality assessment without borders: Adaptation of the MMPI-2 across cultures. *Journal of Personality Assessment, 83(2),* 90–104.

Butcher, J. N. (2009). How to use computer-based reports. In J. N. Butcher (Ed), *Oxford handbook of personality assessment* (pp. 693–706). New York: Oxford University Press.

Butcher, J. N. (2010). Personality assessment from the nineteenth to the early twenty-first century: Past achievements and contemporary challenges. *Annual Review of Clinical Psychology, 6,* 1–20.

Butcher, J. N. (2011). *A beginner's guide to the MMPI-2, 3rd Ed.* Washington, DC: American Psychological Association Press.

Butcher, J. N. (2013). Computerized psychological assessment. In J. R. Graham, & J. Naglieri (Eds), *Handbook of psychology* (pp. 165–191). New York: Wiley Press.

Butcher, J. N., Arbisi, P. A., Atlis, M. M., & McNulty, J. L. (2003). The construct validity of the Lees-Haley Fake Bad Scale: Does this measure somatic malingering and feigned emotional distress? *Archives of Clinical Neuropsychology, 18,* 473–485.

Butcher, J. N., Cheung, F. M., & Lim, J. (2003). Use of the MMPI-2 with Asian populations. *Psychological Assessment, 15(3),* 248–256.

Butcher, J. N., Dahlstrom, W. G., Graham, J. R., Tellegen, A., & Kaemmer, B. (1989). *Minnesota Multiphasic Personality Inventory–2 (MMPI-2): Manual for administration and scoring.* Minneapolis, MN: University of Minnesota Press.

Butcher, J., Derksen, J., Sloore, H., & Sirigatti, S. (2003). Objective personality assessment of people in diverse cultures: European adaptations of the MMPI-2. *Behaviour Research and Therapy, 41(7),* 819–840.

Butcher, J. N., Gass, C. S., Cumella, E., Kally, Z., & Williams, C. L. (2008). Potential for bias in MMPI-2 assessments using the Fake Bad Scale (FBS). *Psychological Injury and Law, 1,* 191–209.

Butcher, J. N., & Graham, J. R. (1989). *Topics in MMPI-2 interpretation.* Minneapolis, MN: University of Minnesota, Department of Psychology.

Butcher, J. N., Graham, J. R., Ben-Porath, Y. S., Tellegen, A., Dahlstrom, W. G., & Kaemmer, B.(2001). *MMPI-2: Manual for administration and scoring (Revised Edition).* Minneapolis, MN: University of Minnesota Press.

Butcher, J. N., Graham, J. R., Williams, C. L., & Ben-Porath, Y. S. (1990). *Development and use of the MMPI-2 content scales.* Minneapolis, MN: University of Minnesota Press.

Butcher, J. N., Hamilton, C. K., Rouse, S. V., & Cumella, E. J. (2006). The deconstruction of the Hy Scale of MMPI-2: Failure of RC3 in measuring somatic symptom expression. *Journal of Personality Assessment, 87,* 186–192.

Butcher, J. N., & Han, K. (1995). Development of an MMPI-2 scale to assess the presentation of self in a superlative manner: The S scale. In J. N. Butcher & C. D. Spielberger (Eds.), *Advances in personality assessment* (pp. 25–50). Hillsdale, NJ: Lawrence Erlbaum Associates.

Butcher, J. N., & Hostetler, K. (1990). Abbreviating MMPI item administration: What can be learned from the MMPI for the MMPI-2? *Psychological Assessment: A Journal of Consulting and Clinical Psychology, 2,* 12–21.

Butcher, J. N., Keller, L. S., & Bacon, S. F. (1985). Current developments and future directions in computerized personality assessment. *Journal of Consulting and Clinical Psychology, 53,* 803–815.

Butcher, J. N., Morfitt, R. C., Rouse, S. V., & Holden, R. R. (1997). Reducing MMPI-2 defensiveness: The effect of specialized instructions on retest validity on a job applicant sample. *Journal of Personality Assessment, 68,* 385–401.

Butcher, J. N., Ones, D. S., & Cullen, M. (2006). Personnel screening with the MMPI-2. In J. N. Butcher (Ed.), *MMPI-2: The Practitioner's Handbook* (pp. 381–406). Washington, DC: American Psychological Association.

Butcher, J. N., & Pancheri, P. (1976). *A handbook of cross-national MMPI research.* Minneapolis, MN: University of Minnesota Press.

Butcher, J. N., Perry, J. N., & Atlis, M. (2000). Validity and utility of computer-based test interpretation. *Psychological Assessment, 12(1),* 6–18.

Butcher, J. N., Perry, J., & Dean, B. L. (2009). Computer-based assessment with the MMPI-2. In J. N. Butcher (Ed). *Oxford handbook of personality assessment* (pp. 163–182). New York: Oxford University Press.

Butcher, J. N., Perry, J., & Hahn, J. (2004). Computers in clinical assessment: Historical developments, present status, and future challenges. *Journal of Clinical Psychology, 60,* 331–346.

Butcher, J. N., & Williams, C. L. (1992). *Essentials of MMPI-2 and MMPI-A interpretation.* Minneapolis, MN: University of Minnesota Press.

Butcher, J. N., & Williams, C. L. (2000). *Essentials of MMPI-2 and MMPI-A interpretation* (2nd ed.). Minneapolis, MN: University of Minnesota Press.

Butcher, J. N., & Williams, C. L. (2012). Problems with using the MMPI-2-RF in forensic evaluations: A clarification to Ellis. *Journal of Child Custody: Research, Issues, and Practices, 9(4),* 217–222.

Butcher, J. N., Williams, C. L., Graham, J. R., Archer, R. P., Tellegen, A., Ben-Porath, Y. S., & Kaemmer, B. (1992). *MMPI-A (Minnesota Multiphasic Personality Inventory – Adolescent):*

Manual for administration, scoring, and interpretation. Minneapolis, MN: University of Minnesota Press.

Caldwell, A. B. (1969). *MMPI critical items.* Los Angeles, CA: Author.

Caldwell, A. B. (1971, April). *Recent advances in automated interpretation of the MMPI.* Paper presented at the 6th Annual MMPI Symposium, Minneapolis, MN.

Caldwell, A. B. (1974, February). *Characteristics of MMPI pattern types.* Paper presented at the Ninth Annual Symposium on the MMPI, Los Angeles, CA.

Caldwell, A. B. (1977). *Questions people ask when taking the MMPI* (Special Bulletin No. 3). Available from Caldwell Report, 1545 Sawtelle Boulevard, Suite 14, Los Angeles, CA 90025.

Caldwell, A. B. (1984, April). *Clinical decision making with the MMPI.* Workshop sponsored by the Advanced Psychological Studies Institute and Northwestern University, Chicago, IL.

Caldwell, A. B. (1988). *MMPI supplemental scale manual.* Los Angeles, CA: Caldwell Report.

Caldwell, A. B. (1991). Commentary on the Minnesota Multiphasic Personality Inventory-2: A review. *Journal of Counseling and Development, 69,* 568–569.

Caldwell, A. B. (1997). *Forensic questions and answers on the MMPI/MMPI-2.* Los Angeles, CA: Caldwell Report.

Caldwell, A. B. (1998). Advanced MMPI/MMPI-2 theory and interpretation seminar. Unpublished materials.

Caldwell, A. B. (1999). Personal communication (D. S. Nichols, June 25, 1999).

Caldwell, A. B. (2003). How can the MMPI-2 help child custody examiners? *Journal of Child Custody, 2(1/2),* 88–117.

Caldwell, A. B. (2006). Maximal measurement or meaningful measurement: The interpretive challenges of the MMPI-2 Restructured Clinical (RC) scales. *Journal of Personality Assessment, 87,* 193–201.

Caldwell, A. B. (2007a). [MMPI-2 data research file for child custody litigants.] Unpublished raw data.

Caldwell, A. B. (2007b). [MMPI-2 data research file for clinical clients.] Unpublished raw data.

Caldwell, A. B. (2007c). [MMPI-2 data research file for pain patients.] Unpublished raw data.

Caldwell, A. B. (2007d). [MMPI-2 data research file for personnel applicants.] Unpublished raw data.

Calvin, J. (1975). *A replicated study of the concurrent validity of the Harris subscales for the MMPI.* Unpublished doctoral dissertation, Kent State University, Kent, OH.

Carkhuff, R. R., Barnett, L., & McCall, J. N. (1965). *The counselor's handbook: Scale and profile interpretations of the MMPI.* Urbana, IL: R. W. Parkinson.

Carr, A. C., & Ghosh, A. (1983). Response of phobic patients to direct computer assessment. *British Journal of Psychiatry, 142,* 60–65.

Carr, G. D., Moretti, M. M., & Cue, B. J. H. (2005). Evaluating parenting capacity: Validity problems with the MMPI-2, PAI, CAPI, and ratings of child adjustment. *Professional Psychology: Research and Practice, 36(2),* 188–196.

Carson, R. C. (1969). Interpretive manual to the MMPI. In J. N. Butcher (Ed.), *MMPI: Research developments and clinical applications* (pp. 279–296). New York: McGraw-Hill.

Castlebury, F. D., & Durham, T. W. (1997). The MMPI-2 GM and GF scales as measures of psychological well-being. *Journal of Clinical Psychology, 53,* 879–893.

Caviaola, A. A., Strohmetz, D. B., Wolf, J. M., & Lavender, N. J. (2003). Comparison of DWI offenders with non-DWI individuals on the MMPI-2 and the Michigan Alcoholism Screening Test. *Addictive Behaviors, 28,* 971–977.

Chang, A. F., Caldwell, A. B., & Moss, T. (1973). Stability of personality traits in alcoholics during and after treatment as measured by the MMPI: A one-year follow-up study. *Proceedings of the American Psychological Association, 8,* 387–388.

Chapman, L. J., Chapman, J. P., & Raulin, M. L. (1978). Body-image aberration in schizophrenia. *Journal of Abnormal Psychology, 87,* 399–407.

Childs, R. A., Dahlstrom, W. G., Kemp, S. M., & Panter, A. T. (1992). *Item response theory in personality assessment: The MMPI-2 Depression scale* (Research Report No. 92–1). Chapel Hill, NC: University of North Carolina, C. C. Thurstone Psychometric Laboratory.

Chisholm, S. M., Crowther, J. H., & Ben-Porath, Y. S. (1997). Selected MMPI-2 scales' ability to predict premature termination and outcome from psychotherapy. *Journal of Personality Assessment, 69*, 127–144.

Chojnacki, J. T., & Walsh, W. B. (1994). The consistency between scores of the Harris-Lingoes subscales of the MMPI and MMPI-2. *Journal of Personality Assessment, 62*, 157–165.

Christian, W. L., Burkhart, B. R., & Gynther, M. D. (1978). Subtle-obvious ratings of MMPI items: New interest in an old concept. *Journal of Consulting and Clinical Psychology, 46*, 1178–1186.

Clark, L. A. (1993). *The schedule for nonadaptive and adaptive personality (SNAP).* Minneapolis, MN: University of Minnesota Press.

Clark, L. A., & Watson, D. (1995). Constructing validity: Basic issues in objective scale development. *Psychological Assessment, 7*, 309–319.

Clark, M. E. (1994). Interpretive limitations of the MMPI-2 Anger and Cynicism content scales. *Journal of Personality Assessment, 63*, 89–96.

Clark, M. E. (1996). MMPI-2 Negative Treatment Indicators Content and Content Component Scales: Clinical correlates and outcome prediction for men with chronic pain. *Psychological Assessment, 8*, 32–38.

Clavelle, P. R., & Butcher, J. N. (1977). An adaptive typological approach to psychiatric screening. *Journal of Consulting and Clinical Psychology, 45*, 851–859.

Clayton, S. (2011). Malingering detection among accommodation-seeking university students. *Dissertation Abstracts International: Section B: The Sciences and Engineering, 71* (12-B), 7719.

Clements, R., & Heintz, J. M. (2002). Diagnostic accuracy and factor structure of the AAS and APS scales of the MMPI-2. *Journal of Personality Assessment, 79*, 564–582.

Clopton, J. R. (1979). The MMPI and suicide. In C. S. Newmark (Ed.), *MMPI: Clinical and research trends* (pp. 149–166). New York: Praeger.

Clopton, J. R., & Neuringer, C. (1977). MMPI Cannot Say scores: Normative data and degree of profile distortion. *Journal of Personality Assessment, 41*, 511–513.

Cofer, C. N., Chance, J. E., & Judson, A. J. (1949). A study of malingering on the MMPI. *Journal of Psychology, 27*, 491–499.

Coffield, S. B. (2007). Prediction of treatment-related variables using the MMPI-2 (Doctoral dissertation, Kent State University). *Dissertation Abstracts International, 67*(7-B), 4099.

Colby, F. (1989). Usefulness of the *K* correction in MMPI profiles of patients and non-patients. *Psychological Assessment: A Journal of Consulting and Clinical Psychology, 1*, 142–145.

Colligan, R. C., & Offord, K. P. (1987a). The MacAndrew Alcoholism scale applied to a contemporary normative sample. *Journal of Clinical Psychology, 43*, 291–293.

Colligan, R. C., & Offord, K. P. (1987b). Resiliency reconsidered: Contemporary MMPI normative data for Barron's Ego Strength scale. *Journal of Clinical Psychology, 43*, 467–472.

Colligan, R. C., & Offord, K. P. (1988a). The risky use of the MMPI Hostility Scale in assessing risk for coronary heart disease. *Psychosomatics: Journal of Consultation Liaison Psychiatry, 29*, 188–196.

Colligan, R. C., & Offord, K. P. (1988b). Contemporary norms for the Wiggins content scales: A 45-year update. *Journal of Clinical Psychology, 44*, 23–32.

Colligan, R. C., & Offord, K. P. (1991). Adolescents, the MMPI, and the issue of *K* correction: A contemporary normative study. *Journal of Clinical Psychology, 47*, 607–631.

Colligan, R. C., & Offord, K. P. (1992). Age, stage, and the MMPI: Changes in response patterns over an 85-year age span. *Journal of Clinical Psychology, 48*, 476–493.

Colligan, R. C., Osborne, D., & Offord, K. P. (1980). Linear transformation and the interpretation of MMPI *T* scores. *Journal of Clinical Psychology, 36*, 162–165.

Colligan, R. C., Osborne, D., Swenson, W. M., & Offord, K. P. (1983). *The MMPI: A contemporary normative sample.* New York: Praeger.

Colligan, R. C., Osborne, D., Swenson, W. M., & Offord, K. P. (1984). The MMPI: Development of contemporary norms. *Journal of Clinical Psychology, 40,* 100–107.

Colligan, R. C., Osborne, D., Swenson, W. M., & Offord, K. P. (1989). *The MMPI: A contemporary normative study of adults* (2nd ed.). Odessa, FL: Psychological Assessment Resources.

Colligan, R. C., Rasmussen, N. H., Agerter, D. C., Offord, K. P., Malinchoc, M., O'Byrne, M. M., & Benson, J. T. (2008). The MMPI-2: A contemporary normative study of Midwestern family medicine outpatients. *Journal of Clinical Psychology in Medical Settings, 15,* 98–119.

Collins, L. J. (1999). Select MMPI-2 scales and consistency of physical effort during trunk extension exercise as predictors of treatment outcome for functional restoration rehabilitation in chronic back pain patients (Doctoral dissertation, University of Detroit Mercy). *Dissertation Abstracts International,* 5573.

Comrey, A. L. (1958). A factor analysis of items on the MMPI Psychasthenia scale. *Educational and Psychological Measurement, 18,* 293–300.

Constantinople, A. (1973). Masculinity-femininity: An exception to a famous dictum? *Psychological Bulletin, 80,* 389–407.

Cook, W. W., Leeds, C. H., & Callis, R. (1951). *Minnesota Teacher Attitude Inventory.* New York: The Psychological Corporation.

Cook, W. W., & Medley, D. M. (1954). Proposed hostility and Pharisaic-Virtue scales for the MMPI. *Journal of Applied Psychology, 38,* 414–418.

Cooke, G. C. (2010). MMPI-2 defensiveness in child custody evaluations: The role of education and socioeconomic level. *American Journal of Forensic Psychology, 28(2),* 5–16.

Costa, P. T., Jr., & McCrae, R. R. (1992a). *NEO PI-R: Professional manual.* Odessa, FL: Psychological Assessment Resources.

Costa, P. T., Jr., & McCrae, R. R. (1992b). Normal personality assessment in clinical practice: The NEO Personality Inventory. *Psychological Assessment: A Journal of Consulting and Clinical Psychology, 4,* 5–13.

Costa, P. T., Jr., & McCrae, R. R. (1992c). Reply to Ben-Porath and Waller. *Psychological Assessment: A Journal of Consulting and Clinical Psychology, 4,* 20–22.

Costa, P. T., Jr., & McCrae, R. R. (1992d). *Revised NEO Personality Inventory (NEO–PI-R) and NEO Five-Factor Inventory (NEO–FFI): Professional manual.* Odessa, FL: Psychological Assessment Resources.

Costa, P. T., Zonderman, A. B., McCrae, R. R., & Williams, R. B. (1985). Content and comprehensiveness in the MMPI: An item factor analysis in a normal adult sample. *Journal of Personality and Social Psychology, 48(4),* 925–933.

Costa, P. T., Zonderman, A. B., McCrae, R. R., & Williams, R. B. (1986). Cynicism and paranoid alienation in the Cook and Medley HO Scale. *Psychosomatic Medicine, 48,* 283–285.

Cox, A. C., Weed, N. C., & Butcher, J. N. (2009). The MMPI-2: History, interpretation, and clinical issues. In J. N. Butcher (Ed), *Oxford Handbook of Personality Assessment.* New York: Oxford University Press.

Coyle, F A., Jr., & Heap, R. F. (1965). Interpreting the MMPI L scale. *Psychological Reports, 17,* 722.

Craig, R. J. (1984a). A comparison of MMPI profiles of heroin addicts based on multiple methods of classification. *Journal of Personality Assessment, 48,* 115–120.

Craig, R. J. (1984b). MMPI substance abuse scales on drug addicts with and without concurrent alcoholism. *Journal of Personality Assessment, 48,* 495–499.

Craig, R. J. (1984c). Personality dimensions related to premature termination from an inpatient drug abuse treatment program. *Journal of Clinical Psychology, 40,* 351–355.

Craig, R. J. (1988). Psychological functioning of cocaine free-basers derived from objective psychological tests. *Journal of Clinical Psychology, 44,* 599–606.

Craig, R. J. (2005). Assessing contemporary substance abusers with the MMPI MacAndrews Alcoholism Scale: A review. *Substance Use & Misuse, 40*, 427–450.

Craig, R. J., & Olson, R. E. (2004). Predicting methadone maintenance treatment outcomes using the Addiction Severity Index and the MMPI-2 Content Scales (Negative Treatment Indicators and Cynism Scales). *The American Journal of Drug and Alcohol Abuse, 30*, 823–839.

Cramer, K. M. (1995). Comparing three new MMPI-2 randomness indices in a novel procedure for random profile derivation. *Journal of Personality Assessment, 65*, 514–520.

Cronbach, L. J. (1951). Coefficient alpha and the internal structure of tests. *Psychometrika, 16*, 297–334.

Cross, O. H. (1945). Braille edition of the MMPI for use with the blind. *Journal of Applied Psychology, 31*, 341–353.

CTB McGraw-Hill. (2000). *California Achievement Test—sixth edition survey*. Monterey, CA: CTB McGraw-Hill.

Cuadra, C. (1956). A scale for control in psychological adjustment *(Cn)*. In G. S. Welsh & W. G. Dahlstrom (Eds.), *Basic readings on the MMPI in psychology and medicine* (pp. 235–254). Minneapolis, MN: University of Minnesota Press.

Cumella, E., Kally, Z., & Butcher, J. N. (2009, March). *MMPI-2 restructured (RC) scales with eating disorder patients*. Chicago, IL: Society for Personality Assessment.

Dahlstrom, W. G. (1969). Recurrent issues in the development of the MMPI. In J. N. Butcher (Ed.), *MMPI: Research developments and clinical applications* (pp. 1–40). New York: McGraw-Hill.

Dahlstrom, W. G. (1991). *Subtle-Obvious subscale correlates derived from partner ratings used in the MMPI-2 restandardization*. Unpublished manuscript. University of North Carolina, Chapel Hill, NC.

Dahlstrom, W. G. (1992a). Comparability of two-point high-point code patterns from original MMPI norms to MMPI-2 norms for the restandardization sample. *Journal of Personality Assessment, 59*, 153–164.

Dahlstrom, W. G. (1992b). The growth in acceptance of the MMPI. *Professional Psychology: Research and Practice, 23*, 1–4.

Dahlstrom, W. G. (1993). *Manual supplement: The items in the MMPI-2. Alterations in the wording, patterns of interrelationship and changes in endorsements*. Minneapolis, MN: University of Minnesota Press.

Dahlstrom, W. G., & Archer, R. P. (2000). A shortened version of the MMPI-2. *Assessment, 7*, 131–137.

Dahlstrom, W. G., Archer, R. P., Hopkins, D. G., Jackson, E., & Dahlstrom, L. E. (1994). *Assessing the readability of the Minnesota Multiphasic Personality Inventory instruments—The MMPI, MMPI-2, MMPI-A* (MMPI-2/MMPI-A Test Report No. 2). Minneapolis, MN: University of Minnesota Press.

Dahlstrom, W. G., & Dahlstrom, L. E. (Eds.). (1980). *Basic readings on the MMPI: A new selection on personality measurement*. Minneapolis, MN: University Minnesota Press.

Dahlstrom, W. G., Lachar, D., & Dahlstrom, L. E. (1986). *MMPI patterns of American minorities*. Minneapolis, MN: University of Minnesota Press.

Dahlstrom, W. G., & Moreland, K. L. (1983). Teaching the MMPI: APA-approved clinical internships. *Professional Psychology: Research and Practice, 14*, 563–569.

Dahlstrom, W. G., & Tellegen, A. (1993). *Manual supplement: Socioeconomic status and the MMPI-2. The relation of MMPI-2 patterns to levels of education and occupation*. Minneapolis, MN: University of Minnesota Press.

Dahlstrom, W. G., & Welsh, G. S. (1960). *An MMPI handbook: A guide to use in clinical practice and research*. Minneapolis, MN: University of Minnesota Press.

Dahlstrom, W. G., Welsh, G. S., & Dahlstrom, L. E. (1972). *An MMPI handbook: Vol I. Clinical interpretation* (Rev. ed.). Minneapolis, MN: University of Minnesota Press.

Dahlstrom, W. G., Welsh, G. S., & Dahlstrom, L. E. (1975). *An MMPI handbook: Vol. II. Research applications* (Rev. ed.). Minneapolis, MN: University of Minnesota Press.

Damarin, R., & Messick, S. (1965). *Response styles as personality variables: A theoretical integration* (Technical Report No. ETS RB 65–10). Princeton, NJ: Educational Testing Service.

Davis, K. R. (1971). The actuarial development of a female 4'3 MMPI profile (Doctoral dissertation, Saint Louis University). *Dissertation Abstracts International, 32,* 1207B.

Davis, K. R., & Sines, J. (1971). An antisocial behavior pattern associated with a specific MMPI profile. *Journal of Consulting and Clinical Psychology, 36,* 229–234.

Davis, R. D., & Rostow, C. D. (2004). Using MMPI special scale configurations to predict law enforcement officers fired for cause. *Applied H. R. M. Research, 9(2),* 57–58.

Davis, R. D., Rostow, C. D., Pinkston, J. B., Combs, D. R., & Dixon, D. R. (2004). A re-examination of the MMPI-2 Aggressiveness and Immaturity Indices in law enforcement screening. *Journal of Police and Criminal Psychology, 19,* 17–26.

Davis v. Bellsouth Short Term Disability Plan for Non-Salaried Employees, 2012 U.S.Dist.LEXIS 33395 (M.D.N.C. March 12, 2012).

Davidson v. Strawberry Petroleum et al., Case No. 05-4320 (Hillsborough County, Fla. 2007)

Dean, A. C., Boone, K. R., Kim, M. S., Curiel, A. R., Martin, D. J., Victor, T. L., Zeller, M. A., & Lang, Y. K. (2008). Examination of the impact of ethnicity on the Minnesota Multiphasic Personality Inventory -2 (MMPI-2) Fake Bad Scale. *The Clinical Neuropsychologist, 1,* 1–7.

Deiker, T. E. (1974). A cross-validation of MMPI scales of aggression on male criminal criterion groups. *Journal of Consulting and Clinical Psychology, 42,* 196–202.

Demir, B., Uluğ, B., Batur, S., & Mercan, S. (2002). Alkol bağımlilarinda MMPI-2 bağimlilik alt ölçeklerinin psikometrik özellikleri [The psychometric properties of MMPI-2 Addiction Related Supplementary Scales on alcoholic patients]. *Türk Psikiyatri Dergisi, 13,* 265–272.

Derogatis, L. R. (1983). *SCL-90-R: administration scoring and procedures manual.* Baltimore, MD: Clinical Psychometric Research.

Detrick, P., & Chibnall, J. T. (2008). Positive response distortion by police officer applicants: Association of Paulhus Deception Scales with MMPI-2 and Inwald Personality Inventory Validity Scales. *Assessment,* March, *15(1),* 87–96. doi: 10.1177/107319110730608.

DeViva, J. C., & Bloem, W. D. (2003). Symptom exaggeration and compensation seeking among combat veterans with posttraumatic stress disorder. *Journal of Traumatic Stress, 16,* 503–507.

Devlin, K. S. (1998). The MMPI-2's Addiction Potential Scale and Addiction Acknowledgement Scale: Discriminating between women with substance dependence diagnosis and those without (Doctoral dissertation, Wisconsin School of Professional Psychology, Inc.). *Dissertation Abstracts International, 58(9-B),* 5112.

DiLalla, D. L., Carey, G., Gottesman, I. I., & Bouchard, T. J., Jr. (1996). Heritability of MMPI personality indicators of psychopathology in twins reared apart. *Journal of Abnormal Psychology, 105,* 491–499.

DiLalla, D. L., Gottesman, I. I., Carey, G., & Bouchard, T. J., Jr. (1999). Heritability of MMPI Harris-Lingoes and Subtle-Obvious subscales in twins reared apart. *Assessment, 6(4),* 353–364.

Drake, L. E. (1946). A social I.E. scale for the Minnesota Multiphasic Personality Inventory. *Journal of Applied Psychology, 30,* 51–54.

Drake, L. E., & Oetting, E. R. (1959). *An MMPI codebook for counselors.* Minneapolis, MN: University of Minnesota Press.

Drake, L. E., & Thiede, W. B. (1948). Further validation of the Social I.E. scale for the Minnesota Multiphasic Personality Inventory. *Journal of Educational Research, 41,* 51–56.

Dubinsky, S., Gamble, D. J., & Rogers, M. L. (1985). A literature review of subtle-obvious items on the MMPI. *Journal of Personality Assessment, 49,* 62–68.

Duckworth, J. C. (1979). *MMPI interpretation manual for counselors and clinicians.* Muncie, IN: Accelerated Development.

Duckworth, J. C. (1991a). The Minnesota Multiphasic Personality Inventory 2: A review. *Journal of Counseling and Development, 69*, 564–567.

Duckworth, J. C. (1991b). Response to Caldwell and Graham. *Journal of Counseling and Development, 69*, 572–573.

Duckworth, J. C., & Anderson, W. (1986). *MMPI interpretation manual for counselors and clinicians* (3rd ed.). Muncie, IN: Accelerated Development.

Duckworth, J. C., & Anderson, W. (1995). *MMPI interpretation manual for counselors and clinicians* (4th ed.). Muncie, IN: Accelerated Development.

Duckworth, J. C., & Barley, W. D. (1988). Within-normal-limit profiles. In R. L. Greene (Ed.), *The MMPI: Use with specific populations* (pp. 278–315). Philadelphia, PA: Grune & Stratten.

Dwyer, S. A. (1996). The validity of the Addiction Potential and Addiction Acknowledgement Scales of the MMPI-2 in a dual diagnosis population: An improvement over the MAC-R? (Doctoral dissertation, Kent State University). *Dissertation Abstracts International, 56(12-B)*, 7088.

Earleywine, M., & Finn, P. R. (1991). Sensation seeking explains the relation between behavioral disinhibition and alcohol consumption. *Addictive Behaviors, 16*, 123–128.

Eckblad, M. B., & Chapman, L. J. (1983). Magical ideation as an indicator of schizotypy. *Journal of Consulting and Clinical Psychology, 51*, 215–225.

Edwards, A. L. (1957). *The social desirability variable in personality assessment and research.* New York: Dryden Press.

Edwards, A. L., Diers, C. J., & Walker, J. N. (1962). Response sets and factor loadings on sixty-one personality scales. *Journal of Applied Psychology, 46*, 220–225.

Edwards, D. W., Morrison, T. L., & Weissman, H. N. (1993). Uniform versus linear *T* scores on the MMPI-2/MMPI in an outpatient psychiatric sample: Differential contributions. *Psychological Assessment: A Journal of Consulting and Clinical Psychology, 5*, 499–500.

Edwards, D. W., Weissman, H. N., & Morrison, T. L. (1993). *Forensic case studies with additional data to resolve critical MMP1-2/MMPI differences.* Paper presented at the 101st Annual Convention of the American Psychological Association, Toronto, Ontario, Canada.

Edwards, E. L., Holmes, C. B., & Carvajal, H. H. (1998). Oral and booklet presentation of the MMPI-2. *Journal of Clinical Psychology, 54*, 593–596.

Egger, J. I. M., Delsing, P. A. M., & De Mey, H. R. A. (2003). Differential diagnosis using the MMPI-2: Goldberg's index revisited. *European Psychiatry, 18*, 409–411.

Egger, J. I. M., De Mey, H. R. A., Derksen, J. J. L., & van der Staak, C. P. F. (2003). Cross-cultural replication of the five-factor model and comparison of the NEO-PI-R and MMPI-2 PSY–5 scales in a Dutch psychiatric sample. *Psychological Assessment, 15*, 81–88.

Ehrenworth, N. V., & Archer, R. P. (1985). A comparison of clinical accuracy ratings of interpretative approaches for adolescent MMPI responses. *Journal of Personality Assessment, 49*, 413–421.

Eichman, W. J. (1961). Replicated factors on the MMPI with female NP patients. *Journal of Consulting Psychology, 25(1)*, 55–60.

Eichman, W. J. (1972). Minnesota Multiphasic Personality Inventory: Computerized scoring and interpreting services. In O. K. Buros (Ed.), *Seventh mental measurement yearbook* (pp. 253–255). Highland Park, NJ: Gryphon Press.

Einhorn, J. H., & Hogarth, R. M. (1978). Confidence in judgment: Persistence of the illusion of validity. *Psychological Review, 85*, 395–416.

Elhai, J. D., Ruggiero, K. J., Frueh, B. C., Beckham, J. C., & Gold, P. B. (2002). The Infrequency-Posttraumatic Stress Disorder Scale (Fptsd) for the MMPI-2: Development and initial validation with veterans presenting with combat-related PTSD. *Journal of Personality Assessment, 79*, 531–549.

Elhai, J. D., Naifeh, J. A., Zucker, I. S., Gold, S. N., Deitsch, S. E., & Frueh, B. C. (2004a). Discriminating malingered from genuine civilian posttraumatic stress disorder: A validation of three MMPI-2 infrequency scales (F, Fp, and Fptsd). *Assessment, 11(2)*, 139–144.

Elhai, J. D., Naifeh, J. A., Zucker, I. S., Gold, S. N., Deitsch, S. E., & Frueh, B. C. (2004b). Discriminating malingered from genuine civilian posttraumatic stress disorder: A validation of three MMPI-2 infrequency scales (F, Fp, and Fptsd): Erratum. *Assessment, 11,* 271–271.

Emons, W. H. M., Sijtsma, K., & Meijer, R. R. (2007). On the consistency of individual classification using short scales. *Psychological Methods, 12,* 105–120.

Endicott, N. A., Jortner, S., & Abramoff, E. (1969). Objective measures of suspiciousness. *Journal of Abnormal Psychology, 74,* 26–32.

Erdberg, P. (1979) A systematic approach to providing feedback from the MMPI. In C. S. Newmark (Ed.), *MMPI clinical and research trends* (pp. 238–342). New York: Praeger.

Estes, W. K. (1976). The cognitive side of probability learning. *Psychological Review, 83,* 37–64.

Evans, C., & McConnell, T. R. (1941). A new measure of introversion-extroversion. *Journal of Psychology, 12,* 111–124.

Evans, R. G. (1984). Normative data for two MMPI critical item sets. *Journal of Clinical Psychology, 40,* 512–515.

Eysenck, H. J. (1967). *The biological basis of personality.* Springfield, IL: Thomas.

Eysenck, H. J., & Eysenck, M. W. (1985). *Personality and individual differences.* New York: Plenum.

Eysenck, H. J., & Eysenck, S. B. G. (1975). *Manual: Eysenck Personality Questionnaire* (junior and adult). San Diego, CA: Edits.

Eysenck, H. J., Wakefield, J. A., & Friedman, A. F. (1983). Diagnosis and clinical assessment: The *DSM–III. Annual Review of Psychology, 34,* 167–193.

Fine, H. K. (1973). Studying schizophrenia outside the psychiatric setting. *Journal of Youth and Adolescence, 2,* 291–301.

Finn, S. E. (1996). *Manual for using the MMPI-2 as a therapeutic intervention.* Minneapolis, MN: University of Minnesota Press.

Finn, S. E., & Tonsager, M. E. (1992). Therapeutic effects of providing MMPI-2 test feedback to college students awaiting therapy. *Psychological Assessment: A Journal of Consulting and Clinical Psychology, 4,* 278–287.

Finney, J. C., Smith, D. F., Skeeters, D. E., & Auvenshine, C. D. (1971). MMPI alcoholism scales: Factor structure and content analysis. *Quarterly Journal of Studies on Alcohol, 32,* 1055–1060.

Fjordbak, T. (1985). Clinical correlates of high Lie scale elevations among forensic patients. *Journal of Personality Assessment, 49,* 252–255.

Foerstner, S. B. (1986). *The factor structure and stability of selected Minnesota Multiphasic Personality Inventory (MMPI) subscales: Harris and Lingoes subscales, Wiggins content scales, Wiener subscales, and Serkownek subscales.* Unpublished doctoral dissertation. University of Akron, Akron, OH.

Forbey, J. D., & Ben-Porath, Y. S. (2007a). Computerized Adaptive Personality Testing: A review and illustration with the MMPI-2 computerized adaptive version. *Psychological Assessment, 19(1),* 14–24.

Forbey, J. D., & Ben-Porath, Y. S. (2007b). A comparison of the MMPI-2 restructured clinical (RC) and clinical scales in a substance abuse treatment sample. *Psychological Services, 4,* 46–58.

Forbey, J. D., & Ben-Porath, Y. S. (2008). Empirical correlates of the MMPI-2 Restructures Clinical (RC) scales in a nonclinical setting. *Journal of Personality Assessment, 90,* 136–141.

Forbey, J. D., Ben-Porath, Y. S., & Gartland, D. (2009). Validation of the MMPI-2 Computerized Adaptive Version (MMPI-2-CA) in a correctional intake facility. *Psychological Services, 6,* 279–292. doi: 10.1037/a0016195.

Fowler, R. D. (1966). *The MMPI notebook: A guide to the clinical use of the automated MMPI.* Nutley, NJ: Roche Psychiatric Service Institute.

Fowler, R. D. (1967). Computer interpretation of personality tests: The automated psychologist. *Comprehensive Psychiatry, 8,* 455–467.

Fowler, R. D. (1969). Automated interpretation of personality test data. In J. N. Butcher (Ed.), *MMPI: Research developments and clinical applications* (pp. 105–126). New York: McGraw-Hill.

Fowler, R. D. (1975). *A method for the evaluation of the abuse prone patient.* Paper presented at the meeting of the American Academy of Family Physicians, Chicago, IL.

Fowler, R. D. (1985). Landmarks in computer-assisted psychological assessment. *Journal of Consulting and Clinical Psychology, 53,* 748–759.

Fowler, R. D., & Butcher, J. N. (1986). Critique of Matarazzo's views on computerized testing: All signs and no meaning. *American Psychologist, 41,* 94–96.

Franklin, C. L., Repasky, S., Thompson, K. E., Shelton, S. A., & Uddo, M. (2003). Assessment of response style in combat veterans seeking compensation for posttraumatic stress disorder. *Journal of Traumatic Stress, 16,* 251–255.

Friedman, A. F. (1982). Review of extraversion and introversion: An interactional perspective by Larry W. Morris. *Journal of Personality Assessment, 46,* 185–187.

Friedman, A. F. (1990, March). MMPI-2 concerns. *The APA Monitor,* p. 2.

Friedman, A. F. (2008). Basic principles and concepts in threat assessment evaluations. In Mark A. Lies, II (Ed.), *Preventing and managing workplace violence: Legal and strategic guidelines,* American Bar Association, Chicago, IL.

Friedman, A. F., Archer, R. P., & Handel, R. W. (2005). Minnesota Multiphasic Personality Inventories (MMPI/MMPI-2, MMPI-A) and suicide. In R. Yufit and D. Lester (Eds.), *Assessment, treatment, and prevention of suicidal behavior.* Hoboken, NJ: John Wiley & Sons, Inc.

Friedman, A. F., Gleser, G. C., Smeltzer, D. J., Wakefield, J. A., Jr., & Schwartz, M. S. (1983). MMPI overlap item scales for differentiating psychotics, neurotics, and nonpsychiatric groups. *Journal of Consulting and Clinical Psychology, 51,* 629–631.

Friedman, A. F., & Jaffe, A. M. (1993). *Disability applicants' scores on the MMPI-2 converted to MMPI linear T-scores.* Unpublished manuscript.

Friedman, A. F., Lewack, R., Nichols, D. S. & Webb, J.T. (2001) *Pyschological Assessment with the MMPI-2,* Mahwah, NJ: Lawrence Erlbaum.

Friedman, A. F., Sasek, J., & Wakefield, J. A., Jr. (1976). Subjective ratings of Cattell's 16 personality factors. *Journal of Personality Assessment, 40,* 302–305.

Friedman, A. F., Wakefield, J. A., Jr., Boblitt, W. E., & Surman, G. (1976). Validity of psychoticism scale of the EPQ. *Psychological Reports, 39,* 1309–1310.

Friedman, A. F., Webb, J. T., & Lewak, R. (1989). *Psychological assessment with the MMPI.* Hillsdale, NJ: Lawrence Erlbaum Associates.

Friedman, A. F., Webb, J. T., Smeltzer, D. J., & Lewak, R. (1989). *Workbook for psychological assessment with the MMPI.* Hillsdale, NJ: Lawrence Erlbaum Associates.

Friedman, H. S., & Booth-Kewley, S. (1987). Personality, Type A behavior, and coronary heart disease: The role of emotional expression. *Journal of Personality and Social Psychology, 53,* 783–792.

Frueh, B. C., Gold, P. B., & de Arellano, M. A. (1997). Symptom overreporting in combat veterans evaluated for PTSD: Differentiation on the basis of compensation seeking status. *Journal of Personality Assessment, 68,* 369–384.

Frueh, B. C., Smith, D. W., & Barker, S. E. (1996). Compensation seeking status and psychometric assessment of combat veterans seeking treatment for PTSD. *Journal of Traumatic Stress, 9,* 427–440.

Frye v. United States. 293 F. 1013 (D.C. Cir. 1923).

Fulkerson, S. C., & Willage, D. E. (1980). Decisional ambiguity as a source of "cannot say" responses on personality questionnaires. *Journal of Personality Assessment, 44,* 381–386.

Gallagher, B. J., & Jones, D. J. (1987). The attitudes of psychiatrists toward etiological theories of schizophrenia: 1975–1985. *Journal of Clinical Psychology, 43,* 438–443.

Gallucci, N. T. (1986). General and specific objections to the MMPI. *Educational and Psychological Measurement, 46,* 985–988.

Gallucci, N. T., Kay, D. C., & Thornby, J. I. (1989). The sensitivity of 11 substance abuse scales from the MMPI to change in clinical status. *Psychology of Addictive Behaviors, 3*, 29–33.

Garcia, H. A., Kelley, L. P., Rentz, T. O., & Lee, S. (2011). Pretreatment predictors of dropout from cognitive behavioral therapy for PTSD in Iraq and Afghanistan war veterans. *Psychological Services, 8*, 1–11.

Gass, C. S., & Gonzalez, C. (2003). MMPI-2 short-form proposal: CAUTION. *Archives of Clinical Neuropsychology, 18*, 521–527.

Gass, C. S., & Luis, C. A. (2001). MMPI-2 Scale F(p) and symptom feigning: Scale refinement. *Assessment, 8*, 425–429.

Gass, C. S., Williams, C. L., Cumella, E., Butcher, J. N., & Kally, Z. (2010). Ambiguous measures of unknown constructs: The MMPI-2 Fake Bad Scale (aka Symptom Validity Scale, FBS, FBS-r). *Psychological Injury and Law, 3*, 81–85.

Gearing, M. L. (1979). The MMPI as a primary differentiator and predictor of behavior in prison: A methodological critique and review of the recent literature. *Psychological Bulletin, 86*, 929–963.

Gentry, T. A., Wakefield, J. A., Jr., & Friedman, A. F. (1985). MMPI scales for measuring Eysenck's personality factors. *Journal of Personality Assessment, 49*, 146–149.

Gervais, R. O., Ben-Porath, Y. S., & Wygant, D. B. (2009). Empirical correlates and interpretation of the MMPI-2-RF Cognitive Complaints (COG) scale. *The Clinical Neuropsychologist, 23(6)*, 996–1015.

Gervais, R. O., Ben-Porath, Y. S., Wygant, D. B., & Green, P. (2007). Development and validation of a Response Bias Scale (RBS) for the MMPI-2. *Assessment, 14(2)*, 196–208.

Gervais, R. O., Ben-Porath, Y. S., Wygant, D. B., & Green, P. (2008). Differential sensitivity of the RBS and MMPI-2 validity scales to memory complaints. *The Clinical Neuropsychologist, 22*, 1061–1079.

Gervais, R. O., Ben-Porath, Y. S., Wygant, D. B., & Sellbom, M. (2010). Incremental validity of the MMPI-2-RF over-reporting scales and RBS in assessing the veracity of memory complaints. *Archives of Clinical Neuropsychology, 25(4)*, 274–284.

Gilberstadt, H., & Duker, J. (1965). *A Handbook for clinical and actuarial MMPI interpretation.* Philadelphia, PA: W. B. Saunders.

Gilmore, J. D., Lash, S. J., Foster, M. A., & Blosser, S. L. (2001). Adherence to substance abuse treatment: Clinical utility of two MMPI-2 scales. *Journal of Personality Assessment, 77*, 524–540.

Glaros, A. G., & Kline, R. B. (1988). Understanding the accuracy of tests with cutting scores: The sensitivity, specificity, and predictive value model. *Journal of Clinical Psychology, 44*, 1013–1023.

Glassmire, D. M., Stolberg, R. A., Greene, R. L., & Bongar, B. (2001). The utility of MMPI-2 suicide items for assessing suicidal potential: Development of a suicidal potential scale. *Assessment, 8*, 281–290.

Gold, P. B., & Frueh, C. B. (1999). Compensation-seeking and extreme exaggeration of psychopathology among combat veterans evaluated for posttraumatic stress disorder. *Journal of Nervous and Mental Disease, 187*, 680–684.

Goldberg, L. R. (1965). Diagnosticians vs. diagnostic signs: The diagnosis of psychosis vs. neurosis from the MMPI. *Psychological Monographs: General & Applied, 79*, 29.

Goldberg, L. R., & Slovic, P. (1967). The importance of test item content: An analysis of a corollary of the deviation hypothesis. *Journal of Counseling Psychology, 14*, 462–472.

Gordon, R., Stoffey, R., & Perkins, B. (2013). Comparing the sensitivity of the MMPI-2 clinical scales and the MMPI-RC scales to clients rated as psychotic, borderline or neurotic on the psychodiagnostic chart. *Psychology, 4*, 12–16.

Gosling, F. G. (1987). *Before Freud: Neurasthenia and the American medical community, 1870–1910.* Urbana, IL: University of Illinois Press.

Gottesman, I. I., & Prescott, C. A. (1989). Abuses of the MacAndrew MMPI Alcoholism scale: A critical review. *Clinical Psychology Review, 9*, 223–242.

Gotts, E. E., & Knudsen, T. E. (2005). *The clinical interpretation of the MMPI 2: A content cluster approach.* Mahwah, NJ: Erlbaum.

Gough, H. G. (1948a). A new dimension of status: I. Development of a personality scale. *American Sociological Review, 13,* 401–409.

Gough, H. G. (1948b). A new dimension of status: II. Relationship of the *St* scale to other variables. *American Sociological Review, 13,* 534–537.

Gough, H. G. (1950). The F minus K dissimulation index for the Minnesota Multiphasic Personality Inventory. *Journal of Consulting Psychology, 14,* 408–413.

Gough, H. G. (1951). Studies of social intolerance: III. Relationship of the Pr scale to other variables. *Journal of Social Psychology, 33,* 257–262.

Gough, H. G. (1954). Some common misconceptions about neuroticism. *Journal of Consulting Psychology, 18,* 287–292.

Gough, H. G. (1957). *Manual for the California Psychological Inventory.* Palo Alto, CA: Consulting Psychologists Press.

Gough, H. G., & Heilbrun, A. B. (1983). *The adjective check list manual.* Palo Alto, CA: Consulting Psychologists Press.

Gough, H. G., McClosky, H., & Meehl, P. E. (1951). A personality scale for dominance. *Journal of Abnormal and Social Psychology, 46,* 360–366.

Gough, H. G., McClosky, H., & Meehl, P. E. (1952). A personality scale for social responsibility. *Journal of Abnormal and Social Psychology, 47,* 73–80.

Gough, H. G., McKee, M. G., & Yandell, R. J. (1955). *Adjective check list analyses of a number of selected psychometric and assessment variables,* Officer Education Research Laboratory (Technical Memorandum No. OERL-TM-55-10).

Graham, J. R. (1978, March). *MMPI characteristics of alcoholics, drug abusers, and pathological gamblers.* Paper presented at the 13th Annual Symposium on Recent Developments in the Use of the MMPI, Puebla, Mexico.

Graham, J. R. (1987). *The MMPI: A practical guide.* New York: Oxford University Press.

Graham, J. R. (1990). *MMPI-2: Assessing personality and psychopathology.* New York: Oxford University Press.

Graham, J. R. (1993). *MMPI-2: Assessing personality and psychopathology* (2nd ed.). New York: Oxford University Press.

Graham, J. R. (2011). *MMPI-2: Assessing personality and psychopathology, 5th Ed.* New York: Oxford University Press.

Graham, J. R., Ben-Porath, Y. S., & McNulty, J. L. (1997). Empirical correlates of low scores on MMPI-2 scales in an outpatient mental health setting. *Psychological Assessment: A Journal of Consulting and Clinical Psychology, 9,* 386–391.

Graham, J. R., Ben-Porath, Y. S., & McNulty, J. L. (1999). *MMPI-2 correlates for outpatient community mental health settings.* Minneapolis, MN: University of Minnesota Press.

Graham, J. R., & Butcher, J. N. (1988, March). *Differentiating schizophrenic and major affective disorders with the revised form of the MMPI.* Paper presented at the 23rd Annual Symposium on Recent Developments in the Use of the MMPI, St. Petersburg, FL.

Graham, J. R., & McCord, G. (1985). Interpretation of moderately elevated MMPI scores for normal subjects. *Journal of Personality Assessment, 49,* 477–484.

Graham, J. R., Schroeder, H. E., & Lilly, R. S. (1971). Factor analysis of items on the Social Introversion and Masculinity-Femininity scales of the MMPI. *Journal of Clinical Psychology, 27,* 367–370.

Graham, J. R., & Strenger, V. E. (1988). MMPI characteristics of alcoholics: A review. *Journal of Consulting and Clinical Psychology, 56,* 197–205.

Graham, J. R., Timbrook, R. E., Ben-Porath, Y. S., & Butcher, J. N. (1991). Code-type congruence between MMPI and MMPI-2: Separating fact from artifact. *Journal of Personality Assessment, 57,* 205–215.

Graham, J. R., & Tisdale, M. J. (1983, April). *Interpretation of low 5 scores for women of high educational levels*. Paper presented at the 18th Annual Symposium on Recent Developments in the Use of the MMPI, Minneapolis, MN.

Graham, J. R., Watts, D., & Timbrook, R. E. (1991). Detecting fake-good and fake-bad MMPI-2 profiles. *Journal of Personality Assessment, 57*, 264–277.

Gravitz, M. A. (1968). Normative findings for the frequency of MMPI critical items. *Journal of Clinical Psychology, 24*, 220.

Grayson, H. M. (1951). *A psychological admissions testing program and manual*. Los Angeles, CA: Veterans Administration Center, Neuropsychiatric Hospital.

Grayson, H. M., & Olinger, L. B. (1957). Simulation of "normalcy" by psychiatric patients on the MMPI. *Journal of Consulting Psychology, 21*, 73–77.

Green, B. A., Handel, R. W., & Archer, R. P. (2006). External correlates of the MMPI-2 Content Component Scales in mental health inpatients. *Assessment, 13*, 80–97.

Green, P. (2004). *Memory complaints inventory*. Edmonton, Canada: Green's Publishing.

Greenblatt, R. L., & Davis, W. E. (1999). Differential diagnosis of PTSD, schizophrenia, and depression with the MMPI-2. *Journal of Clinical Psychology, 55*, 217–223.

Greene, R. L. (1978). An empirically derived MMPI Carelessness scale. *Journal of Clinical Psychology, 34*, 407–410.

Greene, R. L. (1980). *The MMPI: An interpretive manual*. New York: Grune & Stratton.

Greene, R. L. (1982). Some reflections on "MMPI Short Forms: A Review." *Journal of Personality Assessment, 46*, 486–487.

Greene, R. L. (1985). New norms, old norms: What norms for the MMPI? [Review of the book *The MMPI: A Contemporary Normative Sample*]. *Journal of Personality Assessment, 49*, 108–110.

Greene, R. L. (1987). Ethnicity and MMPI performance: A review. *Journal of Consulting and Clinical Psychology, 55*, 497–512.

Greene R. L. (1988a). The relative efficacy of *F-K* and the obvious and subtle scales to detect overreporting of psychopathology on the MMPI. *Journal of Clinical Psychology, 44*, 152–159.

Greene, R. L. (1988b). Summary. In R. L. Greene (Ed.), *The MMPI: Use with specific populations* (pp. 316–321). Philadelphia, PA: Grune & Stratton.

Greene, R. L. (1990a, March). *The effects of age, education, gender, and specific MMPI codetypes on the MacAndrew Alcoholism scale*. Paper presented at the annual meeting of the Society for Personality Assessment, San Diego, CA.

Greene, R. L. (1990b). Stability of MMPI scales scores across four codetypes over four decades. *Journal of Personality Assessment, 55*, 1–6.

Greene, R. L. (1991a). *The MMPI/MMPI-2: An interpretive manual*. Boston, MA: Allyn & Bacon.

Greene, R. L. (1991b, July). *Some issues in assessing consistency of item endorsement on the MMPI-2*. Paper presented at the MMPI-2 Summer Institute, Colorado Springs, CO.

Greene, R. L. (1994). Relationships among MMPI codetype, gender, and setting and the MacAndrew Alcoholism scale. *Assessment, 1*, 39–46.

Greene, R. L. (2000). *The MMPI-2: An interpretive manual* (2nd ed.). Boston, MA: Allyn & Bacon.

Greene, R. L. (2011). *The MMPI-2/MMPI-2-RF: An interpretive manual*—3rd Edition. Boston, MA: Allyn & Bacon.

Greene, R. L., & Brown, R., Jr. (1990). MMPI-2 adult interpretive program [Computer Software] Lutz, FL: Psychological Assessment Resources.

Greene, R. L., & Garvin, R. D. (1988). Substance abuse/dependence. In R. L. Greene (Ed.), *The MMPI: Use with specific populations* (pp. 159–197). San Antonio, TX: Grune & Stratton.

Greene R. L., Gwin, R., & Staal, M. (1997). Current status of MMPI-2 research: A methodologic overview. *Journal of Personality Assessment, 68*, 20–36.

Greene, R. L., & Nichols, D. S. (1995). *MMPI-2 structural summary interpretive manual*. Odessa, FL: Psychological Assessment Resources.

Greene, R. L., Rouse, S. V., Butcher, J. N., Nichols, D. S., & Williams, C. L. (2009). The MMPI-2 Restructured Clinical (RC) Scales and redundancy: Response to Tellegen, Ben-Porath, and Sellbom. *Journal of Personality Assessment, 91*, 222–226.

Greene, R. L., Weed, N. C., Butcher, J. N., Arredondo, R., & Davis, H. G. (1992). A cross-validation of MMPI-2 substance abuse scales. *Journal of Personality Assessment, 58*, 405–410.

Greenfield, N. S., Alexander, A. A., & Roessler, R. (1963). Ego strength and physiological responsivity: II. The relationship between the Barron Ego Strength scale to the temporal and recovery characteristics of skin resistance, finger blood volume, heart rate, and muscle potential responses to sound. *Archives of General Psychiatry, 9*, 129–141.

Greenfield, N. S., Roessler, R., & Crosley, A. P. (1959). Ego strength and length of recovery from infectious mononucleosis. *The Journal of Nervous and Mental Disease, 128*, 125–128.

Greiffenstein, M. F., Fox, D., & Lees-Haley, P. R. (2007). The MMPI-2 Fake Bad Scale in detection of noncredible brain injury claims. In K. B. Boone (Ed.), *Assessment of feigned cognitive impairment: A neuropsychological perspective* (pp. 210–235). New York: Guilford Press.

Greist, J. H., Klein, M. H., Erdman, H. P., & Jefferson, J. W. (1983). Computers and psychiatric diagnosis. *Psychiatric Annals, 13*, 785–792.

Greve, K. W., & Bianchini, K. J. (2004). Response to Butcher et al., The construct validity of the Lees-Haley Fake-Bad Scale. *Archives of Clinical Neuropsychology, 19*, 337–339.

Gripshover, D. L., & Dacey, C. M. (1994). Discriminative validity of the MacAndrew Scale in settings with a high base rate of substance abuse. *Journal of Studies on Alcohol, 55*, 303–308.

Gross, K. (2002). The incremental validity of the MMPI-2 and demographic variables in assessing major depression (Doctoral dissertation, Pacific Graduate School of Psychology). *Dissertation Abstracts International, 62(12-B)*, 5963.

Gross, K., Keyes, M. D., & Greene, R. L. (2000). Assessing depression with the MMPI and MMPI-2. *Journal of Personality Assessment, 75*, 464–477.

Groth-Marnat, G. (2009). *Handbook of psychological assessment* (5th ed.). Hoboken, NJ: John Wiley & Sons, Inc.

Grove, W. M., & Meehl, P. E. (1996). Comparative efficiency of informal (subjective, impressionistic) and formal (mechanical, algorithmic) prediction procedures: The clinical statistical controversy. *Psychology, Public Policy and Law, 2*, 293–323.

Grove, W. M., Zald, D. H., Lebow, B. S., Snitz, B. E., & Nelson, C. (2000). Clinical versus mechanical prediction: A meta-analysis. *Psychological Assessment, 12(1)*, 19–30.

Grubaugh, A. L., Elhai, J. D., Monnier, J., & Frueh, B. C. (2004). Service utilization among compensation-seeking veterans. *Psychiatric Quarterly, 75*, 333–341.

Guastello, S. J., & Rieke, M. L. (1990). The Barnum effect and validity of computer-based test interpretations: The human resource development report. *Psychological Assessment: A Journal of Consulting and Clinical Psychology, 2*, 186–190.

Gucker, D. K., Kreuch, T., & Butcher, J. N. (2009, March). *Insensitivity of the MMPI-2 Restructured Clinical (RC) scales.* Chicago, IL: Society for Personality Assessment.

Guéz, M., Brännström, R., Nyberg, L., Toolanen, G., & Hildingsson, C. (2005). Neuropsychological Functioning and MMPI-2 profiles in chronic neck pain: A comparison of whiplash and nontraumatic groups. *Journal of Clinical and Experimental Neuropsychology, 27*, 151–163.

Guilford, J. P. (1936). *Psychometric methods.* New York: McGraw-Hill.

Gulas, I. (1973). MMPI-2 point codes for a "normal" college population: A replication study. *Journal of Psychology, 84*, 319–322.

Gynther, M. D. (1979). Aging and personality: An update. In J. N. Butcher (Ed.), *New developments in the use of the MMPI* (pp. 39–68). Minneapolis, MN: University of Minnesota Press.

Haas, G., & Saborio, C. (2012, March). *The psychological functioning of sexually assaulted women through the MMPI-2 and Restructured Clinical Scales.* Chicago, IL: Society for Personality Assessment.

Hall, G., Bansal, A., & Lopez, I. R. (1999). Ethnicity and psychopathology: A meta-analytic review of 31 years of comparative MMPI/MMPI-2 research. *Psychological Assessment, 11(2)*, 186–197.

Halligan, P. W., Bass, C., Marshall, J. C. (2001). *Contemporary approaches to the study of hysteria: Clinical and theoretical perspectives.* New York: Oxford University Press.

Hampton, P. J. (1951). A psychometric study of drinkers. *Journal of Psychology, 15*, 501–504.

Han, K., Weed, N. C., Calhoun, R. F., & Butcher, J. N. (1995). Psychometric characteristics of the MMPI—2 Cook-Medley Hostility Scale. *Journal of Personality Assessment, 65*, 567–585.

Handel, R. W., & Archer, R. P. (2008). An investigation of the psychometric properties of the MMPI-2 Restructured Clinical (RC) Scales with mental health inpatients. *Journal of Personality Assessment, 90*, 239–249.

Handel, R. W., Ben-Porath, Y. S., Tellegen, A., & Archer, R. P. (2010). Psychometric functioning of the MMPI-2-RF VRIN-r and TRIN-r scales with varying degrees of randomness, acquiescence, and counter-acquiescence. *Psychological Assessment, 22(1)*, 87–95.

Hanvik, L. (1949). *Some psychological dimensions of low back pain.* Unpublished doctoral dissertation, University of Minnesota, Minneapolis.

Hare, R. (1991). *Manual for the revised psychopathy checklist.* Toronto, Canada: Multi-Health Systems.

Harkness, A. R. (1990). Phenotypic dimensions of the personality disorders (Doctoral dissertation, University of Minnesota, 1989). *Dissertation Abstracts International, 50(12B)*, 5880B.

Harkness, A. R., Finn, J. A., McNulty, J. L., & Shields, S. M. (2012). The Personality Psychopathology–Five (PSY–5): Recent constructive replication and assessment literature review. *Psychological Assessment, 24(2)*, 432–443.

Harkness, A. R., Levenson, M. R., Butcher, J. N., Spiro, A., Ben-Porath, Y. S., & Crumpler, C. A. (1995, March). *Drinking and personality: MMPI-2 PSY-5 scales in the Boston VA's Normative Aging Study.* Paper presented at the 30th Annual MMPI-2 and MMPI-A Symposia, St. Petersburg, FL.

Harkness, A. R., & McNulty, J. L. (1994). The Personality Psychopathology Five (PSY-5): Issue from the pages of a diagnostic manual instead of a dictionary. In S. Strack & M. Lorr (Eds.), *Differentiating normal and abnormal personality* (pp. 291–315). New York: Springer.

Harkness, A. R., & McNulty, J. L. (2007, August). *Restructured version of the MMPI-2 Personality Psychopathology Five (PSY–5) Scale.* Paper presented at the meeting of the American Psychological Association, San Francisco, CA.

Harkness, A. R., McNulty, J. L., & Ben-Porath, Y. S. (1995). The Personality Psychopathology Five (PSY–5): Constructs and MMPI-2 scales. *Psychological Assessment: A Journal of Consulting and Clinical Psychology, 7*, 104–114.

Harkness, A. R., Spiro, A., Butcher, J. N., & Ben-Porath, Y. S. (1995). *Personality Psychopathology Five (PSY-5) in the Boston VA Normative Aging Study.* Paper presented at the 103rd Annual Convention of the American Psychological Association, New York, NY

Harrell, T H., Honaker, L. M., & Parnell, T. (1992). Equivalence of the MMPI-2 with the MMPI in psychiatric patients. *Psychological Assessment: A Journal of Consulting and Clinical Psychology, 4*, 460–465.

Harris, R. E., & Lingoes, J. C. (1955). Subscales for the Minnesota Multiphasic Personality Inventory: An aid to profile interpretation. (Mimeographed materials.) San Francisco, CA: University of California, Langley Porter Neuropsychiatric Institute.

Harris, R. E., & Lingoes, J. C. (1968). *Subscales for the Minnesota Multiphasic Personality Inventory: An aid to profile interpretation* (Rev. ed.). (Mimeographed materials.) San Francisco, CA: University of California, Langley Porter Neuropsychiatric Institute.

Hartshorne, H., & May, M. A. (1928). *Studies in deceit.* New York: Macmillan.

Hase, H. D., & Goldberg, L. R. (1967). Comparative validity of different strategies of constructing personality inventory scales. *Psychological Bulletin, 67*, 231–248.

Hathaway, S. R. (1939). The personality inventory as an aid in the diagnosis of psychopathic inferiors. *Journal of Consulting Psychology, 3*, 112–117.

Hathaway, S. R. (1947). A coding system for MMPI profiles. *Journal of Consulting Psychology, 11*, 334–337.

Hathaway, S. R. (1956). Scales 5 (masculinity-femininity), 6 (paranoia), and 8 (schizophrenia). In G. S. Welsh & W. G. Dahlstrom (Eds.), *Basic readings on the MMPI in psychology and medicine* (pp. 104–111). Minneapolis, MN: University of Minnesota Press.

Hathaway, S. R. (1964). MMPI: Professional use by professional people. *American Psychologist, 19*, 204–210.

Hathaway, S. R. (1965). Personality inventories. In B. B. Wolman (Ed.), *Handbook of clinical psychology* (pp. 451–476). New York: McGraw-Hill.

Hathaway, S. R. (1980). Scales 5 (Masculinity-Femininity), 6 (Paranoia), and 8 (Schizophrenia). In W. G. Dahlstrom & L. Dahlstrom (Eds.), *Basic readings on the MMPI: A new selection on personality measurement* (pp. 65–75). Minneapolis, MN: University of Minnesota Press. (Original work published 1956.)

Hathaway, S. R., & Briggs, P. F. (1957). Some normative data on new MMPI scales. *Journal of Clinical Psychology, 131*, 364–368.

Hathaway, S. R., & McKinley, J. C. (1940). A multiphasic personality schedule (Minnesota): I. Construction of the schedule. *Journal of Psychology, 10*, 249–254.

Hathaway, S. R., & McKinley, J. C. (1942). A multiphasic personality schedule (Minnesota): III. The measurement of symptomatic depression. *Journal of Psychology, 14*, 73–84.

Hathaway, S. R., & McKinley, J. C. (1943). *The Minnesota Multiphasic Personality Inventory Manual.* Minneapolis, MN: University of Minnesota Press.

Hathaway, S. R., & McKinley, J. C. (1983). *The Minnesota Multiphasic Personality Inventory Manual* (Rev. ed.). New York: Psychological Corporation.

Hathaway, S. R., & Meehl, P. E. (1944). An atlas for the clinical use of the MMPI. Minneapolis, University of Minnesota Press. *Journal of Applied Psychology, 28*, 153–174.

Hathaway, S. R., & Meehl, P. E. (1951). *An atlas for the clinical use of the MMPI.* Minneapolis, MN: University of Minnesota Press.

Hathaway, S. R., & Meehl, P. E. (1952). Adjective check list correlates of MMPI scores. Unpublished materials.

Health Insurance Portability and Accountability Act of 1996, 42 U.S.C. § 1320d-9 (2010).

Hearn, M. D., Murray, D. M., & Luepker, R. V. (1989). Hostility, coronary heart disease, and total mortality: A 33-year follow-up study of university students. *Journal of Behavioral Medicine, 12*, 105–121.

Heaton, R., Grant, L., & Matthews, C. (1991). *Comprehensive norms for an expanded Halstead-Reitan Battery.* Odessa, FL: Psychological Assessment Resources.

Hedlund, J. L. (1977). MMPI clinical scale correlates. *Journal of Consulting and Clinical Psychology, 45*, 739–750.

Hedlund, J. L., & Won Cho, D. (1979). [MMPI data research tape for Missouri Department of Mental Health Patients.] Unpublished raw data.

Helmes, E., & Reddon, J. R. (1993). A perspective on developments in assessing psychopathology: A critical review of the MMPI and MMPI-2. *Psychological Bulletin, 113*, 453–471.

Hjemboe, S., Butcher, J. N., & Almagor, M. (1992). Empirical assessment of marital distress: The Marital Distress scale (MDS) for the MMPI-2. In C. D. Spielberger & J. N. Butcher (Eds.), *Advances in personality assessment* (Vol. 9, pp. 141–152). Hillsdale, NJ: Lawrence Erlbaum Associates.

Hoffman, G. A., & Pietrzak, D. R. (2012). Nonclinical correlates of the MMPI-2 Supplementary Scales using the Adjective Check List. *The International Journal of Educational and Psychological Assessment, 11*, 77–107.

Hoffmann, H., Loper, R. G., & Kammeier, M. L. (1974). Identifying future alcoholics with MMPI alcoholism scales. *Quarterly Journal of Studies on Alcohol, 35,* 490–498.

Hollrah, J. L., Schlottmann, R. S., Scott, A. B., & Brunetti, D. G. (1995). Validity of the MMPI subtle items. *Journal of Personality Assessment, 65,* 278–299.

Holmes, T. H., & Rahe, R. H. (1967). The Social Readjustment Rating Scale. *Journal of Psychosomatic Research, 77,* 213–218.

Holmes, W. O. (1953). *The development of an empirical MMPI scale for addiction.* Unpublished manuscript, San Jose State College, San Jose, CA.

Holroyd, R. G. (1964). Prediction of defensive paranoid schizophrenics using the MMPI (Doctoral dissertation, University of Minnesota). *Dissertation Abstracts, 25,* 2048.

Hovey, H. B., & Lewis, E. G. (1967). Semiautomatic interpretation of the MMPI. *Journal of Clinical Psychology, 23,* 123–134.

Hoyt, D. P., & Sedlacek, G. M. (1958). Differentiating alcoholics from normals and abnormals with the MMPI. *Journal of Clinical Psychology, 14,* 69–74.

Huber, N. A., & Danahy, S. (1975). Use of the MMPI in predicting completion and evaluating changes in a long-term alcoholism treatment program. *Journal of Studies on Alcohol, 36,* 1230–1237.

Humm, D. G., & Wadsworth, G. W., Jr. (1935). The Humm-Wadsworth Temperament Survey. *American Journal of Psychiatry, 92,* 163–200.

Humphrey, D. H., & Dahlstrom, W. G. (1995). The impact of changing from the MMPI to the MMPI-2 of profile configurations. *Journal of Personality Assessment, 64,* 428–439.

Humphrey, M. D. (1999). A structural analysis of personality factors and their causal relationships with drinking problems (Kent State University). *Dissertation Abstracts International, 59(7-B),* 3754.

Hungerford, L. (2004). Clinical correlates of high scale 2 (D) and low scale 9 (Ma) on the MMPI-2 (Doctoral dissertation, Pacific Graduate School of Psychology). *Dissertation Abstracts International, 65(4-B),* 2095.

Hunsley, J., Hanson, R. K., & Parker, C. H. K. (1988). A summary of the reliability and stability of MMPI scales. *Journal of Clinical Psychology, 44,* 44–46.

Hunt, H. (1948). The effect of deliberate deception on MMPI performance. *Journal of Consulting Psychology, 12,* 396–402.

Hutton, H. E., Miner, M. H., Blades, J. R., & Langfeldt, V. C. (1992). Ethnic differences on the MMPI Overcontrolled-Hostility Scale. *Journal of Personality Assessment, 58,* 260–268.

Ihilevich, D., & Gleser, G. C. (1986). *Defense mechanisms: Their classification, correlates, and measurement with the Defense Mechanism Inventory.* Owasso, MI: DMI.

Ihilevich, D., & Gleser, G. C. (1991). *Defenses in psychotherapy: The clinical application of the Defense Mechanism Inventory.* Owosso, MI: DMI.

Ingram, P. B., Kelso, K. M., & McCord, D. M. (2011). Empirical correlates and expanded interpretation of the MMPI-2-RF Restructured Clinical Scale 3 (Cynicism). *Assessment, 18,* 95–101.

Iverson, G. L., & Barton, E. (1999). Interscorer reliability of the MMPI-2: Should *TRIN* and *VRIN* be computer scored? *Journal of Clinical Psychology, 55,* 65–69.

Iverson, G., Franzen, M., & Hammond, J. (1993, August). *Examination of inmates' ability to malinger on the MMPI-2.* Poster session presented at the 101st Annual Convention of the American Psychological Association, Toronto, Ontario, Canada.

Iverson, G. L., Henrichs, T. F., Barton, E. A., & Allen, S. (2002). Specificity of the MMPI-2 Fake Bad Scale as a marker for personal injury malingering. *Psychological Reports, 90,* 131–136.

Jackson, D. N. (1971). The dynamics of personality tests. *Psychological Review, 78,* 239–248.

Jaffe, A. M. (1992). Psychoanalytic approach to addictive disorders. In C. E. Stout, J. C. Levitt, & D. H. Ruben (Eds.), *Handbook for assessing and treating addictive disorders* (pp. 41–57). Westport, CT: Greenwood.

Jaffe, A. M., & Jaffe, K. L. (1992). Countertransference in the treatment of addictive disorders. In C. E. Stout, J. L. Levitt, & D. H. Ruben (Eds.), *Handbook for assessing and treating addictive disorders* (pp. 301–311). Westport, CT: Greenwood.

Jenkins, C. D., Rosenman, R. H., & Friedman, M. (1967). Development of an objective psychological test for the determination of the coronary-prone behavior pattern in employed men. *Journal of Chronic Disease, 20,* 371–379.

Jenkins, W. L. (1952). The MMPI applied to the problem of prognosis in schizophrenia (Doctoral dissertation, University of Minnesota). *Dissertation Abstracts, 72,* 381.

Jensen, S. (2004). Descriptive and developmental characteristics of chronically overcontrolled hostile women offenders (The Florida State University). *Dissertation Abstracts International, 64(10-B),* 5220.

Johnson, J. H., Butcher, J. N., Null, C., & Johnson, K. N. (1984). Replicated item level factor analysis of the full MMPI. *Journal of Personality and Social Psychology, 47(1),* 105–114.

Johnson, M. E., Jones, G., & Brems, C. (1996). Concurrent validity of the MMPI-2 feminine gender role (GF) and masculine gender role (GM) scales. *Journal of Personality Assessment, 66,* 153–168.

Jones, A., Ingram, M. V., & Ben-Porath, Y. S. (2012). Scores on the MMPI-2-RF Scales as a function of increasing levels of failure on cognitive symptom validity tests in a military sample. *The Clinical Neuropsychologist, 26,* 790–815.

Kahneman, D., & Tversky, A. (1973). On the psychology of prediction. *Psychological Review, 80,* 237–251.

Katz, M. M. (1968). A phenomenological typology of schizophrenia. In M. M. Katz, J. O. Cole, & W. E. Barton (Eds.), *The role and methodology of classification in psychiatry and psychopathology* (PHS Publication No. 1584, pp. 300–320). Washington, DC: U.S. Government Printing Office.

Kawachi, I., Sparrow, D., Kubzansky, L. D., Spiro, A., Vokonas, P. S., & Weiss, S. T. (1998). Prospective study of a self-report Type A scale and risk of coronary heart disease: Test of the MMPI-2 Type A scale. *Circulation, 98,* 405–412.

Kawachi, I., Sparrow, D., Spiro, A., Vokonas, P. S., & Weiss, S. T. (1996). A prospective study of anger and coronary heart disease: The Normative Aging Study. *Circulation, 94,* 2090–2095.

Keane, S. P., & Gibbs, M. (1980). Construct validation of the Sc scale of the MMPI. *Journal of Clinical Psychology, 36,* 152–158.

Keane, T. M., Malloy, P. F., & Fairbank, J. A. (1984). Empirical development of an MMPI subscale for the assessment of combat-related posttraumatic stress disorder. *Journal of Consulting and Clinical Psychology, 52,* 888–891.

Keiller, S. W., & Graham, J. R. (1993). The meaning of low scores on MMPI-2 clinical scales of normal subjects. *Journal of Personality Assessment, 61,* 211–223.

Kendrick, S., & Hatzenbuehler, L. (1982). The effect of oral administration by a live examiner on the MMPI: A split-half design. *Journal of Clinical Psychology, 38,* 788–792.

Kimlicka, T. M., Sheppard, P. L., Wakefield, J. A., & Cross, H. J. (1987). Relationship between psychological androgyny and self-actualization tendencies. *Psychological Reports, 61,* 443–446.

Kimlicka, T. M., Wakefield, J. A., & Friedman, A. F. (1980). Comparison of factors from the Bem Sex-Role Inventory for male and female college students. *Psychological Reports, 46,* 1011–1017.

Kimlicka, T. M., Wakefield, J. A., & Goad, N. A. (1982). Sex-roles of ideal opposite sexed persons for college males and females. *Journal of Personality Assessment, 46,* 519–521.

Kleinmuntz, B. (1960). Identification of maladjusted college students. *Journal of Counseling Psychology, 7,* 209–211.

Kleinmuntz, B. (1961a). The College Maladjustment scale (*Mt*): Norms and predictive validity. *Educational and Psychological Measurement, 21,* 1029–1033.

Kleinmuntz, B. (1961b). Screening: Identification or prediction? *Journal of Counseling Psychology, 8,* 279–280.

Knowles, E. E., & Schroeder, D. A. (1990). Concurrent validation of the MacAndrew Alcoholism scale. *Journal of Studies on Alcohol, 51*, 257–262.

Kohvtek, K. J. (1992a). The location of items of the Wiggins content scales on the MMPI-2. *Journal of Clinical Psychology, 48*, 617–620.

Kohvtek, K. J. (1992b). Wiggins content scales and the MMPI-2. *Journal of Clinical Psychology, 48*, 215–218.

Koss, M. P. (1979). MMPI item content: Recurring issues. In J. N. Butcher (Ed.), *New development in the use of the MMPI* (pp. 3–38). Minneapolis, MN: University of Minnesota Press.

Koss, M. P., & Butcher, J. N. (1973). A comparison of psychiatric patients' self-report with other sources of clinical information. *Journal of Research in Personality, 7*, 225–236.

Koss, M. P., Butcher, J. N., & Hoffmann, N. (1976). The MMPI critical items: How well do they work? *Journal of Consulting and Clinical Psychology, 44*, 921–928.

Kotjahasan, Y. (2005). The TRT as a predictor of attrition from therapeutic services at a youth program (Doctoral dissertation, Carlos Albizu University). *Dissertation Abstracts International, 65(10-B)*, 5407.

Kraepelin, E. (1893). *Psychiatrie* (4th ed.). Leipzig, Germany: Abel.

Kraepelin, E. (1919). *Dementia praecox and paraphrenia*. Edinburg, NY: Churchill Livingstone.

Kranitz, L. (1972). Alcoholics, heroin addicts and nonaddicts: Comparisons on the MacAndrew Alcoholism scale of the MMPI. *Quarterly Journal of Studies on Alcohol, 33*, 807–809.

Krishnamurthy, R., Archer, R. P., & Huddleston, E. N. (1995). Clinical research note on psychometric limitations of two Harris-Lingoes subscales for the MMPI-2. *Assessment, 2*, 301–304.

Krueger, R. F., Eaton, N. R., Clark, L. A., Watson, D., Markon, K. E., Derringer, J., Skodol, A., & Livesley, W. J. (2011). Deriving an empirical structure of personality pathology for DSM-5. *Journal of Personality Disorders, 25*, 170–191.

Kruyen, P. M., Emons, W. H. M., & Sijtsma, K. (2012). Test length and decision quality in personnel selection: When is short too short? *International Journal of Testing, 12*, 321–344.

Kunce, J., & Anderson, W. (1976). Normalizing the MMPI. *Journal of Clinical Psychology, 32*, 776–780.

Kunce, J., & Anderson, W. (1984). Perspectives on uses of the MMPI in nonpsychiatric settings. In P. McReynolds & G. J. Chelvne (Eds.), *Advances in psychological assessment* (Vol. 6, pp. 41–76). San Francisco, CA: Jossey-Bass.

Kwapil, T. R., Chapman, L. J., & Chapman, J. (1999). Validity and usefulness of the Wisconsin Manual for assessing psychotic-like experiences. *Schizophrenia Bulletin, 25*, 363–375.

Lachar, D. (1974). *The MMPI: Clinical assessment and automated interpretation*. Los Angeles, CA: Western Psychological Services.

Lachar, D., & Alexander, R. S. (1978). Veridicality of self-report: Replicated correlates of the Wiggins MMPI content scales. *Journal of Consulting and Clinical Psychology, 46*, 1349–1356.

Lachar, D., Berman, W., Grisell, J. L., & Schoof, K. (1976). The MacAndrew Alcoholism scale as a general measure of substance abuse. *Journal of Studies on Alcohol, 37*, 1609–1615.

Lachar, D., Dahlstrom, W. G., & Moreland, K. L. (1986). Relationship of ethnic background and other demographic characteristics to MMPI patterns in psychiatric samples. In W. G. Dahlstrom, D. Lachar, & L. E. Dahlstrom (Eds.), *MMPI patterns of American minorities* (pp. 139–187). Minneapolis, MN: University of Minnesota Press.

Lachar, D., & Wrobel, T. A. (1979). Validating clinicians' hunches: Construction of a new MMPI critical item set. *Journal of Consulting and Clinical Psychology, 47*, 1349–1356.

Ladd, J. S. (1998). The *F(p)* Infrequency-Psychopathology scale with chemically dependent inpatients. *Journal of Clinical Psychology, 54*, 665–671.

Lamb, D. G., Berry, D. T. R., Wetter, M. W., & Baer, R. A. (1994). Effects of two types of information on malingering of closed head injury on the MMPI-2: An analog investigation. *Psychological Assessment: A Journal of Consulting and Clinical Psychology, 6*, 8–13.

Landis, C., & Katz, S. E. (1934). The validity of certain questions which purport to measure neurotic tendencies. *Journal of Applied Psychology, 8,* 343–356.

Landis, C., Zubin, J., & Katz, S. E. (1935). Empirical evaluation of three personality adjustment inventories. *Journal of Educational Psychology, 26,* 321–330.

Lane, J. B., & Lachar, D. (1979). Correlates of broad MMPI categories. *Journal of Clinical Psychology, 35,* 560–566.

Lane, P. J., & Kling, J. S. (1979). Construct validation of the Overcontrolled Hostility scale of the MMPI. *Journal of Consulting and Clinical Psychology, 47,* 781–782.

Lanyon, R. I. (1968). *A handbook of MMPI group profiles.* Minneapolis, MN: University of Minnesota Press.

Lanyon, R. I., Dannebaum, S. E., Wolf, L. I., & Brown, A. (1989). Dimensions of deceptive responding in criminal offenders. *Psychological Assessment: A Journal of Consulting and Clinical Psychology, 1,* 300–304.

Larrabee, G. (1998). Somatic malingering on the MMPI and MMPI-2 in personal injury litigants. *The Clinical Neuropsychologist, 12,* 179–188.

Larrabee, G. J. (2003). Detection of symptom exaggeration with the MMPI-2 in litigants with malingered neurocognitive dysfunction. *The Clinical Neuropsychologist, 17(1),* 54–68.

Lawton, M. P., & Kleban, M. H. (1965). Prisoners' faking on the MMPI. *Journal of Clinical Psychology, 27,* 269–271.

Leary, T. (1956). *Multilevel measurement of interpersonal behavior.* Berkeley, CA: Psychological Consultation Service.

Leary, T. (1957). *Interpersonal diagnosis of personality.* New York: Ronald Press.

Leboyer, M., Henry, C., Paillere-Martinot, M. L., & Bellivier, F. (2005). Age at onset in bipolar affective disorders: A review. *Bipolar Disorders, 7,* 111–118.

Lee, T. T. C., Graham, J. R., Sellbom, M., & Gervais, R. O. (2012). Examining the potential for gender bias in the prediction of non-credible responding by MMPI-2 Symptom Validity (FBS) Scale Scores. *Psychological Assessment, 24,* 618–627.

Lee v. Northwestern University: Case No. 10 C 1157, 2012, WL 1899329 (N. D. ILL May 24, 2012).

Lees-Haley, P. R. (1988). Litigation Response Syndrome. *American Journal of Forensic Psychology, 6,* 3–12.

Lees-Haley, P. R. (1992). Efficacy of MMPI-2 validity scales and MCMI-II modifier scales for detecting spurious PTSD claims: F, F-K, Fake Bad scale, Ego Strength, Subtle-Obvious subscales, DIS, and DEB. *Journal of Clinical Psychology, 48,* 681–689.

Lees-Haley, P. R., English L.T., & Glenn, W. J. (1991). A Fake Bad Scale on the MMPI-2 for personal injury claimants. *Psychological Reports, 68,* 203–210.

Leiker, M., & Hailey, B. J. (1988). A link between hostility and disease: Poor health habits? *Behavioral Medicine, 14,* 129–133.

Leon, G. R., Finn, S. E., Murray, D., & Bailey, J. M. (1988). Inability to predict cardiovascular disease from hostility scores or MMPI items related to Type A behavior. *Journal of Consulting and Clinical Psychology, 56,* 597–600.

Leon, G. R., Finn, S. E., Murray, D., & Bailey, J. M. (1990). "Inability to predict cardiovascular disease from hostility scores or MMPI items related to Type A behavior": Correction to Leon et al. *Journal of Consulting and Clinical Psychology, 58,* 553.

Leonard, C. V. (1977). The MMPI as a suicide predictor. *Journal of Consulting and Clinical Psychology, 45,* 367–377.

Levak, R. W., Siegel, L., Nichols, D. S., & Stolberg, R. A. (2011). *Therapeutic feedback with the MMPI-2: A positive psychology approach.* New York: Routledge.

Levinson, M. R., Aldwin, C. M., Butcher, J. N., de Labry, L., Workman-Daniels, K., & Bosse, R. (1990). The MAC scale in a normal population: The meaning of "false positives." *Journal of Studies on Alcohol, 51,* 457–462.

Levitt, E. E. (1989). *The clinical application of MMPI special scales.* Hillsdale, NJ: Lawrence Erlbaum Associates.

Levitt, E. E. (1990). A structural analysis of the impact of MMPI-2 on MMPI-1. *Journal of Personality Assessment, 55,* 562–577.

Lewak, R. (1993, March). *Low scores on Scale 6: A case history.* Paper presented at the annual convention of the Society of Personality Assessment, San Francisco, CA

Lewak, R. W., Marks, P. A., & Nelson, G. E. (1990). *Therapist guide to the MMPI and MMPI-2: Providing feedback and treatment.* Muncie, IN: Accelerated Development.

Lewis, J. L., Simcox, A. M., & Berry, D. T. R. (2002). Screening for feigned psychiatric symptoms in a forensic sample by using the MMPI-2 and the structured inventory of malingered symptomatology. *Psychological Assessment, 14(2),* 170–176.

Lilienfeld, S. O. (1996). The MMPI—2 Antisocial Practices Content Scale: Construct validity and comparison with the Psychopathic Deviate Scale. *Psychological Assessment, 8,* 281–293.

Lilienfeld, S. O. (1999). The relation of the MMPI-*2 Pd* Harris-Lingoes subscales to psychopathy, psychopathy facets, and antisocial behavior: Implications for clinical practice. *Journal of Clinical Psychology, 55,* 241–255.

Limbaugh-Kirker v. Dicosta, Case No. Ca 000706, 2/10/09, Transcript Ft. Meyers, FL.

Little, J. W. (1949). *An analysis of the MMPI.* Unpublished master's thesis, University of North Carolina, Chapel Hill, NC.

Little, K. B., & Fisher, J. (1958). Two new experimental scales of the MMPI. *Journal of Consulting Psychology, 22,* 305–306.

Litz, B. T., Orsillo, S. M., Friedman, M., Ehlich, P., & Batres, A. (1997). Posttraumatic stress disorder associated with peacekeeping duty in Somalia for U.S. military personnel. *American Journal of Psychiatry, 154,* 178–184.

Locke, D. C., Kirlin, K. A., Thomas, M. L., Osborne, D., Hurst, D. F., Drazkowski, J. F., Sirven, J. I., & Noe, K. H. (2010). The Minnesota Multiphasic Personality Inventory-2-Restructured Form in the epilepsy monitoring unit. *Epilepsy & Behavior, 17(2),* 252–258.

Long, K. A., & Graham, J. R. (1991). The Masculinity-Femininity scale of MMPI-2: Is it useful with normal men? *Journal of Personality Assessment, 57,* 46–51.

Lubin, B., Larsen, R. M., & Matarazzo, J. (1984). Patterns of psychological test usage in the United States 1935–1982. *American Psychologist, 39,* 451–454.

Lubin, B., Larsen, R. M., Matarazzo, J. D., & Seever, M. F. (1985). Psychological test usage patterns in five professional settings. *American Psychologist, 40,* 857–861.

Lucio, E., & Reyes-Lagunes, I. (1994). MMPI-2 for Mexico: Translation and adaptation. *Journal of Personality Assessment, 63,* 105–116.

MacAndrew, C. (1965). The differentiation of male alcoholic outpatients from nonalcoholic psychiatric patients by means of the MMPI. *Quarterly Journal of Studies on Alcohol, 26,* 238–246.

MacAndrew, C. (1981). What the MAC scale tells us about men alcoholics: An interpretive review. *Journal of Studies on Alcohol, 42,* 604–625.

Maiello, L., Salviati, M., De'Fornari, M. A. C., Del Casale, A., Rreli, A., Rusconi, A. C., & Piccione, M. (2007). Psicoterapia Breve: Valutazione con test MMPI-2 e scala VGF di esperienze individuali e di gruppo [Brief psychotherapy: Evaluation of individual and group experiences with the MMPI-2 test and GAF scale]. *Rivista di Psichiatria, 42,* 247–254.

Maloney, M. P., & Ward, M. P. (1976). *Psychological assessment: a conceptual approach.* New York: Oxford University Press.

Marion, B. E., Sellbom, M., & Bagby, R. (2011). The detection of feigned psychiatric disorders using the MMPI-2-RF over-reporting validity scales: An analog investigation. *Psychological Injury and Law, 4(1),* 1–12.

Marks, P. A., & Seeman, W. (1963). *The actuarial description of abnormal personality: An atlas for use with the MMPI.* Baltimore, MD: Williams & Wilkins.

Marks, P. A., Seeman, W., & Haller, D. (1974). *The actuarial use of the MMPI with adolescents and adults.* Baltimore, MD: Williams & Wilkins.

Marshall, M. B., & Bagby, R. M. (2006). The incremental validity and clinical utility of the MMPI-2 Infrequency Posttraumatic Stress Disorder Scale. *Assessment, 13*, 417–429.

Martin, E. H. (1993). *Masculinity-femininity and the MMPI-2.* Unpublished doctoral dissertation, University of Texas, Austin.

Martin, E. H., & Finn, S. E. (1992). *Masculinity-femininity and the MMPI-2.* Unpublished manuscript.

Martin, H., & Finn, S. E. (2010). *Masculinity and femininity in the MMPI-2 and MMPI-A.* Minneapolis, MN: University of Minnesota Press.

Matarazzo, J. D. (1955). MMPI validity scores as a function of increasing levels of anxiety. *Journal of Consulting Psychology, 19*, 213–217.

Matarazzo, J. D. (1986). Computerized psychological test interpretations: Unvalidated plus all mean and no sigma. *American Psychologist, 41*, 14–24.

Mattson, C., Powers, B., Halfaker, D., Akeson, S., & Ben-Porath, Y. (2012). Predicting drug court treatment completion using the MMPI-2-RF. *Psychological Assessment, 24(4),* 937–943.

Matz, P. A., Altepeter, T. S., & Perlman, B. (1992). MMPI-2: Reliability with college students. *Journal of Clinical Psychology, 48*, 330–334.

McCrae, R. R., Costa, P. T., Dahlstrom, W. G., Barefoot, J. C., Siegler, I. C., & Williams, R. B. (1989). A caution on the use of the MMPI K-correction in research on psychosomatic medicine. *Psychosomatic Medicine, 51*, 58–65.

McCranie, E. W., Watkins, L. O., Brandsma, J. M., & Sisson, B. D. (1986). Hostility, coronary heart disease (CHD) incidence, and total mortality: Lack of association in a 25-year follow-up study of 478 physicians. *Journal of Behavioral Medicine, 9*, 119–125.

McGrath, R. E., Powis, D., & Pogge, D. L. (1998). Code type-specific tables for interpretation of MMPI-2 Harris and Lingoes subscales: Consideration of gender and code type definition. *Journal of Clinical Psychology, 54*, 655–664.

McGrath, R. E., Rashid, T., Hayman, J., & Pogge, D. L. (2002). A comparison of MMPI-2 high-point coding strategies. *Journal of Personality Assessment 79(2):* 243–56.

McGrath, R. E., Terranova, R., Pogge, D. L., & Kravic, C. (2003). Development of a short form for the MMPI-2 based on scale elevation congruence. *Assessment,* 10/1, (13–28), 1073–1911.

McKenna, T., & Butcher, J. N. (1987, May). *Continuity of the MMPI with alcoholics.* Paper presented at the 22rd Annual Symposium on Recent Developments in the Use of the MMPI, Seattle, WA.

McKinley, J. C. (Ed.). (1944). *An outline of neuropsychiatry.* St. Louis, MO: John S. Swift.

McKinley, J. C., & Hathaway, S. R. (1940). A multiphasic personality schedule (Minnesota): II. A differential study of hypochondriasis. *Journal of Psychology, 10*, 255–268.

McKinley, J. C., & Hathaway, S. R. (1942). A multiphasic personality schedule (Minnesota): IV. Psychasthenia. *Journal of Applied Psychology, 26*, 614–624.

McKinley, J. C., & Hathaway, S. R. (1943). The identification and measurement of the psycho-neuroses in medical practice. *Journal of the American Medical Association, 122*, 161–167.

McKinley, J. C., & Hathaway, S. R. (1944). The MMPI: V. Hysteria, hypomania, and psychopathic deviate. *Journal of Applied Psychology, 28*, 153–174.

McKinley, J. C., & Hathaway, S. R. (2000). The MMPI V. Hysteria, hypomania, and psychopathic deviate. In J. N. Butcher (Ed.), *Basic sources on the MMPI-2* (pp. 31–48). Minneapolis, MN: University of Minnesota Press.

McKinley, J. C., Hathaway, S. R., & Meehl, P. E. (1948). The MMPI: VI. The *K* scale. *Journal of Consulting Psychology, 12*, 20–31.

McLaughlin, J. F., Helmes, E., & Howe, M. G. (1983). Note on the reliability of three MMPI short forms. *Journal of Personality Assessment, 47*, 357–358.

McNulty, J. L., Ben-Porath, Y. S., & Graham, J. R. (1998). An empirical examination of the correlates of well-defined and not defined MMPI-2 code types. *Journal of Personality Assessment, 71*, 393–410.

Meehl, P. E. (1945a). The dynamics of "structured" personality tests. *Journal of Clinical Psychology, 1*, 296–304.

Meehl, P. E. (1945b). An investigation of a general normality or control factor in personality testing. *Psychological Monographs, 59*(4, Whole No. 274).

Meehl, P. E. (1954). *Clinical versus statistical prediction: A theoretical analysis and a review of the evidence*. Minneapolis, MN: University of Minnesota Press.

Meehl, P. E. (1956). Wanted—A good cookbook. *American Psychologist, 11*, 262–272.

Meehl, P. E. (1959). Some ruminations on the validation of clinical procedures. *Canadian Journal of Psychology/Revue Canadienne De Psychologie, 13*, 102–128.

Meehl, P. E. (1962). Schizotaxia, schizotypy, schizophrenia. *American Psychologist, 17*, 827–838.

Meehl, P. E. (1970). Psychology and criminal law. *University of Richmond Law Review, 5*, 1–30.

Meehl, P. E. (1971). Prefatory comment. In L. D. Goodstein & R. I. Lanyon (Eds.), *Readings in personality assessment* (pp. 245–246). New York: Wiley.

Meehl, P. E. (1972). Reactions, reflections, projections. In J. N. Butcher (Ed.), *Objective personality assessment* (pp. 131–189). New York: Academic Press.

Meehl, P. E. (1973). Why I do not attend case conferences. In P. E. Meehl (Ed.), *Psychodiagnosis: Selected papers* (pp. 225–302). Minneapolis, MN: University of Minnesota Press.

Meehl, P. E. (1975). Hedonic capacity: Some conjectures. *Bulletin of the Menninger Clinic, 39*, 295–307.

Meehl, P. E. (1987). "Hedonic capacity" ten years later: Some clarifications. In D. C. Clark & J. Fawcett (Eds.), *Anhedonia and affect deficit states* (pp. 47–50). New York: PMA.

Meehl, P. E. (1989). Paul E. Meehl. In G. Linzey (Ed.), *A history of psychology in autobiography* (Vol. 3, pp. 337–389). Stanford, CA: Stanford University Press.

Meehl, P. E. (1997). Credentialed persons, credential knowledge. *Clinical Psychology: Science and Practice, 4*(2), 91–98.

Meehl, P. E., & Dahlstrom, W. G. (1960). Objective configural rules for discriminating psychotic from neurotic MMPI profiles. *Journal of Consulting Psychology, 24*, 375–387.

Meehl, P. E., & Hathaway, S. R. (1946). The K factor as a suppressor variable in the MMPI. *Journal of Applied Psychology, 30*, 525–564.

Megargee, E. I. (1972). *The California Psychological Inventory handbook*. San Francisco, CA: Jossey-Bass.

Megargee, E. I. (1985). Assessing alcoholism and drug abuse with the MMPI: Implications for screening. In C. D. Spielberger & J. N. Butcher (Eds.), *Advances in personality assessment* (Vol. 5, pp. 1–39). Hillsdale, NJ: Lawrence Erlbaum Associates.

Megargee, E. I. (2006). *Use of the MMPI-2 in criminal justice and correctional settings*. Minneapolis, MN: University of Minnesota Press.

Megargee, E. I., & Cook, P. E. (1975). Negative response bias and the MMPI Overcontrolled-Hostility scale: A response to Deiker. *Journal of Consulting and Clinical Psychology, 43*, 725–729.

Megargee, E. I., Cook, P. E., & Mendelsohn, G. A. (1967). Development and validation of an MMPI scale of assaultiveness in overcontrolled individuals. *Journal of Abnormal Psychology, 72*, 519–528.

Megargee, E. I., & Mendelsohn, G. A. (1962). A cross-validation of twelve MMPI indices of hostility and control. *Journal of Abnormal and Social Psychology, 65*, 431–438.

Meloy, J. R., & Gacono, C. (1995). Assessing the psychopathic personality. In J. Butcher (Ed.), *Clinical personality assessment: Practical approaches* (pp. 410–422). New York: Oxford University Press.

Merskey, H. (1995). *The analysis of hysteria: Understanding conversion and dissociation* (2nd ed.). London, England: Gaskell/Royal College of Psychiatrists.

Meyer, R. G. (1983). *The clinician's handbook: The psychopathology of adulthood and late adolescence.* Boston, MA: Allyn & Bacon.

Miller, H. R., Goldberg, J. O., & Streiner, D. L. (1995). What's in a name? The MMPI-2 PTSD scales. *Journal of Clinical Psychology, 51*, 626–631.

Miller, H .R., & Streiner, D. L. (1985). The Harris-Lingoes subscales: Fact or fiction? *Journal of Clinical Psychology, 41*, 45–51.

Miller, H. R., & Streiner, D. L. (1986). Differences in MMPI profiles with the norms of Colligan et al. *Journal of Consulting and Clinical Psychology, 54*, 843–845.

Minnix, J. A., Reitzel, L. R., Repper, K. A., Burns, A. B., Williams, F., Lima, E. N., Cukrowicz, K. C., Kirsch, L., & Joiner, T. E., Jr. (2005). Total number of MMPI-2 clinical scale elevations predicts premature termination after controlling for intake symptom severity and personality disorder diagnosis. *Personality and Individual Differences, 38*, 1745–1755.

Mittag, O., & Maurischat, C. (2004). Die Cook-Medley Hostility Scale (Ho-Skala) im Vergleich zu den Inhaltsskalen "Zynismus", "Ärger" sowie "Typ A" aus dem MMPI-2: Zur zukünftigen Operationalisierung von Feindseligkeit [A comparison of the Cook-Medley Hostility Scale (Ho-scale) and the content scales "cynicism", "anger", and "type A" out of the MMPI-2: On the future assessment of hostility]. *Zeitschrift für Medizinische Psychologie, 13*, 7–12.

Moreland, K. L. (1985). Validation of computer-based test interpretations: Problems and prospects. *Journal of Consulting and Clinical Psychology, 53*, 816–825.

Moreland, K. L. (1990). Some observations on computer-assisted psychological testing. *Journal of Personality Assessment, 55*, 820–823.

Moreland, K. L., & Dahlstrom, W. G. (1983). Professional training with and use of the MMPI. *Professional Psychology: Research and Practice, 14*, 218–223.

Morey, L. C., & Smith, M. R. (1988). Personality disorders. In R. L. Greene (Ed.), *The MMPI: Use with specific populations* (pp. 110–158). Philadelphia, PA: Grune & Stratton.

Morey, L. C., Waugh, M. H., & Blashfield, R. K. (1985). MMPI scales for DSM-III personality disorders: Their derivation and correlates. *Journal of Personality Assessment, 49*, 245–251.

Muench, J. L. (1996). Negative indicators in psychotherapy: The assessment of client difficulty and its relationship to therapist behavior and the working alliance (Doctoral dissertation, Kent State University). *Dissertation Abstracts International, 57(5-B)*, 3417.

Munley, P. H. (2002). Compatibility of MMPI-2 scales and profiles over time. *Journal of Personality Assessment, 78(1)*, 145–160.

Munley, P. H., Busby, R. M., & Jaynes, G. (1997). MMPI-2 findings in schizophrenia and depression. *Psychological Assessment, 9*, 508–511.

Munley, P. H., Germain, J. M., Tovar-Murray, D., & Borgman, A. L. (2004). MMPI-2 profile codetypes and measurement error. *Journal of Personality Assessment, 82(2)*, 179–188.

Nason v. Shafranski, 33 So. 3d 117 (Fla. 4th DCA 2010).

Navran, L. (1954). A rationally derived MMPI scale for dependence. *Journal of Consulting Psychology, 18*, 192.

Nelson, L. D. (1987). Measuring depression in a clinical population using the MMPI. *Journal of Consulting and Clinical Psychology, 55*, 788–790.

Nelson, L. D., & Cicchetti, D. (1991). Validity of the MMPI Depression scale for outpatients. *Psychological Assessment: A Journal of Consulting and Clinical Psychology, 3*, 55–59.

Nelson, N. W., Hoelzle, J. B., Sweet, J. J., Arbisi, P. A., & Demakis, G. J. (2010). Updated meta-analysis of the MMPI-2 Symptom Validity Scale (FBS): Verified utility in forensic practice. *The Clinical Neuropsychologist, 24(4)*, 701–724.

Nelson, N. W., Sweet, J. J., Berry, D. T. R., Bryant, F. B., & Granacher, R. P. (2007). Response validity in forensic neuropsychology: Exploratory factor analytic evidence of distinct cognitive and psychological constructs. *Journal of the International Neuropsychological Society, 13*, 440–449.

Nelson, N. W., Sweet, J. J., & Demakis, G. J. (2006). Meta-analysis of the MMPI-2 Fake Bad Scale: Utility in forensic practice. *The Clinical Neuropsychologist, 20(1)*, 39–58.

Nelson, S. E. (1952). The development of an indirect, objective measure of social status and its relationship to certain psychiatric syndromes (Doctoral dissertation, University of Minnesota). *Dissertation Abstracts, 12*, 782.

Newmark, C. S., Chassin, P., Evans, D., & Gentry, L. (1984). "Floating" MMPI profiles revisited *Journal of Clinical Psychology, 40*, 199–201.

Nichols, D. S. (1988). Mood disorders. In R. L. Greene (Ed.), *The MMPI: Use with specific populations* (pp. 74–109). Philadelphia, PA: Grune & Stratton.

Nichols, D. S. (1992a). Development and use of the MMPI-2: Content scales [Review of the book] *Journal of Personality Assessment, 58*, 434–437

Nichols, D. S. (1992b). Review of the Minnesota Multiphasic Personality Inventory–2. In J. J. Kramer & J. C. Conoley (Eds.), *The eleventh mental measurements yearbook* (pp. 562–565). Lincoln, NE: University of Nebraska, Buros Institute of Mental Measurements.

Nichols, D. S. (1994). *A digest of the MMPI-2 PSY–5: Harkness, McNulty, and Ben-Porath's Personality Psychopathology Five (PSY–5).* Unpublished manuscript.

Nichols, D. S. (2006). The trials of separating bath water from baby: A review and critique of the MMPI-2 Restructured Clinical scales. *Journal of Personality Assessment, 87(2)*, 121–138.

Nichols, D. S. (2008). Differentiating normal-range cognitive difficulty from psychotic disruption with the MMPI-2: The cognitive problems and disorganization scales. (Unpublished manuscript.)

Nichols, D. S. (2009). *Construction of more inclusive and less overlapping subscales for Scale 2 (Depression).* Unpublished manuscript.

Nichols, D. S. (2010). *A potential predictor of suicide risk: An MMPI-2 Hopelessness Scale.* Unpublished manuscript.

Nichols, D. S. (2011). *Essentials of MMPI-2 assessment* (2nd ed.). Hoboken, NJ: John Wiley & Sons, Inc.

Nichols, D. S., & Crowhurst, B. (2006). The use of the MMPI-2 in inpatient metal health settings. In J. N. Butcher (Ed.), *MMPI-2: A practitioner's guide* (pp. 195–252). Washington, DC: APA Press.

Nichols, D. S., & Greene, R. L. (1988, March). *Adaptive or defensive: An evaluation of Paulhus' two-factor model of social desirability responding in the MMPI with non-college samples.* Paper presented at the 23rd Annual Symposium on Recent Developments in the Use of the MMPI, St. Petersburg, FL.

Nichols, D. S., & Greene, R. L. (1991, March). *New measures for dissimulation on the MMPI/MMPI-2.* Paper presented at the 26th Annual Symposium on Recent Developments in the Use of the MMPI (MMPI-2/MMPI-A), St. Petersburg Beach, FL.

Nichols, D. S., & Greene, R. L. (1995). *MMPI-2 structural summary: Interpretive manual.* Odessa, FL: Psychological Assessment Resources.

Nichols, D. S., & Greene, R. L. (1997). Dimensions of deception in personality assessment: The example of the MMPI-2. *Journal of Personality Assessment, 68*, 251–266.

Nicholson, R. A., Mouton, G. J., Bagby, R. M., Buis, T., Peterson, S. A., & Buigas, R. A. (1997). Utility of MMPI-2 indicators of response distortion: Receiver operating characteristic analysis. *Psychological Assessment: A Journal of Consulting and Clinical Psychology, 9*, 471–479.

Osberg, T. M., Haseley, E. N., & Kamas, M. M. (2008). The MMPI-2 Clinical Scales and Restructured Clinical (RC) Scales: Comparative psychometric properties and relative diagnostic efficiency in young adults. *Journal of Personality Assessment, 90*, 81–92.

Osberg, T. M., & Poland, D. L. (2001). Validity of the MMPI-2 Basic and Harris-Lingoes Subscales in a forensic sample. *Journal of Clinical Psychology, 57(12)*, 1369–1380.

Osborne, D. (1979). Use of the MMPI with medical patients. In J. N. Butcher (Ed.), *New developments in the use of MMPI* (pp. 141–163). Minneapolis, MN: University of Minnesota Press.

Osborne, D., Colligan, R., & Offord, K. (1986). Normative tables for the *F – K* index of the MMPI based on a contemporary normal sample. *Journal of Clinical Psychology, 42*, 593–595.

Otto, R. K., Lang, A. R., Megargee, E. I., & Rosenblatt, A. I. (1988). Ability of alcoholics to escape detection by the MMPI. *Journal of Consulting and Clinical Psychology, 56*, 452–457.

Overall, J. E., & Gorham, D. R. (1988). Introduction: The Brief Psychiatric Rating Scale (BPRS): Recent developments in ascertainment and scaling. *Psychopharmacology Bulletin, 24*, 97–98.

Ownby, R. L. (1987). *Psychological reports: A guide to report writing in professional psychology.* Brandon, VT: Clinical Psychology.

Page, J., Landis, C., & Katz, S. E. (1934). Schizophrenic traits in the functional psychoses and in normal individuals. *American Journal of Psychiatry, 13*, 1213–1225.

Pancoast, D. L., & Archer, R. P. (1988). MMPI adolescent norms: Patterns and trends across 4 decades. *Journal of Personality Assessment, 52*, 691–706.

Pancoast, D. L., & Archer, R. P. (1989). Original adult MMPI norms in normal samples: A review with implications for future developments. *Journal of Personality Assessment, 53*, 376–395.

Pancoast, D. L., Archer, R. P., & Gordon, R. A. (1988). The MMPI and clinical diagnosis: A comparison of classification system outcomes with discharge diagnoses. *Journal of Personality Assessment, 52*, 81–90.

Paolo, A. M., Ryan, J. J., & Smith, A. J. (1991). Reading difficulty of MMPI-2 subscales. *Journal of Clinical Psychology, 47*, 529–532.

Patton, D., Barnes, G. E., & Murray, R. P. (1993). Personality characteristics of smokers and ex-smokers. *Personality and Individual Differences, 15*, 653–664.

Paulhus, D. L. (1984). Two-component models of socially desirable responding. *Journal of Personality and Social Psychology, 46*, 598–609.

Paulhus, D. L. (1986). Self-deception and impression management in test responses. In A. Angleitner & J. S. Wiggins (Eds.), *Personality assessment via questionnaires: Current issues in theory and measurement* (pp. 143–165). Berlin: Springer-Verlag.

Payne, F. D., & Wiggins, J. S. (1972). MMPI profile types and the self-report of psychiatric patients. *Journal of Abnormal Psychology, 79*, 1–8.

Persons, R., & Marks, P. (1971). The violent 4-3 MMPI personality type. *Journal of Consulting and Clinical Psychology, 36*, 189–196.

Peterson, C. D. (1991). *Masculinity and femininity as independent dimensions on the MMPI.* Unpublished doctoral dissertation, University of North Carolina, Chapel Hill, NC.

Peterson, C. D., & Dahlstrom, W. G. (1992). The derivation of gender-role scales *GM* and *GF* for the MMPI-2 and their relationship to Scale 5 *(Mf). Journal of Personality Assessment, 59*, 486–499.

Pizitz, T., & McCullaugh, J. (2011). An overview of male stalkers' personality profiles using the MMPI-2. *American Journal of Forensic Psychiatry, 32*, 31–46.

Plante, T. G., Manuel, G., & Bryant, C. (1996). Personality and cognitive functioning among hospitalized sexual offending Roman Catholic priests. *Pastoral Psychology, 45*, 129–139.

Pope, H. G., & Lipinski, J. F. (1978). Diagnosis in schizophrenia and manic-depressive illness: A reassessment of the specificity of schizophrenic symptoms in the light of current research. *Archives of General Psychiatry, 35*, 811–828.

Pope, K. S. (1992). Responsibilities in providing psychological test feedback to clients. *Psychological Assessment: A Journal of Consulting and Clinical Psychology, 4*, 268–271.

Pope, K. S., Butcher, J. N., & Seelen, J. (2006). *The MMPI, MMPI-2, and MMPI-A in court.* Washington, DC: American Psychological Association.

Pope, M. K., Smith, T. W., & Rhodewalt, F. (1990). Cognitive, behavioral, and affective correlates of the Cook and Medley Hostility Scale. *Journal of Personality Assessment, 54*, 501–514.

Prokop, C. K. (1986). Hysteria scale elevations in low back pain patients: A risk factor for misdiagnosis? *Journal of Consulting and Clinical Psychology, 54*, 558–562.

Prokop, C. K. (1988). Chronic pain. In R. C. Greene (Ed.), *The MMPI: Use with specific populations* (pp. 22–49). Philadelphia, PA: Grune & Stratton.

Purdon, S. E., Purser, S. M., & Goddard, K. M. (2011). MMPI-2 Restructured Form over-reporting scales in first-episode psychosis. *The Clinical Neuropsychologist, 25(5)*, 829–842.

Putnam, S. H., Kurtz, J. E., & Houts, D. C. (1996). Four-month test–retest reliability of the MMPI-2 with normal male clergy. *Journal of Personality Assessment, 67*, 341–353.

Putzke, J. D., Williams, M. A., Daniel, F. J., & Boll, T. J. (1999). The utility of *K*-correction to adjust for a defensive response set on the MMPI. *Psychological Assessment, 6*, 61–70.

Quilty, L. C., & Bagby, R. M. (2007). Psychometric and structural analysis of the MMPI-2 Personality Psychopathology Five (PSY-5) facet subscales. *Assessment, 14*, 375–384.

Quinsey, V. L., Harris, G. T., Rice, M. E., & Cormier, C. A. (1998). *Violent offenders: Appraising and managing risk*. Washington, DC: American Psychological Association.

Quinsey, V. L., Maguire, A., & Varney, G. W. (1983). Assertion and overcontrolled hostility among mentally disordered offenders. *Journal of Consulting and Clinical Psychology, 51*, 550–556.

Ranson, M. B., Nichols, D. S., Rouse, S. V., & Harrington, J. L. (2009). Changing or replacing an established psychological assessment standard: Issues, goals, and problems with special reference to recent developments in the MMPI-2. In J. N. Butcher (Ed.), *Oxford library of psychology. Oxford handbook of personality assessment* (pp. 112–139). New York: Oxford University Press.

Rapport, L. J., Todd, R. M., Lumley, M. A., & Fisicaro, S. A. (1998). The diagnostic meaning of "nervous breakdown" among lay populations. *Journal of Personality Assessment, 71*, 242–252.

Raskin, R., & Novacek, J. (1989). An MMPI description of the narcissistic personality. *Journal of Personality Assessment, 53*, 66–80.

Rathvon, N., & Holmstrom, R. W. (1996). An MMPI-2 portrait of narcissism. *Journal of Personality Assessment, 66*, 1–19.

Reise, S. P., & Haviland, M. G. (2005). Item response theory and the measurement of clinical change. *Journal of Personality Assessment, 84*, 228–238.

Rhodes, R. J., & Chang, A. F. (1978). A further look at the Institutionalized Chronic Alcoholic scale. *Journal of Clinical Psychology, 34*, 779–780.

Robin, R. W., Greene, R. L., Albaugh, B., Caldwell, A., & Goldman, D. (2003). Use of the MMPI-2 in American Indians: I. Comparability of the MMPI-2 between two tribes and with the MMPI-2 normative group. *Psychological Assessment, 15(3)*, 351–359.

Rodgers, D. A. (1972). Review of the MMPI. In O. K. Buros (Ed.), *Seventh mental measurements yearbook* (pp. 243–250). Highland Park, NJ: Gryphon Press.

Roessler, R., Alexander, A. A., & Greenfield, N. S. (1963). Ego strength and physiological responsivity: I. The relationship of the Barron *Es* scale to skin resistance. *Archives of General Psychiatry, 8*, 142–154.

Roessler, R., Burch, N. R., & Childers, H. E. (1966). Personality and arousal correlates of specific galvanic skin responses. *Psychophysiology, 3*, 115–130.

Roessler, R., Burch, N. R., & Mefford, R. B. (1967). Personality correlates of catecholamine excretion under stress. *Journal of Psychosomatic Research, 11*, 181–185.

Roessler, R., & Collins, F. (1970). Personality correlates of physiological responses to motion pictures. *Psychophysiology, 6*, 732–739.

Roessler, R., Greenfield, N. S., & Alexander, A. A. (1964). Ego strength and response stereotypy. *Psychophysiology, 1*, 142–150.

Rogers, R., Bagby, R. M., & Chakraborty, D. (1993). Feigning schizophrenia disorders on the MMPI-2: Detection of coached simulators. *Journal of Personality Assessment, 60*, 215–226.

Rogers, R., Gillard, N. D., Berry, D. R., & Granacher, R. P., Jr. (2011). Effectiveness of the MMPI-2-RF validity scales for feigned mental disorders and cognitive impairment: A known-groups study. *Journal of Psychopathology and Behavioral Assessment, 33(3)*, 355–367.

Rogers, R., & Sewell, K. W. (2006) MMPI-2 at the crossroads: Aging technology or radical retrofitting? *Journal of Personality Assessment, 87*, 175–178.

Rogers, R., Sewell, K. W., Harrison, K. S., & Jordan, M. J. (2006). The MMPI-2 Restructured Clinical Scales: A paradigmatic shift in scale development. *Journal of Personality Assessment, 87*, 139–147.

Rogers, R., Sewell, K. W., Martin, M. A., & Vitacco, M. J. (2003). Detection of feigned mental disorders: A meta-analysis of the MMPI-2 and malingering. *Assessment, 10*, 160–177.

Rogers, R., Sewell, K. W., & Salekin, R. T. (1994). A meta-analysis of malingering on the MMPI-2. *Assessment, 1*, 227–237.

Rohan, W. P. (1972). MMPI changes in hospitalized alcoholics: A second study. *Quarterly Journal of Studies on Alcohol, 33*, 65–76.

Rohan, W. P., Tatro, R. L., & Rotman, S. R. (1969). MMPI changes in alcoholics during hospitalization. *Quarterly Journal of Studies on Alcohol, 30*, 389–400.

Rome, H. P., Swenson, W. M., Mataya, P., McCarthy, C. E., Pearson, J. S., Keating, F. R., & Hathaway, S. T. (1962). Symposium on automation procedures in personality assessment. *Proceedings of the Staff Meetings of the Mayo Clinic, 37*, 61–82.

Romney, D. M., & Bynner, J. M. (1992). A simplex model of five *DSM-III* personality disorders. *Journal of Personality Disorders, 6*, 34–39.

Roper, B. L., Ben-Porath, Y. S., & Butcher, J. N. (1991). Comparability of computerized adaptive and conventional testing with the MMPI-2. *Journal of Personality Assessment, 65*, 358–371.

Rosen, A. (1962). Development of MMPI scales based on a reference group of psychiatric patients. *Psychological Monographs, 76(8*, Whole No. 527).

Rosik, C. H., & Borisov, N. I. (2010). Can specific MMPI-2 scales predict treatment response among missionaries? *Journal of Psychology and Theology, 38*, 195–204.

Rostami, R., Nosratabadi, M., & Mohammadi, F. (2007). Primary evaluation of the diagnostic accuracy of the AAS, MAC-R, and APS. *Psychological Research, 10*, 11–28.

Rothke, S. E., & Friedman, A. F. (1994). Response to Fox: Comment and clarification. *Assessment, 1*, 421–422.

Rothke, S. E., Friedman, A. F., Dahlstrom, W. G., Greene, R. L., Arrendondo, R., & Mann, A. W. (1994). MMPI-2 normative data for the *F–K* index: Implications for clinical, neuropsychological, and forensic practice. *Assessment, 1*, 1–15.

Rothke, S. E., Friedman, A. F., Jaffe, A. M., Greene, R. G., Wetter, M. W., Cole, P., & Baker, K. (2000). Normative data for the F(p) Scale of the MMPI-2: Implications for clinical and forensic assessment of malingering. *Psychological Assessment, 12(3)*, 355–340.

Rouse, S. L., Butcher, J. N., & Miller, K. B. (1999). Assessment of substance abuse in psychotherapy clients: The effectiveness of the MMPI-2 substance abuse scales. *Psychological Assessment: A Journal of Consulting and Clinical Psychology, 11*, 101–107.

Rouse, S. V., Greene, R. L., Butcher, J. N., Nichols, D. S., & Williams, C. L. (2008). What do the MMPI-2 Restructured Clinical scales reliably measure? Answers from multiple research settings. *Journal of Personality Assessment, 90*, 435–442.

Russell, J. A. (1980). A circumplex model of affect. *Journal of Personality and Asocial Psychology, 39*, 1161–1178.

Sawrie, S. M., Kabat, M. H., Dietz, C. B., Greene, R. L., Arredondo, R., & Mann, A. W. (1996). Internal structure of the MMPI-2 Addiction Potential Scale in alcoholic and psychiatric inpatients. *Journal of Personality Assessment, 66*, 177–193.

Sawyer, J. (1966). Measurement and prediction, clinical and statistical. *Psychological Bulletin, 66*, 178–200.

Scarr, S. (1969). Social introversion-extraversion as a heritable response. *Child Development, 40(3)*, 823–832.

Schill, T., & Wang, S. (1990). Correlates of the MMPI-2 anger content scale. *Psychological Reports, 67*, 800–802.

Schinka, J. A., & Borum, R. (1993). Readability of adult psychopathology inventories. *Psychological Assessment: A Journal of Consulting and Clinical Psychology, 5,* 384–386.

Schinka, J. A., & LaLone, L. (1997). MMPI-2 norms: Comparisons with a census-matched subsample. *Psychology Assessment, 9(3),* 307–311.

Schlenger, W. E., & Kulka, R. A. (1987, August–September). *Performance of the Keane-Fairbank MMPI scale and other self-report measures in identifying post-traumatic stress disorder.* Paper presented at the 95th Annual Convention of the American Psychological Association, New York.

Schlenger, W. E., Kulka, R. A., Fairbank, J. A., Hough, R. L., Jordan, B. K., Marmar, C. R., & Weiss, D. S. (1989). *The prevalence of post-traumatic stress disorder in the Vietnam generation: Findings from the National Vietnam Veterans Readjustment Study.* Research Triangle Park, NC: Research Triangle Institute.

Schmalz, B. J., Fehr, R. C., & Dalby, J. T. (1989). Distinguishing forensic, psychiatric and inmate groups with the MMPI. *American Journal of Forensic Psychology, 7,* 37–47.

Schneider, K. (1959). *Clinical psychopathology.* New York: Grune and Stratton.

Schroeder, R. W., Baade, L. E., Peck, C. P., VonDran, E. J., Brockman, C. J., Webster, B. K., & Heinrichs, R. J. (2012). Validation of MMPI-2-RF Validity Scales in criterion group neuropsychological samples. *The Clinical Neuropsychologist, 26(1),* 129–146.

Schuldberg, D. (1990). Varieties of inconsistency across test occasions: Effects of computerized test administration and repeated testing. *Journal of Personality Assessment, 55,* 168–182.

Schwartz, M. R., & Graham, J. R. (1979). Construct validity of the MacAndrew Alcoholism scale. *Journal of Consulting and Clinical Psychology, 47,* 1090–1095.

Seligman, M. E. P. (1990). *Learned optimism: how to change your mind and your life.* New York: Knopf.

Sellbom, M., & Bagby, R. (2010). Detection of over-reported psychopathology with the MMPI-2 RF form validity scales. *Psychological Assessment, 22(4),* 757–767.

Sellbom, M., Ben-Porath, Y. S., & Bagby, R. (2008). Personality and psychopathology: Mapping the MMPI-2 Restructured Clinical (RC) Scales onto the Five Factor Model of Personality. *Journal of Personality Disorders, 22,* 291–312.

Sellbom, M., Ben-Porath, Y. S., & Graham, J. R. (2006). Correlates of the MMPI-2 restructured clinical (RC) scales in a college counseling setting. *Journal of Personality Assessment, 86,* 89–99.

Sellbom, M. & Ben-Porath, Y. S. (2005) Mapping the MMPI-2 Restructured Clinical scales onto normal personality traits: Evidence of construct validity. *Journal of Personality Assessment, 85,* 179–187.

Sellbom, M., Ben-Porath, Y. S., McNulty, J. L., Arbisi, P. A., & Graham, J. R. (2006). Elevation differences between MMPI-2 Clinical and Restructured Clinical (RC) Scales: Frequency, origins, and interpretive implications. *Assessment, 13,* 430–441.

Sellbom, M., Graham, J. R., & Schenk, P. W. (2005). Symptom correlates of MMPI-2 scales and code types in a private-practice setting. *Journal of Personality Assessment, 84,* 163–171.

Sellbom, M., Graham, J. R., & Schenk, P. W. (2006). Incremental validity of the MMPI-2 restructured clinical (RC) scales in a private practice sample. *Journal of Personality Assessment, 86,* 196–205.

Sellbom, M., Wygant, D., & Bagby, M. (2012). Utility of the MMPI-2-RF in detecting non-credible somatic complaints. *Psychiatry Research, 197(3),* 295–301.

Sepaher, I., Bongar, B., & Greene, R. L. (1999). Codetype base rates for the "I Mean Business" suicide items on the MMPI-2. *Journal of Clinical Psychology, 55(9),* 1167–1173.

Serkownek, K. (1975). *Subscales for Scales 5 and 0 of the MMPI.* Unpublished manuscript.

Sham, P. C., MacLean, C. J., & Kendler, K. S. (1994). A typological model of schizophrenia based on age at onset, sex and familial morbidity. *Acta Psychiatrica Scandinavica, 89,* 35–41.

Shapiro, D. (1965). *Neurotic styles.* New York: Basic Books.

Sharland, M. J., & Gfeller, J. D. (2007). A survey of neuropsychologists' beliefs and practices with respect to the assessment of effort. *Archives of Clinical Neuropsychology, 22*, 213–223.

Sharpe, J. P., & Desai, S. (2001). The revised NEO Personality Inventory and the MMPI-2 Psychopathology Five in the prediction of aggression. *Personality and Individual Differences, 31*, 505–518.

Shea, C. (2006). A comparison of performance on malingering assessments between neuropsychological patients involved in litigation and non-litigious neuropsychological patients. *Dissertation Abstracts International: Section B: The Sciences and Engineering, 67(1-B)*, 560.

Shekelle, R. B., Gale, M., Ostfeld, A. M., & Paul, O. (1983). Hostility, risk of coronary heart disease, and mortality. *Psychosomatic Medicine, 45*, 109–114.

Sherwood, N. E., & Ben-Porath, Y. S. (1991). The MMPI-2 content component scales. *MMPI-2 News and Profiles, 2*, 9–11.

Shondrick, D. D., Ben-Porath, Y. S., & Stafford, K. P. (1992, May). *Forensic applications of the MMPI-2.* Paper presented at the 27th Annual Symposium on Recent Developments in the Use of the MMPI (MMPI-2 and MMPI-A), Minneapolis, MN.

Sieber, K. O., & Meyers, L. S. (1992). Validation of the MMPI-2 Social-Introversion subscales. *Psychological Assessment: A Journal of Consulting and Clinical Psychology, 4*, 185–189.

Simms, L. J., Casillas, A., Clark, L., Watson, D., & Doebbeling, B. N. (2005). Psychometric evaluation of the restructured clinical scales of the MMPI-2. *Psychological Assessment, 17*, 345–358.

Sines, J. O. (1977). M-F: Bipolar and probably multidimensional. *Journal of Clinical Psychology, 33*, 1038–1041.

Sivec, H. J., Lynn, S. J., & Garske, J. P. (1994). The effect of somatoform disorder and paranoid psychotic role-related dissimulations as a response set on the MMPI-2. *Assessment, 1*, 69–81.

Smith, S. R., & Hilsenroth, M. J. (2001). Discriminative validity of the MacAndrew Alcoholism Scale with Cluster B personality disorders. *Journal of Clinical Psychology, 57*, 801–813.

Smith, S. R., Hilsenroth, M. J., Castlebury, F. D., & Durham, T. W. (1999). The clinical utility of the MMPI-2 Antisocial Practices Content Scale. *Journal of Personality Disorders, 13*, 385–393.

Smith, T. W., & Frohm, K. D. (1985). What's so unhealthy about hostility? Construct validity and psychosocial correlates of the Cook and Medley Ho scale. *Health Psychology, 4*, 503–520.

Solomon & Solomon v. T. K. Power & Goodwin (2008). Case No. 06-CA-00388, Florida 4th Circuit, in and for Duval County, Fla.

Southwick, S. M., Morgan, C. A., III, Nicolaou, A. C., & Charney, D. S. (1997). Consistency of memory for combat-related traumatic events in veterans of Operation Desert Storm. *American Journal of Psychiatry, 154*, 173–177.

Spanier, G. B. (1976). Measuring dyadic adjustment: New scales for assessing the quality of marriage and similar dyads. *Journal of Marriage and the Family, 38*, 15–28.

Spielberger, C. D., & Piotrowski, C. (1990). Clinician's attitudes toward computer-based testing. *The Clinical Psychologist, 43*, 60–63.

Spinhoven, P., Labbe, M. R., & Rombouts, R. (1993). Feasibility of computerized psychological testing with psychiatric outpatients. *Journal of Clinical Psychology, 49*, 440–447.

Staal, M. A., & Greene, R. L. (1998). Classification accuracy in the measurement of MMPI/MMPI-2: Profile similarity. *Journal of Personality Assessment, 71*, 70–83.

Stanley, J. C. (1971). Reliability. In R. L. Thorndike (Ed.), *Educational measurement* (2nd ed., pp. 356–442). Washington, DC: American Council on Education.

Steffan, J. S., Morgan, R. D., Lee, J., & Sellbom, M. (2010). A comparative analysis of MMPI-2 malingering detection models among inmates. *Assessment, 17(2)*, 185–196.

Stein, K. B., (1968). The TSC scales: The outcome of a cluster analysis of the 550 MMPI items. In P. McReynolds (Ed.), *Advances in Psychological Assessment* (Vol. 1, pp. 80–104). Palo Alto, CA: Science and Behavior Books.

Stein, L. A. R., Graham, J. R., Ben-Porath, Y. S., & McNulty, J. L. (1999). Using the MMPI-2 to detect substance abuse in an outpatient mental health setting. *Psychological Assessment: A Journal of Consulting and Clinical Psychology, 11*, 94–100.

Stith v. State Farm Mutual Insurance, Case No. 50-2003 CA 010945AG, Palm Beach County, Fla. 2008.

Stronoberg, D. S. (1991) Interpretive dilemmas created by the Minnesota Multiphasic Personality Inventory-2 (MMPI-2). *Journal of Psychopathology and Behavioral Assessment, 13*, 53–59.

Streiner, D. L., & Miller, H. R. (1986). Can a short form of the MMPI ever be developed? *Journal of Clinical Psychology, 42*, 109–113.

Strong, D. R., Glassmire, D. M., Frederick, R. I., & Greene, R. L. (2006). Evaluating the latent structure of the MMPI-2 Fp scale in a forensic sample: A taxometric analysis. *Psychological Assessment, 118*, 250–261.

Sutker, P. B., Archer, R. P., Brantley, P. J., & Kilpatrick, D. G. (1979). Alcoholics and opiate addicts: Comparison of personality characteristics. *Journal of Studies on Alcohol, 40*, 635–644.

Svanum, S., & Ehrmann, L. C. (1992). Alcoholic subtypes and the MacAndrew Alcoholism Scale. *Journal of Personality Assessment, 58*(2), 411–422.

Svanum, S., & Ehrmann, L. C. (1993). The validity of the MMPI in identifying alcoholics in a university setting. *Journal of Studies on Alcohol, 54*, 722–729.

Svanum, S., McGrew, J., & Ehrmann, L. (1994). Validity of the substance abuse scales of the MMPI-2 in a college student sample. *Journal of Personality Assessment, 62*, 427–439.

Sweet, J. J., Malina, A., & Ecklund-Johnson, E. (2006). Application of the new MMPI-2 Malingered Depression Scale to individuals undergoing neuropsychological evaluation: Relative lack of relationship to secondary gain and failure on validity indices. *The Clinical Neuropsychologist, 20*: 541–551.

Swenson, W. M., & Pearson, J. S. (1964). Automation techniques in personality assessment: A frontier in behavioral science and medicine. *Methods of Information in Medicine, 3*(1), 34–36.

Swenson, W. M., Pearson, J. S., & Osborne, D. (1973). *An MMPI source book: Basic item, scale and pattern data on 50,000 medical patients*. Minneapolis, MN: University of Minnesota.

Tallent, N. (1983). *Psychological report writing* (2nd ed.). Englewood Cliffs, NJ: Prentice-Hall.

Tallent, N. (1987). Computer-generated psychological reports: A look at the modern psychometric machine. *Journal of Personality Assessment, 51*, 95–108.

Tanner, B. A. (1990). Composite descriptions associated with rare MMPI two-point codetypes: Codes that involve Scale 5. *Journal of Clinical Psychology, 46*, 425–431.

Tarter, R. E., McBride, H., Buonpane, N., & Schneider, D. U. (1978). Differentiation of alcoholics: Childhood history of minimal brain dysfunction, family history, and drinking pattern. *Archives of General Psychiatry, 34*, 761–768.

Tarter, R. E., & Perley, R. N. (1975). Clinical and perceptual characteristics of paranoids and paranoid schizophrenics. *Journal of Clinical Psychology, 31*, 42–44.

Taylor, J. A. (1953). A personality scale of manifest anxiety. *Journal of Abnormal and Social Psychology, 48*, 285–290.

Taylor, S. E., & Brown, J. D. (1988). Illusion and well-being: A social psychological perspective on mental health. *Psychological Bulletin, 103*, 193–210.

Tedeschi, R. G., & Calhoun, L. G. (1995). *Trauma and transformation*. Thousand Oaks, CA: Sage.

Tedeschi, R. G., Park, C. L., & Calhoun, L. G. (Eds). (1998). *Posttraumatic growth: Positive changes in the aftermath of crisis*. Mahwah, NJ: Lawrence Erlbaum Associates.

Tellegen, A. (1985). Structures of mood and personality and their relevance to assessing anxiety, with an emphasis on self-report. In A. Tuma, & J. D. Maser (Eds.), *Anxiety and the anxiety disorders* (pp. 681–706). Hillsdale, NJ: Lawrence Erlbaum Associates, Inc.

Tellegen, A., & Ben Porath, Y. S. (1992). The new uniform *T* scores for the MMPI 2: Rationale, derivation, and appraisal. *Psychological Assessment: A Journal of Consulting and Clinical Psychology, 4*, 145–155.

Tellegen, A., & Ben-Porath, Y. S. (1993). Code type comparability of the MMPI and MMPI-2: Analysis of recent findings and criticisms. *Journal of Personality Assessment, 61*, 489–500.

Tellegen, A., & Ben-Porath, Y. S. (1996). Evaluating the similarity of MMPI-2 and MMPI profiles: Reply to Dahlstrom and Humphrey. *Journal of Personality Assessment, 66*, 640–644.

Tellegen, A., & Ben-Porath, Y. S. (2011). *Minnesota Multiphasic Personality Inventory – 2 Restructured Form: Technical manual.* Minneapolis, MN: University of Minnesota Press.

Tellegen, A., Ben-Porath, Y. S., McNulty, J., Arbisi, P., Graham, J. R., & Kaemmer, B. (2003). *MMPI-2: Restructured Clinical (RC) Scales: Development, validation, and interpretation.* Minneapolis, MN: University of Minnesota Press.

Tellegen, A., Ben-Porath, Y. S., & Sellbom, M. (2009). Construct validity of the MMPI-2 Restructured Clinical (RC) Scales: Reply to Rouse, Greene, Butcher, Nichols, and Williams. *Journal of Personality Assessment, 91*, 211–221.

Tellegen, A., Ben-Porath, Y. S., Sellbom, M., Arbisi, P. A., McNulty, J. L., & Graham, J. R. (2006). Further evidence on the validity of the MMPI-2 Restructured Clinical (RC) Scales: Addressing questions raised by Rogers, Sewell, Harrison, and Jordan and Nichols. *Journal of Personality Assessment, 87*, 148–171.

Terman, L. M., & Miles, C. C. (1936). *Sex and personality: Studies in masculinity and femininity.* New York: McGraw-Hill.

Thomas, M. L., & Youngjohn, J. R. (2009). Let's not get hysterical: Comparing the MMPI-2 validity, clinical, and RC scales in TBI litigants tested for effort. *The Clinical Neuropsychologist, 23*, 1067–1084.

Tolin, D. F., Maltby, N., Weathers, F. W., Litz, B. T., Knight, J., & Keane, T. M. (2004). The use of the MMPI-2 infrequency-psychopathology scale in the assessment of posttraumatic stress disorder in male veterans. *Journal of Psychopathology and Behavioral Assessment, 26*, 23–29.

Tolin, D. F., Steenkamp, M. M., Marx, B. P., & Litz, B. T. (2010). Detecting symptom exaggeration in combat veterans using the MMPI-2 symptom validity scales: A mixed group validation. *Psychological Assessment, 22*, 729–736.

Trull, T. J., Useda, J. D., Costa, P. T., & McCrae, R. R. (1995). Comparison of the MMPI-2 Personality Psychopathology Five (PSY–5), the NEO-PI, and the NEO-PI (R). *Psychological Assessment: A Journal of Consulting and Clinical Psychology, 7*, 508–516.

Truscott, D. (1990). Assessment of overcontrolled hostility in adolescence. *Psychological Assessment: A Journal of Consulting and Clinical Psychology, 2*, 145–148.

Tsai, D. C., & Pike, P. L. (2000). Effects of acculturation on the MMPI-2 scores of Asian American students. *Journal of Personality Assessment, 74(2)*, 216–230.

Tsushima, W. T., & Tsushima, V. G. (2001). Comparison of the Fake Bad Scale and other MMPI-2 validity scales with personal injury litigants. *Assessment, 8*, 205–212.

Tydlaska, M., & Mengel, R. (1953). A scale for measuring work attitude for the MMPI. *Journal of Applied Psychology, 37*, 474–477.

Upchurch v. School Board of Broward Co. (2009). OJCC Case No. 98-024122KSP, Florida Division of Administrative Hearings, Judges of Compensation Claims, Broward District.

Van Atta, R. E. (1999). Psychology: A study of the validity of the MMPI post-traumatic stress disorder scale: Implications for forensic clinicians. *The Forensic Examiner, 8*, 20–23.

Van de Riet, V. W., & Wolking, W. D. (1969). *Interpretive hypotheses for the MMPI* [Mimeograph]. Gainesville, FL: University of Florida.

Vandergracht v. Progressive Express et al., Case No. 02-04552 (Fla. 2005).

Van der Heijden, P. T., Egger, J. I. M., & Derksen, J. J. L. (2008). Psychometric evaluation of the MMPI-2 Restructured Clinical scales in two Dutch samples. *Journal of Personality Assessment, 90*, 456–464.

Van der Heijden, P. T., Egger, J. I. M., & Derksen, J. J. L. (2010). Comparability of scores on the MMPI-2-RF scales generated with the MMPI-2 and MMPI-2-RF booklets. *Journal of Personality Assessment, 92(3),* 254–259.

Venn, J. (1988). Low scores on MMPI Scales 2 and 0 as indicators of character pathology in men. *Psychological Reports, 62,* 651–657.

Ventre, N. D., & Watson, C. G. (1972). Behavioral correlates of the MMPI Paranoia scale. *Psychological Reports, 31,* 851–854.

Voelker, T. L., & Nichols, D. S. (1999, March). *Can the MMPI-2 predict Psychopathology Checklist-Revised (PCL-R) scores?* New Orleans, LA: Society for Personality Assessment.

Wakefield, J. A., Jr., Bradley, P. E., Doughtie, E. B., & Kraft, I. A. (1975). Influence of overlapping and nonoverlapping items on the theoretical interrelationships of MMPI scales. *Journal of Consulting and Clinical Psychology, 43,* 851–856.

Wakefield, J. A., Sasek, J., Friedman, A. F., & Bowden, J. D. (1976). Androgyny and other measures of masculinity-femininity. *Journal of Consulting and Clinical Psychology, 44,* 766–770.

Wakefield, J. A., Wood, K. A., Wallace, R. F., & Friedman, A. F. (1978). A curvilinear relationship between extraversion and performance for adult retardates. *Psychological Reports, 43,* 387–392.

Wales, B., & Seeman, W. (1968). A new method for detecting the fake good response set on the MMPI. *Journal of Clinical Psychology, 24,* 211–216.

Wallace, A., & Liljequist, L. (2005). A comparison of the correlational structures and elevation patterns of the MMPI-2 Restructured Clinical (RC) and Clinical Scales. *Assessment, 12,* 290–294.

Waller, N. G. (1999). Searching for structure in the MMPI. In S. E. Embretson & S. L. Hershberger (Eds.), *The new rules of measurement: What every psychologist and educator should know* (pp. 185–217). Mahwah, NJ: Lawrence Erlbaum Associates.

Walters, G. D. (1984). Identifying schizophrenia by means of Scale 8 (Sc) of the MMPI. *Journal of Personality Assessment, 48,* 390–391.

Walters, G. D. (1988). Schizophrenia. In R. L. Greene (Ed.), *The MMPI: Use in specific populations* (pp. 50–73). Philadelphia, PA: Grune & Stratton.

Walters, G. D., & Greene, R. L. (1983). Factor structure of the Overcontrolled-Hostility scale of the MMPI. *Journal of Clinical Psychology, 39,* 560–562.

Walters, G. D., Greene, R. L., & Solomon, G. S. (1982). Empirical correlates of the Overcontrolled-Hostility scale and the MMPI 4-3 high-point pair. *Journal of Consulting and Clinical Psychology, 50,* 213–218.

Walters, G. D., Solomon, G. S., & Greene, R. L. (1982). The relationship between the Overcontrolled-Hostility scale and the MMPI 4-3 high-point pair. *Journal of Clinical Psychology, 38,* 613–615.

Walters, G. D., White, T. W., & Greene, R. L. (1988). Use of the MMPI to identify malingering and exaggeration of psychiatric symptomatology in male prison inmates. *Journal of Consulting and Clinical Psychology, 56,* 111–117.

Wang, L., Zhang, J., Shi, Z., Zhou, M., & Li, Z. (2010). Internal consistencies and structural analysis of the MMPI-2 PSY–5 facet subscales in Chinese population. *Journal of Psychopathology and Behavioral Assessment, 32,* 150–155.

Ward, L. C. (1991). A comparison of T scores from the MMPI and the MMPI-2. *Psychological Assessment: A Journal of Consulting and Clinical Psychology, 3,* 688–690.

Ward, L. C. (1994). MMPI-2 assessment of positive attributes: A methodological note. *Journal of Personality Assessment, 62,* 559–561.

Ward, L. C., & Dillon, E. A. (1990). Psychiatric symptoms of the Minnesota Multiphasic Personality Inventory (MMPI) Masculinity-Femininity scale. *Psychological Assessment: A Journal of Consulting and Clinical Psychology, 2,* 286–288.

Ward, L. C., & Jackson, D. B. (1990). A comparison of primary alcoholics, secondary alcoholics, and nonalcoholic psychiatric patients on the MacAndrew Alcoholism scale. *Journal of Personality Assessment, 54,* 729–735.

Ward, L. C., Kersh, B. C., & Waxmonsky, J. A. (1998). Factor structure of the Paranoia scale of the MMPI-2 in relation to the Harris-Lingoes subscales and Comrey factor analysis. *Psychological Assessment: A Journal of Consulting and Clinical Psychology, 10,* 292–296.

Ward, L. C., & Perry, M. S. (1998). Measurement of social introversion by the MMPI-2. *Journal of Personality Assessment, 70,* 171–182.

Ward, L. C., & Ward, J. W. (1980). MMPI readability reconsidered. *Journal of Personality Assessment, 44,* 387–389.

Watkins, C. E., Jr. (1991). What have surveys taught us about the teaching and practice of psychological assessment? *Journal of Personality Assessment, 56,* 426–437.

Watkins, C. E., Jr., Campbell, V. L., Nieberding, R., & Hallmark, R. (1995). Contemporary practice of psychological assessment by clinical psychologists. *Professional Psychology: Research and Practice, 26,* 54–60.

Watson, C. G., Juba, M., Anderson, P. E. D., & Manifold, V. (1990). What does the Keane et al. PTSD scale for the MMPI measure? *Journal of Clinical Psychology, 46,* 600–606.

Watson, C. G., Thomas, D., & Anderson, P. (1992). Do computer-administered Minnesota Multiphasic Personality Inventories underestimate booklet-based scores? *Journal of Clinical Psychology, 48,* 744–748.

Watson, D., Clark, L. A., & Carey, G. (1988). Positive and negative affectivity and their relation to anxiety and depressive disorders. *Journal of Abnormal Psychology, 97,* 346–353.

Watson, D., & Tellegen, A. (1985). Toward a consensual structure of mood. *Psychological Bulletin, 98,* 219–235.

Webb, J. T. (1970a, April). *The relation of MMPI two-point codes to age, sex and education in a representative nationwide sample of psychiatric outpatients.* Paper presented at the convention of the Southeastern Psychological Association, Louisville, KY.

Webb, J. T. (1970b). Validity and utility of computer-produced MMPI reports with Veterans Administration psychiatric populations. *Proceedings of the 78th Annual Convention of the American Psychological Association, 5,* 541–542.

Webb, J. T. (1971). Regional and sex differences in MMPI scale high-point frequencies of psychiatric patients. *Journal of Clinical Psychology, 27,* 483–486.

Webb, J. T., Fowler, R. D., & Miller, M. L. (1971, May). *Frequency of critical items by sex, age and education in psychiatric patients.* Paper presented at the meeting of the Midwestern Psychological Association, Detroit, MI.

Webb, J. T., Levitt, E. E., & Rojdev, R. S. (1993, March). *A comparison of the clinical use of MMPI-1 and MMPI-2.* Paper presented at the meeting for the Society of Personality Assessment, San Francisco, CA.

Webb, J. T., McNamara, K. M., & Rodgers, D. A. (1986). *Configural interpretations of the MMPI and CPI.* Columbus, OH: Ohio Psychology Publishing. (Original work published 1981.)

Webb, J. T., Miller, M. L., & Fowler, R. D. (1969). Validation of a computerized MMPI interpretation system. *Proceedings of the 77th Annual Convention of the American Psychological Association, 4,* 523–524.

Webb, J. T., Miller, M. L., & Fowler, R. D. (1970). Extending professional time: A computerized MMPI interpretation service. *Journal of Clinical Psychology, 26,* 210–214.

Wechsler, D. (2009). *Wechsler Individual Achievement Test,* 3rd edition. San Antonio, TX: Pearson.

Weed, N. C. (2006). Syndromal complexity, paradigm shifts, and the future of validation research: Comments on Nichols and Rogers, Sewell, Harrison, and Jordan. *Journal Of Personality Assessment, 87,* 217–222.

Weed, N. C., Ben-Porath, Y. S., & Butcher, J. N. (1990). Failure of Weiner and Harmon Minnesota Multiphasic Personality Inventory (MMPI) Subtle scales as personality descriptors and as validity indicators. *Psychological Assessment: A Journal of Consulting and Clinical Psychology, 2,* 281–285.

Weed, N. C., Butcher, J. N., & Ben-Porath, Y. S. (1995). MMPI-2 measures of substance abuse. In J. N. Butcher & C. D. Spielberger (Eds.), *Advances in personality assessment* (Vol. 10, pp. 121–145). Hillsdale, NJ, England: Lawrence Erlbaum Associates.

Weed, N. C., Butcher, J. N., McKenna, T., & Ben-Porath, Y. S. (1992). New measures for assessing alcohol and drug abuse with the MMPI-2: The *APS* and *AAS. Journal of Personality Assessment, 58,* 389–404.

Weisenburger, S. M., Harkness, A. R., McNulty, J. L., Graham, J. R., & Ben-Porath, Y. S. (2008). Interpreting low Personality Psychopathology-Five Aggressiveness scores on the MMPI-2: Graphical, robust, and resistant data analysis. *Psychological Assessment, 20,* 403–408.

Weiss, P. A., Vivian, J. E., Weiss, W. V., Davis, R. D., & Rostow, C. D. (2013). The MMPI-2 *L* Scale, reporting uncommon virtue and predicting police performance. *Psychological Services, 10(1),* 123–130. Doi: 10.1037/a0029062.

Weiss, W. V., Davis, R., Rostow, C., & Kinsman, S. (2003). The MMPI-2 *L* Scale as a tool in police selection. *Journal of Police and Criminal Psychology, 18(1),* 57–60.

Weissman, H. N. (1990). Distortions and deceptions in self-presentation: Effects of protracted litigation in personal injury cases. *Behavioral Sciences and the Law, 8,* 67–74.

Welsh, G. S. (1948). An extension of Hathaway's MMPI profile coding system. *Journal of Consulting Psychology, 12,* 343–344.

Welsh, G. S. (1952). An anxiety index and an internalization ratio for the MMPI. *Journal of Consulting Psychology, 16(1),* 65–72.

Welsh, G. S. (1956). Factor dimensions A and R. In G. S. Welsh & W. G. Dahlstrom (Eds.), *Basic readings on the MMPI in psychology and medicine* (pp. 264–281). Minneapolis, MN: University of Minnesota Press.

Welsh, G. S., & Dahlstrom, W. G. (Eds.) (1956). *Basic readings on the MMPI in psychology and medicine.* Minneapolis, MN: University of Minnesota Press.

Werner, P. D., Becker, J. M., & Yesavage, J. A. (1983). Concurrent validity of the Overcontrolled Hostility scale for psychotics. *Psychological Reports, 52,* 93–94.

Wetter, M. W., Baer, R. A., Berry, D. T. R., Robison, L. H., & Sumpter, J. (1993). MMPI-2 profiles of motivated fakers given specific symptom information: A comparison to matched patients. *Psychological Assessment: A Journal of Consulting and Clinical Psychology, 5,* 317–323.

Wetter, M. W., Baer, R. A., Berry, D., Smith, G. T., & Larsen, L. H. (1992). Sensitivity of MMPI-2 validity scales to random responding and malingering. *Psychological Assessment: A Journal of Consulting and Clinical Psychology, 4,* 369–374.

Wetzler, S., Khadivi, A., & Moser, R. K. (1998). The use of the MMPI-2 for the assessment of depressive and psychotic disorders. *Assessment, 5,* 249–261.

White, A. J., & Heilbrun, K. (1995). The classification of overcontrolled hostility: Comparison of two diagnostic methods. *Criminal Behaviour and Mental Health, 5,* 106–123.

White, W. C. (1975). Validity of the Overcontrolled-Hostility (0-H) scale: A brief report. *Journal of Personality Assessment, 39,* 587–590.

White, W. C., McAdoo, W. G., & Megargee, E. I. (1973). Personality factors associated with over- and under-controlled offenders. *Journal of Personality Assessment, 37,* 473–478.

Whitworth, R. H., & McBlaine, D. D. (1993). Comparison of the MMPI and MMPI-2 administered to Anglo and Hispanic-American university students. *Journal of Personality Assessment, 61,* 19–27.

Wiederholt, J. L., & Bryant, B. R. (1986). *Gray oral reading test* (Rev. ed.). Austin, TX: PROED.

Wiederstein, M. (1986). *Construct validity for measuring Eysenck's dimensions of psychoticism and neuroticism with the MMPI.* Unpublished doctoral dissertation, California School of Professional Psychology, Fresno.

Wiener, D. N. (1948). Subtle and obvious keys for the MMPI. *Journal of Consulting Psychology, 12,* 164–170.

Wiener, D. N. (1956). Subtle and obvious keys for the MMPI. In G. S. Welsh & W. G. Dahlstrom (Eds.), *Basic readings on the MMPI in psychology and medicine* (pp. 195–204). Minneapolis, MN: University of Minnesota Press.

Wiener, D. N., & Harmon, L. R. (1946). *Subtle and obvious keys for the MMPI: Their development* (VA Advisement Bulletin No. 16.). Minneapolis, MN: Regional Veterans Administration Office.

Wiggins, J. S. (1959). Interrelationships among MMPI measures of dissimulation under standard and social desirability instructions. *Journal of Consulting Psychology, 23,* 419–427.

Wiggins, J. S. (1964). Convergences among stylistic response measures from objective personality tests. *Educational and Psychological Measurement, 24,* 551–562.

Wiggins, J. S. (1966). Substantive dimensions of self-report in the MMPI item pool. *Psychological Monographs, 80(22,* Whole No. 630).

Wiggins, J. S. (1969). Content dimensions in the MMPI. In J. N. Butcher (Ed.), *MMPI: Research developments and clinical applications* (pp. 127–180). New York: McGraw-Hill.

Wiggins, J. S. (1973). *Personality and prediction: Principles of personality assessment.* Don Mills, Ontario, Canada: Addison-Wesley.

Wiggins, J. S., Goldberg, L. R., & Applebaum, M. (1971). MMPI content scales: Interpretive norms and correlations with other scales. *Journal of Consulting and Clinical Psychology, 37,* 403–410.

Williams v. CSX Transportation, Inc. Case No. 04-CA-008892 (13th Cir. 2007).

Williams, C. L. (1983). Further investigation of the *Si* scale of the MMPI: Reliabilities, correlates, and subscale utility. *Journal of Clinical Psychology, 39,* 951–957.

Williams, C. L., Butcher, J. N., Gass, C. S., Cumella, E., & Kally, Z. (2009). Inaccuracies about the MMPI-2 Fake Bad Scale in the reply by Ben-Porath, Greve, Bianchini, and Kaufman (2009). *Psychological Injury and Law, 2(2),* 182–197.

Williams, H. L. (1952). The development of a caudality scale for the MMPI. *Journal of Clinical Psychology, 8,* 293–297.

Williams, J. E., & Weed, N. C. (2004). Relative user ratings of MMPI-2 computer-based test interpretations. *Assessment, 11(4),* pp. 316–329.

Williams, J. S. (2002). Psychopathy in instrumental and reactive violent offenders using MMPI-2 scales as predictors (Doctoral dissertation, Spalding University). *Dissertation Abstracts International, 62(9-B),* 4243.

Williams, R. B., Haney, T. L., Lee, K. L., Kong, Y.-H., Blumenthal, J. A., & Whalen, R. E. (1980). Type A behavior, hostility, and coronary atherosclerosis. *Psychosomatic Medicine, 42,* 539–549.

Wong, M. R. (1984). MMPI Scale 5: Its meanings or lack thereof. *Journal of Personality Assessment, 48,* 279–284.

Woo, M., & Oei, T. P. S. (2008). Empirical investigations of the MMPI-2 Gender-Masculine and Gender-Feminine scales. *Journal of Individual Differences, 29,* 1–10.

Wood, H. L. (2008). Cultural validity of the MMPI-2 substance abuse scales with American Indians (Pacific Graduate School of Psychology). *Dissertation Abstracts International, 68(7-B),* 4852.

Woodcock, R. W., McGrew, K. S., & Mather, N. (2001). *Woodcock–Johnson III Test of Achievement Examiners Manual (Standard and Extended Batteries)* Itasco, IL: Riverside Publishing.

Woodworth, R. S. (1920). *Personal data sheet.* Chicago, IL: Stoelting.

Wrobel, T. A. (1992). Validity of Harris and Lingoes MMPI subscale descriptions in an outpatient sample. *Journal of Personality Assessment, 59,* 14–21.

Wrobel, T. A., & Lachar, D. (1982). Validity of the Weiner subtle and obvious scales for the MMPI: Another example of the importance of inventory-item content. *Journal of Consulting and Clinical Psychology, 50*, 469–470.

Wygant, D. B. (2007). *Validation of the MMPI-2 infrequent somatic complaints (Fs) scale.* Unpublished doctoral dissertation, Kent State University, Kent, OH.

Wygant, D. B. (2008). Validation of the MMPI-2 infrequent somatic complaints (Fs) scale. *Dissertation Abstracts International: Section B: The Sciences and Engineering, 687(10-B)*, 6989.

Wygant, D. B., Anderson, J. L., Sellbom, M., Rapier, J. L., Allgeier, L. M., & Granacher, R. P. (2011). Association of the MMPI-2 restructured form (MMPI-2-RF) validity scales with structured malingering criteria. *Psychological Injury and Law, 4(1)*, 13–23.

Wygant, D. B., Ben-Porath, Y. S., & Arbisi, P. A. (2004, May). *Development and initial validation of a scale to detect somatic over-reporting.* Paper presented at the 39th Annual Symposium on Recent Developments in the Use of the MMPI-2 and MMPI-A, Minneapolis, MN.

Wygant, D. B., Ben-Porath, Y. S., Arbisi, P. A., Berry, D. T. R., Freeman, D. B., & Heilbronner, R. L. (2009). Examination of the MMPI-2 Restructured Form (MMPI-2-RF) validity scales in civil forensic settings: Findings from simulation and known group samples. *Archives of Clinical Neuropsychology, 24*, 671–680.

Wygant, D. B., Boutacoff, L. I., Arbisi, P. A., Ben-Porath, Y. S., Kelly, P. H., & Rupp, W. M. (2007). Examination of the MMPI-2 Restructured Clinical (RC) scales in a sample of bariatric surgery candidates. *Journal of Clinical Psychology in Medical Settings, 14*, 197–205.

Wygant, D. B., & Sellbom, M. (2012). Viewing psychopathy from the perspective of the personality psychopathology five model: Implications for DSM-5. *Journal of Personality Disorders, 26*, 717–726.

Wygant, D. B., Sellbom, M., Ben-Porath, Y. S., Stafford, K. P., Freeman, D. B., & Heilbronner, R. L. (2007). The relation between symptom validity testing and MMPI-2 scores as a function of forensic evaluation context. *Archives of Clinical Neuropsychology, 22*, 489–499.

Wygant, D. B., Sellbom, M., Gervais, R. O., Ben-Porath, Y. S., Stafford, K. P., Freeman, D. B., & Heilbronner, R. L. (2010). Further validation of the MMPI-2 and MMPI-2-RF Response Bias Scale: Findings from disability and criminal forensic settings. *Psychological Assessment, 22(4)*, 745–756.

Yehuda, R., & McFarlane, A. C. (1995). Conflict between current knowledge about posttraumatic stress disorder and its original conceptual basis. *American Journal of Psychiatry, 152*, 1705–1713.

Young, A. (1995). *The harmony of illusions: Inventing post-traumatic stress disorder.* Princeton, NJ: Princeton University Press.

Young, K. R., & Weed, N. C. (2006). Assessing alcohol- and drug-abusing clients with the MMPI-2. In J. N. Butcher (Ed.), *MMPI-2: A practitioner's guide* (pp. 361–379). Washington, DC: American Psychological Association.

Youngjohn, J. R., Wershba, R., Stevenson, M., Sturgeon, J., & Thomas, M. L. (2011). Independent validation of the MMPI-2-RF somatic/cognitive and validity scales in TBI litigants tested for effort. *The Clinical Neuropsychologist, 25(3)*, 463–476.

Author Index

Subject Index

Made in the USA
Middletown, DE
16 March 2016